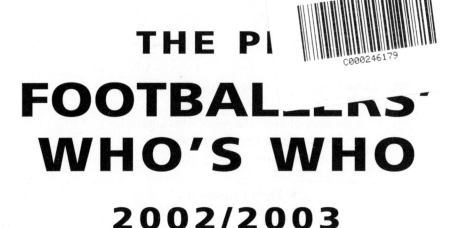

THE PREMIERSHIP FOOTBALLERS' WHO'S WHO

2002/2003

Editor and Statistician
Barry J Hugman

Assistant Editor
Ian Nannestad

Photographs by
Allsport UK

QUEEN ANNE PRESS

First published in Great Britain in 2002 by
Queen Anne Press
a division of Lennard Associates Limited
Mackerye End, Harpenden
Hertfordshire AL5 5DR

© Barry J Hugman

A CIP catalogue record for this book
is available from the British Library

ISBN 1 85291 648 6

Typeset and designed by
Typecast (Artwork & Design)
8 Mudford Road
Yeovil, Somerset BA21 4AA

Printed and bound in Great Britain by
Butler & Tanner, London and Frome

Acknowledgements

Eight years on, and formerly known as the *Factfile*, the *Who's Who* has, hopefully, become invaluable as a part-work which, in due course, will cover the season-by-season record of every player's complete career. To this end, I would once again like to express my thanks to **Gordon Taylor**, the chief executive, and all those at the PFA who are genuinely supporting and helping to establish the *Who's Who*. Their help is invaluable and much appreciated.

I am grateful to **Mark Baber**, **Dave Riley** and all the staff at AFS Enterprises, who allowed me the use of club line ups on their *llvll.co.uk* site. In return, I audited their records in concert with the contributors.

The massive task of editing the text this year was again carried out by the assistant editor, **Ian Nannestad**, who has been a long-standing contributor to the publication for his own club, Lincoln City. Co-author of two books on the history of the Imps, he was previously editor of the AFS Report before establishing a new quarterly magazine, *Soccer History*, in April 2002.

The editorial team were also lucky to be able to call upon **David Barber** (English FA), **Sandy Bryson** (Scottish FA), **Zoe Ward** (FA Premier League), **Ceri Stennett** (FA of Wales), and **Marshall Gillespie** (editor of the Northern Ireland Football Yearbook). Others who gave their time were **Alan Platt** (Where Did They Go?) and **Jenny Hugman** (proof reading), and many Premier and Football League members up and down the country.

For the eigth year, **Jonathan Ticehurst**, managing director of Windsor Insurance Brokers' Sports Division, has thrown his weight behind the publication, both financially and vocally. His and Windsor's support, as with the *British Boxing Board of Control Yearbook*, is greatly appreciated.

For details provided on players, I have listed below, in alphabetical order, the names of the team, without whose help this book would not have been possible to produce. Once again, I thank every one of them for all the hard work they put in.

Audrey Adams *(Watford):* Producer and statistician for BBC Radio Sport and a Watford supporter since the days of Cliff Holton, Audrey was the club statistician for the *Ultimate Football Guide*. Regardless of how the club performed last season her devotion to the Hornets remains undimmed.

Geoff Allman *(Walsall):* A university lecturer by trade, he saw his first ever game in February 1944, Walsall versus Wolves. Has written for Walsall's programme for over 30 seasons and, at one time or another, has provided articles for more than half of the clubs currently in the Premiership and Football League. Geoff is also a Methodist local preacher and press officer.

Mark Barrowclough *(Manchester City):* Mark has been a City supporter since 1965, getting his first season ticket in the 1973-74 season and having one ever since. He met his wife, Dawn, who was working for City in the commercial department at the time. Mark has done matchball sponsorship and sponsored reserve team football matches, and has also produced some match reports for the City programme. Dawn gave birth to their second child in September, a little girl – Sophie, who was made a Junior Blue before she was ten hours old. Would have been sooner but the office isn't open at 2

o'clock in the morning. The same fate had been inflicted on Sophie's elder brother, Joe, four years before.

Stuart Basson *(Chesterfield):* Stuart is pleased to have contributed to the publication since its inception. He is Chesterfield's Club Historian and has had three successful books on the club published – most recently, his *Official History* sold out within months of its publication. Stuart contributes to the historical section of the club's website and is a life-member of the Chesterfield Football Supporters Society, the fans' group that saved the club, and ran it through the 2001-02 season.

Ian Bates *(Bradford):* Ian passed the 50-year mark of watching City last December, the high spot being the club's rise to the Premiership. His main hobby is City, but he also enjoys cricket as well, and has been umpiring for 17 years and loves it. Ian had to stop refereeing, which he did at local level for 19 years, after injuring his back.

David Batters *(York City):* A supporter since 1948, David is the club historian and a contributor to the matchday programme. He is also the author of *York City, the Complete Record 1922-1990*, the compiler of *Images of Sport - York City FC* and commentates on matches for York Hospital Radio.

Harry Berry *(Blackburn Rovers):* Harry has now completed 50 years of following Blackburn Rovers, having been born only three miles from Ewood Park, living within 15 miles all his life, and a season ticket holder ever since starting work. Has been for many years a road runner and has completed a few marathons. By profession he is a financial director and works for the largest manufacturer in Blackburn.

Eddie Brennan *(Sunderland):* A season ticket holder at the Stadium of Light, and a former contributor to the *Carling Ultimate Football Guide*, Eddie has been a regular supporter since 1976.

Jim Brown *(Coventry City):* The club's official statistician and historian and contributor to the programme, he also pens a weekly column in the *Coventry Evening Telegraph* answering readers queries. He is the author of *Coventry City-the Elite Era (1998 and 2001)* and *The Illustrated History (2000)*, in addition to being the co-author of the *Breedon Complete Record (1991)*. He has been a Coventry fan since 1962 and has almost a complete collection of Coventry programmes since the war. During 2002 he has been technical consultant to *Sky Blue Heaven*, an exhibition on the history of the club at the Coventry Museum. Has a large library of football writings and carries out research for a number of commercial bodies.

Mark Brown *(Plymouth Argyle):* Helped on the *PFA Factfile* profiles by his wife Nicola, Mark has been supporting the club for over 25 years, having been introduced to them at the tender age of five by his Argyle-mad family. Follows most of their games, whether home or away, and is a member of the travel club.

Andrew Bubeer *(Rushden & Diamonds):* Andrew is the Diamonds' Communications Manager during their first season in the Football League, a role which includes being Editor of the matchday programme. He was previously Assistant Editor of Manchester United's matchday programme before taking up the post of Managing Editor at Leicester City. Despite these associations with three different clubs, he still manages to maintain an unhealthy interest in the fortunes of a fourth - Plymouth Argyle!

Trevor Bugg *(Hull City):* A supporter of the Tigers for over 30 years, Trevor contributes to Hull City's official web site as well as the matchday programme. He also played a starring role, information wise, for Exxus, prior to their demise.

Bob Cain *(Fulham):* Bob has supported Fulham for 31

years, during which time he has not missed a single home match in any first-team competition. In all he has clocked up almost 1,500 first team games. A strong advocate of all-seater stadiums, he is looking forward to returning to the new Craven Cottage following the groundshare at QPR. Has been a contributor to the club programme for over a decade.

Wallace Chadwick *(Burnley):* A Clarets' supporter for over 40 years, and programme contributor for the last fifteen, Wallace has assisted on several publications about the club. Was a member of the AFS from 1980 until its recent untimely demise. An accountant by profession, statistician by nature, and a supporter by unbreakable habit.

Gary Chalk *(Southampton):* A member of the hagiology group of Saints' historians committed to the collection and dissemination of accurate information on the history of Southampton FC. Currently the club's official co-Historian and Statistician, Gary co-authored *Saints: A Complete History 1885-1987* and *The Alphabet of the Saints 1992* with Duncan Holley, and more recently contributed to the successful *Match of the Millenium* project published by Hagiology Publishing.

Paul Clayton *(Charlton Athletic):* Author of the book *The Essential History of Charlton Athletic*, Paul wrote a regular feature in the club programme between 1993 and 1998, having previously written other articles for the now defunct *Charlton Athletic* magazine and *Valiant's Viewpoint* (Supporters Club newsletter/fanzine). He has also provided the Charlton statistics for a number of publications, including the *Ultimate Football Guide* from 1987 to its final publication in 1999, along with the Charlton player information for the *Factfile/Who's Who* since its inception in 1995. A member of the AFS, he is a long-standing season ticket holder at The Valley and rarely misses a game, home or away, despite living in Wiltshire.

Grant Coleby *(Exeter City):* A member of both the Exeter City Supporters' Club and the Association of Football Statisticians, he has been the contributor for Exeter since the book's conception and a member of the Exeter Supporter's Club.

Eddie Collins *(Nottingham Forest):* A Forest supporter since 1956, and a member of the Associated Football Statisticians, this is the first publication he has been involved in and derives much enjoyment from it.

David Copping *(Barnsley):* David is a life-long Barnsley fan who has been a regular columnist in the Club matchday programme for many seasons. He also did live match commentaries to local hospitals before becoming the 'voice' on the club videos.

Frank Coumbe *(Brentford):* Hasn't missed a competitive Brentford home game since December 1977, a club record. He has also been Brentford's statistician for this book since it began and acted in a similar capacity for the *Ultimate Football Guide* until its demise. 2001-02 was a wonderful season to be a Griffin Park regular thanks to Steve Coppell's tactical awareness and a willing group of players. However, the Bees' fourth Play-Off failure could see more cost cutting and 2002-03 could well be a real struggle for the supporters.

Peter Cullen *(Bury):* Married, aged 42. Peter has supported the Shakers for the last 30 years and seen the club play on all but five league grounds. A former Secretary of the Supporters Assocation, Peter also worked at Bury FC for two and a half years as Ticket office Manager/Programme Editor and has written in the club programme on a voluntary basis since 1980. He has also written three books on the club, including the definitive history, *Bury FC 1983-1999*.

Mick Cunningham *(Bournemouth):* Has been a Bournemouth supporter since 1966, founded the AFC Bournemouth Exiles Club in 1985, edited the magazine and started the AFCB fanzine *Not The 8502* in 1988, which ran until 1996. Mick has been the programme editor at Bournemouth since 1995 and is also the official club photographer. He is 42, born in Bournemouth, and served in the RAF for 12 years.

John Curtis *(Scunthorpe United):* A life-long Scunthorpe fan, John reports on the club in his role as deputy sports editor at the *Scunthorpe Telegraph* and is a former editor of the award-winning club matchday programme.

Carol Dalziel *(Tranmere Rovers):* Has been watching Tranmere for over 30 years, is a regular contributor to the matchday programme, and operates the club's electronic scoreboard.

Denise Dann *(Aston Villa):* In her own words, Denise is a mad, crazy Villa supporter, who follows them up and down the country without fail. Her only previous football work was to help with the club's profiles required for the *Premier League: The Players* publication.

Gareth Davies and **Geraint Parry** *(Wrexham):* Gareth is the co-author of *Who's Who* on Welsh International Footballers (1991) with Ian Garland; editor/compiler of *Coast of Soccer Memories:* Centenary publication of the North Wales Coast FA (1994); co-author of *The Racecourse Robins* with Peter Jones: *Who's Who of Wrexham FC 1921-99* (1999); co-author of *Tempus Images of Sport. Wrexham FC 1872-1950* (2000) with Peter Jones and *Wrexham FC 1950-2001* (2001) with Peter Jones. He is also a contributor to the Wrexham official programme, the *Holyhead Hotspur* (Cymru Alliance) the *Welsh Football* magazine and various articles and info to other magazines and books.

David Downs *(Reading):* David has been a Reading supporter for over 50 years and a programme contributor for the last 25. He is currently employed as the club's Academy Welfare & Child Protection Officer, a part-time employment which he combines with supply teaching. Reading's promotion to Division One takes David one step closer to his lifetime's ambition, that of seeing his club win the European Cup.

Ray Driscoll *(Chelsea):* A life-long Blues' fan, born and bred two miles away from Stamford Bridge, whose more than 40 years spectating encompasses the era from Jimmy Greaves to Jimmy Floyd Hasselbaink. An all-round sports 'nut', he has contributed to many football books as well as other sports books, such as cricket, golf, rugby and tennis. He has also contributed to more 'cerebral' literature, such as reference books.

Brian Ellis *(Luton Town):* One of the co-authors of *The Definitive Luton Town*, Brian is a regular contributor to the Luton Town Fans Newsletter. A former member of The Association of Football Statisticians, he was responsible for many articles over the years. Brian went to his first Luton match in 1967 and has been a regular attender of Luton matches ever since, home and away, but more unusually he is a keen devotee of Luton's reserve side.

Mark Evans *(Leeds United):* Has supported United for over 30 years and describes his association with the club as one of the loves of his life. The Leeds' statistician for the *Ultimate Football Guide* for nearly nine years, he was also involved in my two editions of the *FA Carling Premiership: The Players*.

Colin Faiers *(Cambridge United):* A Cambridge United fan for over 30 years, Colin has witnessed their rise from non-league football. A chartered accountant in the day, he is the club statistician and occasional contributor to the club programme and web site.

Harold Finch *(Crewe Alexandra):* Club historian for Alexandra, Harold has now completed 68 years of supporting them. Although no longer programme editor he is still a regular

4

contributor to the programme and provides all club statistics. His publication, *Crewe Alexandra FC – A Pictorial History of the Club* has proved to be extremely popular with collectors.

Mick Ford and **Richard Lindsey** *(Millwall):* A life-long Millwall fan, Mick has now followed the club for more than 50 years and was justifiably disappointed when they failed to gain promotion from the play-offs last season. Despite living in Worcester, he only misses a handful of games a season and without the understanding of his wife, Sue, would find it difficult to continue his passion. Has an extensive memorabilia collection which he adds to when the right items come up. Meanwhile, his *Who's Who* partner, Richard, the author of *Millwall: The Complete Record*, continues to help establish the Millwall FC Museum at the New Den.

Andrew Frazier *(Kidderminster Harriers):* Has been following the Harriers since 1978, and hasn't missed a game, home or away, for over eight years. Is a contributor to the club programme, is the club statistician, and a member of the Association of Football Statisticians.

Jon Gibbes *(Torquay United):* Saw his first game on Boxing Day 1970 aged seven, the beginning of an unhealthy obsession with Torquay United which at times leads to the woeful neglect of wife, Julie, and children, Rosie and Tommy. After having disproved the long-held belief that the club was formed in 1898, Jon co-wrote the club's *Official Centenary History 1899-1999* with Leigh Edwards and John Lovis.

Paul Godfrey *(Cheltenham Town):* Paul watched his first Cheltenham Town game at the age of ten – the Robins lost 2-1 to Yeovil Town in an FA Cup Fourth Qualifying Round match. He followed similar near misses and disappointments religiously before events took a dramatic turn in the late 1990s. Having become the club's Programme Editor in 1990, he was able to witness at first hand the transformation at Whaddon Road brought about by Steve Cotterill and the Board, headed by Chairman Paul Baker. He joined the club on a full-time basis in 2001 and now combines managing the club's website with his role as Football Secretary. He is still struggling manfully with the task of compiling the club history.

Dave Goody *(Southend United):* A season ticket holder and life-long Shrimpers fan, Dave has now put his large collection of Southend United programmes and memorabilia to good use, co-authoring a series of books in Tempus Publishing's *Archive Photograph Series* with noted football author and fellow fan, Peter Miles. This brings the total of Southend United books authored by him to four.

Frank Grande *(Northampton Town):* Author of *The Cobblers, A History of Northampton Town FC* and a *Who's Who*, Frank also compiled the *Definitive History* of the club and the *Centenary History*. Now working on a biography of Tommy Fowler, the club's longest serving player, he has been a contributor to the club programme for over 20 years.

Roy Grant *(Oxford United):* A life-long Oxford United fan, Roy previously produced the Oxford United matchday programme and had a spell as club statistician. A contributor in the *Footballer's Factfile* (now *Who's Who*) since its first issue, Roy has also written for several football club programmes as well as contributing to football websites and productions such as the *Official Football League Yearbook* and the *Ultimate Football Guide*.

Michael Green *(Bolton Wanderers):* Despite being a fanatical Newcastle United supporter, Michael covers Bolton for the *Who's Who* and his excellent efforts are much appreciated. Having a yearning to get involved in the area of freelance journalism, preferably concerning football or popular entertainment (music, films etc), he has been on a substantial writing course to further himself in this field. Has also formed a

band called Pub Monkey with some friends, playing lead guitar.

Alan Harding *(Swindon Town):* Alan has been supporting Swindon Town since 1968, is a season ticket holder, travels home and away, and has been researching match stats and line-up details, plus details of players since 1981. Is also a member of the AFS and this is the first time he has assisted with anything like this.

Roger Harrison *(Blackpool):* A life-long supporter who has seen the Pool play every other league side, both home and away, and joint programme editor and club statistician, Roger has contributed to other publications, including *Rothmans* and the *Ultimate Football Guide*.

Richard and **Janey Hayhoe** *(Tottenham Hotspur):* Janey and Richard long for the day that their team can fill them with the same pride and show the same progress as their daughter Holly, now four-years old. Richard hopes that another new arrival will bring them similar fulfilment ... that arrival being Glenn Hoddle of course!

Des Hinks *(Stockport County):* Des, who has been following his beloved Hatters for 38 years, independently covers every game, at home and abroad, for the club's website. He also edits and produces their award-winning reserve-team match programme.

Mike Jay *(Bristol Rovers):* Mike, the club's official historian and programme contributor, has had three books published on Bristol Rovers, namely *The Complete Record (1883-1987) Pirates in Profile, A Who's Who of Players 1920-94* and *Bristol Rovers FC Images of England Photographic History 1999*. Mike is currently working in conjunction with Stephen Byrne on a detailed history of the club, which is due to be published in the near future.

Darran and **Chris Jennison** *(Wimbledon):* Darran and Chris are family stand season ticket holders, where they sit with their sons Daniel & Elliott. Chris has supported Wimbledon for over 25 years and everyone is hoping and working towards stopping the Dons move to MK and a return to Merton.

Colin Jones *(Swansea City):* A fan since the early 1960s, and a contributor to the club programme during the last six years, Colin played non-league football before being involved in training and coaching. He will be starting his third season as programme editor, a role which can be classed as 'more of a labour of love' than the money received in expenses! Prior to the start of the 2000/2001 season, he also made a significant contribution in setting out all the stats in grid form for David Farmer's recent book, *The Swans, Town & City*.

Andrew Kirkham *(Sheffield United):* A Blades' supporter since 1953, and a regular contributor to the club programme and handbook since 1984, Andrew is a member of the AFS and 92 Club. He was a contributor to *Sheffield United: The First 100 Years*, and co-author of *A Complete Record of Sheffield United Football Club, 1889-1999*.

Geoff Knights *(Macclesfield Town):* Following a career move to Cheshire, Geoff started following Macclesfield Town in the late '80s and rarely misses a match these days, whether it be home or away. Describing himself as an ordinary supporter who stands on the terraces, and one who enjoys the friendly atmosphere of a small club, he keeps detailed statistics and records on the club, which are used in response to media and other enquiries. He is a contributor to the Macclesfield FC matchday programme (last season he wrote some major articles and this coming season will have his own page) and has recently chaired a number of shareholders' meetings.

Geoffrey Lea *(Wigan Athletic):* A life-long supporter for over 30 seasons who first started watching the club during the non-league days. Editor for the matchday programme for the last seven seasons, Geoff is also the official matchday clubcall reporter and, as the club's statistician, he performs a number of jobs for the club as a labour of love. Has missed only a handful of games over the last ten seasons and has also worked for a number of local radio stations and newspapers following the club's progress.

Gordon Macey *(Queens Park Rangers):* Has supported Queens Park Rangers since the early 1960s and has been collecting and compiling statistics on the club, at all levels, for many seasons. He is a life member of the Association of Football Statisticians and is recognised by many areas of the media as the 'expert' on QPR. In 1993, Gordon was appointed as the club's official historian, following the publication of his successful *Complete Record of Queens Park Rangers* book, and to mark the Millennium he published an update of the club history in August 1999. His three children are all regular attendees at the Rangers' games and help with some of the research at newspaper and local archives. Gordon's work, as an implementer of Financial and Logistic Business Systems, involves travel throughout Europe and other parts of the world. This gives him the opportunity of watching football (and his other interest of ice hockey) in a number of different countries.

John Maguire *(Manchester United):* A one-club man since the *Factfile* (now *Who's Who*) began, John has been working on several sports related booklets in 2002. The result of those efforts may be found in *Sportspages*, both in Manchester and London, and on the bookshops website, usually under the headings of Manchester United. He once again thanks *Sportspages* for their continued support.

Carl Marsden *(Oldham Athletic):* A life-long supporter, Carl has been involved with his beloved Athletic on several levels. He was chairman of SAFE (Secure Athletic's Future Existence), a website editor and regular fanzine contributor. He has now embarked on a career as a freelance football journalist (email: carl@oafc.co.uk).

Carl Marston *(Colchester United):* Has been reporting on the fortunes of Colchester United since they regained their Football League status in 1992, both for the *East Anglian Daily Times* and the *Green 'Un* newspapers. Carl has only missed a handful of games during the last ten years, usually when away, running for Suffolk in cross country races.

Wade Martin *(Stoke City):* A Stoke supporter since birth, he has written numerous books on the club, including the Definitive History – *A Potter's Tale* – and a Who's Who series – *The Master Potters*. Wade acts as the club's historian and was a contributor to the club's programme for many years.

Tony Matthews *(West Bromwich Albion):* The Official statistician and curator at The Hawthorns, his 60 plus publications include complete records/histories of *Aston Villa, Birmingham City, Stoke City, Walsall, West Bromwich Albion* and *Wolverhampton Wanderers;* the essential *Histories of Leicester City and Wolverhampton Wanderers*, also assisting with same on *Aston Villa* and *West Bromwich Albion* (published 2002); full A-Z encyclopaedias of *Aston Villa, Birmingham City, Manchester United* (published 2002), *Stoke City, Tottenham Hotspur, West Bromwich Albion, Wolverhampton Wanderers & Devon Football* (featuring *Exeter City, Plymouth Argyle & Torquay United* - published 2002); *Who's Who of Villa, Blues, Manchester United (1945-85), Albion and Wolves; Who's Who of England World Cup Players/Managers (and World Cup History: 1930-2002);* wartime and photographic books; *Smokin' Joe (The Cyrille Regis Story* - published 2002);and also contributes to programmes of Premiership/Nationwide League clubs. His next projects include *encyclopaedias of Arsenal, Bolton Wanderers and Sheffield United* and up-dated *Who's Whos on Aston Villa, Blues and West Bromwich Albion* as well as a *Who's Who on England International Players: 1872-2003.*

Paul Morant *(Leyton Orient):* Working for an insurance company in London, Paul is an out-and-out Orient fan who rarely misses a game, home or away, and, whenever possible, also attends youth and reserve-team games.

Ian Nannestad *(Lincoln City):* Ian has followed the Imps for more than 35 years and is co-author with his brother Donald of *A Who's Who of Lincoln City, 1892-1994* and *Lincoln City: The Official History.* A freelance writer and book editor, he recently established a new quarterly magazine devoted to the history of the game titled *Soccer History.* Readers wishing to know more about the *Soccer History* magazine can contact Ian by writing to 52 Studland Road, Hall Green, Birmingham, B28 8NW.

Adrian and **Caroline Newnham** and **Tim Carder** *(Brighton & Hove Albion):* Caroline and Adrian are life-long supporters who met through watching the Albion and are actively involved in the campaign to secure the Seagulls a permanent stadium at Falmer (the local council have just provided their approval of the plans- we now await the government!). Adrian undertakes the matchday tours at the Albion's temporary ground at Withdean. Tim is chairman of both the Supporters' Club and the Albion's Collectors' and Historians' Society. Along with Roger Harris, he co-authored *Seagulls:The story of Brighton and Hove Albion FC* and *Albion A-Z: A Who's Who of Brighton and Hove Albion FC.* Tim is also a respected local historian on matters ranging far beyond the Albion. Having waited so long to see a championship winning side (36 years before the Div 3 win in 2001), the wait this time was not nearly as long, and all three watched with pride (and amazement) as the Albion went one better in winning the Div 2 title in 2002.

John Northcutt *(West Ham United):* Has supported the Hammers since 1959 and is the co-author of West Ham books, *The Complete Record* and the *Illustrated History.* A regular contributor to the club programme, John was the club adviser to the *Ultimate Football Guide.* He also answers all the questions put to the Vintage Claret section on the club's web site.

Richard Owen *(Portsmouth):* A life-long supporter and official club historian for Portsmouth, Richard performs several jobs for the club as labour of love and has been a regular contributor to the club programme for the past 24 years, missing only a handful of away games in the past 26 years, having watched Pompey on 105 league grounds. An avid programme collector, with almost a complete set of post-war Portsmouth home and away issues, he co-published in 1998 the *Centenary Pictorial History of Portsmouth FC* and *A team collection,* which featured every team picture of Pompey since 1898, and is due to publish his third book, *100 Pompey Legends* in Autumn 2002. Has now built up a full library of club histories on all British Football League clubs.

Steve Peart and **Dave Finch** *(Wycombe Wanderers):* A former programme editor of the club and a supporter for over 20 years, Steve put together the player profiles, while the club statistics were supplied by Dave, the official Wycombe statistician. Both were authors of *Wycombe Wanderers 1887-1996 - The Official History,* published in 1996. Dave has supported Wycombe regularly since 1964 and is the club's statistician, having been part of their programme editorial team since 1990.

Steve Phillipps *(Rochdale):* A Rochdale supporter for nearly 40 years, and the club's official historian, Steve is the author of *The Survivors, The story of Rochdale AFC* (1990), *The Definitive Rochdale* (1995) and, more recently, *The Official History of Rochdale AFC.* A founder member of the AFS, away from football he is a university lecturer.

6

Terry Phillips *(Cardiff City):* Chief soccer writer for the *South Wales Echo* since 1994, and a sports journalist for over 30 years – *Kent Evening Post* (1970-1977), *Derby Evening Telegraph* (1977-1986), *Gloucester Citizen* (1986-1994) – Terry has previously covered clubs at all levels, including Brian Clough's Nottingham Forest, Derby County, Gillingham, and Gloucester City. His specialist subjects are Cardiff City FC and Cardiff Devils (Ice Hockey).

Andrew Pinfield *(Halifax Town):* The club's Commercial Manager besides being the Programme Editor, Andrew has a keen interest in football memorabilia, something which saw him open his own business in February, trading in the football memorabilia market. Never misses a first-team Halifax Town fixture, both home and away.

Alan Platt *(Liverpool):* Is a dedicated football statistician and a follower of Liverpool FC since 1960, and whilst resident in London, a member and official of the London branch of the LFC Supporters Club. He has assisted Barry Hugman in an editorial capacity on all his football publications since 1980, namely the four updates of the *Football League Players Records*, the two editions of *Premier League Players* and, for the last seven years, the *PFA Who's Who* (formerly the *Factfile*) when not working overseas in his profession of transport planner. Now resident in Manchester, his main interest today is in non-league football and he keeps detailed records on all the senior semi-professional leagues, having compiled a database of over 6,000 players participating in that level of football.

Kevan Platt *(Norwich City):* Kevan has now completed 22 years employ with Norwich City FC, fulfilling a number of roles, before being appointed Club Secretay in December 1998. A keen amateur statistician, he is a former programme editor and contributor to the club's annual handbook and more recently had the pleasure of co-authoring the club's official centenary publication *Canary Citizens - Centenary Edition*. The club's centenary year has kept him really busy, allowing him to trace almost every former Norwich City player. A regular supporter of some 34 years standing, Kevan is no less enthusiastic about his team's progress now than when he was a regular attendee on the Barclay End terrace.

Dave Prentice *(Everton):* As the Everton correspondent for the *Liverpool Echo* since 1993 and author of a club history five years earlier, when he was reporting on both Everton and Liverpool for the *Daily Post*, Dave completed his Mersey set when reporting on Tranmere Rovers for three years from 1990.

Mike Purkiss *(Crystal Palace):* Having supported Palace since 1950 and producing stats on them since 1960, Mike is the author of the *Complete History of Crystal Palace, 1905-1989*. Was the club statistician for the *Ultimate Football Guide* and also contributed to *Premier League: The Players*.

Mick Renshaw *(Sheffield Wednesday):* Has followed Wednesday for over 40 years and is a great supporter of European soccer. Mick also produced the club section for the *Ultimate Football Guide*.

Mick Robinson *(Peterborough United):* Another life-long fan, for a number of years Mick has contributed to the club programme and was the joint editor of the *Official Peterborough History*. Was also club statistician for the *Ultimate Football Guide*.

Phil Sherwin *(Port Vale):* Phil is the Port Vale club statistician and has been a fan since 1968, when they had to seek re-election to the old Fourth Division. Travelling to away games since 1973, he has only missed a handful of games since then and has contributed to the club programme, various books on the club, the now defunct *League Directory*, and the local newspaper, as well as radio and television.

Mike Slater *(Wolverhampton Wanderers):* The Wolves'

contributor to this publication since its inception, Mike wrote a book on the club's history called *Molineux Memories*, which he published in 1988. Well-known as the eight-time compiler of the *Brain of Wolves' Quiz*, he also produced a booklet in 1996 containing all of Wolves' competitive results and records against every other club.

Gordon Small *(Hartlepool United):* Has supported Pools since October 1965, experiencing two promotions, two relegations, and several close calls. He found 2001-02 to be particularly memorable, as it was the first time that Hartlepool had managed three successive above average seasons since he began supporting them.

Dave Smith *(Leicester City):* Dave has been the official Leicester City statistician and historian for many years. He is a regular contributor to both the club programme and the local press. Is also the co-author of a number of succesful hardback books on the club history, notably *Of Fossils & Foxes* which was comprehensively updated and redesigned in 2001 and *The Foxes Alphabet*, which was last published in 1995. He also edited the 2002 publication *Farewell to Filbert Street*, which was published by the club to mark the end of an era at the Foxes' traditional home.

Gerry Somerton *(Rotherham United):* A contributor to the *Factfile* (now *Who's Who*) since its inception, Gerry is the deputy sports editor of the *Rotherham Advertiser* and has followed the club now for over 50 years. He is co-editor of the club's matchday programme and has written three books about the club with his latest venture – *The Ronnie Moore Story* — becoming the town's best selling book last year. He is the club's historian and also acts as summariser for the Millers' games on BBC Radio Sheffield.

Paul Stead *(Huddersfield Town):* A life-long supporter of his hometown football club, and a regular spectator home and away, Paul is now in his fifth year with the publication.

David Steele *(Carlisle United):* David has been involved with the *Who's Who* since its inception in 1995. Has also been a regular contributor to the Carlisle matchday programme since 1989, as well as giving assistance to a wide variety of publications on matters connected with the club's history.

Richard Stocken *(Shrewsbury Town):* Still following Shrewsbury Town for almost 50 years through thick and mostly thin, Richard is a collector of club programmes and memorabilia and has contributed to a number of publications over the years. Due to write a best seller on Shrewsbury come retirement, he is a senior manager with one of the big four banks in his spare time.

Bill Swann *(Newcastle United):* A supporter since the Jackie Milburn days of the early 1950s, and a long-term shareholder in the club, along with his wife and three children (all season ticket holders), he is a keen collector of memorabilia connected with the club, and a member of the AFS. Has consolidated his information on club matches, teams, scorers, and players into a data base for easy access and analysis. Bill assisted in the production of the club's volume in the *Complete Record* series, and this is his seventh year as a contributor to this publication. His 16 year-old son Richard, also a Newcastle fanatic, supplied much of the 'anorak' information in the player biographies.

Colin Tattum *(Birmingham City):* Colin is the chief sports writer of the Birmingham Evening Mail newspaper and as the paper's Birmingham City correspondent, he has covered the fortunes of the club for almost ten years.

Paul Taylor *(Mansfield Town):* A Mansfield Town supporter of over 30 years standing, Paul has contributed to many publications over the last few years, including the club's centenary history published in 1997. He is the club's official historian, the Official Mansfield Town Statistician for the AFS and is also President of the Stags Supporters Association (formed this season from the old Stags Supporter's Club and Support Our Stags members club).

Richard and **Sarah Taylor** and **Ian Mills** *(Notts County):* Richard is a life-long Notts County fan from a Notts County family, travelling the length and breadth of the land in following the Magpies, and has seen them on all but a few current league grounds and many non-current grounds too. In the summer, he umpires cricket matches to while away the close season. Sarah, like her father and two brothers, became a dedicated fan at an early age and has made regular excursions home from university to support the Magpies. Having seen his first game at Gay Meadow in 1959-60, Ian, who ran the matchday programme sales, has been hooked ever since, missing just one match since 1970.

Les Triggs *(Grimsby Town):* A retired librarian, Les first saw the Mariners in a wartime league match whilst the club was in exile at Scunthorpe's Old Show Ground, and has been a regular supporter since their days as a then First Division club. Became involved in the historical side of the club when asked to assist in the staging of the Centenary Exhibition in 1978. The co-author of the Grimsby Town volume in the *Complete Record* series, and the Grimsby statistician for the former *Ultimate Football Guide*, he is also an occasional contributor to the club fanzine.

Roger Triggs *(Gillingham):* Roger has been a Gillingham supporter for over 40 years and has been collecting statistics and records on the club since he was a schoolboy. Co-author of the highly acclaimed centenary book *Home of the Shouting Men*, produced in 1993, Roger has since produced his images collection in conjunction with Tempus Publishing Company and in August 2001 brought out a complete *Who's Who of Gillingham's Football League Players 1920-1938 & 1950-2001*.

Frank Tweddle *(Darlington):* The club's official historian and statistician, Frank has contributed articles to the Darlington programme for the last 27 seasons and has avidly supported the Quakers for well over 40 years. As well as being a member of the 92 Club and the AFS, he is the author of *Darlington's Centenary History* published in 1983 and *The Definitive Darlington 1883 - 2000*, as well as producing work for various other football publications.

Paul Voller *(Ipswich Town):* Has been a life-long Ipswich

Town fan and started attending matches at Portman Road in 1963. A member of the Ipswich Town Supporters Media Committee, he edits the supporters page in the matchday magazine and the supporters weekly page in the local *Evening Star*. Was the Ipswich statistician for the *Rothmans Yearbooks* and the *Football Club Directories* during the 1990's. Joint Author of *The Essential History of Ipswich Town*, published last year.

Tony Woodburn and **Martin Atherton** *(Preston North End):* Both North End fans for over 30 years, Tony and Martin provide statistical and historical information on the club for the National Football Museum's permanent Preston North End collection, as well as writing for the club programme and, of course, the *Who's Who*. Tony is a member of the Association of Football Statisticians, the 92 Club and the Scottish 38 Club, whilst Martin has recently written a history regarding the theft of the Jules Rimet trophy in 1966 on behalf of the National Football Museum.

David Woods *(Bristol City):* An Ashton Gate regular since March 1958, and a shareholder since 1972, David has written four books on Bristol City, the most recent being *Bristol City – The Modern Era 1967-2000*, published by Desert Island. A life-member of the recently defunct Association of Football Statisticians as well as belonging to the 92 Club after first completing visiting all the Football League grounds at Lincoln on 18 April 1970. Recently approached to take on the role of Official Club Historian, a position that he formerly held from 1982-1986, David was the Bristol City Statistician to *Rothmans Football Yearbook* in 1983-84 and the *Football Club Directory* from 1985 to 1998. He has had two spells (1982-86 and 1995-97) of writing regularly in the Bristol City programme, as well as featuring in the Bristol Rovers' publication from 1987-1993. Currently researching in regard to a possible book on ex-City great, John Atyeo, he has also written articles for the *Footballer Magazine* and has recently had published a history on *Bristol Bulldogs Speedway*. A graduate of the Open University, David's other interests include geology, history, cricket (Gloucestershire), rugby (Bristol) and tennis.

Finally, on the production side of the book, my thanks go to Jean Bastin, of Typecast (Artwork & Design) for her patience and diligent work on the typesetting and design, which again went far beyond the call of normal duty and was much appreciated.

The Windsor Insurance Group, through this excellent publication, continues its close association with professional football that was first established nearly 30 years ago. Together with the Professional Footballers' Association, we manage the Players' Permanent Disablement Fund, whereby every registered player in the English leagues receives an insurance benefit if his career is ended through injury or sickness.

Our close links with the Professional Footballers' Association and our knowledge of the game, give us a unique position from which to offer advice on insurance-related matters to all in football. As in years gone by, we are more than happy to continue to support the *Who's Who*, formerly known as the *Factfile*.

Jonathan Ticehurst
Managing Director of the Sports Division, Windsor Insurance Brokers Ltd

PROFESSIONAL FOOTBALLERS' ASSOCIATION

PFA

PENSIONS

TRANSFERS

LEGAL ADVICE

FINANCIAL HELP

CONTRACTS

ACCIDENT INSURANCE

EDUCATION

YOUTH TRAINING

PERSONAL REPRESENTATION

COMMERCIAL AFFAIRS

PLAYERS UNITED

THE OUTCASTS FC

THE PFA SAYS LET'S KICK RACISM OUT OF FOOTBALL

it's only the colour of the shirt that counts

FOUNDED AT THE IMPERIAL HOTEL, MANCHESTER IN 1907, THE PROFESSIONAL FOOTBALLERS' ASSOCIATION TODAY COMMANDS AN ENVIABLE REPUTATION AS THE WORLD'S LONGEST-ESTABLISHED PROFESSIONAL SPORTSMEN'S UNION.

This status stands as testament to the unswerving determination, dedication and commitment of all its contributors, from its earliest forefathers such as Billy Meredith right through to its current Management Committee.

The result is that the PFA is now involved in every aspect of a player's career, from financial management and pensions, to education and training, coaching, commercial, accident insurance and medical & benevolent assistance.

The PFA is also a key factor in both the Youth Training/Football Scholarship Scheme and Football In The Community Programme, ensuring that the players of tomorrow receive the best possible start to their careers.

20 Oxford Court, Bishopsgate, Manchester M2 3WQ

Panasonic

Foreword

I am extremely pleased to give the PFA's full endorsement and recommendation to *Footballers' Who's Who*. In this modern age of such tremendous interest in the professional football game it is good to have at hand the definitive book on statistics and profiles for every one of our members playing in first-team football throughout the Premier League and Football League in England and Wales.

This book gives the background to what the game is all about – the players. Having to deal with 4,000 PFA members, the book gives me a valuable source of information in an easily accessible, attractive and enjoyable format. It is a must for anybody involved in the game as an administrator, player, manager, spectator and commentator and is especially invaluable for any football 'Brain of Britain' or football quiz aspirant!

The World Cup in Japan and Korea had more players from our leagues than any other country in the world – they are all in here giving the book a truly international flavour.

The publication has been compiled by Barry Hugman, whose record in this field is unsurpassed. Barry has a team of over 90 people who provide him with the invaluable aspects of local information which gives this book such credibility.

Gordon Taylor
Chief Executive, The Professional Footballers' Association

Editorial Introduction

Following on from last year's edition which was published as the *Factfile*, the *Who's Who* portrays the statistical career record of every FA Barclaycard Premiership and Nationwide League player who made an appearance in 2001-02, whether it be in league football, the Football League Cup (Worthington Cup), FA Cup (Sponsored by AXA), Charity Shield, European Cup, UEFA Cup, Inter-Toto Cup, or in the Play Offs. Not included are Welsh Cup matches. It goes beyond mere statistics, however, with a write up on all of the 2,300 plus players involved, and also records faithfully last season's playing records separately by club.

The work falls into three sections, all inter-relating. Firstly, the main core, PFA Footballers' Who's Who: A-Z (pages 13 to 452); secondly, FA Barclaycard Premiership and Nationwide League Clubs: Summary of Appearances and Goals for 2001-02 (pages 453 to 474); and thirdly, Where Did They Go? (pages 475 to 479); lists all players shown in the previous edition who either moved on or did not play in 2001-02. Below is an explanation on how to follow the *PFA Footballers' Who's Who*.

As the title suggests, all players are listed in alphabetical order and are shown by Surnames first, followed by full Christian names, with the one the player is commonly known by shown in **bold**. Any abbreviation or pseudonym is bracketed.

Birthplace/date: You will note that several players who would be predominately classified as British, were born in places like Germany and India, for example. My book, *Premier and Football League Players' Records*, which covers every man who has played league football since the war, has, in the past, used the family domicile as a more realistic "birthplace". But, for our purposes here, I have reverted to that which has been officially recorded.

Height and Weight: Listed in feet and inches, and stones and pounds, respectively. It must be remembered that a player's weight can frequently change and, on that basis, the recorded data should be used as a guide only, especially as they would have been weighed several times during the season.

Club Honours: Those shown, cover careers from the Conference and FA Trophy upwards. For abbreviations, read:- European Honours: EC (European Cup), ESC (European Super Cup), ECWC (European Cup Winners' Cup) and UEFAC. English Honours: FAC (FA Cup), FLC (Football League Cup), CS (Charity Shield), FMC (Full Members Cup, which takes in the Simod and Zenith Data sponsorships), AMC (Associated Members Cup - Freight Rover, Sherpa Van, Leyland DAF, Autoglass, Auto Windscreens and LDV Vans), AIC (Anglo-Italian Cup), GMVC (GM Vauxhall Conference), FC (Football Conference), NC (Nationwide Conference), FAT (FA Trophy), FAYC (FA Youth Cup). Scottish Honours: SPD (Scottish Premier Division), S Div 1/2 (Scottish Leagues), SC (Scottish Cup), SLC (Scottish League Cup). Welsh Honours: WC (Welsh Cup). Please note that medals awarded to P/FL, FLC, and AMC winners relate to players who have appeared in 25%, or over, of matches, while FAC, EC, and UEFAC winners medals are for all-named finalists, including unused subs. For our purposes,

however, Charity Shield winners' medals refer to men who either played or came on as a sub. Honours applicable to players coming in from abroad are not shown at present, but the position will be reviewed in future editions.

International Honours: For abbreviations, read:- E (England), NI (Northern Ireland), S (Scotland), W (Wales) and Ei (Republic of Ireland). Under 21 through to full internationals give total appearances (inclusive of subs), while schoolboy (U16s and U18s) and youth representatives are just listed. The cut-off date used for appearances was up to and including 30 June.

Player Descriptions: Gives position and playing strengths and, in keeping the work topical, a few words on how their season went in 2001-02. This takes into account, in a positive fashion, key performances, along with value to the team, injuries, honours, and other points of interest, etc.

Career Records: Full appearances, plus substitutes and goals, are given for all Carling Premiership and Nationwide League games and, if a player who is in the book has played in any of the senior Scottish Leagues, his appearances with the club in question will also be recorded at the point of signing. Other information given, includes the origination of players (clubs in the non-leagues, junior football, or from abroad), registered signing dates (if a player signs permanently following a loan spell, for our purposes, we have shown the initial date as being the point of temporary transfer. Also, loan transfers are only recorded if an appearance is made), transfer fees (these are the figures that have been reported in newspapers and magazines and should only be used as a guide to a player's valuation). Last season's appearances, substitutions and goals are recorded by P/FL (Premiership and Football League), PL (Premier League), FL (Football League), FLC (Football League Cup), FAC (FA Cup), and Others. Other matches took in the Play Offs, LDV Vans Trophy, Charity Shield, and European competitions, such as the European Cup, UEFA Cup, European Super Cup and Intertoto Cup. All of these matches are lumped together for reasons of saving space. Scottish appearances for players on loan to P/FL clubs in 2001-02 are shown at the point of transfer and do not include games following their return to Scotland. That also applies to players transferred from England to Scotland.

Career statistics are depicted as
Appearances + Substitutes/Goals

Whether you wish to analyse someone for your fantasy football team selection or would like to know more about a little-known player appearing in the lower reaches of the game, the *PFA Footballers' Who's Who* should provide you with the answer.

Barry J. Hugman, Editor, PFA Footballers' Who's Who

Match Winning Tackle?

OR

Career Ending Injury?

ABBEY George Peterson
Born: Port Harcourt, Nigeria, 20 October 1978
Height: 5'10" **Weight:** 10.10
George's opportunities for Macclesfield Town were limited during the earlier part of the 2001-02 season due to the form of Steve Hitchen at right back. He put in some useful performances during a spell of 12 consecutive matches, but rarely featured after the appointment of David Moss. An attacking full back who always plays enthusiastically, is capable of making long accurate passes and again showed improvement in his overall game.
Macclesfield T (Signed from Sharks FC, Port Harcourt, Nigeria on 20/8/1999) FL 40+13 FLC 4+1 FAC 2+2 Others 1

ABBEY Nathanael (Nathan)
Born: Islington, 11 July 1978
Height: 6'1" **Weight:** 12.0
Nathan joined Chesterfield shortly before the start of the 2001-02 campaign and after working with coach Andy Leaning his performances in goal improved immeasurably. His all-round game – handling, kicking and concentration – came on to such an extent that he assumed near-hero status among supporters until his refusal of a new contract offer led to his release in May.
Luton T (From trainee on 2/5/1996) FL 54+1 FLC 3 FAC 8 Others 2
Chesterfield (Free on 10/8/2001) FL 46 FLC 1 FAC 3 Others 3

ABBEY Zema
Born: Luton, 17 April 1977
Height: 6'1" **Weight:** 12.11
Zema is an athletic front-runner possessing great pace. Unfortunately, after making a promising start to his first full season at Carrow Road he suffered a serious cruciate ligament injury at Rotherham in mid-September that ended his campaign. He recovered well to feature in the last reserve match of the campaign and will be very eager for season 2002-03 to arrive.
Cambridge U (Signed from Hitchin T on 11/2/2000) FL 16+6/5 FLC 1+1 FAC 1 Others 1
Norwich C (£350,000 on 15/12/2000) FL 17+9/2 FLC 1

ACHTERBERG John
Born: Utrecht, Holland, 8 July 1971
Height: 6'1" **Weight:** 13.8
John again shared the goalkeeping duties with his younger rival Joe Murphy for Tranmere in the early part of the 2001-02 season, before becoming a fixture in the line-up from early December. He deserved his extended run, as his calm efficiency and good handling skills kept the team in several matches, while he achieved ten clean sheets during the campaign.
Tranmere Rov (Free from PSV Eindhoven, Holland, ex NAC Breda, on 22/9/1998) FL 97+3 FLC 11+1 FAC 11

ACUNA Donoso Clarence Williams
Born: Coya Rancagua, Chile, 8 February 1975
Height: 5'8" **Weight:** 11.6
International Honours: Chile: 59; Yth
After spending the summer recovering from tendonitis this, Newcastle midfielder missed the early Inter Toto Cup ties, although he was in the starting line-up for the opening Premiership game at Chelsea when he scored a late equaliser to earn the club's first point of the season. Thereafter he was used mostly as a substitute, although his best game probably came when he started the home FA Cup quarter final against Arsenal in which he had an excellent game. He is a stocky, energetic ballwinner who rarely tries anything extravagant, and as a result he is very reliable and consistent and is clearly an important part of Newcastle's first-team squad.
Newcastle U (£900,000 from Universidad de Chile, ex O'Higgins, on 25/10/2000) PL 33+9/6 FLC 2+1 FAC 5+2/1 Others 0+1

ADAMCZUK Dariusz
Born: Szczecin, Poland, 21 October 1969
Height: 5'10" **Weight:** 12.0
Club Honours: S Div 1 '98; SPD '00
International Honours: Poland 11
Dariusz joined Wigan Athletic at the start of the 2001-02 season on a three-month loan spell from Glasgow Rangers, making his debut in the opening match. Unfortunately he suffered an ankle injury after just three League matches and returned to Ibrox before his loan spell had expired. He is a versatile and experienced right-sided defensive midfield player who can also play in a full-back position.
Dundee (Signed from Pogan Szczecin, Poland on 18/1/1996) SL 95+7/8 SLC 7 SC 8+1 Others 3
Glasgow R (Free on 13/7/1999) SL 6+7 SLC 1 Others 5

Wigan Ath (Loaned on 10/8/2001) FL 3 FLC 1

ADAMS Daniel (Danny) Benjamin
Born: Manchester, 3 January 1976
Height: 5'8" **Weight:** 13.8
Danny is a firm favourite of the Macclesfield fans for his forceful play, a feature that was well to the fore during the FA Cup third round tie against West Ham. He missed several matches last autumn with a groin strain but made the left-back position his own, although he performed equally well in a wing-back role when required. A gritty and determined player especially when tackling, he is an accurate passer of the ball and won the Macclesfield 'Player of the Year' award.
Macclesfield T (£25,000 from Altrincham on 31/8/2000) FL 74+2 FLC 2+1 FAC 5 Others 1

ADAMS Stephen (Steve) Marc
Born: Plymouth, 25 September 1980
Height: 6'0" **Weight:** 11.10
Club Honours: Div 3 '02
Steve had an excellent season at Plymouth in 2001-02, playing a part in every game for the Third Division champions. Quiet and unassuming he was a revelation in the holding midfield role and manager Paul Sturrock described his contribution as "immense". He scored two goals including a thunderous 12-yard header against Southend in November. Steve was voted 'Young Player of the Season' for the second year running by the Argyle supporters.
Plymouth Arg (From trainee on 6/7/1999) FL 53+11/2 FLC 1 FAC 3+2 Others 2+1

ADAMS Tony Alexander
Born: Romford, 10 October 1966
Height: 6'3" **Weight:** 13.11
Club Honours: Div 1 '89, '91; PL '98, '02; FLC '87, '93; FAC '93, '98. '02; ECWC '94; CS '98
International Honours: E: 66; B-4; U21-5; Yth
Now very much in the veteran stage of his career, Tony continued to captain Arsenal and provide inspiration to the side. Niggling injuries and manager Arsene Wenger's plans to reduce the average age of the Gunners' back line combined to restrict his appearances, but he remained as dominant as ever - strong in the tackle and very effective in the air.
Arsenal (From apprentice on 30/1/1984) F/PL 500+4/32 FLC 58+1/5 FAC 53+1/8 Others 55/4

ADAMSON Christopher (Chris)

Born: Ashington, 4 November 1978
Height: 5'1" **Weight:** 11.0
Chris spent most of the 2001-02 season as third choice 'keeper at West Bromwich Albion but joined Plymouth on loan in January to cover for an injury crisis. He played in the 2-1 win against Scunthorpe when he made several crucial saves to keep Argyle's title charge going.
West Bromwich A (From trainee on 2/7/1997) FL 12 FAC 2
Mansfield T (Loaned on 30/4/1999) FL 2
Halifax T (Loaned on 1/7/1999) FL 7
Plymouth Arg (Loaned on 10/1/2001) FL 1

ADEBOLA Bamberdele (Dele)

Born: Lagos, Nigeria, 23 June 1975
Height: 6'3" **Weight:** 12.8
After being sidelined for 11 months with a knee injury, Dele agreed to drop a division and spent a month on loan at Oldham last March. Birmingham sanctioned the move to provide first-team football and get the player back to fitness. After making a promising debut in the 2-2 draw at Reading, he went on to make a total of five appearances for Athletic without scoring.
Crewe Alex (From trainee on 21/6/1993) FL 98+26/39 FLC 4+3/2 FAC 8+2/3 Others 10+1/2
Birmingham C (£1,000,000 on 6/2/1998) FL 86+43/31 FLC 13+4/8 FAC 2+1/2 Others 1+2/1
Oldham Ath (Loaned on 20/3/2002) FL 5

AFFUL Leslie (Les) Samuel

Born: Liverpool, 4 February 1984
Height: 5'4" **Weight:** 9.12
Les made his debut in senior football for Exeter City as a substitute in the dying minutes of the FA Cup first round tie against Cambridge City and also saw first-team action again in the final two league games of the 2001-02 season. A very promising young striker he impressed manager John Cornforth enough to be handed a professional deal at the end of the campaign.
Exeter C (Trainee) FL 0+2 FAC 0+1

AGGREY James (Jimmy) Emmanuel

Born: Hammersmith, 26 October 1978
Height: 6'3" **Weight:** 13.6
Torquay's 'Player of the Season' in 2000-01, Jimmy looked set to mature into a commanding central defender. However, he was dropped by Gulls' manager Roy McFarland following the home defeat by

York and never regained his first-team place. His contract was subsequently cancelled by mutual consent and in December he signed for Conference outfit Dover.
Fulham (From trainee at Chelsea on 2/7/1997)
Airdrieonians (Free on 30/6/1998)
Torquay U (Free on 22/10/1998) FL 87+8/2 FLC 4 FAC 5+1 Others 5

AGOGO Manuel (Junior)

Born: Accra, Ghana, 1 August 1979
Height: 5'10" **Weight:** 11.7
This speedy striker returned to England last March after spending two seasons in the MLS. He joined Queen's Park Rangers on non-contract forms and made appearances from the subs' bench in the end-of-season games at Swindon and Oldham.
Sheffield Wed (Signed from Willesden Constantine on 8/10/1996) PL 0+2 FAC 0+1 (Free to Colorado Rapids, USA on 2/2/2000)
Oldham Ath (Loaned on 18/7/1999) FL 2
Chester C (Loaned on 3/9/1999) FL 10/6
Chesterfield (Loaned on 11/11/1999) FL 3+1
Lincoln C (Loaned on 17/12/1999) FL 3/1
Queens Park R (Free from San Jose Earthquakes, USA on 28/3/2002) FL 0+2

AGYEMANG Patrick

Born: Walthamstow, 29 September 1980
Height: 6'1" **Weight:** 12.0
Patrick proved to be an adequate replacement striker for Wimbledon last term. His big strength is his pace, which enables him to leave defenders in his wake. He proved to be at his most dangerous playing out wide where his challenging runs left the opposition defence in tatters.
Wimbledon (From trainee on 11/5/1999) FL 33+29/8 FLC 1+2 FAC 6+2/1
Brentford (Loaned on 18/10/1999) FL 3+9 FAC 1

AINSWORTH Gareth

Born: Blackburn, 10 May 1973
Height: 5'9" **Weight:** 12.5
Gareth had another season plagued by injury in 2001-02, and only managed to play 32 minutes of football for Wimbledon. Due to financial constraints he was advised that he wouldn't be offered a new contract and was loaned to Preston, where he impressed with some strong wing play. He is a player who rolls his sleeves up and makes things happen for the team and will be remembered with fondness for his barnstorming runs down the right flank. Gareth proved he is a top man by supporting Lincoln in their

time of need, by buying seats and offering items for auction.
Preston NE (Signed from Northwich Vic, ex Blackburn Rov YTS, on 21/1/1992) FL 2+3 Others 1/1
Cambridge U (Free on 17/8/1992) FL 1+3/1 FLC 0+1
Preston NE (Free on 23/12/1992) FL 76+6/12 FLC 3+2 FAC 3+1 Others 8+1/1
Lincoln C (£25,000 on 31/10/1995) FL 83/37 FLC 8/3 FAC 2 Others 4/1
Port Vale (£500,000 on 12/9/1997) FL 53+2/10 FLC 2/1 FAC 2
Wimbledon (£2,000,000 on 3/11/1998) P/FL 13+11/4 FAC 5+1/1
Preston NE (Loaned on 28/3/2002) FL 3+2/1

AISTON Samuel (Sam) James

Born: Newcastle, 21 November 1976
Height: 6'1" **Weight:** 12.10
Club Honours: Div 1 '96
International Honours: E: Sch
The skilful left winger had his pre-season interrupted by injury last term and did not make his first full appearance for Shrewsbury until September. He never really had a significant run of games and made most of his contribution from the bench, often coming on to partner one of the strikers. He was placed on the transfer list in January but showed a greater consistency in the latter stages of the campaign.
Sunderland (Free from Newcastle U juniors on 14/7/1995) P/FL 5+15 FLC 0+2 FAC 0+2
Chester C (Loaned on 21/2/1997) FL 14 FLC 1 Others 2
Chester C (Loaned on 27/11/1998) FL 11 Others 1
Stoke C (Loaned on 6/8/1999) FL 2+4 FLC 1
Shrewsbury T (Loaned on 24/12/1999) FL 10
Shrewsbury T (Free on 21/7/2000) FL 62+15/4 FLC 2 FAC 1+1

AKINBIYI Adeola (Ade) Peter

Born: Hackney, 10 October 1974
Height: 6'1" **Weight:** 12.9
International Honours: Nigeria: 1
This strong and speedy striker cost Leicester a club record fee in July 2000 but never really seemed settled at Filbert Street. Although he never gave less than 100 per cent in effort, his confidence in front of goal was gradually eroded as the campaign progressed. He was eventually sold to Crystal Palace where he impressed with his work rate but still found goals hard to come by.
Norwich C (From trainee on 5/2/1993) P/FL 22+27/3 FLC 2+4/2 FAC 1+2 Others 0+1
Hereford U (Loaned on 21/1/1994) FL 3+1/2
Brighton & Hove A (Loaned on 24/11/1994) FL 7/4

Colin Alcide

Gillingham (£250,000 on 13/1/1997) FL 63/28 FLC 2 FAC 2/1 Others 0+1
Bristol C (£1,200,000 on 28/5/1998) FL 47/21 FLC 5/4 FAC 1
Wolverhampton W (£3,500,000 on 7/9/1999) FL 36+1/16
Leicester C (£5,000,000 on 28/7/2000) PL 49+9/11 FLC 1/1 FAC 5+1/1 Others 2
Crystal Palace (£2,200,000 + on 6/2/2002) FL 9+5/2

ALCIDE Colin James
Born: Huddersfield, 14 April 1972
Height: 6'2" **Weight:** 13.10
This tall powerful striker joined Cambridge United during the 2001 close season, linking up again with his former boss John Beck. Although he made the starting line-up in the opening games an achilles injury ruled him out and soon further injury problems meant that he made no further appearances after the end of November.
Lincoln C (£15,000 from Emley on 5/12/1995) FL 105+16/26 FLC 7+2/2 FAC 3+3/2 Others 3+1
Hull C (Loaned on 4/2/1999) FL 5/1
Hull C (£50,000 on 10/3/1999) FL 22+2/3 FLC 3+1/2 FAC 0+2
York C (£80,000 on 23/11/1999) FL 33+20/7 FLC 1 FAC 2+1/1 Others 2
Cambridge U (£30,000 on 8/6/2001) FL 7+1 FLC 1/1 FAC 1 Others 1

ALDERTON Rio Kevin
Born: Colchester, 12 August 1982
Height: 6'0" **Weight:** 12.0
After failing to make a breakthrough at Millwall, Rio joined Southend United on a short-term contract just before last season's transfer deadline. A tall and well-built central midfielder, his performances in the reserve team earned him two substitute appearances in the final two games of the campaign.
Millwall (From trainee on 23/7/2001)
Southend U (Free on 28/3/2002) FL 0+2

ALEXANDER Gary George
Born: Lambeth, 15 August 1979
Height: 5'11" **Weight:** 13.0
Gary moved north in the 2001 close season to form a productive attacking partnership with Hull's new record signing Lawrie Dudfield. He went on to become the first Tiger to net 20 goals in a season since 1996-97 and won City's 'Player of the Year' award. Big, brave, extremely hardworking and always prepared to shoot on sight, he also bagged the club's 'Goal of the Season' prize with a sensational 30-yard effort at Rushden in October.

Graham Alexander

West Ham U *(From trainee on 6/7/1998)*
Exeter C *(Loaned on 19/8/1999) FL 37/16
FLC 1 FAC 3/1 Others 4/2*
Swindon T *(£300,000 on 11/8/2000) FL
30+7/7 FLC 3 FAC 2+1 Others 2+1/2*
Hull C *(£160,000 on 21/6/2001) FL 43/17
FLC 2/1 FAC 2/2 Others 3/3*

ALEXANDER Graham
Born: Coventry, 10 October 1971
Height: 5'10" **Weight:** 12.7
Club Honours: Div 2 '00
International Honours: S: 3
Preston's regular right-back made his
400th Football League appearance on the
opening day of 2001-02 and went on to
miss only one game all season. Sound in
defence, Graham loves to get forward,
from where he can deliver telling crosses
and long-range strikes at goal. He also
remained the first-choice penalty taker,
and his successes included a first minute
spot kick against Norwich. Graham
became North End's first full Scottish
international for over 40 years when he
came on as a second-half substitute
against Nigeria and was also selected for
the PFA's Division One team.
Scunthorpe U *(From trainee on 20/3/1990)
FL 149+10/18 FLC 11+1/2 FAC 12/1 Others
13+3/3*
Luton T *(£100,000 on 8/7/1995) FL
146+4/15 FLC 17/2 FAC 6+1 Others 6+2*
Preston NE *(£50,000 on 25/3/1999) FL
135/17 FLC 11/3 FAC 9/4 Others 6*

ALEXANDER Neil
Born: Edinburgh, 10 March 1978
Height: 6'1" **Weight:** 11.0
Club Honours: S Div 2 '99; S Div 1 '01
International Honours: S: U21-10
After helping Livingston earn promotion
to the Scottish Premier League in 2000-
01, Neil joined Cardiff City in the close
season and went on to become the
Bluebirds only ever-present last term. A
promising young 'keeper he was called up
by Scotland manager Bertie Vogts for the
tour to the Far East where he sat on the
bench in all three matches.
Stenhousemuir *(Free from Edina Hibs on
8/8/1996) SL 48 SLC 1 SC 1 Others 1*
Livingston *(Signed on 22/8/1998) SL 60 SLC
2 SC 8 Others 5*
Cardiff C *((£200,000 on 6/8/2001) FL 46 FLC
1 FAC 4 Others 2*

ALEXANDERSSON Niclas
Born: Halmstad, Sweden, 29 December
1971
Height: 6'2" **Weight:** 11.8
International Honours: Sweden: 63
A hard-working right winger with the
ability to deliver telling crosses, as well as
tackle back and protect his full back,
Niclas has long been a fixture in the
Swedish national team. He was absent
from Everton's team on only a handful of
occasions last season, but had to wait
until March for his first goal.
Sheffield Wed *(£750,000 from Gothenburg,
Sweden, ex Halmstad, on 9/12/1997) PL
73+2/8 FLC 4+1/2 FAC 8/2*
Everton *(£2,500,000 on 20/7/2000) PL
45+6/4 FLC 2 FAC 4+1*

ALIADIERE Jeremie
Born: Rambouillet, France, 30 March
1983
Height: 6'0" **Weight:** 11.8
Club Honours: FAYC '01
This promising young striker made his
senior debut for Arsenal in the
Worthington Cup tie against Grimsby
Town and also featured in the same
competition against Blackburn. He played
his first Premiership game for the Gunners
when he came on as a late substitute for
Thierry Henry against Fulham in February.
Arsenal *(From trainee on 4/4/2000) PL 0+1
FLC 0+2*

ALLAN Jonathan (Jonny)
Michael
Born: Carlisle, 24 May 1983
Height: 5'10" **Weight:** 11.12
Jonny was one of several youngsters who
forced their way into regular contention
at Carlisle during the 2001-02 campaign.
A promising striker, the majority of his 28
League appearances were off the bench
but he showed considerable aplomb in
the manner in which he scored his two
goals.
Carlisle U *(From trainee on 24/5/2000) FL
10+19/2 FLC 0+1 FAC 0+1 Others 0+1*

ALLEN Bradley James
Born: Romford, 13 September 1971
Height: 5'8" **Weight:** 11.0
International Honours: E: U21-8; Yth
2001-02 proved another frustrating
season for Bradley as a combination of
injuries and increased competition for
places limited his opportunities for
Grimsby and he spent much of his time
on the substitutes' bench. A change of
manager midway through the campaign
saw an upturn in his fortunes and he
developed a fine partnership up front
with Mick Boulding, which helped pull
the Mariners from almost certain
relegation to First Division safety. Bradley
is a lively striker capable of scoring
opportunist goals.
Queens Park R *(From juniors on 30/9/1988)*

F/PL 56+25/27 FLC 5+2/5 FAC 3+2 Others 1
Charlton Ath *(£400,000 on 28/3/1996) FL
30+10/9 FLC 3+1/2 FAC 0+2 Others 1+1*
Colchester U *(Loaned on 24/2/1999) FL 4/1*
Grimsby T *(Free on 12/7/1999) FL 46+34/15
FLC 5+6/4 FAC 0+2/1*

ALLEN Graham
Born: Bolton, 8 April 1977
Height: 6'1" **Weight:** 12.8
International Honours: E: Yth
Graham's appearances for Tranmere
were restricted by a series of niggling
injuries last season. The worst of these
was a cracked bone at the side of his
face, which effectively ended his season
in March. A tall and composed
defender, who can play equally well at
right back or centre back, he made no
secret of the fact that the latter is his
favoured position. Uncompromising
when in defence, Graham likes to go
forward when the opportunity
presents.
Everton *(From trainee on 10/12/1994) PL
2+4*
Tranmere Rov *(Free on 28/8/1998) FL
113+5/6 FLC 10+2 FAC 10*

ALLISON Wayne Anthony
Born: Huddersfield, 16 October 1968
Height: 6'1" **Weight:** 12.6
Club Honours: Div 2 '96
Wayne had a disappointing season for
Tranmere last term, when he was often
used from the subs' bench, particularly in
the second half of the campaign. He has
all the attributes of a traditional centre
forward, being powerful in the air and
creative with the ball at his feet, but
managed a tally of just five senior goals.
At the time of writing his future was
uncertain, but it seemed likely that he
would be leaving Prenton Park during the
summer.
Halifax T *(From trainee on 6/7/1987) FL
74+10/23 FLC 3/2 FAC 4+1/2 Others 8+1/3*
Watford *(£250,000 on 26/7/1989) FL 6+1*
Bristol C *(£300,000 on 9/8/1990) FL
149+46/48 FLC 4+5/2 FAC 12+1/5 Others
6+2/2*
Swindon T *(£475,000 on 22/7/1995) FL
98+3/31 FLC 9/3 FAC 7/2 Others 3*
Huddersfield T *(£800,000 on 11/11/1997)
FL 71+3/15 FLC 3+1/2 FAC 6/2*
Tranmere Rov *(£300,000 on 3/9/1999) FL
85+18/26 FLC 4+3/1 FAC 6+1/5 Others 1*

ALLOTT Mark Stephen
Born: Manchester, 3 October 1977
Height: 5'11" **Weight:** 12.6
Mark began the 2001-02 season in good
form at Oldham netting early on with

goals against Wrexham and Chesterfield before falling out of favour. He subsequently joined Chesterfield on loan where he was brought to lead the forward line. He is an effective striker who holds the ball up well and lays it off accurately to his colleagues. Mark achieved the unusual feat of scoring for each of his clubs against the other during the campaign.

Oldham Ath (From trainee on 14/10/1995) FL 105+49/31 FLC 7+3/2 FAC 8+7 Others 1+3
Chesterfield (Free on 19/12/2001) FL 19+2/4

ALLSOP Daniel (Danny)
Born: Australia, 10 August 1978
Height: 6'1" **Weight:** 12.0
International Honours: Australia: U23-7; Yth
This young Notts County striker had a golden season for the Magpies in 2001-02, scoring goals galore in a campaign which, for the most part, was something of a struggle for his club. He was always a threat from anywhere over the halfway line, often leaving opponents in his wake with a sharp turn of heel. Given a successful team who knows what he might achieve.
Manchester C (£10,000 from Port Melbourne, Australia on 7/8/1998) P/FL 3+26/4 FLC 0+7/1 Others 1+1/1
Notts Co (Loaned on 5/11/1999) FL 3/1
Wrexham (Loaned on 25/2/2000) FL 3/4
Bristol Rov (Loaned on 12/10/2000) FL 4+2
Notts Co (£300,000 on 22/11/2000) FL 69+3/32 FLC 2/4 FAC 7/2 Others 2+1/3

[ALPAY] OZALAN Fehmi
Born: Izmir, Turkey, 29 May 1973
Height: 6'2" **Weight:** 13.7
International Honours: Turkey: 67
This tough-tackling defender is equally adept in the air and on the ground and has become a firm favourite of the Aston Villa fans for his wholehearted level of commitment. Playing as a central defender in a back-four formation, he was ever present in the side until a bad ankle injury resulted in him being stretchered off against Leicester at the beginning of December. This turned out to be far more serious than first thought and he failed to make another appearance for the rest of the season.
Aston Villa (£5,600,000 from Fenerbahce, Turkey, ex Altay, Besiktas, on 31/7/2000) PL 47 FLC 3 FAC 2 Others 8

ALSOP Julian Mark
Born: Nuneaton, 28 May 1973
Height: 6'4" **Weight:** 14.0
Club Honours: Div 3 '00

Julian was one of the undoubted success stories of Cheltenham Town's promotion season last term. He emerged as a slimmer, sharper striker who could not only hold the ball up well and menace defenders, but was also capable of finding the net. He went on to accumulate 26 goals for the season, his best return since stepping out of non-league football in 1995. His fine performances won him the supporter's 'Player of the Year' award and he crowned a memorable season with the second goal in the Division Three play-off final.
Bristol Rov (£15,000 from Halesowen on 14/2/1997) FL 20+13/4 FLC 2/1 FAC 1/1 Others 2
Swansea C (Loaned on 20/1/1998) FL 5/2
Swansea C (£30,000 on 12/3/1998) FL 73+12/14 FLC 4+2 FAC 6+1/1 Others 5
Cheltenham T (Free on 3/7/2000) FL 67+13/25 FLC 2+1 FAC 6+1/5 Others 5/2

AMANKWAAH Kevin
Born: Harrow, 19 May 1982
Height: 6'1" **Weight:** 12.0
International Honours: E: Yth
A series of injuries disrupted this accomplished young defender's campaign at Bristol City in 2001-02. He looked about to have a good run in the side towards the end of the season, but then suffered a broken neck in a car crash, raising a question mark against his future career, even though he was awarded a two-year extension to his contract.
Bristol C (From trainee on 16/6/2000) FL 30+13/1 FLC 1+1/1 FAC 0+1 Others 4+1/1

AMBROSE Darren Paul
Born: Harlow, 29 February 1984
Height: 5'11" **Weight:** 10.5
International Honours: E: Yth
An influential midfield member of Ipswich Town's championship-winning reserve team last season, Darren made his first-team debut when coming on as a late substitute at Highbury in April.
Ipswich T (From trainee on 3/7/2001) PL 0+1

AMEOBI Foluwashola (Shola)
Born: Zaria, Nigeria, 12 October 1981
Height: 6'2" **Weight:** 12.0
International Honours: E: U21-10
With Alan Shearer and Carl Cort both injured, Shola began only his second year of Premiership football carrying much weight on his young shoulders leading Newcastle's attack for a couple of months. Shearer's return inevitably saw

him move to the bench, but he continued to make frequent substitute appearances. Tall and displaying a maturity beyond his years, he has excellent close control which he uses adeptly to extricate himself from tight situations. His season was cut short when he was injured in a reserve match in March necessitating surgery for a torn cartilage in the right knee.
Newcastle U (From trainee on 19/10/1998) PL 16+19/2 FLC 2+1/2 FAC 2+1 Others 6/3

AMPADU Patrick Kwame
Born: Bradford, 20 December 1970
Height: 5'10" **Weight:** 11.10
Club Honours: AMC '94
International Honours: RoI: U21-4; Yth
Kwame firmly established himself in the defensive midfield position for Exeter City last term. Although he failed to get his name on the score sheet he was a key figure in the centre of the park for the Grecians, his experience proving particularly effective in helping to bring on some of the club's younger players.
Arsenal (From trainee on 19/11/1988) FL 0+2
Plymouth Arg (Loaned on 31/10/1990) FL 6/1 Others 1
West Bromwich A (£50,000 on 24/6/1991) FL 27+22/4 FLC 6+1 FAC 1 Others 5/1
Swansea C (£15,000 on 16/2/1994) FL 128+19/12 FLC 8+1/1 FAC 5+1/1 Others 16/1
Leyton Orient (Free on 30/7/1998) FL 69+3/1 FLC 8 FAC 4+1/1 Others 1
Exeter C (Free on 18/7/2000) FL 62+10 FLC 2/1 FAC 3+1

ANDERSEN Trond
Born: Kristiansand, Norway, 6 January 1975
Height: 6'2" **Weight:** 12.8
International Honours: Norway: 18; B-1; U21-30; Yth
2001-02 proved to be another good season for Trond at Wimbledon and he was again a model of consistency. Suited to playing either in the centre of midfield or in defence, he is extremely hard working and constantly challenges and bustles the opposition, but he is equally comfortable with the ball at his feet looking to make the play. He was a regular squad member for the Norwegian national team.
Wimbledon (£2,500,000 from Molde, Norway, ex Clausenengen, on 9/8/1999) P/FL 102+6/5 FLC 6 FAC 10/1

ANDERSON Iain
Born: Glasgow, 23 July 1977
Height: 5'8" **Weight:** 9.10
Club Honours: Div 2 '00
International Honours: S: U21-14

Iain finally began to capture some consistent form for Preston in 2001-02. His first goal of the season proved to be the winner against Millwall, while his second at Molineux on Boxing Day was a cracker as he beat three defenders before finishing in the corner. Able to play as a wide attacker on either side, he produced his trademark ploy, cutting-in from the left and shooting, to score an equaliser at Walsall in January, a match that saw him complete 90 minutes for the first time in ten months. Iain will be hoping to build on this progress in the coming season.
Dundee (From juniors on 10/8/1994) SL 90+37/16 SLC 3+5 SC 6+3/2 Others 6+1/2 (Signed by Toulouse, France on 28/7/1999)
Preston NE (£500,000 from Toulouse, France on 18/2/2000) FL 46+28/13 FLC 4 FAC 3 Others 1+2

ANDERSON Ijah Massai
Born: Hackney, 30 December 1975
Height: 5'8" **Weight:** 10.6
Club Honours: Div 3 '99
After being out for the previous 12 months, Brentford's attacking left back returned to action on the opening day of the 2001-02 season as if he'd never been away. His solid defending and forays down the flank played a big part in the Bees' impressive season. He suffered two short spells out of action as a result of a pulled muscle (August) and a thigh strain (November).
Southend U (From trainee at Tottenham H on 2/8/1994)
Brentford (Free on 31/7/1995) FL 187+6/4 FLC 17/1 FAC 5+3 Others 12+1

ANDERSON Mark James
Born: Scunthorpe, 7 October 1981
Height: 5'11" **Weight:** 12.8
Mark signed professional forms for Scunthorpe United last season and became a regular in the reserves. A hard-working centre forward, his only first-team appearance came as a late substitute in the home game with Oxford in February when he helped create the winning goal. He spent the final month of the campaign on loan to non-league Winterton Rangers and was released in the summer.
Scunthorpe U (From trainee on 3/7/2001) FL 0+1

ANDERTON Darren Robert
Born: Southampton, 3 March 1972
Height: 6'1" **Weight:** 12.5
Club Honours: FLC '99
International Honours: E: 30; B-1; U21-12; Yth

Darren returned from injury to start the 2001-02 season in fine form cementing his place for both club and country. He looked to have regained his pace and awareness as both creator and finisher in attack, but alas, a dip in late-season form meant that despite a late opportunity to prove himself, he didn't make the final squad or the trip to Dubai and on to Korea and Japan. He will be looking forward to a solid season for Tottenham in 2002-03 and to improve upon his five goals scored last term.
Portsmouth (From trainee on 5/2/1990) FL 53+9/7 FLC 3+2/1 FAC 7+1/5 Others 2
Tottenham H (£1,750,000 on 3/6/1992) PL 239+20/33 FLC 27/6 FAC 25+1/6

ANDRE Carlos Paulino de Oli
Born: Lisbon, Portugal, 28 November 1971
Height: 5'9" **Weight:** 11.10
This midfielder made a bright debut in Walsall's New Year's Day draw at Norwich, impressing with his use of the ball. He played in seven successive games including the FA Cup wins over Bradford City and Charlton, but he was substituted on each of his appearances. Many Saddlers fans felt that they haven't yet seen the best of him.
Walsall (Free from FC Vitoria Guimaraes, Portugal, ex Estoril, Beira Mer, Gil Vicente on 28/12/2001) FL 5 FAC 2

ANDREWS Keith Joseph
Born: Dublin, 13 September 1980
Height: 5'11" **Weight:** 11.5
The early season form of Carl Robinson, coupled with the signings of Alex Rae and Colin Cameron, left Keith fourth in Molineux's midfield pecking order. He had captained Wolves in the last match of 2000-01, but had no first-team action last term until the final four minutes at Barnsley in January. He then played an entire second half at Palace before starting the following match. He was involved in the next seven, strongly challenging Cameron for one of only two spots available. He continues to look very assured for a youngster, is a good passer, and has tremendous vision. A knee injury brought his season to a premature end.
Wolverhampton W (From trainee on 26/9/1997) FL 24+11 FAC 2
Oxford U (Loaned on 10/11/2000) FL 4/1 Others 1

ANDREWS Lee David
Born: Carlisle, 23 April 1983
Height: 6'0" **Weight:** 10.12

Lee made his senior debut at right back for Carlisle in the opening match of the 2001-02 season and soon became an automatic choice in the line-up. Quick and positive in the tackle, his performances demonstrated maturity beyond his years. He spent most of the campaign in his best position of central defender but as he grew in confidence, he became more willing to foray upfield with some long-range shooting, while he also added a long throw to his armoury.
Carlisle U (From trainee on 27/6/2001) FL 37+2 FAC 3

ANELKA Nicolas
Born: Versailles, France, 14 March 1979
Height: 6'0" **Weight:** 12.3
Club Honours: PL '98; FAC '98; CS '98
International Honours: France: 28
This mercurial striker joined Liverpool on loan from PSG shortly before Christmas and made his debut in the Boxing Day victory at Villa Park. He scored his first goal for the Reds in the FA Cup victory over Birmingham and by netting the equaliser in the local 'derby' with Everton in February he ensured his acceptance by the Anfield faithful. Despite scoring a number of quality goals no permanent deal could be agreed in the summer and he was subsequently reported to have signed for Manchester City.
Arsenal (£500,000+ from Paris St Germain on 6/3/1997) PL 50+15/23 FLC 3 FAC 13+1/3 Others 7+1/2 (£22,900,000 to Real Madrid, Spain on 20/8/1999)
Liverpool (Loaned from Paris St Germain on 24/12/2001) PL 13+7/4 FAC 2/1

ANGEL Juan Pablo Aranzo
Born: Medellin, Colombia, 24 October 1975
Height: 6'0" **Weight:** 11.6
International Honours: Colombia: 17; Yth
Having struggled to adapt to the English game the previous season, Juan Pablo sprung into life last term, earning the respect and admiration of the Aston Villa fans with a hatful of goals. He started out in sensational form as both goal-scorer and provider and after producing six goals in six starts he quickly became Villa's first choice striker. He featured in the majority of games and finished the campaign as the club's leading scorer.
Aston Villa (£9,500,000 + from River Plate, Argentina, ex Atletico Nacional, on 19/1/2001) PL 33+5/13 FLC 1 FAC 2 Others 2+2/4

ANGELL Brett Ashley Mark
Born: Marlborough, 20 August 1968
Height: 6'2" **Weight:** 13.11
Club Honours: Div 2 '00
This experienced striker began his second season at Walsall on the transfer list, but was brought into the side in time to score against his former club Stockport. He continued to give of his best whenever called upon until his transfer to Rushden in March, holding the ball up well and being a handful for any defence. He made an immediate impact for the Diamonds, scoring on his debut at Mansfield and then in the home game with Swansea two days later. Despite appearing in the Third Division play-off final against Cheltenham, he wasn't offered a long-term deal at Nene Park.
Portsmouth (From trainee on 1/8/1986)
Derby Co (£40,000 from Cheltenham T on 19/2/1988)
Stockport Co (£33,000 on 20/10/1988) FL 60+10/28 FLC 3 FAC 3/1 Others 8/4
Southend U (£100,000 on 2/8/1990) FL 109+6/47 FLC 7+1/4 FAC 3/2 Others 9+1/10
Everton (£500,000 on 17/1/1994) PL 16+4/1 FLC 0+1
Sunderland (£600,000 on 23/3/1995) FL 10 FLC 1/1
Sheffield U (Loaned on 30/1/1996) FL 6/2
West Bromwich A (Loaned on 28/3/1996) FL 0+3
Stockport Co (£120,000 on 19/8/1996) FL 122+4/50 FLC 16+3/7 FAC 7/4 Others 4+1/1
Notts Co (Loaned on 9/12/1999) FL 6/5
Preston NE (Loaned on 24/2/2000) FL 9+6/8
Walsall (Free on 27/7/2000) FL 36+25/16 FLC 2+1 FAC 2+3/2 Others 0+1
Rushden & Diamonds (Free on 8/2/2002) FL 3+2/2 Others 0+2

ANGUS Stevland Dennis
Born: Westminster, 16 September 1980
Height: 6'0" **Weight:** 12.0
Club Honours: FAYC '99
Stevland's form provided one of the few bright spots in an otherwise bleak campaign for Cambridge United in 2001-02. The tall and pacy defender slotted comfortably into the back line and was a near ever present for the U's. Although primarily a centre half he can take any of the back positions and will be looking to build on his successful start at the Abbey Stadium in 2002-03.
West Ham U (From trainee on 2/7/1999)
Bournemouth (Loaned on 11/8/2000) FL 7+2
Cambridge U (Free on 19/7/2001) FL 41 FLC 1 FAC 1 Others 5+1

ANTONELIUS Tomas Emil Rune
Born: Stockholm, Sweden, 7 May 1973
Height: 5'10" **Weight:** 11.8
International Honours: Sweden: 6
The Swedish international full-back changed his name from Gustaffson following his marriage in the summer of 2001. He recovered from a serious cruciate ligament injury sustained in Euro 2000 but failed to win a regular place in the Coventry first team last term. He managed only four starts and was released to join FC Copenhagen in February.
Coventry C (£250,000 from AIK Stockholm, Sweden, ex Brommapojkarna, on 17/12/1999) FL 3+2 FAC 1

APPLEBY Matthew (Matty) Wilfred
Born: Middlesbrough, 16 April 1972
Height: 5'8" **Weight:** 11.12
Matty underwent another hernia operation last October, before joining Oldham on loan and then signing permanently in a two-year deal. He made a positive early impact and Mick Wadsworth, impressed with his leadership qualities, made him team captain. However, he failed to maintain his early promise and will be looking for a return to form in 2002-03.
Newcastle U (From trainee on 4/5/1990) F/PL 18+2 FLC 2+1 FAC 2 Others 2+2
Darlington (Loaned on 25/11/1993) FL 10/1 Others 1
Darlington (Free on 15/6/1994) FL 77+2/7 FLC 2 FAC 4 Others 8/3
Barnsley (£200,000 on 19/7/1996) F/PL 131+8/7 FLC 10+3 FAC 6+2 Others 3
Oldham Ath (Free on 15/11/2002) FL 16+1/2

APPLEBY Richard (Richie) Dean
Born: Middlesbrough, 18 September 1975
Height: 5'9" **Weight:** 11.4
Club Honours: Div 3 '00
International Honours: E: Yth
Richie began the 2001-02 season at Swansea and made a number of appearances early on until a hamstring injury put him out of contention. Soon afterwards he rejoined his former boss Jan Molby at Kidderminster in a loan deal that was to become permanent. He scored on his debut at Leyton Orient and his hard work and creative ability soon made him an indispensable member of the Harriers midfield, although he continued to suffer problems with his hamstring.
Newcastle U (From trainee on 12/8/1993) Others 2
Ipswich T (Free on 12/12/1995) FL 0+3 Others 1
Swansea C (Free on 16/8/1996) FL 90+30/11 FLC 4+4 FAC 5+1/2 Others 3+4/1
Kidderminster Hrs (Free on 9/11/2001) FL 18+1/4 FAC 1

APPLETON Michael Antony
Born: Salford, 4 December 1975
Height: 5'9" **Weight:** 12.4
Club Honours: Div 2 '00
This hard-tackling midfielder tore his posterior cruciate ligament in his right knee last November during the away League game against Birmingham City. The surgeon informed the club that he would be out of action for at least nine months. This was as a massive blow to West Bromwich Albion boss Gary Megson, for at the time Michael was playing exceptionally well in the engine-room.
Manchester U (From trainee on 1/7/1994) FLC 1+1
Wimbledon (Loaned on 22/6/1995) Others 4
Lincoln C (Loaned on 15/9/1995) FL 4 Others 1
Grimsby T (Loaned on 17/1/1997) FL 10/3
Preston NE (£500,000 on 8/8/1997) FL 90+25/12 FLC 7+1/1 FAC 9+1/1 Others 6+1/1
West Bromwich A (£750,000 on 19/1/2001) FL 33 FLC 3 Others 2

ARANALDE Zigor
Born: Guipuzcoa, Spain, 28 February 1973
Height: 6'1" **Weight:** 13.5
Zigor has missed only two games in his first two seasons with Walsall and maintained his reputation as an exciting left wing back, linking well with fellow Spaniard Pedro Matias. He strengthened his defensive qualities during 2001-02 and also opened his goal-scoring account with two goals, one of them a candidate for 'Goal of the Season' when he hammered home a 30-yard thunderbolt against Barnsley.
Walsall (Free from CD Logrones, Spain, ex Albacete, Marbella, Seville, on 11/8/2000) FL 88+2/2 FLC 6 FAC 6 Others 3

ARCA Julio Andres
Born: Quilmes Bernal, Argentine, 31 January 1981
Height: 5'10" **Weight:** 11.6
International Honours: Argentina: Yth (World Yth '01)
An exciting left-sided midfielder or winger, Julio returned to the Stadium of Light a fortnight after his team-mates last summer, having captained Argentina to victory in the U20s World Cup. Skilful and

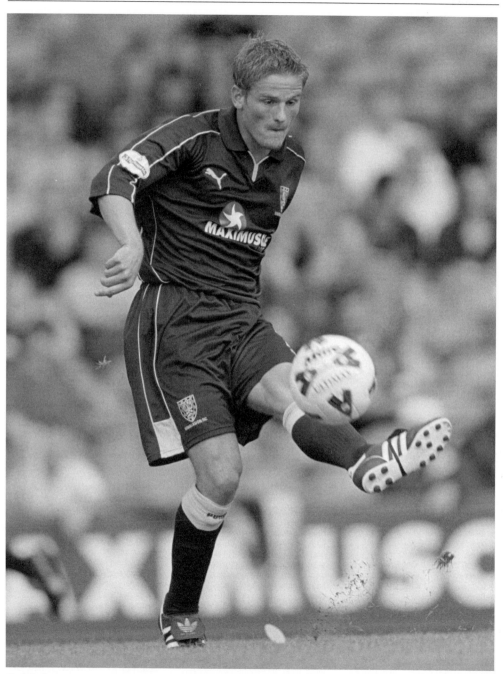

Neil Ardley

strong in the tackle, he is immensely popular with the Sunderland fans and when he was hampered by a persistent groin injury from February onwards, his ability to unlock defences and provide the Black Cats with an element of surprise was sorely missed.

Sunderland (£3,500,000 from Argentinos Juniors, Argentine on 31/8/2000) PL 46+3/3 FLC 3/1 FAC 2

ARDLEY Neal Christopher

Born: Epsom, 1 September 1972
Height: 5'11" **Weight:** 11.9
International Honours: E: U21-10
Neal had another quality year with Wimbledon in 2001-02, playing some of the best football of his career in the centre of midfield. He always led by example and gave his all, but he was out of contract in the summer and his future had yet to be decided at the time of writing.

Wimbledon (From trainee on 29/7/1991) F/PL 212+33/18 FLC 22+3/5 FAC 27+4/3

ARMSTRONG Alun

Born: Gateshead, 22 February 1975
Height: 6'1" **Weight:** 11.13
Club Honours: Div 1 '98
Alun's season at Ipswich was disrupted by a niggling back injury and the manager's rotation of his strikers as he sought to find a successful striking combination. The goals he did score underlined that he has not lost his touch nor his power in the air. The highlight of his season has to be scoring in both legs of the UEFA Cup tie with Inter Milan. His powerful header sealed a famous home win, while his penalty conversion in the San Siro proved to be just a consolation.

Newcastle U (From trainee on 1/10/1993) Stockport Co (£50,000 on 23/6/1994) FL 151+8/48 FLC 22/8 FAC 10+1/5 Others 7 Middlesbrough (£1,500,000 on 16/2/1998) P/FL 10+19/9 FLC 4 Huddersfield T (Loaned on 23/3/2000) FL 4+2 Ipswich T (£500,000 + on 8/12/2000) PL 36+17/11 FLC 2/1 FAC 2+1/1 Others 1+2/2

ARMSTRONG Christopher (Chris)

Born: Newcastle, 5 August 1982
Height: 5'10" **Weight:** 10.8
International Honours: E: Yth
Chris was a regular for Bury at the beginning of the 2001-02 campaign and provided the Shakers with both width and attacking flair down the left flank. When the club's financial problems reached a head in October he was sold to Oldham in a bargain deal. He quickly established

himself as first choice at left back, linking up effectively with the evergreen David Eyres down the flank. His progress was so impressive that he earned international recognition with a late call into the England U20 squad that competed in the Toulon Tournament in France in the summer.

Bury (From trainee on 2/3/2001) FL 33/1 FLC 1 Others 3
Oldham Ath (£200,000 on 22/10/2001) FL 31+1 FAC 3 Others 3

ARMSTRONG Steven Craig

Born: South Shields, 23 May 1975
Height: 5'11" **Weight:** 12.10
Craig started the 2001-02 campaign in midfield for Huddersfield. The left-sided player impressed with some strong tackling and accurate passing but then suffered a nasty ankle injury at Peterborough, which kept him out for over three months. He returned to the fold in mid-January with some 'Man of the Match' displays before being sold to Sheffield Wednesday the following month. He featured at left back and on the left side of midfield adding balance to the Owls' line-up. However, just when he had settled into the team a knock kept him out of the vital run-in to the end of the season.

Nottingham F (From trainee on 2/6/1992) P/FL 24+16 FLC 6+2/2 FAC 1
Burnley (Loaned on 29/12/1994) FL 4
Bristol Rov (Loaned on 8/11/1996) FL 4
Bristol Rov (Loaned on 28/3/1996) FL 9+1
Gillingham (Loaned on 18/10/1996) FL 10 FLC 2 Others 1
Watford (Loaned on 24/1/1997) FL 3
Watford (Loaned on 14/3/1997) FL 12
Huddersfield T (£750,000 on 26/2/1999) FL 101+6/5 FLC 7+1 FAC 2 Others 1+1
Sheffield Wed (£100,000 on 15/2/2002) FL 7+1

ARMSTRONG Gordon Ian

Born: Newcastle, 15 July 1967
Height: 6'0" **Weight:** 12.11
Club Honours: Div 3 '88
A squad member these days rather than an automatic choice, Gordon actually started 2001-02 as a regular in the Burnley defence before giving way to Arthur Gnohere. During that spell he weighed in two goals against Wimbledon and Norwich, and his experience and composure ensured that he never let the side down. Later on he was a regular presence on the bench, and when called on could always be relied upon to tighten things up at the back or shore up the midfield.

Sunderland (From apprentice on 10/7/1985) FL 331+18/50 FLC 25+4/3 FAC 19/4 Others 18+1/4
Bristol C (Loaned on 24/8/1995) FL 6
Northampton T (Loaned on 5/1/1996) FL 4/1 Others 1
Bury (Free on 16/7/1996) FL 49+22/4 FLC 5+2/2 FAC 2+1 Others 1+1
Burnley (Free on 27/8/1998) FL 87+12/5 FLC 2 FAC 3+2

ARMSTRONG Ian

Born: Kirkby, 16 November 1981
Height: 5'7" **Weight:** 10.2
International Honours: E: Yth
This talented left winger showed plenty of promise for Port Vale last term and although a succession of niggling hamstring injuries limited his involvement he scored five goals, including an excellent strike against Colchester. A pacy player who is particularly effective when running at defenders, he has the potential to be one of the outstanding players in the lower divisions. He was a joint-winner of the club's 'Young Player of the Year' award.

Liverpool (From trainee on 16/12/1998)
Port Vale (Free on 2/7/2001) FL 20+11/3 FAC 1 Others 2/2

ARNDALE Neil Darren

Born: Bristol, 26 April 1984
Height: 5'9" **Weight:** 10.0
International Honours: E: Yth
This tough-tackling England youth international right was a regular in Bristol Rovers U19 and reserve teams last season. He produced some impressive performances and stepped up to make his senior debut from the subs' bench in the final match of the campaign at Rochdale when he produced a composed and mature display.

Bristol Rov (Trainee) FL 0+1

ARNISON Paul Simon

Born: Hartlepool, 18 September 1977
Height: 5'10" **Weight:** 10.12
Paul is a strong-running right back who can also play in midfield. He was out of favour at Hartlepool for much of 2001-02, but got back into the first-team squad in the second half of the season. He was the Pool's star player in the play-off game at Cheltenham, scoring the goal which briefly gave the fans hope of a place in the final at the Millennium Stadium.

Newcastle U (From trainee on 1/3/1996)
Hartlepool U (Free on 10/3/2000) FL 42+12/2 FLC 1 FAC 1 Others 7/2

ARPHEXAD Pegguy Michel

Born: Abymes, Guadeloupe, 18 May 1973
Height: 6'2" **Weight:** 13.5

Club Honours: FLC '00, '01; FAC '01; UEFAC '01; ESC '01

Liverpool's reserve 'keeper had an unexpected call-up to first-team duty at the start of the 2001-02 season when he deputised for Sander Westerveld on three occasions. His luck appeared to have changed but the arrival of new signings, Jerzy Dudek and Chris Kirkland, pushed him back in the pecking order of 'keepers at Anfield. He was then loaned out to Stockport County to cover for injuries before making a surprise re-appearance in the Premiership, substituting for the injured Dudek in the second half of the Reds' crushing 6-0 victory at Ipswich.

Leicester C (Free from Lens, France on 20/8/1997) PL 17+4 FLC 4 FAC 3+1
Liverpool (Free on 13/7/2000) PL 1+1 FLC 2 Others 2
Stockport Co (Loaned on 29/9/2001) FL 3

ASABA Carl Edward
Born: London, 28 January 1973
Height: 6'2" **Weight:** 13.4

A lack of goals early on affected Carl's confidence for Sheffield United in the 2001-02 season. He netted his first of the campaign after coming off the subs' bench against Wolves but then suffered knee ligament damage at Maine Road, which meant he missed five matches. He worked very hard for the team but after picking up a niggling achilles injury in mid February he rarely featured, but still finished as the club's leading scorer in league matches. A big powerful striker who creates chances with effective running, he played with a series of different partners and was often used as the target man, not his natural position.

Brentford (Free from Dulwich Hamlet on 9/8/1994) FL 49+5/25 FLC 5 FAC 4 Others 7/2
Colchester U (Loaned on 16/2/1995) FL 9+3/2
Reading (£800,000 on 7/8/1997) FL 31+2/8 FLC 7+2/4 FAC 3/1
Gillingham (£600,000 on 28/8/1998) FL 65+12/36 FLC 3/2 FAC 1+1 Others 9/2
Sheffield U (£92,500 + on 8/3/2001) FL 36+3/12 FLC 2 FAC 2

ASAMOAH Derek
Born: Ghana, 1 May 1981
Height: 5'6" **Weight:** 10.12

Derek joined Northampton Town during the 2001 close season and made his debut from the subs' bench in the home defeat by Bristol City in August. He went on to feature regularly from the subs' bench, delighting the Sixfields faithful with some sterling performances and well-taken goals. He is a promising young

striker who upsets defenders with his pace and skill.

Northampton T (Free from Slough T, ex Barking, Hampton & Richmond Borough, on 26/7/2001) FL 3+37/3 FLC 0+2 FAC 0+1 Others 0+2

ASHBEE Ian
Born: Birmingham, 6 September 1976
Height: 6'1" **Weight:** 13.7
International Honours: E: Yth

One of the more experienced players at Cambridge, Ian had a solid, but by his own high standards, slightly disappointing 2001-02 campaign. Played mainly in midfield, but also used in defence, he took on the poisoned chalice of penalty taker at Oldham and successfully scored, one of two League goals in the season. He was out of contract in the summer and his future was uncertain at the time of writing.

Derby Co (From trainee on 9/11/1994) FL 1
Cambridge U (Free on 13/12/1996) FL 192+11/11 FLC 7 FAC 15 Others 9+1

ASHBY Barry John
Born: Park Royal, 2 November 1970
Height: 6'2" **Weight:** 13.8
Club Honours: FAYC '89

Barry had another fine season in the heart of the Gillingham defence last term, although he lost his place to Guy Butters in September following his dismissal against Wolves. In the latter part of the season, he struggled with a knee ligament strain, but came back for the final three games and will be looking forward to re-establishing himself in the side in 2002-03.

Watford (From trainee on 1/12/1988) FL 101+13/3 FLC 6 FAC 4 Others 2+1
Brentford (Signed on 22/3/1994) FL 119+2/4 FLC 11 FAC 9/1 Others 11+1
Gillingham (£140,000 on 8/8/1997) FL 188+2/6 FLC 12 FAC 15/1 Others 9/1

ASHCROFT Lee
Born: Preston, 7 September 1972
Height: 5'10" **Weight:** 11.10
International Honours: E: U21-1

This versatile striker had a disappointing season with Wigan Athletic in 2001-02, suffering a frustrating time with injuries and a change in management. After starting as a regular, his failure to produce consistent form saw him struggle to keep his place. He netted three goals during the campaign including two from the penalty spot. Lee is at his best with the ball at his feet so he can run at defenders and release one of his powerful shots.

Preston NE (From trainee on 16/7/1991) FL 78+13/13 FLC 3 FAC 5 Others 6+2/1
West Bromwich A (£250,000 on 1/8/1993) FL 66+24/17 FLC 2+3 FAC 3+1/1 Others 8+3
Notts Co (Loaned on 28/3/1996) FL 4+2
Preston NE (£150,000 on 5/9/1996) FL 63+1/22 FLC 4 FAC 5/5 Others 2+1
Grimsby T (£500,000 on 12/8/1998) FL 52+9/15 FLC 7/2 FAC 1
Wigan Ath (£250,000 on 9/8/2000) FL 37+9/8 FLC 1 FAC 3+1/1 Others 0+2

ASHDOWN Jamie Lawrence
Born: Wokingham, 30 November 1980
Height: 6'3" **Weight:** 14.10

Jamie had a brief run of first-team games in goal for Reading last December following an injury to Phil Whitehead. However, despite producing some competent displays, each of the games was lost, and he was replaced by a succession of loan goalkeepers. Towards the end of the campaign he was loaned to Arsenal as cover and made a number of reserve-team appearances for the Gunners.

Reading (From trainee on 26/11/1999) FL 1+1 FAC 1 Others 2

ASHER Alistair Andrew
Born: Leicester, 14 October 1980
Height: 6'0" **Weight:** 11.6

Alistair started the 2001-02 campaign as the reserve right back for Mansfield Town, coming on from the bench when the manager wanted to change things around. His chances of a regular first-team place were limited due to the fine form of Bobby Hassell and he managed just a single start all season. He is a versatile defender who is cool under pressure and distributes the ball accurately.

Mansfield T (From trainee on 23/6/1999) FL 53+20 FLC 2+2 FAC 1+3 Others 3+1

ASHFORD Ryan Marc
Born: Honiton, 13 October 1981
Height: 5'11" **Weight:** 11.13

This young left-sided midfielder was released by Southampton in March when he joined Torquay United on a short-term contract. He did fairly well in his two appearances for the Gulls, scoring a well-taken goal against Halifax, but did not secure a longer deal.

Southampton (From trainee on 15/1/2001) FLC 1
Torquay U (Free on 28/3/2002) FL 1+1/1

ASHTON Dean
Born: Crewe, 24 November 1983
Height: 6'1" **Weight:** 13.11

Dean Ashton

International Honours: E: Yth
This exciting young striker was a first-team regular for Crewe Alexandra last term. Although he missed the start of the season through injury he went on to net a total of ten goals and also represented England at U19 level.
Crewe Alex (From trainee on 6/2/2001) FL 41+11/15 FLC 0+1 FAC 4+2/3

ASHTON Jonathan (Jon) James
Born: Nuneaton, 4 October 1982
Height: 6'2" **Weight:** 13.7
This promising young defender made his first-team debut for Leicester City in the home defeat by Leeds in March as an emergency left back. He did not let anyone down with a steady performance and impressed the crowd with a prodigious long throw. He retained his place to play a full role in the home win over Blackburn at Easter and gained some further useful experience in the final few fixtures.
Leicester C (From trainee on 29/1/2001) PL 3+4

ASKEY John Colin
Born: Stoke, 4 November 1964
Height: 6'0" **Weight:** 12.2
Club Honours: GMVC '95, '97; FAT '96
International Honours: E: SP-1
Last season was an eventful one for Macclesfield's longest serving player. The majority of his senior appearances came from the subs' bench but he still made a useful contribution, always using the ball intelligently and scoring the winner at Darlington. Also a member of the club's backroom staff, he made good use of his UEFA-'B' coaching certificate and was acting assistant manager for a month prior to the appointment of David Moss. His managerial role for the club's reserves provided the highlight of his campaign as he led his team to the Avon Insurance League Division Two title.
Macclesfield T (Free from Milton U during 1985-86) FL 135+37/29 FLC 9+3/2 FAC 7+1/1 Others 2+1

ASTAFJEVS Vitalijs
Born: Riga, Latvia, 3 April 1971
Height: 5'11" **Weight:** 12.5
International Honours: Latvia: 83
This experienced midfielder was transfer-listed by Bristol Rovers at the beginning of the 2001-02 campaign and had brief trials at Walsall and with a number of Scottish clubs. He eventually regained his first-team place in November and produced some eye-catching

performances including scoring the winner in an FA Cup replay against Aldershot. He later suffered a rib injury, which sidelined him for a while but a future away from Bristol looks probable. He continued to captain Latvia during the season.

Bristol Rov (£150,000 from Skonto Riga, Latvia on 28/1/2000) FL 61+15/8 FLC 5 FAC 5+1/1 Others 4/2

[ATANGANA] MVONDO Simon Pierre

Born: Cameroon, 10 July 1979
Height: 5'11" **Weight:** 12.4
This promising striker found himself surplus to requirements at Dundee United last term and in January he joined Port Vale on loan. He made a good start with an appearance from the subs' bench against Oldham but then his world came crashing down in the next game, when he was forced off the field with a torn hamstring after just half an hour of the game with Wycombe. He subsequently returned to Scotland to recuperate.

Dundee U (Signed from Tonnerre Kalara, Cameroon, ex Olympic, Alfath, on 31/8/2001) SL 8+3 SLC 0+1
Port Vale (Loaned on 18/1/2002) FL 1+1

ATHERTON Peter

Born: Orrell, 6 April 1970
Height: 5'11" **Weight:** 13.12
International Honours: E: U21-1; Sch
This experienced Bradford City defender had a horrendous time with knee problems in 2001-02. He initially injured the knee in a friendly at Huddersfield in pre-season, and after surgery in mid-August he was then picked for the game at Norwich in November. However, he was carried off on a stretcher after breaking down again after just 61 minutes, and another operation meant his campaign was over. When fully fit he is a solid central defender who is effective in the tackle.

Wigan Ath (From trainee on 12/2/1988) FL 145+4/1 FLC 8 FAC 7 Others 12+1
Coventry C (£300,000 on 23/8/1991) F/PL 113+1 FLC 4 FAC 2
Sheffield Wed (£800,000 on 1/6/1994) PL 214/9 FLC 16 FAC 18 Others 3
Bradford C (Free on 6/7/2000) P/FL 26 FLC 3 FAC 1 Others 4
Birmingham C (Loaned on 15/2/2001) FL 10 Others 2

ATKINS Mark Nigel

Born: Doncaster, 14 August 1968
Height: 6'0" **Weight:** 13.2
Club Honours: PL '95

International Honours: E: Sch
This experienced midfield player provided the guidance that the young Shrewsbury squad needed last season. He was always looking to be involved and his control on the ball did much to shore up the back-bone of the midfield area. Despite being in the twilight of his career he was a near ever present, contributing two goals, both in the December victory at Halifax.

Scunthorpe U (From juniors on 9/7/1986) FL 45+5/2 FLC 3+1 FAC 5 Others 6+1
Blackburn Rov (£45,000 on 16/6/1988) F/PL 224+33/35 FLC 20+2/4 FAC 11+3 Others 17+2/1
Wolverhampton W (£1,000,000 on 21/9/1995) FL 115+11/8 FLC 12+1/2 FAC 11+1 Others 2/1
York C (Free on 5/8/1999) FL 10/2 FLC 2 (Free to Doncaster Rov on 4/11/1999)
Hull C (Free on 21/3/2001) FL 8 Others 1+1
Shrewsbury T (Free on 5/7/2001) FL 42/2 FLC 1 FAC 1 Others 1

ATKINSON Brian

Born: Darlington, 19 January 1971
Height: 5'10" **Weight:** 12.5
International Honours: E: U21-6
Brian was again an important figure in the Darlington side last term, when his ability to hold the ball in midfield and prompt the attack was much appreciated. He managed to remain fairly free from injury and is now approaching 200 games for the Quakers. He is the uncle of team-mate Danny Mellanby.

Sunderland (From trainee on 21/7/1989) FL 119+22/4 FLC 8+2 FAC 13/2 Others 2+3
Carlisle U (Loaned on 19/1/1996) FL 2 Others 1
Darlington (Free on 10/8/1996) FL 174+19/11 FLC 9 FAC 14+1/2 Others 6+1/1

ATKINSON Graeme

Born: Hull, 11 November 1971
Height: 5'8" **Weight:** 11.6
Club Honours: Div 3 '96
After missing the whole of the 2000-01 season with a cruciate ligament injury, Graeme returned to the Rochdale line-up last September, adding his class to the left side of their midfield. However, his joy was short lived as a further, unrelated, injury ruled him out of the side until the turn of the year. Yet another injury ensured that he was restricted to just a handful more outings from the subs' bench. At his best he is a direct and dangerous winger with a good eye for goal.

Hull C (From trainee on 6/5/1990) FL 129+20/23 FLC 6+3/2 FAC 4+1/1 Others 5/2
Preston NE (£80,000 on 7/10/1994) FL

63+16/6 FLC 5/1 FAC 2+1 Others 5/2
Rochdale (Loaned on 12/12/1997) FL 5+1
Brighton & Hove A (Free on 5/3/1998) FL 16 FLC 1
Scunthorpe U (Free on 2/11/1998) FL 0+1
Scarborough (Free on 18/2/1999) FL 15/1
Rochdale (Free on 1/7/1999) FL 40+11/5 FLC 2 FAC 3+1/1 Others 4+1

AUSTIN Dean Barry

Born: Hemel Hempstead, 26 April 1970
Height: 5'11" **Weight:** 12.4
Dean was the Crystal Palace team captain last term and started the season as a first choice defender before Steve Vickers came in on loan. He returned to the side when Trevor Francis became manager and played some of the best football of his time at Selhurst Park in the centre of the defence.

Southend U (£12,000 from St Albans C on 22/3/1990) FL 96/2 FLC 4/1 FAC 2 Others 7
Tottenham H (£375,000 on 4/6/1992) PL 117+7 FLC 7+2 FAC 16+1
Crystal Palace (Free on 8/7/1998) FL 127+12/6 FLC 17+2 FAC 3 Others 2

AUSTIN Kevin Levi

Born: Hackney, 12 February 1973
Height: 6'0" **Weight:** 14.0
International Honours: Trinidad & Tobago:1
After finally recovering from a serious injury suffered the previous February, Kevin signed non-contract forms for Cambridge United last November. A tall central defender, he made an impressive debut as substitute at Queen's Park Rangers in February but after a handful of games he was released.

Leyton Orient (Free from Saffron Walden on 19/8/1993) FL 101+8/3 FLC 4 FAC 6 Others 7
Lincoln C (£30,000 on 31/7/1996) FL 128+1/2 FLC 9 FAC 6 Others 4
Barnsley (Free on 5/7/1999) FL 3 FLC 2+1
Brentford (Loaned on 27/10/2000) FL 3
Cambridge U (Free on 21/11/2001) FL 4+2 Others 1

AYRES Lee Terence

Born: Birmingham, 28 August 1982
Height: 6'1" **Weight:** 10.10
Young central defender Lee had a roller coaster ride to the start of his professional career last term when he was thrown into the Kidderminster defence for his debut in the Worthington Cup tie against Preston. Two games later he broke a bone in his foot and spent the next four months on the sidelines after which he was unable to force his way back into the line-up.

Kidderminster Hrs (Free from Evesham U on 12/6/2001) FL 5+1 FLC 1

Espen Baardsen

B

BAARDSEN Per Espen
Born: San Rafael, USA, 7 December 1977
Height: 6'5" **Weight:** 13.13
Club Honours: FLC '99
International Honours: Norway: 4; U21-31; Yth USA: Yth
Espen started the 2001-02 season as Watford's first-choice goalkeeper, but lost his place to Alec Chamberlain in October. His shot-stopping abilities were not in doubt, and he saved a penalty against Rotherham, but he paid the price for some jittery defending in front of him and the extra assurance and organisation of the experienced Chamberlain was preferred. He was transfer-listed in February with a view to seeking regular first-team football elsewhere.
Tottenham H (Free from San Francisco All Blacks, USA, on 16/7/1996) PL 22+1 FLC 3 FAC 2+1
Watford (£1,250,000 on 3/8/2000) FL 41 FLC 5

BABAYARO Celestine
Born: Kaduna, Nigeria, 29 August 1978
Height: 5'8" **Weight:** 11.0
Club Honours: FLC '98; ESC '98; FAC '00; CS '00
International Honours: Nigeria: 26; U23 (OLYM '96); Yth (World-U17 '93)
This excellent left back had a truncated season, starting just half of Chelsea's fixtures during 2001-02. He was away on African Nations' Cup duty with Nigeria in the new year and in March picked up a thigh strain which caused him to miss eight of the last nine matches, his only outing being the first half of the FA Cup final, before being unable to continue.
Chelsea (£2,250,000 from Anderlecht, Belgium on 20/6/1997) PL 94+9/3 FLC 8+2 FAC 11+1 Others 26+3/3

BABBEL Markus
Born: Munich, Germany, 8 September 1972
Height: 6'3" **Weight:** 12.10
Club Honours: UEFAC '01; FLC '01; FAC '01; ESC '01; CS '01
International Honours: Germany: 51
After a highly successful first campaign for Liverpool holding down the right-back slot, Markus started the 2001-02 season in fine form playing the first six games. However in the August Bank Holiday match at Bolton he was withdrawn at half time feeling unwell and was eventually diagnosed as suffering from Guillain-Barre syndrome. A cool and composed defender who can play anywhere in the back four and, until recently a mainstay of the German national team, it would be a tragedy for both player and club if his distinguished career was brought to a premature end by illness.
Liverpool (Free from Bayern Munich, Germany, ex SV Hamburg, on 10/7/2000) PL 40/3 FLC 4/1 FAC 5/1 Others 16+1/1

BACON Daniel (Danny) Stephen
Born: Mansfield, 20 September 1980
Height: 5'10" **Weight:** 10.12
Danny had a frustrating time with injuries at Mansfield last term and his campaign eventually ended in March when an operation was necessary. The highlight of his season was coming off of the bench against Shrewsbury to turn the match around by scoring the first goal and setting up the winner to put the Stags into second place in the table. When fully fit he is a skilful striker who causes problems for defenders with his pace.
Mansfield T (From trainee on 5/11/2000) FL 14+24/4 FLC 1+3 FAC 1+2 Others 1/1

BAILEY Mark
Born: Stoke, 12 August 1976
Height: 5'8" **Weight:** 10.12
Mark gave some steady performances at right back for Lincoln after signing from Conference club Northwich Victoria last October. In his second spell as a full-time pro he quickly settled into the Imps' back four and suffered from niggling injuries and missed the final eight games of the campaign after damaging his achilles in the home match with Cheltenham Town.
Stoke C (From trainee on 12/7/1994)
Rochdale (Free on 10/10/1996) FL 49+18/1 FLC 3+1 FAC 1 Others 4 (Free to Winsford U during 1999 close season)
Lincoln C (Free from Northwich Vic, ex Lancaster C, on 8/10/2001) FL 18 FAC 2 Others 1

BAIRD Andrew (Andy) Crawford
Born: East Kilbride, 18 January 1979
Height: 5'10" **Weight:** 12.6
Andy finally made his comeback for Wycombe last February after a year out with cruciate damage to his knee, but managed only one start and five substitute appearances. At peak fitness he is a fast, powerful and unselfish striker capable of scoring spectacular goals. However, the frequent periods of injury over the last few years have taken their toll, and he was released at the end of the season.
Wycombe W (From trainee on 18/3/1998) FL 55+24/13 FLC 2+7/2 FAC 8+2/2 Others 3+1

BAK Arkadiusz (Arek)
Born: Poland, 6 January 1974
Height: 5'9" **Weight:** 11.12
International Honours: Poland: 13
Arek joined Birmingham City on loan last December and made his debut as a substitute in the 3-0 win at Stockport. His first start came in the 3-0 FA Cup defeat at Liverpool. He is a small but energetic midfielder who is busy on the ball and likes to get forward. His loan was cancelled by mutual consent as he struggled to adapt to the English game.
Birmingham C (Loaned from Polonia Warsaw, Poland on 21/12/2001) FL 2+2 FAC 1

BAKKE Eirik
Born: Sogndal, Norway, 13 September 1977
Height: 6'2" **Weight:** 12.9
International Honours: Norway: 17; U21-34; Yth
Eirik has proved to be one of David O'Leary's most inspired signings for Leeds United. A strong and forceful midfielder, he was another player to suffer from injury last term, causing him to miss three months of the campaign. He began the season well, scoring three goals in four games early on. Eirik is very highly thought of at Elland Road.
Leeds U (£1,000,000 + from Sogndal, Norway on 13/7/1999) PL 68+17/6 FLC 5/1 FAC 5/4 Others 25+3/4

BALABAN Bosko
Born: Croatia, 15 October 1978
Height: 5'11" **Weight:** 11.10
International Honours: Croatia: 13
A proven goal-scorer at international level, Bosko has yet to make any significant impact at Villa Park. He came to England with a huge reputation, having scored the goals that fired Croatia towards the World Cup finals, but endured a very disappointing season when he only managed to make two starts and a further handful of substitute appearances during the whole campaign. He is a natural predator and is likely to hit the net with some regularity once he establishes a run in the side.
Aston Villa (£6,000,000 from Dinamo Zagreb, Croatia, ex NK Rijeka, on 24/8/2001) PL 0+8 FLC 1+1 Others 1

BALDRY Simon Jonathan
Born: Huddersfield, 12 February 1976
Height: 5'10" **Weight:** 11.6
A pre-season injury kept this Huddersfield

midfielder on the sidelines last term until the televised match against Wycombe Wanderers. A strong and accurate crosser of the ball, Town benefited from his skilful displays. Used frequently from the substitutes' bench, Simon suffered a recurring ankle injury that dogged him throughout the season.
Huddersfield T (From trainee on 14/7/1994) FL 73+51/6 FLC 3+5 FAC 2+2 Others 2+3/1
Bury (Loaned on 8/9/1998) FL 0+5

BALIS Igor
Born: Czechoslovakia, 5 January 1970
Height: 5'11" **Weight:** 11.4
International Honours: Slovakia: 41
It took this tall, rangy right wing back almost four months before he finally displaced the experienced Des Lyttle in the West Bromwich Albion side, and once in he became a key member of Gary Megson's team, having an excellent season. He scored his first goal for the club in a comprehensive 5-0 home win over Portsmouth in February and then netted a dramatic injury-time penalty in the penultimate League game of the season away to Bradford City.
West Bromwich A (£150,000 from Slovan Bratislava, Slovakia, ex Spartak Trnava, on 14/12/2000) FL 33+8/2 FLC 0+1 FAC 3+1

BALL Kevin Anthony
Born: Hastings, 12 November 1964
Height: 5'10" **Weight:** 12.6
Club Honours: Div 1 '96, '99
Burnley's second season back in the First Division saw a more positive approach than the first, and Kevin's gritty midfield talents were perhaps less crucial to the cause than in the previous campaign. Even so, he appeared in all but four of the side's League games and continued to provide the bite sometimes lacking in other areas of the team, complementing the more elegant skills of Tony Grant or Paul Cook. He was released at the end of the season.
Portsmouth (From apprentice at Coventry C on 6/10/1982) FL 96+9/4 FLC 8+1 FAC 8 Others 6
Sunderland (£350,000 on 16/7/1990) P/FL 329+10/21 FLC 23+3/4 FAC 16 Others 7/2
Fulham (£200,000 on 9/12/1999) FL 15+3 FAC 2
Burnley (Free on 24/7/2000) FL 77+5/2 FLC 5 FAC 3

BALMER Stuart Murray
Born: Falkirk, 20 September 1969
Height: 6'0" **Weight:** 12.11
Club Honours: AMC '99
International Honours: S: Yth; Sch

Stuart joined Oldham in the summer of 2001and quickly established himself in the team in the centre of the defence. He enjoyed a fruitful goal-scoring spell, netting in three consecutive games in September. However, injuries and the additions of David Beharall, Fitz Hall and Julien Baudet to the squad meant he found first-team appearances increasingly hard to come by as the season progressed. His tally of six League goals was the most prolific of his career to date.
Glasgow Celtic (From juniors in 1987)
Charlton Ath (£120,000 on 24/8/1990) FL 201+26/8 FLC 15 FAC 9+1 Others 11+1
Wigan Ath (£200,000 on 18/9/1998) FL 99+2/4 FLC 7 FAC 8 Others 12/1
Oldham Ath (Free on 20/7/2001) FL 35+1/6 FLC 2 FAC 4 Others 2

BANGER Nicholas (Nicky) Lee
Born: Southampton, 25 February 1971
Height: 5'9" **Weight:** 11.6
Nicky arrived at Plymouth on a three-month contract last August after a short trial. He played as a striker in 11 league matches, scoring twice – the most significant being his equaliser against former club Oxford in October. However he was not retained and moved on to Merthyr before returning to League action with Torquay United in March. He made his debut against Mansfield, but still looked short of match fitness and no deal was pursued.
Southampton (From trainee on 25/4/1989) F/PL 18+37/8 FLC 2+2/3 FAC 0+2 Others 1
Oldham Ath (£250,000 on 4/10/1994) FL 44+20/10 FLC 6/1 FAC 2+1 Others 0+1
Oxford U (Free on 24/7/1997) FL 41+22/8 FLC 6+2/1 FAC 3
Dundee (Free on 9/11/1999) SL 2+4 SLC 0+1 SC 1+1
Scunthorpe U (Loaned on 3/11/2000) FL 0+1
Plymouth Arg (Free on 24/8/2001) FL 3+7/2 Others 1
Torquay U (Free on 22/3/2002) FL 1

BANKOLE Ademola (Ade)
Born: Abeokuta, Nigeria, 9 September 1969
Height: 6'3" **Weight:** 12.10
This experienced 'keeper was a regular for Crewe Alexandra for much of the 2001-02 season. Now in the second season of his current spell at Gresty Road, he took over the number one spot from Jason Kearton, and also featured as a member of Nigeria's international squad during the campaign.

Doncaster Rov (Free from Shooting Stars, Ibadan, Nigeria on 30/11/1995)
Leyton Orient (Free on 27/12/1995)
Crewe Alex (Free on 25/9/1996) FL 6 FLC 1
Queens Park R (£50,000 on 2/7/1998) FL 0+1
Crewe Alex (£50,000 on 19/7/2000) FL 49 FLC 1+1 FAC 5

BANKS Christopher (Chris) Noel
Born: Stone, 12 November 1965
Height: 5'11" **Weight:** 12.2
Club Honours: NC '99
International Honours: E: SP-2
This long-serving Cheltenham Town defender and club captain enjoyed another highly consistent season in 2001-02. A superb reader of the game with excellent positional sense, his partnership with Michael Duff was one of the key factors in the club's promotion campaign. He also starred in the Robins' record-breaking FA Cup run and produced an outstanding individual performance in the fourth round victory over Burnley. Sadly he missed out on the clubs' end-of-season triumph after suffering a knee injury in the closing weeks of the campaign.
Port Vale (From juniors on 3/12/1982) FL 50+15/1 FLC 3+3 FAC 4 Others 8+4
Exeter C (Free on 24/6/1988) FL 43+2/1 FLC 2 FAC 1 Others 2 (Free to Bath C during 1989 close season)
Cheltenham T (Free on 11/8/1994) FL 119+1/1 FLC 5 FAC 9 Others 5

BANKS Steven (Steve)
Born: Hillingdon, 9 February 1972
Height: 6'0" **Weight:** 13.2
Last season was a somewhat frustrating one for Steve. With Jussi Jaaskelainen having firmly established himself as Bolton's first choice goalkeeper, he saw his first-team chances limited to just two starts. He spent three months on loan at Rochdale around the turn of the year, where he won rave reviews for his performances. A competent and reliable 'keeper, he is now at the stage in his career where he must decide if first-team football is a more attractive option than being a Premiership squad member.
West Ham U (From trainee on 24/3/1990) Others 1
Gillingham (Free on 25/3/1993) FL 67 FAC 7 Others 2
Blackpool (£60,000 on 18/8/1995) FL 150 FLC 13 FAC 8 Others 10
Bolton W (£50,000 on 25/3/1999) P/FL 20+1 FLC 7 FAC 5 Others 3
Rochdale (Loaned on 14/12/2001) FL 15

BARACLOUGH Ian Robert

Born: Leicester, 4 December 1970
Height: 6'1" **Weight:** 12.2
Club Honours: Div 3 '98
International Honours: E: Yth

Ian returned to Notts County in the 2001 close season to take over the troublesome left-back slot. He is a highly capable, experienced and determined left-sided player who is also capable of playing in midfield where he has even greater scope to deliver his crosses and shots.

Leicester C *(From trainee on 15/12/1988) FAC 1 Others 0+1*
Wigan Ath *(Loaned on 22/3/1990) FL 8+1/2*
Grimsby T *(Loaned on 21/12/1990) FL 1+3*
Grimsby T *(Free on 13/8/1991) FL 1*
Lincoln C *(Free on 21/8/1992) FL 68+5/10 FLC 7/1 FAC 4 Others 7*
Mansfield T *(Free on 6/6/1994) FL 47/5 FLC 7 FAC 4 Others 4*
Notts Co *(Signed on 13/10/1995) FL 107+4/10 FLC 5+1/1 FAC 8 Others 2*
Queens Park R *(£50,000 on 19/3/1998) FL 120+5/1 FLC 7 FAC 6*
Notts Co *(Free on 5/7/2001) FL 30+3/3 FLC 2 FAC 3 Others 3*

BARKER Christopher (Chris) Andrew

Born: Sheffield, 2 March 1980
Height: 6'0" **Weight:** 11.8

After over 100 appearances Chris netted his first goal for Barnsley at Norwich and repeated the feat in the next match. Up to Christmas he was without doubt the club's most improved. His link with Darren Barnard provided the team with a number of goal-scoring opportunities and he produced some committed displays in the left-back position.

Barnsley *(Signed from Alfreton on 24/8/1998) FL 110+3/3 FLC 11+1 FAC 4 Others 0+1*

BARKER Richard (Richie) Ian

Born: Sheffield, 30 May 1975
Height: 6'0" **Weight:** 13.5
International Honours: E: Yth; Sch

There was no more willing worker than Richie as Rotherham United defied the odds to survive in their first season in Division One last term. He is a strong-running and hard-working striker who is good in the air and he endeared himself to the supporters when he scored a last-minute winner at near-neighbours Sheffield Wednesday. He mainly had to be content with a role as a substitute but he proved to be a valuable member of the squad.

Sheffield Wed *(From trainee on 27/7/1993) Others 1+1 (Free to Linfield on 22/8/1996)*

Doncaster Rov *(Loaned on 29/9/1995) FL 5+1 Others 0+1*
Brighton & Hove A *(Free on 19/12/1997) FL 48+12/12 FLC 1+1/1 FAC 1/1 Others 1*
Macclesfield T *(Free on 5/7/1999) FL 58/23 FLC 6/2 FAC 3 Others 1/1*
Rotherham U *(£60,000 on 3/1/2001) FL 18+36/4 FLC 1+1 FAC 2/1*

BARLOW Martin David

Born: Barnstaple, 25 June 1971
Height: 5'7" **Weight:** 10.3

Martin was a regular in the centre of midfield for Exeter City last term and performed consistently well throughout the season. His close ball control and ability to deliver both long and short passes made him a virtual first-choice in the line-up. However, niggling injuries and a need to reduce the wage bill contributed to him being released in the summer.

Plymouth Arg *(From trainee on 1/7/1989) FL 294+35/24 FLC 11+1/2 FAC 19 Others 17+1*
Exeter C *(Free on 9/7/2001) FL 26+4 FLC 1 FAC 3 Others 1*

BARLOW Stuart

Born: Liverpool, 16 July 1968
Height: 5'10" **Weight:** 11.0
Club Honours: AMC '99

This popular striker finished the 2001-02 campaign as Tranmere's leading scorer with 14 Second Division goals, which included hat-tricks against Notts County and Wrexham within the space of four days last September. His acceleration and control continued to make him a constant menace to opposing defenders, while great things are expected when he renews his striking partnership with former Wigan colleague Simon Haworth in 2002-03.

Everton *(Free from Sherwood Park on 6/6/1990) F/PL 24+47/10 FLC 3+5/1 FAC 4+3/2 Others 0+2*
Rotherham U *(Loaned on 10/1/1992) Others 0+1*
Oldham Ath *(£450,000 on 20/11/1995) FL 78+15/31 FLC 5+1 FAC 6+1/1 Others 1*
Wigan Ath *(£45,000 on 26/3/1998) FL 72+11/40 FLC 6/3 FAC 5/3 Others 9+3/6*
Tranmere Rov *(Free on 5/7/2000) FL 43+22/16 FLC 4+3/3 FAC 3+5/2*

BARMBY Nicholas (Nick) Jonathan

Born: Hull, 11 February 1974
Height: 5'7" **Weight:** 11.3
Club Honours: FLC '01; UEFAC '01; CS '01
International Honours: E: 23; B-2; U21-4; Yth; Sch

If his first season at Anfield was frustrating, after missing out on the climax to Liverpool's trophy laden 2000-01 campaign, then Nick's second season was doubly so. Ironically, in the opening months of the new season he found himself a regular place in the England national team, whilst unable to hold down the left-midfield slot at his club. He then picked up an ankle injury, which sidelined him for four months, and after returning to action in March he made a handful of appearances from the subs' bench before returning to the sidelines once more.

Tottenham H *(From trainee on 9/4/1991) PL 81+6/20 FLC 7+1/2 FAC 12+1/5*
Middlesbrough *(£5,250,000 on 8/8/1995) PL 42/8 FLC 4/1 FAC 3/1*
Everton *(£5,750,000 on 2/11/1996) PL 105+11/18 FLC 2/2 FAC 12/3*
Liverpool *(£6,000,000 on 19/7/2000) PL 23+9/2 FLC 3+4/1 FAC 2+3/1 Others 10+4/4*

BARNARD Darren Sean

Born: Rintein, Germany, 30 November 1971
Height: 5'9" **Weight:** 12.3
International Honours: W: 16; E: Sch

Darren was again employed on the left-hand side of midfield player by Barnsley in the early part of the 2001-02 season, but he was not at his best under Nigel Spackman as the team struggled. With the change of manager and the improvement in the team's fortunes, he returned to form and his 30-yard right-foot strike against Blackburn in the FA Cup provided a special moment. However, as the team fell back into relegation trouble he found himself more on the fringes of the squad and was released in the summer.

Chelsea *(£50,000 from Wokingham T on 25/7/1990) F/PL 18+11/2 FLC 1+1 FAC 1+1*
Reading *(Loaned on 18/11/1994) FL 3+1*
Bristol C *(£175,000 on 6/10/1995) FL 77+1/15 FLC 4/1 FAC 6 Others 6/1*
Barnsley *(£750,000 on 8/8/1997) P/FL 151+19/28 FLC 16+3/5 FAC 9/3 Others 3*

BARNARD Donny Gary

Born: Forest Gate, 1 July 1984
Height: 6'0" **Weight:** 11.3

Donny began the 2001-02 campaign in Leyton Orient's U17 team, but came through to make his senior debut against Rushden and featured in a handful more games during the season. He is a promising right back who has good pace and is crisp in the tackle. His best performance came in the FA Cup tie at Portsmouth when he controlled the opposing winger superbly.

Leyton Orient *(Trainee) FL 6+4 FAC 0+1*

BARNES Philip (Phil) Kenneth
Born: Sheffield, 2 March 1979
Height: 6'1'' **Weight:** 11.1
Club Honours: AMC '02
Phil was the number one goalkeeper for Blackpool for the majority of the 2001-02 season, despite losing his place for a while to on-loan James Pullen. He grew in confidence as the season progressed and with age on his side he is expected to get even better in 2002-03.
Rotherham U (From trainee on 25/6/1997) FL 2
Blackpool (£100,000 on 22/7/1997) FL 78 FLC 5 FAC 4 Others 12

BARNESS Anthony
Born: Lewisham, 25 March 1973
Height: 5'10" **Weight:** 13.1
Club Honours: Div 1 '00
Once again, Anthony showed that he was a valuable member of the Bolton squad. Despite not being the club's first choice right back, he managed 19 Premiership starts last season, his appearances mainly coming before the arrival of Bruno N'Gotty, and later on in the season, when N'Gotty was employed as a centre half. A solid and dependable player, he showed great skill and determination when called into the team and is one of the most reliable members in the squad.
Charlton Ath (From trainee on 6/3/1991) FL 21+6/1 FLC 2 FAC 3 Others 1+1/1
Chelsea (£350,000 on 8/9/1992) PL 12+2 FLC 2 Others 2+1
Middlesbrough (Loaned on 12/8/1993) Others 1
Southend U (Loaned on 2/2/1996) FL 5
Charlton Ath (£165,000 on 8/8/1996) P/FL 83+13/3 FLC 5 FAC 3+1 Others 1+1
Bolton W (Free on 6/7/2000) P/FL 36+9 FLC 4 FAC 4 Others 3

BARNETT Jason Vincent
Born: Shrewsbury, 21 April 1976
Height: 5'9" **Weight:** 11.6
This right-sided player was used both in the back four and in midfield by Lincoln last season. Jason started the campaign as first choice at right back but lost his place in October following the arrival of Mark Bailey and then suffered a groin injury which continued to trouble him until the summer break. He was one of five out-of-contract players released by the Imps in May after the club went into administration.
Wolverhampton W (From trainee on 4/7/1994)
Lincoln C (£5,000 on 26/10/1995) FL 189+18/6 FLC 8 FAC 8+1 Others 13+1

BAROS Milan
Born: Czechoslovakia, 28 October 1981
Height: 6'0" **Weight:** 11.12
International Honours: Czech Republic: 10; U21: Yth
This young striker joined Liverpool last December, clearly as a player with great potential but as yet unready for regular first-team action. He made his debut, and to date his only first-team appearance, as a substitute for Emile Heskey in the Champions' League match in Barcelona in March.
Liverpool ((£3,400,000 from Banik Ostrava, Czechoslovakia, on 24/12/2001) Others 0+1

BARR Hamid
Born: Lewisham, 29 September 1976
Height: 5'11" **Weight:** 12.7
This central midfielder joined Queen's Park Rangers on a free transfer in the summer of 2001. He made a good impression in the pre-season but suffered a number of injuries during the campaign and his only first-team appearance came in the LDV Vans Trophy defeat at Yeovil in October.
Queens Park R (Free from Fisher Ath, ex Crockenhill, on 17/7/2001) Others 0+1

BARRAS Anthony (Tony)
Born: Billingham, 29 March 1971
Height: 6'0" **Weight:** 13.0
This central defender opened the 2001-02 season with a match-winning header against West Brom, a further two goals against Crystal Palace early in November left him as Walsall's leading scorer up to then! A hip injury just before Christmas was a setback but he returned to play a tremendous game in the goalless draw against leaders Manchester City in March. Tony is the personification of the brave defender who is always to be found in the thick of the action.
Hartlepool U (From trainee on 6/7/1989) FL 9+3 FLC 2 FAC 1 Others 1
Stockport Co (Free on 23/7/1990) FL 94+5/5 FLC 2 FAC 7 Others 19+1
Rotherham U (Loaned on 25/2/1994) FL 5/1
York C (£25,000 on 18/7/1994) FL 167+4/11 FLC 16/2 FAC 10/1 Others 8+1/1
Reading (£20,000 on 19/3/1997) FL 4+2/1
Walsall (£20,000 on 16/7/1999) FL 77+9/9 FLC 9/2 FAC 4/1 Others 4

BARRASS Matthew (Matt) Robert
Born: Bury, 28 February 1980
Height: 5'11" **Weight:** 12.0
This young Bury right back had another unfortunate time with injuries in 2001-02. He featured regularly early on before suffering cruciate ligament damage at

Wrexham in September. He fought back bravely and it was a massive psychological boost for player and club alike when he was fit to start the final two fixtures against Colchester and Peterborough.
Bury (From trainee on 19/5/1999) FL 34+3/1 FLC 1+1 Others 1

BARRETT Adam Nicholas
Born: Dagenham, 29 November 1979
Height: 5'10" **Weight:** 12.0
Adam was still recovering from an ankle injury at the start of the 2001-02 campaign and it was not until October that he returned to action. Although a little rusty at first, he soon hit form and established a solid central defensive partnership with Stuart Reddington. He is a strong tackler who likes to play the ball out of defence.
Plymouth Arg (Free from USA football scholarship on 13/1/1999) FL 47+5/3 FLC 4 FAC 6+1 Others 1
Mansfield T (£10,000 on 1/12/2000) FL 34+3/1 FAC 3 Others 2

BARRETT Graham
Born: Dublin, 6 October 1981
Height: 5'10" **Weight:** 11.7
Club Honours: FAYC '00
International Honours: RoI: U21-15; Yth (UEFA-U16 '98); Sch
This Arsenal youngster spent most of the 2001-02 season out on loan to gain experience of first-team football. He spent a month at Crewe in the early part of the campaign, featuring in a handful of games on the left wing without registering a goal. In December he joined Colchester United in a long-term arrangement, and quickly developed into the U's most effective attacking force. Operating down the right flank, and occasionally as a striker, he scored a vital double in the Boxing Day win at Northampton, but his season was cut short by a knee injury picked up at Wycombe in March.
Arsenal (From trainee on 14/10/1998) PL 0+2 FLC 1
Bristol Rov (Loaned on 15/12/2000) FL 0+1
Crewe Alex (Loaned on 11/9/2001) FL 2+1 FLC 0+1
Colchester U (Loaned on 14/12/2001) FL 19+1/4

BARRETT Neil William
Born: Tooting, 24 December 1981
Height: 6'0" **Weight:** 11.12
Neil joined Portsmouth in the summer of 2001, after playing a handful of reserve games at Fratton Park the previous season on trial. Known to Graham Rix from his days at Chelsea, the 18-year-old forced his way into the first team and impressed

many with his busy work rate, commitment and skill, chasing everything and closing opponents down quickly. An attacking midfielder who weighed in with two goals, an injury restricted his progress in the latter part of the season.
Portsmouth (Free from Chelsea juniors on 5/7/2001) FL 23+3/2

BARRETT Paul David
Born: Newcastle, 13 April 1978
Height: 5'11" **Weight:** 11.5
International Honours: E: Yth
This industrious Wrexham player again struggled to establish himself as a regular at first-team level in 2001-02, although he was not helped by a series of niggling injuries. He made the starting line-up for the final nine games and the improved form he showed persuaded manager Denis Smith to offer him a new one-year contract.
Newcastle U (From trainee on 20/6/1996)
Wrexham (Free on 24/3/1999) FL 57+10/2 FLC 0+1 FAC 2+1 Others 1+1

BARRETT Scott
Born: Ilkeston, 2 April 1963
Height: 6'0" **Weight:** 14.4
Club Honours: GMVC '92; FAT '92
Scott started the 2001-02 season as reserve to Ashley Bayes for Leyton Orient, but when Bayes suffered a shoulder injury Scott regained his first-team place and kept it for most of the remainder of the campaign. He is still an agile 'keeper despite his age, and his fine performances earned him the 'Away Player of the Year' and 'Captain's Player of the Year' awards.
Wolverhampton W (Signed from Ilkeston T on 27/9/1984) FL 30 FLC 1 FAC 1 Others 3
Stoke C (£10,000 on 24/7/1987) FL 51 FLC 2 FAC 3 Others 4
Colchester U (Loaned on 10/1/1990) FL 13
Stockport Co (Loaned on 22/3/1990) FL 10 Others 2
Gillingham (Free on 14/8/1992) FL 51 FLC 7 FAC 4 Others 4
Cambridge U (Free on 2/8/1995) FL 119 FLC 6 FAC 7 Others 3
Leyton Orient (Free on 25/11/1999) FL 88 FLC 2 FAC 5 Others 3

BARRON Michael James
Born: Chester le Street, 22 December 1974
Height: 5'11" **Weight:** 11.9
Michael skippered Hartlepool to their third consecutive appearance in the Division Three play-offs last term. He is a versatile player who rarely has an off day, and has now made over 200 appearances for the club. At his best as a central defender, he

also featured in midfield and at right back in 2001-02.
Middlesbrough (From trainee on 2/2/1993) P/FL 2+1 FLC 1 Others 3+3
Hartlepool U (Loaned on 6/9/1996) FL 16
Hartlepool U (Free on 8/7/1997) FL 176+2/2 FLC 6 FAC 6 Others 18

BARRY Gareth
Born: Hastings, 23 February 1981
Height: 6'0" **Weight:** 12.6
International Honours: E: 6; U21-18; Yth
Gareth has developed in to a versatile defender who can slot into any position in the back line. However, with the arrival of Alpay and Olof Mellberg, he struggled to gain a regular place in the team. His season took a dramatic turn for the better when injuries forced the manager to reshuffle his pack and Gareth found himself plunged into midfield, but this was only a brief interlude and he was soon back on the bench. He received a new lease of life when Graham Taylor was appointed manager and quickly established himself on the left side of midfield. Gareth was voted as Villa's 'Young Player of the Season' for his efforts.
Aston Villa (From trainee on 27/2/1998) PL 103+11/3 FLC 9 FAC 10+2 Others 13+1/1

BARRY-MURPHY Brian
Born: Cork, Ireland, 27 July 1978
Height: 6'0" **Weight:** 12.4
International Honours: RoI: U21-6; Yth
Brian was a peripheral figure at Preston in 2001-02, only making two starts and three substitute appearances in all, despite captaining the title-winning reserve side. In February he was loaned to Southend to gain more first-team experience and scored in his final appearance against Leyton Orient. A combative player who is an excellent tackler and possesses a powerful shot, he is able to play on the left flank either in defence or midfield.
Preston NE (Free from Cork C on 3/8/1999) FL 4+15 FLC 1+3 FAC 1+1 Others 1
Southend U (Loaned on 11/2/2002) FL 8/1

BART-WILLIAMS Christopher (Chris) Gerald
Born: Freetown, Sierra Leone, 16 June 1974
Height: 5'11" **Weight:** 11.6
Club Honours: Div 1 '98
International Honours: E: B-1; U21-16; Yth
Chris began the 2001-02 season on the transfer list at Nottingham Forest and after turning down a number of moves he was dropped from the team in November.

He subsequently joined Charlton on a month's loan, which was extended to a contract until the end of the campaign. He immediately slotted into the side and put in some useful performances, getting on the score sheet against Derby County at the Valley with a well-taken free kick. An excellent passer of the ball, and a good tackler, Chris was used mainly as a defensive midfield player and made up for his lack of pace with good vision and positional awareness.
Leyton Orient (From trainee on 18/7/1991) FL 34+2/2 FLC 4 Others 2
Sheffield Wed (£275,000 on 21/11/1991) F/PL 95+29/16 FLC 14+2/4 FAC 9+3/2 Others 1+3/2
Nottingham F (£2,500,000 on 1/7/1995) F/PL 200+7/30 FLC 16/3 FAC 14/2 Others 7+1
Charlton Ath (Free on 3/12/2001) PL 10+6/1 FAC 2

BARTHEZ Fabien Alain
Born: Lavelanet, France, 28 June 1971
Height: 5'11" **Weight:** 12.8
Club Honours: PL '01
International Honours: France: 51
Fabien had quite a traumatic time in goal for Manchester United last term, not helped by the fact that the defence leaked goals following the departure of Jaap Stam to Lazio. He conceded 30 goals in just 19 games, but United also scored 40 at the other end! Sir Alex Ferguson called it 'roller-coaster football designed to give supporters a heart attack,' and Fabien certainly subscribed to that view. Fortunately the defence switched to mean mode as the New Year began, and Fabien's solid performances were just one of the reasons why the Reds mounted a title challenge which in the end was too little, too late. He is the son of the former French international rugby union player, Alain Barthez.
Manchester U (£7,800,000 from AS Monaco, France, ex Toulouse, Olympique Marseille, on 7/6/2000) PL 62 FAC 2 Others 29

BARTLETT Thurston **Shaun**
Born: Cape Town, South Africa, 31 October 1972
Height: 6'1" **Weight:** 12.4
International Honours: South Africa: 60
After previously being on loan, Shaun joined Charlton on a permanent basis in the 2001 close season. He was first choice striker in the early part of the campaign, but only managed a single goal, in the home win over Leicester, however his overall play was very good. He has good close control and is quick, strong and excellent in the air. He sustained a calf

Jon Bass

injury in the opening game of the African Nations' Cup in January, which took a long time to clear up, and then suffered an achilles injury and took no further part in the season.

Charlton Ath (Loaned from FC Zurich, Switzerland, ex Cape Town Spurs, Colorado Rapids, NY/NJ Metro Stars, Cape Town Spurs, on 1/12/2000) PL 26+6/8 FLC 2 FAC 2+1

BARTON Warren Dean
Born: Stoke Newington, 19 March 1969
Height: 6'0" **Weight:** 12.0
International Honours: E: 3; B-3
Warren started last season as first choice right back for Newcastle, and after nine games he was rested for the Worthington Cup tie against Brentford, but he rarely featured afterwards. He eventually joined Premiership strugglers Derby County in February, but was unable to prevent them from being relegated. A versatile player who also featured in midfield, he is strong in the tackle and can deliver an accurate cross from the flank.
Maidstone U (£10,000 from Leytonstone on 28/7/1989) FL 41+1 FLC 0+2 FAC 3/1 Others 7
Wimbledon (£300,000 on 7/6/1990) F/PL 178+2/10 FLC 16/1 FAC 11 Others 2
Newcastle U (£4,500,000 on 5/6/1995) PL 142+22/4 FLC 12/1 FAC 19+3 Others 20+2
Derby Co (Signed on 1/2/2002) PL 14

BARTRAM Vincent (Vince) Lee
Born: Birmingham, 7 August 1968
Height: 6'2" **Weight:** 13.4
After appearing in 103 consecutive games for Gillingham, Vince lost his place to youngster Jason Brown last March. The big 'keeper had another impressive season between the posts, and although he lost out to Brown on the run-in, he will be back in 2002-03 more determined than ever to regain his first-team spot.
Wolverhampton W (From juniors on 17/8/1985) FL 5 FLC 2 FAC 3
Blackpool (Loaned on 27/10/1989) FL 9 Others 2
Bournemouth (£65,000 on 24/7/1991) FL 132 FLC 10 FAC 14 Others 6
Arsenal (£400,000 on 10/8/1994) PL 11 FLC 0+1
Huddersfield T (Loaned on 17/10/1997) FL 12
Gillingham (Free on 20/3/1998) FL 178 FLC 11 FAC 13 Others 10

BARWICK Terence (Terry) Patrick
Born: Doncaster, 11 January 1983
Height: 5'11" **Weight:** 11.2
Terry featured regularly in the Scunthorpe

United senior squad during the first half of last season. A tigerish ball winner in the centre of midfield, he started seven League matches during the campaign, including four of the first seven matches. He signed a professional contract at the end of the season and should get more first-team opportunities next term.
Scunthorpe U (Trainee) FL 7+4 FLC 1 Others 0+1

BASHAM Michael (Mike)
Born: Barking, 27 September 1973
Height: 6'2" **Weight:** 13.9
Club Honours: AMC '94
International Honours: E: Yth; Sch
Mike's strengths in the heart of the York City's defence last season were his steadiness and distribution of the ball. He netted twice – in a 3-0 win at Torquay and when coming on as a substitute in a 2-0 home success over Darlington. He is a cultured defender who is close to reaching 200 senior appearances.
West Ham U (From trainee on 3/7/1992)
Colchester U (Loaned on 18/11/1993) FL 1
Swansea C (Free on 24/3/1994) FL 27+2/1 FAC 6 Others 8+2
Peterborough U (Free on 18/12/1995) FL 17+2/1 FLC 1 FAC 0+1
Barnet (Free on 5/8/1997) FL 74+1/2 FLC 2 FAC 0+1 Others 7+1
York C (Free on 14/3/2001) FL 32+4/3 FLC 1 FAC 4 Others 0+1

BASHAM Steven (Steve) Brian
Born: Southampton, 2 December 1977
Height: 5'11" **Weight:** 12.0
Club Honours: Div 2 '00
Steve finally returned to the Preston first team last August after a ten-month lay-off with a badly broken leg. He was brought back earlier than expected due to an injury crisis, but he became a regular on the bench from November onwards, with his only start coming in the FA Cup win over Sheffield United. Everyone at Deepdale was pleased to see the skilful striker complete his recovery when he scored the winner at Walsall. Possessing a surprisingly powerful shot for one so slight, his future may lie elsewhere following his reported rejection of a new contract.
Southampton (From trainee on 24/5/1996) PL 1+18/1 FLC 0+1
Wrexham (Loaned on 6/2/1998) FL 4+1
Preston NE (£200,000 on 5/2/1999) FL 37+31/15 FLC 5+2/1 FAC 1+2

BASS Jonathan (Jon) David
Born: Weston super Mare, 1 January 1976

Height: 6'0" **Weight:** 12.2
International Honours: E: Sch
This stylish right back joined Hartlepool in the 2001 close season. He had some good games early on, but then struggled with the faster pace of Division Three football. He lost his place in mid-season, and was subsequently restricted to reserve football. He enjoyed success off the field, gaining a degree in economics from the Open University.
Birmingham C (From juniors on 27/6/1994) FL 60+8 FLC 7+1 FAC 5
Carlisle U (Loaned on 11/10/1996) FL 3
Gillingham (Loaned on 23/3/2000) FL 4+3
Hartlepool U (Free on 17/7/2001) FL 19+1/1 FLC 1 FAC 1

BASSEDAS Christian Gustavo
Born: Buenos Aires, Argentine, 16 February 1973
Height: 5'9" **Weight:** 11.7
International Honours: Argentina: 23
Christian is an accomplished left-sided midfielder with good close control and tidy distribution. After a first year finding his feet in the Premiership he began the new season looking to establish himself in the Newcastle midfield, and started in the first three Inter Toto Cup games. However, on the return to fitness of Rob Lee he lost his place in the side and made only another two starts plus a couple of substitute appearances, after which he joined Spanish club Tenerife at the end of 2001 on loan to the end of the season.
Newcastle U (£4,100,000 from Velez Sarsfield, Argentine on 6/7/2000) PL 18+6/1 FLC 2+1 FAC 2 Others 3+1

BATTERSBY Anthony (Tony)
Born: Doncaster, 30 August 1975
Height: 6'0" **Weight:** 12.7
After signing a new three-year contract in the summer of 2001 Tony began the season alongside Lee Thorpe in the Lincoln starting line-up. He scored at Grimsby Town in the Worthington Cup but then found goals difficult to come by and ended up fighting it out with Dave Cameron for a first-team place. At his best he worked well with Thorpe holding the ball up well and providing a handful of spectacular goals.
Sheffield U (From trainee on 5/7/1993) FL 3+7/1 FLC 1+1 Others 2+1/1
Southend U (Loaned on 23/3/1995) FL 6+2/1
Notts Co (£200,000 on 8/11/1996) FL 20+19/8 FLC 1 FAC 0+3 Others 4
Bury (£125,000 on 3/3/1997) FL 37+11/8 FLC 3+1/1 FAC 2

Peter Beagrie

Lincoln C *(£75,000 on 8/8/1998) FL 94+35/21 FLC 5/2 FAC 3+3/1 Others 8+1/2*
Northampton T *(Loaned on 24/9/1999) FL 0+3/1*

BATTY David

Born: Leeds, 2 December 1968
Height: 5'8" **Weight:** 12.0
Club Honours: Div 2 '90, Div 1 '92; CS '92
International Honours: E: 42; B-5; U21-7
David's return to full fitness has been remarkable after a nightmare period with injuries. He has consistently proved to be an inspiration to the younger players around him, and had another excellent season for Leeds last term. His calm approach, tactical awareness and ability to read the game have again come to the fore and epitomise his authoritative performances. He remains a model professional, still as strong and aggressive as ever.
Leeds U *(From trainee on 3/8/1987) F/PL 201+10/4 FLC 17 FAC 12 Others 17*
Blackburn Rov *(£2,750,000 on 26/10/1993) PL 53+1/1 FLC 6 FAC 5 Others 6*
Newcastle U *(£3,750,000 on 2/3/1996) PL 81+2/3 FLC 6 FAC 9/1 Others 16*
Leeds U *(£4,400,000 on 9/12/1998) PL 69+9 FLC 3 FAC 3 Others 16+2*

BAUDET Julien

Born: St-Martin-d'Hyeres, France, 13 January 1979
Height: 6'3" **Weight:** 14.2
This former Toulouse player initially arrived at Boundary Park on a trial. He did enough to earn a permanent deal by October and became the first Frenchman to play for Oldham when making his debut against Barrow in the FA Cup. Powerful displays both at centre half and in midfield established him as a first-team regular and he made over 20 appearances. Julien capped a fine season by scoring his first goal for the club in the last-day home win over Queen's Park Rangers.
Oldham Ath *(Free from Toulouse, France on 9/10/2001) FL 13+7/1 FAC 1+2 Others 1*

BAYES Ashley John

Born: Lincoln, 19 April 1972
Height: 6'1" **Weight:** 13.5
International Honours: E: Yth
Ashley was again first-choice 'keeper for Leyton Orient at the start of the 2001-02 campaign, but then suffered a shoulder injury and spent a long period out of action. He eventually returned to the line-up towards the end of the season before being released on a free transfer. He is an

effective shot stopper who is good in the air and possesses a long kick out. He was reported to have signed for League of Ireland club Bohemians in the summer.
Brentford *(From trainee on 5/7/1990) FL 4 FLC 5 FAC 2 Others 1*
Torquay U *(Free on 13/8/1993) FL 97 FLC 7 FAC 9 Others 6*
Exeter C *(Free on 31/7/1996) FL 127 FLC 6 FAC 8 Others 4*
Leyton Orient *(Free on 5/7/1999) FL 68+1 FLC 7 FAC 5 Others 5*

BAYLISS David (Dave) Anthony

Born: Liverpool, 8 June 1976
Height: 5'11" **Weight:** 12.4
Dave was a regular for Rochdale in the opening matches of the 2001-02 campaign but was then sidelined by injury and was unable to regain his place. After a spell on the bench he was allowed to join promotion rivals Luton who required cover due to an injury crisis, and went on to feature regularly for the Hatters. His enthusiasm and experience brought stability to a leaking defence and he proved to be an excellent reader of the game.
Rochdale *(From trainee on 10/6/1995) FL 169+17/9 FLC 11 FAC 5+3 Others 12+1*
Luton T *(Free on 7/12/2001) FL 15+3*

BEAGRIE Peter Sydney

Born: Middlesbrough, 28 November 1965
Height: 5'8" **Weight:** 12.0
International Honours: E: B-2; U21-2
Peter joined Scunthorpe in the summer of 2001 as player-coach and became a key figure on the left wing, using his dazzling skills to beat his man and deliver pinpoint crosses. His fitness held up well until a calf injury in February ruled him out for a month and hampered his progress when he returned for the last six games. He scored 13 goals, including five penalties and two direct from corners, and won a place in the PFA Division Three team for the season.
Middlesbrough *(From juniors on 10/9/1983) FL 24+9/2 FLC 1 Others 1+1*
Sheffield U *(£35,000 on 16/8/1986) FL 81+3/11 FLC 5 FAC 5 Others 4*
Stoke C *(£210,000 on 29/6/1988) FL 54/7 FLC 4 FAC 3/1*
Everton *(£750,000 on 2/11/1989) F/PL 88+26/11 FLC 7+2/3 FAC 7+2 Others 5+1/1*
Sunderland *(Loaned on 26/9/1991) FL 5/1*
Manchester C *(£1,100,000 on 24/3/1994) F/PL 46+6/3 FLC 8/1 FAC 4+1/1*
Bradford C *(£50,000 on 2/7/1997) P/FL 113+18/20 FLC 9/3 FAC 5+1 Others 0+1*
Everton *(Loaned on 26/3/1998) PL 4+2*

Wigan Ath *(Free on 16/2/2001) FL 7+3/1 Others 2*
Scunthorpe U *(Free on 12/7/2001) FL 39+1/11 FLC 1 FAC 3 Others 2/2*

BEALL Matthew (Billy) John

Born: Enfield, 4 December 1977
Height: 5'7" **Weight:** 10.12
Billy made a few first-team appearances in midfield for Leyton Orient last autumn before falling out of favour. He was subsequently released from his contract in February and moved on to Dr Martens League club Cambridge City. He is a determined midfield player who is strong in the tackle.
Cambridge U *(From trainee on 28/3/1996) FL 73+8/7 FLC 2 FAC 6/2 Others 1+1*
Leyton Orient *(Signed on 26/10/1998) FL 62+22/3 FLC 2 FAC 6+2 Others 5*

BEARD Mark

Born: Roehampton, 8 October 1974
Height: 5'10" **Weight:** 11.6
Mark returned to Southend United shortly after the start of the 2001-02 campaign, bringing much needed experience to the defence and midfield. Unfortunately, his combative style led to a suspension early in the new year and this, combined with some niggling injuries, meant he failed to manage a sustained period in the team.
Millwall *(From trainee on 18/3/1993) FL 32+13/2 FLC 3+1 FAC 4/1*
Sheffield U *(£117,000 on 18/8/1995) FL 22+16 FLC 2+1 FAC 2+2*
Southend U *(Loaned on 24/10/1997) FL 6+2 Others 1*
Southend U *(Free on 6/7/1998) FL 74+4/1 FLC 1 FAC 2 Others 1 (Released during 2000 close season)*
Southend U *(Free from Kingstonian on 11/10/2001) FL 5+9 FAC 0+1 Others 1+1*

BEASANT David (Dave) John

Born: Willesden, 20 March 1959
Height: 6'4" **Weight:** 14.3
Club Honours: Div 4 '83, Div 2 '89; Div 1 '98; FAC '88; FMC '90
International Honours: E: 2; B-7
Dave is an 'evergreen' among professional footballers and joined Portsmouth in May 2001 on a three-month contract after being released by Nottingham Forest. After a short run in the team at the beginning of 2001-02 he lost his place and moved on to Tottenham Hotspur as cover for Neil Sullivan. However, he returned to Pompey on another temporary contract to play the remainder of the 2001-02 season as the club's number one 'keeper. His vast experience and considerable presence in defence

were great assets to the team and he pulled off many magnificent saves to prevent heavier defeats.
Wimbledon (£1,000 from Edgware T on 7/8/1979) FL 340 FLC 21 FAC 27 Others 3
Newcastle U (£800,000 on 13/6/1988) FL 20 FLC 2 FAC 2 Others 1
Chelsea (£725,000 on 14/1/1989) F/PL 133 FLC 11 FAC 5 Others 8
Grimsby T (Loaned on 24/10/1992) FL 6
Wolverhampton W (Loaned on 12/1/1993) FL 4 FAC 1
Southampton (£300,000 on 4/11/1993) PL 86+2 FLC 8 FAC 9
Nottingham F (Free on 22/8/1997) P/FL 139 FLC 8+1 FAC 6
Portsmouth (Free on 9/8/2001) FL 8 FLC 1
Tottenham H (Free on 16/11/2001)
Portsmouth (Free on 11/1/2002) FL 19

BEATTIE James Scott
Born: Lancaster, 27 February 1978
Height: 6'1" **Weight:** 12.0
International Honours: E: U21-5
Despite starting the 2001-02 campaign on the bench at Southampton, James quickly regained the previous season's goal-scoring form with a brace against Middlesborough at the Riverside. The big striker's main qualities lie in his ability in the air linked with a powerful shot, and he proved to be the perfect foil for his partner Marian Pahars. A brilliant 35-yard goal from a free kick at Chelsea started the new year on the right note, but a serious ankle injury sustained soon after sidelined him for two months.
Blackburn Rov (From trainee on 7/3/1995) PL 1+3 FLC 2 FAC 0+1
Southampton (£1,000,000 on 17/7/1998) PL 83+35/28 FLC 7+3/3 FAC 6+1/1

BEAUCHAMP Joseph (Joey) Daniel
Born: Oxford, 13 March 1971
Height: 5'10" **Weight:** 12.11
Joey had a disappointing season for Oxford United in 2001-02 when he was absent for several months with a broken toe that took many months to heal. When he eventually appeared at the U's new Kassam Stadium he volleyed home a fine goal – picked by many as the best goal at the ground to date. An experienced winger, he only made the starting line-up on two occasions during the campaign.
Oxford U (From trainee on 16/5/1989) FL 117+7/20 FLC 6+1/2 FAC 8/3 Others 5+1
Swansea C (Loaned on 30/10/1991) FL 5/2 Others 1
West Ham U (£1,000,000 on 22/6/1994)

Swindon T (£850,000 on 18/8/1994) FL 39+6/3 FLC 7+2/1 FAC 2 Others 4
Oxford U (£75,000 on 4/10/1995) FL 203+35/43 FLC 22+2/8 FAC 12+3/1 Others 2+4

BECKETT Luke John
Born: Sheffield, 25 November 1976
Height: 5'11" **Weight:** 11.6
Luke seemed to lose his edge as a striker for Chesterfield last term, although frequent changes of role up front didn't help, and the opportunity to move presented a fresh start for player and club. He was sold to Stockport County where he added some much needed firepower in the latter stages of the season, netting seven goals in 19 appearances. The clever front man is expected to lead the charge for County's return to Division One next season.
Barnsley (From trainee on 20/6/1995)
Chester C (Free on 11/6/1998) FL 70+4/25 FLC 5/5 FAC 4/2 Others 1
Chesterfield (£75,000 on 19/7/2000) FL 58+4/22 FLC 4/2 FAC 3/2 Others 5
Stockport Co (£100,000 on 14/12/2001) FL 17+2/7

BECKHAM David Robert Joseph
Born: Leytonstone, 2 May 1975
Height: 6'0" **Weight:** 11.12
Club Honours: FAYC '92; PL '96, '97, '99, '00, '01; FAC '96, '99; CS '96, '97; EC '99
International Honours: E: 54; U21-9; Yth
David finally found himself hailed as the hero of the national side last term, in sharp contrast to attitudes towards him following the France '98 World Cup finals. He led England to a crushing victory over Germany in September and followed this up with a brilliant late strike in the vital match against Greece. His displays in the final tournament were competent, but no more, although he was never fully fit after breaking a bone in his foot earlier in the campaign. At club level he seemed to have a dip in fortunes in the late autumn, as much as anything due to a general weariness. After a spell on the bench he returned in the new year only to suffer that broken metatarsal in a Champions' League encounter with Deportivo La Coruna which so nearly kept him out of Englands squad for Japan/Korea.
Manchester U (From trainee on 29/1/1993) PL 210+24/55 FLC 5+2 FAC 19+2/5 Others 77+3/14
Preston NE (Loaned on 28/2/1995) FL 4+1/2

BEDEAU Anthony (Tony) Charles Osmond
Born: Hammersmith, 24 March 1979
Height: 5'10" **Weight:** 11.0
2001-02 proved to be another season of unfulfilled potential for this speedy striker at Torquay. Never given a regular run in the first team, although self-confidence continued to dog him. The fact that First Division Barnsley took him on loan with a view to a signing served as a reminder of the qualities which had previously attracted the attention of many scouts and which should deliver rewards when the self-belief returns.
Torquay U (From trainee on 28/7/1997) FL 125+50/40 FLC 6+1/3 FAC 8+3/1 Others 1+8
Barnsley (Loaned on 1/2/2002) FL 0+3

BEECH Christopher (Chris)
Born: Congleton, 5 November 1975
Height: 5'10" **Weight:** 11.12
International Honours: E: Yth; Sch
A left-sided defender who can always be relied upon to give his best, Chris made just three starts for Rotherham last term. His main contribution to the club's cause was when he smashed home the winning goal against Portsmouth from the edge of the penalty area. He was captain of the Millers' successful reserve team.
Manchester C (From trainee on 12/11/1992)
Cardiff C (Free on 7/8/1997) FL 46/1 FLC 2 FAC 6
Rotherham U (Free on 30/6/1998) FL 39+14/1 FLC 6 FAC 0+1

BEECH Christopher (Chris) Stephen
Born: Blackpool, 16 September 1974
Height: 5'11" **Weight:** 11.12
The 2001-02 campaign started brightly for this industrious Huddersfield Town midfielder, and he produced some fine performances in the middle of the park. With a keen eye for goal and strong tackling, Chris was an important member of the starting eleven. However, after only nine games an achilles injury cut short his season, until a surprise return to the bench for the final match.
Blackpool (From trainee on 9/7/1993) FL 53+29/4 FLC 4+4 FAC 1 Others 3+3/2
Hartlepool U (Free on 18/7/1996) FL 92+2/23 FLC 5/1 FAC 3/1 Others 3/1
Huddersfield T (£65,000 on 27/11/1998) FL 63+8/12 FLC 6/1 FAC 2/2

BEHARALL David Alexander
Born: Jarrow, 8 March 1979
Height: 6'0" **Weight:** 11.12
This central defender began the 2001-02 season on loan at Grimsby, where he was

needed to help solve the Mariners' continuing problems in the back line following the departure of Peter Handyside and the long-term injury to Steve Livingstone. In November he began a loan spell at Oldham where he quickly established himself as a first-team regular. He eventually signed permanent forms for Athletic before tendonitis in a knee prematurely ended his season in March. He is an effective defender who has a real aerial presence.

Newcastle U (From trainee on 4/7/1997) PL 4+2
Grimsby T (Loaned on 10/8/2001) FL 13+1 FLC 1
Oldham Ath (£150,000 on 19/11/2001) FL 18+1 FAC 2 Others 2

BELGRAVE Barrington
Born: Bedford, 16 September 1980
Height: 5'9" **Weight:** 11.8
Barrington joined Southend United last September and was initially asked to fill-in in an unfamiliar wide-midfield role. He came into his own when moved to his favoured forward position by new manager, Rob Newman. Never one to give less than 100 per cent, his ability to hold the ball up and lay it off plus his fine surging runs proved to be plus points in an otherwise disappointing season for the Blues.

Plymouth Arg (From trainee at Norwich C on 28/7/1999) FL 2+13 FLC 0+1 FAC 0+2
(Free to Yeovil T on 2/8/2000)
Southend U (£40,000 on 13/9/2001) FL 32+2/5 FAC 2+1/2 Others 2

BELL David Anthony
Born: Kettering, 21 April 1984
Height: 5'10" **Weight:** 11.6
David is one of a number of exciting prospects to have come through the ranks at Rushden. A central midfielder who loves to get forward at every opportunity, he played a major part in the club's successful first season in the Football League Youth Alliance, and got his first senior opportunity when appearing as a substitute in the 1-0 reverse at Plymouth Argyle in the final game of 2001. He received the club's 'Most Improved Young Player of the Year' award.

Rushden & Diamonds (From juniors on 24/7/2001) FL 0+1 Others 0+1

BELL Michael (Mickey)
Born: Newcastle, 15 November 1971
Height: 5'9" **Weight:** 11.4
2001-02 proved to be a somewhat disappointing season for this Bristol City player, despite the fact that he was selected in the PFA divisional team for the

third successive year. A stylish left-sided defender, he eventually came good towards the end of the campaign. He netted some superb goals including a terrific strike, his second of the game, in the home clash with Cambridge United in March.

Northampton T (From trainee on 1/7/1990) FL 133+20/10 FLC 7+1 FAC 5/1 Others 9+2/1
Wycombe W (£45,000 on 21/10/1994) FL 117+1/5 FLC 5 FAC 9/2 Others 3+1
Bristol C (£150,000 on 2/7/1997) FL 193+3/31 FLC 12 FAC 13 Others 9/1

BELL Stuart
Born: Carlisle, 15 March 1984
Height: 5'10" **Weight:** 10.7

Another product of the Carlisle United youth ranks, forward Stuart Bell made his first-team debut against Macclesfield on Easter Monday. He impressed sufficiently to feature in all but one of the season's remaining fixtures and will be hoping to build on this promising foundation in 2002-03.

Carlisle U (Trainee) FL 3+2

BELLAMY Craig Douglas
Born: Cardiff, 13 July 1979
Height: 5'9" **Weight:** 10.12
International Honours: W: 16; U21-8; Yth; Sch

Craig Bellamy

Ali Benarbia

Craig made a major contribution to Newcastle becoming an exciting force near the top of the Premiership. His searing pace, instinctive reactions, and huge appetite for involvement made him a constant menace to opposition defences, and he formed a fine striking partnership with Alan Shearer. He settled quickly into goal-scoring mode and when rested for the Worthington Cup tie at home to Brentford he came off the bench to net a hat-trick, making him the first United player to score a three both in extra-time and when coming on as a substitute. In February he was diagnosed as suffering from a tear in the patella tendon plus a touch of tendonitis, forcing him to rest. His performances throughout the season earned him the PFA 'Young Player of the Year' award.

Norwich C *(From trainee on 20/1/1997) FL 71+13/32 FLC 6/2 FAC 1*
Coventry C *(£6,500,000 on 17/8/2000) PL 33+1/6 FLC 3/1 FAC 2/1*
Newcastle U *(£6,000,000 on 11/7/2001) PL 26+1/9 FLC 2+1/4 FAC 3 Others 6/1*

BELLION David
Born: Sevres, France, 27 November 1982
Height: 5'11" **Weight:** 11.5
This young right winger, made his debut for Sunderland as a substitute against Fulham in August, immediately forcing a brilliant save from Edwin van der Sar. Lightning quick and never afraid to take defenders on, he will have gained vital experience from his limited appearances from the bench, especially his showing against Manchester United at the Stadium of Light when he immediately rounded three Reds' defenders before losing his footing.
Sunderland *(Free from AS Cannes, France on 17/8/2001) PL 0+9 FLC 1*

BENALI Francis Vincent
Born: Southampton, 30 December 1968
Height: 5'10" **Weight:** 11.0
International Honours: E: Sch
A loyal servant and model professional, Francis remains a valuable member of the Saints' squad although first-team appearances are now rare due to the outstanding form of Wayne Bridge. The left-side defender signed a new one year deal in January.
Southampton *(From apprentice on 5/1/1987) F/PL 269+40/1 FLC 24+7 FAC 21 Others 3+1*
Nottingham F *(Loaned on 12/1/2001) FL 15*

BENARBIA Ali
Born: Oran, Algeria, 8 October 1968
Height: 5'7" **Weight:** 10.7
Club Honours: Div 1 '02
Ali made an immediate impact after arriving at Maine Road last September, having a hand in two of Manchester City's three goals on his debut against Birmingham. He went on to produce some breathtaking performances throughout the season when he missed only a handful of games. A midfielder with the vision to deliver a defence-splitting pass, he was deservedly voted in to the PFA First Division team for the season.
Manchester C *(Free from Paris St Germain, France, ex Martigues, AS Monaco, Bordeaux, on 14/9/2001) FL 38/8 FLC 2 FAC 2*

BEN ASKAR Aziz
Born: Chateau Gontier, France, 30 March 1976
Height: 6'2" **Weight:** 13.5
This central defender joined Queen's Park Rangers from Laval on a year's loan. He was a regular in the line-up at the start of the 2001-02 season before getting injured and it was not until February that he regained his place. He was subsequently dropped when manager Ian Holloway changed the defensive formation.
Queens Park R *(Loaned from Stade Lavallois, France, on 11/8/2001) FL 18 FLC 1 Others 1*

BENEFIELD James (Jimmy) Patrick
Born: Torbay, 6 May 1983
Height: 5'10" **Weight:** 11.2
A product of Torquay's youth scheme, Jimmy is a creative midfielder of great promise. First-team appearances last term were restricted due to an ongoing relegation struggle requiring experienced heads, but the fact that a short-term contract was quickly replaced by a longer deal clearly demonstrates that the club hold him in high regard.
Torquay U *(From trainee on 12/7/2001) FL 3+6 FLC 0+1 FAC 0+1 Others 0+1*

BENJAMIN Trevor Junior
Born: Kettering, 8 February 1979
Height: 6'2" **Weight:** 13.2
International Honours: E: U21-1
This powerfully built striker was looking to make a Premiership breakthrough at Leicester last season but it never really happened for him. A brief run in the team in the autumn coincided with the Foxes last realistic chance of avoiding relegation, but he was unable to make a major impact and was subsequently loaned to Crystal Palace, Norwich City and West Brom in an attempt to boost his confidence and experience whilst, at the same time, reducing the wage bill at Filbert Street.
Cambridge U *(From trainee on 21/2/1997) FL 96+27/35 FLC 7+3/4 FAC 9+1/5 Others 3/2*
Leicester C *(£1,000,000 + on 14/7/2000) PL 11+21/1 FLC 0+2 FAC 2+2*
Crystal Palace *(Loaned on 20/12/2001) FL 5+1/1*
Norwich C *(Loaned on 8/2/2002) FL 3+3*
West Bromwich A *(Loaned on 27/3/2002) FL 0+3/1*

BENNETT Daniel (Danny) Mark
Born: Great Yarmouth, 7 January 1978
Height: 6'0" **Weight:** 12.0
Danny arrived at Wrexham last February after trials with a number of Football League clubs. His credentials were interesting – a former player in the S-League, he had been voted Singapore's 'Player of the Year' in 2001 and had also featured for Team Singapore in friendlies against Manchester United and Liverpool. A central defender who can also play in midfield, he showed composure and confidence on the ball and gave a fine performance against Stoke in April. He signed for Singapore Armed Forces FC in May, but may yet be back at the Racecourse for the 2002-03 campaign.
Wrexham *(Free from Tanjong Pager U, Malaysia on 31/1/2002) FL 5+1*

BENNETT Dean Alan
Born: Wolverhampton, 13 December 1977
Height: 5'10" **Weight:** 11.0
Club Honours: NC '00
International Honours: E: SP-1
Dean began the 2001-02 campaign on Kidderminster's transfer list, but his performances improved to such an extent that he was rewarded with a new contract midway through the season. He is a lively midfield player whose strengths lie in his ability to run at defenders with the ball.
West Bromwich A *(Free from Aston Villa juniors on 19/12/1996) FL 0+1 (Free to Bromsgrove Rov on 14/9/98)*
Kidderminster Hrs *(£30,000 on 29/1/1999) FL 74+10/12 FLC 2 FAC 2+2 Others 3*

BENNETT Ian Michael
Born: Worksop, 10 October 1971
Height: 6'0" **Weight:** 12.10
Club Honours: Div 2 '95; AMC '95
Ian missed the start of the 2001-02 season because of a fractured finger, but

Henning Berg

was restored to the Birmingham City line-up in November by caretaker managers Mick Mills and Jim Barron and kept a clean sheet in a 2-0 win against Coventry. He performed capably, stopping shots well and also becoming more dominant on crosses. A hand injury allowed Nico Vaesen to reclaim the goalkeeper's jersey in March.
Newcastle U (From trainee at Queens Park R on 20/3/1989)
Peterborough U (Free on 22/3/1991) FL 72 FLC 10 FAC 3 Others 4
Birmingham C (£325,000 on 17/12/1993) FL 271 FLC 36 FAC 16 Others 13

BENNETT Thomas (Tom)
McNeill
Born: Falkirk, 12 December 1969
Height: 5'11" **Weight:** 11.8
Walsall skipper for most of 2001-02, Tom battled on tirelessly in a 'holding' role in midfield. He always gave of his best and scored the opening goal in the FA Cup win over Bradford City. He was rather unlucky to be sent off in a late-season game against Barnsley and ended the campaign with substitute appearances in the last two games before being released after just over two seasons at Bescot.
Aston Villa (From apprentice on 16/12/1987)
Wolverhampton W (Free on 5/7/1988) FL 103+12/2 FLC 7 FAC 5+2 Others 3+1
Stockport Co (£75,000 on 23/6/1995) FL 105+5/5 FLC 20/2 FAC 10 Others 6+1
Walsall (Loaned on 30/12/1999) FL 4/1
Walsall (Free on 23/3/2000) FL 75+10/7 FLC 1+1 FAC 5/1 Others 3

BENT Darren Ashley
Born: Wandsworth, 6 February 1984
Height: 5'11" **Weight:** 11.7
International Honours: E: Yth
Darren is another graduate from the Ipswich Town academy and played a starring role in the reserve team's championship-winning season as their leading scorer. He made his first-team debut against Bolton and his only Premiership goal was the winner against Middlesbrough. A striker with a good turn of speed and a powerful right foot, he was capped by England at U19 level during the season.
Ipswich T (From trainee on 2/7/2001) PL 2+3/1 FLC 0+1/1 Others 0+1

BENT Jason
Born: Toronto, Canada, 8 March 1977
Height: 5'9" **Weight:** 11.7
Club Honours: Div 3 '02
International Honours: Canada: 29; Yth

Jason joined Plymouth last September and made his long-awaited debut as a substitute in the home win against Macclesfield. The midfielder showed his class in the centre of the park by using and distributing the ball well. He added a further four caps for Canada during his time with Argyle, but suffered a hamstring injury in the Gold Cup semi-final against USA which kept him out of action for a while. However he returned towards the end of the campaign and scored the final goal in the win at Darlington in April.
Plymouth Arg (Free from Colorado Rapids, USA on 21/9/2001) FL 16+5/3 FAC 2+1/1 Others 1

BENT Marcus Nathan
Born: Hammersmith, 19 May 1978
Height: 6'2" **Weight:** 12.4
International Honours: E: U21-2
Marcus had few chances at Blackburn last season and joined Ipswich in November, initially to cover for Marcus Stewart. He had to wait until Boxing Day to open his account, against Leicester City, and then proceeded to score six goals in six games. He has the ability to do the unexpected and get away from defenders either through a quick turn in the box or a deft change of pace as was demonstrated against Tottenham when his speed earned a corner which he promptly headed into the net.
Brentford (From trainee on 21/7/1995) FL 56+14/8 FLC 7/1 FAC 8/3 Others 5+1
Crystal Palace (£150,000 + on 8/11/1998) P/FL 13+15/5 FLC 0+2 FAC 0+1
Port Vale (£375,000 on 15/1/1999) FL 17+6/1 FLC 1
Sheffield U (£300,000 on 28/10/1999) FL 48/20 FLC 5/3 FAC 3/1
Blackburn Rov (£1,300,000 + on 24/11/2000) P/FL 22+15/8 FLC 0+1 FAC 5+1/3
Ipswich T (£3,000,000 on 23/11/2001) PL 22+3/9 FAC 2/1

BERESFORD David
Born: Middleton, 11 November 1976
Height: 5'5" **Weight:** 11.4
International Honours: E: Yth; Sch
After previously trying to sign the diminutive winger for Hull, Tigers boss Brian Little got his man in the 2001 close season. David put his earlier injury problems behind him and went on to play a key role in the Boothferry Park revolution. Primarily right footed, he was used on the left with the added bonus of being able to switch flanks. Reputed to be one of the fastest wingmen outside of the Premiership, the former FA School of

Excellence pupil was a constant threat to Division Three defences.
Oldham Ath (From trainee on 22/7/1994) P/FL 32+32/2 FLC 3+3 FAC 0+1 Others 3
Swansea C (Loaned on 11/8/1995) FL 4+2
Huddersfield T (£350,000 on 27/3/1997) FL 24+11/3 FLC 2+3 FAC 1+1
Preston NE (Loaned on 17/12/1999) FL 1+3 FAC 0+1 Others 1
Port Vale (Loaned on 15/9/2000) FL 4
Hull C (Free on 4/7/2001) FL 33+8/1 FLC 2 FAC 1 Others 3

BERESFORD Marlon
Born: Lincoln, 2 September 1969
Height: 6'1" **Weight:** 13.6
Marlon made just one first-team appearance last term, replacing Mark Crossley soon after the start of Boro's visit to Liverpool in December. He later spent two months on loan at Burnley as cover for regular 'keeper Nik Michopoulos. He hardly put a foot wrong between the posts for the Clarets, his sure handling and sometimes spectacular shot stopping certainly being worth a few points to the side. His contract was due to expire in the summer and at the time of writing his future was uncertain.
Sheffield Wed (From trainee on 23/9/1987)
Bury (Loaned on 25/8/1989) FL 1
Northampton T (Loaned on 27/9/1990) FL 13 Others 2
Crewe Alex (Loaned on 28/2/1991) FL 3
Northampton T (Loaned on 15/8/1991) FL 15
Burnley (£95,000 on 28/8/1992) FL 240 FLC 18 FAC 20 Others 16
Middlesbrough (£500,000 on 10/3/1998) P/FL 8+2 FLC 3
Sheffield Wed (Loaned on 12/1/2000) FL 4
Burnley (Loaned on 31/1/2002) FL 13

BERG Henning
Born: Eidsvell, Norway, 1 September 1969
Height: 6'0" **Weight:** 12.7
Club Honours: PL '95, '99, '00; FLC '02
International Honours: Norway: 89; U21-15; Yth
This commanding central defender is approaching the end of an illustrious career, but he remains an immense competitor, strong, aggressive and bruising to play against. There is never a doubt that he hates to lose, that he plays with his heart on his sleeve and that he organises and instructs those around him. Although the Worthington Cup final was not his best game, it demonstrated everything about him. Captain for the day he held together an experimental and inexperienced defence, and when the pressure intensified he was a lion where the action was fiercest.

Blackburn Rov (£400,000 from Lillestrom, Norway, ex VIF, on 26/11/1993) PL 154+5/4 FLC 16 FAC 10 Others 9
Manchester U (£5,000,000 on 12/8/1997) PL 49+17/2 FLC 3 FAC 7 Others 22+5/1
Blackburn Rov (£1,750,000 on 8/9/2000) P/FL 75/2 FLC 3 FAC 5

BERGER Patrik

Born: Prague, Czechoslovakia, 10 November 1973
Height: 6'1" **Weight:** 12.6
Club Honours: FAC '01; UEFAC '01; CS '01
International Honours: Czech Republic: 44; U21-1; Czechoslovakia: 2; Yth (UEFA-U16 '90)
After spending most of the previous campaign on the sidelines with a serious ankle injury, Patrik desperately needed a trouble-free season last term, but it was not to be. After only two games he suffered problems with his knee that kept him out of action until October. He eventually resumed his customary position on the left side of midfield and heralded his comeback with a trademark goal from outside the penalty area against Middlesbrough at Anfield. However the injury jinx struck again at the end of January when a groin strain sidelined him for two months, and it was not until the closing stages that he returned to fitness once more.
Liverpool (£3,250,000 from Borussia Dortmund, Germany, ex Slavia Prague, on 15/8/1996) PL 106+40/28 FLC 8+2/2 FAC 4+4 Others 17+11/4

BERGKAMP Dennis

Born: Amsterdam, Holland, 18 May 1969
Height: 6'0" **Weight:** 12.5
Club Honours: PL '98, '02; FAC '02; CS '98
International Honours: Holland: 79; U21
Barring the odd injury, Denis featured regularly for Arsenal last term, although the policy of rotating the club's strikers meant that he spent much of the time on the subs' bench. A talented player with the ability to score and create goals out of nothing, he netted a total of 14 in all competitions during the season.
Arsenal (£7,500,000 from Inter Milan, Italy, ex Ajax, on 3/7/1995) PL 181+24/69 FLC 15/8 FAC 24+3/11 Others 23+5/9

BERGSSON Gudni

Born: Reykjavik, Iceland, 21 July 1965
Height: 6'1" **Weight:** 12.3
Club Honours: Div 1 '97
International Honours: Iceland: 77; U21-4; Yth

Phenomenal. No other word can sum up 'The Iceman' better. Gudni delayed his retirement for 12 months when Bolton achieved promotion to the Premiership and, whilst the doubters stated that he might be too slow and too old for a full campaign in the top flight, he enjoyed yet another outstanding season. He generally played in the centre of the defence and his experience showed in every game. A superb reader of the game with excellent distribution, he showed that even the finest centre forwards in the Premiership would struggle against this hugely influential player.
Tottenham H (£100,000 from Valur, Iceland on 15/12/1988) F/PL 51+20/2 FLC 4+2 FAC 2+2 Others 5+1
Bolton W (£115,000 on 21/3/1995) P/FL 232+7/22 FLC 23+2/1 FAC 12/1 Others 8+2/2

BERHALTER Gregg

Born: Tenafly, New Jersey, USA, 1 August 1973
Height: 6'1" **Weight:** 12.7
International Honours: USA: 29
This tall left back never established himself as a regular in the Crystal Palace line-up last season, although he scored his first goal for the club at Bradford City. He also continued to be a member of the USA international squad throughout the campaign.
Crystal Palace (Free from Cambuur, Holland, ex University of North Carolina, FC Zwolle, Sparta Rotterdam, on 16/2/2001) FL 10+9/1 FLC 1+1

BERKLEY Austin James

Born: Dartford, 28 January 1973
Height: 5'10" **Weight:** 11.6
Austin joined Carlisle on a short-term contract early last season and featured in a handful of matches before being released and returning to Barnet. He is an experienced left-sided midfield player who showed some neat touches.
Gillingham (From trainee on 13/5/1991) FL 0+3 Others 0+3
Swindon T (Free on 16/5/1992) FL 0+1 FLC 0+1 Others 3+1/1
Shrewsbury T (Free on 29/7/1995) FL 152+20/12 FLC 5+2 FAC 6+1 Others 12+1/1
Barnet (Free on 4/7/2000) Others 1+1
Carlisle U (Loaned on 21/8/2001) FL 2+3 FLC 0+1

BERKOVIC Eyal

Born: Haifa, Israel, 2 April 1972
Height: 5'7'' **Weight:** 10.6
Club Honours: SLC '00; Div 1 '02
International Honours: Israel: 73; U21

It was widely expected that Eyal would stay on at Ewood Park last season, but Manchester City boss Kevin Keegan stepped in to sign the creative midfielder in the close season. Right from his debut in the opening game against Watford, he made the home crowd aware of his undoubted skills. He won the 'Man of the Match' award and scored a goal in City's 3-0 win, but then suffered a torn hamstring in the following game against Norwich. On his return he blossomed alongside Ali Benarbia, and scored a memorable volley in the 4-1 win at Ipswich in the FA Cup. He was deservedly voted into the PFA's First Division team for the season.
Southampton (Loaned from Maccabi Tel Aviv, Israel on 11/10/1996) PL 26+2/4 FLC 5+1/2 FAC 1
West Ham U (£1,700,000 on 30/7/1997) PL 62+3/10 FLC 6 FAC 7+1/2
Glasgow Celtic (£5,500,000 on 20/7/1999) SL 29+3/9 SLC 0+2 SC 1 Others 3+3
Blackburn Rov (Loaned on 9/2/2001) FL 4+7/2 FAC 3
Manchester C (£1,500,000 on 2/8/2001) 20+5/6 FLC 2+1 FAC 3/1

BERNARD Olivier

Born: Paris, France, 14 October 1979
Height: 5'9" **Weight:** 12.6
A series of outstanding displays in the reserves' pre-season friendlies earned Olivier a call up to the Newcastle first-team squad for the Inter Toto Cup matches, and he impressed when called from the bench in three of the games. He was awarded his first start in the Worthington Cup tie at Barnsley in October and a few weeks later made his Premiership bow as a substitute in the home win over Villa. Olivier became a regular squad member, mostly as a substitute with occasional starts. A powerful, stocky player with a good turn of speed and a fine left foot, he was used primarily as an understudy to Laurent Robert on the left wing.
Newcastle U (Signed from Lyon, France, on 26/10/2000) PL 4+12/3 FLC 2 FAC 2 Others 0+3
Darlington (Loaned on 13/3/2001) FL 9+1/2

BERTOS Leonida (Leo) Christos

Born: Wellington, New Zealand, 20 December 1981
Height: 6'0" **Weight:** 12.6
International Honours: New Zealand: Sch
Leo damaged a knee in pre-season and

his first-team chances at Barnsley looked remote. The introduction of new manager Steve Parkin brought him back into contention and he made his first ever start in Parkin's second game in charge at Norwich. Unfortunately he then suffered a bout of glandular fever that put him out of action until the season was nearly over. He is a hard-running wide midfield player who can power past defenders and has a strong shot.

Barnsley (Signed from Wellington Olympic, New Zealand on 1/9/2000) FL 2+4 FAC 0+1

BESWETHERICK Jonathan (Jon) Barry
Born: Liverpool, 15 January 1978
Height: 5'11" **Weight:** 11.4
Club Honours: Div 3 '02
Jon started the 2001-02 season as first choice left back in Plymouth's back four. His surging runs, timely tackles and left wing crosses ensured he remained a firm favourite with the Argyle fans. Although he lost his place to Brian McGlinchey midway through the campaign, he came back and played a major role in the final push for promotion. Jon was out of contract in the summer and at the time of writing was considering the offer of a two-year contract.

Plymouth Arg (From trainee on 27/7/1996) FL 133+13 FLC 3 FAC 14+2 Others 4

BETSY Kevin Eddie Lewis
Born: Seychelles, 20 March 1978
Height: 6'1" **Weight:** 11.12
International Honours: E: SP-1
After making what proved his only Premiership appearance of the season for Fulham as a substitute at Old Trafford in the opening game, Kevin drifted back into the reserve team where he remained a regular although he failed to find the target as often as in previous seasons. At the end of February he was loaned to Barnsley where he made a good impression and signed permanent forms shortly before the transfer deadline. He is a talented midfielder who normally operates in a wide-right role.

Fulham (£80,000 + from Woking on 16/9/1998) P/FL 3+12/1 FLC 2+1 FAC 0+1 Others 1
Bournemouth (Loaned on 3/9/1999) FL 1+4
Hull C (Loaned on 26/11/1999) FL 1+1 Others 1
Barnsley (£200,000 on 28/2/2002) FL 10

BETTS Robert
Born: Doncaster, 21 December 1981
Height: 5'10" **Weight:** 11.0

This young central midfield player joined Lincoln City on loan from Coventry last October as cover for injuries. He made his Imps' debut in a bad-tempered clash with Oxford United and subsequently only featured from the bench. He returned to Highfield Road where he made the starting line-up in the new year as cover for Youssef Safri and regularly featured on the bench thereafter. Robert received the Sky Blues' 'Most Improved Player' award for some promising displays.

Doncaster Rov (Trainee) FL 2+1
Coventry C (From trainee on 23/12/1998) P/FL 4+8 FAC 1
Plymouth Arg (Loaned on 16/2/2001) FL 3+1
Lincoln C (Loaned on 11/10/2001) FL 1+2 Others 0+1

BETTS Simon Richard
Born: Middlesbrough, 3 March 1973
Height: 5'7" **Weight:** 11.6
This experienced defender returned to his native north-east in the 2001 close season and immediately settled into the Darlington team operating in either full-back position with equal ease. His quick tackling and sure distribution established him as a key member of the defence until a nasty knee injury sustained at Carlisle in February ruled him out for a lengthy spell, but he managed to return for the final game of the season.

Ipswich T (From trainee on 2/7/1991)
Colchester U (Free, via trials at Wrexham and Scarborough, on 11/12/1992) FL 182+9/11 FLC 9 FAC 8+2 Others 14/2 (Free to Scarborough during 1999 close season)
Darlington (Free from Yeovil T on 26/7/2001) FL 29 FLC 1 FAC 4 Others 2

Kevin Betsy

BHUTIA Bhaichung
Born: Gangtok, Sikkim, India, 15 December 1976
Height: 5'8" **Weight:** 10.2
International Honours: India: 46
This diminutive Bury striker suffered another frustrating season wrecked by injury in 2001-02. He started pre-season in goal-scoring form and earned a first-team shirt in the opening weeks, but then injured his knee and although he gamely played on, it became obvious that he had a cartilage problem. He initially underwent keyhole surgery in September and made a comeback at reserve level the following month, but suffered a reaction and underwent another operation in November. He gradually battled back towards fitness in March but did not progress beyond the reserve team and was eventually released in the summer.
Bury (Signed from East Bengal, India on 29/9/1999) FL 20+17/3 FLC 2 FAC 2+3 Others 2

BIAGINI Leonardo Angel
Born: Arroyo Seco, Argentina, 13 April 1977
Height: 5'11" **Weight:** 11.7
Leonardo is a talented midfielder with an excellent first touch, good awareness and very speedy down the flanks. He scored twice in six appearances for Portsmouth last season but suffered from hamstring problems in the closing stages of the campaign.
Portsmouth (Loaned from Real Mallorca, Spain, ex Newells, Atletico Madrid, Merida, on 12/2/2002) FL 6+2/2

BIANCALINI Frederic
Born: Villerupt, France, 21 July 1974
Height: 6'0" **Weight:** 11.5
Frederic joined Walsall after a pre-season trial with Huddersfield but was handicapped by a training ground eye injury in the first few weeks of the campaign. After a couple of games in defence he settled into midfield around the turn of the year, contributing opportunist goals and accurate crosses, but suffered a setback when sent off against Preston in January. He came back to set up Darren Byfield's vital late-season match winner against Barnsley.
Walsall (Free from Nancy, France on 17/8/2001) FL 13+5/2 FLC 0+1 FAC 2

BIGNOT Marcus
Born: Birmingham, 22 August 1974
Height: 5'10" **Weight:** 11.2
International Honours: E: SP-1
Marcus is a wholehearted player who can perform equally well on the right-hand side of midfield or as a left wing back. He was one of the few regular players for Queen's Park Rangers last term, and contributed a cracking last-minute goal against Bury.
Crewe Alex (£150,000 + from Kidderminster Hrs on 1/9/1997) FL 93+2 FLC 8 FAC 3
Bristol Rov (Free on 7/8/2000) FL 26/1 FLC 5/2 FAC 1 Others 3
Queens Park R (Signed on 16/3/2001) FL 49+5/1 FLC 1 FAC 1 Others 1

BILLY Christopher (Chris) Anthony
Born: Huddersfield, 2 January 1973
Height: 5'11" **Weight:** 11.8
Bury's utility man began the 2001-02 season as a regular on the right side of midfield but was stretchered off with a knee injury in the game at Brentford in October. The injury required an operation and it was not until January that he returned to first-team duties. He ruptured his groin with his first touch and as a result missed the next three months before making another comeback in April, ironically at home to Brentford, when he put his troubles behind him by scoring both goals in a 2-0 win.
Huddersfield T (From trainee on 1/7/1991) FL 76+18/4 FLC 8+2 FAC 5 Others 15+2/2
Plymouth Arg (Signed on 10/8/1995) FL 107+11/9 FLC 5 FAC 8/1 Others 5+1
Notts Co (Free on 2/7/1998) FL 3+3 FLC 2
Bury (Free on 17/9/1998) FL 132+8/7 FLC 4 FAC 6/1 Others 1+1

BIMSON Stuart James
Born: Liverpool, 29 September 1969
Height: 5'11" **Weight:** 11.12
Stuart suffered from a niggling calf injury early in the 2001-02 season but quickly won back his place on the left side of Lincoln's four-man defensive system. He worked hard throughout the campaign earning the respect of his team colleagues and was appointed as stand-in captain during John Finnigan's absences due to injury.
Bury (£12,500 from Macclesfield T on 6/2/1995) FL 36 FLC 5 Others 3
Lincoln C (Free on 29/11/1996) FL 116+17/3 FLC 1 FAC 6+2 Others 9+1/1

BINGHAM Michael James
Born: Leyland, 21 May 1981
Height: 6'0" **Weight:** 12.10
Michael joined Mansfield Town in the summer of 2001 as understudy to goalkeeper Kevin Pilkington and was given his senior debut in the LDV Vans Trophy match against Blackpool. He later made his first League appearance as a substitute at Swansea in March when he replaced Pilkington, who had been sent off.
Blackburn Rov (From trainee on 15/7/1998)
Mansfield T (Free on 19/7/2001) FL 1+1 Others 1

BIRCH Gary Stephen
Born: Birmingham, 8 October 1981
Height: 5'10" **Weight:** 11.6
Gary spent the first three months of the 2001-02 season on loan at Exeter where he featured regularly, although mostly from the subs' bench. On his return to Walsall, his first-team chances were limited to a substitute appearance at Rotherham in October, but he remained popular with reserve-team fans for his enthusiastic front running and eye for goal. He scored some useful goals around the turn of the year whilst on loan to Nuneaton in the Conference.
Walsall (From trainee on 31/10/1998) FL 0+1 Others 2/1
Exeter C (Loaned on 22/3/2001) FL 6+3/2
Exeter C (Loaned on 10/8/2001) FL 5+10 Others 1

BIRCH Mark
Born: Stoke, 5 January 1977
Height: 5'10" **Weight:** 12.5
Mark was a near ever present for Carlisle last term featuring at both right wing back and right midfield. A dependable defender, his game continued to improve and he can look back with satisfaction on his performances during the season. A solid tackler with good pace, he was always willing to move up to support the attack.
Stoke C (From trainee on 8/7/1995. Free to Northwich Vic on 22/7/98)
Carlisle U (£10,000 on 10/8/2000) FL 86 FLC 3 FAC 6 Others 2

BIRCHALL Christopher (Chris)
Born: Stafford, 5 May 1984
Height: 5'9" **Weight:** 12.12
Still a trainee with Port Vale, this all-action right winger made his debut as a substitute in the Worthington Cup tie at Charlton Athletic last season and did reasonably well considering he was facing Premiership defenders. He then returned to a mixture of youth and reserve-team games before being recalled to the first team, also from the bench, for the final game of the season against Brighton when he again shone.
Port Vale (Trainee) FL 0+1 FLC 0+1

BIRCHAM Marc Stephen John
Born: Wembley, 11 May 1978
Height: 5'10'' **Weight:** 12.4
Club Honours: Div 2 '01
International Honours: Canada: 13;
U23-1
Marc had a frustrated season at Millwall last term due to the excellent central midfield partnership established by Tim Cahill and David Livermore. He spent most of the campaign on the bench and also featured in a wide role where he put in some excellent performances. Marc is a hard-working, strong-running midfielder who always gives 100 per cent, which goes down well with the Millwall faithful.
Millwall (From trainee on 22/5/1996) FL 86+18/3 FLC 3+1 FAC 6+1/1 Others 5+1

BIRD Anthony (Tony)
Born: Cardiff, 1 September 1974
Height: 5'10" **Weight:** 12.8
Club Honours: Div 3 '00
International Honours: W: U21-8; Yth
Tony spent the whole of the 2001-02 campaign on the transfer list at Kidderminster despite having a productive pre-season and then scoring four times in the first five games. The goals dried up after that, however, and he soon found himself on the sidelines. Even though he is a strong centre forward, Tony was used in a variety of positions when he did force his way back into the squad usually on the right hand side of midfield. He left the club at the end of the season when his contract expired.
Cardiff C (From trainee on 4/8/1993) FL 44+31/13 FLC 8/2 FAC 4+1/1 Others 12+4/3 (Free to Barry T in January 1996)
Swansea C (£40,000 on 8/8/1997) FL 51+35/18 FLC 5+2/1 FAC 2+1 Others 3+3/3
Kidderminster Hrs (Free on 14/7/2000) FL 30+21/3 FLC 3/2 FAC 2+1/1 Others 2+1/1

BIRMINGHAM David Paul
Born: Portsmouth, 16 April 1981
Height: 5'6" **Weight:** 10.0
David signed non-contract forms for Bournemouth in the closing stages of the 2000-01 campaign and was invited to train with the club at the start of last season. He found himself on the bench on a couple of occasions early on and made his full debut against Torquay in the Worthington Cup. He also played for Bognor Regis Town throughout the campaign but apart from a short run in the side around Christmas, he rarely featured for the Cherries. A left-sided defender who is quick and hard working, he was released in the summer.

Portsmouth (From trainee at Bournemouth on 4/8/1999) FL 1+1 FLC 0+1
Bournemouth (Free on 22/3/2001) FL 3+1 FLC 1

BISCAN Igor
Born: Yugoslavia, 4 May 1978
Height: 6'3" **Weight:** 12.8
Club Honours: FLC '01; ESC '01; CS '01
International Honours: Croatia: 15
Although a valued member of the Liverpool squad, Igor has yet to make his mark at Anfield. 2001-02 started promisingly with four outings in the first five games of the season, but thereafter his appearances in the first team were fleeting, deputising occasionally when Steven Gerrard or Dietmar Hamann were unavailable. His progress was disrupted by a short-term ankle injury in October but a pallid performance at Stamford Bridge in the 4-0 defeat by Chelsea in December proved to be his last first-team appearance of the season, bar a late substitute appearance in the Champions' League at home to Roma in March.
Liverpool (£3,500,000 from Dynamo Zagreb, Croatia, ex Samobar, on 7/12/2000) PL 12+6 FLC 4/1 FAC 3+1 Others 1+4

BJORKLUND Joachim
Born: Vaxjo, Sweden, 15 February 1971
Height: 6'1" **Weight:** 12.10
Club Honours: SPD '97; SLC '96
International Honours: Sweden: 75
A former Swedish international, centre back Joachim joined Sunderland in January and endured a real baptism of fire at Old Trafford as a rampant Manchester United hit the Black Cats for four, but he soon settled at the Stadium of Light, forming a solid partnership with Jody Craddock in the back four. His main asset is his pace and he turned in excellent performances against quality strikers such as Alan Shearer and Michael Owen in an overworked defence.
Glasgow R (Signed from Vicenza, Italy, ex Osters, Brann Bergen, Goteborg, on 15/7/1996) SL 59 SLC 5 SC 8 Others 13 (Transferred to Valencia, Spain during 1998 close season)
Sunderland ((£1,500,000 on 1/2/2002) PL 11+1

BJORNEBYE Stig Inge
Born: Elverum, Norway, 11 December 1969
Height: 5'10" **Weight:** 11.9
Club Honours: FLC '95, '02
International Honours: Norway: 76; B-1; U21; Yth
The solid defender's place in the Blackburn line-up came under challenge

last term, but he faced the threat with his usual calm approach and retained a regular place in the starting line-up. A master of sensing danger on the edge of the area and making the last ditch tackle, he was occasionally outpaced but remained cool under pressure. His distribution has faded but he still possesses the ability to deliver a pass with inch perfection. He fractured an eye socket in late April and could be out for some time.
Liverpool (£600,000 from Rosenborg, Norway, ex Strommen, Kongsvinger, on 18/12/1992) PL 132+7/2 FLC 16 FAC 11+2 Others 16/2
Blackburn Rov (£300,000 on 28/6/2000) P/FL 53+3/1 FLC 6 FAC 4+1

BLACK Kingsley Terence
Born: Luton, 22 June 1968
Height: 5'9" **Weight:** 11.2
Club Honours: FLC '88; FMC '92; AMC '98
International Honours: E: Sch. NI: 30; B-3; U21-1
This former Northern Ireland international gave Lincoln some quality on the right side of their midfield four after signing from neighbours Grimsby Town. City manager Alan Buckley also used him as a striker playing off Lee Thorpe and he contributed a number of goals including a spectacular long-range free kick at Carlisle United. Niggling injuries caused him to miss several games in the second half of the season.
Luton T (From juniors on 7/7/1986) FL 123+4/26 FLC 16+2/1 FAC 5+1/2 Others 3+2/1
Nottingham F (£1,500,000 on 2/9/1991) F/PL 80+18/14 FLC 19+1/5 FAC 4 Others 4+2/1
Sheffield U (Loaned on 2/3/1995) FL 8+3/2
Millwall (Loaned on 29/9/1995) FL 1+2/1 FLC 0+1
Grimsby T (£25,000 on 16/7/1996) FL 91+50/8 FLC 14+2 FAC 5+2 Others 2+5/1
Lincoln C (Loaned on 13/10/2000) FL 5
Lincoln C (Free on 2/7/2001) FL 30+1/5 FLC 1 FAC 1+1 Others 1

BLACK Thomas (Tommy)
Robert
Born: Chigwell, 26 November 1979
Height: 5'7" **Weight:** 11.4
Tommy began the 2001-02 season in good form for Crystal Palace, scoring two goals in the Worthington Cup tie at Leyton Orient. A hard-working right winger he had a couple of spells out through suspension, but mostly featured from the subs' bench.

Michael Blackwood (right)

Arsenal (From trainee on 3/7/1998) PL 0+1 FLC 1
Carlisle U (Loaned on 25/8/1999) FL 5/1
Bristol C (Loaned on 17/12/1999) FL 4
Crystal Palace (£250,000 + on 21/7/2000) FL 35+30/4 FLC 9+1/3 FAC 0+1

BLACKWOOD Michael Andrew
Born: Birmingham, 30 September 1979
Height: 5'10" **Weight:** 11.10
Michael looked impressive when in full flight and bearing down on goal, unfortunately, his positive runs often fizzled out to nothing. However the pacy left winger made some useful contributions for the Robins, scoring the only goal in Denis Smith's first game in charge against Queen's Park Rangers and producing a cracker in the 3-2 success at Peterborough. He was rarely included in the line-up in the closing stages of the campaign and was released in the summer.
Aston Villa (From trainee on 14/4/1998)
Chester C (Loaned on 3/9/1999) FL 9/2
Wrexham (Free on 18/7/2000) FL 24+22/2 FLC 1 FAC 1+1 Others 1

BLAKE Mark Antony
Born: Nottingham, 16 December 1970
Height: 5'11" **Weight:** 13.0
International Honours: E: U21-9; Yth; Sch
Tough tackling, all-action midfielder Mark came to Kidderminster in the 2001 close season and was immediately handed the captain's armband. His combative style caused him problems with referees and he was also dogged by an ankle injury. After a spell out he returned to the team in February, but then snapped his achilles tendon and missed the remainder of the campaign.
Aston Villa (From trainee on 1/7/1989) FL 26+5/2 FLC 1+1 FAC 2 Others 2
Wolverhampton W (Loaned on 17/1/1991) FL 2
Portsmouth (£400,000 on 5/8/1993) FL 15 Others 4+1
Leicester C (£360,000 on 24/3/1994) P/FL 42+7/4 FLC 4 Others 3
Walsall (Free on 23/8/1996) FL 51+10/5 FLC 2 FAC 0+4 Others 2+2/1
Mansfield T (Free on 13/8/1999) FL 78+6/9 FLC 4 FAC 3/1 Others 3
Kidderminster Hrs (Free on 23/7/2001) FL 23+1/4 FLC 1 FAC 1 Others 1+1

BLAKE Nathan Alexander
Born: Cardiff, 27 January 1972
Height: 5'11" **Weight:** 13.2
Club Honours: WC '92, '93; Div 3 '93, Div 1 '97

International Honours: W: 22; B-1; U21-5; Yth
This striker was on the bench for Blackburn at the start of last term and came on to score a well-struck goal against Derby County. However he was sold to Wolves soon afterwards where he found the net in his first two matches before the goals dried up. He held the ball up well and was effective when laying it off, indeed he seemed happier playing with his back to goal.
Cardiff C (From trainee at Chelsea on 20/8/1990) FL 113+18/35 FLC 6+2 FAC 10/4 Others 13+2/1
Sheffield U (£300,000 on 17/2/1994) P/FL 55+14/34 FLC 3+1/1 FAC 1 Others 1
Bolton W (£1,500,000 on 23/12/1995) F/PL 102+5/38 FLC 10+1/8 FAC 6/2
Blackburn Rov (£4,250,000 on 30/10/1998) P/FL 37+17/13 FLC 3/1 FAC 5+3/2
Wolverhampton W (£1,400,000 on 13/9/2001) FL 38+1/11 FAC 1 Others 2

BLAKE Robert (Robbie) James
Born: Middlesbrough, 4 March 1976
Height: 5'9" **Weight:** 12.6
Robbie started the 2001-02 season on the bench for Bradford City, but once in the starting line-up he showed the fans that he had not lost his goal-scoring touch, and finished the campaign with 12 goals. He established a good partnership with Ashley Ward, but it came to an end when he was transferred to Burnley in January. However, a series of niggling injuries restricted his involvement at Turf Moor and he had little chance to impress. He is a tricky and skilful striker who clearly knows the way to goal.
Darlington (From trainee on 1/7/1994) FL 54+14/21 FLC 4+2/1 FAC 3+1 Others 3+1/1
Bradford C (£300,000 on 27/3/1997) P/FL 109+44/40 FLC 8+3/4 FAC 7/1 Others 3+1/2
Nottingham F (Loaned on 22/8/2000) FL 9+2/1 FLC 1
Burnley (£1,000,000 + on 25/1/2002) FL 1+9

BLANC Laurent Robert
Born: Ales, France, 19 November 1965
Height: 6'4" **Weight:** 13.9
International Honours: France: 97
This world-class central defender was brought to Old Trafford by Manchester United manager Sir Alex Ferguson as a replacement for the departed Jaap Stam. Although unlikely to be a long-term solution to the problem, he was a regular in the line-up and particularly effective in the Champions' League fixtures. His

experience proved invaluable and he contributed three goals, netting both home and away against Boavista and with a well-placed header against Spurs. Having announced his retirement at the end of the campaign, Laurent's time at Old Trafford might have had its traumas, but overall, he emerged very much a winner.
Manchester U (Free from Inter Milan, Italy, ex Montpelier, Napoli, Nimes, St Etienne, Auxerre, Barcelona, Marseilles, on 3/9/2001) PL 29/1 FAC 2 Others 15/2

BLATHERWICK Steven (Steve) Scott
Born: Hucknall, 20 September 1973
Height: 6'1" **Weight:** 14.6
The unfortunate Chesterfield centre back missed almost all of the 2001-02 season with a recurrence of a previous back injury, which was aggravated in the 6-3 home defeat by Colchester in the opening game. He was finally able to return to action in March and immediately made an impact in an otherwise inexperienced defence.
Nottingham F (From trainee at Notts Co on 2/8/1992) FL 10 FLC 2 FAC 1 Others 2
Wycombe W (Loaned on 18/2/1994) FL 2 Others 1
Hereford U (Loaned on 11/9/1995) FL 10/1 Others 2
Reading (Loaned on 27/3/1997) FL 6+1
Burnley (£150,000 on 18/7/1997) FL 16+8 FLC 5 FAC 1+1 Others 3
Chesterfield (Loaned on 18/9/1998) FL 2
Chesterfield (£50,000 on 1/12/1998) FL 85+6/2 FLC 6 FAC 2 Others 7/2

BLATSIS Con
Born: Melbourne, Australia, 6 July 1977
Height: 6'3" **Weight:** 13.7
International Honours: Australia: 2; U23; Yth
Out of favour at Derby, Con eventually joined Colchester United in a short-term deal towards the end of the 2001-02 season. He immediately shored up a suspect defence and his debut coincided with a vital 3-1 win over Queen's Park Rangers, which effectively guaranteed Second Division football at Layer Road for another year. Employed as a centre half alongside skipper Scott Fitzgerald, he featured in the final seven games of the campaign.
Derby Co (£150,000 from South Melbourne, Australia on 15/8/2000) PL 2
Sheffield Wed (Loaned on 29/12/2000) FL 6 FAC 2
Colchester U (Free on 15/3/2002) FL 7

BLEIDELIS Imants
Born: Latvia, 16 August 1975
Height: 5'10" **Weight:** 11.11
International Honours: Latvia: 58
This speedy, dangerous right winger has rarely featured at first-team level for Southampton since his arrival in December 1999. Imants made a very brief appearance as a substitute against West Ham United in January and manned the bench on several occasions towards the end of the season.
Southampton (£600,000 from Skonto Riga, Latvia on 10/2/2000) PL 0+2 FLC 1+1 FAC 0+1

BLINKHORN Matthew David
Born: Blackpool, 2 March 1985
Height: 5'11" **Weight:** 10.10
A first-year trainee with Blackpool, this young striker made his League debut as a substitute at Wrexham last October, coming in the closing stages of the match. He spent most of the 2001-02 season developing in the reserve and youth teams where he had a good goal-scoring record, but also added three more senior appearances from the bench.
Blackpool (Trainee) FL 0+3 Others 0+1

BLOMQVIST Lars Jesper
Born: Umea, Sweden, 5 February 1974
Height: 5'9" **Weight:** 11.6
Club Honours: EC '99; FAC '99; PL '99
International Honours: Sweden: 30
A classy winger, equally at home on the left or right, Jesper was crushed to learn he had been omitted from Sweden's World Cup squad in May. That he had even been considered, however, was testimony to one of the bravest comebacks of recent years. After missing the previous two years with a serious knee injury he returned to action with Everton and seized his opportunity with both hands, a match-winning goal against Sunderland proving to be the culmination of a stirring comeback.
Manchester U (£4,400,000 from Parma, Italy, ex Goteborg, AC Milan, on 31/7/1998) PL 20+5/1 FLC 0+1 FAC 3+2 Others 6+1
Everton (Free on 10/11/2001) PL 10+5/1 FAC 2+1

BLONDEAU Patrick
Born: Marseilles, France, 27 January 1968
Height: 5'9" **Weight:** 11.10
International Honours: France: 2
This experienced right back joined Watford on a free transfer in the summer of 2001 and went straight into the first team making a good impression,

especially with his attacking forays down the right wing. However he seemed to fall prey to a long list of niggling injuries and was seldom able to string consecutive appearances together.
Sheffield Wed ((£1,800,000 from AS Monaco on 10/7/1997) PL 5+1 (Transferred to Bordeaux, France on 15/1/1998)
Watford (Free from Marseilles, France on 19/7/2001) FL 24+1 FLC 2 FAC 1

BLOOMER Matthew (Matt) Brian
Born: Grimsby, 3 November 1978
Height: 6'0" **Weight:** 13.0
Matt spent most of the 2001-02 season in Hull's reserves before joining Lincoln City on loan under an agreement by which the Tigers continued to pay his wages. He was introduced to the Imps' first team at York before being left out of the final game against his parent club. A right-sided defender, he was mostly used at centre back but also made one appearance at right back. The third generation of a footballing family, he completed a unique double as grandfather Jimmy also played for both Hull and Grimsby.
Grimsby T (From juniors on 3/7/1997) FL 3+9 FLC 0+2 Others 0+1
Hull C (Free on 5/7/2001) FL 0+3 FLC 1
Lincoln C (Loaned on 22/3/2002) FL 4+1

BOA MORTE Luis Pereira
Born: Lisbon, Portugal, 4 August 1977
Height: 5'10" **Weight:** 11.5
Club Honours: PL '98; Div 1 '01; CS '98, '99
International Honours: Portugal: 4; U21; Yth
Luis joined Fulham on a permanent basis in the summer of 2001 following a season-long loan from Southampton. He is a tricky player who can hold the ball up well and is capable of scoring spectacular goals. His pace and close ball control, significant features of his game, continued to cause trouble for opposition defences in the Premiership. Although a fairly regular choice, initially he found himself unable to regain his place in the starting line-up following an injury at Sunderland in January. However, he continued to win further international recognition with Portugal.
Arsenal (£1,750,000 + from Sporting Lisbon, Portugal on 25/6/1997) PL 6+19 FLC 3/2 FAC 2+3/1 Others 2+4/1
Southampton (£500,000 + on 27/8/1999) PL 6+8/1 FLC 0+2 FAC 1
Fulham (£1,700,000 on 31/7/2000) P/FL 36+26/19 FLC 7+2/4 FAC 3+1

BOATENG George
Born: Nkawkaw, Ghana, 5 September 1975
Height: 5'9" **Weight:** 11.7
International Honours: Holland: 2; U21-18
George is the workhorse of the Villa team. He is a committed tackler who can run non-stop and is always in the thick of the action, displaying class, composure and an array of passing skills in the midfield. He had an excellent season last term, when he missed only one Premiership match and was in influential form throughout the campaign. He scored just one goal, a shot into the roof of the net from an acute angle, after a fine over-lapping run at Southampton. He stepped up to make his full debut for Holland during the season.
Coventry C (£250,000 from Feyenoord, Holland, ex Excelsior, on 19/12/1997) PL 43+4/5 FLC 3/1 FAC 8/1
Aston Villa (£4,500,000 on 22/7/1999) PL 96+7/4 FLC 9+1/1 FAC 9 Others 12

BOBIC Fredi
Born: Maribor, Slovenia, 30 October 1971
Height: 6'1" **Weight:** 12.3
International Honours: Germany: 19
Fredi signed for Bolton last January, initially on loan until the end of the season. A vastly experienced striker, both at club and international level, it was hoped that he would deliver the goals that would keep the club in the Premiership. He made his debut as a substitute in the home game against Chelsea and his first goal eventually came in the home win against Aston Villa, to be swiftly followed by a first-half hat-trick in the 4-1 demolition of Ipswich in April, which virtually assured Wanderers of their place in the Premiership for another season.
Bolton W (Loaned from Borussia Dortmund, Germany, ex Cannstat, VFB Stuttgart, Ditzingen, Stuttgarter Kickers, VFB Stuttgart, on 11/1/2002) PL 14+2/4

BOERTIEN Paul
Born: Haltwhistle, 21 January 1979
Height: 5'10" **Weight:** 11.2
This young left-footed midfield player did well in Derby County's reserve team and went on to establish himself as a regular in the Premiership club's starting line-up in the second half of the 201-02 season.
Carlisle U (From trainee on 13/5/1997) FL 16+1/1 FLC 0+2 FAC 1 Others 1
Derby Co (£250,000 on 25/3/1999) PL 30+13/1 FLC 1+1 FAC 2+2
Crewe Alex (Loaned on 11/2/2000) FL 2

BOKSIC Alen
Born: Makarska, Yugoslavia, 31 January 1970
Height: 6'1" **Weight:** 12.8
International Honours: Croatia: 39
This experienced striker again struggled to combat niggling injuries for much of the 2001-02 season. Nevertheless, he still finished as Middlesbrough's leading scorer with eight Premiership goals and contributed his share of vital strikes to preserve top-flight football at the Riverside for another season. He was a member of the Croatia squad for the 2002 World Cup finals.
Middlesbrough (£2,500,000 from Lazio, Italy, ex Hajduk Split, AS Cannes, Olympique Marseille, Lazio, Juventus, on 11/8/2000) PL 46+4/20 FLC 1+1 FAC 4+2

BOLAND William (Willie)
John
Born: Ennis, Ireland, 6 August 1975
Height: 5'9" **Weight:** 11.2
International Honours: RoI: B-1; U21-11; Yth; Sch
The tenacious defensive midfield player enjoyed by far his best season to date for Cardiff City in 2001-02. He worked hard, showing good movement and passing ability and formed a powerful midfield trio with Graham Kavanagh and Mark Bonner. His consistent performances won him several individual awards: 'Carling Player of the Year' (an award decided after monthly votes through the season), the club's official website 'Player of the Year' and the Cardiff Valley RAMS (Rhondda Aberdare Merthyr Supporters) award.
Coventry C (From juniors on 4/11/1992) PL 43+20 FLC 6+1 FAC 0+1
Cardiff C (Free on 24/6/1999) FL 85+10/3 FLC 5 FAC 6+4 Others 3

BOLDER Adam Peter
Born: Hull, 25 October 1980
Height: 5'8" **Weight:** 11.0
This tenacious young midfielder made excellent progress with Derby County reserves last term. He broke through to make his first appearances in the starting line-up and also featured a number of times from the subs' bench.
Hull C (From trainee on 9/7/1999) FL 18+2 Others 2+1
Derby Co (Signed on 3/4/2000) PL 2+11 FAC 1

BOLLAND Paul Graham
Born: Bradford, 23 December 1979
Height: 5'11" **Weight:** 11.0

2001-02 proved to be a frustrating season at Notts County for this accomplished young midfield dynamo. Totally out of favour in the Scott regime, he quickly re-established himself after the change of management only to suffer an injury lay-off. The best is yet to come from this hard-running and determined young man.
Bradford C (From trainee on 20/3/1998) FL 4+8 FLC 2
Notts Co (£75,000 on 14/1/1999) FL 53+11/1 FLC 1+4 FAC 3+1 Others 1+2

BOLLAND Philip (Phil)
Christopher
Born: Liverpool, 26 August 1976
Height: 6'2" **Weight:** 13.8
Phil rejoined his former boss Mark Wright at Oxford during the 2001 close season. He initially struggled a little for pace but was just finding his feet when Wright departed. A big, ball playing centre back, he scored his only first-team goal against Rushden, but ended the campaign back in the Conference when Wright again signed him for Chester.
Oxford U (Free from Southport, ex Altrincham, Knowsley, on 9/7/2001) FL 20/1 FLC 1 FAC 1 Others 1

BONNER Mark
Born: Ormskirk, 7 June 1974
Height: 5'10" **Weight:** 11.0
This gutsy and tenacious midfield player played a major role in Cardiff City's surge into the play-offs in 2001-02. Mark played alongside Willie Boland and Graham Kavanagh in the centre of the park for much of the season and the three worked well together. His only goal came in the 7-1 demolition of Rushden in the LDV Vans Trophy. He finished the campaign strongly and was awarded a new contract by the Bluebirds.
Blackpool (From trainee on 18/6/1992) FL 156+22/14 FLC 15+3 FAC 11 Others 10+3/1
Cardiff C (Free on 17/7/1998) FL 92+17/2 FLC 6 FAC 7+1 Others 6/1
Hull C (Loaned on 8/1/1999) FL 1/1

BONNOT Alexandre (Alex)
Born: Paris, France, 31 July 1973
Height: 5'8" **Weight:** 11.6
Alex was one of a number of players to join Queen's Park Rangers after being associated with assistant-manager Kenny Jackett's previous club, Watford. A left-central midfield player he arrived on a three-month contact in the summer of 2001 and played well enough to have the contract extended on a month-by-month basis until financial considerations led to his being released at the end of February.

Watford (Free from SCO Angers, France on 10/11/1998) P/FL 8+8
Queens Park R (Free on 9/8/2001) FL 17+5/1 FLC 1 FAC 1 Others 1

BONVIN Pablo Facundo
Born: Argentina, 15 April 1981
Height: 5'8" **Weight:** 11.8
Pablo joined Sheffield Wednesday on a year's loan from Boca Juniors. A skilful attacker, although not very robust, he spent some time adjusting to the English game. He showed the potential to become more of a schemer than a striker although where his future lies was uncertain at the time of writing.
Sheffield Wed (Loaned from Boca Juniors, Argentina on 15/8/2001) FL 7+16/4 FLC 2+4/1 FAC 0+1

BOOK Steven (Steve) Kim
Born: Bournemouth, 7 July 1969
Height: 5'11" **Weight:** 11.1
Club Honours: FAT '98; NC '99
International Honours: E: SP-3
Although Steve missed the opening weeks of the 2001-02 season for Cheltenham with a back injury, he quickly re-established himself as the Robins' number one 'keeper for the remainder of the campaign. His main qualities are sharp reflexes and speed of thought, coupled with keen anticipation. He also added extra consistency to his game by eliminating the handling errors that had previously surfaced from time to time.
Cheltenham T (Signed from Forest Green Rov on 23/7/1997) FL 131 FLC 4 FAC 9 Others 7

BOOTH Andrew (Andy) David
Born: Huddersfield, 6 December 1973
Height: 6'0" **Weight:** 13.0
International Honours: E: U21-3
Andy remained mostly injury-free at Huddersfield last term, netting a respectable tally of 14 goals in all competitions. A highlight was his hat-trick in the 3-0 win at Northampton. He is a big target man who leads the attack with confidence and distributes the ball with purpose to create goal-scoring opportunities for others. Andy makes up for his lack of pace with his close-range goal-poaching talents and some excellent skills in the air.
Huddersfield T (From trainee on 1/7/1992) FL 109+14/54 FLC 6+1/3 FAC 8/3 Others 12+1/4
Sheffield Wed (£2,700,000 on 8/7/1996) P/FL 124+9/28 FLC 10+1/1 FAC 9+1/5
Tottenham H (Loaned on 30/1/2001) PL 3+1
Huddersfield T (£200,000 on 22/3/2001) FL 38+6/14 FLC 1 FAC 2 Others 7/3

BOOTY Martyn James
Born: Kirby Muxloe, 30 May 1971
Height: 5'8" **Weight:** 11.2
Martyn emerged as an important team member at Chesterfield last term. Most of his season was spent at right back before a switch to a midfield anchor role was made with some success. Dependable and consistent, Martyn tackles well and is mobile enough to contribute to attack, as he did with some effect at Meadow Lane last August, equalising with a 20-yard shot as the final whistle approached.
Coventry C (From trainee on 30/5/1989) FL 4+1 FLC 2 FAC 2
Crewe Alex (Free on 7/10/1993) FL 95+1/5 FLC 6 FAC 8/1 Others 13
Reading (£75,000 on 18/1/1996) FL 62+2/1 FLC 10+1 FAC 7/1
Southend U (Free on 7/1/1999) FL 78+2 FLC 4 FAC 5 Others 2
Chesterfield (Free on 9/8/2001) FL 40/2 FLC 1 FAC 3 Others 3

BOPP Eugene
Born: Kiev, Ukraine, 5 September 1983
Height: 5'10" **Weight:** 12.4
Widely regarded as one of the brightest talents to emerge from Nottingham Forest's successful academy, this midfielder burst on to the first-team scene during pre-season friendlies, producing a string of performances that showed maturity beyond his teenage years. He then made a handful of appearances from the bench before stepping up to make his full senior debut against Crystal Palace in December. He featured on several occasions in the second half of the campaign and scored his first senior goal against Crewe in the final home game of the season.
Nottingham F (From trainee on 11/9/2000) FL 12+7/1 FLC 0+2

BORLEY David
Born: Newcastle, 14 April 1983
Height: 5'10" **Weight:** 13.5
This 18-year-old made his debut for Bury in an LDV Vans Trophy game against Notts County last October and promptly set up a goal for Ian Lawson. He was so impressive that he was handed his full League debut seven days later, when he marked another stunning performance by scoring in a 3-0 win against Cardiff. An inventive and skilful central midfielder with excellent passing ability, he signed a new two-and-a-half-year contract in February. Only flu and a groin strain kept him out of the side from November onwards.
Bury (From trainee on 16/7/2001) FL 16+5/3 FAC 2 Others 1

BOSHELL Daniel (Danny) Kevin
Born: Bradford, 30 May 1981
Height: 5'11" **Weight:** 11.10
This Bradford-born player came through the youth ranks and has been with Oldham Athletic since July 1997. Danny is a good passer of the ball but has yet to fulfil his undoubted potential as a midfield playmaker. His 2001-02 campaign was dogged by injury problems, which again prevented him from making the breakthrough to regular first-team football. Fierce competition in the Latics' midfield means the 2002-03 season will be a crucial one for Danny's prospects as his contract nears expiry.
Oldham Ath (From trainee on 10/7/1998) FL 17+13/1 FLC 3/1 FAC 2 Others 1

BOSNICH Mark John
Born: Sydney, Australia, 13 January 1972
Height: 6'2" **Weight:** 14.6
Club Honours: FLC '94, '96; PL '00
International Honours: Australia: 17; U23; Yth
Mark Bosnich's exile at Old Trafford was ended in January 2001 when he signed for Chelsea. However, it was a case of déjà vu for Mark as he was stranded behind Ed de Goey and Carlo Cudicini at Stamford Bridge. After kicking his heels for ten months he was pitched into two crucial away games within four days and responded superbly to keep the Blues on an even keel. His long-delayed debut came in the UEFA Cup first leg away tie in Tel Aviv against Hapoel when six first-teamers declined to make the trip. His heroics failed to save the Blues from defeat but he held his place until a freak injury at Goodison in November saw him ousted once more.
Manchester U (Free from Sydney Croatia, Australia on 5/6/1989) FL 3
Aston Villa (Free on 28/2/1992) F/PL 179 FLC 20+1 FAC 17 Others 11
Manchester U (Free on 7/7/1999) PL 23 FLC 1 Others 11
Chelsea (Free on 18/1/2001) PL 5 Others 2

BOTHROYD Jay
Born: London, 7 May 1982
Height: 6'3" **Weight:** 13.6
Club Honours: FAYC '00
International Honours: E: U21-1; Yth; Sch
Jay was a first choice striker for Coventry alongside Lee Hughes for a large part of the 2001-02 season and acquitted himself well. A strong first touch and good close control, allied to outstanding dribbling

and an ability to hold the ball up earned him many plaudits, although some fans found his languid style frustrating. He scored several spectacular goals including long-range shots at Bradford and Millwall and a stunning lob at Crystal Palace. In the final run-in he was hampered by a hernia problem that will necessitate an operation in the summer. He played several times for England U20s.
Arsenal (From trainee on 8/7/1999)
Coventry C (£1,000,000 on 13/7/2000) P/FL 27+12/6 FLC 1+2 FAC 2

BOULDING Michael Thomas
Born: Sheffield, 8 February 1975
Height: 5'10" **Weight:** 11.4
Michael was undoubtedly Grimsby Town's success story of the 2001-02 season. The pacy striker initially found it difficult to establish himself in the senior squad and it was not until the departure of manager Lennie Lawrence at the turn of the year that he became a first choice. He then forged a productive partnership with Bradley Allen as the pair played a major role in saving the club from relegation. He finished the season as leading scorer, mainly as a result of netting seven times in nine games towards the end of the campaign. His tally included a hat-trick against Wimbledon and a brace in the vital 3-1 victory over Burnley. Michael is one of the speediest strikers in the First Division and his pace can upset defenders and create chances.
Mansfield T (Signed from Hallam FC on 2/8/1999) FL 28+38/12 FLC 2+2 FAC 2+1 Others 1+1
Grimsby T (Free on 24/8/2001) FL 24+11/11 FLC 0+2 FAC 0+2

BOUND Matthew Terence
Born: Melksham, 9 November 1972
Height: 6'2" **Weight:** 14.6
Club Honours: Div 3 '00
Matthew missed the start of the 2001-02 season through suspension and when he returned he formed a useful central defensive partnership with Jason Smith. He then joined Oxford on loan shortly before Christmas and this eventually became permanent. Matthew went straight into the U's line-up and was a near ever present for the remainder of the campaign.
Southampton (From trainee on 3/5/1991) F/PL 2+3
Hull C (Loaned on 27/8/1993) FL 7/1
Stockport Co (£100,000 on 27/10/1994) FL 44/5 FLC 1 FAC 3/1 Others 3/1
Lincoln C (Loaned on 11/9/1995) FL 3+1 Others 1

*Swansea C (£55,000 on 21/11/1997) FL
173+1/9 FLC 8/2 FAC 10 Others 8+1/2*
Oxford U (Free on 21/12/2001) FL 22

BOWEN Jason Peter

Born: Merthyr Tydfil, 24 August 1972
Height: 5'7" **Weight:** 11.0
Club Honours: AMC '94
International Honours: W: 2; B-1; U21-
5; Yth; Sch
Jason was mainly used in a role just
behind the front two at Cardiff last term
and showed he has the ability to
dominate matches. He looked far more
comfortable there than as an out-and-out
striker or playing wide on the right. Highly
influential at his best, Jason is a talented
player with good movement and
outstanding awareness.
*Swansea C (From trainee on 1/7/1990) FL
93+31/26 FLC 6+1/2 FAC 9+2/1 Others
15+3/8*
*Birmingham C (£350,000 on 24/7/1995) FL
35+13/7 FLC 4+6/2 FAC 1+4 Others 2/2*
Southampton (Loaned on 2/9/1997) PL 1+2
*Reading (£200,000 on 24/12/1997) FL
12+3/1 FLC 1+1 FAC 5*
*Cardiff C (Free on 12/11/1999) FL 98+23/31
FLC 4/2 FAC 10+2 Others 1+1*

BOWER Mark James

Born: Bradford, 23 January 1980
Height: 5'10" **Weight:** 11.0
Mark had a frustrating time at Bradford
City last term and even when all the
centre backs were out injured, the
manager swapped defenders around or
brought players in on loan. However, he
waited patiently and was rewarded when
he played his first game in March and
stayed in the team for the rest of the
season. He was voted 'Young Player of
the Season' and received three 'Man of
the Match' awards from just ten first-
team starts.
*Bradford C (From trainee on 28/3/1998) P/FL
10+3/2 FLC 2 Others 1+1*
York C (Loaned on 16/2/2000) FL 15/1
*York C (Loaned on 30/11/2000) FL 21/1 FAC
3 Others 0+1*

BOWRY Robert (Bobby) John

Born: Hampstead, 19 May 1971
Height: 5'9" **Weight:** 10.8
Club Honours: Div 1 '94
International Honours: St Kitts & Nevis
After signing for Colchester United in the
summer of 2001, Bobby had to bide his
time during the first two months of the
campaign, when he was used only as a
substitute. His first start came in the
terrific 2-0 home win over Reading in
October and he went on to become a

regular in the team for the remainder of
the season. A defensive central midfield
player, he is adept at breaking up
opposing attacks, while his experience
proved vital in helping to bring on the
youngsters in the U's squad.
*Crystal Palace (Free from Carshalton on
4/4/1992) F/PL 36+14/1 FLC 10 FAC 1*
*Millwall (£220,000 on 5/7/1995) FL
125+15/5 FLC 9+1 FAC 6 Others 4*
*Colchester U (Free on 25/7/2001) FL 27+9/1
FLC 0+2 FAC 1 Others 2*

BOWYER Lee David

Born: London, 3 January 1977
Height: 5'9" **Weight:** 10.6
International Honours: E: U21-13; Yth
Lee had another outstanding season on
the field for Leeds United last term, but
continued to be dogged by a much
publicised off-the-field event and a
seemingly endless round of discussions
over a new contract. Hard working, with
good anticipation which helps close down
the opposition and create goals, he is
nearly always at the centre of United's
endeavours. He again weighed in with his
fair share of goals, although he missed
several games in the autumn owing to
injury. A dynamic and tireless performer in
the centre of the park, he continues to
show he is one of the best midfielders in
the country.
*Charlton Ath (From trainee on 13/4/1994) FL
46/8 FLC 6+1/5 FAC 3/1 Others 2*
*Leeds U (£2,600,000 on 5/7/1996) PL
181+7/35 FLC 6+1/1 FAC 16/3 Others 33/13*

BOXALL Daniel (Danny)
James

Born: Croydon, 24 August 1977
Height: 5'8" **Weight:** 11.10
Club Honours: Div 3 '99
International Honours: RoI: U21-8
After over two years out of action due to
a cruciate ligament injury, this attacking
Brentford right back returned to the first-
team squad last March and was a regular
on the bench until the end of the season.
He made his comeback as a substitute in
the 3-0 victory at Wrexham.
*Crystal Palace (From trainee on 19/4/1995)
F/PL 5+3 FLC 1+1*
*Oldham Ath (Loaned on 21/11/1997) FL 6
Others 1*
Oldham Ath (Loaned on 27/2/1998) FL 12
*Brentford (Free on 9/7/1998) FL 62+6/1 FLC
6 FAC 4 Others 5+1*

BOYCE Emmerson Orlando

Born: Aylesbury, 24 September 1979
Height: 5'11" **Weight:** 11.10
Emmerson is a fast, dependable right-

sided player who can appear at full back,
as a central defender or in midfield. He is
good in the air, very quick, strong in the
tackle and provides plenty of support for
his colleagues. He was rewarded for his
performances with a new contract.
*Luton T (From trainee on 2/4/1998) FL
96+14/4 FLC 7 FAC 2+3 Others 2*

BOYD Adam Mark

Born: Hartlepool, 25 May 1982
Height: 5'9" **Weight:** 10.12
Adam is a talented young striker who is
also able to play in midfield. After two
years of carrying the tag of an outstanding
prospect, he began to realise his true
potential for Hartlepool in 2001-02. A
tireless runner, he showed himself to be a
more than capable goal-scorer, although
he will be a little disappointed not to have
been in the starting line-up more often.
*Hartlepool U (From trainee on 20/9/1999) FL
13+25/10 FAC 0+1 Others 2+2*

BRABIN Gary

Born: Liverpool, 9 December 1970
Height: 5'11" **Weight:** 14.8
International Honours: E: SP-3
After being released by Hull, Gary missed
the start of the 2001-02 season and
looked a little short of match fitness on
turning up at Torquay in early October. His
reputation as a midfield hard man
preceded him, and he was unfortunately
sent off twice in seven matches. Finding
difficulty settling in the south, he
requested the early cancellation of his
contract and subsequently signed for
Chester City.
*Stockport Co (From trainee on 14/12/1989)
FL 1+1 Others 1+1*
*Doncaster Rov (£45,000 from Runcorn on
26/7/1994) FL 58+1/11 FLC 2 FAC 2 Others 4*
Bury (£125,000 on 29/3/1996) FL 5
*Blackpool (£200,000 on 30/7/1996) FL
50+13/5 FLC 7+1 FAC 2 Others 2+2*
*Lincoln C (Loaned on 11/12/1998) FL 3+1
Others 1*
*Hull C (Free on 8/11/1999) FL 89+6/9 FLC 5+1
FAC 5 Others 3 (Free to Boston U during
2001 close season)*
Torquay U (Free on 2/10/2001) FL 6 FAC 1

BRACKSTONE Stephen
(Steve)

Born: Hartlepool, 19 September 1982
Height: 5'11" **Weight:** 11.2
International Honours: E: Yth
Steve was unable to break into the first-
team picture at Middlesbrough and joined
York City in the closing stages of the
2001-02 campaign. He quickly impressed
with his passing ability and composure in

midfield and was rewarded with a contract for 2002-03.

Middlesbrough (From trainee on 7/7/2000)
York C (Signed on 27/2/2002) FL 6+3

BRADBURY Lee Michael
Born: Isle of Wight, 3 July 1975
Height: 6'2" **Weight:** 13.10
International Honours: E: U21-3
Lee's high work rate and tireless running in every match were some of the few positives for Portsmouth fans last season. Unfortunately, he suffered serious knee ligament damage at Millwall in December, bringing his campaign to a premature end. He still managed 7 goals in just 17 games, the majority of them scored with headers. He established good partnerships with Peter Crouch and Mark Burchill, before the latter was injured, and his bustling style was sorely missed in the second half of the campaign.

Portsmouth (Free from Cowes on 14/8/1995) FL 41+13/15 FLC 1+2 FAC 4/2
Exeter C (Loaned on 1/12/1995) FL 14/5
Manchester C (£3,000,000 + on 1/8/1997) FL 34+6/10 FLC 6/1
Crystal Palace (£1,500,000 on 29/10/1998) FL 28+4/6 FLC 3+1/1 FAC 1/1
Birmingham C (Loaned on 25/3/1999) FL 6+1 Others 1+1
Portsmouth (£380,000 on 14/10/1999) FL 87+9/27 FLC 3+2 FAC 2/1

BRADLEY Shayne
Born: Gloucester, 8 December 1979
Height: 5'11" **Weight:** 13.2
International Honours: E: Sch
Shayne looked to be in good form during Mansfield's friendly matches prior to the start of the 2001-02 campaign, but picked up a heel injury that just wouldn't go away and this kept him out of action until October. Thereafter niggling injuries prevented him from establishing a regular place in the line-up, although when fit he always looked likely to score goals. He is a traditional-style centre forward who leads the line well and possesses a powerful shot.

Southampton (From trainee on 16/1/1998) PL 0+4
Swindon T (Loaned on 25/3/1999) FL 6+1
Exeter C (Loaned on 17/9/1999) FL 6+2/1 FAC 1
Mansfield T (£50,000 + on 22/8/2000) FL 28+14/10 FLC 0+1 FAC 2+2 Others 2

BRADSHAW Carl
Born: Sheffield, 2 October 1968
Height: 5'11" **Weight:** 11.11
Club Honours: AMC '99
International Honours: E: Yth

Carl joined Scunthorpe last summer and started the 2001-02 season in centre midfield, adding vital experience to a young team with his excellent range of passing. Injuries then set in, with an achilles problem ruling him out for a month before he underwent surgery on a groin problem. He returned at the end of February but then fell out of favour and appeared only once in the closing two months. He can also play at right back or on the right side of midfield. Carl was released at the end of the season.

Sheffield Wed (From apprentice on 23/8/1986) FL 16+16/4 FLC 2+2 FAC 6+1/3 Others 1
Barnsley (Loaned on 23/8/1986) FL 6/1
Manchester C (£50,000 on 30/9/1988) FL 1+4 FAC 0+1 Others 0+1
Sheffield U (£50,000 on 7/9/1989) F/PL 122+25/8 FLC 10+1/2 FAC 12+1/3 Others 4
Norwich C (£500,000 on 28/7/1994) P/FL 55+10/2 FLC 6+1/1 FAC 2
Wigan Ath (Free on 6/10/1997) FL 109+11/11 FLC 6/1 FAC 5 Others 9+1/1
Scunthorpe U (Free on 12/7/2001) FL 18+3/1 Others 1

BRADSHAW Gary
Born: Hull, 30 December 1982
Height: 5'6" **Weight:** 10.6
Although Gary's first-team involvement was limited in 2001-02, the skilful forward continued to impress by hitting double figures for Hull's reserve and junior teams. He was given a senior run-out when his youth coach, Billy Russell, became the Tigers' caretaker-manager and responded by netting his first League goal in the 4-1 defeat of Mansfield. Further involvement was restricted by a back injury. Gary was also a key figure in City's successful youth team and was deservedly named their 'Young Player of the Year'.

Hull C (From trainee on 14/7/2000) FL 8+9/1 FAC 0+1

BRADY Garry
Born: Glasgow, 7 September 1976
Height: 5'10" **Weight:** 11.0
International Honours: S: Yth; Sch
Garry is a hard-working midfield player whose footwork and accurate distribution stand out as his best assets. However, he managed just one first-team start for Portsmouth last season, with a further five appearances from the subs' bench. An accurate passer of the ball, he was transfer listed by Pompey.

Tottenham H (From trainee on 9/9/1993) PL 0+9 FAC 1+1

Newcastle U (£650,000 on 15/7/1998) PL 3+6 FAC 2+1
Norwich C (Loaned on 22/3/2000) FL 6
Norwich C (Loaned on 4/9/2000) FL 2 FLC 2
Portsmouth (Free on 1/3/2001) FL 9+5

BRADY Jonathan (Jon) Edmund Alexander
Born: Newcastle, Australia, 14 January 1975
Height: 5'8" **Weight:** 11.6
Club Honours: NC '01
This midfielder started Rushden's first season in the Football League as first choice on the right side of midfield after playing a major role in the club's promotion from the Conference. The arrival of Paul Hall in October consigned him to a bit-part role for the rest of the season, yet when injury to others gave him his chance, he demonstrated an ability to move to the left of midfield and even filled in at right back against Oxford United, a game which saw him clinch a 2-1 victory with a stunning free-kick. Out of contract at the end of the season, Jon was allowed to leave the club on a free transfer.

Swansea C (Free from trainee at Brentford on 20/7/1993. Released during 1994 close season)
Rushden & Diamonds (Free from Hayes on 8/7/1998) FL 9+13/1 FLC 2 FAC 1+1 Others 0+1

BRAGSTAD Bjorn Otto
Born: Trondheim, Norway, 15 January 1971
Height: 6'4" **Weight:** 13.5
International Honours: Norway: 15
Bjorn Otto joined Birmingham City on loan last September as cover for injury problems, but found it difficult to settle at St Andrew's. The experienced central defender made just three appearances for the Blues before returning to Pride Park, but failed to make a senior appearance for County during the season.

Derby Co (£1,500,000 from Rosenborg, Norway on 4/8/2000) PL 10+2 FLC 3/2 FAC 1
Birmingham C (Loaned on 7/9/2001) FL 3

BRAMBLE Tesfaye (Tes)
Born: Ipswich, 20 July 1980
Height: 6'1" **Weight:** 13.10
An extremely talented and skilful striker, Tes's 2001-02 season at Southend was ultimately a frustrating one. Fantastic flashes of on-the-ball skill added to a deceptive turn of pace were his key assets, but he unfortunately finished with an eight-game injury spell. After ending the campaign as top scorer with

Titus Bramble

13 goals, Tes will be looking for more consistency in 2002-03. He is the brother of Ipswich defender Titus Bramble.
Southend U (Signed from Cambridge C on 19/1/2001) FL 44+7/15 FLC 0+1 FAC 4/3 Others 4+1/1

BRAMBLE Titus Malachi
Born: Ipswich, 21 July 1981
Height: 6'1" **Weight:** 13.10
International Honours: E: U21-6
Following on from an excellent first season in the Premiership, Titus was expected to really establish himself in the Ipswich Town first team and there was even talk of him being in England's World Cup squad. However, Town's poor start affected his confidence and this, together with a niggling heel injury for which he had an operation once the season had ended, added up to a disappointing season for Titus. His surges up field still thrilled the fans but with the defence under increased pressure they became fewer. His only goal came in the home UEFA Cup tie with Torpedo Moscow and preserved Town's unbeaten European record at Portman Road.
Ipswich T (From trainee on 24/8/1998) P/FL 41+7/1 FLC 4+1/2 FAC 4+1 Others 4/1
Colchester U (Loaned on 29/12/1999) FL 2

BRAMMER David (Dave)
Born: Bromborough, 28 February 1975
Height: 5'10" **Weight:** 12.0
Club Honours: AMC '01
This hard-working midfielder joined Crewe in the 2001 close season and did well in his new surroundings. He made an impact in all his games until an injury in the FA Cup replay against Everton ended his season prematurely. A popular figure with the fans, he was sorely missed in the closing games of the campaign.
Wrexham (From trainee on 2/7/1993) FL 118+19/12 FLC 6+2 FAC 8+2/1 Others 13+2/1
Port Vale (£350,000 + on 24/3/1999) FL 71+2/3 FLC 2 FAC 2/1 Others 7
Crewe Alex (£500,000 on 10/8/2001) FL 29+1/2 FLC 2/1 FAC 4

BRANAGAN Keith Graham
Born: Fulham, 10 July 1966
Height: 6'0" **Weight:** 13.2
Club Honours: Div 1 '97
International Honours: RoI: 1; B-1
Keith found himself third in line for the 'keeper's role at Ipswich last term after the arrival of Andy Marshall and Matteo Sereni. He made his only appearance for the club when he came on as substitute

at Leicester after Sereni had been sent off on the hour. He injured his shoulder in the new year and had an operation to put it right in the close season.
Cambridge U (From juniors on 4/8/1983) FL 110 FLC 12 FAC 6 Others 6
Millwall (£100,000 on 25/3/1988) FL 46 FLC 1 FAC 5 Others 1
Brentford (Loaned on 24/11/1989) FL 2 Others 1
Gillingham (Loaned on 1/10/1991) FL 1
Bolton W (Free on 3/7/1992) P/FL 214 FLC 33 FAC 10 Others 6
Ipswich T (Free on 7/4/2000) PL 2+1 FLC 1

BRANCH Graham
Born: Liverpool, 12 February 1972
Height: 6'2" **Weight:** 12.2
The 2001-02 season began badly for Graham when, just recovered from a knee injury from the previous campaign, he suffered damage to an achilles tendon in a pre-season friendly. It kept him out until November and he struggled on his return, more often than not appearing at left back and looking decidedly short of the pace that was always his major asset. He was sidelined again for the last two months of the season and the emergence of Alan Moore on the Clarets' left side may make a return to his former prominence unlikely.
Tranmere Rov (Free from Heswall on 2/7/1991) FL 55+47/10 FLC 4+8/1 FAC 1+2 Others 2+1
Bury (Loaned on 20/11/1992) FL 3+1/1 Others 1
Wigan Ath (Loaned on 24/12/1997) FL 2+1
Stockport Co (Free on 31/7/1998) FL 10+4/3 FLC 1
Burnley (Free on 31/12/1998) FL 79+30/9 FLC 4+2 FAC 2+4 Others 1

BRANCH Paul Michael
Born: Liverpool, 18 October 1978
Height: 5'10" **Weight:** 11.7
International Honours: E: U21-1; Yth; Sch
The skilful young forward began the 2001-02 season with an injury, and had to wait a while for his first chance at Wolves. He came on as a substitute against Crystal Palace then made four starts, before being used as sub again. After this flurry of action he was then restricted to just one more appearance as stand-in for Shane Newton in January. Michael can play both as a right-sided attacker and as a striker, and was used in both roles. He is yet to fulfil his early promise and was loaned to Reading in March but had little opportunity to impress with the Second Division club.

Everton (From trainee on 24/10/1995) PL 16+25/3 FLC 0+1 FAC 1+2
Manchester C (Loaned on 29/10/1998) FL 4
Wolverhampton W (£500,000 + on 25/11/1999) FL 61+11/10 FLC 2+1 FAC 4
Reading (Loaned on 21/3/2002) FL 0+2

BRANDON Christopher (Chris) William
Born: Bradford, 7 April 1976
Height: 5'7" **Weight:** 10.3
After missing the previous season through injury, Chris returned to the fray at Torquay last term keen to make up for lost time. Back in the attacking midfield role that allows him to use his skill to run at defenders from deep, he had just returned to top form when he suffered a hamstring injury at Tottenham, which led to another lengthy layoff. On his return, he was tried as an out-and-out striker and impressed greatly in his new role.
Torquay U (Free from Bradford PA on 5/8/1999) FL 64+7/8 FLC 4/1 FAC 5/1 Others 3

BRANIFF Kevin Robert
Born: Belfast, 4 March 1983
Height: 5'11" **Weight:** 12.0
International Honours: NI: U21-1; Yth; Sch
Although he only played in a couple of games for Millwall last term, this Northern Ireland U21 international showed great promise. As a centre forward he has tremendous skill and was a regular in the reserves, scoring on many occasions. Not only is he a proven goal-scorer, he is quite at home in the flanks, has a good turn of speed and is a good crosser of the ball.
Millwall (From trainee on 12/4/2000) FL 2+4 FLC 3+1/1 FAC 0+2

BRANNAN Gerard (Ged) Daniel
Born: Prescot, 15 January 1972
Height: 6'0" **Weight:** 12.3
A hard working and versatile player capable of filing a midfield or defensive role, Ged always gave 100 per cent for Wigan Athletic last term. A permanent fixture in the Latics' line-up, he scored his first goal for the club in the Worthington Cup tie against Blackpool in August. At his best he is a strong-running player, solid in the tackle and a good passer of the ball. He missed the final stages of the season after breaking a toe and then suffering a hamstring injury in his reserve-team comeback match.
Tranmere Rov (From trainee on 3/7/1990) FL 227+11/20 FLC 26+1/4 FAC 10+1 Others 26+1/1

Manchester C *(£750,000 on 12/3/1997) FL 38+5/4 FLC 2 FAC 1*
Norwich C *(Loaned on 21/8/1998) FL 10+1/1 FLC 1*
Motherwell *(£378,000 on 28/10/1998) SL 81/16 SLC 3+1 SC 7/2*
Wigan Ath *(£175,000 on 16/2/2001) FL 43+3 FLC 1/1 Others 1*

BRANSTON Guy Peter Bromley
Born: Leicester, 9 January 1979
Height: 6'0" **Weight:** 13.12
After an almost automatic choice the previous season, this strong left-footed central defender found himself pushed down the order following the arrival of Martin McIntosh at Rotherham in 2001-02. Whenever he was called upon he gave his usual wholehearted performance, while he netted the Millers' first goal of the season against Crystal Palace on the opening day.
Leicester C *(From trainee on 3/7/1997)*
Colchester U *(Loaned on 9/2/1998) FL 12/1 Others 1*
Colchester U *(Loaned on 7/8/1998) FL 0+1*
Plymouth Arg *(Loaned on 20/11/1998) FL 7/1 Others 1*
Lincoln C *(Loaned on 10/8/1999) FL 4 FLC 2*
Rotherham U *(£50,000 on 15/10/1999) FL 81/11 FLC 2+1 FAC 3 Others 2*

BRASS Christopher (Chris) Paul
Born: Easington, 24 July 1975
Height: 5'10" **Weight:** 12.6
York City's captain appeared in midfield for much of the 2001-02 season but switched to the centre of defence in the closing weeks and showed outstanding form. An inspirational leader both on and off the field, he played a big part in City's eventual climb to safety. He scored four times, including strikes in the Worthington Cup tie at home to Crewe and in the FA Cup at Colchester.
Burnley *(From trainee on 8/7/1993) FL 120+14/1 FLC 8+1 FAC 6+1 Others 8+2*
Torquay U *(Loaned on 14/10/1994) FL 7 FAC 2 Others 1*
Halifax T *(Loaned on 22/9/2000) FL 6*
York C *(Free on 15/3/2001) FL 49+2/3 FLC 1/1 FAC 5/1 Others 1*

BRAYLEY Albert (Bertie) Patrick
Born: Basildon, 5 September 1981
Height: 5'9" **Weight:** 12.7
Club Honours: FAYC '99
Bertie became new Swindon Town manager Roy Evans' first signing when he arrived at the County Ground last August. He is a keen striker who was used as a

substitute on a number of occasions without ever making the starting line-up. The return of Andy King saw Bertie go to Southend on trial and he was released shortly before the end of the season.
Queens Park R *(Free from trainee at West Ham U on 12/8/2000)*
Swindon T *(Free on 10/8/2001) FL 0+7 FLC 0+1 FAC 0+1 Others 0+1*

BRAYSON Paul
Born: Newcastle, 16 September 1977
Height: 5'7" **Weight:** 10.10
International Honours: E: Yth
This tricky right-footed striker was played wide on the left and at times just behind the front two for Cardiff City last term, although he was often used from the subs' bench. He featured in the memorable FA Cup victory over Leeds United but was out of contract at the end of the season and somewhat unlucky to be released by the Bluebirds.
Newcastle U *(From trainee on 1/8/1995) FLC 1+1*
Swansea C *(Loaned on 30/1/1997) FL 11/5*
Reading *(£100,000 on 26/3/1998) FL 15+26/1 FLC 0+2 FAC 1+1 Others 2*
Cardiff C *(Free on 16/3/2000) FL 48+36/19 FLC 2 FAC 3+4/1 Others 1*

BRAZIER Matthew (Matt) Ronald
Born: Leytonstone, 2 July 1976
Height: 5'8" **Weight:** 11.6
It seemed a crying shame that when Cardiff City needed a left-sided player they did not turn to Matt last season. He managed just a single appearance for the Bluebirds before moving on to Leyton Orient with Kevin Nugent in January. He was mainly used as a left winger by the O's but he can also play at left back if required. Injuries ended his campaign early but he will be looking to regain his position in 2002-03 and form an effective partnership with Matt Lockwood on the left hand side.
Queens Park R *(From trainee on 1/7/1994) P/FL 36+13/2 FLC 3+2/1 FAC 3*
Fulham *(£65,000 on 20/3/1998) FL 4+5/1 FAC 2+1 Others 1*
Cardiff C *(Loaned on 28/8/1998) FL 11/2*
Cardiff C *(£100,000 on 9/7/1999) FL 43+13/3 FLC 2+3/1 FAC 5+1/1 Others 2*
Leyton Orient *(Free on 31/1/2002) FL 8*

BRECKIN Ian
Born: Rotherham, 24 February 1975
Height: 6'0" **Weight:** 12.9
Club Honours: AMC '96
Chesterfield's classiest defender was consistently linked with moves to bigger

clubs last term. Given the Spireites' financial situation, a move is more likely than not, but the buyers will have to do better than the derisory offers received to date. Ian's great reading ability and timing made him excellent both on the ground and in the air, and he held the Spireites' defence together. Unsurprisingly, Ian skippered the side.
Rotherham U *(From trainee on 1/11/1993) FL 130+2/6 FLC 6 FAC 5 Others 11*
Chesterfield *(£100,000 on 25/7/1997) FL 208+4/8 FLC 16/1 FAC 9/1 Others 12/1*

BREEN Gary Patrick
Born: Hendon, 12 December 1973
Height: 6'2" **Weight:** 12.0
International Honours: Rol: 47; U21-9
Gary is a skilful right-footed central defender who likes to bring the ball out of defence and is also very good in the air. Previously a cult figure with the Coventry fans, his refusal to discuss a new contract somewhat soured that relationship. He regained his first-team place after the departure of Gordon Strachan and was a major reason for the dramatic turnaround in the club's fortunes at that time. He suffered a twisted knee at Birmingham and was out for a month. Gary was first choice for the Republic of Ireland throughout the season adding four more caps to bring his total to 42.
Maidstone U *(From Charlton Ath juniors on 6/3/1991) FL 19*
Gillingham *(Free on 2/7/1992) FL 45+6 FLC 4 FAC 5 Others 1*
Peterborough U *(£70,000 on 5/8/1994) FL 68+1/1 FLC 6 FAC 6 Others 6/1*
Birmingham C *(£400,000 on 9/2/1996) FL 37+3/2 FLC 4 FAC 1*
Coventry C *(£2,400,000 on 1/2/1997) P/FL 138+8/2 FLC 10+3 FAC 12*

BRENNAN Dean James Gary
Born: Dublin, 17 June 1980
Height: 5'9" **Weight:** 11.8
Made only one first-team appearance for Luton Town, featuring in the LDV Vans Trophy tie at Dagenham & Redbridge, when he scored one of the Hatters' goals. A left-sided midfielder who can also play in a striking role, he was converted to a left back in the reserves for whom he was made captain. He left the club in the new year and after a trial with Clyde and a brief spell at Wingate & Finchley he signed for Hitchin Town.
Sheffield Wed *(Signed from Stella Maris YC on 21/11/1997)*
Luton T *(Free on 11/8/2000) FL 2+7 FLC 1+2 FAC 1 Others 1/1*

Wayne Bridge

BRENNAN James (Jim) Gerald
Born: Toronto, Canada, 8 May 1977
Height: 5'9" **Weight:** 12.5
International Honours: Canada: 31
(Gold Cup 2000); U23-1
After finishing the 2000-01 season on loan at Huddersfield, Jim had a much better campaign with Nottingham Forest last term. Playing either at left back or left wing back he firmly established himself in the line-up and rarely missed a match all season.
Bristol C (Free from Sora Lazio, Canada on 25/10/1994) FL 51+4/3 FLC 6 FAC 1
Nottingham F (£1,500,000 on 29/10/1999) FL 72+6 FLC 5 FAC 5
Huddersfield T (Loaned on 21/3/2001) FL 0+2

BRESLAN Geoffrey (Geoff)
Francis
Born: Torquay, 4 June 1980
Height: 5'8" **Weight:** 11.0
Geoff was in and out of the starting line-up at Exeter last term, but featured in the squad for well over half the games, reflecting the progress made over the season. A left-sided midfield player with a good touch on the ball his great enthusiasm made him a favourite of the Grecians' fans. He netted two goals during the campaign (against Oxford and Bristol Rovers) and both turned out to be winning strikes.
Exeter C (From trainee on 7/1/1999) FL 61+38/6 FLC 4+1 FAC 3+4 Others 7/1

BREVETT Rupis (Rufus)
Emanuel
Born: Derby, 24 September 1969
Height: 5'8" **Weight:** 11.6
Club Honours: Div 2 '99; Div 1 '01
This attacking left back signed a new two-year contract for Fulham prior to the start of the 2001-02 season and held off the challenge of new signing Jon Harley to retain his place, giving a succession of resolute displays in the left-back position. Strong and committed in the tackle he often found time to join in the attack and excited the Craven Cottage faithful with his dashes down the left flank. Rufus scored a rare but vital goal in the closing minutes of the Worthington Cup tie at Rochdale. The turn of the year brought mixed fortunes for him. He captained the side in the absence of skipper Andy Melville but also found himself left out on the odd occasion.
Doncaster Rov (From trainee on 8/7/1988) FL 106+3/3 FLC 5 FAC 4 Others 10+1
Queens Park R (£250,000 on 15/2/1991)
F/PL 141+11/1 FLC 9+1 FAC 8
Fulham (£375,000 on 28/1/1998) P/FL 151+2/1 FLC 14+2/1 FAC 14 Others 2

BRIDGE Wayne Michael
Born: Southampton, 5 August 1980
Height: 5'10" **Weight:** 11.11
International Honours: E: 7; U21-8; Yth
Wayne's continued improvement at club level for Southampton reaped rewards with a well-deserved call up to the full England side last term. He was a star performer for Saints, with his impressive forward running and excellent pin point crosses. An ever present once again, he has featured in every minute of Premiership football for the club since March 1999 and was rewarded with a place in the PFA's Premiership team for the season.
Southampton (From trainee on 16/1/1998) PL 106+12/1 FLC 8+1 FAC 7

BRIDGE-WILKINSON Marc
Born: Nuneaton, 16 March 1979
Height: 5'6" **Weight:** 11.8
Club Honours: AMC '01
This diminutive Port Vale midfield player spent a large part of the 2001-02 campaign out injured. A foot problem meant that he was rarely seen until the new year and his first start was in the local 'derby' victory at Stoke City in February. The team then embarked on their best run of the season with Marc playing no small part. He is arguably the best finisher in the club and scored six goals in just 15 games including a brilliant free kick at Huddersfield Town and two in injury time against Chesterfield.
Derby Co (From trainee on 26/3/1997) PL 0+1
Carlisle U (Loaned on 5/3/1999) FL 4+3
Port Vale (Free on 4/7/2000) FL 55+6/15 FLC 1/1 FAC 2/1 Others 7/3

BRIDGES David Stephen
Born: Huntingdon, 22 September 1982
Height: 6'0" **Weight:** 12.0
A product of Cambridge United's youth system, David stepped up to make his senior debut from the subs' bench against Huddersfield Town last March. He went on to feature as a substitute on several occasions, notably when he came on at half time against Tranmere and altered the course of the game. A classy midfielder he was rewarded with a first start at Northampton in the final match of the season.
Cambridge U (From trainee on 20/3/2002) FL 1+6/1

BRIGGS Keith
Born: Ashton under Lyne, 11 December 1981
Height: 5'10" **Weight:** 11.6
A product of the Stockport County youth system, Keith had a fantastic season at Edgeley Park last term, thoroughly deserving his awards for 'Internet Player of the Year' and Supporters' Club 'Young Player of the Year'. He was switched from right back to a midfield role by new manager Carlton Palmer to devastating effect, for he proved to be one of the few midfield players at County to be able to run with the ball at opposing defences.
Stockport Co (From trainee on 27/8/1999) FL 34+5/1 FLC 2/1 FAC 1+1

BRIGHTWELL David John
Born: Lutterworth, 7 January 1971
Height: 6'2" **Weight:** 13.5
This experienced central defender helped give the Darlington defence a more solid look last season. Strong in the air and uncompromising in the tackle he produced a series of resolute displays, especially when deputising for club captain Craig Liddle. However, he suffered from injury problems himself that restricted his total of appearances during the campaign.
Manchester C (From juniors on 11/4/1988) F/PL 35+8/1 FLC 2+1 FAC 5+2/1
Chester C (Loaned on 22/3/1991) FL 6
Lincoln C (Loaned on 11/8/1995) FL 5 FLC 2
Stoke C (Loaned on 11/9/1995) FL 0+1 Others 1
Bradford C (£30,000 on 22/12/1995) FL 23+1 FAC 1 Others 2
Blackpool (Loaned on 12/12/1996) FL 1+1
Northampton T (Free on 29/7/1997) FL 34+1/1 FLC 2 FAC 5 Others 2+1
Carlisle U (Free on 10/7/1998) FL 78/4 FLC 4 FAC 2 Others 3
Hull C (Free on 27/6/2000) FL 24+3/2 FLC 2 FAC 2 Others 1
Darlington (Free on 15/2/2001) FL 34+2 FLC 1 FAC 4 Others 1

BRIGHTWELL Ian Robert
Born: Lutterworth, 9 April 1968
Height: 5'10" **Weight:** 12.5
International Honours: E: U21-4; Yth
Ian was as steady and dependable as ever when called upon in defence by Walsall last term and excelled in the FA Cup win at Charlton. A fortnight later, however, he was injured early in the game against Sheffield Wednesday and soon after returning to the side moved to Stoke on transfer deadline day. Whilst he featured principally on the bench his experience

was seen as invaluable as the play-offs beckoned.

Manchester C *(From juniors on 7/5/1986) F/PL 285+36/18 FLC 29+2 FAC 19+4/1 Others 4+3*
Coventry C *(Free on 2/7/1998) FLC 1*
Walsall *(Free on 11/2/2000) FL 77+4 FLC 6 FAC 5 Others 3*
Stoke C *(Free on 28/3/2002) FL 3+1 Others 0+1*

BRISCO Neil Anthony
Born: Wigan, 26 January 1978
Height: 6'0" **Weight:** 11.5
Club Honours: AMC '01
This tough-tackling midfield player had a steady but unspectacular season with Port Vale in 2001-02. He missed around a dozen games largely through a knee injury sustained mid season. His own personal highlight was his performance in the local 'derby' victory at Stoke City in which he totally nullified the home midfielders. Although he possesses a decent shot he was unable to get on to the score sheet last term, largely because he was playing deeper than previously.
Manchester C *(From trainee on 4/3/1997)*
Port Vale *(Free on 7/8/1998) FL 62+5/1 FLC 2 FAC 3 Others 7+1*

BRISCOE Lee Stephen
Born: Pontefract, 30 September 1975
Height: 5'11" **Weight:** 11.12
International Honours: E: U21-5
After his first injury-disrupted season at the Turf, Lee's second Burnley campaign saw him firmly established in the side. Although he is usually considered a natural left back, Stan Ternent often preferred to play him further forward, and he certainly seemed to enjoy displaying the more attacking side of his game. His tackling and distribution skills improved and he regularly provided good service to the men up front. His most memorable day came in the 5-2 home win against Walsall when he scored twice after coming on from the bench.
Sheffield Wed *(From trainee on 22/5/1994) PL 48+30/1 FLC 5+2 FAC 0+2 Others 2+1*
Manchester C *(Loaned on 20/2/1998) FL 5/1*
Burnley *(Free on 14/7/2000) FL 68+5/5 FLC 3 FAC 2*

BRKOVIC Ahmet
Born: Dubrovnik, Croatia, 23 September 1974
Height: 5'7" **Weight:** 10.8
This skilful right-sided midfielder filled in very well in an ever-changing Luton Town side at the start of last season. He created numerous chances for his colleagues, but

injury plagued him towards the end of the campaign.
Leyton Orient *(Free from HNK Dubrovnik, Croatia on 14/10/1999) FL 59+10/8 FLC 3/2 FAC 4+2 Others 2+2*
Luton T *(Free on 4/10/2001) FL 17+4/1 FAC 1/1*

BROAD Joseph (Joe) Reginald
Born: Bristol, 24 August 1982
Height: 5'11" **Weight:** 12.7
A promising young midfielder, Joe made his debut for Plymouth as a substitute in the first away game of 2001-02 at Hull and then came on to make an impact in the Worthington Cup tie at Watford. His only starting appearance was in the 3-2 victory at Rushden, the first game of Argyle's record-breaking run of 18 League games without defeat. He was loaned to Conference club Yeovil Town in November but was later included on first-team duties in the closing weeks of the campaign.
Plymouth Arg *(From trainee on 15/2/2002) FL 1+6 FLC 0+1*

BROAD Stephen
Born: Epsom, 10 June 1980
Height: 6'0" **Weight:** 11.5
A solid and dependable full back, Stephen struggled to show his best form early on last season, but eventually won a regular place in the Southend United line-up in November. A fine tackler with good positional sense, he also likes to overlap, although his crossing skills need to be worked on. A good disciplinary record showed his fine attitude and he can only go on to greater things.
Chelsea *(From trainee on 9/2/1998)*
Southend U *(Free on 31/3/2001) FL 40+2/2 FLC 1 FAC 3 Others 1*

BROADHURST Karl Matthew
Born: Portsmouth, 18 March 1980
Height: 6'1" **Weight:** 11.7
2001-02 proved to be a frustrating season for Karl as injuries ruled him out of the Bournemouth line-up for a number of games. Ankle problems kept him out early on and he then suffered a badly broken nose in a training ground accident, which meant that he missed the vital run-in. He is a right-sided central defender who can also operate at right back.
Bournemouth *(From trainee on 3/7/1998) FL 63+6 FLC 3+1 FAC 5 Others 3*

BROCK Stuart Alan
Born: West Bromwich, 26 September 1976
Height: 6'1" **Weight:** 13.8
Club Honours: NC '00

Stuart was one of Kidderminster's most consistent performers last term and a good spell in mid-season earned him an extension to his contract. Despite some hiccups in the two games against Luton Town he remained the Harriers' first choice 'keeper throughout the season.
Aston Villa *(From trainee on 10/5/1995)*
Northampton T *(Free on 27/3/1997. Free to Solihull Borough during 1997 close season)*
Kidderminster Hrs *(Free on 17/9/1997) FL 63 FLC 2 FAC 4 Others 1*

BRODIE Stephen (Steve) Eric
Born: Sunderland, 14 January 1973
Height: 5'7" **Weight:** 10.10
Steve was reunited with his former manager Colin Addison after joining Swansea from Conference outfit Scarborough last November. He showed up well when used in an attacking central midfield role, but played most of his games on the right-hand side. He showed a good awareness on the ball and worked hard in the centre of the park.
Sunderland *(From trainee on 1/7/1991) FL 1+11*
Doncaster Rov *(Loaned on 31/8/1995) FL 5/1*
Scarborough *(Free on 20/12/1996) FL 109+2/27 FLC 4 FAC 3 Others 2+1*
Swansea C *(Free on 16/11/2001) FL 21+5/2 FAC 1*

BROMBY Leigh
Born: Dewsbury, 2 June 1980
Height: 6'0" **Weight:** 11.8
International Honours: E: Sch
This terrific prospect had a good season for Sheffield Wednesday in 2001-02. He is a solid and reliable young central defender who also shows plenty of skill on the ball. A knee injury eventually put him out for the remainder of the campaign and gave the Owls a real problem as they sought to replace him.
Sheffield Wed *(Free from Liversedge on 9/7/1998) FL 43+1/1 FLC 6 FAC 2+1*
Mansfield T *(Loaned on 10/12/1999) FL 10/1 Others 1*

BROOKER Paul
Born: Hammersmith, 25 November 1976
Height: 5'8" **Weight:** 10.0
Club Honours: Div 3 '01; Div 2 '02
Paul had another fine season with Brighton in 2001-02 and is now very much a cult hero of the club's supporters. A player who thrives on confidence, he clearly benefited from Peter Taylor's influence and one of the highlights of his campaign was a tremendous equaliser at Bournemouth when he hit a curling effort

from 20 yards with his weaker left foot. He is a talented winger with good pace and excellent ball control.

Fulham *(From trainee on 1/7/1995) FL 13+43/4 FLC 1+2/1 FAC 1+3/1 Others 3+3*
Brighton & Hove A *(£25,000 on 18/2/2000) FL 70+27/9 FLC 3+1 FAC 2+3 Others 3/1*

BROOKER Stephen Michael Lord
Born: Newport Pagnell, 21 May 1981
Height: 5'10" **Weight:** 12.4
Club Honours: AMC '01
This burly striker was a regular in the Port Vale line-up for virtually the whole of the 2001-02 season. After a slow start he led the line well and often brought other players into the game through his hard work in holding the ball up. Despite providing an awkward presence for opposing defenders he failed to score as many goals as he would have liked and will be looking to improve upon that in 2002-03.

Watford *(From trainee on 9/7/1999) PL 0+1 FAC 0+1*
Port Vale *(£15,000 on 5/1/2001) FL 61+3/17 FLC 2 FAC 2/1 Others 8/3*

BROOKS Jamie Paul
Born: Oxford, 12 August 1983
Height: 5'9" **Weight:** 10.9
Jamie was without doubt the star of the Oxford side in what was a troubled 2001-02 campaign. The winger/striker won all four individual club awards on offer (Sponsors', Players', Supporters' and Young Player) and scored ten goals from just 18 starts. He had a few knocks and was used sparingly at times, but his class shone through when he appeared. He also had the distinction of scoring United's first goal at the new Kassam Stadium. During the 2002 close season he was rushed to hospital after contracting a virus, but at the time of writing he seemed to be on the way to recovery.

Oxford U *(From trainee on 13/12/2000) FL 21+8/11 FAC 1 Others 1*

BROOMES Marlon Charles
Born: Birmingham, 28 November 1977
Height: 6'0" **Weight:** 12.12
International Honours: E: U21-2; Yth; Sch
Marlon joined Grimsby Town on loan at the start of the 2001-02 season as the Mariners sought to solve their problems in central defence. He appeared sound at the back and was capable of the odd goal from set pieces, netting in the shock 2-1 Worthington Cup defeat of Liverpool at Anfield. Unfortunately, the board were

unable to finance a permanent move and he was eventually signed by Sheffield Wednesday. He made an excellent impression at Hillsborough, and looked very assured in everything he did. He filled in at full back initially, then made the centre-half spot his own and helped the Owls look more solid defensively.

Blackburn Rov *(From trainee on 28/11/1994) P/FL 24+7/1 FLC 3 FAC 4*
Swindon T *(Loaned on 22/1/1997) FL 12/1*
Queens Park R *(Loaned on 25/10/2000) FL 5*
Grimsby T *(Loaned on 7/9/2001) FL 13+2 FLC 3/2*
Sheffield Wed *(Free on 13/12/2001) FL 18+1 FAC 1*

BROUGH John Robert
Born: Ilkeston, 8 January 1973
Height: 6'0" **Weight:** 13.0
Club Honours: NC '99
John returned to first-team action for Cheltenham Town last term after missing most of the previous campaign with a serious knee injury, but had to content himself with a place on the substitutes' bench for most of the campaign. A strong competitive central defender, he was a regular selection during the closing weeks of the season but lost his place to the predominantly left-footed Richard Walker for the play-off matches. Nevertheless, he remained an important member of the squad and was offered a new contract in the summer.

Notts Co *(From trainee on 9/7/1991)*
Shrewsbury T *(Free on 6/7/1992) FL 7+9/1 FLC 1+1 FAC 1 Others 1 (Free to Telford during 1994 close season)*
Hereford U *(Free on 4/11/1994) FL 70+9/3 FLC 5 FAC 4/1 Others 4+3*
Cheltenham T *(Signed on 16/7/1998) FL 28+40/3 FLC 1+1 FAC 2+2/1 Others 0+1*

BROUGH Michael
Born: Nottingham, 1 August 1981
Height: 6'0" **Weight:** 11.7
This young midfield terrier was still learning his trade at Notts County last season, but impressed with some energetic running. Other aspects of his game also began to develop and he gradually showed more composure when in possession.

Notts Co *(From trainee on 1/7/1999) FL 36+12/1 FAC 3+3 Others 2*

BROUGH Scott
Born: Scunthorpe, 10 February 1983
Height: 5'6" **Weight:** 9.10
This young winger was involved in most of Scunthorpe United's games in the first half of last season and scored on his full

League debut at Rochdale in September. Very quick and with two good feet, he can operate down either flank but fell out of favour at the end of January and only made one substitute appearance during the final three months of the season. He signed a new one-year contract at the end of the campaign.

Scunthorpe U *(From juniors on 9/11/2000) FL 5+18/1 FLC 0+1 FAC 0+1 Others 1+3*

BROUGHTON Drewe Oliver
Born: Hitchin, 25 October 1978
Height: 6'3" **Weight:** 12.10
Drewe found that much of his contribution to Kidderminster's second Football League season came from the subs' bench. A big, strong traditional-style centre forward he still managed to chip in with goals, scoring eight times in the Third Division, thus making him Harriers' record aggregate Football League scorer to date. Most notable were the two that he scored in the 4-1 win over York in October which began Harriers' climb up the table.

Norwich C *(From trainee on 6/5/1997) FL 3+6/1*
Wigan Ath *(Loaned on 15/8/1997) FL 1+3*
Brentford *(£100,000 on 30/10/1998) FL 1*
Peterborough U *(£100,000 on 17/11/1998) FL 19+16/8 FLC 2 Others 1+1/1*
Kidderminster Hrs *(£50,000 on 22/1/2001) FL 42+15/15 FLC 1 Others 2*

BROWN Aaron Wesley
Born: Bristol, 14 March 1980
Height: 5'10" **Weight:** 11.12
International Honours: E: Sch
Despite his pace and skill Aaron still found it hard to make his mark as a goal-scorer for Bristol City last term. As in the previous campaign he failed to register a goal until the final League game of the season when he equalised in the 1-1 home draw with Stoke City. Aaron was involved in the car crash in which his club colleague Kevin Amankwaah received serious injuries, although he was more fortunate and only missed a few games. He is the older brother of City's Marvin Brown.

Bristol C *(From trainee on 7/11/1997) FL 85+13/5 FLC 2+2 FAC 7 Others 8+1*
Exeter C *(Loaned on 6/1/2000) FL 4+1/1*

BROWN David Alistair
Born: Bolton, 2 October 1978
Height: 5'10" **Weight:** 12.6
The former Hull striker was one of a string of central strikers tried out by Torquay on short-term contracts last term. He put in a few tidy performances, but did not find the net and after failing to

secure a longer deal he moved on to Chester City.
Manchester U (From trainee on 27/10/1995)
Hull C (Free on 26/3/1998) FL 108+23/23 FLC 9+1/5 FAC 10/3 Others 5+1
Torquay U (Free on 9/11/2001) FL 2 FAC 1

BROWN Grant Ashley
Born: Sunderland, 19 November 1969
Height: 6'0" **Weight:** 11.12
Grant experienced mixed emotions in a season that saw him break Lincoln's Football League appearance record only to be released at the end of the campaign after 12 years at Sincil Bank. He spent pre-season continuing his recovery from a fractured left leg but made such good progress that he was on the subs' bench for the opening League game. He quickly won his place back in the centre of a four-man defence and produced some sterling performances which earned him the supporters' 'Player of the Year' award. He made his record-breaking 403rd League appearance at York in late March and went on to play a further four games before the end of the season.
Leicester C (From trainee on 1/7/1988) FL 14 FLC 2
Lincoln C (Loaned on 20/8/1989) FL 14/1 FLC 2 Others 1
Lincoln C (£60,000 on 4/1/1990) FL 387+6/14 FLC 20/1 FAC 18 Others 20+1/2

BROWN Jason Roy
Born: Southwark, 18 May 1982
Height: 5'11" **Weight:** 13.3
This former Charlton trainee got his chance in March when he replaced the experienced Vince Bartram between the posts for Gillingham. In his first two games he pulled off some remarkable saves as he helped the club reach 50 points to keep them safe from relegation. A regular for the reserves before getting his first-team chance, he was called up for training with the Wales U21 team just before the end of the season.
Gillingham (Free from trainee at Charlton Ath on 19/3/2001) FL 10

BROWN Marvin Robert
Born: Bristol, 6 July 1983
Height: 5'9" **Weight:** 11.1
International Honours: E: Yth
Despite all the acclaim this skilful forward still has to follow his elder brother Aaron and cement a regular first-team place for Bristol City. The club's youngest-ever player when making his debut back in 1999, he appeared to have arrived in the away game at Wycombe, but he was

given no further opportunities to build on his great display that day. He is the younger brother of Ashton Gate colleague Aaron.
Bristol C (From trainee on 18/7/2000) FL 1+16 FLC 0+1 FAC 0+2 Others 2+3

BROWN Michael Robert
Born: Hartlepool, 25 January 1977
Height: 5'9" **Weight:** 11.8
International Honours: E: U21-4
Michael had an excellent season for Sheffield United in 2001-02. The hard-working left-sided midfielder proved an effective ball winner, and his vision and passing created opportunities for others. His pace and control going forward down the left flank created openings and his improved tally of six goals came mainly from long-range efforts. A groin problem brought his season to an end when he went off injured in the abandoned game against West Bromwich Albion. In November he signed a year's extension to his contract and in April he was voted Supporters' Club 'Player of the Year'.
Manchester C (From trainee on 13/9/1994) F/PL 67+22/2 FLC 2+4 FAC 10+1/2 Others 4
Hartlepool U (Loaned on 27/3/1997) FL 6/1
Portsmouth (Loaned on 19/11/1999) FL 4
Sheffield U (Signed on 17/12/1999) FL 93+3/9 FLC 6/1 FAC 2/1

BROWN Simon James
Born: Chelmsford, 3 December 1976
Height: 6'2" **Weight:** 15.0
Simon was second choice 'keeper to Andy Woodman at Colchester in the first half of the 2001-02 season. Given a surprise start at Tranmere in January, he seized the opportunity with both hands, producing a 'Man-of-the-Match' performance. He missed only one more game and Woodman eventually moved on to Oxford. Simon is sill liable to make the odd error, but his confidence has improved and he showed the capacity to dominate his area.
Tottenham H (From trainee on 1/7/1995)
Lincoln C (Loaned on 19/12/1997) FL 1
Colchester U (Free on 20/7/1999) FL 75 FLC 5 FAC 2 Others 3

BROWN Steven (Steve) Byron
Born: Brighton, 13 May 1972
Height: 6'1" **Weight:** 13.10
Club Honours: Div 1 '00
A reliable central defender or right back, Steve was a regular in the Charlton side in the early part of last season, but lost his place to Jon Fortune in December and with the signing of Jorge Costa the same

month, only made further appearances from the substitutes' bench. Strong and commanding in the air, he distributes the ball well and possesses a powerful right-foot shot. He also scored valuable goals at Sunderland and Arsenal, both with headers.
Charlton Ath (From trainee on 3/7/1990) P/FL 194+45/9 FLC 12+3/1 FAC 19+1/1 Others 3+2

BROWN Steven (Steve) Ferold
Born: Northampton, 6 July 1966
Height: 6'0" **Weight:** 11.8
This tenacious and cultured left-footed midfielder was again a popular figure with the Wycombe fans last term for his committed displays. He showed remarkable fitness levels for his age and worked tirelessly in a central-midfield role, always looking to take on opponents and start attacks. He scored nine goals, including a spectacular narrow-angled effort at Colchester in the League, and was the club's second highest scorer.
Northampton T (From juniors on 11/8/1983) FL 14+1/3 (Free to Irthlingborough T in December 1985)
Northampton T (Free on 21/7/1989) FL 145+13/19 FLC 10/1 FAC 12/2 Others 10+1/1
Wycombe W (£60,000 on 9/2/1994) FL 281+28/29 FLC 21+2/3 FAC 23+6/3 Others 10+2/1

BROWN Wayne Lawrence
Born: Barking, 20 August 1977
Height: 6'0" **Weight:** 12.6
Wayne spent much of the 2001-02 campaign out on loan. He proved a big asset during his spell at Wimbledon where he organised the defence well and was always dangerous at set pieces. He subsequently spent time at Watford in the new year where he also proved to be a great success. Initially used at left back, he laid on a goal for Gifton Noel-Williams at Preston with his very first touch. However, he really came into his own playing in central defence alongside Filippo Galli, where he looked calm and assured. Wayne scored three goals during his stay at Vicarage Road, including a double against Coventry. His only appearance for Ipswich came in the FA Cup third round tie against Dagenham & Redbridge.
Ipswich T (From trainee on 16/5/1996) P/FL 21+10 FLC 2 FAC 2 Others 1+1
Colchester U (Loaned on 16/10/1997) FL 0+2
Queens Park R (Loaned on 22/3/2001) FL 2
Wimbledon (Loaned on 14/9/2001) FL 17/1
Watford (Loaned on 30/1/2002) FL 10+1/3

Marcus Browning

BROWN Wesley (Wes)
Michael
Born: Manchester, 13 October 1979
Height: 6'1" **Weight:** 12.4
Club Honours: EC '99; PL '99; '01
International Honours: E: 6; U21-8;
Yth; Sch
This solid central defender had a
somewhat difficult season at Old Trafford
last term. The departure of Jaap Stam to
Lazio put a huge weight of expectation
on his shoulders and at the same time
the Manchester United defence began to
leak goals. A sublime performance in the
European Champions' League against
Bayern Munich suggested better things
before he was sidelined with a training
ground injury in early December that
kept him out of action for several
months.
*Manchester U (From trainee on 13/11/1996)
PL 52+9 FLC 1+1 FAC 3 Others 17+5*

BROWNING Marcus Trevor
Born: Bristol, 22 April 1971
Height: 6'0" **Weight:** 12.10
International Honours: W: 5
Without a doubt Marcus had his best
season in Gillingham's colours since
joining the club. A hard-working
midfielder, he started out in explosive
form by scoring twice in the 5-0 home
victory over Preston. A player approaching
the peak of his career, he still has the
potential to force his way back into the
full squad for Wales.
*Bristol Rov (From trainee on 1/7/1989) FL
152+22/13 FLC 7+3 FAC 8/1 Others 13+5/3
Hereford U (Loaned on 18/9/1992) FL 7/5
Huddersfield T (£500,000 on 17/2/1997) FL
25+8 FLC 2+2
Gillingham (Loaned on 20/11/1998) FL 1
Gillingham (£150,000 on 25/3/1999) FL
60+17/3 FLC 6+1 FAC 3+3 Others 0+1*

BRUCE Paul Mark
Born: Lambeth, 18 February 1978
Height: 5'11" **Weight:** 12.0
A left-sided wingback or midfield player,
Paul was a regular choice for Queen's
Park Rangers at the start of last season.
However, although he was injured in the
middle of September, he was able to
regain his place when he recovered
fitness. He held on until the middle of
November when Danny Murphy replaced
him and was never really in contention for
a starting place for the remainder of the
campaign.
*Queens Park R (From trainee on 15/7/1996)
FL 30+7/3 FLC 1+1 FAC 3+2 Others 1
Cambridge U (Loaned on 25/3/1999) FL 2+2*

BRUMWELL Phillip (Phil)
Born: Darlington, 8 August 1975
Height: 5'8" **Weight:** 11.0
Phil continued to occupy various positions
in defence and midfield for Darlington
last term, although he often found
himself on the subs' bench. He is a local
lad who really relishes playing for his
hometown club and always produces
committed displays whenever he is called
upon. He has now completed over 200
games for the Quakers.
*Sunderland (From trainee on 30/6/1994)
Darlington (Free on 11/8/1995) FL 106+50/1
FLC 5+2 FAC 7+5/2 Others 8+3
Hull C (Free on 10/8/2000) FL 1+3 FLC 1+1
Darlington (Free on 30/11/2000) FL 35+8
FAC 3+2 Others 3+2/1*

BRYAN Derek (Del) Kirk
Born: Hammersmith, 11 November 1974
Height: 5'10" **Weight:** 11.10
Club Honours: Div 3 '99
After 21 months out of action this right
winger returned to the Brentford first
team last October when he came off the
bench against Peterborough in a match
where the club let in all supporters for
free. This marked Del's 50th League
appearance for the club. Unfortunately
the cruciate ligament injury that had kept
him out of action for so long forced him
out of League football later in the season
and he moved on to Ryman League club
Gravesend & Northfleet in March.
*Brentford (£50,000 from Hampton Borough
on 28/8/1997) FL 16+34/7 FLC 1+1 FAC 0+4
Others 1+2/1*

BRYAN Marvin Lee
Born: Paddington, 2 August 1975
Height: 6'0" **Weight:** 12.2
Marvin played for the first two months of
the 2001-02 season on the right-hand
side of the back four for Rotherham, but
he was then troubled by an achilles injury
that kept him out of first-team action for
some time. When he returned in February
he produced his best form since joining
the club and was on course to make the
position his own, before his injury
problem returned. It is hoped that an
operation at the end of the season will
see him return to full fitness in 2002-03.
*Queens Park R (From trainee on 17/8/1992)
Doncaster Rov (Loaned on 8/12/1994) FL
5/1
Blackpool (£20,000 on 10/8/1995) FL
172+10/4 FLC 10+3 FAC 8 Others 12
Bury (Free on 23/3/2000) FL 6+3
Rotherham U (Free on 10/7/2000) FL 42+5
FLC 2+1 FAC 1 Others 1*

BRYANT Simon Christopher
Born: Bristol, 22 November 1982
Height: 5'9" **Weight:** 10.7
This battling midfielder had a season to
forget at Bristol Rovers last term, making
just eight starts. He suffered a succession
of injuries, affected by back trouble early
on and then a knee problem that
sidelined him for four months. On his
return he suffered another knee injury
against Exeter City in March and did not
play again.
*Bristol Rov (From trainee on 17/1/2000) FL
44+9/1 FLC 5+3 FAC 1 Others 3+1*

BRYNGELSSON Fredrik
Born: Sweden, 10 April 1975
Height: 6'3" **Weight:** 13.0
The tall central defender made only three
appearances for Stockport County at the
end of October prior to the dismissal of
former manager Andy Kilner. He did not
feature at all in the plans of new boss
Carlton Palmer and was released in
February when he returned to Sandinavia.
*Stockport Co (£80,000 from BK Hacken,
Sweden, ex IFK Goteborg, Norrby IF, on
25/7/2000) FL 7+1 FLC 2*

BUBB Alvin Ryan
Born: Paddington, 11 October 1980
Height: 5'6" **Weight:** 10.7
This young winger followed Gerry Francis
to Bristol Rovers and spent much of the
2001-02 season on the substitutes'
bench, starting on just three occasions.
He netted regularly for Rovers' reserve
side but failed to get on the score sheet
in the first team, although he enjoyed a
'Man of the Match' performance in the
LDV Vans Trophy victory over Yeovil Town.
He was one of 14 Rovers players whose
contracts were not renewed in the
summer.
*Queens Park R (From trainee on
16/11/1998) FL 0+1
Bristol Rov (Free on 18/7/2001) FL 3+10 FAC
0+1 Others 0+2*

BUCHANAN Wayne Bernard
Born: Banbridge, 12 January 1982
Height: 6'1" **Weight:** 13.2
International Honours: NI: U21-1; Yth;
Sch
A product of Bolton's academy, this young
central defender made his first-team
debut in the FA Cup defeat at Spurs,
coming on as a second half substitute. He
spent the closing stages of the campaign
on loan at Chesterfield where he
impressed with his composure and some
fine skills on the ground.
*Bolton W (From trainee on 7/7/2001) FAC 0+1
Chesterfield (Loaned on 22/3/2002) FL 3*

BUCKLE Paul John
Born: Hatfield, 16 December 1970
Height: 5'8" **Weight:** 11.10
Club Honours: Div 3 '92
Paul had a stop-start season at Exeter in 2001-02, spending time on the sidelines as a result of suffering a shoulder injury in August and a broken ankle in December. Used in midfield or as a wing back, his experience and versatility made him one of the first names on manager John Cornforth's team sheet. His only goal of the campaign proved to be the winner in the home match against York in March.
Brentford (From trainee on 1/7/1989) FL 42+15/1 FLC 5+1 FAC 3+1 Others 6+5
Torquay U (Free on 3/2/1994) FL 57+2/9 FLC 8 FAC 3 Others 1
Exeter C (Free on 13/10/1995) FL 22/2 FAC 1 Others 2
Northampton T (Free on 30/8/1996)
Wycombe W (Free on 18/10/1996)
Colchester U (Free on 28/11/1996) FL 96+9/7 FLC 4 FAC 2 Others 10/3
Exeter U (Free on 2/7/1999) FL 85+8/5 FAC 6+1 Others 7/1

BUCKLEY Adam Christian
Born: Nottingham, 2 August 1979
Height: 5'9" **Weight:** 11.6
This left-sided midfield player developed into a regular member of Lincoln City's first-team squad after moving from Grimsby Town in the summer of 2001. Adam showed plenty of spirit in his first season at Sincil Bank. He possesses an excellent cross and his balls into the box created some good chances. He is the son of the former Imps' manager Alan Buckley.
Grimsby T (Free from West Bromwich A juniors on 7/8/1997) FL 8+7 FLC 0+1 FAC 2
Lincoln C (Free on 23/7/2001) FL 19+12 FAC 3 Others 0+1

BUKRAN Gabor
Born: Hungary, 16 November 1975
Height: 5'11" **Weight:** 12.2
International Honours: Hungary: 1; U21; Yth
This stylish central midfielder joined Wigan Athletic on a non-contract basis last summer. He made an immediate impression scoring with a spectacular volley in a pre-season match against Everton. His only League appearance came in the opening match of the season against Brentford, but he then turned down the offer of a permanent contract. He later signed for Austrian club SV Salzburg.
Walsall (Free from Xerex CD, Spain, ex

Honved, Charleroi, Cordoba, on 5/8/1999) FL 63+10/4 FLC 8/3 FAC 3+1 Others 1+1
Wigan Ath (Free on 10/8/2001) FL 1

BULL Ronald (Ronnie) Rodney
Born: Hackney, 26 December 1980
Height: 5'8" **Weight:** 10.12
A product of the Millwall youth set-up, Ronnie spent much of last season on the bench due to the excellent form of Robbie Ryan. When he came on he acquitted himself excellently but couldn't maintain a regular spot until an injury to Ryan late in the campaign gave him an opportunity to prove his worth. He produced some confident performances in the closing stages and was voted as the club's 'Young Player of the Season'.
Millwall (From trainee on 12/5/1999) FL 28+10 FLC 0+1 Others 3

BULLARD James (Jimmy) Richard
Born: Newham, 23 October 1978
Height: 5'10" **Weight:** 11.10
Jimmy joined Peterborough in the summer of 2001 and started last season in a wide position, but as soon as he was moved into central midfield he blossomed. He delivered some fine defence-splitting passes and waded in with some great goals. He missed part of the campaign after suffering a broken toe.
West Ham U (£30,000 from Gravesend & Northfleet on 10/2/1998)
Peterborough U (Free on 6/7/2001) FL 36+4/8 FLC 1 FAC 5/1 Others 2/2

BULLOCK Darren John
Born: Worcester, 12 February 1969
Height: 5'9" **Weight:** 12.10
Bury's tough tackling midfield player struggled to gain a first-team place in the early weeks of the 2001-02 season, and although he made the starting line-up on two occasions he was released in October. He subsequently joined Dr Martens League club Worcester City, his hometown club.
Huddersfield T (£55,000 from Nuneaton Borough on 19/11/1993) FL 127+1/16 FLC 11/1 FAC 8/2 Others 9/1
Swindon T (£400,000 on 24/2/1997) FL 55+11/2 FLC 2 FAC 1
Bury (£150,000 + on 15/2/1999) FL 45+8/5 FLC 4/2 FAC 5/1 Others 1/1
Sheffield U (Loaned on 22/3/2001) FL 6

BULLOCK Lee
Born: Stockton, 22 May 1981
Height: 5'9" **Weight:** 11.7
Lee was a virtual ever present in York's

midfield in 2001-02 when he had a fine season and made excellent progress. He finished third-top scorer for City with nine goals and signed an extended contract during the campaign. He has excellent all-round skills in tackling, passing and heading and consistently supported the front men.
York C (From trainee on 29/6/1999) FL 84+13/11 FLC 3+1/1 FAC 7+2/1

BULLOCK Martin John
Born: Derby, 5 March 1975
Height: 5'5" **Weight:** 10.7
Club Honours: AMC '02
International Honours: E: U21-1
Martin joined Blackpool in the 2001 close season and was a regular in the line-up throughout the 2001-02 campaign. A pacy attacking midfielder with good close control, he scored the 'golden goal' at Huddersfield Town in the LDV Vans Trophy semi-final to take the Tangerines through to the final at the Millenium Stadium.
Barnsley (£15,000 from Eastwood T on 4/9/1993) F/PL 108+77/4 FLC 14+3 FAC 4+11/3 Others 1
Port Vale (Loaned on 14/1/2000) FL 6/1
Blackpool (Free on 10/8/2001) FL 37+6/2 FLC 1+1 FAC 4 Others 6/3

BULLOCK Matthew
Born: Stoke, 1 November 1980
Height: 5'8" **Weight:** 11.6
International Honours: E: Yth
Matthew began the 2001-02 campaign in Stoke City's reserve team before joining Macclesfield on loan in October. He made a promising debut against Hartlepool when he looked impressive on the right wing but was then surprisingly dropped and only made two further appearances before returning to the Britannia Stadium. He was released in January and signed for Unibond outfit Leek Town soon afterwards.
Stoke C (From trainee on 21/11/1997) FL 4+3 FAC 0+1
Macclesfield T (Loaned on 22/10/2001) FL 2+1

BULMAN Dannie
Born: Ashford, Surrey, 24 January 1979
Height: 5'10" **Weight:** 12.3
This central midfielder was unexpectedly dropped by Wycombe Wanderers seven weeks into the 2001-02 season after falling short of his usual high standards. However, by mid-November he was restored to the side and became a permanent fixture. He has extremely high stamina levels and a fearsome tackle that

remarkably only produced two yellow cards. He also possesses the hardest shot at the club and chipped in with six goals, the pick being a looping thunderbolt from 20 yards in the second game of the season against Wrexham.

Wycombe W *(£5,000 + from Ashford T on 17/6/1998) FL 88+34/11 FLC 6+1 FAC 11+5/1 Others 6*

BUNJEVCEVIC Goran Petar
Born: Karlovac, Croatia, 17 February 1973
Height: 6'3" **Weight:** 12.6
International Honours: Yugoslavia: 14

Injury wrecked Goran's chances of impressing on the Spurs' faithful just what a good buy he had been. In early-season opportunities he looked pacy and solid when bringing the ball out of defence.

Too early to form an opinion but his credentials are sound and Goran will be hoping to return to full fitness and to regain his place as a regular in the Spurs back line.

Tottenham H *(£1,400,000 from Red Star Belgrade, Yugoslavia, ex FK Crvena, Zuezda, on 25/7/2001) PL 5+1 FLC 1+1*

BURCHILL Mark James
Born: Broxburn, 18 August 1980
Height: 5'8" **Weight:** 10.2
Club Honours: SLC '00
International Honours: S: 6; U21-15; Sch

Mark scored twice on his debut for Portsmouth against Grimsby, and netted four goals in just five matches before a freak training ground accident resulted in damage to a cruciate ligament and

sidelined him for the remainder of the season. When fully fit he is a striker who possesses a blinding streak of pace, has an excellent first touch and a great eye for goal.

Glasgow Celtic *(From Celtic BC on 3/6/1997) SL 17+34/21 SLC 3+2 SC 1+2/1 Others 4+1/3*
Birmingham C *(Loaned on 22/9/2000) FL 4+9/4 FLC 3+1/1*
Ipswich T *(Loaned on 22/1/2001) PL 2+5/1*
Portsmouth *(£600,000 on 24/8/2001) FL 5+1/4*

BURGESS Andrew (Andy) John
Born: Bozcat, 10 August 1981
Height: 6'2" **Weight:** 11.6
Club Honours: NC '01

A series of niggling injuries interrupted Andy's season with Rushden last term,

Martin Bullock

but on his day he remained one of the most exciting prospects in the Third Division. A genuine left winger who possesses the ability to get to the dead-ball line and put in dangerous crosses. He scored one of the goals of the season in the Third Division – a spectacular 30-yard effort against Hull City from just inside the touchline. But his season ended in heartache when suspension kept him out of the play-off final against Cheltenham.
Rushden & Diamonds (From juniors on 3/7/1999) FL 28+4/4 FLC 1 FAC 1+1 Others 2+1

BURGESS Benjamin (Ben)
Born: Buxton, 9 November 1981
Height: 6'3" **Weight:** 14.4
International Honours: RoI: U21-2; Yth
Ben joined Brentford on loan in the first week of the 2001-02 campaign, and eventually stayed all season. A tall striker with a cultured left foot, good close control and neat flicks, he netted with a wonderfully curled left-foot shot on his debut against Port Vale. He was a regular scorer until the end of February, including doubles against Brighton and Oldham, but failed to find the net in his last 13 appearances as the Bees lost the Second Division play-off final to Stoke. He also made his debut for the Republic of Ireland at U21 level, scoring against Denmark.
Blackburn Rov (From trainee on 25/11/1998) FL 1+1 FLC 1
Brentford (Loaned on 16/8/2001) FL 43/17 FLC 2 FAC 2/1 Others 4

BURGESS Daryl
Born: Birmingham, 24 January 1971
Height: 5'11" **Weight:** 12.4
Daryl missed most of the early part of the 2001-02 campaign for Northampton through injury but eventually returned to the line-up towards the end of September, settling into one of the centre back spots. Despite playing alongside a series of partners due to the club's injury problems he always maintained a steady level of performance.
West Bromwich A (From trainee on 1/7/1989) FL 317+15/10 FLC 19+3/3 FAC 9 Others 14
Northampton T (Free on 5/7/2001) FL 36/1 FAC 2 Others 2

BURGESS Oliver David
Born: Bracknell, 12 October 1981
Height: 5'10" **Weight:** 11.7
This right-sided midfield player, was a member of Queen's Park Rangers'

successful U19 side in 2000-01. He broke into the first team against Northampton Town last October and retained his place after an impressive performance. Unfortunately, he suffered a cruciate ligament injury in only his fourth game against Swindon which resulted in him missing the remainder of the season.
Queens Park R (Trainee) FL 4+1/1 FAC 0+1

BURGESS Richard Daniel
Born: Bromsgrove, 18 August 1978
Height: 5'8" **Weight:** 11.4
This diminutive Port Vale striker spent the majority of his time in the reserves last season. He made his only start in Vale colours in a 1-0 home defeat by Northampton Town and his other appearances both came from the bench. He has a sharp turn of pace and scored his only senior goal in the FA Cup tie against Aylesbury after replacing the injured Steve McPhee. That game turned out to be his final appearance and in December he joined the Conference club Nuneaton Borough on a free transfer.
Aston Villa (From trainee on 5/7/1996)
Stoke C (Free on 17/5/1997. Free to Worcester C on 31/3/2000)
Port Vale (Free from Bromsgrove Rov on 22/3/2001) FL 1+2 FAC 0+1/1

BURLEY Craig William
Born: Irvine, 24 September 1971
Height: 6'1" **Weight:** 13.0
Club Honours: SLC '97; SPD '98
International Honours: S: 45; U21-7; Yth; Sch
Derby County's midfield schemer was appointed club captain at the start of the 2001-02 season but went on to have a frustrating campaign. He was a regular in the line-up early on but suffered a knee injury in November. A cartilage operation followed and then he was troubled by further achilles problems, preventing him from playing a full role in the Rams struggle against relegation.
Chelsea (From trainee on 1/9/1989) P/FL 85+28/7 FLC 8 FAC 12+5/4 Others 3
Glasgow Celtic (£2,500,000 on 24/7/1997) SL 61+3/20 SLC 7 SC 6/1 Others 12/1
Derby Co (£3,000,000 on 2/12/1999) PL 53/7 FLC 5/3 FAC 2

BURNELL Joseph (Joe) Michael
Born: Bristol, 10 October 1980
Height: 5'10" **Weight:** 11.1
With Bristol City's injury problems of the previous season showing no sign of abating in 2001-02, this accomplished performer was able to add to his senior

experience with the club. When injury robbed City of Matt Hill's services for a lengthy spell Joe stepped in, but despite his dogged determination he never looked comfortable on the left side of defence. No one could doubt his commitment though and he looks certain to feature more often in 2002-03.
Bristol C (From trainee on 24/7/1999) FL 60+10 FLC 0+2 FAC 0+3 Others 9/1

BURNETT Wayne
Born: Lambeth, 4 September 1971
Height: 5'11" **Weight:** 12.6
Club Honours: AMC '98
International Honours: E: Yth
Wayne was once again plagued by injury problems in the 2001-02 season and after having a long spell out he returned to the Grimsby Town line-up in November He then had a somewhat chequered campaign, finding himself in and out of the squad and sometimes on the substitutes' bench. When fully fit he is a speedy and creative midfielder who plays with grit and determination.
Leyton Orient (From trainee on 13/11/1989) FL 34+6 FLC 3+1/1 FAC 3+1 Others 4
Blackburn Rov (£90,000 on 19/8/1992)
Plymouth Arg (Signed on 9/8/1993) FL 61+9/3 FLC 3 FAC 8 Others 4+1
Bolton W (£100,000 on 12/10/1995) F/PL 0+2
Huddersfield T (Signed on 6/9/1996) FL 44+6 FLC 6+1/1 FAC 1+1
Grimsby T (£100,000 on 9/1/1998) FL 80+26/6 FLC 5+2 FAC 2+2 Others 8/3

BURNS Liam
Born: Belfast, 30 October 1978
Height: 6'0" **Weight:** 12.12
International Honours: NI: U21-13; Yth
This strong Port Vale central defender had his best season so far for the club, featuring regularly and producing some effective no-nonsense displays. It was not until the visit to Bristol City in September that he won a place in the side, but thereafter he was a fixture in the line-up. Never afraid to go in where it hurts, he is effective in the air but still awaits his first senior goal. He played for Northern Ireland in a friendly match with Macclesfield Town during the campaign.
Port Vale (From trainee on 2/7/1997) FL 61+14 FLC 1 FAC 3+1 Others 2+1

BURROWS David
Born: Dudley, 25 October 1968
Height: 5'9" **Weight:** 11.8
Club Honours: CS '89; Div 1 '90; FAC '92

International Honours: E: B-3; U21-7
In his second season at Birmingham, David played with assurance and was an asset to the defence. He unluckily lost his place to Martin Grainger and later joined Sheffield Wednesday on a short-term contract in March. He did well at Hillsborough and proved to be a useful defender who is composed on the ball and a good passer.
West Bromwich A (From apprentice on 8/11/1986) FL 37+9/1 FLC 3+1 FAC 2 Others 1
Liverpool (£550,000 on 20/10/1988) F/PL 135+11/3 FLC 16 FAC 16+1 Others 14
West Ham U (Signed on 17/9/1993) PL 29/1 FLC 3/1 FAC 3
Everton (Signed on 6/9/1994) PL 19 FLC 2 FAC 2

Coventry C (£1,100,000 on 2/3/1995) PL 106+5 FLC 9 FAC 9
Birmingham C (Free on 4/7/2000) FL 17+8 FLC 1+3 FAC 1
Sheffield Wed (Free on 8/3/2002) FL 8

BURROWS Mark
Born: Kettering, 14 August 1980
Height: 6'3" **Weight:** 12.8
This tall and effective central defender was overlooked by Exeter City for virtually the whole of 2001-02 and it seemed a certainty that he would be on his way out of St James' Park. However after a loan spell with Dr Martens League club Merthyr Town he returned to claim his place in the line-up. He went on to produce some excellent performances in

the final few games of the season, adding some much needed pace at the back. Mark was rewarded for his efforts when he was offered a new short-term contract by Grecians' manager John Cornforth.
Coventry C (From trainee on 19/1/1998)
Exeter C (Free on 18/7/2000) FL 27+11 FLC 2 FAC 1

BURT Jamie Paul
Born: Blyth, 29 September 1979
Height: 5'10" **Weight:** 12.0
Jamie joined Whitby from neighbours Scarborough in the 2001 close season and was a key figure in their FA Cup run before moving on to Chesterfield in December. His early performances for the Spireites were eye opening: pacy on either

Deon Burton

side, difficult to dispossess and willing to shoot from anywhere. However, he felt the physical pressure of an immediate introduction to full-time football and was rested more as the season neared its climax, but will be a forward to be feared with a full pre-season under his belt.
Chesterfield (Free from Whitby T, ex Bridlington T, Scarborough, on 14/12/2001) FL 18+6/7

BURTON Deon John
Born: Ashford, 25 October 1976
Height: 5'9" **Weight:** 11.9
International Honours: Jamaica: 40
This experienced striker made little impact at Derby County last term and joined Stoke City on loan in the new year. He proved an inspired signing for the Britannia Stadium club, for whom he added mobility and options to the strike force. His goal in the home leg of the play-off semi-final against Cardiff City kept the club's hopes alive and they eventually went on to win promotion.
Portsmouth (From trainee on 15/2/1994) FL 42+20/10 FLC 3+2/2 FAC 0+2/1
Cardiff C (Loaned on 24/12/1996) FL 5/2 Others 1
Derby Co (£1,000,000 + on 9/8/1997) PL 74+44/22 FLC 7+2/3 FAC 9+1/3
Barnsley (Loaned on 14/12/1998) FL 3
Stoke C (Loaned on 21/2/2002) FL 11+1/2 Others 2+1/2

BURTON-GODWIN Osagyefo (Sagi) Lenin Ernesto
Born: Birmingham, 25 November 1977
Height: 6'2" **Weight:** 13.6
Club Honours: AMC '01
This solid central defender had a useful season at the heart of the Port Vale defence in 2001-02. Big and strong, he always let the opposition strikers know that he was around despite the odd mistake. Although primarily a defender he began the campaign in a trial midfield role without too much success before reverting to the defence. He was also tried out front for one game! He was out of contract in the summer and looked set to leave Vale Park.
Crystal Palace (From trainee on 26/1/1996) P/FL 19+6/1 FLC 1 FAC 0+1 Others 0+1
Colchester U (Free on 26/5/1999) FL 9 FLC 2
Sheffield U (Free on 19/11/1999)
Port Vale (Free on 14/1/2000) FL 76+10/2 FLC 3/1 FAC 3 Others 6+1/1

BUSHELL Stephen (Steve) Paul
Born: Manchester, 28 December 1972
Height: 5'9" **Weight:** 11.6

Steve began the 2001-02 season playing with Stalybridge Celtic in the Conference before joining Halifax Town on a month-to-month contract in November. He proved to be an instant hit at the Shay and was soon given a contract through to the end of the season. A hard-working no-nonsense midfield player he impressed to such an extent that he was made team captain towards the end of the campaign. He managed just a solitary goal, netting in the Boxing Day game at Macclesfield.
York C (From trainee on 25/2/1991) FL 156+18/10 FLC 8+1/2 FAC 5 Others 11+2/1
Blackpool (Free on 2/7/1998) FL 64+15/6 FLC 8 FAC 5+1 Others 3+1 (Free to Stalybridge Celtic during 2001 close season)
Halifax T (Free on 23/11/2001) FL 25/1

BUSSCHER Robby
Born: Leischenden, Holland, 23 November 1982
Height: 5'8" **Weight:** 11.5
International Honours: Holland: Yth
This young midfielder joined Grimsby Town in the 2001 close season but although previously capped by Holland at U18 level he failed to make much impression at Blundell Park. He made a solitary appearance from the subs' bench during the opening match of the campaign and was released by the Mariners in January.
Grimsby T (Free from Feyenoord, Holland on 23/7/2001) FL 0+1

BUTLER Philip Anthony (Tony)
Born: Stockport, 28 September 1972
Height: 6'2" **Weight:** 12.0
Tony began the 2001-02 season at the heart of the West Bromwich Albion defence, alongside Larus Sigurdsson and Phil Gilchrist. However, he was sent off in the away game at Watford and his subsequent absence through suspension let in Darren Moore. After that although determined and hard-working as ever, he never really got a look in, acting mainly as a substitute, although he did return briefly when Moore was sidelined.
Gillingham (From trainee on 13/5/1991) FL 142+6/5 FLC 12 FAC 12+1 Others 5+1/1
Blackpool (£225,000 on 30/7/1996) FL 98+1 FLC 7 FAC 4 Others 4/1
Port Vale (£115,000 on 25/3/1999) FL 19
West Bromwich A (£140,000 on 23/3/2000) FL 65+5/1 FLC 7 FAC 1+1 Others 2

BUTLER Lee Simon
Born: Sheffield, 30 May 1966
Height: 6'2" **Weight:** 13.6
Club Honours: Div 3 '97

Lee began the 2001-02 season as Halifax Town's first-choice goalkeeper but a persistent knee injury eventually forced him to announce his retirement from the full-time game at the end of December. He subsequently joined Conference club Doncaster Rovers, ironically as a replacement for Barry Richardson who moved to the Shay around the same time.
Lincoln C (Free from Haworth Colliery on 16/6/1986) FL 30 FLC 1 FAC 1
Aston Villa (£100,000 on 21/8/1987) FL 8 Others 2
Hull C (Loaned on 18/3/1991) FL 4
Barnsley (£165,000 on 22/7/1991) FL 118+2 FLC 5 FAC 9 Others 4
Scunthorpe U (Loaned on 5/2/1996) FL 2
Wigan Ath (Free on 5/7/1996) FL 63 FLC 3 FAC 2 Others 2
Dunfermline Ath (Free on 3/7/1998) SL 35 SLC 1 SC 2
Halifax T (Signed on 24/9/1999) FL 92+1 FLC 1 FAC 7 Others 4

BUTLER Martin Neil
Born: Wordsley, 15 September 1974
Height: 5'11" **Weight:** 11.9
Although he failed to reproduce his goal-scoring exploits of the previous season, Martin was a vital and regular part of the Reading strike force in 2001-02 until suffering a serious ankle injury. A typically brave challenge in the home game against Wrexham saw him sidelined for five months. He did not return until the last two games of the campaign, when his excellent link-up play enabled the team to force draws against Tranmere and Brentford, which secured promotion.
Walsall (From trainee on 24/5/1993) FL 43+31/8 FLC 2+4 FAC 2+5/2 Others 2+2/2
Cambridge U (£22,500 on 8/8/1997) FL 100+3/41 FLC 9/5 FAC 9+2/5 Others 3+1/1
Reading (£750,000 + on 1/2/2000) FL 73+6/30 FLC 3+1 FAC 3/2 Others 4+1/2

BUTLER Paul John
Born: Manchester, 2 November 1972
Height: 6'2" **Weight:** 13.0
Club Honours: Div 2 '97; Div 1 '99
International Honours: RoI: 1; B-1
Paul was made captain at Molineux last season and it seemed to suit him from the start. He led by example as Wolves topped the table after 11 matches. They had the best defence in the division for some time, and it was often when Paul's form dipped that the team had bad results. He was virtually an ever present and often joined the attack, being rewarded with a fine headed goal at Birmingham in March. Like many of the team he was not at his best in the closing

Darren Byfield

stages of the campaign. Paul is a towering central defender, who is strong in the tackle and in the air.

Rochdale (From trainee on 5/7/1991) FL 151+7/10 FLC 8+1 FAC 6+2 Others 12+1
Bury (£100,000 on 22/7/1996) FL 83+1/4 FLC 8 FAC 2 Others 3/1
Sunderland (£600,000 + on 15/7/1998) P/FL 78+1/3 FLC 11+1/1 FAC 4
Wolverhampton W (Loaned on 17/11/2000) FL 5
Wolverhampton W (£1,000,000 on 31/1/2001) FL 50/1 FLC 1 FAC 1 Others 2

BUTLER Thomas Anthony
Born: Dublin, Ireland, 25 April 1981
Height: 5'8" **Weight:** 10.8
International Honours: RoI; U21-8; Yth
This diminutive left-sided midfielder, made a handful of substitute appearances for Sunderland last term and continued to impress fans at the Stadium of Light. A Republic of Ireland U21 international, he did not look out of his depth in the Premiership, despite being asked to play wide on the left wing, and his confidence and ability on the ball should see him playing a bigger part for the Black Cats in 2002-03.

Sunderland (From trainee on 25/6/1998) PL 2+10 FLC 0+2
Darlington (Loaned on 13/10/2000) FL 8 FAC 2

BUTT Nicholas (Nicky)
Born: Manchester, 21 January 1975
Height: 5'10" **Weight:** 11.3
Club Honours: FAYC '92; CS '96, '97; PL '96, '97, '99, '00, 01; FAC '96; EC '99
International Honours: E: 22; U21-7; Yth; Sch
This gritty midfielder possesses some neat skills combined with a hardened edge to match. The arrival of Juan Sebastian Veron over the summer put more pressure on his prospects of regular first team football, but he took it all in his stride, and went on to produce some outstanding midfield performances in the opening half of last season. Stepping in admirably for skipper, Roy Keane in October he combined so well with Veron, that the Irishman's absence went almost unnoticed. He eventually lost his place in the side due to hamstring problems, but was back in contention at the end of January. His club form continued to show improvement and it was no surprise when he had a fine World Cup tournament for England over the summer.

Manchester U (From trainee on 29/1/1993) PL 184+47/20 FLC 5 FAC 20+2/1 Others 54+12/3

BUTTERFIELD Daniel (Danny) Paul
Born: Boston, 21 November 1979
Height: 5'10" **Weight:** 11.10
Club Honours: AMC '98
International Honours: E: Yth
The 2001-02 campaign was one of Danny's best since turning professional with Grimsby Town. Now playing permanently in midfield, he showed great consistency and made the squad for all of the Mariners' 52 competitive games. A tenacious tackler with excellent distribution, he settled well into his new role.

Grimsby T (From trainee on 7/8/1997) FL 100+24/3 FLC 13+1 FAC 5+2 Others 1+1/1

BUTTERS Guy
Born: Hillingdon, 30 October 1969
Height: 6'3" **Weight:** 14.2
International Honours: E: U21-3
Guy re-established himself at the heart of the Gillingham defence last October following Barry Ashby's suspension and later appeared for the final 11 games, when his astute positional play and experience helped the club end on a high note with a comfortable mid-table position.

Tottenham H (From trainee on 5/8/1988) FL 34+1/1 FLC 2+1 FAC 1
Southend U (Loaned on 13/1/1990) FL 16/3 Others 2
Portsmouth (£375,000 on 28/9/1990) FL 148+6/6 FLC 15+1/1 FAC 7 Others 7+2
Oxford U (Loaned on 4/11/1994) FL 3/1 Others 1
Gillingham (£225,000 on 18/10/1996) FL 155+4/16 FLC 9 FAC 14/1 Others 11

BUTTERWORTH Garry Jeffrey
Born: Whittlesey, 8 June 1969
Height: 5'10" **Weight:** 12.0
Club Honours: NC '01
Garry's superb loyalty to Rushden was rewarded with a testimonial season in 2001-02, which started with a game in his honour against West Ham United. A central midfielder who rarely grabbed the headlines, he could be relied upon to turn in solid performances week-in, week-out. Dropped after the first month of the season, Garry was placed on the transfer list, but knuckled down to reclaim his place. Although never the most prolific of goal-scorers, his 25-yard equaliser against Rochdale in the first leg of the play-off semi-final was an absolute screamer. He was given a free transfer at the end of the season, and subsequently joined Farnborough Town.

Peterborough U (From trainee on 20/6/1988) FL 101+22/3 FLC 8+1 FAC 8+1 Others 6+3 (Free to Dagenham & Redbridge during 1992 close season)
Rushden & Diamonds (Signed on 2/8/1994) FL 28+1/1 FLC 1 FAC 2 Others 3/1

BUXTON Lewis Edward
Born: Newport, IoW, 10 December 1983
Height: 6'1" **Weight:** 13.10
Lewis was just still a trainee at Portsmouth when he made his first-team debut as a central defender at Stockport last August. A regular in the line-up since January, he impressed all with his composure, touch and distribution. He reads the game well and plays with a maturity well beyond his years.

Portsmouth (From trainee on 9/4/2001) FL 27+2

BYFIELD Darren
Born: Sutton Coldfield, 29 September 1976
Height: 5'11" **Weight:** 11.11
After his sensational winning goal in the 2000-01 play-off final, Darren was a key figure in Walsall's First Division struggles last season, whether starting games or when used as a substitute. He scored some fine goals such as the volley against Norwich in October, but in March he moved to relegation rivals Rotherham. The speedy striker made an immediate impact, scoring the goal that gave the team a point at West Bromwich Albion, and he was on target in the next match to earn another point against Birmingham.

Aston Villa (From trainee on 14/2/1994) PL 1+6 FLC 1 FAC 0+1 Others 1
Preston NE (Loaned on 6/11/1998) FL 3+2/1 Others 1
Northampton T (Loaned on 13/8/1999) FL 6/1 FLC 1/1
Cambridge U (Loaned on 17/9/1999) FL 3+1
Blackpool (Loaned on 6/3/2000) FL 3
Walsall (Free on 21/6/2000) FL 45+32/13 FLC 2+3/2 FAC 4+2/1 Others 2+2/1
Rotherham U (£50,000 on 27/3/2001) FL 3/2

BYRNE Christopher (Chris) Thomas
Born: Manchester, 9 February 1975
Height: 5'9" **Weight:** 10.4
Club Honours: GMVC '97
International Honours: E: SP-1
Chris signed a two-year contract with Macclesfield Town during the 2001 close season. No stranger to the Moss Rose, having been instrumental in the club's promotion to Football League status, he

soon settled into a midfield role. He scored eight well taken goals, including lobbing the 'keeper, lashing home volleys and the occasional header, and, to his credit, he played on with a hernia injury in the closing stages of the campaign before undergoing surgery in April.

Crewe Alex (From trainee on 21/6/1993. Free to Flixton on 1/8/1994)
Sunderland (Signed from Macclesfield T on 11/6/1997) FL 4+4 FLC 1+1
Stockport Co (£200,000 on 21/11/1997) FL

Chris Byrne

43+13/11 FLC 3/1 FAC 1+1
Macclesfield T (Loaned on 27/8/1999) FL 5
Macclesfield T (Free on 16/7/2001) FL 26+6/6 FLC 1 FAC 4/2

BYRNE Desmond (Dessie)
Born: Dublin, 10 April 1981
Height: 6'1" **Weight:** 12.8
International Honours: RoI: Yth
Dessie began the 2001-02 season on loan at Cambridge United for whom he made five early-season appearances. A

promising left back with a good turn of pace and a useful left foot, he mostly featured for Wimbledon reserves on his return, but stepped up to make his first-team debut in the final game of the campaign when he came off the bench for the last three minutes.

Stockport Co (Trainee) FL 2 (Free to St Patricks Ath on 1/2/1999)
Wimbledon (£20,000 on 2/8/2000) FL 0+1
Cambridge U (Loaned on 8/8/2001) FL 3+1 FLC 1

BYRNE Mark John
Born: Billinge, 8 May 1983
Height: 5'9" **Weight:** 11.1
This young striker negotiated his release from Blackburn Rovers and within days the player who had not even featured for Rovers' reserve side was setting up Stockport County's memorable winner against neighbours Manchester City in front of a full house at Edgeley Park! He was given a new 12-month contract by County after impressing in a handful of senior appearances.

Blackburn Rov (From trainee on 5/7/2001)
Stockport Co (Free on 14/3/2002) FL 1+4

BYRNE Paul
Born: Newcastle, Natal, South Africa, 26 November 1982
Height: 5'9" **Weight:** 11.0
This left-sided midfield player made steady progress at Port Vale last term. His first appearance of the season came as a substitute at Rochdale in the LDV Vans Trophy tie, and he was then chosen for the starting line-up at Peterborough in January. His only other taste of first-team action came on the final day of the season when he was again on the bench against Brighton.

Port Vale (Trainee) FL 2+1 Others 0+1

BYRNE Shaun Ryan
Born: Chesham, 21 January 1981
Height: 5'9" **Weight:** 11.12
International Honours: RoI: U21-10; Yth (UEFA-U16 '98)
This left-sided midfielder has been beset with injuries over the last two years. He came on as substitute for West Ham against Everton in September at Goodison. Unfortunately more niggling injuries followed and he only just returned to action for the reserves just before the season ended.

West Ham U (From trainee on 2/7/1999) PL 0+2
Bristol Rov (Loaned on 7/1/2000) FL 1+1 Others 2

C

CACERES Adrian Claudio
Born: Buenos Aires, Argentina, 10 January 1982
Height: 5'10" **Weight:** 12.5
Adrian failed to make the Saints' first team last season and in September he went on loan to Brentford. He impressed with some neat ball control at Griffin Park but after returning to Southampton he was eventually released in March. The skilful striker then spent the closing weeks of the campaign on a short-term contract at Third Division Hull after scoring twice in a reserve-team fixture.

Southampton (£25,000 from Perth Glory, Australia on 19/9/2000)
Brentford (Loaned on 7/9/2001) FL 5
Hull C (Free on 20/3/2002) FL 1+3

CADAMARTERI Daniel (Danny) Leon
Born: Bradford, 12 October 1979
Height: 5'7'' **Weight:** 11.12
Club Honours: FAYC '98
International Honours: E: U21-3; Yth
A powerful and pacy striker, Danny started only two matches for Everton in 2001-02 before he was allowed to join Bradford City. A hard-working and unselfish player, he established a useful partnership with Ashley Ward for the

Bantams and impressed in his brief time at Valley Parade.
Everton (From trainee on 15/10/1996) PL 38+55/13 FLC 6+3/2 FAC 6+3
Fulham (Loaned on 4/11/1999) FL 3+2/1
Bradford C (Free on 22/2/2002) FL 14/2

CAHILL Timothy (Tim)
Born: Sydney, Australia, 6 December 1979
Height: 5'10" **Weight:** 10.11
Club Honours: Div 2 '01
This Australian-born midfielder was a crucial figure for Millwall last season when his running and determination resulted in him getting into some great goal-scoring positions. His aerial ability was a tremendous asset to the team, and his late runs led to him getting on the end of many a cross. Operating mainly in central midfield he scored a creditable tally of 13 goals for the Lions.
Millwall (Signed from Sydney U, Australia on 31/7/1997) FL 163+3/40 FLC 8+1/1 FAC 3+2 Others 10+1/1

CALDWELL Gary
Born: Stirling, 12 April 1982
Height: 5'11" **Weight:** 12.0
International Honours: S: 4; U21-5; Yth; Sch
This classy young defender joined Darlington on loan last November when injuries had ruled out all but one of the central defenders and he immediately formed a formidable partnership with David Brightwell in the heart of the defence. His quickness of thought and sure distribution of the ball stood out in the Third Division, but after just four games he returned to Tyneside only to go out on loan again in the Scottish Premier League with Hibernian. He went on to make his full debut for Scotland against France in March and added further caps on the tour of Asia during the summer.
Newcastle U (From trainee on 19/4/1999)
Darlington (Loaned on 20/11/2001) FL 4
Hibernian (Loaned on 31/1/2002) SL 10+1 SLC 1

CALDWELL Stephen (Steve)
Born: Stirling, 12 September 1980
Height: 6'0" **Weight:** 11.5
International Honours: S: 1; U21-7; Yth
This young Newcastle centre back started on the bench for the Inter Toto Cup games, making three substitute appearances, but Andy O'Brien's return to fitness saw him displaced and he did not make the team again all season. Steve is a strong tackler who reads the game well, and to further his experience of senior

Tim Cahill

football he was loaned out to Blackpool in October and then Bradford City over the turn of the year. He featured both at right back and in the centre of the defence at Valley Parade and soon became a big favourite of the City supporters after some fine displays.

Newcastle U (From trainee on 30/10/1997) PL 5+4 FLC 1/1 Others 0+3
Blackpool (Loaned on 12/10/2001) FL 6 Others 1/1
Bradford C (Loaned on 7/12/2001) FL 9

CALVO-GARCIA Alexander (Alex)

Born: Ordizia, Spain, 1 January 1972
Height: 5'10'' **Weight:** 11.12

A knee ligament injury pre-season ruled Alex out of the Scunthorpe United line-up until last October but he returned to the team better than ever in the centre of midfield. Hard-working with good ball skills, he netted eight times and was an ever-present for the remainder of the campaign. He deservedly won the club's 'Player of the Season' award and was rewarded with a new two-year deal in the summer.

Scunthorpe U (Free from Eibar, Spain on 4/10/1996) FL 169+17/27 FLC 9/3 FAC 18/4 Others 10/2

CAMARA Aboubacar (Titi) Sidiki

Born: Guinea, 17 November 1972
Height: 6'1" **Weight:** 12.8
International Honours: Guinea

It was a very disappointing campaign for the former Liverpool striker. Due to injuries and loss of form he was only able to play in a handful of games for West Ham reserves. He did however figure as a substitute in the Hammers fine away win against Manchester United in December.

Liverpool (£2,600,000 from Olympique Marseille, France, ex St Etienne, RC Lens, on 14/6/1999) PL 22+11/9 FLC 0+2 FAC 2/1
West Ham U (£1,500,000 on 21/12/2000) PL 5+2 FAC 1

CAMARA Mohamed

Born: Conakry, Guinea, 25 June 1975
Height: 5'11" **Weight:** 11.6

Mohamed played in a Worthington Cup-tie for Wolves last term, but was initially more of a squad player. However, further chances gradually came his way, and he began a run in the team in January, and was an ever-present from then onwards. His lively attacking forays down the flank delighted the crowd, and he was not averse to waving at them if one of his 'tricks' worked. More importantly, his

defensive play tightened up, although he could still be unpredictable at times.
Wolverhampton W (Signed from Le Havre, France, ex AS Beauvais, on 11/8/2000) FL 27+18 FLC 2+1 FAC 1+1 Others 2

CAME Shaun Raymond

Born: Crewe, 15 June 1983
Height: 6'3" **Weight:** 11.12

Shaun made only one senior appearance for Macclesfield in 2001-02, and that at a time when the side was depleted due to injury and suspensions. Nevertheless he performed well in both the reserve and youth teams and continued to show promise as a central defender who is good in the air. He missed two months in the autumn after breaking his hand in training. Shaun is the son of former Bolton Wanderers player Mark Came.
Macclesfield T (From trainee on 5/7/2000) FL 4+4 Others 0+1

CAMERON Colin

Born: Kirkcaldy, 23 October 1972
Height: 5'6" **Weight:** 10.6
Club Honours: S: 11; S Div 1 '93, '95; SLC '94; SC '98
International Honours: Scotland: 15

Wolves were pleased to sign Colin from Hearts last August. After a few games he proved to be a hard-working midfielder, and helped inspire the team to five successive wins. He got in some telling tackles and interceptions, but the signing of Alex Rae reduced his attacking exploits somewhat. As the season wore on Colin's form dipped slightly, but he came good again in the closing weeks. He added a further cap for Scotland against world champions France in March.
Raith Rov (Signed from Lochore Welfare on 13/7/1990) SL 106+16/23 SLC 8+1/5 SC 6/3 Others 9/2
Heart of Midlothian (£400,000 on 31/3/1996) SL 154+3/48 SLC 13/6 SC 17+1/6 Others 6+3/1
Wolverhampton W (£1,750,000 on 24/8/2001) FL 38+3/4 FAC 1 Others 2

CAMERON David (Dave) Anthony

Born: Bangor, Wales, 24 August 1975
Height: 6'1" **Weight:** 13.8

Dave's hard work up front won him the backing of Lincoln's fans in a disappointing season for the Third Division club. He was undeterred by spending the entire campaign on the transfer list and his tenacity in the box was an inspiration to everyone at Sincil Bank. He produced a healthy supply of

goals in the first half of the season but netted just once in 2002. He signed for Conference club Chester City in the summer.
Falkirk (Signed from Dunipace Juniors on 17/8/1994)
East Stirling (Free on 31/8/1995) SL 0+8 (Free to Pencaitland & Ormiston during 1997 close season)
St Mirren (Signed from Whitehall Welfare on 2/2/1999) SL 3+8
Brighton & Hove A (Free from British Army on 8/7/1999) FL 6+11 FLC 0+1 Others 0+1 (Free to Worthing on 31/3/2000)
Lincoln C (Free on 5/7/2000) FL 33+27/8 FLC 2+1 FAC 3+1/1 Others 1+5/1

CAMERON Martin George William

Born: Dunfermline, 16 August 1978
Height: 6'1" **Weight:** 12.11
Club Honours: SCC '00

The Bristol Rovers striker scored two spectacular early-season goals against York City and Oxford in successive home matches but then suffered a pulled hamstring that put him out of action. The arrival of Sergio Ommel in November put him further out of the picture and he was mostly restricted to appearances from the subs' bench after this. He spent the last few months of the season on loan at Partick Thistle.
Alloa Ath (Signed from Craigmillar Thistle on 11/10/1997) SL 60+27/39 SLC 3+3/3 SC 7+2/3 Others 5/3
Bristol Rov (£100,000 on 11/7/2000) FL 16+23/6 FLC 1+2/1 FAC 3+1 Others 2+1/1
Partick Thistle (Loaned on 27/2/2002) SL 6+2/1 SC 0+1

CAMM Mark Liam

Born: Mansfield, 1 October 1981
Height: 5'8" **Weight:** 10.12

Mark continued to build up his first-team experience last term and was rewarded when Lincoln gave him a new contract for the 2002-03 campaign. He patiently waited for his chance before injuries gave him the opportunity in November, making his first appearance of the season as a half-time substitute in the memorable home win over Hull City. By the end of the campaign he was a regular member of the first-team squad although mostly on the subs' bench. Mark was mainly used at right back but also made appearances on the right side of midfield where his busy style and enthusiasm proved effective.
Sheffield U (From trainee on 5/7/1999)
Lincoln C (Free on 14/8/2000) FL 8+11 FAC 1+2 Others 0+2

CAMPBELL Andrew (Andy) Paul

Born: Stockton, 18 April 1979
Height: 5'11" **Weight:** 11.7
International Honours: E: U21-4; Yth
This skilful young striker never made the starting line-up for Middlesbrough last term, despite scoring the winner in the FA Cup triumph over Manchester United. He joined Cardiff City on loan at the end of February and after netting on his debut at Northampton Town he hit seven goals in his first six matches. He quickly became a favourite with the Ninian Park faithful and in April he joined the Bluebirds permanently.
Middlesbrough (From trainee on 4/7/1996) F/PL 28+28/4 FLC 5+5/1 FAC 2+3/2
Sheffield U (Loaned on 10/12/1998) FL 5/1
Sheffield U (Loaned on 25/3/1999) FL 6/2
Bolton W (Loaned on 9/3/2001) FL 3+3
Cardiff C (£950,000 on 25/2/2002) FL 8/7 Others 0+2

CAMPBELL Jamie

Born: Birmingham, 21 October 1972
Height: 6'1" **Weight:** 12.11
Jamie found himself somewhat out in the cold at Exeter last term as new boss John Cornforth preferred Chris Curran and Alex Watson as his centre-back pairing. An unfortunate training ground incident was followed by his departure and he subsequently linked up with Conference outfit Stevenage. At his best he is an effective defender who is always dangerous when going forward at set pieces.
Luton T (From trainee on 1/7/1991) FL 10+26/1 FLC 1+1 FAC 1+3 Others 1+2
Mansfield T (Loaned on 25/11/1994) FL 3/1 FAC 2
Cambridge U (Loaned on 10/3/1995) FL 12
Barnet (Free on 11/7/1995) FL 50+17/5 FLC 3+3/1 FAC 4+2/1 Others 1
Cambridge U (Free on 8/8/1997) FL 91/6 FLC 7 FAC 6/1 Others 4
Brighton & Hove A (Free on 7/7/1999) FL 22+1/1 FLC 2 FAC 3 Others 2
Exeter C (Free on 11/7/2000) FL 56+2/3 FLC 2 FAC 2+1 Others 2

CAMPBELL Kevin Joseph

Born: Lambeth, 4 February 1970
Height: 6'1" **Weight:** 13.8
Club Honours: FAYC '88; FLC '93; FAC '93; ECWC '94; Div 1 '98
International Honours: E: B-1; U21-4
A powerful and intelligent leader of the forward line, Kevin kicked off Everton's season as captain. With four goals in his first eight appearances he also looked set to finish the season as top scorer for the

fourth successive campaign. A painful back injury put paid to that ambition, though, as he spent almost three months on the sidelines. Asked to lead the line on his own on his return he struggled to make the same impact and further niggling injuries reduced his effectiveness before he was succeeded as skipper by strike-partner Duncan Ferguson.
Arsenal (From trainee on 11/2/1988) F/PL 124+42/46 FLC 14+10/6 FAC 13+6/2 Others 15+4/5
Leyton Orient (Loaned on 16/1/1989) FL 16/9
Leicester C (Loaned on 8/11/1989) FL 11/5 Others 1/1
Nottingham F (£3,000,000 on 1/7/1995) F/PL 79+1/32 FLC 2 FAC 11/3 Others 3 (£2,500,000 to Trabzonspor, Turkey on 7/8/1998)
Everton (£3,000,000 on 25/3/1999) PL 82+4/34 FLC 2+3/1 FAC 9/3

CAMPBELL Paul Andrew

Born: Middlesbrough, 29 January 1980
Height: 6'1" **Weight:** 11.0
This promising young player made only a limited number of appearances for Darlington in 2001-02 mainly due to injury. He scored on his first appearance of the season at Halifax in November and had a brief six-game run before being ruled out again. He showed creative ability in midfield and an eye for goal although he only found the net twice during the campaign.
Darlington (From trainee on 8/7/1998) FL 32+24/6 FLC 1+4/1 FAC 2+1/1 Others 3+1

CAMPBELL Stuart Pearson

Born: Corby, 9 December 1977
Height: 5'10" **Weight:** 10.8
Club Honours: FLC '97, '00
International Honours: S: U21-14
Stuart was dogged by injury during the 2001-02 campaign and he was out of the Grimsby Town line-up for almost two months in November and December and again during the closing weeks of the season. A strong and skilful midfielder who loves to run forward into the box, his tireless efforts made an invaluable contribution to the Mariners' annual struggle for First Division survival.
Leicester C (From trainee on 4/7/1996) PL 12+25 FLC 2+5 FAC 3+3
Birmingham C (Loaned on 23/3/2000) FL 0+2
Grimsby T (£200,000 on 15/9/2000) FL 70+1/5 FLC 4 FAC 3

CAMPBELL Sulzeer (Sol) Jeremiah

Born: Newham, 18 September 1974
Height: 6'2" **Weight:** 14.1

Club Honours: FLC '99; PL '02; FAC '02
International Honours: E: 51; B-1; U21-11; Yth (UEFA-U18 '93)
After making the controversial move from Tottenham to North London rivals during the 2001 close season, Sol soon settled in to become a rock solid figure in the centre of defence for the Gunners and was one of the cornerstones of their double triumph. He was also a key figure for the England national team, forging an extremely effective partnership with Rio Ferdinand as the national team battled through to the quarter-finals of the 2002 World Cup.
Tottenham H (From trainee on 23/9/1992) PL 246+9/10 FLC 28/4 FAC 28+2/1 Others 2
Arsenal (Free on 10/7/2001) PL 29+2/2 FAC 7/1 Others 10

CANHAM Marc David

Born: Weburg, Germany, 11 September 1982
Height: 5'11" **Weight:** 12.3
Marc had an outstanding season for the Colchester youth and reserve teams last term and was rewarded with his senior debut when he came on from the subs' bench in the penultimate home game of the season against Cardiff. A cultured central midfielder, he was offered a one-year professional contract for the 2002-03 campaign.
Colchester U (Trainee) FL 0+1

CANHAM Scott Walter

Born: Newham, 5 November 1974
Height: 5'9" **Weight:** 11.10
Scott returned to Leyton Orient in the 2001 close season after impressing Tommy Taylor whilst training with the club during the summer break. He broke into the team in December, scoring in the 5-0 win over Lincoln and went on to add further goals including one in the FA Cup tie at Everton. He was rewarded with a new contract at the end of the season.
West Ham U (From trainee on 2/7/1993)
Torquay U (Loaned on 3/11/1995) FL 3
Brentford (Loaned on 19/1/1996) FL 14
Brentford (£25,000 + on 29/8/1996) FL 24+11/1 FLC 4+2 FAC 1+1 Others 1+2
Leyton Orient (Free on 10/8/1998) FL 3+6 FLC 0+1 Others 1 (Free to Chesham U on 8/9/2000)
Leyton Orient (Free on 9/7/2001) FL 23+1/4 FAC 1/1 Others 0+1

CANOVILLE Lee

Born: Ealing, 14 March 1981
Height: 6'1" **Weight:** 11.3
International Honours: E: Yth; Sch

Kevin Campbell

A product of Arsenal's youth system Lee signed for Torquay last September. After some lively early displays on the right-hand side of midfield, he fell victim to shin splints, which ruled him out of action for four months. He returned towards the end of the season, capping his best performance to date against Rochdale with a goal in a 3-0 victory.

Arsenal (From trainee on 3/7/1998 earlier been transferred from Millwall juniors for an undisclosed fee on 9/7/1997) FLC 0+1
Northampton T (Loaned on 26/1/2001) FL 2
Torquay U (Free on 14/9/2001) FL 10+2/1 Others 1

CARASSO Cedric
Born: Avignon, France, 30 December 1981
Height: 6'4" **Weight:** 13.11
This French 'keeper had a brief trial at Crystal Palace before returning on a six-month contract last December. Small and stocky, his only first-team appearance was as a second-half substitute against Birmingham City.

Crystal Palace (Loaned from Avignon, ex Marseilles, France, on 14/12/2001) FL 0+1

CARBON Matthew (Matt)
Phillip
Born: Nottingham, 8 June 1975
Height: 6'2" **Weight:** 13.6
International Honours: E: U21-4
Matt joined Walsall during the summer of 2001, but after looking good in a pre-season game at Livingston was kept out of action by off-the-field matters and injury until making his debut at Stockport in November. His power in the air and speed along the ground were evident as the Saddlers won two and drew one of his first three games. He had two more spells out with injury, but each time returned to hit top form immediately. He headed a splendid late match-winner against Wimbledon in Colin Lee's first League game in charge in January, and was a tower of strength in the late run that kept the club in Division One.

Lincoln C (From trainee on 13/4/1993) FL 66+3/10 FLC 4/1 FAC 3 Others 4+3
Derby Co (£385,000 on 8/3/1996) P/FL 11+9 FLC 1 FAC 0+1
West Bromwich A (£800,000 on 26/1/1998) FL 106+7/5 FLC 7+2 FAC 4
Walsall (Free on 23/7/2001) FL 22/1 FAC 2

CARBONARI Horacio Angel
Born: Argentina, 2 May 1973
Height: 6'3" **Weight:** 13.4
Derby County's central defender suffered a groin injury shortly before the start of

the 2001-02 campaign and it was some time before he recovered full fitness. However he never managed to win a regular place for the Rams and in March he was loaned to Coventry City, linking up with his former boss Jim Smith once more. He looked impressive on his debut for the Sky Blues against Birmingham but thereafter struggled in the back four and eventually returned to Pride Park at the end of the season.

Derby Co (£2,700,000 from Athletico Rosario Central, Argentina on 1/7/1998) PL 87+1/8 FLC 2 FAC 9
Coventry C (Loaned on 22/3/2002) FL 5

CARBONE Benito (Beni)
Born: Begnara, Italy, 14 August 1971
Height: 5'6" **Weight:** 10.8
International Honours: Italy: U21 (UEFA-U21 '94)
One of the greatest players ever to wear a Bradford City shirt, Beni was unfortunately too expensive for the club to afford and spent much of the 2001-02 season out on loan. He spent three months at Derby in the autumn, linking up with Fabrizio Ravanelli, played a couple of times for the Bantams on his return and was then loaned out to Middlesbrough until the end of the season. A supremely talented player, he is particularly effective running at opposition defences when his pace and tight control can cause havoc.

Sheffield Wed (£3,000,000 from Inter Milan, Italy, ex Torino, Reggina, Casert, Ascoli, Napoli, on 18/10/1996) PL 86+10/25 FLC 3+1 FAC 7/1
Aston Villa (Signed on 21/10/1999) PL 22+2/3 FAC 6/5
Bradford C (Free on 10/8/2000) P/FL 39+3/10 FLC 3/2 FAC 0+1
Derby Co (Loaned on 18/10/2001) PL 13/1 FAC 1
Middlesbrough (Loaned on 8/2/2002) PL 13/1

CAREY Brian Patrick
Born: Cork, 31 May 1968
Height: 6'3" **Weight:** 14.4
International Honours: RoI: 3; U21-1
Brian suffered a frustrating time with injuries throughout the 2001-02 campaign and these restricted his appearances for Wrexham. A hernia operation in September was followed by a stress fracture of the foot in March and his season never really got out of first gear. Always a commanding figure in the centre of defence, he is dangerous when going up for set-pieces in opponents' penalty areas and his experience was sorely missed by the Robins last term.

Manchester U (£100,000 from Cork C on 2/9/1989)
Wrexham (Loaned on 17/1/1991) FL 3
Wrexham (Loaned on 24/12/1991) FL 13/1 FAC 3 Others 3
Leicester C (£250,000 on 16/7/1993) F/PL 51+7/1 FLC 3 FAC 0+1 Others 4
Wrexham (£100,000 on 19/7/1996) FL 209+2/9 FLC 10 FAC 20 Others 8+1

CAREY Louis Anthony
Born: Bristol, 20 January 1977
Height: 5'10" **Weight:** 11.10
International Honours: S: U21-1
This cool and cultured defender again captained Bristol City in 2001-02. His mazy runs forward offered City attacking options, and he confidently led the back line. Already approaching 250 Football League appearances for City despite his young age, he is expected to be a regular once more in 2002-03.

Bristol C (From trainee on 3/7/1995) FL 239+8/3 FLC 13+1 FAC 16 Others 10+2

CAREY Shaun Peter
Born: Kettering, 13 May 1976
Height: 5'9" **Weight:** 10.12
Club Honours: NC '01
International Honours: RoI: U21-2
This central midfielder appeared for Rushden in the first ten games of last season, but didn't make another competitive first-team appearance. The arrival of Richie Hanlon from Peterborough United denied him further opportunities and he languished in the reserves before moving to Chester City in February.

Norwich C (From trainee on 1/7/1994) FL 50+18 FLC 5+2 FAC 1+1
Rushden & Diamonds (Free on 18/8/2000) FL 7+1 FLC 2

CARLISLE Wayne Thomas
Born: Lisburn, 9 September 1979
Height: 6'0" **Weight:** 11.6
International Honours: NI: U21-9; Yth; Sch
Wayne made a single first-team appearance for Crystal Palace last term, coming on from the subs' bench in the Worthington Cup tie against Leyton Orient before moving on loan to Swindon. A fast-running, attacking midfielder with a ferocious shot he did well with the Second Division club, scoring spectacularly in the 1-1 draw at Wycombe in what was his first appearance in the starting line-up. He subsequently accepted a short-term contract at Bristol Rovers but had the

Jamie Carragher

misfortune to be red carded on his debut for the club.
Crystal Palace (From trainee on 18/9/1996) FL 29+17/3 FLC 4+3 FAC 1
Swindon T (Loaned on 12/10/2001) FL 10+1/2 FAC 2
Bristol Rov (Free on 28/3/2002) FL 5

CARPENTER Richard

Born: Sheerness, 30 September 1972
Height: 6'0" **Weight:** 13.0
Club Honours: Div 3 '01; Div 2 '02
Richard really came into his own for Brighton during the promotion run-in last term. He is the type of cultured midfield player whose efforts are not always widely appreciated but who is a vital member of the squad. He again showed some excellent distribution, particularly following the arrival of Junior Lewis which gave the midfield a much better shape. He shared the free-kick duties with Paul Watson and scored two in the 4-1 victory at Colchester.
Gillingham (From trainee on 13/5/1991) FL 107+15/4 FLC 2+1 FAC 9+1 Others 7/1
Fulham (£15,000 on 26/9/1996) FL 49+9/7 FLC 4/1 FAC 2/1 Others 2
Cardiff C (£35,000 on 29/7/1998) FL 69+6/2 FLC 3+1 FAC 8+1 Others 1
Brighton & Hove A (Free on 4/7/2000) FL 87/9 FLC 4 FAC 5/1 Others 1

CARR Darren John

Born: Bristol, 4 September 1968
Height: 6'2" **Weight:** 13.7
This experienced central defender was released from his contract at Brighton last August and eventually signed for Conference outfit Dover in October. His appearances were restricted by injury and he was allowed to leave early in the new year. Following a brief trial at Oxford he signed non-contract forms for Rushden in time to play at Hartlepool. Unfortunately Diamonds slumped to their worst league defeat of the season, and he was released soon afterwards. At his best he is a no-nonsense centre half who is effective in the air.
Bristol Rov (From trainee on 20/8/1986) FL 26+4 FLC 2+2 FAC 3 Others 2
Newport Co (Loaned on 30/10/1987) FL 4
Newport Co (£3,000 on 28/11/1988) FL 5
Sheffield U (£8,000 on 10/3/1988) FL 12+1/1 FLC 1 FAC 3+1 Others 1
Crewe Alex (£35,000 on 18/9/1990) FL 96+8/5 FLC 8 FAC 12/2 Others 10
Chesterfield (£30,000 on 21/7/1993) FL 84+2/4 FLC 9 FAC 6+3 Others 8
Gillingham (£75,000 on 7/8/1998) FL 22+8/2 FLC 2 FAC 1 Others 3+1

Brighton & Hove A (£25,000 on 14/7/1999) FL 18+3 FAC 3 Others 2 (Free to Dover on 17/8/2001)
Rotherham U (Loaned on 30/11/2000) FL 1 Others 1
Lincoln C (Loaned on 19/1/2001) FL 3
Carlisle U (Loaned on 9/2/2001) FL 10
Rushden & Diamonds (Free on 25/1/2002) FL 1

CARRAGHER James (Jamie)
Lee Duncan
Born: Bootle, 28 January 1978
Height: 6'1" **Weight:** 13.0
Club Honours: FAYC '96; FLC '01; FAC '01; UEFAC '01; ESC '01; CS '01
International Honours: E: 6; B-2; U21-27; Yth
This versatile Liverpool and England defender had another outstanding season in 2001-02. Early on he played some games at right back in place of Markus Babbel, before switching to a more familiar place on the left flank after the arrival of Abel Xavier. Apart from suspension he was a near ever present for the Reds, and also featured regularly for England but missed out on the World Cup finals due to an impending knee operation.
Liverpool (From trainee on 9/10/1996) PL 148+11/2 FLC 13+1 FAC 12 Others 35+1

CARRAGHER Matthew (Matt)

Born: Liverpool, 14 January 1976
Height: 5'9" **Weight:** 11.4
Club Honours: Div 3 '97; AMC '01
Port Vale's captain had another steady season in the back four last season. His role varied between full back, centre half and sweeper depending on the chosen formation, but as usual he gave his all for the cause wherever he played. He missed only six games, mostly due to a leg injury, but when he returned for the local 'derby' against Stoke City he slotted back in as if he had never been away. He is now Vale's longest serving player.
Wigan Ath (From trainee on 25/11/1993) FL 102+17 FLC 6+1/1 FAC 10+1/2 Others 7+1
Port Vale (Free on 3/7/1997) FL 156+3/1 FLC 8 FAC 4 Others 9

CARRATT Philip (Phil)

Born: Stockport, 22 October 1981
Height: 5'10" **Weight:** 12.7
A product of the Stockport County youth system, Phil only appeared as a substitute last season. A promising young striker, he was released in the summer after failing

to impress new manager Carlton Palmer.
Stockport Co (From trainee on 28/9/2000) FL 0+4

CARRICK Michael

Born: Wallsend, 28 July 1981
Height: 6'0" **Weight:** 11.10
Club Honours: FAYC '99
International Honours: E: 2; U21-8; Yth
This talented young left-sided midfielder added to his admirers, after some brilliant displays for West Ham last season. He has amazing vision and has excellent distribution with both feet. He tackles well and has a good understanding with Joe Cole in the centre of the park, the two complementing each other's talents. Michael missed several weeks of the campaign after undergoing surgery in the new year to resolve a groin problem.
West Ham U (From trainee on 25/8/1998) PL 66+5/4 FLC 5 FAC 5 Others 0+1
Swindon T (Loaned on 12/11/1999) FL 6/2
Birmingham C (Loaned on 23/2/2000) FL 1+1

CARROLL David (Dave)
Francis
Born: Paisley, 20 September 1966
Height: 6'0" **Weight:** 12.0
Club Honours: FAT '91, '93; GMVC '93
International Honours: E: Sch
After 14 years as a highly influential midfielder at Wycombe, Dave's career finally came to an end last March when he was released early to enable him to find another club. He immediately signed for Aldershot Town and scored on his debut. The rigours of professional football finally caught up with him and his season was a long struggle against niggling injuries, notably a groin strain. Used mostly from the bench he made just four starts and left Adams Park with a record of 100 goals in 602 appearances. Dave will be fondly remembered as the most skilful player at Wycombe in the 1990s.
Wycombe W (£6,000 from Ruislip Manor in 1988 close season) FL 277+25/41 FLC 21+2/1 FAC 30+5/6 Others 16/3

CARROLL Roy Eric

Born: Enniskillen, 30 September 1977
Height: 6'2" **Weight:** 12.9
Club Honours: AMC '99
International Honours: NI: 11; U21-11; Yth
This highly accomplished goalkeeper settled down as Fabien Barthez's deputy at Old Trafford with the minimum of fuss last term. He endured something of a baptism of fire when Aston Villa's, Darius Vassell beat him after just four minutes of

his Premiership debut in September, but Roy gave a stirring performance thereon in. His record was quite impressive throughout the campaign and he more than justified Sir Alex Ferguson's faith in him.
Hull C (From trainee on 7/9/1995) FL 46 FLC 2 FAC 1 Others 1
Wigan Ath (£350,000 on 16/4/1997) FL 135 FLC 11 FAC 8 Others 15
Manchester U (£2,500,000 on 27/7/2001) PL 6+1 FLC 1 FAC 1 Others 1

CARRUTHERS Christopher (Chris) Paul
Born: Kettering, 19 August 1983
Height: 5'10" **Weight:** 12.3
This attacking left back came on tremendously with Northampton Town last term, seeming to grow in confidence with every game. Although he missed a lot of the season through injury, he capped his return with his first goal in senior football against Wycombe Wanderers in April.
Northampton T (From trainee on 9/4/2002) FL 7+9/1 Others 1

CARRUTHERS Martin George
Born: Nottingham, 7 August 1972
Height: 5'11" **Weight:** 11.9
Martin finished top scorer for Scunthorpe United with 17 goals last season, an impressive return considering that he missed two months in the new year following a knee cartilage operation. A hard-working centre forward with good finishing ability, he benefited from playing alongside a big target man and celebrated his 100th career goal in the defeat at Plymouth in January.
Aston Villa (From trainee on 4/7/1990) F/PL 2+2 FAC 0+1 Others 0+1
Hull C (Loaned on 31/10/1992) FL 13/6 Others 3
Stoke C (£100,000 on 5/7/1993) FL 60+31/13 FLC 7+3/1 FAC 3+1 Others 10+4/6
Peterborough U (Signed on 18/11/1996) FL 63+4/21 FLC 5+1/2 FAC 6/4 Others 6
York C (Loaned on 29/11/1999) FL 3+3
Darlington (Signed on 25/3/1999) FL 11+6/2
Southend U (£50,000 on 17/9/1999) FL 69+1/26 FLC 2 FAC 5 Others 5+1/3
Scunthorpe U (£20,000 on 22/3/2001) FL 38+3/14 FLC 1 FAC 2/3 Others 3/1

CARSLEY Lee Kevin
Born: Birmingham, 28 February 1974
Height: 5'10" **Weight:** 11.11
International Honours: RoI: 20; U21-1
This combative midfielder turned in some impressive performances in the first half of the 2001-02 season for Coventry before he was sold to Everton in February.

Although used regularly on the right of midfield, he is much more effective in the centre – as he showed on the final day of the season when he scored a splendid goal at Arsenal. An uncompromising tackler, diligent worker and a steady passer, Lee was delighted when he helped the Goodison Park club avoid relegation.
Derby Co (From trainee on 6/7/1992) P/FL 122+16/5 FLC 10+3 FAC 12 Others 3
Blackburn Rov (£3,375,000 on 23/3/1999) P/FL 40+6/10 FLC 4/1 FAC 4/1
Coventry C (£2,500,000 on 1/12/2000) P/FL 46+1/4 FLC 2/1 FAC 3
Everton (£1,950,000 on 8/2/2002) PL 8/1

CARSS Anthony (Tony) John
Born: Alnwick, 31 March 1976
Height: 5'10" **Weight:** 12.0
A bargain free-transfer signing from Carlisle United, Tony had swept the 'Player of the Season' awards at Oldham Athletic in season 2000-01 and was looking forward to the new campaign with relish. However, injuries disrupted his season meaning he missed several months' action and only returned to full fitness in March. His tigerish presence and industrious work were sorely missed in midfield. Supporters and management alike hope he can now stay injury-free and quickly re-establish himself as the driving force in the side.
Blackburn Rov (From trainee at Bradford C on 29/8/1994)
Darlington (Free on 11/8/1995) FL 33+24/2 FLC 5/1 FAC 2+1 Others 4
Cardiff C (Free on 28/7/1997) FL 36+6/1 FLC 2 FAC 5+1 Others 1
Chesterfield (Free on 7/9/1998) FL 26+9/1 FLC 2 FAC 1 Others 1+1
Carlisle U (Free on 11/8/2000) FL 6+1 FLC 2
Oldham Ath (Free on 13/10/2000) FL 42+7/3 FLC 1 FAC 3

CARTER Darren Anthony
Born: Solihull, 18 December 1983
Height: 6'2" **Weight:** 12.5
International Honours: E: Yth
Darren was the landslide choice as Birmingham City's 'Young Player of the Year' last season. He made his debut in the January 'derby' at West Brom and played fearlessly. A strong box-to-box midfielder who tackles hard, he scored his first goal as a pro in the 3-1 win over Crewe in April that propelled Blues into the play-off places. Darren became the hero of Blues' fans everywhere when he netted the decisive kick in the penalty shoot-out at the end of the play-off final against Norwich, thus taking the club into the Premiership.

Birmingham C (From trainee on 13/11/2001) FL 12+1/1 Others 1+1

CARTWRIGHT Lee
Born: Rawtenstall, 19 September 1972
Height: 5'8" **Weight:** 11.0
Club Honours: Div 3 '96; Div 2 '00
Lee started the 2001-02 campaign with a testimonial against Middlesbrough in pre-season before playing his 400th senior game for Preston in September, the first North End player to reach this mark since the early 1980s. Employed largely on the right flank, he briefly returned to his original central midfield role and showed this may be where his future lies. His slight frame belies the tenacity of his tackling, while he distributes the ball accurately. Never a prolific scorer, his first goal for over two years was an even rarer header, which turned out to be the winner at Portsmouth. Rested in January with shin splints, he recovered to challenge for his place back.
Preston NE (From trainee on 30/7/1991) FL 297+66/22 FLC 18+2/2 FAC 18+5/1 Others 20+5/1

CARTWRIGHT Mark Neville
Born: Chester, 13 January 1973
Height: 6'2" **Weight:** 13.6
Club Honours: Div 3 '01
Mark joined Shrewsbury Town during the summer of 2001 and made his debut with a clean sheet in the opening day victory at eventual champions Plymouth. He is a reliable 'keeper who soon became a favourite of the crowd with a series of solid displays and gained the confidence of his defensive colleagues playing in front of him. However an injury in October and then a suspension saw him lose out to Ian Dunbavin and he never regained his first-team place for the remainder of the season.
Stockport Co (From trainee at York C on 17/8/1991. Freed during 1992 close season)
Wrexham (Signed following a USA soccer scholarship on 5/3/1994) FL 37 FLC 2 FAC 6 Others 6
Brighton & Hove A (Free on 10/8/2000) FL 12+1 FLC 2
Shrewsbury T (Free on 4/7/2001) FL 14 FLC 1

CAS Marcel
Born: Breda, Holland, 30 April 1972
Height: 6'1" **Weight:** 12.8
Marcel was a near ever present for Notts County last term, showing pace and talent to burn. The nearest thing to a good old-fashioned winger seen at Meadow Lane in years, he often had the beating of opposition defenders. His

Luigi Cennamo

sorties down the right flank could end with him crossing, losing the ball or scoring a spectacular goal!
Notts Co (Free from RBC Roosendaal, Holland on 4/7/2001) FL 39+1/6 FLC 2 FAC 2 Others 2

CASEY Ryan Peter
Born: Coventry, 3 January 1979
Height: 6'1'' **Weight:** 11.2
International Honours: RoI: Yth
Ryan was again troubled by injuries at Swansea in 2001-02. His problems included a knee injury, fractured skull, and damaged ligaments and broken bone in his ankle in the penultimate League match at Hartlepool. After a loan spell early on with Merthyr he enjoyed his best run in the first team showing signs of establishing himself as a regular in the line-up. He is a skilful left winger with the ability to deliver quality crosses from the flank.
Swansea C (From trainee on 7/5/1997) FL 19+43/2 FLC 1+1 FAC 0+2 Others 2+1

CASH Brian Dominick
Born: Dublin, 24 November 1982
Height: 5'9" **Weight:** 12.0
International Honours: RoI: U21-3; Yth
Another product of the Nottingham Forest youth academy to make his mark at first-team level in 2001-02, Brian operated on the right-hand side of midfield. He has the ability to ghost past players and provide quality crosses, and also possesses a keen eye for goal himself. All his appearances last term came from the subs' bench and he will be looking to make the starting line-up in 2002-03.
Nottingham F (From trainee on 15/12/1999) FL 0+5

CASKEY Darren Mark
Born: Basildon, 21 August 1974
Height: 5'8" **Weight:** 11.9
International Honours: E: Yth (UEFA-U18 '93); Sch
There was a huge burden of expectation placed on Darren's shoulders when he arrived at Notts County in the summer of 2001. A talented midfield playmaker, it was rather unfortunate that a leaky defence behind him undermined much of his excellent work going forward. He was handed the captain's armband and eventually orchestrated the team away from the bottom of the table with some inspired leadership.
Tottenham H (From trainee on 6/3/1992) PL 20+12/4 FLC 3+1/1 FAC 6+1
Watford (Loaned on 27/10/1995) FL 6/1

Reading (£700,000 on 28/2/1996) FL 180+22/35 FLC 10+2/4 FAC 9+1/5 Others 8+1/1
Notts Co (Free on 4/7/2001) FL 39+3/5 FLC 2 FAC 3 Others 2+1/1

CASTLE Stephen (Steve) Charles
Born: Barkingside, 17 May 1966
Height: 5'11" **Weight:** 12.10
This experienced midfield player began the 2001-02 campaign as a reserve for Leyton Orient and made a couple of appearances from the subs' bench before going out on loan to Stevenage Borough. On his return he eventually succumbed to a knee injury that led him to announce his retirement from the game.
Leyton Orient (From apprentice on 18/5/1984) FL 232+11/55 FLC 15+1/5 FAC 23+1/6 Others 18+2
Plymouth Arg (£195,000 on 30/6/1992) FL 98+3/35 FLC 5/1 FAC 8/2 Others 6/1
Birmingham C (£225,000 on 21/7/1995) FL 16+7/1 FLC 11 FAC 1 Others 3/1
Gillingham (Loaned on 15/2/1996) FL 5+1/1
Leyton Orient (Loaned on 3/2/1997) FL 4/1
Peterborough U (Free on 14/5/1997) FL 96+6/17 FLC 7+1 FAC 4+1/2 Others 6+1/1
Leyton Orient (Free on 10/7/2000) FL 2+8 FLC 0+1 FAC 0+1 Others 2+1

CAVILL Aaran
Born: Bedford, 5 March 1984
Height: 5'11" **Weight:** 11.8
Aaran came on as a substitute for the final two minutes of Northampton Town's game against Oldham last August to establish a record as the shortest Football League career to date for the club. He is a promising young midfield player who will be aiming to feature more regularly in the first-team squad during 2002-03.
Northampton T (Trainee) FL 0+1

CENNAMO Luigi
Born: Germany, 11 February 1980
Height: 6'2" **Weight:** 12.13
Goalkeeper Luigi joined Burnley from Olympiakos in the 2001 close season, and he was a fixture on the bench up to being given his first-team baptism following Nik Michopoulos' injury in the FA Cup tie at Cheltenham. Unfortunately for Luigi, virtually his first two tastes of action comprised picking the ball out of the net, as the Clarets joined the ranks of victims of cup giant-killers. Stan Ternent's response was to bring in Marlon Beresford on loan to stand in for Michopoulos and Luigi was not retained at the end of the season.
Burnley (Free from Olympiakos, Greece on 20/7/2001) FAC 0+1

CHADWICK Luke Harry
Born: Cambridge, 18 November 1980
Height: 5'11" **Weight:** 11.0
Club Honours: PL '01
International Honours: E: U21-12; Yth
Despite his classy wing play and penchant for netting outstanding goals, Luke carries the burden of being David Beckham's understudy at Old Trafford. He started the 2001-02 season in sparkling fashion for both England U21s and United, and was in mesmerising form in the Premiership match against then leaders Everton at Old Trafford. Although not yet considered ready for European Champions' League action, it was still clear that he had come on in leaps and bounds over the previous 12 months.
Manchester U (From trainee on 8/2/1999) PL 11+13/2 FLC 4 FAC 1+2 Others 1+2

CHADWICK Nicholas (Nicky) Gerald
Born: Market Drayton, 26 October 1982
Height: 6'0" **Weight:** 12.8
A powerful, deceptively quick centre forward, Nicky had scored bucket-loads of goals at every level he had appeared for Everton. After making an impressive appearance from the subs' bench at Aston Villa in January, he then showed he was just as capable of scoring regularly in the Premiership. His first senior strike was no more than a tap-in against Bolton, but a header against Leicester was more difficult, then a third strike against Blackburn – a masterly piece of improvisation to back-heel in from six yards – showed his natural goal instinct.
Everton (From trainee on 29/10/1999) PL 2+7/3 FLC 0+1 FAC 0+1

CHALK Martyn Peter Glyn
Born: Swindon, 30 August 1969
Height: 5'6" **Weight:** 10.0
Martyn enjoyed an extended run in the Wrexham side from last October up until around Christmas time. However, injuries again hampered him in his bid to establish a regular place within the line-up. A busy little player who looks more at home in the hub of central midfield, he notched an important goal in the 3-2 defeat of Northampton Town in December. He failed to feature from February onwards and with his contract up for renewal he was released in the summer.
Derby Co (£10,000 from Louth U on 23/1/1990) FL 4+3/1 FAC 3/1 Others 0+1
Stockport Co (£40,000 on 30/6/1994) FL 29+14/6 FLC 7+1/2 FAC 2+3 Others 2+2
Wrexham (£25,000 on 19/2/1996) FL 136+48/13 FLC 4+3 FAC 13+3 Others 8

Nicky Chadwick

CHALLINOR David (Dave) Paul

Born: Chester, 2 October 1975
Height: 6'1" **Weight:** 12.6
International Honours: E: Yth; Sch
After recovering from a broken leg suffered during the previous season, Dave did not seem to figure in new Tranmere manager Dave Watson's plans last term and in January he moved on to Stockport County. A no-nonsense centre-half, his trademark long throws came into play on his debut against Crystal Palace and immediately caused problems for the opposition defence. After an inconsistent start to his Edgeley Park career Dave was back to his dominant best by the season's end and has been entrusted with the captain's armband for the new campaign.

Tranmere Rov (Signed from Brombrough Pool on 18/7/1994) FL 124+16/6 FLC 17+1 FAC 9+2 Others 1
Stockport Co (£120,000 on 11/1/2002) FL 18

CHALLIS Trevor Michael

Born: Paddington, 23 October 1975
Height: 5'9" **Weight:** 11.4
International Honours: E: U21-2; Yth
Trevor began the 2001-02 season in his accustomed left-back position at Bristol Rovers. However, he suffered a series of niggling shin, hip and ankle injuries which restricted his ability to hold down a regular place. He eventually returned to produce some sparkling performances as a wing back in the final third of the campaign. Not one to shirk a challenge, his wholehearted attitude won him many admirers amongst the Pirates' supporters.

Queens Park R (From trainee on 1/7/1994) F/PL 12+1 FAC 2
Bristol Rov (Free on 15/7/1998) FL 121+8/1 FLC 6 FAC 12+1 Others 5

CHAMBERLAIN Alec Francis Roy

Born: March, 20 June 1964
Height: 6'2" **Weight:** 13.9
Club Honours: Div 1 '96; Div 2 '98
Alec started the 2001-02 campaign as second-choice goalkeeper behind Espen Bardsen at Watford, but regained the first-team jersey at Sheffield United in October and went on to have one of his best seasons. Alec himself modestly credited goalkeeping coach Kevin Hitchcock for his excellent form, but manager Luca Vialli preferred to draw attention to his professionalism and communication skills behind a somewhat shaky defence. In January he signed a one-year extension to his contract and in the following month he passed the

milestone of 700 senior appearances. He finished a memorable campaign by being voted Watford's 'Player of the Year' for the second time.

Ipswich T (Free from Ramsey T on 27/7/1981)
Colchester U (Free on 3/8/1982) FL 188 FLC 11 FAC 10 Others 12
Everton (£80,000 on 28/7/1987)
Tranmere Rov (Loaned on 1/11/1987) FL 15
Luton T (£150,000 on 27/7/1988) FL 138 FLC 7 FAC 7 Others 7
Sunderland (Free on 8/7/1993) FL 89+1 FLC 9 FAC 8 Others 1
Watford (£40,000 on 10/7/1996) P/FL 174+2 FLC 13+1 FAC 9 Others 3

CHAMBERS Adam Craig

Born: West Bromwich, 20 November 1980
Height: 5'10" **Weight:** 11.8
International Honours: E: Yth
Twin brother of James, Adam came to the fore in November following an injury to West Bromwich Albion's hard-tackling midfielder Michael Appleton. He stepped confidently into the breach and did exceedingly well, his eager approach and tremendous work-rate receiving high praise from his team-mates and manager alike.

West Bromwich A (From trainee on 8/1/1999) FL 28+15/1 FLC 4+1 FAC 4 Others 0+1

CHAMBERS James Ashley

Born: West Bromwich, 20 November 1980
Height: 5'10" **Weight:** 11.8
International Honours: E: Yth
Twin brother of Adam, the versatile James Chambers was given very few opportunities during the course of the season as West Bromwich Albion were blessed with several experienced and capable defenders. He started only one game – the 2-0 away defeat at Norwich City in October.

West Bromwich A (From trainee on 8/1/1999) FL 38+10 FLC 4+1 FAC 1

CHAMBERS Triston

Born: Enfield, 25 December 1982
Height: 5'8" **Weight:** 11.5
This promising striker scored on a regular basis for the Colchester U19s last term, helping them to win the Youth Alliance South-East Conference title. With the first team safe from relegation, he was handed his senior debut as a second-half substitute against Cardiff in April. He has been given a three-month professional contract for the start of 2002-03.

Colchester U (Trainee) FL 0+1

CHAPMAN Benjamin (Ben)

Born: Scunthorpe, 2 March 1979
Height: 5'7" **Weight:** 11.0
2001-02 proved to be another disappointing season for this young Grimsby Town full back. Despite being made available on a free transfer during the close season, he was unable to find a new club and returned to Blundell Park to fulfil the remaining year of his contract. Once again his opportunities were limited due to the consistent form of regular defenders, but spells of injury to both Tony Gallimore and John McDermott enabled him to notch up a few more appearances.

Grimsby T (From trainee on 11/7/1997) FL 13+8 FLC 3 FAC 3 Others 0+1

CHARLTON Simon Thomas

Born: Huddersfield, 25 October 1971
Height: 5'8" **Weight:** 11.10
International Honours: E: Yth
A solid and dependable left back, Simon has now become a firm favourite of the Reebok fans and deservedly won one of Bolton's 'Player of the Year' awards last season. Firm in the tackle and seeming to have the ability to run all day, he is now the club's first choice left back, and his foraging runs up field have brought him quite a few goal assists.

Huddersfield T (From trainee on 1/7/1989) FL 121+3/1 FLC 9/1 FAC 10 Others 14
Southampton (£250,000 on 8/6/1993) PL 104+10/2 FLC 9+4/1 FAC 8+1
Birmingham C (£250,000 on 5/12/1997) FL 69+3 FLC 3 FAC 3
Bolton W (Free on 12/7/2000) P/FL 53+5 FLC 1 FAC 3+1 Others 3

CHARNOCK Philip (Phil) Anthony

Born: Southport, 14 February 1975
Height: 5'11" **Weight:** 11.2
This hard-working player was again somewhat unlucky with injuries at Crewe last term and only managed to appear in around half the first-team fixtures. Normally featuring on the left-hand side of midfield, he scored a spectacular goal in the away win at Portsmouth.

Liverpool (From trainee on 16/3/1993) FLC 1 Others 0+1
Blackpool (Loaned on 9/2/1996) FL 0+4
Crewe Alex (Signed on 30/9/1996) FL 136+21/8 FLC 13+2 FAC 5 Others 6

CHARVET Laurent Jean

Born: Beziers, France, 8 May 1973
Height: 5'10" **Weight:** 12.3
Club Honours: ECWC '98
After having a difficult time the previous

season, Laurent forced his way into Kevin Keegan's plans for the start of the 2001-02 campaign. He made the starting line up for City's opening game at home to Watford and gave what was probably his best performance to date in a Manchester City shirt. However, he only featured twice more before being sidelined with an achilles injury, which kept him out for over a month, and on his return he only saw reserve-team action.
Chelsea (Loaned from Cannes, France on 22/1/1998) PL 7+4/2 FLC 0+1 Others 0+1
Newcastle U (£750,000 on 23/7/1998) PL 37+3/1 FLC 3 FAC 6 Others 4
Manchester C (£1,000,000 + on 26/10/2000) P/FL 19+4 FAC 0+1

CHETTLE Stephen (Steve)
Born: Nottingham, 27 September 1968
Height: 6'1" **Weight:** 13.3
Club Honours: FMC '89, '92; FLC '89, '90; Div 1 '98
International Honours: E: U21-12
After starting the season as Barnsley's regular centre half and club captain Steve lost his place in mid-September when manager Nigel Spackman changed the formation to three centre backs. He was loaned to Walsall shortly afterwards where his sterling qualities were never more in evidence than in the game at Hillsborough, when he continued to battle away despite twice having to leave the field for running repairs. He returned to Oakwell and briefly acted as player-coach until new boss Steve Parkin was installed. He retained his place for the remainder of the campaign before being released in the summer.
Nottingham F (From apprentice on 28/8/1986) F/PL 398+17/11 FLC 49+3/1 FAC 36+1 Others 21+2/2
Barnsley (Free on 26/11/1999) FL 91+1/2 FLC 4 FAC 3 Others 3
Walsall (Loaned on 25/9/2001) FL 6

CHILLINGWORTH Daniel Thomas
Born: Cambridge, 13 September 1981
Height: 6'0" **Weight:** 12.6
This tall, pacy striker began the 2001-02 campaign on loan at Cambridge City again, before joining Darlington on a similar basis in November. He made an immediate impact by scoring twice in five appearances before being recalled to the Abbey Stadium. He went on to feature regularly for the Cambridge United in the second half of the campaign, and should prove a problem for Division Three defences in 2002-03.

Cambridge U (From trainee on 14/2/2000) FL 10+6/2 Others 3+2/1
Darlington (Loaned on 19/11/2001) FL 2+2/1 FAC 1/1

CHILVERS Liam Christopher
Born: Chelmsford, 6 November 1981
Height: 6'1" **Weight:** 13.5
Club Honours: FAYC '00
This promising Arsenal centre half joined Notts County on loan last November and his classy background was clearly evident. A tall strong defender, he showed good positional sense and was quietly confident in possession. His loan spell was unfortunately interrupted by injury, but he left behind him a first-class impression.
Arsenal (From trainee on 18/7/2000)
Northampton T (Loaned on 22/12/2000) FL 7
Notts Co (Loaned on 1/11/2001) FL 9/1 FAC 2

CHIPPO Youssef
Born: Boujaad, Morocco, 10 June 1973
Height: 5'10" **Weight:** 10.10
International Honours: Morocco
Youssef had a much better season at Coventry last term and was generally first choice as a flank player in midfield. His early-season appearances were mainly on the left wing where his passing and ball winning ability were used effectively. Later he played in central midfield and on the right wing, although he missed several games whilst playing for Morocco in the African Nations Cup in January. On his return he hit a strong vein of form scoring a stunning winner against Walsall and then netting after just 14 seconds against Barnsley for the club's goal of the season.
Coventry C (£1,200,000 from FC Porto, Portugal, ex Al Arabi, on 16/7/1999) P/FL 80+19/6 FLC 6/2 FAC 3/2

CHRISTIE Iyseden
Born: Coventry, 14 November 1976
Height: 6'0" **Weight:** 12.6
Iyseden missed the first half of the 2001-02 campaign as he was still recovering from a ruptured knee ligament suffered the previous season. He returned to the Leyton Orient line-up in time to make an appearance from the subs' bench in the FA Cup tie at Portsmouth when he scored the final goal in O's shock 4-1 win. He regained his starting place the following month but despite scoring three more goals he was released during the summer break.
Coventry C (From trainee on 22/5/1995) PL 0+1 FLC 0+1
Bournemouth (Loaned on 18/11/1996) FL 3+1
Mansfield T (Loaned on 7/2/1997) FL 8

Mansfield T (Free on 16/6/1997) FL 44+37/18 FLC 4/5 FAC 0+4 Others 2+1
Leyton Orient (£40,000 on 2/7/1999) FL 32+26/12 FLC 4+1/1 FAC 1+2/1 Others 1

CHRISTIE Jeremy John
Born: Whangarei, New Zealand, 22 May 1983
Height: 5'10" **Weight:** 10.12
International Honours: New Zealand: Yth
Another product of the Barnsley academy, Jeremy progressed to become a regular in the reserves last season and made his senior debut as a substitute in the FA Cup replay at Blackburn. A midfielder who can play either through the centre or wide, he is a hard-working player with an eye for goal. He made his second first-team appearance on the final day of the season when again coming on as a substitute.
Barnsley (Trainee) FL 0+1 FAC 0+1

CHRISTIE Malcolm Neil
Born: Stamford, 11 April 1979
Height: 5'6" **Weight:** 11.4
International Honours: E: U21-11
This talented young striker was once again a regular for Derby County last term and finished the season as the club's joint-top scorer with nine Premiership goals. A fast and direct player, he was in devastating form in the home game with Manchester United, scoring twice and coming close to a hat-trick.
Derby Co (£50,000 + from Nuneaton Borough on 2/11/1998) PL 66+26/22 FLC 4+2/2 FAC 4/2

CLAPHAM James (Jamie) Richard
Born: Lincoln, 7 December 1975
Height: 5'9" **Weight:** 10.11
Jamie continued to be a valuable member of the Ipswich Town first-team squad last term and when he did make the line-up he played in left midfield more often than left wing back. He played in all the club's European games and scored two goals, both after he had come on as a substitute, against Sunderland and at Bolton. He is the son of the former Shrewsbury Town and Chester player Graham Clapham.
Tottenham H (From trainee on 1/7/1994) PL 0+1 Others 4
Leyton Orient (Loaned on 29/1/1997) FL 6
Bristol Rov (Loaned on 27/3/1997) FL 4+1
Ipswich T (£300,000 on 9/11/1998) P/FL 161+20/9 FLC 16+1/3 FAC 3+3 Others 10+2/1

CLARE Robert
Born: Belper, 28 February 1983
Height: 6'1" **Weight:** 11.7

Youssef Chippo

Stockport County's young centre half made a first-team place his own last season. At only 19 years of age Robert hardly put a foot wrong in the defence and already performs like an experienced defender. He nearly capped off a great season with his first ever goal, but his looping header at Norwich on the final day bounced to safety off the underside of the crossbar. He was an unused substitute for the England U19 team during the qualifying stages of the UEFA Championships.
Stockport Co (From trainee on 10/3/2000) FL 40+5 FLC 1 FAC 3

CLARIDGE Stephen (Steve) Edward
Born: Portsmouth, 10 April 1966
Height: 5'11" **Weight:** 12.10
Club Honours: Div 3 '91, Div 2 '95; AMC '95; FLC '97
This journeyman striker was named Millwall's 'Player of the Season' and was also the leading goal-scorer, a great achievement from this true professional. The image of Steve, arms and legs pumping with his socks round his ankles is one that has endeared him to supporters up and down the country. With his non-stop running he is a credit to the team while his control is outstanding, and as a role model for youngsters he is second to none. Steve sustained a foot injury, which sidelined him for three weeks and during this time he was sorely missed.
Bournemouth (Signed from Fareham on 30/11/1984) FL 3+4/1 Others 1 (£10,000 to Weymouth in October 1985)
Crystal Palace (Signed on 11/10/1988)
Aldershot (£14,000 on 13/10/1988) FL 58+4/19 FLC 2+1 FAC 6/1 Others 5/2
Cambridge U (£75,000 on 8/2/1990) FL 56+23/28 FLC 2+4/2 FAC 1 Others 6+3/1
Luton T (£160,000 on 17/7/1992) FL 15+1/2 FLC 2/3 Others 2/1
Cambridge U (£195,000 on 20/11/1992) FL 53/18 FLC 4/3 FAC 4 Others 3
Birmingham C (£350,000 on 7/11/1994) FL 86+2/35 FLC 14+1/2 FAC 7 Others 9+1/5
Leicester C (£1,200,000 on 1/3/1996) P/FL 53+10/17 FLC 8/2 FAC 4/1 Others 3+1/1
Portsmouth (Loaned on 23/1/1998) FL 10/2
Wolverhampton W (£400,000 on 26/3/1998) FL 4+1 FAC 1
Portsmouth (£200,000 on 10/8/1998) FL 94+10/34 FLC 4+2 FAC 2+2/1
Millwall (Free on 21/3/2001) FL 45+2/20 FLC 1+1/1 FAC 0+1 Others 1+1

CLARK Anthony Carl
Born: London, 5 October 1984
Height: 5'11" **Weight:** 8.10

This young Southend United trainee produced some impressive displays in a wide midfield role for the reserve and U19 teams last season. He eventually stepped up to make his senior debut from the subs' bench at Kidderminster in March.
Southend U (Trainee) FL 0+2

CLARK Ian David
Born: Stockton, 23 October 1974
Height: 5'11" **Weight:** 11.7
Ian began the 2001-02 campaign as Hartlepool's first choice left back, but the emergence of Mark Robinson and the signing of Paul Smith saw his first-team opportunities limited. He subsequently made the rare move to local rivals Darlington, where he became new manager Tommy Taylor's first signing. He immediately endeared himself to the Feethams fans with an outstanding display on his debut against Rochdale, capped by scoring the only goal of the game. He appeared in a variety of roles but was best used attacking down the left flank where his tricky footwork and direct running were particularly effective. He ended the season as leading scorer for the Quakers.
Doncaster Rov (Free from Stockton on 11/8/1995) FL 23+22/3 FLC 1+2 FAC 1+1 Others 4/1
Hartlepool U (Free on 24/10/1997) FL 109+29/17 FLC 4 FAC 4+2 Others 11+2/1
Darlington (£10,000 on 14/11/2001) FL 28/13 FAC 2+1

CLARK Lee Robert
Born: Wallsend, 27 October 1972
Height: 5'8" **Weight:** 11.7
Club Honours: Div 1 '93, '99, '01
International Honours: E: U21-11; Yth; Sch
Lee gave some wholehearted displays in midfield for Fulham last season. He is a ball winner who helped influence games and often created goal-scoring opportunities for others with his excellent distribution of the ball. Sadly his own goal-scoring touch, so much in evidence during the previous season, deserted him. Lee picked up an injury against Charlton on Boxing Day that kept him out for several weeks, and he was injured again on his return against Liverpool ruling him out for the rest of the campaign.
Newcastle U (From trainee on 9/12/1989) F/PL 153+42/23 FLC 17 FAC 14+2/3 Others 7+5/1
Sunderland (£2,750,000 on 25/6/1997) FL 72+1/16 FLC 4+1 FAC 4 Others 3
Fulham (£3,000,000 on 13/7/1999) P/FL 92+4/15 FLC 13/1 FAC 5

CLARK Peter James
Born: Romford, 10 December 1979
Height: 6'1" **Weight:** 12.7
2001-02 proved to be an injury-plagued season for Stockport County's popular left-sided defender and he was restricted to just a handful of appearances after damaging both his ankle and knee during the campaign. He only made one start for the club during the opening three months after collecting an injury in a reserve game at Scunthorpe, but eventually returned to the side towards the end of the season and played in the morale-boosting 2-1 victory over Watford.
Carlisle U (From trainee at Arsenal on 6/8/1998) FL 77+2/1 FLC 2 FAC 2 Others 3
Stockport Co (£75,000 on 7/7/2000) FL 45+6/2 FLC 2 FAC 3

CLARK Simon
Born: Boston, 12 March 1967
Height: 6'1" **Weight:** 12.12
Simon began the 2001-02 season as Colchester United's skipper and featured regularly in the line-up before surprisingly announcing his decision to quit the club. In January he moved to Singapore to begin a new career with S-League team Woodlands Wellington. The U's missed him badly, winning just one of the next 12 games following his departure. He is a reliable left-sided central defender, who can feature equally well in a back three or back four.
Peterborough U (Free from Stevenage Borough on 25/3/1994) FL 102+5/4 FLC 5 FAC 12 Others 7+1/1
Leyton Orient (£20,000 on 16/6/1997) FL 98/9 FLC 6 FAC 9 Others 5
Colchester U (Free on 5/7/2000) FL 52+3 FLC 6 FAC 0+1 Others 2

CLARK Steven (Steve) Terence
Born: Stepney, 10 February 1982
Height: 6'1" **Weight:** 12.4
Steve initially joined Southend on loan last November and did well enough to earn a permanent transfer early in the new year. He showed his undoubted class in patches on the wing, but he only managed 12 appearances in five months due to a combination of injury and suspension. Amazingly tricky and skilful, his game is based on confidence, and he can rip opposition defences apart when truly on form.
West Ham U (From trainee on 21/7/2001)
Southend U (£12,000 + on 19/11/2001) FL 9+3/1

CLARKE Andrew (Andy)
Weston
Born: Islington, 22 July 1967
Height: 5'10" **Weight:** 11.7
Club Honours: GMVC '91
International Honours: E: SP-2
Andy had a somewhat disappointing season at Peterborough last term when he missed a couple of months due to suspension. He is an experienced striker with good pace who is able to upset opposition defences with his excellent close control.
Wimbledon (£250,000 from Barnet on 21/2/1991) F/PL 74+96/17 FLC 13+12/4 FAC 9+8/2
Port Vale (Loaned on 28/8/1998) FL 2+4
Northampton T (Loaned on 15/1/1999) FL 2+2
Peterborough U (Free on 4/5/1999) FL 88+19/29 FLC 2+1/2 FAC 11+1/4 Others 6/2

CLARKE Christopher (Chris)
Edward
Born: Leeds, 18 December 1980
Height: 6'3" **Weight:** 12.10
Chris enjoyed another productive season at Halifax last term and it was no surprise when Blackpool came in and signed him in the new year. A powerful young defender, he scored for the Tangerines in the LDV Vans Trophy final victory over Cambridge United. He is the twin brother of Halifax defender Matthew Clarke.
Halifax T (From trainee at Wolverhampton W on 5/7/1999) FL 50+1/1 FLC 2 FAC 3 Others 1
Blackpool (£120,000 on 18/2/2002) FL 10+1 Others 1/1

CLARKE Clive Richard
Born: Dublin, 14 January 1980
Height: 6'1" **Weight:** 12.3
Club Honours: AMC '00
International Honours: RoI: U21-11; Yth
Clive had another excellent season at Stoke last term, firmly establishing himself at left back following the departure of Tony Dorigo. His distribution from the left side of defence was of a high quality and he turned in a series of 'Man of the Match' performances.
Stoke C (From trainee on 25/11/1997) FL 95+13/2 FLC 8+3 FAC 5+1 Others 17/1

CLARKE Darrell James
Born: Mansfield, 16 December 1977
Height: 5'10" **Weight:** 11.6
A close season signing for Hartlepool, Darrell began 2001-02 with a thigh strain, and it took some time for his season to get going. A skilful midfielder, his game steadily picked up and he played his best

football towards the end of the campaign as the club's fortunes also improved. He became a useful goal-scorer, and in April hit a hat-trick in a 7-1 win over Swansea.
Mansfield T (From trainee on 3/7/1996) FL 137+24/24 FLC 7/2 FAC 4+1/1 Others 2+2
Hartlepool U (Signed on 17/7/2001) FL 24+9/7 FLC 0+1 FAC 1/1 Others 2

CLARKE James (Jamie)
William
Born: Sunderland, 18 September 1982
Height: 6'2" **Weight:** 12.9
This left-footed defender was Mansfield Town's 'Youth Team Player of the Year' for 2001 and was knocking on the first-team door for most of the season. He eventually made his debut at Luton on Easter Monday as manager Stuart Watkiss rang in the changes after some poor showings. He is a confident youngster who will be looking to gain further senior experience in 2002-03.
Mansfield T (Trainee) FL 1

CLARKE Lee
Born: Peterborough, 28 July 1983
Height: 5'11" **Weight:** 10.10
Lee joined Peterborough from United Counties League club Yaxley last October and played regularly in the reserves. A slightly built striker, he made his senior debut in the closing stages of the LDV Vans Trophy tie against Bristol City and also featured as a substitute at Colchester. He is the son of the former Northern Ireland international Colin Clarke.
Peterborough U (Signed from Yaxley on 15/10/2001) FL 0+1 Others 0+1

CLARKE Matthew (Matt)
John
Born: Sheffield, 3 November 1973
Height: 6'4" **Weight:** 13.10
Steve Bruce paid a substantial fee for this experienced 'keeper last September in a bid to shore up a leaky defence, and after conceding seven himself in his first two games, Matt began to show his undoubted class. He remained as the club's first choice, and was awarded the 'Nationwide Save of the Month' in October for a stop against his old club.
Rotherham U (From trainee on 28/7/1992) FL 123+1 FLC 4 FAC 3 Others 11
Sheffield Wed (£325,000 + on 10/7/1996) PL 2+2
Bradford C (Free on 5/7/1999) PL 38 FLC 2 FAC 2 Others 3
Bolton W (Loaned on 20/3/2001) FL 8 Others 3
Crystal Palace (£1,350,000 on 7/9/2001) FL 28 FLC 2

CLARKE Matthew Paul
Born: Leeds, 18 December 1980
Height: 6'3" **Weight:** 12.7
Matthew continued to develop at Halifax last season and looked more than comfortable in his new role as a central defender. He also helped out at left back during an injury crisis and scored his only goal in Town's final away game of the campaign to help secure a fine 4-2 win at Torquay. He is the twin brother of the Blackpool defender Chris Clarke.
Halifax T (From trainee at Wolverhampton W on 5/7/1999) FL 42+27/2 FAC 5+1 Others 2+2

CLARKE Nathan
Born: Halifax, 30 November 1983
Height: 6'2" **Weight:** 11.5
This promising Huddersfield Town youngster had a whirlwind start to his football career, stepping up from the juniors into first-team football at Stoke last September and collecting the 'Man of the Match' award. He also shone in the following game at home to Blackpool when he scored the opening goal. A classy and impressive central defender with a powerful long throw, he subsequently retained his place in the team for much of the remainder of the campaign.
Huddersfield T (From trainee on 6/9/2001) FL 36/1 FAC 1 Others 4

CLARKE Peter Michael
Born: Southport, 3 January 1982
Height: 6'0" **Weight:** 12.0
International Honours: E: Yth; Sch
Captain of England's U20 team during the end of season Toulon tournament, Peter is a solid, powerful and sharp-tackling centre half. Unfortunately the majority of his eight appearances for Everton last season came at right back. He applied himself enthusiastically to the unfamiliar role, and always gave 100 per cent never letting the team down.
Everton (From juniors on 19/1/1999) PL 5+3 FAC 3

CLARKE Ryan James
Born: Bristol, 30 April 1982
Height: 6'1" **Weight:** 12.0
A first-year professional at Bristol Rovers, this young goalkeeper spent most of the 2001-02 campaign developing in the club's reserve team. He made his League debut for the Pirates from the subs' bench in the final match of the season at Rochdale. Despite being on the pitch for just 14 minutes he pulled off several saves before conceding a late penalty. He kept

out the resultant spot kick but it was ordered to be retaken, and this time he was beaten.
Bristol Rov (From trainee on 4/7/2001) FL 0+1

CLARKSON Ian Stewart
Born: Solihull, 4 December 1970
Height: 5'10" **Weight:** 12.12
Club Honours: AMC '91; NC '00
Ian began the 2001-02 season as Kidderminster's back-up at right back but soon found himself in the line-up when Parfait Medou-Otyé was suspended. He responded with some excellent form and was a near ever-present for the rest of the campaign. When manager Jan Molby resigned late in the season, Ian was promoted to assistant-manager to work alongside caretaker Ian Britton for the final weeks of the campaign. At the end of the season, however, he was one of four out-of-contract players released by the club.
Birmingham C (From trainee on 15/12/1988) FL 125+11 FLC 12 FAC 5+1 Others 17+1
Stoke C (£40,000 on 13/9/1993) FL 72+3 FLC 6 FAC 5 Others 8+2
Northampton T (Free on 2/8/1996) FL 91+3/1 FLC 7+2 FAC 6 Others 10/1
Kidderminster Hrs (Free on 5/11/2000) FL 73+4 FLC 2 FAC 4 Others 3

CLARKSON Philip (Phil) Ian
Born: Garstang, 13 November 1968
Height: 5'10" **Weight:** 12.5
Phil was on the fringe of the first team at Blackpool last season and managed only three appearances before moving on to Bury on a short-term contract on transfer deadline day. A central midfield battler capable of ghosting into the box and scoring goals, he played in four of the five closing fixtures for the Shakers but was unable to prevent them from dropping into the Third Division.
Crewe Alex (£22,500 from Fleetwood T on 15/10/1991) FL 76+22/27 FLC 6+2/1 FAC 3+2/2 Others 7+4/1
Scunthorpe U (Loaned on 30/10/1995) FL 4/1
Scunthorpe U (Free on 13/2/1996) FL 45+3/18 FLC 2/1 FAC 3/2 Others 1
Blackpool (£80,000 on 6/2/1997) FL 154+17/35 FLC 10+1/2 FAC 6+2/4 Others 11/2
Bury (Free on 28/3/2002) FL 4

CLEGG George Gerald
Born: Manchester, 16 November 1980
Height: 5'10" **Weight:** 11.12
This left-sided striker joined Bury on a short-term contract last summer, but

failed to impress during his early time at Gigg Lane. After a prolonged spell on the subs' bench, injuries to other players eventually gave him a first-team chance in December and he grasped the opportunity with both hands. A determined and wholehearted player with a tremendous work-rate and an eye for goal, he was rewarded with an extended contract in January. A permanent fixture in the side from December onwards, he scored four important goals and was able to slot back into a deeper left-sided role during games when required.
Manchester U (From trainee on 5/7/1999)
Wycombe W (Loaned on 2/3/2001) FL 2+8 FAC 1
Bury (Free on 10/8/2001) FL 25+6/4 FAC 0+1 Others 0+1

CLEGG Michael Jaime
Born: Ashton under Lyne, 3 July 1977
Height: 5'8" **Weight:** 11.8
Club Honours: FAYC '95
International Honours: E: U21-2
This very able full back was again mostly confined to the reserve team at Old Trafford last season, his only senior action coming in the Worthington Cup tie against Arsenal in November. In February he moved on a free transfer to near neighbours Oldham Athletic where he was immediately installed at right back, but he struggled to adjust to the requirements of lower division football and after just five starts he found himself out of favour.
Manchester U (From trainee on 1/7/1995) PL 4+5 FLC 7+1 FAC 3+1 Others 1+2
Ipswich T (Loaned on 16/2/2000) FL 3
Wigan Ath (Loaned on 23/3/2000) FL 6
Oldham Ath (Free on 19/2/2002) FL 5+1

CLELAND Alexander (Alex)
Born: Glasgow, 10 December 1970
Height: 5'8" **Weight:** 11.6
Club Honours: SPL '95, '96, '97; SC '94, '96
International Honours: S: B-2; U21-11; Sch
Plagued for some time by a series of calf injuries, Alex made just three substitute appearances in 2001-02 and was released by Everton at the end of the campaign. A tidy and technically accomplished right back, he can also play centre half and in midfield.
Dundee U (From juniors on 18/6/1987) SL 131+20/8 SLC 10+1 SC 7+2 Others 8+1/1
Glasgow R (Signed on 26/1/1995) SL 90+6/4 SLC 8+2 SC 13+1 Others 13+1
Everton (Free on 3/7/1998) PL 21+14 FLC 5+2 FAC 2

CLEMENCE Stephen Neal
Born: Liverpool, 31 March 1978
Height: 5'11" **Weight:** 11.7
Club Honours: FLC '99
International Honours: E: U21-1; Yth; Sch
Injury halted Stephen's progression for Tottenham last term after he had cemented a regular first-team spot in midfield. Returning late in the season, it was encouraging to see that he had lost little of the enthusiasm and maturity that had began to be amongst his greatest assets. A great prospect for Spurs still, he will be aiming for a return to full fitness as Glenn Hoddle looks for both youth and experience in his bid for European qualification next season.
Tottenham H (From trainee on 3/4/1995) PL 68+22/2 FLC 6+1 FAC 7+1/1 Others 2+1

CLEMENT Neil
Born: Reading, 3 October 1978
Height: 6'0" **Weight:** 12.3
International Honours: E: Yth; Sch
This left wing back had another exceptionally fine season at West Bromwich Albion in 2001-02. Positive and stylish, his brilliant left-foot crosses and free kicks produced several scoring chances for his colleagues, and he netted some stunning goals himself. Among his best scoring efforts were a brilliant equaliser to salvage a point in the local 'derby' with Wolves at the Hawthorns and one of two in a 4-0 defeat of Manchester City. Neil was named in the PFA Division One team of the season. He is the son of former Queen's Park Rangers defender Dave Clement.
Chelsea (From trainee on 8/10/1995) PL 1 FLC 0+2 FAC 0+1
Reading (Loaned on 19/11/1998) FL 11/1 Others 1
Preston NE (Loaned on 25/3/1999) FL 4
Brentford (Loaned on 23/11/1999) FL 7+1
West Bromwich A (£100,000 + on 23/3/2000) FL 97+1/11 FLC 7/2 FAC 5/2 Others 2

CLEMENTS Matthew (Matt) Carlton
Born: Birmingham, 17 September 1977
Height: 6'0" **Weight:** 12.6
Matt was very much on the fringes of the first-team squad at Cambridge last term and managed only one senior appearance, coming on from the subs' bench at Peterborough in September. He spent much of the season on loan at Stalybridge and then King's Lynn and was eventually released. He was previously one

of the top junior hurdlers in the country, but although a very pacy striker he found it difficult to adapt to the full-time game.

Cambridge U (Free from Mildenhall T on 9/8/2001) FL 0+1

CLIST Simon James
Born: Shaftesbury, 13 June 1981
Height: 5'9" **Weight:** 11.0
This talented Bristol City midfielder fell by the wayside at Ashton Gate last term. Despite tremendous technical ability on the ball, with some deft touches and intelligent running, he was placed on the transfer list at the end of the season.

Bristol C (From trainee at Tottenham H on 24/7/1999) FL 53+14/5 FLC 2/1 FAC 6+1/2 Others 4+3

COATES Jonathan Simon
Born: Swansea, 27 June 1975
Height: 5'8" **Weight:** 10.4
Club Honours: Div 3 '00
International Honours: W: B-1; U21-5; Yth
Jonathan missed just one Third Division game for Swansea last term and contributed five valuable goals. The best of these were his chip over the goalkeeper's head from outside the penalty area at Scunthorpe, and an audacious 45-yard strike against Shrewsbury. He featured regularly in the centre of midfield, where his ability to create extra space allowed him to find more goal-scoring opportunities than in previous seasons.

Swansea C (From trainee on 8/7/1993) FL 218+32/23 FLC 11+2/1 FAC 10 Others 11+3/1

COBIAN Juan Manuel
Born: Buenos Aires, Argentine, 11 September 1975
Height: 5'9" **Weight:** 12.0
This neat and tidy right wing back found his first-team opportunities very limited at Swindon last season. He made just one appearance from the subs' bench, coming on in injury time at Stoke, and did not even have the opportunity to touch the ball!

Sheffield Wed (Signed from Boca Juniors, Argentine on 13/8/1998) PL 7+2 FLC 1
Charlton Ath (Free on 5/8/1999)

Neil Clement

Aberdeen *(Free on 1/11/1999) SL 2+1 SLC 1*
Swindon T *(Free on 27/7/2000) FL 3+1 FLC 2 FAC 1 Others 0+2*

COID Daniel (Danny) John
Born: Liverpool, 3 October 1981
Height: 5'11" **Weight:** 11.7
Club Honours: AMC '02
This versatile Blackpool player who can feature both in defence and midfield appeared regularly in the line-up last term. He scored a tremendous goal against Wigan at Bloomfield Road, but missed out on a place in the LDV Vans Trophy triumph over Cambridge United.
Blackpool *(From trainee on 24/7/2000) FL 82+13/5 FLC 5 FAC 8 Others 10+1*

COLDICOTT Stacy
Born: Redditch, 29 April 1974
Height: 5'8" **Weight:** 11.8
This competitive and hard-tackling midfielder was absent from the Grimsby Town line-up for the first few weeks of last season, and on his return to fitness he spent much of his time on the substitutes' bench. The change of manager bought a slight upturn in his fortunes but it was not until the closing weeks of the campaign that he won a regular place in the team, when his combative play contributed to the Mariners retaining their First Division status.
West Bromwich A *(From trainee on 4/3/1992) FL 64+40/3 FLC 8+1 FAC 2+2/1 Others 7+3*
Cardiff C *(Loaned on 30/8/1996) FL 6*
Grimsby T *(£125,000 on 6/8/1998) FL 130+14/3 FLC 11/2 FAC 5+1*

COLE Andrew (Andy) Alexander
Born: Nottingham, 15 October 1971
Height: 5'11" **Weight:** 11.12
Club Honours: Div 1 '93; PL '96, '97, '99, '00, '01; FAC '96, '99; CS '97; EC '99; FLC '02
International Honours: E: 15; B-1; U21-8; Yth, Sch
Although Andy began the 2001-02 season in goal-scoring form for Manchester United, the summer signing of Ruud van Nistelroy seemed to put his prospects in some jeopardy. A rare appearance in the early stages of the Champions' League brought a goal against Olympiakos in October, once again confirming his status as Britain's leading European club scorer, but it was to be his last for United and in December he was sold to Blackburn Rovers. He found the transition to life at Ewood Park

rather difficult and struggled to get into the side, although he more than compensated for any possible shortcomings by netting the winner in the Worthington Cup final against Tottenham.
Arsenal *(From trainee on 18/10/1989) FL 0+1 Others 0+1*
Fulham *(Loaned on 5/9/1991) FL 13/3 Others 2/1*
Bristol C *(£500,000 on 12/3/1992) FL 41/20 FLC 3/4 FAC 1 Others 4/1*
Newcastle U *(£1,750,000 on 12/3/1993) F/PL 69+1/55 FLC 7/8 FAC 4/1 Others 3/4*
Manchester U *(£6,000,000 on 12/1/1995) PL 161+34/93 FLC 2 FAC 19+2/9 Others 49+8/19*
Blackburn Rov *(£7,500,000 on 29/12/2001) PL 15/9 FLC 3/3 FAC 2/1*

COLE Ashley
Born: Stepney, 20 December 1980
Height: 5'8" **Weight:** 10.8
Club Honours: FAC '02; PL '02
International Honours: E: 13; U21-3; Yth
Ashley made further progress at Arsenal last term and firmly established himself on the left side of defence. His season was disrupted by a knee ligament injury, but he returned and went on to feature for England in the 2002 World Cup finals. He is a talented left back, effective in the tackle and capable of making surging runs down the flank.
Arsenal *(From trainee on 23/11/1998) PL 45+2/5 FLC 1+1 FAC 9+1 Others 14+2*
Crystal Palace *(Loaned on 25/2/2000) FL 14/1*

COLE Carlton
Born: Croydon, 12 November 1983
Height: 6'3" **Weight:** 13.4
International Honours: E: Yth
During the 2001-02 season Chelsea gave first-team debuts to four of their brightest young English stars, the latest of whom, 18-year-old striker Carlton Cole, made a tremendous impact. Originally given a 15-minute run out as a substitute against Everton in April, three weeks later he made his full debut at Middlesbrough as a late replacement and scored a superb goal. The England U19 centre forward is a prolific scorer in reserve and youth-team football and coach Ranieri has described him as 'a Young Lion'.
Chelsea *(From trainee on 23/10/2000) PL 2+1/1*

COLE Joseph (Joe) John
Born: Islington, 8 November 1981
Height: 5'9" **Weight:** 11.0
Club Honours: FAYC '99
International Honours: E: 7; U21-4; Yth; Sch

West Ham's young central midfielder is now the most exciting prospect in British football. He was troubled by a foot injury at the start of the 2001-02 season but once recovered he set the game alight. He has brilliant dribbling skills and was 'Man of the Match' on numerous occasions. Joe has terrific determination and the confidence to succeed at the very top. He scored in the FA Cup at Macclesfield, but needs to find the net more often to be recognised as a complete player. He appeared for England U21s at the start of the campaign but his stunning displays elevated him to the senior team and he travelled to the World Cup finals as a member of England's 23-man squad.
West Ham U *(From trainee on 11/12/1998) PL 72+18/6 FLC 5+1/1 FAC 8+1/1 Others 2+3*

COLEMAN Simon
Born: Worksop, 13 March 1968
Height: 6'0" **Weight:** 11.8
Simon looked to have shrugged off his injury problems at the beginning of the 2001-02 campaign and started out in terrific form for Rochdale. He scored the winning goal in the opening day game at Oxford before another long-term injury ruled him out once more. He was subsequently restricted to just a handful more appearances in the new year and became Dale's regular defensive substitute for the remainder of the term. A commanding central defender, he was released in the summer.
Mansfield T *(From juniors on 29/7/1985) FL 96/7 FLC 9 FAC 7 Others 7/1*
Middlesbrough *(£600,000 on 26/9/1989) FL 51+4/2 FLC 5 Others 10/1*
Derby Co *(£300,000 on 15/8/1991) FL 62+8/2 FLC 5+1 FAC 5 Others 12*
Sheffield Wed *(£250,000 on 20/1/1994) PL 11+5/1 FLC 3 FAC 2*
Bolton W *(£350,000 on 5/10/1994) P/FL 34/5 FLC 4 FAC 2*
Wolverhampton W *(Loaned on 2/9/1997) FL 3+1*
Southend U *(Free on 20/2/1998) FL 98+1/9 FLC 6 FAC 2 Others 2*
Rochdale *(Free on 10/7/2000) FL 13+3/1 FLC 1 Others 0+1*

COLES Daniel (Danny) Richard
Born: Bristol, 31 October 1981
Height: 6'1" **Weight:** 11.5
Danny made great progress with Bristol City in 2001-02, making a huge impression after taking over one of the central defensive berths. Cool, calm and collected, he looks like a good prospect for the future although perhaps more as a sweeper than as a dominating centre half.

Andy Cole

Bristol C (From trainee on 7/6/2000) FL 21+5 FAC 1 Others 7

COLLETT Andrew (Andy)
Alfred
Born: Stockton, 28 October 1973
Height: 6'0" **Weight:** 12.10
Andy had another season interrupted by injury at Darlington last term, sustaining cracked ribs in the home game with Lincoln City in January and later suffering a collapsed lung. As a result he missed the remainder of the campaign. Up until this unfortunate mishap he had been in outstanding form in goal for the Quakers and was solely responsible for the team obtaining all three points on more than one occasion.
Middlesbrough (From trainee on 6/3/1992) PL 2 Others 3
Bristol Rov (Loaned on 18/10/1994) FL 4

Bristol Rov (£10,000 on 23/3/1995) FL 103 FLC 4 FAC 7 Others 8
Darlington (Free on 6/8/1999) FL 78 FLC 5 FAC 8 Others 3

COLLINS James Michael
Born: Newport, 23 August 1983
Height: 6'2" **Weight:** 13.0
International Honours: W: Yth
The Cardiff City coaching staff were unsure for some time whether James should be playing in attack or defence. However, all his best performances came at centre half and that is likely to remain his permanent position for the future. A young player with a lot of potential, manager Lennie Lawrence had no hesitation in plunging him into the first team during the run-in last season. He also featured for Wales U19s during the campaign.

Cardiff C (From trainee on 5/4/2001) FL 2+8/1 FAC 0+4 Others 2+2

COLLINS John Angus Paul
Born: Galashiels, 31 January 1968
Height: 5'7" **Weight:** 10.10
Club Honours: SC '95; Div 1 '01
International Honours: S: 58; U21-8; Yth
This vastly experienced player who again proved a vital influence in the Fulham midfield in 2001-02. He is a creative player who is often able to play a killer pass when the opposition least expect it. Predictions that he would find it difficult to last the pace in the top flight proved unfounded and he made more than 30 Premiership appearances. His only goal of the season came in the Worthington Cup win against Derby.
Hibernian (Free from Hutchison Vale BC on 9/8/1984) SL 155+8/16 SLC 7+3/1 SC 17/3 Others 4/1
Glasgow Celtic (Signed on 13/7/1990) SL 211+6/47 SLC 22/3 SC 21/3 Others 13/1 (Free to AS Monaco, France on 2/7/1996)
Everton (£2,500,000 on 7/8/1998) PL 52+3/3 FLC 3+2/1 FAC 4
Fulham (£2,000,000 on 21/7/2000) P/FL 54+7/3 FLC 2/1 FAC 5

COLLINS Lee
Born: Bellshill, 3 February 1974
Height: 5'8" **Weight:** 11.6
Club Honours: AMC '02
This hard-tackling midfielder was a regular member of the first-team squad at Blackpool in 2001-02. He played some of the best football of his career and scored a memorable late equaliser against Brighton in December. His performances earned him a new contract with the Tangerines.
Albion Rov (Signed from Pollock on 25/11/1993) SL 43+2/1 SLC 2 SC 2 Others 2
Swindon T (£15,000 on 15/11/1995) FL 52+11/2 FAC 4 Others 1
Blackpool (Free on 24/7/2000) FL 47+13/2 FLC 3 FAC 4 Others 4+1

COLLINS Samuel (Sam) Jason
Born: Pontefract, 5 June 1977
Height: 6'3" **Weight:** 14.0
This old-fashioned 'stopper' centre half started the 2001-02 season in Bury's back five but lost his place in September following the arrival of George Syros at the club. He battled gamely on and was in and out of the side for the next four months before regaining his place in the line-up in January.
Huddersfield T (From trainee on 6/7/1994) FL 34+3 FLC 6+1 FAC 3

Lee Collins (left)

Bury (£75,000 on 2/7/1999) FL 78+4/2 FLC 5 FAC 0+2 Others 1

COLLINS Wayne Anthony
Born: Manchester, 4 March 1969
Height: 6'0" **Weight:** 12.0
Club Honours: Div 2 '97
This stylish player returned to Crewe for a second spell in the summer of 2001 after being released by Fulham. Although not a regular in the first team during 2001-02, he still made a useful contribution to the campaign in his role on the right-hand side of midfield.
Crewe Alex (£10,000 from Winsford U on 29/7/1993) FL 102+15/14 FLC 5/1 FAC 8+1 Others 14+1/2
Sheffield Wed (£600,000 on 1/8/1996) PL 16+15/6 FLC 2 FAC 1
Fulham (£400,000 + on 23/1/1998) FL 37+21/4 FLC 10+1/2 FAC 6+2/2 Others 4
Crewe Alex (Free on 9/8/2001) FL 13+7 FLC 2 FAC 1

COLOSIMO Simon
Born: Australia, 24 August 1980
Height: 6'1" **Weight:** 12.6
International Honours: Australia: 13; Yth
This highly rated right back saw little first-team action for Manchester City last term and made the starting line-up on just one occasion, for the Worthington Cup second round tie at Notts County. He also featured on around half-a-dozen occasions from the subs' bench but he was released in January and soon afterwards signed for Belgian club KRC Genk.
Manchester C (£800,000 from South Melbourne, Australia on 19/7/2001) FL 0+6 FLC 1

COLUSSO Christian Daniel
Born: Argentina, 2 July 1977
Height: 5'9" **Weight:** 11.2
International Honours: Argentina: Yth
This stylish midfielder joined Oldham Athletic last January on a trial thanks to manager Mick Wadsworth's South American contacts. It did not take him long to impress with spectacular goals against Tranmere and Bury quickly endearing him to the fans. The former Argentinian U20 international had hoped a stint at Boundary Park would earn him a contract with a higher division club, but nothing transpired. He returned home without agreeing a new deal and it appears unlikely he will return the club.
Oldham Ath (Free from Rosario Central, Argentina on 7/2/2002) FL 6+7/2

COMBE Alan
Born: Edinburgh, 3 April 1974
Height: 6'1" **Weight:** 12.6

Alan was one of four goalkeepers used by Bradford City during the 2001-02 season. Unable to get in the Dundee United line-up, he joined City on loan for the closing months of the campaign and had an outstanding time at Valley Parade. He dominated the six-yard box and his distribution of the ball was outstanding.
Cowdenbeath (Signed from Kelty Hearts on 13/7/1992) SL 20 SLC 1
St Mirren (Signed on 7/8/1993) SL 123+1 SLC 6 SC 4 Others 4
Dundee U (Signed on 17/6/1998) SL 68 SLC 7 SC 4
Bradford C (Loaned on 1/2/2002) FL 16

COMMONS Kristian (Kris) Arran
Born: Mansfield, 30 August 1983
Height: 5'6" **Weight:** 9.8
This promising Stoke City youngster received his break in the LDV Vans Trophy game at Blackpool last season. A left-sided player who is equally at home at full back or in midfield, he has the ability to break forward into attacking positions. Blessed with a terrific shot and crossing abilities, he is expected to feature more regularly in 2002-03.
Stoke C (From trainee on 25/1/2001) Others 1

CONLON Barry John
Born: Drogheda, 1 October 1978
Height: 6'3" **Weight:** 13.7
International Honours: Rol: U21-7
Barry proved to be an excellent target man for Darlington after signing during the 2001 close season. He offered a strong physical presence and showed the ability to hold up the ball and bring others into the game. He also displayed an eye for goal, netting 11 times to finish second-top scorer for the Quakers. A combination of injury and suspension saw him play in only three of the last ten games, but he scored in each.
Manchester C (From trainee at Queens Park R on 14/8/1997) FL 1+6 FLC 0+1
Plymouth Arg (Loaned on 26/2/1998) FL 13/2
Southend U (Loaned on 4/9/1998) FL 28+6/7 FAC 1 Others 1
York C (£100,000 on 20/7/1999) FL 33+15/11 FLC 2+2 FAC 1 Others 0+1
Colchester U (Loaned on 9/11/2000) FL 23+3/8 FAC 1 Others 1
Darlington (£60,000 on 6/7/2001) FL 35/10 FLC 1 FAC 1/1 Others 1

CONNELL Lee Anthony
Born: Bury, 24 June 1981
Height: 6'0" **Weight:** 12.0
Bury's home-grown utility man finally made an impression at first-team level in

the 2001-02 season. Able to play at right back or in central midfield, Lee found himself on the subs' bench for most of the first half of the campaign, but was given his chance in January when he made a couple of appearances during an injury crisis. He played a further seven games in the closing months, mainly deputising at right back for Lee Unsworth and his strong running set up a goal for Gareth Seddon at Wycombe.
Bury (From trainee on 9/7/1999) FL 10+6/1 FAC 0+1 Others 1

CONNELLY Sean Patrick
Born: Sheffield, 26 June 1970
Height: 5'10" **Weight:** 11.10
Sean became a permanent signing for Wolves in the close season after previously being on loan, and played in a Worthington Cup tie early on. The steady right back was then out of contention until Kevin Muscat was away with the Australian team, and he had a run in the team then. A good tackler and not easily ruffled, he even kept his place for another match after Muscat was available again. He looked set to take advantage of another absence by the same player in the spring, but a knee injury at Burnley brought his season to a premature end.
Stockport Co (Free from Hallam on 12/8/1991) FL 292+10/6 FLC 29/1 FAC 15+2 Others 15+1
Wolverhampton W (Free on 21/3/2001) FL 11+3 FLC 1

CONNOLLY David James
Born: Willesden, 6 June 1977
Height: 5'8" **Weight:** 11.4
International Honours: Rol: 34; U21
David was out of contract with Feyenoord in the summer of 2001 and joined Wimbledon on a free transfer in July. He immediately formed an impressive partnership with Neil Shipperley that benefited both strikers throughout the season. David is nippy, good with both feet and works well off the big front man, and scored an impressive 18 goals for the Dons last term.
Watford (From trainee on 15/11/1994) FL 19+7/10 FLC 1 FAC 3+3/4 Others 1/1 (Free to Feyenoord during 1997 close season)
Wolverhampton W (Loaned on 21/8/1998) FL 18+14/6 FLC 2 FAC 0+1
Wimbledon (Free from Feyenoord, Holland on 27/7/2001) FL 35/18 FLC 1 FAC 2

CONNOLLY Karl Andrew
Born: Prescot, 9 February 1970
Height: 5'10" **Weight:** 11.2
Club Honours: WC '95

This left-sided midfielder was one of the few consistent players for Queen's Park Rangers last term. Although not starting every game he was rarely absent before suffering a serious leg injury against Wrexham in February. The injury kept him out for the remainder of the season.
Wrexham (Free from Napoli, in local Sunday League, on 8/5/1991) FL 337+21/88 FLC 22/4 FAC 37+1/16 Others 32+1/6
Queens Park R (Free on 31/5/2000) FL 41+15/8 FLC 1 FAC 3+1 Others 1

CONNOR Daniel (Dan) Brian
Born: Dublin, 31 January 1981
Height: 6'2" **Weight:** 12.9
International Honours: Rol: Yth
Dan was once again second choice to Mark Tyler at Peterborough last term and spent most of the time on the bench – in fact he now holds the club record of 106 appearances as an unused substitute. He played twice at first-team level, coming on from the bench for the second half of the home game against Cardiff and also playing in the Worthington Cup tie at Swansea. The promising 'keeper kept a clean sheet on both occasions.
Peterborough U (From trainee on 29/4/1998) FL 2+2 FLC 1 Others 2

CONNOR Paul
Born: Bishop Auckland, 12 January 1979
Height: 6'1" **Weight:** 11.5
Club Honours: AMC '00
Paul had a frustrating time at Rochdale last term when he was beset by a succession of injuries that kept him out of action for much of the time. His eventual reappearance could not have been in more dramatic circumstances, as he was thrown on for the final ten minutes of the play-off semi-final in a desperate, but unsuccessful, attempt to grab an equalising goal.
Middlesbrough (From trainee on 4/7/1996)
Hartlepool U (Loaned on 6/2/1998) FL 4+1
Stoke C (Free on 25/3/1999) FL 18+18/7 FLC 3+3/3 FAC 0+1 Others 2+3
Cambridge U (Loaned on 9/11/2000) FL 12+1/5 FAC 1
Rochdale (£100,000 on 9/3/2001) FL 25+6/11 FLC 1 FAC 2+1 Others 0+1

CONSTANTINE Leon
Born: Hackney, 24 February 1978
Height: 6'2" **Weight:** 11.10
Leon was unable to make a breakthrough at Millwall last term and spent most of the first half of the campaign on loan at Leyton Orient. He added pace and power to the O's forward line, but after Paul Brush

replaced Tommy Taylor as manager he returned to the New Den. He later spent time on loan with Partick Thistle where he featured in a handful of first-team games before being released by the Lions at the end of the season.
Millwall (Signed from Edgware T on 31/8/2000) FL 0+1 Others 1
Leyton Orient (Loaned on 27/8/2001) FL 9+1/3 Others 0+1
Partick Thistle (Loaned on 11/1/2002) SL 2 SC 1

CONVERY Mark Peter
Born: Newcastle, 29 May 1981
Height: 5'6" **Weight:** 10.5
Mark found his first-team opportunities limited at Darlington last season following the arrival of Neil Wainwright. He is a busy midfield player who covers every blade of grass in his efforts to support the attack and keep possession. He was particularly effective wide on the right where his excellent crosses led to a number of goals for the Quakers.
Sunderland (From trainee on 24/3/1999)
Darlington (Free on 30/1/2001) FL 11+17/1 FLC 1 FAC 0+2 Others 1

COOK Lee
Born: Hammersmith, 3 August 1982
Height: 5'9" **Weight:** 11.7
Lee missed the start of the 2001-02 season at Watford with a serious cruciate ligament injury sustained in the last match of the previous campaign. After a period of rehabilitation at Lilleshall and a stint in the reserves, he returned to the first team at Preston in January and soon demonstrated that he had lost none of his tricky dribbling skills. A left-footed player, Lee also appeared on the right wing, but was less effective there.
Watford (Signed from Aylesbury U on 19/11/1999) FL 8+6

COOK Paul Anthony
Born: Liverpool, 22 June 1967
Height: 5'11" **Weight:** 11.0
One of Stan Ternent's more surprising decisions of 2001-02 came in December when he let Paul Cook go on loan to Wigan. Up to then, Paul had played in every League game and was considered by many to be playing the best football of his Burnley career, with a more aggressive edge added to his well-established passing skills. He was also scoring goals, including a spectacular lob in the 5-2 home win against Walsall which was certainly one of the goals of the season at Turf Moor. He impressed during his time at Wigan, where he

never finished on the losing side, but he was unable to break back into the Clarets' side on his return and frequently failed to make the bench.
Wigan Ath (Signed from Marine on 20/7/1984) FL 77+6/14 FLC 4 FAC 6+1 Others 5+1/1
Norwich C (£73,000 on 23/5/1988) FL 3+3 Others 1+1
Wolverhampton W (£250,000 on 1/11/1989) FL 191+2/19 FLC 7/1 FAC 5+2 Others 6+1/1
Coventry C (£600,000 on 18/8/1994) PL 35+2/3 FLC 3 FAC 3
Tranmere Rov (£250,000 on 29/2/1996) FL 54+6/4 FLC 8 FAC 1
Stockport Co (£250,000 on 24/10/1997) FL 48+1/3 FLC 1+1 FAC 2
Burnley (Free on 12/3/1999) FL 119+5/12 FLC 4+2 FAC 6+1/2
Wigan Ath (Loaned on 30/11/2001) FL 6

COOKE Andrew (Andy) Roy
Born: Shrewsbury, 20 January 1974
Height: 6'0" **Weight:** 12.8
There was again no faulting Andy's work rate and commitment to the cause for Stoke City during the 2001-02 season. An honest hard-working striker he became a firm favourite with the supporters and his haul of goals underscored a string of fine performances, even though he undoubtedly suffered as the management team regularly shuffled the front men to find a fruitful blend.
Burnley (Signed from Newtown on 1/5/1995) FL 134+37/52 FLC 8+2/6 FAC 7+3/2 Others 9+2/2
Stoke C (£350,000 on 1/12/2000) FL 47+10/15 FLC 0+1 FAC 2+2/1 Others 4+4/1

COOKE Stephen Lee
Born: Walsall, 15 February 1983
Height: 5'8" **Weight:** 9.8
International Honours: E: Yth
Stephen spent much of last season developing at Aston Villa, but his only senior action came during a loan spell with Second Division Bournemouth. Despite his slight frame, he was a real success with the Cherries and quickly became popular with the club's fans. He enjoyed a remarkable debut when he met his new team-mates just an hour before the Northampton game and played a starring role in a 5-1 win. A talented creative midfielder, he was a regular with the England U19s and is clearly a player with a great future in front of him.
Aston Villa (From trainee on 22/2/2000) Others 0+1
Bournemouth (Loaned on 8/3/2002) FL 6+1

COOKE Terence (Terry) John
Born: Birmingham, 5 August 1976
Height: 5'7" **Weight:** 11.4
Club Honours: FAYC '95
International Honours: E: U21-4; Yth
Out of favour at Maine Road, this fast and skilful right winger joined Grimsby Town on loan on the transfer deadline and this was converted to a short-term contract soon afterwards. He created an immediate impression with the Mariners' fans, scoring in the 1-1 draw at Norwich and contributing to the club's struggle to avoid relegation. Although he has expressed a wish to make the move permanent his future remained in doubt at the time of writing.
Manchester U (From trainee on 1/7/1994) PL 1+3 FLC 1+2/1 Others 0+1
Sunderland (Loaned on 29/1/1996) FL 6
Birmingham C (Loaned on 29/11/1996) FL 1+3
Wrexham (Loaned on 30/10/1998) FL 10 Others 1
Manchester C (£1,000,000 on 13/11/1999) FL 27+7/7 FLC 3+1/1 Others 3
Wigan Ath (Loaned on 7/3/2000) FL 10/1
Sheffield Wed (Loaned on 21/9/2000) FL 12+1/1
Sheffield Wed (Loaned on 15/12/2000) FL 4
Grimsby T (Free on 28/3/2002) FL 3/1

COOPER Colin Terence
Born: Sedgefield, 28 February 1967
Height: 5'10" **Weight:** 11.9
Club Honours: Div 1 '98
International Honours: E: 2; U21-8
This experienced defender began last season at left back for Middlesbrough, but lost his place through injury in October. He was back in action by the end of the year, but then faced personal tragedy following the death of his young son. The popular Boro' player eventually returned to first-team duties before the end of the campaign.
Middlesbrough (From juniors on 17/7/1984) FL 183+5/6 FLC 18 FAC 13 Others 19+1/2
Millwall (£300,000 on 25/7/1991) FL 77/6 FLC 6 FAC 2 Others 4
Nottingham F (£1,700,000 on 21/6/1993) F/PL 179+1/20 FLC 14/2 FAC 12/1 Others 7
Middlesbrough (£2,500,000 on 22/8/1998) PL 97+6/5 FLC 8+1 FAC 4

COOPER Kevin Lee
Born: Derby, 8 February 1975
Height: 5'7" **Weight:** 10.7
This hard-working left winger scored ten goals for Wimbledon from midfield last term, but although the Dons were in contention for a play-off place he was sold to promotion rivals Wolves in March.

Required at Molineux as a replacement for the injured Mark Kennedy, he scored his first goal for his new club in style when he netted from 30 yards against Norwich in the play-offs.
Derby Co (From trainee on 2/7/1993) FL 0+2 FLC 0+2 Others 0+1
Stockport Co (£150,000 on 24/3/1997) FL 146+22/21 FLC 7+5/2 FAC 6 Others 1
Wimbledon (£800,000 + on 15/3/2001) FL 50+1/13 FLC 1 FAC 2
Wolverhampton W (£1,000,000 on 26/3/2002) FL 4+1 Others 2/1

COOPER Richard Anthony
Born: Nottingham, 27 September 1977
Height: 5'9" **Weight:** 10.12
International Honours: E: Yth; Sch
Richard was an ever present for York City in 2001-02 until breaking his leg in the victory over Hull in January. He recovered well and made a substitute appearance in the final game of the campaign. Mostly at home on the right-hand side of the defence or midfield, his tenacity and enthusiasm made him a firm favourite with the fans. He notched his first senior goal in the 2-2 draw at Bristol Rovers last September.
Nottingham F (From trainee on 2/10/1996) FL 0+3
York C (Free on 2/3/2001) FL 37+2/1 FLC 1 FAC 5+1 Others 1

COOPER Shaun David
Born: Isle of Wight, 5 October 1983
Height: 5'10" **Weight:** 10.10
Shaun has come up through the ranks at Portsmouth after being spotted playing in the Isle of Wight Schools team and groomed in the club's School of Excellence. A right back of immense promise, he made his full debut at Crystal Palace last March and featured regularly in the closing weeks of the campaign.
Portsmouth (From trainee on 7/4/2001) FL 3+4

COOTE Adrian
Born: Great Yarmouth, 30 September 1978
Height: 6'2" **Weight:** 12.0
International Honours: NI: 6; B-1; U21-14
Adrian was unable to win a place in the Norwich City line-up last season and in December he moved the short distance down the A12 to become Colchester United's joint-most expensive signing. He was employed mostly as a substitute, but netted four goals, including a double at Bury after coming on late in the game. He is a tall striker who has a commanding presence in the air.

Norwich C (From trainee on 3/7/1997) FL 20+34/3 FLC 1+5 FAC 0+1
Colchester U (£50,000 on 21/12/2001) FL 5+14/4

COPPINGER James
Born: Middlesbrough, 10 January 1981
Height: 5'7" **Weight:** 10.6
International Honours: E: Yth
This promising youngster was restricted to reserve-team football at Newcastle last season before linking up once again with neighbours Hartlepool in a three-month loan deal. He was an instant success scoring on his debut in a 5-1 win over Rushden. Previously employed as a striker, he adopted a deeper role in his second spell at Victoria Park. Although there was talk of a permanent move he returned to Tyneside when his loan spell was over.
Newcastle U (£250,000 + from trainee at Darlington on 27/3/1998) PL 0+1
Hartlepool U (Loaned on 10/3/2000) FL 6+4/3 Others 1
Hartlepool U (Loaned on 25/1/2002) FL 14/2

CORAZZIN Giancarlo (Carlo) Michele
Born: Canada, 25 December 1971
Height: 5'10" **Weight:** 12.7
International Honours: Canada: 54 (Gold Cup '00)
Carlo's second season at Boundary Park was another solid yet unspectacular one. Although a tireless worker up front, putting in unselfish runs and crosses for team-mates, his form did not translate into a prolific vein of goal-scoring. He was transfer listed in December as part of a clearout, but manager Mick Wadsworth had a rethink and the Canadian international returned to first-team action again in the new year. Oldham scored freely in 2001-02 but, given his promise, Carlo's return of nine goals was a disappointment.
Cambridge U (£20,000 from Vancouver 86ers, Canada on 10/12/1993) FL 104+1/39 FLC 4/2 FAC 5 Others 3/2
Plymouth Arg (£150,000 on 28/3/1996) FL 61+13/22 FLC 1+1 FAC 0+2/1 Others 2+1
Northampton T (Free on 2/7/1998) FL 63+15/30 FLC 5+2/1 FAC 3 Others 1/1
Oldham Ath (Free on 31/7/2000) FL 61+10/16 FLC 3+1/1 FAC 5/1 Others 1

CORBETT Andrew (Andy) John
Born: Worcester, 20 February 1982
Height: 6'0" **Weight:** 11.4
A young striker who can also play in midfield, Andy only managed to make two substitute appearances for

Kidderminster in 2001-02 and he is yet to score his first senior goal. With Harriers expected to operate with a smaller squad next season, he will hope to have more opportunities to show what he is capable of.
Kidderminster Hrs (From juniors on 4/7/2000) FL 3+5

CORBO Mateo Andres
Born: Montevideo, Uruguay, 21 April 1976
Height: 5'11" **Weight:** 12.7
An attacking left-sided midfield player, Matteo was limited to just one appearance from the subs' bench for Barnsley last term. In November he suffered knee ligament damage during a testimonial game and was out of action until mid-January. By this stage the team had a settled look about it and he did not get another game. He left the club in February by mutual consent.
Barnsley (£250,000 from Real Oviedo, Spain, ex Racing Club, on 29/8/2000) FL 10+8 FLC 2/1 FAC 0+1

CORDEN Simon **Wayne**
Born: Lee, 1 November 1975
Height: 5'9" **Weight:** 11.3
The summer signing of Allen Tankard at left back kick-started Wayne's career at Mansfield as he was able to switch from playing as a wing back to a role in an out-and-out winger. He is a skilful player who likes to cut in and shoot, as was demonstrated by the goals he scored to earn the Stags some much-needed points.
Port Vale (From trainee on 20/9/1994) FL 30+36/1 FLC 4 FAC 2+1/1
Mansfield T (Free on 3/7/2000) FL 77+3/11 FLC 5/2 FAC 4/1 Others 2

CORICA Stephen (Steve) Christopher
Born: Queensland, Australia, 24 March 1973
Height: 5'8" **Weight:** 11.0
International Honours: Australia: 31; U23; Yth
Steve was quickly snapped up by Colin Lee whose appointment as Walsall's manager coincided with his return from a spell in the J-League. He immediately looked the part when taking the field as a substitute in the FA Cup tie against Fulham and held his place for the final 13 games of the season, playing successfully both in the space behind the front men and as a striker. Always seeming to have time and space, he ended the season on a high note when netting twice in the last game against Bradford City.

Leicester C (£325,000 from Marconi, Australia on 11/8/1995) FL 16/2 FAC 2
Wolverhampton W (£700,000 on 16/2/1996) FL 80+20/5 FLC 5+1 FAC 3+1 (Free to Sanfrecce Hiroshima, Japan on 20/3/2000)
Walsall (Free on 8/2/2002) FL 13/3 FAC 0+1

CORREIA Albano Joao Soares
Born: Guinea-Bissau, 18 October 1981
Height: 6'2" **Weight:** 12.13
This skilful young striker spent most of last season developing in Bristol City's reserve team. He stepped up to make his senior debut in the 2-0 success at Southend in the LDV Vans Trophy last October.
Bristol C (Signed from Oriental Lisbon, Portugal on 18/9/2000) Others 0+1

CORT Carl Edward Richard
Born: Southwark, 1 November 1977
Height: 6'4" **Weight:** 12.7
International Honours: E: U21-12
Carl spent the summer recovering from a serious ligament strain in his right ankle incurred in a friendly at Exeter the previous season, then four days before the start of the 2001-02 campaign he strained a ligament in his left knee during a practice match which delayed his return to the side, and a further set back led to minor surgery in December. It was not until March that he appeared in the first team, as a substitute in the home game with Arsenal, following which he was selected as a regular in the starting line-up, scoring a stunning goal at home to Everton.
Wimbledon (From trainee on 7/6/1996) PL 54+19/16 FLC 8+2/7 FAC 6+4/2
Lincoln C (Loaned on 3/2/1997) FL 5+1/1
Newcastle U (£7,000,000 on 6/7/2000) PL 19+2/7 FLC 2/1 FAC 2

CORT Leon Terence Anthony
Born: Bermondsey, 11 September 1979
Height: 6'2" **Weight:** 13.4
After making his League debut in the opening game of the 2001-02 season, Leon went on to become a near ever present for Southend United. Tall and elegant in the air, he also improved his skills on the ground immensely, and his fine record of only one yellow card all season showed him to be mature beyond his years. He is the brother of Newcastle's Carl Court.
Millwall (Free from Dulwich Hamlet on 23/1/1998)
Southend U (Free on 11/7/2001) FL 43+2/4 FLC 1 FAC 4 Others 1

COSTA Jorge Paulo Almeida
Born: Porto, Portugal, 4 October 1971
Height: 6'2" **Weight:** 13.5
International Honours: Portugal: 50; U21; Yth
This central defender joined Charlton on loan from Porto in December and immediately slotted into the middle of the Addicks' defence alongside Mark Fish and Jon Fortune. Strong and powerful with good vision and commanding in the air, he fully lived up to his nickname 'The Tank'. He was a revelation in marshalling the back line and showed his qualities with some match-winning performances, looking completely at ease in the Premiership. He linked up well with Richard Rufus in the last few games of the season as the latter returned to the side after his long-term injury.
Charlton Ath (Loaned from Porto, Portugal on 4/12/2001) PL 22+2 FAC 2

COTTERILL James Michael
Born: Barnsley, 3 August 1982
Height: 6'0" **Weight:** 12.4
Injuries continued to affect this young defender's progress at Scunthorpe during 2001-02. Having broken into the first team in October, he was hampered by a groin problem which needed an operation and kept him sidelined for three months. Equally at home at right back or in the centre of defence, he is a solid player who can expect more opportunities next season after signing a new one-year deal.
Scunthorpe U (From trainee on 3/7/2001) FL 12+2 Others 1

COUGHLAN Graham
Born: Dublin, 18 November 1974
Height: 6'2" **Weight:** 13.6
Club Honours: S Div 1 '01; Div 3 '02
Graham was Plymouth manager Paul Sturrock's only signing during the 2001 close season. He soon established himself as an extremely popular centre back and did not miss one single minute of the action, despite some horrific facial injuries. His outstanding performances at the heart of the defence ensured that the goals against tally was reduced, providing the base for Argyle to win the Third Division title. Surprisingly for a defender he also finished as the club's leading scorer netting 11 goals, mainly from within the six-yard box. He was voted 'Player of the Season' by the fans and also won a place in the PFA Division Three team of the season.

Blackburn Rov *(£100,000 from Bray W on 14/10/1995)*
Swindon T *(Loaned on 25/3/1997) FL 3*
Livingston *(Free on 29/3/1999) SL 53+3/2 SLC 4 SC 2 Others 5*
Plymouth Arg *(Free on 21/6/2001) FL 46/11 FLC 1 FAC 4 Others 1*

COUNAGO Pablo Gonzalez

Born: Pontevedra, Spain, 9 August 1979
Height: 5'11" **Weight:** 11.12
Pablo joined Ipswich in the close season but took time to adjust to the English game. He was used mainly as a substitute in the Premiership, making just the one start – against Bolton. As a striker he holds the ball up well and can turn defenders with ease. However, he is yet to open his scoring account for the first team although he regularly found the net for the title-winning reserves' side.
Ipswich T *(Free from Celta Vigo, Spain on 19/7/2001) PL 1+12 FLC 1 FAC 0+1 Others 2+2*

COURTOIS Laurent

Born: Lyon, France, 11 September 1978
Height: 5'8" **Weight:** 11.2
This left-sided midfielder or winger arrived at West Ham in the summer of 2001. He came on as substitute on the opening day at Anfield, but saved his best performance on his home debut against Newcastle, when he set up the opening goal for Don Hutchison. Laurent has pace and skill on the ball and proved to be an excellent signing, however due to the form of Trevor Sinclair the Hammers fans did not see too much of him during the campaign.
West Ham U *(Free from Toulouse, France, ex Lyon, Ajaccio, on 15/8/2001) PL 5+2 FLC 0+1*

COUSINS Jason Michael

Born: Hayes, 14 October 1970
Height: 5'11" **Weight:** 12.4
Club Honours: GMVC '93; FAT '93
Jason began the 2001-02 season as a first choice central defender at Wycombe but lost his place in mid-September in a back-four reshuffle. He returned for a six-match run at the turn of the year due to an injury crisis, and once again displayed a wholehearted enthusiasm for the game, excellent in the air and a great timer of tackles. A serious achilles injury then saw him miss two months of the season, before returning to the bench for the last weeks. He was granted a testimonial game against Celtic's first team due to be held in July 2002 to finally end 11 years with the Chairboys.
Brentford *(From trainee on 13/7/1989) FL 20+1 Others 2+2*

Wycombe W *(Free on 1/7/1991) FL 270+26/6 FLC 19+2/1 FAC 34+3 Others 19*

COWAN Thomas (Tom)

Born: Bellshill, 28 August 1969
Height: 5'9" **Weight:** 11.10
This experienced left back found himself out of favour at Cambridge United for most of last season. In January he joined neighbours Peterborough United on loan, where one of his main contributions was his powerful long throw. On his return to the Abbey Stadium he was recalled to the team and scored at Bournemouth in March. He was reported to have signed for York City during the summer.
Clyde *(Free from Netherdale BC on 11/7/1988) SL 16/2 SC 2*
Glasgow R *(Signed on 9/2/1989) SL 8+4 SC 0+1 Others 2*
Sheffield U *(£350,000 on 1/8/1991) F/PL 45 FLC 5 FAC 2 Others 1*
Stoke C *(Loaned on 1/10/1993) FL 14 FLC 1 Others 3*
Huddersfield T *(£150,000 on 24/3/1994) FL 137/8 FLC 13/1 FAC 9/1 Others 6*
Burnley *(£20,000 on 12/3/1999) FL 17+3/1 FLC 2 Others 0+1*
Cambridge U *(Loaned on 22/2/2000) FL 4*
Cambridge U *(Free on 20/7/2000) FL 44+2/3 FLC 1 FAC 1*
Peterborough U *(Loaned on 18/1/2002) FL 4+1/1*

COX Ian Gary

Born: Croydon, 25 March 1971
Height: 6'0" **Weight:** 12.2
International Honours: Trinidad & Tobago: 5
This classy central defender began the 2001-02 season partnering Steve Davis at the back for Burnley, and subsequently lined up alongside Arthur Gnohere following Davis' injury. Ian had two spells out injured and missed the ultimately disappointing end to the campaign. At his best a cultured centre-back with pace, sureness in the tackle and good distribution, he seemed to struggle as the Clarets' fortunes declined, although he did score one of the goals of the season, a spectacular shot from outside the area at Stockport.
Crystal Palace *(£35,000 from Carshalton on 8/3/1994) F/PL 2+13 FAC 1+2/1*
Bournemouth *(Free on 28/3/1996) FL 172/16 FLC 14 FAC 10 Others 11/1*
Burnley *(£500,000 on 4/2/2000) FL 84+5/4 FLC 5 FAC 4*

COX Neil James

Born: Scunthorpe, 8 October 1971
Height: 6'0" **Weight:** 13.7

Club Honours: FLC '94; Div 1 '95
International Honours: E: U21-6
Neil was transfer listed during the summer of 2001, and started the new season without as much as a squad number. He seemed to have no future at Watford, but an injury crisis led to a first-team recall at the end of August, and he ended up making more appearances than anyone else, playing at either right back or in central defence. Manager Luca Vialli commended his excellent attitude and had the good grace to admit his earlier misjudgement when he took Neil off the transfer list in October and made him captain at Bradford. By the end of the campaign he had made more than 400 senior appearances and enjoyed one of his finest seasons at the club.
Scunthorpe U *(From trainee on 20/3/1990) FL 17/1 FAC 4 Others 4+1*
Aston Villa *(£400,000 on 12/2/1991) F/PL 26+16/3 FLC 5+2 FAC 4+2/1 Others 2*
Middlesbrough *(£1,000,000 on 19/7/1994) P/FL 103+3/3 FLC 14+1 FAC 5/1 Others 2*
Bolton W *(£1,200,000 on 27/5/1997) FL 77+3/7 FLC 9/1 FAC 1+1 Others 3*
Watford *(£500,000 on 5/11/1999) P/FL 102+3/7 FLC 9 FAC 3*

COYNE Christopher (Chris) John

Born: Brisbane, Australia, 20 December 1978
Height: 6'1" **Weight:** 13.10
Chris began the 2001-02 season at Dundee where he featured in their Inter Toto Cup games before joining Luton Town in September. A commanding central defender who is good in the air and can tackle well, he soon established himself as a regular alongside Russ Perrett in the heart of the Hatters' defence.
West Ham U *(£150,000 from Perth SC, Australia on 13/11/1996) PL 0+1*
Brentford *(Loaned on 21/8/1998) FL 7 FLC 1*
Southend U *(Loaned on 25/3/1999) FL 0+1*
Dundee *(Free on 31/3/2000) SL 16+4 SLC 0+2 SC 4 Others 2*
Luton T *(£50,000 on 18/9/2001) FL 29+2/3*

COYNE Daniel (Danny)

Born: Prestatyn, 27 August 1973
Height: 5'11" **Weight:** 13.0
International Honours: W: 2; B-1; U21-9; Yth; Sch
Danny enjoyed yet another successful season in goal for Grimsby Town last term. His best performance was undoubtedly at Anfield when he produced a number of world-class saves to help the Mariners eliminate holders Liverpool from the Worthington Cup. His

consistent form meant that he missed only one of the club's 52 senior competitive games and he was rewarded with a second full cap for Wales when he came on as a second half substitute against Czech Republic in March. He also became the first Grimsby player in a decade to be voted 'Player of the Year' in two successive seasons.
Tranmere Rov (From trainee on 8/5/1992) FL 110+1 FLC 13 FAC 2 Others 2
Grimsby T (Free on 12/7/1999) FL 135 FLC 9 FAC 5

CRADDOCK Jody Darryl
Born: Redditch, 25 July 1975
Height: 6'1" **Weight:** 12.4
The Sunderland centre back can look back on season 2001-02 with a great deal of satisfaction as he firmly established himself as one of the key players at the Stadium of Light. In the eyes of most supporters, Jody was easily the club's player of the season; his pace, strength in the air, and tackling prowess rescuing his side on numerous occasions. Despite a succession of different partners in back four, he turned in consistently solid performances and had the pleasure of opening his goal-scoring account for the Black Cats when he headed home Julio Arca's free kick in a vital win at Bolton.
Cambridge U (Free from Christchurch on 13/8/1993) FL 142+3/4 FLC 3/1 FAC 6 Others 5
Sunderland (£300,000 + on 4/8/1997) P/FL 115+6/1 FLC 7+2 FAC 3+2 Others 3
Sheffield U (Loaned on 27/8/1999) FL 10

CRANE Anthony (Tony) Steven
Born: Liverpool, 8 September 1982
Height: 6'1" **Weight:** 12.6
2001-02 proved to be a disappointing season at Sheffield Wednesday for this tall, well-built midfielder. Young enough to still command a regular first-team spot in the future, he was unable to force his way into the team. His strengths were his heading and tackling, while he also gave the line-up a better shape, but nevertheless most of his appearances came from the subs' bench.
Sheffield Wed (From trainee on 15/9/1999) FL 11+19/2 FLC 3+5/1 FAC 0+3

CRESSWELL Richard Paul Wesley
Born: Bridlington, 20 September 1977
Height: 6'0" **Weight:** 11.8
International Honours: E: U21-4
Signed during the summer of 2001, Richard soon became a crowd favourite at Preston with his high work rate, determined running and close control. He

was a regular on the bench in the early part of the season and showed his worth by scoring four times in three substitute appearances, also making goals in two other matches. Having established himself as a starter he suffered a hamstring injury in December that kept him out for six weeks, but he returned to assume the mantle of main striker following Jon Macken's transfer and ended the campaign as leading scorer with 16 goals.
York C (From trainee on 15/11/1995) FL 72+23/21 FLC 3+3 FAC 4+2/3 Others 4
Mansfield T (Loaned on 27/3/1997) FL 5/1
Sheffield Wed (£950,000 + on 25/3/1999) PL 7+24/2 FLC 1+1/1 FAC 0+3
Leicester C (£750,000 on 5/9/2000) PL 3+5 FLC 1 FAC 0+2/1 Others 0+2
Preston NE (£500,000 on 12/3/2001) FL 32+19/15 FLC 1+1/1 FAC 1+1/2 Others 1+2

CRICHTON Paul Andrew
Born: Pontefract, 3 October 1968
Height: 6'1" **Weight:** 12.2
Paul was signed by Norwich in the summer of 2001 to create real competition for the number one spot with Robert Green. A vastly experienced goalkeeper, he found it difficult to displace an extremely consistent Green, but when called upon he didn't let the side down. An excellent shot stopper, he is a tremendous enthusiast and a real character within the squad. Paul is a good organiser of his defence and has proved an excellent acquisition.
Nottingham F (From juniors on 23/5/1986)
Notts Co (Loaned on 19/9/1986) FL 5
Darlington (Loaned on 30/1/1987) FL 5
Peterborough U (Loaned on 27/3/1987) FL 4
Darlington (Loaned on 28/9/1987) FL 3 FLC 1 Others 1
Swindon T (Loaned on 24/12/1987) FL 4
Rotherham U (Loaned on 9/3/1988) FL 6
Torquay U (Loaned on 25/8/1988) FL 13 FLC 2
Peterborough U (Signed on 3/11/1988) FL 47 FAC 5 Others 3
Doncaster Rov (Free on 25/8/1990) FL 77 FLC 5 FAC 3 Others 5
Grimsby T (Free on 9/7/1993) FL 133 FLC 7 FAC 8 Others 2
West Bromwich A (£250,000 on 9/9/1996) FL 32 FLC 1 FAC 1
Burnley (Loaned on 7/8/1998) FL 1
Burnley (£100,000 on 19/11/1998) FL 81+1 FLC 4 FAC 4 Others 2
Norwich C (£150,000 on 25/6/2001) FL 5+1

CROFT Gary
Born: Burton on Trent, 17 February 1974
Height: 5'9" **Weight:** 11.8
International Honours: E: U21-4
After failing to win a Premier League

place at Ipswich this defender joined Wigan Athletic on loan last January in order to gain some first-team action. He is a steady but unspectacular full back with stamina and excellent crossing ability, who can play on either flank. Ironically his last home match for the Latics was against Cardiff City, who he later joined for a loan spell on transfer deadline day. He featured eight times for the Bluebirds, scoring at Tranmere in the final game of the regular season, but was unable to inspire the team to promotion in the Second Division play-offs.
Grimsby T (From trainee on 7/7/1992) FL 139+10/3 FLC 7 FAC 8+2/1 Others 3
Blackburn Rov (£1,700,000 on 29/3/1996) PL 33+7/1 FLC 6 FAC 4+2
Ipswich T (£800,000 on 21/9/1999) P/FL 20+9/1 FLC 3+1 FAC 1 Others 2+1
Wigan Ath (Loaned on 17/1/2002) FL 7
Cardiff C (Loaned on 28/3/2002) FL 3+3/1 Others 2

CRONIN Glenn
Born: Dublin, 14 September 1981
Height: 5'8" **Weight:** 11.4
International Honours: RoI: Yth
This promising youngster broke through into the Exeter City first team last term and went on to produce a series of captivating performances in midfield. After establishing himself in the squad towards the end of 2001 he formed a formidable midfield partnership with Kwame Ampadu. If Glenn can add some goals to his repertoire he is likely to gain a place in the Republic of Ireland U21 squad and attract the attention of much bigger clubs.
Exeter C (From trainee on 18/7/2000) FL 24+6 FAC 0+2 Others 0+1

CROOKES Peter
Born: Liverpool, 7 May 1982
Height: 6'2" **Weight:** 12.7
International Honours: E: Yth
Peter signed for Halifax on a 12-month contract during the summer of 2001, but spent virtually all the 2001-02 season on the subs' bench as deputy for Lee Butler and then Barry Richardson. He made a dramatic entrance to League football in the home game with Shrewsbury in December when he was shown the red card ten minutes from time for a professional foul.
Halifax T (Free from trainee at Liverpool on 22/3/2001) FL 1

CROOKS Lee Robert
Born: Wakefield, 14 January 1978
Height: 6'0" **Weight:** 12.1

International Honours: E: Yth
Although he signed for Barnsley towards the end of the 2000-01 campaign Lee had to wait until the opening game of last season to make his debut for the Reds due to a knee injury. He immediately made a position his own firstly at right back and then as one of three central defenders until he damaged a hamstring that saw him out of action for a fortnight and he returned in the right back position. Under new manager Steve Parkin he was used as a utility player but illness and niggling injuries saw his opportunities limited.
Manchester C (From trainee on 14/1/1995) P/FL 52+24/2 FLC 5+2 FAC 5 Others 3
Northampton T (Loaned on 26/12/2000) FL 3
Barnsley (£190,000 on 2/3/2001) FL 20+6 FLC 2 FAC 1

CROSBY Andrew (Andy)
Keith
Born: Rotherham, 3 March 1973
Height: 6'2" **Weight:** 13.7
Club Honours: Div 3 '01
Following the arrival of Simon Morgan, opportunities were few and far between for Andy at Brighton last term. He played in two LDV Vans Trophy matches and also came on from the subs' bench a couple of times before moving on to Oxford United in December where he was new manager Ian Atkins' first signing. Here he proved to be a steadying influence at the back, forming an effective partnership with Matthew Bound in the centre of defence and contributing a vital goal in the 3-3 draw with Torquay. He is a solid and dependable defender who is good in the air and a strong tackler.
Doncaster Rov (From trainee at Leeds U on 4/7/1991) FL 41+10 FLC 1+1 FAC 2 Others 4+1/1
Darlington (Free on 10/12/1993) FL 179+2/3 FLC 10 FAC 11/1 Others 9
Chester C (Free on 8/7/1998) FL 41/4 FLC 3 FAC 1 Others 1
Brighton & Hove A (£10,000 on 28/7/1999) FL 64+8/5 FLC 3 FAC 1+1 Others 7
Oxford U (Free on 13/12/2001) FL 22+1/1

CROSSLEY Mark Geoffrey
Born: Barnsley, 16 June 1969
Height: 6'0" **Weight:** 16.0
International Honours: W: 5; B-1; E: U21-3
Mark never managed to establish himself as Middlesbrough's first choice 'keeper last term and spent much of the campaign as deputy to Mark Schwarzer, most of his appearances coming during a run at the turn of the year. Powerfully

built, he is a brave and confident shot stopper.
Nottingham F (From trainee on 2/7/1987) F/PL 301+2 FLC 39+1 FAC 32 Others 18
Millwall (Loaned on 20/2/1998) FL 13
Middlesbrough (Free on 25/7/2000) PL 21+2 FLC 3 FAC 3

CROUCH Peter James
Born: Macclesfield, 30 January 1981
Height: 6'7" **Weight:** 11.12
International Honours: E: U21-4; Yth
This giant centre forward had a fine season at Portsmouth last term and showed tremendous ball control and the ability to run at and beat defenders. He was eventually sold to Aston Villa in March, thus becoming the tallest striker in the Premiership. He scored on his debut for Villa against Newcastle and was voted as Pompey's 'Player of the Season', despite his departure.
Tottenham H (From trainee on 2/7/1998)
Queens Park R (£60,000 on 28/7/2000) FL 38+4/10 FLC 1+1 FAC 3/2
Portsmouth (£1,250,000 on 11/7/2001) FL 37/18 FLC 1/1 FAC 1
Aston Villa (£4,000,000 + on 28/3/2002) PL 7/2

CROUDSON Steven (Steve)
David
Born: Grimsby, 14 September 1979
Height: 6'0" **Weight:** 12.4
Once again the consistent form of Grimsby's first-choice 'keeper Danny Coyne kept Steve very much in the shadows at Blundell Park and he made only one senior appearance for the Mariners, deputising when Coyne was called up to the Welsh squad. He joined neighbours Scunthorpe on loan in August and played five matches as cover for the injured Tommy Evans. He looked a good shot-stopper but only managed one clean sheet and lost his place after a 4-3 defeat at Macclesfield Town. On his return he was hampered by a nagging shoulder problem in the second half of the campaign and was due to receive corrective treatment during the close season.
Grimsby T (From trainee on 6/7/1998) FL 5+1 FLC 1 FAC 1
Scunthorpe U (Loaned on 16/8/2001) FL 4 FLC 1

CROWE Dean Anthony
Born: Stockport, 6 June 1979
Height: 5'5" **Weight:** 11.3
Dean was loaned to Plymouth Argyle at the start of the 2001-02 campaign but after appearing from the bench in the

opening game against Shrewsbury he returned to the Britannia Stadium. He subsequently joined Luton Town at the end of September and got off to a great start scoring on his debut, ironically against Plymouth. A quick and pacy striker, he went on to find the net regularly for the Hatters and finished the season as the club's second-top scorer with 15 goals.
Stoke C (From trainee on 5/9/1996) FL 29+31/12 FLC 2+3 Others 2/1
Northampton T (Loaned on 11/2/2000) FL 3+2
Bury (Loaned on 23/3/2000) FL 4/1
Bury (Loaned on 11/8/2000) FL 1+6/1
Plymouth Arg (Loaned on 11/8/2001) FL 0+1
Luton T (Free on 29/9/2001) FL 32+2/15 FAC 1

CROWE Jason William
Born: Sidcup, 30 September 1978
Height: 5'9" **Weight:** 10.9
International Honours: E: Yth
Jason's 2001-02 season was shortened by a foot injury in February which sidelined him for the remainder of the campaign. He is a talented right wing back with good man-to-man marking skills and a dead ball specialist. He will be looking to settle in a regular place in Harry Redknapp's Portsmouth team in 2002-03.
Arsenal (From trainee on 13/5/1996) FLC 0+2 FAC 0+1
Crystal Palace (Loaned on 10/11/1998) FL 8
Portsmouth (£750,000 + on 7/7/1999) FL 60+10/1 FLC 3 FAC 1+2
Brentford (Loaned on 12/9/2000) FL 9 FLC 2

CRYAN Colin
Born: Dublin, 23 March 1981
Height: 5'10" **Weight:** 13.4
Colin was a regular in Sheffield United's reserve line-up last term where he had an impressive season as a central defender after switching from his previous role in midfield. A powerfully built fearless competitor, he found it difficult to break into the first team but made an appearance for the final 15 minutes of the last game of the season at Birmingham. He was rewarded for his progress with a new two-year contract towards the end of the campaign.
Sheffield U (From trainee on 6/8/1999) FL 0+2 FLC 0+2

CUDICINI Carlo
Born: Milan, Italy, 6 September 1973
Height: 6'1" **Weight:** 12.3
Club Honours: FAC '00; CS '00
Chelsea were fortunate to have three top-

class goalkeepers to choose from last term. Ed de Goey began the season as first choice, playing in the opening eight matches, before suffering a knee injury and to the chagrin of Mark Bosnich, the 'keeper's jersey was handed to Carlo Cudicini, who embarked on an amazing run of conceding just one goal in his first ten matches. This rubber-stamped his burgeoning reputation as one of the best 'keepers in the Premiership. Carlo is the perfect example of the modern goalkeeper: agile, confident, a good shot-stopper, comfortable kicker (either from hand or back pass) and able to act as an auxiliary sweeper to clear dangerous situations just outside the penalty area.
Chelsea (£160,000 from Castel di Sangro, Italy, ex AC Milan, Prato, Lazio, on 6/8/1999) PL 51+2 FLC 6 FAC 11 Others 2+1

CULLEN David **Jonathan (Jon)**
Born: Durham City, 10 January 1973
Height: 6'0" **Weight:** 12.0
Jon had an unfortunate time with injuries last season and never managed to get a regular run at first-team level for Peterborough. An elegant midfield player who can play either in the centre or wide on the left, he was released by Posh in the summer.
Doncaster Rov (From trainee on 16/9/1991) FL 8+1 FLC 2+1/1 FAC 0+1 Others 1 (Free to Spennymoor in September 1993)
Hartlepool U (Free from Morpeth on 27/3/1997) FL 33+1/12 FLC 2 FAC 1 Others 2
Sheffield U (£250,000 on 26/11/1998) FL 0+4
Shrewsbury T (Loaned on 10/9/1999) FL 10/1
Halifax T (Loaned on 17/12/1999) FL 11/5
Peterborough U (£35,000 on 3/3/2000) FL 34+10/5 FLC 1+1 FAC 1+2 Others 4/1
Carlisle U (Loaned on 16/3/2001) FL 10+1

CULLIP Daniel (Danny)
Born: Bracknell, 17 September 1976
Height: 6'1" **Weight:** 12.7
Club Honours: Div 3 '01; Div 2 '02
Danny is a no-nonsense centre half who formed a successful partnership with Simon Morgan at the heart of Brighton's defence last term. He rocked the Seagulls with a transfer request soon after the arrival of Peter Taylor, but then stayed to play a key part in the championship-winning side, captaining the team for much of the latter part of the campaign. He scored a tremendous goal in the FA Cup victory over Rushden and capped a fine season by being nominated to the PFA Division Two representative team.
Oxford U (From trainee on 6/7/1995)
Fulham (Free on 5/7/1996) FL 41+9/2 FLC 8 FAC 2 Others 1

Brentford (£75,000 on 17/2/1998) FL 15 FLC 2
Brighton & Hove A (£50,000 on 17/9/1999) FL 114+1/4 FLC 3 FAC 9/2 Others 3/1

CUMMINGS Warren
Born: Aberdeen, 15 October 1980
Height: 5'9" **Weight:** 11.8
International Honours: S: U21-9
Once again this talented player acted as cover for Neil Clement for West Bromwich Albion, and only got the occasional outing in the senior side, being mainly used as a substitute. He added two further Scottish U21 caps to his collection.
Chelsea (From trainee on 5/7/1999)
Bournemouth (Loaned on 20/10/2000) FL 10/1 Others 1
West Bromwich A (Loaned on 21/3/2001) FL 1+2
West Bromwich A (Loaned on 25/7/2001) FL 6+8 FLC 0+2

CUMMINS Michael Thomas
Born: Dublin, 1 June 1978
Height: 6'0" **Weight:** 11.11
Club Honours: AMC '01
International Honours: RoI: U21-2; Yth
This adaptable midfield player became Port Vale's first ever present for eight years last term. He usually occupied the right-hand side of midfield but also sometimes played at right back. Good in the air, he scored a career-best nine goals, including two in one game against Chesterfield and the only goal in the local 'derby' victory at Stoke City to propel him into local folklore. Even a broken nose didn't spoil his record as a waterlogged pitch at Cambridge gave him another week's grace.
Middlesbrough (From trainee on 1/7/1995) PL 1+1
Port Vale (Free on 17/3/2000) FL 101+2/11 FLC 4 FAC 4/1 Others 10/1

CUNNINGHAM Kenneth (Kenny) Edward
Born: Dublin, 28 June 1971
Height: 6'0" **Weight:** 11.8
International Honours: RoI: 40; B-2; U21-4; Yth
'Captain Dependable' missed the start of the 2001-02 season through injury, returning to action for Wimbledon in the 4-0 thumping of Manchester City at Maine Road. Kenny provided invaluable experience and consistency in a Dons defence that has undergone a lot of change. Generally used as a central defender, he won the club's 'Player of the Year' award for his outstanding performances.

Millwall (Signed from Tolka Rov on 18/9/1989) FL 132+4/1 FLC 10 FAC 1 Others 5+1/1
Wimbledon (£650,000 on 9/11/1994) P/FL 249+1 FLC 22+1 FAC 32+1

CURETON Jamie
Born: Bristol, 28 August 1975
Height: 5'8" **Weight:** 10.7
International Honours: E: Yth
Jamie only played the full 90 minutes in 11 of his 41 first-team appearances for Reading last term, but still finished as second-top goal-scorer behind Nicky Forster. His pace, composure and exquisite first touch brought him the majority of his goals, none more vital than the 77th minute equaliser at Brentford on the last day of the season, which ensured Royals returned to Division One. His high goals-per-game ratio suggests he will remain a vital part of the strike force in 2002-03.
Norwich C (From trainee on 5/2/1993) P/FL 13+16/6 FLC 0+1 FAC 0+2
Bournemouth (Loaned on 8/9/1995) FL 0+5 Others 0+1
Bristol Rov (£250,000 on 20/9/1996) FL 165+9/72 FLC 7+1/2 FAC 10/2 Others 6/2
Reading (£250,000 on 21/8/2000) FL 61+20/41 FLC 3+1/1 FAC 4+1/2 Others 5/2

CURLE Keith
Born: Bristol, 14 November 1963
Height: 6'1" **Weight:** 12.12
Club Honours: AMC '86; FMC '88
International Honours: E: 3; B-4
Sheffield United's player-coach was probably more involved at first-team level than he anticipated in the 2001-02 campaign. Starting the season at left back, he later replaced Shaun Murphy in the centre of defence and was also made team captain. He made up for his lack of pace with anticipation and experience, being decisive under pressure and constructive when playing out of defence. His only goal, against Bradford City, was volleyed in after a one-two with Bobby Ford. At the time of writing Keith has been offered just a playing contract for the 2002-03 season and his future at Bramall Lane is uncertain.
Bristol Rov (From apprentice on 20/11/1981) FL 21+11/4 FLC 3 FAC 1
Torquay U (£5,000 on 4/11/1983) FL 16/5 FAC 1/1 Others 1
Bristol C (£10,000 on 3/3/1984) FL 113+8/1 FLC 7+1 FAC 5 Others 14+1
Reading (£150,000 on 23/10/1987) FL 40 FLC 8 Others 5
Wimbledon (£500,000 on 21/10/1988) FL 91+2/3 FLC 7 FAC 5 Others 6/1

Manchester C *(£2,500,000 on 14/8/1991)*
F/PL 171/11 FLC 18/2 FAC 14 Others 1
Wolverhampton W *(£650,000 on 2/8/1996)*
FL 148+2/9 FLC 7/1 FAC 11/1 Others 2
Sheffield U *(Free on 10/7/2000) FL 53+4/1
FLC 3 FAC 1*

CURRAN Christopher (Chris)
Born: Birmingham, 17 September 1971
Height: 5'11" **Weight:** 12.4
Club captain Chris was the bedrock in the
Exeter City defence last term when he
established an effective partnership with
Alex Watson and was responsible for
halting the leakage of goals after John
Cornforth took over as manager. He is a
hard working and committed defender
who reads the game well.
Torquay U *(From trainee on 13/7/1990) FL
144+8/4 FLC 15 FAC 8 Others 10/1*
Plymouth Arg *(£40,000 on 22/12/1995) FL
26+4 FLC 1+1 FAC 1 Others 4*
Exeter C *(£20,000 on 31/7/1997) FL 136+8/6
FLC 7 FAC 10/1 Others 6*

Darren Currie

CURRIE Darren Paul
Born: Hampstead, 29 November 1974
Height: 5'11" **Weight:** 12.7
Darren immediately showed the
Wycombe fans why he had such a big
reputation. Blessed with two wonderfully
skilful feet he was used on both midfield
wings from where he delivered accurate
inswinging crosses. His six goals were
almost all spectacular, the pick being his

25-yard left footer at Colchester and a
similar goal in front of the cameras at
Hayes in the FA Cup when he also
dribbled his way in to the box to score a
second. He figured in every League game,
only rested for two cup games, and has
already shown the ability to stay free of
injury. Highly regarded by his manager,
only a lack of pace has prevented him
from playing at a much higher level.
West Ham U *(From trainee on 2/7/1993)*
Shrewsbury T *(Loaned on 5/9/1994) FL
10+2/2*
Shrewsbury T *(Loaned on 3/2/1995) FL 5*
Leyton Orient *(Loaned on 16/11/1995) FL
9+1*
Shrewsbury T *(£70,000 on 7/2/1996) FL
46+20/8 FLC 2+1/1 FAC 3*
Plymouth Arg *(Free on 26/3/1998) FL 5+2*
Barnet *(Free on 13/7/1998) FL 120+7/19 FLC
5/1 FAC 3/2 Others 6*
Wycombe W *(£200,000 on 11/7/2001) FL
44+2/3 FLC 1 FAC 4/3*

CURTIS John Charles
Born: Nuneaton, 3 September 1978
Height: 5'10" **Weight:** 11.9
Club Honours: FAYC '95; FLC '02
International Honours: E: B-1; U21-16;
Yth; Sch
This young right-sided defender struggled
with leg injuries at Blackburn last term
and was sidelined early on. He
subsequently lost his place to Lucas Neill
and thereafter was restricted to
infrequent appearances.
Manchester U *(From trainee on 3/10/1995)
PL 4+9 FLC 5 Others 0+1*
Barnsley *(Loaned on 19/11/1999) FL 28/2
Others 1+1*
Blackburn Rov *(£2,250,000 on 1/6/2000)
P/FL 56 FLC 9 FAC 6*

CURTIS Thomas (Tom) David
Born: Exeter, 1 March 1973
Height: 5'8" **Weight:** 11.7
Tom returned to fitness last August
following his broken ankle, but was
unable to gain first-team football with
Portsmouth. He had a brief loan spell at
Walsall but had the misfortune to come
up against Wolves and Manchester City in
top form and returned south after just
four games. He subsequently featured
occasionally for Pompey in the second
half of the campaign before being made
available for transfer in the summer. He is
a reliable midfield player who always gives
100 per cent.
Derby Co *(From juniors on 1/7/1991)*
Chesterfield *(Free on 12/8/1993) FL
235+5/12 FLC 20+1 FAC 14/1 Others 11+1*

Portsmouth *(£150,000 on 4/8/2000) FL 7+6
FLC 1+1*
Walsall *(Loaned on 20/9/2001) FL 3+1*

CUSACK Nicholas (Nicky)
John
Born: Maltby, 24 December 1965
Height: 6'0" **Weight:** 12.8
Club Honours: Div 3 '00
Nicky was as active off the field as on it
last season. He played a key role in
assisting his fellow players through the
various crises faced at Swansea
throughout the campaign and eventually
took on the role of joint-caretaker
manager with Roger Freestone. On the
field he again showed his versatility
during the season, playing as a striker, in
midfield, and even in a central defensive
role.
Leicester C *(Signed from Alvechurch on
18/6/1987) FL 5+11/1 FAC 0+1 Others 1+1*
Peterborough U *(£40,000 on 29/7/1988) FL
44/10 FLC 4/1 FAC 4/1 Others 2*
Motherwell *(£100,000 on 2/8/1989) SL
68+9/17 SLC 5/4 SC 3+1/2 Others 1+1/1*
Darlington *(£95,000 on 24/1/1992) FL 21/6*
Oxford U *(£95,000 on 16/7/1992) FL
48+13/10 FLC 3/2 FAC 4+2/1 Others 2+1*
Wycombe W *(Loaned on 24/3/1994) FL
2+2/1*
Fulham *(Free on 4/11/1994) FL 109+7/14
FLC 6+4/1 FAC 7+1/1 Others 5+2/3*
Swansea C *(£50,000 on 30/10/1997) FL
180+13/12 FLC 5+1/1 FAC 11/3 Others 5+1*

CUTLER Neil Anthony
Born: Birmingham, 3 September 1976
Height: 6'1" **Weight:** 12.0
International Honours: E: Yth; Sch
It was assumed that Neil was to be
second choice to Gavin Ward as Stoke
City's goalkeeper following his arrival in
the 2001 close season, but he received an
early chance and grabbed it with both
hands. A fine shot stopper, the defence
had much to thank Neil for and he can be
proud of an outstanding contribution to
the club's promotion challenge. It was
fitting that prior to the end of the season
he was rewarded with a longer contract.
West Bromwich A *(From trainee on
7/9/1993)*
Chester C *(Loaned on 27/3/1996) FL 1*
Crewe Alex *(Signed on 30/7/1996)*
Chester C *(Loaned on 30/8/1996) FL 5*
Chester C *(Free on 8/7/1998) FL 23 FLC 1
FAC 1 Others 1*
Aston Villa *(Signed on 30/11/1999) PL 0+1*
Oxford U *(Loaned on 15/12/2000) FL 11*
Stoke C *(Free on 24/7/2001) FL 36 FLC 1 FAC
3 Others 3*

D

DABIZAS Nikolaos (Nikos)
Born: Amyndaeo, Greece, 3 August 1973
Height: 6'1" **Weight:** 12.7
International Honours: Greece: 51;
U21; Yth
Nikos demonstrated his value to
Newcastle by being a regular choice at
the centre of the back four throughout
the season, playing with wholehearted
commitment and assurance. One of his
rare absences occurred after the away
game at Leeds in December, in which he
broke his nose and suffered a seriously
gashed leg, but he was back in the team
a couple of weeks later. He enjoys joining
the attack whenever the opportunity
arises, and he scored goals against both
Middlesbrough and Sunderland. A regular
in the Greek national side he won his
50th cap in the home game against
Sweden.
*Newcastle U (£1,300,000 from Olympiakos,
Greece on 13/3/1998) PL 106+8/10 FLC 5
FAC 17/2 Others 14/1*

DACOURT Olivier
Born: Montreuil-sous-Bois, France, 25
September 1974
Height: 5'9" **Weight:** 11.12
International Honours: France: 3; U21
After an excellent first season at Elland
Road, Olivier was dogged by injury last
term. He picked up a bad shoulder injury
in December, and then a hamstring
problem forced him to sit out the closing
stages of the campaign. A talented and
tireless midfield player, his contributions
were widely recognised across Europe and
he was constantly linked with transfers
elsewhere.
*Everton (£4,000,000 from Strasbourg,
France, ex Thovars, on 7/8/1998) PL 28+2/2
FLC 4/1 FAC 2 (£6,500,000 to RC Lens,
France on 29/6/99)*
*Leeds U (£7,200,000 on 18/7/2000) PL
49+1/3 FLC 2 FAC 1 Others 20*

DADASON Rikhardur (Rikki)
Born: Reykjavik, Iceland, 26 April 1972
Height: 6'4" **Weight:** 12.0
International Honours: Iceland: 40;
U21-10; Yth
The 2001-02 campaign was unfortunately
another season of might-have-beens for
this cultured Icelandic international at
Stoke City. He again missed a full pre-
season, this time because of a serious
knee injury that saw him succumb to the
surgeon's knife twice. He scored four

goals from six starts, but it is without
question that City fans have yet to see
the best from him.
*Stoke C (Free from Viking, Norway, ex Fram
Reykjavik, Kalamata, KR Reykjavik, on
31/10/2000) FL 19+20/10 FLC 0+1/1 FAC 0+3
Others 3+3/1*

DAILLY Christian Eduard
Born: Dundee, 23 October 1973
Height: 6'0" **Weight:** 12.10
Club Honours: SC '94
International Honours: S: 34; B-1; U21-
34; Yth; Sch
This central defender enjoyed an excellent
season in 2001-02, being the only ever
present in the West Ham line-up. His
partnership with Tomas Repka blossomed
into one of the best in the Premiership.
He is very consistent and strong in the air
and was unlucky not to have scored a
couple of goals from set pieces. Christian
was the most improved player at Upton
Park and his performances helped the
Hammers in finishing in a creditable
position in the table.
*Dundee U (From juniors on 2/8/1990) SL
110+33/18 SLC 9/1 SC 10+2 Others 8+1/1*
*Derby Co (£1,000,000 on 12/8/1996) PL
62+5/4 FLC 6 FAC 4+1*
*Blackburn Rov (£5,300,000 on 22/8/1998)
P/FL 60+10/4 FLC 5+1 FAC 4 Others 2*
*West Ham U (£1,750,000 on 18/1/2001) PL
49+1 FLC 1 FAC 6*

DAINO Daniele (Danny)
Born: Alessandria, Italy, 8 September 1979
Height: 5'11" **Weight:** 11.11
This young AC Milan defender joined
Derby County in a long-term loan deal
during the 2001 close season. He played
in the first two Premiership games and in
a couple of Worthington Cup ties, but
faded from the scene afterwards and
returned to Italy in November.
*Derby Co (Loaned from AC Milan, Italy, ex
AC Milan, Napoli, Perugia, on 10/8/2001) PL
2 FLC 1+1*

DALGLISH Paul
Born: Glasgow, 18 February 1977
Height: 5'10" **Weight:** 10.0
International Honours: S: U21-7
Recruited at the start of the 2001-02
season by Wigan Athletic, Paul has
perhaps suffered under the expectation of
being the son of Kenny Dalglish. A direct
mobile striker with pace to burn, he is at
his best when playing down the right
where his strong running causes
defenders real problems. He netted two
goals including a stunning strike in the 6-1
thrashing of Stoke City, but struggled to

hold down his place in the side in the
new year following the arrival of Gary
Teale. Released at the end of his contract,
Paul later had a trial with MLS club DC
United.
Glasgow Celtic (From juniors on 20/7/1995)
Liverpool (Free on 14/8/1996)
*Newcastle U (Free on 21/11/1997) PL 6+5/1
FLC 2/1*
Bury (Loaned on 21/11/1997) FL 1+11 FAC 1
*Norwich C (£300,000 on 25/3/1999) FL
25+18/2 FLC 3+1 FAC 1*
*Wigan Ath (Free on 22/3/2001) FL 22+13/2
FAC 1*

**DALLA BONA Samuelle
(Sam)**
Born: Venice, Italy, 6 February 1981
Height: 6'1" **Weight:** 12.0
International Honours: Italy: Yth
The promising Chelsea career of young
Italian midfielder Sam Dalla Bona seemed
to be ending prematurely in the summer
of 2001 as he initially refused to commit
his long-term future to the Blues and the
club brought in a series of expensive
signings. However against all the odds
Sam battled back to make an influential
contribution to the Blues' season. An
energetic, all-action midfielder who covers
every blade of grass and bursts
dangerously into the penalty area, Sam's
first goal of the season was a sensational
injury-time 30-yard winner against Ipswich
Town.
*Chelsea (Signed from Atalanta, Italy on
16/10/1998) PL 42+13/6 FLC 3+2 FAC 5+2
Others 1+5*

DALY Jonathan (Jon) Marvin
Born: Dublin, Ireland, 8 January 1983
Height: 6'1" **Weight:** 12.4
International Honours: RoI: U21-3; Yth
Jon was given his first extended run in the
Stockport County team by Carlton Palmer
and responded with goals against Bolton
Wanderers in the FA Cup and at
Wimbledon. A player of immense
promise, he needs to work hard at
improving his temperament as he missed
no fewer than 12 games through
suspension. He won three U21 caps for
the Republic of Ireland in the prestigious
Toulon tournament and was expected to
play a key role for the U19s at the UEFA
Championship finals to be held in Norway
in July.
*Stockport Co (From trainee on 18/1/2000) FL
11+6/1 FLC 1 FAC 1/1*

DALY Wesley (Wes) James
Patrick
Born: Hammersmith, 7 March 1984
Height: 5'9" **Weight:** 11.2

Wes is a combative young midfielder who came up through the ranks at Queen's Park Rangers. He spent much of last season developing in the reserves but stepped up to make his League debut at Colchester in March.
Queens Park R (Trainee) FL 1

DANBY John Robert
Born: Stoke, 20 September 1983
Height: 6'2" **Weight:** 14.7
John began the 2001-02 season in Kidderminster's successful youth team, but after the departure of Brendan Murphy he was promoted to second choice 'keeper for the senior side. He was handed a surprise debut away at Luton in March when Stuart Brock was sent off and his next senior appearance also came as a substitute when Gary Montgomery was red-carded.
Kidderminster Hrs (From juniors on 14/12/2001) FL 0+2

DANIELSSON Helgi Valur
Born: Rejkjavic, Iceland, 13 July 1981
Height: 6'0" **Weight:** 12.0
International Honours: Iceland: 1; U21-11; Yth
Helgi struggled to find his best form for Peterborough at the beginning of last season, but after a spell in the reserves he returned to produce some good performances. A promising young midfield player who is talented on the ball and has excellent distribution, he scored his first senior goals during the campaign.
Peterborough U (Free from Fylkir, Iceland on 16/10/1998) FL 23+14/2 FLC 1 FAC 1/1 Others 2

DARBY Duane Anthony
Born: Birmingham, 17 October 1973
Height: 5'11" **Weight:** 12.6
Club Honours: NC '01
The 2001-02 season promised so much for Duane, whose striking partnership with Justin Jackson had taken Rushden into the Football League. But a pre-season injury, combined with the arrival of Warren Patmore, left him on the bench for the first game. He came off it to score in the shock Worthington Cup win at Burnley, and then scored both goals in the 2-3 defeat by Plymouth. Ankle ligament damage kept him sidelined for another spell, and then the arrival of Onandi Lowe restricted him mainly to substitute appearances. His season came to a premature end when he sustained another ankle injury at Mansfield Town in March 2001.
Torquay U (From trainee on 3/7/1992) FL

60+48/26 FLC 4+3/1 FAC 1+4 Others 5+3/2
Doncaster Rov (£60,000 on 19/7/1995) FL 8+9/4 FLC 2 FAC 0+1 Others 1+1
Hull C (Signed on 27/3/1996) FL 75+3/27 FLC 5/1 FAC 4/6 Others 4/2
Notts Co (Free on 2/7/1998) FL 22+6/5 FLC 3+1/1
Hull C (Loaned on 25/3/1999) FL 4+4
Rushden & Diamonds (Free on 21/6/2000) FL 17+13/7 FLC 0+1/1 FAC 1

DARLINGTON Jermaine Christopher
Born: Hackney, 11 April 1974
Height: 5'7" **Weight:** 10.10
Signed for a bargain fee from Queen's Park Rangers last July, Jermaine is comfortable with the ball at his feet and fitted in at both left and right-back positions for Wimbledon last term. As he has previously played in midfield he likes to push forward and join in the attacks and his speed and vision make him a handful to control.
Charlton Ath (From trainee on 30/6/1992) FL 1+1 (Free to Dover Ath on 23/9/1993)
Queens Park R (£25,000 from Aylesbury U on 25/3/1999) FL 70+1/2 FLC 2 FAC 6
Wimbledon (£200,000 on 16/7/2001) FL 25+4 FLC 1

DARLOW Kieran Brian
Born: Bedford, 9 November 1982
Height: 6'0" **Weight:** 13.12
This promising young left winger was unable to break into the York City side on a regular basis in 2001-02 and made only a couple of senior appearances. He was released at the end of the season.
York C (Trainee) FL 1+4

D'AURIA David Alan
Born: Swansea, 26 March 1970
Height: 5'10" **Weight:** 12.6
Club Honours: WC '94
International Honours: W: Yth
David missed a sizeable chunk of the 2001-02 campaign for Chesterfield after suffering an ankle injury in a pre-season friendly. When fit, his opportunities were limited by the presence of Marcus Ebdon and Mark Innes. He is a creative midfielder who passes intelligently and uses a dead ball well, and has the ability to switch from creating to stopping if possession is lost.
Swansea C (From trainee on 2/8/1988) FL 27+18/6 FLC 2+2 FAC 1 Others 4 (Free transfer to Merthyr Tydfil during 1991 close season)
Scarborough (Signed from Barry T on 22/8/1994) FL 49+3/8 FLC 3+2/1 FAC 4+1 Others 2

Scunthorpe U (£40,000 on 6/12/1995) FL 103+4/18 FLC 6 FAC 7/1 Others 4+1
Hull C (Free on 16/7/1998) FL 52+2/4 FLC 5+2 FAC 5 Others 2/1
Chesterfield (£50,000 on 25/11/1999) FL 18+7/1 FAC 3+1/1 Others 3+1/1

DAVENPORT Calum Raymond Paul
Born: Bedford, 1 January 1983
Height: 6'4" **Weight:** 14.4
International Honours: E: Yth
A product of Coventry's youth scheme, Calum made one start and two substitute appearances in 2001-02. The young centre half won plaudits for his cool and assured performance against Burnley and looks to have a bright future in the game. Strong in the air and comfortable on the ball, he was a regular in the reserve team.
Coventry C (From trainee on 6/1/2000) P/FL 1+3

DAVIDSON Callum Iain
Born: Stirling, 25 June 1976
Height: 5'10" **Weight:** 11.8
Club Honours: S Div 1 '97
International Honours: S: 15; U21-2
This left-sided full back or wing back had a mixed season last term, adding to his tally of caps in the World Cup qualifier against Latvia, but only spasmodically showed his best form for Leicester. Oddly, perhaps his best performance came when asked to operate in an unfamiliar central midfield role due to the Foxes' mounting injury crisis. He showed that he still knows how to strike a fierce shot, but with little luck this campaign. The club's injury jinx finally caught up with him in March when a training mishap sidelined him for a while, but he returned after Easter.
St Johnstone (From juniors on 8/6/1994) SL 39+5/4 SLC 1 Others 3
Blackburn Rov (£1,750,000 on 12/2/1998) P/FL 63+2/1 FLC 3+1 FAC 6 Others 1+1
Leicester C (£1,700,000 on 12/7/2000) PL 54+4/1 FLC 2+1 FAC 2+1 Others 0+1

DAVIES Benjamin (Ben) James
Born: Birmingham, 27 May 1981
Height: 5'6" **Weight:** 10.7
Ben began the 2001-02 season as first choice in the centre of Kidderminster's midfield, and his hard-working style and accurate passing made him one of the best performers in the team's opening games. He lost his place when Danny Williams returned from suspension and he made only one more appearance after the end of September. He was one of four

Callum Davidson (right)

out-of-contract players who were released by the club at the end of the campaign.
Walsall *(From trainee at Stoke C on 11/8/1999)*
Kidderminster Hrs *(Free on 1/3/2000) FL 11+1 FLC 1 Others 1*

DAVIES Gareth Melville
Born: Hereford, 11 December 1973
Height: 6'1" **Weight:** 11.12
International Honours: W: U21-8
Gareth returned for Swindon Town against Colchester last September after a lengthy absence through injury, featuring in an unfamiliar midfield role. He made a further outing from the bench at Chesterfield later that same month but this proved to be his final League appearance as he was subsequently forced to announce his retirement from the professional game in January due to continuing problems with his knees. He subsequently joined Dr Martens League outfit Chippenham Town until the end of the season.
Hereford U *(From trainee on 10/4/1992) FL 91+4/1 FLC 5+2 FAC 4 Others 5*
Crystal Palace *(£120,000 on 1/7/1995) F/PL 22+5/2 FAC 2 Others 1*
Cardiff C *(Loaned on 21/2/1997) FL 6/2*
Reading *(£100,000 on 12/12/1997) FL 18+1 FLC 1 FAC 3*
Swindon T *(Free on 2/3/1999) FL 24+2 FLC 1 FAC 0+1*

DAVIES Kevin Cyril
Born: Sheffield, 26 March 1977
Height: 6'0" **Weight:** 13.6
International Honours: E: U21-3; Yth
Kevin began the 2001-02 season operating on the right-hand side of midfield for Southampton, but when Gordon Strachan arrived he found himself out in the cold after the new manager brought in Paul Telfer. It wasn't until the unfortunate injury to James Beattie that he found himself back in favour in a more advanced striking role. Goals against Liverpool and West Ham went a long way to boost his confidence but unfortunately his form dipped towards the end of season and found himself out the team once more.
Chesterfield *(From trainee on 18/4/1994) FL 113+16/22 FLC 7+2/1 FAC 10/6 Others 9+2/1*
Southampton *(£750,000 on 14/5/1997) PL 20+5/9 FLC 3+1/3 FAC 1*
Blackburn Rov *(£7,250,000 on 2/6/1998) P/FL 11+12/1 FLC 3 FAC 2/1 Others 1*
Southampton *(Signed on 18/8/1999) PL 58+15/9 FLC 3+2/1 FAC 3+1/1*

DAVIES Simon
Born: Haverfordwest, 23 October 1979
Height: 5'10" **Weight:** 11.4
International Honours: W: 8; B-1; U21-10; Yth
This young midfielder had a great season for Tottenham last term and he is fast proving to be one of the hottest prospects in the Premiership. Strong and intelligent in midfield, he likes nothing better than to attack with the ball at his feet and loves to score goals. He adds width and pace to the Spurs midfield and has a confidence equal to that of his Premiership counterparts.
Peterborough U *(From trainee on 21/7/1997) FL 63+2/6 FLC 4 FAC 3 Others 3*
Tottenham H *(£700,000 on 10/1/2000) PL 32+15/6 FLC 6+2/3 FAC 3+1/2*

DAVIS James (Jimmy) Roger William
Born: Redditch, 9 February 1982
Height: 5'8" **Weight:** 11.10
International Honours: E: Yth
Jimmy is a strong, direct striker who can operate on the right-hand side or at centre forward. After two years as a professional at Old Trafford he stepped up to make his senior performance in the Worthington Cup tie against Arsenal last November. He offered ample proof that United still have plenty of strength in reserve, but received no further chances and will be looking to gain more senior action in 2002-03.
Manchester U *(From trainee on 9/9/1999) FLC 1*

DAVIS Kelvin Geoffrey
Born: Bedford, 29 September 1976
Height: 6'1" **Weight:** 14.0
International Honours: E: U21-3; Yth
2001-02 was another outstanding season for Wimbledon's number six goalkeeper. Kelvin missed a few games with niggling injuries, but his ability at shot stopping will be hard to better in the Football League and he wouldn't look out of place in the Premiership – indeed a transfer to a bigger club seems likely in the near future.
Luton T *(From trainee on 1/7/1994) FL 92 FLC 7 FAC 2 Others 6*
Torquay U *(Loaned on 16/9/1994) FL 2 FLC 1 Others 1*
Hartlepool U *(Loaned on 8/8/1997) FL 2 FLC 1 Others 1*
Wimbledon *(£600,000 + on 14/7/1999) FL 85 FLC 4 FAC 6*

DAVIS Sean
Born: Clapham, 20 September 1979
Height: 5'10" **Weight:** 12.0

Club Honours: Div 1 '01
International Honours: E: U21-12
England U21 star Sean had a mixed season in 2001-02 having initially suffered a loss of form during the autumn, which saw him named as a substitute on several occasions. After overcoming this he re-established himself in the side only to be hit by a series of niggling injuries. He returned to full fitness late in the campaign when he was back to his impressive best. Sean mostly operated in a 'holding' role linking the defence to attack. Crisp in the tackle, he is an excellent passer of the ball and possesses a strong shot.
Fulham *(From trainee on 2/7/1998) P/FL 78+25/6 FLC 9+4/3 FAC 5+2/1*

DAVIS Solomon (Sol) Sebastian
Born: Cheltenham, 4 September 1979
Height: 5'8" **Weight:** 11.0
Sol's 2001-02 campaign was disrupted by groin injuries prior to Christmas. When he returned to the Swindon Town line-up he gave his usual hard working and committed performances on the left-hand side both at full back and wing back. Although mainly known for his tackling ability, he is capable of making surging runs down the left flank and delivering telling crosses. However, a further injury during March brought a premature end to his season.
Swindon T *(From trainee on 29/5/1998) FL 99+17 FLC 7 FAC 4+1 Others 1*

DAVIS Stephen (Steve) Mark
Born: Hexham, 30 October 1968
Height: 6'2" **Weight:** 14.7
Club Honours: Div 4 '92
2001-02 was a frustrating season for Burnley's captain – a player rarely troubled by injuries previously – Steve was absent for half of the campaign with knee trouble and was missed not only for his defensive dominance and surging forward runs, but also for his leadership of the side. After nearly four months out he returned in February but looked a little short of pace on occasions and was sidelined again, before coming back for the final three games.
Southampton *(From trainee on 6/7/1987) FL 5+1*
Burnley *(Loaned on 21/11/1989) FL 7+2*
Notts Co *(Loaned on 28/3/1991) FL 0+2*
Burnley *(£60,000 on 17/8/1991) FL 162/22 FLC 10/2 FAC 18/1 Others 13*
Luton T *(£750,000 on 13/7/1995) FL 137+1/21 FLC 19/3 FAC 5/2 Others 10/1*
Burnley *(£800,000 on 21/12/1998) FL 127+1/16 FLC 6/1 FAC 6 Others 1*

Nick Daws

DAVISON Aidan John
Born: Sedgefield, 11 May 1968
Height: 6'1" **Weight:** 13.12
Club Honours: AMC '98
International Honours: NI: 3; B-1
Aidan was the substitute 'keeper for
Bradford City for the first three months of
the 2001-02 season, but when Gary
Walsh was injured he took his chance well
and played in nine League games before
he tore his groin muscle and was out of
action for the rest of the campaign. Aidan
is dominant in his penalty area, brilliant at
high crosses, and very good at catching
the ball with one hand.
*Notts Co (Signed from Billingham Synthonia
on 25/3/1988) FL 1*
Bury (£6,000 on 7/10/1989)
*Millwall (Free on 14/8/1991) FL 34 FLC 3
FAC 3 Others 2*
*Bolton W (£25,000 on 26/7/1993) P/FL 35+2
FAC 8 Others 4*
Hull C (Loaned on 29/11/1996) FL 9 Others 1
Bradford C (Free on 14/3/1997) FL 10
*Grimsby T (Free on 16/7/1997) FL 77 FLC 10
FAC 7 Others 10*
Sheffield U (Free on 6/8/1999) FL 1+1
*Bradford C (Free on 4/1/2000) P/FL 16+1 FLC
5 Others 2+1*

DAWS Nicholas (Nick) John
Born: Manchester, 15 March 1970
Height: 5'11" **Weight:** 13.2
Club Honours: Div 2 '97
This experienced midfielder found it
difficult to win a regular place at
Rotherham in the first half of the 2001-02
season, and mostly had to be content
with sitting on the subs' bench. It was not
until the middle of February that he
established himself as an automatic
choice, and from then on he produced
the form that had been expected of him.
Accurate with free kicks and corners, his
only goal of the campaign proved to be
the winner against Gillingham.
*Bury (£10,000 from Altrincham on
13/8/1992) FL 356+13/16 FLC 25+3/3 FAC
19/1 Others 15+4/3*
*Rotherham (Free on 16/7/2001) FL
21+14/1 FLC 2 FAC 0+1*

DAWSON Andrew (Andy)
Born: Northallerton, 20 October 1978
Height: 5'9" **Weight:** 10.2
Andy continued to underline his
reputation as one of Division Three's top
left backs with another solid campaign for
Scunthorpe in 2001-02. Very quick, his
tackling and willingness to get forward
saw Norwich City have a bid for him
rejected during the season. He only
missed three matches – all through

suspensions – but surprisingly failed to
get on the score sheet. He was out of
contract in the summer but was offered a
new three-year deal by the club.
*Nottingham F (From trainee on 31/10/1995)
FLC 1*
*Scunthorpe U (£70,000 on 18/12/1998) FL
149+3/6 FLC 5 FAC 8/1 Others 9/1*

DAWSON Kevin Edward
Born: Northallerton, 18 June 1981
Height: 6'0" **Weight:** 10.10
Kevin received few first-team
opportunities at Nottingham Forest last
term and only managed three senior
appearances, but never let the side down
when called upon. He is a tough tackling,
no-nonsense central defender who likes
to get forward for set pieces and corners.
He was released by the club in the
summer. He is the older brother of
Forest's Mike Dawson.
*Nottingham F (From trainee on 25/6/1998)
FL 8+3 FAC 1*
Barnet (Loaned on 9/3/2001) FL 5

DAWSON Michael (Mike)
Richard
Born: Northallerton, 18 November 1983
Height: 6'2" **Weight:** 12.12
International Honours: E: Yth
A promising central defender like his older
brother Kevin, Mike spent most of the
2001-02 campaign developing in the
Nottingham Forest reserve team. He
stepped up to make a useful debut in the
Easter Monday home game against
Walsall, as yet his only senior appearance.
He is a tough-tackling defender who will
be looking to feature more regularly in
2002-03.
*Nottingham F (From trainee on 23/11/2000)
FL 1*

DAY Christopher (Chris)
Nicholas
Born: Walthamstow, 28 July 1975
Height: 6'3" **Weight:** 13.6
International Honours: E: U21-6; Yth
(UEFA-U18 '93)
Chris quickly became a crowd favourite
after joining Queen's Park Rangers in the
summer of 2001. He was an automatic
choice for the 'keeper's jersey and
produced some outstanding performances
in early-season games. Unfortunately, he
suffered a double fracture of the right leg
during the home game with Oldham in
November and this kept him out of action
for the remainder of the season.
*Tottenham H (From trainee on 16/4/1993)
Others 4*
*Crystal Palace (£225,000 + on 9/8/1996) FL
24 FLC 2 FAC 2*

*Watford (£225,000 on 18/7/1997) PL 11 FLC
1 Others 1*
*Lincoln C (Loaned on 4/12/2000) FL 14
Others 4*
*Queens Park R (Free on 24/7/2001) FL 16
FLC 1 Others 1*

DAY Rhys
Born: Bridgend, 31 August 1982
Height: 6'2" **Weight:** 13.6
Club Honours: AMC '02
International Honours: W: U21-8; Yth
This young Manchester City defender
joined Blackpool in a long-term loan deal
last December to gain some experience of
senior football. He made his League
debut against Stoke City on New Year's
Day and featured in around a dozen
games, although he was often used from
the subs' bench.
Manchester C (From trainee on 21/9/1999)
*Blackpool (Loaned on 31/12/2001) FL 4+5
FAC 0+1 Others 3*

DEANE Brian Christopher
Born: Leeds, 7 February 1968
Height: 6'3" **Weight:** 12.7
International Honours: E: 3; B-3
This experienced striker was never a first
choice for Middlesbrough last season and
in November he signed for Leicester City
as the Foxes sought to boost their strike
force. He opened his account for City on
his debut at Elland Road debut, when he
earned 'Man of the Match' plaudits, but it
was not quite such plain sailing thereafter.
However he also managed to add a
twisting bullet header at Southampton
and actually ended the campaign as the
club's leading Premiership goal-scorer.
*Doncaster Rov (From juniors on 14/12/1985)
FL 59+7/12 FLC 3 FAC 2+1/1 Others 2+2*
*Sheffield U (£30,000 on 19/7/1988) F/PL
197/82 FLC 16/11 FAC 23+1/11 Others 2/2*
*Leeds U (£2,900,000 on 14/7/1993) PL
131+7/32 FLC 8+3/2 FAC 13+3/4 Others 3*
*Sheffield U (£1,500,000 on 29/7/1997) PL
24/11 FLC 4/2 FAC 1 (£1,000,000 to Benfica,
Portugal on 15/1/1998)*
*Middlesbrough (£3,000,000 on
16/10/1998) PL 72+15/18 FLC 4+1 FAC 3/1*
*Leicester C (£150,000 on 30/11/2001) PL
13+2/6 FAC 1*

DEARDEN Kevin Charles
Born: Luton, 8 March 1970
Height: 5'11" **Weight:** 13.4
A close season signing from Wrexham,
this experienced 'keeper was a
commanding and confident presence in
the Torquay goal last term. He did not
miss a League or cup game all season,
kept a club record of six consecutive clean

Kevin Dearden

sheets and deservedly won the 'Player of the Season' award.

Tottenham H (From trainee on 5/8/1988) PL 0+1 FLC 1
Cambridge U (Loaned on 9/3/1989) FL 15
Hartlepool U (Loaned on 31/8/1989) FL 10
Swindon T (Loaned on 23/3/1990) FL 1
Peterborough U (Loaned on 24/8/1990) FL 7
Hull C (Loaned on 10/1/1991) FL 3
Rochdale (Loaned on 16/8/1991) FL 2
Birmingham C (Loaned on 19/3/1992) FL 12
Brentford (Free on 30/9/1993) FL 205 FLC 17 FAC 13 Others 19
Barnet (Loaned on 5/2/1999) FL 1
Wrexham (Free on 4/6/1999) FL 81 FLC 3 FAC 6
Torquay U (Free on 9/8/2001) FL 46 FLC 2 FAC 1 Others 1

DEBEVE Michael
Born: Abbeville, France, 1 December 1970
Height: 6'0" **Weight:** 12.8
This experienced right-sided midfield player joined Middlesbrough last February and made his debut in the FA Cup quarter-final tie against Everton. However, he never managed to establish himself in the line-up and started just twice for Boro', although he featured on a number of occasions as a substitute.
Middlesbrough (Free from RC Lens, France, ex Toulouse, Le Havre, on 28/2/2002) PL 1+3 FAC 1+1

DEFOE Jermain Colin
Born: Beckton, 7 October 1982
Height: 5'7" **Weight:** 10.4
International Honours: E: U21-14; Yth; Sch
The young West Ham striker boasts both quality and deadly instinct in front of the goal. He is a natural born goal-scorer and was used mainly as a substitute, to be unleashed towards the end of games when he came on and scored vital goals. He scored a dramatic winner against Manchester United at Old Trafford in December and finished the season with a tally of 14 goals. He deservedly won the fans 'Young Player of the Year' award.
West Ham U (£400,000 + from trainee at Charlton Ath on 15/10/1999) PL 14+22/10 FLC 1+1/1 FAC 2+1/4
Bournemouth (Loaned on 26/10/2000) FL 27+2/18 FAC 1/1 Others 1

DE GOEY Eduard (Ed)
Franciscus
Born: Gouda, Holland, 20 December 1966
Height: 6'6" **Weight:** 15.0
Club Honours: FLC '98; ECWC '98; ESC '98; FAC '00; CS '00

International Honours: Holland: 31; U21-17
Most Stamford Bridge observers felt that Mark Bosnich would take over as Chelsea's first-choice goalkeeper when the 2001-02 season opened but Claudio Ranieri kept faith in Dutch international Ed de Goey who had finished the previous season as understudy to Carlo Cudicini. Despite a sticky moment in the opening match, Ed justified his restoration as number one 'keeper with some solid displays during an eight-match unbeaten spell until he sustained a knee injury which required a cartilage operation in October. Cudicini and Bosnich in turn took over between the posts leaving Ed to occupy the subs' bench for the rest of the season.
Chelsea (£2,250,000 from Feyenoord, Holland, ex Sparta Rotterdam, on 10/7/1997) PL 121 FLC 5 FAC 13 Others 37

DELANEY Damien
Born: Cork, 20 July 1981
Height: 6'3" **Weight:** 13.10
International Honours: RoI: U21-1; Yth
Damien is a left-sided midfielder or defender of immense promise and undoubted class. He had a quiet season last term, spending much of his time gaining experience on loan to struggling Stockport County where he impressed in the centre of the park. When he did return to the Foxes' line-up it was as an emergency left back due to the massive injury crisis at Filbert Street, and not surprisingly, he was occasionally caught out at Premiership level. He later joined Second Division Huddersfield on loan on transfer deadline day.
Leicester C (£50,000 from Cork C on 9/11/2000) PL 5+3 FLC 1 FAC 1+1
Stockport Co (Loaned on 15/11/2001) FL 10+2/1
Huddersfield T (Loaned on 28/3/2002) FL 1+1

DELANEY Dean
Born: Dublin, 15 September 1980
Height: 6'1" **Weight:** 13.2
Club Honours: FAYC '98
International Honours: RoI: U21-6
Dean was second choice goalkeeper with Port Vale last term and made only a handful of appearances thanks to the consistency of Mark Goodlad. After an outing from the bench at Queen's Park Rangers, Dean's first start came at Wycombe in September, but it all went wrong for him as Vale went 3-0 down in the first quarter of an hour. Two further appearances followed later in the

campaign but after a 4-0 defeat at Blackpool he spent the rest of the season in the reserves.
Everton (From trainee on 23/9/1997)
Port Vale (Free on 16/6/2000) FL 10+2 Others 1

DELANEY Mark Anthony
Born: Fishguard, 13 May 1976
Height: 6'1" **Weight:** 11.7
International Honours: W: 15
Mark was Aston Villa's regular right back last season, playing in a back-four formation and cementing his place with a string of assured performances. He is a hard-working, committed player and his consistency has earned him high praise from the Villa faithful. He suffered one or two minor injuries during the campaign, most notably damage to his medial ligaments at West Ham in December, which kept him out for six games.
Cardiff C (Free from Carmarthen on 3/7/1998) FL 28 FLC 2 FAC 5/1
Aston Villa (£250,000 + on 10/3/1999) PL 67+12/1 FLC 2+3 FAC 4+1 Others 9

DELAP Rory John
Born: Sutton Coldfield, 6 July 1976
Height: 6'0" **Weight:** 12.10
Club Honours: AMC '97
International Honours: RoI: 7; B-1; U21-4
A club record fee was paid to bring Rory to St Mary's in the summer of 2001. Although starting the new season in the right-back berth he struggled with his form and despite being quick to join the attack his lack of speed showed when getting back to a defensive position. The return of Jason Dodd to the side pushed him in to a more successful midfield berth and with it a more settled position and his form in the latter part of the campaign was a revelation.
Carlisle U (From trainee on 18/7/1994) FL 40+25/7 FLC 4+1 FAC 0+3 Others 12+2
Derby Co (£500,000 + on 6/2/1998) PL 97+6/11 FLC 7/2 FAC 2+1
Southampton (£3,000,000 + on 21/7/2001) PL 24+4/2 FLC 1

DELGADO Chala Agustin
Born: Ibarra, Ecuador, 23 December 1974
Height: 6'3" **Weight:** 14.2
International Honours: Ecuador: 49
A national hero in Ecuador Agustin, or 'The Tin Man' as he is affectionately known, helped his country to its first World Cup finals scoring the only goal in a famous win over Brazil along the way. He joined Saints in November but almost immediately needed surgery on a knee injury. It was not until January that the

Mark Delaney

club's supporters saw him come off the bench to give an impressive display against Manchester United. Problems with the knee reappeared soon after and it remains to be seen whether he will stay at St Mary's.
Southampton (£3,500,000 from Necaxa, Mexico on 13/11/2001) PL 0+1 FAC 1

DELORGE Laurent Jan
Born: Leuven, Belgium, 21 July 1979
Height: 5'10" **Weight:** 12.0
International Honours: Belgium: U21; Yth
This young right winger was given an early chance by new Coventry City boss Roland Nilsson and rose to the challenge. He scored the winning goal with his first touch in League football at Bramall Lane and appeared in every game from then until Christmas. He picked up a back injury in February and was sidelined for the last two months of the season, making only one further substitute appearance. He scored four goals including two in the 6-1 win at Crewe where he had his most influential game. His speed and dribbling ability caused many headaches for left backs and his crossing was a strong feature of his game.
Coventry C (£1,250,000 from KAA Gent, Belgium, ex Maleisen, Wavre, on 12/11/1998) FL 21+7/4 FLC 0+1 FAC 0+1

DEMPSEY Paul
Born: Birkenhead, 3 December 1981
Height: 5'11" **Weight:** 12.0
Paul had a disappointing season with Northampton Town in 2001-02, losing his place to new signing Gerard Lavin and then finding Chris Marsh took over the right-back position when Lavin was injured. Having eventually won his place back he was then injured himself and was released at the end of the season. He was later reported to be considering a move to New Zealand's Auckland Kingz.
Sheffield U (From trainee on 7/7/2000) Northampton T (Free on 12/3/2001) FL 18+8 FLC 1+1 Others 1

DEMPSTER John
Born: Kettering, 1 April 1983
Height: 6'0" **Weight:** 11.10
John is another of the promising crop of youngsters at Rushden who made his senior bow in 2001-02, his debut coming as substitute at Carlisle in January. A very promising centre half, he signed a new one-year deal for the Diamonds.
Rushden & Diamonds (From juniors on 24/7/2001) FL 0+2

DE ORNELAS Fernando
Born: Caracas, Venezuela, 29 July 1976
Height: 6'0" **Weight:** 11.10
International Honours: Venezuela: 13
This established Venezuelan international joined Queen's Park Rangers on a monthly contract last October. A wide right-sided midfield player he made only one first-team appearance before leaving Loftus Road. He subsequently signed for the Portuguese club CS Maritimo.
Crystal Palace (Free from Happy Valley, Hong Kong, ex Deportivo Chacao, South China, on 30/9/1999) FL 5+4
Glasgow Celtic (Free on 31/3/2000) SL 0+2
Queens Park R (Free on 25/10/2001) FL 1+1

DERRY Shaun Peter
Born: Nottingham, 6 December 1977
Height: 5'10" **Weight:** 10.13
Club Honours: Div 3 '98
Recurring hamstring and groin injuries sidelined Shaun for most of last season, but he returned to regular action in the final third of the campaign. He is a composed defender who has a good first touch and an excellent turn of pace.
Notts Co (From trainee on 13/4/1996) FL 76+3/4 FLC 4+1 FAC 6+1/1 Others 3
Sheffield U (£700,000 on 26/11/1998) FL 62+10 FLC 4 FAC 7/1
Portsmouth (£300,000 + on 16/3/2000) FL 48+1/1 FLC 4 FAC 1+1

DESAILLY Marcel
Born: Accra, Ghana, 7 September 1968
Height: 6'1" **Weight:** 13.5
Club Honours: ESC '98; FAC '00; CS '00
International Honours: France: 97 (WC '98, UEFA '00); B-1; U21
'The bigger the occasion, the better he plays'. That has always been the hallmark of a great footballer and the superb Marcel Desailly personifies this maxim perfectly. FA Cup semi-final, FA Cup final, Premiership clashes with top-six rivals - he was magnificent in these high profile encounters. He lost November and December through tendonitis but came back as strong as ever. His only goal of the season was the last-minute winner, which kept alive Chelsea's long unbeaten Premiership sequence at White Hart Lane. Marcel has now overtaken Dan Petrescu's record of winning most caps whilst a Chelsea player.
Chelsea (£4,600,000 from AC Milan, Italy, ex Nantes, Marseilles, on 14/7/1998) PL 111+1/4 FLC 4 FAC 20 Others 28/1

DEVANEY Martin Thomas
Born: Cheltenham, 1 June 1980
Height: 5'10" **Weight:** 11.12
Martin's versatility enables him to play either up front or in a wide-midfield role, but he was unable to hold down a regular place for Cheltenham in either position last term. However, there were some notable highlights to his season including the stunning individual goal he scored in the league game at Hartlepool and his man-of-the-match performance in the Division Three play-off final. Martin is at his best when running at defenders with the ball at his feet and can both excite and frustrate crowds at the same time.
Coventry C (From trainee on 4/6/1997)
Cheltenham T (Free on 5/8/1999) FL 50+35/17 FLC 4 FAC 1+3/1 Others 3+2/1

DEVINE Sean Thomas
Born: Lewisham, 6 September 1972
Height: 6'0" **Weight:** 13.6
Club Honours: FAYC '91
International Honours: RoI: B-1
After missing the whole of the previous season with a knee injury, Sean finally made his long awaited return for Wycombe at Wrexham last January. It was sooner than planned, due to a lack of fit strikers at the club, and after an anxious few games he scored his first goal in 22 months against Bristol City. He netted in the next two games as well before a long barren spell, but ended the season with a goal in each of the last two games. It will obviously take time to recover his best form, but his desire to score goals is undiminished and his abrasive, forceful style of front play is as unsettling to defences as it ever was. He likes to shoot hard and often with either foot and aims to be top scorer once more in 2002-03.
Millwall (From trainee on 4/5/199. Free to Bromley during the 1992 close season)
Barnet (£10,000 from Famagusta, Cyprus on 5/10/1995) FL 112+14/47 FLC 9/3 FAC 5/5 Others 6
Wycombe W (£220,000 + on 18/3/1999) FL 69+2/36 FLC 4/1 FAC 5+1/1

DEVLIN Paul John
Born: Birmingham, 14 April 1972
Height: 5'9" **Weight:** 11.5
Club Honours: AIC '95
Paul was unsettled at Sheffield United at the start of last season and was placed on the transfer list. A spell on the subs' bench followed, before an injury crisis meant a return to the starting line-up. However he failed to create the openings he had found the previous season and in February he moved to Birmingham City

Martin Devaney

on loan with a view to a permanent transfer. He provided a spark on the right wing and his crosses accounted for several goals during the club's run to the play-offs. He scored a spectacular volley with the outside of his foot against Wolves in March to send Blues on a ten-game unbeaten end to the regular season.

Notts Co (£40,000 from Stafford R on 22/2/1992) FL 132+9/25 FLC 11+1/1 FAC 8/1 Others 17+2/4
Birmingham C (Signed on 29/2/1996) FL 61+15/28 FLC 8+1/4 FAC 3+1/2
Sheffield U (£200,000 + on 13/3/1998) FL 122+25/24 FLC 9+3/4 FAC 8/1 Others 2
Notts Co (Loaned on 23/10/1998) FL 5
Birmingham C (£200,000 on 8/2/2002) FL 11+2/1 Others 2

DE VOGT Wilko
Born: Breda, Holland, 17 September 1975
Height: 6'2" **Weight:** 12.13
After medical doubts about a knee problem had been resolved, goalkeeper Wilko joined Sheffield United last August from NAC Breda as cover for Simon Tracey. Some fine performances in the reserves earned him his debut at home to Grimsby Town, where he performed competently making use of his long throw and even longer kick. His opportunities were somewhat limited by Tracey's excellent form but he did enough to earn a new one-year deal in March. Wilko is a good shot stopper although he tends to stay on his line rather than go for crosses.
Sheffield U (Free from NAC Breda, Holland on 10/7/2001) FL 5+1 FAC 2

DE VOS Jason Richard
Born: Ontario, Canada, 2 January 1974
Height: 6'4" **Weight:** 13.7
International Honours: Canada: 38 (Gold Cup 2000); U23-14
This tall commanding Wigan centre back broke two bones in his foot in the Worthington Cup tie against Blackpool early on last term and it was not until the turn of the year that he was back in action. He netted his first goal for the club coming off the bench in the 2-2 draw at Bristol City. He then missed much of January on Gold Cup duty with Canada, appearing in all five games as they secured the bronze medal position. He subsequently formed an effective partnership at the heart of the defence alongside Arjan De Zeeuw. A very solid defender, effective in the tackle, he used his height and strength to good use when pushing forward at corners.

Darlington (Free from Montreal Impact, Canada on 29/11/1996) FL 43+1/5 FLC 3/1 FAC 4 Others 1
Dundee (£400,000 on 12/10/1998) SL 91+2/2 SLC 5+1 SC 12
Wigan Ath (£500,000 on 8/8/2001) FL 19+1/5 FLC 1

DE-VULGT Leigh Stewart
Born: Swansea, 17 March 1981
Height: 5'9" **Weight:** 11.2
International Honours: W: U21-2; Yth
Leigh had a somewhat roller coaster time at Swansea in 2001-02. In the early part of the season he featured as a substitute for Wales U21s against Armenia, then went on loan to Dr Martens League club Merthyr where he suffered a fractured foot. He recovered by the new year and after another loan spell at Llanelli to recover match fitness he enjoyed a decent run in the team at right back. However, he then suffered knee ligament and cartilage damage during a Welsh U-21 training camp just before the campaign ended.
Swansea C (From trainee on 5/7/1999) FL 13+6 Others 4

DE ZEEUW Adrianus (Arjan) Johannes
Born: Castricum, Holland, 16 April 1970
Height: 6'1" **Weight:** 13.11
This classy and composed central defender produced some excellent performances for Wigan Athletic last season and was rewarded when he was again named in the PFA Second Division team. A virtual ever present, he scored two goals, both coming from corners, against Cardiff City and Stoke City. He captained the Latics team showing total commitment with his excellent tackling and positional sense, and forming an effective partnership alongside Jason De Vos at the heart of the defence. Arjan again swept the board at the club's end-of-season awards but was reported to have signed for Portsmouth during the summer.
Barnsley (£250,000 from Telstar, Holland, ex Vitesse 22, on 3/11/1995) F/PL 138/7 FLC 12 FAC 14
Wigan Ath (Free on 2/7/1999) FL 126/6 FLC 8 FAC 6 Others 6

DIALLO Cherif
Born: Dakar, Senegal, 23 December 1976
Height: 5'8" **Weight:** 10.11
This well-travelled striker joined Exeter City on non-contract forms in the early part of the 2001-02 campaign but managed just two brief outings from the

subs' bench. Although he looked enthusiastic he was released when John Cornforth was appointed as manager and eventually signed for Conference club Hayes early in the new year.
Exeter C (Free from Scarborough, ex Draguignan and trial at Brighton & Hove A, on 4/9/2001) FL 0+2

DIAWARA Djibril
Born: Dakar, Senegal, 3 January 1975
Height: 6'1" **Weight:** 12.3
Djibril was signed by Bolton on a season-long loan deal at the start of the 2001-02 campaign. A tall defensive midfielder, he showed the occasional glimpse of brilliance, but appeared to find the Premiership going quite tough and not suited to his relaxed style of play. He appeared in the centre of midfield and as a centre back, but didn't look entirely comfortable in either role. He eventually returned to Torino in the new year.
Bolton W (Loaned from Torino, Italy, ex Le Havre, AS Monaco, on 17/7/2001) PL 4+5 FLC 2

DIBBLE Andrew (Andy) Gerald
Born: Cwmbran, 8 May 1965
Height: 6'3" **Weight:** 16.8
International Honours: W: 3; U21-3; Yth; Sch
This veteran goalkeeper came into action for Stockport County during the second half of last season and made some fantastic saves along the way for a team that were already heading out of the First Division. He was released by the club at the end of the season and was reported to have signed for Wrexham over the summer.
Cardiff C (From apprentice on 27/8/1982) FL 62 FLC 4 FAC 4
Luton T (£125,000 on 16/7/1984) FL 30 FLC 4 FAC 1 Others 1
Sunderland (Loaned on 21/2/1986) FL 12
Huddersfield T (Loaned on 26/3/1987) FL 5
Manchester C (£240,000 on 1/7/1988) P/FL 113+3 FLC 14 FAC 8+1 Others 2
Aberdeen (Loaned on 20/10/1990) SL 5
Middlesbrough (Loaned on 20/2/1991) FL 19 Others 2
Bolton W (Loaned on 6/9/1991) FL 13 Others 1
West Bromwich A (Loaned on 27/2/1992) FL 9
Glasgow R (Signed on 11/3/1997) SL 7
Luton T (Free on 15/9/1997) FL 1 FLC 2
Middlesbrough (Free on 30/11/1998) FL 2 (Free to Altrincham during 1998 close season)
Hartlepool U (Free on 25/3/1999) FL 6 FLC 2 Others 2+1

Paolo Di Canio

Carlisle U (Loaned on 8/10/1999) FL 2
Stockport Co (Free on 10/8/2000) FL 22+1
FLC 0+1 FAC 1

DI CANIO Paolo

Born: Rome, Italy, 9 July 1968
Height: 5'9" **Weight:** 11.9
The maestro had another fine season at West Ham. Once again the fans were treated to some amazing skills and goals. Who would have the audacity to chip a penalty? Paolo did at Liverpool and Leicester to leave the keepers floundering. Then there were the memorable goals, a low eight-yarder against Newcastle, a 15-yard volley against Ipswich and on Boxing Day he tucked home from 18 yards to help the Hammers win 4-0 against Derby County. He is a playmaker, a goal-scorer and a unique showman. Unfortunately during the game with Charlton in April he suffered a bad ligament injury, which forced him to miss the remaining games of the season.
Glasgow Celtic (Signed from AC Milan, Italy, ex AC Milan, Lazio, Ternana, Juventus, Napoli, on 3/7/1996) SL 25+1/12 SLC 2 SC 6/3 Others 2+1
Sheffield Wed (£3,000,000 on 8/8/1997) PL 39+2/15 FLC 4/2 FAC 3
West Ham U (£1,700,000 on 28/1/1999) PL 98+2/38 FLC 7/2 FAC 5/1 Others 10/1

DICHIO Daniele (Danny)
Salvatore Ernest
Born: Hammersmith, 19 October 1974
Height: 6'3" **Weight:** 12.3
Club Honours: Div 1 '99
International Honours: E: U21-1; Sch
Danny initially joined West Bromwich Albion on loan last August and scored in his first two games. Although lacking pace, he battled on bravely and when he returned to the Hawthorns on a permanent basis, he netted some more vitally important goals, including the only one of the game in a promotion encounter with Norwich City. Strong in the air, especially inside the penalty area, he was the perfect foil to the darting Scott Dobie and Jason Roberts, and played well at times with Bob Taylor, always proving a handful to the marking defenders.
Queens Park R (From trainee on 17/5/1993) P/FL 56+19/20 FLC 6/2 FAC 3+3 (Free to Sampdoria, Italy during 1997 close season)
Barnet (Loaned on 24/3/1994) FL 9/2
Sunderland (£750,000, via loan spell at Lecce, Italy on 28/1/1998) P/FL 20+56/11 FLC 11+1/6 FAC 3+3/1 Others 1+2

West Bromwich A (Loaned on 23/8/2001) FL 3/2
West Bromwich A (£1,250,000 on 30/11/2001) FL 23+1/7 FAC 4/1

DICKINSON Michael James
Born: Newcastle, 4 May 1984
Height: 5'11" **Weight:** 10.8
This promising young forward, made his first-team debut for Carlisle United when he came on as a substitute at Hartlepool last September. He was subsequently offered a further one-year contract by the club and will be aiming to feature more regularly in 2002-03.
Carlisle U (Trainee) FL 0+1

DICKOV Paul
Born: Livingston, 1 November 1972
Height: 5'6" **Weight:** 11.9
Club Honours: ECWC '94
International Honours: S: 3; U21-4; Yth; Sch
This busy striker had little chance to prove himself at Manchester City last season, partly due to a prolonged achilles injury. He scored his only goal away at Notts County in the Worthington Cup, before moving on to Premiership strugglers Leicester City at the end of February. Here he began to forge a useful partnership with Brian Deane, adding enthusiasm and experience to the Foxes' front line.
Arsenal (From trainee on 28/12/1990) PL 6+15/3 FLC 2+2/3
Luton T (Loaned on 8/10/1993) FL 8+7/1
Brighton & Hove A (Loaned on 23/3/1994) FL 8/5
Manchester C (£1,000,000 on 23/8/1996) P/FL 105+51/33 FLC 9+4/5 FAC 5+4/1 Others 3/2
Leicester C (Signed on 22/2/2002) PL 11+1/4

DIGBY Fraser Charles
Born: Sheffield, 23 April 1967
Height: 6'1" **Weight:** 13.10
Club Honours: Div 2 '96
International Honours: E: U21-5; Yth; Sch
This experienced goalkeeper joined Queen's Park Rangers last November in a deal that lasted until the end of the season. Signed as a replacement for the injured Chris Day, he was a regular in the line-up until becoming an injury victim himself in February.
Manchester U (From apprentice on 25/4/1985)
Swindon T (£32,000 on 25/9/1986) F/PL 417 FLC 33 FAC 21 Others 33+1
Crystal Palace (Free on 8/8/1998) FL 56 FLC 7 FAC 1 (Released on 31/10/2000)

Huddersfield T (Free from Barry T on 16/8/2001)
Queens Park R (Free on 11/10/2001) FL 19 FAC 1

DINNING Tony
Born: Wallsend, 12 April 1975
Height: 6'0" **Weight:** 12.11
Tony made a sound start to the 2001-02 season, playing in the opening five matches and for Wolves before being surprisingly transferred to Wigan in September. An attacking central midfield player he set up the opening goal on his debut for the Latics at Bury. Hard working and strong in the tackle, he produced a man of the match performance in the home match against Queen's Park Rangers when he also scored his first goal for the club. Shortly before the transfer deadline day he was loaned to Stoke as cover for the injured Brynjar Gunnarsson and played his part in securing a place for them in the Second Division play-offs.
Newcastle U (From trainee on 1/10/1993)
Stockport Co (Free on 23/6/1994) FL 159+32/25 FLC 12+5/3 FAC 5+7 Others 6+1/2
Wolverhampton W (£600,000 + on 22/9/2000) FL 35/6 FLC 1/1 FAC 1
Wigan Ath (£750,000 on 7/9/2001) FL 32+1/5 FAC 1
Stoke C (Loaned on 27/3/2002) FL 5 Others 3

DIOMEDE Bernard
Born: St Doulchard, France, 23 January 1974
Height: 5'7" **Weight:** 11.4
International Honours: France: 8
Very much a forgotten man at Anfield, the former French international midfielder was even more invisible in 2001-02 than the previous season, despite no apparent injury problems. He made his only first-team appearance early in the season in the second leg of Liverpool's Champions' League qualifying round tie at home to Haka of Finland along with several other reserves following the emphatic first-leg victory.
Liverpool (£3,000,000 from Auxerre, France on 5/7/2000) PL 1+1 Others 3

DI PIEDI Michele
Born: Italy, 4 December 1980
Height: 6'6" **Weight:** 13.7
This energetic, enthusiastic Sheffield Wednesday striker endured an injury-wrecked campaign in 2001-02. The Owls could certainly have used his hard-running, all-action approach and he remained very popular with the

supporters. He was not always in the 16-man squad even when fit and managed just two starts all season.

Sheffield Wed *(Free from Perugia, Italy on 15/8/2000) FL 8+29/5 FLC 1+4/2*

DISLEY Craig Edward
Born: Worksop, 24 August 1981
Height: 5'10" **Weight:** 11.0
Craig made a storming start to the 2001-02 season, celebrating his 20th birthday by scoring his first two League goals at Cheltenham. He repeated the dose against Macclesfield the following match where, but for a missed penalty, he would have registered his first hat-trick. He is a lively central midfield player who likes to get forward and is not afraid to have a crack at goal.

Mansfield T *(From trainee on 23/6/1999) FL 49+16/7 FLC 1 FAC 4 Others 1*

DISTIN Sylvain
Born: Paris, France, 16 December 1977
Height: 6'4" **Weight:** 13.10
Sylvain joined Newcastle last September on loan until the end of the season. He made his debut as a last-minute substitute in the home victory over Manchester United, following which he became a regular in the first-team squad, primarily as a substitute with occasional starts, until establishing himself in the starting line-up primarily at left back. A fine athlete who is very quick over the ground his long throws have added to his side's attacking options, and at 6'4" he is one of the tallest players ever to represent the club.

Newcastle U *(Loaned from Paris St Germain, France, ex Tours, Guegnon, on 14/9/2001) PL 20+8 FLC 2 FAC 5*

DIXON Lee Michael
Born: Manchester, 17 March 1964
Height: 5'9" **Weight:** 11.8
Club Honours: Div 1 '89, '91; PL '98, '02; FAC '93, '98, '02; ECWC '94; CS '98, '99
International Honours: E: 22; B-4
Now very much at the veteran stage of his career, Lee found himself a victim of Arsene Wenger's attempts to reduce the average age of the Gunners' defence last term. He started just three Premiership games, although he was often used as a substitute, and announced his retirement in the summer. A tough-tackling right back, he is equally comfortable moving forward and creating attacking moves.

Burnley *(From juniors on 21/7/1982) FL 4 FLC 1*
Chester C *(Free on 16/2/1984) FL 56+1/1 FLC 2 FAC 1 Others 3*

Bury *(Free on 15/7/1985) FL 45/5 FLC 4 FAC 8/1 Others 1*
Stoke C *(£40,000 on 18/7/1986) FL 71/5 FLC 6 FAC 7 Others 4*
Arsenal *(£400,000 on 29/1/1988) F/PL 439+19/25 FLC 45 FAC 52+2/1 Others 64/2*

D'JAFFO Laurent
Born: Aquitane, France, 5 November 1970
Height: 6'0" **Weight:** 13.5
Although he was not expected to be a first-choice striker Laurent was a key figure for Sheffield United for much of the 2001-02 season, often playing when not fully fit because of injuries to others. Mainly used as a target man he always worked hard for the team and scored some vital goals, his best being a 25-yard screamer in the 3-0 defeat of Burnley. The final few games of the campaign saw Laurent have possibly his best spell at Bramall Lane, showing excellent control, awareness and tenacity and he was unlucky not to score more. He was out of contract in the summer and at the time of writing his future was uncertain.

Ayr U *(Signed from Red Star Paris, France on 13/10/1997) SL 21+3/10 SC 2+1*
Bury *(Free on 28/7/1998) FL 35+2/8 FLC 4+1/1 FAC 1*
Stockport Co *(£100,000 on 13/8/1999) FL 20+1/7 FLC 2/1*
Sheffield U *(£100,000 + on 4/2/2000) FL 45+24/11 FLC 0+2/1 FAC 1+2*

DJORDJIC Bojan
Born: Belgrade, Yugoslavia, 6 February 1982
Height: 5'10" **Weight:** 11.5
International Honours: Sweden: U21-5
This talented young Manchester United midfielder received his only first-team chance last season in the Worthington Cup tie against Arsenal in November. He moved on loan to Sheffield Wednesday soon afterwards where he gave some lively performances down the left flank before returning to Old Trafford to continue his development. Bojan is the son of former Red Star Belgrade and Yugoslavia player, Branko Djordjic.

Manchester U *(£1,000,000 from Bromma Pojkarna, Sweden on 18/2/1999) PL 0+1 FLC 1*
Sheffield Wed *(Loaned on 7/12/2001) FL 4+1*

DJORKAEFF Youri
Born: Lyon, France, 9 March 1968
Height: 5'11" **Weight:** 11.6
International Honours: France: 82
The arrival of this talented player at Bolton last February turned out to be a

truly inspirational move by manager Sam Allardyce. Playing in his favoured role just behind an out-and-out striker, Youri quickly turned on the skill and showed just why he has won virtually every major trophy in international and European club football. When on the ball he gave defenders a torrid time with his precision passing and close control, he also worked tirelessly to regain possession when the ball was lost. He was particularly outstanding when scoring a double at Charlton at the end of March.

Bolton W *(Loaned from Kaiserslautern, Germany, ex Grenoble, Strasbourg, AS Monaco, Paris St Germain, on 15/2/2002) PL 12/4*

DOANE Benjamin (Ben) Nigel David
Born: Sheffield, 22 December 1979
Height: 5'10" **Weight:** 12.0
A pre-season knee ligament injury kept Ben out of action until the end of September when he returned to the Sheffield United reserves line-up. He then seemed to have made the right-back spot his own following Rob Kozluk's injury, producing some solid performances. Quick into the tackle and showing good anticipation, he linked well down the right wing. However suspension brought his run to an end and he did not regain his place in the line-up until Gus Uhlenbeek moved to Walsall in March. Ben marked his return with his first goal for the club – a 25-yarder – to earn the Blades a point at Crewe.

Sheffield U *(From trainee on 15/7/1998) FL 17+1/1 FLC 0+1*

DOBIE Robert Scott
Born: Workington, 10 October 1978
Height: 6'1" **Weight:** 12.8
International Honours: S: 2
A snip-of-a-signing by manager Gary Megson, striker Scott Dobie, sharp and decisive, took over from the departed Lee Hughes in style, scoring nine times in his first 12 matches for Albion. Unfortunately the goals somehow dried up, but he was always grafting for an opening, never giving less than 100 per cent effort out on the park. Gradually his scoring touch returned as Albion surged on towards promotion, and when the season ended Scott was the Baggies' leading marksman with 12 goals.

Carlisle U *(From trainee on 10/5/1997) FL 101+35/24 FLC 2+6 FAC 4+1/2 Others 6+1*
Clydebank *(Loaned on 3/11/1998) SL 6*
West Bromwich A *(£125,000 + on 11/7/2001) FL 32+11/10 FLC 3/2 FAC 1+3*

DOBSON Michael William
Born: Isleworth, 9 April 1981
Height: 5'11" **Weight:** 12.4
Michael established himself as Brentford's regular right back last season. His solid defending and overlapping runs forward endeared him to the Bees' fans and he was one of the team's most consistent players throughout the campaign. He missed a few games due to a groin injury in October and scored his only goal in the FA Cup match against Scunthorpe. He is the son of former Brentford winger George Dobson.
Brentford (From trainee on 30/6/1999) FL 61+4 FLC 2+1 FAC 2/1 Others 10/3

DODD Ashley Michael
Born: Stafford, 7 January 1982
Height: 5'10" **Weight:** 10.2
International Honours: E: Sch
This stylish Port Vale midfield player spent the majority of the 2001-02 campaign in the reserves. It all began rather well as he scored on the opening day with a cracking shot against Notts County, but as the team struggled Ashley was in and out of the side. He played in the local 'derby' against Stoke City in October but little was seen of him after that. He is good on the ball but probably needs to add more strength to his game. He was released on a free transfer in the summer.
Manchester U (From trainee on 9/9/1999)
Port Vale (Free on 22/3/2001) FL 8+4/1 FLC 0+1 FAC 1+1 Others 1

DODD Jason Robert
Born: Bath, 2 November 1970
Height: 5'10" **Weight:** 12.3
International Honours: E: U21-8
A summer knee operation sidelined the Saints' skipper until October of last season, but his return coincided with a change in fortunes for the side. A technically sound defender, his experience more than makes up for a lack of speed. Now in his 13th season with the club he was as dependable as ever.
Southampton (£50,000 from Bath C on 15/3/1989) F/PL 327+23/9 FLC 38+2/1 FAC 30/3 Others 5

DOHERTY Gary Michael Thomas
Born: Carndonagh, 31 January 1980
Height: 6'2" **Weight:** 13.1
International Honours: RoI: 9; U21-7; Yth
Gary had an injury-ravaged season at Tottenham last term and managed only a handful of first-team appearances. He is a versatile player who can perform equally well in the centre of defence or as a

striker, but he was disappointed to miss out on a place in the Republic of Ireland squad for the World Cup finals.
Luton T (From trainee on 2/7/1997) FL 46+24/12 FLC 0+3/1 FAC 6+2/2 Others 1+1
Tottenham H (£1,000,000 on 22/4/2000) PL 22+9/3 FLC 1 FAC 5/3

DOHERTY Thomas (Tommy) Edward
Born: Bristol, 17 March 1979
Height: 5'8" **Weight:** 9.13
This promising youngster put his injury problems behind him last season and featured regularly at first-team level for Bristol City. He produced some terrier-like performances in midfield adding some much needed bite, although he was rarely able to last the full 90 minutes. He will be looking forward to gain even more senior experience in 2002-03.
Bristol C (From trainee on 8/7/1997) FL 64+24/4 FLC 4+1/1 FAC 2+1 Others 4

DOIG Christopher (Chris) Ross
Born: Dumfries, 13 February 1981
Height: 6'2" **Weight:** 12.6
International Honours: S: U21-6; Yth; Sch
Chris started the 2001-02 season at centre back for Nottingham Forest, and was beginning to establish a useful partnership with Jon Hjelde but suffered a serious knee injury at Wolves, and this put him out for the remainder of the campaign. Earlier the classy defender had scored his first senior goal for the club at home to Rotherham. He started light training in April and hopefully should be fit for the start of 2002-03.
Queen of the South (Associated Schoolboy) SL 2+2
Nottingham F (From trainee on 7/3/1998) P/FL 31+5/1 FLC 4+1 FAC 1

DONNELLY Paul Michael
Born: Stoke, 16 February 1981
Height: 5'7" **Weight:** 11.10
This adaptable Port Vale defender was mainly a reserve in 2001-02, starting just two games, both at left back, against Carlisle United in the LDV Vans Trophy and then in the Second Division match at Peterborough United in January. Unfortunately the latter was arguably the team's worst display of the season and Paul did not make the first eleven again. He always tried his best but a lack of opportunity led to him being given a free transfer in the summer.
Port Vale (From trainee on 1/7/1999) FL 5+6 Others 1+1

DONNELLY Simon Thomas
Born: Glasgow, 1 December 1974
Height: 5'9" **Weight:** 11.0
Club Honours: SC '95; SPD '98
International Honours: S: 10; U21-11
Injury once again blighted Simon's career at Sheffield Wednesday last term. He eventually managed to come back and become a regular member of the squad, but still appeared lightweight. He is very skilful, and could still make it at Hillsborough, but as a schemer rather than a striker.
Glasgow Celtic (From juniors on 27/5/1993) SL 113+33/30 SLC 11+6/4 SC 8+5/2 Others 13+7/6
Sheffield Wed (Free on 9/7/1999) P/FL 17+21/6 FLC 3+2 FAC 0+3

DONOVAN Kevin
Born: Halifax, 17 December 1971
Height: 5'8" **Weight:** 11.2
Club Honours: AMC '98
After joining Barnsley in the summer of 2001, Kevin made his debut for the Reds on the opening day of the season. He was a regular starter until he suffered a damaged knee in a training ground accident that ended his campaign at the beginning of March. A thoughtful wide player he found it difficult to win over the Oakwell fans, but he was playing in a struggling team for most of the season.
Huddersfield T (From trainee on 11/10/1989) FL 11+9/1 FLC 1+1 FAC 1/2 Others 4
Halifax T (Loaned on 13/2/1992) FL 6
West Bromwich A (£70,000 on 1/10/1992) FL 139+29/19 FLC 9+2/6 FAC 7+1/3 Others 15+1/4
Grimsby T (£300,000 on 29/7/1997) FL 150+6/24 FLC 13+1/2 FAC 11/1 Others 9/3
Barnsley (Free on 2/7/2001) FL 28+4/1 FLC 2+1 FAC 2

DORRIAN Christopher (Chris) Stewart
Born: Harlow, 3 April 1982
Height: 5'9" **Weight:** 10.0
Chris spent three months on loan with Conference outfit Dover Athletic at the start of the 2001-02 campaign but was still unable to win a regular place in the Leyton Orient line-up on his return. He deputised a couple of times for the injured Matthew Joseph before being released in March. He subsequently had a brief trial at Southend before joining Chelmsford City. Chris is a promising young right back who is solid in the tackle and distributes the ball accurately.
Leyton Orient (From trainee on 10/7/2000) FL 4+1 FLC 1 FAC 2

[DOUDOU] MBOMBO
Aziana Ebele
Born: Kinshasha, Zaire, 11 September 1980
Height: 5'5" **Weight:** 9.11
Doudou joined Queen's Park Rangers last August in an unusual deal. With the club in administration they could not afford his wages but two supporters agreed to finance the deal. A quick player who featured on the right side of midfield or as a striker, he become a favourite with the fans for his wholehearted efforts. Although not a prolific scorer himself, he made numerous chances for his colleagues.
Queens Park R (Free from AS Monaco, France on 17/8/2001) FL 20+16/3 FLC 1 FAC 1 Others 0+1

DOUGHTY Matthew (Matt)
Liam
Born: Warrington, 2 November 1981
Height: 5'8" **Weight:** 10.8
Matt began the 2001-02 season on a high for Rochdale, netting the first ever goal scored at Oxford's Kassam Stadium in the opening game. Although initially playing on the left of midfield, he later settled in at left back after both Lee Todd and Sean McAuley were injured. Very much a fans' favourite at Spotland he impressed with his spirited bursts from the by-line from where he delivered some useful crosses.
Chester C (Trainee) FL 19+14/1 FLC 2 FAC 4
Rochdale (Free on 20/7/2001) FL 32+4/1 FLC 0+1 FAC 3/1 Others 4

DOUGLAS Jonathan
Born: Monaghan, 22 November 1981
Height: 5'10" **Weight:** 12.12
International Honours: RoI: U21-1 Yth
That Jonathan re-appeared for Blackburn at all was something of a miracle following post-season surgery on a medial and cruciate ligament injury that threatened to ruin his career. Coming back with the reserves in February he immediately scored a hat-trick, came on as substitute in the FA Cup defeat at Middlesbrough and was made reserve-team captain. He was called up for the Republic of Ireland U21 team in the Toulon tournament during the summer.
Blackburn Rov (From trainee on 10/2/2000) FLC 0+1 FAC 0+2

DOUGLAS Stuart Anthony
Born: Enfield, 9 April 1978
Height: 5'9" **Weight:** 11.5
Stuart had a frustrating season in 2001-02

when he was plagued by hamstring injuries. He featured from the subs' bench on several occasions early on, but he found himself well down the pecking order of strikers and in October he joined Oxford United on loan. However he made little impact at the Kassam Stadium, nor did he impress in another loan spell at Rushden in the new year. He is a small, nippy striker who works hard and is always willing to chase lost causes.
Luton T (From trainee on 2/5/1996) FL 104+42/18 FLC 11+3/3 FAC 8+2/2 Others 1+1
Oxford U (Loaned on 23/10/2001) FL 1+3
Rushden & Diamonds (Loaned on 18/1/2002) FL 4+5

DOUGLIN Troy Alexander
Born: Coventry, 7 May 1982
Height: 6'0" **Weight:** 11.8
As a succession of new central defenders arrived at Torquay, Troy found his first-team opportunities limited last season. A powerful and confident young centre back, whose qualities had greatly interested Celtic during the previous campaign, his chance will surely come.
Torquay U (From trainee on 4/7/2000) FL 8+1 FLC 4 FAC 1 Others 1

DOWNER Simon
Born: Romford, 19 October 1981
Height: 5'11" **Weight:** 12.0
Simon started the 2001-02 season as first-choice centre half for Leyton Orient but he suffered a serious knee injury in the away game at Mansfield in October that ruled him out for the remainder of the campaign. He showed what a valuable asset he is in the early season games when his pace and timing of tackle were particularly impressive.
Leyton Orient (From trainee on 4/10/1999) FL 55+13 FLC 3+2 FAC 3+1 Others 5

DOWNING Stewart
Born: Middlesbrough, 22 July 1984
Height: 5'11" **Weight:** 10.6
International Honours: E: Yth
This promising Middlesbrough youngster stepped up to the professional ranks last September and went on to make his Premiership bow at Ipswich in April. A talented left-sided player, he went on to feature twice more in the closing stages of the campaign.
Middlesbrough (From trainee on 6/9/2001) PL 2+1

DOYLE Daire Michael
Born: Dublin, 18 October 1980
Height: 5'11" **Weight:** 11.12
Daire is a talented midfielder but found

his chances extremely limited at Kidderminster last season, although he spent time out injured in the early part of the campaign. His contribution to the cause was limited to just two substitute appearances – against Preston in the Worthington Cup and then in the League against Macclesfield in February. He made the starting line-up for the Worcestershire Senior Cup matches, scoring his first goal for Harriers in the first leg of the final.
Coventry C (Signed from Cherry Orchard on 15/9/1998)
Kidderminster Hrs (Free on 12/1/2001) FL 13+3 FLC 0+1

DOYLEY Lloyd Collin
Born: Whitechapel, 1 December 1982
Height: 6'0" **Weight:** 11.10
A graduate of the Watford academy, Lloyd made his debut at the age of 18 as a substitute centre half at home to Birmingham. He also added a handful of further appearances at right back, where he looked more at ease, and impressed with his enthusiasm and willingness to learn.
Watford (From trainee on 8/3/2001) FL 11+9 FLC 1

DRAPER Craig James Edwin
Born: Swansea, 4 December 1982
Height: 5'10" **Weight:** 9.7
A graduate of Swansea's youth policy, Craig made his League debut as substitute against Rochdale at the Vetch Field, but apart from a substitute outing in an FAW Premier Cup tie at Newport, his only other first-team appearance was from the bench in the final game of the season against Torquay. Highly rated by the Swans for his clever midfield play, he will be looking to improve his stamina levels over the coming season.
Swansea C (From trainee on 4/7/2001) FL 0+2

DRAPER Mark Andrew
Born: Long Eaton, 11 November 1970
Height: 5'10" **Weight:** 12.4
Club Honours: FLC '96
International Honours: E: U21-3
This experienced midfielder had a frustrating time at Southampton last term. He managed one senior appearance at West Ham in October before a serious knee injury put him on the sidelines for four months. Despite returning to action in March he never really got another chance.
Notts Co (From trainee on 12/12/1988) FL 206+16/40 FLC 14+1/2 FAC 10/2 Others 21+2/5

117

Leicester C *(£1,250,000 on 22/7/1994) PL 39/5 FLC 2 FAC 2*
Aston Villa *(£3,250,000 on 5/7/1995) PL 108+12/7 FLC 11+1/2 FAC 10/2 Others 12+1*
Southampton *(£1,500,000 on 21/7/2000) PL 17+7/1 FLC 1+1 FAC 3+1*

DRURY Adam James
Born: Cambridge, 29 August 1978
Height: 5'10" **Weight:** 11.8
Adam proved to be one of the most consistent performers in the Norwich City line-up last season, solving the club's long-term left-back problem. A reliable and solid defender, he is an excellent timer of tackles and is more than useful in the air, having often played at centre back for his previous club, Peterborough United. His distribution is good and his attacking skills will improve with experience.
Peterborough U *(From trainee on 3/7/1996) FL 138+10/2 FLC 8 FAC 9 Others 10+1*
Norwich C *(£275,000 on 21/3/2001) FL 41 FLC 1 FAC 1 Others 3*

DRYDEN Richard Andrew
Born: Stroud, 14 June 1969
Height: 6'0" **Weight:** 13.12
Club Honours: Div 4 '90
This experienced left-sided central defender made only two first-team starts for Luton Town last term and spent two months on loan at Scarborough at the turn of the year. He made quite an impact at Seamer Road, scoring on his debut, but was unable to force his way back into the reckoning on his return to Kenilworth Road and was freed at the end of the season.
Bristol Rov *(From trainee on 14/7/1987) FL 12+1 FLC 2+1 FAC 0+2 Others 2*
Exeter C *(Loaned on 22/9/1988) FL 6*
Exeter C *(£10,000 on 8/3/1989) FL 86/13 FLC 7/2 FAC 2 Others 4*
Notts Co *(£250,000 on 9/8/1991) FL 30+1/1 FLC 1+1 FAC 2+1 Others 2*
Plymouth Arg *(Loaned on 18/11/1992) FL 5 Others 1*
Birmingham C *(£165,000 on 19/3/1993) FL 48 FLC 5 FAC 1*
Bristol C *(£10,000 on 16/12/1994) FL 32+5/2 FLC 4 FAC 1+1 Others 2*
Southampton *(£150,000 on 6/8/1996) PL 44+3/1 FLC 7/3*
Stoke C *(Loaned on 3/11/1999) FL 3*
Stoke C *(Loaned on 23/3/2000) FL 8+2 Others 1+1*
Northampton T *(Loaned on 8/9/2000) FL 9+1*
Swindon T *(Loaned on 24/11/2000) FL 7 FAC 1*
Luton T *(Free on 2/2/2001) FL 22+1 FLC 0+1 FAC 1 Others 1*

DRYSDALE Leon Anthony
Born: Walsall, 3 February 1981
Height: 5'9" **Weight:** 11.6
This right-sided defender is one of the exciting squad of youngsters being developed by Kevin Ratcliffe at Shrewsbury. He is strong in the tackle, always gives 100 per cent and likes to push forward. He initially took his chance following an injury to Iain Jenkins but then found himself restricted by injuries that limited his appearances.
Shrewsbury T *(From trainee on 2/7/1999) FL 40+6 FLC 1+1 FAC 1*

DSANE Roscoe
Born: Epsom, 16 October 1980
Height: 5'8" **Weight:** 11.2
After trials with Plymouth and Brentford during the summer of 2001, Roscoe had brief associations with non-league clubs Slough and Woking before joining Southend on non-contract forms last November. Brought in to try and solve the team's wide-midfield problem, he managed only one full plus one substitute appearance before being released. He subsequently returned to Woking.
Crystal Palace *(From trainee on 29/6/1999. Free to Woking during 2001 close season)*
Southend U *(Free from Slough T on 8/11/2001) FL 1+1*

DUBERRY Michael Wayne
Born: Enfield, 14 October 1975
Height: 6'1" **Weight:** 13.6
Club Honours: FLC '98; ECWC '98; ESC '98
International Honours: E: U21-5
Michael has suffered a stop-start to his career at Elland Road since his move from Chelsea. Just when he was beginning to prove himself he damaged an achilles at Derby in September 2000, missing the rest of that season. The 2001-02 campaign saw him primarily in a squad role making limited first-team appearances, and having to endure the club's much publicised off-field problem.
Chelsea *(From trainee on 7/6/1993) PL 77+9/1 FLC 8 FAC 12/2 Others 9*
Bournemouth *(Loaned on 29/9/1995) FL 7 Others 1*
Leeds U *(£4,000,000 + on 29/7/1999) PL 20+1/1 FLC 0+3 FAC 1+1 Others 6*

DUBLIN Dion
Born: Leicester, 22 April 1969
Height: 6'1" **Weight:** 12.4
Club Honours: Div 3 '91
International Honours: E: 4
Dion is a powerful target man who is good in the air and at holding the ball up

with a defender on his back. He had a somewhat disappointing season for Villa last term, and often found himself on the subs' bench once the strike partnership between Darius Vassell and Juan Pablo Angel had been established. He joined Millwall on loan just before the transfer deadline day and scored on his debut against Stockport before going on to become an influential figure for the Lions in the closing stages of the campaign.
Norwich C *(Free from Oakham U on 24/3/1988)*
Cambridge U *(Free on 2/8/1988) FL 133+23/52 FLC 8+2/5 FAC 21/11 Others 14+1/5*
Manchester U *(£1,000,000 on 7/8/1992) PL 4+8/2 FLC 1+1/1 FAC 1+1 Others 0+1*
Coventry C *(£2,000,000 on 9/9/1994) PL 144+1/61 FLC 11+1/4 FAC 13/7*
Aston Villa *(£5,750,000 on 6/11/1998) PL 85+19/35 FLC 6+1/4 FAC 4+2/1 Others 8+2/2*
Millwall *(Loaned on 28/3/2002) FL 5/2 Others 2/1*

DUCROCQ Pierre
Born: Pontoise, France, 18 December 1976
Height: 5'11" **Weight:** 11.12
This experienced midfielder found himself out of favour at PSG last term and in October he joined Derby County on loan until the end of the season. Although he featured regularly for the Rams he failed to prevent them from being relegated and returned across the Channel in the summer.
Derby Co *(Loaned from Paris St Germain, France on 18/10/2001) PL 19*

DUCROS Andrew (Andy) John
Born: Evesham, 16 September 1977
Height: 5'4" **Weight:** 10.6
International Honours: E: Sch
Andy was blighted by injuries last term which restricted him to just a handful of appearances. When fit, his flair and creativity from a position just behind the strikers are more than a match for any defence in the Third Division. The highpoint of his season was probably the goal scored direct from a free kick to win the game against Scunthorpe on the opening day.
Coventry C *(From trainee on 16/9/1994) PL 2+6 FLC 0+1(Free to Nuneaton Borough on 6/8/99)*
Kidderminster Hrs *(£100,000 on 24/7/2000) FL 36+12/4 FLC 1 FAC 3+1*

DUDEK Jerzy
Born: Rybnik, Poland, 23 March 1973
Height: 6'2" **Weight:** 12.10

International Honours: Poland: 23
Jerzy was signed by Liverpool at the end
of last August and went on to become
the regular first-choice 'keeper last term,
his outstanding form contributing
significantly to the tightest defence in the
Premier League. After an unfortunate
debut in a shock home defeat by Aston
Villa, for which he could not be held
responsible, he went on to keep 26 clean
and in total let in only 39 goals. Despite
the occasional misjudgement none of the
goals conceded by Liverpool could be
attributed to him.
*Liverpool (£4,850,000 from Feyenoord,
Holland, ex GKS Tychy, Sokol Tychy, on
31/8/2001) PL 35 FAC 2 Others 12*

DUDFIELD Lawrence (Lawrie) George
Born: Southwark, 7 May 1980
Height: 6'1" **Weight:** 13.9
Hull smashed a 12-year-old club record
transfer fee to sign Lawrie in the 2001
close season. A skilful right-sided forward,
he proved the perfect foil for fellow new
boy Gary Alexander. They became the first
Tigers' striking duo to both hit a double-
figure goals tally in League action since
Dean Windass and Linton Brown in 1994-
95. Lawrie totalled 14 goals in all
competitions. His form dipped a little in
mid-term but soon recovered to prove his
value to the team.
*Leicester C (Signed from Kettering T on
6/6/1997) PL 0+2*
Lincoln C (Loaned on 15/9/2000) FL 2+1
*Chesterfield (Loaned on 14/12/2000) FL
4+10/3 Others 3+1/1*
*Hull C (£210,000 on 2/7/2001) FL 32+6/12
FLC 2 FAC 2/2 Others 3*

DUDLEY Craig Bryan
Born: Ollerton, 12 September 1979
Height: 5'10'' **Weight:** 11.2
Club Honours: Div 3 '98
International Honours: E: Yth
This pacy striker made around a dozen
senior appearances for Oldham last term,
but found the net just once – against
former club, Notts County. He then fell
out of favour following a change in
management and was transfer listed in
December. A one-month loan spell at
Scunthorpe United followed in February,
but he failed to impress and returned to
Boundary Park.
*Notts Co (From trainee on 2/4/1997) FL
11+20/3 FLC 1+2/1 FAC 1+2*
Shrewsbury T (Loaned on 8/1/1998) FL 3+1
Hull C (Loaned on 10/11/1998) FL 4+3/2
*Oldham Ath (Free on 25/3/1999) FL
34+26/10 FLC 2+1 FAC 5+3/3 Others 0+2*

Chesterfield (Loaned on 20/8/1999) FL 0+2
Scunthorpe U (Loaned on 1/2/2002) FL 1+3

DUFF Damien Anthony
Born: Dublin, Ireland, 2 March 1979
Height: 5'10" **Weight:** 9.7
Club Honours: FLC '02
International Honours: RoI: 30; B-1;
Yth; Sch
Although hampered by a hamstring injury
in the first half of last season Damien
began to emerge as a true star at
Blackburn. If adequately protected by
referees he is almost impossible to stop.
He has both pace and quick feet and an
ability to keep moving despite any body
contact short of taking his legs from
under him. Full of quick feints that only
great ball control will permit he is doubly
dangerous because he can use speed to
go outside but show him the inside and
his quick feet will permit him to make
huge inroads into the penalty area. He
covered the left side assiduously, tackling
and covering well and also contributed
some memorable goals.
*Blackburn Rov (Signed from Lourdes Celtic
on 5/3/1996) P/FL 131+27/18 FLC 14+1/4
FAC 13+5/2 Others 1*

DUFF Michael James
Born: Belfast, 11 January 1978
Height: 6'1" **Weight:** 11.8
Club Honours: FAT '98; NC '99
International Honours: NI: 1
One of the key success stories of a
remarkable season for Cheltenham Town
last term was the blossoming of Michael
Duff into one of the most highly regarded
young defenders in the lower divisions.
He was moved from his previous roles of
right back or right midfield to the centre
of defence and took to the new position
immediately, combining the art of man-
marking with a growing awareness and
ability to read the game. He also
provided a threat from set pieces and
contributed some important goals. His
reward came with a first full cap for
Northern Ireland against Poland in
February and a place in the PFA Division
Three team of the season.
*Cheltenham T (From trainee on 17/8/1996)
FL 115/10 FLC 3 FAC 9 Others 7*

DUFFIELD Peter
Born: Middlesbrough, 4 February 1969
Height: 5'6" **Weight:** 10.4
Peter had an unfortunate time with
injuries at York City in 2001-02 during
which he suffered a broken leg on two
occasions. In the handful of games he
played mid-term he showed excellent

form, scoring in the wins over Hull City at
Bootham Crescent and at Leyton Orient.
A busy striker who holds the ball up well,
he will be hoping for better fortunes in
2002-03.
*Middlesbrough (From apprentice on
4/11/1986)*
*Sheffield U (Free on 20/8/1987) FL
34+24/14 FLC 3+5/2 FAC 6+2/1 Others 3+2/3*
*Halifax T (Loaned on 7/3/1988) FL 12/6
Others 1*
Rotherham U (Loaned on 7/3/1991) FL 17/4
*Blackpool (Loaned on 23/7/1992) FL 3+2/1
FLC 0+1*
*Crewe Alex (Loaned on 15/1/1993) FL 0+2
FAC 0+1*
*Stockport Co (Loaned on 19/3/1993) FL
6+1/4 Others 2+1*
*Hamilton Ac (Signed on 24/9/1993) SL
69+3/39 SLC 2/1 SC 2 Others 3/3*
*Airdrie (Signed on 21/7/1995) SL 19+5/6 SLC
2+2/2 SC 3/3 Others 1*
*Raith Rov (Signed on 2/3/1996) SL 37+14/11
SLC 2+1/3 SC 2 Others 1+1*
*Morton (Signed on 8/11/1997) SL 25/9 SLC 1
SC 1*
Falkirk (Signed on 27/8/1998) SL 10+7/3
*Darlington (Signed on 15/11/1999) FL
31+16/14 FLC 0+2 FAC 2/1 Others 3*
*York C (Free on 3/7/2000) FL 13+4/6 FLC 1
FAC 0+1*

DUFFY Lee
Born: Oldham, 24 July 1982
Height: 5'7" **Weight:** 10.7
Lee made a tremendous impact in
Rochdale's reserves last season and made
his senior debut as a substitute at Hull. He
went on to make his full debut in the LDV
Vans Trophy and also made the starting
line-up for the Third Division game
against champions-to-be Plymouth, when
he acquitted himself splendidly. A
promising right back with a fierce shot, he
was offered a new two-year contract in
May.
*Rochdale (From trainee on 6/9/2001) FL 1+5
Others 1+1*

DUFFY Richard Michael
Born: Swansea, 30 August 1985
Height: 5'10" **Weight:** 10.4
A first-year scholar at the Vetch Field,
Richard made his debut for Swansea as a
substitute in an FA Cup tie at Macclesfield
in mid-December at the age of 16 years
and 99 days. An assured defender with
the youth team, he has good pace and
distribution. Unfortunately it was
discovered that he had a stress fracture in
his back, and this brought his season to a
premature end.
Swansea C (Trainee) FAC 0+1

Carl Duguid

DUFFY Robert James
Born: Swansea, 2 December 1982
Height: 6'1" **Weight:** 12.6
This young striker made his senior debut
for Rushden in the Worthington Cup
defeat at Crewe Alexandra last
September. A prolific scorer in the club's
reserve and youth sides, he demonstrates
excellent control and uses his height
effectively. He scored a consolation goal in
the 5-1 defeat at Hartlepool in January.
*Rushden & Diamonds (From juniors on
7/7/2000) FL 1+7/1 FLC 0+1 FAC 0+1*

DUGUID Karl Anthony
Born: Letchworth, 21 March 1978
Height: 5'11" **Weight:** 11.7
Karl bounced back from an indifferent
time the previous season to sweep the
board at Colchester United last term,
receiving the 'Home Supporters', 'Away
Supporters' and 'Players' Player of the
Year' awards. He looked more at home in
his new role as a roving right wing back
and attacked well down the flanks,
delivering some fine crosses. Highlights
included scoring a vital goal in the home
draw against Huddersfield, and netting a
last-minute equaliser in the FA Cup replay
at York.
*Colchester U (From trainee on 16/7/1996) FL
156+57/32 FLC 6+3 FAC 7+3/2 Others 3+5*

DUKE David
Born: Inverness, 7 November 1978
Height: 5'10" **Weight:** 11.3
David was a regular member of the
Swindon Town side during 2001-02 when
he showed himself to be a steady, hard-
working player. He showed his versatility,
featuring in both wing-back positions and
also in the centre and on the left-hand
side of midfield. Although not known as a
prolific scorer he netted twice during the
season, the highlight being a fine late
effort at Bury to round off a 3-0 win.
*Sunderland (Free from Redby CA on
3/7/1997)*
*Swindon T (Free on 10/8/2000) FL 60+14/3
FLC 6 FAC 4+2 Others 4*

DUNBAVIN Ian Stuart
Born: Huyton, 27 May 1980
Height: 6'2" **Weight:** 13.0
This young Shrewsbury goalkeeper came
off the bench to replace the injured Mark
Cartwright at Leyton Orient last October
and did so well that he was involved in
every game until the end of the season.
He grasped the opportunity with both
hands making the number one shirt his
own with a string of assured
performances, being particularly

impressive in the December games
against Halifax and Macclesfield when he
produced some vital saves.
Liverpool (From trainee on 26/11/1998)
*Shrewsbury T (Free on 17/1/2000) FL 58+5
FLC 2 FAC 2 Others 1*

DUNCAN Andrew (Andy)
Born: Hexham, 20 October 1977
Height: 5'11" **Weight:** 13.0
International Honours: E: Sch
This experienced central defender
featured fairly regularly for Cambridge
United in 2001-02. He established useful
central defensive partnerships with both
Dean Walling and Adam Tann during the
campaign but was unable to prevent the
U's from being relegated to the Third
Division.
Manchester U (From trainee on 10/7/1996)
*Cambridge U (£20,000 on 9/1/1998) FL
135+5/3 FLC 9+1 FAC 6 Others 12*

DUNN David John Ian
Born: Blackburn, 27 December 1979
Height: 5'10" **Weight:** 12.3
Club Honours: FLC '02
International Honours: E: U21-10; Yth
David's 2001-02 season at Blackburn
started badly with an injury on the
opening day that saw him kept on the
sidelines for two months. He returned
straight into the first team when fit, but
for most of the year alternated between
his preferred role in the centre of
midfield and a wide right role. The
season also saw him start to make the
transition to completeness, using his
natural body strength to tackle and cover
in midfield. He is still not the most
assiduous at tracking back, but
nevertheless he is a man of immense
talent. His goal against Aston Villa,
taking a cross-field pass on the wide
right, cutting in and producing a
thundering left-foot finish, was a classic.
Blackburn Rov (From trainee on 30/9/1997)
P/FL 94+14/22 FLC 12+3/5 FAC 9+2/3

DUNNE Alan James
Born: Dublin, 23 August 1982
Height: 5'10" **Weight:** 12.0
After a long-term injury this young
defender proved what a quality full back
he was last term by getting back to full
fitness and playing in most of Millwall's
reserve games, where he put in some
excellent performances. He was given his
senior debut at right back at Sheffield
United when he showed considerable
potential.
Millwall (From trainee on 17/3/2000) FL 0+1

DUNNE Joseph (Joe) John
Born: Dublin, 25 May 1973
Height: 5'9" **Weight:** 11.6
International Honours: RoI: U21-1; Yth;
Sch
Injuries effectively ruined Joe's 2001-02
season for Colchester. He started with a
bang, scoring the U's first goal of the
campaign in a remarkable 6-3 win at
Chesterfield in the opening game, but a
burst blood vessel in his leg then kept
him on the sidelines. He returned to
action, but in November he damaged
cruciate knee ligaments in the home
match with Bury and was sidelined for
the rest of the season. A tenacious right
back who is renowned for his wholehearted displays, he is a big favourite
with supporters.
*Gillingham (From trainee on 9/8/1990) FL
108+7/1 FLC 7 FAC 5+1 Others 4+2*
*Colchester U (Free on 27/3/1996) FL
79+22/3 FLC 3+1/1 FAC 5+1 Others 7+1
(Free to Dover Ath during 1999 close season)*
*Colchester U (Free on 14/12/1999) FL
56+6/3 FLC 4 FAC 0+2 Others 1*

DUNNE Richard Patrick
Born: Dublin, 21 September 1979
Height: 6'1'' **Weight:** 14.0
Club Honours: FAYC '98, Div 1 '02
International Honours: RoI: 14; B-1;
U21-4; Yth (UEFA-U18 '98); Sch
The solid Manchester City defender was a
regular in the first team last term. He was
a cornerstone of the defence, rarely
putting a foot wrong and if he did, he
seemed able to quickly recover the
situation. He has blossomed under Kevin
Keegan, using the attacking tactics to get
forward and deliver some fine balls into
the box from the flank.
*Everton (From trainee on 8/10/1996) PL
53+7 FLC 4 FAC 8*
*Manchester C (£3,000,000 on 20/10/2000)
P/FL 65+3/1 FLC 3 FAC 6*

DUNNING Darren
Born: Scarborough, 8 January 1981
Height: 5'6" **Weight:** 11.12
Darren again captained Blackburn's
reserve team last term and made only one
senior appearance for Rovers, playing in
the Worthington Cup tie against Oldham
when he scored his first goal for the club.
The young midfielder subsequently had
spells on loan with both Rochdale and
Blackpool to gain further experience of
senior football.
*Blackburn Rov (From trainee on 25/2/1999)
FL 1 FLC 2/1 FAC 1*

Richard Dunne

Bristol C (Loaned on 12/8/2000) FL 9
Rochdale (Loaned on 29/11/2001) FL 4+1
Blackpool (Loaned on 28/3/2002) FL 5

DURKAN Keiron John
Born: Chester, 1 December 1973
Height: 5'11" **Weight:** 12.10
Club Honours: WC '95
International Honours: RoI: U21-3
Keiron took the wide-left midfield
position for Rochdale at the start of the
2001-02 campaign, but then fell out of
favour only to reappear in a more familiar
right-wing role after Tony Ford left.
However he was again left out following
the emergence of Paddy McCourt and
most of his appearances in the second
half of the season came from the
substitutes' bench. He is an experienced
winger capable of beating defenders and
delivering quality crosses.
Wrexham (From trainee on 16/7/1992) FL
43+7/3 FLC 3+1 FAC 4+2/2 Others 15/1
Stockport Co (£95,000 on 16/2/1996) FL
52+12/4 FLC 10+1 FAC 4/3 Others 4+2
Macclesfield T (£15,000 on 25/3/1998) FL
92+11/13 FLC 4+3 FAC 2+3 Others 1+1
York C (Loaned on 5/10/2000) FL 7
Rochdale (Free on 4/7/2001) FL 16+14/1 FLC
2 FAC 3 Others 1

DURNIN John Paul
Born: Bootle, 18 August 1965
Height: 5'10" **Weight:** 12.3
This experienced midfield player began
the 2001-02 campaign with League of
Wales club Rhyl before signing for Port
Vale in December. He soon settled in,
despite being the oldest player in the
team by over ten years, and his ability to
pass the ball well engineered the club's
rise up the league table from relegation
candidates to the top half. John scored
one goal, a wind assisted free-kick
against Wycombe, before being released
in April.
Liverpool (Free from Waterloo Dock on
29/3/1986) FLC 1+1
West Bromwich A (Loaned on 20/10/1988)
FL 5/2
Oxford U (£225,000 on 10/2/1989) FL
140+21/44 FLC 7/1 FAC 7/1 Others 4+1/1
Portsmouth (£200,000 on 15/7/1993) FL
118+63/31 FLC 14+3/2 FAC 5+2 Others 4+2
Blackpool (Loaned on 1/11/1999) FL 4+1/1
FAC 1/1
Carlisle U (Free on 3/12/1999) FL 20+2/2
Others 1
Kidderminster Hrs (Free on 13/10/2000) FL
28+3/9 FAC 1 (Released during 2001 close
season)
Port Vale (Free from Rhyl on 14/12/2001) FL
18+1/1

DUXBURY Lee Edward
Born: Keighley, 7 October 1969
Height: 5'10" **Weight:** 11.13
Although officially club captain, Lee
found himself in and out of Oldham's
first team in late 2001-02. The 32-year-
old midfielder lost the armband to new
signing Matty Appleby and found
himself restricted to the substitutes'
bench on several occasions. A tenacious
midfielder with an impressive goal-
scoring record, Lee has made over 200
appearances for Athletic and will look
to reaffirm his first-team place in 2002-
03. However, much will depend on
how he fits into the plans of new
manager Iain Dowie.
Bradford C (From trainee on 4/7/1988) FL
204+5/25 FLC 18+1/3 FAC 11 Others 13
Rochdale (Loaned on 18/1/1990) FL 9+1
FAC 1
Huddersfield T (£250,000 on 23/12/1994)
FL 29/2 FLC 1 Others 3
Bradford C (£135,000 on 15/11/1995) FL
63/7 FLC 2 FAC 5 Others 3
Oldham Ath (£350,000 on 7/3/1997) FL
206+8/28 FLC 11/1 FAC 16/5 Others 5/1

DYCHE Sean Mark
Born: Kettering, 28 June 1971
Height: 6'0" **Weight:** 13.10
Club Honours: Div 2 '01
Sean formed an excellent partnership with
Stuart Nethercott in the centre of defence
for Millwall last term, which was one of
the main reasons for the club's fine
defensive record. An experienced
defender who reads the game well, he is
at ease with either foot and is a true
professional. He missed a few games last
season with niggling injuries but was
always the first choice to partner
Nethercott.
Nottingham F (From trainee on 20/5/1989)
Chesterfield (Free on 1/2/1990) FL 219+12/8
FLC 9 FAC 13/1 Others 16
Bristol C (£350,000 on 11/7/1997) FL 14+3
FLC 2+1
Luton T (Loaned on 4/1/1999) FL 14/1
Others 1
Millwall (£150,000 on 5/7/1999) FL 69/3 FLC
2+1 FAC 4

DYER Bruce Antonio
Born: Ilford, 13 April 1975
Height: 6'0" **Weight:** 11.3
International Honours: E: U21-11
Bruce took on the mantle of Barnsley's
main striker with relish after the
transfer in the summer of Neil
Shipperley and deservedly finished the
campaign with the club's 'Player of the

Season' award. He always gave 100 per
cent and his 18-goal haul was a
justification of the skill, ability and total
commitment that he showed in what
was a poor season for the club. The
two goals he scored against West Brom
at Oakwell were particularly memorable.
A 25-yard volley and then a cool finish
having run through from the half-way
line.
Watford (From trainee on 19/4/1993) FL
29+2/6 FLC 4/2 FAC 1 Others 2/1
Crystal Palace (£1,100,000 on 10/3/1994)
F/PL 95+40/37 FLC 9+5/1 FAC 7+3/6 Others
3+2
Barnsley (£700,000 on 23/10/1998) FL
110+32/42 FLC 10+1/4 FAC 4+2/2 Others
2+1/3

DYER Kieron Courtney
Born: Ipswich, 29 December 1978
Height: 5'7" **Weight:** 9.7
International Honours: E: 12; B-2; U21-
11; Yth
This talented and versatile Newcastle
midfield player spent the summer of 2001
recovering from a bone graft operation in
which he had a pin inserted in his leg.
However, during pre-season training he
suffered a muscle reaction in the calf
surrounding the bone, which required
surgery and it was December before he
appeared in the first team. He soon
returned to the starting line-up and
performed as if he had been playing all
season, showing terrific energy, an
impressive change of pace, and tight
control of the ball while moving at speed.
Unfortunately in January he suffered a
stress fracture in his left foot and was
sidelined for another two and a half
months.
Ipswich T (From trainee on 3/1/1997) FL
79+12/9 FLC 11/1 FAC 5 Others 5+1/2
Newcastle U (£6,000,000 on 16/7/1999) PL
67+11/11 FLC 4+1/1 FAC 8+1/1 Others 3

DYSON Jonathan (Jon) Paul
Born: Mirfield, 18 December 1971
Height: 6'1" **Weight:** 12.12
This long-serving Huddersfield Town
defender was hampered by a back
injury throughout the 2001-02
campaign and made just a single first-
team appearance in the FA Cup tie at
Mansfield. When fully fit he is an
assured centre half who is strong in the
tackle and distributes the ball
accurately.
Huddersfield T (From juniors on
29/12/1990) FL 182+31/9 FLC 17+4 FAC 11
Others 7+4

Robbie Earnshaw

E

EADEN Nicholas (Nicky) Jeremy
Born: Sheffield, 12 December 1972
Height: 5'9" **Weight:** 12.8
Nicky was a regular in midfield for Birmingham during the early part of last season under Trevor Francis. He worked the right flank unselfishly and delivered pin-point passes and crosses, hardly wasting a ball. He was also used on the odd occasion at right back. However, when new manager Steve Bruce took over he found his chances limited and was only ever on the fringes of the squad.
Barnsley (From juniors on 4/6/1991) F/PL 281+12/10 FLC 18+3/3 FAC 20 Others 4+1
Birmingham C (Free on 6/7/2000) FL 68+6/3 FLC 13/1 FAC 1 Others 1+1/1

EARNSHAW Robert (Robbie)
Born: Zambia, 6 April 1981
Height: 5'8" **Weight:** 10.10
International Honours: W: 1; U21-10; Yth
Robbie had a somewhat frustrating time with injuries at Cardiff last term, but still finished the season with a respectable tally of 15 goals in all competitions. He faced calls from his new boss Lennie Lawrence to alter his celebrations after scoring for fear of injury – his customary elaborate routine begins with a somersault. Undoubtedly the highlight of his campaign came on his senior debut for Wales against Germany at the Millenium Stadium, when he produced an outstanding display and scored the winner.
Cardiff C (From trainee on 4/8/1998) FL 54+28/32 FLC 1+2/1 FAC 7+1/8 Others 2+1/1
Greenock Morton (Loaned on 20/1/2000) SL 3/2 SC 1

EASTER Jermaine Maurice
Born: Cardiff, 15 January 1982
Height: 5'8" **Weight:** 12.4
International Honours: W: Yth
2001-02 proved to be a frustrating season for this young Hartlepool prospect who was expected to make his big breakthrough. The campaign began well with him being named in the Wales Under-21 squad, but he then seemed to lose his appetite for the game. He was restricted to substitute appearances, but at least had the satisfaction of opening his goal-scoring account. He is a promising striker with a fine turn of speed.

Wolverhampton W (From trainee on 6/7/2000)
Hartlepool U (Free on 17/3/2001) FL 0+16/2 Others 0+2

EASTON Clint Jude
Born: Barking, 1 October 1977
Height: 5'11" **Weight:** 10.8
Club Honours: Div 2 '98
International Honours: E: Yth
Clint is a left-sided midfield player who joined Norwich in the 2001 close season and only figured peripherally until the latter stages of the campaign when he won a regular place in Nigel Worthington's line-up. A skilful player with good passing skills, he has the potential to develop in a more central role. He scored a vital goal in the home match against Gillingham and offered a real goal threat from that position often coming in unnoticed at the far post.
Watford (From trainee on 5/7/1996) P/FL 50+14/1 FLC 4+4/1 FAC 3+1 Others 3
Norwich C (£200,000 on 19/6/2001) FL 10+4/1 FAC 0+1 Others 3

EATON Adam Paul
Born: Wigan, 2 May 1980
Height: 5'11" **Weight:** 11.2
Club Honours: FAYC '98
A sound left back, Adam continued to make steady progress with Preston. His first full game came in the Worthington Cup win at Kidderminster, and he later appeared as a substitute on several occasions before replacing the injured Rob Edwards in January. Adam is a firm favourite with the fans for his steady play and his willingness to join the attack, and he was unlucky not to score his first senior goal for the club on a few occasions. A regular place in the line-up for the promising youngster cannot be far away.
Everton (From trainee on 2/6/1997)
Preston NE (Free on 29/6/1999) FL 7+6 FLC 1 FAC 1 Others 0+1

EBDON Marcus
Born: Pontypool, 17 October 1970
Height: 5'10" **Weight:** 12.4
International Honours: W: U21-2; Yth
Marcus again looked like Chesterfield's most creative midfielder last season. Another Spireite to suffer from hernia problems, Marcus missed most of December and January. He was best used when given a central role, with a ball-winner playing around him. He later returned from injury to link well with Martyn Booty and new signing Mark Innes as the central unit of a midfield five.

Everton (From trainee on 16/8/1989)
Peterborough U (Free on 15/7/1991) FL 136+11/15 FLC 14+2 FAC 12+3/1 Others 11+1
Chesterfield (£100,000 on 21/3/1997) FL 159+9/9 FLC 10+1/1 FAC 7 Others 7/3

EDDS Gareth James
Born: Sydney, Australia, 3 February 1981
Height: 5'11" **Weight:** 10.12
International Honours: Australia: Yth
Gareth was out of the first-team picture at Nottingham Forest last season and managed just a single appearance from the subs' bench. A versatile player who can feature at full back or in midfield, he is strong in the tackle and possesses a fierce shot. He was released at the end of the season after being told his contract was not being renewed.
Nottingham F (From trainee on 19/2/1998) FL 11+5/1 FAC 1

EDGE Roland
Born: Gillingham, 25 November 1978
Height: 5'9" **Weight:** 11.6
Although he started 2001-02 as the regular left back, Roland missed most of the season for Gillingham with hamstring problems. It did not help being dismissed twice during the campaign and although he made a comeback in March, he then went down with a sciatic nerve complaint. When fit he always added a different dimension down the left-hand side of the park.
Gillingham (From trainee on 10/7/1997) FL 59+9/1 FLC 5 FAC 10+1 Others 5

EDGHILL Richard Arlon
Born: Oldham, 23 September 1974
Height: 5'9" **Weight:** 11.5
International Honours: E: B-1; U21-3
Once captain of Manchester City, Richard found it difficult to win a regular place in the line-up last term. After eventually forcing his way in to the line-up he tore the medial ligaments in his left knee and it was not until December that he returned to first-team action once more. He rarely featured after Christmas and a ten-year association with the Maine Road club ended when he was released in the summer.
Manchester C (From trainee on 15/7/1992) P/FL 178+3/1 FLC 17 FAC 8+1 Others 3
Birmingham C (Loaned on 14/11/2000) FL 3

EDINBURGH Justin Charles
Born: Basildon, 18 December 1969
Height: 5'10" **Weight:** 12.0
Club Honours: FAC '91; FLC '99
This tenacious defender scored his first

Andy Edwards

goal in ten years last season to earn Portsmouth a valuable 1-0 home win over Sheffield United. He was hampered by achilles and calf muscle injuries throughout the campaign and eventually accepted medical advice and announced his retirement.

Southend U (From trainee on 5/8/1988) FL 36+1 FLC 2+1 FAC 2 Others 4+1/1
Tottenham H (£150,000 on 30/7/1990) F/PL 190+23/1 FLC 25+4 FAC 27+1 Others 4+2
Portsmouth (£175,000 on 6/3/2000) FL 34+1/1 FLC 3

EDMONDSON Darren Stephen
Born: Coniston, 4 November 1971
Height: 6'0" **Weight:** 12.11
Club Honours: Div 3 '95; AMC '97
This hard tackling and fully committed right back had an excellent season in York City's defence during 2001-02. He always looked strong pushing forward from a wing-back position and linked up well with midfield to become a vital cog in the Minstermen's team.

Carlisle U (From trainee on 17/7/1990) FL 205+9/9 FLC 15/1 FAC 15/3 Others 22/3
Huddersfield T (£200,000 + on 3/3/1997) FL 28+9 FLC 2 FAC 2+2
Plymouth Arg (Loaned on 11/9/1998) FL 4
York C (Free on 23/3/2000) FL 63+3 FLC 3 FAC 7

[EDU] EDUARDO Cesar Gaspar
Born: Sao Paulo, Brazil, 15 May 1978
Height: 6'1" **Weight:** 11.4
Club Honours: FAC '02; PL '02
This skilful Arsenal midfielder had another frustrating time at Highbury in 2001-02 when he again failed to win a regular place in the starting line-up. However, his season finished on a high when he came on as a substitute in the closing stages of the FA Cup final victory over Chelsea. He thus became the first Brazilian to gain an FA Cup winners' medal.

Arsenal (£6,000,000 from Corinthians, Brazil on 18/1/2001) PL 10+9/1 FLC 3/1 FAC 4+1/1 Others 2+3

EDWARDS Andrew (Andy) David
Born: Epping, 17 September 1971
Height: 6'3" **Weight:** 12.10
Andy had another fine season as captain of Peterborough last term, and has now moved into the top-ten all-time appearance list for Posh. He rarely missed a game and also contributed a couple of invaluable goals. He is a commanding central defender who is strong in the tackle and comfortable on the ball.

Southend U (From trainee on 14/12/1989) FL 141+6/5 FLC 5 FAC 4 Others 9/2
Birmingham C (£400,000 on 6/7/1995) FL 37+3/1 FLC 12/1 FAC 2 Others 5/1
Peterborough U (Signed on 29/11/1996) FL 243/9 FLC 12 FAC 20/1 Others 16/1

EDWARDS Akenhaton Carlos
Born: Port of Spain, Trinidad, 24 October 1978
Height: 5'11" **Weight:** 11.9
International Honours: Trinidad & Tobago: 15
Carlos continued to be somewhat enigmatic at Wrexham last term. A talented wide-right midfield player, he can unsettle the best of defences with his darting runs down the flank, although he has a tendency to overdo things. After commencing the season in the starting line-up he was confined to the bench for much of the campaign. He scored a fine goal on the volley from far out against Colchester United at the end of August but needs to find greater consistency. He was used as a wing back in the closing matches and looked impressive in this new role.

Wrexham (£125,000 from Defence Force, Trinidad on 8/8/2000) FL 41+21/9 FLC 1+2 FAC 1

EDWARDS Christian (Chris) Nicholas Howells
Born: Caerphilly, 23 November 1975
Height: 6'2" **Weight:** 12.8
International Honours: W: 1; B-2; U21-7
After being a regular for Nottingham Forest the previous season, this Welsh international centre back hardly got a look in during 2001-02, making just three full senior appearances. He joined Crystal Palace on loan in November with a view to a permanent move and did well in a two-month spell at Selhurst Park, but the deal fell through and he returned to the City Ground. He is a big no-nonsense defender who is good in the air and brave in the tackle.

Swansea C (From trainee on 20/7/1994) FL 113+2/4 FLC 5 FAC 9+1
Nottingham F (£175,000 + on 26/3/1998) P/FL 44+10/3 FLC 1 FAC 1
Bristol C (Loaned on 11/12/1998) FL 3
Oxford U (Loaned on 24/2/2000) FL 5/1
Crystal Palace (Loaned on 16/11/2001) FL 9

EDWARDS Michael
Born: Hessle, 25 April 1980
Height: 6'1" **Weight:** 12.0
The modest, unassuming defender is probably the first name on Hull's team sheet as Michael has barely missed a game since the end of 1998. Being a local

lad, he is also widely appreciated by the Tigers' faithful. Fully capable of playing central defence and strong on either foot, he was employed in both full back berths in 2001-02 – mainly on the right. His consistent displays earned him third place in the Tigers' 'Player of the Year' awards.

Hull C (From trainee on 16/7/1998) FL 162+10/6 FLC 8+1 FAC 11/2 Others 9+1

EDWARDS Nathan Mark
Born: Lincoln, 8 April 1983
Height: 5'11" **Weight:** 12.10
This second-year trainee made his League debut for Swindon as a substitute against Cardiff last October and started an LDV Vans Trophy tie at Colchester two days later. Thereafter he began to appear on the bench with increasing regularity, before making his first League start at the Britannia Stadium in April. Nathan usually takes a holding midfield role and signed a 12-month professional contract at the end of the season.

Swindon T (Trainee) FL 2+5 Others 1

EDWARDS Neil Ryan
Born: Aberdare, 5 December 1970
Height: 5'9" **Weight:** 11.10
International Honours: W: U21-1; Yth; Sch
Rochdale's club captain and goalkeeper was expected to be a key figure during the 2001-02 campaign but he injured a knee early on in the season. His absence stretched from weeks into months and apart from an attempted comeback in November his appearances were restricted to the last four league games and the play-offs, when he demonstrated all his old shot-stopping skills.

Leeds U (From trainee on 10/3/1989) Others 1
Stockport Co (£5,000 on 3/9/1991) FL 163+1 FLC 11 FAC 11 Others 31
Rochdale (£25,000 on 3/11/1997) FL 163 FLC 7 FAC 9+1 Others 11

EDWARDS Paul
Born: Manchester, 1 January 1980
Height: 5'11" **Weight:** 10.12
Paul had a trial with Conference club Leigh RMI during the 2001 close season before joining Swindon Town on a 12-month contract last August. An attacking left wing back who likes to run at defenders, he made his Town debut as a substitute in the 2-2 draw at home to Tranmere in September and followed this up with a series of star performances. A knee injury curtailed his progress and he was just coming back into form when a bizarre collision with goalkeeper Bart Griemink put him out of action until the end of February. His future at the County

Ground was unclear at the time of writing.
***Doncaster Rov** (Free from Ashton U on 2/2/1998) FL 5+4 (Released during 1998 close season)*
***Swindon T** (Free from Altrincham, ex Knutsford T, on 17/8/2001) FL 14+6 FLC 0+1 FAC 1/1 Others 1*

EDWARDS Robert (Rob)
Born: Manchester, 23 February 1970
Height: 5'9" **Weight:** 12.4
Rob struggled a little to match the faster pace of Second Division football last term and often came into midfield when Chesterfield employed a back three. After Nicky Law's departure, new manager Dave Rushbury used him up front, where he had performed with distinction for Crewe, and he began playing some of his best football of the season. However a double hernia then became too much, and he was forced to sit out all but the last match of the campaign.
***Crewe Alex** (From trainee on 11/7/1988) FL 110+45/44 FLC 8/5 FAC 13+5/5 Others 9+8/4*
***Huddersfield T** (£150,000 on 8/3/1996) FL 109+29/14 FLC 12+1/1 FAC 7+1/1*
***Chesterfield** (£20,000 on 8/9/2000) FL 64+1/5 FLC 2 FAC 4 Others 7*

EDWARDS Robert (Rob)
William
Born: Kendal, 1 July 1973
Height: 6'0" **Weight:** 12.2
Club Honours: Div 2 '00
International Honours: W: 4; B-2; U21-17; Yth
Another consistent season saw Preston's left back receive a call up for Wales in August 2001, only to miss out due to injury. He is effective both as a defender and when overlapping down the flank to help out with the attack. His first goal for 18 months proved to be the winner at Birmingham, and he also scored in the very next match before a broken rib and punctured lung put him out for five games at the turn of the year. He later showed his versatility by playing as an emergency centre half on several occasions, and even filled in effectively at right back against West Bromwich Albion.
***Carlisle U** (From trainee on 10/4/1990) FL 48/5 FLC 4 FAC 1 Others 2+1*
***Bristol C** (£135,000 on 27/3/1991) FL 188+28/5 FLC 16+3/1 FAC 13+2 Others 12+1/2*
***Preston NE** (Free on 5/8/1999) FL 114+5/4 FLC 10 FAC 9 Others 5/1*

EDWORTHY Marc
Born: Barnstaple, 24 December 1972
Height: 5'8" **Weight:** 11.10

After being out of favour with the old regime Marc was recalled to the Coventry City first team under Roland Nilsson, firstly as a left back before switching to his preferred right-back position. Unquestionably the best right back at the club, he displayed his overlapping talents and man-marking ability with several steady performances during City's strong pre-Christmas run. A knee operation in January virtually ended his season although he appeared in the final game at Burnley. He was out of contract in the summer and was not expected to stay at Highfield Road.
***Plymouth Arg** (From trainee on 30/3/1991) FL 52+17/1 FLC 5+2 FAC 5+2 Others 2+2*
***Crystal Palace** (£350,000 on 9/6/1995) F/PL 120+6 FLC 8+1/1 FAC 8 Others 8*
***Coventry C** (£850,000 + on 28/8/1998) P/FL 62+14/1 FLC 5 FAC 4*

EHIOGU Ugochuku (Ugo)
Born: Hackney, 3 November 1972
Height: 6'2" **Weight:** 14.10
Club Honours: FLC '96
International Honours: E: 4; B-1; U21-15
Middlesbrough's powerful central defender had a useful season last term. The high point was undoubtedly adding a further two caps for England in the friendly fixtures against Holland and Italy. Despite being hampered by a niggling groin injury he appeared regularly for Boro' during the campaign.
***West Bromwich A** (From trainee on 13/7/1989) FL 0+2*
***Aston Villa** (£40,000 on 12/7/1991) F/PL 223+14/12 FLC 23+1/1 FAC 22+2/1 Others 18/1*
***Middlesbrough** (£8,000,000 on 20/10/2000) PL 50/4 FLC 2 FAC 5/1*

EKOKU Efangwu (Efan)
Goziem
Born: Manchester, 8 June 1967
Height: 6'2" **Weight:** 12.0
International Honours: Nigeria:
Efan had a reasonable campaign for Sheffield Wednesday in 2001-02, despite playing in a struggling side, never an easy situation for a striker. A leg injury just into the season saw him miss about a dozen matches. He has never really looked the bustling centre forward he could be, but continued to score a decent ratio of goals per game.
***Bournemouth** (£100,000 from Sutton U on 11/5/1990) FL 43+19/21 FLC 0+2 FAC 5+2/2 Others 3+1/2*
***Norwich C** (£500,000 on 26/3/1993) PL

26+11/15 FLC 3/1 FAC 1+1 Others 3/1
***Wimbledon** (£900,000 on 14/10/1994) PL 102+21/37 FLC 11+2/4 FAC 16+1/3 (£500,000 to Grasshopper Zurich, Switzerland on 27/8/99)*
***Sheffield Wed** (Free on 20/10/2000) FL 52+7/14 FLC 8+1/7 FAC 2+1*

EL KHALEJ Tahar
Born: Morocco, 16 June 1968
Height: 6'3" **Weight:** 13.8
International Honours: Morocco
Tahar figured regularly in defence for Southampton after the departure of Dean Richards but then injury and the arrival of Paul Williams limited his opportunities. He subsequently replaced the injured Claus Lundekvam and gave some faultless displays. Never frightened to go where the feet are, his brave efforts and steady play make him an important member of Gordon Strachan's side.
***Southampton** (£300,000 from Benfica, Portugal, ex KAC Marrakesh, Uniao Leiria, on 10/3/2000) PL 48+9/3 FLC 2+3/1 FAC 1+1*

ELLINGTON Nathan Levi
Fontaine
Born: Bradford, 2 July 1981
Height: 5'10" **Weight:** 12.10
This talented striker started the 2001-02 season scoring regularly for Bristol Rovers before being sidelined with an ankle injury. He returned to net a superb hat-trick, which knocked Derby County out of the FA Cup at Pride Park. He added further trebles against Leyton Orient and Swansea and it was no real surprise when he became Wigan Athletic's first million pound signing on transfer deadline day. Despite his move he won a place in the PFA Third Division team for the season.
***Bristol Rov** (£150,000 from Walton & Hersham on 18/2/1999) FL 76+40/35 FLC 7/2 FAC 6+1/4 Others 6+1/3*
***Wigan Ath** (£750,000 + on 28/3/2002) FL 3/2*

ELLIOTT Matthew (Matt)
Stephen
Born: Wandsworth, 1 November 1968
Height: 6'3" **Weight:** 14.10
Club Honours: FLC '00
International Honours: S: 18
A right-footed central defender and Leicester City's club captain, Matt had something of a mixed season last term, starting in below-par fashion before finding his best form shortly after Dave Bassett took over. Conceding a penalty at home to West Ham in December, the

aftermath of which led to a red card, seemed to knock his confidence and his form again suffered as the Foxes generally struggled during the second half of the campaign. Unusually, Matt's goal supply also dried up and this was another factor in Leicester's decline last season. He added three caps to his Scottish total before being omitted from Berti Vogts younger-looking squad in March.

Charlton Ath (£5,000 from Epsom & Ewell on 9/5/1988) FLC 1
Torquay U (£10,000 on 23/3/1989) FL 123+1/15 FLC 9/2 FAC 9/2 Others 16/1
Scunthorpe U (£50,000 on 26/3/1992) FL 61/8 FLC 6 FAC 2 Others 8
Oxford U (£150,000 on 5/11/1993) FL 148/21 FLC 16/1 FAC 11/2 Others 6
Leicester C (£1,600,000 on 18/1/1997) PL 192/22 FLC 17+1/3 FAC 16/2 Others 4

ELLIOTT Robert (Robbie) James

Born: Newcastle, 25 December 1973
Height: 5'10" **Weight:** 11.6
International Honours: E: U21-2; Yth
Local boy Robbie rejoined his hometown club Newcastle in the summer of 2001 on a 'Bosman' style free transfer, and immediately established himself at left

back in the team. Confident and strong in the tackle he found time to supplement his attack when the occasion warranted, scoring the equaliser in the 4-4 draw in the Inter Toto Cup final home leg, and the vital goal at Leeds which sparked a revival as United turned a 3-1 deficit into a 4-3 victory. He was disappointed to lose his place for the visit of his former club Bolton in February and the form of Sylvain Distin kept him on the bench for much of the remainder of the season.

Newcastle U (From trainee on 3/4/1991) F/PL 71+8/9 FLC 5 FAC 7+3 Others 5+1
Bolton W (£2,500,000 + on 2/7/1997) P/FL 71+15/5 FLC 4+2/2 FAC 5 Others 5+2
Newcastle U (Free on 11/7/2001) PL 26+1/1 FLC 2+1 FAC 3+1 Others 6/1

ELLIOTT Steven (Steve) William

Born: Swadlincote, 29 October 1978
Height: 6'1" **Weight:** 14.0
International Honours: E: U21-2
This young Derby County central defender made just two Premiership starts last term, although he also appeared on the bench on a number of occasions. A player who is strong in the tackle and has good

distribution skills, he will be looking to become a regular in the line-up in 2002-03.

Derby Co (From trainee on 26/3/1997) PL 35+11 FLC 7+1 FAC 2+2

ELLIOTT Stuart Thomas

Born: Willesden, 27 August 1977
Height: 5'9" **Weight:** 12.0
This much-travelled midfielder was one of several players to sign short-term deals for Carlisle United at the start of last season. Despite some impressive contributions, notably against his former club Darlington, he was not kept on at the end of his one-month contract. He later featured for Durham City and Scarborough before joining Exeter City on non-contract forms in the new year. His only appearance for the Grecians came when he played the final 12 minutes of the game against Macclesfield and he was released soon afterwards.

Newcastle U (From trainee on 28/8/1995)
Hull C (Loaned on 28/2/1997) FL 3
Swindon T (Loaned on 20/2/1998) FL 1+1
Gillingham (Loaned on 23/10/1998) FL 4+1
Hartlepool U (Loaned on 29/1/1999) FL 5
Wrexham (Loaned on 22/3/1999) FL 8+1 Others 1

Nathan Ellington

Bournemouth *(Loaned on 3/12/1999) FL 6+2*
Stockport Co *(Loaned on 25/2/2000) FL 4+1*
Darlington *(Free on 21/7/2000) FL 20+4 FLC 3+1/3 FAC 1+1 Others 3/1*
Plymouth Arg *(Free on 7/3/2001) FL 11+1*
Carlisle U *(Free on 16/8/2001) FL 6 FLC 1*
Exeter C *(Free on 1/2/2002) FL 0+1*

ELLIOTT Wade Patrick
Born: Eastleigh, 14 December 1978
Height: 5'9" **Weight:** 11.1
International Honours: E: Sch
Wade's second full season as a professional for Bournemouth proved to be more difficult than the first and a dip in form saw him relegated to the substitutes' bench on occasions. He still weighed in with eight goals including three that were candidates for 'Goal of the Season'. He showed great character after missing a vital last-minute penalty at Reading to net two more from the spot after that and will be hoping for success in Division Three in the coming season.
Bournemouth *(£5,000 from Bashley on 4/2/2000) FL 73+21/20 FLC 1+1 FAC 5/2 Others 1+1*

ELLIS Anthony (Tony) Joseph
Born: Salford, 20 October 1964
Height: 5'11" **Weight:** 11.0
It was a surprise when this veteran striker signed for Burnley in the summer of 2001, and there were certainly more than a few sceptics among the supporters. They were silenced early on in the campaign, though, when Tony scored a stunning late winner at Bradford City, turning and shooting to give the Clarets three points that took them to the top of the First Division. He left Turf Moor at the end of the season to play in Australia.
Oldham Ath *(Free from Horwich RMI on 22/8/1986) FL 5+3 FLC 1 Others 1*
Preston NE *(£23,000 on 16/10/1987) FL 80+6/26 FLC 3 FAC 5 Others 11+1/5*
Stoke C *(£250,000 on 20/12/1989) FL 66+11/19 FLC 5+1/1 FAC 1+4 Others 3+2*
Preston NE *(£140,000 on 14/8/1992) FL 70+2/48 FLC 4/2 FAC 6/3 Others 6/3*
Blackpool *(£165,000 on 25/7/1994) FL 140+6/54 FLC 10+1/6 FAC 7/1 Others 8/3*
Bury *(£75,000 on 12/12/1997) FL 24+14/8 FLC 2+2*
Stockport Co *(£25,000 on 3/2/1999) FL 17+3/6 FLC 1+1*
Rochdale *(Free on 1/11/1999) FL 55+4/17 FLC 1/1 FAC 1+1 Others 5+1*
Burnley *(Free on 20/7/2001) FL 0+11 FLC 1*

ELLISON Kevin
Born: Liverpool, 23 February 1979
Height: 6'1" **Weight:** 12.8

This competitive left-sided midfielder was one of the first signings made for Stockport County by new manager Carlton Palmer, arriving initially on loan from Premiership outfit Leicester City in early December before he made the move permanently. Although his appearances were restricted due to a niggling hamstring injury, his powerful displays down the left touchline showed plenty of promise for the coming campaign.
Leicester C *(£50,000 + from Altrincham on 13/2/2001) FL 0+1*
Stockport Co *(£55,000 on 30/11/2001) FL 6+5 FAC 1*

EMANUEL Lewis James
Born: Bradford, 14 October 1983
Height: 5'8" **Weight:** 11.12
Lewis made his first-team debut for Bradford City in the Worthington Cup tie against Macclesfield last August and played his first League game against Grimsby the following month. He then made sporadic appearances during the season and was also selected for the England U19 squad. He usually featured at right back but occasionally played on the right-hand side of midfield.
Bradford C *(From trainee on 5/7/2001) FL 8+1 FLC 2 FAC 0+1*

EMBERSON Carl Wayne
Born: Epsom, 13 July 1973
Height: 6'2" **Weight:** 14.7
Club Honours: FAYC '91
Carl joined Luton Town as their back-up 'keeper in the 2001 close season but found himself making his debut at the start of the campaign. A reliable shot stopper with a good command of his area, he went on to make the first-team place his own in the new year with a series of fine performances.
Millwall *(From trainee on 4/5/1991) Others 1*
Colchester U *(Loaned on 17/12/1992) FL 13*
Colchester U *(£25,000 on 6/7/1994) FL 178+1 FLC 9 FAC 8 Others 16*
Walsall *(Free on 28/6/1999) FL 6+2 FLC 1 Others 2*
Luton T *(Free on 13/7/2001) FL 33 FLC 1 FAC 1*

EMBLEN Neil Robert
Born: Bromley, 19 June 1971
Height: 6'1" **Weight:** 13.11
The 2001-02 season was a major disappointment for Neil, who signed for Norwich in the 2001 close season. This experienced utility player, who has played regularly in midfield, defence and attack for his previous clubs, was brought in to give some real strength to the City midfield and performed well in pre-

season, so much so that he was soon appointed club captain. However, a persistent and niggling hamstring injury, sustained less than 35 minutes into his first-day debut at Millwall, totally disrupted his campaign. Neil made just one more solitary substitute appearance, in late September, before being ruled out for the rest of the season.
Millwall *(£175,000 from Sittingbourne on 8/11/1993) FL 12 Others 1*
Wolverhampton W *(£600,000 on 14/7/1994) FL 80+8/9 FLC 2+2/1 FAC 7+2 Others 2+1*
Crystal Palace *(£2,000,000 on 21/8/1997) PL 8+5 FAC 1+1/2*
Wolverhampton W *(£900,000 on 26/3/1998) FL 102+12/7 FLC 8+1/1 FAC 6+1*
Norwich C *(£500,000 + on 12/7/2001) FL 1+1*

EMBLEN Paul David
Born: Bromley, 3 April 1976
Height: 5'11" **Weight:** 12.5
This Wycombe midfielder/striker started in the opening home game of last season against Wrexham and scored an opportunistic goal. It was a triumphant return after missing the previous 21 months with serious injuries. Although he gave an impressive performance he was unable to hold down a place in the line-up, starting just eight games. His strengths are his great stamina and two good feet and, although not a natural goal-scorer, his high work rate often earned him a forward role. He was released towards the end of the campaign more due to economic reasons in the wake of the financial crisis affecting the game.
Charlton Ath *(£7,500 + from Tonbridge on 16/5/1997) FL 0+4*
Brighton & Hove A *(Loaned on 4/11/1997) FL 15/4*
Wycombe W *(£60,000 on 28/8/1998) FL 45+18/3 FLC 4+3 FAC 3+5 Others 3/1*

EMMERSON Scott
Born: Durham, 10 October 1982
Height: 5'9" **Weight:** 12.7
This young striker had an unlucky time with injuries last season and was unable to establish himself in the York City attack. He managed just seven first-team appearances, all from the subs' bench, before being released in the summer.
York C *(Trainee) FL 3+11/1 FLC 0+1*

ENCKELMAN Peter
Born: Turku, Finland, 10 March 1977
Height: 6'2" **Weight:** 12.5
International Honours: Finland: 3; U21

Peter was once again the second choice 'keeper for Aston Villa last term. He made his first Premiership appearance of the season against West Ham in December when he saved a penalty, then a shoulder injury to Peter Schmeichel enabled him to start three games at the end of January. Always reliable when called upon, he received a ray of hope that he might possibly see regular first-team action in 2002-03 following Schmeichel's decision to join Manchester City.
Aston Villa (£200,000 from TPS Turku, Finland on 1/2/1999) PL 18+1 FLC 3 FAC 1 Others 4+1

ERIBENNE Chukwunyeaka (Chukki) Osondu
Born: Westminster, 2 November 1980
Height: 5'10" **Weight:** 11.12
Chukki made the starting line-up for Bournemouth at the beginning of the 2001-02 campaign, but without a goal his confidence and belief soon ebbed away. He showed far more to his game though with his strong, bustling style, which unsettled defences. He is a powerful young striker who generally featured from the subs' bench during the season.
Coventry C (From trainee on 19/1/1998)
Bournemouth (Free on 4/7/2000) FL 12+29/1 FLC 2 FAC 0+3 Others 2+1

ESPARTERO Mario
Born: Frejus, France, 17 January 1978
Height: 5'6" **Weight:** 11.1
This tough-tackling midfielder joined Bolton last February in a loan deal covering the rest of the season. He made his debut as a substitute in the home game against Southampton, and went on to make just two more appearances from the bench before he left the Reebok.
Bolton W (Loaned from Metz, France, ex Louhans-Cuiseaux, on 22/2/2002) PL 0+3

ETHERINGTON Matthew
Born: Truro, 14 August 1981
Height: 5'10" **Weight:** 11.2
International Honours: E: U21-2; Yth
Cameo appearances for this youthful forward last season allowed Matthew the opportunity to gain vital experience at the top level which will bode well for him in Spurs longer term plans. He looks comfortable on the ball and quick, although he managed just one FA Cup goal. In October he went on loan to Bradford City where he impressed with some fast and skilful wing play. He scored on his debut against Watford and

received 'Man of the Match' awards on six separate occasions.
Peterborough U (From trainee on 15/8/1998) FL 43+8/6 FLC 1+1 FAC 2+1 Others 2
Tottenham H (£500,000 on 10/1/2000) PL 5+17 FLC 1+1 FAC 1+1/1
Bradford C (Loaned on 23/10/2001) FL 12+1/1

ETUHU Dixon Paul
Born: Kano, Nigeria, 8 June 1982
Height: 6'2" **Weight:** 13.4
Club Honours: Div 1 '02
Dixon made his first-team debut for Manchester City against Birmingham last September, when he linked up with another new boy, Ali Benarbia. He then had a run of 11 games in midfield for City before losing his place at the end of October. However, he was sold to Preston North End in January where he became instantly popular with the fans for his powerful tackling and strong running in the centre of the park.
Manchester C (From trainee on 23/12/1999) FL 11+1 FLC 1
Preston NE (£300,000 on 24/1/2002) FL 16/3

EUELL Jason Joseph
Born: Lambeth, 6 February 1977
Height: 6'0" **Weight:** 12.7
International Honours: E: U21-6
Signed from Wimbledon for Charlton's record fee during the summer, Jason was initially played in midfield before moving to striker where he looked much more comfortable. He is quick and strong, good in the air and holds the ball up well. His unselfish play brings others into the game, and he set up numerous chances for his colleagues. He scored some brilliant goals including Charlton's fourth in the great win over Arsenal at Highbury. Jason finished as top scorer for the Addicks with 13 goals in his first season at the Valley.
Wimbledon (From trainee on 1/6/1995) P/FL 118+23/41 FLC 15+2/4 FAC 14+5/2 Others 2+2
Charlton Ath (£4,750,000 on 16/7/2001) PL 31+5/11 FLC 2/1 FAC 2/1

EUSTACE John Mark
Born: Solihull, 3 November 1979
Height: 5'11" **Weight:** 11.12
This young midfielder was appointed club captain by Coventry City boss Gordon Strachan prior to the start of the 2001-02 campaign. However, he suffered a knee injury during pre-season training and apart from one early appearance against

Grimsby he missed the whole of the season up until Easter. He played in the last five games but his all-action style and big heart were insufficient to get the club into the play-off positions.
Coventry C (From trainee on 5/11/1996) P/FL 39+15/3 FLC 5+1/2 FAC 2+2/1
Dundee U (Loaned on 17/2/1999) SL 8+3/1 SC 2

EVANS Gareth Joseph
Born: Leeds, 15 February 1981
Height: 6'0" **Weight:** 11.12
International Honours: E: Yth
Gareth joined Huddersfield Town shortly before the start of the 2001-02 campaign and made his debut against Bournemouth in the opening game. He adapted well to first-team football and became a regular in the line-up at left back. Strong in the tackle and a confident passer of the ball, he missed a number of games through a hamstring injury.
Leeds U (From trainee on 26/3/1998) PL 0+1 Others 0+1
Huddersfield T (Free on 9/8/2001) FL 35 FLC 1 Others 5

EVANS Gary Lee
Born: Doncaster, 13 September 1982
Height: 5'9" **Weight:** 12.8
A third-year scholar with Bury, Gary can play at left back or on the left side of midfield, and made such progress last term that he was rewarded with an occasional glimpse of first-team action. He was initially named as a non-playing substitute in the home game against Wrexham in March before making his full League debut in the final fixture of the season at Peterborough when he came through the full 90 minutes with distinction.
Bury (From trainee on 4/3/2002) FL 1

EVANS Mark Graham
Born: Chester, 16 September 1982
Height: 6'0" **Weight:** 12.0
A third year scholar at Wrexham, Mark made his debut for the Robins when replacing Steve Roberts against Port Vale last September. He added another three appearances from the bench during the season, and more than held his own. A confident central defender with plenty of pace he can also perform up front and scored a number of goals for the reserves last term.
Wrexham (Trainee) FL 0+4

EVANS Michael
Born: Venlo, Holland, 21 July 1976
Height: 6'0" **Weight:** 12.2

Wayne Evans

After being released following several seasons with VVV Venlo, Michael had a trial with Bradford City during the 2001 close season before joining York on a monthly contract in September. He made a big impression when coming on as a substitute at Hull and made his full debut in the following game at home to Luton. A lively right-sided midfield player he was then sidelined by a long-term hamstring injury and after being released he returned to Holland.

York C (Free from VVV Venlo, Holland, via a trial at Bradford C, on 7/9/2001) FL 1+1

EVANS Michael (Micky)
James
Born: Plymouth, 1 January 1973
Height: 6'1" **Weight:** 13.4
Club Honours: Div 3 '02
International Honours: Rol: 1
Micky made an invaluable contribution to Plymouth's Division Three championship success last season. An extremely hard working striker, he was often played as the sole forward in Argyle's 4-5-1 away formation. This meant that the team relied on Micky holding the ball up, a task in which he proved to be very successful. He also weighed in with his share of goals including a strike against Devon rivals Exeter City in September and another in the 4-1 success away at Darlington to clinch the title on that unforgettable night in April.

Plymouth Arg (From trainee on 30/3/1991) FL 130+33/38 FLC 8+1 FAC 10+2/3 Others 10/2
Southampton (£500,000 on 4/3/1997) PL 14+8/4 FLC 2+1/1
West Bromwich A (£750,000 on 27/10/1997) FL 35+28/6 FLC 3+3/2 FAC 2+2/1
Bristol Rov (£250,000 on 18/8/2000) FL 19+2/4 FLC 2 Others 3/2
Plymouth Arg (£30,000 on 22/3/2001) FL 40+8/11 FLC 1 FAC 3 Others 0+1

EVANS Paul Simon
Born: Oswestry, 1 September 1974
Height: 5'8" **Weight:** 11.6
Club Honours: Div 3 '94, '99
International Honours: W: 1; U21-4; Yth
Brentford's inspirational captain, midfield ball-winner and scorer of spectacular goals had an amazing start to the 2001-02 season netting nine times in the first 11 League games. He then injured a hamstring at Wycombe in the LDV Vans Trophy tie, missing six games before returning to lead the side to the heartbreaking play-off final defeat by

Stoke. He had a 100 per cent record from the penalty spot with six out of six, and was voted into the PFA Second Division team. He won his first cap for Wales when replacing Robbie Savage against the Czech Republic in March.

Shrewsbury T (From trainee on 2/7/1993) FL 178+20/26 FLC 12+2/4 FAC 12+1/2 Others 12/4
Brentford (£110,000 on 3/3/1999) FL 130/31 FLC 8 FAC 3 Others 13/3

EVANS Rhys Karl
Born: Swindon, 27 January 1982
Height: 6'1" **Weight:** 12.2
International Honours: E: Yth; Sch
Rhys joined Queen's Park Rangers on loan last November in a deal that was to last until the end of the season. He was initially the club's second choice 'keeper behind Fraser Digby, but stepped into the action when Digby was injured in February. He did sufficiently well to retain his place until the end of the campaign, even after his rival had returned to fitness.

Chelsea (From trainee on 8/2/1999)
Bristol Rov (Loaned on 25/2/2000) FL 4
Queens Park R (Loaned on 6/11/2001) FL 11

EVANS Stephen (Steve)
James
Born: Caerphilly, 25 September 1980
Height: 6'1" **Weight:** 11.6
International Honours: W: U21-2; Yth
Steve joined Swansea on loan from Crystal Palace last November and made his debut in the 2-1 win at Torquay. An attacking left wing back, he showed good ball skills and the ability to deliver telling crosses from the flanks. However he returned to Selhurst Park after a successful month at the Vetch Field.

Crystal Palace (From trainee on 31/10/1998) FL 0+6 FLC 0+1
Swansea C (Loaned on 9/11/2001) FL 4 FAC 2
Brentford (Free on 27/3/2002)

EVANS Terence (Terry)
Born: Pontypridd, 8 January 1976
Height: 5'8" **Weight:** 11.0
International Honours: W: U21-4
Terry signed for Swansea from League of Wales club Barry Town last October and proved to be a useful addition to the Swans squad when employed either at right back or in a right wing-back position. Possessing good defensive qualities, he is also capable of delivering quality crosses from the flanks when pushing forward. His season ended prematurely after he suffered a double

fracture of the jaw against Leyton Orient in mid-February.

Cardiff C (From trainee on 8/7/1994) FL 12+2 FLC 2+1 FAC 1 Others 2+2 (Free to Barry T in February 1996)
Swansea C (Free on 30/10/2001) FL 16 FAC 2

EVANS Thomas (Tommy)
Raymond
Born: Doncaster, 31 December 1976
Height: 6'0" **Weight:** 13.2
International Honours: NI: Yth
Tommy was again Scunthorpe United's first choice 'keeper last term and had a solid campaign, enhancing his reputation as one of the Third Division's best shot-stoppers. His season started badly when he sustained a knee cartilage injury on the opening day at Kidderminster and was returned in September and was an ever-present from then on, making two crucial penalty saves during the campaign.

Sheffield U (From trainee on 3/7/1995)
Crystal Palace (Free on 14/6/1996)
Scunthorpe U (Free on 22/8/1997) FL 144+1 FLC 5 FAC 10 Others 6

EVANS Duncan Wayne
Born: Abermule, 25 August 1971
Height: 5'10" **Weight:** 12.5
Wayne was his usual dependable self at right back for Rochdale last term when he was a near ever-present in the line-up. A difficult man for opposing wingers to get past, he is equally good covering his central defensive partners. His consistency and reassuring presence at the back went a long way to providing the defensive stability Dale needed to maintain their charge into the play-offs.

Walsall (Free from Welshpool on 13/8/1993) FL 173+10/1 FLC 14+1/1 FAC 15+1 Others 12+3
Rochdale (Free on 2/7/1999) FL 134/3 FLC 6/1 FAC 7 Others 9

EVATT Ian Ross
Born: Coventry, 19 November 1981
Height: 6'3" **Weight:** 13.11
Ian enjoyed a successful loan period at Northampton last term when he mostly featured in the centre of the defence. He returned to Pride Park after two months and after a couple of appearances from the bench stepped up to receive his first Premiership start in the final game of the season at Sunderland. He is a versatile youngster who can also play in midfield.

Derby Co (From trainee on 3/12/1998) PL 1+3
Northampton T (Loaned on 10/8/2001) FL 10+1 FLC 2

EVERS Sean Anthony
Born: Hitchin, 10 October 1977
Height: 5'9" **Weight:** 9.11
Sean was in the Plymouth starting line-up for three of the first four games last season, but then only made the team on one more occasion, for the visit to Shrewsbury in January. Towards the end of the campaign he was loaned to Conference side Stevenage Borough, appearing in their FA Trophy final defeat at Villa Park. He is a busy central midfielder with a neat touch on the ball.

Luton T (From trainee on 16/5/1996) FL 43+9/6 FLC 9/1 FAC 2 Others 6
Reading (£500,000 on 25/3/1999) FL 8+10 FLC 1+1 FAC 4 Others 2+1
St Johnstone (Loaned on 13/10/2000) SL 5+1
Plymouth Arg (Free on 8/3/2001) FL 5+9 FLC 1 FAC 0+1

EYRE John Robert
Born: Hull, 9 October 1974
Height: 6'0" **Weight:** 12.7

David Eyres

John rejoined the club where he started his career when signing for Oldham Athletic in the summer of 2001. He was brought back to Boundary Park by former team-mate Andy Ritchie and was a first-team regular in the early part of the campaign, but became more of a squad player after Ritchie's departure. Used chiefly as a target man, he had notched six goals by January before injury prematurely ended his season.

Oldham Ath (From trainee on 16/7/1993) P/FL 4+6/1 FLC 0+2
Scunthorpe U (Loaned on 15/12/1994) FL 9/8
Scunthorpe U (£40,000 on 4/7/1995) FL 151+13/43 FLC 9/2 FAC 12/3 Others 8+1/3
Hull C (Free on 5/7/1999) FL 43+9/13 FLC 5/3 FAC 4+1/2 Others 3+2/1
Oldham Ath (Free on 25/7/2001) FL 11+9/5 FLC 2 FAC 2+1 Others 2+1/1

EYRE Richard Paul
Born: Poynton, 15 September 1976
Height: 5'11" **Weight:** 11.6
Richard joined Macclesfield on a short-term contract at the start of the 2001-02 season and was given the role of operating on the left side of midfield. He always adopted an enthusiastic approach but found it difficult to perform at a consistent level and was released at the end of January.

Port Vale (From trainee on 29/6/1995) FL 26+22/1 FLC 1+2 FAC 1 Others 0+1
Macclesfield T (Free on 9/8/2001) FL 12+2 FLC 1 Others 1

EYRES David
Born: Liverpool, 26 February 1964
Height: 5'11" **Weight:** 11.8
Club Honours: Div 2 '00
David had an outstanding season for Oldham Athletic in 2001-02. A late starter, this evergreen 37-year-old produced a series of dazzling and tireless performances on Athletic's left flank. A near ever present, his ample supply of goals and countless assists ensured he swept the club's 'Player of the Season' awards. A key man at set pieces, Athletic hope he will continue to roll back the years in 2002-03 and inspire promotion.

Blackpool (£10,000 from Rhyl on 15/8/1989) FL 147+11/38 FLC 11+1/1 FAC 11/2 Others 13+2/4
Burnley (£90,000 on 29/7/1993) FL 171+4/37 FLC 17/7 FAC 14/8 Others 9/3
Preston NE (£80,000 on 29/10/1997) FL 85+23/19 FLC 3+4 FAC 10/3 Others 5/3
Oldham Ath (Free on 13/10/2000) FL 70+5/12 FLC 2 FAC 7/3 Others 2/1

F

FACEY Delroy Michael
Born: Huddersfield, 22 April 1980
Height: 5'11' **Weight:** 13.10
A back injury forced this young Huddersfield Town striker to miss the majority of the 2001-02 season. When he returned to action he made an immediate impact as a second half substitute in the win at Blackpool. He subsequently gained a regular place in the starting line-up scoring at Wrexham and in the final home game of the campaign to help Town qualify for the play-offs.
Huddersfield T (From trainee on 13/5/1997) FL 40+35/15 FLC 1+1 FAC 1+2 Others 2

FALCONER William (Willie) Henry
Born: Aberdeen, 5 April 1966
Height: 6'1" **Weight:** 12.0
Club Honours: SC '95
The veteran Scot began the 2001-02 campaign on trial with Clydebank before signing terms with St Johnstone where he featured regularly in first-team action. He subsequently joined Grimsby Town on a short-term contract on the transfer deadline. However he made little impact with the Mariners, featuring in just two games, both away from home, and at the time of writing it seemed unlikely that he would remain at Blundell Park for the start of 2002-03.
Aberdeen (From juniors on 20/4/1983) SL 49+28/14 SLC 5+5/1 SC 3+2/1 Others 5+5/2
Watford (£300,000 on 17/6/1988) FL 85+13/12 FLC 5 FAC 6/1 Others 4+3
Middlesbrough (£305,000 on 16/8/1991) FL 47+6/10 FLC 2+1 FAC 3/2
Sheffield U (£425,000 on 12/8/1993) FL 21+2/3 FLC 2
Glasgow Celtic (£375,000 on 9/2/1994) SL 33+9/5 SLC 1+1 SC 4+2/3 Others 0+1
Motherwell (£200,000 on 16/1/1996) SL 57+1/10 SLC 3/1 SC 5 Others 1
Dundee (Free on 7/7/1998) SL 70+8/18 SLC 5/4 SC 3+2 Others 4
Clydebank (Free on 1/8/2001) SL 1
St Johnstone (Free on 10/8/2001) SL 16+9/3 SLC 1+1 SC 0+1
Grimsby T (Free on 27/3/2002) FL 1+1

FALLON Rory Michael
Born: Gisbourne, New Zealand, 20 March 1982
Height: 6'2" **Weight:** 11.10
International Honours: E: Yth
Rory began last season in the Barnsley reserve team but soon found himself in the first-team squad both as a substitute and also in the starting line up. He is a tall striker who has a good range of skills. However the change of manager at Oakwell saw his chances diminish and he went out on loan to Shrewsbury where he did well in a two-month spell, despite failing to register a goal. On returning to the club he found himself back in the reserves where he was a regular scorer.
Barnsley (From trainee on 23/3/1999) FL 3+7 FLC 1
Shrewsbury T (Loaned on 14/12/2001) FL 8+3

FARRELL Andrew (Andy)
Born: Easington, 21 December 1983
Height: 6'0" **Weight:** 11.0
The emergence of Andy Farrell from the youth team was one of the high spots in a disappointing season for Halifax Town last term. The youngster earned himself praise for his willingness and work rate up front and was unfortunate not to find himself with a goal to his credit.
Halifax T (Trainee) FL 7+2

FARRELL David (Dave) William
Born: Birmingham, 11 November 1971
Height: 5'10" **Weight:** 11.9
Dave had a rather disappointing season for Peterborough in 2001-02, although he featured regularly in the line-up. The highlight of his campaign was his goal in the FA Cup tie against Newcastle when the television cameras captured him singing along with the Posh fans in celebration. A wide-left sided midfield player who continued to cause problems for Second Division defences with his blistering pace.
Aston Villa (£45,000 from Redditch U on 6/11/1992) F/PL 5+1 FLC 2
Scunthorpe U (Loaned on 25/1/1993) FL 4+1/1 Others 2
Wycombe W (£100,000 on 14/9/1995) FL 44+16/6 FLC 6 FAC 3+2 Others 2
Peterborough U (Free on 21/7/1997) FL 175+21/26 FLC 9+2/2 FAC 14/3 Others 9/4

FARRELLY Gareth
Born: Dublin, 28 August 1975
Height: 6'0" **Weight:** 13.0
International Honours: RoI: 6; B-1; U21-11; Yth; Sch
Having promised so much in the previous season, Gareth will have been disappointed at how last season turned out. A catalogue of injuries, plus severe competition for midfield places, restricted him to only 11 Premiership starts, although he did register an additional seven substitute appearances. A valuable squad member, who is very comfortable

when on the ball, he will be looking to make much more of an impression when the 2002-03 season gets underway.
Aston Villa (From trainee on 21/1/1992) PL 2+6 FLC 0+1
Rotherham U (Loaned on 21/3/1995) FL 9+1/2
Everton (£700,000 + on 9/7/1997) PL 18+9/1 FLC 2/1 FAC 1
Bolton W (Free on 12/11/1999) P/FL 55+15/4 FLC 4 FAC 4+2 Others 3/1

FAULCONBRIDGE Craig Michael
Born: Nuneaton, 20 April 1978
Height: 6'1" **Weight:** 13.0
Wrexham's leading goal-scorer led the line well last term, also earning praise for his work rate. A tall energetic front man he got on the score sheet in the first three games of the campaign, and added an important strike in the 1-1 home encounter with promotion-chasing Huddersfield Town at the end of March. He was left out of the final four games after previously turning down a new contract and announcing his intention of leaving the Racecourse Ground.
Coventry C (From trainee on 5/7/1996)
Dunfermline Ath (Loaned on 27/3/1998) SL 1+12/1 SLC 0+1
Hull C (Loaned on 18/12/1998) FL 4+6 FAC 1 Others 1+1
Wrexham (Free on 6/8/1999) FL 92+19/30 FLC 4+1/1 FAC 4+2/1 Others 4/1

FEENEY Warren
Born: Belfast, 17 January 1981
Height: 5'10" **Weight:** 11.6
International Honours: NI: 2; U21-2 Yth; Sch
Warren was one of the true successes in an otherwise disappointing 2001-02 season for Bournemouth. After serving the club on loan during the tail end of the previous season he signed permanently in the summer and quickly established himself as a crowd favourite, going on to sweep the board for the 'Player of the Year' awards. A young and pacy striker, he was top scorer with 13 goals and also won his first full caps for Northern Ireland.
Leeds U (Signed from St Andrew's BC on 26/1/1998)
Bournemouth (Free on 22/3/2001) FL 38+9/17 FLC 1 FAC 2

FENN Neale Michael Charles
Born: Edmonton, 18 January 1977
Height: 5'10" **Weight:** 12.8
International Honours: RoI: B-1; U21-9; Yth
A close season signing for Peterborough,

Nicky Fenton

Neale quickly became a crowd favourite at London Road last term. A striker with excellent close control, an eye for the defence-splitting pass and the ability to hold the ball up to bring midfield into play, the only thing missing from his game is pace. He was a regular before Christmas, but seemed to spend most of the second half of the campaign on the bench.
Tottenham H *(From trainee on 1/7/1995)* PL 0+8 FLC 1/1 FAC 1
Leyton Orient *(Loaned on 30/1/1998)* FL 3
Norwich C *(Loaned on 26/3/1998)* FL 6+1/1
Swindon T *(Loaned on 13/11/1998)* FL 4
Lincoln C *(Loaned on 31/12/1998)* FL 0+4 Others 1
Peterborough U *(Free on 6/7/2001)* FL 25+11/6 FLC 1+1/1 FAC 6/1 Others 2

FENTON Graham Anthony
Born: Wallsend, 22 May 1974
Height: 5'10" **Weight:** 12.10
Club Honours: FLC '94, '96, '00; AMC '02
International Honours: E: U21-1
This experienced striker joined Blackpool in the summer of 2001, but had a frustrating time with injuries at Bloomfield Road. A skilful player who can hold the ball up and lay it off well, he still managed to net five times from six starts.
Aston Villa *(From trainee on 13/2/1992)* PL 16+16/3 FLC 2+5
West Bromwich A *(Loaned on 10/1/1994)* FL 7/3
Blackburn Rov *(£1,500,000 on 7/11/1995)* PL 9+18/7 FLC 0+2 FAC 0+1
Leicester C *(£1,100,000 on 8/8/1997)* PL 13+21/3 FLC 3+2/1 FAC 0+4 Others 0+2
Walsall *(Loaned on 20/3/2000)* FL 8+1/1
Stoke C *(Free on 11/8/2000)* FL 2+3/1 FLC 2
St Mirren *(Free on 29/9/2000)* SL 26/2 SLC 2 SC 1
Blackpool *(Free on 20/8/2001)* FL 6+9/5 FLC 0+1 FAC 1 Others 3

FENTON Nicholas (Nicky) Leonard
Born: Preston, 23 November 1979
Height: 5'10" **Weight:** 10.4
International Honours: E: Yth
This very talented and capable defender joined Notts County as a centre half, but appeared regularly at right back for a while last season. However his best form returned when he was restored to his rightful central-defensive slot in the final third of the campaign when some of his performances were truly inspirational.
Manchester C *(From trainee on 26/11/1996)* FL 15 FLC 3+1 Others 1
Notts Co *(Loaned on 7/10/1999)* FL 13/1 Others 1

Bournemouth *(Loaned on 23/3/2000)* FL 8
Bournemouth *(Loaned on 11/8/2000)* FL 4+1
Notts Co *(£150,000 on 18/9/2000)* FL 71+1/5 FLC 3 FAC 8 Others 2

FERDINAND Leslie (Les)
Born: Acton, 8 December 1966
Height: 5'11" **Weight:** 13.5
Club Honours: FLC '99
International Honours: E: 17; B-1
2001-02 was undoubtedly Les' best season yet for Spurs. He looked sharp, lean and athletic and instilled a real threat in the attack. Consistently the team's most formidable player up front, he netted a total of 15 goals in all competitions. He developed a fine partnership with Teddy Sheringham and benefited from the support of Gus Poyet.
Queens Park R *(£15,000 from Hayes on 12/3/1987)* F/PL 152+11/80 FLC 11+2/7 FAC 6+1/3 Others 1
Brentford *(Loaned on 24/3/1988)* FL 3
Newcastle U *(£6,000,000 on 7/6/1995)* PL 67+1/41 FLC 6/3 FAC 4+1/2 Others 5/4
Tottenham H *(£6,000,000 on 5/8/1997)* PL 93+14/31 FLC 10+3/5 FAC 15+1/1

FERDINAND Rio Gavin
Born: Peckham, 8 November 1978
Height: 6'2" **Weight:** 12.1
International Honours: E: 27; U21-5; Yth
There were many raised eyes when Leeds paid £18 million for Rio, which made him the world's most costliest defender. However, he has proved everyone wrong, his leadership qualities impressing David O'Leary so much that he was made club captain last season. Although he had several partners in defence, he remained a shining beacon with some outstanding displays. Positive in everything he does, he reads the game superbly well. Rio is regarded as the best ball-playing centre half in the country and seems certain to get even better in years to come. A factor underlined by some superb performances for England in the World Cup finals over the summer. He was also deservedly named in the PFA's Premiership team for the season.
West Ham U *(From trainee on 27/11/1995)* PL 122+5/2 FLC 12+1 FAC 9 Others 9
Bournemouth *(Loaned on 8/11/1996)* FL 10 Others 1
Leeds U *(£18,000,000 on 27/11/2000)* PL 54/2 FLC 2 FAC 3 Others 14/1

FERGUSON Darren
Born: Glasgow, 9 February 1972
Height: 5'10" **Weight:** 11.10

Club Honours: PL '93
International Honours: S: U21-5; Yth
Darren continued to provide the midfield 'engine room' for Wrexham last term. Although perhaps less effective than in previous seasons, his passing and set-piece skills were again features of his performance, as demonstrated by the remarkable late free kick that secured three points in the relegation encounter with Northampton at the Racecourse.
Manchester U *(From trainee on 11/7/1990)* F/PL 20+7 FLC 2+1
Wolverhampton W *(£250,000 on 13/11/1994)* FL 94+23/4 FLC 13+2/3 FAC 9+2/3 Others 6
Wrexham *(Free on 17/9/1999)* FL 117+1/16 FLC 3/1 FAC 7/1 Others 3

FERGUSON Duncan
Born: Stirling, 27 December 1971
Height: 6'4" **Weight:** 14.6
Club Honours: SL '94; SLC '94; FAC '95
International Honours: S: 7; B; U21-7; Yth; Sch
An Everton talisman, Duncan was once again stricken by injuries on his second season back at his spiritual home. But there was a ray of sunshine in the shape of a new fitness adviser who gave him tips on posture and pre-match preparation. Some observers suggested it was a psychological coup by new boss David Moyes in appointing him as captain, but the player gave the credit to his new fitness guru for the most consistent spell of goal-scoring in his Goodison career. Everton supporters will hope his injury worries are finally behind him.
Dundee U *(Signed from Carse Thistle on 1/2/1990)* SL 75+2/28 SLC 2+1/2 SC 6/4
Glasgow R *(£4,000,000 on 20/7/1993)* SL 8+6/2 SLC 2+2/3 SC 0+3 Others 1
Everton *(£4,400,000 on 4/10/1994)* PL 110+6/37 FLC 8/1 FAC 8+1/4
Newcastle U *(£7,000,000 + on 25/11/1998)* PL 24+6/8 FLC 6+2/3 Others 2+1/1
Everton *(£3,750,000 on 19/8/2000)* PL 26+8/12 FLC 1/1 FAC 3/1

FERNANDES Fabrice
Born: Paris, France, 29 October 1979
Height: 5'9" **Weight:** 11.7
Club Honours: Div 1 '01
International Honours: France: U21
Fabrice joined Southampton last December for a bargain fee and immediately impressed the club's supporters, opening his goal account with a spectacular 20-yard free kick against West Ham. Although lightweight

Les Ferdinand

his agility, speed and imagination gave Saints an extra dimension on the left flank.

Fulham *(Loaned from Rennes, France on 3/8/2000) FL 23+6/2 FLC 4+2/1 FAC 1*
Southampton *(£1,100,000 from Rennes, France on 27/12/2001) PL 6+5/1 FAC 1*

FERRARI Carlos Eduardo
Born: Brazil, 19 February 1979
Height: 6'0" **Weight:** 12.2
This young striker signed for Birmingham City from Mirassol, a second-level club from Sao Paulo, on a season-long loan, which was terminated after he broke his foot just before Christmas. He earned his call-up to the substitutes' bench under caretaker managers Mick Mills and Jim Barron. Carlos always showed great willingness and an eye for goal in the reserves. He was more of a traditional English forward than Brazilian, ready to handle himself against physical defenders.
Birmingham C *(Loaned from Mirassol, Brazil on 24/8/2001) FL 0+4*

FERRER Albert Llopes
Born: Barcelona, Spain, 6 June 1970
Height: 5'7" **Weight:** 10.6
Club Honours: ESC '98
International Honours: Spain: 36; U23 (OLYM '92)
After being marooned on 99 first-team appearances, this popular right back finally broke the century barrier for Chelsea with his first outing of the 2001-02 season from the subs' bench at Fulham in September. However the campaign as a whole proved frustrating with niggling injuries and the form of Mario Melchiot keeping his appearances down to a handful.
Chelsea *(£2,200,000 from Barcelona, Spain on 15/8/1998) PL 68+5 FLC 1+2 FAC 10+1 Others 22/1*

FESTA Gianluca
Born: Cagliari, Italy, 15 March 1969
Height: 6'0" **Weight:** 13.6
This experienced defender was very much on the fringes of the first team at Middlesbrough last season and it was not until the new year that he appeared in Premiership action. Soon after his return he received a red card, and he never really settled in the side, making the starting line-up only 11 times during the campaign.
Middlesbrough *(£2,700,000 from Inter Milan, Italy, ex Cagliari, on 18/1/1997) F/PL 132+6/10 FLC 18/1 FAC 14+1/1*

FETTIS Alan William
Born: Belfast, 1 February 1971
Height: 6'1" **Weight:** 12.10
International Honours: NI: 25; B-3; Yth; Sch
Alan had another outstanding campaign in goal for York City during 2001-02 and for the second successive season he won the 'Clubman of the Year' award. The ever-popular 'keeper missed his first League match since joining the Minstermen when injury kept him out of the final game of the season at Scunthorpe.
Hull C *(£50,000 from Ards on 14/8/1991) FL 131+4/2 FLC 7+1 FAC 5 Others 7*
West Bromwich A *(Loaned on 20/11/1995) FL 3*
Nottingham F *(£250,000 on 13/1/1996) PL 4 FLC 1 FAC 0+1*
Blackburn Rov *(£300,000 on 12/9/1997) P/FL 9+2 FAC 1*
York C *(Free on 1/3/2000) FL 104 FLC 2 FAC 10*

FEUER Anthony Ian
Born: Las Vegas, Nevada, USA, 20 May 1971
Height: 6'7" **Weight:** 15.6
International Honours: USA: 1
This giant goalkeeper found it impossible to dislodge Kelvin Davies as the club's number one last season. He made a couple of appearances during a loan spell at Derby, replacing the injured Andy Oakes, but his outings for the Dons were few and far between. He was out of contract in the summer and looked set to leave the Selhurst Park club.
West Ham U *(£70,000 from Los Angeles Salsa, USA on 23/3/1994)*
Peterborough U *(Loaned on 20/2/1995) FL 16*
Luton T *(£580,000 on 11/9/1995) FL 97 FLC 7 FAC 5 Others 5 (Free to New England Revolution, USA on 24/3/1998)*
Cardiff C *(Free from Colorado Rapids, USA on 10/1/2000)*
West Ham U *(Free on 23/2/2000) PL 3*
Wimbledon *(Free on 28/6/2000) FL 2+2 FLC 1 FAC 2*
Derby Co *(Loaned on 12/10/2001) PL 2*

FIELDING John Robert
Born: Billingham, 7 April 1982
Height: 6'1" **Weight:** 14.0
In his first season as a professional the young central defender was thrust into the York City senior side early in the 2001-02 campaign and he enjoyed an extended run in the line-up. He impressed with a number of solid displays but then suffered a serious ankle injury from which

he struggled to recover. He was released at the end of the season.
York C *(From trainee on 6/7/2001) FL 9/1 FLC 1 Others 1*

FILAN John Richard
Born: Sydney, Australia, 8 February 1970
Height: 5'11" **Weight:** 13.2
International Honours: Australia: 1; U23
This experienced 'keeper made only one Worthington Cup outing for Blackburn Rovers last term and then moved on to Wigan Athletic. He celebrated his second appearance for the Latics by saving a penalty in the away match at Reading and producing further 'Man of the Match' performances in the away match at Queen's Park Rangers and at home to Wycombe. An outstanding shot stopper with good reflexes, he was an ever-present following his arrival. He collected the Second Division club's 'Players' Player of the Year' award.
Cambridge U *(£40,000 from Budapest St George, Australia on 12/3/1993) FL 68 FLC 6 FAC 3 Others 3*
Coventry C *(£300,000 on 2/3/1995) PL 15+1 FLC 2*
Blackburn Rov *(£700,000 on 10/7/1997) P/FL 61+1 FLC 6 FAC 5*
Wigan Ath *(£450,000 on 14/12/2001) FL 25*

FINCH Keith John
Born: Easington, 6 May 1982
Height: 6'0" **Weight:** 12.2
Keith made his first senior appearance for Darlington for over two years when he came off the subs' bench to replace the injured Andy Collett against Lincoln City last January. An agile and fearless shot stopper he made his full debut in the following match at Rushden and went on to play eleven times before Chris Porter was brought in for the closing games of the season.
Darlington *(From trainee on 9/7/2001) FL 11+1 FAC 0+1*

FINNAN Stephen (Steve) John
Born: Limerick, 20 April 1976
Height: 5'10" **Weight:** 11.6
Club Honours: Div 3 '98; Div 2 '99; Div 1 '01
International Honours: RoI: 19; B-1; U21-8
An ever present in the Fulham line-up last term, Steve once again proved a consistent performer in the right-back position. He is an attack-minded defender who links well with the midfield and provides high quality crosses into the box.

Darryl Flahavan

When called upon to defend he often makes crucially timed interceptions to break up the opposition attacks. A fine season saw him named the fans 'Player of the Season', selected for the PFA's Premiership team and named in the Republic of Ireland squad for the World Cup finals.
Birmingham C (£100,000 from Welling U on 12/6/1995) FL 9+6/1 FLC 2+2 Others 2+1
Notts Co (Loaned on 5/3/1996) FL 14+3/2 Others 3/1
Notts Co (£300,000 on 31/10/1996) FL 71+9/5 FLC 4 FAC 7/1 Others 1
Fulham (£600,000 on 13/11/1998) P/FL 139+1/6 FLC 10+1 FAC 15/1 Others 1

FINNIGAN John Francis
Born: Wakefield, 29 March 1976
Height: 5'8" **Weight:** 10.11
Lincoln's skipper had a frustrating time at Sincil Bank last season, with his appearances restricted first of all by the recurrence of an old neck problem and then by a toe injury. His passing ability and battling qualities in the centre of midfield were a key part of Lincoln's game and after his departure to Cheltenham in early March the Imps failed to win another game. He went straight into the Robins' first team effectively as a replacement for the injured Lee Howells and having failed to score in his previous 77 games for the Imps he netted on his debut in the 4-0 win over York. He went on to find the net twice more including the spectacular third goal in the Division Three play-off final.
Nottingham F (From trainee on 10/5/1993)
Lincoln C (£50,000 on 26/3/1998) FL 139+4/3 FLC 7 FAC 8+1/1 Others 7
Cheltenham T (Free on 7/3/2002) FL 12/2 Others 3/1

FISH Mark Anthony
Born: Capetown, South Africa, 14 March 1974
Height: 6'3" **Weight:** 13.2
International Honours: South Africa: 60 (ANC '96)
Mark was a regular in the Charlton Athletic side in 2001-02 until a knee injury finished his season in February. Used primarily as a central defender, he also played several games at right back, and looked a class act wherever he appeared. Strong and very good in the air, he is also extremely comfortable in possession and loves to run with the ball into the opponents half. Mark was building a great partnership with Jorge Costa in the centre of the Addicks' defence before his injury.

Bolton W (£2,500,000 from Lazio, Italy, ex Orlando Pirates, on 16/9/1997) P/FL 102+1 FLC 12+1/1 FAC 6 Others 5
Charlton Ath (£700,000 on 10/11/2000) PL 49/1 FLC 1 FAC 3

FISKEN Gary Stewart
Born: Watford, 27 October 1981
Height: 6'0" **Weight:** 12.7
Gary worked his way up through the Watford academy teams and made his first-team debut at the age of 19 against Wimbledon. A combative and hard-working midfield player, he made several appearances during the season without ever pinning down a regular place. He scored a memorable first senior goal with a spectacular 25-yard lob at Walsall.
Watford (From trainee on 8/2/2000) FL 12+5/1 FLC 2+2 FAC 1

FITZGERALD Brian Maurice
Born: Perivale, 23 October 1983
Height: 5'9" **Weight:** 12.2
International Honours: RoI: Yth
After being a member of Queen's Park Rangers' successful U19 side the previous season Brian continued his development at the club in 2001-02. Following several good performances for the reserves he made his senior debut as a substitute against Bury in January.
Queens Park R (From trainee on 27/10/2000) FL 0+1

FITZGERALD Scott Brian
Born: Westminster, 13 August 1969
Height: 6'0" **Weight:** 12.12
International Honours: RoI: B-1; U21-4
Scott was appointed Colchester United skipper following Simon Clark's surprise departure last January and did not miss a game for the remainder of the season. An experienced defender, who was mostly used at centre half, he acted as a calming influence on the youngsters around him.
Wimbledon (From trainee on 13/7/1989) F/PL 95+11/1 FLC 13 FAC 5 Others 1
Sheffield U (Loaned on 23/11/1995) FL 6
Millwall (Loaned on 11/10/1996) FL 7
Millwall (£50,000 + on 28/7/1997) FL 79+3/1 FLC 4 FAC 2 Others 5
Colchester U (Free on 17/10/2000) FL 66+1 FLC 2 FAC 3 Others 2

FITZPATRICK Ian Matthew
Born: Manchester, 22 September 1980
Height: 5'9" **Weight:** 10.6
International Honours: E: Yth; Sch
Ian Fitzpatrick was out of favour at Halifax under Paul Bracewell but when a new management team was installed he was

given the opportunity to display his obvious talents. A striker who can also play wide on the left or just behind the front two, he scored seven times during the season and had the distinction of netting Town's final goal in the Football League.
Manchester U (From trainee on 8/7/1998)
Halifax T (Free on 2/3/2000) FL 37+12/10 FLC 1+1 FAC 3

FLACK Steven (Steve) Richard
Born: Cambridge, 29 May 1971
Height: 6'2" **Weight:** 13.2
Now the longest serving player on Exeter City's books, Steve enjoyed another fine season in 2001-02. He was generally a first-choice striker and played alongside a combination of front players as the best attacking formation was considered. Although out of action for two months with an ankle injury, he still managed to bag six goals – and what City fan can forget his celebration after scoring at Macclesfield!
Cardiff C (£10,000 from Cambridge C on 13/11/1995) FL 6+5/1
Exeter C (£10,000 on 13/9/1996) FL 174+54/50 FLC 8+1 FAC 10+4/5 Others 6+2/2

FLAHAVAN Darryl James
Born: Southampton, 28 November 1978
Height: 5'10" **Weight:** 12.1
Voted the fans 'Player of the Year', Darryl had an excellent season between the Southend posts in 2001-02, proving himself to be capable of playing at a higher grade, especially after having to cope with the tragic loss of his goalkeeping brother, Aaron, during the close season. Although small in build for a 'keeper, he proved a very able shot stopper, but his season soured a little towards the end after he was dropped when he turned down a new contract.
Southampton (From trainee on 14/5/1996. Free to Woking on 13/8/1998)
Southend U (Free on 16/10/2000) FL 70 FLC 1 FAC 8 Others 8

FLEMING Craig
Born: Halifax, 6 October 1971
Height: 6'0" **Weight:** 12.10
Craig was an ever-present for Norwich City in 2001-02, producing yet another series of incredibly consistent performances at the heart of the Norwich defence. He seldom makes a mistake and his best work often goes unnoticed as he makes a crucial block here or a vital interception there. He clocked up his

Gary Fletcher

200th senior appearance for Norwich and the 400th League game of his career during the season.

Halifax T *(From trainee on 21/3/1990)* FL 56+1 FLC 4 FAC 3 Others 3+2
Oldham Ath *(£80,000 on 15/8/1991)* F/PL 158+6/1 FLC 12+1 FAC 11 Others 4
Norwich C *(£600,000 on 30/6/1997)* FL 178+5/7 FLC 16 FAC 5+1 Others 3

FLEMING Curtis

Born: Manchester, 8 October 1968
Height: 5'11" **Weight:** 12.8
Club Honours: Div 1 '95
International Honours: RoI: 10; U23-2; U21-5; Yth

Curtis featured a number of times for Middlesbrough in the early part of 2001-02, but in November he was loaned to Birmingham City. He played the last five games of caretaker managers' Mick Mills and Jim Barron's reign, but returned north soon after Steve Bruce took over. He subsequently joined former Blues' boss Trevor Francis at Crystal Palace at the end of December and was a regular in the line-up in the second half of the campaign. A hard-tackling defender, he is particularly effective when pushing forward.

Middlesbrough *(£50,000 from St Patricks on 16/8/1991)* F/PL 248+18/3 FLC 24+2/1 FAC 16+1 Others 7+1
Birmingham C *(Loaned on 16/11/2001)* FL 6
Crystal Palace *(£100,000 on 31/12/2001)* FL 17

FLEMING Terence (Terry)
Maurice

Born: Marston Green, 5 January 1973
Height: 5'9" **Weight:** 10.9
This combative midfield player featured regularly for Cambridge United last term. A versatile player who can also appear at full back, he possesses a useful long throw but failed to register a goal for the U's during the season.

Coventry C *(From trainee on 2/7/1991)* F/PL 8+5 FLC 0+1
Northampton T *(Free on 3/8/1993)* FL 26+5/1 FLC 2 FAC 0+1 Others 0+1
Preston NE *(Free on 18/7/1994)* FL 25+7/2 FLC 4 FAC 0+1 Others 3+2
Lincoln C *(Signed on 7/12/1995)* FL 175+8/8 FLC 11+1/2 FAC 11/2 Others 4
Plymouth Arg *(Free on 4/7/2000)* FL 15+2 FLC 2 FAC 2 Others 0+2
Cambridge U *(Free on 8/3/2001)* FL 37+7/1 FLC 1 FAC 1 Others 3+1

FLETCHER Carl Neil

Born: Camberley, 7 April 1980
Height: 5'10" **Weight:** 11.7

This combative midfielder firmly established himself in the Bournemouth side last season and became the Cherries' youngest ever captain when he led the side out against Blackpool in January. He managed to hone his fiery nature during the season, but still picked up too many disciplinary points.

Bournemouth *(From trainee on 3/7/1998)* FL 98+7/14 FLC 3 FAC 6+1/1 Others 1+1

FLETCHER Gary

Born: Widnes, 4 June 1981
Height: 5'10" **Weight:** 11.7
Gary joined Leyton Orient during the 2001 close season but had a frustrating time with injuries and took time to adjust to full-time football. He had a spell on loan with Ryman League club Grays Athletic at the turn of the year before returning to the O's line-up towards the end of the season. He is a promising young striker who possesses both pace and power.

Hull C *(Loaned from Northwich Vic on 16/3/2001)* FL 1+4
Leyton Orient *(£150,000 on 9/7/2001)* FL 3+6

FLETCHER Steven (Steve)
Mark

Born: Hartlepool, 26 June 1972
Height: 6'2" **Weight:** 14.9
2001-02 proved a frustrating time for Steve at Bournemouth. He missed the start of the season due to a knee injury, but recovered to make an appearance as a substitute against Worksop in the FA Cup, marking the occasion with a goal in the 3-0 win. He then made his first start the following Saturday against Chesterfield but a recurrence of the injury ruled him out of the rest of the campaign. The big target man was sorely missed as the side failed in their bid to avoid relegation, but he is expected to be fit for pre-season training for what is his testimonial year in 2002-03.

Hartlepool U *(From trainee on 23/8/1990)* FL 19+13/4 FLC 0+2/1 FAC 1+2 Others 2+2/1
Bournemouth *(£30,000 on 28/7/1992)* FL 294+19/60 FLC 26/3 FAC 17+1/4 Others 13/2

FLITCROFT David (Dave) John

Born: Bolton, 14 January 1974
Height: 5'11" **Weight:** 13.5
Dave missed the start of the 2001-02 season through suspension and was then unable to oust Michael Oliver from the centre of Rochdale's midfield, generally starting only when a five-man midfield was employed. More often than not on the bench, he was offered the chance of

a move to Shrewsbury but turned it down to fight for his place. His chance came when new boss John Hollins restored him to the side, and though he sometimes had to play wide on the right, his determined performances saw him remain in the side for the rest of the campaign. He is the younger brother of Gary Flitcroft.

Preston NE *(From trainee on 2/5/1992)* FL 4+4/2 FLC 0+1 Others 0+1
Lincoln C *(Loaned on 17/9/1993)* FL 2 FLC 0+1
Chester C *(Free on 9/12/1993)* FL 146+21/18 FLC 10+1 FAC 7 Others 8/1
Rochdale *(Free on 5/7/1999)* FL 101+18/2 FLC 4+2 FAC 2+3 Others 9+1

FLITCROFT Garry William

Born: Bolton, 6 November 1972
Height: 6'0" **Weight:** 12.2
Club Honours: FLC '02
International Honours: E: U21-10; Yth; Sch

Garry brings muscle, commitment and belief to the Blackburn midfield and when they face a physically strong team he is essential. He is not a creative player, his passing is safe rather than constructive and although permitted the freedom to get forward he seldom used his penalty area surges to maximum effect. He missed the Worthington Cup final through suspension and scored his only goal with a splendid header against West Ham.

Manchester C *(From trainee on 2/7/1991)* PL 109+6/13 FLC 11+1 FAC 14/2
Bury *(Loaned on 5/3/1992)* FL 12
Blackburn Rov *(£3,200,000 on 26/3/1996)* P/FL 151+10/9 FLC 7+2/1 FAC 9+1/2 Others 2/1

FLOWERS Timothy (Tim)
David

Born: Kenilworth, 3 February 1967
Height: 6'2" **Weight:** 14.0
Club Honours: PL '95; FLC '00
International Honours: E: 11; U21-3; Yth

This experienced goalkeeper played in the opening two fixtures of 2001-02 for Leicester City, whilst new signing Ian Walker served a suspension, but hardly got a look in thereafter. He had loan spells with both Stockport County and Coventry City during the season as cover for injuries and even had one game as temporary coach of the Foxes after Peter Taylor was sacked. Although he had the misfortune to concede a number of goals in his few senior appearances, things picked up a little and he registered a

notable clean sheet against the free-scoring Newcastle attack when replacing the injured Walker early in the match.
Wolverhampton W *(From apprentice on 28/8/1984) FL 63 FLC 5 FAC 2 Others 2*
Southampton *(£70,000 on 13/6/1986) F/PL 192 FLC 26 FAC 16 Others 8*
Swindon T *(Loaned on 23/3/1987) FL 2*
Swindon T *(Loaned on 13/11/1987) FL 5*
Blackburn Rov *(£2,400,000 on 4/11/1993) PL 175+2 FLC 14 FAC 13+1 Others 12*
Leicester C *(£1,100,000 + on 30/7/1999) PL 54+1 FLC 5+1 FAC 2 Others 2*
Stockport Co *(Loaned on 26/10/2001) FL 4*
Coventry C *(Loaned on 19/2/2002) FL 5*

FLYNN Michael (Mike)
Anthony
Born: Oldham, 23 February 1969
Height: 6'0" **Weight:** 11.0
After missing the opening day defeat by Coventry, Stockport County's captain missed only one further game up until the start of January. However, he was then allowed to go out on loan to Stoke, where he acquitted himself well whether in a back three or four. Although he initially agreed to stay for a third month he eventually joined Barnsley on a permanent move. Brought in to add his experience to the Reds' defence. He became a regular until the season's end, but his effort and organisational skills were not enough to save the team from relegation. He has already shown his strength in the air and in the tackle for the Oakwell club.
Oldham Ath *(From apprentice on 7/2/1987) FL 37+3/1 FLC 1+1/1 FAC 1 Others 2*
Norwich C *(£100,000 on 22/12/1988)*
Preston NE *(£125,000 on 4/12/1989) FL 134+2/7 FLC 6 FAC 6+1/1 Others 13*
Stockport Co *(£125,000 on 25/3/1993) FL 386+1/16 FLC 34/2 FAC 20/1 Others 19*
Stoke C *(Loaned on 12/1/2002) FL 11+2*
Barnsley *(Free on 15/3/2002) FL 7*

FLYNN Sean Michael
Born: Birmingham, 13 March 1968
Height: 5'8" **Weight:** 11.8
This diligent right-sided or central midfielder contributed a valuable ten goals for Tranmere in 2001-02, including a double in the home game against Blackpool. A determined and enthusiastic player, he missed the last few games of the season with a broken toe but is now out of contract and his future at Prenton Park was still uncertain at the time of writing. He was voted as the supporters' 'Player of the Season'.

Coventry C *(£20,000 from Halesowen T on 3/12/1991) F/PL 90+7/9 FLC 5/1 FAC 3*
Derby Co *(£250,000 on 11/8/1995) F/PL 39+20/3 FLC 3 FAC 3*
Stoke C *(Loaned on 27/3/1997) FL 5*
West Bromwich A *(£260,000 on 8/8/1997) FL 99+10/8 FLC 11/1 FAC 0+2*
Tranmere Rov *(Free on 18/7/2000) FL 65+1/6 FLC 8/2 FAC 8/3*

FOLAN Caleb Colman
Born: Leeds, 26 October 1982
Height: 6'1" **Weight:** 12.12
This promising young Leeds United striker was loaned to Rushden last October to gain experience of senior football. A tall, gangly player he made seven appearances in total for the League's newcomers, six of them as substitute. He subsequently had another loan spell at Hull where he proved well suited to the physical demands of Third Division football before returning to Elland Road to continue his development.
Leeds U *(From trainee on 2/11/1999)*
Rushden & Diamonds *(Loaned on 5/10/2001) FL 1+5 Others 1*
Hull C *(Loaned on 30/11/2001) FL 0+1*

FOLETTI Patrick
Born: Switzerland, 27 May 1974
Height: 6'2" **Weight:** 14.8
Patrick joined Derby County on loan from Luzern last October as cover for regular 'keeper Andy Oakes. He made his Premiership bow for the injured Oakes in a rare win at Leicester in February and appeared in the starting line-up for the home game with Everton soon afterwards.
Derby Co *(Loaned from FC Luzern, Switzerland. ex Coldrerio, Mandrisio, Grasshopper, Schaffhausen, on 22/2/2002) PL 1+1*

FOLEY Dominic Joseph
Born: Cork, 7 July 1976
Height: 6'1" **Weight:** 12.8
International Honours: RoI: 6; U21-8
Dominic began the 2001-02 season in the Watford first-team squad, after signing a new contract in July. Manager Luca Vialli felt the tall striker had potential, but he failed to convert his promise into goals in the first team, despite a hat trick for the reserves against Wimbledon in October. Later that month he was loaned to Queen's Park Rangers, but that arrangement was curtailed when he tore a hamstring after 20 minutes of his debut. After recovering, Dominic went on loan to Swindon where he scored with a coolly-taken 25-yard lob on his debut but

otherwise failed to impress. Finally he returned to Loftus Road for a second loan spell and once again scored in his first outing.
Wolverhampton W *(£35,000 from St James' Gate on 31/8/1995) FL 4+16/3 FLC 0+3 FAC 0+1 Others 0+2*
Watford *(Loaned on 24/2/1998) FL 2+6/1*
Notts Co *(Loaned on 7/12/1998) FL 2 Others 1*
Watford *(Free on 11/6/1999) P/FL 6+12/2 FLC 3+3*
Queens Park R *(Loaned on 25/10/2001) FL 1*
Swindon T *(Loaned on 11/1/2002) FL 5+2/1*
Queens Park R *(Loaned on 28/3/2002) FL 2+2/1*

FOLLAND Robert (Rob)
William
Born: Swansea, 16 September 1979
Height: 5'9" **Weight:** 11.0
International Honours: W: U21-1; Yth
Rob was very much on the fringe of the first-team squad at Oxford in the first half of the 2001-02 campaign. He made just one start (and that in an LDV Vans Trophy game) but appeared on the subs' bench on a number of occasions. He dropped out of the reckoning altogether under new boss Ian Atkins and was released at the end of the season. He appeared in a variety of roles during his time with the U's including striker, midfield and wing back but never really seemed to find his best position.
Oxford U *(From trainee on 3/7/1998) FL 18+22/3 FLC 4+3 FAC 4+1/1 Others 2*

FORAN Mark James
Born: Aldershot, 30 October 1973
Height: 6'4" **Weight:** 14.3
Mark added valuable experience and an aerial presence at the centre of Bristol Rovers defence in 2001-02. He started the season on the sub's bench but quickly established himself in the side and scored his first goal for the Pirates, a firm header against Southend United. He could always be relied upon to give a good account of himself and produced an outstanding performance in the FA Cup tie against Premiership club Derby County.
Millwall *(From trainee on 3/11/1990)*
Sheffield U *(£25,000 on 28/8/1993) FL 10+1/1 FLC 1 Others 0+1*
Rotherham U *(Loaned on 26/8/1994) FL 3*
Wycombe W *(Loaned on 11/8/1995) FL 5 FLC 2*
Peterborough U *(£40,000 on 8/2/1996) FL 22+3/1 FAC 1 Others 2*
Lincoln C *(Loaned on 22/1/1997) FL 1+1*
Oldham Ath *(Loaned on 3/3/1997) FL 0+1*
Crewe Alex *(£25,000 + on 12/12/1997) FL 25+6/1 FLC 2 FAC 1*

Bristol Rov (Free on 11/8/2000) FL 39+4/2 FLC 2+1 FAC 4 Others 4

FORAN Richard (Richie)
Born: Dublin, 16 June 1980
Height: 6'1" **Weight:** 12.9
International Honours: RoI: U21-2
Richie joined Carlisle United during the 2001 close season and impressed with his work rate and unselfishness on his debut against Rochdale, going on to score his first goal a week later at Darlington. A powerful striker who wins more than his share of aerial duels, he had an excellent season and finished as the club's top scorer with 16 goals. In one remarkable spell he scored in the last minute in three consecutive fixtures, converting a potential two draws and a defeat into two wins and a draw.

Terrell Forbes

Carlisle U (£20,000 from Shelbourne on 31/8/2001) FL 37/14 FAC 3/1 Others 1/1

FORBES Adrian Emmanuel
Born: Ealing, 23 January 1979
Height: 5'8'' **Weight:** 11.10
International Honours: E: Yth
This speedy versatile right winger became something of a 'Super Sub' at Luton last term, scoring three of his four goals after coming off the bench. He featured in almost every match, although he made 25 appearances from the bench, and his best performance came at Halifax when he scored one and made two more.
Norwich C (From trainee on 21/1/1997) FL 66+46/8 FLC 1+4 FAC 2+2
Luton T (£60,000 on 16/7/2001) FL 15+25/4 FLC 1 FAC 1/1

FORBES Scott Hugh
Born: Canewdon, 3 December 1976
Height: 5'8" **Weight:** 11.2
With the Southend team struggling throughout for a natural wide-man, 2001-02 really should have been Scott's season, but it turned into a miserable time with injuries restricting him to just three starts and ended with him being released. Much was expected of him after his excellent introduction the previous campaign, but the Blues' faithful were left with just memories of his darting runs and excellent team play.
Southend U (Free from Saffron Walden T on 10/8/2000) FL 30+17/3 FLC 0+1 FAC 5+1/1 Others 4

FORBES Terrell
Born: Southwark, 17 August 1981
Height: 6'0" **Weight:** 12.8
Club Honours: FAYC '99
This right-sided defender was one of the finds of the 2001-02 season by Queen's Park Rangers. He soon become a favourite for his runs down the right wing invariably followed by the delivery of a good cross. He was a near ever present, although he failed to find the net all season. Terrell was voted 'Player of the Year' by one of the club's supporters' associations.
West Ham U (From trainee on 2/7/1999)
Bournemouth (Loaned on 18/10/1999) FL 3 FAC 1
Queens Park R (Free on 24/7/2001) FL 43 FLC 1 FAC 1

FORD James Anthony
Born: Portsmouth, 23 October 1981
Height: 5'8" **Weight:** 11.0
The 2001-02 season started off well for James as he made his full debut for Bournemouth against Blackpool and then had a run of four starts in September before being dropped to the bench. However the tidy midfielder failed to make another start in the side, his last appearance coming as a substitute against Brighton in February, and he was released in the summer.
Bournemouth (From trainee on 12/4/2000) FL 5+7 FLC 1

FORD Mark Stuart
Born: Pontefract, 10 October 1975
Height: 5'8" **Weight:** 10.10
Club Honours: FAYC '93
International Honours: E: U21-2; Yth
Mark started the 2001-02 season as a key member of the Darlington team but was sidelined for almost two months in the autumn due to injury. Extremely quick

into the tackle and an accurate passer of the ball, he is also capable of getting forward and grabbing spectacular goals from the edge of the box. There is no doubt that the Quakers' midfield needs his vision and experience and he also contributed seven valuable goals.
Leeds U (From trainee on 5/3/1993) PL 27+2/1 FLC 7 FAC 5 Others 0+1
Burnley (£250,000 on 18/7/1997) FL 43+5/1 FLC 2 FAC 1+1 Others 5+1 (Free to KFC Lommelse, Belgium during 1999 close season)
Torquay U (Free on 17/7/2000) FL 28/3 FLC 2 FAC 2/1 Others 1
Darlington (£15,000 on 19/2/2001) FL 45+1/9 FLC 1 FAC 2

FORD Robert (Bobby) John
Born: Bristol, 22 September 1974
Height: 5'9" **Weight:** 11.0
Bobby started the 2001-02 season as a first choice in midfield for Sheffield United before giving way to teenager Michael Tonge. He also enjoyed a brief run in the line-up in January and February but generally featured much less than in the previous campaign. A hard-working player who was involved in both defence and attack, he was out of contract in the summer and at the time of writing his future was uncertain.
Oxford U (From trainee on 6/10/1992) FL 104+12/7 FLC 14+2/1 FAC 10/2 Others 7/1
Sheffield U (£400,000 on 28/11/1997) FL 138+17/6 FLC 10+2/1 FAC 14+4 Others 2

FORD Simon Gary
Born: Newham, 17 November 1981
Height: 6'0" **Weight:** 11.6
A former Charlton Athletic trainee, Simon proved to be one of the finds of the 2001-02 season for Grimsby Town. The young central defender impressed with the Mariners' reserves before receiving a surprise call up to the senior squad. Nurtured by the experienced Paul Groves he created such an impression that he was voted Grimsby's 'Young Player of the Year'. Strong both in the air and on the ground, he has attracted the attention of several bigger clubs but hopes are high that he can be persuaded to remain at Blundell Park to provide a long-term solution to the club's problems in the centre of defence.
Grimsby T (Free from trainee at Charlton Ath on 12/7/2001) FL 8+5/1 FLC 0+1 FAC 2

FORD Tony
Born: Grimsby, 14 May 1959
Height: 5'10" **Weight:** 13.0
Club Honours: Div 3 '80; FLGC '82

International Honours: E: B-2
The Rochdale assistant manager continued as an automatic choice on the right-hand side of midfield last term, his accurate crosses helping Dale race to the top of the table and dump Huddersfield out of the Worthington Cup. An ever present until November, Tony then decided to hang up his boots and move with manager Steve Parkin to Barnsley, ending a phenomenal career of well over 1000 games in total. The Oakwell club had to pay a fee of around £70,000 in compensation, partly because he was still a registered player – surely making him the most expensive 42-year-old ever!
Grimsby T (From apprentice on 1/5/1977) FL 321+34/55 FLC 31+3/4 FAC 15+4/2 Others 2
Sunderland (Loaned on 27/3/1986) FL 8+1/1
Stoke C (£35,000 on 8/7/1986) FL 112/13 FLC 8 FAC 9 Others 6/1
West Bromwich A (£145,000 on 24/3/1989) FL 114/14 FLC 7 FAC 4/1 Others 2+1
Grimsby T (£50,000 on 21/11/1991) FL 59+9/3 FLC 1 FAC 3
Bradford C (Loaned on 16/9/1993) FL 5 FLC 2
Scunthorpe U (Free on 2/8/1994) FL 73+3/9 FLC 4/1 FAC 7/1 Others 4 (Free to Barrow on 22/8/1996)
Mansfield T (Free on 25/10/1996) FL 97+6/7 FLC 4/1 FAC 4/1 Others 5
Rochdale (Free on 6/7/1999) FL 81+8/6 FLC 6/1 FAC 4 Others 4+1

FORINTON Howard Lee
Born: Boston, 18 September 1975
Height: 5'11" **Weight:** 11.4
Howard had another rather frustrating season at Peterborough in 2001-02 when he was never really able to claim a first-team place for his own. At his best he is a bustling all-action striker with a good goal-scoring record. He was released by Posh in the summer.
Birmingham C (Signed from Yeovil T on 14/7/1997) FL 0+4/1 FLC 1+1
Plymouth Arg (Loaned on 18/12/1998) FL 8+2/3 FLC 1+2
Peterborough U (£250,000 on 17/9/1999) FL 34+16/10 FLC 1 FAC 2+5 Others 2

FORLAN Corazo Diego
Born: Montevideo, Uruguay, 19 May 1979
Height: 5'8" **Weight:** 11.11
International Honours: Uruguay: 5
This gifted young striker chose Manchester United ahead of Premiership rivals Middlesbrough last January and was soon in Premiership action. He made his debut against Bolton at the Reebok and soon emerged as a truly exciting prospect

with a scintillating performance against Boavista in the Champions' League. Although mostly featuring from the bench he can be satisfied with his progress since arriving at Old Trafford. Diego's father, Pablo Forlan represented Uruguay in the 1960s and 1970s, and played in two World Cup final tournaments.
Manchester U (£7,500,000 from Independiente, Uruguay on 23/1/2002) PL 6+7 Others 1+4

FORREST Martyn William
Born: Bury, 2 January 1979
Height: 5'10" **Weight:** 12.2
Martyn enjoyed a superb season for Bury in central midfield in 2001-02, and visibly grew in stature and confidence as the campaign progressed. He took over the captaincy in October and hung on to it thereafter. It was a blow when he broke his foot in the game at Colchester in November, but he returned after a two-month absence. He signed a new long-term contract in February and was ever-present in the closing 18 games. The fans voted Martyn as runner-up in their 'Player of the Year' poll.
Bury (From trainee on 16/7/1997) FL 60+17/1 FLC 1+2 FAC 1+1 Others 3

FORRESTER Jamie Mark
Born: Bradford, 1 November 1974
Height: 5'6" **Weight:** 11.0
Club Honours: FAYC '93
International Honours: E: Yth (UEFA-U18 '93); Sch
Jamie had another useful season at Northampton in 2001-02, hitting his best form at the turn of the year, when he netted 11 goals in a 16-match spell, and once again finishing as the club's leading scorer. He is a lively striker with a keen eye for goal and also took on the role of penalty taker during the campaign. He has a double target to chase in 2002-03 as he is closing in on his 100th first-class goal and his 50th for the Cobblers.
Leeds U (£60,000 from Auxerre, France on 20/10/1992) PL 7+2 FAC 1+1/2
Southend U (Loaned on 1/9/1994) FL 3+2
Grimsby T (Loaned on 10/3/1995) FL 7+2/1
Grimsby T (Signed on 17/10/1995) FL 27+14/6 FLC 0+2 FAC 3+1/3
Scunthorpe U (Signed on 21/3/1997) FL 99+2/37 FLC 6/2 FAC 7/4 Others 7 (Free to FC Utrecht, Holland on 1/6/1999)
Walsall (Free on 30/12/1999) FL 2+3
Northampton T (£150,000 on 21/3/2000) FL 91+5/40 FLC 4/1 FAC 4/2 Others 1

FORSSELL Mikael
Born: Steinfurt, Germany, 15 March 1981
Height: 6'1" **Weight:** 12.8
International Honours: Finland: 19; U21; Yth
Mikael returned from a season-long loan spell at Crystal Palace to score in his second appearance back in Chelsea colours - a towering header to clinch the Worthington Cup third round tie at Coventry. He has established a reputation as a 'Super Sub' and in an 11-day period in January scored goals from four consecutive appearances off the bench. The young Finn finished the campaign with the remarkable tally of nine goals, - all scored as a substitute! He was sorely missed in the climax of the season when he joined fellow-strikers Jimmy-Floyd Hasselbaink and Eidur Gudjohnsen on the injury list.
Chelsea (Free from HJK Helsinki, Finland on 18/12/1998) PL 6+26/5 FLC 1+4/2 FAC 3+6/5 Others 1+3
Crystal Palace (Loaned on 23/2/2000) FL 44+8/16 FLC 8/2 FAC 1+1

FORSTER Nicholas (Nicky) Michael
Born: Caterham, 8 September 1973
Height: 5'10" **Weight:** 11.5
International Honours: E: U21-4
Nicky was the spearhead of Reading's 4-4-2 formation last season, and despite working with a number of fellow strikers, his own pace and guile enabled him to finish as the team's leading scorer. He also owed much of his success to the work done with him by fitness coach Niall Clark. He netted a superb hat-trick in the 3-0 home win over Blackpool, and was deservedly selected for the PFA Division Two team of the season.
Gillingham (Signed from Horley T on 22/5/1992) FL 54+13/24 FLC 3+2 FAC 6/2
Brentford (£100,000 on 17/6/1994) FL 108+1/39 FLC 11/3 FAC 8/1 Others 7+1/4
Birmingham C (£700,000 on 31/1/1997) FL 24+44/11 FLC 2+2/1 FAC 3+1
Reading (£650,000 on 23/6/1999) FL 67+20/30 FLC 5 FAC 3 Others 3+4/1

FORSYTH Richard Michael
Born: Dudley, 3 October 1970
Height: 5'11" **Weight:** 13.0
Club Honours: GMVC '94
International Honours: E: SP-3
Richard was the hub of the Peterborough United team last season when he was a regular in the line-up. An influential central midfield player, he rarely does anything extravagant but exerts a controlling influence in the centre of the park.

Birmingham C (£50,000 from Kidderminster Hrs on 13/7/1995) FL 12+14/2 FLC 7+2 FAC 2 Others 3+1
Stoke C (£200,000 on 25/7/1996) FL 90+5/17 FLC 7/1 FAC 4 Others 1+1
Blackpool (Free on 5/7/1999) FL 10+3 FAC 0+2 Others 0+1
Peterborough U (Free on 14/7/2000) FL 55+7/2 FLC 4/1 FAC 9/1 Others 1+1

FORTUNE Clayton Alexander
Born: Forest Gate, 10 November 1982
Height: 6'3" **Weight:** 13.10
This tall young defender made his senior debut for Bristol City against Peterborough in an LDV Vans Trophy match last season and also featured from the bench in the 3-0 win at Cambridge shortly afterwards. He did well in both games and will be aiming to make further progress in 2002-03.
Bristol C (Free from trainee at Tottenham H on 22/3/2001) FL 0+1 Others 0+1

FORTUNE Jonathan (Jon) Jay
Born: Islington, 23 August 1980
Height: 6'2" **Weight:** 11.4
Having gained valuable experience on loan to Mansfield the previous season, Jon eventually made his Premiership debut for Charlton Athletic when he came on as a substitute in the opening game of the 2001-02 campaign against Everton. He went on to establish himself as a regular squad member and progressed very quickly into an accomplished central defender, coping adequately with the Premiership's best strikers. Good in the air and very quick, Jon is strong and has learnt a lot from playing alongside established internationals such as Jorge Costa and Mark Fish. He scored his first senior goal for the Addicks against Port Vale in the Worthington Cup.
Charlton Ath (From trainee on 2/7/1998) PL 14+5 FLC 2/1 FAC 2
Mansfield T (Loaned on 18/2/2000) FL 4
Mansfield T (Loaned on 31/8/2000) FL 14

FORTUNE Quinton
Born: Cape Town, South Africa, 21 May 1977
Height: 5'11" **Weight:** 11.11
International Honours: South Africa: 43
This pacy striker or midfielder stepped out of the shadows to earn a warm tribute from Sir Alex Ferguson at the start of the 2001-02 campaign, after initially suffering from a dislocated shoulder, and expressing a wish to leave Old Trafford during the summer. He took full advantage of an opportunity to play

against Everton in September and scored in United's 4-1 win. Thereafter he had a short run in the side producing some quality performances, particularly in the Champions' League.
Manchester U (£1,500,000 from Atletico Madrid, Spain on 27/8/1999) PL 18+9/5 FLC 2 Others 5+8/2

FORTUNE-WEST Leopold (Leo) Paul Osborne
Born: Stratford, 9 April 1971
Height: 6'3" **Weight:** 13.10
This big striker was a prominent figure for Cardiff last season as they came close to a second successive promotion. He produced a series of above average displays, playing on the left-hand side of the attack alongside Peter Thorne and Robbie Earnshaw. Under contract, but tipped to be among those on their way out of Ninian Park, don't be surprised if Leo proves people wrong again. He is a gritty, committed player who is a threat in attack and useful in defence.
Gillingham (£5,000 from Stevenage Borough on 12/7/1995) FL 48+19/18 FLC 3+1/2 FAC 3+1/2
Leyton Orient (Loaned on 27/3/1997) FL 1+4
Lincoln C (Free on 6/7/1998) FL 7+2/1 FLC 2
Rotherham U (Loaned on 8/10/1998) FL 5/4
Brentford (£60,000 on 17/11/1998) FL 2+9 FAC 0+1 Others 2+1/1
Rotherham U (£35,000 on 26/2/1999) FL 59/26 FLC 4 FAC 2 Others 2
Cardiff C (£300,000 on 11/9/2000) FL 46+27/21 FLC 1 FAC 6+2/2 Others 3/1

FOSTER James Ian
Born: Liverpool, 11 November 1976
Height: 5'7" **Weight:** 11.0
Club Honours: NC '00
International Honours: E: SP-1; Sch
After missing most of the previous season through injury, it was a fit Ian Foster who showed Kidderminster supporters what he is capable of by finishing 2001-02 as the leading scorer in all competitions. Being small of stature, Ian's strengths lie in his speed and his finishing, and it was his pace that was a key feature of Harriers' attacking style throughout the second part of the season. At the end of the campaign he was rewarded with a one-year extension to his contract.
Hereford U (Free from Liverpool juniors on 15/7/1996) FL 4+15 FLC 2+1 Others 0+1 (Free to Barrow during 1998 close season)
Kidderminster Hrs (Free on 13/8/1999) FL 30+13/10 FLC 2 FAC 2 Others 3

FOSTER Stephen (Steve)
Born: Mansfield, 3 December 1974
Height: 6'1" **Weight:** 12.0
Club Honours: FAT '97
This experienced central defender began the 2001-02 season brightly, netting the winner for Bristol Rovers in their opening match against Torquay United. He remained a regular in the side until December, but was then absent following a groin operation and on his return he received a red card against Luton. Although he was the Pirates' longest-serving player he was expected to leave the club in the summer.
Mansfield T (From trainee on 15/7/1993) FL 2+3 FLC 2 (Free to Telford on 22/1/1994)
Bristol Rov (£150,000 from Woking on 23/5/1997) FL 193+4/7 FLC 14 FAC 13 Others 11

FOSTER Stephen (Steve) John
Born: Warrington, 10 September 1980
Height: 5'11" **Weight:** 11.8
International Honours: E: Sch
Steve is one of a number of young players who have developed through the ranks at Crewe. He is a versatile player who has appeared both in a central defensive role and also at right back. The 2001-02 season saw him continue to make progress in his development, and he emerged as a danger from set pieces, as his tally of six goals proved.
Crewe Alex (From trainee on 19/9/1998) FL 50+15/5 FLC 3+1/1 FAC 5+1/1

FOTIADIS Panos Andrew
Born: Hitchin, 6 September 1977
Height: 5'11" **Weight:** 11.7
International Honours: E: Sch
Andrew did well to get over a string of minor injuries that have dogged him over the last two seasons to become a regular on the substitutes' bench for Luton in 2001-02. Tall, very quick on the turn and with a powerful shot, he has all the skills required to be the perfect striker. However, the form of the Hatters' regular strikers saw him reduced to the level of a squad player for the majority of the second half of the campaign.
Luton T (From juniors on 26/7/1996) FL 42+64/12 FLC 2+6/1 FAC 4+1/1 Others 4+2

FOWLER Jason Kenneth
Born: Bristol, 20 August 1974
Height: 6'3" **Weight:** 11.12
After long-term illness had led to his losing his place in Cardiff's first-team squad, Jason made a fresh start at Torquay last November. A tall and elegant

midfielder, he possesses excellent vision, passes the ball well and is very dangerous at set pieces. Unfortunately, the injury jinx struck and groin and ligament injuries ruled him out of much of the run-in.
Bristol C (From trainee on 8/7/1993) FL 16+9 FLC 1+2 Others 1+1
Cardiff C (Signed on 19/6/1996) FL 138+7/14 FLC 8/1 FAC 12+2/4 Others 3/1
Torquay U (Free on 30/11/2001) FL 14/1

FOWLER Lee Anthony
Born: Cardiff, 10 June 1983
Height: 5'7" **Weight:** 10.8
International Honours: W: Yth
This youngster broke into the Coventry City first-team squad last November, making an impressive debut after coming on in the Burnley home game when he was named 'Man of the Match'. His tenacious, battling qualities and strong passing skills won him a lot of admirers and he earned a regular place as a substitute for the next three months. His performance on his full debut at West Brom was impressive but after five starts he returned to the bench. He ended the season with some useful displays for the reserves and will undoubtedly be knocking on the first-team door next season.
Coventry C (From trainee on 7/7/2000) FL 5+8

FOWLER Robert (Robbie) Bernard
Born: Liverpool, 9 April 1975
Height: 5'11" **Weight:** 11.10
Club Honours: FLC '95, '01; FAC '01; UEFAC '01; ESC '01
International Honours: E: 26; B-1; U21-8; Yth (UEFA-U18 '93)
Although Robbie netted a hat-trick for Liverpool against Leicester last October, his career at Anfield seemed to have entered a cul-de-sac following injuries and off-the-field incidents. It was still a major surprise, however, when he was off-loaded to Premiership rivals Leeds United in the autumn. He made a quiet debut, but scored a fine hat-trick at Bolton on Boxing Day and after establishing a productive partnership with Mark Viduka he went on to finish as leading scorer for United with 12 goals. Although no longer a first choice for England, he remained in the squad and featured in the World Cup finals over the summer.
Liverpool (From trainee on 23/4/1992) P/FL 210+26/120 FLC 32/27 FAC 21+3/12 Others 26+12/12
Leeds U (£11,000,000 on 30/11/2001) PL 22/12 FAC 1

FOX Christian
Born: Stonehaven, 11 April 1981
Height: 5'10" **Weight:** 11.5
This highly rated young York City midfielder again struggled with injuries during 2001-02 and these restricted him to just a handful of senior appearances. He went on loan to Larne in March and on his return won a place back on the bench for the final games of the season.
York C (From trainee on 29/6/1999) FL 36+18/1 FLC 1 FAC 2 Others 3

FOX Ruel Adrian
Born: Ipswich, 14 January 1968
Height: 5'6" **Weight:** 10.10
Club Honours: FLC '99
International Honours: E: B-2
Ruel was used sparingly by West Bromwich Albion manager Gary Megson throughout the 2001-02 season. Frequently named as substitute, he started only two matches but his experience showed through when called into action. He pounced to score a dramatic late equaliser in the home game with Sheffield Wednesday shortly before Christmas.
Norwich C (From apprentice on 20/1/1986) F/PL 148+24/22 FLC 13+3/3 FAC 11+4 Others 12+4
Newcastle U (£2,250,000 on 2/2/1994) PL 56+2/12 FLC 3/1 FAC 5 Others 4/1
Tottenham H (£4,200,000 on 6/10/1995) PL 95+11/13 FLC 7+3/1 FAC 11+1/1 Others 1
West Bromwich A (£200,000 on 26/8/2000) FL 38+20/2 FLC 3+1 FAC 1+2 Others 2

FOXE Hayden
Born: Australia, 23 June 1977
Height: 6'4" **Weight:** 13.5
International Honours: Australia: 10; U23; Yth
The 2001-02 season started badly for Hayden as a broken finger forced him to miss the first six weeks. The stylish central defender came into the side in October and played well for West Ham against Ipswich and Fulham but he had few other opportunities.
West Ham U (Free from Sanfrecce Hiroshima, Japan, ex Ajax, Arminia Bielefeld, on 14/3/2001) PL 7+4 FAC 0+1

FOY Keith Patrick
Born: Dublin, 30 December 1981
Height: 5'11" **Weight:** 12.3
International Honours: RoI: U21-7; Yth (UEFA-U16 '98)
This promising young wing back appeared in the first two games of last season for Nottingham Forest but then lost his place to Jim Brennan and never got back into

the side. Skilful on the ball, he likes to push forward and deliver crosses into the box. He was placed on the transfer list at the end of the campaign.
Nottingham F (From trainee on 8/1/1999) FL 19+3/1

FOYEWA Amos
Born: Nigeria, 26 December 1981
Height: 5'8" **Weight:** 11.13
After joining Bournemouth during the 2001 close season, Amos had a most frustrating time last term. A lightning-quick forward, he made his Football League debut on the opening day and earned a first start at the end of August at Cardiff when he unfortunately broke his leg. He was then out of action for several months, but recovered to make a few fleeting appearances from the subs' bench towards the end of the campaign.
Bournemouth (Free from trainee at West Ham U on 12/7/2001) FL 1+7 FLC 0+1

FRADIN Karim
Born: St Martin d'Hyeres, France, 2 February 1972
Height: 5'10" **Weight:** 13.0
Karim scored Stockport County's first goal of the 2001-02 campaign with a bullet header in a 4-1 defeat away to Crystal Palace and many within Edgeley Park feel that, on his day, he remains the best midfield player at the club. However, he is very much an enigma. Dominating one week, anonymous the next, and a source of frustration to manager Carlton Palmer in the process.
Stockport Co (Free from OGC Nice, France on 19/11/1999) FL 64+8/9 FLC 1 FAC 3+1/1

FRAIN John William
Born: Birmingham, 8 October 1968
Height: 5'9" **Weight:** 11.9
Club Honours: AMC '91
John captained Northampton in 2001-02, leading the team by example. Equally at home as a left wing back or in the centre of midfield, he always gave a 100 per cent performance and was generally to be seen in the thick of the action. Although he spent two months out injured he returned in time to lead the Cobblers to safety from relegation.
Birmingham C (From apprentice on 10/10/1986) FL 265+9/23 FLC 28/1 FAC 12 Others 22/2
Northampton T (Free on 24/1/1997) FL 190+3/4 FLC 10 FAC 10/1 Others 15/2

FRAMPTON Andrew (Andy) James Kerr
Born: Wimbledon, 3 September 1979
Height: 5'11" **Weight:** 10.10

This tall and pacy left back again spent most of the season in the reserves at Crystal Palace, and had to wait until April before he received his two first-team outings. A product of the club's youth system, he needs to gain regular senior action to progress his career.
Crystal Palace (From trainee on 8/5/1998) FL 19+8 FLC 3 FAC 2

FRANCIS Damien Jerome
Born: Wandsworth, 27 February 1979
Height: 6'1" **Weight:** 11.2
Damien missed the start of the 2001-02 season while still recovering from the knee ligament injury he suffered the previous season. He made his first appearance as sub away at Coventry and went on to feature regularly for Wimbledon. Unfortunately, his goal tally wasn't up to his efforts in 2000-01, but the same tenacity and desire to win was there. Damien is a real powerhouse in the centre of midfield and a good injury-free pre-season should see him scoring again.
Wimbledon (From trainee on 6/3/1997) P/FL 51+12/9 FLC 5+3 FAC 7

FRANDSEN Per
Born: Copenhagen, Denmark, 6 February 1970
Height: 6'1" **Weight:** 12.6
Club Honours: Div 1 '97
International Honours: Denmark: 22; U21; Yth
It was back to business as usual for Per last season when he really found his form of old, establishing an impressive midfield partnership with Kevin Nolan. He missed a handful of games following a nasty leg injury sustained in the game at Middlesbrough in January, but he returned for the season's run-in in fine form. He also contributed his share of trademark free kicks, notably in the 5-0 drubbing of Leicester at the start of the season, when he notched two set-piece stunners.
Bolton W (£1,250,000 from FC Copenhagen, Denmark, ex Lille, on 7/8/1996) F/PL 129+1/17 FLC 15+1/4 FAC 4+1 Others 3/1
Blackburn Rov (£1,750,000 + on 22/9/1999) FL 26+5/5 FAC 4/1
Bolton W (£1,600,000 on 24/7/2000) P/FL 60+8/10 FLC 2+1 FAC 2+2 Others 2+1/1

FRASER Stuart James
Born: Cheltenham, 1 August 1978
Height: 6'0" **Weight:** 12.6
Stuart began the 2001-02 campaign as second choice 'keeper at Exeter City, but stepped up to first-team action when

Arjan van Heusden was injured. He performed well when called upon and as a result he was rewarded with a new contract by the Grecians.
Stoke C (Signed from Cheltenham T on 8/7/1996) FL 0+1
Exeter C (Free on 18/7/2000) FL 15+3 FLC 1 Others 1

FRASER Stuart Thomas
Born: Edinburgh, 9 January 1980
Height: 5'9" **Weight:** 11.4
International Honours: S: U21-5
After making a gradual come back from his broken fibula, Stuart turned in some fine performances for Luton reserves last term, but made only one-first team appearance, at right back in the LDV Vans Trophy tie against Dagenham & Redbridge. He eventually left the club in the new year and after a trial with Dundee United he signed for Stevenage Borough, later appearing for them in their FA Trophy final defeat by Yeovil Town.
Luton T (From trainee on 2/4/1998) FL 36+8/1 FLC 6 FAC 9 Others 4

FREEDMAN Douglas (Dougie) Alan
Born: Glasgow, 21 January 1974
Height: 5'9" **Weight:** 11.2
International Honours: S: 2; B-1; U21-8; Sch
Dougie had an excellent season at Crystal Palace last term, forging a productive partnership with Clint Morrison which yielded over 40 goals for the Eagles. He is an intelligent striker who turns defenders well and has a great eye for goal. His progress was recognised when he was awarded his first full Scottish cap against Latvia at Hampden Park and won a place in the PFA's First Division team.
Queens Park R (From trainee on 15/5/1992)
Barnet (Free on 26/7/1994) FL 47/27 FLC 6/5 FAC 2 Others 2
Crystal Palace (£800,000 on 8/9/1995) F/PL 72+18/31 FLC 3+2/1 FAC 2+1 Others 3+2/2
Wolverhampton W (£800,000 on 17/10/1997) FL 25+4/10 FAC 5+1/2
Nottingham F (£950,000 on 12/8/1998) P/FL 50+20/18 FLC 8+1/4 FAC 3+1/1
Crystal Palace (£600,000 on 23/10/2000) FL 55+11/31 FLC 2/1 FAC 1+1

FREESTONE Christopher (Chris) Mark
Born: Nottingham, 4 September 1971
Height: 5'11" **Weight:** 11.7
Club Honours: AMC '97
Chris had a disappointing time at Shrewsbury last term and after featuring in only a handful of games he was

John Frain

released in November. He subsequently joined Dr Martens League club Rugby United and also had a brief association with Forest Green Rovers in the new year. He is an experienced striker who scored freely after stepping down into non-league football.

Middlesbrough *(£10,000 from Arnold T on 2/12/1994) P/FL 2+7/1 FLC 1+1/1 FAC 0+2*
Carlisle U *(Loaned on 3/3/1997) FL 3+2/2 Others 2*
Northampton T *(£75,000 on 8/12/1997) FL 40+17/13 FLC 4/3 FAC 1+2 Others 6+1/3*
Hartlepool U *(£75,000 on 25/3/1999) FL 24+13/7 FLC 2 FAC 2 Others 3*
Cheltenham T *(Loaned on 11/2/2000) FL 5/2*
Shrewsbury T *(Free on 21/7/2000) FL 19+8 FLC 2+1/1 FAC 1/1 Others 0+1*

FREESTONE Roger
Born: Newport, 19 August 1968
Height: 6'3" **Weight:** 14.6
Club Honours: Div 2 '89; Div 3 '00; AMC '94
International Honours: W: 1; U21-1; Yth; Sch
Despite a season of turmoil off the field at Swansea last term, Roger was his usual consistency in goal, even playing through the pain barrier when needed. Early March saw him take on the role of joint caretaker-manager with Nick Cusack, and when injury eventually forced him on to the sidelines, Roger was a strange sight to see bellowing out instructions from the dugout. He has been awarded a testimonial for long service and his former team Chelsea are due to visit the Vetch Field prior to the start of the 2002-03 season.

Newport Co *(From trainee on 2/4/1986) FL 13 Others 1*
Chelsea *(£95,000 on 10/3/1987) FL 42 FLC 2 FAC 3 Others 6*
Swansea C *(Loaned on 29/9/1989) FL 14 Others 1*
Hereford U *(Loaned on 9/3/1990) FL 8*
Swansea C *(£45,000 on 5/9/1991) FL 481+1/3 FLC 27 FAC 29 Others 43*

FRENCH Daniel John
Born: Peterborough, 25 November 1979
Height: 5'11" **Weight:** 11.4
This talented young winger mostly featured from the subs' bench for Peterborough last season, managing just one appearance in the starting line-up. He scored his first senior goal minutes after coming on in the home game against Bournemouth to seal an impressive 6-0 victory. A speedy player who crosses the ball well, he will be aiming to feature more regularly in 2002-03.

Peterborough U *(From trainee on 6/7/1998) FL 2+16/1 FAC 0+1 Others 1+2*

FREUND Steffen
Born: Brandenburg, Germany, 19 January 1970
Height: 5'11" **Weight:** 11.6
Club Honours: FLC '99
International Honours: Germany: 21; U21; Yth
This gutsy, committed player generally played in a 'holding' midfield role for Tottenham last term. His determination and enthusiasm have made him a favourite at White Hart Lane and his influence in the centre of the park adds stability to the line-up. Injury hit Steffen in mid-season and the team's form suffered as a direct result.

Tottenham H *(£750,000 from Borussia Dortmund, Germany, ex Motor Sud, Stahl Brandenburg, Schalke 04, on 29/12/1998) PL 79+6 FLC 13 FAC 10 Others 4*

FRIARS Sean Martin
Born: Londonderry, 15 May 1979
Height: 5'8" **Weight:** 10.12
International Honours: NI: U21-14
After being released by Ipswich Town Sean signed for Newry Town during the 2001 close season. He subsequently had a trial at Carlisle in the autumn but his only first-team appearance was as a substitute against Mansfield. Unfortunately this earned the club a substantial fine for a breach of the registration rules. The left-sided midfielder was released soon afterwards.

Liverpool *(From juniors on 22/5/1996)*
Ipswich T *(Free on 6/7/1998) FL 0+1 (Free to Newry T during 2001 close season)*
Carlisle U *(Free on 1/11/2001) FL 0+1*

FRIEDEL Bradley (Brad) Howard
Born: Lakewood, USA, 18 May 1971
Height: 6'3" **Weight:** 14.7
Club Honours: FLC '02
International Honours: USA: 68
An excellent stop stopper, Brad has great ability to improvise as best demonstrated at Leeds when in a one-on-one he was forced to go down to his right to cover the angle but still retained the presence and athleticism to move against his momentum when chipped to the left and got a hand to the ball. Some fine saves in the Worthington Cup final earned him the 'Man of the Match' award. He committed few errors and regained his place as USA's number one goalkeeper during the season.

Liverpool *(£1,000,000 from Columbus Crew, USA on 23/12/1997) PL 25 FLC 4 Others 1+1*
Blackburn Rov *(Free on 7/11/2000) P/FL 63 FLC 6 FAC 9*

FRIIO David
Born: Thionville, France, 17 February 1973
Height: 6'0" **Weight:** 11.7
Club Honours: Div 3 '02
This extremely popular central midfield player had an excellent season in 2001-02 and was one of the main reasons for Plymouth's success. He shone in the hustle and bustle of Division Three football showing a classy touch and always seeming to have time on the ball. His energetic runs into goal-scoring positions helped turn draws into wins on several occasions and his goals included late strikes in the 1-0 victories against Darlington in December and in the top-of-the-table clash against Mansfield in March. His outstanding performances throughout the campaign resulted in him being voted into the PFA Division Three team of the season by his fellow professionals.

Plymouth Arg *(Free from ASOA Valence, France, ex Epinal, Nimes, on 30/11/2000) FL 67/13 FLC 1 FAC 4/2 Others 2/1*

FURLONG Paul Anthony
Born: Wood Green, 1 October 1968
Height: 6'0" **Weight:** 13.8
Club Honours: FAT '88
International Honours: E: SP-5
This experienced striker was plagued by injury last season, despite working hard in the summer to get himself in excellent shape. He scored his only goal for Birmingham in Trevor Francis's last game, a 3-1 win at Barnsley in October. He later spent time on loan at Sheffield United as cover for injuries where he started off well, scoring twice in his first game. However, his season ended on a sour note with an operation to repair a torn thigh muscle that had come away from the bone.

Coventry C *(£130,000 from Enfield on 31/7/1991) FL 27+10/4 FLC 4/1 FAC 1+1 Others 1*
Watford *(£250,000 on 24/7/1992) FL 79/37 FLC 7/4 FAC 2 Others 4*
Chelsea *(£2,300,000 on 26/5/1994) PL 44+20/13 FLC 3+1 FAC 5+4/1 Others 7/3*
Birmingham C *(£1,500,000 on 17/7/1996) FL 104+27/50 FLC 11+2/3 FAC 5/3 Others 4*
Queens Park R *(Loaned on 18/8/2000) FL 3/1*
Sheffield U *(Loaned on 8/2/2002) FL 4/2*

Marco Gabbiadini

G

GAARDSOE Thomas
Born: Randers, Denmark, 23 November 1979
Height: 6'2" **Weight:** 12.8
International Honours: Denmark: U21-7
Thomas joined Ipswich last August and made his debut against West Ham at Portman Road. His appearances were restricted by minor but niggling injuries and the competition for defensive places, but he impressed the fans with his attitude and skills and an ability to keep calm in pressure situations. He scored against Sunderland when he headed home a corner unchallenged. He was a Danish U21 international when he joined Ipswich and has earned more caps since his arrival in England.
Ipswich T (£1,300,000 from AAB Aalborg on 31/8/2001) PL 3+1/1 FLC 0+1 Others 0+1

GABBIADINI Marco
Born: Nottingham, 20 January 1968
Height: 5'10" **Weight:** 13.4
Club Honours: Div 3 '88
International Honours: E: B-1; U21-2
Marco spent much of the 2001-02 season at Northampton in an unfamiliar midfield role due to the injury crisis at the club. He looked comfortable there, creating as well as scoring goals and although in the veteran stages of his career he showed that he still posed a threat to opposition defences. He reached two milestones during the campaign, 700 first-class games and 250 first-class goals.
York C (From apprentice on 5/9/1985) FL 42+18/14 FLC 4+3/1 Others 4/3
Sunderland (£80,000 on 23/9/1987) FL 155+2/74 FLC 14/9 FAC 5 Others 9/4
Crystal Palace (£1,800,000 on 1/10/1991) FL 15/5 FLC 6/1 FAC 1 Others 3/1
Derby Co (£1,000,000 on 31/1/1992) F/PL 163+25/50 FLC 13/7 FAC 8+1/3 Others 16+1/8 (Free to Panionios, Greece during 1997 close season)
Birmingham C (Loaned on 14/10/1996) FL 0+2
Oxford U (Loaned on 31/1/1997) FL 5/1
Stoke C (Free on 24/12/1997) FL 2+6 FAC 1/1
York C (Free on 20/2/1998) FL 5+2/1
Darlington (Free on 8/7/1998) FL 81+1/47 FLC 4/1 FAC 4/1 Others 5+1/3
Northampton T (Free on 28/6/2000) FL 64+15/13 FLC 3/1 FAC 3+1/2 Others 2+1

GABBIDON Daniel (Danny)
Leon
Born: Cwmbran, 8 August 1979
Height: 6'1" **Weight:** 11.2

International Honours: W: 1; U21-17; Yth
This cool and composed defender was a near ever present for Cardiff City last term. A versatile player who can operate at left back, right back or wing back on either side, his best position is considered to be in the centre of defence. A highlight of his campaign was his impressive senior debut for Wales in the goalless draw against the Czech Republic at the Millennium Stadium. He signed a new long-term contract for the Bluebirds during the season.
West Bromwich A (From trainee on 3/7/1998) FL 20 FLC 4+1 FAC 2
Cardiff C (£175,000 + on 10/8/2000) FL 86+1/6 FLC 3 FAC 8

GADSBY Matthew John
Born: Sutton Coldfield, 6 September 1979
Height: 6'1" **Weight:** 11.12
Matthew began the 2001-02 season on the right side of defence for Walsall and though he didn't hold down a regular place, he played resourcefully whenever called upon, whether in defence or midfield, and his accurate crossing was a strong feature of his game.
Walsall (From trainee on 12/2/1998) FL 23+14 FLC 2 FAC 0+1 Others 2+5

GAIN Peter Thomas
Born: Hammersmith, 11 November 1976
Height: 6'1" **Weight:** 11.0
International Honours: RoI: U21-1; Yth
Peter was first choice for Lincoln on the left side of a four-man midfield although he was also occasionally called on to fill the left-back role. He had a steady season saving one of his better performances for the final game at Hull when he was switched to the right side of the pitch with great effect. His skill on the ball showed up in what proved a difficult season with the Imps struggling near the foot of the table for much of the campaign.
Tottenham H (From trainee on 1/7/1995)
Lincoln C (Loaned on 31/12/1998) FL 0+1 Others 1
Lincoln C (£15,000 on 26/3/1999) FL 74+27/9 FLC 4+1 FAC 6+1/1 Others 4+1

GALL Kevin Alexander
Born: Merthyr Tydfil, 4 February 1982
Height: 5'9" **Weight:** 11.1
International Honours: W: U21-2; Yth; Sch
This lively striker began the 2001-02 campaign in an unfamiliar midfield role for Bristol Rovers, but still managed to

score three goals in his first nine starts. He featured regularly in the side in the first half of the season but then fell out of favour and although he scored a number of goals for the reserves he appeared in the starting line-up just four more times. Kevin made his debut for Wales at U21 level against Norway and Belarus.
Newcastle U (From trainee on 29/4/1999)
Bristol Rov (Free on 22/3/2001) FL 28+13/5 FLC 2 FAC 2+1 Others 2+1

GALLACHER Kevin William
Born: Clydebank, 23 November 1966
Height: 5'8" **Weight:** 11.6
International Honours: S: 53; B-2; U21-7; Yth
Kevin had something of a lost season at Preston last term, mainly due to persistent injury problems. Hamstring trouble reduced him to just a handful of first-team appearances and he eventually moved on to Sheffield Wednesday on the transfer deadline day. Although he clearly showed his experience as a wing man at Hillsborough, he made little impact during his spell with the club.
Dundee U (Signed from Duntocher BC on 2/9/1983) SL 118+13/27 SLC 13/5 SC 20+3/5 Others 15+6/3
Coventry C (£900,000 on 29/1/1990) F/PL 99+1/28 FLC 11/7 FAC 4 Others 2
Blackburn Rov (£1,500,000 on 22/3/1993) P/FL 132+12/46 FLC 8+2/3 FAC 13/4 Others 1+1
Newcastle U (£700,000 on 1/10/1999) PL 27+12/4 FLC 2/1 FAC 5+1/1
Preston NE (Free on 17/8/2001) FL 1+4/1 FLC 0+1/1
Sheffield Wed (Free on 28/3/2002) FL 0+4

GALLAS William
Born: Paris, France, 17 August 1977
Height: 6'1" **Weight:** 12.7
International Honours: France: U21
The latest in a chain of top-quality French central defenders to appear for Chelsea, this impressive young player had a sensational first season in English football. Comfortable anywhere in defence, he began the campaign at right back but when the mercurial Marcel Desailly contracted an achilles tendon injury in October he was switched to central defence to partner John Terry and the youngsters formed a formidable barrier and were an integral component in the Blues' vastly-improved defensive record. His season appeared to be over when, on Easter Saturday, he picked up a stress fracture of the leg against Derby County which ruled him out of the FA

Cup semi-final but he made a remarkable recovery and was pressed into service as an emergency left back for the final.
Chelsea (£6,200,000 from Marseilles, France, ex SM Caen, on 4/7/2001) PL 27+3/1 FLC 4 FAC 4/1 Others 3

GALLEN Kevin Andrew
Born: Chiswick, 21 September 1975
Height: 5'11" **Weight:** 12.10
International Honours: E: U21-4; Yth (UEFA-U18 '93); Sch
Kevin made his debut for Barnsley on the opening day of the 2001-02 season, but soon afterwards he suffered a torn hamstring and was out until early October. He played when fit and scored 'Goal of the Season' contender for the Reds with a volley from outside the penalty area against local rivals Sheffield Wednesday. Soon after Steve Parkin was installed as manager he was transferred to Queen's Park Rangers where he made an immediate impact, scoring two on his debut. He kept his place for the remainder of the season and established a good understanding with fellow striker Andy Thomson.
Queens Park R (From trainee on 22/9/1992) P/FL 126+45/36 FLC 9+3/2 FAC 6+2/2
Huddersfield T (Free on 10/8/2000) FL 30+8/10 FAC 1
Barnsley (Free on 27/7/2001) FL 8+1/2 FLC 0+1
Queens Park R (Free on 20/11/2001) FL 25/7

GALLI Filippo
Born: Monza, Italy, 19 May 1963
Height: 6'0" **Weight:** 11.7
Filippo joined Watford on a free transfer before the start of the 2001-02 season and was promptly elected team captain. A player with a distinguished pedigree – he won three European Cups during his 14 years with AC Milan – Filippo lived up to his billing with a series of polished performances in central defence and endeared himself to the fans with his effort and commitment. He even scored a rare goal against Walsall. At 38, Filippo was the oldest Watford first-team debutant since Taffy Davies in the 1950s, but unfortunately his age also made him prone to niggling injuries, especially a hamstring strain that kept him out during November and December, and a broken collarbone at Stockport in April. He was released at the end of the campaign.
Watford (Free from Brescia, Italy, AC Milan, Pesara, Reggiana, on 19/7/2001) FL 27+1/1 FLC 1

GALLIMORE Anthony (Tony) Mark
Born: Crewe, 21 February 1972
Height: 5'11" **Weight:** 12.6
Club Honours: Div 3 '95; AMC '98
Tony recovered from the injury problems that had dogged his 2000-01 campaign and re-established himself as one of Grimsby Town's most consistent players. A strong defender with a powerful left foot, his uncompromising style earned him some yellow cards, but he was a valued team member as the Mariners fought successfully to avoid the drop.
Stoke C (From trainee on 11/7/1990) FL 6+5
Carlisle U (Loaned on 3/10/1991) FL 8
Carlisle U (Loaned on 26/2/1992) FL 8
Carlisle U (£15,000 on 25/3/1993) FL 124/9 FLC 8/1 FAC 8 Others 24/1
Grimsby T (£125,000 on 28/3/1996) FL 225+10/4 FLC 19/2 FAC 13 Others 10

GALLOWAY Michael (Mick) Anthony
Born: Nottingham, 13 October 1974
Height: 5'11" **Weight:** 12.4
The 2001-02 season was a very disappointing one for Carlisle's skilful midfielder. Sidelined with a cartilage injury in October, he marked his return to full fitness with a late appearance off the bench at Port Vale in the LDV Vans Trophy tie. It proved to be his only first-team game of the campaign and he eventually went to Gretna on loan. He remains on the books at Brunton Park where he will hope to make more impact in 2002-03.
Notts Co (From trainee on 15/6/1993) FL 17+4 FLC 2 FAC 0+1 Others 4
Gillingham (£10,000 + on 27/3/1997) FL 58+17/5 FLC 3+1 FAC 1+2 Others 5
Lincoln C (Loaned on 29/9/1999) FL 5
Chesterfield (£15,000 on 5/11/1999) FL 18+2/1 FLC 2+1 Others 3
Carlisle U (Free on 9/11/2000) FL 26/1 FAC 2 Others 0+1

GAMBLE Joseph (Joe) Finbar
Born: Cork, 14 January 1982
Height: 5'7" **Weight:** 11.2
International Honours: RoI: U21-5; Yth
Joe completed his first 90 minutes of League action for Reading when he starred in the 1-0 away victory at Huddersfield last January, and made a handful of other senior appearances to add to his total. A slim but tough and skilful midfielder, his ability was recognised by the Republic of Ireland U21 selectors, and he rewarded them by coming off the bench to score the winner in a 3-2 victory over Denmark in his

hometown of Cork. Joe signed an extension to his contract that will keep him at the Madejski Stadium until 2004.
Reading (Free from Cork C on 8/8/2000) FL 2+5 FLC 0+2 FAC 1+1 Others 2

GARCIA Richard
Born: Perth, Australia, 4 September 1981
Height: 6'1" **Weight:** 11.2
Club Honours: FAYC '99
International Honours: Australia: Yth
Richard recovered from a cruciate knee ligament injury to finally make his West Ham debut last September against Reading in the Worthington Cup. However, it was not until February that he made his bow in the Premiership, against Bolton at the Reebok Stadium. The central midfielder generally featured from the subs' bench, but managed two starts during the campaign.
West Ham U (From trainee on 16/9/1998) PL 2+6 FLC 0+1
Leyton Orient (Loaned on 11/8/2000) FL 18/4 FLC 3

GARDEN Stuart Robertson
Born: Dundee, 10 February 1972
Height: 6'0" **Weight:** 12.5
Stuart joined Notts County during the 2001 close season and was expected to be the second choice 'keeper last term. However when given the opportunity of a place in the senior line-up he seized it with both hands. His form was such that it was impossible to leave him out and his contribution of clean sheets became an essential part of the club's late-season revival.
Dundee (Signed from Dundee NE on 1/3/1993)
Brechin C (Free on 1/9/1995) SL 91+2 SLC 4 SC 8 Others 3
Forfar Ath (Free on 4/8/1999) SL 67 SLC 1 SC 1 Others 1
Notts Co (Free on 5/7/2001) FL 21 Others 2

GARDNER Anthony
Born: Stone, 19 September 1980
Height: 6'5" **Weight:** 13.8
International Honours: E: U21-1
This towering young Spurs defender is extremely agile and skilful for one of such height. He looks composed on the ball and a real prospect to fill the hole left by the departure of the likes of Sol Campbell at the back. Pacy, intelligent and confident in his abilities, Anthony has a great future at White Hart Lane.
Port Vale (From trainee on 31/7/1998) FL 40+1/4 FLC 2 FAC 1
Tottenham H (£1,000,000 on 28/1/2000) PL 16+7 FLC 3 FAC 1

GARDNER Ricardo Wayne
Born: Jamaica, 25 September 1978
Height: 5'9" **Weight:** 11.0
International Honours: Jamaica: 40
A real livewire on the left-hand side of
midfield, Ricardo was a vital part of the
team that secured Premiership survival for
Bolton last season. Despite a niggling foot
injury which caused him to miss the last
four games, he played some lovely
football and caused endless problems for
opposing defenders who struggled to
cope with his mazy runs and effortless
trickery when on the ball. He also
notched some crucial goals, notably the
winner in the game against West Ham at
the Reebok in February.
*Bolton W (£1,000,000 from Harbour View,
Jamaica on 17/8/1998) P/FL 101+21/13 FLC
11+2/2 FAC 6+3 Others 6/2*

GARNER Glyn
Born: Pontypool, 9 December 1976
Height: 6'2" **Weight:** 13.6
Bury's second choice goalkeeper made his
debut in the Shakers' LDV Vans Trophy
game against Notts County and also
played in an FA Cup replay against Lincoln
City before finally making his Football
League debut against Brighton in
December. One of his more dramatic
performances was at home to Cambridge
when he entered the fray after Paddy
Kenny was dismissed and immediately
saved a penalty. After creating a
favourable impression with some
confident performances he was rewarded
with his fifth and final League start in the
closing fixture of the season.
*Bury (Free from Llanelli on 7/7/2000) FL 5+2
FAC 1 Others 1*

GARNETT Shaun Maurice
Born: Wallasey, 22 November 1969
Height: 6'2" **Weight:** 13.4
Club Honours: AMC '90
After falling out of favour, Shaun was one
of 14 players transfer listed by new
Oldham boss Mick Wadsworth last
December. The 32-year-old centre-half
then suffered cruciate ligament damage
that ruled him out for the season and
beyond the expiry date of his existing
contract. In recognition of past services,
Athletic offered the player a new deal
enabling him to make a full recovery and
challenge for a first-team place in the
2002-03 campaign.
*Tranmere Rov (From trainee on 15/6/1988)
FL 110+2/5 FLC 13/1 FAC 4 Others 15+2*
Chester C (Loaned on 1/10/1992) FL 9
*Preston NE (Loaned on 11/12/1992) FL 10/2
Others 1*

Wigan Ath (Loaned on 26/2/1993) FL 13/1
*Swansea C (£200,000 on 11/3/1996) FL 15
FLC 2*
*Oldham Ath (£150,000 on 19/9/1996) FL
165+8/9 FLC 7 FAC 12 Others 4*

GARROCHO Carlos Miguel
Born: Angola, 26 January 1974
Height: 5'11" **Weight:** 12.2
A former team-mate of Jorge Leitao,
Carlos had accumulated a career total of
more than 100 senior goals in Portugal
before trying his luck at Walsall. He
showed some neat touches as a wide
man in pre-season games but had only
the occasional first-team outing before
sustaining a serious training ground
injury in March. He underwent keyhole
surgery in April to clear up cruciate
ligament damage and should be fit in
time for the start of the 2002-03
campaign.
*Walsall (Free from Leca, Portugal, ex CD
Feirense, on 9/8/2001) FL 2+2 FLC 0+1*

GASCOIGNE Paul John
Born: Gateshead, 27 May 1967
Height: 5'10" **Weight:** 11.12
Club Honours: FAYC '85; FAC '91. SPL
'96, '97; SLC '97; SC '96
International Honours: E: 57; B-4; U21-
13; Yth
A fleetingly intermittent figure at Everton,
Paul still produced a few flashes of the
old superstar. He scored what will almost
certainly be his final Premiership goal in a
draw at Bolton in November, then in an
FA Cup tie against Leyton Orient
produced a hat-trick of goal-creating
passes. Always close to Walter Smith,
when his mentor was sacked he quickly
followed him out of the Goodison exit
door to First Division Burnley. He arrived
at Turf Moor in a blaze of publicity, but
after a solid debut against Bradford City
he soon found himself on the bench and
he failed to inspire the Clarets to a place
in the play-offs before leaving in the
summer.
*Newcastle U (From apprentice on
13/5/1985) FL 83+9/21 FLC 8/1 FAC 4/3
Others 2+1*
*Tottenham H (£2,000,000 on 18/7/1988) FL
91+1/19 FLC 14+1/8 FAC 6/6 (£5,500,000 to
Lazio, Italy on 1/5/1992)*
*Glasgow R (£4,300,000 on 10/7/1995) SL
64+10/30 SLC 7/4 SC 7+1/3 Others 16/2*
*Middlesbrough (£3,450,000 on 27/3/1998)
P/FL 39+2/4 FLC 3+2 FAC 2*
*Everton (Free on 20/7/2000) PL 18+14/1 FLC
1+1 FAC 3+1*
Burnley (Free on 18/3/2002) FL 3+3

GAVIN Jason Joseph
Born: Dublin, 14 March 1980
Height: 6'1" **Weight:** 12.7
International Honours: RoI: U21-6; Yth
(UEFA-U18 '98)
This promising Middlesbrough youngster
continued his development at the
Riverside last term, making around a
dozen first-team appearances spread over
the season. He is a tough and
uncompromising defender who is very
effective in the air and never shirks a
tackle.
*Middlesbrough (From trainee on 26/3/1997)
PL 19+12 FLC 4+1 FAC 1+2*

GAY Daniel (Danny) Karl
Born: Norwich, 5 August 1982
Height: 6'1" **Weight:** 12.8
Danny joined Southend during the 2001
close season, but spent most of the
campaign as deputy 'keeper to Darryl
Flahavan. He made his first appearance
for the Blues from the subs' bench at
Rochdale after Flahavan had received a
red card. Commanding for his size, he
proved a very able deputy and went on to
make his full debut against League
leaders Luton. Called upon again later in
the campaign, his shot-stopping ability
meant that the Blues' defence retained
full confidence whichever custodian they
played in front of.
*Southend U (Free from trainee at Norwich C
on 6/7/2001) FL 5+1*

GAYLE Marcus Anthony
Born: Hammersmith, 27 September 1970
Height: 6'1" **Weight:** 12.9
Club Honours: Div 3 '92
International Honours: E: Yth.
Jamaica: 14
Marcus joined Watford for a substantial
fee in the summer of 2001. An
experienced support striker, he made an
excellent start, netting with a beautifully
struck free kick against Plymouth, and
also had the pleasure of scoring against
his old club Wimbledon. However a run
of 25 League games without a goal –
including two missed penalties – sapped
his confidence, although he did find the
net against Arsenal in the FA Cup.
Manager Luca Vialli continued to select
him, mainly in an out-and-out striking
role, but placed him on the transfer list in
February.
*Brentford (From trainee on 6/7/1989) FL
118+38/22 FLC 6+3 FAC 6+2/2 Others
14+6/2*
*Wimbledon (£250,000 on 24/3/1994) P/FL
198+38/37 FLC 23+1/7 FAC 18+7/3*

155

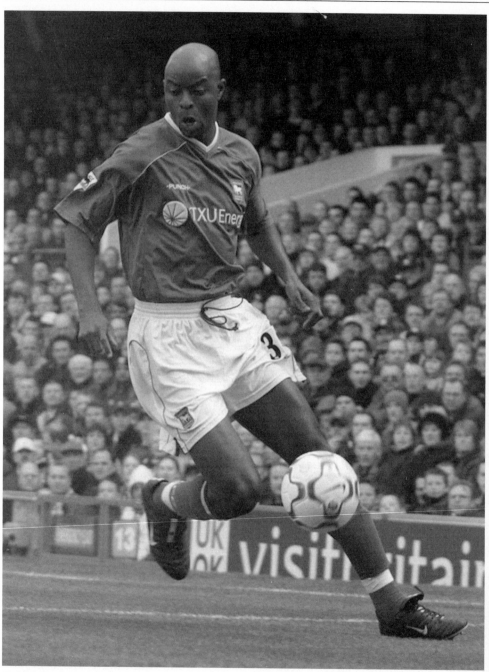

Finidi George

Glasgow R (£900,000 on 9/3/2001) SL 28+8/4
Watford (£900,000 on 8/8/2001) FL 28+8/4 FLC 3+1/2 FAC 1/1

GEARY Derek Peter
Born: Dublin, 19 June 1980
Height: 5'6" **Weight:** 10.8
This young enthusiastic full back was happy to play on either flank for Sheffield Wednesday last term and always gave 100 per cent. Right back is his preferred position but his attacking forays help the side out on either side of the pitch, although he still needs to tighten up defensively.
Sheffield Wed (Signed from Cherry Orchard on 17/11/1997) FL 30+7 FLC 10+1 FAC 1

GEMMILL Scot
Born: Paisley, 2 January 1971
Height: 5'11" **Weight:** 11.6
Club Honours: FMC '92; Div 1 '98
International Honours: S: 22; B-2; U21-4
An industrious and perceptive midfielder, the arrival of Berti Vogts as Scottish boss finally gave Scot greater opportunities to show his talents at international level. He claimed a spectacular strike against Middlesbrough early in the season to take Everton temporarily top of the table, but his fortunes dipped like those of his club, as the season progressed. But for a five game absence through injury in September he was almost ever present, without ever quite hitting the form he had shown earlier in his Goodison career. He is the son of former Scotland international Archie Gemmill.
Nottingham F (From trainee on 5/1/1990) F/PL 228+17/21 FLC 29+2/3 FAC 19+2/1 Others 13+1/4
Everton (£250,000 on 25/3/1999) PL 69+12/5 FLC 2 FAC 6+2

GEORGE Finidi
Born: Port Harcourt, Nigeria, 15 April 1971
Height: 6'2" **Weight:** 12.7
International Honours: Nigeria:
Finidi made an immediate impact on his home debut for Ipswich against Derby, scoring twice and producing an outstanding performance. He received a setback at Fulham in October when he broke his jaw and was out for five weeks but came back with a mini-scoring streak before disappearing for African Nations' Cup duty. Before he left he scored the goal of the season at Portman Road against Sunderland when he ran on to Matt Holland's through ball and chipped

into the net from the right-hand corner of the penalty area. He was unable to recapture his form on his return from Mali and consequently was in and out of the side.
Ipswich T (£3,100,000 from Real Mallorca, Spain, ex Port Harcourt, Calabar Rov, Ajax, on 17/8/2001) PL 21+4/6 Others 4/1

GEORGE Liam Brendan
Born: Luton, 2 February 1979
Height: 5'9" **Weight:** 11.3
International Honours: RoI: U21-4; Yth (UEFA-U18 '98)
After failing to sign a new contract at the start of last season Liam found himself out of favour at Luton and he rarely featured at first-team level. He was released in January and after a number of trials in England he moved north of the border and made two appearances for Clyde as a trialist, before signing forms for Conference outfit Stevenage Borough.
Luton T (From trainee on 20/1/1997) FL 81+21/20 FLC 3+6 FAC 9+1/4 Others 2+1

GERRARD Paul William
Born: Heywood, 22 January 1973
Height: 6'2" **Weight:** 14.4
International Honours: E: U21-18
On his day a talented shot-stopper, Paul's season effectively ended in October when he was dropped in favour of Steve Simonsen after a run of 25 consecutive appearances and only regained his place for a brief spell at the end of the campaign when the youngster was injured. Despite this he will be hoping to regain his place under new boss David Moyes in 2002-03.
Oldham Ath (From trainee on 2/11/1991) P/FL 118+1 FLC 7 FAC 7 Others 2+1
Everton (£1,000,000 + on 1/7/1996) PL 87+1 FLC 6 FAC 3
Oxford U (Loaned on 18/12/1998) FL 16

GERRARD Steven George
Born: Huyton, 30 May 1980
Height: 6'2" **Weight:** 12.4
Club Honours: FLC '01; FAC '01; UEFAC '01; ESC '01
International Honours: E: 10; U21-4; Yth
After a relatively injury-free season for Liverpool it was ironic for player and country that this midfielder was declared unavailable for the 2002 World Cup finals when it was announced that he had a recurrence of a groin strain requiring an operation. Steven started the campaign in outstanding form with a majestic display for England in the historic 5-1 victory over Germany in Munich. However on his own

admission his form through the season was inconsistent, especially during the Reds' mid-season slump. He is the complete midfield player, composed on the ball, tigerish in the tackle and immaculate with his long passes.
Liverpool (From trainee on 26/2/1998) PL 85+17/11 FLC 4 FAC 6+2/1 Others 24+1/3

GHENT Matthew Ian
Born: Burton, 5 October 1980
Height: 6'3" **Weight:** 14.1
International Honours: E: Yth; Sch
After signing for Barnsley at the start of the 2001-02 campaign Matthew was sidelined for six weeks with knee ligament damage. He finally made his debut for the Reds at Wimbledon on the last day of the season. He managed to keep a clean sheet, giving an excellent display of shot stopping that was capped when he saved a penalty to maintain Barnsley's lead.
Aston Villa (From trainee on 13/10/1997)
Lincoln C (Free on 1/12/2000) FL 0+1 FAC 1 (Free to Forest Green Rovers in January 2001)
Barnsley (Free on 10/8/2001) FL 1

GIBB Alistair (Ally) Stuart
Born: Salisbury, 17 February 1976
Height: 5'9" **Weight:** 11.7
Ally featured in all but six of Stockport County's games last term and excited the fans with his energetic, storming runs down the right-hand side. He was also the only player at Edgeley Park to feature regularly for both Andy Kilner and new boss Carlton Palmer. Although his crossing can at times be erratic, and he is yet to score a goal after more than 100 County appearances, his popularity deservedly earned him the Supporters Club 'Player of the Year' award.
Norwich C (From trainee on 1/7/1994)
Northampton T (Loaned on 22/9/1995) FL 9/1
Northampton T (£30,000 on 5/2/1996) FL 51+7/3 FLC 8+4 FAC 5+3 Others 6+3
Stockport Co (£50,000 on 18/2/2000) FL 91+3 FLC 4 FAC 3

GIBBS Nigel James
Born: St Albans, 20 November 1965
Height: 5'7" **Weight:** 11.11
Club Honours: FAYC '82; Div 2 '98
International Honours: E: U21-5; Yth
Nigel came on as a substitute in the last game of the 2001-02 season and was greeted with a standing ovation – fitting reward for a full back who had spent the whole of his career with Watford and was retiring after 20 seasons of stalwart service. A groin operation in July precluded any earlier appearances and prevented him from adding to his 491

Ryan Giggs

senior games, a total exceeded only by Luther Blissett, although Nigel has made more starts for Watford than anyone. Voted club captain at the start of the season, Nigel was appointed Chief Scout in December and has deservedly been granted a second testimonial.
Watford (From apprentice on 23/11/1983)
P/FL 385+23/5 FLC 25/2 FAC 39+2 Others 17

GIBBS Paul Derek
Born: Gorleston, 26 October 1972
Height: 5'10" **Weight:** 11.10
A fine player down the Brentford left, Paul alternated between left back and the left side of midfield throughout the season. He scored a scorching 25-yarder against Morecambe in November before being sidelined with a hernia the following month. In March he was sold to Barnsley as new boss Steve Parkin sought to strengthen his defence and in his brief spell with the Reds he showed himself to be a specialist with dead-ball kicks.
Colchester U (Signed from Diss T on 6/3/1995) FL 39+14/3 FAC 1+1 Others 8+1
Torquay U (Free on 26/7/1997) FL 40+1/7 FLC 4/1 FAC 3/1 Others 3/1
Plymouth Arg (Free on 7/7/1998) FL 30+4/3 FLC 2
Brentford (Free on 10/7/2000) FL 49+5/3 FLC 3 FAC 3/1 Others 6+1
Barnsley (Free on 15/3/2002) FL 4

GIBSON Alexander (Alex) Jonathan
Born: Plymouth, 12 August 1982
Height: 5'9" **Weight:** 10.4
Alex joined Port Vale during the 2001 close season and made his League debut in September in the 1-1 draw at Chesterfield. He held his place for the next game, the LDV Vans Trophy tie with Carlisle, but was confined to the subs' bench or the reserves thereafter. A strong running right wing back, he was released at the end of the campaign.
Port Vale (Free from trainee at Stoke C on 2/7/2001) FL 1 Others 1

GIBSON Robin John
Born: Crewe, 15 November 1979
Height: 5'6" **Weight:** 10.7
This busy, mobile winger again failed to establish himself at Wrexham last season. A player who always battles for his side, his competitiveness was much appreciated by the Racecourse fans, but nevertheless he was released in the summer.
Wrexham (From trainee on 3/7/1998) FL 49+28/3 FLC 1+1 FAC 2+2/1 Others 2+4

GIER Robert (Rob) James
Born: Bracknell, 6 January 1980
Height: 5'9" **Weight:** 11.7
Last season was a frustrating time for Rob at Wimbledon and he received few opportunities at first-team level. He made just three appearances, all at the beginning of the campaign, but was a regular in the reserves, captaining the side. He mostly featured at right back but can also play as a central defender, his pace and tackling abilities being suitable for either role.
Wimbledon (From trainee on 11/5/1999) FL 16+1 FLC 1+2

GIGGS Ryan Joseph
Born: Cardiff, 29 November 1973
Height: 5'11" **Weight:** 10.9
Club Honours: ESC '91; FAYC '92; FLC '92; PL '93, '94, '96, '97, '99, '00, '01; CS '93, '94, '96, '97; FAC '94, '96, '99; EC '99
International Honours: W: 36; U21-1; Yth. E: Sch
This talented left winger has such an influence on United's fortunes these days that when he was absent with hamstring trouble last autumn the team entered something resembling a slump. He returned to partner Ruud van Nistelrooy and the two won plenty of plaudits for some top-class striking performances. United won seven matches on the trot after his return, but in the end they were not quite good enough to win any of the major trophies last term. Whether he will remain as out-and-out striker is unclear but he certainly has plenty of top-class football left in him. Ryan was again honoured by his fellow professionals with a place in the PFA's Premiership team for the season.
Manchester U (From trainee on 1/12/1990)
F/PL 309+37/71 FLC 17+4/6 FAC 36+4/7 Others 74+4/15

GILCHRIST Philip (Phil) Alexander
Born: Stockton on Tees, 25 August 1973
Height: 5'11" **Weight:** 13.12
Club Honours: FLC '00
Playing on the left side of West Bromwich Albion's mean defence, Phil showed excellent positional sense and a positive approach, enjoying a superb season. Always composed, solid in the tackle, and hard working, he suffered a broken wrist at Barnsley early in the season and then received a nasty facial injury just before Christmas in the home game with Sheffield Wednesday, but he bounced back each time,
Nottingham F (From trainee on 5/12/1990)
Middlesbrough (Free on 10/11/1992)
Hartlepool U (Free on 27/11/1992) FL 77+5 FLC 4+1 FAC 4 Others 5
Oxford U (£100,000 on 17/2/1995) FL 173+4/10 FLC 16 FAC 9/1 Others 3
Leicester C (£500,000 on 10/8/1999) PL 23+16/1 FLC 6+1 FAC 4+1
West Bromwich A (£500,000 on 22/3/2001) FL 51 FLC 3 FAC 4 Others 2

GILES Martyn
Born: Cardiff, 10 April 1983
Height: 6'0" **Weight:** 12.0
International Honours: W: Yth
Martyn made two senior appearances for Cardiff during his first season as a senior professional, netting his first goal in the 7-1 LDV Vans Trophy win over Rushden. He is a talented left-sided player.
Cardiff C (From trainee on 23/3/2001) FL 1+4 Others 0+2/1

GILKS Matthew (Matty)
Born: Oldham, 4 June 1982
Height: 6'1" **Weight:** 12.7
Matty could reasonably have expected to spend his first season as a professional understudying Rochdale's undisputed number one 'keeper, Neil Edwards, but circumstances conspired to pitch him straight into the limelight. Playing in the first two games as Edwards was suspended, he was immediately thrust back into Dale's table-topping side when his mentor was injured. Although he was later given a breather when on-loan 'keepers were brought in, he continued to pull out excellent performances when called upon and won the Nationwide League 'Save of the Month' for a spectacular effort in a goalless draw at York in January.
Rochdale (From trainee on 4/7/2001) FL 21+1 FLC 1 FAC 2

GILL Jeremy (Jerry) Morley
Born: Clevedon, 8 September 1970
Height: 5'7" **Weight:** 11.0
International Honours: E: SP-1
Jerry began the 2001-02 season as first choice for Birmingham City, and performed in his usual dedicated and hard-working manner. Never one to get too carried away, he was steady and nothing but professional. He found favour only once under Steve Bruce, who signed Jeff Kenna to play right back, in the FA Cup defeat at Liverpool.
Leyton Orient (Free from Trowbridge T on 16/12/1988). Free to Weston super Mare on 1/7/1990)
Birmingham C (£30,000 from Yeovil T on 14/7/1997) FL 43+17 FLC 11+1 FAC 3 Others 1

GILL Matthew James
Born: Cambridge, 8 November 1980
Height: 5'11" **Weight:** 12.10
Matthew spent most of last season recovering from a serious knee injury suffered the previous March. It was not until late February that he returned to action but he settled in immediately and performed as if he had never been away. His performance belittled the length of his lay off and it was as if he had never been out injured. He was used at full back rather than in his preferred midfield role, but adapted well to the change.
Peterborough U (From trainee on 2/3/1998) FL 53+24/4 FLC 2 FAC 4 Others 2+3

GILL Wayne John
Born: Chorley, 28 November 1975
Height: 5'9" **Weight:** 11.0
Out of favour at Tranmere, Wayne joined Oldham last October. His debut came in the home defeat by Bristol City and he made just two further appearances before injuries struck. After damaged ankle ligaments sidelined him for over two months, Wayne broke down with a recurrence of another old ankle injury in March. He played no further part in Athletic's campaign.
Blackburn Rov (From trainee on 12/7/1994) FLC 3
Blackpool (Signed on 6/3/2000) FL 12/7
Tranmere Rov (Free on 5/7/2000) FL 7+9/2 FLC 3+2/1 FAC 0+1
Oldham Ath (£70,000 on 12/10/2001) FL 3

GILLESPIE Keith Robert
Born: Bangor, 18 February 1975
Height: 5'10" **Weight:** 11.3
Club Honours: FAYC '92; FLC '02
International Honours: NI: 41; U21-1; Yth; Sch
Keith emerged from being written out of Blackburn's plans to becoming an integral part of the team on the right hand side last term, but remained as enigmatic and frustrating as ever. He regained the confidence to take on his man on the outside but occasionally looked to have lost half-a-yard of his once explosive pace. An occasional goal-scorer, he produced a glorious effort against Manchester United, when he cut inside and unleashed a rocket shot with his left foot.
Manchester U (From trainee on 3/2/1993) PL 3+6/1 FLC 3 FAC 1+1/1
Wigan Ath (Loaned on 3/9/1993) FL 8/4 Others 2
Newcastle U (£1,000,000 on 12/1/1995) PL 94+19/11 FLC 7+1/1 FAC 9+1/2 Others 11+5

Blackburn Rov (£2,250,000 on 18/12/1998) P/FL 57+31/5 FLC 6+1 FAC 6+2/1
Wigan Ath (Loaned on 1/12/2000) FL 4+1 FAC 2

GILLMAN Robert
Born: London, 26 April 1984
Height: 6'2" **Weight:** 13.8
A second-year trainee at Luton, Robert can play in defence or midfield with equal ability. Called up to play in the reserves, he scored a goal in the Bedfordshire Premier Cup and then made the starting line-up for the LDV Vans Trophy tie against Dagenham & Redbridge. He performed very well that night but picked up a serious injury in March and this ruled him out of further contention.
Luton T (Trainee) Others 1

GILROY David Miles
Born: Yeovil, 23 December 1982
Height: 5'11" **Weight:** 11.3
This trainee striker made his League debut for Bristol Rovers early on last season when he came off the subs' bench against Luton Town and then started in the following match at Darlington. A regular reserve-team goal-scorer, he later had loan spells with Dr Martens League clubs Clevedon Town and Bath City to gain further experience of senior football. He was rewarded with a full professional contract and will be aiming to claim a regular first-team place with the Pirates in the near future.
Bristol Rov (Trainee) FL 2+2

GINOLA David Desire Marc
Born: Gassin, France, 25 January 1967
Height: 6'0" **Weight:** 11.10
Club Honours: FLC '99
International Honours: France: 17; B-2; U21
At his best David is an extremely talented footballer, who provides a danger to even the tightest defences with his tricky dribbling and excellent crosses. He rarely featured for Aston Villa last term, appearing only as a substitute in Premiership action and in February he made a surprise move to Everton. He enjoyed an influential debut in a televised game against Arsenal, which the Blues unluckily lost, but after four starts was relegated to the substitutes' bench and didn't start again.
Newcastle U (£2,500,000 from Paris St Germain, France, ex Toulon, Racing Paris, Brest, on 6/7/1995) PL 54+4/6 FLC 6 FAC 4 Others 7+1/1
Tottenham H (£2,000,000 on 18/7/1997) PL 100/12 FLC 13/4 FAC 11/5 Others 2+1

Aston Villa (£3,000,000 on 1/8/2000) PL 14+18/3 FLC 1+1 FAC 1 Others 3+3/2
Everton (Free on 8/2/2002) PL 2+3 FAC 2

GIVEN Seamus (Shay) John
Born: Lifford, 20 April 1976
Height: 6'0" **Weight:** 13.4
Club Honours: Div 1 '96
International Honours: RoI: 43; U21-5; Yth
Shay had a wonderful season as the last line of defence at Newcastle. Quick and agile with safe hands he has become a more complete custodian, excellent in one-on-one situations, and ready and able to patrol outside his area to quell any emerging threat. He barely made an error all season, and his performances at Everton and Sunderland were outstanding, while the home fans will remember his full length save of a Fabrizio Ravanelli penalty to secure a win against Derby. He was rewarded for his efforts with a place in the PFA Premiership team for the season.
Blackburn Rov (From Glasgow Celtic juniors on 8/8/1994) PL 2 FLC 0+1
Swindon T (Loaned on 4/8/1995) FL 5
Sunderland (Loaned on 19/11/1996) FL 17
Newcastle U (£1,500,000 on 14/7/1997) PL 141 FLC 4+1 FAC 17 Others 14

GLASS Stephen
Born: Dundee, 23 May 1976
Height: 5'9" **Weight:** 11.0
Club Honours: SLC '96
International Honours: S: 1; B-2; U21-11; Sch
Stephen arrived at Watford on a summer free transfer, although an injury at the start of the season delayed his debut until September. The archetypal left winger, with fine ball-playing skills and an accurate cross, he was a first-team regular for much of the campaign, although he seemed to fade towards the end. Highlights included two goals against Coventry and he will be looking to score more often in the 2002-03 campaign.
Aberdeen (Free from Crombie Sports on 25/10/1994) SL 93+13/7 SLC 10/2 SC 7+2 Others 3/2
Newcastle U (£650,000 on 22/7/1998) FL 24+19/7 FLC 3 FAC 3+4 Others 2+3
Watford (Free on 5/7/2001) FL 29+2/3 FLC 2

GLENNON Matthew (Matty) William
Born: Stockport, 8 October 1978
Height: 6'2" **Weight:** 14.9
Matty became a part of Hull's summer 2001 spending spree and soon

established himself as a popular figure around Boothferry Park. The confident keeper faced familiar competition at City as he had been Paul Musselwhite's understudy during his loan at Port Vale in 1999. The tables were turned in the first half of the campaign as Matt took over in the Tigers goal, and his impressive form helped Hull establish a top-three placing. However, his season was halted in December by a thigh injury and it was not until the last three games that he returned to the side.

Bolton W (From trainee on 3/7/1997)
Bristol Rov (Loaned on 15/9/2000) FL 1
Carlisle U (Loaned on 10/11/2000) FL 29 FAC 3 Others 1
Hull C (£50,000 on 20/6/2001) FL 26 FLC 2 FAC 2 Others 2

GLOVER Edward **Lee**
Born: Kettering, 24 April 1970
Height: 5'11" **Weight:** 12.1
Club Honours: FLC '89; FMC '92
International Honours: S; U21-3; Yth
Top goal scorer for the second consecutive season and Macclesfield's penalty taker, it was appropriate that Lee should score the decider in the record-breaking penalty shoot-out in the FA Cup first round replay against Forest Green. Lee played in the majority of the matches in the 2001-02 campaign and coped well with a series of different partners up front. He is particularly effective with his back to the goal when he can collect the ball, skilfully turn and shoot all in one action. He completed the UEFA-'B' coaching certificate during the season.
Nottingham F (From apprentice on 2/5/1987) F/PL 61+15/9 FLC 6+5/2 FAC 8+2/1 Others 4+1/1
Leicester C (Loaned on 14/9/1989) FL 3+2/1
Barnsley (Loaned on 18/1/1990) FL 8 FAC 4
Luton T (Loaned on 2/9/1991) FL 1
Port Vale (£200,000 on 2/8/1994) FL 38+14/7 FLC 5+1/4 FAC 0+2 Others 3+2/2
Rotherham U (£150,000 on 15/8/1996) FL 70+15/29 FLC 5 FAC 9+1/3 Others 1+1
Huddersfield T (Loaned on 3/3/1997) FL 11
Macclesfield T (Free on 5/7/2000) FL 67+13/17 FLC 1+1/1 FAC 4+1/2 Others 2/3

GNOHERE David **Arthur**
Born: Yamoussoukro, Ivory Coast, 20 November 1978
Height: 6'2" **Weight:** 12.13
Every so often, an improbable cult hero emerges at Burnley, and in 2001-02 it was this man-mountain who arrived just before the start of the season and made an instant impression. A central or left-sided defender, he was a player it was

impossible to ignore. Strong in the tackle, effective in the air and on the ground, and a sight to behold when charging forward, his sheer enthusiasm communicated itself to the crowd, who christened him 'King Arthur' after his two goals helped the Clarets to a 3-2 victory at local rivals Preston. The return of Steve Davis ended his guarantee of a first-team start, but the best of Arthur is surely yet to come.
Burnley (Free from Caen, France, ex AS Cannes, on 9/8/2001) FL 31+3/3 FLC 1 FAC 2

GOATER Leonard **Shaun**
Born: Hamilton, Bermuda, 25 February 1970
Height: 6'1" **Weight:** 12.0
Club Honours: AMC '96; Div 1 '02
International Honours: Bermuda: 19; Yth
The 2001-02 campaign proved to be a season that Shaun will never forget. Sharing the attacking duties for Manchester City with Paulo Wanchope, Darren Huckerby and latterly Jon Macken, he was a member of a strike force that scored 108 goals to equal a club record. He went on to record a tally of 32 goals in all competitions, the highlights of which included hat-tricks at Burnley and at home to Gillingham. His performances won him a place in the PFA's First Division team for the season.
Manchester U (Free from North Village, Bermuda on 8/5/1989)
Rotherham U (Free on 25/10/1989) FL 169+40/70 FLC 13+4/4 FAC 12+3/7 Others 15+5/5
Notts Co (Loaned on 12/11/1993) FL 1
Bristol C (£175,000 on 17/7/1996) FL 67+8/40 FLC 7/2 FAC 5 Others 5+1/1
Manchester C (£400,000 on 26/3/1998) P/FL 150+8/77 FLC 11/9 FAC 9+2/9 Others 3/1

GOFF Shaun **John**
Born: Tiverton, 13 April 1984
Height: 5'10" **Weight:** 11.10
This young left back impressed during his appearances for Exeter City reserves last term and the club rated him highly enough to offer him a professional deal. He went on to make his senior debut at Southend in April and will be aiming to feature more regularly in 2002-03.
Exeter C (Trainee) FL 2

GOLDBAEK Bjarne
Born: Nykobing Falster, Denmark, 6 October 1968
Height: 5'10" **Weight:** 12.4
Club Honours: Div 1 '01

International Honours: Denmark: 28; B-1; U21; Yth
Although Bjarne did not claim a regular place for Fulham during the 2001-02 season he did not disappoint when called upon. An excellent tackler and passer of the ball he is also not afraid to try his luck on goal from distance. A dead-ball specialist, he continued to display his ability with free kicks with excellent efforts in the FA Premier Reserve League games at Charlton and West Ham. His two-goal burst against the latter earned him a recall to the side and he returned to score a magnificent goal in the 3-0 home win over Bolton. Bjarne continued to represent Denmark for whom he was also more of a squad player rather than a first choice.
Chelsea (£350,000 from FC Copenhagen, Denmark, ex Naestved, FC Schalke, Kaiserslautern, Tennis Borussia, FC Koln, on 10/11/1998) PL 15+14/5 FLC 3 FAC 2+4 Others 1+1
Fulham (£500,000 + on 18/1/2000) P/FL 65+10/6 FLC 5 FAC 2+2

GOMA Alain
Born: Sault, France, 5 October 1972
Height: 6'0" **Weight:** 13.0
International Honours: France: 2; B-1; U21; Yth
After arriving at the end of the previous season when injury had restricted his appearances, Alain again found himself on the sidelines at Fulham with injury after just three Premiership games last term. His return to the side in mid-October coincided with an upturn in the team's fortunes and he established himself as a regular in the starting line-up for the remainder of the campaign. He is a commanding figure in the heart of defence where his excellent positional play and ability to read the game gave Fulham one of the meanest defences in the Premiership.
Newcastle U (£4,750,000 from Paris St Germain, France, on 9/7/1999) PL 32+1/1 FLC 4 FAC 2 Others 2
Fulham (£4,000,000 on 16/3/2001) P/FL 35+1 FLC 1 FAC 6

GOODEN Ty **Michael**
Born: Canvey Island, 23 October 1972
Height: 5'8" **Weight:** 12.6
Club Honours: Div 2 '96
Ty missed over half the 2001-02 season with a string of injuries, which included groin, calf, hip and ankle. The Gillingham midfielder showed when he was fit that he was an important member of the side with his cultured play on the left-hand

Shaun Goater

side of the pitch. The highlight of his season was undoubtedly his wonder goal at Arsenal in the FA Cup, which won the award by a local newspaper for 'Goal of the Season'.
Swindon T *(Free from Wycombe W on 17/9/1993) P/FL 118+28/9 FLC 6+1/1 FAC 7+1/1 Others 3+1*
Gillingham *(£75,000 on 4/1/2000) FL 52+7/5 FLC 4 FAC 2+1/1 Others 3/1*

GOODFELLOW Marc David
Born: Burton, 20 September 1981
Height: 5'8" **Weight:** 10.6
Marc had a terrific season with Stoke City last season, performing either in a central striking role or more usually wide on the left. His blistering pace caught out many Second Division defences who at times resorted to physical challenges as the only way to stop him. He is a fine prospect whose development will surely continue in 2002-03.
Stoke C *(From juniors on 29/1/1999) FL 11+19/5 FLC 1+2/1 FAC 1+3 Others 4/1*

GOODHIND Warren Ernest
Born: Johannesburg, South Africa, 16 August 1977
Height: 5'11" **Weight:** 11.6
Warren began the 2001-02 campaign in the Conference with newly relegated Barnet, but quickly made a return to League action with Cambridge United. Unfortunately he was badly affected by hamstring problems that subsequently restricted his appearances. He is an effective central defender who also appeared at full back for the U's last term.
Barnet *(From trainee on 3/7/1996) FL 73+20/3 FLC 5+1 FAC 2 Others 4/1*
Cambridge U *(£80,000 on 21/9/2001) FL 11+3 Others 1+3*

GOODING Scott Osmond
Born: Croydon, 2 January 1982
Height: 5'10" **Weight:** 11.7
This young Crystal Palace defender spent most of the 2001-02 season developing in the reserves. He received a belated Christmas present when given his first-team debut at Millwall on Boxing Day, coming on from the bench to replace Jamie Smith for the final quarter of an hour.
Crystal Palace *(From trainee on 4/7/2001) FL 0+1*

GOODISON Ian
Born: Jamaica, 21 November 1972
Height: 6'3" **Weight:** 12.10
International Honours: Jamaica

Ian was employed in the unfamiliar left-back role in the early stages of Hull's 2001-02 campaign. Having given some typically reliable performances, his season suffered a major setback in September when he suffered nasty cuts to his leg and knee in a road accident when back home on international duty. While struggling to recapture the previous season's form, the stylish defender's progress was further hampered by a knee injury. Ian rejected the offer of a new two-year contract in February and was released when his contract ended at the close of the season. He won 26 full international caps whilst with the Tigers.
Hull C *(Free from Olympic Gardens, Jamaica on 22/10/1999) FL 67+3/1 FLC 2 FAC 6+1 Others 5*

GOODLAD Mark
Born: Barnsley, 9 September 1979
Height: 6'0" **Weight:** 13.2
Club Honours: AMC '01
Port Vale's first choice goalkeeper had another excellent campaign between the posts in 2001-02. A deserved winner of the supporters' 'Player of the Year' award. A very good shot stopper with a bright future, he saved a twice-taken penalty at Peterborough and was instrumental in Vale's rise up the league table in the new year. He signed a new three-year contract just before the end of the season.
Nottingham F *(From trainee on 2/10/1996)*
Scarborough *(Loaned on 5/2/1999) FL 3*
Port Vale *(Free on 23/3/2000) FL 83+1 FLC 4 FAC 4 Others 9*

GOODMAN Donald (Don) Ralph
Born: Leeds, 9 May 1966
Height: 5'10" **Weight:** 13.2
Club Honours: Div 3 '85
After suffering a nagging injury in an early-season game against Wolves, Don came back strongly in the last two months of the season, inspiring his Walsall colleagues with his non-stop efforts and scoring a vital late winner against Barnsley after coming on as substitute. The Bescot faithful are hoping that at 36 he will have at least one more season in a Saddlers' shirt.
Bradford C *(Free from Collingham on 10/7/1984) FL 65+5/14 FLC 5+1/2 FAC 2+3/4 Others 4+1/2*
West Bromwich A *(£50,000 on 27/3/1987) FL 140+18/60 FLC 11/1 FAC 7/1 Others 5/1*
Sunderland *(£900,000 on 6/12/1991) FL 112+4/40 FLC 9/1 FAC 3/1 Others 4/2*

Wolverhampton W *(£1,100,000 on 6/12/1994) FL 115+10/33 FLC 8+1/4 FAC 16+1/2 Others 3 (Free to Hiroshima Antlers, Japan during 1998 close season)*
Barnsley *(Loaned on 25/11/1998) FL 5+3 FAC 2*
Motherwell *(Signed on 30/3/1999) SL 39+16/9 SLC 4+1 SC 4/3*
Walsall *(Free on 22/3/2001) FL 15+10/3 FLC 1 Others 3/1*

GOODRIDGE Gregory (Greg) Ronald St Clair
Born: Barbados, 10 July 1971
Height: 5'6" **Weight:** 10.0
International Honours: Barbados
This talented winger, was again rarely considered for Bristol City's first team last season. He joined Torquay United on a short-term contract and initially demonstrated the trickery and skill on the right flank that had endeared him to the fans at Plainmoor first time around. However, a decision to revert to a 5-3-2 formation meant that there was no place for him in the line-up and he did not earn an extended deal.
Torquay U *(Free from Lambada, St Vincent on 24/3/1994) FL 32+6/4 FLC 4/1 FAC 2+1 Others 3+1/1*
Queens Park R *(£350,000 on 9/8/1995) PL 0+7/1 FLC 0+1 FAC 0+1*
Bristol C *(£50,000 on 19/8/1996) FL 76+43/14 FLC 10+2/1 FAC 5+4/1 Others 3+5/1*
Cheltenham T *(Loaned on 24/2/2001) FL 10+1/1*
Torquay U *(Free on 30/11/2001) FL 9+8/1*

GORAM Andrew (Andy) Lewis
Born: Bury, 13 April 1964
Height: 5'11" **Weight:** 12.6
Club Honours: SPD '92, '93, '95, '96, '97; SLC '93, '97; SC '92, '93, '96
International Honours: S: 43; U21-1
Andy joined Coventry City on a month's loan just after the start of last season as cover for the reserve goalkeepers. Before the month was over however he was called up for first-team action after the sale of Chris Kirkland and an injury to Magnus Hedman. His experience was invaluable to the City defence and he rarely looked troubled. He eventually signed a one-year contract but a knee injury required keyhole surgery in January and soon afterwards he signed a short-term deal for Oldham. Unfortunately he made his debut in the 7-1 home defeat by Cardiff City and after making three more appearances he was released by the Latics.

Oldham Ath (Free from West Bromwich A juniors on 22/8/1981) FL 195 FLC 10 FAC 7 Others 3
Hibernian (£325,000 on 9/10/1987) SL 138/1 SLC 7 SC 13 Others 4
Glasgow R (£1,000,000 on 27/6/1991) SL 184 SLC 19 SC 26 Others 31
Notts Co (Free on 3/9/1998) FL 1
Sheffield U (Free on 7/9/1998) FL 7 FLC 2
Motherwell (Free on 12/1/1999) SL 57 SLC 4 SC 8
Manchester U (£100,000 on 22/3/2001) PL 2
Coventry C (Free on 28/8/2001) FL 6+1
Oldham Ath (Free on 14/3/2002) FL 4

GORDON Dean Dwight
Born: Croydon, 10 February 1973
Height: 6'0" **Weight:** 13.4
Club Honours: Div 1 '94
International Honours: E: U21-13
Dean was very much on the fringe of the first-team squad for Middlesbrough last term and in November he joined Cardiff City on loan. He made his debut for the Bluebirds in a goalless draw at Notts County and went on to score with two cracking free kicks against Blackpool and Stoke. On his return to the Riverside he made a single Premiership appearance from the subs' bench at Sunderland in January and was reported to have joined Coventry City over the summer. He is a pacy, exciting winger who is very effective pushing down the flank to deliver crosses into the box.
Crystal Palace (From trainee on 4/7/1991) F/PL 181+20/20 FLC 16+3/2 FAC 14+1/1 Others 5+1
Middlesbrough (£900,000 on 17/7/1998) PL 53+10/4 FLC 5 FAC 3
Cardiff C (Loaned on 23/11/2001) FL 7/2

GORDON Kenyatta Gavin
Born: Manchester, 24 June 1979
Height: 6'1" **Weight:** 12.0
Gavin suffered a frustrating time with injuries at Cardiff in 2001-02. A thorough medical examination eventually identified posture problems as a root cause and he has been given a programme to put that right. The experts are confident that after following the programme throughout the summer, he will have left the injuries behind him by the start of 2002-03. At his best, Gavin is a bustling striker who works hard to harass defenders and is good in the air. The highlight of his campaign was undoubtedly the five goals he scored in City's 7-1 LDV Vans Trophy win over Rushden.
Hull C (From trainee on 3/7/1996) FL 22+16/9 FLC 1+4/1 Others 1+1

Lincoln C (£30,000 on 7/11/1997) FL 87+12/28 FLC 2/1 FAC 9/2 Others 4+1
Cardiff C (£275,000 + on 18/12/2000) FL 16+9/2 FLC 0+1 FAC 2/1 Others 1/5

GORE Shane Stephen
Born: Ashford, Kent, 28 October 1981
Height: 6'1" **Weight:** 12.1
Shane almost joined the small band of elite goalkeepers that have saved a penalty on their senior debut. He came on with ten minutes to go at Grimsby after Ian Feuer had been sent off and saved the resultant spot kick with his first touch of the ball in League soccer, but was harshly adjudged to have moved and a re-take was ordered. It then turned out to be a bit of miserable start as another two goals were put past him in the final ten minutes. He has been offered a one-year contract for 2002-03.
Wimbledon (From trainee on 29/6/2001) FL 0+1

GORRE Dean
Born: Surinam, 10 September 1970
Height: 5'8" **Weight:** 11.7
International Honours: Holland: U21
Dean made his debut for Barnsley on the opening day of the 2001-02 season and after an unsure start he began to find his feet when given the role in the 'hole' behind the forwards. However, when the system changed back to 4-4-2 he found himself on the sidelines. A change of manager saw him totally out of favour until near the end of the season when, after a number of impressive performances in the reserves, he forced his way back into the first team. He is a skilful midfielder who will be looking to play a more prominent role in 2002-03.
Huddersfield T (£330,000 from Ajax, Holland on 16/9/1999) FL 49+13/6 FLC 4/1 FAC 1+1
Barnsley (£50,000 on 24/7/2001) FL 14+5/2 FLC 2

GOTTSKALKSSON Olafur
Born: Keflavik, Iceland, 12 March 1968
Height: 6'3" **Weight:** 13.12
Club Honours: S Div 1 '99
International Honours: Iceland: 9; U21-7; Yth
This fine shot stopper started the 2001-02 season as Brentford's first choice goalkeeper turning in a number of impressive performances. However he suffered a bout of tendonitis at the turn of the year and was eventually left out of the side while he recovered. Once fully fit,

however, he was unable to dislodge Paul Smith from the 'keeper's jersey.
Hibernian (Signed from Keflavik, Iceland, ex IA Akranes, KR Reykjavik, on 29/7/1997) SL 64 SLC 4 SC 2
Brentford (Free on 11/7/2000) FL 73 FLC 6 FAC 3 Others 7

GOUGH Neil
Born: Harlow, 1 September 1981
Height: 5'11" **Weight:** 12.0
Neil appeared mainly as a substitute for Leyton Orient last season as a winger and scored his only goal for the club at home to Bristol Rovers, but fell out of favour when Paul Brush was appointed manager. He joined Chelmsford City on loan at the end of December and was released by the O's in March when he signed for Ryman League outfit Hampton & Richmond Borough.
Leyton Orient (From trainee on 10/7/2000) FL 2+13/1 FLC 0+1

GRABBI Corrado
Born: Turin, Italy, 29 July 1975
Height: 5'11" **Weight:** 12.12
Club Honours: FLC '02
This experienced striker showed plenty of energy at Blackburn last term, but only managed one goal, despite hitting the woodwork on a number of occasions. He also sustained four different injuries in a short period of time before returning to Italy to join Messina on loan.
Blackburn Rov (£6,750,000 from Ternana, Italy on 12/7/2001) PL 10+4/1 FLC 1+2 FAC 1+1/1

GRAHAM David
Born: Edinburgh, 6 October 1978
Height: 5'10" **Weight:** 11.5
International Honours: S: U21-8
David possesses far more natural skill than most Third Division players. He started the 2001-02 season as a central striker for Torquay and scored six times before Christmas with every goal being a cracker. However, a tendency to drift out of matches when the team began to struggle meant that he lost his place in the new year, but he returned later in a free attacking-midfield role where his ability was harnessed to create chances for others.
Glasgow R (From juniors on 1/7/1995) SL 0+3 Others 1+1
Dunfermline Ath (Signed on 15/11/1998) SL 17+23/4 SLC 1 SC 3/1 Others 0+1
Inverness Caledonian Thistle (Loaned on 5/1/2001) SL 0+2 SC 0+2
Torquay U (Free on 22/3/2001) FL 36+5/10 FLC 2/1 FAC 1

GRAINGER Martin Robert

Born: Enfield, 23 August 1972
Height: 5'11" **Weight:** 12.0
Martin took a while to find his rhythm for Birmingham City last season, when transfer speculation early on did not help him settle. He faced a battle with David Burrows for a full-back slot as the campaign wore on and towards the close was back to his best form, scoring with brilliant free-kicks in the last two games to help earn Blues a play-off spot. Aggressive in the tackle, Martin hit many telling centres and cross-field passes with accuracy.
Colchester U (From trainee on 28/7/1992) FL 37+9/7 FLC 3 FAC 3+2 Others 3/1
Brentford (£60,000 on 21/10/1993) FL 100+1/12 FLC 6/1 FAC 9/1 Others 8/2
Birmingham C (£400,000 on 25/3/1996) FL 194+19/24 FLC 21+2/2 FAC 8+1/1 Others 7

GRANT Anthony (Tony) James

Born: Liverpool, 14 November 1974
Height: 5'10" **Weight:** 10.2
Club Honours: CS '95
International Honours: E: U21-1
Tony was unable to establish himself as a regular in Manchester City's midfield last season and made only three appearances in the starting line-up. In October he moved on to First Division rivals Burnley, where he had a more comfortable time. He added something new for the Clarets in the centre of the park and became a key man in the line-up. Strong in the tackle, skilful on the ball and with immaculate distribution, his form slipped a little after Christmas.
Everton (From trainee on 8/7/1993) PL 43+18/2 FLC 5+1 FAC 4+4 Others 2+2/1
Swindon T (Loaned on 18/1/1996) FL 3/1
Tranmere Rov (Loaned on 2/9/1999) FL 8+1 FLC 1/1
Manchester C (£450,000 on 24/12/1999) P/FL 11+10 FLC 1 FAC 2+1
West Bromwich A (Loaned on 1/12/2000) FL 3+2
Burnley (£250,000 on 11/10/2001) FL 26+2 FAC 2

GRANT Gareth Michael

Born: Leeds, 6 September 1980
Height: 5'9" **Weight:** 10.4
Gareth was used sparingly by Bradford City in 2001-02. He usually played on the left side of midfield and occasionally at centre forward, and scored in his first League game of the season at home to Portsmouth. He has lightning speed and his approach work is first class, but he occasionally seems to lack confidence in front of goal. He was one of several

players released by the Bantams in the summer.
Bradford C (From trainee on 28/4/1998) P/FL 6+18/1 FLC 5+4/1 FAC 0+1 Others 0+2/1
Halifax T (Loaned on 12/2/1999) FL 0+3 Others 0+1
Lincoln C (Loaned on 9/2/2001) FL 3 Others 1/1

GRANT John Anthony Carlton

Born: Manchester, 9 August 1981
Height: 5'11" **Weight:** 11.0
Another graduate of the Crewe Alexandra youth scheme, John made the starting line-up for the opening game of the 2001-02 season at Grimsby and also featured on a handful of occasions from the subs' bench. The young striker also had spells out on loan at Rushden (where he made no senior appearances) and Northwich Victoria to further his footballing education.
Crewe Alex (From trainee on 7/7/1999) FL 2+5 FLC 1+3

GRANT Kimberley (Kim) Tyrone

Born: Ghana, 25 September 1972
Height: 5'10" **Weight:** 11.6
International Honours: Ghana:
Kim joined Scunthorpe United on trial at the start of last season and made the squad for the opening fixture, before going on to score his first goal in the 4-0 away win at Exeter at the end of August. A fast and direct striker, he struggled to stay match fit and was released after two months, joining Conference outfit Yeovil Town.
Charlton Ath (From trainee on 6/3/1991) FL 74+49/18 FLC 3+9/1 FAC 8+5/5 Others 5+2/1
Luton T (£250,000 on 15/3/1996) FL 18+17/5 FLC 4/2 FAC 0+2 Others 2+1/1
Millwall (£185,000 on 29/8/1997) FL 35+20/11 FLC 3/1 FAC 0+1 Others 2+1/1
(£65,000 to KFC Lommel,Belgium on 11/8/1999)
Notts Co (Loaned on 24/12/1998) FL 6/1
Scunthorpe U (Free from FC Marco, Portugal on 10/8/2001) FL 3+1/1 FLC 1

GRANT Lee

Born: York, 31 December 1985
Height: 6'2" **Weight:** 11.0
Lee became the second youngest player ever to appear for York City after coming on as a substitute in the home game against Bristol Rovers in April – the club had to get special permission from his school to allow him to play. The highly promising central defender has taken up the offer of a three-year scholarship with the Minstermen.
York C (Associated Schoolboy) FL 0+1

GRANVILLE Daniel (Danny) Patrick

Born: Islington, 19 January 1975
Height: 5'11" **Weight:** 12.5
Club Honours: FLC '98; ECWC '98; Div 1 '02
Danny started the 2001-02 season in Manchester City's line-up and missed only one game until the middle of October. He seemed to relish the left-wing-back role, getting forward at every opportunity in Kevin Keegan's attack-minded team. He scored his only goal of the season for the Blues in an emphatic 6-2 away win at Hillsborough against Sheffield Wednesday, but with competition for first-team places intense at Maine Road he departed for Crystal Palace at the end of December. He went on to become a regular at left back for the Selhurst Park club for the remainder of the season.
Cambridge U (From trainee on 19/5/1993) FL 89+10/7 FLC 3+2 FAC 2+2 Others 4+2
Chelsea (£300,000 + on 21/3/1997) PL 12+6 FLC 3 Others 4+1/1
Leeds U (£1,600,000 on 8/7/1998) PL 7+2 FLC 1 FAC 3 Others 0+1
Manchester C (£1,000,000 on 7/8/1999) P/FL 56+14/3 FLC 1+4 FAC 5
Norwich C (Loaned on 27/10/2000) FL 6
Crystal Palace (£500,000 on 28/12/2001) FL 16 FAC 1

GRAVES Wayne Alan

Born: Scunthorpe, 18 September 1980
Height: 5'8" **Weight:** 12.10
After starting the first six League games of the 2001-02 season for Scunthorpe, Wayne suffered a major blow when he broke a bone in his foot in early September and was ruled out for virtually four months. He returned to net three goals in two games in February before a knee ligament injury kept him out for another month. He was used mainly as a central midfielder, although he can also play on the right-hand side, his ball-winning ability, great pace and darting runs were missed whenever he was ruled out.
Scunthorpe U (From trainee on 24/3/1999) FL 50+23/5 FLC 3+2 FAC 1+4 Others 2

GRAVESEN Thomas

Born: Vejle, Denmark, 11 March 1976
Height: 5'10" **Weight:** 12.4
International Honours: Denmark: 27; U21-6
A talented midfielder with all the qualities to become the complete player, Thomas does not always do himself justice. At his best in the centre of

Danny Granville

...idfield, it was from this position that ...e scored a memorable goal in the 5-0 ...hrashing of West Ham in September. ...ut the fact he often fills a sweeper role ...or Denmark points to his versatility. He ...ourished under new Everton manager ...David Moyes. Technically excellent, a ...ood passer, and possessing a powerful ...hot, only his tendency to drift through ...ome games prevents him from ...ecoming a major Premiership star.
...verton (£2,500,000 from SV Hamburg, ...iermany, ex Vejle BK, on 9/8/2000) PL ...i2+5/4 FLC 1 FAC 2+1

GRAY Andrew (Andy) David
Born: Harrogate, 15 November 1977
Height: 6'1" **Weight:** 13.0
International Honours: S: Yth
This right-sided midfielder or wing back ...gain struggled to make an impact for ...Nottingham Forest last season and was ...ever a regular in the line-up. Although ...e scored his first goal for the club, he ...vas one of several players released in the ...ummer.
...eeds U (From trainee on 1/7/1995) PL 13+9 ...LC 3+1 FAC 0+2
...ury (Loaned on 11/12/1997) FL 4+2/1
...Nottingham F (£175,000 on 2/9/1998) P/FL ...i4+30/1 FLC 3+4 FAC 4+1
...Preston NE (Loaned on 23/2/1999) FL 5
...Oldham Ath (Loaned on 25/3/1999) FL 4

GRAY Ian James
Born: Manchester, 25 February 1975
Height: 6'2" **Weight:** 13.0
This likeable goalkeeper was first choice ...at Rotherham in 2000-01, but the return ...of Mike Pollitt saw him drop back to the ...eserves last term. His only appearance ...ame on at Preston when he came on in the ...36th minute to replace the injured Pollitt. ...The latter part of the season saw him ...undergo a double hernia operation from ...vhich he has now fully recovered.
...Oldham Ath (From trainee on 16/7/1993)
...Rochdale (Loaned on 18/11/1994) FL 12 ...Others 3
...Rochdale (£20,000 on 17/7/1995) FL 66 FLC ...4 FAC 5 Others 4
...Stockport Co (£200,000 + on 30/7/1997) FL ...4+2 FLC 3
...Rotherham U (Free on 10/7/2000) FL 33+1 ...FLC 2 FAC 3 Others 1

GRAY Julian Raymond
Born: Lewisham, 21 September 1979
Height: Weight:
This former Arsenal junior blossomed into ...a gifted left winger at Crystal Palace last ...season and was a regular in the squad ...throughout the campaign. A pacy player,

he not only had the beating of opposition defenders, but could also supply accurate crosses for his strikers. He scored twice – in the away games at Barnsley and Grimsby.
Arsenal (From trainee on 13/7/1998) PL 0+1
Crystal Palace (£250,000 + on 21/7/2000) FL 47+19/3 FLC 4+4 FAC 1

GRAY Kevin John
Born: Sheffield, 7 January 1972
Height: 6'0" **Weight:** 14.0
Kevin is a natural leader and gritty defender who missed only one game for Huddersfield Town last season, when he often captained the side. The committed defender celebrated his 200th League appearance for the club against Tranmere Rovers and managed to find the score sheet once, in the away win at Wycombe Wanderers. Always in the thick of the action with his strong tackling and heading of the ball, he won several 'Man of the Match' awards during the campaign.
Mansfield T (From trainee on 1/7/1990) FL 129+12/3 FLC 8/1 FAC 6+1 Others 12+2/2
Huddersfield T (Signed on 18/7/1994) FL 214+16/6 FLC 12+1 FAC 15 Others 11
Stockport Co (Loaned on 11/8/2000) FL 1

GRAY Michael
Born: Sunderland, 3 August 1974
Height: 5'7" **Weight:** 10.10
Club Honours: Div 1 '96, '99
International Honours: E: 3
Sunderland's left back and team captain, Michael endured a frustrating season as the Black Cats struggled to find any consistent form. Quick and attack minded, Michael was also required to fill in on the right side of midfield as injuries and suspensions took hold before he himself was laid low by a back injury, forcing him to miss much of the run-in. Although he will probably be glad to see the back of 2001-02, he will be looking forward to a lucrative testimonial against Celtic at the Stadium of Light in the summer.
Sunderland (From trainee on 1/7/1992) P/FL 309+21/15 FLC 22+4 FAC 13+1/1 Others 2

GRAY Philip (Phil)
Born: Belfast, 2 October 1968
Height: 5'10" **Weight:** 12.5
International Honours: NI: 26; U23-1; Yth; Sch
An experienced striker, Phil was used only sparingly by Oxford United last term and never really gained a regular spot in the line-up. His best performance came against Mansfield when he came on as a

substitute and showed predatory instincts to score twice and help gain a rare win. He spent a month on loan at Conference outfit Boston United in the autumn and was eventually released in the summer when his contract expired.
Tottenham H (From apprentice on 21/8/1986) FL 4+5 FAC 0+1
Barnsley (Loaned on 17/1/1990) FL 3 FAC 1
Fulham (Loaned on 8/11/1990) FL 3 Others 2/1
Luton T (£275,000 on 16/8/1991) FL 54+5/22 FLC 4/3 FAC 2/1 Others 2
Sunderland (£800,000 on 19/7/1993) FL 108+7/34 FLC 9/4 FAC 8/3 Others 2 (Free to Nancy, France during 1996 close season)
Luton T (£400,000 from Fortuna Sittard, Holland on 19/9/1997) FL 74+7/21 FLC 9/3 FAC 3/3 Others 0+1
Burnley (Free on 20/7/2000) FL 5/1 FLC 2+1
Oxford U (Free on 10/11/2000) FL 35+9/11 FLC 1 FAC 2/2 Others 1

GRAY Stuart Edward
Born: Harrogate, 18 December 1973
Height: 5'11" **Weight:** 11.2
International Honours: S: U21-7
Stuart started his first full season with Rushden operating either at left back or in left midfield, and all was going well until he sustained a calf injury at the end of August. Initial hopes of a short-term lay-off were soon put to rest and it wasn't until the final game of 2001 that he reappeared. He then played through the pain barrier for the next eight games before he bowed to the inevitable and underwent a clean-up operation on his achilles. He finally made his comeback for the play-off final against Cheltenham at Cardiff. He is the son of former Leeds United star Eddie Gray.
Glasgow Celtic (Signed from Giffnock North AFC on 7/7/1992) SL 19+9/1 SC 1 Others 2+1
Reading (£100,000 on 27/3/1998) FL 46+6/2 FLC 8 FAC 1+1 Others 2
Rushden & Diamonds (Free on 23/3/2001) FL 12 FLC 1 Others 1+1

GRAY Wayne William
Born: Camberwell, 7 November 1980
Height: 5'10" **Weight:** 12.10
Wayne was unable to break into the first team at Wimbledon last term and at the end of November he joined Leyton Orient on loan for a three-month period. He used his pace to good effect and quickly became a fans' favourite during his spell at Brisbane Road. In March he went to Brighton, also on loan, where he was used as cover for the injured Bobby Zamora. He made an impressive debut scoring in the 4-1 away victory at

Stuart Green

Colchester, but following Zamora's recovery he took on the role of a squad player. He is a promising striker with good pace and an eye for goal.
Wimbledon (From trainee on 10/2/1999) P/FL 1+11 FAC 0+4/1
Swindon T (Loaned on 3/3/2000) FL 8+4/2
Port Vale (Loaned on 6/10/2000) FL 2+1
Leyton Orient (Loaned on 30/11/2001) FL 13+2/5 FAC 2/1
Brighton & Hove A (Loaned on 27/3/2002) FL 3+1/1

GRAYSON Neil
Born: York, 1 November 1964
Height: 5'10" **Weight:** 12.10
Club Honours: NC '99
International Honours: E: SP-4
It was the end of an era at Cheltenham Town when folk-hero striker Neil Grayson was released at the end of the 2001-02 season. He was used mainly as a substitute during the campaign, unable to break up the Julian Alsop /Tony Naylor partnership, but still managed to contribute the crucial equalising goal in the play-off semi-final first leg. Strong, fit and still capable of scoring goals, he performed with the enthusiasm of someone half his age.
Doncaster Rov (Free from Rowntree Mackintosh on 22/3/1990) FL 21+8/6 FAC 1+1 Others 2+1/1
York C (Free on 28/3/1991) FL 0+1
Chesterfield (Free on 16/8/1991) FL 9+6 FLC 2 FAC 1 Others 1 (Free to Gateshead during 1992 close season)
Northampton T (Free from Boston U on 19/6/1994) FL 103+17/31 FLC 7+1 FAC 3 Others 10/3 (Transferred to Hereford U on 4/8/1997)
Cheltenham T (£15,000 on 5/3/1998) FL 75+33/24 FLC 3/2 FAC 3+5/2 Others 3+3/1

GRAYSON Simon Nicholas
Born: Ripon, 16 December 1969
Height: 6'0" **Weight:** 13.7
Club Honours: FLC '97
Simon was out of the first-team picture at Blackburn last term and in September he joined Notts County on loan. He featured in a variety of roles for the Magpies, giving his most accomplished performances at Ewood Park, but returned to Ewood Park when Gary Brazil took over as boss. He subsequently joined Bradford City, also on loan, in February. He quickly became a crowd favourite at Valley Parade with his crunching tackles and exciting runs down the flank before returning to Blackburn once more.
Leeds U (From trainee on 13/6/1988) FL 2 Others 1+1

Leicester C (£50,000 on 13/3/1992) F/PL 175+13/4 FLC 16+2/2 FAC 9 Others 13+1
Aston Villa (£1,350,000 on 1/7/1997) PL 32+16 FLC 1+1 FAC 4+1/2 Others 6+3
Blackburn Rov (£750,000 + on 29/7/1999) FL 31+3 FLC 1+1 FAC 2+1
Sheffield Wed (Loaned on 11/8/2000) FL 5
Stockport Co (Loaned on 12/1/2001) FL 13 FAC 1
Notts Co (Loaned on 6/9/2001) FL 10/1 FLC 1 Others 2
Bradford C (Loaned on 15/2/2002) FL 7

GRAZIOLI Giuliano Stefano Luigi
Born: Marylebone, 23 March 1975
Height: 5'11" **Weight:** 12.11
Ever popular with the Swindon fans, Giuliano finished the 2001-02 season as the club's leading scorer in League matches with eight goals. A predatory forward who is keen and very dangerous in the box, the highlight of his season was his double in the home game against Cambridge during October, which included a spectacular late volley to seal the victory. Unfortunately injury brought an early close to his season and he was released in April.
Peterborough U (Free from Wembley on 19/10/1995) FL 23+18/16 FLC 1+2 FAC 0+3/1 Others 0+2
Swindon T (Free on 15/7/1999) FL 45+33/18 FLC 3+4 FAC 1+1 Others 1

GREAVES Mark Andrew
Born: Hull, 22 January 1975
Height: 6'1" **Weight:** 13.0
Mark made a fantastic start to the 2001-02 campaign, holding down a regular slot in the middle of Hull's new-look midfield. Unfortunately, he suffered a double fracture of the lower leg and dislocated ankle in a freak accident in the last minute of the home game with Kidderminster at the end of August. With typical determination, he fought his way back to fitness well ahead of schedule and made the side for the return fixture with Harriers in December. Although quite prepared to give of his best in any role, right-footed Mark admits centre-back is his preferred position.
Hull C (Free from Brigg T on 17/6/1996) FL 149+25/10 FLC 8/1 FAC 11/1 Others 6+2

GREEN Francis James
Born: Nottingham, 25 April 1980
Height: 5'9" **Weight:** 11.6
Francis was probably disappointed not to get more of a run out at Peterborough last season, but only managed 4 goals from his 15 starts. He is a quick and

powerful young striker who needs to have an extended run in the team to prove himself.
Peterborough U (£25,000 + from Ilkeston T on 2/3/1998) FL 43+43/12 FLC 3+2 FAC 5 Others 3+3/2

GREEN Robert Paul
Born: Chertsey, 18 January 1980
Height: 6'2" **Weight:** 12.2
International Honours: E: Yth
Following the departure of Andy Marshall to Ipswich, Robert soon established himself as Norwich City's first choice goalkeeper and a real favourite with the Carrow Road faithful. Often having to endure quiet matches, especially at Carrow Road, his levels of concentration remained particularly high as the Canaries enjoyed one of the best home records in Division One. He made several truly great saves during the course of the campaign, displaying fantastic agility and tremendous technique.
Norwich C (From juniors on 3/7/1997) FL 50+1 FLC 1 FAC 2 Others 3

GREEN Ryan Michael
Born: Cardiff, 20 October 1980
Height: 5'8" **Weight:** 11.0
International Honours: W: 2; U21-16; Yth
Ryan joined Millwall last October as cover for the injured Matty Lawrence, thus rejoining his former boss Mark McGhee and acquitted himself well when he was called upon. He is a compact full back with good distribution who is effective both when defending and getting forward to support the attack.
Wolverhampton W (From trainee on 25/10/1997) FL 6+2 FLC 2 FAC 0+2
Torquay U (Loaned on 2/3/2001) FL 10
Millwall (Free on 19/10/2001) FL 12+1

GREEN Scott Paul
Born: Walsall, 15 January 1970
Height: 5'10" **Weight:** 12.5
Club Honours: Div 1 '97; AMC '99
Scott featured both as an attacking right back and on the left side of the midfield for Wigan Athletic last term. He showed lots of confidence on the ball, and his goal at Stoke demonstrated his ability to run at defenders, finishing with a powerful strike from the edge of the box. A tireless worker with a good engine, he also produced a 'Man of the Match' performance in the game at Swindon Town, when he was rewarded with a goal.

Derby Co (From trainee on 20/7/1988)
Bolton W (£50,000 on 17/3/1990) P/FL
166+54/25 FLC 19+4/1 FAC 20+3/4 Others
16+4/1
Wigan Ath (£300,000 on 30/6/1997) FL
163+19/8 FLC 13 FAC 14 Others 13+1

GREEN Stuart
Born: Carlisle, 15 June 1981
Height: 5'10" **Weight:** 11.4
This young Newcastle prospect spent a
profitable three months on loan at
Carlisle United last season. He soon
made his presence felt as an attacking
midfielder, scoring on his second
appearance at Rushden and
demonstrating a vision and authority
that often belied his years. His finest
performance was perhaps the return
match against the Diamonds when he
was involved in setting up two goals for
United after opening the scoring
himself with a thrilling volley. He was
reported to have signed a 12-month
loan deal with Hull City for the 2002-03
campaign.
Newcastle U (From trainee on 8/7/1999)
Carlisle U (Loaned on 14/12/2001) FL 16/3

GREENACRE Christopher
(Chris) Mark
Born: Halifax, 23 December 1977
Height: 5'11" **Weight:** 12.8
Chris started the 2001-02 season in fine
form for Mansfield and was soon
banging in the goals. His performances
attracted a host of scouts to Field Mill
to review his progress before he
eventually pledged himself to the Stags
for the immediate future. Quick off the
mark and with an eye for goal he had
notched 20 goals before Christmas
including a spectacular overhead winner
against Shrewsbury in September and a
superb hat-trick against Huddersfield in
the FA Cup. His form dipped slightly
afterwards but he was still selected for
the PFA Division Three side.
Manchester C (From trainee on 1/7/1995) FL
3+5/1 FAC 0+1
Cardiff C (Loaned on 22/8/1997) FL 11/2
Blackpool (Loaned on 5/3/1998) FL 2+2
Scarborough (Loaned on 10/12/1998) FL
10+2/2 Others 1
Mansfield T (Free on 5/11/1999) FL
120+1/49 FLC 5/3 FAC 5/6 Others 2+1

GREENING Jonathan
Born: Scarborough, 2 January 1979
Height: 5'11" **Weight:** 11.7
Club Honours: EC '99

International Honours: E: U21-10; Yth
Jonathan had an excellent first season
for Middlesbrough last term after
following new boss Steve McClaren
over from Old Trafford. Operating either
out wide or in a central midfield role he
was a near ever present for Boro'
during the season and scored his first
ever Premiership goal at Leicester in
October.
York C (From trainee on 23/12/1996) FL
5+20/2 FLC 0+1 Others 1
Manchester U (£500,000 + on 25/3/1998)
PL 4+10 FLC 6 FAC 0+1 Others 3+3
Middlesbrough (£2,000,000 on 9/8/2001)
PL 36/1 FLC 1 FAC 3+1

GREER Gordon
Born: Glasgow, 14 December 1980
Height: 5'10" **Weight:** 12.4
Signed by Blackburn as a prospect for
development prospect, Gordon received
only the one early Worthington Cup
game last term, when he played as the
right-hand man in a back three. A
threat at set pieces he showed a
pleasing strength in the tackle and
commitment in his reserve
appearances. He will be looking to
feature more regularly in the 2002-03
campaign.
Clyde (Free from Port Glasgow on
28/6/2000) SL 27+3 SLC 0+1 SC 1 Others 1
Blackburn Rov (£200,000 on 23/5/2001)
FLC 1

GREGAN Sean Matthew
Born: Guisborough, 29 March 1974
Height: 6'2" **Weight:** 14.7
Club Honours: Div 2'00
Like his team-mates, Preston's captain
suffered something of a hangover from
the previous season's playoff
disappointment at the start of the
2001-02 campaign. Mainly seen as a
combative midfielder nowadays, Sean
returned to a defensive role at Wolves
on Boxing Day and promptly scored his
first goal of the season for the winner.
Out for four weeks with a knee injury,
he spent most of the remainder of the
campaign in the heart of the defence
where his uncompromising tackling and
forceful headers were often vital. This
talismanic figure made his 400th senior
career appearance in February and he
remains a firm favourite with fans and
management alike.
Darlington (From trainee on 20/1/1991) FL
129+7/4 FLC 8 FAC 7 Others 10+1/1
Preston NE (£350,000 on 29/11/1996) FL
206+6/12 FLC 14 FAC 15/1 Others 10

GREGG Matthew (Matt)
Stephen
Born: Cheltenham, 30 November 1978
Height: 5'11" **Weight:** 12.0
Matt began the 2001-02 campaign in
the Crystal Palace reserve team but an
injury crisis at St James' Park saw him
join Exeter City on loan, where he made
two first-team appearances. He was
released by the Eagles shortly after his
return and signed for Bray Wanderers
soon afterwards. An experienced
'keeper, he finally gained regular first-
team action with the League of Ireland
club after spending the last few seasons
as a second choice at Selhurst Park.
Torquay U (From trainee on 4/7/1997) FL 32
FLC 5 FAC 1 Others 1
Crystal Palace (£400,000 on 24/10/1998) FL
7 FLC 2+1
Swansea C (Loaned on 12/2/1999) FL 5
Exeter C (Loaned on 14/9/2001) FL 2

GREGORY David Spencer
Born: Hadleigh, 23 January 1970
Height: 5'10" **Weight:** 12.8
David started 11 of the first 13 League
games for Colchester last season, but
was then laid low by a series of
injuries, culminating in a knee
operation before Christmas. He briefly
returned in March before another knee
problem brought his campaign to a
premature close. A central midfielder
who can also play as an emergency
centre half or right back, he has been
offered a short-term contract to prove
his fitness for 2002-03.
Ipswich T (From trainee on 31/3/1987) F/PL
16+16/2 FLC 3+2 FAC 1 Others 3+2/4
Hereford U (Loaned on 9/1/1995) FL 2
Others 1
Peterborough U (Free on 4/7/1995) FL 0+3
FLC 1 FAC 1 Others 2
Colchester U (Free on 8/12/1995) FL
211+14/20 FLC 10+1/2 FAC 8/2 Others 15/2

GRENET Francois
Born: Bordeaux, France, 8 March 1975
Height: 5'11" **Weight:** 11.11
This experienced right back joined
Derby County last November and
enjoyed a useful run in the line-up.
However he rarely featured in the
second half of the campaign and will be
looking to re-establish himself in the
side next term.
Derby Co (£3,000,000 from Bordeaux,
France on 6/11/2001) PL 12+3 FAC 1

GREYLING Anton
Born: Pretoria, South Africa, 5 November
1977
Height: 6'0" **Weight:** 11.9

International Honours: South Africa: U23-11

A South Africa under-23 international midfielder, Anton came to Torquay on loan from the Pretoria-based Sunsport United but departed after just two substitute appearances.

Torquay U (Free from Supersport U, South Africa on 17/8/2001) FL 0+2

GRIEMINK Bart

Born: Holland, 29 March 1972
Height: 6'4" **Weight:** 15.4
Bart had a fine season with Swindon last term, making the goalkeeper's jersey his own with some consistent performances throughout the campaign. A superb shot-stopper he made some wonderful saves to help Town reach a much-improved position in the Second Division table. His confidence and handling improved, although his kicking can still be erratic at times.

Birmingham C (Free from WK Emmen, Holland on 9/11/1995) FL 20 FLC 3 FAC 1 Others 1+1
Peterborough U (£25,000 on 11/10/1996) FL 58 FLC 1 FAC 4 Others 4
Swindon T (Loaned on 5/2/2000) FL 4
Swindon T (Free on 27/7/2000) FL 69+1 FLC 6 FAC 5 Others 3

GRIFFIN Adam

Born: Salford, 26 August 1984
Height: 5'7" **Weight:** 10.5
Adam is a recent graduate of Oldham Athletic's youth system. The Salford-born midfielder was rewarded for an outstanding season in the youth and reserve sides with a first-team call-up for the final game of 2001-02 at home to Queen's Park Rangers. A promising left winger, he appeared as a second-half substitute replacing David Eyres. He contributed a couple of dangerous crosses and did enough to suggest he will be a fine option for the future. Adam signed professional terms in April 2002.

Oldham Ath (Trainee) FL 0+1

GRIFFIN Andrew (Andy)

Born: Billinge, 7 March 1979
Height: 5'9" **Weight:** 10.10
International Honours: E: U21-2; Yth
Andy is a talented Newcastle right back who is a forceful tackler able to subdue even the most skilled of wingers. His pace enables him to join the attack, while his stamina ensures that he is quick to regain his position after such sorties. After recovering from a hernia operation during the summer of 2001

he began the season as a substitute in the opening Premiership game at Chelsea. Brought into Newcastle's starting line up for the Worthington Cup tie against Brentford in September he played well enough to retain his place for the visit of Manchester United, but only managed a couple more starts and was then restricted by a groin injury.

Stoke C (From trainee on 5/9/1996) FL 52+5/2 FLC 4+1 FAC 2
Newcastle U (£1,500,000 + on 30/1/1998) PL 36+8/1 FLC 6 FAC 5 Others 1

GRIFFIN Antony Richard

Born: Bournemouth, 22 March 1979
Height: 5'11" **Weight:** 11.2
Having recovered from the injury problems that troubled him in the previous season, Antony suffered a further setback at the start of last term when he was involved in a car accident. On regaining match fitness he then had to wait patiently for a place in the line-up before going on to establish himself as Cheltenham's first-choice right back. He is a very quick player whose tackling and positional sense improved as the campaign progressed.

Bournemouth (From trainee on 7/7/1997) FL 1+5
Cheltenham T (£20,000 on 27/7/1999) FL 49+21/1 FLC 2+1 FAC 5 Others 3+1

GRIFFITHS Carl Brian

Born: Welshpool, 15 July 1971
Height: 5'11" **Weight:** 11.10
International Honours: W: B-1; U21-2; Yth
Carl had a great start to the 2001-02 season at Luton, scoring on his debut and establishing a fine partnership up front with Steve Howard. He netted a brilliant hat-trick against Torquay United, but then had the misfortune to suffer a broken leg against his former team, Leyton Orient. The injury was serious enough to threaten his career, but thankfully he was on his way to a full recovery at the time of writing.

Shrewsbury T (From trainee on 26/9/1988) FL 110+33/54 FLC 7+4/3 FAC 6/2 Others 7+3/3
Manchester C (£500,000 on 29/10/1993) PL 11+7/4 FLC 0+1 FAC 2
Portsmouth (£200,000 on 17/8/1995) FL 2+12/2 FLC 0+1
Peterborough U (£225,000 on 28/3/1996) FL 6+10/2 FLC 0+2/1 FAC 1+1/1 Others 0+1
Leyton Orient (Loaned on 31/10/1996) FL 5/3

Leyton Orient (£100,000 on 7/3/1997) FL 60+5/29 FLC 7+1/3 FAC 5/2 Others 2
Wrexham (Loaned on 13/1/1999) FL 4/3 Others 1/1
Port Vale (£100,000 on 25/3/1999) FL 3+5/1 FLC 0+2/1
Leyton Orient (£80,000 on 16/12/1999) FL 46+2/18 FLC 2+1 FAC 3/4
Luton T (£65,000 on 10/7/2001) FL 10/7 FLC 1

GRIFFITHS Gareth John

Born: Winsford, 10 April 1970
Height: 6'4" **Weight:** 14.0
One of Rochdale's main summer signings, Gareth was virtually ever present at centre half in the 2001-02 season and formed a solid defensive partnership with the experienced Richard Jobson. His determined attitude also made him an obvious choice as the Dale skipper following Gary Jones' departure. Tremendous in the air, he dominated most opposing strikers and netted his share of goals at set pieces, including a brace of headers against Kidderminster and a crucial late winner against Shrewsbury.

Port Vale (£1,000 from Rhyl on 8/2/1993) FL 90+4/4 FLC 8 FAC 7/1 Others 7
Shrewsbury T (Loaned on 31/10/1997) FL 6
Wigan Ath (Free on 2/7/1998) FL 44+9/2 FLC 4/1 FAC 5 Others 5+1
Rochdale (Free on 18/7/2001) FL 41/4 FLC 2 FAC 2 Others 3

GRIFFITHS Leroy

Born: London, 30 December 1976
Height: 5'11" **Weight:** 13.5
A tall striker who can also play in a wide-left position, Leroy joined Queen's Park Rangers after a successful trial at the end of the 2000-01 campaign. He won over the fans immediately with a superb goal in the pre-season friendly against Chelsea and featured regularly in the Second Division last term.

Queens Park R (£40,000 from Hampton & Richmond Borough, ex Corinthian Casuals, on 30/5/2001) FL 23+7/3 FAC 1

GRIMANDI Gilles

Born: Gap, France, 11 November 1970
Height: 6'0" **Weight:** 12.7
Club Honours: PL '98, '02; FAC '98; CS '98, '99
Gilles once again proved a valuable member of the Arsenal first-team squad last term, without ever establishing himself as a regular in the line-up. A versatile player who can appear in defence or midfield, he is effective at

171

Jesper Gronkjaer

breaking up opposition attacks and can deliver accurate long-range passes.
Arsenal (£1,500,000 from Monaco, France, ex FC Gap, on 25/6/1997) PL 85+29/4 FLC 9 FAC 10+7/1 Others 24+6/1

GRITTON Martin
Born: Glasgow, 1 June 1978
Height: 6'1" **Weight:** 12.7
This tall and pacy striker, appeared from the substitutes' bench on three occasions for Plymouth at the start of the 2001-02 season but then failed to make the senior team again during the remainder of the campaign. He was loaned out to Conference side Yeovil Town to gain regular first-team football and when he returned he moved to League of Ireland club Shelbourne, also on loan. At the time of writing his future with Argyle was uncertain.
Plymouth Arg (Free from Porthleven on 7/8/1998) FL 15+29/7 FLC 2+2/1 FAC 0+4 Others 3/1

GRONKJAER Jesper
Born: Nuuk, Denmark, 12 August 1977
Height: 6'1" **Weight:** 12.8
International Honours: Denmark: 30; U21-13
Yet again Chelsea fans have only had fleeting glimpses of this Danish winger as he was sidelined with injury once more, this time through a cartilage operation on his left knee. This was particularly frustrating in view of his promising start to the season as Claudio Ranieri opted for an attack-minded four-man midfield. Jesper on the right and Boudewijn Zenden on the left provided the pace and subtlety on the flanks upon which Jimmy-Floyd Hasselbaink, in particular, relished. Chelsea's compelling start to the season was compromised by Jesper's injury, which he sustained in September after only four Premiership matches. Absent for a lengthy spell following his knee operation, he made a welcome return as a late substitute at Charlton in March.
Chelsea (£7,800,000 from Ajax, Holland, ex Aalborg BK, on 21/12/2000) PL 17+10/1 FAC 4+1/2

GROSS Marcus John
Born: Barnstaple, 15 December 1982
Height: 6'0" **Weight:** 12.0
A young trainee defender with Exeter City, Marcus made his senior debut in the 2-0 reverse at Rochdale in August. He

will be looking to gain more experience in the reserves before staking a claim for a first-team berth during the 2002-03 campaign.
Exeter C (Trainee) FL 1

GROVES Paul
Born: Derby, 28 February 1966
Height: 5'11" **Weight:** 11.5
Club Honours: AMC '98
The 2001-02 season proved to be an eventful time for Grimsby Town's most consistent player. With the Mariners facing almost certain relegation he was promoted to player-manager at the turn of the year and produced a transformation in the club's fortunes. The added responsibility appeared to enhance his performances on the field despite the fact that he found himself playing alongside a constantly changing series of partners in central defence. Paul reached another milestone in his career in March when he became only the fourth Grimsby player to make 400 League appearances for the club.
Leicester C (£12,000 from Burton A on 18/4/1988) FL 7+9/1 FLC 1/1 FAC 0+1 Others 0+1
Lincoln C (Loaned on 20/8/1989) FL 8/1 FLC 2
Blackpool (£60,000 on 25/1/1990) FL 106+1/21 FLC 6/1 FAC 9/4 Others 13/3
Grimsby T (£150,000 on 12/8/1992) FL 183+1/38 FLC 10+1/2 FAC 12/2 Others 4/1
West Bromwich A (£600,000 on 8/7/1996) FL 27+2/4 FLC 2/1 FAC 1
Grimsby T (£250,000 on 21/7/1997) FL 223/30 FLC 24/5 FAC 11/1 Others 10/2

GUDJOHNSEN Eidur Smari
Born: Reykjavik, Iceland, 15 September 1978
Height: 6'1" **Weight:** 13.0
Club Honours: CS '00
International Honours: Iceland: 16; U21-11; Yth
This livewire Icelandic striker began the 2001-02 season on the bench as Ranieri paired veteran Gianfranco Zola upfront with Jimmy Floyd Hasselbaink but once given his chance alongside Hasselbaink, Eidur became a permanent fixture in the starting line-up. He announced his arrival with two superb goals against Levski Spartak, which turned the UEFA Cup-tie in the Blues' favour and from then on scored consistently and also created goals for Hasselbaink as the Chelsea duo became the most potent pairing in the Premiership. He hit a

purple patch either side of the new year with 11 goals in 14 matches and finished with a tally of 23 goals in all competitions.
Bolton W (Free from KR Reykjavik, Iceland, ex Valur, PSV Eindhoven, on 6/8/1998) FL 48+7/18 FLC 8+1/4 FAC 4+1/4 Others 4/1
Chelsea (£4,000,000 on 12/7/2000) PL 43+19/24 FLC 5+1/3 FAC 7+3/6 Others 3+3/3

GUDJONSSON Bjarni
Born: Iceland, 26 February 1979
Height: 5'9" **Weight:** 11.9
Club Honours: AMC '00
International Honours: Iceland: 8; U21-20; Yth
Bjarni was a permanent fixture on the right side of Stoke's midfield four last season. On his day he is capable of turning in match-winning performances and is the key to most of the team's dead-ball moves. The son of former Stoke boss Gudjon Thordarson, he can look back with satisfaction on an excellent campaign.
Newcastle U (£500,000 from Akranes, Iceland on 14/7/1997) . £125,000 to KRC Genk on 12/11/1998)
Stoke C (£250,000 on 10/3/2000) FL 94+2/10 FLC 6/2 FAC 6/1 Others 9+4/2

GUDJONSSON Thordur
Born: Akranes, Iceland, 14 October 1973
Height: 5'9" **Weight:** 12.5
International Honours: Iceland: 42; U21-10; Yth
Thordur joined Preston on a short-term contract last January, but his debut was delayed due to a dispute between his former club, Las Palmas, and the Spanish FA. His first three appearances came from the bench, and he showed himself to be an attacking wide player with an eye for a shot, although his lack of match fitness was an obvious hindrance to him achieving his full potential. He failed to win a longer contract at Deepdale and was released before the end of the campaign. Thordur is the son of the former Stoke manager Gudjon Thordarson.
Derby Co (Loaned from Las Palmas, Spain, ex IA Akranes, KA Akureyrar, VFL Bochum, RC Genk, on 2/3/2001) PL 2+8/1
Preston NE (Loaned from Las Palmas, Spain on 8/2/2002) FL 4+3 FAC 0+1

GUERET Willy July
Born: Guadeloupe, 3 August 1973
Height: 6'1" **Weight:** 13.5

Eidur Gudjohnsen

Willy was limited to just a single first-team appearance for Millwall last term, mainly due to the excellent form of Tony Warner. This French goalkeeper was a rock, being excellent in the air and also a good shot stopper. His one start came against Blackburn in the FA Cup, and he proved what an excellent 'keeper he was when playing against Premiership opposition.
Millwall *(Free from Le Mans, France on 31/7/2000) FL 11+1 FAC 1 Others 2*

GUERRERO Mario **Ivan**
Born: Honduras, 30 November 1977
Height: 5'7" **Weight:** 10.3
International Honours: Honduras
This young left wing back was given very few opportunities to display his talents for Coventry City last term. He made three starts and produced an impressive contribution against Barnsley. A few days later a quiet game at Portsmouth saw him relegated to the reserves again. Good going forward and comfortable on the ball his defensive talents were rarely put to the test.
Coventry C *(Signed from Motagua, Honduras on 24/10/2000) P/FL 6+1 FLC 1*

GUINAN Stephen (Steve)
Anthony
Born: Birmingham, 24 December 1975
Height: 6'1" **Weight:** 13.7
Steve found himself out of favour at Plymouth last season and after failing to make a single first-team appearance he moved on to Shrewsbury Town on transfer deadline day. He made his debut from the subs' bench in the home defeat by Torquay when he seemed to lack match fitness, but made the starting line-up for the last four games when he appeared to be establishing a useful partnership with leading scorer Luke Rodgers. He is a tall strong striker who holds the ball up well.
Nottingham F *(From trainee on 7/1/1993) F/PL 2+5 FLC 2/1*
Darlington *(Loaned on 14/12/1995) FL 3/1*
Burnley *(Loaned on 27/3/1997) FL 0+6*
Crewe Alex *(Loaned on 19/3/1998) FL 3*
Halifax T *(Loaned on 16/10/1998) FL 12/2*
Plymouth Arg *(Loaned on 24/3/1999) FL 11/7*
Scunthorpe U *(Loaned on 10/9/1999) FL 2+1/1*
Cambridge U *(Free on 24/12/1999) FL 4+2 FAC 0+2 Others 1*
Plymouth Arg *(Free on 23/3/2000) FL 15+15/3 FLC 2 FAC 2 Others 0+1*
Shrewsbury T *(Free on 28/3/2002) FL 4+1*

GUNBY Stephen (Steve)
Robert
Born: Boston, 13 April 1984
Height: 5'11" **Weight:** 13.3
This second-year scholarship student was drafted into Bury's senior squad last season due to injuries and suspension. Able to perform on either side of the midfield he is a no-nonsense player who will always battle for the ball. He received his first taste of senior action when he came off the subs' bench in the final fixture at Peterborough.
Bury *(Trainee) FL 0+1*

GUNNARSSON Brynjar Bjorn
Born: Iceland, 16 October 1975
Height: 6'1" **Weight:** 11.12
International Honours: Iceland: 29; U21-8; Yth
Injury ravaged Brynjar's season at Stoke in 2001-02 and after he had established himself in the central-midfield role where he is seen to best advantage, he twice suffered broken bones in his foot. His late runs into the key areas ensured he scored the majority of his goals with his head but he possesses a tremendous shot and his tackling abilities were there for all to see.
Stoke C *(£600,000 from Orgryte IS, Sweden on 4/1/2000) FL 88+3/11 FLC 6/1 FAC 4/2 Others 12+1/1*

GUNNLAUGSSON Arnar (Arnie) Bergmann
Born: Akranes, Iceland, 6 March 1973
Height: 6'0" **Weight:** 11.10
Club Honours: FLC '00
International Honours: Iceland: 30; U21-6; Yth
This left-footed midfielder and occasional striker remained as popular as ever with the Filbert Street faithful last term, but only managed a couple of substitute outings before eventually joining Stoke City on a free transfer in February. Arriving at the Britannia Stadium on a short-term contract he added some much needed quality to the line up, playing either wide on the left or in the 'hole' behind the front two. His 25-yard volley against Chesterfield was arguably Stoke's goal of the season.
Bolton W *(£100,000 from IA Akranes, Iceland, ex Feyenoord, IFC Nuremberg,*

Sochaux, on 7/8/1997) P/FL 24+18/13 FLC 6+3/2 FAC 1+1*
Leicester C *(£2,000,000 on 5/2/1999) PL 10+20/3 FLC 1+2 FAC 2+4/1 Others 0+1*
Stoke C *(Loaned on 3/3/2000) FL 10+3/2 Others 5/1*
Stoke C *(Free on 22/2/2002) FL 9/3 Others 2*

GURNEY Andrew (Andy)
Robert
Born: Bristol, 25 January 1974
Height: 5'10" **Weight:** 11.6
Andy had a successful season for Swindon Town in 2001-02 after his short move down the M4. He featured in a variety of positions playing as part of a back three or back four, as a central defender, right back or in midfield as required. The return of Andy King seemed to bring the best out of him. A versatile player, he looked comfortable bringing the ball out of defence and contributed seven vital goals.
Bristol Rov *(From trainee on 10/7/1992) FL 100+8/9 FLC 7/1 FAC 5 Others 15*
Torquay U *(Free on 10/7/1997) FL 64/10 FLC 6 FAC 5/1 Others 3*
Reading *(£100,000 on 15/11/1999) FL 55+12/3 FLC 5 FAC 5+1 Others 5+1*
Swindon T *(Free on 2/7/2001) FL 43/6 FLC 2 FAC 2 Others 1*

GUTTRIDGE Luke
Born: Barnstaple, 27 March 1982
Height: 5'5" **Weight:** 9.7
This busy combative midfielder broke into the Cambridge United first team last November and was virtually ever present from then onwards. He netted goals in the games at Brighton and Oldham and will be looking to build on this promising start in 2002-03.
Torquay U *(Trainee) FL 0+1*
Cambridge U *(Free on 15/8/2000) FL 28+2/3 FLC 0+1 FAC 1 Others 4+2/1*

GUYETT Scott Barry
Born: Ascot, 20 January 1976
Height: 6'2" **Weight:** 13.2
Scott followed manager Mark Wright to Oxford during the 2001 close season and settled in reasonably well playing in a back three. He appeared to be developing into an effective centre back when Ian Atkins was appointed as the U's new boss and he rarely featured after this. He is a big defender who is nevertheless comfortable on the ball.
Oxford U *(Free from Southport, ex Brisbane C, Gresley Rov, on 9/7/2001) FL 20+2 FLC 1 FAC 1 Others 1*

Scott Guyett

H

HAALAND Alf-Inge (Alfie)
Rasdal
Born: Stavanger, Norway, 23 November 1972
Height: 5'10" **Weight:** 12.12
International Honours: Norway: 34; U21-29; Yth
The season 2001-02 will be remembered by most people connected with Manchester City as a wonderful time, with flowing football and records being created regularly, but for Alfie Haaland it will be a time to forget as he battled to regain fitness after undergoing two cartilage operations, which caused him to miss the first half of the campaign. When he returned to action the knee flared up again and he withdrew to the sidelines once more.
Nottingham F (Signed from Bryne, Norway on 25/1/1994) F/PL 66+9/7 FLC 2+5 FAC 5+1 Others 2+3
Leeds U (£1,600,000 on 17/7/1997) PL 57+17/8 FLC 3 FAC 5+1 Others 7+2
Manchester C (£2,500,000 on 16/6/2000) P/FL 35+3/3 FLC 5 FAC 3+1

HAAS Bernt
Born: Vienna, Austria, 8 April 1978
Height: 6'1" **Weight:** 12.8
International Honours: Switzerland: 13
This right back arrived at Sunderland in the 2001 close season and impresses early on with his blistering pace and attacking prowess. He initially looked like being one of the bargains of the year, but as the campaign wore on a combination of fatigue and loss of form saw him lose his place in the side. He was also unfortunate with injuries, suffering a badly gashed head at Newcastle in August (although he gamely battled on) and a hamstring pull in March.
Sunderland (£750,000 from Grasshopper Zurich, Switzerland on 10/8/2001) PL 27 FLC 0+1 FAC 1

HACKETT Christopher (Chris) James
Born: Oxford, 1 March 1983
Height: 6'0" **Weight:** 11.6
2001-02 proved to be a disappointing season for the speedy winger and he did not make the breakthrough to regular first-team action with Oxford that was hoped for. He missed several weeks with an injury and when he did appear it was normally from the bench. He possesses

tremendous speed which few defenders in the Third Division can match, but this was not used as much as it could have been. He remains a bright prospect and will be hoping for more first-team action in the new campaign. Chris was also occasionally used as a wing back and central striker.
Oxford U (From trainee on 20/4/2000) FL 15+18/2 FAC 1+1 Others 0+2

HACKWORTH Anthony (Tony)
Born: Durham, 19 May 1980
Height: 6'1" **Weight:** 13.7
International Honours: E: Yth
Notts County invested quite heavily in this youngster who had been leading scorer in the Premier Reserve League in the 2000-01 season. He took some time to adjust to Second Division football and was mainly used from the subs' bench last term, but will surely develop further when the goals start to flow.
Leeds U (From trainee on 23/5/1997) FLC 0+1 Others 0+2
Notts Co (£150,000 on 16/7/2001) FL 9+24/1 FLC 0+1 FAC 2+1 Others 3/1

HADDOW Alexander (Alex)
Born: Aldershot, 8 January 1982
Height: 5'8" **Weight:** 11.2
Alex was one of manager Roddy Collins' first signings when he took over at Carlisle United last August. However, he had only limited chances to show his ability in left midfield before sustaining an injury to the cruciate ligaments that sidelined him for the rest of the season.
Reading (From trainee on 18/3/2000) FL 1+2 FLC 1
Carlisle U (Free on 20/8/2001) FL 4 FLC 0+1

Tony Hackworth

HADJI Moustapha

Born: Ifrane, Morocco, 16 November 1971
Height: 6'0" **Weight:** 11.10
International Honours: Morocco
Moustapha is a creative midfielder who can turn a game with a flick of the ball or an ingenious pass. An athletic and inventive player, he likes to attack from deep and can conjure up some spectacular goals. After joining Aston Villa in the close season, he had mixed fortunes last term. He was restricted to a sub's role for the first few matches, but by September had established himself as a key figure in the side until he was laid low with a knee injury which kept him out of action for the best part of two months. He went on to became one of Villa's biggest threats, constantly putting opposition defences under pressure with his pace and direct approach.
Coventry C (£4,000,000 from Deportivo La Coruna, Spain, ex Nancy, Sporting Lisbon, on 3/8/1999) PL 61+1/12 FLC 4+1 FAC 3/1
Aston Villa (£4,500,000 on 6/7/2001) PL 17+6/2 FLC 2 FAC 0+1 Others 3+3/1

HADLAND Phillip (Phil) Jonathan

Born: Warrington, 20 October 1980
Height: 5'11" **Weight:** 11.8
Phil began the 2001-02 season at Leyton Orient, but struggled to win a place in the first-team squad and shortly before Christmas he joined Carlisle United on loan. He added width to the attack and netted with an emphatic strike against Scunthorpe before returning to Brisbane Road. In March he moved on to Brighton where he made his debut from the subs' bench against Bristol City on Easter Monday. He is an orthodox winger who likes to run at defenders and is difficult to shake off the ball.
Reading (From trainee on 22/6/1999) FLC 1
Rochdale (Free on 8/8/2000) FL 12+20/2 FLC 0+1 FAC 1 Others 1
Leyton Orient (Free on 9/7/2001) FL 0+5/1 FLC 0+1
Carlisle U (Loaned on 19/11/2001) FL 4/1 FAC 1
Brighton & Hove A (Free on 19/3/2002) FL 0+2

HADLEY Stewart

Born: Dudley, 30 December 1973
Height: 6'0" **Weight:** 13.2
Club Honours: NC '00
Stewart was one of several senior players who found opportunities limited at Kidderminster last season. A lack of goals meant that the striker was soon relegated

to the substitutes' bench and in December he was loaned out to local rivals Worcester City of the Dr Martens League, a move that was later made permanent.
Derby Co (Free from Halesowen T on 6/7/1992)
Mansfield T (Signed on 9/2/1994) FL 100+24/31 FLC 6+2 FAC 7/1 Others 5+1/3
Kidderminster Hrs (Free on 24/6/1998) FL 23+20/6 FLC 2+1/1 FAC 2+1/2 Others 1+1

HADRAVA David Leo

Born: Ilford, 26 February 1983
Height: 5'10" **Weight:** 12.0
This promising young right back did well with Colchester's reserve team in 2001-02 before stepping up to make his senior debut when he came off the bench for the final 35 minutes of the LDV Vans Trophy tie against Reading in October.
Colchester U (Trainee) Others 0+1

HAHNEMANN Marcus Stephen

Born: Seattle, USA, 15 June 1972
Height: 6'3" **Weight:** 16.2
International Honours: USA: 4
Fulham's third choice 'keeper, became an instant cult hero after joining Rochdale on loan last October. Hoping to catch the eye of the USA selectors ahead of the World Cup, Marcus kept four clean sheets in five League games before returning to Craven Cottage. He subsequently had another loan spell, this time at Second Division Reading where he arrived just before Christmas. He again impressed with a series of clean sheets and in the way he dominated the penalty area, but then went back to the Premiership club to see out the season.
Fulham (£80,000 from Colorado Rapids, USA on 9/7/1999) FL 2 FLC 2
Rochdale (Loaned on 12/10/2001) FL 5 Others 2
Reading (Loaned on 14/12/2001) FL 6

HAINING William (Will) Wallace

Born: Glasgow, 2 October 1982
Height: 5'11" **Weight:** 10.10
Glasgow-born Will has progressed through the Boundary Park youth system. He made his debut at Blackpool on Boxing Day, appearing as a late substitute for Paul Murray. The versatile 19-year-old, who can play at left back, central defence or in midfield, is highly rated by the coaching staff and signed professional forms last October. Will made his full debut in the final game of the 2001-02 campaign, impressing

alongside centre half Fitz Hall in a 1-0 win over QPR.
Oldham Ath (From trainee on 17/10/2001) FL 1+3

HALL Fitz

Born: Leytonstone, 20 December 1980
Height: 6'1" **Weight:** 13.4
Oldham Athletic unearthed a bargain when signing Fitz Hall from Ryman League outfit Chesham United last March 2002. The 21-year-old central defender was thrust into first-team action unexpectedly soon – making his debut in a 0-0 draw at Huddersfield on Easter Monday. A former West Ham trainee, he produced an outstanding performance and bettered it by scoring the last-gasp winner in the next game at home to Stoke City. Fitz is assured on the ball and provides a big aerial presence.
Oldham Ath (£20,000 + from Chesham U, ex Staines T, on 15/3/2002) FL 4/1

HALL Laurence Washington

Born: Nottingham, 26 March 1984
Height: 6'0" **Weight:** 12.0
Laurence made great progress with Stoke City last term and was duly rewarded when he made his senior debut as a substitute in the LDV Vans Trophy against Blackpool. A strong athletic striker of whom much is expected, he ended the season in a rich vein of goal-scoring form for the club's reserve and U-19 sides.
Stoke C (Trainee) Others 0+1

HALL Marcus Thomas

Born: Coventry, 24 March 1976
Height: 6'1" **Weight:** 12.2
International Honours: E: B-1; U21-8
A veteran of several relegation campaigns, Marcus is now the longest serving Coventry City player. This was the last season of his present contract and it is fair to say he struggled to adapt to life in the Nationwide League. Niggling injuries undoubtedly played their part in his performances that lacked the swashbuckling forays to support his attack which were very much his trademark in the past. One of his best performances came at Crystal Palace when he looked confident and scored an excellent goal.
Coventry C (From trainee on 1/7/1994) P/FL 113+19/2 FLC 14+1/2 FAC 8+2

HALL Paul Anthony

Born: Manchester, 3 July 1972
Height: 5'9" **Weight:** 11.0
International Honours: Jamaica: 36
Paul found his first-team opportunities at

Walsall limited to a substitute appearance in the Worthington Cup game at Bolton and soon afterwards moved on to Rushden. The right midfielder proved a revelation and his form played no small part in the team's push for an end-of-season play-off berth. He chipped in with his fair share of goals as well, 11 in all, including a stunning solo run and strike against Darlington at Nene Park. A tremendous effort levelled the scores in the play-off final against Cheltenham Town even though it proved to be in vain.
Torquay U (From trainee on 9/7/1990) FL 77+16/1 FLC 7 FAC 4+1/2 Others 5+1/1
Portsmouth (£70,000 on 25/3/1993) FL 148+40/37 FLC 10+3/1 FAC 7+1/2 Others 6+2/2
Coventry C (£300,000 on 10/8/1998) PL 2+8 FLC 2+1/1
Bury (Loaned on 18/2/1999) FL 7
Sheffield U (Loaned on 17/12/1999) FL 1+3/1
West Bromwich A (Loaned on 10/2/2000) FL 4
Walsall (Free on 17/3/2000) FL 46+6/10 FLC 4+1 FAC 3/1 Others 3
Rushden & Diamonds (Free on 11/10/2001) FL 34/8 FAC 2 Others 4/3

HALLE Gunnar
Born: Larvik, Norway, 11 August 1965
Height: 5'11" **Weight:** 11.2
Club Honours: Div 2 '91
International Honours: Norway: 64; U21-23; Yth
The 2001-02 season proved to be Gunnar's best at Bradford City and he was outstanding when overlapping and crossing the ball, which led to plenty of chances for the forwards. He also played at centre back before joining Wolves on loan in the closing stages of the campaign. He settled in fairly quickly at Molineux and showed his experience during the tense play-off matches. He was released by the Bantams in the summer and signed for Lillestrom.
Oldham Ath (£280,000 from Lillestrom, Norway on 15/2/1991) F/PL 185+3/17 FLC 16/2 FAC 8/2 Others 4
Leeds U (£400,000 on 13/12/1996) PL 65+5/4 FLC 3+1 FAC 8+1 Others 2
Bradford C (£200,000 on 11/6/1999) P/FL 78+5/1 FLC 5+1/1 FAC 2 Others 2
Wolverhampton W (Loaned on 28/3/2002) FL 4+1 Others 2

HALLIDAY Kevin Joseph
Born: Swindon, 8 July 1983
Height: 5'11" **Weight:** 12.0
Kevin is a second-year trainee with

Swindon Town who made just one senior appearance last term, coming on as a late substitute in the LDV Vans Trophy game at Colchester. An attacking left-footed midfielder, he was a regular in Town's reserve side throughout the season and was rewarded with a one-year professional contract.
Swindon T (Trainee) Others 0+2

HALLIDAY Stephen (Steve) William
Born: Sunderland, 3 May 1976
Height: 5'10" **Weight:** 12.12
A clever and determined forward, Steve played in all but a handful of Carlisle's games in 2001-02. Although he has never quite recovered the goal-scoring form he showed on his first spell at Brunton Park, his close control and competitive attitude continued to pose a threat to opposing defenders. He scored both United's goals at Kidderminster but his most notable effort was the neat flick that secured all three points against Bristol Rovers.
Hartlepool U (From trainee on 5/7/1994) FL 111+29/25 FLC 8+3 FAC 4+1/1 Others 5+1
Motherwell (Free on 7/7/1998) SL 3+6 SLC 3+2/2 (Free to Doncaster Rov on 26/7/2000)
Carlisle U (Loaned on 14/2/2000) FL 16/7 Others 2/1
Carlisle U (Free on 20/10/2000) FL 31+36/7 FLC 1 FAC 1+2 Others 2

HALLS John
Born: Islington, 14 February 1982
Height: 6'0" **Weight:** 11.4
Club Honours: FAYC '00
International Honours: E: Yth
This promising Arsenal youngster made three senior appearances for the Gunners last term, all from the subs' bench in Worthington Cup ties, before spending a month on loan at Colchester in the new year. He filled a number of positions for the U's including centre half, left back and central midfield and showed some neat touches to demonstrate his Premiership pedigree.
Arsenal (From trainee on 18/7/2000) FLC 0+3
Colchester U (Loaned on 18/1/2002) FL 6

HAMANN Dietmar
Born: Waldsasson, Germany, 27 August 1973
Height: 6'3" **Weight:** 12.2
Club Honours: FLC '01; FAC '01; UEFA '01; ESC '01; CS '01
International Honours: Germany: 46; U21; Yth
The defensive anchor man in Liverpool's midfield Dietmar enjoyed another consistent but unspectacular season for

the Reds, protecting the back four by breaking up opposition attacks with his timely tackles and interceptions, before setting up attacking moves with short passes out of defence. Generally an automatic choice for club and country, he made the German squad for Japan and Korea and was a member of the team that reached the final only to fall to Brazil.
Newcastle U (£4,500,000 from Bayern Munich, Germany, ex Wacker Munchen, on 5/8/1998) PL 22+1/4 FLC 1 FAC 7/1
Liverpool (£8,000,000 on 23/7/1999) PL 84+5/4 FLC 3+3 FAC 9/1 Others 27

HAMILTON Derrick (Des) Vivian
Born: Bradford, 15 August 1976
Height: 5'11" **Weight:** 13.0
International Honours: E: U21-1
This powerful midfield player was frustrated by injuries during his first season with Cardiff City and eventually finished the campaign with a thigh strain, which kept him out of the Second Division play-offs. When fully fit he is a reliable figure in the centre of the park who tackles forcefully and loves getting forward. He can also play at right back if required.
Bradford C (From trainee on 1/6/1994) FL 67+21/5 FLC 6/1 FAC 6 Others 4+1/2
Newcastle U (£1,500,000 + on 27/3/1997) PL 7+5 FLC 1+1/1 FAC 1 Others 2+1
Sheffield U (Loaned on 16/10/1998) FL 6
Huddersfield T (Loaned on 15/2/1999) FL 10/1
Norwich C (Loaned on 22/3/2000) FL 7
Tranmere Rov (Loaned on 25/10/2000) FL 2 FLC 1
Tranmere Rov (Loaned on 10/1/2001) FL 3+1 FAC 3
Cardiff C (Free on 3/7/2001) FL 14+5 FAC 2/1 Others 2

HAMILTON Ian Richard
Born: Stevenage, 14 December 1967
Height: 5'9" **Weight:** 11.3
This experienced midfielder had a brief spell of first-team action for Notts County early in the 2001-02 season but was released soon after Gary Brazil took temporary charge of the club. He subsequently joined Third Division Lincoln City where he was a regular in the line-up, although he struggled to reach his best form at a club that was finding life difficult both on and off the pitch. Ian was mainly used on the right side of a midfield four by the Imps but also played in a more central role on occasions.
Southampton (From apprentice on 24/12/1985)

*Cambridge U (Signed on 29/3/1988) FL
23+1/1 FLC 1 FAC 2 Others 2*
*Scunthorpe U (Signed on 23/12/1988) FL
139+6/18 FLC 6 FAC 6+1 Others 14+1/3*
*West Bromwich A (£160,000 on 19/6/1992)
FL 229+11/23 FLC 13+2/1 FAC 10+1/1 Others
14+2/3*
*Sheffield U (Signed on 26/3/1998) FL
38+7/3 FLC 6/1 FAC 2+3 Others 2*
Grimsby T (Loaned on 4/11/1999) FL 6/1
*Notts Co (Free on 18/8/2000) FL 29+5 FLC
3+2 FAC 3+1 Others 2+1*
Lincoln C (Free on 9/11/2001) FL 26 FAC 3/1

HAMMOND Elvis Zark
Born: Accra, Ghana, 6 October 1980
Height: 5'10" **Weight:** 10.10
This young Fulham striker enjoyed a one-
month loan spell at Bristol Rovers early on
last season. He produced a 'Man of the
Match performance on his debut against
Shrewsbury Town but was unable to get
on the score sheet during his time at the
Memorial Stadium despite showing some
good close control. He subsequently
returned to Craven Cottage to continue
his development.
Fulham (From trainee on 1/7/1999) FLC 0+1
*Bristol Rov (Loaned on 31/8/2001) FL 3+4
FLC 0+1*

HAMSHAW Matthew Thomas
Born: Rotherham, 1 January 1982
Height: 5'9" **Weight:** 11.9
International Honours: E: Yth; Sch
Matthew made a quiet start to the
2001-02 season for Sheffield
Wednesday, but did much better in the
second half of the campaign. He is a
pacy, skilful wide midfield player and
having built on the breakthrough he
made in 2000-01 he will be aiming to
win a regular place in the line-up in
2002-03. He scored a really excellent
individual goal against Watford and also
earned call-ups to the England U20
squad.
*Sheffield Wed (From trainee on 5/11/1999)
FL 22+17 FLC 6+1/2 FAC 2/2*

HANCOCK Glynn Roy
Born: Biddulph, 24 May 1982
Height: 6'0" **Weight:** 12.2
Although Glynn's total first- team action
for Stockport County in 2001-02
amounted to just two minutes, when he
replaced Andrew Thomas at Rotherham in
February, he was still offered an extension
to his contract. A strong and powerful
central defender, he captained the club's
reserve team during the season.
*Stockport Co (From trainee on 27/8/1999) FL
1+2*

HAND Jamie
Born: Uxbridge, 7 February 1984
Height: 5'11" **Weight:** 11.10
A second-year Watford academy scholar,
Jamie made a confident debut at the age
of 17 when he came on as a substitute
against Arsenal in the FA Cup. A hard-
working and combative midfield player,
he made a handful more first-team
appearances, as well as being prominent
with the reserves.
Watford (Trainee) FL 4+6 FAC 0+1

HANDYSIDE Peter David
Born: Dumfries, 31 July 1974
Height: 6'1" **Weight:** 13.8
Club Honours: AMC '98
International Honours: S: U21-7
Peter was one of Stoke City's best pre-
season signings last term and was
immediately installed as captain. He led
the team supremely well, indeed when a
foot injury interrupted his season City's
form slid worryingly. A cultured defender
who is capable of bringing the ball out of
defence and setting up attacks, his
partnership with Sergei Shtaniuk was a
major plus point for the club.
*Grimsby T (From trainee on 21/11/1992) FL
181+9/4 FLC 18+1 FAC 12+1 Others 13+1*
*Stoke C (Free on 10/7/2001) FL 34 FLC 1 FAC
3/1 Others 3*

HANKIN Sean Anthony
Born: Camberley, 28 February 1981
Height: 5'11" **Weight:** 12.4
This young defender joined Torquay
initially on loan as a replacement when
David Woozley moved back to Crystal
Palace, but went on to sign a permanent
deal. Playing on the left side of a three-
centre-back system, he looked
comfortable on the ball, he benefited
from the freedom the system afforded
him to push forward.
*Crystal Palace (From trainee on 29/6/1999)
FL 0+1*
*Torquay U (£20,000 on 15/10/2001) FL 27
FAC 1 Others 1*

HANLON Richard (Richie) Kenneth
Born: Wembley, 26 May 1978
Height: 6'1" **Weight:** 13.7
Richie only managed a single appearance
from the subs' bench for Peterborough
last term before moving on to Rushden.
He made the transition into the first
team at Nene Park seamlessly. A superb
dead-ball specialist, he quickly
established himself as the club penalty
taker, four of his nine goals coming from
the 12-yard mark. A real box-to-box

player, he quickly won over the
supporters but his season finished on a
sour note, a hamstring injury sustained
at Scunthorpe United forcing him out of
the last five games of the campaign,
including the play-off final.
*Southend U (From trainee at Chelsea on
10/7/1996) FL 1+1 (Free to Welling U during
1997 close season)*
*Peterborough U (Signed from Rushden &
Diamonds on 9/12/1998) FL 0+4/1 Others 1
(Free to Welling U on 12/8/1999)*
*Peterborough U (From trainee on 17/12/1999) FL
30+13/2 FLC 1+1 FAC 0+1 Others 3+2*
*Rushden & Diamonds (£30,000 on
10/9/2001) FL 33+2/6 FLC 0+1 FAC 2/2
Others 1*

HANSEN Bo
Born: Denmark, 16 June 1972
Height: 5'11" **Weight:** 11.10
International Honours: Denmark: 1
Last season was something of a
frustrating one for Bo. After playing in the
vast majority of Bolton's games during the
promotion-winning campaign, he was
hoping for an extended run in the first
team either as a winger or at centre
forward. He began in the starting line-up,
but a series of niggling injuries and the
arrival of big name players such as Fredi
Bobic and Youri Djorkaeff meant that he
spent much of the time either in the
treatment room or on the bench. He did,
however, score a wonderful goal at
Middlesbrough in January, whilst wearing
a pair of Michael Ricketts' golden boots.
*Bolton W (£1,000,000 from Brondby,
Denmark on 12/2/1999) P/FL 64+32/15 FLC
7+2/1 FAC 4+2/1 Others 3+5*

HANSON Christian
Born: Middlesbrough, 3 August 1981
Height: 6'1" **Weight:** 11.5
International Honours: E: Yth; Sch
Christian joined Torquay United on loan
last season to gain further experience of
senior football. He performed steadily as
an orthodox left back when the Gulls
returned to a flat back four, but his stay
was terminated prematurely. He will be
aiming to make a breakthrough at the
Riverside in 2002-03.
Middlesbrough (From trainee on 5/8/1998)
Cambridge U (Loaned on 22/3/2001) FL 8
Torquay U (Loaned on 23/11/2001) FL 6

HARDIKER John David
Born: Preston, 17 February 1982
Height: 6'0" **Weight:** 11.4
John arrived at Stockport County for a
record fee for a Conference defender and
it didn't taken him long to achieve

legendary status at Edgeley Park. He scored on his debut at Rotherham – his first-ever Football League goal – and then added two more during the final five, pulsating minutes when County memorably came from behind to beat neighbours Manchester City 2-1 at Edgeley Park.
Stockport Co *(£150,000 from Morecambe on 28/1/2002) FL 11+1/3*

HARDY Lee
Born: Blackpool, 26 November 1981
Height: 6'0" **Weight:** 11.12
Pacy prospect Lee had a frustrating 2001-02 campaign at Oldham. After signing on a free from Blackburn during the summer, the 21-year-old left-winger struggled to break into the first team. He made just one appearance as a late substitute against Port Vale in December and was one of 14 players transfer-listed later that month by new boss Mick Wadsworth. A free transfer switch to Macclesfield Town was agreed in May, but the deal fell through.
Blackburn Rov *(From trainee on 3/7/2000)*
Oldham Ath *(Free on 19/7/2001) FL 0+1*

HARDY Neil John Paul
Born: Manchester, 29 December 1973
Height: 6'2" **Weight:** 14.0
Neil only managed a handful of appearances for Stockport County last season after suffering a bad injury to his ankle. He scored his first Football League goals when he netted twice in the 3-3 draw with Grimsby, but started just one game under Carlton Palmer and was subsequently released at the end of the campaign.
Stockport Co *(£15,000 + from Radcliffe Borough, ex Northwich Vic, Hyde U, Altrincham, Morecambe, on 13/6/2001) FL 4+6/2 FLC 1+1*

HARDY Philip (Phil)
Born: Ellesmere Port, 9 April 1973
Height: 5'8" **Weight:** 11.8
Club Honours: WC '95
International Honours: RoI: U21-9
This experienced left back missed the start of the 2001-02 season for Port Vale due to a niggling hamstring injury. He had previously spent 11 years with Wrexham, scoring just the one goal from the penalty spot, but lo and behold on his League debut for Vale he scored from open play with a crisp finish against Peterborough! Often used in an unfamiliar wing-back role, he was in and out of the team and was eventually released on a free transfer in the summer.

Wrexham (From trainee on 24/11/1990) FL 346+3/1 FLC 19 FAC 36 Others 38
Port Vale (Free on 30/7/2001) FL 8/1 FLC 2

HAREWOOD Marlon Anderson
Born: Hampstead, 25 August 1979
Height: 6'1" **Weight:** 11.0
This determined striker had another good season for Nottingham Forest in 2001-02 and finished the campaign as the club's second-top scorer with 11 goals. Big and strong, he has pace to burn and can give defenders a yard or two start and still overtake them. With all the key attributes for a goal-scorer, the only thing lacking from his game is consistency.
Nottingham F (From trainee on 9/9/1996) P/FL 63+56/19 FLC 8+4/3 FAC 2+2
Ipswich T (Loaned on 28/1/1999) FL 5+1/1

HARGREAVES Christian (Chris)
Born: Cleethorpes, 12 May 1972
Height: 5'11" **Weight:** 12.2
This live wire midfield player was outstanding for Northampton Town throughout the 2001-02 campaign. His 'never say die' attitude plus a higher-than-average work rate made him a firm favourite with the Sixfields' faithful. A high point was his double in the home game against Wycombe and he finished the season by being voted 'Player of the Year' by both the supporters and the travelling fans.
Grimsby T (From trainee on 6/12/1989) FL 15+36/5 FLC 2+2/1 FAC 1+2/1 Others 2+4
Scarborough (Loaned on 4/3/1993) FL 2+1
Hull C (Signed on 26/7/1993) FL 34+15 FLC 1 FAC 2+1/1 Others 3+1
West Bromwich A (Free on 13/7/1995) FL 0+1 Others 0+1
Hereford U (Free on 19/2/1996) FL 57+4/6 FLC 3+1 FAC 1 Others 2
Plymouth Arg (Free on 20/7/1998) FL 74+2/5 FLC 4 FAC 11/2 Others 1
Northampton T (Free on 7/7/2000) FL 67+3/3 FLC 3 FAC 3 Others 2

HARKIN Maurice (Mo) Presley
Born: Londonderry, 16 August 1979
Height: 5'9" **Weight:** 11.11
International Honours: NI: U21-9; Yth
This midfield playmaker joined Carlisle United on a monthly contract at the start of the 2001-02 campaign, but made only a handful of appearances before moving on to Aldershot Town and then Conference outfit Nuneaton Borough.
Wycombe W (From trainee on 14/2/1997) FL 26+47/2 FLC 5+2/1 FAC 4+4 Others 4/1
Carlisle U (Free on 20/8/2001) FL 2+2 FLC 1

HARLEY Jonathan (Jon)
Born: Maidstone, 26 September 1979
Height: 5'9" **Weight:** 10.3
Club Honours: FAC '00
International Honours: E: U21-3; Yth
Jon arrived at Fulham at the start of the 2001-02 campaign and made his debut in the opening game at Old Trafford. However he failed to remove Rufus Brevett from the left-back spot and was unable to establish himself, although he did on occasion appear on the left side of midfield, a role in which he looked more comfortable. He is a positive player who likes to join the attack and has the ability to try his luck on goal from distance.
Chelsea (From trainee on 20/3/1997) PL 19+11/2 FLC 0+1 FAC 7 Others 1+3
Wimbledon (Loaned on 20/10/2000) FL 6/2
Fulham (£3,500,000 on 8/8/2001) PL 5+5 FLC 2 FAC 0+1

HARPER James (Jamie) Alan John
Born: Chelmsford, 9 November 1980
Height: 5'10" **Weight:** 11.7
Jamie was a regular in Reading's midfield from the start of last season until mid-November, when he missed the home game against Bristol City with a bout of influenza. Thereafter he was mainly confined to the substitutes' bench, but continued to give evidence of his ability as a perceptive passer of the ball. His only goal brought a 1-0 home win over Cambridge United, and he was unlucky to see a 30-yard free kick disallowed for offside against Queen's Park Rangers.
Arsenal (From trainee on 8/7/1999)
Cardiff C (Loaned on 29/12/2000) FL 3
Reading (£400,000 on 28/2/2001) FL 28+10/2 FLC 3 FAC 1 Others 2+2

HARPER Kevin Patrick
Born: Oldham, 15 January 1976
Height: 5'6" **Weight:** 10.10
International Honours: S: B-1; U21-7; Sch
Kevin was a near ever present for Portsmouth last season playing either on the wing or in midfield. His greatest asset is his pace from out wide, but he adapted well when temporarily asked to play at wing back, showing defensive qualities to add to his attacking strengths. His one goal in 2001-02 was a spectacular 20-yard curling right-foot shot against Norwich.
Hibernian (Signed from Hutchison Vale BC on 3/8/1992) SL 73+23/15 SLC 4+5 SC 9+1/3
Derby Co (£300,000 + on 11/9/1998) PL 6+26/1 FLC 1+5 FAC 0+3/1
Walsall (Loaned on 17/12/1999) FL 8+1/1

Portsmouth (£300,000 on 6/3/2000) FL
64+11/5 FLC 0+1 FAC 2

HARPER Lee Charles Phillip
Born: Chelsea, 30 October 1971
Height: 6'1" **Weight:** 13.11
Lee kept a clean sheet in both his first
Worthington Cup game and his first
League game for Walsall. He lost his
place, however, after successive tough
games against Wolves and Manchester
City and was unable to regain it on
account of the tremendous form shown
by Jimmy Walker. He nonetheless
continued to excel in reserve games.
*Arsenal (£150,000 from Sittingbourne on
16/6/1994) PL 1*
*Queens Park R (£125,000 + on 11/7/1997)
FL 117+1 FLC 8+1 FAC 4*
Walsall (Free on 20/7/2001) FL 3 FLC 2

HARPER Stephen (Steve)
Alan
Born: Easington, 14 March 1975
Height: 6'2" **Weight:** 13.0
Newcastle are fortunate to have such a
fine second goalkeeper as Steve who
remains at the club despite enjoying only
limited opportunities for first-team
football. Locally born he is the longest-
serving player on the club's books and has
the doubtful distinction of having been
on the bench more often than any other
player in United's history. He made only
three first-team appearances last season,
all in the Worthington Cup, but when
called upon he demonstrated that he is a
fine keeper in his own right.
*Newcastle U (Free from Seaham Red Star on
5/7/1993) PL 29+2 FLC 7 FAC 7+1 Others 6*
Bradford C (Loaned on 18/9/1995) FL 1
Hartlepool U (Loaned on 29/8/1997) FL 15
*Huddersfield T (Loaned on 18/12/1997) FL
24 FAC 2*

HARPER Steven (Steve)
James
Born: Newcastle under Lyme, 3 February
1969
Height: 5'10" **Weight:** 11.12
Club Honours: Div 4 '92
This experienced utility player was used
mainly as a substitute by Darlington last
term. He made the starting line-up for the
first seven games of the season, operating
mainly as an attacking left-sided
midfielder and using his speed and
trickery to good advantage. He scored his
first and so far only goal for the club after
coming on from the bench against Leyton
Orient in September.
*Port Vale (From trainee on 29/6/1987) FL
16+12/2 FLC 1+2 Others 1+1*

Preston NE (Signed on 23/3/1989) FL
57+20/10 FLC 1+1 FAC 1+2 Others 6+1/1
*Burnley (Free on 23/7/1991) FL 64+5/8 FLC
1+2 FAC 10/3 Others 8*
*Doncaster Rov (Free on 7/8/1993) FL
56+9/11 FLC 2+1/1 FAC 3 Others 4*
*Mansfield T (£20,000 on 8/9/1995) FL
157+3/18 FLC 6 FAC 8/1 Others 7*
*Hull C (Free on 13/7/1999) FL 63+2/4 FLC 5
FAC 7 Others 3*
*Darlington (Free on 15/2/2001) FL 32+8/1
FLC 1 Others 0+1*

HARRIS Andrew (Andy) David
Douglas
Born: Springs, South Africa, 26 February
1977
Height: 5'10" **Weight:** 11.11
Andy featured mainly in central midfield
for Leyton Orient in 2001-02 but was also
used as a right back when needed. A
near ever present for the O's, he scored
his first ever League goal away at
Hartlepool in December. He is a good
tackler and an effective box-to-box player,
breaking up attacks and making surging
runs to counter attack.
Liverpool (From trainee on 23/3/1994)
*Southend U (Free on 10/7/1996) FL 70+2
FLC 5 FAC 3*
*Leyton Orient (Free on 5/7/1999) FL
100+4/1 FLC 9 FAC 8 Others 2+1*

HARRIS Jason Andre Sebastian
Born: Sutton, 24 November 1976
Height: 6'1" **Weight:** 11.7
A very fast and agile forward, Jason did
well with Southend's reserve team in the
early part of last season, but only
managed five senior appearances before
being released. He subsequently had a
spell with Unibond League outfit
Harrogate Town before joining Nuneaton
Borough in the new year. He is the older
brother of Wycombe's Richard Harris.
*Crystal Palace (From trainee on 3/7/1995) FL
0+2 FLC 0+2*
*Bristol Rov (Loaned on 22/11/1996) FL
5+1/2 Others 1/1*
Lincoln C (Loaned on 11/8/1997) FL 0+1
*Leyton Orient (Loaned on 23/9/1997) FL
22+15/7 FLC 1 FAC 2 Others 1+1*
*Preston NE (Signed on 28/8/1998) FL 9+25/6
FAC 2+1/1 Others 2+2*
*Hull C (£30,000 + on 12/7/1999) FL 19+19/4
FLC 0+3 FAC 0+1 Others 1+2*
*Shrewsbury T (Loaned on 16/3/2001) FL
1+3*
Southend U (Free on 11/7/2001) FL 2+3

HARRIS Neil
Born: Orsett, 12 July 1977
Height: 5'11" **Weight:** 12.9

Club Honours: Div 2 '01
Neil had a somewhat frustrating season at
Millwall last term after recovering from a
serious illness. He came back earlier than
expected but after a couple of games got
a virus, which sidelined him again. He
made most of his appearances from the
bench and scored four times during the
campaign. As an out-and-out striker Neil
will be waiting for the start of the 2002-
03 season, so he can do what he likes
doing most – scoring goals.
*Millwall (£30,000 from Cambridge C on
26/3/1998) FL 121+22/71 FLC 4+1 FAC 5+2/1
Others 11+1/3*

HARRIS Richard
Born: Croydon, 23 October 1980
Height: 5'11" **Weight:** 10.9
This young Crystal Palace striker joined
Mansfield on loan last September, making
his debut in the 3-1 defeat at Rochdale.
Used mostly as a substitute, his
appearances were restricted by the
management who preferred the more
experienced Jason White. Later in the
season he also went on loan to Wycombe
where despite suffering a hamstring injury
he earned himself a 12-month contract.
He is a bustling striker with an effective
long throw. Richard is the younger
brother of Jason Harris.
*Crystal Palace (From trainee on 22/12/1997)
FL 2+7 FLC 2+2*
Mansfield T (Loaned on 28/9/2001) FL 0+6
Wycombe W (Free on 26/3/2002) FL 2+1

HARRISON Craig
Born: Gateshead, 10 November 1977
Height: 6'0" **Weight:** 11.13
Craig had another season plagued with
injuries at Crystal Palace last term. When
fit he was mainly a reserve player and
managed just four starts in the campaign.
He had the misfortune to suffer a double
fracture to his leg playing for the second
string at Reading in January and he had
not recovered match fitness by the
summer break.
*Middlesbrough (From trainee on 4/7/1996)
F/PL 19+5 FLC 4+2 FAC 2*
*Preston NE (Loaned on 15/1/1999) FL 6
Others 1*
*Crystal Palace (£200,000 on 11/8/2000) FL
34+4 FLC 8 FAC 2*

HARRISON Daniel (Danny)
Robert
Born: Liverpool, 4 November 1982
Height: 5'11" **Weight:** 12.5
Danny worked his way up through the
ranks to sign his first professional contract
for Tranmere in the summer of 2001. A

regular in the reserves, he made his bow in senior football in the home game with Wigan in October and also played in the LDV Vans Trophy tie at Oldham soon afterwards. A reliable and mature midfielder, he leads by example and is more than capable of finding the back of the net when helping out in attack.
Tranmere Rov (From trainee on 16/5/2002) FL 1 Others 1

HARSLEY Paul
Born: Scunthorpe, 29 May 1978
Height: 5'9" **Weight:** 11.5
After joining Halifax Town during the 2001 close season, Paul was simply a revelation throughout the 2001-02 campaign. He missed just one game, through suspension, and his displays earned him the club's 'Player of the Season' award. Playing mostly in midfield, although occasionally at right back, he finished the season as Town's leading scorer with 12 goals.
Grimsby T (From trainee on 16/7/1996)
Scunthorpe U (Free on 7/7/1997) FL 110+18/5 FLC 6 FAC 4+2/1 Others 5+1
Halifax T (Free on 1/7/2001) FL 45/11 FLC 1 FAC 3/1 Others 1

HART Gary John
Born: Harlow, 21 September 1976
Height: 5'9" **Weight:** 12.8
Club Honours: Div 3 '01; Div 2 '02
Gary continued to operate in a wide-right role for Brighton in 2001-02, although he occasionally also appeared in his former position of centre midfield. Very much a favourite of the Albion fans, he could always be relied upon to give 100 per cent and netted important winners at Huddersfield and at home to Tranmere. However, his season ended in frustration when he suffered a broken leg at Peterborough in the game that effectively sealed the club's promotion. He is expected to have recovered sufficiently to return for pre-season training in the summer.
Brighton & Hove A (£1,000 from Stansted on 13/6/1998) FL 161+10/32 FLC 5+3 FAC 7 Others 4+1/1

HARTE Ian Patrick
Born: Drogheda, 31 August 1977
Height: 5'10" **Weight:** 11.8
International Honours: RoI: 44; U21-3
This talented defender now seems firmly established in the left-back role for Leeds United and is still recognised as one of the deadliest exponents of the dead-ball situation. In fact his tremendous power with either foot means that he is capable

of switching play with a range of excellent long passes. He again weighed in with his share of goals, including a superb free kick in the 4-3 defeat by Manchester United and continued to feature regularly for the Republic of Ireland.
Leeds U (From trainee on 15/12/1995) PL 154+9/24 FLC 7+2/1 FAC 12+2/3 Others 40/6

HASLAM Steven Robert
Born: Sheffield, 6 September 1979
Height: 5'11" **Weight:** 10.10
International Honours: E: Yth; Sch
This local born lad enjoyed a good, steady season for Sheffield Wednesday last term. He was a regular in the 'holding' midfield position, but can also play at right back if required. A solid performer, he tends to play the simple ball rather than try the unexpected. He passed the landmark figure of 100 appearances for Wednesday during the campaign.
Sheffield Wed (From trainee on 12/9/1996) P/FL 81+12/1 FLC 10+1 FAC 6

HASSELBAINK Jerrel (Jimmy Floyd)
Born: Surinam, 27 March 1972
Height: 6'2" **Weight:** 13.4
Club Honours: CS '00
International Honours: Holland: 19
Following on from his exploits of the previous season when his cannonball shooting earned him the Golden Boot, Jimmy Floyd started 2001-02 with a bang. He opened his account in the second match of the season with a milestone goal, the first Premiership goal to be scored at Southampton's St Mary's ground. His burgeoning partnership with Eidur Gudjohnsen developed into the most lethal in the country. Recognised as an out-and-out goal-scorer par excellence, his all-round game has improved dramatically as his movement off the ball and intuitive passing have created an abundance of chances for his fellow strikers. His final tally of 29 included a hat-trick against Tottenham, although he was absent at the very end of the campaign with a calf injury.
Leeds U (£2,000,000 from Boavista, Portugal, ex Campomaiorense, on 18/7/1997) PL 66+3/34 FLC 5/2 FAC 9/5 Others 4/1
(£12,000,000 to Atletico Madrid, Spain on 20/8/1999)
Chelsea (£15,000,000 on 12/7/2000) PL 70/46 FLC 5/3 FAC 9/5 Others 5/1

HASSELL Robert (Bobby) John Francis
Born: Derby, 4 June 1980
Height: 5'9" **Weight:** 12.6

Bobby started the 2001-02 season as Mansfield Town's regular right back, producing some tremendous performances right from the opening matches. His strong tackling and assured distribution helped steady a rather shaky rearguard, while he was also effective pushing down the flank in support of the attack. Consistent throughout the campaign, he was rewarded with the supporters' 'Player of the Year' award.
Mansfield T (From trainee on 3/7/1998) FL 99+7/3 FLC 5+1 FAC 5 Others 1

HATCHER Daniel (Danny) Ian
Born: Newport, IoW, 24 December 1983
Height: 5'10" **Weight:** 11.8
Danny continued to develop with Leyton Orient's reserve and junior teams last season and made a handful of appearances for the senior side from the subs' bench. He started the last two games of the campaign and showed he has the pace to unsettle Third Division defences. He is a quick and direct striker who will be looking to appear more regularly in the first team in 2002-03.
Leyton Orient (Trainee) FL 2+8 FAC 0+1 Others 0+1

HATSWELL Wayne Mervin
Born: Swindon, 8 February 1975
Height: 6'0" **Weight:** 13.10
Wayne started the 2001-02 season playing on the left of a back three for Oxford United under Mark Wright. He performed steadily and was winning over supporters with his determination to succeed, but he lost his place in the side when Ian Atkins took over as manager. He played his last game for the U's on Boxing Day and was subsequently released with a few weeks of the season remaining. He was reported to have joined Chester City during the summer.
Oxford U (£35,000 from Forest Green Rov on 1/12/2000) FL 47+1 FLC 1 FAC 1 Others 2

HAWKINS Peter Steven
Born: Maidstone, 19 September 1978
Height: 6'0" **Weight:** 11.6
Peter can feel proud of himself following a very successful year at left back for Wimbledon. His confidence grew as the season went on and his performances became more solid. With the departure of other players he has the ability and experience to make this position his own. He is equally comfortable distributing the ball with his left or right foot and he has a good work rate.
Wimbledon (From trainee on 6/3/1997) FL 54+5 FLC 3 FAC 7
York C (Loaned on 22/2/2000) FL 14

Jimmy Floyd Hasselbaink

HAWLEY Karl Leon
Born: Walsall, 6 December 1981
Height: 5'7" **Weight:** 12.0
In his first full season as a professional this young striker was popular with the Walsall reserve-team fans with his lively front running. He showed neat touches and a sharp turn of speed in his solitary first-team substitute appearance against Gillingham in March.
Walsall (From trainee on 26/1/2001) FL 0+1 Others 0+2

HAWORTH Simon Owen
Born: Cardiff, 30 March 1977
Height: 6'2" **Weight:** 13.8
Club Honours: AMC '99
International Honours: W: 5; B-1; U21-12; Yth
A tall striker with an eye for goal, Simon finished the 2001-02 season as second-top scorer for Wigan despite being sold to Tranmere at the start of March. His tally of ten goals for the Latics included superb strikes in the away wins at Northampton and Peterborough. At Prenton Park he resumed his old striking partnership with Stuart Barlow with some success, netting five times in the closing fixtures. A confidence player with the ability to score spectacular goals, he is effective in the air and has a great touch for such a tall player.
Cardiff C (From trainee on 7/8/1995) FL 27+10/9 FLC 4 FAC 0+1 Others 4/1
Coventry C (£500,000 on 4/6/1997) PL 5+6 FLC 2/1 FAC 0+1
Wigan Ath (£600,000 on 2/10/1998) FL 99+18/44 FLC 8/6 FAC 4/4 Others 12+1/4
Tranmere Rov (£125,000 on 28/2/2002) FL 12/5

HAY Alexander (Alex) Neil
Born: Birkenhead, 14 October 1981
Height: 5'10" **Weight:** 11.5
This enthusiastic striker made his senior debut for Tranmere at Brentford last September and added a handful more early-season appearances. He then seemed to fade from the manager's plans, and early in the new year he had a spell on loan with Conference club Morecambe. He refused to be discouraged and featured regularly for Rovers reserves, for whom he scored prolifically.
Tranmere Rov (From trainee on 24/3/2000) FL 2+1 FLC 1 Others 1

HAY Christopher (Chris) Drummond
Born: Glasgow, 28 August 1974
Height: 5'11" **Weight:** 12.5

Chris found himself the main front man for Huddersfield Town at the start of the 2001-02 season and was later often used in a wide-attacking role after coming on from the subs' bench. A striker with close control and able to deliver a useful cross, he is always willing to chase lost causes.
Glasgow Celtic (Free from Giffnock North AFC on 27/5/1993) SL 9+16/4 SC 0+3 Others 0+2/1
Swindon T (£330,000 on 6/8/1997) FL 73+21/30 FLC 2+2 FAC 2+1
Huddersfield T (£70,000 on 23/3/2000) FL 21+21/5 FLC 3 FAC 0+1 Others 2+4/1

HAYLES Barrington (Barry) Edward
Born: Lambeth, 17 May 1972
Height: 5'9" **Weight:** 13.0
Club Honours: GMVC '96; Div 2 '99; Div 1 '01
International Honours: Jamaica: 8; E: SP-2
This excellent striker has now completed the difficult journey from non-league to Premiership in a matter of a few years. An opportunist who is always likely to get a goal, he once again managed double figures in League and cup last season, despite not being a consistent first choice once Steve Marlet returned from injury around the turn of the year. Excellent in the air, he also uses his pace and an ability to shield the ball to hold up play to allow others to join the attack. Included in his goal tally were a spectacular winner at Walsall in the FA Cup, a double against Everton and a notable effort in the home draw against Chelsea.
Bristol Rov (£250,000 from Stevenage Borough on 4/6/1997) FL 62/32 FLC 4/1 FAC 5/2 Others 3+2/2
Fulham (£2,100,000 on 17/11/1998) P/FL 102+33/39 FLC 9+2/5 FAC 9+4/5

HAYTER James (Jamie) Edward
Born: Sandown, IoW, 9 April 1979
Height: 5'9" **Weight:** 11.2
Jamie was a regular in the Bournemouth line-up in 2001-02 when he was usually employed in a role just behind the front two strikers. He again showed himself to be an industrious player and scored a total of eight goals. The highlight of his season was a tremendous individual goal in the first game at the Cherries' new Fitness First Stadium.
Bournemouth (From trainee on 7/7/1997) FL 109+33/22 FLC 2+2/1 FAC 6/2 Others 3+2/1

HAZELL Reuben
Born: Birmingham, 24 April 1979
Height: 5'11" **Weight:** 12.0
A pacy and cultured full back, Reuben made several first-team appearances for Tranmere at the beginning of the 2001-02 season, but after a successful loan spell at Torquay, he made a permanent move. He quickly settled into a position on the right-hand side of a three-centre-back system for the Gulls and showed excellent positional sense and an ability to read the game. Reuben is the nephew of the former Queen's Park Rangers star Bob Hazell.
Aston Villa (From trainee on 20/3/1997)
Tranmere Rov (Free on 5/8/1999) FL 38+4/1 FLC 8 FAC 3 Others 1
Torquay U (Free on 10/1/2002) FL 19

HEALD Paul Andrew
Born: Wath on Dearne, 20 September 1968
Height: 6'2" **Weight:** 14.0
Paul was second choice 'keeper at Wimbledon last term and managed only four starts. He joined Sheffield Wednesday on an extended loan due to an injury crisis in the goalkeeping department. A day or so later he made his Owls debut in the League Cup semi-final against Blackburn in his next game he shut out Sheffield United, and played very well until Kevin Pressman regained his place when fit again. Paul was out of contract with the Dons in the summer and his future remained uncertain at the time of writing.
Sheffield U (From trainee on 30/6/1987)
Leyton Orient (Signed on 2/12/1988) FL 176 FLC 13 FAC 9 Others 21
Coventry C (Loaned on 10/3/1992) PL 2
Swindon T (Loaned on 24/3/1994) PL 1+1
Wimbledon (£125,000 on 25/7/1995) P/FL 26+2 FLC 7
Sheffield Wed (Loaned on 22/1/2002) FL 5 FLC 1

HEALY Brian
Born: Glasgow, 27 December 1968
Height: 6'1" **Weight:** 12.10
International Honours: E: SP-1
Having missed the previous season through injury, Brian understandably looked somewhat rusty in the opening two matches of last season. Surprisingly he was not given the opportunity to regain full match fitness and had his contract terminated allowing him to return to the North East to try his luck with Darlington. He immediately became a hero for the Quakers when he headed the only goal of the game against Oxford United at Feethams on his debut. He

showed himself to be a shrewd passer of the ball from the centre of midfield, but was soon released and joined Northern League club Shildon.

Torquay U (£25,000 from Morecambe on 16/12/1998) FL 55+4/11 FLC 1 Others 3
Darlington (Free on 9/11/2001) FL 1+1/1 FAC 1

HEALY Colin

Born: Cork, 14 March 1980
Height: 5'11" **Weight:** 9.12
International Honours: RoI: 3; U21-10
This young Celtic midfield player joined Coventry City on loan last January and was an ever present for the remainder of the season. After a quiet start he emerged as a fine attacking central midfielder with good feet and a bite in the tackle. He showed an eye for goal with fine efforts in successive games against Sheffield Wednesday and Birmingham. His form earned him a call-up to Mick McCarthy's Republic of Ireland squad and his first cap, and he narrowly failed to force his way into the final 23 for the World Cup finals.

Glasgow Celtic (Signed from Wilton U, Ireland on 7/7/1998) SL 16+13/1 SLC 5+1/2 SC 0+1 Others 1+4
Coventry C (Loaned on 29/1/2002) FL 17/2

HEALY David Jonathan

Born: Downpatrick, 5 August 1979
Height: 5'8" **Weight:** 11.0
International Honours: NI: 18; B-1; U21-5; Yth; Sch
Preston's record signing had an inconsistent season in 2001-02, which is to be expected in a young player who is still learning his trade. After opening his account at Grimsby he failed to add to his tally for ten games, then managed to hit the net in two successive matches, before scoring his first senior hat-trick in the first half of the 6-0 win over Stockport. A classic treble (left foot, right foot, header) was his seasonal high spot, as tiredness began to creep into his play and the goals largely dried up. Despite this, he played successfully in an attacking midfield role on several occasions, when his pace led to several goal-scoring opportunities. A player with huge potential, David continued to appear regularly for Northern Ireland with whom he performed as a lone striker.

Manchester U (From trainee on 28/11/1997) PL 0+1 FLC 0+2
Port Vale (Loaned on 25/2/2000) FL 15+1/3
Preston NE (£1,500,000 on 29/12/2000) FL 54+12/19 FLC 2 FAC 3+1 Others 3/1

HEANEY Neil Andrew

Born: Middlesbrough, 3 November 1971
Height: 5'9" **Weight:** 11.10
Club Honours: FAYC '88
International Honours: E: U21-6; Yth
Neil was Plymouth manager Paul Sturrock's final permanent signing of the 2001-02 season. Arriving from SPL club Dundee United in December he added pace and experience in midfield but his appearances were restricted by injury. He was due to undergo surgery on his troublesome knee during the summer break and will be aiming to be fit in time to take part in Argyle's Second Division campaign in 2002-03.

Arsenal (From trainee on 14/11/1989) F/PL 4+3 FLC 0+1
Hartlepool U (Loaned on 3/1/1991) FL 2+1
Cambridge U (Loaned on 9/1/1992) FL 9+4/2 FAC 1
Southampton (£300,000 on 22/3/1994) PL 42+19/5 FLC 4+2 FAC 6/2
Manchester C (£500,000 on 25/11/1996) FL 13+5/1 FAC 2/1 Others 1
Charlton Ath (Loaned on 26/3/1998) FL 4+2 Others 3
Bristol C (Loaned on 12/3/1999) FL 2+1
Darlington (Free on 6/8/1999) FL 33+3/5 FLC 1 FAC 3 Others 3
Dundee U (£175,000 on 25/7/2000) SL 7+5 SLC 1 SC 0+1
Plymouth Arg (Free on 5/12/2001) FL 1+7

HEARN Charles (Charley) Richard

Born: Ashford, Kent, 5 November 1983
Height: 5'11" **Weight:** 11.9
Another product of Millwall's youth policy, this 19-year-old midfielder is an excellent prospect. He was outstanding in the U19s and reserves and came on as substitute for the final ten minutes at Walsall when he showed glimpses of what he is capable of doing.

Millwall (From trainee on 27/4/2001) FL 0+2

HEARY Thomas Mark

Born: Dublin, 14 February 1978
Height: 5'10" **Weight:** 11.12
International Honours: RoI: U21-4; Yth; (UEFA-U18 '98); Sch
Thomas enjoyed his most fruitful season to date with Huddersfield Town last term, when he featured both at full back and in a central midfield role. The promotion challenge seemed to inspire him and he grew in stature as the campaign progressed. He gave some astute displays in defence with a no-frills approach and some strong tackling and provided an extra dimension to the midfield engine room.

Huddersfield T (From trainee on 17/2/1996) FL 54+18 FLC 3+1 FAC 4 Others 8

HEATH Matthew Philip

Born: Leicester, 1 November 1981
Height: 6'4" **Weight:** 13.13
This promising young defender was thrust into the Leicester City first team on a handful of occasions last term when the injury situation demanded and he found it a tough baptism in the Premiership. Nevertheless, the experience should prove invaluable as he challenges for a regular place 2002-03. He continued to earn rave reviews in the reserves throughout.

Leicester C (From trainee on 17/2/2001) PL 3+2 FAC 0+1

HEATHCOTE Michael (Mick)

Born: Kelloe, 10 September 1965
Height: 6'2" **Weight:** 12.5
Mick proved to be an inspirational signing for Shrewsbury boss Kevin Ratcliffe on the eve of the 2001-02 season. He quickly formed a strong central defensive partnership with Matt Redmile bringing some much needed experience and composure to the back line. His influence on the team was evident during his absence at the turn of the year when they managed just three wins in an 11-match spell.

Sunderland (£15,000 from Spennymoor on 19/8/1987) FL 6+3 Others 0+1
Halifax T (Loaned on 17/12/1987) FL 7/1 FAC 1
York C (Loaned on 4/1/1990) FL 3 Others 1
Shrewsbury T (£55,000 on 12/7/1990) FL 43+1/6 FLC 6 FAC 5 Others 4
Cambridge U (£150,000 on 12/9/1991) FL123+5/13 FLC 7/1 FAC 5+2/2 Others 7/2
Plymouth Arg (£70,000 on 27/7/1995) FL 195+4/13 FLC 9/1 FAC 18/3 Others 9
Shrewsbury T (Free on 8/8/2001) FL 33+1/2 FLC 1 FAC 1 Others 1

HECKINGBOTTOM Paul

Born: Barnsley, 17 July 1977
Height: 5'11" **Weight:** 12.0
After missing the first half dozen games of the 2001-02 season Paul established himself regularly in the Darlington side for the rest of the campaign, featuring mainly at left back but also in the centre of the defence when necessary. He is strong in the tackle and makes penetrating runs down the flank, but is also effective in the air and showed great composure when playing in the heart of the defence. He weighed in with three valuable goals during the season.

Sunderland (From trainee at Manchester U on 14/7/1995)

Scarborough (Loaned on 17/10/1997) FL 28+1 Others 1

Hartlepool U (Loaned on 25/9/1998) FL 5/1
Darlington (Free on 25/3/1999) FL 111+4/5 FLC 4 FAC 8/1 Others 8

HEDMAN Magnus Carl

Born: Stockholm, Sweden, 19 March 1973
Height: 6'4" **Weight:** 13.10
International Honours: Sweden: 49; B-1; U21; Yth
Sweden's number one 'keeper was expected to leave Coventry in the summer of 2001, but when a move to Everton broke down the club were forced to sell Chris Kirkland and he stayed at Highfield Road. He had several injury frustrations with chest, calf and back injuries and missed 12 games. His shot-stopping skills were as brilliant as ever, and whilst he was less reluctant to stay on his line at corners this remained an area of his game that needed improvement. His performances for his country were of a high class and he rarely conceded a goal for them.
Coventry C (£500,000 from AIK Solna, Sweden on 24/7/1997) P/FL 134 FLC 6 FAC 11

HEFFERNAN Paul

Born: Dublin, Ireland, 29 December 1981
Height: 5'10" **Weight:** 10.7
International Honours: RoI: U21-3
This talented young striker is a born predator with a great eye for goal. He stepped up to become a regular in the Notts County first team last season following an injury to Mark Stallard and quickly established a productive partnership up front with Danny Allsop.
Notts Co (Signed from Newtown, Co Wicklow on 22/10/1999) FL 18+8/6 FLC 0+1 FAC 1 Others 0+3

HEINEMANN Nicholas (Nicky)

Born: Bradford, 4 January 1985
Height: 6'0" **Weight:** 12.0
Nicky is one of the talented crop of youngsters on the books of Halifax Town. A left-footed centre back, he was introduced to first-team action once Town's relegation was confirmed. He made his debut at left back against Hartlepool United when he was outstanding, picking up all the sponsors' 'Man of the Match' awards.
Halifax T (Trainee) FL 3

HELGUSON Heidar

Born: Iceland, 22 August 1977
Height: 6'0" **Weight:** 12.2

International Honours: Iceland: 20; U21-6; Yth
Watford's own super sub, Heidar had the doubtful distinction of setting a new club record with 29 substitute appearances last term. A hard-working and aggressive forward who is particularly effective in the air, he had a creditable return of seven goals, which left the fans wondering what might have been had he enjoyed more starts.
Watford (£1,500,000 from SK Lillestrom, Norway, ex Throttur, on 13/1/2000) P/FL 48+35/20 FLC 2+7/2 FAC 0+2

HELIN Petri Juhani

Born: Helsinki, Finland, 13 December 1969
Height: 5'11" **Weight:** 13.2
International Honours: Finland: 24
This experienced right-sided midfielder spent the last three months of the 2001-02 season on loan in Turkey with Denizlispor after being told by new Stockport County manager Carlton Palmer that he did not feature in his plans. He has since been released by the club after agreeing to terminate his contract which still had twelve months to run and is expected to return to his native country.
Luton T (Free from FC Jokerit, Finland, ex Ikast, PPT Pon, HJK Helsinki, on 2/11/2000) FL 23/1 FAC 3 Others 1
Stockport Co (Free on 30/7/2001) FL 10+3 FLC 1+1 FAC 0+1

HENCHOZ Stephane

Born: Billens, Switzerland, 7 September 1974
Height: 6'1" **Weight:** 12.10
Club Honours: FLC '01; FAC '01; UEFAC '01; ESC '01; CS '01
International Honours: Switzerland: 53; U21; Yth
2001-02 was another outstanding season for this central defender, as together with his partner Sami Hyypia, he provided a frequently impenetrable barrier to opposition attacks and confirmed Liverpool's reputation for being the tightest defence in the Premiership. He was a model of consistency throughout the campaign, preventing many certain goals with his block tackles and goal-line clearances.
Blackburn Rov (£3,000,000 from Hamburg, Germany, ex FC Bulle, Neuchatel Xamax, on 14/7/1997) PL 70 FLC 3+1 FAC 6 Others 2
Liverpool (£3,750,000 on 20/7/1999) PL 98 FLC 8 FAC 9 Others 27

HENDERSON Darius Alexis

Born: Sutton, 7 September 1981
Height: 6'0" **Weight:** 12.8
Darius set a club record for Reading by making 39 appearances as a playing substitute last season. The burly striker enhanced his reputation as an incisive finisher, and led the goal-scorers for the first half of the campaign. He also had the distinction of netting Reading's 5,000th Football League goal when he headed the first in the 2-0 defeat of Wycombe Wanderers in September. But his finest performance came at Peterborough when he came off the bench to score twice and earn his team a 2-1 victory.
Reading (From trainee on 15/12/1999) FL 4+44/7 FLC 2+2/2 FAC 1+1 Others 2+1/2

HENDERSON Kevin Malcolm

Born: Ashington, 8 June 1974
Height: 6'3" **Weight:** 13.2
This hard-working striker had an unfortunate time with injuries in 2001-02, and had a lengthy spell out with knee trouble. He returned to first-team action in the closing stages of the season but was not able to win a regular place, being used as substitute.
Burnley (Signed from Morpeth T on 17/12/1997) FL 0+14/1 FLC 0+2 Others 0+4/1
Hartlepool U (Free on 2/7/1999) FL 76+22/27 FLC 3+1 FAC 1+1 Others 5+3/3

HENDON Ian Michael

Born: Ilford, 5 December 1971
Height: 6'0" **Weight:** 12.10
Club Honours: FAYC '90; CS '91; Div 3 '98
International Honours: E: U21-7; Yth
Although the first choice at right back for Sheffield Wednesday last term, Ian's season was ruined by two separate injuries. He was restricted to just ten first-team appearances and the Owls looked very uncertain at the back in his absence.
Tottenham H (From trainee on 20/12/1989) FL 0+4 FLC 1 Others 0+2
Portsmouth (Loaned on 16/11/1992) FL 1+3
Leyton Orient (Loaned on 26/3/1992) FL 5+1
Barnsley (Loaned on 17/3/1993) FL 6
Leyton Orient (£50,000 on 9/8/1993) FL 130+1/5 FLC 8 FAC 7 Others 12/1
Birmingham C (Loaned on 23/3/1995) FL 4
Notts Co (£50,000 on 24/2/1997) FL 82/6 FLC 5/1 FAC 8+1
Northampton T (£30,000 on 25/3/1999) FL 60/3 FLC 4 FAC 1/1 Others 1
Sheffield Wed (£40,000 + on 12/10/2000) FL 40/2 FLC 1 FAC 2

Lee Hendrie

HENDRIE Lee Andrew
Born: Birmingham, 18 May 1977
Height: 5'10" **Weight:** 10.3
International Honours: E: 1; B-1; U21-13; Yth
Lee is a quick-witted midfielder, perhaps better in a 'holding' role, who also has the feet to make things happen when moving forward. He was an ever present in the team up to February and produced a number of consistent performances until he was forced to miss out with a hamstring injury. He then lost his place to Thomas Hitzlsperger, and now needs to force his way back into the manager's thoughts.
Aston Villa (From trainee on 18/5/1994) PL 116+30/15 FLC 6+2/3 FAC 7+8 Others 13+3/2

HENDRY Edward Colin James
Born: Keith, 7 December 1965
Height: 6'1" **Weight:** 12.7
Club Honours: FMC '87; PL '95; SLC '98; SPD '99; SC '99
International Honours: S: 51; B-1
This experienced central defender was a valued member of the Bolton Wanderers squad last term, although he only played in a handful of first games. In February he joined Preston on loan as cover for injuries and made an uncompromising debut against Birmingham. Sadly, that was virtually it as far as his North End career was concerned, for a first-half calf injury at Millwall in the next game meant he was unavailable for the rest of his month's loan.
Dundee (Signed from Islavale on 1/7/1983) SL 17+24/2 SC 2+3/1
Blackburn Rov (£30,000 on 11/3/1987) FL 99+3/22 FLC 4 FAC 3 Others 13/1
Manchester C (£700,000 on 16/11/1989) FL 57+6/5 FLC 4+1/1 FAC 5/2 Others 4/2
Blackburn Rov (£700,000 on 8/11/1991) P/FL 229+5/12 FLC 23 FAC 17+1 Others 11
Glasgow R (£4,000,000 on 5/8/1998) SL 18+3 SLC 3+1 SC 3 Others 4+1
Coventry C (£750,000 on 3/3/2000) PL 10+1
Bolton W (£250,000 on 15/12/2000) P/FL 25/3 FLC 4 FAC 1 Others 3
Preston NE (Loaned on 28/2/2002) FL 2

HENRIKSEN Bo
Born: Denmark, 7 February 1975
Height: 5'10" **Weight:** 11.10
A pony-tailed Emmanuel Petit look-alike, Bo left Denmark to join his boyhood idol Jan Molby at Kidderminster and soon became a fans' favourite after scoring on his debut at Leyton Orient. Despite playing with a troublesome groin injury he managed to weigh in with a further seven goals including strikes in the Christmas victories over Rochdale and Hull. Although essentially a striker, his passing skills and vision also saw him employed in midfield.
Kidderminster Hrs (Free from Herfolge, Denmark, ex Odense BK, on 9/11/2001) FL 24+1/8 FAC 1

HENRY Karl Levi Daniel
Born: Wolverhampton, 26 November 1982
Height: 6'1" **Weight:** 10.13
International Honours: E: Yth
Karl was one of the youngsters who made the Stoke City first-team squad last season, and whether in the starting line-up or used from the bench he turned in a string of good performances that marked him out as an outstanding prospect. His vision is exciting for one so young and his promotion to the England U-20 side on two occasions suggests he has a bright future in front of him.
Stoke C (From trainee on 30/11/1999) FL 9+15 FLC 1 FAC 2 Others 1+1

HENRY Nicholas (Nick) Ian
Born: Liverpool, 21 February 1969
Height: 5'6" **Weight:** 10.12
Club Honours: Div 2 '91
A keen tackling, committed and energetic midfielder, Nick was a regular for Tranmere in the 2001-02 campaign. He is a natural leader whose tackling is as sharp as his on the field verbal encouragement to his colleagues, while his intelligent passing of the ball provided many a scoring opportunity for them.
Oldham Ath (From trainee on 6/7/1987) F/PL 264+9/19 FLC 30+4/3 FAC 21 Others 5
Sheffield U (£500,000 on 28/2/1997) FL 13+3 FAC 2+1 Others 2
Walsall (Free on 25/3/1999) FL 8
Tranmere Rov (Free on 5/7/1999) FL 84+5/2 FLC 12+1/2 FAC 10+3/1 Others 0+1

HENRY Thierry
Born: Paris, France, 17 August 1977
Height: 6'1" **Weight:** 12.2
Club Honours: FAC '02; PL '02
International Honours: France: 38 (UEFA '00); Yth; (UEFA-U18 '96)
Thierry enjoyed yet another superb season for Arsenal last term, netting a total of 32 first-team goals including 24 from 31 Premiership starts. A striker with lightning pace, tricky ball skills and an eye for goal he was a crucial figure for the Gunners in their amazing double season. He also featured regularly for France but was unable to inspire them to a successive World Cup victory over the summer. Thierry's talent was again recognised when he was selected by his fellow professionals for the PFA's Premiership team for the season.
Arsenal (£8,000,000 from Juventus, Italy, ex Monaco, on 6/8/1999) PL 84+15/58 FLC 2/1 FAC 10+2/2 Others 32+5/19

HERBERT Robert
Born: Durham, 29 August 1983
Height: 5'8" **Weight:** 11.0
Robert did not quite make the breakthrough that was expected of him at Halifax last term, but nonetheless continued to develop steadily and appeared in around a quarter of the Shaymen's fixtures. One or two minor injury problems did not help his cause but on his day he is an effective midfielder with a tremendous burst of acceleration.
Halifax T (From trainee on 28/10/2000) FL 15+10/1 FLC 0+1 FAC 0+3 Others 0+1

HERIVELTO Moriera
Born: Brazil, 23 August 1975
Height: 5'10" **Weight:** 11.6
This speedy attacker impressed with some mazy runs early on for Walsall last term and crossed for Jorge Leitao's opening goal in the first game of the season against West Brom. He scored in three successive early-season games, and although after that he made more substitute appearances than starts, he was consistently a handful for defences.
Walsall (Free from Cruzeiro, Brazil, ex CS Maritimo, on 9/8/2001) FL 11+13/4 FLC 2/1 FAC 1+1

HERRERA Roberto (Robbie)
Born: Torquay, 12 June 1970
Height: 5'7" **Weight:** 10.6
After being released at the end of the 2000-01 season, Torquay's failure to find a new left back meant Robbie was given another chance on short-term contracts last term. He eventually moved on to Leyton Orient in October where he was needed as cover for the injured Matt Lockwood. However he was released by the O's and signed for Dr Martens League club Merthyr Tydfil.
Queens Park R (From trainee on 1/3/1988) FL 4+2 FLC 1+2 Others 1+1
Torquay U (Loaned on 17/3/1992) FL 11
Torquay U (Loaned on 24/10/1992) FL 5
Fulham (Signed on 29/10/1993) FL 143+2/1 FLC 15 FAC 13 Others 7+1
Torquay U (£30,000 on 4/8/1998) FL 104+3/1 FLC 5 FAC 5 Others 3
Leyton Orient (Free on 4/10/2001) FL 2 FAC 0+1 Others 1

HERRING Ian

Born: Swindon, 14 February 1984
Height: 6'1" **Weight:** 11.12
This young midfielder, who is still a member of Swindon's youth squad, was rewarded for his hard work last season when he was given his League debut as an injury-time substitute in the final game of the season against Wycombe. He still had time to make one quality pass and will be looking to gain further senior experience in 2002-03.
Swindon T (Trainee) FL 0+1

HESKEY Emile William Ivanhoe

Born: Leicester, 11 January 1978
Height: 6'2" **Weight:** 13.12
Club Honours: FLC '97, '00, '01; FAC '01; UEFAC '01; ESC '01; CS '01
International Honours: E: 29; B-1; U21-16; Yth
Already established as a first choice striker for Liverpool, last season saw Emile establish himself in the England squad as the regular partner to Michael Owen. A powerful, mobile, almost traditional centre forward, he wins most aerial battles with defenders, holds the ball up well and can also perform on the flanks to whip in low crosses into the heart of the penalty area. Although never a prolific goal-scorer, he still contributed 14 goals in the campaign.
Leicester C (From trainee on 3/10/1995) PL 143+11/40 FLC 25+2/6 FAC 11 Others 5
Liverpool (£11,000,000 on 10/3/2000) PL 71+12/26 FLC 3+2 FAC 4+3/5 Others 27+2/8

HESSENTHALER Andrew (Andy)

Born: Dartford, 17 June 1965
Height: 5'7" **Weight:** 11.5
International Honours: E: SP-1
Gillingham's player-manager, Andy took a back seat during the course of the 2001-02 season and was only involved in a few matches. However, he was a regular for the reserves in the Avon Combination where he was able to help bring on the youngsters and at the same time keep himself fit, in case of emergencies, for the League team.
Watford (£65,000 from Redbridge Forest on 12/9/1991) FL 195/12 FLC 13/1 FAC 5/2 Others 4
Gillingham (£235,000 on 7/8/1996) FL 186+15/16 FLC 19+1/2 FAC 13+2/2 Others 9+1/3

HEWITT James (Jamie) Robert

Born: Chesterfield, 17 May 1968
Height: 5'10" **Weight:** 12.0
This long-serving Chesterfield right back decided to forego first-team football to concentrate on training for a career as a physio last season. He was plunged back into action for one game, in an injury crisis, and produced the sort of experienced display that made him the club's second-highest appearance-maker. Immediately after this, manager Nicky Law left and in the subsequent reshuffle Jamie was promoted to first-team physio.
Chesterfield (From trainee on 22/4/1986) FL 240+9/14 FLC 10/1 FAC 8+1 Others 11+2
Doncaster Rov (Free on 1/8/1992) FL 32+1 FLC 3+1/1 FAC 1 Others 3
Chesterfield (Free on 8/10/1993) FL 248+9/12 FLC 18 FAC 15/1 Others 14/1

HEWLETT Matthew (Matt) Paul

Born: Bristol, 25 February 1976
Height: 6'2" **Weight:** 11.3
International Honours: E: Yth
Matt finally opened his goal-scoring account for Swindon in the 2-0 victory at Port Vale last September. A regular on the left side of the Town midfield throughout the 2001-02 campaign, he showed himself as a steady, composed player who works hard and can battle when required.
Bristol C (From trainee on 12/8/1993) FL 111+16/9 FLC 10+2 FAC 4+1/2 Others 7+2/1
Burnley (Loaned on 27/11/1998) FL 2 Others 1
Swindon T (Free on 27/7/2000) FL 63+2/1 FLC 6 FAC 1 Others 1

HEWS Chay

Born: Norkopping, Sweden, 30 September 1976
Height: 5'10" **Weight:** 12.7
This experienced right-sided midfield player joined Carlisle United on a short-term contract shortly after the start of the 2001-02 season. He scored both on his full debut against York, in which he also set up Carlisle's opening goal, and in his final match at Hartlepool. Despite this he was released the following month.
Carlisle U (Free from IF Sylvia, Sweden, via trial at Halifax T, ex Brisbane Strikers, Bellmare Hiratsuka, on 10/9/2001) FL 4+1/2

HEYWOOD Matthew (Matty) Stephen

Born: Chatham, 26 August 1979
Height: 6'2" **Weight:** 14.0
This solid, unflappable central defender produced some fine displays for Swindon Town and deservedly won no less than six 'Player of the Season' awards. Tough and uncompromising, he adapted well to the different systems used, featuring in left, right and central positions in either a three or four-man defensive line. He played the whole of the game at Stoke as an emergency forward. Matty weighed in with four goals during the campaign including the equaliser in the final game against Wycombe.
Burnley (From trainee on 6/7/1998) FL 11+2 FAC 1 Others 1
Swindon T (Free on 22/1/2001) FL 63+2/5 FLC 2 FAC 3/1 Others 3

HIBBERT Anthony (Tony) James

Born: Liverpool, 20 February 1981
Height: 5'8" **Weight:** 11.3
Club Honours: FAYC '98
A sharp and crisp-tackling right back, Tony added to his Premiership experience with several starts last term. Unfortunately, each time he looked set to enjoy a run of appearances, an ankle injury flared up. He spent the summer working back towards full fitness and will be looking to make a prolonged impact during 2002-03.
Everton (From trainee on 1/7/1998) PL 8+5 FLC 0+1 FAC 1

HIGGINBOTHAM Daniel (Danny) John

Born: Manchester, 29 December 1978
Height: 6'1" **Weight:** 12.6
Danny had an excellent season for Derby County last term, firmly establishing himself in the line-up as a left-sided central defender partnering Chris Riggott. He scored his only goal at Bolton and was deservedly rewarded for a fine campaign when he was selected as the Rams' 'Player of the Year'.
Manchester U (From trainee on 10/7/1997) PL 2+2 FLC 1 Others 1+1
Derby Co (£2,000,000 on 12/7/2000) PL 60+3/1 FLC 5+1 FAC 3+1

HIGGS Shane Peter

Born: Oxford, 13 May 1977
Height: 6'2" **Weight:** 12.12
Shane was once again forced to watch nearly all of Cheltenham Town's first-team games last term from the sidelines as third-choice 'keeper behind Steve Book and Carl Muggleton. His consistent performances for the reserves eventually earned him a place on the substitutes' bench and he made his only senior appearance in the defeat at Halifax in March when he came on after Steve Book had been sent off. A tall, strong goalkeeper, his handling and shot stopping have improved during his time with the Robins and he was awarded a new contract at the end of the season.

Bristol Rov (From trainee on 17/7/1995) FL 10 Others 2 (Free to Worcester C on 11/7/1998)
Cheltenham T (£10,000 on 21/6/1999) FL 0+2 Others 1

HIGNETT Craig John
Born: Prescot, 12 January 1970
Height: 5'9" **Weight:** 11.10
Club Honours: Div 1 '95; FLC '02
Craig spent much of last term on the subs' bench for Blackburn, but for a time after Christmas he was included instead of Keith Gillespie on the right wing. He struck a golden spell when he scored in four consecutive games and his composure when in the danger area enabled him to exploit his scoring potential. His last-minute winner at Southampton brought the club its first away win and his patience in waiting for the ball to fall and then placing his chip was a classic example of a cool head. Still troubled by an old achilles tendon injury his season ended early with an operation.
Crewe Alex (From trainee at Liverpool on 11/5/1988) FL 108+13/42 FLC 9+1/4 FAC 11+1/8 Others 6+1/3
Middlesbrough (£500,000 on 27/11/1992) F/PL 126+30/33 FLC 19+3/12 FAC 9+2/3 Others 5+1
Aberdeen (Free on 1/7/1998) SL 13/2 SLC 2
Barnsley (£800,000 on 26/11/1998) FL 62+4/28 FLC 2 FAC 6/5 Others 3/2
Blackburn Rov (£2,250,000 on 14/7/2000) P/FL 19+31/7 FLC 5+1/3 FAC 4+4/3

HILEY Scott Patrick
Born: Plymouth, 27 September 1968
Height: 5'9" **Weight:** 11.5
Club Honours: Div 4 '90
This consistent defender played over 30 games for Portsmouth last season, many of them as captain, but lost his place after a run of bad results. A right back or central defender, he was later placed on the transfer list by Pompey.
Exeter C (From trainee on 4/8/1986) FL 205+5/12 FLC 17 FAC 14 Others 16+2
Birmingham C (£100,000 on 12/3/1994) FL 49 FLC 7 FAC 1 Others 2
Manchester C (£250,000 on 23/2/1996) P/FL 4+5
Southampton (Free on 4/8/1998) PL 30+2 FAC 1
Portsmouth (£200,000 on 3/12/1999) FL 66+9 FLC 2 FAC 3

HILL Clinton (Clint) Scott
Born: Huyton, 19 October 1978
Height: 6'0" **Weight:** 11.6
Clint's appointment as club captain by Tranmere manager Dave Watson last term

was partly a tribute to his vastly improved disciplinary record. A rugged, no-nonsense yet also very creative central defender, he is a product of Rovers' youth scheme and he was a key figure in his side's attempt to reach a play-off position. He was out of contract in the summer and looked set to move on.
Tranmere Rov (From trainee on 9/7/1997) FL 138+2/16 FLC 18/3 FAC 11+1/1

HILL Keith John
Born: Bolton, 17 May 1969
Height: 6'0" **Weight:** 12.6
This experienced central defender joined Cheltenham Town in the summer of 2001, but after a couple of early-season appearances he lost his place in the team and moved on to Wrexham on loan in October. He made a dozen appearances for the Racecourse Robins for whom he looked solid and efficient, bringing out the best in his defensive partner Steve Roberts. He subsequently returned to Whaddon Road and was placed on the transfer list.

HILL Kevin
Born: Exeter, 6 March 1976
Height: 5'8" **Weight:** 10.3
Although his skills of arriving unmarked in the penalty area and grabbing goals are better suited to a free-ranging midfield role, Kevin was predominantly used in a left-wing-back role by Torquay last term, and after a shaky start to the campaign his understanding improved during the season. He always gave total commitment wherever he was asked to play.
Torquay U (Free from Torrington on 8/12/1997) FL 175+28/25 FLC 10+1/1 FAC 12/2 Others 7+1/1

Blackburn Rov (From juniors on 9/5/1987) F/PL 89+7/3 FLC 6/1 FAC 5+1 Others 3+2
Plymouth Arg (Signed on 23/9/1992) FL 117+6/2 FLC 9 FAC 10 Others 9
Rochdale (Free on 3/7/1996) FL 171+5/6 FLC 10 FAC 8 Others 6/1
Cheltenham T (Free on 27/6/2001) FL 2+3
Wrexham (Loaned on 11/10/2001) FL 12/1 FAC 1 Others 2

Matt Hill

HILL Matthew (Matt) Clayton
Born: Bristol, 26 March 1981
Height: 5'7" **Weight:** 12.6
Not the most elegant of performers, Matt's tigerish tackling, speedy recovery, and honest commitment, endeared him to the Bristol City fans last term. A good header of the ball, despite a lack of inches, this left-sided defender cemented his place in the first team during the campaign. Twice voted the 'PFA Second Division Player of the Month' (January and February), he scooped further awards at the end of the season, winning the supporters' club's 'Player of the Year' and 'Young Player of the Year' titles. Unfortunately, knee ligament damage suffered in the 3-1 win at Bournemouth in March ruled him out until the summer.
Bristol C (From trainee on 22/2/1999) FL 80+11/1 FLC 3 FAC 7 Others 7+3

HILL Nicholas (Nicky) Damien
Born: Accrington, 26 February 1981
Height: 6'0" **Weight:** 12.3
This Bury youngster struggled to gain a first-team place throughout the 2001-02 season, finding himself well down the pecking order of central defenders at Gigg Lane. He had to wait until early in the new year when Steve Redmond was suspended before he made a breakthrough, but suffered a broken nose in his first game against Wrexham and was then sidelined by an ankle injury soon afterwards.
Bury (From trainee on 9/7/1999) FL 15+5 Others 2+1

HILLIER David
Born: Blackheath, 19 December 1969
Height: 5'10" **Weight:** 12.5
Club Honours: FAYC '88; Div 1 '91
International Honours: E: U21-1
This experienced central midfielder recovered from his knee injury problems to regain a place in Bristol Rovers starting line-up at the beginning of last season. He ended his own personal three-year goal drought in style with a Worthington Cup winner at Wycombe, and followed this up with another strike in the next match against Luton. A specialist with free kicks and corners, he held down a regular place until the closing stages of the campaign and was released in the summer.
Arsenal (From trainee on 11/2/1988) F/PL 82+22/2 FLC 13+2 FAC 13+2 Others 5+4
Portsmouth (£250,000 on 2/11/1996) FL 62+5/4 FLC 3/2 FAC 4/1
Bristol Rov (£15,000 on 24/2/1999) FL 82+1/1 FLC 6/1 FAC 5 Others 1+1

HILLIER Ian Michael
Born: Neath, 26 December 1979
Height: 6'0" **Weight:** 11.10
International Honours: W: U21-5
Ian signed for Luton at the start of the 2001-02 campaign and made his debut at left back at Bristol Rovers. He scored his first League goal away at York City, but after the turn of the year his chances in the senior team became fewer and fewer, but he is sure to be in the reckoning for the start of the 2002-03 campaign.
Tottenham H (From trainee on 2/7/1998)
Luton T (Free on 18/8/2001) FL 11+12/1 FAC 1

HILLS John David
Born: Blackpool, 21 April 1978
Height: 5'9" **Weight:** 11.2
Club Honours: AMC '02
This popular Blackpool player had a fine season in 2001-02 and was deservedly voted as the club's 'Player of the Year'. He was mostly used in a midfield role and his tally of seven goals included a memorable strike in the FA Cup tie at Charlton.
Blackpool (From trainee on 27/10/1995)
Everton (£90,000 on 4/11/1995) PL 1+2
Swansea C (Loaned on 30/1/1997) FL 11/1
Swansea C (Loaned on 22/8/1997) FL 7
Blackpool (£75,000 on 16/1/1998) FL 126+9/11 FLC 4 FAC 10/1 Others 12+1/2

HINCHCLIFFE Andrew (Andy) George
Born: Manchester, 5 February 1969
Height: 5'10" **Weight:** 13.7
Club Honours: FAC '95; CS '95
International Honours: E: 7; U21-1; Yth
An achilles injury ended this polished former England international left back's career. He managed just two first-team appearances for Sheffield Wednesday last term, one as a substitute, and it was a bitter blow when he announced his retirement. His experience and cool play under pressure would have had a big impact in Division One but he now looks set to go into coaching.
Manchester C (From apprentice on 13/2/1986) FL 107+5/8 FLC 11/1 FAC 12/1 Others 4/1
Everton (£800,000 on 17/7/1990) F/PL 170+12/7 FLC 21+2/1 FAC 12+2/1 Others 8
Sheffield Wed (£2,850,000 on 30/1/1998) P/FL 86/7 FLC 4+1 FAC 6

HINDS Richard Paul
Born: Sheffield, 22 August 1980
Height: 6'2" **Weight:** 11.0
Richard had a somewhat disappointing season for Tranmere in 2001-02 when he was in and out of the line-up and only started a handful of games. He prefers to

play at centre back but is sufficiently versatile to deputise in any of the midfield roles. Unruffled and mature, he can pass accurately and is blessed with a calm temperament which makes him walk away from potential trouble rather than provoke it.
Tranmere Rov (From juniors on 20/7/1998) FL 36+11 FLC 3+4 FAC 5 Others 1

HINTON Craig
Born: Wolverhampton, 26 November 1977
Height: 6'0" **Weight:** 12.0
Club Honours: NC '00
Craig continued to be rock steady in the centre of the Kidderminster defence in 2001-02 and deservedly retained the supporters' 'Player of the Season' award. Having been the only ever present the previous season, his run was halted by injury for five games in September, but he played in all of the remaining fixtures to maintain his record as Harriers' top Football League appearance maker.
Birmingham C (From trainee on 5/7/1996)
Kidderminster Hrs (Free on 12/8/1998) FL 87/2 FLC 3 FAC 4 Others 4

HISLOP Neil **Shaka**
Born: Hackney, 22 February 1969
Height: 6'4" **Weight:** 14.4
Club Honours: Div 2 '94
International Honours: E: U21-1. Trinidad & Tobago: 14; E: U21-1
Shaka was able to start the 2001-02 season as the number one goalkeeper at West Ham following a bad injury to David James. He is a good shot stopper and his early-season displays at Liverpool and Derby proved crucial. He was also the star man when playing against his old club Reading in the Worthington Cup where he kept a clean sheet. He played in the first 12 Premiership games until James returned to the side in November.
Reading (Signed from Howard University, USA on 9/9/1992) FL 104 FLC 10 FAC 3 Others 9
Newcastle U (£1,575,000 on 10/8/1995) PL 53 FLC 8 FAC 6 Others 4
West Ham U (Free on 8/7/1998) PL 105 FLC 11 FAC 7 Others 9

HITCHEN Steven (Steve) James
Born: Salford, 28 November 1976
Height: 5'8" **Weight:** 11.8
Macclesfield's automatic choice for the right-back position in 2001-02, Steve is an attacking player who distributes the ball accurately and is equally at home as a wing back. It was in this role that he

scored his first senior goal away at Scunthorpe when he collected the ball wide on the right, cut in past defenders and cracked it home. He missed several matches through injury (ankle, knee and hamstring) but was nevertheless a valuable member of the first-team squad.
Blackburn Rov (From trainee on 4/7/1995)
Macclesfield T (Free on 14/7/1997) FL 103+6/1 FLC 5+1 FAC 8 Others 2

HITZLSPERGER Thomas
Born: Munich, Germany, 5 April 1982
Height: 6'0" **Weight:** 12.5
International Honours: Germany: U21-4; Yth
This classy left-sided midfield player joined Chesterfield on loan at the start of the 2001-02 campaign to gain some experience of senior football. He impressed greatly during his spell with the Spireites before returning to Aston Villa for whom he made his first senior appearance of the season coming on as a sub away at Manchester United in February. He showed no signs of being overawed, and his performance was so impressive he earned a full debut against West Ham the following week when he was 'Man of the Match'. He subsequently retained his place in the closing stages of the campaign, producing some high quality performances.
Aston Villa (Free from Bayern Munich, Germany on 8/8/2000) PL 11+2/1
Chesterfield (Loaned on 27/10/2001) FL 5 Others 1

HJELDE Jon Olav
Born: Levanger, Norway, 30 April 1972
Height: 6'1" **Weight:** 13.7
Club Honours: Div 1 '98
This big centre back probably had his best season to date for Nottingham Forest in 2001-02. A tall central defender who is strong in the air and solid on the ground, he coped with numerous defensive partners, but looked most effective alongside Riccardo Scimeca.
Nottingham F (£600,000 from Rosenborg, Norway on 8/8/1997) P/FL 117+14/4 FLC 10/2 FAC 5

HOBSON Gary
Born: Hull, 12 November 1972
Height: 6'1" **Weight:** 13.3
Gary was again troubled by injury problems at York last season and these severely restricted his senior opportunities. When fit the experienced central defender showed great composure and he played an important role in the memorable FA Cup ties against Grimsby Town and Fulham.

Hull C (From trainee on 17/7/1991) FL 135+7 FLC 13+1 FAC 2+2/1 Others 6
Brighton & Hove A (£60,000 on 27/3/1996) FL 92+6/1 FLC 7 FAC 4+1 Others 3
Chester C (Signed on 7/11/2000) FL 20
York C (Free on 17/7/2000) FL 22+5 FLC 1 FAC 4

HOCKING Matthew (Matt)
James
Born: Boston, 30 January 1978
Height: 5'11" **Weight:** 11.12
Matt was a regular in the York City side in 2001-02 and showed consistent form throughout. He was best employed on the right-hand side of defence where his pace and powers of recovery were put to good use. He was one of several players released by the Minstermen in the summer.
Sheffield U (From trainee on 16/5/1996)
Hull C (£25,000 on 19/9/1997) FL 55+2/2 FLC 6 FAC 4 Others 4
York C (£30,000 on 25/3/1999) FL 83+14/2 FLC 2+1 FAC 6+2 Others 2

HOCKLEY Matthew (Matt)
Born: Paignton, 5 June 1982
Height: 5'10" **Weight:** 11.7
This dedicated young professional had limited opportunities for Torquay last term, but filled in efficiently when called upon. Equally at home as a right back or a centre back, Matt is particularly adept at man-marking.
Torquay U (From trainee on 4/7/2000) FL 16+2/1 FAC 3 Others 1

HODGE John
Born: Skelmersdale, 1 April 1969
Height: 5'7" **Weight:** 11.12
Club Honours: AMC '94
John spent much of the 2001-02 campaign on the substitutes' bench for Northampton, making the starting line-up on just a handful of occasions. The right-sided midfield player is probably one of the fastest players on the Cobbler's books and he can also deliver an accurate cross into the box. John has a reputation as the club comedian and his antics have helped to calm nerves in the dressing room.
Exeter C (Signed from Falmouth T on 12/9/1991) FL 57+8/10 FLC 3/1 FAC 2 Others 8+2/1
Swansea C (Signed on 14/7/1993) FL 87+25/10 FLC 6+2/3 FAC 6 Others 13+4
Walsall (Free on 23/9/1996) FL 67+9/12 FLC 5 FAC 7+1/2 Others 5+2
Gillingham (Free on 10/7/1998) FL 8+41/1 FLC 4+1 FAC 3+2/1 Others 2+4
Northampton T (£25,000 on 7/3/2000) FL 33+27/2 FLC 0+2 FAC 0+1 Others 0+2

HODGES Lee Leslie
Born: Plaistow, 2 March 1978
Height: 5'5" **Weight:** 10.2
International Honours: E: Sch
Lee had a mixed 2001-02 season, winning a place in the PFA Division Three team for the second successive year but struggling to keep his place in the Scunthorpe side. Two summer knee operations hampered his progress but he returned to the team in September and ended the campaign with eight goals. Still very skilful on the ball, he played most of the campaign on the right but his best, and preferred, position is the left wing where he can cut inside and show off his thunderous shooting. He was surprisingly released in the summer.
West Ham U (From trainee on 2/3/1995) PL 0+3 FAC 0+3
Exeter C (Loaned on 13/9/1996) FL 16+1
Leyton Orient (Loaned on 28/2/1997) FL 3
Plymouth Arg (Loaned on 6/11/1997) FL 9 Others 1
Ipswich T (Loaned on 20/11/1998) FL 0+4
Southend U (Loaned on 25/3/1999) FL 10/1
Scunthorpe U (£50,000 on 8/7/1999) FL 97+16/20 FLC 4 FAC 9/2 Others 4/2

HODGES Lee Leslie
Born: Epping, 4 September 1973
Height: 6'0" **Weight:** 12.1
Club Honours: Div 3 '02
International Honours: E: Yth
After training with Northampton Town during the 2001 close season, Lee joined Plymouth following the opening day defeat at home to Shrewsbury Town. The left-sided midfield player subsequently appeared in every remaining game of the campaign. He was particularly effective in the air from dead-ball situations and his headers set up many chances for his colleagues. He also scored six times himself, including the final goal at Rochdale in March to clinch Argyle's promotion back to Division Two.
Tottenham H (From trainee on 29/2/1992) PL 0+4
Plymouth Arg (Loaned on 26/2/1993) FL 6+1/2
Wycombe W (Loaned on 31/12/1993) FL 2+2 FAC 1 Others 1
Barnet (Free on 31/5/1994) FL 94+11/26 FLC 6+1 FAC 6+1/4 Others 3+1
Reading (£100,000 on 29/7/1997) FL 58+21/10 FLC 7+3 FAC 7+1/1 Others 0+2
Plymouth Arg (Free on 17/8/2001) FL 42+3/6 FLC 1 FAC 4 Others 1

HODGSON Richard James
Born: Sunderland, 1 October 1979
Height: 5'10" **Weight:** 11.8

Chris Holland (right)

Richard is a direct left winger who loves to run at defenders and provides accurate crosses for his team-mates. He has the knack of tricking defenders and cutting inside from a wide berth to shoot at goal and he found the net twice in this fashion last season. However, he failed to win a regular place in the Darlington line-up and often found himself on the subs' bench.

Nottingham F (From trainee on 8/10/1996)
Scunthorpe U (Free on 9/3/2000) FL 1
Darlington (Free on 7/8/2000) FL 44+27/4 FLC 3+1 FAC 5+1/2 Others 4+1/1

HOEKSTRA Peter
Born: Groningen, Holland, 4 April 1973
Height: 6'3" **Weight:** 12.8
International Honours: Holland: 5
Peter produced some sensational form for Stoke City in the early part of the 2001-02 campaign, and his skills were particularly breathtaking in the game against Bury. It is many years since a City player created so much anticipation in the hearts and minds of supporters, but unfortunately he suffered an injured ankle in the FA Cup second round tie at Halifax and this decimated his season. A fully fit Peter Hoekstra would surely grace the Premiership.

Stoke C (Free from Ajax, Holland, ex PSV Eindhoven, on 27/7/2001) FL 20+4/3 FLC 1 FAC 2+1

HOGG Lewis James
Born: Bristol, 13 September 1982
Height: 5'8" **Weight:** 10.8
This ball-winning midfielder had to be patient in the first part of the 2001-02 season but was rewarded when he was appointed as Bristol Rovers' captain at Christmas by new manager Garry Thompson. His own performances improved and he inspired his team-mates, none more so than in the 3-1 FA Cup victory at Premiership Derby County. He turned down the opportunity to represent Northern Ireland at U21 level, preferring to devote his efforts to helping Rovers pull away from the lower reaches of the Third Division.

Bristol Rov (From trainee on 14/9/1999) FL 53+4/3 FLC 5/1 FAC 5/1 Others 3/1

HOLDEN Dean Thomas John
Born: Salford, 15 September 1979
Height: 6'0" **Weight:** 11.0
International Honours: E: Yth
A product of the Bolton academy, Dean made one Worthington Cup appearance for Wanderers last term before joining Oldham Athletic on loan and the deal was

eventually extended until the end of the season. His form at right back steadily improved and a personal high came when he scored his first goals for Athletic against Cambridge in March. He was reported to have joined the Boundary Park club permanently during the summer.

Bolton W (From trainee on 23/12/1997) FL 7+6/1 FLC 3 FAC 3+1
Oldham Ath (Loaned on 12/10/2001) FL 20+3/2 FAC 1 Others 3

HOLDSWORTH David Gary
Born: Walthamstow, 8 November 1968
Height: 6'1" **Weight:** 12.10
International Honours: E: U21-1; Yth
David stepped briefly into the Birmingham City line-up when Darren Purse was injured towards the end of Trevor Francis's time in charge. He performed calmly but failed to appear on the winning side, and had a torrid time in the 6-0 Worthington Cup defeat at Manchester City in October. He was loaned to Walsall in February and looked assured in defence from the start of his debut at West Brom, then excelled in the shock FA Cup win at Charlton a week later, and continued to give of his best whenever called upon. He is the twin brother of Dean Holdsworth.

Watford (From apprentice on 8/11/1986) FL 249+9/11 FLC 20/2 FAC 14+1/1 Others 8+2
Sheffield U (£450,00 on 8/10/1996) FL 93/4 FLC 7 FAC 13/3 Others 5
Birmingham C (£1,200,000 on 22/3/1999) FL 78+7/7 FLC 10/1 FAC 1 Others 4+1
Walsall (Loaned on 18/1/2002) FL 9/1 FAC 2

HOLDSWORTH Dean Christopher
Born: Walthamstow, 8 November 1968
Height: 5'11" **Weight:** 11.13
Club Honours: Div 3 '92
International Honours: E: B-1
Last season saw Dean taking on the role of 'Super Sub' at the Reebok, as he made a total of 24 appearances from the bench. While his game now involves a lot more link-up play with other strikers, he still has that predatory goal-scoring instinct. He popped up with one of the most important Bolton goals of the campaign, in the 2-1 home win over Liverpool in August. He is a firm favourite of the fans for his wholehearted displays and willingness to run until he drops. Dean is the twin brother of David Holdsworth.

Watford (From apprentice on 12/11/1986) FL 2+14/3 Others 0+4
Carlisle U (Loaned on 11/2/1988) FL 4/1
Port Vale (Loaned on 18/3/1988) FL 6/2
Swansea C (Loaned on 25/8/1988) FL 4+1/1

Brentford (Loaned on 13/10/1988) FL 2+5/1
Brentford (£125,000 on 29/9/1989) FL 106+4/53 FLC 7+1/6 FAC 6/7 Others 12+2/9
Wimbledon (£720,000 on 20/7/1992) PL 148+21/58 FLC 16+3/11 FAC 13+7/7
Bolton W (£3,500,000 on 3/10/1997) P/FL 92+57/39 FLC 11+4/4 FAC 5+2/3 Others 5/3

HOLLAND Christopher (Chris) James
Born: Clitheroe, 11 September 1975
Height: 5'9" **Weight:** 11.5
International Honours: E: U21-10; Yth
This committed Huddersfield Town midfielder was a regular in the first team in the 2001-02 campaign. He impressed with some strong running and purposeful passing and was always willing to help out in defence. A high spot was being named in the Nationwide 'Team of the Week' after outstanding displays against Cardiff City and Chesterfield.

Preston NE (Trainee) FL 0+1 Others 1
Newcastle U (£100,000 on 20/1/1994) PL 2+1 FLC 0+1
Birmingham C (£600,000 on 5/9/1996) FL 39+31 FLC 7+5 FAC 4 Others 1+1
Huddersfield T (£150,000 on 3/2/2000) FL 80+3/2 FLC 2 FAC 3 Others 7+1/1

HOLLAND Matthew (Matt) Rhys
Born: Bury, 11 April 1974
Height: 5'9" **Weight:** 11.12
International Honours: RoI: 23; B-1
Matt continued to lead Ipswich Town with spirit and wholehearted endeavour last term and felt the pain of relegation deeply. Once again he played in all the team's Premiership games although he was rested for a couple of domestic cup ties. He equalled his goal tally of the previous season, three, but would have hoped to have scored more as he is able to get into the opposing penalty area in support of his forwards on a regular basis. On the international scene, Matt remained a regular member of the Republic of Ireland squad and was picked to go to the World Cup.

West Ham U (From trainee on 3/7/1992)
Bournemouth (Signed on 27/1/1995) FL 97+7/18 FLC 6 FAC 3 Others 3
Ipswich T (£800,000 on 31/7/1997) P/FL 214/31 FLC 22+1/6 FAC 10 Others 13/2

HOLLIGAN Gavin Victor
Born: Lambeth, 13 June 1980
Height: 5'10" **Weight:** 12.0
Wycombe signed this diminutive striker in the summer of 2001 but his season was punctuated by a number of minor injuries. His 14 starts produced five goals,

the best being at Northampton in April when, receiving with his back to goal, he beat two defenders and coolly scored from the edge of the box. The manner of that finish was probably the fans first glimpse of his renowned ability to score spectacular goals and bodes well for the coming season.
West Ham U (£100,000 from Kingstonian on 5/3/1999) PL 0+1
Leyton Orient (Loaned on 17/9/1999) FL 1 FLC 1
Exeter C (Loaned on 17/10/2000) FL 3
Wycombe W (Free on 9/8/2001) FL 11+9/4 FAC 2 Others 2/1

HOLLOWAY Darren
Born: Crook, 3 October 1977
Height: 5'10" **Weight:** 12.2
International Honours: E: U21-1
Darren had another good season for Wimbledon last term and was deservedly awarded the title of 'Most Improved Player of the Year'. He made the right-back role his own with some hard-working performances and enjoyed the odd raid forward, his first goal for the Dons can't be too far off!
Sunderland (From trainee on 12/10/1995) P/FL 46+12 FLC 3 FAC 2 Others 3
Carlisle U (Loaned on 29/8/1997) FL 5
Bolton W (Loaned on 14/12/1999) FL 3+1
Wimbledon (£1,250,000 on 2/10/2000) FL 62+1 FAC 6

HOLLUND Martin
Born: Stord, Norway, 11 August 1974
Height: 6'0" **Weight:** 12.9
International Honours: Norway: U21
Martin had another frustrating time at Hartlepool in 2001-02 when for the second successive season he began as first-choice 'keeper only to lose his place to Anthony Williams. He was subsequently restricted to the substitutes' bench for the remaining 47 first-team games of the campaign, and was released on a free transfer in the close season.
Hartlepool U (Free from SK Brann Bergen, Norway on 21/11/1997) FL 117 FLC 4 FAC 4 Others 8

HOLMES Derek
Born: Lanark, 18 October 1978
Height: 6'0" **Weight:** 13.2
Derek began the 2001-02 campaign with Ross County before moving south to join Bournemouth on loan and did well enough to secure a permanent transfer, becoming manager Sean O'Driscoll's only ever purchase. He took a while to adapt to English football but enjoyed a good run in front of goal in the latter stages of

the season, scoring five times in eight games. With a pre-season behind him, much is expected of the big striker in 2002-03.
Heart of Midlothian (From juniors on 5/1/1995) SL 1+6/1 SLC 0+2/2 Others 0+3/1
Ross Co (Free on 15/10/1999) SL 39+19/14 SLC 1+1/1 SC 1+1 Others 3
Bournemouth (£40,000 on 14/9/2001) FL 34+3/9 FAC 0+1 Others 1

HOLMES Paul
Born: Stocksbridge, 18 February 1968
Height: 5'10" **Weight:** 11.3
After a poor 2000-01 season, this experienced Torquay campaigner missed the first half of last season through injury. However, he eventually returned to fitness and regained the right-wing-back spot from Steve Tully for the latter half of the campaign.
Doncaster Rov (From apprentice on 24/2/1986) FL 42+5/1 FAC 3+1/1 Others 1
Torquay U (£6,000 on 12/8/1988) FL 127+12/4 FLC 9 FAC 9+2 Others 13+3
Birmingham C (£40,000 on 5/6/1992) FL 12 FAC 1
Everton (£100,000 on 19/3/1993) PL 21 FLC 4 FAC 1 Others 0+2
West Bromwich A (£80,000 on 12/1/1996) FL 102+1/1 FLC 5 FAC 4 Others 3
Torquay U (Free on 11/11/1999) FL 75+5/2 FLC 2 FAC 3 Others 1+1

HOLMES Peter James
Born: Bishop Auckland, 18 November 1980
Height: 5'10" **Weight:** 10.6
International Honours: E: Yth; Sch
Peter had another frustrating season at Luton last term when he failed to win a regular place in the first team. However, with another season left on his contract, he has more chances to prove his ability. He is a young midfield player who possesses two good feet and excellent ball control, and it seems only a matter of time before he makes a first-team place his own.
Sheffield Wed (From trainee on 2/12/1997)
Luton T (Free on 1/8/2000) FL 16+9/2 FLC 2+2 FAC 2 Others 1

HOLMES Richard
Born: Grantham, 7 November 1980
Height: 5'10" **Weight:** 10.7
Although he burst on the League scene some four years ago, Richard is still very much a youngster and developing all the time as a right wing back. His best performances for Notts County last season came when he featured as an orthodox right back with the licence to overlap and cause mayhem in opponents'

penalty areas. He had a brief spell on loan with Conference club Hereford United in the new year.
Notts Co (From trainee on 23/3/1999) FL 45+10 FLC 3+1 FAC 2+2 Others 2

HOLMES Shaun Paul
Born: Derry, 27 December 1980
Height: 5'9" **Weight:** 11.3
International Honours: NI: 1; U21-13; Yth; Sch
Shaun enjoyed an excellent first season in the Football League for Wrexham in 2001-02. A promising defender, he was a near ever present for the Robins and won his first full cap for Northern Ireland when he appeared as a substitute in the friendly against Liechtenstein.
Manchester C (From trainee on 10/1/1998)
Wrexham (Free on 9/8/2001) FL 39+1 FLC 1 FAC 1 Others 1

HOLMES Steven (Steve) Peter
Born: Middlesbrough, 13 January 1971
Height: 6'2" **Weight:** 13.0
Steve again proved an effective central defender in the first half of Lincoln's 2001-02 campaign before injury brought his season to an end in November. Although always starting at the back he was sometimes pushed up as an emergency striker in the latter stages of games and responded by netting dramatic late equalisers against Bury in the FA Cup and a week later at Rochdale. His injury problems began with a knee ligament strain in the replay at Gigg Lane. He then contracted an infection after undergoing a minor operation, a second op followed and at the end of the season he was still working his way back to fitness. Steve was one of a number of out-of-contract players released by the Imps in the summer.
Lincoln C (From trainee on 17/7/1989)
Preston NE (£10,000 from Guisborough T, ex Gainsborough Trinity, on 14/3/1994) FL 13/1 FAC 3 Others 1
Hartlepool U (Loaned on 10/3/1995) FL 5/2
Lincoln C (Loaned on 20/10/1995) FL 12/1 Others 2
Lincoln C (£30,000 on 15/3/1996) FL 185+4/32 FLC 9/2 FAC 10/2 Others 8/1

HOLNESS Dean Thomas
Born: Lewisham, 25 July 1976
Height: 5'5" **Weight:** 10.13
After starring in the Sky TV soap 'Dream Team', Dean's dream seemed to have come true when he was given a short-term contract by Southend manager Dave Webb for the start of the 2001-02 season. A slightly built winger, he made his debut in the opening match, but failed

to bring his on-screen skills to the Third Division. His game certainly did not lack effort, but after only one further substitute appearance he was released.
Southend U (Free from Dulwich Hamlet, ex Kingstonian, on 7/8/2001) FL 1+1

HOLT Andrew (Andy)
Born: Stockport, 21 May 1978
Height: 6'1" **Weight:** 12.7
Andy became the fourth most expensive signing in Hull's history when he became a permanent Tiger during the 2001 close season. A talented left back with considerable stature, he missed the opening weeks after dropping a box of bathroom tiles on his big toe! His return was further delayed by a calf muscle problem. With a struggle to make up for lost time, he found it difficult to recapture his best form, however he impressed in the final games of the season when new boss Jan Molby selected him in a left-midfield role.
Oldham Ath (From trainee on 23/7/1996) FL 104+20/10 FLC 8 FAC 6+4 Others 3
Hull C (£150,000 on 15/3/2001) FL 34+6/2 FLC 1 Others 4+1

HOLT David Arthur
Born: Manchester, 18 November 1984
Height: 5'7" **Weight:** 10.2
David became Stockport County's 13th home-grown player to appear in the First Division last season when he replaced the flu'-stricken Carlton Palmer in the 63rd minute at Walsall in April. He immediately came close to creating an equaliser with an accurate corner, but Rob Clare's header was deflected wide. Still a second-year trainee, the young striker is highly thought of at Edgeley Park.
Stockport Co (Trainee) FL 0+1

HOLT Gary James
Born: Irvine, 9 March 1973
Height: 6'0" **Weight:** 12.11
Club Honours: SC '98
International Honours: S: 4
Gary was recalled for Norwich from March 2001 and his first few weeks at Carrow Road gave little hint as to the massive influence he would have at the club. His main attributes are his ability to break forward at pace when in possession of the ball and his capacity to work back to deny the opposition time and space when he hasn't got the ball. His performances won him a recall to the full Scottish squad and he came on as a substitute in Berti Vogts' first game in charge of Scotland away at France. He scored two goals, at home to Burnley and away at Sheffield Wednesday,

both spectacular candidates for anyone's 'Goal of the Season'. He was also voted the club's 'Player of the Season' for 2001-02.
Stoke C (Free from Glasgow Celtic N/C on 20/10/1994)
Kilmarnock (Free on 18/8/1995) SL 138+13/9 SLC 10+1 SC 13 Others 8
Norwich C (£100,000 on 22/3/2001) FL 49+1/2 FLC 1 FAC 2 Others 3

HOOPER Dean Raymond
Born: Harefield, 13 April 1971
Height: 5'11" **Weight:** 11.6
International Honours: E: SP-1
Dean was used sparingly by Peterborough United last season and spent the closing months of the campaign on loan with Conference high flyers Dagenham & Redbridge. A tough tackling right back who is comfortable on the ball, he was reported to have signed for Ryman League club Aldershot Town in the summer.
Swindon T (£15,000 from Hayes on 3/3/1995) FL 0+4 FLC 0+2 Others 2 (Free to Hayes on 4/10/1996)
Peterborough U (Loaned on 15/12/1995) FL 4
Peterborough U (Signed from Kingstonian on 6/8/1998) FL 99+14/2 FLC 6 FAC 7+4 Others 5+1

HOPE Christopher (Chris) Jonathan
Born: Sheffield, 14 November 1972
Height: 6'1" **Weight:** 12.7
For the second consecutive season, Chris was an ever present in the heart of the Gillingham defence and was deservedly voted runner-up in the club's 'Player of the Year' competition. A cool and unruffled central defender, he led by example and was always capable of notching the odd goal at the other end from set pieces. He is now considered one of the finest centre halves outside of the Premier Division.
Nottingham F (From Darlington juniors on 23/8/1990)
Scunthorpe U (£50,000 on 5/7/1993) FL 278+9/19 FLC 13+1 FAC 18/1 Others 18/2
Gillingham (£250,000 on 12/7/2000) FL 92/6 FLC 7 FAC 5/1

HOPE Richard Paul
Born: Stockton, 22 June 1978
Height: 6'2" **Weight:** 12.6
After failing to score a single goal in over 70 first-team appearances for Northampton, Richard netted twice in the 4-2 defeat at Oldham last October, making him temporarily the club's leading scorer! The Cobblers' injury crisis forced

him to play left back, centre back and even emergency centre forward during the campaign. Richard is the son of John Hope, the former Sheffield United and Hartlepool 'keeper.
Blackburn Rov (From trainee on 9/8/1995)
Darlington (Free on 17/1/1997) FL 62+1/1 FLC 3 FAC 1 Others 0+1
Northampton T (Signed on 18/12/1998) FL 96+16/6 FLC 3 FAC 4+1 Others 6

HOPKIN David
Born: Greenock, 21 August 1970
Height: 5'9" **Weight:** 11.0
International Honours: S: 7; B-1
This tall Crystal Palace midfielder spent long periods in the treatment room last season and these restricted his appearances at first-team level. A hard-tackling and combative figure in the centre of the park, he scored with a brilliant volley in the final home game against Preston.
Greenock Morton (Signed from Port Glasgow BC on 7/7/1989) SL 33+15/4 SLC 2/2 SC 2/1
Chelsea (£300,000 on 25/9/1992) PL 21+19/1 FLC 0+1 FAC 3+2
Crystal Palace (£850,000 on 29/7/1995) FL 79+4/21 FLC 6/6 FAC 3 Others 4/2
Leeds U (£3,250,000 on 23/7/1997) PL 64+9/6 FLC 7 FAC 6 Others 6+1
Bradford C (£2,500,000 on 12/7/2000) PL 8+3 FLC 1 Others 3+1
Crystal Palace (£1,500,000 on 15/3/2001) FL 21+8/4 FLC 0+1 FAC 1

HOPKINS Gareth
Born: Cheltenham, 14 June 1980
Height: 6'2" **Weight:** 13.8
Gareth faced the difficult task of trying to break up the prolific strike partnership of Julian Alsop and Tony Naylor last term and found himself restricted to just a handful of first-team outings from the subs' bench for Cheltenham. He later spent time on loan at Bath City and Forest Green Rovers and was released in the summer. He is a big, strong centre forward with good pace but despite showing plenty promise at youth and reserve levels he never managed to establish himself in the Robins' first team.
Cheltenham T (From trainee on 27/7/1998) FL 1+7 FLC 0+1 FAC 0+1 Others 1

HOPPER Tony
Born: Carlisle, 31 May 1976
Height: 5'11" **Weight:** 12.8
Club Honours: AMC '97
Tony was the one Carlisle player who had already played under new manager Roddy Collins when he arrived at Brunton Park.

Geoff Horsfield

A footballer whose commitment to the United cause is never in doubt, he gave a series of whole-hearted displays whenever he was selected for the side. Primarily used as a defensive midfielder, he only occasionally featured on the score sheet but his spectacular overhead kick at Southend produced one of the club's goals of the season.

Carlisle U (From trainee on 18/7/1994) FL 75+25/1 FLC 2+1 FAC 3+1/1 Others 7+4 (Free to Bohemians during 2000 close season)
Carlisle U (Free from Workington on 14/2/2001) FL 24+14/1 FLC 1 FAC 1

HORE John
Born: Liverpool, 18 August 1982
Height: 5'11" **Weight:** 11.12
John is a product of Carlisle's youth system but the 19-year-old striker managed just three substitute appearances last term. He was later loaned to Workington for a spell but not before he had netted four times for United's reserves in a 20-0 Cumberland Cup victory.

Carlisle U (From trainee on 12/6/2000) FL 2+3 Others 1

HORLOCK Kevin
Born: Erith, 1 November 1972
Height: 6'0" **Weight:** 12.0
Club Honours: Div 2 '96; Div 1 '02
International Honours: NI: 29; B-2
After finishing the previous season with a broken bone in his foot, Kevin's future at Maine Road had a question mark over it last term. However, there were only two games in the entire season when he was not involved, either on the substitute's bench or in the actual starting line-up. The Northern Ireland international went on to have probably his best season to date. Playing a 'holding' role in the centre of the park alongside the creative Ali Benarbia and Eyal Berkovic, the midfield was the main reason why City went on to equal their record for goals in one season.

West Ham U (From trainee on 1/7/1991)
Swindon T (Free on 27/8/1992) F/PL 151+12/22 FLC 15+2/1 FAC 12/3 Others 5+2
Manchester C (£1,250,000 on 31/11/1997) P/FL 162+12/37 FLC 14/3 FAC 8/1 Others 3/1

HORRIGAN Darren
Born: Middlesbrough, 2 June 1983
Height: 6'4" **Weight:** 12.7
Darren continued his development as a 'keeper in his final year as a scholar and was a regular on the Lincoln bench in the second half of last season. He made his Football League debut against Southend United in March when he came on as a

half-time replacement for the injured Alan Marriott. He kept a clean sheet and made a couple of important saves and was rewarded at the end of the season with a one-year professional contract. He also received the club's 'Young Player of the Year' award. Darren is the grandson of the former Middlesbrough and Southend 'keeper Paddy Nash.

Lincoln C (Trainee) FL 0+1

HORSFIELD Geoffrey (Geoff) Malcolm
Born: Barnsley, 1 November 1973
Height: 5'10" **Weight:** 11.0
Club Honours: FC '98; Div 2 '99
This bustling striker had an excellent season for Birmingham City in 2001-02. He was a constant threat to defences and was the most fouled player in Division One. He held possession well and when he turned and ran at opponents there was always danger. Geoff scored vital goals, including the winner at Sheffield Wednesday on Boxing Day after a mazy dribble, and the vital breakthrough in the last game against Sheffield United, which Blues needed to win to make the play-offs.

Scarborough (From juniors on 10/7/1992) FL 12/1 FAC 1 Others 0+2 (Free to Halifax T on 31/3/1994)
Halifax T (Free from Witton A on 8/5/1997) FL 10/7 FLC 4/1
Fulham (£325,000 on 12/10/1998) FL 54+5/22 FLC 6/6 FAC 8+1/3
Birmingham C (£2,000,000 on 12/7/2000) FL 58+16/18 FLC 8+1/3 FAC 1+1 Others 5/2

HOTTE Mark Stephen
Born: Bradford, 27 September 1978
Height: 5'11" **Weight:** 11.1
Mark was one of 14 players transfer-listed by Oldham Athletic last December after making just two substitute appearances in the 2001-02 season. The 23-year-old central defender had spent nine years at Athletic, rising through the ranks to first-team level. The Bradford-born player, whose chief asset is his pace, fell down the pecking order and his contract was eventually cancelled by mutual consent in January. He subsequently joined Conference side Scarborough, linking up again with former team-mate Paul Shepherd in defence.

Oldham Ath (From trainee on 1/7/1997) FL 59+6 FLC 2+2 FAC 2+1 Others 2

HOUGHTON Scott Aaron
Born: Hitchin, 22 October 1971
Height: 5'7" **Weight:** 12.4
Club Honours: FAYC '90

International Honours: E: Yth; Sch
Scott was Leyton Orient's leading goal-scorer in the early part of the 2001-02 campaign, but lost his place in the team following a change of manager at Brisbane Road. He was eventually released in February when he joined struggling Halifax Town on a short-term contract. He added width and experience to the Shaymen's midfield but was soon on his way back south, signing for Conference club Stevenage Borough. He is a diminutive left winger who can deliver a superb cross.

Tottenham H (From trainee on 24/8/1990) FL 0+10/2 FLC 0+2 Others 0+2
Ipswich T (Loaned on 26/3/1991) FL 7+1/1
Gillingham (Loaned on 17/12/1992) FL 3
Charlton Ath (Loaned on 26/2/1993) FL 6
Luton T (Free on 10/8/1993) FL 7+9/1 FLC 2+1 FAC 0+1 Others 2
Walsall (£20,000 on 2/9/1994) FL 76+2/14 FLC 0+1/1 FAC 10/3 Others 4
Peterborough U (£60,000 + on 12/7/1996) FL 57+13/13 FLC 6+2 FAC 7/1 Others 1+1/1
Southend U (Signed on 20/11/1998) FL 75+4/9 FLC 3+1 FAC 1 Others 1
Leyton Orient (Free on 6/10/2000) FL 27+15/6 FLC 1/1 FAC 3/1 Others 4/1
Halifax T (Free on 1/2/2002) FL 7

HOULT Russell
Born: Ashby de la Zouch, 22 November 1972
Height: 6'3" **Weight:** 14.9
Regarded by many as one of the best goalkeepers outside the Premiership, Russell had a wonderful season for West Bromwich Albion, establishing a new club record by keeping 27 clean sheets. He also blanked out his opponents in seven successive games during January and February - another club record. Cool and composed with excellent reflexes and strong kick, he commanded his area with confidence and produced some stunning saves, including a vital last-minute penalty stop at Watford which ended in a vital 2-1 win for the Baggies. He was chosen for the PFA's Division One side for the season and was also voted as Albion's 'Player of the Year'.

Leicester C (From trainee on 28/3/1991) FL 10 FLC 3 Others 1
Lincoln C (Loaned on 27/8/1991) FL 2 FLC 1
Bolton W (Loaned on 3/11/1993) FL 3+1 Others 1
Lincoln C (Loaned on 12/8/1994) FL 15 Others 1
Derby Co (£300,000 on 17/2/1995) F/PL 121+2 FLC 8 FAC 7
Portsmouth (£300,000 + on 21/11/2000) FL 40 FLC 4

West Bromwich A (£500,000 on 5/1/2001)
FL 58 FLC 3 FAC 4 Others 2

HOWARD Jonathan (Jon)
Born: Sheffield, 7 October 1971
Height: 5'11" **Weight:** 12.6
Jon was not among the first choice strikers at Chesterfield last season, and often appeared on the right side of a midfield five. Despite this, his tally of five goals from 12 starts was more prolific than in previous seasons. Although approaching the twilight of his career his ability and willingness to operate in two quite different areas has made him more of an asset, and he has been offered a contract for 2002-3.
Rotherham U (From trainee on 10/7/1990) FL 25+11/5 FLC 0+1 FAC 4/2 Others 3+1 (Free to Buxton on 11/11/94)
Chesterfield (Free on 9/12/1994) FL 151+76/39 FLC 11+3/1 FAC 14+2/2 Others 10+3/2

HOWARD Michael (Mike)
Anthony
Born: Birkenhead, 2 December 1978
Height: 5'9" **Weight:** 11.13
Club Honours: Div 3 '00
This gritty, dependable full back made numerous appearances as a left wing back when the Swans defence was switched to a three-man unit. Capable of delivering accurate crosses from the flanks, Mike scored his first League goal for three years at Southend last September. He displayed excellent form in the second half of the campaign when he was encouraged to attack more, and set up numerous opportunities with his raiding down the flank.
Tranmere Rov (From trainee on 9/7/1997)
Swansea C (Free on 6/2/1998) FL 160+5/2 FLC 8 FAC 9 Others 6

HOWARD Steven (Steve)
John
Born: Durham, 10 May 1976
Height: 6'2" **Weight:** 14.6
Steve got off to a somewhat slow start for Luton last term, but once he scored in the 5-1 hammering of Torquay the goals began to flow. A high point was a fine hat-trick against Hull City and he went on to finish the campaign as the Hatters' leading scorer with 24 goals. A strong and powerful centre forward who holds the ball up well, he was voted as the club's 'Player of the Season' and 'Player's Player of the Season'.
Hartlepool U (Free from Tow Law on 8/8/1995) FL 117+25/27 FLC 7+1/1 FAC 5/2 Others 7/3

Northampton T (£120,000 on 22/2/1999) FL 67+19/18 FLC 4 FAC 2+1 Others 2
Luton T (£50,000 on 22/3/2001) FL 54/27 FLC 1

HOWARTH Neil
Born: Farnworth, 15 November 1971
Height: 6'2" **Weight:** 13.6
Club Honours: GMVC '95, '97; FAT '96
International Honours: E: SP-1
Neil was Cheltenham's regular right back for the first half of the 2001-02 season, but lost his place through injury and then failed to dislodge Antony Griffin in the latter stages of the campaign. He is a tall and experienced defender who has the versatility to operate in a variety of roles within a back four or five.
Burnley (From trainee on 2/7/1990) FL 0+1
Macclesfield T (Free on 3/9/1993) FL 49+11/3 FLC 3 FAC 2+2 Others 2
Cheltenham T (£7,000 on 24/2/1999) FL 80+13/6 FLC 5 FAC 4+1/1 Others 4

HOWARTH Russell Michael
Born: York, 27 March 1982
Height: 6'1" **Weight:** 13.10
International Honours: E: Yth
Although capped for England U20s during the 2001-02 season this highly rated young 'keeper again played understudy to Alan Fettis at York. His senior appearances were limited to an LDV Vans Trophy tie at Notts County, when he gave an outstanding display, and end-of-season matches against Bristol Rovers and Scunthorpe. Senior clubs continued to track his progress and a big future is predicted for him.
York C (From trainee on 26/8/1999) FL 6+2 FLC 3 Others 2

HOWE Edward (Eddie) John
Frank
Born: Amersham, 29 November 1977
Height: 5'10" **Weight:** 11.10
International Honours: E: U21-2
Eddie was again the key member of the Bournemouth defence last term when he captained the side. His distribution, aerial ability, and leadership were great assets to the Cherries in an otherwise disappointing season and it came as no surprise when he was sold to Portsmouth on transfer deadline day. He went straight into the first team for Pompey and impressed on his debut only for a long-term knee injury to return, causing him to miss the last few games of the campaign.
Bournemouth (From trainee on 4/7/1996) FL 183+17/10 FLC 12+1/1 FAC 12/2 Others 8+2
Portsmouth (£400,000 on 28/3/2002) FL 1

HOWE Stephen Robert (Bobby)
Born: Cramlington, 6 November 1973
Height: 5'7" **Weight:** 10.4
International Honours: E: Yth
The 2001-02 season was probably Bobby's best in a Swindon Town shirt. A hard-working and strong-running central midfielder with good passing skills, he produced many of his best performances away from home. Highlights of the season included a 25-yard screamer in the Worthington Cup win at Wolves and a tremendous display in atrocious conditions at Tranmere. He was released at the close of the season.
Nottingham F (From trainee on 5/12/1990) P/FL 6+8/2 FLC 2 Others 1+1
Ipswich T (Loaned on 17/1/1997) FL 2+1 FLC 1
Swindon T (£30,000 on 16/1/1998) FL 103+19/6 FLC 5+1/2 FAC 6/3 Others 1

HOWELLS Lee David
Born: Perth, Australia, 14 October 1968
Height: 5'11" **Weight:** 11.12
Club Honours: FAT '98; NC '99
International Honours: SP-2
Cheltenham Town's longest serving player enjoyed arguably his best season with the club, before suffering a broken leg in the game at Bristol Rovers in March. An athletic box-to-box midfield player, his partnership with Mark Yates in the centre of the park was a key feature of the Robins successful season. Ironically his injury came only days after signing a new contract, but he was out of plaster by mid-May and was expected to be fit for the start of the 2002-03 campaign.
Bristol Rov (From apprentice on 17/10/1986. Freed on 1/7/1988)
Cheltenham T (Signed from Brisbane Lions, Australia on 1/12/1991) FL 112/6 FLC 2 FAC 9/2 Others 4

HOWEY Stephen (Steve)
Norman
Born: Sunderland, 26 October 1971
Height: 6'2" **Weight:** 11.12
Club Honours: Div 1 '93, '02
International Honours: E: 4
After having previously played under Kevin Keegan at Newcastle, Steve proved to be one of the cornerstones at the heart of the Manchester City defence last term. Keegan tried two systems during the campaign, one with three at the back and using wingbacks, the other with a flat back four. Whichever formation was used Steve did a fine job, and formed excellent understandings with Richard Dunne and Lucien Mettomo. Rarely absent from the

line-up throughout the campaign, he finished off in style by scoring a fine header in the last match of the season against Portsmouth.
Newcastle U (From trainee on 11/12/1989) F/PL 167+24/6 FLC 14+2/1 FAC 21+2 Others 10+2
Manchester C (£2,000,000 + on 14/8/2000) P/FL 70/9 FLC 4 FAC 3

Steve Howey

HOWIE Scott
Born: Motherwell, 4 January 1972
Height: 6'2" **Weight:** 13.7
Club Honours: S Div 2 '93
International Honours: S: U21-5
Scott joined Bristol Rovers during the 2001 close season and immediately established himself as the club's first choice 'keeper with some consistent performances. Personal highlights included a penalty save from Scunthorpe winger Peter Beagrie and his assist from a huge goal kick for Nathan Ellington to score Rovers' first goal in the FA Cup victory at Derby County. Unflappable under pressure, he won many 'Man of the Match' awards and was the only ever-present in the team.
Clyde (Signed from Ferguslie U on 7/1/1992) SL 55 SLC 3 SC 4 Others 1
Norwich C (£300,000 on 12/8/1993) PL 1+1
Motherwell (£300,000 on 13/10/1994) SL 69 SLC 4 SC 5 Others 1
Reading (£30,000 on 26/3/1998) FL 84+1 FLC 6 FAC 4 Others 7
Bristol Rov (Free on 2/8/2001) FL 46 FLC 2 FAC 6 Others 3

HOWSON Stuart Leigh
Born: Chorley, 30 September 1981
Height: 6'1" **Weight:** 12.12
Signed by Chesterfield last February, Stuart quickly established himself in the centre of defence where he displayed more ability, composure and game-reading skills than might be expected of one so young. He proved completely unflappable and has yet to lose out to an opponent in tests of skill or courage. Dave Rushbury's excellent discovery will hopefully form a keystone of the Spireites' defence for seasons to come.
Blackburn Rov (From trainee on 22/7/1999)
Chesterfield (Free on 15/2/2002) FL 13/1

HREIDARSSON Hermann
Born: Iceland, 11 July 1974
Height: 6'1" **Weight:** 13.1
Club Honours: Div 3 '99
International Honours: Iceland: 41; U21-6
Hermann was the only Ipswich Town player, apart from Matt Holland, to play in every Premiership game and was made captain in the FA Cup match that Matt missed. A versatile defender who can play as centre back or as a wing back, he was used mainly in the latter capacity as George Burley adopted a 4-4-2 formation, rather than the 5-3-2 style of the previous season. He is a good tackler and is dangerous on the attack as an overlapping full back. Hermann scored the equaliser in Helsingborg with a volley that set his team on the way to UEFA Cup victory.
Crystal Palace (Signed from IBV, Iceland on 9/8/1997) P/FL 32+5/2 FLC 5/1 FAC 4 Others 2
Brentford (£850,000 on 24/9/1998) FL 41/6 FLC 2 FAC 2/1 Others 3/1

Wimbledon (£2,500,000 on 14/10/1999)
P/FL 25/1 FAC 2
Ipswich T (£4,000,000 + on 19/8/2000) PL
73+1/2 FLC 8 FAC 4 Others 6/1

HUCK William Roger Fernend
Born: Paris, France, 17 March 1979
Height: 5'10" **Weight:** 11.13
William had another disappointing season
with Bournemouth in 2001-02, his only
start coming in the LDV Vans Trophy
game against Barnet. Although he made
a number of appearances from the subs'
bench towards the end of the campaign
he was released in the summer. He is a
left-sided midfielder capable of delivering
useful crosses into the box.
Arsenal (Signed from Monaco, France on
6/11/1998)
Bournemouth (£50,000 on 25/3/1999) FL
11+29 FLC 0+6/1 Others 3

HUCKERBY Darren Carl
Born: Nottingham, 23 April 1976
Height: 5'10" **Weight:** 11.12
Club Honours: Div 1 '02
International Honours: E: B-1; U21-4
The 2001-02 campaign was probably a
season that Darren never wanted to end.
Although it was tough competing
for the two front places, he finally got his
chance and seized it with both hands. He
went on to form a good understanding
with Shaun Goater and the two got
better as the season progressed. His pace
and 100 per cent commitment caused
many defences problems throughout the
campaign. He found the net 26 times in
all competitions, including four against
Birmingham City in the Worthington Cup
and hat-tricks in consecutive home games
against Nottingham Forest and Barnsley.
Even when record signing Jonathan
Macken arrived from Preston, Darren's
form made it almost impossible for the
manager to drop him.
Lincoln C (From trainee on 14/7/1993) FL
20+8/5 FLC 2 Others 1/2
Newcastle U (£400,000 on 10/11/1995) PL
0+1 FAC 0+1
Millwall (Loaned on 6/9/1996) FL 6/3
Coventry C (£1,000,000 on 23/11/1996) PL
85+9/28 FLC 2+1 FAC 12/6
Leeds U (£4,000,000 on 12/8/1999) PL
11+29/2 FLC 1+1/2 FAC 1+2 Others 1+11/2
Manchester C (£2,250,000 + on
29/12/2000) P/FL 38+15/21 FLC 2+1/5 FAC
6/2

HUDSON Daniel (Danny)
Robert
Born: Doncaster, 25 June 1979
Height: 5'9" **Weight:** 10.3

A young midfield player who developed
through the ranks at Rotherham, Danny
was rarely in contention for a first-team
place last term and featured just twice
as a substitute in the Worthington Cup
ties. He was a regular in the reserve
team for whom he scored some
spectacular goals.
Rotherham U (From trainee on 25/6/1997)
FL 29+19/5 FLC 0+4 FAC 3+2/2 Others 3+1

HUDSON Mark
Born: Bishop Auckland, 24 October 1980
Height: 5'10" **Weight:** 11.3
Mark is another of the promising
youngsters on the books at
Middlesbrough. A cultured midfield
player, he made a further two
appearances as a substitute in the
Premiership last season, coincidentally
these were in the home and away fixtures
against struggling Ipswich Town.
Middlesbrough (From trainee on 5/7/1999)
PL 0+5 FAC 0+1

HUGHES Aaron William
Born: Magherafelt, 8 November 1979
Height: 6'0" **Weight:** 11.2
International Honours: NI: 24; B-2; Yth
Aaron opened Newcastle's season at
centre back, but then man-marked
Thomas Hassler out of the Inter Toto Cup
games against TSV Munich in which he
even found time to score a rare goal. He
then settled in the centre of the back
four until he picked up a groin injury in
September. After missing five games he
returned at right back and struck such a
rich vein of form that he made the
position his own. A fine reader of the
game and very comfortable on the ball
he grew in assurance and increasingly
lent his weight to the attack. He was a
regular in the Northern Ireland team, and
showed he has a social conscience with
his involvement as a patron of the
Newcastle United Disabled Supporters'
Association.
Newcastle U (From trainee on 11/3/1997) PL
106+8/2 FLC 8 FAC 8+2/1 Others 6+2/1

HUGHES Andrew (Andy) John
Born: Manchester, 2 January 1978
Height: 5'11" **Weight:** 12.1
Club Honours: Div 3 '98
It took Andy the first two months of the
2001-02 season to establish his place in
the Reading midfield, but once he had
recovered from a series of niggling injuries
he became a vital component in the
promotion campaign. He looked more
comfortable playing in the central-
midfield berth rather than wide on the

right, and also filled in as an emergency
right back when the occasion demanded.
He weighed in with some important and
well-taken goals too, and fully justified
the large fee the club had paid to Notts
County for him.
Oldham Ath (From trainee on 20/1/1996) FL
18+15/1 FLC 1+1 FAC 3+1 Others 1+2
Notts Co (£150,000 on 29/11/1998) FL
85+25/17 FLC 6+1/1 FAC 10/2 Others 2
Reading (Free on 16/7/2001) FL 34+5/6 FAC
2 Others 1

HUGHES Bryan
Born: Liverpool, 19 June 1976
Height: 5'10" **Weight:** 11.2
Club Honours: WC '95
This talented midfielder started the 2001-
02 season with six goals in 11 games for
Birmingham City then broke his foot at
Nottingham Forest in October. On
returning Steve Bruce was in charge and
he revelled in a central midfield role.
Bryan added a competitive edge to his
game and adapted to a deeper role
alongside Darren Carter. He remained a
threat breaking late into the area and was
Blues most consistent performer under
Bruce.
Wrexham (From trainee on 7/7/1994) FL
71+23/12 FLC 2 FAC 13+3/7 Others 14+1/3
Birmingham C (£750,000 + on 12/3/1997)
FL 170+30/29 FLC 16+5/3 FAC 5+3/2 Others
6+2/1

HUGHES Robert David
Born: Wrexham, 1 February 1978
Height: 6'4" **Weight:** 14.0
International Honours: W: B-2 ; U21-
13; Yth
This tall, commanding central defender
had a difficult time with Cardiff City in
2001-02, battling against injuries that
restricted him to just two Second
Division appearances. He went on as a
substitute in the first match of the
season, started the second, but then did
not play again as injuries hit him hard.
The long-throw expert finished the
season fully fit and will hope to make a
major impact in 2002-03.
Aston Villa (From trainee on 5/7/1996) PL
4+3
Carlisle U (Loaned on 26/3/1998) FL 1
Shrewsbury T (Free on 22/9/1999) FL
42+4/3 FLC 1 FAC 4 Others 2
Cardiff C (£450,000 on 9/2/2001) FL 12+2
FLC 1 Others 2

HUGHES Ian
Born: Bangor, 2 August 1974
Height: 5'10" **Weight:** 12.8
Club Honours: Div 2 '97; AMC '02

International Honours: W: U21-12; Yth Blackpool's club captain began the 2001-02 season in the starting line-up but suffered a series of niggling injuries that restricted his appearances. Although in and out of the side he gained a winners' medal in the LDV Vans Trophy after coming on as a substitute. He is a hard-tackling central defender who is very effective in the air.

Bury (From trainee on 19/11/1991) FL 137+24/1 FLC 13+3 FAC 6+2 Others 14+4/1
Blackpool (£200,000 on 12/12/1997) FL 126+16/3 FLC 11/1 FAC 8 Others 7+4/1

HUGHES Lee
Born: Smethwick, 22 May 1976
Height: 5'10" **Weight:** 11.6
International Honours: E: SP-4
Lee had a dream start for Coventry City, netting on his debut at Stockport but generally found goals hard to come by in the first half of last season, managing only five in 24 League games, including two penalties. Goals started to flow between Christmas and February when he netted seven in seven games including a hat-trick at Crewe. This was probably down to the signing of Lee Mills with whom he struck up a useful partnership. Despite his patchy form Lee's work-rate was always high and his commitment could not be faulted.

West Bromwich A (£250,000 + from Kidderminster Hrs on 19/5/1997) FL 137+19/10 FLC 10+3/4 FAC 6/2 Others 2/1
Coventry C (£5,000,000 on 9/8/2001) FL 35+3/14 FLC 1+1

HUGHES Leslie **Mark**
Born: Wrexham, 1 November 1963
Height: 5'11" **Weight:** 13.0
Club Honours: FAC '85, '90, '94, '97; ECWC '91, '98; ESC '91; FLC '92, '98, '02; PL '93, '94; CS '93, '94
International Honours: W: 72; U21-5; Yth; Sch
What do you say about a 38-year-old who was brought in for a major cup final, produced his best game for the club, stayed on for all 90 minutes and was generally acknowledged as the man whose muscle made the difference in the encounter? Although he can seldom last a full game, looks increasingly less mobile and appears at the end of his career this manager rarely took him off the team sheet, bringing him on both as a mid-field player and a striker. He also contributed a goal in the Worthington Cup tie against Arsenal.
Manchester U (From apprentice on 5/11/1980) FL 85+4/37 FLC 5+1/4 FAC 10/4

Others 14+2/2 (£2,500,000 to Barcelona on 1/7/86)
Manchester U (£1,500,000 on 20/7/1988) F/PL 251+5/82 FLC 32/12 FAC 34+1/13 Others 27+1/8
Chelsea (£1,500,000 on 6/7/1995) PL 88+7/25 FLC 7+3/3 FAC 13+1/9 Others 1+3/2
Southampton (£650,000 on 15/7/1998) PL 50+2/2 FLC 5 FAC 2+2
Everton (Free on 14/3/2000) PL 15+3/1 FLC 1
Blackburn Rov (Free on 2/10/2000) P/FL 25+25/6 FLC 4+2/1 FAC 4+4

HUGHES Michael Eamonn
Born: Larne, 2 August 1971
Height: 5'7" **Weight:** 10.13
International Honours: NI: 63; U23-2; U21-1; Yth; Sch
Michael proved again what a class player he is either through the middle of the park or playing wide in midfield for Wimbledon last term. He scored a spectacular goal in the demolition of Birmingham at St Andrew's and later in the season he was loaned to Blues where he impressed with some neat, clever passing before a stress fracture of the ankle put him on the sidelines.
Manchester C (From trainee on 17/8/1988) FL 25+1/1 FLC 5 FAC 1 Others 1 (£450,000 to RS Strasbourg, France in 1992 close season)
West Ham U (Loaned on 29/11/1994) PL 15+2/2 FAC 2
West Ham U (Loaned on 2/10/1995) PL 28 FLC 2 FAC 3/1
West Ham U (Free on 12/8/1996) PL 33+5/3 FLC 5 FAC 2
Wimbledon (£1,600,000 on 25/9/1997) P/FL 99+16/13 FLC 5+1/2 FAC 8+1/2
Birmingham C (Loaned on 28/3/2002) FL 3

HUGHES John **Paul**
Born: Hammersmith, 19 April 1976
Height: 6'0" **Weight:** 12.10
International Honours: E: Sch
If there were an award for the unluckiest player in the League, Paul would be amongst the contenders! After a promising start to his career minor injuries limited his chances of first-team football and then a serious groin injury kept him out of the game for eight months. Released by Southampton at the end of the 2000-01 campaign, he had a brief association with Burnley before joining Luton Town at the start of last season. His career seemed to be finally getting back on track, with two goals in eight first-team starts, but then injury struck again in the guise of an ankle ligament. Out for two

months, he returned to action but was always on the fringes of the squad. He is an attacking midfield player with plenty of creativity.
Chelsea (From trainee on 11/7/1994) PL 13+8/2 FAC 2 Others 1
Stockport Co (Loaned on 17/12/1998) FL 7
Norwich C (Loaned on 24/3/1999) FL 2+2/1
Southampton (Free on 23/3/2000)
Luton T (Free, via trial at Burnley, on 10/8/2001) FL 12+10/1 FLC 1

HUGHES Richard
Born: Glasgow, 25 June 1979
Height: 5'9" **Weight:** 9.12
International Honours: S: U21-8; Yth
This highly creative and influential midfielder endured a frustrating season at Bournemouth in 2001-02 as injuries restricted his appearances and halted his progress with the Scotland U21 squad. When fit, Richard is capable of running games and has a keen eye for goal. He is out of contract in the summer, and at the time of writing it was unclear where his future lies.
Arsenal (Free from Atalanta, Italy on 11/8/1997)
Bournemouth (£20,000 on 5/8/1998) FL 123+8/14 FLC 9+1 FAC 8/2 Others 5

HUGHES Stephen John
Born: Reading, 18 September 1976
Height: 6'0" **Weight:** 12.12
Club Honours: FAYC '94; PL '98; CS '98
International Honours: E: U21-8; Yth; Sch
The former England U21 midfielder arrived at Watford during the summer of 2001 and seemed likely to become a key element of manager Vialli's team rebuilding. A left-footed player, he made a good early impression but had his season severely disrupted by injury. He was concussed at Crewe in September, and then suffered a groin injury in November which required surgery in January and prevented any further appearances.
Arsenal (From trainee on 15/7/1995) PL 22+27/4 FLC 5+3/1 FAC 7+7/1 Others 2+4/1
Fulham (Loaned on 26/7/1999) FL 3 FLC 1
Everton (£500,000 + on 10/3/2000) PL 27+2/1 FLC 1+1 FAC 2/1
Watford (Free on 12/7/2001) FL 11+4 FLC 2

HULBERT Robin James
Born: Plymouth, 14 March 1980
Height: 5'9" **Weight:** 10.5
International Honours: E: Yth; Sch
Robin continued to make steady progress at Bristol City in 2001-02 and featured fairly often in the squad, most of his

Steve Hunt

appearances coming from the bench. A hard-tackling player who operates on the right-hand side of midfield, he will be looking to win a regular place in the starting line-up in 2002-03.
Swindon T (From trainee on 25/9/1997) FL 12+17 FLC 1+1 FAC 2
Bristol C (£25,000 on 23/3/2000) FL 19+13 FLC 0+2 Others 3+2

HULSE Robert (Rob) William
Born: Crewe, 25 October 1979
Height: 6'1" **Weight:** 11.4
The 2001-02 season saw Rob consolidate his place as one of the main strikers for Crewe Alexandra. A hard-working player who came up through the ranks, he headed the club's list of scorers with a total of 12 in League and cup competitions.
Crewe Alex (From trainee on 25/6/1998) FL 62+16/24 FLC 5+1/1 FAC 4+1

HUME Iain
Born: Brampton, Ontario, Canada, 31 October 1983
Height: 5'7" **Weight:** 11.2
International Honours: Canada: Yth
Iain continued to develop at a steady pace with Tranmere last term, when he again featured mostly from the subs' bench, although also making the starting line-up on a couple of occasions. Assured and unflappable, he has the ability to kick with both feet. He was a mainstay of the reserve team and must surely feature in Dave Watson's plans for 2002-03.
Tranmere Rov (From juniors on 6/11/2000) FL 1+26 FLC 0+2 FAC 0+1 Others 1

HUMPHREYS Richard (Richie) John
Born: Sheffield, 30 November 1977
Height: 5'11" **Weight:** 14.6
International Honours: E: U21-3; Yth
A close-season signing for Hartlepool, Richie soon became popular with the supporters for his positive attitude. He is a stocky young striker, but achieved greater success playing in a deeper role. He was the only Pool player to feature in all 51 first-team games during the season.
Sheffield Wed (From trainee on 8/2/1996) P/FL 34+33/4 FLC 4+2 FAC 5+4/4
Scunthorpe U (Loaned on 13/8/1999) FL 6/2
Cardiff C (Loaned on 22/11/1999) FL 8+1/2 FAC 1 Others 1
Cambridge U (Free on 2/2/2001) FL 7/3
Hartlepool U (Free on 18/7/2001) FL 42+4/5 FLC 1 FAC 1 Others 3

HUNT James Malcolm
Born: Derby, 17 December 1976
Height: 5'8" **Weight:** 10.3
James had another solid season for Northampton Town last term. A reliable central midfield player who operates from box to box, he had one of his best goal tallies for the club and he twice netted winners to help secure some valuable points in the fight against relegation.
Notts Co (From trainee on 15/7/1994) FL 15+4/1 FAC 0+1 Others 2+2/1
Northampton T (Free on 7/8/1997) FL 150+22/8 FLC 8+2 FAC 7+3/1 Others 10+1/1

HUNT Stephen (Steve)
Born: Port Laoise, Ireland, 1 August 1980
Height: 5'7" **Weight:** 12.6
International Honours: RoI: U21-1
Steve is an extremely enthusiastic Brentford winger with a useful left foot. In his first season at Griffin Park he soon established himself on the wing, his speed worrying many full backs, and he created a number of goals for his colleagues. His most eventful match of the campaign came at Bournemouth where he scored both goals, his first for the club, in the 2-0 victory before being sent off.
Crystal Palace (From trainee on 29/6/1999) FL 0+3
Brentford (Free on 6/8/2001) FL 34+1/4 FLC 0+1 FAC 1 Others 4

HUNTER Barry Victor
Born: Coleraine, 18 November 1968
Height: 6'3" **Weight:** 13.2
International Honours: NI: 15; B-2; Yth
This experienced centre half initially moved from Reading to Rushden last September 2001 in a one-month loan deal, but that was soon extended to the end of the season. He deputised for the suspended Jim Rodwell but soon made the place his own with a series of assured displays. He is not the quickest defender around but compensated for his lack of pace with an acute awareness of the play. He was eventually forced on to the sidelines with a fractured foot, but made it back to the subs' bench by the end of the campaign. Barry followed up his appearance on television's 'The Weakest Link' by appearing on 'Britain's Brainiest Footballer'.
Newcastle U (Signed from Coleraine on 2/11/1987. Freed during 1988 close season)
Wrexham (£50,000 from Crusaders on 20/8/1993) FL 88+3/4 FLC 6 FAC 7+1/1 Others 15/1

Reading (£400,000 on 12/7/1996) FL 76+8/4 FLC 5/1 FAC 3+1/1 Others 6+1
Southend U (Loaned on 12/2/1999) FL 5/2
Rushden & Diamonds (Free on 14/9/2001) FL 23/1 FAC 2

HUNTER Roy Ian
Born: Saltburn, 29 October 1973
Height: 5'10" **Weight:** 12.8
After finally recovering from his injury problems Roy switched from a midfield role to the right-wing-back slot for Northampton Town last term. He adapted well to the new position and also took over as team captain. A highlight of his season came in the 4-1 win over Wrexham when he tucked away two goals from the penalty spot in the absence of Jamie Forrester.
West Bromwich A (From trainee on 4/3/1992) FL 3+6/1 Others 4+1
Northampton T (Free on 2/8/1995) FL 149+28/17 FLC 10 FAC 11/2 Others 13/1

HURST Glynn
Born: Barnsley, 17 January 1976
Height: 5'10" **Weight:** 11.10
Glynn didn't feature as much as expected for Stockport County last term and although he scored four goals early on he fell out of favour following the arrival of new manager Carlton Palmer. He subsequently joined Chesterfield the day after Luke Beckett moved in the opposite direction. A quick-witted striker who is lively on his feet, he is good in the air, too. His brace of goals in the 4-2 win over Oldham were a header from 12 yards and a powerful shot after a run from the halfway line. In that respect, Glynn scores many different sorts of goals, and that makes him a handful for any defence.
Barnsley (From trainee at Tottenham H on 13/7/1994) FL 0+8 FLC 1 (Freed on 27/3/1997)
Swansea C (Loaned on 15/12/1995) FL 2/1
Mansfield T (Loaned on 18/11/1996) FL 5+1 Others 0+1
Ayr U (£30,000 from Emley on 23/3/1998) SL 78/49 SLC 6/2 SC 10 Others 1+2
Stockport Co (£150,000 on 16/2/2001) FL 22+4/4 FLC 0+1
Chesterfield (Free on 14/12/2001) FL 22+1/9

HURST Paul Michael
Born: Sheffield, 25 September 1974
Height: 5'4" **Weight:** 9.4
Club Honours: AMC '96
Paul made the left-back position at

Rotherham his own in 2001-02, enjoying his best ever season for the club. A near ever present, his only regret was that he didn't get on the score sheet but he was voted as the Supporters' Club 'Player of the Year'.
Rotherham U (From trainee on 12/8/1993) FL 230+38/11 FLC 6+1 FAC 17+2/2 Others 14+1

HUTCHINGS Carl Emil
Born: Hammersmith, 24 September 1974
Height: 5'11" **Weight:** 11.0
Carl signed a new deal for Southend United the day before the 2001-02 season started. A dominant, driving force in midfield, he seemed to cover every blade of grass at times, forming a fine midfield partnership with Kevin Maher. A strong tackler and talented passer, he accepted a long-term deal with Leyton Orient early in the new year. Injuries restricted his appearances at Brisbane Road but he will be looking to regain his place in the team for the start of the 2002-03 campaign.
Brentford (From trainee on 12/7/1993) FL 144+18/7 FLC 9+1 FAC 11+1 Others 11+3
Bristol C (£130,000 on 6/7/1998) FL 33+9/3 FLC 4+1/2 FAC 2+2 Others 1
Brentford (Loaned on 11/2/2000) FL 7+1
Exeter C (Loaned on 30/11/2000) FL 2 Others 1
Southend U (Free on 29/12/2000) FL 42+1/4 FLC 1 FAC 4 Others 2/1
Leyton Orient (Free on 13/2/2002) FL 9+1/1

HUTCHINSON Edward (Eddie) Stephen
Born: Kingston, 23 February 1982
Height: 6'1" **Weight:** 12.7
The 2001-02 season was a disappointing one for Eddie as he spent most of the time on the fringes of the first team at Brentford. He started just two League games although he was often one of the nominated substitutes. The neat midfielder put in a number of consistent performances in the reserves and will be hoping to feature more often at senior level in 2002-03.
Brentford (£75,000 from Sutton U on 21/7/2000) FL 7+9 FAC 0+1 Others 1

HUTCHINSON Jonathan (Jon)
Born: Middlesbrough, 2 April 1982
Height: 6'0" **Weight:** 12.0
Jon made his senior debut for Birmingham City in the Worthington Cup tie at Bristol Rovers last September and impressed with determined headers and sensible use of ball. Then he came off the

bench at Manchester City at half time and was unfazed. He is a promising defender who is comfortable in possession and quick to read situations.
Birmingham C (From trainee on 1/7/2000) FL 0+3 FLC 1

HUTCHISON Donald (Don)
Born: Gateshead, 9 May 1971
Height: 6'1" **Weight:** 11.8
International Honours: S: 19; B-1
This right-sided midfielder played his final match for Sunderland in the local 'derby' encounter with Newcastle at the start of last season before returning to West Ham at the end of August. He soon settled back into life at Upton Park. He had a superb game at Manchester United in December and was one of the stars in the Hammers 1-0 win. However, he had the misfortune to suffer a torn cruciate ligament against Middlesboro in February and this ruled him out until the end of the campaign.
Hartlepool U (From trainee on 20/3/1990) FL 19+5/2 FLC 1+1 FAC 2 Others 1
Liverpool (£175,000 on 27/11/1990) F/PL 33+12/7 FLC 7+1/2 FAC 1+2 Others 3+1/1
West Ham U (£1,500,000 on 30/8/1994) PL 30+5/11 FLC 3/2 FAC 0+1
Sheffield U (£1,200,000 on 11/1/1996) FL 70+8/5 FLC 3+2 FAC 5/1 Others 2+1
Everton (£1,000,000 + on 27/2/1998) PL 68+7/10 FLC 4+1/1 FAC 9
Sunderland (£2,500,000 on 19/7/2000) FL 32+2/8 FLC 2/2 FAC 3
West Ham U (£5,000,000 on 31/8/2001) PL 24/1 FLC 1 FAC 3

HUTH Robert
Born: Berlin, Germany, 18 August 1984
Height: 6'2" **Weight:** 12.12
This commanding central defender made his first-team debut in Chelsea's final Premiership match of last season, the fifth youngster to be blooded by the Blues during the 2001-02 campaign. He replaced Graeme Le Saux for the second half against Aston Villa and gave an assured performance. Robert is powerfully built and dominant in the air and is another for whom youth coach Steve Clarke predicts a very bright future.
Chelsea (From trainee on 23/8/2001) PL 0+1

HYDE Graham
Born: Doncaster, 10 November 1970
Height: 5'8" **Weight:** 11.11
Graham had a loan spell at Chesterfield in the early part of the 2001-02 campaign and looked very effective playing in a

midfield anchor role. His presence allowed Marcus Ebdon to demonstrate his full range of skills and the team won three on the trot, with Graham scoring at Swindon. He returned to St Andrew's but remained out of favour and his only start for Birmingham came against Nottingham Forest on New Year's Day.
Sheffield Wed (From trainee on 17/5/1988) F/PL 126+46/11 FLC 17+3/2 FAC 13+5/2 Others 8/1
Birmingham C (Free on 5/2/1999) FL 35+17/1 FLC 2+2/1 FAC 2
Chesterfield (Loaned on 18/8/2001) FL 8+1/1

HYDE Micah Anthony
Born: Newham, 10 November 1974
Height: 5'9" **Weight:** 11.5
Club Honours: Div 2 '98
International Honours: Jamaica: 5
A combative and skilful midfield player, Micah was a regular in the Watford first team in 2001-02 and prospered from the passing philosophy encouraged by new manager Gianluca Vialli. Although he had a purple patch in October, scoring four times in three matches, his overall return of six goals was disappointing for such a clean striker of the ball.
Cambridge U (From trainee on 19/5/1993) FL 89+18/13 FLC 3 FAC 7+2 Others 4+1
Watford (£225,000 on 21/7/1997) P/FL 170+13/19 FLC 14/4 FAC 7 Others 3

HYYPIA Sami
Born: Porvoo, Finland, 7 October 1973
Height: 6'4" **Weight:** 13.5
Club Honours: FLC '01; FAC '01; UEFAC '01; ESC '01; CS '01
International Honours: Finland: 44; U21; Yth
Outstanding in his first season at Anfield, Sami continued to grow in stature last term and must now be considered one of the most assured central defenders in the Premiership, if not in Europe. His partnership with Stephane Henchoz was the bedrock on which most opposition attacks floundered and compares favourably with almost any of the great defensive pairings from the past at Anfield. Commanding in the air, decisive in the tackle with the composure to carry the ball out of defence and always a threat at set pieces he is a manager's dream. He was selected by his fellow professionals for the PFA's Premiership team for the season.
Liverpool (£2,600,000 from Willem II, Holland, ex MyPa, on 7/7/1999) PL 110+3/5 FLC 9/1 FAC 10 Others 28/2

I

IBEHRE Jabo Oshevire
Born: Islington, 28 January 1983
Height: 6'2" **Weight:** 12.10
Jabo is a quick and strong centre forward who is both skilful and unpredictable. He started the 2001-02 season as a first choice for Leyton Orient and continued to score his share of goals whilst creating chances for others. He missed two months with a groin injury but returned to the line-up before the end of the campaign.
Leyton Orient (From trainee on 18/7/2001) FL 22+14/6 FLC 1+1 FAC 2+1/1 Others 3+1

IFIL Jerel Christopher
Born: Wembley, 27 June 1982
Height: 6'1" **Weight:** 12.11
Jerel was a regular in the Watford reserve team last season and in March he joined Second Division Huddersfield Town to gain some experience of senior football. Signed by the Terriers as additional cover for the defence, he made a brief substitute appearance in the 1-1 draw at Wrexham, subsequently making his full League debut against Notts County, before appearing in both legs of the play-off semi-final against Brentford. He is a promising youngster who produced some cool and collected displays in his spell at the McAlpine Stadium.
Watford (From trainee on 8/2/2000)
Huddersfield T (Loaned on 28/3/2002) FL 1+1 Others 2

IFILL Paul
Born: Brighton, 20 October 1979
Height: 6'0" **Weight:** 12.10
Club Honours: Div 2 '01
Paul has had another good season for Millwall in 2001-02. A very tricky pacy forward, he caused many a problem to opposition defences. He has a good shot with either foot and scored some excellent goals especially when he chose to cut inside. A good crosser of the ball, he was the Lions' main provider of goal-scoring opportunities from the flanks.
Millwall (From trainee on 2/6/1998) FL 105+29/22 FLC 4/1 FAC 5 Others 8+1

IGOE Samuel (Sammy) Gary
Born: Staines, 30 September 1975
Height: 5'6" **Weight:** 10.0
Sammy was a permanent feature in the Reading midfield last term, except for a brief spell following the embarrassing home defeat by Swindon Town in

October. He proved to be the most prolific crosser of the ball from his position on the wide right, and scored his only goal in the 1-1 home draw against Bury. Despite his consistency and determination, securing a new contract with Reading became a problem at the end of the season, the club claiming they were unable to offer improved terms until the Nationwide League's dispute with ITV Digital could be resolved.
Portsmouth (From trainee on 15/2/1994) FL 100+60/11 FLC 8+5 FAC 2+3
Reading (£100,000 on 23/3/2000) FL 45+27/7 FLC 4 FAC 2+2 Others 6+1

ILIC Sasa
Born: Melbourne, Australia, 18 July 1972
Height: 6'4" **Weight:** 14.0
International Honours: Yugoslavia: 2
Unable to get a game at Charlton, Sasa joined Portsmouth on loan last September as cover for the injured Dave Beasant. He played seven games for Pompey, impressing with his command over the area, reflex saves and shot-stopping skills but returned to the Valley the following month.
Charlton Ath (Free from St Leonards Stamcroft on 5/10/1997) P/FL 51 FLC 3 FAC 2 Others 3
West Ham U (Loaned on 24/2/2000) PL 1
Portsmouth (Loaned on 7/9/2001) FL 7

IMPEY Andrew (Andy) Rodney
Born: Hammersmith, 13 September 1971
Height: 5'8" **Weight:** 11.2
Club Honours: FLC '00
International Honours: E: U21-1
This right-sided winger or wing back seemed to flourish at Leicester under Peter Taylor in 2000-01 but had much less impact as the team struggled last season. He played mostly on the right of a midfield four, occasionally filling in at right back, but will tend to remember this campaign as steady but unspectacular. He finally succumbed to the Foxes' injury jinx in February and only returned for the closing day win over Tottenham.
Queens Park R (£35,000 from Yeading on 14/6/1990) F/PL 177+10/13 FLC 15+1/3 FAC 7+3/1 Others 0+2/1
West Ham U (£1,300,000 on 26/9/1997) PL 25+2 FLC 4 FAC 3
Leicester C (£1,600,000 on 25/11/1998) PL 94+13/1 FLC 5+4 FAC 8+1 Others 2

INAMOTO Junichi
Born: Kagashima, Japan,, 18 September 1979
Height: 5'11" **Weight:** 11.13
International Honours: Japan: 27

This hard-tackling all-action midfield player had a rather disappointing season at Arsenal in 2001-02 and rarely seemed to feature in manager Arsene Wenger's first-team plans. His only senior appearances came in the Worthington Cup and as a late substitute in European Champions' League matches. Nevertheless he went on to prove a revelation for Japan in the World Cup finals, prompting speculation of a move away from Highbury.
Arsenal (£4,000,000 from Gamba Osaka, Japan on 24/7/2001) FLC 2 Others 0+2

INCE Clayton
Born: Trinidad, 13 July 1972
Height: 6'3" **Weight:** 14.2
International Honours: Trinidad & Tobago
After spending two seasons as a reserve 'keeper at Crewe, Clayton finally came into the first-team picture more during the 2001-02 campaign. He made his first full appearance for Crewe in the Worthington Cup tie against Rushden in September and made the starting line-up on more than 20 occasions. He will be aiming to establish himself as the club's number one custodian in 2002-03.
Crewe Alex (£50,000 from Defence Force, Trinidad on 21/9/1999) FL 18+3 FLC 2 FAC 2

INCE Paul Emerson Carlyle
Born: Ilford, 21 October 1967
Height: 5'11" **Weight:** 12.2
Club Honours: CS '93, '94; FAC '90, '94; ECW '91; ESC '91; FLC '92; PL '93, '94
International Honours: E: 53; B-1; U21-2; Yth
Paul was once again an inspirational figure in central midfield for Middlesbrough last term, when he was a near ever present in the team. A combative tenacious figure in the centre of the park, he also contributed two goals for Boro'.
West Ham U (From apprentice on 18/7/1985) FL 66+6/7 FLC 9/3 FAC 8+2/1 Others 4/1
Manchester U (£1,000,000 on 14/9/1989) F/PL 203+3/24 FLC 23+1/2 FAC 26+1/1 Others 24/1 (£8,000,000 to Inter Milan, Italy on 13/7/1995)
Liverpool (£4,200,000 on 22/7/1997) PL 65/14 FLC 6/1 FAC 3/1 Others 7/1
Middlesbrough (£1,000,000 on 3/8/1999) PL 93/7 FLC 6/1 FAC 7/1

INGHAM Michael
Born: Preston, 9 September 1980
Height: 6'4" **Weight:** 13.12
International Honours: NI: U21-4; Yth

This young goalkeeper, Michael made his full Sunderland debut in the Worthington Cup tie at Sheffield Wednesday last September. Although he gave away a penalty in an eventual 4-2 defeat, at times he kept the score down single-handedly and will have only benefited from the experience.
Sunderland *(£30,000 from Cliftonville on 28/7/1999) FLC 1*
Carlisle U *(Loaned on 1/10/1999) FL 7*

INGIMARSSON Ivar
Born: Iceland, 20 August 1978
Height: 6'0" **Weight:** 12.7
International Honours: Iceland: 2; U21-14; Yth
This cool and composed Brentford centre back came of age as a footballer during the 2001-02 season. Previously a midfielder Ivar formed a superb central defensive pairing with Darren Powell. He was ever present and wasn't cautioned in any game throughout the season, a remarkable achievement for a defender. Selected as the Bees' 'Player of the Season', he even chipped in with six goals, including efforts home and away against champions Brighton. He also won another cap for Iceland, playing the full 90 minutes against Kuwait.
Torquay U *(Loaned from IBV Vestmannaeyjar, Iceland on 21/10/1999) FL 4/1*
Brentford *(£150,000 on 18/11/1999) FL 109+4/10 FLC 6 FAC 3 Others 13/1*

INGLEDOW Jamie Graeme
Born: Barnsley, 23 August 1980
Height: 5'6" **Weight:** 9.7
Injury prevented this hustling midfielder making a sustained impact upon the Chesterfield team in 2001-02. He cracked a bone in his left foot in February and that finished his season. Jamie undoubtedly has ability; he gets forward well and always demonstrates great competitiveness, but the stop-start nature of his campaign led to his being freed in April.
Rotherham U *(From trainee on 1/7/1998) FL 17+8/2 FLC 3 FAC 5 Others 2+1*
Chesterfield *(Free on 19/7/2000) FL 26+15/3 FLC 1+1 FAC 1 Others 5*

INGRAM Rae
Born: Manchester, 6 December 1974
Height: 5'11" **Weight:** 12.8
This tall defender featured both at centre half and left back for Port Vale last term. He was a regular in the side until going off injured against Cardiff City in October and another injury at Oldham just before

Christmas led to a further spell on the sidelines. Three months later he got back in the side, but after coming on as a substitute against Wigan he was forced to leave the field after only seven minutes when a collision with Sagi Burton caused him to bite a piece off his tongue. He returned to the fray before the end of the

campaign though and will be hoping for a more regular role in 2002-03.
Manchester C *(From trainee on 9/7/1993) P/FL 18+5 FLC 1 FAC 4*
Macclesfield T *(Free on 19/3/1998) FL 95+8/1 FLC 6 FAC 4+1 Others 1+1*
Port Vale *(Free on 2/7/2001) FL 22+2 FLC 2 FAC 2 Others 2*

Ivar Ingimarsson

INNES Mark
Born: Glasgow, 27 September 1978
Height: 5'10" **Weight:** 12.1
Mark only made the starting line-up for Oldham in the LDV Vans Trophy games and after being transfer listed he joined Chesterfield, initially on loan, before signing permanently the following month. Comfortable at left back or in midfield, he has a wide range of passing skills and is an accurate striker of a dead ball.
Oldham Ath *(From trainee on 10/10/1995)*
FL 52+21/1 FLC 4+3 FAC 4+2 Others 3+1
Chesterfield *(Free on 19/12/2001) FL 22+1/2*

INVINCIBILE Daniel (Danny)
Born: Australia, 31 March 1979
Height: 6'4" **Weight:** 12.2
International Honours: Australia: Sch
Danny was used mainly as a striker by Swindon Town last season, but also featured at both left and right wing back and in a wide-right midfield position. He consolidated his position as a crowd favourite by finishing as joint-leading scorer with a tally of eight goals. His opener in the 2-0 win at Vale Park was a particularly memorable effort. He picked up the ball just inside the Port Vale half, evaded four challenges and buried a great shot into the left corner.
Swindon T *(Free from Marconi Stallions, Australia on 10/8/2000) FL 72+14/15 FLC 3+1/1 FAC 6/2 Others 2*

IPOUA Gui (Guy)
Born: Douala, Cameroon, 14 January 1976
Height: 6'1" **Weight:** 12.0
A record of 25 appearances as substitute for Gillingham last term showed that Guy was always capable of changing the course of a game when called upon. He has electric pace, good close control and tremendous upper body strength, but on the other hand can often be frustrating in front of goal.
Bristol Rov *(Free from Seville, Spain on 7/8/1998) FL 15+9/3 FLC 1+1 FAC 3+1 Others 1*
Scunthorpe U *(Free on 27/8/1999) FL 50+15/23 FAC 5/4 Others 2*
Gillingham *(£25,000 on 19/3/2001) FL 20+29/8 FLC 1+2 FAC 0+3*

IRELAND Craig
Born: Dundee, 29 November 1975
Height: 6'3" **Weight:** 13.9
Craig is a classical big centre half, brought south by former Notts County boss Jocky Scott. A no-nonsense player, he is a colossus in the air and possesses a strong left foot. Last season he proved himself to

Danny Invincibile

be the Magpies' best-left sided central defender and his partnership with Nick Fenton was one of the best seen at Meadow Lane in a decade.
Aberdeen *(From juniors on 5/10/1994) SLC 1*
Dunfermline Ath *(Free on 12/2/1996) SL 61+6/2 SLC 0+2 SC 0+1*
Dundee *(Free on 27/10/1999) SL 14/1 SC 1*
Airdrieonians *(Loaned on 12/10/2000) SL 12/2 Others 1*
Notts Co *(£50,000 on 2/2/2001) FL 42+1/1 FLC 1*

IRONS Kenneth (Kenny)
Born: Liverpool, 4 November 1970
Height: 5'10" **Weight:** 12.2
This central midfielder made an explosive start for Huddersfield Town last term, netting with a thunderous volley in the opening game against Bournemouth. He appeared to have the ability to win any match with his close control and accurate passing, while his role in delivering set pieces helped him find the net seven times during the season.
Tranmere Rov *(From trainee on 9/11/1989) FL 313+39/54 FLC 24+7/7 FAC 14+2/3 Others 28+3/3*
Huddersfield T *(£450,000 on 18/6/1999) FL 91+23/10 FLC 8/2 FAC 3 Others 7*

IRWIN Joseph Denis
Born: Cork, 31 October 1965
Height: 5'8" **Weight:** 11.0
Club Honours: CS '93, '96, '97; ECWC '91; ESC '91; FLC '92; PL '93, '94, '96, '97, '99, '00, '01; FAC '94, '96; EC '99
International Honours: Rol: 56; B-1; U23-1; U21-3; Yth; Sch
Although he only featured sporadically in Premiership action last term, Denis still remained very much part of Sir Alex Ferguson's plans at Old Trafford last term. He was a model of consistency at full back for United, even when the rest of the defence seemed to be leaking goals, and established a new club record with his 70th appearance in European competition against Deportivo La Coruna in October.
Leeds U *(From apprentice on 3/11/1983) FL 72/1 FLC 5 FAC 3 Others 2*
Oldham Ath *(Free on 22/5/1986) FL 166+1/4 FLC 19/3 FAC 13 Others 5*
Manchester U *(£625,000 on 20/6/1990) F/PL 356+12/22 FLC 28+3 FAC 42+1/7 Others 85+2/4*

ISSA Pierre
Born: Johannesburg, South Africa,, 11 September 1975
Height: 6'4" **Weight:** 13.6
International Honours: South Africa: 43

Pierre arrived at Watford on a free transfer last September. A two-footed player, he started in midfield, but looked far more comfortable when he switched to central defence. He achieved an unusual moment of fame when he was carried off with a shoulder injury against Birmingham and was dropped by the stretcher bearers – an episode that featured as a 'What Happened Next' on a television programme. Pierre represented South Africa at the African Nations Cup in January, but seemed to have trouble readjusting to life in England on his return and made no further appearances. He was transfer-listed in February.
Watford *(Free from Marseilles, France, ex Dunkerque, on 13/9/2001) FL 12+3/1 FLC 2 FAC 1*

ITONGA Carlin Daniel
Born: Zaire, 11 December 1982
Height: 5'9" **Weight:** 11.9
Club Honours: FAYC '01
This young Arsenal striker signed professional forms for the club in August 2001 and stepped up to make his senior debut as a substitute in the Worthington Cup game against Manchester United last November. He has scored regularly for the U19s team for whom he netted seven goals in a 9-1 victory over Ipswich.
Arsenal *(From trainee on 9/8/2001) FLC 0+1*

IVERSEN Steffen
Born: Oslo, Norway, 10 November 1976
Height: 6'1" **Weight:** 11.10
Club Honours: FLC '99
International Honours: Norway: 31; U21-23; Yth
Steffen battled back from injury to regain a place in the Spurs attack last season. A player with great aerial ability and a powerful strike, he was sorely missed by the team and his absence was a factor in the lack of goals, for he netted seven goals from 14 starts once back in action.
Tottenham H *(£2,700,000 from Rosenborg, Norway, ex Nationalkam, on 7/12/1996) PL 104+20/35 FLC 10+3/6 FAC 10+4/4 Others 4/1*

IWELUMO Christopher (Chris) Robert
Born: Coatbridge, 1 August 1978
Height: 6'3" **Weight:** 13.8
Chris made remarkable progress at Stoke City last the season and although not one of the most likely to break into a regular first-team spot he took his chances with both hands. A powerful striker who is fearless in the air, he won the hearts of

the City fans with some fine all-round play while his tally of 10 goals was the key to the club earning their third successive appearance in the play-offs. A call up for the Scotland training squad at the end of the season was due recognition for a fine season.
St Mirren *(From juniors on 5/8/1996) SL 7+19 SLC 0+3/1 SC 1+1/1 Others 0+2 (Free to Aarhus Fremad, Denmark during 1998 close season)*
Stoke C *(£25,000 from AGF Aarhus, Denmark on 1/3/2000) FL 22+21/11 FLC 0+3/1 FAC 3+1/1 Others 4+1/1*
York C *(Loaned on 10/11/2000) FL 11+1/2 FAC 4/1*
Cheltenham T *(Loaned on 13/2/2001) FL 2+2/1*

IZZET Kemal (Kem)
Born: Whitechapel, 29 September 1980
Height: 5'8" **Weight:** 10.5
Kem came of age with an excellent first full campaign of senior football for Colchester in 2001-02. He was particularly impressive early on in the season, scoring some vital goals, including the winner at Portsmouth in the Worthington Cup, and further strikes against Oldham and Reading. He tired a little at the turn of the year, but finished the campaign with a flourish. Kem is a battling midfield player with boundless energy. The younger brother of Muzzy Izzet, he was deservedly named as the U's 'Young Player of the Year'.
Charlton Ath *(From trainee on 11/1/1999)*
Colchester U *(Signed on 22/3/2001) FL 41+5/4 FLC 2/1 FAC 1 Others 2/1*

IZZET Mustafa (Muzzy)
Kemal
Born: Mile End, 31 October 1974
Height: 5'10" **Weight:** 10.12
Club Honours: FLC '97, '00
International Honours: Turkey: 7
This right-footed midfielder continued to look the class performer of the squad but could not turn Leicester's fortunes around single-handedly last term. He scored the winning injury-time penalty at Pride Park but, unusually, missed a couple of spot kicks during the season. His vision led to one of City's more unusual goals, at St Mary's, where a return volley of goalkeeper Paul Jones' header struck the woodwork before Brian Deane netted the follow-up. He was recalled for Turkey for the friendly against Ecuador that was played in Breda in February.
Chelsea *(From trainee on 19/5/1993)*
Leicester C *(£650,000 + on 28/3/1996) P/FL 197+4/32 FLC 21+1/3 FAC 14/4 Others 7/1*

JAASKELAINEN Jussi
Born: Vaasa, Finland, 19 April 1975
Height: 6'3" **Weight:** 12.10
International Honours: Finland: 7; U21; Yth
Jussi took the opportunity last season to firmly establish himself as one of the top goalkeepers in the Premiership. A fine shot stopper, he still has some minor flaws in his game, Bolton fans will have been particularly pleased to see Jussi become a lot more aggressive in the box, but there can be no doubt that he is an integral part of the Wanderers team and is likely to remain so for the near future.
Bolton W (£100,000 + from VPS Vaasa, Finland, ex MPS, on 14/11/1997) P/FL 128+1 FLC 10 FAC 5 Others 2

JACK Michael Lawrence
Born: Carlisle, 2 October 1982
Height: 5'8" **Weight:** 10.5
A product of Carlisle's youth system, Michael made his debut in mid-September as a substitute. By the end of the season he had featured in the majority of United's matches, giving a series of solid if unspectacular performances in midfield. Although regarded as one of the more promising youngsters at the club he was surprisingly released in the summer.
Carlisle U (From trainee on 27/6/2001) FL 16+16 FAC 2+1 Others 0+1

JACK Rodney Alphonso
Born: Kingstown, St Vincent, 28 September 1972
Height: 5'7" **Weight:** 10.9
International Honours: St Vincent & Grenadines
This versatile striker has played in a number of roles since joining Crewe back in 1998. A skilful player with a fine turn of speed, he can also score spectacular goals. He finished the 2001-02 season with seven goals and passed the landmark of 100 League appearances for the Railwaymen during the campaign.
Torquay U (Free from Lambada, St Vincent on 10/10/1995) FL 82+5/24 FLC 6/1 FAC 6 Others 6/3
Crewe Alex (£650,000 on 14/8/1998) FL 105+20/24 FLC 10/2 FAC 6+2

JACKMAN Daniel James
Born: Worcester, 3 January 1983
Height: 5'5" **Weight:** 10.2
This diminutive left-sided midfielder joined

Cambridge United on loan early in the new year, making his senior debut at Bury in February. In the few games that he played he showed plenty of class before returning to Villa Park to continue his development in the reserves.
Aston Villa (From trainee on 4/4/2001)
Cambridge U (Loaned on 14/2/2002) FL 5+2/1 Others 1+1

JACKSON Justin Jonathan
Born: Nottingham, 10 December 1974
Height: 6'0" **Weight:** 11.6
Club Honours: Div 3 '98; NC '01
International Honours: E: SP-2
This Rushden striker was the first casualty of the club's indifferent start to their first season in the Football League. Despite scoring 20 goals in the Conference-winning season, he failed to find the target in the first six games last term, but it was still a surprise to many supporters when he accepted a move to Doncaster Rovers. He is a quick-footed striker with a great turn of pace who has the ability to 'spin' his marker.
Notts Co (£30,000 from Woking on 26/9/1997) FL 7+18/1 FAC 3+2 Others 1
Rotherham U (Loaned on 21/1/1999) FL 2/1
Halifax T (£30,000 on 11/2/1999) FL 16+1/4 (Transferred to Morecambe on 24/8/1999)
Rushden & Diamonds (£180,000 on 16/6/2000) FL 5 FLC 1

JACKSON Kirk Stewart
Born: Doncaster, 16 October 1976
Height: 5'11" **Weight:** 12.0
Kirk never really lived up to his reputation as a goal-scorer after joining Darlington from Worksop Town in February 2001, scoring only once during his career with the Quakers. He made only one League start last term, although he featured several times from the subs' bench, but despite some strong running and plenty of effort he failed to find the net. He moved on to Stevenage Borough early in the new year and went on to appear for them in the FA Trophy final against Yeovil Town at the end of the season.
Sheffield Wed (From trainee on 15/5/1995)
Scunthorpe U (Free on 23/7/1996) FL 0+4/1 Others 0+1
Chesterfield (Free on 6/8/1997) FL 0+3 FLC 0+1 FAC 0+1 Others 1 (Free to Grantham T on 7/8/1998)
Darlington (£30,000 from Worksop T on 1/3/2001) FL 6+15/1 FLC 0+1 FAC 1+1 Others 2

JACKSON Mark Graham
Born: Barnsley, 30 September 1977
Height: 6'0" **Weight:** 11.12

International Honours: E: Yth
Mark established himself as Scunthorpe United's top defender during the 2001-02 season. Strong in the air and comfortable on the floor, he became a defensive rock for the Iron and was rewarded with the captaincy on occasions. He scored with a stunning 20-yard free kick to win the local 'derby' against Hull and only missed one match all season. He signed a new three-year contract during the campaign.
Leeds U (From trainee on 1/7/1995) PL 11+8 FAC 4
Huddersfield T (Loaned on 29/10/1998) FL 5
Barnsley (Loaned on 14/1/2000) FL 1
Scunthorpe U (Free on 9/3/2000) FL 79+4/4 FLC 1 FAC 8 Others 4

JACKSON Matthew (Matt) Alan
Born: Leeds, 19 October 1971
Height: 6'1" **Weight:** 12.12
Club Honours: FAC '95
International Honours: E: U21-10; Sch
This experienced defender initially joined Wigan Athletic on loan last October before signing permanently soon afterwards. He showed his versatility by appearing at right back and also occasionally in the centre of defence as cover for injuries. A composed performer who copes well under pressure, he is comfortable on the ball and dangerous at set pieces. He missed several matches after suffering a dislocated kneecap in the home win over Brighton in January.
Luton T (From juniors on 4/7/1990) FL 7+2 FLC 2 Others 0+1
Preston NE (Loaned on 27/3/1991) FL 3+1 Others 1
Everton (£600,000 on 18/10/1991) F/PL 132+6/4 FLC 9 FAC 14/2 Others 4
Charlton Ath (Loaned on 26/3/1996) FL 8 Others 2
Queens Park R (Loaned on 20/8/1996) FL 7
Birmingham C (Loaned on 31/10/1996) FL 10
Norwich C (£450,000 on 24/12/1996) FL 158+3/6 FLC 6 FAC 5
Wigan Ath (Free on 19/10/2001) FL 26

JACKSON Michael Douglas
Born: Cheltenham, 26 June 1980
Height: 5'7" **Weight:** 10.10
Michael was a near ever-present for Cheltenham reserves in 2001-02, but only managed a single senior outing when he replaced Mark Yates at half time in the 'derby' match against Kidderminster last October. He later had a loan spell with Dr Martens League outfit Weston-super-Mare before being released in the summer. He is a young central midfielder who works

David James

hard and gets forward to support the attack.
Cheltenham T (From trainee on 1/8/1997) FL 2+7 FLC 0+2 FAC 0+1 Others 1

JACKSON Michael James
Born: Runcorn, 4 December 1973
Height: 6'0" **Weight:** 13.8
Club Honours: Div 2 '97, '00
International Honours: E: Yth
After scoring the winning goal for Preston at Kidderminster in the Worthington Cup tie, Michael's 2001-02 season quickly went flat. He subsequently lost his regular place at centre half to Chris Lucketti and then after being recalled due to Colin Murdock's injury he himself suffered an ankle injury at Portsmouth that required an operation. His recovery was much slower than anticipated and he did not return to the first team until the end of the campaign. At his best, Michael is an uncomplicated defender who takes no chances when in possession, and who poses a serious threat in the opposition box.
Crewe Alex (From trainee on 29/7/1992) FL 5 FLC 1 FAC 1 Others 2
Bury (Free on 13/8/1993) FL 123+2/9 FLC 9/1 FAC 3 Others 12
Preston NE (£125,000 on 26/3/1997) FL 175+5/16 FLC 14/1 FAC 13 Others 8

JACKSON Richard
Born: Whitby, 18 April 1980
Height: 5'8" **Weight:** 10.12
Richard only managed sporadic first-team appearances for Derby County in 2001-02, before stepping forward to feature in each of the last four games of the season. A promising young right-sided defender, he will be looking to win a regular place in the line-up in 2002-03.
Scarborough (From trainee on 27/3/1998) FL 21+1 FLC 2
Derby Co (£30,000 + on 25/3/1999) PL 7+4 FLC 1

JACOBS Wayne Graham
Born: Sheffield, 3 February 1969
Height: 5'9" **Weight:** 11.2
Bradford City's longest serving player had another outstanding campaign in 2001-02 when he mostly featured at right back and occasionally on the left side of midfield. He missed three games with a groin injury, but was recalled when fit and scored his only goal of the season at Rotherham in a 1-1 draw. Wayne also works hard in the community and is always available to talk to schools and supporters' associations.

Sheffield Wed (From apprentice on 3/1/1987) FL 5+1 FLC 3 Others 1
Hull C (£27,000 on 25/3/1988) FL 127+2/4 FLC 7 FAC 8 Others 6
Rotherham U (Free on 5/8/1993) FL 40+2/2 FLC 4 FAC 1 Others 2
Bradford C (Free on 5/8/1994) P/FL 259+9/12 FLC 17+2 FAC 12/2 Others 7

JAGIELKA Philip (Phil)
Nikodem
Born: Manchester, 17 August 1982
Height: 5'11" **Weight:** 12.8
International Honours: E: Yth
Phil had the misfortune to suffer a broken nose in his first start of the 2001-02 season for Sheffield United and it was not until February that he received the opportunity of an extended run in the team. He went on to produce some excellent performances, netting his first goals against Burnley when he scored in each half. A hard-working athletic midfielder, he tackles well in defence, looks comfortable on the ball and confidently moves up to support the attack. He signed a one-year contract extension in April, and also represented England at U20 level during the campaign.
Sheffield U (From trainee on 8/5/2000) FL 17+22/3 FLC 4

JAGIELKA Stephen (Steve)
Born: Manchester, 10 March 1978
Height: 5'8" **Weight:** 11.5
Steve was used mainly in a right-sided midfield role by Shrewsbury in 2001-02. He continued to show improvement in his game although his appearances were restricted by injuries. The 100 per cent commitment he offers in every game makes him a favourite with the fans and his skills were much missed in the vital run-in to try and secure a play-off spot. At the time of writing he looked to face a spell on the sidelines until early 2003 as he faced surgery to solve a cruciate ligament problem.
Stoke C (From trainee on 15/7/1996)
Shrewsbury T (Free on 30/7/1997) FL 77+65/14 FLC 4+3 FAC 4+1/1 Others 2+1/1

JAMES David Benjamin
Born: Welwyn Garden City, 1 August 1970
Height: 6'5" **Weight:** 14.5
Club Honours: FAYC '89; FLC '95
International Honours: E: 8; B-1; U21-10; Yth
The West Ham supporters were impressed when they heard their club had bought David from Aston Villa, unfortunately he suffered a bad knee injury playing for

England against Holland at White Hart Lane in August before he had even made his debut. He finally made the line-up against Tottenham at Upton Park at the end of November. He soon showed everyone why he is one of the best goalkeepers in the country with his confidence when coming for crosses and his assured kicking. He was the Hammers star man on many occasions, notably in the 1-0 win at Manchester United and against his old club Aston Villa in March.
Watford (From trainee on 1/7/1988) FL 89 FLC 6 FAC 2 Others 1
Liverpool (£1,000,000 on 6/7/1992) PL 213+1 FLC 22 FAC 19 Others 22
Aston Villa (£1,800,000 on 23/6/1999) PL 67 FLC 6 FAC 8 Others 4
West Ham U (£3,500,000 on 17/7/2001) PL 26 FAC 3

JAMES Kevin Ernest
Born: Southwark, 3 January 1980
Height: 5'9" **Weight:** 10.7
A near ever present for Gillingham's reserves in the Avon Combination, Kevin never made a full start for the first team in 2001-02, but still made the occasional appearance as substitute when he played down the middle or in a right back wing position.
Charlton Ath (From trainee on 2/7/1998)
Gillingham (Free on 21/8/2000) FL 1+16 FLC 0+1

JANSEN Matthew (Matt)
Brooke
Born: Carlisle, 20 October 1977
Height: 5'11" **Weight:** 10.13
Club Honours: AMC '97; FLC '02
International Honours: E: U21-6; Yth
Despite playing the last part of the 2001-02 campaign needing a hernia operation, Matt had an immense season at Blackburn. One of the club's leading tacklers, he plays all over the field, although he is strongest on the left. Deceptively good in the air, he has the trickery and ball skills to take on any defender, never shirks a challenge, can be knocked down but still not beaten as he has amazing balance that enables him to extricate himself from impossible situations. As the club's only reliable goal-scorer, he was asked to play either alone up front, or with a partner, but adapted well no matter what the occasion.
Carlisle U (From trainee on 18/11/1996) FL 26+16/10 FLC 4+1/3 FAC 1+3 Others 3+3
Crystal Palace (£1,000,000 + on 12/2/1998) P/FL 23+3/10 FLC 4 FAC 0+1 Others 2
Blackburn Rov (£4,100,000 on 19/1/1999) P/FL 91+25/40 FLC 7+2/8 FAC 6+4/2

JARRETT Jason Lee Mee
Born: Bury, 14 September 1979
Height: 6'0" **Weight:** 12.4
This all-action attacking midfielder was a fixture in the Bury side last season. A skilful player who glides past opponents with ease he sometimes struggled to maintain a level of consistency. He scored two goals for the Shakers but with the club in financial difficulties he was sold to Wigan in a bargain deal. He featured in a handful of games for the Latics, showing a liking for the hard-work and decisive tackling required for a central midfield berth, and produced a superb display in the final home match of the season against Northampton Town.
Blackpool *(From trainee on 3/7/1998) FL 2 FAC 0+1 Others 1*
Wrexham *(Free on 8/10/1999) FL 1*
Bury *(Free on 13/7/2000) FL 45+17/4 FLC 0+1 FAC 2+2 Others 3/1*
Wigan Ath *(£75,000 on 27/3/2002) FL 5*

JASZCZUN Antony (Tommy) John
Born: Kettering, 16 September 1977
Height: 5'10" **Weight:** 10.10
Club Honours: AMC '02
This left-sided defender had another good campaign for Blackpool in 2001-02 and was again a regular in the first-team squad throughout the campaign. A hard-working player who likes to get forward and support the attack, his only goal of the season came in the FA Cup tie against Newport County.
Aston Villa *(From trainee on 5/7/1996) FLC 0+1*
Blackpool *(£30,000 on 20/1/2000) FL 87+7 FLC 6 FAC 3/1 Others 9/1*

JAVARY Jean-Phillipe
Born: Montpellier, France, 10 January 1978
Height: 6'0" **Weight:** 12.6
International Honours: France: Yth (UEFA-U18 '96)
Jean-Phillipe had a trial with Partick Thistle in the early part of the 2001-02 campaign before moving back to Raith where he made a number of first-team appearances. He subsequently signed a short-term contract for Sheffield United in March. A combative midfielder he made an immediate impression with his non-stop running. Always looking to be involved and appearing comfortable when in possession, he showed himself to be a good winner of the ball, helping out in defence and supporting the attack. His efforts endeared him to the fans and

earned him a two-year contract at Bramall Lane.
Raith Rov *(Signed from Montpellier, France, ex ASOA Valence, RCD Espanyol, on 20/1/2000) SL 11+1*
Brentford *(Free on 18/8/2000) FL 4+2 FLC 2 Others 1*
Plymouth Arg *(Free on 28/2/2001) FL 4 (Freed during 2001 close season)*
Partick Thistle *(Free on 27/10/2001) SL 0+1*
Raith Rov *(Free on 24/11/2001) SL 7 SC 1*
Sheffield U *(Free on 15/3/2002) FL 6+1/1*

JEANNE Leon Charles
Born: Cardiff, 17 November 1980
Height: 5'8" **Weight:** 11.1
International Honours: W: U21-8; Yth
Although Leon made a couple of early-season appearances for Cardiff City last term, he spent much of the campaign battling against well-publicised off-the-field problems. However, he finished on a positive note and after a string of fine performances for the club's reserves he produced a useful display to help the Bluebirds to a 1-0 win over Swansea City in the FA Wales Premier Cup final. At his best he is a pacy and skilful winger or wide front man.
Queens Park R *(From trainee on 18/11/1997) FL 8+4*
Cardiff C *(Free on 12/7/2001) FL 0+2*

JEANNIN Alexandre (Alex)
Born: France, 30 December 1970
Height: 6'1" **Weight:** 11.12
This commanding left-sided central defender started the 2001-02 season on the bench for Darlington but forced his way into the side in September and had a run of 13 successive games forming a formidable partnership with club captain Craig Liddle. However he was out of favour with new manager Tommy Taylor his contract was cancelled in November and he returned to France.
Darlington *(Free from Troyes, France on 22/3/2001) FL 22 Others 2*

JEFFERS Francis
Born: Liverpool, 25 January 1981
Height: 5'10" **Weight:** 10.7
Club Honours: FAYC '98
International Honours: E: U21-9; Yth; Sch
After signing for Arsenal in a big money deal during the 2001 close season, Francis had a somewhat disappointing campaign at Arsenal last term, when he spent much of the time struggling with an ankle problem that eventually required surgery over the summer. He scored twice from two starts for the Gunners, but will be

looking to see much more regular Premiership action in 2002-03.
Everton *(From trainee on 20/2/1998) PL 37+12/18 FLC 2+2/1 FAC 6+1/1*
Arsenal *(£8,000,000 + on 27/6/2001) PL 2+4/2 FAC 1+1 Others 0+2*

JEFFREY Michael (Mike) Richard
Born: Liverpool, 11 August 1971
Height: 5'11" **Weight:** 11.6
Club Honours: AMC '96
The 2001-02 campaign proved to be another less than satisfactory season for this much travelled striker who found himself further down the pecking order at Grimsby Town. His appearances were mostly from the bench during the first half of the season and after the mid-season change of manager he found himself completely left out in the cold. He joined neighbours Scunthorpe United on loan in March and scored on his debut against Carlisle. He started another three matches up front for the Iron and showed a good work-rate and the ability to lead the line.
Bolton W *(From trainee on 9/2/1989) FL 9+6 FLC 1+2 FAC 1 Others 2+1*
Doncaster Rov *(£20,000 on 5/3/1992) FL 48+1/19 FLC 4 Others 2/1*
Newcastle U *(£60,000 on 4/10/1993) PL 2 FLC 1/1 Others 0+2*
Rotherham U *(£80,000 on 22/6/1995) FL 22/5 FLC 3/1 FAC 1 Others 3 (£205,000 to Fortuna Sittard, Holland on 16/1/1996)*
Kilmarnock *(Signed on 14/7/1999) SL 10+8/2 SLC 3+2/1 SC 1 Others 1+3*
Grimsby T *(Free on 10/8/2000) FL 19+28/3 FLC 4+2/1 FAC 1+1/1*
Scunthorpe U *(Loaned on 14/3/2002) FL 4+2/1*

JELLEYMAN Gareth Anthony
Born: Holywell, 14 November 1980
Height: 5'10" **Weight:** 10.6
International Honours: W: U21-1; Yth
Gareth had another frustrating time with injuries at Peterborough last season and never managed to stay fit long enough to establish himself in the side. A pacy young left back who is quick in the tackle, he will be hoping to enjoy an injury-free time in the 2002-03 campaign.
Peterborough U *(From trainee on 5/8/1998) FL 26+12 FAC 2+2 Others 7+1*

JEMSON Nigel Bradley
Born: Hutton, 10 October 1969
Height: 5'11" **Weight:** 12.10
Club Honours: FLC '90; AMC '96
International Honours: E: U21-1

Shrewsbury Town's club captain managed ten goals in 2001-02, despite the fact that this season ended prematurely after suffering a dislocated shoulder in the 2-2 home draw against Scunthorpe in February. He is an experienced striker who holds the ball up well and set up some excellent chances for his partner up front, Luke Rodgers.

Preston NE (From trainee on 6/7/1987) FL 28+4/8 FAC 2/1 Others 5+1/5
Nottingham F (£150,000 on 24/3/1988) FL 45+2/13 FLC 9/4 FAC 3+1/3 Others 1
Bolton W (Loaned on 23/12/1988) FL 4+1
Preston NE (Loaned on 15/3/1989) FL 6+3/2 Others 2/1
Sheffield Wed (£800,000 on 17/9/1991) F/PL 26+25/9 FLC 3+4 FAC 3+3/1 Others 2+2/1
Grimsby T (Loaned on 10/9/1993) FL 6/2 Others 1
Notts Co (£300,000 on 8/9/1994) FL 7+7/1 FLC 2+2/1 Others 1
Watford (Loaned on 12/1/1995) FL 3+1
Rotherham U (Loaned on 15/2/1996) FL 16/5 Others 3/4
Oxford U (£60,000 on 23/7/1996) FL 68/27 FLC 12/6 FAC 2
Bury (£100,000 on 5/2/1998) FL 17+12/1 FLC 0+2 FAC 0+1
Ayr U (Free on 21/7/1999) SL 9+3/5 SLC 1
Oxford U (Free on 27/11/2000) FL 13+5
Shrewsbury T (Free on 21/7/2000) FL 69/25 FLC 3/1 FAC 2 Others 2

JENAS Jermaine Anthony

Born: Nottingham, 18 February 1983
Height: 5'11" **Weight:** 11.2
International Honours: E: U21-3; Yth
Jermaine showed real class in central midfield or out wide on the left for Nottingham Forest last term and in January he was sold to Newcastle United. He made his full debut for the Magpies in the white heat of the 'derby' at Sunderland and then settled down to a regular place in the side, looking fully at home at the higher level. Tall and willowy he is elegant and athletic with a fine turn of pace and seems mature beyond his years.

Nottingham F (From trainee on 19/2/2000) FL 29/4 FLC 2 FAC 2
Newcastle U (£5,000,000 on 5/2/2002) PL 6+6

JENKINS Iain

Born: Prescot, 24 November 1972
Height: 5'9" **Weight:** 11.12
International Honours: NI: 5; B-1
After recovering from long-term injury Iain began the 2001-02 season with hopes of an injury-free run for Shrewsbury Town. However the left-sided defender struggled to find his best form and he soon moved on to Chester City, initially on loan and then permanently.

Everton (From trainee on 4/6/1991) PL 3+2 FLC 0+1
Bradford C (Loaned on 31/12/1992) FL 6 Others 1
Chester C (Free on 13/8/1993) FL 155+5/1 FLC 7+2 FAC 11+1 Others 12
Dundee U (Signed on 27/3/1998) SL 13+1 SLC 1 SC 2
Shrewsbury T (Free on 11/7/2000) FL 19+2 FLC 2 FAC 1+1 Others 1

JENKINS Lee David

Born: Pontypool, 28 June 1979
Height: 5'9" **Weight:** 11.0
Club Honours: Div 3 '00
International Honours: W: U21-9; Yth; Sch
Lee started the 2001-02 season at right wing back for Swansea, but then suffered a medial ligament injury to the left knee in October. He eventually made a come back but encountered further problems which sidelined him for the remainder of the season. His goal at Kidderminster in September was his first for the Swans since November 1996.

Swansea C (From trainee on 20/12/1996) FL 91+34/3 FLC 2+1 FAC 2+1 Others 8

JENKINS Stephen (Steve) Robert

Born: Merthyr Tydfil, 16 July 1972
Height: 5'11" **Weight:** 12.3
Club Honours: AMC '94
International Honours: W: 16; U21-2; Yth
Huddersfield's skipper was on the verge of being sold to Birmingham City at the beginning of the 2001-02 season, but the deal fell through. He went on to prove a revelation in the back four for the Terriers with only minor injuries and suspension keeping him out of the line-up. He was best used at right back where he was responsible for leading many an attack down the flanks. He scored a wonderful long-range effort in the 2-2 draw with Notts County. Steve continued to be a member of the Wales national squad during the campaign.

Swansea C (From trainee on 1/7/1990) FL 155+10/1 FLC 12+1 FAC 10+1 Others 26
Huddersfield T (£275,000 on 3/11/1995) FL 231+1/4 FLC 16 FAC 13 Others 5
Birmingham C (Loaned on 15/12/2000) FL 3 FLC 1

JENSEN Brian

Born: Copenhagen, Denmark, 8 June 1975
Height: 6'1" **Weight:** 12.4
Nicknamed the 'Beast', Brian acted as second fiddle to the in-form Russell Hoult in goal for West Bromwich Albion last term. He made only one first-team appearance during the season, in the 2-0 home defeat by Millwall in October.

West Bromwich A (£100,000 from AZ Alkmaar, Holland, ex B93, Hvidovre, on 3/3/2000) FL 46 FLC 4

JENSEN Claus William

Born: Nykobing, Denmark, 29 April 1977
Height: 5'11" **Weight:** 12.6
International Honours: Denmark: 15; U21-17
Now established in the Danish international side, Claus was absent for most of the second half of Charlton's season with a knee injury and he was sorely missed. Whilst in the side he put in some outstanding displays in midfield. Extremely comfortable on the ball, he is able to run with ease with the ball at his feet, and is not afraid to hit a 40-yard pass. He is also extremely dangerous at corners and set pieces, having the ability to bend a free kick into the goal from the edge of the penalty area. He only scored one goal during the campaign, but his delightful chip against Arsenal at Highbury was voted 'Goal of the Season' by the Addicks' supporters.

Bolton W (£1,600,000 from Lyngby, Denmark, ex Naestved, on 14/7/1998) FL 85+1/8 FLC 12/2 FAC 6 Others 5
Charlton Ath (£4,000,000 on 21/7/2000) PL 53+3/6 FLC 4 FAC 2

JENSEN Niclas

Born: Denmark, 17 August 1974
Height: 5'11" **Weight:** 12.3
Club Honours: Div 1 '02
International Honours: Denmark: 11
Niclas joined Manchester City in January, arriving from FC Copenhagen, where he had played in the left-back position. At Maine Road he slotted in as a left wing back making his debut at Watford. Thereafter he featured in every game for City, linking well with the midfield and making intelligent runs down the left flank. His only goal for the Blues was at St Andrew's when he converted a Darren Huckerby cross to equalise on the stroke of half time against Birmingham City.

Manchester C (£700,000 from FC Copenhagen, Denmark, ex Lyngby, on 16/1/2002) FL 16+2/1 FAC 2

215

Eoin Jess

JERVIS David John
Born: Retford, 18 January 1982
Height: 5'9" **Weight:** 11.3
David played well when called upon by Mansfield Town in 2001-02 but his opportunities were restricted due to the form of Martin Pemberton and AllenTankard. He made his first appearance of the season in the LDV Vans Trophy defeat by Blackpool and eventually got off the bench to produce some impressive performances in the Third Division, playing in his regular left full back position. Although relatively small in stature he is strong in the tackle and distributes the ball well. His campaign effectively ended in February following an injury on the training ground.
Mansfield T (From trainee on 3/7/2000) FL 17+8 FAC 2 Others 0+1

JESS Eoin
Born: Aberdeen, 13 December 1970
Height: 5'9" **Weight:** 11.10
Club Honours: SLC '89
International Honours: S: 18; B-2; U21-14
Eoin was Bradford City's leading scorer last term with 14 goals, an excellent tally for a midfielder. He had an outstanding campaign and played in more first-team games for the Bantams than anyone else. He is very strong in tackle yet also shows some silky passing skills. He played a few games up front to cover for injuries but his preferred role was in the centre of midfield.
Aberdeen (Free from Glasgow R juniors on 13/11/1987) SL 167+34/50 SLC 19+2/4 SC 14+2/3 Others 8+2/6
Coventry C (£1,750,000 on 24/2/1996) PL 28+11/1 FLC 1 FAC 4/2
Aberdeen (£700,000 on 3/7/1997) SL 108+3/29 SLC 8+1/1 SC 6/1
Bradford C (Free on 29/12/2000) P/FL 60+2/17 FLC 2 FAC 2

JEVONS Philip (Phil)
Born: Liverpool, 1 August 1979
Height: 5'11" **Weight:** 11.10
Club Honours: FAYC '98
Signed by Grimsby Town in the 2001 close season, this young striker proved an instant hit at Blundell Park, forming a useful partnership up front with local product Jonny Rowan. He went on to become the Mariners top scorer in the first half of the campaign netting eight times including a volley in the dying seconds of extra time at Anfield to knock Liverpool out of the Worthington Cup. The new year saw a loss of form and his appearances were largely on the

substitutes' bench under the new management. He was due to undergo surgery for a long-standing cartilage problem during the summer break but will be seeking to re-establish his place in the line-up during 2002-03.
Everton (From trainee on 10/11/1997) PL 2+6 FLC 1
Grimsby T (£150,000 + on 26/7/2001) FL 25+6/6 FLC 4/2 FAC 2

JIHAI Sun
Born: Dalian, China, 30 September 1977
Height: 5'10" **Weight:** 10.12
International Honours: China: 59
This versatile defender arrived at Manchester City last February to aid the final push for the First Division title and promotion. He featured on a number of occasions in a wing-back role, but with competition for places fierce, he soon found himself dropping back to the bench. Solid in defence and creative coming forward, he was included in China's squad for the World Cup finals.
Crystal Palace (£500,000 from Dalian Wanda, China on 10/9/1998) FL 22+1 FLC 1 FAC 1 (£500,000 to Dalian Wanda, China on 27/7/1999)
Manchester C (£2,000,000 on 26/2/2002) FL 2+5

JOACHIM Julian Kevin
Born: Boston, 20 September 1974
Height: 5'6" **Weight:** 12.2
International Honours: E: U21-9; Yth; (UEFA-U18 '93)
Julian had a miserable season at Coventry last term after suffering a serious ankle injury in the first pre-season friendly in Ireland. He recovered sufficiently to make three appearances in early September but in the third game his ankle problems returned and he was on the sidelines again until late November. Several substitute appearances failed to demonstrate his full fitness despite a well-taken goal, his only one of the season, against Bradford and he made only three further starts during the campaign.
Leicester C (From trainee on 15/9/1992) F/PL 77+22/25 FLC 7+2/3 FAC 4+1/1 Others 4+2/2
Aston Villa (£1,500,000 on 24/2/1996) PL 90+51/40 FLC 10+1/3 FAC 8+4/2 Others 6+3/1
Coventry C (Signed on 11/7/2001) FL 4+12/1 FLC 1 FAC 1

JOB Josephe-Desire
Born: Lyon, France, 1 December 1977
Height: 5'10" **Weight:** 11.3
International Honours: Cameroon: 37 (ANC '00)

This pacy striker received a few early-season outings for Middlesbrough last term, but then faded from the first-team picture. In January he joined Metz on loan and this seemed to kick-start his campaign, for he went on to win a return for the Cameroon national team and made the final 23 for the 2002 World Cup finals.
Middlesbrough (£3,000,000 from RC Lens, France, ex Lyon, on 7/8/2000) PL 11+5/3 FLC 1+2

JOBSON Richard Ian
Born: Holderness, 9 May 1963
Height: 6'1" **Weight:** 13.5
Club Honours: Div 2 '91
International Honours: E: B-2
This veteran central defender made just a single appearance for Tranmere at the beginning of last season before moving on to Rochdale where he soon forged a successful partnership with Gareth Griffiths. Not the fastest of defenders, he more than made up for this with his reading of the game and proved a steadying influence at the back for Dale. He missed only one game after his arrival and even netted a brace of goals against York, but he was injured early on in the second leg of the play-off semi-final that ended in defeat.
Watford (£22,000 from Burton A on 5/11/1982) FL 26+2/4 FLC 2 FAC 0+1 Others 5+1
Hull C (£40,000 on 7/2/1985) FL 219+2/17 FLC 12 FAC 13/1 Others 9
Oldham Ath (£460,000 on 30/8/1990) P/FL 188+1/10 FLC 19/1 FAC 13 Others 4
Leeds U (£1,000,000 on 26/10/1995) PL 22/1 FLC 3 FAC 1
Southend U (Loaned on 23/1/1998) FL 8/1
Manchester C (Free on 12/3/1998) FL 49+1/4 FLC 4+1 FAC 2
Watford (Loaned on 7/11/2000) FL 2
Tranmere Rov (Free on 28/12/2000) FL 17 FAC 5
Rochdale (Free on 28/9/2001) FL 34+1/3 FAC 3 Others 4

JOHANSSON Jonatan (JJ) Lillebror
Born: Stockholm, Sweden, 16 August 1975
Height: 6'1" **Weight:** 12.8
Club Honours: SPL '99, '00; SLC '99
International Honours: Finland: 39
JJ couldn't quite repeat his scoring record of the previous season but nevertheless had a good season playing up front for Charlton last term. The Finnish international is very quick, possesses a powerful shot and is able to set up goals

Phil Jevons

for other players using his pace and ability to turn defenders. Although used mainly as a striker, he can also play wide on the left, a position he sometimes occupies for his international side. He linked up well with Shaun Bartlett and Jason Euell, and found the net on five occasions including a spectacular overhead kick against West Ham at the Valley.

Glasgow R (From FC Flora Tallinn, Estonia, ex TPS Turku, on 13/8/1997) SL 22+25/14 SLC 4/1 SC 2+4/3 Others 9+8/7
Charlton Ath (£3,250,000 + on 1/8/2000) PL 48+13/16 FLC 4/3 FAC 1+1

JOHANSSON Nils-Eric
Born: Stockholm, Sweden, 13 January 1980
Height: 6'1" **Weight:** 12.7
Club Honours: FLC '02
International Honours: Sweden: U21-21
This young central defender joined Blackburn mid-way through the 2001-02 season and initially received his opportunities in the Worthington Cup where his goal against Manchester City qualifies as one of the club's goals of the season. Loping elegantly out of the left side of defence he brilliantly left an opponent for dead on the edge of the area before producing a deadly finish. Quick and strong in the tackle he is less assured in the air and has a high degree of consistency about his play, being removed from the first team after a disastrous display at Leicester.
Blackburn Rov (£2,700,000 from Nuremburg, Germany, ex Brommapojkarna, AIK Solna, Bayern Munich, on 5/10/2001) PL 14+6 FLC 5/1 FAC 3/1

JOHN Stern
Born: Trinidad, 30 October 1976
Height: 6'1" **Weight:** 12.12
International Honours: Trinidad & Tobago
This big striker was to some extent a victim of the small print of his transfer deal from Columbus Crew last term for after it was revealed that Nottingham Forest would have to pay his previous club £90,000 a goal once he had netted 15 times he was allowed to join Birmingham City for a cut-price fee. He made an immediate impact at St Andrew's by scoring the winner on his debut against Barnsley and went on to net seven in 15 appearances. His poise, close control and ability on the ball provided the team with a new dimension for the run-in and he played his part in the play-off final against Norwich, netting the vital first spot kick for Blues in the decisive penalty shoot-out.

Nottingham F (£1,500,000 + from Columbus Crew, USA on 22/11/1999) FL 49+23/18 FLC 3/2 FAC 4+1
Birmingham C (Free on 8/2/2002) FL 15/7 Others 3/1

JOHNROSE Leonard (Lenny)
Born: Preston, 29 November 1969
Height: 5'10" **Weight:** 12.6
Club Honours: Div 2 '97
Injuries contributed in large part to what was virtually a wasted year for Lenny, Burnley's midfield ball-winner. The first three months of the season saw him sidelined with an achilles problem from the previous campaign, and he made no more than cameo appearances before further injury left him frustrated again. Lenny was released at the end of the season.
Blackburn Rov (From trainee on 16/6/1988) FL 20+22/11 FLC 2+1/1 FAC 0+3 Others 2
Preston NE (Loaned on 21/1/1992) FL 1+2/1
Hartlepool U (£50,000 on 28/2/1992) FL 59+7/11 FLC 5+1/4 FAC 5/1 Others 5
Bury (Signed on 7/12/1993) FL 181+7/19 FLC 16+2/2 FAC 9/1 Others 9/1
Burnley (£225,000 on 12/2/1999) FL 46+26/4 FLC 2 FAC 1+2/1 Others 1

JOHNSEN Jean Ronny
Born: Norway, 10 June 1969
Height: 6'2" **Weight:** 13.2
Club Honours: PL '97, '99, '01; CS '97; FAC '99; EC '99
International Honours: Norway: 48
This classy midfielder or central defender made a welcome return to first-team action for Manchester United following a horrific catalogue of knee problems. More importantly, he showed that he had lost none of his razor-sharp reflexes in dealing with the most elusive of attackers. With a steady partnership blossoming with Wes Brown in early August, and a goal against Ipswich in the Premiership to add to his tally in September, the injury jinx struck again during the Champions' League qualifier against Deportivo in October and he was forced into another lengthy lay-off. He returned to a regular place in the line-up in February before being sidelined again with hamstring trouble.
Manchester U (£1,200,000 from Besiktas, Turkey, ex Lyn, Lillestrom, on 26/7/1996) PL 85+14/7 FLC 3 FAC 8+2/1 Others 35+3/1

JOHNSON Andrew (Andy)
Born: Bedford, 10 February 1981
Height: 5'9" **Weight:** 9.7
International Honours: E: Yth
This young striker began the 2001-02 season in electric form for Birmingham

City, using his pace and direct style to good effect. He scored four goals in as many games including two in a scintillating performance against Burnley at St Andrew's. Unfortunately he then pulled his hamstring and lost out firstly to Marcelo and later on to Stern John.
Birmingham C (From juniors on 11/3/1998) FL 44+39/8 FLC 6+9/5 FAC 1 Others 1+3

JOHNSON Andrew (Andy) James
Born: Bristol, 2 May 1974
Height: 6'0" **Weight:** 13.0
Club Honours: Div 1 '98
International Honours: E: Yth. W: 7
Andy began the 2001-02 campaign at Nottingham Forest but was sold to West Brom in a cut-price deal at the beginning of September. He slotted straight into Albion's style of play and went on to produce a series of outstanding performances, scoring some vital goals, including the winner in the League game against rivals Birmingham City at St Andrew's and a great header which earned Albion an FA Cup victory at Premiership Sunderland. He was injured in the abandoned League game at Sheffield United, but recovered full fitness after a four-match absence to help the Baggies storm through to promotion.
Norwich C (From trainee on 4/3/1992) F/PL 56+10/13 FLC 6+1/2 FAC 2
Nottingham F (£2,200,000 on 4/7/1997) P/FL 102+17/9 FLC 6+1/1 FAC 2
West Bromwich A (£200,000 on 19/9/2001) FL 28+4/4 FAC 4/1

JOHNSON Damien Michael
Born: Lisburn, 18 November 1978
Height: 5'9" **Weight:** 11.2
Club Honours: FLC '02
International Honours: NI: 16; U21-11; Yth
Damien falls between two positions in that he appears best suited to central midfield, particularly as he never pulls out of a tackle, but his speed makes him equipped to play wide right. He scored twice for Blackburn, including a devastating finish in the Worthington Cup tie against Manchester City. He was surprisingly allowed to join Birmingham City in the new year where he impressed by scoring on his home debut against Grimsby and won a quick return to the Premiership via the play-offs.
Blackburn Rov (From trainee on 2/2/1996) P/FL 43+17/3 FLC 12+3/1 FAC 3+4 Others 0+1

Nottingham F (Loaned on 29/1/1998) FL 5+1
Birmingham C (Signed on 8/3/2002) FL 5+4/1 Others 1

JOHNSON David Anthony

Born: Kingston, Jamaica, 15 August 1976
Height: 5'6" **Weight:** 12.3
Club Honours: FAYC '95; Div 2 '97
International Honours: E: B-1; Sch. Jamaica: 4

David never seemed to settle at Nottingham Forest last season and in February he joined Sheffield Wednesday on loan. He failed to score in his first five games for the Owls but then netted in consecutive matches before an injury saw him return to the City Ground. He later joined Burnley, also on loan, where he linked up with his former manager Stan Ternent. He got off to a great start, netting against local rivals Preston and equalling a club record by scoring in each of his first four games at Turf Moor. A fast and extremely tricky striker, he was told he could leave Forest on a free transfer in the summer.

Manchester U (From trainee on 1/7/1994) Bury (Free on 5/7/1995) FL 72+25/18 FLC 8+3/4 FAC 1+1 Others 3+2/1
Ipswich T (£800,000 on 14/11/1997) P/FL 121+10/55 FLC 13/5 FAC 7/2 Others 7
Nottingham F (£3,000,000 + on 12/1/2001) FL 36+5/5 FLC 2 FAC 0+1
Sheffield Wed (Loaned on 5/2/2002) FL 7/2
Burnley (Loaned on 12/3/2002) FL 8/5

JOHNSON Gavin

Born: Stowmarket, 10 October 1970
Height: 5'11" **Weight:** 12.0
Club Honours: Div 2 '92; Div 3 '97
This left-sided player enjoyed a 14-game run in Colchester United's starting line-up during the first half of the 2001-02 season, cracking home a delightful left-footed goal from long range in the 3-1 home win over Cambridge. However he hardly figured after November due to a succession of injuries to his groin and hip. An experienced campaigner, either as a left-back or central midfielder, his distribution is rarely wasteful.

Ipswich T (From trainee on 1/3/1989) P/FL 114+18/11 FLC 10+1/2 FAC 12/2 Others 3+1/1
Luton T (Free on 4/7/1995) FL 4+1
Wigan Ath (£15,000 on 15/12/1995) FL 82+2/8 FLC 4 FAC 3 Others 1
Dunfermline Ath (Free on 1/7/1998) SL 18 SC 0+1
Colchester U (Free on 12/11/1999) FL 76+8/3 FLC 3+1 FAC 3 Others 2

JOHNSON Jermaine

Born: Kingston, Jamaica, 25 June 1980
Height: 5'9" **Weight:** 11.5
International Honours: Jamaica: Jermaine only figured in ten Premiership games for Bolton last term, but he showed enough to suggest that he may well become an important player for the club. A pacy and tricky midfielder, he did well against Newcastle and Arsenal and is certainly not afraid to take on the very best players.

Bolton W (£750,000 from Tivoli Gardens, Jamaica on 19/9/2001) PL 4+6 FLC 2 FAC 1+1

JOHNSON Leon Dean

Born: Shoreditch, 10 May 1981
Height: 6'0" **Weight:** 12.4
After featuring in the Southend United midfield for the first 20 games of the 2001-02 season, Leon lost his place and eventually ended up being released by the club. He also played at full back on occasions, but never really established himself in either position despite some strong-tackling displays.

Southend U (From trainee on 17/11/1999) FL 43+5/3 FLC 1 FAC 1+3 Others 8

JOHNSON Marvin Anthony

Born: Wembley, 29 October 1968
Height: 6'0" **Weight:** 13.6
A rare commodity in the modern game, Marvin has spent his entire career with one club and when he appeared for Luton in the opening game of the 2001-02 season he became one of a handful of players to have played in every division. Club captain, he is popular with his fellow players and fans, but a long-standing neck problem and a series of niggling leg injuries saw the veteran defender mostly confined to the bench last term. The highlight of his season was when he scored the equalising goal after coming off the bench against Hartlepool to earn the Hatters a valuable point.

Luton T (From apprentice on 12/11/1986) FL 352+21/7 FLC 27+2/2 FAC 19+1/1 Others 14

JOHNSON Michael Owen

Born: Nottingham, 4 July 1973
Height: 5'11" **Weight:** 11.12
Club Honours: AIC '95
International Honours: Jamaica: 7
Michael feared for his future at Birmingham City when Steve Bruce took over as manager because he couldn't get in the team. He decided to undergo a gruelling personal fitness regime and lost weight. When his chance came he was excellent, attacking the ball with

determination and marking opponents out of the game. He is a quick and skilful defender and although small he compensates for his lack of inches with a prodigious leap.

Notts Co (From trainee on 9/7/1991) FL 102+5 FLC 9 FAC 4 Others 15+1
Birmingham C (£225,000 on 1/9/1995) FL 222+34/13 FLC 25+6/5 FAC 6+3 Others 11

JOHNSON Roger

Born: Ashford, 28 April 1983
Height: 6'3" **Weight:** 11.0
This tall defender became Wycombe's find of the season in 2001-02 when unexpectedly called into action in January as cover for the injured first choice central defenders. The maturity of his dominating performances was astonishing given his 19 years and lack of previous experience. He scored his first goal for the club at home to Notts County, taking advantage of a goalkeeping error, and was a constant threat at set pieces. His run in the team was cut short by a knee cartilage problem but he will be hoping to return to the line-up in 2002-03.

Wycombe W (From trainee on 10/7/2001) FL 7+2/1 Others 1+1

JOHNSON Ross Yorke

Born: Brighton, 2 January 1976
Height: 6'0" **Weight:** 12.12
The highlight of the 2001-02 season for Ross was drilling home a dramatic winner in Colchester United's 3-2 victory at Wigan in November, his only goal for the club. Injury caused him to miss the start of the campaign, but he was a regular in the U's back four from October until the turn of the year. He only started two more games and was released shortly before the end of the campaign. He is a right-sided central defender with a powerful long throw.

Brighton & Hove A (From trainee on 22/7/1994) FL 113+19/2 FLC 3+3 FAC 4 Others 4+1
Colchester U (Free on 12/1/2000) FL 47+5/1 FAC 2 Others 1

JOHNSON Seth Art Maurice

Born: Birmingham, 12 March 1979
Height: 5'10" **Weight:** 11.0
International Honours: E: 1; U21-15; Yth
Seth was a regular for Derby County early on last season before making a big-money move to Leeds United in October. Unfortunately he then suffered from the Elland Road 'injury jinx' as a blood clot on the knee kept him out of the first-

team picture in the first two months of the new year. A gifted young player, he was mostly used in a central midfield role by United.
Crewe Alex (From trainee on 12/7/1996) FL 89+4/6 FLC 5 FAC 2/1 Others 0+3
Derby Co (£3,000,000 on 21/5/1999) PL 73/2 FLC 6+1 FAC 0+1
Leeds U (£7,000,000 + on 19/10/2001) PL 12+2

JOHNSON Thomas (Tommy)
Born: Newcastle, 15 January 1971
Height: 5'11" **Weight:** 12.8
Club Honours: FLC '96; SPD '01; SLC 00; SC '01
International Honours: E: U21-7
This experienced striker was out of the first-team picture at Celtic and joined Sheffield Wednesday on loan shortly after the start of the 2001-02 campaign. He never really made much impact for the First Division club and in December he moved on to Kilmarnock where he went on to record a respectable tally of seven goals from ten appearances.
Notts Co (From trainee on 19/1/1989) FL 100+18/47 FLC 7+2/5 FAC 3+2/1 Others 14+3/4
Derby Co (£1,300,000 on 12/3/1992) FL 91+7/30 FLC 9+1/2 FAC 5/1 Others 16/8
Aston Villa (£1,450,000 on 6/1/1995) PL 38+19/13 FLC 5/2 FAC 5+2/1 Others 1+1/1
Glasgow Celtic (£2,400,000 on 27/3/1997) SL 23+12/18 SLC 3+1/3 SC 2+4 Others 0+3/1
Everton (Loaned on 24/9/1999) PL 0+3
Sheffield Wed (Loaned on 8/9/2001) FL 8/3 FLC 1

JOHNSSON Julian (JJ) Schantz
Born: Faroe Islands, 24 February 1975
Height: 6'1" **Weight:** 12.10
International Honours: Faroe Isles: 43
'JJ' became the first Faroe Islands international to play in the English Football League when he joined Hull, and also became the third current international at the Third Division club. Although born in Denmark, Julian qualifies for the Islands through parentage. A strong, mobile, right-footed central midfielder, his height was used to good effect in the middle of the park as well as further forward.
Hull C (£50,000 from Sogndal, Norway on 5/7/2001) FL 38+2/4 FLC 2 FAC 2/1 Others 2+1

JOHNSTON Allan
Born: Glasgow, 14 December 1973
Height: 5'9" **Weight:** 11.0
Club Honours: Div 1 '99
International Honours: S: 15; B-2; U21-3

This tricky winger began the 2001-02 season with Rangers before signing for Middlesbrough at the beginning of September. He was a regular in the line-up in his early days at the Riverside, scoring in his second game for Boro' when they defeated West Ham 2-0. He later returned for another run in the side towards the end of the campaign.
Heart of Midlothian (Free from Tynecastle BC on 23/6/1990) SL 46+38/12 SLC 3+2/2 SC 4+1 (Signed for Rennes, France during 1996 close season)
Sunderland (£550,000 on 27/3/1997) FL 82+4/19 FLC 8+1/1 FAC 3 Others 3
Birmingham C (Loaned on 15/10/1999) FL 7+2 FLC 1
Bolton W (Free on 21/1/2000) FL 17+2/3 FAC 2 Others 2/1
Glasgow R (Free on 13/6/2000) SL 10+4 SLC 0+2 SC 2+1/1
Middlesbrough (£1,000,000 on 5/9/2001) PL 13+4/1 FLC 1 FAC 2+1

JOKANOVIC Slavisa
Born: Novi Sad, Yugoslavia, 16 August 1968
Height: 6'3" **Weight:** 13.10
International Honours: Yugoslavia: 64
The 2001-02 season was another difficult one for the tall Chelsea midfielder who found himself behind new signings Frank Lampard and Emmanuel Petit and also the emerging Sam Dalla Bona, and was mainly confined to a utility role. Slavisa has tried valiantly to win over a sceptical crowd and cannot be faulted for effort as his wholehearted approach demonstrates, even if he lacks the pace and subtlety of some Premiership opponents.
Chelsea (£1,700,000 from Deportivo la Coruna, Spain, ex Novi Sad, Vojvodina, Partizan Belgrade, Real Oviedo, Tenerife, on 16/10/2000) PL 19+20 FLC 3+1 FAC 3+4 Others 3

JONES Darren Lee
Born: Newport, 26 August 1983
Height: 6'0" **Weight:** 12.6
International Honours: W: Yth; Sch
This young Bristol City defender impressed when coming on as substitute in the defeat at Blackpool last April, and again took the eye on making his full debut in the final game of the season, when Stoke were held 1-1 at Ashton Gate. He also featured in a couple of LDV Vans Trophy games and was rewarded with a new two-year contract at the end of the campaign.
Bristol C (From trainee on 22/9/2000) FL 1+2 Others 0+3

JONES Gary
Born: Huddersfield, 6 April 1969
Height: 6'1" **Weight:** 12.9
Club Honours: Div 3 '98
This hard-working striker had a disappointing season at Halifax in 2001-02 and never really hit top form throughout the campaign. He netted just four goals, although these included two well-taken efforts in the Shaymen's fine 3-0 home victory against Lincoln City in January.
Doncaster Rov (Free from Rossington Main on 26/1/1989) FL 10+10/2 FLC 1 (Free to Grantham on 1/11/1989)
Southend U (£25,000 from Boston U, ex Kettering T, on 3/6/1993) FL 47+23/16 FLC 3/1 FAC 2 Others 6+1/2
Lincoln C (Loaned on 17/9/1993) FL 0+4/2 Others 0+1
Notts Co (£140,000 on 1/3/1996) FL 103+14/38 FLC 5+1/1 FAC 9+1/7 Others 2+1
Scunthorpe U (Loaned on 21/2/1997) FL 9+2/5
Hartlepool U (Signed on 10/3/1999) FL 42+3/7 FLC 2 FAC 2/1 Others 2+2
Halifax T (Free on 23/3/2000) FL 58+18/10 FLC 2+1 FAC 2+2 Others 3/2

JONES Gary Roy
Born: Birkenhead, 3 June 1977
Height: 5'10" **Weight:** 12.0
The Rochdale skipper was in fine form in central midfield last term, netting key goals in victories over Plymouth and Mansfield, and with a thunderous strike at Bristol Rovers. He subsequently followed Dale boss Steve Parkin to Barnsley where he went straight in the first team and remained there for the rest of the season. He is a hard-working midfielder who chases and harrasses opponents and is not afraid to shoot.
Swansea C (Signed from Caernarfon T on 11/7/1997) FL 3+5 FLC 0+1
Rochdale (Free on 15/1/1998) FL 123+17/22 FLC 4+1 FAC 6+3 Others 7+2/3
Barnsley (£175,000 on 30/11/2001) FL 25/1

JONES Gary Steven
Born: Chester, 10 May 1975
Height: 6'3" **Weight:** 14.0
Gary arrived at the City Ground with a reputation for being a versatile performer and underlined that in the 2000-01 season by producing a highly competent performance in a string of positions, but last season he had to wait until February before he made the first team. He only added one further appearance, although he had a few outings from the subs' bench.

Lee Jones (Stockport County)

Essentially a midfielder or defender, he is very strong in the tackle.
Tranmere Rov (From trainee on 5/7/1993) FL 117+61/28 FLC 17+2/2 FAC 9+2/3 Others 1+1
Nottingham F (Free on 3/7/2000) FL 24+12/2 FLC 1+1 FAC 1

JONES Thomas **Gethin**
Born: Llanbyther, 8 August 1981
Height: 5'11" **Weight:** 12.4
Gethin made steady progress after his recovery from a broken leg suffered in September 2000. He was a regular for Cardiff's reserve team in the Avon Insurance Combination last season and made three senior appearances – coming on from the subs' bench in the amazing 7-1 victory at Oldham and also appearing in two LDV Vans Trophy ties. He is a promising young central defender who will be looking to feature more regularly in 2002-03.
Cardiff C (Free from Carmarthen on 11/8/2000) FL 0+3 FLC 1 Others 1+1

JONES Jason Andrew
Born: Wrexham, 10 May 1979
Height: 6'2" **Weight:** 12.7
International Honours: W: U21-3; Yth
With no reserve-team fixtures at Swansea last term, Jason was limited to work on the training ground for most of the season apart from a substitute appearance for Wales U21s against Belarus in October. However he came into the side in the closing weeks of the campaign as a replacement for the injured Roger Freestone and although he conceded a number of goals, many of these were down to failings in the defensive unit in front of him.
Swansea C (From trainee at Liverpool on 29/12/1997) FL 10

JONES Keith Aubrey
Born: Dulwich, 14 October 1965
Height: 5'8" **Weight:** 11.2
Club Honours: Div 1 '00
International Honours: E: Yth; Sch
2001-02 was not the happiest of seasons for this veteran Reading midfielder, who had a run of four consecutive first-team games in September and again in December, but was otherwise confined to the substitutes' bench and reserve-team football. He lost his place to younger players, and it seemed his long and distinguished career in the Football League was coming to an end when he was given a free transfer at the end of the campaign. His final appearance came as a late substitute in the 2-2 draw at Cambridge United in March.

Chelsea (From apprentice on 16/8/1983) FL 43+9/7 FLC 9+2/3 FAC 1 Others 4+1
Brentford (£40,000 on 3/9/1987) FL 167+2/13 FLC 15/2 FAC 13/4 Others 16/1
Southend U (£175,000 on 21/10/1991) FL 88+2/11 FLC 4 FAC 5 Others 9/1
Charlton Ath (£150,000 on 16/9/1994) P/FL 142+16/6 FLC 6+1 FAC 4+3/1 Others 3
Reading (Free on 7/7/2000) FL 28+11 FAC 4/1 Others 2

JONES Lee
Born: Pontypridd, 9 August 1970
Height: 6'3" **Weight:** 14.4
Club Honours: AMC '94
Stockport County's first choice goalkeeper suffered a season blighted with injury problems in 2001-02 and spent long periods out of action. A freak training ground injury on Christmas Day put him out for two months and he hadn't been back in the side long when he suffered a broken collarbone in a collision with former County striker Laurent D'Jaffo at Sheffield United which effectively ended his season in early March. However, he remains Carlton Palmer's number-one 'keeper and is expected to be fully fit when the 2002-03 season begins.
Swansea C (£7,500 from AFC Porth on 24/3/1994) FL 6 Others 1
Bristol Rov (Signed on 7/3/1998) FL 76 FLC 6 FAC 7 Others 4
Stockport Co (£50,000 on 19/7/2000) FL 48+3 FLC 4 FAC 2

JONES Philip Lee
Born: Wrexham, 29 May 1973
Height: 5'9" **Weight:** 10.8
International Honours: W: 2; B-1; U21-14; Yth
Lee was hampered by hamstring trouble throughout the 2001-02 campaign and only rarely made the starting line-up for Barnsley, his contract being cancelled by mutual consent in March. Joining Wrexham on transfer deadline day, the return of the 'prodigal son' against Cambridge United was a five-star event and the five goals he scored equalled the club record set up 68 years earlier by Tommy Bamford. Sadly, the 'nap hand' was not enough to prevent the Robins from being relegated the same day. He also set another record by becoming the first player to have joined Wrexham on four separate occasions. Used mainly on the left side of midfield at Oakwell, he featured as an out-and-out striker for Wrexham where his explosive pace and eye for goal were readily apparent.
Wrexham (From trainee on 5/7/1991) FL 24+15/10 FLC 2 FAC 1+2/1 Others 4+1/2

Liverpool (£300,000 on 12/3/1992) PL 0+3 FLC 0+1
Crewe Alex (Loaned on 3/9/1993) FL 4+4/1
Wrexham (Loaned on 26/11/1996) FL 20/9
Wrexham (Loaned on 31/1/1997) FL 2+4
Tranmere Rov (£100,000 on 27/3/1997) FL 58+28/16 FLC 7+3/2 FAC 0+1
Barnsley (Free on 3/7/2000) FL 17+23/5 FLC 3+4/2 FAC 0+1 (Free to Oswestry T on 27/3/2002)
Wrexham (Loaned on 28/3/2002) FL 3+1/5

JONES Mark Andrew
Born: Walsall, 7 September 1979
Height: 5'9" **Weight:** 11.7
International Honours: E: Yth; Sch
Mark was unable to make much impression at Chesterfield last season, despite fairly regular run-outs from the bench. Although a willing and eager chaser, it became clear that he would be unable to give the team the guile they were lacking up front, and others were brought in. He moved on to Raith Rovers in November.
Wolverhampton W (From trainee on 25/9/1996) FL 0+3 FLC 0+2
Cheltenham T (Loaned on 4/10/1999) FL 3
Chesterfield (Free on 9/8/2000) FL 1+8 FAC 0+1 Others 1+2/1

JONES Matthew Graham
Born: Llanelli, 1 September 1980
Height: 5'11" **Weight:** 11.5
Club Honours: FAYC '97
International Honours: W: 11; B-1; U21-7; Yth
This central midfield player netted his first Leicester City goal in the home fixture with Middlesbrough, but generally suffered injuries whenever he threatened to establish himself in the team last season. He took a while to earn selection under Dave Bassett, who questioned the fitness levels of the whole squad, then suffered cruciate ligament damage at Anfield in January to put him on the sidelines for a year just when he had looked set for a longer run in the team.
Leeds U (From trainee on 3/9/1997) PL 11+12 FLC 1+1 FAC 0+2 Others 4+2
Leicester C (£3,250,000 on 13/12/2000) PL 16+5/1 FLC 1+1 FAC 4

JONES Nathan Jason
Born: Rhondda, 28 May 1973
Height: 5'7" **Weight:** 10.12
Club Honours: Div 3 '01
Nathan predominantly played as a winger for Brighton last season, but also covered for Kerry Mayo at left back on occasions. He was effective when attacking

Paul Jones

defenders and often adopted a roaming role, coming infield from the flank. He possesses neat footwork, a jinking run and has also developed an effective long throw. He scored twice during the campaign including a strike from the edge of the box in the 1-1 draw at Wycombe. He spent much of the last quarter of the season on the bench but was rewarded with a new contract by manager Peter Taylor.

Luton T (£10,000 from Merthyr Tydfil on 30/6/1995. Freed on 20/12/1995)
Southend U (Free from Numancia, Spain on 5/8/1997) FL 82+17/2 FLC 6+2 FAC 3+1/1 Others 0+3
Scarborough (Loaned on 25/3/1999) FL 8+1
Brighton & Hove A (Free on 7/7/2000) FL 56+20/6 FLC 3+1/1 FAC 4+1 Others 3

JONES Paul Steven
Born: Chirk, 18 April 1967
Height: 6'3" **Weight:** 14.8
International Honours: W: 25
Paul has been Southampton's number one keeper since his arrival in 1997 and again produced some exceptional performances between the posts last season. He was an ever present until suffering a training ground injury two games before the end of the campaign, resulting in a minor operation on his right knee.

Wolverhampton W (£40,000 from Kidderminster Hrs on 23/7/1991) FL 33 FLC 2 FAC 5 Others 4
Stockport Co (£60,000 on 25/7/1996) FL 46 FLC 11 FAC 4 Others 4
Southampton (£900,000 on 28/7/1997) PL 171 FLC 16 FAC 10

JONES Scott
Born: Sheffield, 1 May 1975
Height: 5'10" **Weight:** 12.8
This utility defender started the 2001-02 season at left back for Bristol Rovers, but after losing his place had to be content with brief substitute appearances until a change of management in January saw him return to his preferred central defensive role. He was one of five Rovers players placed on the transfer list in March and he welcomed the opportunity to return to his native Yorkshire for an end-of-season loan spell at York City. He made a big impression at Bootham Crescent playing on the left side of the defence and scored the winner against Swansea with a fine header.

Barnsley (From trainee on 1/2/1994) F/PL 6+7/4 FLC 7/1 FAC 4+3/2
Mansfield T (Loaned on 7/8/1997) FL 6 FLC 2

Bristol Rov (£200,000 on 10/8/2000) FL 51+7/3 FLC 5 FAC 2 Others 2+1
York C (Loaned on 26/3/2002) FL 7+1/1

JONES Stephen (Steve) Gary
Born: Cambridge, 17 March 1970
Height: 6'1" **Weight:** 12.12
Steve was in excellent form for Bristol City at the start of the 2001-02 campaign, producing some scintillating displays although he never looked like becoming a regular goal-scorer. His battling qualities were sorely missed when a leg injury brought about a lengthy lay off. Strangely he wasn't afforded many first-team chances thereafter as City's season drifted into obscurity and with the club seeking to lower their wage bill he was put on the transfer list in the summer.

West Ham U (£22,000 from Billericay T on 16/11/1992) PL 8+8/4 FAC 2+2/1 Others 1+1
Bournemouth (£150,000 on 21/10/1994) FL 71+3/26 FLC 4/3 FAC 3/1 Others 3
West Ham U (Signed on 16/5/1996) PL 5+3 FLC 0+1 FAC 2 Others 1
Charlton Ath (£400,000 on 14/2/1997) P/FL 28+24/8 FLC 3+1 FAC 1 Others 1+2
Bournemouth (Loaned on 24/12/1997) FL 5/4 Others 1/1
Bristol C (£425,000 + on 10/9/1999) FL 29+7/7 FLC 4/1 FAC 2+1 Others 0+1
Brentford (Loaned on 21/1/2000) FL 6+2 Others 2
Southend U (Loaned on 17/3/2000) FL 9/2
Wycombe W (Loaned on 17/7/2000) FL 5 FLC 1

JONES Stephen (Steve) Graham
Born: Derry, 25 October 1976
Height: 5'4" **Weight:** 10.9
A close season signing from Leigh RMI, Steve joined Crewe with a reputation as a goal-scorer who could operate on either flank. He made his debut for the Railwaymen at Sheffield United in October 2001 and also made a further five appearances from the subs' bench. In the new year he went on loan to Rochdale, making his first appearance in the sensational 5-4 victory over York. Thereafter he appeared mainly in a wide role before being recalled to Gresty Road as cover.

Blackpool (Free from Chadderton on 30/10/1995)
Bury (Free on 23/8/1996. Free to Sligo Rov during 1997 close season)
Crewe Alex (£75,000 + from Leigh RMI, ex Bray W, Chorley, on 4/7/2001) FL 1+5
Rochdale (Loaned on 5/2/2002) FL 6+3/1

JONES Stephen (Steve) Robert
Born: Bristol, 25 December 1970
Height: 5'10" **Weight:** 12.2
Club Honours: Div 3 '00
Steve returned to Cheltenham during the 2001 close season, but after making the starting line-up for the first two games of the new campaign he suffered a serious ankle injury that kept him out of action for more than three months. On returning to match fitness he found that the central defensive partnership between Chris Banks and Michael Duff was firmly established and he rarely featured at first-team level before the end of the season. Steve is a solid defender who can play either at right back or in a more central role.

Swansea C (£25,000 from Cheltenham T on 14/11/1995) FL 140+6/4 FLC 2+1 FAC 9 Others 8
Cheltenham T (Free on 11/7/2001) FL 2+3

JONES William (Billy) Kenneth
Born: Chatham, 26 March 1983
Height: 6'0" **Weight:** 11.7
Billy had a lengthy spell in the Leyton Orient line-up last term as a replacement for the injured Matt Lockwood at left back. He showed a maturity beyond his age, always looking comfortable on the ball and with the vision to spray passes around the pitch. He is seen by many at Brisbane Road as an exciting prospect for the future.

Leyton Orient (From trainee on 10/7/2001) FL 17 FAC 3+1

[JORDAO] BATISTA Adelion Jose Martins
Born: Malange, Angola, 30 August 1971
Height: 6'3" **Weight:** 12.10
This tall, powerful midfielder has no real preference where he plays: right, centre or down the left. He was not always a first-choice selection by West Bromwich Albion manager Gary Megson last term, but when called upon he gave some excellent performances. He volleyed in the only goal of the League game against Wolves at Molineux and netted twice in a vital 4-1 home win over Crewe Alexandra in late March.

West Bromwich A (£350,000 from Sporting Braga, Portugal, ex Estrela Amadora, Campomaiorense, Lece, on 25/8/2000) FL 47+13/6 FLC 3+1/2 FAC 1 Others 0+2

JORGENSEN Claus Beck
Born: Denmark, 24 April 1979
Height: 5'11" **Weight:** 11.0

Claus joined Bradford City as a midfielder in the summer of 2001, but occasionally featured at right back last season, where he certainly didn't look out of place. Although used sparingly at the beginning of the campaign, he was a regular in the closing stages. Strong in the tackle and with good positional sense, he never seemed to get flustered and always gave 100 per cent whatever position he was playing in.
Bournemouth *(Free from AC Horsens, Denmark on 12/7/1999) FL 77+10/14 FLC 6/1 FAC 6 Others 1+1*
Bradford C *(Free on 23/7/2001) FL 13+5/1 FLC 2*

JORGENSEN Henrik
Born: Denmark, 12 January 1979
Height: 6'2" **Weight:** 14.0
This skilful and accomplished central defender found it impossible to win a regular place in the Notts County first-team squad last term and was restricted to a single start in the LDV Vans Trophy and four outings from the subs' bench. He was eventually released in the new year and returned to his former club B1909.
Notts Co *(Signed from B1909, Denmark, ex Odense BK, on 27/10/2000) FL 3+4 FLC 0+1 FAC 0+2 Others 2*

JOSEPH Marc Ellis
Born: Leicester, 10 November 1976
Height: 6'0" **Weight:** 12.10
Marc joined Peterborough United during the 2001 close season as a centre back but often featured as a full back last term. He was a near ever present in the team and finally broke his goal-scoring duck, netting in two consecutive matches. A calm and assured defender, he is strong in the tackle and distributes the ball accurately.
Cambridge U *(From trainee on 23/5/1995) FL 136+17 FLC 7 FAC 5+2 Others 7+1*
Peterborough U *(Free on 3/7/2001) FL 44/2 FLC 2 FAC 5 Others 2*

JOSEPH Matthew Nathanial
Born: Bethnal Green, 30 September 1972
Height: 5'8" **Weight:** 10.7
International Honours: E: Yth. Barbados: 2
Matthew was mainly used at right back by Leyton Orient last term, but he can also play in midfield and, despite his height, as a centre half. He was particularly effective moving forward, producing some surging runs and excellent crosses to set up chances for the forwards. A highlight of his season was

scoring with a diving header in the home game with Rochdale.
Arsenal *(From trainee on 17/11/1990)*
Gillingham *(Free on 7/12/1992)*
Cambridge U *(Signed on 19/11/1993) FL 157+2/6 FLC 6+1 FAC 7 Others 5*
Leyton Orient *(£10,000 on 22/1/1998) FL 159+4/2 FLC 8+1 FAC 13+1 Others 5+1*

Matthew Joseph

JOY Ian Paul
Born: San Diego, USA, 14 July 1981
Height: 5'10" **Weight:** 11.1
Ian provided much needed left-sided cover at Kidderminster and gave regular left back Scott Stamps some genuine competition. The form of Stamps meant that his opportunities were limited, but he never let the team down when called upon and became one of the most dependable members of the squad. Diminutive in stature, he is tigerish in the tackle and offers an extra attacking option when he makes overlapping runs on the left wing.
Tranmere Rov *(From trainee on 29/7/1998)*
Stirling A *(Free on 3/8/2000) SL 0+2 Others 1*
Montrose *(Free on 27/9/2000) SL 24+2/2 SC 3+1*
Kidderminster Hrs *(Free on 6/8/2001) FL 13+3 Others 1*

[JUAN] MALDONDO Duarte
Born: Sao Paulo, Brazil, 6 February 1982
Height: 5'6" **Weight:** 9.7
This young Arsenal defender stepped up to make his debut in senior football for

Arsenal in their Worthington Cup tie against Grimsby Town last November. He also made the starting line-up for the FA Cup tie against Gillingham and will be aiming to feature more regularly in 2002-03.
Arsenal *(Signed from Sao Paulo, Brazil on 9/7/2001) FLC 1 FAC 1*

[JUANJO] PEREZ Juanjo Carricondo
Born: Barcelona, Spain, 4 May 1977
Height: 5'7" **Weight:** 10.10
Juanjo joined Bradford City last November, but was overlooked for much of the time and spent long spells on the subs' bench. He is a live-wire striker whose dribbling and close control cause problems for the best of defenders. He scored in his first game for City with a header at Walsall but made just five starts for the Bantams.
Heart of Midlothian *(Free from Barcelona, Spain on 9/10/1998) SL 32+40/9 SLC 3+3 SC 4+3/2 Others 3*
Bradford C *(Free on 31/10/2001) FL 5+12/1 FAC 1*

JULES Mark Anthony
Born: Bradford, 5 September 1971
Height: 5'8" **Weight:** 11.1
Mark had another consistent season at full back for Halifax Town in 2001-02 and featured regularly throughout the campaign. He had plenty of work to do both on and off the field, and was called into action as the PFA's representative when the club went into administration in April.
Bradford C *(From trainee on 3/7/1990) FLC 0+1*
Scarborough *(Free on 14/8/1991) FL 57+20/16 FLC 6+2/2 FAC 1+1 Others 6/4*
Chesterfield *(£40,000 on 21/5/1993) FL 155+31/4 FLC 12+3/2 FAC 13+2 Others 10+*
Halifax T *(Free on 5/7/1999) FL 88+9/1 FLC FAC 3+1 Others 2*

JUPP Duncan Alan
Born: Guildford, 25 January 1975
Height: 6'0" **Weight:** 12.12
International Honours: S: U21-9
Duncan was very much a fringe first-team player at Wimbledon last season and only started one senior game, adding a couple more appearances from the subs' bench. An attack-minded right back, he deserved other chances to prove himself as he played consistently well in the reserves.
Fulham *(From trainee on 12/7/1993) FL 101+4/2 FLC 10+2 FAC 9+1/1 Others 9+1/1*
Wimbledon *(£125,000 + on 27/6/1996) P/F 23+7 FLC 8+2 FAC 3+2*

K

KABBA Stephen (Steve)
Born: Lambeth, 7 March 1981
Height: 5'10" **Weight:** 11.12
With Dougie Freedman and Clint
Morrison in such good form, this tall,
speedy and skilful striker only made the
Crystal Palace bench in mid-season last
term, despite scoring a double-figure tally
for the reserves. He then went on loan to
Luton Town on transfer deadline day and
did well in a couple of appearances from
the subs' bench.
*Crystal Palace (From trainee on 29/6/1999)
FL 2+4 FLC 0+1*
Luton T (Loaned on 28/3/2002) FL 0+3

KACHLOUL Hassan
Born: Agadir, Morocco, 19 February 1973
Height: 6'1" **Weight:** 11.12
International Honours: Morocco
Hassan arrived at Villa Park on a 'Bosman'
free transfer during the summer. He is a
hard-working creative midfielder with a
tremendous eye for goal. He experienced
mixed fortunes following his arrival. He
managed to secure a regular place in the
side, having only missed one game
through a hamstring problem until his
fortune changed in a Worthington Cup
tie at the end of November. Although he
completed the game he suffered
concussion, which subsequently ruled him
out of the next four games, and after the
turn of the year he struggled to secure a
regular place in the side.
*Southampton (£250,000 from St Etienne,
France, ex Nimes, Dunkerque, Metz, on
20/10/1998) PL 73+13/14 FLC 5 FAC 4+2/1*
*Aston Villa (Free on 1/7/2001) PL 17+5/2
FLC 2 Others 6+1*

KANDOL Tresor Osmar
Born: Zaire, 30 August 1981
Height: 6'2" **Weight:** 11.7
This tall striker joined Cambridge United
during the 2001 close season, but after a
couple of senior appearances he was
loaned out to Ryman League club
Heybridge Swifts. He was eventually
released in October and signed non-
contract forms for Bournemouth. He
made his debut at Wycombe soon
afterwards, but despite scoring in the LDV
Vans Trophy tie against Barnet he never
established himself in the line-up and was
released in the summer.
*Luton T (From trainee on 26/9/1998) FL
9+12/3 FLC 3+1/2 Others 0+1*

Cambridge U (Free on 24/8/2001) FL 2+2
*Bournemouth (Free on 12/10/2001) FL 3+9
FAC 0+2 Others 1/1*

KANOUTE Frederic
Born: Sainte Foy Les Lyon, France, 2
September 1977
Height: 6'4" **Weight:** 12.10
International Honours: France: B-1; U21
This West Ham striker is a handful for any
defence with his power and pace. He was
awesome in October when scoring a total
of four goals in successive wins against
Southampton, Chelsea and Ipswich. In
November he suffered a hamstring injury,
which forced him to miss several games
but he returned against Arsenal to score
with a brilliant volley. His pace and
trickery also helped set up goals for his
young partner Jermain Defoe. He again
finished as the club's top scorer in
Premiership matches with 11 goals.
*West Ham U (£4,000,000 from Lyon, France
on 23/3/2000) PL 67/24 FLC 3 FAC 5/4*

KANU Nwankwo
Born: Owerri, Nigeria, 1 August 1976
Height: 6'4" **Weight:** 13.3
Club Honours: CS '99; FAC '02; PL '02
International Honours: Nigeria: 38; U23
(OLYM '96); Yth (World-U17 '93)
This talented striker was again very much
on the edge of the Arsenal first-team
squad last term, making more
appearances from the subs' bench than in
the starting line-up. He went on to
feature for Nigeria in both the African
Nations' Cup and World Cup finals and
gained an FA Cup winners' medal as a
late substitute for Thierry Henry during
the Gunners' 2-0 victory over Chelsea.
*Arsenal (£4,500,000 from Inter Milan, Italy,
ex Fed Works, Iwuanyanwu National, Ajax,
on 4/2/1999) PL 51+42/24 FLC 3/2 FAC
3+10/3 Others 25+14/6*

KARLSSON Par
Born: Sweden, 29 May 1978
Height: 5'8" **Weight:** 10.10
International Honours: Sweden: U21
Par found his chances wide on the left
limited at Wimbledon last season due to
strong competition within the squad. He
came highly recommended from
Gothenburg but to date hasn't played the
best football of his career, although he
featured regularly in the club's reserves.
However, following Kevin Cooper's
departure he should get more
opportunities in the 2002-03 campaign.
*Wimbledon (£40,000 from IFK Gothenburg,
Sweden, ex Karlskoya, on 7/9/2000) FL 8+15
FLC 1 FAC 5/1*

KAVANAGH Graham Anthony
Born: Dublin, 2 December 1973
Height: 5'10" **Weight:** 12.11
Club Honours: AMC '00
International Honours: RoI: 3; B-1; U21-
9; Yth; Sch
Cardiff City's big-money signing lived up
to his reputation in 2001-02 and scored
several magnificent goals for the
Bluebirds. His tally of 15 included a
number of 'Goal of the Season'
contenders from long-range efforts and
free kicks, and the important first goal in
the memorable FA Cup win over Leeds
United. He accumulated a number of
bookings, but won wider recognition
from his colleagues when he was selected
for the PFA divisional team for the fourth
year in succession.
*Middlesbrough (Signed from Home Farm on
16/8/1991) F/PL 22+13/3 FLC 1 FAC 3+1/1
Others 7*
Darlington (Loaned on 25/2/1994) FL 5
*Stoke C (£250,000 + on 13/9/1996) FL
198+8/35 FLC 16+2/7 FAC 6 Others 15/4*
*Cardiff C (£1,000,000 on 6/7/2001) FL 43/13
FLC 1 FAC 4/2 Others 2*

KAWAGUCHI Yoshikatsu (Yoshi)
Born: Shizuoka, Japan, 15 August 1975
Height: 5'11" **Weight:** 12.5
International Honours: Japan: 43
This experienced international goalkeeper
joined Portsmouth for a substantial fee
last October and immediately attracted
enormous media attention from his home
country. He had the misfortune to concede
a goal after just 26 seconds on his debut
against Sheffield Wednesday, but after a
brief run behind an insecure defensive line
he gave way to the more experienced
Dave Beasant. An agile 'keeper who
distributes the ball well he made Japan's
squad for the World Cup finals.
*Portsmouth (£1,800,000 from Yokohama
Antlers, Japan on 24/10/2001) FL 11 FAC 1*

KAY Antony Roland
Born: Barnsley, 21 October 1982
Height: 5'11" **Weight:** 11.8
International Honours: E: Yth
Last season proved to be a frustrating
time for Antony and he rarely featured in
the first-team squad at Barnsley, playing
most of his football in the reserves. A
stylish midfielder he had a trial with
Northampton Town in mid-February. He
was tried as a centre back in the second
string on a number of occasions by new
boss Steve Parkin.
*Barnsley (From trainee on 25/10/1999) FL
3+5*

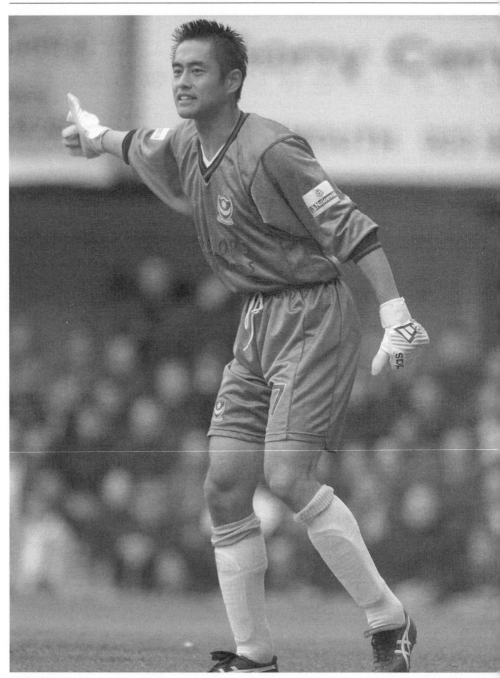

Yoshi Kawaguchi

KEANE Michael Thomas Joseph
Born: Dublin, 29 December 1982
Height: 5'7" **Weight:** 10.10
International Honours: RoI: U21-5; Yth
Young Irishman Michael strode onto the first-team scene at Preston late in the 2000-01 campaign and has become a fixture ever since. An all-action terrier in midfield, he progressed through the Republic of Ireland ranks, being called up by the U21s whilst only 18, and his club form followed a similar path. He scored his first goal against Wimbledon when his celebratory run will be long remembered. An exuberant player, he is raw and strongly left-sided, but the fans adore his total commitment and he has the potential to go far in the game. Michael was rested on the bench in late season to protect him from burn out, but he has done enough to cement his squad place for the foreseeable future.
Preston NE (From trainee on 7/8/2000) FL 17+5/2 FLC 0+1 FAC 3

KEANE Robert (Robbie) David
Born: Dublin, 8 July 1980
Height: 5'9" **Weight:** 11.10
International Honours: RoI: 37; B-1; Yth UEFA-U18 '98)
Signed initially on loan from Inter Milan, Robbie made the switch to Leeds permanently last summer in a multi-million pound deal. An immensely talented young striker, he started the 2001-02 season alongside Mark Viduka and began brightly, scoring a hat-trick in the 6-0 Worthington Cup victory at Leicester in October. He appeared to keep his best performances for the UEFA Cup and netted in the opening two rounds including a superb opening goal at Elland Road against Maritimo. However, after the arrival of Robbie Fowler in November, he was confined to substitute appearances, although he continued to be a crucial figure for the Republic of Ireland.
Wolverhampton W (From trainee on 26/7/1997) FL 66+7/24 FLC 7+2/3 FAC 3+2/2
Coventry C (£6,000,000 on 20/8/1999) PL 30+1/12 FAC 3 (£13,000,000 to Inter Milan, Italy on 31/7/1999)
Leeds U (£12,000,000 on 22/12/2000) PL 28+15/12 FLC 2/3 FAC 2 Others 6/3

KEANE Roy Maurice
Born: Cork, 10 August 1971
Height: 5'10" **Weight:** 12.10
Club Honours: FMC '92; CS '93, '96, '97; PL '94, '96, '97, '99, '00, '01; FAC '94, '96, '99

International Honours: RoI: 58; U21-4; Yth; Sch
If further proof was needed of that commonly held belief that Manchester United are an engine short of a dynamo without Roy Keane, his absence from late September to early November was a classic case in point. The team stumbled in the absence of his battling skills in midfield, although on his return he was initially deployed in the back four to stem the flow of goals conceded. A hamstring injury ruled him out in April, and then came the well-publicised spat that saw him ruled out of the World Cup finals. The inspirational midfield general received recognition from his fellow professionals for his efforts with a place in the PFA's Premiership team for the season.
Nottingham F (£10,000 from Cobh Ramblers on 12/6/1990) F/PL 114/22 FLC 17/6 FAC 18/3 Others 5/2
Manchester U (£3,750,000 on 22/7/1993) PL 233+8/29 FLC 9+2 FAC 33+1/1 Others 74+1/16

KEARNEY Thomas (Tom) James
Born: Liverpool, 7 October 1981
Height: 5'9" **Weight:** 11.0
Tom joined Bradford City last March on a one-year contract following a successful trial period. Despite being a bit light in stature he proved to be fearless in the tackle and won the 'Man of the Match' award on his first-team debut at Watford. He is a talented young midfielder with excellent distribution. His older sister Gillian is a well-known actress who has appeared in the film Shirley Valentine and also in Brookside.
Everton (From trainee on 15/10/1999)
Bradford C (Free on 21/3/2002) FL 5

KEATES Dean Scott
Born: Walsall, 30 June 1978
Height: 5'6" **Weight:** 10.10
This brave little midfielder suffered an achilles injury in an early-season game for Walsall at Crewe and on his recovery found it difficult to win back a regular place. When called upon he always gave of his best and banged home a penalty in the vital late-season draw at Millwall. Dean follows in the tradition of the Saddlers' home-grown diminutive 100 per cent midfielders.
Walsall (From trainee on 14/8/1996) FL 125+34/9 FLC 15+1/1 FAC 10+4 Others 14+1/3

KEEGAN Michael Jerard
Born: Wallasey, 12 May 1981
Height: 5'10" **Weight:** 11.0
Michael was only on the fringe of the first-team squad at Swansea last season and managed just two outings from the subs' bench. In November he had a trial at Kidderminster, where he featured in the reserves and early in the new year he went on loan to Merthyr. He was released by the Swans in February. He is a wide-right midfield player with neat control and the ability to cross a ball accurately.
Swansea C (From trainee on 5/7/1999) FL 7+3 FLC 1+1 FAC 1+1 Others 4

KEEN Kevin Ian
Born: Amersham, 25 February 1967
Height: 5'8" **Weight:** 10.10
International Honours: E: Yth; Sch
Despite the fact that he is now approaching veteran status, Kevin inspired the Macclesfield midfield for most of the 2001-02 season although he missed several weeks with a calf strain. A hard-working attacking midfielder he completed his 600th senior appearance during the campaign. Kevin was acting manager for a month prior to the appointment of David Moss and also gained his UEFA-'A' coaching certificate.
West Ham U (From apprentice on 8/3/1984) FL 187+32/21 FLC 21+1/5 FAC 15+7/1 Others 14+2/3
Wolverhampton W (£600,000 on 7/7/1993) FL 37+5/7 FLC 2+1 FAC 5/1 Others 4/1
Stoke C (£300,000 on 19/10/1994) FL 147+30/10 FLC 13+3/2 FAC 6 Others 3+1
Macclesfield T (Free on 11/9/2000) FL 59+3/2 FLC 2+1 FAC 4+1/1 Others 1

KEEN Peter Alan
Born: Middlesbrough, 16 November 1976
Height: 6'0" **Weight:** 12.0
Peter began 2001-02 as understudy to Luke Weaver at Carlisle and did not see first-team action until the end of September. Thereafter he kept his place with some confident performances. A good all-round 'keeper, who was voted the club's most improved player, he won several 'Man of the Match' citations during the season.
Newcastle U (From trainee on 25/3/1996)
Carlisle U (Free on 4/8/1999) FL 45/1 FAC 3 Others 1
Darlington (Loaned on 13/3/2001) FL 7

KEENAN Joseph (Joe) John
Born: Southampton, 14 October 1982
Height: 5'7" **Weight:** 10.8
International Honours: E: Yth
After a handful of unused substitute

outings this young left-sided midfielder finally made his first-team bow for Chelsea in February in the Premiership fixture at Villa Park. A week later he came on against Preston in the FA Cup fifth round tie and created Chelsea's third goal with a beautiful cross field ball which was put away by Mikael Forssell. He was one of five debutants during the season and with Claudio Ranieri's brief to lower the average age of the Blues' squad - Joe is well positioned to make a significant contribution over the coming seasons.
Chelsea (From trainee on 15/10/1999) PL 0+1 FAC 0+1

KEITH Joseph (Joe) Richard
Born: Plaistow, 1 October 1978
Height: 5'7" **Weight:** 10.6
Joe again made progress at Colchester last season, featuring regularly in the line at left back, left wing back or on the left-hand side of midfield. Not afraid to take on defenders, his mazy runs often brought him into the opposing penalty area, while he was also useful in dead-ball situations. He contributed five goals during the campaign including vital ones in the home win over Port Vale and the draws against Queen's Park Rangers and Blackpool.
West Ham U (From trainee on 9/7/1997)
Colchester U (Free on 5/7/1999) FL 99+14/8 FLC 5+2/2 FAC 3 Others 2+1

KEITH Marino
Born: Peterhead, 16 December 1974
Height: 5'10" **Weight:** 12.11
Club Honours: SCC '98; Div 3 '02
Marino made a couple of appearances for Livingston in the early part of the 2001-02 season before moving on to join Plymouth in November. A pacy attacker he contributed several valuable goals including a brace against Devon rivals Exeter City in February, a 'goal of the season' contender against Carlisle in April (a 20-yard first time volley from over his shoulder with his left foot) and finally a brace in the championship clinching victory away to Darlington.
Dundee U (Free from Fraserburgh on 11/10/1995) SL 0+4 SC 0+1
Falkirk (Free on 9/9/1997) SL 53+8/27 SLC 2/1 SC 7/1 Others 1+1
Livingston (Signed on 30/7/1999) SL 15+5/7 SLC 1+3 SC 2/3 Others 2
Plymouth Arg (Free on 8/11/2001) FL 13+10/9 FAC 0+2

KELL Richard
Born: Bishop Auckland, 15 September 1979
Height: 6'1" **Weight:** 10.13

International Honours: E: Sch
Turned down a new deal at Torquay to join Scunthorpe in mid-September after a successful trial. He became a key player in the centre of the Iron midfield with good passing skills, an excellent work rate and an eye for getting forward. He opened his goal account in the 7-1 victory over Darlington at the end of November but his season ended prematurely the following month when he suffered a broken leg against Hull. It is hoped that he will be fit enough to return to action pre-season.
Middlesbrough (From trainee on 2/7/1998)
Torquay U (Free on 8/2/2001) FL 15/3
Scunthorpe U (Free on 12/9/2001) FL 16/1 FAC 2 Others 3

KELLER Kasey C
Born: Washington DC, USA, 27 November 1969
Height: 6'2" **Weight:** 13.12
Club Honours: FLC '97
International Honours: USA: 60
Kasey joined Spurs in the 2001 close season as a back up to regular 'keeper Neil Sullivan. He eventually got his chance late in the campaign when Sullivan was sidelined by injury and made nine consecutive appearances, impressing the White Hart Lane faithful with his agility and sharp reflexes.
Millwall (Free from Portland University on 20/2/1992) FL 176 FLC 14 FAC 8 Others 4
Leicester C (£900,000 on 17/8/1996) PL 99 FLC 16 FAC 8 Others 2 (Signed for Rayo Vallecano, Spain during 1999 close season)
Tottenham H (Free on 16/8/2001) PL 9 FLC 2

KELLY Alan Thomas
Born: Preston, 11 August 1968
Height: 6'2" **Weight:** 14.3
International Honours: Rol: 34; U23-1; Yth
Alan began the 2001-02 season on loan at Birmingham as cover for injuries and made a superb debut against Walsall. He provided an assured presence behind the defence at St Andrew's, but much of the remainder of his campaign was blighted by a knee injury. His only senior appearance for Blackburn came in the FA Cup as Brad Friedel firmly kept a grip on the 'keeper's jersey.
Preston NE (From apprentice on 25/9/1985) FL 142 FLC 1 FAC 8 Others 13
Sheffield U (£200,000 on 24/7/1992) P/FL 213+3 FLC 15 FAC 22 Others 2
Blackburn Rov (£675,000 on 30/7/1999) P/FL 38+1 FLC 4 FAC 4
Stockport Co (Loaned on 3/4/2001) FL 2
Birmingham C (Loaned on 24/8/2001) FL 6

KELLY David Thomas
Born: Birmingham, 25 November 1965
Height: 5'11" **Weight:** 12.1
Club Honours: Div 1 '93
International Honours: Rol: 26; B-3; U23-1; U21-3
David joined Mansfield Town last February after being released by Motherwell and soon settled in, scoring two goals in only his second full appearance. His experience was invaluable during the run-in when the Stags were going for promotion and players were missing through injury and suspension. He is a hard-working striker who has a good goals-per-game record.
Walsall (Signed from Alvechurch on 21/12/1983) FL 115+32/63 FLC 11+1/4 FAC 12+2/3 Others 14+3/10
West Ham U (£600,000 on 1/8/1988) FL 29+12/7 FLC 11+3/5 FAC 6 Others 2+1/2
Leicester C (£300,000 on 22/3/1990) FL 63+3/22 FLC 6/2 FAC 1 Others 2/1
Newcastle U (£250,000 on 4/12/1991) FL 70/35 FLC 4/2 FAC 5/1 Others 4/1
Wolverhampton W (£750,000 on 23/6/1993) FL 76+7/26 FLC 5/2 FAC 11/6 Others 4/2
Sunderland (£1,000,000 on 19/9/1995) P/FL 32+2/2 FLC 2+1 FAC 3
Tranmere Rov (£350,000 on 5/8/1997) FL 69+19/21 FLC 16+1/13 FAC 11+1/3
Sheffield U (Free on 21/7/2000) FL 21+14/6 FLC 4/2 FAC 1
Motherwell (Free on 30/7/2001) SL 19/6 SLC 1/1 SC 1
Mansfield T (Free, via trial at Stoke, on 31/1/2002) FL 11+6/4

KELLY Garry
Born: Drogheda, 9 July 1974
Height: 5'8" **Weight:** 11.8
International Honours: Rol: 50; U21-5; Yth; Sch
Although Garry remained an important squad member at Elland Road last term, he received few senior opportunities due to the form of Danny Mills. He remains one of the quickest defenders in the Premiership, a solid and adventurous full back, although his best game last season came at Blackburn Rovers in December when he played on the right side of midfield and produced some excellent crosses to set up Harry Kewell in the 2-1 victory.
Leeds U (Signed from Home Farm on 24/9/1991) PL 255+10/2 FLC 21+2 FAC 24+1 Others 29+1

KELLY Gary Alexander
Born: Preston, 3 August 1966
Height: 5'11" **Weight:** 13.6
Club Honours: FAYC '85

International Honours: Rol: B-1; U23-1; 21-8
...ary had a frustrating 2001-02 campaign
: Oldham. After starting the season as
...rst choice he was hit by injury, which
...sulted in Paul Rachubka joining on loan
...om Manchester United. The veteran
...eeper was subsequently unable to oust
...achubka and did not return to first-team
...ction February. An unfortunate ankle
...jury then ended his season in mid-
...1arch. His best moment came in August
...hen he saved and scored a penalty in
...thletic's Worthington Cup penalty shoot-
...ut triumph.
...ewcastle U (From apprentice on
...)/6/1984) FL 53 FLC 4 FAC 3 Others 2
...lackpool (Loaned on 7/10/1988) FL 5
...ury (£60,000 on 5/10/1989) FL 236 FLC 14
...1C 13 Others 29
...Idham Ath (£10,000 on 27/8/1996) FL
...24+1 FLC 13 FAC 19 Others 6

...ELLY Leon Michael
...orn: Coventry, 26 June 1978
...eight: 6'1" **Weight:** 12.4
...his pacy young striker made his senior
...ebut for Cambridge at Brentford last
...ugust before moving on loan to
...onference outfit Stalybridge Celtic. On
...s return he received a further outing for
...e U's from the subs' bench but that was
...e extent of his first-team involvement.
...e subsequently spent much of the
...mainder of the campaign on loan at
...uneaton Borough and Dover Athletic
...nd was released in the summer.
...ambridge U (£15,000 from Atherstone U
...1 15/8/2001) FL 1+1

...ELTIE Clark
...orn: Newcastle, 31 August 1983
...eight: 6'1" **Weight:** 12.7
...his strong Newcastle-born midfielder
...me from Walker Central at the
...eginning of last season and after
...roducing a series of consistent displays in
...e reserves he went on to make his
...nior debut on the last day of the season
: Oxford. He did not look out of place in
...e team and appears to have a bright
...ture in the game.
...arlington (Free from Walker Central on
...9/9/2001) FL 0+1

...ENDALL Lee Mark
...orn: Newport, 8 January 1981
...eight: 5'11" **Weight:** 14.4
...ternational Honours: W: U21-2; Yth
...e established himself as Cardiff City's
...mber two 'keeper last season, but the
...rm of Neil Alexander meant he was
...stricted to just 90 minutes of first-team

action, coming in the amazing 7-1 win
over Rushden in the LDV Vans Trophy.
Earlier on he kept a number of clean
sheets in pre-season matches, proving
himself to be a more than competent
goalkeeper. He is the son of former Spurs,
Wolves and Newport County goalkeeper
Mark Kendall.
Crystal Palace (From trainee on 13/1/1998)
Cardiff C (£50,000 on 22/12/2000) Others 1

KENNA Jeffrey (Jeff) Jude
Born: Dublin, 27 August 1970
Height: 5'11" **Weight:** 12.2
International Honours: Rol: 27; B-1;
U21-8; Yth; Sch
Unable to make the first team for
Blackburn Rovers, this experienced full
back joined Wigan Athletic on a month's
loan at the start of November to put
himself in the shop window. He was
impressive in his spell with the Latics,
firing home a stunning shot in the
demolition of Stoke City.   He returned to
Ewood Park and made one appearance in
the Worthington Cup before becoming
one of former Wigan boss Steve Bruce's
first signings at Birmingham City. Initially
arriving on loan, a permanent deal soon
followed and he was appointed as Blues'
captain. He worked hard, providing
support down the flank and giving the
defence a much more solid look.
Southampton (From trainee on 25/4/1989)
F/PL 110+4/4 FLC 4 FAC 10+1 Others 3
Blackburn Rov (£1,500,000 on 15/3/1995)
P/FL 153+2/1 FLC 17+2 FAC 13 Others 7
Tranmere Rov (Loaned on 20/3/2001) FL 11
Wigan Ath (Loaned on 2/11/2001) FL 6/1
FAC 1
Birmingham C (Free on 24/12/2001) FL 21
Others 3

KENNEDY Mark
Born: Dublin, 15 May 1976
Height: 5'11" **Weight:** 11.9
International Honours: Rol: 34; U21-7;
Yth; Sch
This left-winger was a summer signing for
Wolves, but made a quiet start to the
2001-02 season. He came to prominence
with a beautiful left-foot strike at Walsall,
and there was a spell in which he seemed
to be involved in every Wolves goal. He
unfortunately pulled a hamstring in the
home match with Burnley, which
restricted him somewhat, but he was
soon back on song, scoring another
superb goal at Stockport. A torn abductor
muscle kept him out for five games, and
after a subdued return in the final League
match he managed only 45 minutes in
the play-offs. Mark continued to represent

Republic of Ireland and was also named in
the PFA First Division team of the year.
Millwall (From trainee on 6/5/1992) FL
37+6/9 FLC 6+1/2 FAC 3+1/1
Liverpool (£1,500,000 on 21/3/1995) PL
5+11 FLC 0+2 FAC 0+1 Others 0+2
Queens Park R (Loaned on 27/1/1998) FL 8/2
Wimbledon (£1,750,000 on 27/3/1998) PL
11+10 FLC 4+1/1 FAC 2
Manchester C (£1,000,000 + on 15/7/1999)
P/FL 56+10/8 FLC 5+4/3 FAC 2
Wolverhampton W (£1,800,000 on
6/7/2001) FL 35/5 FLC 1 FAC 1 Others 0+1

KENNEDY Peter Henry James
Born: Lurgan, 10 September 1973
Height: 5'9" **Weight:** 11.11
Club Honours: Div 2 '98
International Honours: NI: 13; B-1
Peter became Paul Jewell's first signing
for Wigan Athletic and after making a
slow start he soon got to grips with his
new challenge, providing a more
balanced look in the centre of the park. A
left-sided player, he favoured a midfield
role but showed his versatility by playing
at left back to cover for injuries. Blessed
as an excellent crosser of the ball and
dangerous at set pieces, he set up all four
goals from corners in the home win over
Cardiff City in February. However, he
missed the last seven matches of the
season following a knee injury. Peter
continued to appear regularly for
Northern Ireland, adding four more caps.
Notts Co (£100,000 from Portadown on
28/8/1996) FL 20+2 FLC 1 FAC 2+1/1 Others
0+1
Watford (£130,000 on 10/7/1997) P/FL
108+7/18 FLC 9/2 FAC 7/2 Others 3
Wigan Ath (£300,000 on 18/7/2001) FL
29+2 FAC 1 Others 1

KENNY Patrick (Paddy)
Joseph
Born: Halifax, 17 May 1978
Height: 6'1" **Weight:** 14.6
Paddy enjoyed mixed fortunes as Bury's
first choice goalkeeper last season. Once
again he dominated his area and
impressed with his ability as a shot
stopper, however he also suffered at the
hands of the officials, being sent off twice
after clumsy challenges. His most
impressive performance was a one-man
defensive show when his spectacular
saves helped the Shakers to a 1-0 win at
Colchester. He also stopped three
penalties during the campaign. The club's
financial problems saw him transfer-listed
at the end of January.
Bury (£10,000 + from Bradford PA on
28/8/1998) FL 133 FLC 5 FAC 7 Others 5

Paddy Kenny

KENTON Darren Edward
Born: Wandsworth, 13 September 1978
Height: 5'10" **Weight:** 11.11
Darren enjoyed his best season to date at Norwich last term. He has great pace and is strong in the tackle; he can compete with the best in the air, timing his challenges to perfection; and he loves getting forward in attack as his tally of four goals, including two in the home win against Sheffield United testifies. He can play in either full-back position or in central defence (his personal preference), but he seems to be settling in as Norwich City's regular right-back.

Norwich C (From trainee on 3/7/1997) FL 106+15/8 FLC 8+1 FAC 2+2 Others 3

KEOWN Martin Raymond
Born: Oxford, 24 July 1966
Height: 6'1" **Weight:** 12.4
Club Honours: PL '98, '02; FAC '98, '02; CS '98, '99
International Honours: E: 43; B-1; U21-8; Yth
This experienced central defender was again a regular for Arsenal apart from a two-month spell on the sidelines in the new year after he fractured a bone in his right leg playing against Blackburn Rovers.

He returned to action in time to make a brief appearance from the subs' bench in the FA Cup final victory over Chelsea and made the final 23 for England's World Cup squad over the summer.
Arsenal (From apprentice on 2/2/1984) FL 22 FAC 5
Brighton & Hove A (Loaned on 15/2/1985) FL 21+2/1 FLC 2/1 Others 2/1
Aston Villa (£200,000 on 9/6/1986) FL 109+3/3 FLC 12+1 FAC 6 Others 2
Everton (£750,000 on 7/8/1989) F/PL 92+4 FLC 11 FAC 12+1 Others 6
Arsenal (£2,000,000 on 4/2/1993) PL 257+19/4 FLC 18+2/1 FAC 26+3 Others 40+7/3

KERR Brian
Born: Motherwell, 12 October 1981
Height: 5'8" **Weight:** 11.2
International Honours: S: Yth; Sch
Brian had a quiet start to Newcastle's 2001-02 season as he was recovering from a dislocated shoulder and was unable to play competitively until mid-September. He is an energetic midfield player with good control and an eye for goal, and his performances in the reserves earned him the captaincy of the side and he led the team to the top of the table. His first-team exposure was limited to a couple of brief substitute appearances in the FA Cup ties at Peterborough and Arsenal, but if he stays injury free he will expect to be pushing for a place in the first-team squad in 2002-03.
Newcastle U (From trainee on 4/12/1998) PL 0+1 FAC 0+2

KERR Dylan
Born: Valetta, Malta, 14 January 1967
Height: 5'9" **Weight:** 11.4
Club Honours: Div 2 '94
This experienced left back joined Exeter City shortly before the start of 2001-02 and featured in a handful of early-season games, netting once at Halifax. He was released soon after John Cornforth took over as manager of the Grecians and subsequently returned north of the border to sign for Morton where he featured regularly for the remainder of the campaign.
Sheffield Wed (From juniors on 1/9/1984. Freed during 1985 close season)
Leeds U (Free from Arcadia Shepherds, South Africa on 8/2/1989) F/PL 6+7 FLC 2 FAC 1 Others 0+4
Doncaster Rov (Loaned on 22/8/1991) FL 7/1
Blackpool (Loaned on 31/12/1991) FL 12/1 Others 1
Reading (£75,000 on 15/7/1993) FL 84+5/5 FLC 8+1 FAC 2 Others 3+1

Darren Kenton

Martin Keown

Carlisle U *(Free on 16/9/1996) FL 0+1*
Kilmarnock *(Free on 11/10/1996) SL 63 SLC
2 SC 6+1 Others 2*
Kidderminster Hrs *(Free on 7/9/2000) FL
0+1 (Free to Harrogate T in October 2000)*
Hamilton Academical *(Free, via trial at
Clydebank, on 20/1/2001) SL 17/3*
Exeter C *(Free on 6/8/2001) FL 5/1 FLC 1*

KERR James **Stewart**
Born: Motherwell, 13 November 1974
Height: 6'2" **Weight:** 13.4
International Honours: S: U21-10
An outstanding shot stopper who
commands his penalty area and organises
his defence impressively, Stewart joined
Wigan Athletic after a brief trial. He was
immediately thrown into the deep end,
making his debut in the home match
against Bristol City just a day after putting
pen to paper. He produced excellent
performances in the away matches at
Bury and Bournemouth before suffering a
freak spinal injury in training in October.
The injury virtually ended his season,
although he returned on the subs' bench
for the final match of the season against
Colchester United.
Glasgow Celtic *(From juniors on 27/5/1993)
SL 33+1 SLC 1 Others 0+1*
Brighton & Hove A *(Loaned on 1/11/1994)
FL 2*
Wigan Ath *(Free on 24/8/2001) FL 8*

KERRIGAN Daniel (Danny)
Anthony
Born: Basildon, 4 July 1982
Height: 5'7" **Weight:** 10.8
After being on the fringe of the Southend
United first-team squad for most of 2001-
02, Danny finally forced his way into the
reckoning at the end of the season, only
to be released by manager Rob Newman.
A small and bustling midfielder, he was
also asked to play as a full back at times,
although he never looked comfortable in
this role. He was a useful squad man for
the Blues and never gave any less than
100 per cent.
Southend U *(From trainee on 24/7/2000) FL
6+9 FAC 0+1 Others 2+1*

KERRIGAN Steven (Steve)
John
Born: Baillieston, 9 October 1972
Height: 6'1" **Weight:** 12.4
Club Honours: S Div 2 '97
Steve never really got started at Halifax in
the 2001-02 season mainly due to a
niggling groin injury. Despite finishing
leading scorer in the previous campaign
his goal touch seemed to desert him and
he failed to find the net even once. He is

a pacy striker who is powerful in the air
and still an asset to the team.
Albion Rov *(Free from Newmains Juveniles
on 22/7/1992) SL 46+7/14 SLC 2/1 SC 1
Others 1*
Clydebank *(Free on 11/2/1994) SL 17+13
SLC 1+1 Others 2+1/2*
Stranraer *(Signed on 4/11/1995) SL 19+2/5
SC 1*
Ayr U *(£25,000 on 25/6/1996) SL 26+7/17
SLC 2/2 SC 1 Others 2/2*
Shrewsbury T *(£25,000 on 21/1/1998) FL
63+13/15 FLC 2+1 FAC 3/3*
Halifax T *(Signed on 23/3/2000) FL 70+8/22
FLC 2+1 FAC 3 Others 3/1*

KETSBAIA Temuri
Born: Georgia, 18 March 1968
Height: 6'0" **Weight:** 13.0
International Honours: Georgia: 51
This attacking midfielder never really
seemed happy at Molineux, although he
played a brief part in the three of the
opening four matches of the 2001-02
campaign. In October he signed for
Dundee where he achieved a creditable
tally of six goals from 22 appearances
during the season.
Newcastle U *(Free from AEK Athens,
Greece, ex Dynamo Sukhumi, Dynamo Tbilisi,
Anorthosis Famagusta, on 10/7/1997) PL
41+37/8 FLC 1+1 FAC 8+8/4 Others 7+6/2*
Wolverhampton W *(£900,000 on
10/8/2000) FL 14+10/3 FLC 4+1/1*

KEWELL Harold (Harry)
Born: Sydney, Australia, 22 September
1978
Height: 6'0" **Weight:** 11.10
Club Honours: FAYC '97
International Honours: Australia: 13; Yth
Harry returned to action for Leeds United
last term after the woes of the previous
season's injury-wrecked campaign. He
displays lightning pace and skills that
baffle opposing defenders, and is capable
of hitting some spectacular goals – this
was highlighted with his strike against
Grasshoppers in the UEFA Cup when he
picked up a clearance on the edge of his
own goal area before beating defender
after defender and scoring a remarkable
goal. Harry again suffered an injury-
blighted campaign after going out of the
World Cup with Australia in a play-off
defeat at Uruguay.
Leeds U *(Signed from the Australian
Academy of Sport on 23/12/1995) PL
138+12/31 FLC 7/4 FAC 12/5 Others 29+3/7*

KIDD Ryan Andrew
Born: Radcliffe, 6 October 1971
Height: 6'0" **Weight:** 12.10

Club Honours: Div 3 '96, Div 2 '00
Ryan missed the start of 2001-02, his
testimonial season, after undergoing an
operation for the fourth consecutive
summer, this time on his knee. He
returned at left back in September for the
visit of Wolves, but was then out of
action for a further six weeks with a rib
injury. Sadly, in his third game back, he
suffered a recurrence of a neck problem
and was forced to retire on medical
advice. Ryan will be missed by all at
Deepdale where he is remembered for his
consistency over a ten-year period at both
centre half and left back.
Port Vale *(From trainee on 12/7/1990) FL 1
FLC 0+2 Others 0+1*
Preston NE *(Free on 15/7/1992) FL 241+18/9
FLC 17+3/1 FAC 18 Others 19+1/1*

KIELY Dean Laurence
Born: Salford, 10 October 1970
Height: 6'1" **Weight:** 13.5
Club Honours: Div 2 '97; Div 1 '00
International Honours: Rol: 6; B-1; E:
Yth; Sch
2001-02 was a great season for the
Republic of Ireland 'keeper, who was ever
present in the Charlton goal throughout
the campaign. Dean is comfortable at
dealing with crosses and is an excellent
shot stopper who commands his area
well, and must be among the best in the
Premiership on current form. He made
some outstanding saves and kept 14
clean sheets in League and cup matches.
He was voted 'Player of the Year' by the
Addicks' supporters.
Coventry C *(From trainee on 30/10/1987)*
York C *(Signed on 9/3/1990) FL 210 FLC 9
FAC 4 Others 16*
Bury *(£125,000 on 15/8/1996) FL 137 FLC
13 FAC 4 Others 3*
Charlton Ath *(£1,000,000 on 26/5/1999)
P/FL 108 FLC 6 FAC 8*

KILBANE Kevin Daniel
Born: Preston, 1 February 1977
Height: 6'0" **Weight:** 12.10
International Honours: Rol: 37; U21-11
A tall rangy left winger, Kevin has
endured some tough times at Sunderland
but finished the 2001-02 season as one
of the Black Cats' most consistent
performers. On his day, Kevin is a flank
player who can torment opposition full
backs with his pace and crossing ability
and he continued to be a regular for the
Republic of Ireland, helping them to
qualify for the 2002 World Cup. Kevin
bagged his only goal of the campaign in a
3-0 success at Blackburn on Boxing Day.

Steve Kerrigan

Preston NE (From trainee on 6/7/1995) FL 39+8/3 FLC 4 FAC 1 Others 1+1
West Bromwich A (£1,000,000 on 13/6/1997) FL 105+1/15 FLC 12/2 FAC 4/1
Sunderland (£2,500,000 on 16/12/1999) PL 67+11/7 FLC 2 FAC 0+4/1

KILFORD Ian Anthony
Born: Bristol, 6 October 1973
Height: 5'10" **Weight:** 11.0
Club Honours: Div 3 '97; AMC '99
A stylish central-midfielder with good passing ability and fine vision, Ian struggled to force his way into new manager Paul Jewell's plans at Wigan last term. Restricted to just a handful of first-team starts, the hard-running player was used mainly from the subs' bench, but never let the side down when called. Out of contract in the summer, he was not offered a new deal.
Nottingham F (From trainee on 3/4/1991) FL 0+1
Wigan Ath (Loaned on 23/12/1993) FL 2+1/2 FAC 0+1
Wigan Ath (Free on 13/7/1994) FL 175+43/30 FLC 14+2/1 FAC 14+3/2 Others 14+2/2

KILLEEN Lewis Keith
Born: Peterborough, 23 September 1982
Height: 5'10" **Weight:** 10.4
After good performances in the U19 and reserve sides, Lewis was given his first-team chance by Sheffield United when he came on as a substitute in the final home game of last season. A lively striker with an eye for goal he made a promising debut and with a little luck might have scored. He was voted as the Blades' U19 'Player of the Year ' and will be looking to receive more opportunities in the senior team in 2002-03.
Sheffield U (From trainee on 4/7/2001) FL 0+1

KILLEN Christopher (Chris) John
Born: Wellington, New Zealand, 8 October 1981
Height: 5'11" **Weight:** 11.3
International Honours: New Zealand:
This tall striker finally got his chance to be part of the Manchester City first-team squad last season, but failed to make the starting line up. He had a spell on loan at Port Vale in the early part of the season to gain valuable experience, and despite being laid low by a bout of shingles he found the net on a regular basis. He made three substitute appearances at Maine Road altogether and will be looking to gain more senior experience in 2002-03.

Manchester C (Free from Miramar Rangers, New Zealand on 8/3/1999) FL 0+3
Wrexham (Loaned on 8/9/2000) FL 11+1/3
Port Vale (Loaned on 24/9/2001) FL 8+1/6 Others 1

KILTY Mark Thomas
Born: Sunderland, 24 June 1981
Height: 5'11" **Weight:** 12.5
Mark had a frustrating time with injuries at Darlington in 2001-02 which caused him to miss virtually all of the campaign. He returned to action for the FA Cup replay at Peterborough in January but was still not fully fit and made only one more appearance during the season. He is a versatile defender who is tenacious in the tackle and strong in the air.
Darlington (From trainee on 17/7/1999) FL 20+3/1 FLC 1 FAC 1+1 Others 3

KIMBLE Alan Frank
Born: Dagenham, 6 August 1966
Height: 5'9" **Weight:** 12.4
Club Honours: Div 3 '91
Alan had to play second fiddle at Wimbledon last season as the manager opted for a younger back line. He possesses one of the best left feet in the game and his set-piece play is still up to a

Alan Kimble

Kevin Kilbane

good standard, but he made the starting line-up for the Dons only seven times. He finished the campaign on loan at Peterborough and it was announced that his contract would not be renewed in the summer.

Charlton Ath *(From juniors on 8/8/1984) FL 6*
Exeter C *(Loaned on 23/8/1985) FL 1 FLC 1*
Cambridge U *(Free on 22/8/1986) FL 295+4/24 FLC 23+1 FAC 29/1 Others 22*
Wimbledon *(£175,000 on 27/7/1993) P/FL 196+19 FLC 22+3/1 FAC 26*
Peterborough U *(Loaned on 15/3/2002) FL 3*

KINET Christophe
Born: Huy, Belgium, 31 December 1972
Height: 5'8" **Weight:** 10.12
Club Honours: Div 2 '01
This tricky winger received limited opportunities at Millwall last term due to the consistency of the regular first-team members. When he was called upon he caused defenders great problems and struck a candidate for 'Goal of the Season' in the 2-0 victory over Sheffield United at the Den.
Millwall *(£75,000 from Racing Strasbourg, France, ex Germinal, on 9/2/2000) FL 29+18/5 FLC 3+1/1 FAC 1+3 Others 2+2/3*

KING Ledley Brenton
Born: Stepney, 12 October 1980
Height: 6'2" **Weight:** 13.6
International Honours: E: 1; U21-12; Yth
This young defender had a fantastic season for Spurs last term. Filling the gap left by Sol Campbell so admirably, he became a firm favourite at White Hart Lane and with the crowd and his team behind him grew in stature and confidence as the campaign progressed. He looks composed on the ball and likes to get forward. His height makes him a threat at set pieces and his confidence means that he is quick to seize opportunities to get forward and score goals.
Tottenham H *(From trainee on 22/7/1998) PL 52+2/1 FLC 7/1 FAC 7+1/1*

KING Marlon Francis
Born: Dulwich, 26 April 1980
Height: 6'1" **Weight:** 11.12
Marlon finished as Gillingham's top scorer for the second successive season last term, when his work rate and goal poaching ability were exceptional. He improved with every game he played and successfully put off-field problems to the back of his mind. He came close to a call up for the Republic of Ireland U21 squad after being watched by Mick

McCarthy on a few occasions.
Barnet *(From trainee on 9/9/1998) FL 36+17/14 FLC 0+2 FAC 0+1 Others 2+2*
Gillingham *(£255,000 on 28/6/2000) FL 64+16/32 FLC 5+1/2 FAC 4+1/1*

KING Simon Daniel Roy
Born: Oxford, 11 April 1983
Height: 5'11" **Weight:** 12.4
This promising young left back, again had to wait until the closing stages of the season to gain further senior experience with Oxford United in 2001-02. He is well thought of at the Kassam Stadium and after some useful performances in the club's reserves he will be aiming to make a breakthrough to regular first-team action in 2002-03.
Oxford U *(From trainee on 13/12/2000) FL 3+1*

KINKLADZE Georgiou (Georgi)
Born: Tbilisi, Georgia, 6 November 1973
Height: 5'8" **Weight:** 11.2
International Honours: Georgia: 46
Georgi again found himself in a struggling team at Derby last term and only featured occasionally in the first half of the campaign. However he eventually won through to gain a regular place in the line-up in the new year, but still proved unable to prevent the Rams from being relegated. A supremely talented midfield player with excellent vision, he remained a regular for the Georgian national team.
Manchester C *(£2,000,000 from Mretebi Tbilisi, Georgia, ex Mretebi, on 17/8/1995) P/FL 105+1/20 FLC 6 FAC 9/2 (£5,000,000 to Ajax, Holland on 15/5/1998)*
Derby Co *(Signed on 26/11/1999) PL 38+27/3 FLC 3/1 FAC 2*

KINSELLA Mark Anthony
Born: Dublin, 12 August 1972
Height: 5'9" **Weight:** 11.8
Club Honours: GMVC '92; FAT '92; Div 1 '00
International Honours: RoI: 32; B-1; U21-8; Yth
An immensely influential right-sided midfield player, Mark missed a large part of the 2001-02 season through injury. First an operation to cure a double hernia, then a knee problem disrupted his season. A regular member of the Republic of Ireland international side and Charlton's captain, Mark controls the midfield, linking up effectively with Graham Stuart and Scott Parker. He reads the game well and is an excellent passer of the ball. He possesses a thunderous shot, but this was

not seen too often due to his occupying a much deeper midfield role last term.
Colchester U *(Free from Home Farm on 18/8/1989) FL 174+6/27 FLC 11/3 FAC 11/1 Others 9+1/5*
Charlton Ath *(£150,000 on 23/9/1996) P/FL 200+8/19 FLC 4+2 FAC 8+1/3 Others 3*

KIPPE Frode
Born: Oslo, Norway, 17 January 1978
Height: 6'4" **Weight:** 13.10
Club Honours: AMC '00
International Honours: Norway: B-1; U21-27
After over 30 months on the Liverpool playing staff the tall Norwegian central defender finally made his first-team debut as a substitute in the Worthington Cup against Grimsby last October, a game that the Reds surprisingly lost. Plagued by knee injuries since his arrival at Anfield, he returned to his former club Lillestrom in March.
Liverpool *(£700,000 from Lillestrom, Norway, ex Kilbotn, on 7/11/1999) FLC 0+2*
Stoke C *(Loaned on 24/12/1999) FL 15/1 Others 5*
Stoke C *(Loaned on 13/10/2000) FL 15+4 Others 5*

KIRKLAND Christopher (Chris)
Born: Leicester, 2 May 1981
Height: 6'3" **Weight:** 11.7
International Honours: E: U21-5; Yth
Chris appeared for Coventry City in the opening match of the 2001-02 campaign before being sold to Liverpool, where he arrived on the same day as the Polish international 'keeper Jerzy Dudek. He made his debut for the Reds in the Worthington Cup tie with Grimsby and later in the season deputised for the injured Dudek for three games in February, performing competently on each occasion. He also made further appearances for England at U21 level during the campaign.
Coventry C *(From trainee on 6/5/1998) P/FL 24 FLC 3+1 FAC 1*
Liverpool *(£6,000,000 + on 31/8/2001) PL 1 FLC 1 Others 2*

KIROVSKI Jovan
Born: Escondido, California, USA, 18 March 1976
Height: 6'1" **Weight:** 12.4
International Honours: USA: 54
Jovan became Steve Bruce's first signing for Crystal Palace when he arrived on a free transfer shortly before the start of the 2001-02 season. A right-sided midfield player he featured regularly for the Eagles and had a good campaign. However, he

was unable to agree a new contract at the end of the season and his future was uncertain at the time of writing.
Manchester U (Signed from La Jolla Nomads, California, USA on 1/7/1995. Freed during 1996 close season)
Crystal Palace (£350,000 from Sporting Lisbon, Portugal, ex Borussia Dortmund, on 9/8/2001) FL 25+11/5 FLC 2 FAC 1

KISHISHEV Radostin Prodanov
Born: Bulgaria, 30 July 1974
Height: 5'10" **Weight:** 12.4
International Honours: Bulgaria: 45
A gifted right-sided midfielder or wing back Radostin was plagued by knee problems at Charlton in 2001-02. A cruciate ligament injury meant only four substitute appearances in all competitions during the season, although he did start an international game for Bulgaria against Croatia. He is a good tackler, very comfortable on the ball and not afraid to try the unexpected. He is popular with the crowd and never shies away from the action.
Charlton Ath (£300,000 + from Liteks Lovech, Bulgaria, ex Neftokhimik Burgas, Bursapor, on 14/8/2000) PL 25+5 FLC 1 FAC 2+1

KITAMIRIKE Joel Derick
Born: Uganda, 5 April 1984
Height: 5'10" **Weight:** 13.1
This promising young defender made his debut in the most difficult of circumstances. Following the withdrawal of six first teamers for the controversial trip to Tel Aviv for the UEFA Cup tie against Hapoel, Joel was thrown into the proverbial deep end by being selected to play alongside John Terry in central defence. He gave a creditable display and certainly did not let himself or the club down in a match that was decided by two goals in stoppage time. He plays at right back for the youth side and coach Steve Clark forecasts a bright future for this powerfully built youngster.
Chelsea (From trainee on 6/4/2001) Others 1

KITSON David (Dave)
Born: Hitchin, 21 January 1980
Height: 6'3" **Weight:** 12.11
Dave did well with Cambridge United last term, despite the club's poor showing in Division Two. A tall striker who is good in the air, he led the line ably and also showed considerable skill on the ground. He finished the campaign as the U's second-top scorer with a tally of ten goals in all competitions.
Cambridge U (Signed from Arlesey T on 16/3/2001) FL 36+5/10 FLC 1 FAC 2 Others 4/1

KITSON Paul
Born: Murton, 9 January 1971
Height: 5'11" **Weight:** 10.12
International Honours: E: U21-7
This experienced West Ham striker was looking to gain a regular place in the side under new manager Glenn Roeder last term. Once fully fit Paul can be a handful for any back line as the Charlton defenders will tell you. Playing at the Valley in November he scored a sensational hat-trick in the exciting 4-4 draw. He was on the bench for the majority of the season and found it difficult to justify a regular place.
Leicester C (From trainee on 15/12/1988) FL 39+11/6 FLC 5/3 FAC 1+1/1 Others 5/1
Derby Co (£1,300,000 on 11/3/1992) FL 105/36 FLC 7/3 FAC 5/1 Others 13+1/9
Newcastle U (£2,250,000 on 24/9/1994) PL 26+10/10 FLC 3+2/1 FAC 6+1/3 Others 0+1
West Ham U (£2,300,000 on 10/2/1997) FL 46+17/18 FLC 2+3/1 FAC 4+1/1 Others 3+5/2
Charlton Ath (Loaned on 21/3/2000) FL 2+4/1
Crystal Palace (Loaned on 14/9/2000) FL 4

KNIGHT Leon Leroy
Born: Hackney, 16 September 1982
Height: 5'4" **Weight:** 9.10
International Honours: E: Yth
One of the most promising youngsters at Stamford Bridge, Leon finally made his Chelsea first-team debut in Bulgaria in the UEFA Cup-tie against Levski Spartak. He replaced the equally diminutive Franco Zola for the last half-hour before enjoying another successful loan spell, this time at Huddersfield Town. He impressed as a striker with his pace and trickery and became the first loan player to win Town's 'Player of the Year' award. To ward off predatory clubs Chelsea have signed Leon on a long-term contract.
Chelsea (From trainee on 17/9/1999) Others 0+1
Queens Park R (Loaned on 9/3/2001) FL 10+1
Huddersfield T (Loaned on 23/10/2001) FL 31/16 FAC 2/1 Others 4

KNIGHT Richard
Born: Burton, 3 August 1979
Height: 6'1" **Weight:** 14.0
International Honours: E: Yth
Despite being 'Player of the Year' in 2000-01, Richard made just three appearances for Oxford United last season. He started the first game in the line-up before losing out to newcomer Ian McCaldon and then to Andy Woodman. He ended the season on loan at Colchester where he made a single appearance against Bury, producing

a series of fine saves to consolidate a 3-1 win. He subsequently returned to Oxford where he still has another year of his contract to run.
Derby Co (Signed from Burton A on 25/6/1997)
Carlisle U (Loaned on 26/3/1999) FL 6
Birmingham C (Loaned on 4/8/1999) FLC 0+1
Hull C (Loaned on 7/10/1999) FL 1
Macclesfield T (Loaned on 3/12/1999) FL 3
Oxford U (Loaned on 19/1/2000) FL 1+1
Oxford U (Free on 13/3/2000) FL 47 FLC 2 FAC 2
Colchester U (Loaned on 28/3/2002) FL 1

KNIGHT Zatyiah (Zat)
Born: Solihull, 2 May 1980
Height: 6'6" **Weight:** 13.8
International Honours: E: U21-4
Central defender Zat was one of the big success stories at Craven Cottage in the 2001-02 season. The former Rushall Olympic player appeared at Leicester in September, retaining his place for the next three games. As the campaign progressed he operated in more of a midfield role where he showed his willingness to move forward and hit shots from distance. Although not a first choice he never let anyone down when selected and his talent was recognised with England U21 honours.
Fulham (Signed from Rushall Olympic on 19/2/1999) PL 8+2 FLC 5 FAC 3
Peterborough U (Loaned on 25/2/2000) FL 8

KOEJOE Samuel (Sammy)
Born: Paramaribo, Surinam, 17 August 1974
Height: 6'1" **Weight:** 12.2
This big bustling striker made three early-season appearances as a substitute for Queen's Park Rangers before his contract was cancelled by mutual agreement at the end of August. He subsequently had trials at a number of clubs including Stoke and Northampton before returning to Austria to sign for Lustenau, one of his former clubs.
Queens Park R (£250,000 from Salzburg, Austria, ex DWV Amsterdam, Lustenau, on 29/11/1999) FL 13+21/3 FLC 1+2 FAC 3+2

KOLINKO Aleksandrs (Alex)
Born: Latvia, 18 June 1975
Height: 6'3" **Weight:** 13.7
International Honours: Latvia: 28
This tall Crystal Palace 'keeper started the 2001-02 season by conceding seven goals in three games, yet still picked up the 'Nationwide Save of the Month' for his stop against Rotherham on the opening

day. Although soon replaced by Matt Clarke, he later returned for two spells, making a brilliant save in the FA Cup tie at Newcastle. He also continued to represent Latvia during the campaign, but was unable to prevent his club colleague Dougie Freedman scoring against him for Scotland.

Crystal Palace (£600,000 from Skonto Riga, Latvia, ex Metals Riga, on 15/9/2000) FL 53+1 FLC 8 FAC 3

KONCHESKY Paul Martyn

Born: Barking, 15 May 1981
Height: 5'10" **Weight:** 10.12
International Honours: E: U21-5; Yth
2001-02 proved to be a great season for Paul who is a skilful and competitive left-sided defender who can also play in midfield. He is quick, as well as being a strong tackler and improved immensely as the campaign progressed, playing at left back, in the centre of defence and occasionally in midfield. He featured in the majority of Charlton's matches and was called up for the England U21s against Portugal. He has a powerful shot and scored his first senior goal for the club at Everton. Paul has the distinction of being the Addicks' youngest-ever debutant and has the potential to be a top-class player.

Charlton Ath (From trainee on 25/5/1998) P/FL 42+28/1 FLC 4+4/1 FAC 4+1

KONJIC Muhamed (Mo)

Born: Bosnia, 14 May 1970
Height: 6'4" **Weight:** 13.7
International Honours: Bosnia-Herzegovina:
After two seasons of frustration with niggling injuries, Mo became a first choice central defender for Coventry City last term. Although injured in the opening game, he established himself as a regular soon after the departure of Gordon Strachan. His strong physical presence and outstanding heading ability earned him admiration from Sky Blues' fans and his mazy dribbles up field began to win him cult status at Highfield Road. He scored two goals, a looping header in the home win over Manchester City and a tap-in against Rotherham. He was runner-up in most of the club's 'Player of the Year' awards and regained his place in the Bosnian international side.

Coventry C (£2,000,000 from AS Monaco, France, ex Slobada Tuzla, Croatia Belisce, Croatia Zagreb, FC Zurich, on 5/2/1999) P/FL 52+2/2 FLC 4+1 FAC 1

KONSTANTINIDIS Kostas

Born: Greece, 31 August 1972
Height: 6'2" **Weight:** 12.11
International Honours: Greece: 34
Kostas was signed on loan by Bolton last March, to provide defensive cover for an injury-ravaged back line. A tough-tackling, no-nonsense type of player, he made his debut in the home win against Aston Villa but went on to make just two more appearances for Wanderers.

Bolton W (Loaned from Hertha Berlin, Germany, ex Panathinaikos, on 27/3/2002) PL 3

KOUMAS Jason

Born: Wrexham, 25 September 1979
Height: 5'10" **Weight:** 11.0
International Honours: W: 2
Jason was again a key member of the Tranmere Rovers line-up last season. An inventive and classy midfielder, he is hard working and alert, always looking to develop positive attacking moves rather than choosing the safe option. He was rewarded by his fellow professionals with a place in the PFA's Second Division team for the season, but looks likely to leave Prenton Park in the summer.

Tranmere Rov (From trainee on 27/11/1997) FL 92+31/23 FLC 9+5/2 FAC 9/5

KOZLUK Robert (Rob)

Born: Mansfield, 5 August 1977
Height: 5'8" **Weight:** 11.7
International Honours: E: U21-2
Rob's position was uncertain at Sheffield United at the beginning of the 2001-02 campaign after the arrival of Robert Page and at one stage he seemed likely to be on his way to Wigan. However he later broke in to the Blades' line-up and produced some excellent performances in the right-wing-back slot. Quick, with good anticipation in defence, he linked well down the flank and his long throws were always a danger. In October he suffered serious knee ligament damage at Maine Road bringing his season to an end. Although he was out of contract in the summer the club agreed a one-year extension, and with his rehabilitation progressing better than expected, hopes are high that he will be back in action in the early part of the 2002-03 season.

Derby Co (From trainee on 10/2/1996) PL 9+7 FLC 3 FAC 2+1
Sheffield U (Signed on 12/3/1999) FL 75+9 FLC 3 FAC 3
Huddersfield T (Loaned on 7/9/2000) FL 14

KUIPERS Michel

Born: Amsterdam, Holland, 26 June 1974
Height: 6'2" **Weight:** 14.10

Club Honours: Div 3 '01; Div 2 '02
Michel started the 2001-02 season as the undisputed first-choice goalkeeper for Brighton and apart from injuries over the new year he was a near ever-present in the line-up. He kept a total of 19 clean sheets in all competitions his best performance coming when he almost single-handedly earned a point at Tranmere with a fine display of shot stopping. His development as a player was underlined when he came a very close second in the Albion 'Player of the Season' awards.

Bristol Rov (Free from SDW Amsterdam, Holland on 20/11/1999) FL 1
Brighton & Hove A (Free on 4/7/2000) FL 73 FLC 2 FAC 4 Others 5

KUQI Shefki

Born: Albania, 10 November 1976
Height: 6'2" **Weight:** 13.10
International Honours: Finland: 21
This powerful striker played a prominent role in the Stockport County forward line at the beginning of the 2001-02 season, scoring four times in his first ten appearances. His performances declined after the departure of Andy Kilner and his goal on Boxing Day against Barnsley proved to be his last action for the club before Sheffield Wednesday took him to Hillsborough for a substantial fee. He made an immediate impact for the Owls with his bustling style and big things are expected of him in 2002-03.

Stockport Co (£300,000 from FC Jokerit, Finland, ex HJK Helsinki, on 31/1/2001) FL 32+3/11 FLC 2/1 FAC 1
Sheffield Wed (£700,000 + on 11/1/2002) FL 17/6

KYLE Kevin Alistair

Born: Stranraer, 7 June 1981
Height: 6'3" **Weight:** 13.7
International Honours: S: 2; U21-3
This young Scottish striker continues to make progress at Sunderland and is seen as a possible successor to Niall Quinn. Tall and not afraid to compete in the physical stakes, Kevin made a handful of substitute appearances during the campaign and is getting ever closer to that elusive first goal in a red-and-white shirt.

Sunderland (Free from Ayr Boswell on 25/9/1998) PL 0+9 FLC 0+1 FAC 0+1
Huddersfield T (Loaned on 8/9/2000) FL 0+4
Darlington (Loaned on 1/11/2000) FL 5/1 FAC 3/1
Rochdale (Loaned on 26/1/2001) FL 3+3

Kostas Konstantinidis

L

LABANT Vladimir
Born: Slovakia, 8 June 1974
Height: 6'0" **Weight:** 11.7
International Honours: Slovakia: 17
This skilful left back joined West Ham last January and made his debut in the FA Cup tie against Chelsea. A tough tackler who figured prominently in wins against Everton and Fulham, he is a very determined player with a cultured left foot and has been a good addition to the squad.
West Ham U (£900,000 from Sparta Prague, Czechoslovakia, ex Slavia Sofia, on 11/1/2002) PL 7+5 FAC 0+2

LACEY Damian James
Born: Bridgend, 3 August 1977
Height: 5'9'' **Weight:** 11.3
Club Honours: Div 3 '00
Damian continued to suffer with the foot problems that have troubled him in recent seasons and it was not until the FA Cup tie against Queen's Park Rangers that he made the Swansea City starting line-up last term. In the next game at York he scored the Swans second goal, but also received a red card. When fit, Damian is a hard-working midfield player who operates from box to box.
Swansea C (From trainee on 1/7/1996) FL 68+26/2 FLC 3 FAC 3+1 Others 5/1

LAMBERT Rickie Lee
Born: Liverpool, 16 February 1982
Height: 5'10" **Weight:** 11.2
Rickie was promoted to the Macclesfield first-team squad last September after some impressive appearances for the reserve side and soon afterwards won a place in the starting line-up. He scored with two spectacular free kicks in his first ever FA Cup game against Forest Green Rovers and the following week netted a hat-trick in the home win against Luton Town (Macc's only league treble of the season). Rickie is equally effective as a striker or in mid-field and possesses a devastating right-foot shot from set-pieces.
Blackpool (From trainee on 17/7/2000) FL 0+3
Macclesfield T (Free on 2/3/2001) FL 36+8/8 FAC 4/2 Others 1

LAMPARD Frank James
Born: Romford, 20 June 1978
Height: 6'0" **Weight:** 12.6
International Honours: E: 7; B-1; U21-19; Yth
Chelsea drastically revamped their midfield in the summer months of 2001. Out went veteran heroes Dennis Wise and Gustavo Poyet and in came Emmanuel Petit and Frank Lampard. The dismissal of his uncle Harry Redknapp and father Frank senior from the Hammers' managerial set-up put Frank in an invidious position and Chelsea beat off stiff competition for his signature. The loss through injury of Jesper Gronkjaer saw Frank moved to the right flank away from his favoured central midfield position where he established a reputation as a consistent goal-scorer but a switch back to the centre brought a return to his best form.
West Ham U (From trainee on 1/7/1995) PL 132+16/23 FLC 15+1/9 FAC 13/2 Others 10/4
Swansea C (Loaned on 6/10/1995) FL 8+1/1 Others 1+1
Chelsea (£11,000,000 on 3/7/2001) PL 34+3/5 FLC 4 FAC 7+1/1 Others 4/1

LANGLEY Richard Barrington Michael
Born: Harlesden, 27 December 1979
Height: 5'10" **Weight:** 11.4
International Honours: Jamaica: 1; E: Yth
This versatile midfield player, missed over half the 2001-02 season for Queen's Park Rangers whilst recovering from a cruciate ligament injury suffered back in January 2001. On his return he played out wide on the right, and scored some spectacular goals, including a left-foot volley to seal the home win over Blackpool.
Queens Park R (From trainee on 31/12/1996) FL 84+9/8 FLC 4/1 FAC 6

LARKIN Colin
Born: Dundalk, Ireland, 27 April 1982
Height: 5'9" **Weight:** 10.4
International Honours: Rol: Yth
Colin joined Kidderminster in September initially on loan for a month, this was later increased to three months and then to the rest of the season. Normally used in a wide-right role his pace was a key factor in Harriers' improvement in mid-season. He managed to score seven times, but by his own admission would have hit over 20 had his finishing been better.
Wolverhampton W (From trainee on 19/5/1999) FL 1+2 FLC 0+1/1
Kidderminster Hrs (Loaned on 14/9/2001) FL 31+2/6 Others 1+1/1

LARRIEU Romain
Born: Mont-de-Marsan, France, 31 August 1975
Height: 6'4" **Weight:** 13.11
Club Honours: Div 3 '02
This extremely popular goalkeeper made the number one jersey his own at Plymouth in 2001-02 and his magnificent performances helped to ensure that the team had the best defensive record in the whole of the Football League. His main strengths are his commanding presence in the penalty area, shot stopping and an amazing success rate in one-on-ones with opposing attackers. One save that will stick in the mind was a superb close-range double stop against Leyton Orient in March. He was voted into the PFA Division Three team of the year by his fellow professionals.
Plymouth Arg (Free from ASOA Valence, France, ex Montpellier, on 30/11/2000) FL 59+1 FLC 1 FAC 4 Others 3

LASLANDES Lilian
Born: Pavillac, France, 4 September 1971
Height: 6'1" **Weight:** 12.12
International Honours: France: 3
This experienced striker joined Sunderland in the 2001 close season and was expected to form a new strike partnership with Kevin Phillips. The portents looked good following an impressive debut against Ipswich, when his excellent first touch was evident from the off, but a combination of poor form and the team's insistence on playing the long ball saw the Frenchman out of favour. He netted his only Sunderland goal in a Worthington Cup tie at Sheffield Wednesday in September and was loaned out to German club 1FC Koln for the remainder of the season in the new year.
Sunderland (£3,600,000 from Bordeaux, France, ex Saint-Seurin, Axerre, on 18/7/2001) PL 5+7 FLC 0+1/1

[LAUREN] LAUREANO Bisan-Etame Mayer
Born: Lodhji Krib, Cameroon, 19 January 1977
Height: 5'11" **Weight:** 11.4
Club Honours: FAC '02; PL '02
International Honours: Cameroon: 25 (ANC '00, OLYM '00)
Lauren had another good season for Arsenal in 2001-02 when he established himself in the starting line-up at right back in place of Lee Dixon. A skilful and resilient player, he was a key member of the Gunners' squad that won a domestic double during the season. He continued to represent Cameroon, being a member of the team that won the 2002 African Nations' Cup and also featuring in the World Cup finals over the summer.
Arsenal (£7,200,000 from Real Mallorca, Spain, ex Cant Sevilla, Utrera, Seville, Levante, on 16/6/2000) PL 42+3/4 FAC 7 Others 17+5/1

Liam Lawrence

LAURSEN Jacob

Born: Vejle, Denmark, 6 October 1971
Height: 5'11" **Weight:** 12.3
International Honours: Denmark: 25
This experienced defender was tempted back to the Premiership by Leicester boss Dave Bassett in January. However, his lack of recent practice at this level made it difficult for him to shore up an ailing rearguard, as the club were already entrenched in a run of games without a win by the time he joined. He did not really settle at Filbert Street and soon linked up with Wolves on transfer deadline day. No loan appearances accrued however and on his return Jacob returned to Denmark to join AGF Aarhus in another loan deal.
Derby Co (£500,000 from Silkeborg, Denmark, ex Vejle, on 17/7/1996) PL 135+2/3 FLC 9 FAC 7 (Signed for FC Copenhagen on 24/8/2000)
Leicester C (£400,000 on 11/1/2002) PL 10

LAVIN Gerard

Born: Corby, 5 February 1974
Height: 5'10" **Weight:** 11.0
International Honours: S: U21-7
Gerard joined Northampton Town during the 2001 close season to fill the problem right-back position, however he had the misfortune to suffer a broken leg in the Worthington Cup tie against Queen's Park Rangers, in only his third game. He spent the remainder of the campaign recovering fitness but was expected to be back in action by the start of 2002-03.
Watford (From trainee on 11/5/1992) FL 121+5/2 FLC 11/1 FAC 6 Others 2+1
Millwall (£500,000 on 23/11/1995) FL 67+7 FLC 2 FAC 3+1 Others 8/1
Bristol C (Free on 6/8/1999) FL 21+1 FLC 3 FAC 2 Others 1
Wycombe W (Loaned on 19/1/2001) FL 2 Others 1
Northampton T (Free on 5/7/2001) FL 2 FLC 1

LAW Gareth Martin

Born: Torquay, 20 August 1982
Height: 6'0" **Weight:** 12.8
In his second season as a professional, this locally-born central striker who had come through the youth ranks found his first-team chances at Torquay limited to a handful of substitute appearances. He was not retained by the Gulls at the end of the season.
Torquay U (From trainee on 21/11/2000) FL 2+13/1 FAC 0+1 Others 0+1

LAWRENCE Denis William

Born: Trinidad, 1 August 1974
Height: 6'7" **Weight:** 12.7
International Honours: Trinidad & Tobago: 30
'Tall-Man' did not find it easy to convince the Wrexham fans that he was a good investment by former manager Brian Flynn, but by the end of the 2001-02 campaign he seemed to have won them over. He started well, getting on the score sheet in the opener with Oldham Athletic, but was left out at the end of September and failed to figure in Denis Smith's plans until the second half of the season. Once he had returned he did not look back, gaining in confidence with every game and producing some authoritative displays.
Wrexham (£100,000 from Defence Force, Trinidad on 10/3/2001) FL 30+5/2 FLC 1 FAC 0+1

LAWRENCE James (Jamie) Hubert

Born: Balham, 8 March 1970
Height: 5'11" **Weight:** 12.11
Club Honours: FLC '97
International Honours: Jamaica: 12
Jamie won Jamaica's 'Player of the Year' award for his outstanding international appearances, but his season for Bradford City did not start until February, after being out with breaks to his arm, wrist and thumb and then a groin operation! A talented right midfield player who also played at wing back, he won the Supporters' Club's 'Goal of the Season' prize for his effort at Gillingham.
Sunderland (Signed from Cowes on 15/10/1993) FL 2+2 FLC 0+1
Doncaster Rov (£20,000 on 17/3/1994) FL 16+9/3 FLC 2 FAC 1 Others 3
Leicester C (£125,000 on 6/1/1995) P/FL 21+26/1 FLC 3+4/2 FAC 1+1
Bradford C (£50,000 on 17/6/1997) P/FL 118+21/11 FLC 8+1/1 FAC 4+1/1 Others 0+2

LAWRENCE Liam

Born: Retford, 14 December 1981
Height: 5'10" **Weight:** 11.3
Liam is another product of the Mansfield Town youth set-up who became a regular in the first team in 2001-02. Playing wide on the right he supported the attack well and provided some wonderful crosses from that position. He was also not afraid to have a go at goal, although his shooting was often wayward. His season was ended prematurely by injuries received in a car accident in mid-February.
Mansfield T (From trainee on 3/7/2000) FL 39+13/6 FLC 1 FAC 3 Others 0+2

LAWRENCE Matthew (Matty) James

Born: Northampton, 19 June 1974
Height: 6'1" **Weight:** 12.12
Club Honours: Div 2 '01
International Honours: E: Sch
After the departure of Lucas Neill, this tall, hard-tackling defender was the first choice full back for Millwall until suspension, then a bad head injury kept him out of the side for three months. He bounced back and once again became a regular in the side, putting in some excellent performances. His trademark runs forward followed by a quality cross were a thorn in the side of many an opposition defence.
Wycombe W (£20,000 from Grays Ath on 19/1/1996) FL 13+3/1 FLC 4 FAC 1 Others 0+1
Fulham (Free on 7/2/1997) FL 57+2 FLC 4+1 FAC 2 Others 5
Wycombe W (£86,000 + on 2/10/1998) FL 63/4 FLC 4 FAC 6 Others 3
Millwall (£200,000 on 21/3/2000) FL 78+2 FLC 5+1 FAC 5 Others 6

LAWSON Ian James

Born: Huddersfield, 4 November 1977
Height: 5'11" **Weight:** 11.5
Ian rejoined Bury last September and initially played alongside Jon Newby in attack. However he spent much of the season on the subs' bench from where he scored three goals including a last-minute equaliser at Reading. A pacy striker who is good in the air he is expected to make a much bigger impression for the Shakers in 2002-03.
Huddersfield T (From trainee on 26/1/1995) FL 13+29/5 FLC 1+4 FAC 1+1
Blackpool (Loaned on 6/11/1998) FL 5/3
Blackpool (Loaned on 8/1/1999) FL 4
Bury (£75,000 on 16/7/1999) FL 20+5/11 FLC 2 FAC 3+1 Others 1
Stockport Co (£150,000 on 17/2/2000) FL 14+11/4
Bury (Free on 12/9/2001) FL 12+12/4 FAC 1 Others 1/1

LAZARIDIS Stanley (Stan)

Born: Perth, Australia, 16 August 1972
Height: 5'9" **Weight:** 11.12
International Honours: Australia: 55; U23; Yth
When on song, Stan was a real menace last term with his elusive dribbling and crossing. He was often Birmingham City's most creative midfield influence early on in the season until he fell out of favour with Trevor Francis. New manager Steve Bruce often preferred Tommy Mooney wide on the left because of his goal

threat, so Stan had to make do with a substitute role towards the end of the campaign.

West Ham U *(£300,000 from West Adelaide, Australia on 8/9/1995)* PL 53+16/3 FLC 6+1 FAC 9+1 Others 0+1

Birmingham C *(£1,600,000 on 29/7/1999)* FL 74+20/4 FLC 9+3 FAC 1+1 Others 2+5

LEABURN Carl Winston
Born: Lewisham, 30 March 1969
Height: 6'3" **Weight:** 13.0
After being released by Wimbledon, Carl had trials with Charlton, Wycombe and Leyton Orient before joining Queen's Park Rangers on non-contract forms. The lanky striker managed a single appearance from the subs' bench against Reading before being released. He thus created a new record for the shortest first-team career with Rangers, just three minutes.

Charlton Ath *(From apprentice on 22/4/1987)* FL 276+46/53 FLC 19/5 FAC 19+2/4 Others 9+5/4

Northampton T *(Loaned on 22/3/1990)* FL 9
Wimbledon *(£300,000 on 9/11/1998)* P/FL 36+23/4 FLC 5+6/1 FAC 4 *(Released during 2001 close season)*

Queens Park R *(Free, following trials at Charlton Ath, Wycombe W, Leyton Orient, on 31/12/2001)* FL 0+1

LEACH Marc Thomas
Born: Hemel Hempstead, 12 July 1983
Height: 6'1" **Weight:** 11.10
After previous spells at Arsenal and Watford, Wycombe's giant centre forward scored regularly for the U19s last season and was called up for his first-team debut at leaders Brighton in March. Used in his former position of central defender, he coped as well as anyone could against Bobby Zamora but was released in the summer.

Wycombe W *(Trainee)* FL 1

LEE Alan Desmond
Born: Galway, 21 August 1978
Height: 6'2" **Weight:** 13.9
International Honours: RoI: U21-5
A strong and pacy striker Alan adjusted well to the demands of First Division football last term and continued to show what a bargain buy he has been for Rotherham. He didn't score with any great regularity in the early part of the season, but he went on to net some vital goals in the battle against relegation. His strikes against Wolves and Manchester City were particularly important while he maintained his 100 per cent record from the penalty spot when netting a late equaliser against Bradford City.

Aston Villa *(From trainee on 21/8/1995)*
Torquay U *(Loaned on 27/11/1998)* FL 6+1/2 Others 2/1
Port Vale *(Loaned on 2/3/1999)* FL 7+4/2
Burnley *(£150,000 on 8/7/1999)* FL 2+13 FLC 1+1 FAC 0+2 Others 1/1
Rotherham U *(£150,000 on 21/9/2000)* FL 66+3/22 FLC 2/1 FAC 3+1/1 Others 1/1

LEE Andrew (Andy) Jack
Born: Bradford, 18 August 1982
Height: 5'7" **Weight:** 9.7
Andy is one of the most promising youngsters on the books at Bradford City. He spent much of last season developing in the reserves before having a spell on loan at Unibond club Emley, and on his return he stepped up to the senior squad. He was on the bench for the last four games and came on for the last 30 minutes in the final game of the campaign at Walsall when he did well. He is a very speedy left-sided player who can play at full back or in midfield.

Bradford C *(From trainee on 5/7/2001)* FL 0+1

LEE Christian Earl
Born: Aylesbury, 8 October 1976
Height: 6'2" **Weight:** 11.7
Christian began last season in the Conference with Farnborough Town, before joining Rushden on a short-term contract in September. He made just two appearances for the League's new boys, in the 2-1 defeat of Hartlepool, and then in the record 7-1 thrashing at Cardiff City in the LDV Vans Trophy. The striker subsequently joined Eastwood Town before returning to Farnborough at the turn of the year.

Northampton T *(From trainee at Doncaster Rov on 13/7/1995)* FL 25+34/8 FLC 2/2 FAC 3+3 Others 6+2

Gillingham *(£35,000 + on 3/8/1999)* FL 1+2 FLC 1+1
Rochdale *(Loaned on 20/10/2000)* FL 2+3/1
Leyton Orient *(Loaned on 6/3/2001)* FL 2+1
Bristol Rov *(Free on 22/3/2001)* FL 8+1/2
Rushden & Diamonds *(Free on 28/9/2001)* FL 1 Others 1

LEE David John Francis
Born: Basildon, 28 March 1980
Height: 5'11" **Weight:** 11.8
This talented right-sided midfielder moved to Hull in the 2001 close season but struggled to establish his place in the middle of City's new look midfield. He gave the Boothferry Park fans glimpses of his genuine ability – notably a brilliant free kick to complete the 4-0 defeat of York in September. Two months later he

was on his way to Brighton as part of the deal that saw Matthew Wicks make the opposite journey. He made his debut when coming on as sub during the goalless home draw against Wrexham, but did not get another chance until the last day of the season when he again came on from the bench and gave a comfortable performance in central midfield.

Tottenham H *(From trainee on 17/7/1998)*
Southend U *(Free on 2/8/2000)* FL 37+5/8 FLC 2 FAC 3 Others 5/2
Hull C *(Free on 1/6/2001)* FL 2+9/1 FLC 0+1 FAC 0+1 Others 0+1
Brighton & Hove A *(Free on 11/1/2002)* FL 0+2

LEE Graeme Barry
Born: Middlesbrough, 31 May 1978
Height: 6'2" **Weight:** 13.7
Graeme put his injury problems of the previous season behind him at Hartlepool in 2001-02, returning to the kind of form that had attracted the attention of bigger clubs. A central defender who dominates in the air, his consistent play earned him the supporters' 'Player of the Year' award.

Hartlepool U *(From trainee on 2/7/1996)* FL 163+11/17 FLC 6+2/1 FAC 6+1 Others 13+2/2

LEE Martyn James
Born: Guildford, 10 September 1980
Height: 5'6" **Weight:** 9.0
Although much was expected of this skilful and busy left-footed midfielder, Martyn found it very hard to break into the Wycombe midfield last term. After just four starts he was loaned out to Third Division Cheltenham Town in March until the end of the season to gain further experience. He made his debut for the Robins in the 2-1 win at Scunthorpe United and acted as an able deputy for the injured Russell Milton. His cool temperament was demonstrated when he stepped up to take a penalty in the nail biting play-off semi-final shoot-out against Hartlepool.

Wycombe W *(From trainee on 30/1/1999)* FL 20+15/3 FAC 4+2 Others 3+1
Cheltenham T *(Loaned on 28/3/2002)* FL 2+3 Others 1+1

LEE Robert (Rob) Martin
Born: West Ham, 1 February 1966
Height: 5'11" **Weight:** 11.13
Club Honours: Div 1 '93
International Honours: E: 21; B-1; U21-2
Midfielder Rob started the 2001-02 season at Newcastle struggling with a niggling knee injury, but soon settled into

his normal routine as conductor of the side from midfield. He passed the landmark figure of 300 league appearances for the Magpies but was rather surprisingly sold to Derby County in February. He feature regularly for John Gregory's team, although he was unable to prevent them from being relegated.
Charlton Ath (Free from Hornchurch on 12/7/1983) FL 274+24/59 FLC 16+3/1 FAC 14/2 Others 10+2/3
Newcastle U (£700,00 on 22/9/1992) F/PL 292+11/44 FLC 22+1/3 FAC 27/5 Others 28/4
Derby Co (£250,000 + on 7/2/2002) PL 13

LEGG Andrew (Andy)
Born: Neath, 28 July 1966
Height: 5'8" **Weight:** 10.7
Club Honours: WC '89, '91; AIC '95
International Honours: W: 6
Andy was a hugely influential figure at Cardiff City again last season. Reverting to a role on the left-hand side of defence he gave his usual 100 per cent commitment. City's club captain, his effort, enthusiasm and tenacity, earned him a new 12-month contract. He was troubled by a number of injuries during the campaign and was sorely missed in the play-off semi-finals against Stoke City.
Swansea C (Signed from Britton Ferry on 12/8/1988) FL 155+8/29 FLC 9+1 FAC 16/4 Others 15+3/5
Notts Co (£275,000 on 23/7/1993) FL 85+4/9 FLC 11 FAC 7+1 Others 13+2/6
Birmingham C (Signed on 29/2/1996) FL 31+14/5 FLC 3+1 FAC 2+1
Ipswich T (Loaned on 3/11/1997) FL 6/1 FLC 1
Reading (£75,000 on 20/2/1998) FL 12 FLC 1
Peterborough U (Loaned on 15/10/1998) FL 5
Cardiff C (Free on 16/12/1998) FL 126+14/9 FLC 7 FAC 13+3

LEGWINSKI Sylvain
Born: Clermont-Ferrand, France, 6 October 1973
Height: 6'3" **Weight:** 11.7
International Honours: France: U21
Sylvain arrived at Craven Cottage a few days after the start of the 2001-02 season having previously played under Jean Tigana at Monaco. A tough-tackling midfielder he operated mostly in a central role, but seemed to cover most of the pitch during the course of a game. Although not always on top of his form he never gave up and displayed an instinct to pop up in vital positions. He scored in successive games against West Ham and Newcastle and went on to net a total of five goals in all competitions during the season.

Fulham (£3,500,000 from Bordeaux, France, ex AS Monaco, on 22/8/2001) PL 30+3/3 FLC 1+1/1 FAC 5/1

LEHMANN Dirk Johannes
Born: Aachen, Germany, 16 August 1971
Height: 6'0" **Weight:** 11.10
Dirk never really settled on the south coast after joining Brighton from Hibernian in the summer of 2001. His only goal during his time at Withdean was the first in the 2-1 away victory at Swansea in the LDV Vans Trophy and soon after the arrival of Peter Taylor he returned north of the border to sign for Motherwell on a free transfer. At his best he is an useful striker who is particularly effective in the air.
Fulham (£30,000 from Energie Cottbus, Germany, ex Alemannia Aachen, FC Koln, Lierse, RWD Molenbeek, on 7/8/1998) FL 16+10/2 FLC 5/2 FAC 2+2/1 Others 1
Hibernian (Free on 15/7/1999) SL 28+31/9 SLC 4+2/1 SC 5+4/3
Brighton & Hove A (Free on 29/6/2001) FL 3+4 FLC 1+1 Others 3/1
Motherwell (Loaned on 18/1/2002) SL 10+1/4

LEIGERTWOOD Mikele Benjamin
Born: Enfield, 12 November 1982
Height: 6'1" **Weight:** 13.11
Mikele joined Leyton Orient on loan from Wimbledon last November and proved to be a confident centre half who impressed the O's fans with his no-nonsense approach and crisp tackling. On his return to Selhurst Park he had to wait till the final game of the season for his first start in the senior team. He gave a classy performance and will be looking to gain further senior experience in 2002-03.
Wimbledon (From trainee on 29/6/2001) FL 1
Leyton Orient (Loaned on 19/11/2001) FL 8 FAC 2

LEITAO Jorge Manuel Vasconcelos
Born: Oporto, Portugal, 14 January 1974
Height: 5'11" **Weight:** 13.4
Jorge got off to a great start to his second season in English football with a fine headed goal for Walsall in the opening game against West Brom, but was in and out of the side for much of the first half of 2001-02. Colin Lee brought him back immediately after his appointment as manager in January and Jorge responded with two splendidly taken goals in the FA Cup win at Charlton. When on song he was strong, quick and difficult to handle and in the final run-in he netted decisive

goals in successive wins over Stockport and Sheffield United, though not fully match fit, to ensure the Saddlers stayed in Division One.
Walsall (£150,000 from SC Farense, Portugal, ex Avintes, on 10/8/2000) FL 64+18/26 FLC 5/2 FAC 5+1/3 Others 3

LEONHARDSEN Oyvind
Born: Kristiansund, Norway, 17 August 1970
Height: 5'10" **Weight:** 11.2
International Honours: Norway: 78; U21-14; Yth
This plucky Tottenham midfielder missed a large chunk of the 2001-02 season through injury. On the rare occasions that he appeared in the team he looked as sharp and comfortable on the ball as ever. Great with the ball at his feet, Oyvind loves to get forward and was badly missed by the team.
Wimbledon (£660,000 from Rosenborg, Norway, ex Clausenengen, Molde, on 8/11/1994) PL 73+3/13 FLC 7+2/1 FAC 17/2
Liverpool (£3,500,000 on 3/6/1997) PL 34+3/7 FLC 4+2 FAC 1 Others 3+2
Tottenham H (£3,000,000 on 6/8/1999) PL 46+8/7 FLC 6+2/2 FAC 3+3/1 Others 4/1

LE PEN Ulrich
Born: Auray, France, 21 January 1974
Height: 5'8" **Weight:** 9.12
This experienced left winger began last season at Laval before joining Ipswich Town in November. He made his debut from the subs' bench against Bolton soon afterwards but had the misfortune to suffer an ankle injury within a matter of minutes of coming on the pitch. He returned for the FA Cup defeat by Manchester City but made no further appearances during the campaign.
Ipswich T (£1,400,000 from Lorient, France, ex Rennes, Lavallois, on 15/11/2001) PL 0+1 FAC 0+1

LE SAUX Graeme Pierre
Born: Jersey, 17 October 1968
Height: 5'10" **Weight:** 12.2
Club Honours: PL '95; FLC '98; ESC '98; CS '00
International Honours: E: 36; B-2; U21-4
Left back Graeme Le Saux had an outstanding campaign for Chelsea last term, - skippering the side in the absence of Marcel Desailly he proved to be an inspirational leader. With Celestine Babayaro fully fit and claiming the left-back spot Graeme then usurped Bouwedjin Zenden for the wide-left midfield role and played an important

Graeme Le Saux

Joleon Lescott

part in the Blues' new-found defensive solidarity in addition to supplementing the attack and curling over dangerous crosses for the front-men. Graeme picked up an unfortunate injury in the FA Cup semi-final when after just four minutes he pulled up with a calf strain with no other player nearby and was carried off on a stretcher; fortunately he recovered in time for the final against Arsenal after travelling to Germany to receive specialist treatment.

Chelsea *(Free from St Paul's, Jersey on 9/12/1987) F/PL 77+13/8 FLC 7+6/1 FAC 7+1 Others 8+1*
Blackburn Rov *(£750,000 on 25/3/1993) PL 127+2/7 FLC 10 FAC 8 Others 6+1*
Chelsea *(£5,000,000 on 8/8/1997) PL 106+6/2 FLC 8/1 FAC 15+2/2 Others 19+2*

LESCOTT Aaron Anthony
Born: Birmingham, 2 December 1978
Height: 5'8" **Weight:** 10.9
Aaron failed to make a significant breakthrough for Sheffield Wednesday last season and was allowed to join Stockport County in November, becoming Carlton Palmer's first signing for the club. He made his debut in the memorable 2-1 victory over Norwich and became so influential that he was handed the captain's armband when long-term skipper Mike Flynn went out on loan to Stoke. A wholehearted midfield player, he missed the closing months of the campaign after suffering a knee injury.
Aston Villa *(From trainee on 5/7/1996) FAC 0+1*
Lincoln C *(Loaned on 14/3/2000) FL 3+2*
Sheffield Wed *(£100,000 on 3/10/2000) FL 19+18 FLC 3+1 FAC 2*
Stockport Co *(£75,000 on 14/11/2001) FL 17 FAC 1*

LESCOTT Joleon Patrick
Born: Birmingham, 16 August 1982
Height: 6'2" **Weight:** 13.0
International Honours: E: Yth
Joleon rather surprisingly partnered Paul Butler in the heart of the Wolves' defence from the opening day of last season. He was outstanding, making it very difficult for opponents to get by him, and he made fewer mistakes than previously. He also managed a couple of goals s in the opening weeks. When he missed three matches due to suspension, the team did not look so solid at the back. He is excellent at breaking up attacks and his distribution is improving. Joleon made the England U20 team, was again Wolves 'Youth Player of the Season' and was also named in the PFA Division One team for

Jack Lester

2001-02. He is the brother of Stockport's Aaron Lescott.
Wolverhampton W (From trainee on 18/8/1999) FL 75+6/7 FLC 5 FAC 2 Others 2

LESTER Jack William
Born: Sheffield, 8 October 1975
Height: 5'10" **Weight:** 11.8
Club Honours: AMC '98
International Honours: E: Sch
Jack is a striker who always gives 100 per cent and runs his heart out for the team. He had an in-and-out season at Nottingham Forest last term after suffering a groin strain and then breaking his hand. His tally of five goals was a little disappointing, although he sometimes played in a midfield, a role that seemed to suit him.
Grimsby T (From juniors on 8/7/1994) FL 93+40/17 FLC 13+4/6 FAC 7+2/2 Others 4+4
Doncaster Rov (Loaned on 20/9/1996) FL 5+6/1
Nottingham F (£300,000 on 28/1/2000) FL 53+13/14 FLC 2/1 FAC 1

LE TISSIER Matthew (Matt) Paul
Born: Guernsey, 14 October 1968
Height: 6'1" **Weight:** 13.8
International Honours: E: 8; B-6; Yth
Restricted to just four substitute appearances during the season, Matt brought down the curtain on his outstanding playing career by announcing his retirement in March. Without doubt the most skilful to wear the red-and-white strips of Southampton, his testimonial in May marked a well earned reward for his loyal and devoted dedication to keeping Saints in the Premiership. Matt's services though will not be lost as he will remain at St Mary's as an ambassador for the club.
Southampton (From apprentice on 17/10/1986) F/PL 377+66/162 FLC 44+8/27 FAC 30+3/12 Others 11+1/9

LEVER Mark
Born: Beverley, 29 March 1970
Height: 6'3" **Weight:** 13.5
Club Honours: AMC '98
After his injury-hit campaign of the previous season, Mark had a relatively successful time at Bristol City in 2001-02. A tidy accomplished central defender who is powerful in the air and strong in the tackle, he was placed on the transfer list at the end of the campaign.
Grimsby T (From trainee on 9/8/1988) FL 343+18/8 FLC 22+2 FAC 17+3 Others 18
Bristol C (Free on 24/7/2000) FL 28+3/1 FLC 3 FAC 1 Others 1+1

LEWIS Edward (Eddie) James
Born: Cerritos, California, USA, 17 May 1974
Height: 5'9" **Weight:** 11.12
International Honours: USA: 43
This winger appeared only once for the Fulham first team last term, lining up in the final Premiership game of the season. Eddie did not enjoy the best of seasons at club level and was rarely named in the first-team match-day squad. He did however remain very much a part of the national team and secured a place in the USA World Cup squad. A tricky winger who is arguably the best wide player at the club, he enjoys taking on defenders with the ball at his feet. He has an explosive shot and is not frightened to have a go from distance, though sadly his goal-scoring touch deserted him somewhat in the FA Premier Reserve League.
Fulham (£1,300,000 from San Jose Clash, USA on 17/3/2000) P/FL 8+8 FLC 6/1

LEWIS Karl Junior
Born: Wembley, 9 October 1973
Height: 6'5" **Weight:** 12.4
Club Honours: Div 2 '02
This lanky midfielder found his limitations were sometimes exposed at Premiership level and eventually rejoined his former boss Peter Taylor on loan at Brighton where he scored on his home debut against Reading. The Seagulls' midfield took on a better shape following his arrival and the team went on to lose only one more game, which was the televised defeat at Stoke. Junior weighed in with some important goals including the winner against Huddersfield before returning to Filbert Street where he subsequently underwent a hernia operation.
Fulham (From trainee on 3/7/1992) FL 4+1 FAC 1 (Free to Dover Ath during 1993 close season)
Gillingham (Free from Hendon on 3/8/1999) FL 47+12/8 FLC 4+2 FAC 7+2 Others 4
Leicester C (£50,000 on 30/1/2001) PL 19+2 FLC 1
Brighton & Hove A (Loaned on 8/2/2002) FL 14+1/3

LEWIS Matthew Thomas
Born: Coventry, 20 March 1984
Height: 6'1" **Weight:** 11.7
Matthew scored over 50 times for the youth team of Coventry Marconi in the 2000-01 campaign and this attracted the attention of the Kidderminster management who quickly snapped him

up on a three-year contract. A tall and gangly centre forward he was limited to just two substitute appearances last term, but with Harriers set to operate with a smaller squad in 2002-03 he should find himself given more chances.
Kidderminster Hrs (Free from Coventry Marconi on 23/7/2001) FL 0+2

LIBBRA Marc
Born: Toulon, France, 5 August 1972
Height: 6'3" **Weight:** 12.11
Marc is a fantastic showman who is capable of the most brilliant flicks, tricks and moments of skill, but who on other occasions simply does not contribute to his team's performance. He became an instant success with the fans, scoring within 19 seconds of coming off the bench in his debut against Manchester City, with a fantastic volley. He has outstanding control and technique to go past defenders in very tight situations and he has one of the most powerful left feet in the First Division. He seemed to struggle in the mid-season period and was often left out, but he retained the potential to change a game in a single moment with one piece of brilliance.
Hibernian (Loaned from Toulouse, France on 22/2/2000) SL 7+4/5 SC 2+1
Norwich C (£500,000 from Toulouse, France, ex Marseilles, AS Cannes, on 9/8/2001) FL 17+17/7 FLC 1 FAC 2 Others 0+1

LIBURD Richard John
Born: Nottingham, 26 September 1973
Height: 5'9" **Weight:** 11.1
Richard is the sort of player for whom the term 'utility player' was invented – just name the job and give him the shirt! An honest player who carries out the task in hand with a quiet efficiency, his best position is at right back, although he was often found on the opposite flank for Notts County last term. He is capable of turning a game with a quite unpredictable moment of creative genius – leaving Magpies' fans wishing he could produce these more regularly.
Middlesbrough (£20,000 from Eastwood T on 25/3/1993) FL 41/1 FLC 4 FAC 2 Others 5
Bradford C (£200,000 on 21/7/1994) FL 75+3/3 FLC 6+2 FAC 2+2 Others 2
Carlisle U (Free on 26/2/1998) FL 9
Notts Co (Free on 4/8/1998) FL 101+21/7 FLC 4+2 FAC 8+4/2 Others 0+1

LIDDELL Andrew (Andy) Mark
Born: Leeds, 28 June 1973
Height: 5'7" **Weight:** 11.6
Club Honours: AMC '99

Jari Litmanen

International Honours: S: U21-12
A key member of Wigan Athletic's side, Andy finished the 2001-02 season as top scorer with a career-best tally of 18 League goals. A talented right-footed striker with pace, who can make as well as score goals, his unselfish running often unlocked defences for his colleagues. He was out for several weeks after twisting an ankle at Brighton and on his return played in a more advanced striking position. He went on to net the club's 1500th Football League goal in the away win at Brentford, and his first ever hat-trick in the home win over Brighton, followed by another in the 4-1 win against Cambridge United. His performances saw him collect runners-up spot in the supporters' 'Player of the Year' awards, and receive a call up from new Scotland coach Berti Vogts for an end-of-season training camp.
Barnsley (From trainee on 6/7/1991) F/PL 142+56/34 FLC 11+2/3 FAC 5+7/1 Others 2+1
Wigan Ath (£350,000 on 15/10/1998) FL 139+1/45 FLC 6/1 FAC 6/1 Others 13+1

LIDDLE Craig George
Born: Chester le Street, 21 October 1971
Height: 5'11" **Weight:** 12.7
Darlington skipper Craig was playing as well as ever in the centre of the defence at the start of last season before suffering a broken ankle against Hull City in October. When he returned in mid-January he was still not quite fit and was in and out of the side for the next couple of months. However he played the last nine games of the campaign and eventually found his best form. His leadership was sorely missed on the field and the Quakers' fortunes suffered in his absence.
Aston Villa (From trainee on 4/7/1990. Free to Blyth Spartans in August 1991)
Middlesbrough (Free on 12/7/1994) P/FL 20+5 FLC 3+2 FAC 2 Others 2
Darlington (Free on 20/2/1998) FL 180/8 FLC 8 FAC 10 Others 10/3

LIGHTBOURNE Kyle Lavince
Born: Bermuda, 29 September 1968
Height: 6'2" **Weight:** 12.4
Club Honours: AMC '00
International Honours: Bermuda: 22; Yth
After signing for Macclesfield only a fortnight before the start of the 2001-02 campaign Kyle found it difficult to settle. His appearances were further restricted by an ankle injury but he still showed the ability to score spectacular goals,

including a 40-yard pinpoint chip in the home match against Shrewsbury Town. Shortly before the transfer deadline he joined Hull in a loan deal. Arriving at a difficult time for the club, his experience as a striker helped to take the pressure off the shoulders of his young partners. Kyle is a double international having represented Bermuda at both football and cricket.
Scarborough (Signed from Pembroke Hamilton, Bermuda on 11/12/1992) FL 11+8/3 FLC 1 Others 0+1
Walsall (Free on 17/9/1993) FL 158+7/65 FLC 8/3 FAC 16+2/12 Others 7/5
Coventry C (£500,000 + on 18/7/1997) PL 1+6 FLC 3
Fulham (Loaned on 13/1/1998) FL 4/2 Others 1/1
Stoke C (£500,000 on 16/2/1998) FL 83+28/21 FLC 7 FAC 3/1 Others 7+2/3
Swindon T (Loaned on 13/1/2001) FL 2
Cardiff C (Loaned on 20/2/2001) FL 2+1
Macclesfield T (Free on 31/7/2001) FL 22+7/4 FLC 1
Hull C (Loaned on 20/3/2002) FL 3+1

LINDEROTH Tobias
Born: Sweden, 21 April 1979
Height: 5'9" **Weight:** 10.12
International Honours: Sweden: 24; U21-22
A steady, technically sound central midfielder, Tobias likes to sit in front of the back four breaking up opposition attacks and earning his team possession. Snapped up by Walter Smith from Stabaek he suffered when his mentor was sacked and new boss David Moyes didn't use him until the final match of the season, by which time his place on the plane as part of Sweden's World Cup squad had already been assured. Tobias' father Anders played for Sweden in the 1978 World Cup finals in Argentina.
Everton (£2,500,000 + from Stabaek, Norway, ex Hassleholm, Elfsborg, on 1/2/2002) PL 4+4 FAC 2+1

LISBIE Kevin Anthony
Born: Hackney, 17 October 1978
Height: 5'8" **Weight:** 10.12
International Honours: Jamaica: 2; E: Yth
Kevin probably had his best season yet for the Addicks, featuring in over half the games and finishing joint-second-top scorer with five goals. He has electric pace, is very skilful on the ball and can play as a central striker or wide on the right. He holds the ball up well and is a good crosser of the ball. He scored a brilliant late equaliser against Sunderland at the Valley to ensure another Premiership season for Charlton, but his

best performance was against Tottenham at the Valley when he scored twice. He was rewarded for his hard work with a call-up to the Jamaican national team.
Charlton Ath (From trainee on 24/5/1996) P/FL 20+63/7 FLC 2+7/2 FAC 2+4
Gillingham (Loaned on 5/3/1999) FL 4+3/4
Reading (Loaned on 26/11/1999) FL 1+1
Queens Park R (Loaned on 1/12/2000) FL 1+1

LITMANEN Jari Olaui
Born: Lahti, Finland, 20 February 1971
Height: 5'11" **Weight:** 12.12
Club Honours: ESC '01
International Honours: Finland: 75
Jari was expected to have a large influence on Liverpool's team strategy in 2001-02 following an injury troubled first season, but in reality he was used more as a squad player. The system operated by the Reds did not require a player in the 'hole' behind the front two, where Jari excels, so he generally appeared up front as a partner to Emile Heskey or Michael Owen. He scored seven goals during the campaign including long-distance winners against Tottenham in the Premiership and Dynamo Kiev in the Champions' League.
Liverpool (Free from Barcelona, Spain, ex Reipas, HJK Helsinki, MyPa, Ajax, on 18/1/2001) PL 12+14/5 FLC 2+1 FAC 1+2/1 Others 4+7/3

LITTLE Colin Campbell
Born: Wythenshawe, 4 November 1972
Height: 5'10" **Weight:** 11.0
Colin again found it difficult to win a regular place in the Crewe Alexandra line-up last term and appeared in the starting line-up on only ten occasions. When called upon he always gave 100 per cent effort and contributed two goals. He is a quick and lively striker who is capable of causing problems for opposition defenders.
Crewe Alex (£50,000 from Hyde U on 7/2/1996) FL 132+55/33 FLC 15+2/8 FAC 5/1 Others 5/3

LITTLE Glen Matthew
Born: Wimbledon, 15 October 1975
Height: 6'3" **Weight:** 13.0
Some were talking of 'Super Glen' becoming Burnley's first England international for nearly 30 years, so impressive were his performances for the Clarets last autumn. Not only were his pace and trickery on the wing causing untold problems for First Division defences, he was also scoring goals like never before, including a magnificent 20-yard curler in a 3-2 win at Birmingham. Not for the first time, though, injury was

Freddie Ljungberg

to disrupt his season. His nine League goals all came before Christmas, and afterwards he never quite looked at his sharpest although he remained the one Burnley player who appeared capable of turning a game.

Crystal Palace *(From trainee on 1/7/1994. Free to Glentoran on 11/11/1994)*
Burnley *(£100,000 on 29/11/1996) FL 150+29/24 FLC 7+3 FAC 8+3/1 Others 4+1/1*

LITTLEJOHN Adrian Sylvester
Born: Wolverhampton, 26 September 1970
Height: 5'9" **Weight:** 11.0
International Honours: E: Yth
Adrian became a free agent during the summer of 2001 and after trials with a number of clubs he joined Sheffield United on a non-contract basis as cover for injuries. After a run out in the reserves he featured as a striker against Crewe and made substitute appearances in the following two games. Although not match fit, he nevertheless played with his usual directness, making good use of his still impressive pace and, with a little luck, could have scored. He was released by the Blades in December.

Walsall *(From trainee at West Bromwich A juniors on 24/5/1989) FL 26+18/1 FLC 2+1 FAC 1+1 Others 4+1*
Sheffield U *(Free on 6/8/1991) F/PL 44+25/12 FLC 5+1 FAC 3+2/1 Others 2/1*
Plymouth Arg *(£100,000 on 22/9/1995) FL 100+10/29 FLC 6 FAC 6+2/3 Others 6*
Oldham Ath *(Signed on 20/3/1998) FL 16+5/5 FLC 2/1*
Bury *(£75,000 on 13/11/1998) FL 69+30/14 FLC 4/2 FAC 6/1 Others 2+1*
Sheffield U *(Free on 22/10/2001) FL 1+2*

LIVERMORE David
Born: Edmonton, 20 May 1980
Height: 5'11" **Weight:** 12.1
Club Honours: Div 2 '01
This hard-tackling midfielder showed himself to be a true professional at Millwall last term and was a real asset to the side. A near ever present, he never seemed to know when to give up and the only minor criticism is that he failed to get on the score sheet.

Arsenal *(From trainee on 13/7/1998)*
Millwall *(£30,000 on 30/7/1999) FL 111+3/5 FLC 8/1 FAC 5 Others 5*

LIVINGSTONE Stephen (Steve) Carl
Born: Middlesbrough, 8 September 1968
Height: 6'1" **Weight:** 13.6
Club Honours: AMC '98

Steve spent virtually the whole of the 2001-02 campaign on the injury list after suffering a calf injury during a pre-season tour of Northern Ireland which proved more serious than was at first thought. The veteran Grimsby striker/central defender eventually returned for the last few weeks of the season and made three appearances from the subs' bench in the closing matches. After such a difficult time he will be hoping to return to full match fitness for the 2002-03 season and to re-establish himself as part of the senior squad.

Coventry C *(From trainee on 16/7/1986) FL 17+14/5 FLC 8+2/10 Others 0+1*
Blackburn Rov *(£450,000 on 17/1/1991) F/PL 25+5/10 FLC 2 FAC 1/1*
Chelsea *(£350,000 on 23/3/1993) PL 0+1*
Port Vale *(Loaned on 3/9/1993) FL 4+1*
Grimsby T *(£140,000 on 29/10/1993) FL 205+54/40 FLC 15+6/4 FAC 11+5/4 Others 4+3*

LJUNGBERG Fredrik (Freddie)
Born: Sweden, 16 April 1977
Height: 5'9" **Weight:** 11.6
Club Honours: CS '99; PL '02; FAC '02
International Honours: Sweden: 34; U21-12; Yth
Freddie was in excellent form for Arsenal last term and contributed a total of 17 goals including a great strike in the FA Cup final victory over Chelsea. A combative midfield dynamo, he is also an aggressive ball winner. He was a key member of the Gunners' squad that achieved a domestic double in 2001-02 and also featured for Sweden in the 2002 World Cup finals.

Arsenal *(£3,000,000 from BK Halmstad, Sweden on 17/9/1998) PL 81+16/25 FLC 2 FAC 13+2/3 Others 30+7/7*

LLEWELLYN Christopher (Chris) Mark
Born: Swansea, 29 August 1979
Height: 5'11" **Weight:** 11.6
International Honours: W: 2; B-1; U21-14; Yth
Chris had the misfortune to lose his place in the Norwich City line-up through injury early on last season and then struggled to win it back. Predominantly a left-sided midfielder, he can also play as a central striker, a position he played as a youth-team player. A strong-running player with an eye for goal he will be looking to re-establish himself in the senior line-up again in 2002-03.

Norwich C *(From trainee on 21/1/1997) FL 101+36/17 FLC 7+2 FAC 3+3/1*

LOCKE Adam Spencer
Born: Croydon, 20 August 1970
Height: 5'11" **Weight:** 12.7
This vastly experienced midfielder, rarely featured in the Luton Town first team last season. Niggling injuries, the most recent a calf problem, reduced his playing chances even in the reserves. A hard-working player who likes to push forward in support of his strikers, he was out of contract in the summer.

Crystal Palace *(From trainee on 21/6/1988)*
Southend U *(Free on 6/8/1990) FL 56+17/4 FLC 5 FAC 2+1 Others 6+1*
Colchester U *(Loaned on 8/10/1993) FL 4 Others 1*
Colchester U *(Free on 23/9/1994) FL 64+15/8 FLC 5+1 FAC 5 Others 8+5*
Bristol C *(Free on 23/7/1997) FL 61+4/4 FLC 6 FAC 3 Others 2/1*
Luton T *(Free on 24/8/1999) FL 45+17/5 FLC 1+1 FAC 5+2 Others 2*

LOCKE Gary
Born: Edinburgh, 16 June 1975
Height: 5'10" **Weight:** 11.3
International Honours: S: U21-10
Gary started the 2001-02 season in outstanding form for Bradford City, mostly featuring in a central midfield role. However he was plagued by injuries in the second half of the campaign when an ankle problem and then a groin operation effectively sidelined him until the summer. He is a very strong and hard-tackling midfielder and received a number of yellow cards last term – an area of his game where he needs to show improvement.

Heart of Midlothian *(Free from Whitehill Welfare on 31/7/1992) SL 126+29/5 SLC 14+1 SC 10+1/1 Others 8*
Bradford C *(Free on 26/1/2001) P/FL 32+6/2 FLC 1 FAC 1*

LOCKWOOD Matthew (Matt) Dominic
Born: Southend, 17 October 1976
Height: 5'9" **Weight:** 10.12
Matt had another useful season at Leyton Orient last term, although he missed a lengthy spell in the first half of the campaign after suffering a ruptured spleen. He is an attacking left back who is a master at free kicks and penalties. He was rewarded for some fine performances with a new two-year contract for the O's.

Queens Park R *(From trainee at Southend U on 2/5/1995)*
Bristol Rov *(Free on 24/7/1996) FL 58+5/1 FLC 2+1 FAC 6 Others 4+2*
Leyton Orient *(Free on 7/8/1998) FL 128+6/18 FLC 11/2 FAC 11 Others 7/1*

LOGAN Richard Anthony
Born: Barnsley, 24 May 1969
Height: 6'1" **Weight:** 13.3
This experienced central defender had a frustrating season at Lincoln City last term. Richard was on the injured list after suffering a pre-season calf strain and then had a recurrence of the back injury which kept him out for most of the 2000-01 season. When he regained his fitness he found it impossible to get into the Imps' starting line-up. Richard finally got into action as a stoppage time substitute at Oxford United in February but made just one further brief appearance from the bench.
Huddersfield T (Free from Gainsborough Trinity on 15/11/1993) FL 35+10/1 FLC 3 FAC 1 Others 9
Plymouth Arg (£20,000 on 26/10/1995) FL 67+19/12 FLC 4/1 FAC 2+2 Others 8
Scunthorpe U (Free on 2/7/1998) FL 77+3/7 FLC 1 FAC 4 Others 3
Lincoln C (Free on 12/7/2000) FL 4+3 FLC 1

LOGAN Richard James
Born: Bury St Edmunds, 4 January 1982
Height: 6'0" **Weight:** 12.5
International Honours: E: Yth; Sch
Richard spent three months on loan with Torquay last term to gain more experience of senior football. He added shape to the Gulls' line-up playing as a central striker, and he showed the ability to control the ball, hold it up and bring his colleagues into the game. He scored four times in his first ten games but some profligate finishing saw him fail to add to the tally, and his later performances seemed to lack the aggression and commitment required of a target man.
Ipswich T (From trainee on 6/1/1999) FL 0+3 FAC 0+1
Cambridge U (Loaned on 25/1/2001) FL 5/1
Torquay U (Loaned on 13/12/2001) FL 16/4

LOMAS Stephen (Steve) Martin
Born: Hanover, Germany, 18 January 1974
Height: 6'0" **Weight:** 12.8
International Honours: NI: 40; B-1; Yth; Sch
After being out of the game for ten months with a cruciate ligament injury Steve returned to the West Ham team against Charlton last November. His battling qualities and leadership from the right side of midfield had been sorely missed. Unfortunately in the very next game against Spurs he broke his toe and did not play again until January.

He returned again at Chelsea in the FA Cup and earned the Hammers a deserved draw. His enthusiasm was a joy to watch and he was also able to net three goals.
Manchester C (From trainee on 22/1/1991) P/FL 102+9/8 FLC 15/2 FAC 10+1/1
West Ham U (£1,600,000 on 26/3/1997) PL 129+1/9 FLC 10/2 FAC 9+1/1 Others 10

LOPEZ Carlos
Born: Mexico City, 18 April 1970
Height: 6'1" **Weight:** 12.0
This Mexican central defender, reputed to have played for Necaxa, joined Wycombe Wanderers on trial last January. Unexpectedly given his League debut at Cambridge, he was used as a left wing back without impressing and was released after the game.
Wycombe W (Free from Chester City, via trial with Cambridge U, on 17/1/2002) FL 1

LOPEZ Rik Alexander
Born: Harrow, 25 December 1979
Height: 5'10" **Weight:** 11.12
Rik Lopez joined Bristol Rovers as a non-contract player after a short spell in Portuguese football. A pacy attacking left back, he showed early promise but then had to undergo a calf operation, which kept him out of action for three months. Returning to the first team in February, he enjoyed a 'Man of the Match' performance at Oxford but then picked up another injury in the following match, and did not add any further appearances to his total. He was released at the end of the season.
Queens Park R (From trainee on 2/4/1997. Released during 2000 close season)
Bristol Rov (Free from Uniao Leiria, Portugal on 9/8/2001) FL 5+2 FAC 1

LORMOR Anthony (Anth)
Born: Ashington, 29 October 1970
Height: 6'0" **Weight:** 13.6
This proven goal-scorer failed to gain a regular first-team place at Hartlepool during the 2001-02 season. Always prepared to give his best despite often being restricted to substitute appearances, he remained popular with the supporters. In February he was loaned out to Shrewsbury as a replacement for the injured Nigel Jemson. He enjoyed better fortunes at Gay Meadow, scoring in his second game against Mansfield and also against Swansea. He returned to Hartlepool to see out his contract and was released on a free transfer in the close season.

Newcastle U (From trainee on 25/2/1988) FL 6+2/3
Lincoln C (£25,000 on 29/1/1990) FL 90+10/30 FLC 1+2/3 FAC 4/2 Others 6
Peterborough U (Free on 4/7/1994) FL 2+3 FAC 1 Others 1+1
Chesterfield (Free on 23/12/1994) FL 97+16/35 FLC 8/4 FAC 5/3 Others 7+1/3
Preston NE (£130,000 + on 5/11/1997) FL 9+3/3 FAC 3 Others 3
Notts Co (Loaned on 20/2/1998) FL 2+5
Mansfield T (£20,000 on 16/7/1998) FL 68+6/20 FLC 2+1 FAC 3/3 Others 4/1
Hartlepool U (£30,000 on 9/8/2000) FL 26+22/9 FLC 1+1 Others 2+3
Shrewsbury T (Loaned on 15/2/2002) FL 7/2

LOUIS Jefferson Lee
Born: Harrow, 22 February 1979
Height: 6'2" **Weight:** 13.2
Jefferson returned to football with Ryman League outfit Thame United at the start of 2002 and impressed sufficiently to win a trial with Oxford United within a matter of weeks. He subsequently signed non-contract forms with the Third Division club and appeared as a substitute in the last game of the season against Darlington. He is a big and powerful strong-running striker.
Oxford U (Free from Thame U, ex Aylesbury U, on 4/3/2002) FL 0+1

LOUIS-JEAN Matthieu
Born: Mont St Aignan, France, 22 February 1976
Height: 5'9" **Weight:** 10.12
International Honours: France: U21; Yth
This right full back or wing back made the position his own for Nottingham Forest last term, playing in 37 games. Good in the tackle, comfortable on the ball and effective going forward, he scored his first senior goal for the club in the final home game of the season against Crewe.
Nottingham F (Signed from Le Havre, France on 14/9/1998) P/FL 88+6/1 FLC 9+2 FAC 2

LOVELL Stephen (Steve) William Henry
Born: Amersham, 6 December 1980
Height: 6'1" **Weight:** 12.7
Steve scored regularly for Portsmouth's reserves last season, but was in and out of the first team, and mostly featured as a substitute. A two-footed striker with pace, he concentrated hard on his game and scored doubles against Crewe and Stockport, but still needs a longer run in the team to develop consistency. He joined Sheffield United on loan in March

Onandi Lowe

and made a promising start on his debut against Millwall, playing with strength and determination alongside Laurent D'Jaffo.

Bournemouth (From trainee on 15/7/1999) FL 1+7

Portsmouth (£250,000 on 13/8/1999) FL 13+19/3 FLC 2+1/1 FAC 1

Exeter C (Loaned on 20/3/2000) FL 4+1/1

Sheffield U (Loaned on 19/3/2002) FL 3+2/1

LOVETT Jay
Born: Brighton, 22 January 1978
Height: 6'2" Weight: 12.5
This steady Brentford right back had a disappointing season in 2001-02. The previous campaign had seen him a regular in the squad but last term he made just two League appearances. He then spent three months on loan with his former club Crawley before returning to Griffin Park to play for the reserves.

Brentford (£75,000 from Crawley on 27/7/2000) FL 23+4 Others 3+2/1

LOW Joshua (Josh) David
Born: Bristol, 15 February, 1979
Height: 6'1" Weight: 12.0
International Honours: W: U21-4; Yth
Josh was hampered by hamstring injuries at Cardiff last term, but finished the season fully fit and set for a major effort in 2002-03. The speedy right winger occasionally appeared to lack confidence in his own ability, but at his best his searing pace caused defenders problems. He will be hoping to make the wide-right position his own in the coming season.

Bristol Rov (From trainee on 19/8/1996) FL 11+11 FLC 0+2 FAC 2+2 Others 2

Leyton Orient (Free on 27/5/1999) FL 2+3/1 FLC 1

Cardiff C (Free on 20/11/1999) FL 54+21/6 FLC 1+1 FAC 2+3 Others 3+1

LOWE Onandi
Born: Kingston, Jamaica, 2 December 1973
Height: 6'3" Weight: 13.12
International Honours: Jamaica
An inspirational signing by Rushden boss Brian Talbot, Onandi burst onto the Third Division scene towards the end of 2001. Initially recruited on a three-month loan deal, he finally secured a long-term contract after lengthy discussions between the club and the Major League Soccer organisation, which held his Kansas City Wizards registration. In 29 games he hit an incredible 20 goals, including nine in

five games. Without them the club wouldn't have reached the play-offs, if he had been there from August they might well have earned automatic promotion!

Port Vale (Loaned from Rochester Rhinos, USA, ex Harbour View, Montreal Impact, Waterhouse, Richmond Kickers, on 1/2/2001) FL 4+1/1 Others 1/1

Rushden & Diamonds (Free from Kansas Wizards, USA on 30/11/2001) FL 25/19 FAC 1 Others 3/1

LOWE Ryan Thomas
Born: Liverpool, 18 September 1978
Height: 5'11" Weight: 11.10
Ryan made tremendous progress at Shrewsbury in 2001-02, only his second season of senior football. He took some time to get going after suffering a pre-season injury, but showed his best form after Christmas. Playing as a striker or just behind the front two on the right he showed good control on the ball and an excellent turn of pace which made him a constant threat to Division Three defences. He scored seven goals during the season including a vital strike in the 1-0 home win against Carlisle as a play off spot beckoned.

Shrewsbury T (Free from Burscough on 25/7/2000) FL 35+33/11 FLC 0+2 FAC 0+1 Others 2

LOWNDES Nathan Peter
Born: Salford, 2 June 1977
Height: 5'11" Weight: 11.6
Nathan mostly featured from the bench for Livingston last term, and after being tracked for some time by Rotherham manager Ronnie Moore, he moved on loan to Millmoor on transfer deadline day. However, he was unable to make any real impact in his two starts as a striker for the Millers and subsequently returned north of the border.

Leeds U (From trainee on 1/4/1995)

Watford (£40,000 on 3/10/1995) FL 1+6 FLC 0+1 FAC 1+1 Others 1

St Johnstone (£50,000 on 21/8/1998) SL 30+34/14 SLC 2+2/2 SC 4+2 Others 2+1

Livingston (Free on 20/7/2001) SL 7+14/3 SLC 0+2 SC 0+2

Rotherham U (Loaned on 28/3/2002) FL 2

LUA LUA Lomano Tresor
Born: Zaire, 28 December 1980
Height: 5'8" Weight: 12.2
International Honours: DR Congo: 4
The African Nations' Cup in Mali saw Lomana capped by the Democratic Republic of Congo playing in attack

and in midfield. On the domestic front he didn't start many first team matches for Newcastle, but he was on the bench for almost every game, making 28 substitute appearances in the season, a new club record. He broke his scoring duck for United with a spectacular overhead kick at Sporting Lokeren in the Inter Toto Cup, and added an excellent strike in the home game with TSV Munich in the same competition. He is a pacy runner with excellent control and exciting dribbling skills, and he provokes a buzz of excitement around St James' Park whenever he is seen to be preparing to enter a match.

Colchester U (Signed from Leyton College on 25/9/1998) FL 37+24/15 FLC 4/4 FAC 1/1 Others 1

Newcastle U (£2,250,000 on 29/9/2000) PL 7+34/3 FLC 0+3 FAC 0+5 Others 0+6/2

LUCAS David Anthony
Born: Preston, 23 November 1977
Height: 6'2" Weight: 13.10
International Honours: E: Yth
David started the 2001-02 campaign as first-choice 'keeper for Preston before losing his place after dropping a clanger against Wolves. He was back in the team after his replacement Tepi Moilanen suffered an injury, but soon after making a superb penalty save in the FA Cup tie at Brighton he too was injured and lost his place. A superb shot stopper, he demonstrated that his abilities in one-on-one situations have also improved, although he still needs to work at his decision making on crosses. He retained his place for the run-in after Tepi was dropped in February, but was then injured again himself and no doubt the two will continue to contest the goalkeeper's jersey in 2002-03.

Preston NE (From trainee on 12/12/1994) FL 97+2 FLC 6 FAC 7 Others 11

Darlington (Loaned on 14/12/1995) FL 6

Darlington (Loaned on 3/10/1996) FL 7

Scunthorpe U (Loaned on 23/12/1996) FL 6 Others 2

LUCKETTI Christopher (Chris) James
Born: Rochdale, 28 September 1971
Height: 6'0" Weight: 13.6
Club Honours: Div 2 '97
Chris began the 2001-02 campaign at Huddersfield but the club's financial position led to his being sold to First Division Preston North End after just

two games. He established himself as the pivot in the back line at Deepdale, his organisational abilities being appreciated by colleagues and fans alike. A superb debut at Grimsby was followed by his first goal in the home defeat by Wolves. His goal at Coventry was awarded to Richard Cresswell by the club, but he made up for this by scoring in the following match to restore his account, and he remained a fixture until missing the end of the season with a badly gashed foot. A no-nonsense defender, he distributes the ball intelligently and his tackling is strong and decisive.

Rochdale (Trainee) FL 1
Stockport Co (Free on 23/8/1990)
Halifax T (Free on 12/7/1991) FL 73+5/2 FLC 2/1 FAC 2 Others 4
Bury (£50,000 on 1/10/1993) FL 235/8 FLC 16 FAC 11/1 Others 15/1
Huddersfield T (£750,000 + on 14/6/1999) FL 68/1 FLC 7/1
Preston NE (£750,000 on 23/8/2001) FL 40/2 FLC 1 FAC 3

LUDDEN Dominic James
Born: Basildon, 30 March 1974
Height: 5'8" **Weight:** 11.0
International Honours: E: Sch
Dominic joined Halifax Town during the 2001 close season but he had a frustrating time with injuries throughout the 2001-02 campaign. It was not until the end of November that he featured in the first team for the 2-0 home victory over Torquay, but after a short run in the side he dropped out and made no further appearances. When fully fit he is a speedy and experienced left back.

Leyton Orient (Signed from Billericay T on 6/7/1992) FL 50+8/1 FLC 1 FAC 0+1 Others 6/1
Watford (£100,000 on 7/8/1994) FL 28+5 FLC 3 FAC 2+1 Others 2
Preston NE (Free on 31/7/1998) FL 29+8 FLC 2 FAC 2 Others 3
Halifax T (Free on 1/7/2001) FL 2 FAC 1

LUMSDON Christopher (Chris)
Born: Newcastle, 15 December 1979
Height: 5'7" **Weight:** 10.6
This young midfielder initially joined Barnsley on loan last October before signing permanently in December. He made an impressive debut in the Worthington Cup-tie against his hometown club. Despite playing in a struggling team he won over the Reds'

fans with a series of fine displays. His passing, both long and short, was probably his best feature but he also showed an ability to dribble past players and had a destructive shot.
Sunderland (From trainee on 3/7/1997) P/FL 2 FLC 1+1
Blackpool (Loaned on 3/2/2000) FL 6/1
Crewe Alex (Loaned on 11/9/2000) FL 14+2
Barnsley (£350,000 on 8/10/2001) FL 32/7 FLC 1 FAC 1

LUNAN Daniel Dean
Born: Bromley, 14 March 1984
Height: 6'1" **Weight:** 12.12
Having played the majority of last season in Southend United's reserves, Daniel was given the chance of making his debut as a substitute in the 3-1 home victory over Exeter City in April. A well-built centre-half with good distribution qualities, he certainly didn't look uncomfortable playing in the senior team, and will be looking to force himself into the reckoning on a more regular basis in the 2002-03 campaign. His brother Jamie was previously on the Blues' books as a goalkeeper.
Southend U (Trainee) FL 0+1

LUNDEKVAM Claus
Born: Norway, 22 February 1973
Height: 6'3" **Weight:** 12.10
International Honours: Norway: 12; U21-16
Yet to find the net after six years with Southampton, Claus remained a crucial figure at the centre of defence last term, combining well with Paul Williams. Dominant in the air, quick to the tackle and a steadying influence to his team-mates, he picked up several head injuries as a result of his combative approach.
Southampton (£400,000 from SK Brann, Norway on 3/9/1996) PL 186+6 FLC 20+3 FAC 10

LUNT Kenneth (Kenny) Vincent
Born: Runcorn, 20 November 1979
Height: 5'10" **Weight:** 10.0
International Honours: E: Yth; Sch
Kenny was once again a mainstay of the Crewe Alexandra team last season, operating on the right-hand side of midfield. A competitive and skilful player, he was an ever present in First Division matches and contributed five goals for the Railwaymen.
Crewe Alex (From trainee on 12/6/1997) FL 165+28/12 FLC 13+4/1 FAC 8+1

LUNTALA Tresor
Born: Dreux, France, 31 May 1982
Height: 5'9" **Weight:** 11.2
Tresor made his breakthrough at Birmingham City under caretaker managers Mick Mills and Jim Barron last October. He gave Blues some midfield 'legs' due to non-stop running and work. He passed the ball carefully and safely and only after Steve Bruce took over did he fade from the squad as Bryan Hughes and Darren Carter took over the central midfield roles.
Birmingham C (Free from Rennes, France on 4/8/1999) FL 9+6 FLC 1

LUZHNY Oleg
Born: Ukraine, 5 August 1968
Height: 6'1" **Weight:** 12.3
Club Honours: CS '99; PL '02
International Honours: Ukraine: 46; USSR: 8
This vastly experienced Arsenal player had a somewhat disappointing season in 2001-02. Even though Lee Dixon was rarely in contention for the right-back position, he more often than not lost out to Lauren, although he still managed to play in almost half the Gunners' Premiership fixtures.
Arsenal (£1,800,000 from Dinamo Kiev, Ukraine on 9/7/1999) PL 47+11 FLC 3 FAC 7 Others 17+1

LYTTLE Desmond (Des)
Born: Wolverhampton, 24 September 1971
Height: 5'9" **Weight:** 12.13
Club Honours: Div 1 '98
This experienced defender started the 2001-02 season as West Bromwich Albion's first choice right back, but found it difficult to hold down a place after October owing to the form and presence of Igor Balis, and also the 3-5-2 system adopted by manager Gary Megson. Nevertheless, when called into action, he was an effective performer and his usual endeavour and commitment were there for all to see.
Leicester C (From trainee on 1/9/1990)
Swansea C (£12,500 from Worcester C on 9/7/1992) FL 46/1 FLC 2 FAC 5 Others 5
Nottingham F (£375,000 on 27/7/1993) F/PL 177+8/3 FLC 19+1 FAC 16 Others 8
Port Vale (Loaned on 20/11/1998) FL 7
Watford (Free on 28/7/1999) PL 11 FLC 1
West Bromwich A (Free on 21/3/2000) FL 59+13/1 FLC 7 FAC 2+1 Others 2

Jason McAteer

M

McALLISTER Gary
Born: Motherwell, 25 December 1964
Height: 6'1" **Weight:** 11.12
Club Honours: S Div 1 '85; Div 1 '92; CS '92, '02; FLC '01; FAC '01; UEFA '01; ESC '01
International Honours: S: 57; B-2; U21-1
After his heroics of the previous campaign when his goals and creative play were the catalyst for Liverpool's trophy-laden triumphs, it was inevitable that Gary's second season at Anfield would be something of an anti-climax. Nevertheless, despite being first reserve to Steven Gerrard and Dietmar Hamann in central midfield he made an appearance in most of the Reds' matches prior to the new year. Thereafter his contribution was more fleeting with only two starts and eight substitute appearances to the end of the season when he was appointed the new manager of his former club Coventry City.
Motherwell (Signed from Fir Park BC on 5/9/1981) SL 52+7/6 SLC 3+1 SC 7/2
Leicester C (£125,000 on 15/8/1985) FL 199+2/47 FLC 14+1/3 FAC 5/2 Others 4
Leeds U (£1,000,000 on 2/7/1990) F/PL 230+1/31 FLC 26/5 FAC 24/6 Others 14/4
Coventry C (£3,000,000 on 26/7/1996) PL 119/20 FLC 11/5 FAC 10/1
Liverpool (Free on 6/7/2000) PL 35+20/5 FLC 3+3/1 FAC 4+1 Others 10+11/3

McANESPIE Kieran
Born: Gosport, 11 September 1979
Height: 5'8" **Weight:** 10.13
International Honours: S: U21-4
Keiran was again unable to make a breakthrough at Fulham last season and joined Bournemouth on loan in February. The left-sided defender found the pace and physical side of Division Two football hard to adapt to, but he scored his first senior goal in English football against Bristol City and the experience will make him a stronger player. He received a boost when he was called up by new Scotland coach Bertie Vogts for the training match against Dundee United at the end of April.
St Johnstone (From juniors on 14/9/1995) SL 24+26/5 SC 3+2 Othrs 3+1
Fulham (£80,000 on 11/8/2000) FLC 1+1
Heart of Midlothian (Loaned on 22/1/2001) SL 3+2 SC 0+1
Bournemouth (Loaned on 15/2/2002) FL 3+4/1

McANESPIE Stephen (Steve)
Born: Kilmarnock, 1 February 1972
Height: 5'9" **Weight:** 10.7
Club Honours: S Div 1 '95; SLC '95; Div 1 '97
International Honours: S: Yth
Steve again found himself out of favour at Cambridge United last term, and apart from a single appearance as a substitute against Cardiff in September he did not feature at first-team level. He eventually left the Abbey Stadium in March and returned to Scotland to sign for Partick Thistle. He is a positive right back who can also play in midfield.
Aberdeen (From juniors on 12/5/1988) . Transferred to Vaesterhaninge, Sweden on 30/6/93)
Raith Rov (Signed on 25/1/1994) SL 37+3 SLC 4 SC 3 Others 5
Bolton W (£900,000 on 30/9/1995) F/PL 19+5 FLC 6
Fulham (£100,000 on 28/11/1997) FL 3+4 FAC 1 Others 2+1
Bradford C (Loaned on 26/3/1998) FL 7
Cambridge U (Free on 9/8/2000) FL 20+4 FLC 2 FAC 1 Others 2

McANUFF Joel Joshua Frederick
Born: Edmonton, 9 November 1981
Height: 5'11" **Weight:** 11.10
International Honours: Jamaica: 1
Joel acquitted himself very well in his debut season at Wimbledon last term. He is a talented right winger who possesses lightning speed along with the confidence to take on defenders and get past them. He will be looking to consolidate such an excellent start in 2002-03.
Wimbledon (From trainee on 11/7/2000) FL 22+16/4 FAC 0+2

McAREAVEY Paul
Born: Belfast, 3 December 1980
Height: 5'10" **Weight:** 11.6
International Honours: NI: U21-7; Yth
Paul eventually made his full senior debut for Swindon Town in the LDV Vans Trophy tie at Colchester last season. A tough-tackling left sided midfielder with a high work rate, he forced his way into first-team reckoning with increasing regularity in the second half of the season. He was also used as a left back on a couple of occasions. He was released at the end of the season.
Swindon T (From trainee on 10/7/1999) FL 10+14/1 FAC 1+1 Others 1

MACARI Paul
Born: Manchester, 23 August 1976
Height: 5'8" **Weight:** 11.12
Paul occupied the subs' bench for Huddersfield Town for much of last season, making a handful of brief appearances when he was generally brought on late in the match to add pace to the front line. A striker with good close control and a keen eye for goal he will be looking to feature more regularly in 2002-03. He is the son of the former Terriers boss Lou Macari.
Stoke C (From juniors on 26/8/1993) FL 0+3
Sheffield U (Free on 10/12/1998)
Huddersfield T (Free on 1/7/2000) FL 0+6 FLC 0+1 Others 0+2

McATEER Jason Wynn
Born: Birkenhead, 18 June 1971
Height: 5'10" **Weight:** 11.12
International Honours: RoI: 49; B-1
This midfield dynamo was used sparingly by Blackburn boss Graeme Souness at the start of last season and in October he was sold to Sunderland. His undoubted enthusiasm and incredible stamina made an immediate impact at the Stadium of Light and although he was initially employed on the right wing, where his crossing ability was put to good use, he was unquestionably at his best when playing in central midfield, arriving in the box to score vital goals against Bolton and Southampton in March, and his ability to break up the play and launch attacks was vital in Sunderland's relegation fight.
Bolton W (Signed from Marine on 22/1/1992) P/FL 109+5/8 FLC 11/2 FAC 11/3 Others 8+1/2
Liverpool (£4,500,000 on 6/9/1995) PL 84+16/3 FLC 12+1 FAC 11+1/3 Others 12+2
Blackburn Rov (£4,000,000 on 28/1/1999) P/FL 58+14/4 FLC 4 FAC 7
Sunderland (£1,000,000 on 19/10/2001) PL 26/2 FAC 1

McAUGHTRIE Craig James
Born: Burton, 3 March 1981
Height: 6'2" **Weight:** 14.6
A powerfully built player who can perform either in defence or up front, Craig managed only a handful of appearances for Carlisle last season, although his versatility often earned him a place on the bench. One of his few starts was against Macclesfield when he forced home a close range equaliser as United snatched victory from the jaws of defeat with two goals in the last two minutes.
Sheffield U (From trainee on 5/7/1999)
Carlisle U (Free on 7/8/2000) FL 2+8/1 Others 2

McAULEY Hugh Francis
Born: Plymouth, 13 May 1976
Height: 5'10" **Weight:** 11.4

The 2001-2002 season was not a memorable one for Hugh. He began the campaign on the left-hand side of Cheltenham's midfield but soon lost his place and made only one more starting appearance in league matches. A skilful player with good passing ability and vision, he found it difficult to impose himself in the physically demanding arena of Division Three football and was released by the club in the summer.
Cheltenham T (Signed from Leek T on 15/7/1999) FL 55+26/7 FLC 3 FAC 3+1 Others 3+2/1

McAULEY Sean
Born: Sheffield, 23 June 1972
Height: 5'11" **Weight:** 11.12
International Honours: S: U21-1; Yth
After rarely featuring during the previous season, Sean was drafted back into the Rochdale line-up at left back when Lee Todd was injured after only a couple of games of the 2001-02 campaign. He played his part in the side's rise to the top of the table before being injured himself and then an ankle injury in February ruled him out for the rest of the term. In April he crossed the Atlantic to sign for US-A League outfit Portland Timbers.
Manchester U (From trainee on 1/7/1990)
St Johnstone (Signed on 22/4/1992) SL 59+3 SLC 3/1 SC 3 Others 1
Chesterfield (Loaned on 4/11/1994) FL 1/1 FAC 1+1 Others 2
Hartlepool U (Free on 21/7/1995) FL 84/1 FLC 6 FAC 3 Others 3
Scunthorpe U (Signed on 26/3/1997) FL 63+6/1 FLC 5 FAC 5 Others 2
Scarborough (Loaned on 25/3/1999) FL 6+1
Rochdale (Free on 11/2/2000) FL 34+3 FLC 1+1 FAC 3 Others 3

MACAULEY Stephen (Steve) Roy
Born: Lytham, 4 March 1969
Height: 6'1" **Weight:** 12.0
Club Honours: FAYC '86
Steve received a testimonial season at Crewe last term, but after serving the club loyally for a decade, he found few opportunities in the first team. He had two loan spells at Macclesfield, the first during December and the second in February and March, returning to Gresty Road in the intervening period to recover from a fractured hand. He is an experienced central defender who is good in the air and can score vital goals.
Manchester C (From trainee on 5/11/1987. Released during 1988 close season)
Crewe Alex (£25,000 from Fleetwood T on 24/3/1992) FL 247+14/26 FLC 20 FAC 16/1 Others 20/3

Macclesfield T (Loaned on 14/12/2001) FL 4 FAC 1
Macclesfield T (Loaned on 15/2/2002) FL 8

McAVOY Andrew (Andy) David
Born: Middlesbrough, 28 August 1979
Height: 6'0" **Weight:** 12.0
Andy joined Macclesfield on a six-month contract just before the start of the 2001-02 season and did well enough to earn an extension until the end of the campaign. Although mostly a reserve he made a few appearances playing either as a striker or an attacking right-sided midfielder, these included his first ever FA Cup appearance in the home tie against Forest Green Rovers. His future at Moss Rose was uncertain at the time of writing for he had been reported to be seeking a move to another club towards the end of the campaign.
Blackburn Rov (From trainee on 14/7/1997)
Hartlepool U (Free on 24/11/1999) FL 7+14 Others 1+3
Macclesfield T (Free on 9/8/2001) FL 4+6 FLC 0+1 FAC 2+1

McCALDON Ian
Born: Liverpool, 14 September 1974
Height: 6'5" **Weight:** 15.9
Club Honours: S Div 2 '99
Ian came to Oxford in the 2001 close season and was the first-choice 'keeper before picking up a calf injury. By the time he had recovered he had lost his place to Andy Woodman and he then had to compete with Richard Knight for the second-choice spot. A big goalkeeper, he dominated the area and came out well for crosses.
Livingston (Signed from Glenafton Ath on 21/12/1996) SL 79+1 SLC 6 SC 5 Others 5
St Mirren (Loaned on 9/11/2000) SL 4+1
Oxford U (Free on 17/8/2001) FL 28 FLC 1 FAC 1 Others 1

McCALL Andrew Stuart Murray
Born: Leeds, 10 June 1964
Height: 5'7" **Weight:** 12.0
Club Honours: Div 3 '85; SPL '92, '93, '94, '95, '96; SLC '92, '93; SC '92, '93, '96
International Honours: S: 40; U21-2
Stuart is one of Bradford City's all-time greats and had another tremendous season at Valley Parade. A powerful tackler, he ran around in midfield like a youngster and rarely missed a match. After enjoying a testimonial match against Glasgow Rangers he was released in the summer.
Bradford C (From apprentice on 1/6/1982) FL

235+3/37 FLC 16/3 FAC 12/3 Others 12+1/3
Everton (£850,000 on 1/6/1988) FL 99+4/6 FLC 11/1 FAC 16+2/3 Others 8+1
Glasgow R (£1,200,000 on 15/8/1991) SL 186+8/14 SLC 15/3 SC 25+2 Others 28/2
Bradford C (Free on 4/6/1998) P/FL 154+3/8 FLC 5+3/1 FAC 5+1 Others 4

McCAMMON Mark Jason
Born: Barnet, 7 August 1978
Height: 6'5" **Weight:** 14.5
A tall, powerful centre forward, Mark started the 2001-02 campaign for Brentford with an ankle injury and wasn't fit until October. He then spent much of the rest of the season on the substitute's bench, starting just one game, as he was unable to dislodge either Ben Burgess or Lloyd Owusu from the starting line-up. He failed to register a first-team goal during the campaign.
Cambridge U (Free from Cambridge C on 31/12/1996) FL 1+3 FAC 0+1 Others 1
Charlton Ath (Free on 17/3/1999) FL 1+3 FLC 0+1
Swindon T (Loaned on 3/1/2000) FL 4
Brentford (£100,000 + on 18/7/2000) FL 15+23/3 FLC 3/1 FAC 0+1 Others 2+5/2

McCANN Gavin Peter
Born: Blackpool, 10 January 1978
Height: 5'11" **Weight:** 11.0
International Honours: E: 1
An industrious midfielder, Gavin had a somewhat disappointing season for Sunderland last term. At his best, he is a key man in Sunderland's midfield being a real all-rounder with the ability to both win the ball and distribute it with a high level of accuracy. Unfortunately, he also picked up his share of bookings during the season and missed the last two crucial games of the campaign through suspension.
Everton (From trainee on 1/7/1995) PL 5+6
Sunderland (£500,000 on 27/11/1998) P/FL 77+9/7 FLC 2+3/1 FAC 8+1/2

McCANN Grant Samuel
Born: Belfast, 14 April 1980
Height: 5'10" **Weight:** 12.0
International Honours: NI: 3; U21-11
Grant did very well when he came on as substitute in West Ham's opening fixtures against Liverpool and Leeds last term. He normally plays on the left side of midfield but can play at left back if required. However he faded from the scene after appearing in the 7-1 defeat by Blackburn Rovers in October and made no further senior appearances.
West Ham U (From trainee on 6/7/1998) PL 0+4

Livingston (Loaned on 27/8/1999) SL 0+4
Notts Co (Loaned on 11/8/2000) FL 2 FLC 1
Cheltenham T (Loaned on 17/10/2000) FL 27+3/3 FAC 2 Others 1

McCARTHY Jonathan (Jon) David

Born: Middlesbrough, 18 August 1970
Height: 5'9" **Weight:** 11.5
International Honours: NI: 18; B-2
A popular figure, Jon returned to the Birmingham City line-up on Boxing Day against Sheffield Wednesday after breaking the same leg a third time. Steve Bruce then withdrew him from the team after lack of matches caught up with him and went on to sign Paul Devlin and Damien Johnson. A strong-running right winger, he joined Sheffield Wednesday for the closing stages of the campaign and added guile and craft to the flank.
Hartlepool U (From juniors on 7/11/1987) FL 0+1 (Free to Shepshed Charterhouse in March 1989)
York C (Free on 22/3/1990) FL 198+1/31 FLC 8/1 FAC 11/3 Others 15/3
Port Vale (£450,000 on 1/8/1995) FL 93+1/12 FLC 10/2 FAC 7/1 Others 8/2
Birmingham C (£1,500,000 on 11/9/1997) FL 107+17/8 FLC 9+1 FAC 4 Others 3+1
Sheffield Wed (Loaned on 28/3/2002) FL 4

McCARTHY Paul Jason

Born: Cork, 4 August 1971
Height: 5'10" **Weight:** 13.12
International Honours: RoI: U21-10; Yth; Sch
Wycombe's team captain was missing for two months midway through last season with a persistent leg injury which will require a minor operation in the summer. His dominating physical presence and all-round experience were sorely missed in his absence. He formed the left side in a formidable central defensive partnership with Mark Rogers and was one of the first names down on the team sheet. He scored three goals in his 26 League starts, two of these were powerful headers but perhaps most memorably was his injury-time winner at home to Queen's Park Rangers in August.
Brighton & Hove A (From trainee on 26/4/1989) FL 180+1/6 FLC 11/1 FAC 13 Others 12/1
Wycombe W (£100,000 on 5/7/1996) FL 177+11/8 FLC 15+1/3 FAC 20/5 Others 6

McCARTHY Sean Casey

Born: Bridgend, 12 September 1967
Height: 6'1" **Weight:** 12.12
International Honours: W: B-1

Sean joined Exeter City from local rivals Plymouth Argyle, but nevertheless quickly established himself as a cult figure with the Grecians faithful. He performed well as a striker, and although not renowned for his pace he showed he had not lost his eye for goal, his tally of six including a brace in the local 'derby' against Torquay.
Swansea C (Signed from Bridgend T on 22/10/1985) FL 76+15/25 FLC 4+1/3 FAC 5+2/4 Others 9+1/6
Plymouth Arg (£50,000 on 18/8/1988) FL 67+3/19 FLC 7/5 FAC 3/1 Others 0+1/1
Bradford C (£250,000 on 4/7/1990) FL 127+4/60 FLC 10+2/10 FAC 8/2 Others 8+1/7
Oldham Ath (£500,000 on 3/12/1993) P/FL 117+23/42 FLC 10/1 FAC 6+1/1 Others 4/1
Bristol C (Loaned on 26/3/1998) FL 7/1
Plymouth Arg (Free on 7/8/1998) FL 66+16/19 FLC 3+2/3 FAC 8
Exeter C (Free on 3/7/2001) FL 18+8/6 FLC 1 FAC 1

McCARTNEY George

Born: Belfast, 29 April 1981
Height: 6'0" **Weight:** 12.6
International Honours: NI: 5; U21-5; Yth; Sch
This pacy young defender enjoyed an eventful season at Sunderland last term. Primarily a left back who can also operate in central defence, he won his first full cap for Northern Ireland in September and even managed a goal in a 3-0 win over Iceland. He signed a new long-term contract and then enjoyed a run in the side towards the end of the season, impressing supporters with his calm assured play, which belied his relative inexperience.
Sunderland (From trainee on 28/5/1998) PL 13+7 FLC 3+1 FAC 1+1

McCLARE Sean Patrick

Born: Rotherham, 12 January 1978
Height: 5'10" **Weight:** 11.12
International Honours: RoI: U21-3
Unable to win a first-team place at Barnsley, this busy midfielder joined Port Vale on loan in October. He made his first appearance in the local 'derby' against Stoke City and impressed enough to make the move a permanent one six weeks later. He scored one goal, against Oldham, but tended to be in and out of the line-up as Vale struggled for consistency. He was placed on the transfer list at the end of the season.
Barnsley (From trainee on 3/7/1996) FL 29+21/6 FLC 10+3 FAC 5+1/1
Rochdale (Loaned on 22/3/2000) FL 5+4
Port Vale (Free on 20/10/2001) FL 19+4/1 FAC 1 Others 2

McCLEN James (Jamie) David

Born: Newcastle, 13 May 1979
Height: 5'9" **Weight:** 11.3
This neat and tidy midfield player was on the Newcastle bench for the opening three games last season, appearing in two of them, but with the return to fitness of Rob Lee and Clarence Acuna he dropped out of the picture. When the FA Cup came around in January injuries opened the door for him and he played in the tie against Peterborough, scoring his first ever goal for the club and performing well enough to retain his place for five games before the arrival of Jermaine Jenas saw him replaced. He was recalled for the quarter-final against Arsenal when he had a storming game and was voted 'Man of the Match' but then tore a calf muscle.
Newcastle U (From trainee on 4/7/1997) PL 7+6 FAC 3/1 Others 0+5
Motherwell (Loaned on 13/10/2000) SL 1+2

McCOMBE Jamie

Born: Scunthorpe, 1 January 1983
Height: 6'5" **Weight:** 12.6
Youth-team skipper Jamie was thrown into Scunthorpe's first team as a one-off against Darlington in the LDV Vans Trophy at the end of October and impressed so much he kept his place for over two months. He scored both on his debut and in the FA Cup tie at Millwall and finished the season with a trial at Premiership Aston Villa. He is a tall central defender who is very strong in the air and will be looking to win a regular place in the United line-up in 2002-03.
Scunthorpe U (From trainee on 28/11/2001) FL 11+6 FAC 3/1 Others 2/1

McCONNELL Barry

Born: Exeter, 1 January 1977
Height: 5'10" **Weight:** 10.3
Barry continued to make progress at Exeter City last term and went on to establish himself as a regular in the first-team line-up at right back. A series of consistent displays earned him a new contract but his season came to a premature end after suffering a nasty eye injury at Luton. He is expected to be fully fit for the start of the 2002-03 campaign.
Exeter C (From trainee on 4/8/1995) FL 95+46/15 FLC 3+3/1 FAC 5+5 Others 4+1

McCOURT Patrick (Paddy) James

Born: Derry, 16 December 1983
Height: 5'10" **Weight:** 11.0
International Honours: NI: 1; U21-1
Rochdale's teenage sensation made his

senior debut in an LDV Vans Trophy game last October and went on to win a regular place in the first-team squad in the second half of the 2001-02 campaign. His mazy dribbles turned several games and he came up with remarkable winning goals against Luton and at Halifax, as well as a vital one against Hull in the game that guaranteed Dale a place in the play-offs for the first time. Paddy gained his first cap for Northern Ireland at U21 level against Germany and went on to top an amazing season by winning his first full cap against Spain in April.
Rochdale (From trainee on 11/2/2002) FL 10+13/4 FAC 0+2 Others 0+3

McCREADY Christopher (Chris) James
Born: Runcorn, 5 September 1981
Height: 6'0" **Weight:** 11.11
Chris is another youngster to develop through the academy scheme at Crewe. After sitting on the bench on a number of occasions he made his senior debut when he came on in the away game at Millwall at the end of December. He is a versatile player who can take any of the defensive positions.
Crewe Alex (From trainee on 30/5/2000) FL 0+1

McCULLOCH Lee Henry
Born: Bellshill, 14 May 1978
Height: 6'5" **Weight:** 13.6
International Honours: S: U21-14
A tall target man whose main strength is his aerial ability, Lee was on target for Wigan Athletic in the opening two League matches of the 2001-02 campaign. His physical presence enabled him to hold the ball up but he struggled to find his best form. After spending much of the season on the subs' bench he returned to the line-up following the departure of Simon Haworth, leading the line well but without the reward of goals his performances deserved.
Motherwell (Signed from Cumbernauld U on 17/8/1995) SL 75+47/28 SLC 5+2/2 SC 11+3/4
Wigan Ath (£700,000 on 2/3/2001) FL 34+10/9 FAC 1 Others 1+1

McCULLOCH Scott Anderson James
Born: Irvine, 29 November 1975
Height: 6'0" **Weight:** 13.4
International Honours: S: Sch
Scott was very much on the fringe of the first-team squad at Cardiff last season, suffering a number of niggling injuries and being restricted to a single

appearance in the LDV Vans Trophy. In February he returned to Scotland and after a trial period with Airdrie signed for Forfar Athletic.
Glasgow R (From juniors on 1/7/1992)
Hamilton Academical (Signed on 24/3/1995) SL 46+11/4 SLC 1+1 SC 3 Others 4
Dunfermline Ath (Signed on 2/12/1997) SL 37/2 SLC 1 SC 2
Dundee U (Signed on 26/2/1999) SL 19+5 SC 1
Cardiff C (£100,000 on 1/9/2000) FL 9+12/1 FLC 1 FAC 3 Others 2

McDERMOTT John
Born: Middlesbrough, 3 February 1969
Height: 5'7" **Weight:** 11.0
Club Honours: AMC '98
Grimsby Town's senior professional was again a tower of strength at right back during the 2001-02 campaign. He missed a lengthy spell with a serious calf injury and his influence on the team was such that they fell 15 places in the league table in his absence. On his return to the side he was made club captain in succession to Paul Groves who had been promoted to player-manager and played a major role in the Mariners campaign to avoid relegation.
Grimsby T (From trainee on 1/6/1987) FL 479+18/7 FLC 35+2 FAC 29+2/2 Others 21

McDONAGH William (Will)
Born: Dublin, 14 March 1983
Height: 6'1" **Weight:** 11.12
This young midfielder followed Carlisle manager Roddy Collins from Bohemians last October but had the misfortune to receive a red card on his debut in the FA Cup tie at Tranmere. He eventually became a regular member of the squad, scoring his first goal at Scunthorpe in March, and will be looking to make further progress in 2002-03.
Carlisle U (Signed from Bohemians on 16/10/2001) FL 7+5/1 FAC 1

MacDONALD Charles (Charlie) Lea
Born: Southwark, 13 February 1981
Height: 5'9" **Weight:** 11.10
Charlie had limited chances to break into the Charlton Athletic side last season, but did well when called upon, scoring the equaliser against Newcastle United at the Valley to earn a valuable point. Although short for a striker, he has a good first touch, is quick, strong and holds the ball up well. He has a good scoring record at junior and reserve team level, and has always done well when brought into the

side. In order to gain regular first team experience, Charlie was loaned to Torquay United and Colchester United during the season. He did well at Layer Road, and found the net with a rasping shot on the final day of the season against Wigan.
Charlton Ath (From trainee on 10/11/1998) P/FL 1+7/1 FLC 0+3 FAC 1+1/1
Cheltenham T (Loaned on 16/3/2001) FL 7+1/2
Torquay U (Loaned on 15/2/2002) FL 5
Colchester U (Loaned on 27/3/2002) FL 2+2/1

MacDONALD Gary
Born: Germany, 25 October 1979
Height: 6'1" **Weight:** 12.12
Last season proved to be a frustrating time for Gary, for after appearing in the Peterborough United starting line-up five times early on he suffered an injury that restricted him to just a handful more games. He is a promising left-footed central defender who can also play at full back if required.
Portsmouth (From trainee on 3/7/1998. Free to Havant & Waterlooville on 22/7/1999)
Peterborough U (Signed on 16/2/2001) FL 8+1/1 FLC 2 FAC 1

McDONALD Scott
Born: Melbourne, Australia, 21 August 1983
Height: 5'8" **Weight:** 12.4
International Honours: Australia: Yth
Impressive performances by this young striker in the Southampton in the U19 and reserve sides were rewarded with a Worthington Cup debut at Brighton. Quick and agile, his darting runs and off the ball running make him an exciting prospect.
Southampton (Signed from Eastern Pride, Australia on 23/8/2000) PL 0+2 FLC 1

McELHATTON Michael (Mike) Terence
Born: Killarney, Ireland, 16 April 1975
Height: 6'1" **Weight:** 12.12
International Honours: RoI: Sch
Injury has seriously hampered the career development of this attacking midfielder. Having sustained an initial cruciate injury in March 2000 and fighting back magnificently to return to the Rushden first team the following October, soon afterwards he succumbed to a second cruciate problem. Determined to prove the doubters wrong, Mike underwent surgery and set off on the road to recovery once more. His patience was rewarded last December when he returned to first-team action against Luton.

Bournemouth (From trainee on 5/7/1993) FL 21+21/2 FLC 3+1 FAC 1+2/2 Others 1
Scarborough (£15,000 on 20/9/1996) FL 64+6/7 FLC 3 FAC 3+1 Others 4
Rushden & Diamonds (Signed on 16/7/1998) FL 4+3/1

McELHOLM Brendan Anthony
Born: Omagh, 7 July 1982
Height: 5'11" **Weight:** 12.2
International Honours: NI: Yth
Brendan found himself unable to win a place in the Leyton Orient line-up at the start of the 2001-02 season and in September he joined Chelmsford City on loan. He returned to make an appearance in the LDV Vans Trophy match against Dagenham at right back in Paul Brush's first game in charge, and also made a couple of substitute appearances in Third Division games. He was released in January and returned to Northern Ireland to sign for Omagh Town.
Leyton Orient (From trainee on 10/7/2000) FL 6+11 FLC 1+2 Others 2

McEVILLY Lee Richard
Born: Liverpool, 15 April 1982
Height: 6'0" **Weight:** 13.0
International Honours: NI: 1
Lee enjoyed a meteoric rise to fame after signing for Rochdale last December. After a few appearances from the subs' bench, he scored when coming on in the amazing 5-4 victory over York to earn a starting berth in the absence of suspended striker Clive Platt. He featured regularly from then onwards, proving quite a handful for opposition defenders when teamed up with either Platt or Kevin Townson. His last goal of the season was probably the best, a storming run past several defenders culminating in a ferocious shot to give Dale the lead in their play-off semi-final at Rushden. By then he had also become Rochdale's first-ever full international when he came on as substitute for Northern Ireland against Spain in April.
Rochdale (£20,000 from Burscough on 24/12/2001) FL 13+5/4 Others 2/1

McEWEN David (Dave)
Born: Westminster, 2 November 1977
Height: 6'0" **Weight:** 11.0
This promising young striker joined Queen's Park Rangers on a six-month contract last summer. He produced several good performances for the reserves, but made just a handful of first-team appearances and was released in January.
Tottenham H (Free from Dulwich Hamlet on 6/11/2000) PL 0+4
Queens Park R (Free on 17/7/2001) FL 2+3 FLC 0+1

McGHEE David (Dave) Christopher
Born: Worthing, 19 June 1976
Height: 5'11" **Weight:** 12.4
Dave established himself as a regular at centre half for Leyton Orient in 2001-02 following the injury to Simon Downer. He is a commanding defender who has become a fans' favourite with his no-nonsense tackling and whole-hearted approach. He is also dangerous in the air when moving forward at set pieces.
Brentford (From trainee on 15/7/1994) FL 95+22/8 FLC 5+2/1 FAC 9/1 Others 8+1 (Freed on 22/1/1999)
Leyton Orient (Free from Stevenage Borough on 11/11/1999) FL 95+7/6 FLC 4 FAC 8 Others 6

McGIBBON Patrick (Pat) Colm
Born: Lurgan, 6 September 1973
Height: 6'2" **Weight:** 13.12
Club Honours: AMC '99
International Honours: NI: 7; B-5; U21-1; Sch
This long-serving Wigan Athletic defender found his appearances restricted following the arrival of new manager Paul Jewell last season. A regular at the start of the campaign the tall centre half found chances harder to come by once Jason DeVos regained fitness and formed a defensive partnership alongside Arjan De Zeeuw. Quick in the tackle and effective in the air, he showed his versatility by also playing in the right-back berth, a true professional never letting the side down when selected. He joined Scunthorpe on loan in February and did well at Glanford Park, never finishing on the losing side in six matches, but he returned to the Latics when a permanent deal collapsed and was released in the summer.
Manchester U (£100,000 from Portadown on 1/8/1992) FLC 1
Swansea C (Loaned on 20/9/1996) FL 1
Wigan Ath (£250,000 on 3/3/1997) FL 163+10/11 FLC 11+1 FAC 9+1 Others 18
Scunthorpe U (Loaned on 15/2/2002) FL 6

McGILL Brendan
Born: Dublin, 22 March 1981
Height: 5'8" **Weight:** 9.8
International Honours: RoI: Yth (UEFA-U16 '98)
Brendan joined Carlisle United in a long-term loan deal for the whole of the 2001-02 campaign. Operating primarily on the right flank he produced some fine performances, his ability to deliver a telling cross or defence-splitting pass

meant that United always looked more threatening when he was in the line-up. A provider rather than a taker of goals, he finally made the score sheet in the 6-1 defeat of Leyton Orient.
Sunderland (Signed from River Valley Rangers on 29/7/1998) FLC 0+1
Carlisle U (Loaned on 7/9/2001) FL 27+1/2 FAC 3 Others 1

McGLEISH Scott
Born: Barnet, 10 February 1974
Height: 5'9" **Weight:** 11.3
Scott enjoyed his best ever season for Colchester last term, scoring 15 goals for the first time in his career and finishing with a bang when he smashed home a 30-yarder against Wigan on the final day of the campaign. He had also begun in sensational fashion with nine goals in the first 14 Second Division games, including two in the opening day fixture at Chesterfield. A tireless worker, he shone in the air, his tremendous leap yielding him several headed goals.
Charlton Ath (Free from Edgware T on 24/5/1994) FL 0+6
Leyton Orient (Loaned on 10/3/1995) FL 4+2/1 Others 1/1
Peterborough U (Free on 4/7/1995) FL 3+10 FLC 0+1 FAC 0+1 Others 3+1/2
Colchester U (Loaned on 23/2/1996) FL 10+5/6 Others 2
Cambridge U (Loaned on 2/9/1996) FL 10/7 FLC 1
Leyton Orient (£50,000 on 22/11/1996) FL 36/7 FLC 3/1 FAC 1 Others 1
Barnet (£70,000 on 1/10/1997) FL 106+28/36 FLC 5/4 FAC 3 Others 7+2/1
Colchester U (£15,000 on 11/1/2001) FL 55+12/20 FLC 2 FAC 2/1 Others 2

McGLINCHEY Brian Kevin
Born: Londonderry, 26 October 1977
Height: 5'7" **Weight:** 10.2
Club Honours: Div 3 '01
International Honours: NI: B-1; U21-14; Yth
Brian scored possibly Plymouth's most vital goal of the 2001-02 season – the winner against Rushden last August after Argyle had been 2-0 down. This result sent the team on their way to a new club record sequence of unbeaten games. He took over the left-back position from Jon Beswetherick but his season was interrupted by injury when he suffered a broken ankle against Scunthorpe in January. He returned to the subs' bench by the end of the campaign, but will be looking to regain his position in the starting line-up in 2002-03.
Manchester C (From trainee on 4/12/1995)

Brian McGlinchy (right)

Port Vale (Free on 1/7/1998) FL 10+5/1 FLC 0+1 FAC 1
Gillingham *(Free on 3/8/1999) FL 7+7/1 FLC 3+1 FAC 4/1 Others 1*
Plymouth Arg *(Free on 1/12/2000) FL 43+6/1 FLC 1 FAC 3 Others 2+1*

McGOVERN Brian
Born: Dublin, 28 April 1980
Height: 6'3" **Weight:** 12.7
International Honours: RoI: U21-2; Yth
This former Arsenal defender found it difficult to force his way into the Canaries' line-up in season 2001-02, having finished the previous campaign as likely first choice right back. A quick and mobile defender, he can play either centrally or on the right-hand side where his pace enables him to support his attack effectively.
Arsenal *(Signed from Cherry Orchard on 5/9/1997) PL 0+1*
Queens Park R *(Loaned on 24/12/1999) FL 3+2*
Norwich C *(£50,000 + on 27/7/2000) FL 8+13/1 FLC 3+1*

McGREAL John
Born: Liverpool, 2 June 1972
Height: 5'11" **Weight:** 12.8
John continued to be a tower of strength in the centre of the Ipswich defence last term and supported the attack at corner kicks and free kicks. His only goal of the season gave Town a double over Tottenham when he headed home a corner from Mark Venus in the latter stages of the game. John is adept at the last-minute tackle, often than not coming away with the ball following a clean take.
Tranmere Rov *(From trainee on 3/7/1990) FL 193+2/1 FLC 20+1 FAC 8 Others 7+2*
Ipswich T *(£650,000 on 4/8/1999) P/FL 86+3/2 FLC 11 FAC 3 Others 4*

McGREGOR Mark Dale Thomas
Born: Chester, 16 February 1977
Height: 5'11" **Weight:** 11.5
After signing for Burnley in the summer of 2001 Mark was widely expected to step straight into the right-back spot for the Clarets, but the sheer consistency of Dean West kept him out of the first team for almost all of his first season at Turf Moor. He made a scoring debut in the Worthington Cup tie against Rushden, but did not make his League bow until March, when West was suspended. He performed well, looking solid in defence and linking well with the forward players on the right side, but immediately reverted to the reserves on West's return.

Wrexham *(From trainee on 4/7/1995) FL 237+7/11 FLC 9 FAC 24+1 Others 11*
Burnley *(Free on 20/7/2001) FL 1 FLC 1/1*

McGREGOR Paul Anthony
Born: Liverpool, 17 December 1974
Height: 5'10" **Weight:** 11.6
Paul featured in a variety of roles for Northampton Town in 2001-02 – striker, central midfield, and winger. Wherever he played his work rate could not be faulted and he also managed to contribute a handful of goals. He is a skilful player whose main position is wide on the right-hand side either in midfield or attack.
Nottingham F *(From trainee on 13/12/1991) F/PL 7+23/3 FAC 0+3 Others 0+4/1*
Carlisle U *(Loaned on 25/9/1998) FL 3/2*
Carlisle U *(Loaned on 20/11/1998) FL 6+1/1 Others 1*
Preston NE *(Free on 24/3/1999) FL 1+3*
Plymouth Arg *(Free on 6/7/1999) FL 75+2/19 FLC 2+1/1 FAC 9/4 Others 0+1*
Northampton T *(Free on 5/7/2001) FL 37+2/3 FLC 1+1/1 FAC 0+2 Others 2/1*

McGURK David
Born: Middlesbrough, 30 September 1982
Height: 6'0" **Weight:** 11.10
This tall, young reserve defender broke into the Darlington first team because of a crop of injuries to the regular players and made his debut as a half-time substitute in the FA Cup tie at Kidderminster last November. He went on to produce some mature displays and his effective tackling and strength in the air make him a good prospect for the future.
Darlington *(Trainee) FL 10+2 FAC 0+1*

MACHO Jurgen
Born: Vienna, Austria, 24 August 1977
Height: 6'4" **Weight:** 13.10
International Honours: Austria: U21
This tall goalkeeper was understudy to Thomas Sorensen at Sunderland last term when he was restricted to just four senior appearances. Against Spurs in September, he was caught out by a speculative Christian Ziege effort from 35 yards and at Manchester United in February his heroics prevented a 4-1 defeat from being far heavier. Jurgen's reflexes are as sharp as any 'keeper in the Premiership and he remains a capable deputy and useful squad player at the Stadium of Light.
Sunderland *(Free from First Vienna, Austria, ex Sportklub, Casino Vienna, on 24/7/2000) PL 8+1 FLC 1+1*

McINNES Derek John
Born: Paisley, 5 July 1971
Height: 5'8" **Weight:** 12.0
Club Honours: S Div 2 '95; SPL '97
Derek was the anchorman in West Bromwich Albion's efficient midfield last term, where his experience, determination and passing expertise gave the team a purposeful look about it. A tough competitor, he scored a fine goal in the 4-0 demolition of champions-to-be Manchester City at the Hawthorns and whipped in a marvellous right-footed effort in the game at Sheffield United – but it was his creativeness that made him such a huge asset.
Morton *(Signed from Gleniffer Thistle on 13/8/1988) SL 196+25/19 SLC 7+1/1 SC 10+6 Others 10*
Glasgow R *(£250,000 on 13/11/1995) SL 15+20/1 SLC 4+2/1 SC 0+1 Others 7+2/1 (Transferred to Toulouse, France on 27/12/1999)*
Stockport Co *(Loaned on 6/11/1998) FL 13 FAC 2*
West Bromwich A *(£450,000 on 10/8/2000) FL 59/4 FLC 7 FAC 4*

McINTOSH Martin Wyllie
Born: East Kilbride, 19 March 1971
Height: 6'2" **Weight:** 12.0
International Honours: S: B-2; Sch
This commanding left-sided defender proved to be one of Rotherham's best acquisitions for many years following his move from Hibernian. He came initially on loan but his powerful and commanding performances led to a permanent move and he went on to prove to be the key figure in the Millers' defence. Superb in the air, he weighed in with a handful of crucial goals, the pick of which was undoubtedly a magnificent free kick from 20 yards in the last home game of the season against Birmingham City. He deservedly scooped several 'Player of the Season' awards at the end of the campaign.
St Mirren *(From trainee at Tottenham H on 30/11/1988) SL 2+2*
Clydebank *(Signed on 17/8/1991) SL 59+6/10 SLC 2 SC 4+1/1 Others 3/1*
Hamilton Academical *(Signed on 1/2/1994) SL 99/12 SLC 5 SC 5 Others 5/1*
Stockport Co *(£80,000 on 15/8/1997) FL 96+3/5 FLC 5+1 FAC 4*
Hibernian *(£250,000 on 10/2/2000) SL 21 SLC 3 SC 2*
Rotherham U *(£125,000 on 17/8/2001) FL 39/4 FLC 2 FAC 2*

MACKAY Malcolm (Malky) George
Born: Bellshill, 19 February 1972
Height: 6'1" **Weight:** 11.7
Malky enjoyed an excellent season for Norwich, missing just a couple of games and forming an outstanding central defensive partnership with Craig Fleming. A robust central defender who enjoys the confrontation playing against a big centre forward brings, he is strong in the air and brave in the challenge. His aerial ability makes him a threat at set pieces although he didn't score as many goals as he would like. He skippered the Canary line-up in Iwan Roberts' post-Christmas absence from the side and proved himself an excellent leader.
Queens Park (From juniors on 8/12/1989) SL 68+2/6 SLC 3/2 SC 2 Others 2
Glasgow Celtic (Signed on 6/8/1993) SL 32+5/4 SLC 5+1 SC 4/1 Others 4+1
Norwich C (£350,000 on 18/9/1998) FL 118+12/5 FLC 6+1 FAC 4 Others 3/1

McKEEVER Mark Anthony
Born: Londonderry, 16 November 1978
Height: 5'9" **Weight:** 11.8
International Honours: NI: Yth. RoI: U21-4
Mark suffered an ankle injury in pre-season training, which kept him sidelined for over seven months last term. He eventually regained fitness with regular appearances for the reserves before finally returning to the Bristol Rovers first-team starting line-up in February. A talented winger, he added some much needed width and flair for the Pirates in the centre of the park.
Peterborough U (Trainee) FL 2+1 FLC 1
Sheffield Wed (£500,000 + on 15/4/1997) PL 2+3 FLC 0+1 FAC 0+1
Bristol Rov (Loaned on 10/12/1998) FL 5+2
Reading (Loaned on 8/3/1999) FL 6+1/2
Bristol Rov (Free on 8/2/2001) FL 13+7 FAC 0+1

MACKEN Jonathan (Jon) Paul
Born: Manchester, 7 September 1977
Height: 5'10" **Weight:** 12.8
Club Honours: Div 2 '00
International Honours: E: Yth
Jon appeared unsettled at Preston at the beginning of last term and spent some time on the transfer list. He still managed to find the net for North End and netted one of the goals of the season when he hit a looping pile driver over Manchester City 'keeper's head from inside the centre circle. Shortly before the transfer deadline the Maine Road club paid out a new club record fee for his services and he

immediately impressed with his ability to hold the ball up and bring colleagues into play. In all he netted five times from eight appearances for City, including the record-equalling 108th goal against Portsmouth.
Manchester U (From trainee on 10/7/1996)
Preston NE (£250,000 on 31/7/1997) FL 155+29/63 FLC 12+2/8 FAC 10+5/2 Others 9+3/1
Manchester C (£4,000,000 + on 5/3/2002) FL 4+4/5

McKENNA Paul Stephen
Born: Chorley, 20 October 1977
Height: 5'7" **Weight:** 11.12
Club Honours: Div 2 '00
A hernia operation in the summer of 2001 meant Paul started last season in discomfort, but he battled on to play a superb central midfield role in Preston's win over Norwich in September. Normally employed wide on the left, he scored his first goal of the season in his 150th appearance with a trademark rocket from the edge of the area, a feat he repeated several times including a strike after only 20 seconds in the home draw with Crewe. Out for a month from January with a serious foot injury, the creative midfield battler made a surprise return at Chelsea in the FA Cup fifth round tie, and then settled into a central role for the remainder of the campaign.
Preston NE (From trainee on 2/2/1996) FL 136+16/12 FLC 9 FAC 5+2/2 Others 6+2

McKENZIE Leon Mark
Born: Croydon, 17 May 1978
Height: 5'11" **Weight:** 11.2
Although Leon missed a substantial part of the 2001-02 season for Peterborough, he still managed to finish the campaign as the club's leading scorer with 20 goals. He is a pacy front man with an excellent goal-scoring record who is as good as any of the strikers in the Second Division on his day.
Crystal Palace (From trainee on 7/10/1995) F/PL 44+41/7 FLC 5+2/1 FAC 2+4
Fulham (Loaned on 3/10/1997) FL 1+2
Peterborough U (Loaned on 13/8/1998) FL 4/3
Peterborough U (Loaned on 30/11/1998) FL 10/5 Others 1/1
Peterborough U (Free on 13/10/2000) FL 58+2/31 FLC 1 FAC 6+1/1 Others 1/1

MacKENZIE Neil David
Born: Birmingham, 15 April 1976
Height: 6'2" **Weight:** 12.12
Club Honours: AMC '02
Neil signed for Blackpool in the 2001

close season but a hernia problem severely restricted his appearances and caused him to miss the second half of the campaign, including the LDV Vans Trophy final. When fully fit he is a talented central midfielder with a good range of passing skills.
Stoke C (From trainee at West Bromwich A on 9/11/1995) FL 15+27/1 FLC 1+1 FAC 0+1 Others 0+1
Cambridge U (Loaned on 24/3/1999) FL 3+1/1
Cambridge U (£45,000 on 14/10/1999) FL 20+8 FLC 1+1 FAC 5 Others 0+1
Kidderminster Hrs (Free on 24/11/2000) FL 20+3/3 FAC 0+1 Others 2
Blackpool (Free on 9/7/2001) FL 6+8/1 FLC 1+1 FAC 1+3/1 Others 3/2

MACKIE John
Born: London, 5 July 1976
Height: 6'0" **Weight:** 12.6
John progressed from the obscurity of reserve-team football and a trial game with Cambridge United to become one of the best centre backs in the Second Division last season. Injuries to other defenders gave him his first League start of the campaign against Bristol City, and he responded by heading the opening goal in Reading's 3-2 victory. He also netted against Oldham, but it was as a quick, brave and dominant defender that he contributed so materially to the Royals' push for promotion. His passing and awareness improved too, and he now looks to be manager Alan Pardew's best signing.
Reading (Free from Sutton U on 5/11/1999) FL 34+3/2 FLC 1+1 FAC 3+2 Others 1+2

McKINNEY Richard
Born: Ballymoney, 18 May 1979
Height: 6'3" **Weight:** 14.0
Richard joined Swindon Town during the 2001 close season and found it almost impossible to dislodge Bart Griemink from the 'keeper's jersey. He was a near ever present on the subs' bench before stepping up to make his full League debut in the 2-0 defeat at Stoke when he acquitted himself well with two fine saves and some competent handling.
Manchester C (Free from Ballymena U on 25/8/1999)
Swindon T (Free on 18/7/2001) FL 1

McLACHLAN Fraser Malcolm
Born: Manchester, 9 November 1982
Height: 5'11" **Weight:** 12.6
After making his debut for Stockport County at Sheffield United last March, Fraser became an important part of the team's midfield during their better end-of-

season form. He is comfortable on the ball, hard working and with a good range of passing. He rounded off a fine season with a magnificent left-foot volley in the 2-1 victory over Watford at Edgeley Park to register his first Football League goal.
Stockport Co (From trainee on 11/7/2001)
FL 11/1

McLAREN Paul Andrew
Born: High Wycombe, 17 November 1976
Height: 6'0" **Weight:** 13.4
This hard-working midfielder had a solid if unspectacular season in midfield for Sheffield Wednesday last season. A surprise summer signing from Luton Town he adapted quite well on stepping up to Division One. Halfway through the season he had a dip in form but recovered his place and again looked quite impressive.
Luton T (From trainee on 5/1/1994) FL 137+30/4 FLC 10+4/1 FAC 11/2 Others 9
Sheffield Wed (Free on 11/6/2001) FL 29+6/2 FLC 5+1/1 FAC 1

McLEAN Aaron
Born: Hammersmith, 25 May 1983
Height: 5'6" **Weight:** 10.2
Aaron appeared mainly from the subs' bench for Leyton Orient during the 2001-02 season, making only a couple of starts. He is a pacy young striker who can unsettle defenders and has a tremendous leap for one so small. He will be looking to gain a regular starting place for the O's in 2002-03.
Leyton Orient (From trainee on 9/7/2001) FL 5+27/2 FAC 0+3 Others 1+1/1

McLEOD Kevin Andrew
Born: Liverpool, 12 September 1980
Height: 5'11" **Weight:** 11.3
A pacy, aggressive winger with the ability to clip in accurate crosses, Kevin was selected for senior duty just once by Everton last term, appearing at left wing back in the Worthington Cup tie against Crystal Palace. He acquitted himself well, but found himself back in the reserves soon after to continue his education.
Everton (From trainee on 24/9/1998) PL 0+5 FLC 1

McLOUGHLIN Alan Francis
Born: Manchester, 20 April 1967
Height: 5'8" **Weight:** 10.10
International Honours: RoI: 42; B-3
Alan again struggled to find his way into the Wigan Athletic side last term, his only Second Division outing coming in the away draw at Cardiff City. A creative central midfield player he was released from his contract and joined Rochdale for

the second half of the season. After taking some time to regain his match fitness, he came off the bench at Halifax with 20 minutes left and completely transformed the game. A fixture in the centre of the park for Dale thereafter, his passing and creativity were vital factors as the team consolidated fifth place in the Third Division table. His only goal came from a twice-taken penalty in the last game of the regular season. The play-off semi-finals enabled him to reach a tally of 600 senior games, but he failed to win the offer of a further contract.
Manchester U (From apprentice on 25/4/1985)
Swindon T (Free on 15/8/1986) FL 101+5/19 FLC 11+3/5 FAC 4+2 Others 10/1
Torquay U (Loaned on 13/3/1987) FL 21+3/4
Southampton (£1,000,000 on 13/12/1990) FL 22+2/1 FLC 0+1 FAC 4 Others 1
Aston Villa (Loaned on 30/9/1991) Others 1
Portsmouth (£400,000 on 17/2/1992) FL 297+12/54 FLC 27/7 FAC 15+1/7 Others 9/1
Wigan Ath (£250,000 on 9/12/1999) FL 12+10/1 FLC 0+1 Others 4/2
Rochdale (Free on 21/12/2001) FL 15+3/1 Others 2

McMILLAN Stephen (Steve) Thomas
Born: Edinburgh, 19 January 1976
Height: 5'10" **Weight:** 11.10
International Honours: S: U21-4
A pacy left back who loves to push forward down the wing, Steve was one of the most reliable members of the Wigan Athletic squad last term. After missing the start of the season due to a hamstring injury, he returned with a 'Man of the Match' performance in the win at Bury. Unfortunately he then suffered a broken wrist in the away match at Cardiff City, forcing him to miss a couple of months. An ever present on his return he combined surging runs down the flanks with an ability to deliver telling crosses.
Motherwell (Signed from Troon Juniors on 19/8/1993) SL 144+8/6 SLC 9 SC 13+1
Wigan Ath (£550,000 on 2/3/2001) FL 35

McNAMARA Niall Anthony
Born: Limerick, 26 January 1982
Height: 5'11" **Weight:** 11.12
International Honours: RoI: Yth
This quick and skilful young striker joined Notts County during the 2001 close season and eventually made his senior debut as a substitute in the home defeat by Northampton last January. He featured three more times from the bench and was rather unfortunate to be released in the summer.
Nottingham F (From trainee on 2/2/1999)
Notts Co (Free on 5/7/2001) FL 0+4

McNAMEE Anthony
Born: Kensington, 13 July 1984
Height: 5'6" **Weight:** 10.0
One of the few bright spots of an otherwise mediocre season at Watford was the emergence of this young left winger, who won the club's 'Young Player of the Year' award on the strength of only seven first-team appearances. After starring for the juniors and the reserves, Anthony made his debut against Coventry in March and impressed the fans with his vision, ability to beat defenders and fine crossing. Manager Gianluca Vialli described him as a "bright talent", and he was included in the England U18 squad. He scored his first senior goal in the final match of the campaign against Gillingham – a spectacular left-footed drive.
Watford (Trainee) FL 2+5/1

McNEIL Martin James
Born: Rutherglen, 28 September 1980
Height: 6'1" **Weight:** 12.7
Martin was one of several players to follow manager Roy McFarland from Cambridge to Torquay last term. He established himself on the centre right of Torquay's back five for the early part of the season before losing his place due to a pelvic injury. His contract was later terminated following an off-the-field incident and he signed for Dr Martens League club King's Lynn.
Cambridge U (From trainee on 15/12/1998) FL 38+3 FLC 1 FAC 6 Others 1
Torquay U (Free on 9/8/2001) FL 16 FLC 2

McNIVEN Scott Andrew
Born: Leeds, 27 May 1978
Height: 5'10" **Weight:** 12.1
International Honours: S: U21-1; Yth
Scott was released by Oldham Athletic at the end of last season after progressing through the club's youth system. He made over 200 appearances for the club either as a right back or in central defence, including over 40 in the 2001-02 campaign. However, with the recent additions of Michael Clegg and Dean Holden to the squad, Athletic decided he was now surplus to requirements.
Oldham Ath (From trainee on 25/10/1995) FL 204+18/3 FLC 13+1 FAC 18+1/1 Others 9+2

McPHAIL Stephen
Born: Westminster, 9 December 1979
Height: 5'10" **Weight:** 12.0
Club Honours: FAYC '97
International Honours: RoI: 5; U21-7; Yth (UEFA-U18 '98)

Steve McPhee

In a season blighted by serious injury, Stephen failed to make a real impact at Leeds United last term. A talented midfield player with a sweet left foot and superb vision, he was loaned to Millwall in March but unfortunately was sent off in his first game for the Lions and returned to Elland Road.
Leeds U (From trainee on 23/12/1996) PL 37+16/2 FLC 2+3 FAC 3 Others 13+2
Millwall (Loaned on 14/3/2002) FL 3

McPHEE Christopher (Chris) Simon
Born: Eastbourne, 20 March 1983
Height: 5'10" **Weight:** 12.4
Chris is a young striker who emerged from Brighton's Centre of Excellence and stepped up to join the first-team squad for regular training to build up his strength and fitness levels. He came into reckoning for the first team due to Bobby Zamora's suspension in March. He started two games and was unlucky not to score at Bournemouth when he was brought down by the 'keeper early on when clean through. He was rewarded with a two-year professional contract.
Brighton & Hove A (Trainee) FL 2+4 Others 0+1

McPHEE Stephen (Steve)
Born: Glasgow, 5 June 1981
Height: 5'7" **Weight:** 10.8
This pacy striker joined Port Vale in the summer of 2001 and scored on his debut against Notts County, adding three more in the next two home games to begin the season with a bang. Two excellent goals in the 3-1 victory at Wrexham brought him wider acclaim and he made his debut for Scotland at U21 level against Latvia in October. Steve was also sometimes used in midfield, but he nevertheless finished the campaign as the club's leading scorer with 14 goals.
Coventry C (From juniors on 19/11/1998)
St Mirren (Loaned on 30/3/2001) SL 6+1
Port Vale (Free on 30/7/2001) FL 44/11 FLC 2/2 FAC 2 Others 3/1

McSHEFFREY Gary
Born: Coventry, 13 August 1982
Height: 5'8" **Weight:** 10.10
International Honours: E: Yth
Gary was given few opportunities to demonstrate his outstanding speed and shooting ability for Coventry last term. Fully recovered from the injuries that had blighted the previous two seasons, he made a number of substitute appearances before finally receiving his first League start in the final game of the season. He

had a month's loan at Stockport at the turn of the year, scoring on his debut at Burnley. A promising striker, he lifted the crowd with his 100 per cent commitment, first-time shooting and strong-running approach. He was a member of the England U20 squad that played in the Toulon tournament in the summer.
Coventry C (From trainee on 27/8/1999) P/FL 1+11/1 FLC 2+1
Stockport Co (Loaned on 30/11/2001) FL 3+2/1

McSPORRAN Jermaine
Born: Manchester, 1 January 1977
Height: 5'8" **Weight:** 10.10
After a nine-month absence due to a cruciate ligament injury to his left knee, Wycombe fans were relieved when Jermaine started last season without any loss to his truly blistering pace. Used on both wings and as a central striker, he once again tormented defences with his audacious runs. The high point of his season was an eye-catching performance against Fulham in the Worthington Cup third round tie. Described by Jean Tigana as the fastest player Fulham had come up against, he won a penalty with his speed and scored with a brilliant piece of finishing. He had contributed eight goals in 22 starts when, in an April training session, he received a devastating blow, suffering cruciate damage to his other knee and is expected to be out until February 2003.
Wycombe W (Signed from Oxford C on 5/11/1998) FL 82+34/22 FLC 8+1/3 FAC 7+1/1 Others 3+2/2

McSWEENEY David (Dave)
Born: Basildon, 28 December 1981
Height: 5'11" **Weight:** 11.7
After making seven starts in his familiar right-back position, injuries forced Southend manager Rob Newman to play Dave as a centre half towards the end of last season. He responded magnificently, his positional sense and all-round skills enabling him to become very comfortable in his new role, and he will be looking to use the one-year contract he earned to force his way into the side on a more regular basis during 2002-03.
Southend U (From trainee on 30/4/2001) FL 23+9 FLC 0+1 FAC 1+2 Others 5

McSWEGAN Gary John
Born: Glasgow, 24 September 1970
Height: 5'8" **Weight:** 11.2
Club Honours: SC '93
International Honours: S: Yth; Sch
This bustling Hearts striker joined Barnsley on loan last December, soon after Steve

Parkin took over as manager. He made his debut as a late substitute at Sheffield United and was a regular on the bench during his stay at Oakwell. In February he moved south again to join Luton Town on loan but had a disappointing time at Kenilworth Road when he was affected by injuries. He subsequently returned north of the border to Tynecastle after three appearances from the bench.
Glasgow R (From juniors in 1986 on 1/1/1986) SL 9+9/4 SLC 1 SC 0+2 Others 0+3/1
Notts Co (£400,000 on 13/7/1993) FL 47+15/21 FLC 6+1/3 FAC 4+1/1 Others 6/1
Dundee U (£375,000 on 6/10/1995) SL 56+36/32 SLC 4+4/7 SC 4+7/2 Others 3+2/6
Heart of Midlothian (Signed on 9/10/1998) SL 54+27/25 SLC 4 SC 2+5/4 Others 2+2/1
Barnsley (Loaned on 14/12/2001) FL 1+4
Luton T (Loaned on 15/2/2002) FL 2+1

McVEIGH Paul
Born: Belfast, 6 December 1977
Height: 5'6" **Weight:** 10.5
International Honours: NI: 3; U21-11; Yth; Sch
Paul started the 2001-02 season as fourth or fifth choice striker at Norwich but was quick to capitalise on Chris Llewellyn's unfortunate injury in the second game of the season and settled down quickly into an attacking left-sided midfield role. His striker's instinct ensured that he was a regular contributor of goals and he surpassed everyone's expectations with his ability to go past people and deliver telling crosses. As he settled into the role he was also able to improve on his defensive work, occasionally playing as a left wing back. He scored a vital goal in the play-off semi-final against Wolves.
Tottenham H (From trainee on 10/7/1996) PL 2+1/1
Norwich C (Free on 23/3/2000) FL 43+11/9 FLC 1+1 FAC 2 Others 3/1

MADDISON Lee Robert
Born: Bristol, 5 October 1972
Height: 5'11" **Weight:** 12.4
Club Honours: S Div 1 '98
Lee was given few opportunities to shine at Carlisle in 2001-02 and after losing his place in the first-team squad he joined Oxford for a three-month loan spell, linking up with his former boss Ian Atkins. However no permanent deal materialised and he eventually returned to Brunton Park where he made a surprise appearance in the last two matches of the season.
Bristol Rov (From trainee on 18/7/1991) FL 68+5 FLC 4 FAC 2 Others 6+1

Northampton T (£25,000 on 22/9/1995) FL 55 FLC 3+1 FAC 3 Others 4+1
Dundee (Free on 23/7/1997) SL 59+6/1 SLC 3 SC 3/1
Carlisle U (Free on 13/10/2000) FL 39+2 FLC 1 FAC 2
Oxford U (Loaned on 5/2/2002) FL 11

MADDISON Neil Stanley

Born: Darlington, 2 October 1969
Height: 5'10" **Weight:** 12.0
This experienced midfielder joined Darlington with the record of never having played outside the Premiership and made his Third Division debut at Southend on the opening day of last season. A series of niggling injuries prevented him from really establishing himself in the line-up, although his classy passing of the ball was obvious. Towards the end of the season he was forced into playing up front as a striker because of injuries and he grabbed his first goal for the Quakers at Exeter in March.
Southampton (From trainee on 14/4/1988) F/PL 149+20/19 FLC 9+5 FAC 8+5 Others 1
Middlesbrough (£250,000 on 31/10/1997) P/FL 32+24/4 FLC 7+1 FAC 4
Barnsley (Loaned on 4/11/2000) FL 3
Bristol C (Loaned on 16/3/2001) FL 4+3/1
Darlington (Free on 26/7/2001) FL 24+6/1 FLC 1 FAC 1+2 Others 2

MADDIX Daniel (Danny) Shawn

Born: Ashford, 11 October 1967
Height: 5'11" **Weight:** 12.2
International Honours: Jamaica: 2
Signed by Sheffield Wednesday in the summer of 2001, this experienced centre half never really impressed the Hillsborough faithful last season. He rarely looked totally convincing in the centre of defence and often appeared a little shaky under pressure, although he was always playing in a struggling team.
Tottenham H (From apprentice on 25/7/1985)
Southend U (Loaned on 1/11/1986) FL 2
Queens Park R (Free on 23/7/1987) F/PL 259+35/13 FLC 25/3 FAC 21+2/2 Others 2+3
Sheffield Wed (Free on 11/7/2001) FL 33+3/1 FLC 5/1

MAGILTON James (Jim)

Born: Belfast, 6 May 1969
Height: 6'0" **Weight:** 14.2
International Honours: NI: 47; U23-2; U21-1; Yth; Sch
After being a regular first-team player for Ipswich since he joined the club, Jim found that his place in the side was not guaranteed last season – a situation not helped by some minor injuries. He still maintains the ability to let the ball do the work but in a troubled campaign the ball tended to by-pass the midfield at times. He was forced to miss the last few games of the season due to family illness.
Liverpool (From apprentice on 14/5/1986)
Oxford U (£100,000 on 3/10/1990) FL 150/34 FLC 9/1 FAC 8/4 Others 6/3
Southampton (£600,000 on 11/2/1994) PL 124+6/13 FLC 12+2/2 FAC 12/3
Sheffield Wed (£1,600,000 on 10/9/1997) PL 14+13/1 FLC 2 FAC 1
Ipswich T (£682,500 on 15/1/1999) P/FL 100+14/8 FLC 9/1 FAC 3+1/1 Others 10/3

MAHER Kevin Andrew

Born: Ilford, 17 October 1976
Height: 6'0" **Weight:** 12.5
International Honours: RoI: U21-4
A supremely talented midfielder, Kevin was a dominant force at Southend United last season. Excellent control and accurate passing were the hallmarks of his performances, and he created a fine partnership with Carl Hutchings. Although not fully appreciated by all the club's fans, Kevin's contributions cannot be underestimated, and the Blues will be looking to build a promotion challenge around him in 2002-03.
Tottenham H (From trainee on 1/7/1995)
Southend U (Free on 23/1/1998) FL 146+7/12 FLC 8 FAC 9 Others 7+1/1

MAHER Shaun Patrick

Born: Dublin, 20 June 1978
Height: 6'2" **Weight:** 12.6
Shaun initially joined Bournemouth as a non-contract player at the start of last season but signed permanently on a one-year deal soon afterwards. The tall centre half excelled in his first few games for the Cherries, but the rigours of full-time football caught up with him and he found it difficult to adapt. After a spell out injured and then in the reserves, he regained his place in the first team and was ever present during the end-of-season run-in.
Fulham (£35,000 from Bohemians on 18/12/1997) Others 2 (Free to Bohemians on 10/9/1998)
Bournemouth (Free on 23/8/2001) FL 28+3 FLC 1

MAHON Alan Joseph

Born: Dublin, 4 April 1978
Height: 5'10" **Weight:** 11.5
Club Honours: FLC '02
International Honours: RoI: 1; U21-18; Yth; Sch
Signed during the 2001 close season, Alan was never going to be more than a squad player at Blackburn last term and so it proved. Although he likes to play central mid field, he was often used as a deputy for Damien Duff on the left or even at left back. High energy levels allow him to put in plenty of challenges in the centre of the park and he scored a valuable goal in an early game against Tottenham. He missed the final games through injury.
Tranmere Rov (From trainee on 7/4/1995) FL 84+36/13 FLC 12+6/2 FAC 3+2 (Free to Sporting Lisbon, Portugal on 1/7/2000)
Blackburn Rov (£1,500,000 on 14/12/2000) P/FL 24+7/1 FLC 3+3 FAC 9

MAHON Gavin Andrew

Born: Birmingham, 2 January 1977
Height: 6'0" **Weight:** 13.2
Club Honours: Div 3 '99
This skilful Brentford player reverted to a central midfield role in 2001-02 having had a spell in central defence the previous season. He impressed alongside Paul Evans in the early months of the season as the Bees topped the Second Division table but was eventually sold to Watford in March. He soon proved his value at Vicarage Road as a two-footed utility player, appearing both in midfield and the centre of the defence. Unfortunately, he suffered serious knee ligament damage in April that brought his season to an early close.
Wolverhampton W (From trainee on 3/7/1995)
Hereford U (Free on 12/7/1996) FL 10+1/1 FLC 4
Brentford (£50,000 + on 17/11/1998) FL 140+1/8 FLC 8 FAC 5 Others 12
Watford (£150,000 + on 4/3/2002) FL 6

MAKEL Lee Robert

Born: Sunderland, 11 January 1973
Height: 5'10" **Weight:** 11.12
Lee joined Bradford City on a four-month contract last August but with an abundance of midfielders on the club's books he only managed two starts. A midfield playmaker who can put his foot on the ball and spray passes all over the pitch he was released soon after manager Jim Jeffries departed and joined SPL Livingston shortly before the end of the year.
Newcastle U (From trainee on 11/2/1991) FL 6+6/1 FLC 1 Others 0+1
Blackburn Rov (£160,000 on 20/7/1992) PL 1+5 FLC 0+3 Others 1+3
Huddersfield T (£300,000 on 13/10/1995) FL 62+3/5 FLC 7 FAC 6+1

Heart of Midlothian (£75,000 on 13/3/1998) SL 30+19/1 SLC 3+1 SC 2+2 Others 5+1/1
Bradford C (Free on 31/8/2001) FL 2+11 FLC 2

MAKIN Christopher (Chris) Gregory
Born: Manchester, 8 May 1973
Height: 5'10" **Weight:** 11.2
Club Honours: Div 1 '99
International Honours: E: U21-5; Yth; Sch
Chris produced a series of consistent displays at right back for Ipswich Town last term and kept his place in the side throughout the season until an ankle ligament injury in the home game with Aston Villa ended his campaign a month early. He possesses a sufficient turn of speed to keep most opposing wingers in check and is a strong tackler.
Oldham Ath (From trainee on 2/11/1991) F/PL 93+1/4 FLC 7 FAC 11 Others 1+1 (Transferred to Marseille, France during 1996 close season)
Wigan Ath (Loaned on 28/8/1992) FL 14+1/2
Sunderland (£500,000 on 5/8/1997) P/FL 115+5/1 FLC 13 FAC 7+1 Others 1+1
Ipswich T (£1,250,000 on 7/3/2001) PL 40 FLC 2 FAC 1 Others 4+1

MALBRANQUE Steed
Born: Mouscron, Belgium, 6 January 1980
Height: 5'8" **Weight:** 11.7
International Honours: France: U21
Signed from Lyon two weeks before the start of the campaign, this French U21 midfielder immediately established himself as a firm crowd favourite. A tireless worker in midfield he scored a number of vital goals including a double in the 2-1 home win over Southampton and a stunning angled shot in the crucial late-season win at Leeds. His positional sense often sees him link well with the attack and his dead-ball skills are often displayed with accuracy at free kicks and corners. An excellent distributor of the ball he is also very crisp in the tackle.
Fulham (£5,000,000 from Lyon, France on 14/8/2001) PL 33+4/8 FLC 1+2/1 FAC 6/1

MALEY Mark
Born: Newcastle, 26 January 1981
Height: 5'9" **Weight:** 12.3
International Honours: E: Yth; Sch
Unable to break into the first team at Sunderland, Mark spent a lengthy period on loan at York City last term as he continued with his footballing education. The solidly built defender figured at both

right and left back during his time at Bootham Crescent but injuries restricted his appearances.
Sunderland (From trainee on 30/1/1998) FLC 3
Blackpool (Loaned on 6/10/2000) FL 2
Northampton T (Loaned on 24/11/2000) FL 2
York C (Loaned on 27/9/2001) FL 11+2 FAC 2+1 Others 1

MALLON Ryan
Born: Sheffield, 22 March 1983
Height: 5'9" **Weight:** 11.8
After some encouraging displays with Sheffield United reserves, Ryan was picked on the bench against Grimsby Town last October. To his surprise he made a two-minute appearance as a substitute - but failed to touch the ball. A powerful, quick and tricky striker, Ryan has scored goals at youth and reserve-team level and will be challenging for first-team action in 2002-03.
Sheffield U (From juniors on 13/7/2001) FL 0+1

MANSELL Lee Richard Samuel
Born: Gloucester, 28 October 1982
Height: 5'9" **Weight:** 10.10
Despite playing in the opening games of the 2001-02 season for Luton, Lee was unable to build upon the promise he had shown at the end of the 2000-01 season. It was a disappointing campaign for the 19-year-old left-sided or central midfielder, but he still has time to break through to regular first-team football
Luton T (From trainee on 16/5/2001) FL 23+6/6 FLC 1 FAC 1/1 Others 1

MARCELLE Clinton (Clint) Sherwin
Born: Trinidad, 9 November 1968
Height: 5'4" **Weight:** 10.0
International Honours: Trinidad & Tobago
This experienced, diminutive striker never really figured in the first-team plans at Darlington last term and he made only one start, in the LDV Vans Trophy match against Macclesfield Town. He also made three appearances from the subs' bench in Third Division games, but did not feature in the first team after October.
Barnsley (Free from Felgueiras, Portugal on 8/8/1996) F/PL 37+32/8 FLC 3+5 FAC 6+1/1 (Freed on 29/2/2000)
Scunthorpe U (Loaned on 10/10/1999) FL 8+2 FAC 1
Hull C (Free from Goole T on 1/9/2000) FL 16+7/2 FLC 1 FAC 1
Darlington (Free on 23/2/2001) FL 8+7 Others 1

[MARCELO] CIPRIANO DOS SANTOS Marcelo
Born: Niteroi, Brazil, 11 October 1969
Height: 6'0" **Weight:** 13.8
Marcelo did particularly well for Birmingham following the appointment of caretaker managers Mick Mills and Jim Barron, netting a hat-trick in the 4-0 win over Bradford and scoring 12 times in a 15-game spell. A tireless worker, he was deadly on crosses inside the area and was Blues' first choice striker until Steve Bruce decided to buy Stern John and allow him to leave on a free to Walsall. He impressed at Bescot with his high work rate but the expected flow of goals just did not come although he netted a valuable match-winner against Burnley in March.
Sheffield U (£400,000 from Deportivo Alaves, Spain, ex Benfica, on 6/10/1997) FL 47+19/24 FLC 3+1/2 FAC 10+1/5 Others 1+1/1
Birmingham C (£500,000 on 25/10/1999) FL 47+30/24 FLC 2+6/1 FAC 1+3 Others 3+1/1
Walsall (Free on 8/2/2002) FL 9/1

MARGETSON Martyn Walter
Born: Neath, 8 September 1971
Height: 6'0" **Weight:** 14.0
International Honours: W: B-1; U21-7; Yth; Sch
Opportunity knocked for this Welsh 'keeper at Huddersfield last term and he seized the chance to establish himself as the first choice at the McAlpine Stadium. An ever present during the campaign, he grew in confidence as the season progressed. Always capable of making vital saves and handling crosses safely, he kept the opposition at bay on many occasions, none more so than in the away draw at Wrexham, when he made numerous superb saves and blocks.
Manchester C (From trainee on 5/7/1990) F/PL 51 FLC 2+2 FAC 3 Others 1
Bristol Rov (Loaned on 8/12/1993) FL 2+1
Southend U (Free on 3/8/1998) FL 32 FLC 4 FAC 1 Others 1
Huddersfield T (Signed on 6/8/1999) FL 47+1 FLC 1 FAC 2 Others 8

MARINELLI Carlos Ariel
Born: Buenos Aires, Argentina, 14 March 1982
Height: 5'8" **Weight:** 11.6
International Honours: Argentina: Yth
This exciting attacking midfielder continued to make good progress at Middlesbrough last term and featured regularly in the first-team squad. He

Marcelo

scored two goals in the 5-1 victory over Derby County in November and went on to produce some impressive performances.
Middlesbrough *(£1,500,000 from Boca Juniors, Argentina on 27/10/1999) PL 14+21/2 FLC 1+2 FAC 3+2*

MARLET Steve
Born: Pithiviers, France, 10 January 1974
Height: 5'11" **Weight:** 11.5
International Honours: France: 6
Steve became Fulham's record signing when he arrived at Craven Cottage last September. He struggled to assert himself in his first few games before suffering a broken leg, which put him out of action for two months. Upon his return against Manchester United he scored his first goal and went on to prove a valuable goal-scorer in the fight to stay in the Premiership. He is an unselfish striker who works hard off the ball and displays silky skills when on it. He was recalled to the French national side for the game against Scotland in March when he scored the final goal in a 5-0 victory.
Fulham *(£13,500,000 from Lyon, France, ex Paris Red Star, Auxerre, on 3/9/2001) PL 21+5/6 FLC 1 FAC 5+1/3*

MARRIOTT Alan
Born: Bedford, 3 September 1978
Height: 6'1" **Weight:** 12.5
Alan was a virtual ever-present in the Lincoln line-up producing some excellent performances in goal in what was generally a disappointing season for the Third Division club. Although he made occasional errors, his confidence grew as he built on his experience and during the season he completed 100th senior appearance for the Imps.
Tottenham H *(From trainee on 3/7/1997)*
Lincoln C *(Free on 5/8/1999) FL 91 FLC 3 FAC 4 Others 3*

MARRIOTT Andrew (Andy)
Born: Sutton in Ashfield, 11 October 1970
Height: 6'1" **Weight:** 12.6
Club Honours: Div 4 '92; FMC '92; WC '95
International Honours: E: U21-1; Yth; Sch. W: 5
Andy made his debut for Barnsley at Grimsby last September when he came on as a late substitute after the sending off of Kevin Miller. He replaced Miller when he served his suspension and after keeping the Reds' first clean sheet of the campaign retained his place in the team. He fell out of favour when Nigel

Steve Marlet

275

Chris Marsden

Spackman departed before returning to the line-up for the crucial run-in. A good shot stopper he made a couple of excellent penalty saves late in the season but his form could not prevent the Reds from going down.
Arsenal (From trainee on 22/10/1988)
Nottingham F (£50,000 on 20/6/1989) F/PL 11 FLC 1 Others 1
West Bromwich A (Loaned on 6/9/1989) FL 3
Blackburn Rov (Loaned on 29/12/1989) FL 2
Colchester U (Loaned on 21/3/1990) FL 10
Burnley (Loaned on 29/8/1991) FL 15 Others 2
Wrexham (£200,000 on 8/10/1993) FL 213 FLC 10 FAC 22 Others 21
Sunderland (£200,000 + on 17/8/1998) P/FL 2 FLC 3
Wigan Ath (Loaned on 1/1/2001) Others 2
Barnsley (Free on 13/3/2001) FL 17+1 FLC 1

MARSDEN Christopher (Chris)

Born: Sheffield, 3 January 1969
Height: 5'11" **Weight:** 10.12
Chris produced some fine performances for Southampton throughout the 2001-02 season. A no nonsense attitude, combined with non-stop running and motivating skills make him a vital cog in the Saints side. He was appointed captain in the absence of Jason Dodd in March and capped a fine performance at Portman Road with a superb goal, beating two defenders and the keeper diagonally across the Ipswich penalty area. He was selected as the club's 'Player of the Year' in May.
Sheffield U (From apprentice on 6/1/1987) FL 13+3/1 FLC 1 Others 1
Huddersfield T (Signed on 15/7/1988) FL 113+8/9 FLC 15+1 FAC 6+2 Others 10
Coventry C (Loaned on 2/11/1993) PL 5+2
Wolverhampton W (£250,000 on 11/1/1994) FL 8 FAC 3
Notts Co (£250,000 on 15/11/1994) FL 10 FLC 1 Others 1/1
Stockport Co (£70,000 on 12/1/1996) FL 63+2/3 FLC 13 FAC 4 Others 4/1
Birmingham C (£500,000 on 9/10/1997) FL 51+1/3 FLC 5/3 FAC 2
Southampton (£800,000 on 2/2/1999) PL 79+7/5 FLC 4+2 FAC 4

MARSH Adam

Born: Sheffield, 20 February 1982
Height: 5'10" **Weight:** 11.7
This young striker's game is characterised by his tenacious running and chasing to put defenders under constant pressure. However his opportunities at Darlington last season were very limited and he made only one start in a League game against Hull City, and two substitute appearances in the cup ties against Sheffield United and Macclesfield Town. He also had spells on loan at Whitby Town and Hampton & Richmond during the second half of the campaign.
Darlington (Signed from Worksop T on 30/11/2000) FL 2+6 FLC 0+1 Others 2+1/1

MARSH Christopher (Chris) Jonathan

Born: Sedgley, 14 January 1970
Height: 5'11" **Weight:** 13.2
Chris made just one appearance from the subs' bench for Wycombe Wanderers last term before moving on to Northampton Town. A wing back who is equally at home on either side of the field, he was the last player to sign for the Cobblers before a transfer embargo was placed on the club. Unfortunately, no sooner had he arrived than he too was struck by the club's injury curse before bouncing back with a vengeance and playing a large part in the fight for survival.
Walsall (From trainee on 11/7/1988) FL 355+37/23 FLC 23+2/1 FAC 33+3/3 Others 24+1/3
Wycombe W (£30,000 on 23/3/2001) FL 11+1 FLC 0+1
Northampton T (£10,000 on 6/9/2001) FL 26 FAC 1 Others 1

MARSHALL Andrew (Andy) John

Born: Bury St Edmunds, 14 April 1975
Height: 6'2" **Weight:** 13.7
International Honours: E: U21-4; Yth (UEFA-U18 '93)
Andy joined Ipswich from local rivals Norwich on a free transfer, but a back injury in a pre-season friendly meant that he wasn't fit to play at the start of last season. This caused the club to bring in Matteo Sereni and Andy didn't get a sniff of the action until the new year. His first game was at Dagenham & Redbridge in the FA Cup and he kept his place for the next nine games, which coincided with Town's best spell of the season. He returned to the side at Easter following an injury to Sereni and remained in the line-up for the rest of the campaign.
Norwich C (From trainee on 6/7/1993) P/FL 194+1 FLC 18 FAC 5+1
Bournemouth (Loaned on 9/9/1996) FL 11
Gillingham (Loaned on 21/11/1996) FL 5 FLC 1 Others 1
Ipswich T (Free on 4/7/2001) PL 13 FAC 2

MARSHALL Ian Paul

Born: Liverpool, 20 March 1966
Height: 6'1" **Weight:** 13.10
Club Honours: Div 2 '91; FLC '00
A firm favourite with the Bolton fans, Ian's appearances were limited to two Worthington Cup starts and two substitute appearances in the top flight. Desperate for first-team football at this stage in his career, he went on loan to Blackpool in October, in a deal which was made permanent in January. He settled down in defence for the Tangerines and made an appearance in the LDV Vans Trophy final before an injury ended his campaign. He subsequently announced his retirement from playing.
Everton (From apprentice on 23/3/1984) FL 9+6/1 FLC 1+1/1 Others 7
Oldham Ath (£100,000 on 24/3/1988) F/PL 165+5/36 FLC 17 FAC 14/3 Others 2+1/1
Ipswich T (£750,000 on 9/8/1993) P/FL 79+5/32 FLC 4/3 FAC 9/3
Leicester C (£875,000 on 31/8/1996) PL 49+34/18 FLC 4+2/4 FAC 6+2/3 Others 2/1
Bolton W (Free on 11/8/2000) P/FL 13+25/6 FLC 2 FAC 3 Others 0+2
Blackpool (Free on 6/11/2001) FL 21/1 FAC 1 Others 4

MARSHALL Lee Keith

Born: Islington, 21 January 1979
Height: 6'0" **Weight:** 11.11
International Honours: E: U21-1
This promising young full back or midfielder was thrust into Leicester City's first team after Gary Rowett suffered a long-term injury and experienced mixed fortunes last term. Occasional errors at right back were often punished at Premiership level, but he generally performed better as part of a three-man defensive unit, where he gained valuable experience. He produced an excellent performance in the FA Cup tie at the Hawthorns, but his instinctive volley from the edge of the box was tipped to safety by Russell Hoult.
Norwich C (Signed from Enfield on 27/3/1997) FL 95+22/11 FLC 11+1/2 FAC 2
Leicester C (£600,000 on 21/3/2001) PL 36+8 FLC 1 FAC 2

MARSHALL Shaun Andrew

Born: Fakenham, 3 October 1978
Height: 6'1" **Weight:** 12.12
Shaun was once again second choice goalkeeper at Cambridge United last term, making just four starts in the senior team when regular 'keeper Lionel Perez was unavailable. Whenever called upon he proved reliable and competent and at

24 he still has plenty time ahead of him to break through to regular first-team football.
Cambridge U *(From trainee on 21/2/1997)*
FL 59+5 FLC 1 FAC 6 Others 1

MARTEINSSON Petur
Born: Reykjavik, Iceland, 14 July 1973
Height: 6'1" **Weight:** 12.4
International Honours: Iceland: 24; U21-19; Yth
Petur completed his contract with Norwegian club Stabaek before joining Stoke City last January. A training injury to his foot then delayed his debut and after just a couple of games he suffered an ankly injury that brought his campaign to a premature close. When fit he added versatility to the City squad, being able to play either in midfield or defence.
Stoke C *(Free from Stabaek IF, Norway, ex Leftur, Fram, Hammarby, on 10/1/2002) FL 2+1*

MARTIN Andrew (Andy) Peter
Born: Cardiff, 28 February 1980
Height: 6'0" **Weight:** 10.12
International Honours: W: U21-1; Yth
This young striker was released by Crystal Palace last March and moved on to try his luck at Torquay. He looked lively and seemed to possess good control, but failed to find the net and was not offered a long-term deal.
Crystal Palace *(From trainee on 28/2/1997) FL 12+10/2 FLC 0+1*
Torquay U *(Free on 22/3/2002) FL 5*

MARTIN John (Johnny)
Born: Bethnal Green, 15 July 1981
Height: 5'6" **Weight:** 9.12
Johnny had his best season to date for Leyton Orient in 2001-02. Playing on the left-hand side of midfield he excelled under new manager Paul Brush. Although slightly built he is a talented winger and also contributed his first goals for the O's during the campaign.
Leyton Orient *(From trainee on 6/8/1998) FL 53+7/2 FLC 5 FAC 3+1 Others 3+3*

MARTIN Lee Brendan
Born: Huddersfield, 9 September 1968
Height: 6'0" **Weight:** 13.0
Club Honours: FC '98
International Honours: E: Sch
Lee commenced the 2001-02 season as Macclesfield's first choice 'keeper but was dropped after the defeat by Mansfield at the end of August. His only subsequent appearances were early in the new year when Steve Wilson was recovering from a knee injury. However, Lee played an important part for the club's reserve team

who went on to win the Avon Insurance League Division Two championship. He once again proved to be cool, calm and collected even when under the most intense pressure.
Huddersfield T *(From trainee on 1/7/1987) FL 54 FAC 4 Others 5*
Blackpool *(Free on 31/7/1992) FL 98 FLC 8 FAC 4 Others 7*
Rochdale *(Free on 8/11/1996)*
Halifax T *(Free on 12/8/1997) FL 37 FLC 4 FAC 1 Others 1*
Macclesfield T *(Free on 19/7/1999) FL 50+1 FLC 1 FAC 3 Others 1*

MARTINEZ Jairo Manfredo
Born: Honduras, 14 May 1978
Height: 5'9" **Weight:** 12.7
International Honours: Honduras:
The young Coventry City reserve striker made a number of first-team appearances due to injuries and suspensions in the early part of the 2001-02 season. His enthusiasm was infectious and his eye for goal was rewarded with well-taken efforts at Barnsley, Gillingham and Millwall. He slipped out of contention during the winter months and disappointed in two starts in January. Soon afterwards he had a knee operation and spent two months convalescing before a couple of reserve games at the end of the campaign.
Coventry C *(Signed from Motagua, Honduras on 24/10/2000) FL 5+6/3 FLC 1 FAC 0+1*

MARTYN Antony **Nigel**
Born: St Austell, 11 August 1966
Height: 6'2" **Weight:** 14.7
Club Honours: Div 3 '90; FMC '91; Div 1 '94
International Honours: E: 23; B-6; U21-11
Now recognised for many years as one of the most consistent goalkeepers in England, Nigel had another fine season for Leeds United last term. He was an ever present in the Premiership last term but was still unable to wrest the England 'keeper's jersey from David Seaman.
Bristol Rov *(Free from St Blazey on 6/8/1987) FL 101 FLC 6 FAC 6 Others 11*
Crystal Palace *(£1,000,000 on 21/11/1989) F/PL 272 FLC 36 FAC 22 Others 19*
Leeds U *(£2,250,000 on 26/7/1996) PL 207 FLC 12 FAC 18 Others 36*

MATHIE Alexander (Alex)
Born: Bathgate, 20 December 1968
Height: 5'10" **Weight:** 11.7
Club Honours: Div 2 '00
International Honours: S: Yth
This experienced striker again found himself troubled by injuries which limited

his appearances for York City in 2001-02. He found the net twice – once when coming on as a substitute to clinch an important win at Leyton Orient. Alex will be hoping for an injury-free time in 2002-03 when his undoubted skill and experience should prove invaluable to the Third Division club.
Glasgow Celtic *(From juniors on 15/5/1987) SL 7+4 SC 1 Others 0+1*
Morton *(£100,000 on 1/8/1991) SL 73+1/31 SLC 2/1 SC 5/3 Others 7/9*
Port Vale *(Loaned on 30/3/1993) FL 0+3*
Newcastle U *(£285,000 on 30/7/1993) PL 3+22/4 FLC 2+2*
Ipswich T *(£500,000 on 24/2/1995) P/FL 90+19/38 FLC 10+3/8 FAC 2+2 Others 6/1*
Dundee U *(£700,000 on 16/10/1998) SL 13+10/1 SLC 0+1 SC 4+2*
Preston NE *(Loaned on 17/9/1999) FL 5+7/2 FLC 2/2 FAC 1+2 Others 1*
York C *(Free on 27/9/2000) FL 24+18/3 FAC 2+4/1 Others 1+1*

MATIAS Pedro Manuel Miguel
Born: Madrid, Spain, 11 October 1973
Height: 6'0" **Weight:** 12.0
International Honours: Spain: U21
In his third season with Walsall Pedro again impressed with his left-flank raiding during 2001-02, linking splendidly with fellow countryman Zigor Aranalde. He also carried out his fair share of defensive duties and was always liable to pop up with the surprise goal, as when netting a crisp shot and smart header in the opening half hour against Rotherham in October, and when contributing spectacular goals in the vital late-season games at Millwall and Nottingham Forest.
Macclesfield T *(Free from Logrones, Spain, ex Real Madrid, Almeria, on 3/12/1998) FL 21+1/2 FAC 1*
Tranmere Rov *(Free on 5/8/1999) FL 1+3*
Walsall *(Free on 7/10/1999) FL 91+12/20 FLC 4 FAC 6+1/1 Others 4/2*

MATTEO Dominic
Born: Dumfries, 24 April 1974
Height: 6'1" **Weight:** 11.12
International Honours: S: 6; E: B-1; U21-4; Yth
Dominic is a very underrated player who consistently produces good performances for Leeds United. His versatility enables him to fill a variety of positions whether it be left midfield, left back or in central defence. In fact the side's best spell defensively came when he partnered Rio Ferdinand at the back. An intelligent payer with an abundance of vision, skill and athleticism, he has become a regular in the Scotland side.

Liverpool *(From trainee on 27/5/1992)* PL
112+15/1 FLC 9 FAC 6+2/1 Others 10+1
Sunderland *(Loaned on 28/3/1995)* FL 1
Leeds U *(£4,750,000 on 24/8/2000)* PL 62
FLC 2 FAC 2 Others 22/2

MATTHEWS Lee Joseph
Born: Middlesbrough, 16 January 1979
Height: 6'3" **Weight:** 12.6
Club Honours: FAYC '97
International Honours: E: Yth
Lee occasionally looked as though he
could give Bristol City the skill and
firepower that their attack needed, but
niggling injury problems prevented him
enjoying a decent run in the side. His two
great strikes against Bristol Rovers in the
LDV Vans Trophy made him a hero, but he
was never able to build on the acclaim
generated by this feat. He was one of
several City players placed on the transfer
list at the end of the season.
Leeds U *(From trainee on 15/2/1996)* PL 0+3
FLC 0+1
Notts Co *(Loaned on 24/9/1998)* FL 4+1
Gillingham *(Loaned on 23/3/2000)* FL 2+3
Bristol C *(£100,000 on 16/3/2001)* FL
10+18/6 FLC 0+2 Others 2+1/2

MATTHEWS Robert (Rob)
David
Born: Slough, 14 October 1970
Height: 6'0" **Weight:** 13.0
Club Honours: Div 2 '97
International Honours: E: Sch
An experienced midfielder, Rob provided
essential back up to Hull's promotion-
chasing squad in 2001-02. A highlight
was his vital goal in the 1-0 win at Luton
in November. Although preferring the
right, Rob was used on both wings last
season before being made available for
transfer at the end of the term.
Notts Co *(Free from Loughborough
University on 26/3/1992)* FL 23+20/11 FLC
0+2 FAC 3+2/2 Others 4+3
Luton T *(£80,000 on 17/3/1995)* FL 6+5 FLC
0+1
York C *(£90,000 on 8/9/1995)* FL 14+3/1 FAC
1 Others 3
Bury *(£100,000 on 12/1/1996)* FL 54+20/11
FLC 4+5/3 FAC 1 Others 3
Stockport Co *(£120,000 on 12/11/1998)* FL
29+9/4 FAC 2+2
Blackpool *(Loaned on 28/12/1999)* FL 5+1/2
Others 2/1
Halifax T *(Loaned on 9/2/2001)* FL 8/2
Hull C *(£30,000 on 14/3/2001)* FL 17+6/3
FLC 0+1 FAC 2/1 Others 3+1

MATTIS Dwayne Antony
Born: Huddersfield, 31 July 1981
Height: 6'1" **Weight:** 10.10

International Honours: RoI: U21-1; Yth
Dwayne started the 2001-02 campaign
on the subs' bench for Huddersfield
before winning his first start in the defeat
at Wigan. He made a real impact in the
centre of midfield with some keen
tackling and accurate passing to turn
defence into attack. The season's
highlights included scoring his first goal
against Cardiff City in a 2-1 win, and
making his debut for the Republic of
Ireland at U21 level against Denmark.
Huddersfield T *(From trainee on 8/7/1999)*
FL 21+10/1 FLC 0+1 FAC 2 Others 3

MAUGE Ronald (Ronnie)
Carlton
Born: Islington, 10 March 1969
Height: 5'10" **Weight:** 11.10
International Honours: Trinidad &
Tobago: 8
The tough-tackling midfielder announced
his retirement from international football
with Trinidad & Tobago to concentrate on
helping Bristol Rovers regain their Second
Division status last season. He started the
campaign as a regular in the line-up but a
series of injuries including a broken finger
and knee trouble limited his appearances.
He was transfer listed in March and
released on a free transfer in the summer.
Charlton Ath *(From trainee on 22/7/1987)*
Fulham *(Free on 21/9/1988)* FL 47+3/2 FLC 4
FAC 1 Others 2
Bury *(£40,000 on 30/7/1990)* FL 92+16/10
FLC 8+2/2 FAC 8/2 Others 10+2
Manchester C *(Loaned on 26/9/1991)*
Others 0+1
Plymouth Arg *(£40,000 on 22/7/1995)* FL
119+16/14 FLC 6 FAC 11/3 Others 5+1/1
Bristol Rov *(Free on 5/7/1999)* FL 50+3 FLC
6 FAC 4 Others 6

MAWENE Youl
Born: Caen, France, 16 July 1979
Height: 6'2" **Weight:** 12.6
This versatile defender appeared regularly
for Derby County in the first half of last
season, but then lost his place and rarely
featured in the closing stages of the
campaign. A promising player with pace
and vision he can play at right back or in
the centre of the defence.
Derby Co *(£500,000 from RC Lens, France
on 4/8/2000)* PL 24+1/1 FL 2 FAC

MAXWELL Layton Jonathan
Born: Rhyl, 3 October 1979
Height: 5'8" **Weight:** 11.6
International Honours: W: U21-14; Yth
After signing for Cardiff shortly before the
start of last season Layton initially found it
difficult to win a place in the line-up. A

busy, bustling midfield player he often
featured from the subs' bench but his
influence grew as the campaign
progressed. He scored in the 2-1 win at
Northampton and will be hoping to
feature more regularly in 2002-03.
Liverpool *(From trainee on 17/7/1997)*
FLC 1/1
Stockport Co *(Loaned on 17/7/2000)* FL
8+12/2 FLC 1+1 FAC 0+1
Cardiff C *(Free on 7/8/2001)* FL 5+12/1 FAC
0+1 Others 2+1

MAY David
Born: Oldham, 24 June 1970
Height: 6'0" **Weight:** 13.5
Club Honours: CS '94, '96; PL '96, '97,
'99; FAC '96, '99; EC '99
They say that a week can be a long time
in politics, and for David, the same could
be said about his football career at Old
Trafford. Perennially jinxed by injuries over
the past few years, his name came high in
the pecking order when Jaap Stam was
sent packing to Lazio in September.
Although David occupied the back four
when the team kept their first clean sheet
in the Premiership against Ipswich in
September, unfortunately, after two more
outings, the injury jinx struck again, and
he went back to square one. When fully
fit he is a very able central defender with
good recovery skills, and excellent
heading ability to match.
Blackburn Rov *(From trainee on 16/6/1988)*
F/PL 123/3 FLC 12+1/2 FAC 10/1 Others 5
Manchester U *(£1,400,000 on 1/7/1994)* PL
68+16/6 FLC 7/1 FAC 6 Others 15+2/1
Huddersfield T *(Loaned on 24/12/1999)* FL 1

MAYBURY Alan
Born: Dublin, 8 August 1978
Height: 5'11" **Weight:** 11.12
Club Honours: FAYC '97
International Honours: RoI: 2; B-1; U21-
8; Yth
This young defender was again on the
fringes of the Leeds United first-team
squad in 2001-02 and managed just brief
outing from the subs' bench before
moving on to SPL Hearts where he
became a regular in the line-up.
Leeds U *(Free from St Kevin's BC on
17/8/1995)* PL 10+4 FLC 1 FAC 2 Others 1
Reading *(Loaned on 25/3/1999)* FL 8
Crewe Alex *(Loaned on 8/10/2000)* FL 6

MAYE Daniel Peter Christopher
Born: Leicester, 14 July 1982
Height: 5'9" **Weight:** 10.10
This promising left-sided Port Vale player
overcame a leg injury to earn a 12-
month contract with the club. He made

his debut as a substitute in the 5-0 home win over Cambridge and also featured against Carlisle United in the LDV Vans Trophy. A tricky player who looks to have a bright future in the game, his only other senior appearance was as a substitute against Bournemouth in April. At the end of the season he was released on a free transfer.
Port Vale (From trainee on 29/9/2001) FL 0+2 Others 0+1

MAYLETT Bradley (Brad)
Born: Manchester, 24 December 1980
Height: 5'8" **Weight:** 10.10
It was another season on the fringes for Burnley's speedy right-winger. Brad failed to add to his single League start, but was often on the bench and available to add fresh legs when the Clarets appeared to be flagging. His pace is certainly his main asset; he could outrun defenders and often looked dangerous in full flight, but his final ball was not always accurate and the lack of first-team opportunities may be hindering the further development of his game.
Burnley (From trainee on 19/2/1999) FL 2+37 FLC 1+2 FAC 0+1 Others 1

MAYO Kerry
Born: Haywards Heath, 21 September 1977
Height: 5'10" **Weight:** 13.4
Club Honours: Div 3 '01; Div 2 '02
Kerry was out of favour at Brighton for the first few games of 2001-02 but returned to the starting line-up for the first away win of the season at Wrexham and went on to establish himself as the Seagulls' regular left back once more. He is an effective defender and was often seen providing support to the wingers, while his powerful long throw caused panic in opposition defences.
Brighton & Hove A (From trainee on 3/7/1996) FL 184+18/9 FLC 6+1 FAC 6+6/2 Others 4+3

MAYO Paul
Born: Lincoln, 13 October 1981
Height: 5'11" **Weight:** 11.9
Paul found it difficult to break into the Lincoln starting line-up last season, with his favoured left-back position take by the more experienced Stuart Bimson. In the second half of the campaign he was sometimes used as a central defender but was unable to substantially add to his first-team appearance total.
Lincoln C (From trainee on 6/4/2000) FL 56+4 FLC 2 FAC 3+1 Others 3

MAZZINA Jorge Nicolas
Born: Buenos Aires, Argentina, 31 January 1979
Height: 5'10" **Weight:** 11.7
This attacking midfielder arrived at Swansea during the 2001 close season following a spell with Argentinian Second Division club AC Kimberley. He began promisingly but then suffered a knee injury in September and struggled to regain his first-team place. By December he was having trials at a number of other clubs and in February he was released by the Swans.
Swansea C (Free from AC Kimberley, Argentina on 10/8/2001) FL 3 FLC 1

MBOMA Patrick
Born: Douala, Cameroon, 15 November 1970
Height: 6'1" **Weight:** 13.6
International Honours: Cameroon: 23 (ANC '00, OLYM '00)
This powerfully built striker arrived at Sunderland on loan from Italian club Parma last February after helping Cameroon retain their African Nations' Cup title. Extremely quick, athletic and the possessor of a scorching left foot shot, he made his debut as a substitute against Newcastle, before scoring on his full debut a week later in a 2-1 reverse at Tottenham. Unfortunately, knee and ankle injuries restricted his appearances as the Black Cats struggled against relegation and it remains to be seen whether the club will seek to make his transfer permanent.
Sunderland (Loaned from Parma, Italy on 15/2/2002) PL 5+4/1

MEARS Tyrone
Born: Stockport, 18 February 1983
Height: 5'11" **Weight:** 11.10
This 19-year-old defender was only named on the bench for Manchester City once last season, coming on in place of Stuart Pearce for the final six minutes of the home game against Nottingham Forest. He will be looking to gain more senior experience next term.
Manchester C (From juniors on 5/7/2000) FL 0+1

MEDOU-OTYE Andre Parfait
Born: Ekoundendi, Cameroon, 29 January 1976
Height: 5'10" **Weight:** 11.12
International Honours: France: Yth
Parfait began the season as Kidderminster's first choice at right back. However, he lost his place after just one week of the campaign after receiving a red card at Darlington. The form of Ian Clarkson then kept him out of the side before he was

diagnosed as suffering from a rare heart condition that unfortunately forced him into premature retirement.
Morton (Signed from Le Mans, France, ex Le Havre, on 4/8/2000)
Kidderminster Hrs (Free on 23/11/2000) FL 18+1 FLC 1 Others 2

MELCHIOT Mario
Born: Amsterdam, Holland, 4 November 1976
Height: 6'1" **Weight:** 11.8
Club Honours: FAC '00; CS '00
International Honours: Holland: 9; U21-13; Yth
How Mario Melchiot must enjoy playing against Manchester United! His power header was the opener in Chelsea's amazing 3-0 victory at Old Trafford and only his second goal in English football the first coming against the Reds in the 2000 Charity Shield. Now seemingly over the injury hoodoo that dogged his early spell at Stamford Bridge, Mario has developed into one of the most accomplished all-round players in the Premiership. He began the 2001-02 season by playing on the right side of a midfield quartet but moved back to right back in October, in preference to the assured Albert Ferrer. Although Mario is built like a cruiserweight boxer he is a superb athlete, being quick on the turn, comfortable on the ball and has never been embarrassed by a winger.
Chelsea (Free from Ajax, Holland on 5/7/1999) PL 66+7/2 FLC 5 FAC 7+1 Others 5/1

MELLANBY Daniel (Danny)
Born: Bishop Auckland, 17 July 1979
Height: 5'10" **Weight:** 11.9
Danny joined Darlington during the summer of 2001 and made his senior debut on the opening day of last season at Southend. He immediately impressed with his neat control and confidence in taking on defenders. He was rewarded with his first goal on his home debut against Kidderminster and went on to grab another four in the League before injury halted his progress. Although he returned on a number of occasions he was not fully fit and had to sit out the last quarter of the season. He is the nephew of Quakers' team-mate Brian Atkinson.
Darlington (Free from Bishop Auckland, ex West Auckland on 26/7/2001) FL 22+2/4 FLC 1 FAC 3

MELLBERG Erik Olof
Born: Gullspang, Sweden, 3 September 1977
Height: 6'1" **Weight:** 12.10

Olof Mellberg

Andy Melville

International Honours: Sweden: 26
Olof enjoyed a very successful first season
at Villa Park. A tough-tackling defender
who was brought in to fill the void left by
Gareth Southgate, he is cultured enough
to have the ball at his feet and make
things happen. He made an immediate
impact in the opening day draw at
Tottenham and established a solid central
defensive partnership with both Alpay and
Steve Staunton playing as a central
defender in a back-four formation. With
the exception of a seven-match lay-off after
damaging ankle ligaments against NK
Varteks he was an ever present in the team.
*Aston Villa (£5,000,000 from Racing
Santander, Spain, ex Degerfors, AIK Solna, on
25/7/2001) PL 32 FLC 1 FAC 1 Others 2*

MELLIGAN John (JJ) James
Born: Dublin, 11 February 1982
Height: 5'9" **Weight:** 11.4
International Honours: RoI: Yth
This promising youngster joined
Bournemouth on loan from Wolves last
December, but had a rather frustrating
time with the Second Division club as his
arrival coincided with an alarming slump
in form by the team. A left-sided
midfielder with pace and vision, he
unfortunately never tasted victory in his
nine outings for the Cherries.
*Wolverhampton W (From trainee on
11/7/2000)*
*Bournemouth (Loaned on 30/11/2001) FL
7+1 FAC 1*

MELLON Michael (Micky)
Joseph
Born: Paisley, 18 March 1972
Height: 5'10" **Weight:** 12.11
Now in his second spell at Tranmere,
Micky experienced a frustrating season in
2001-02. An accumulation of yellow
cards seemed to affect his first-team
chances, and after appearing in the away
game at Wrexham in February it was not
until the final fixture against Cardiff that
he made the starting line-up again. A
very experienced midfielder, Micky can
instigate attacks and deliver useful passes
to his colleagues up front. As one of the
few senior Rovers players still under
contract, he is likely to provide stability in
what is likely to be a young midfield set-
up at Prenton Park in 2002-03.
*Bristol C (From trainee on 6/12/1989) FL
26+9/1 FLC 3 FAC 1+1 Others 5+3*
*West Bromwich A (£75,000 on 11/2/1993)
FL 38+7/6 FLC 3+2 FAC 0+1 Others 6/1*
*Blackpool (£60,000 on 23/11/1994) FL
123+1/14 FLC 9/1 FAC 4 Others 7/2*
*Tranmere Rov (£285,000 on 31/10/1997) FL
45+12/3 FLC 4 FAC 3+1*

*Burnley (£350,000 on 8/1/1999) FL 72+12/5
FLC 3+1 FAC 5*
*Tranmere Rov (Free on 5/3/2001) FL 34+6/2
FLC 3/1 FAC 2+1 Others 1*

MELTON Stephen (Steve)
Born: Lincoln, 3 October 1978
Height: 5'11" **Weight:** 12.2
Club Honours: Div 3 '01
Steve was blighted by a string of injuries
during the 2001-02 campaign and these
restricted his appearances for Brighton.
He scored three times including the
'golden goal' winner in the LDV Vans
Trophy against Wycombe and a
memorable strike in the 3-1 victory over
then leaders Reading, which was later
voted the Albion's best goal of the season
by ITV's Meridian Tonight viewers. He is a
versatile player who can appear in central
midfield or defence.
*Nottingham F (From trainee on 9/10/1995)
P/FL 2+1 FLC 1*
*Stoke C (Free on 28/2/2000) FL 0+5 Others
0+2*
*Brighton & Hove A (Free on 2/8/2000) FL
15+23/2 FLC 0+2 Others 4+1/2*

MELVILLE Andrew (Andy)
Roger
Born: Swansea, 29 November 1968
Height: 6'0" **Weight:** 13.10
Club Honours: WC '89; Div 1 '96, '01
International Honours: W: 51; B-1; U21-2
This vastly experienced defender
captained both club and country in 2001-
02, leading Wales for the first time on the
occasion of his 50th cap against the
Czech Republic. At club level he provided
the inspiration for a defence that was
amongst the best in the Premiership. A
commanding figure in the air, he has the
ability to read the game in a way which
reassures less experienced defenders
around him. A regular for much of the
season he was left out of the side on a
number of occasions in the new year, but
returned to galvanise the Fulham side in
the face of an unexpected brush with
relegation.
*Swansea C (From trainee on 25/7/1986) FL
165+10/22 FLC 10 FAC 14+1/5 Others 13/2*
*Oxford U (£275,000 on 23/7/1990) FL
135/13 FLC 12/1 FAC 6 Others 6/1*
*Sunderland (£750,000 + on 9/8/1993) P/FL
204/14 FLC 18+1 FAC 11 Others 2*
Bradford C (Loaned on 13/2/1998) FL 6/1
*Fulham (Free on 1/7/1999) P/FL 117+1/4 FLC
10+1 FAC 10+1*

MENETRIER Mickael
Born: Reims, France, 23 August 1978
Height: 6'3" **Weight:** 12.10

Mickael spent virtually the entire 2001-02
campaign either on the bench for
Bournemouth or on trial elsewhere. He
made just one League appearance during
the season, keeping a clean sheet in a 0-0
draw at Tranmere in March, but was
relegated to the bench for the next
match. He is a promising young
goalkeeper but needs to gain more
experience at first-team level.
*Bournemouth (Free from Metz, France on
11/8/2000) FL 12+1 FLC 2 Others 3*

MERSON Paul Charles
Born: Harlesden, 20 March 1968
Height: 6'0" **Weight:** 13.2
Club Honours: Div 1 '89, '91; FLC '93;
FAC '93; ECWC '94
International Honours: E: 21; B-4; U21-
4; Yth
There are few players who command
quite as much respect in the game as Paul
does. He was therefore the obvious
choice to take over the captain's armband
at Aston Villa following Gareth
Southgate's departure. A player of
undoubted talent, he is still an awesome
sight when he is in full flow and spraying
superb passes to all corners of the pitch.
He had a time of mixed fortunes last
term, being hampered by a number of
niggling injuries up to December, securing
a regular place in the side for a three-
month spell up to February, before slowly
disappearing from first-team action. He
was voted both the supporters' and the
club's 'Player of the Year' and also
received the Midlands Football Writers'
Association 'Player of the Year' award.
*Arsenal (From apprentice on 1/12/1985) F/PL
289+38/78 FLC 38+2/9 FAC 28+3/4 Others
27+2/7*
*Brentford (Loaned on 22/1/1987) FL 6+1
Others 1+1*
*Middlesbrough (£4,500,000 + on
15/7/1997) P/FL 48/11 FLC 7/3 FAC 3/1*
*Aston Villa (£6,750,000 on 10/9/1998) PL
101+16/18 FLC 6+2 FAC 11 Others 8/1*

METTOMO Lucien
Born: Cameroon, 19 April 1977
Height: 6'0" **Weight:** 12.7
Club Honours: Div 1 '02
International Honours: Cameroon: 23
(ANC '00)
This versatile defender joined Manchester
City last September as manager Kevin
Keegan sought to strengthen the Blues'
defence. He soon settled down in a
central defensive role, growing in
confidence with every game, before
departing to play for his country in the
African Nations' Cup finals. Although

Paul Merson

Cameroon won the tournament, he spent most of the time on the bench, and in fact this was also his lot on returning to Maine Road, for he managed just one more appearance in the starting line-up.
Manchester C (£1,200,000 from St Etienne, France on 4/10/2001) FL 17+6/1 FLC 1+1

MICHOPOULOS Nikalaos (Nik)
Born: Khardsa, Greece, 20 February 1970
Height: 6'3" **Weight:** 14.5
Solid as ever in Burnley's goal for the first half of the 2001-02 season, Nik remained ever-present until suffering a calf injury in the FA Cup game at Cheltenham. In his absence, Marlon Beresford arrived on loan, and his performances were so impressive that Nik had to wait until Beresford's return to Middlesbrough before resuming between the posts. It seemed some of the confidence had gone from his game when he came back for the last five games of the season, his positioning and handling more suspect than before, although he was still capable of some spectacular shot-stopping.
Burnley (Free from PAOK Salonika, Greece on 25/8/2000) FL 72 FLC 3 FAC 4

MIDDLETON Craig Dean
Born: Nuneaton, 10 September 1970
Height: 5'10" **Weight:** 11.12
Craig had something of a hit and miss season for Halifax Town last term when he featured in a variety of positions including wing back. He hit two goals within the space of a week in November, but then had to wait until the last away game at Torquay to score again, but it was well worth it – a 30-yard screamer into the net.
Coventry C (From trainee on 30/5/1989) F/PL 2+1 FLC 1
Cambridge U (Free on 20/7/1993) FL 55+4/10 FLC 3 FAC 1 Others 1
Cardiff C (Free on 30/8/1996) FL 95+24/8 FLC 3+1 FAC 13+1/3 Others 4+2
Plymouth Arg (Loaned on 27/11/2000) FL 6/2
Halifax T (£25,000 on 16/3/2000) FL 66+10/8 FLC 2+1 FAC 1+1/1 Others 3

MIDGLEY Craig Steven
Born: Bradford, 24 May 1976
Height: 5'8" **Weight:** 11.7
Craig spent much of the 2001-02 campaign on the bench for Halifax Town, but when called upon the tricky forward caused defences problems with his quick footwork. He scored Town's first goal of the season at Lincoln but then had to wait until March until he found the net again, adding further strikes in successive

matches at home to Kidderminster Harriers and Cheltenham Town.
Bradford C (From trainee on 4/7/1995) FL 0+11/1 FAC 0+4 Others 1
Scarborough (Loaned on 7/12/1995) FL 14+2/1
Scarborough (Loaned on 14/3/1997) FL 6/2
Darlington (Loaned on 1/12/1997) FL 1 Others 0+1/1
Hartlepool U (£10,000 on 13/3/1998) FL 61+35/18 FLC 2+2 FAC 3/2 Others 9+1/1
Halifax T (Free on 1/7/2001) FL 12+12/3 FLC 1 FAC 2 Others 0+1

MIGLIORANZI Stefani
Born: Pocos de Caldas, Brazil, 20 September 1977
Height: 6'0" **Weight:** 11.12
An immensely talented but inconsistent midfielder, Stefani rarely featured for Portsmouth last term – a combined result of injuries and strong competition for places within a large squad. He played in the first match of the season at Wolves and came on as a substitute on three occasions, giving him little opportunity to show his close ball-skills and little shimmies. He was one of several Pompey players placed on the transfer list at the end of the season.
Portsmouth (Free from St John's University, NY, USA on 8/3/1999) FL 25+10/2 FLC 2+4 FAC 1

MIKE Leon Jonathan
Born: Manchester, 4 September 1981
Height: 5'10" **Weight:** 12.2
International Honours: E: Yth; Sch
Leon finally got his first-team chance for Manchester City at Fratton Park last season, when he came on to replace Shaun Goater just before the interval. He was unlucky not to get on the score sheet, missing a couple of good chances, and was also on the team sheet the following week against Rotherham, but those were to be his only senior opportunities for City and in February he moved north of the border to sign for Aberdeen. Leon is a cousin of the former City player Adie Mike.
Manchester C (From trainee on 23/9/1998) FL 1+1
Oxford U (Loaned on 21/9/2000) FL 1+2
Halifax T (Loaned on 9/2/2001) FL 2+5

MILD Hakan
Born: Trollhatten, Sweden, 14 June 1971
Height: 6'0" **Weight:** 11.10
International Honours: Sweden: 74
Wimbledon fans didn't see the best of Hakan last season. He was signed when he was carrying an injury and after nine

senior appearances and some outings in the reserves he suffered a further injury shortly before the end of the season. He is a hard-working midfield player who enjoys getting stuck into the thick of the action.
Wimbledon (Signed from IFK Gothenburg, Sweden, ex IFK Gothenburg, Servette, Real Sociedad on 16/11/2001) FL 8+1

MILDENHALL Stephen (Steve) James
Born: Swindon, 13 May 1978
Height: 6'4" **Weight:** 14.0
Steve joined Notts County for a substantial fee in the summer of 2001 and was a regular for the Magpies in the first half of the 2001-02 campaign. However, he lost his place to Stuart Garden early in the new year and was unable to win it back before the end of the season. A tall and commanding 'keeper, he will undoubtedly improve further with experience and when given the chance to play behind a more settled defence.
Swindon T (From trainee on 19/7/1996) FL 29+4 FLC 2 FAC 2 Others 1
Notts Co (£150,000 on 16/7/2001) FL 25+1 FLC 2/1 FAC 3 Others 1

MILES John Francis
Born: Bootle, 28 September 1981
Height: 5'10" **Weight:** 10.8
A graduate of the Liverpool Academy, John was released from his contract after failing to break into the Reds forward line despite being highly regarded by the Anfield coaching staff. He signed a short-term contract for Stoke City on transfer deadline day and made his senior debut as a substitute in the final game of the regular season. He is a promising youngster who is equally at home in attack or midfield.
Liverpool (From trainee on 27/4/1999)
Stoke C (Free on 28/3/2002) FL 0+1

MILLER Kenneth (Kenny)
Born: Edinburgh, 23 December 1979
Height: 5'8" **Weight:** 11.3
International Honours: S: 1; U21-7
This rangy striker made a handful of appearances for Rangers at the beginning of last term before being loaned to Wolves in September. He made a big impression at Molineux but then dislocated a shoulder. He had not recovered when his three-month loan period ended, but after a few twists and turns, he was signed permanently. Ironically, he could not get into the team in January, such was the form of Dean Sturridge and Nathan Blake, and he was

not at his best as a sub. By the last day of the season he had only once played a full match for Wolves and was often playing too deep to get amongst the goals.

Hibernian (Signed from Hutchison Vale BC on 22/5/1996) SL 29+16/12 SLC 1+2/1 SC 5/1
Stenhousemuir (Loaned on 25/11/1998) SL 11/8
Glasgow R (£2,000,000 on 16/7/2000) SL 12+18/8 SLC 1/1 SC 2+1/1 Others 3+2/1
Wolverhampton W (Loaned on 7/9/2001) FL 3+2/2
Wolverhampton W (£3,000,000 on 14/12/2001) FL 2+13 FAC 0+1 Others 0+2

MILLER Kevin
Born: Falmouth, 15 March 1969
Height: 6'1" **Weight:** 13.0
Club Honours: Div 4 '90
Kevin lost his place in the Barnsley line-up after receiving a harsh red card at Grimsby last September and it was not until Steve Parkin was installed as manager that he returned to the line-up. An excellent shot stopper and one of the strong characters in the Reds' team, he was released in the summer.

Exeter C (Free from Newquay on 9/3/1989) FL 163 FLC 7 FAC 12 Others 18
Birmingham C (£250,000 on 14/5/1993) FL 24 FLC 4 Others 2
Watford (£250,000 on 7/8/1994) FL128 FLC 10 FAC 10 Others 3
Crystal Palace (£1,000,000 + on 21/7/1997) P/FL 66 FLC 3 FAC 5 Others 2
Barnsley (£250,000 on 27/8/1999) FL 115 FLC 11 FAC 4 Others 3

MILLER Thomas (Tommy)
William
Born: Easington, 8 January 1979
Height: 6'1" **Weight:** 11.12
After previously being on Ipswich's books as a schoolboy, Tommy returned to Portman Road for a substantial fee. Initially his-first team opportunities were limited as he adjusted to the standards required in the Premiership. He had to wait until Easter Monday for his full Premiership debut and he took full advantage with a 'Man of the Match' performance'. An energetic player, he operates from box to box and is not afraid to take a shot at goal.

Hartlepool U (From trainee on 8/7/1997) FL 130+7/35 FLC 6/3 FAC 5/1 Others 12/5
Ipswich T (£800,000 + on 16/7/2001) PL 5+3 FLC 2 FAC 0+1 Others 0+2

MILLER William (Willie) Nesbit
Born: Edinburgh, 1 November 1969
Height: 5'8" **Weight:** 10.10
Club Honours: SLC '91

International Honours: S: U21-7
Out of favour at Dundee, Willie joined Wrexham in a three-month loan deal last September in a bid to get his career back on track. A solid tackler, he lent his experience to the back line, but was unable to complete his full loan period. After six first-team appearances he suffered a pulled hamstring during training and returned north of the border. He eventually moved on to Raith Rovers towards the end of the season.

Hibernian (Signed from Edina Hibs on 14/3/1987) SL 239+7/1 SLC 21+1 SC 17+1/1 Others 2
Dundee (Signed on 8/7/1998) SL 36+2 SLC 3 SC 1
Wrexham (Loaned on 18/9/2001) FL 5 Others 1

MILLIGAN Jamie
Born: Blackpool, 3 January 1980
Height: 5'6" **Weight:** 9.12
Club Honours: FAYC '98; AMC '02
International Honours: E: Yth
This promising young midfield player was used sparingly by Blackpool last season, although he often found himself on the bench. He is a skilful player with a cultured left foot who is particularly effective when delivering set pieces. He will be looking to win a regular place in the line-up in 2002-03.

Everton (From trainee on 13/6/1997) PL 0+4
Blackpool (Free on 22/3/2001) FL 10+13 FLC 0+1 FAC 1+1 Others 2+4

MILLIGAN Michael (Mike)
Joseph
Born: Manchester, 20 February 1967
Height: 5'8" **Weight:** 11.0
International Honours: RoI: 1; B-2; U23-1; U21-1
Mike found himself out of favour at Blackpool last term and his only first-team outings came during a brief spell in October. He is an experienced central midfield player, who can still perform as a ball-winner in the centre of the park. He was released at the end of the season.

Oldham Ath (From apprentice on 2/3/1985) FL 161+1/17 FLC 19+1/1 FAC 12/1 Others 4
Everton (£1,000,000 on 24/8/1990) FL 16+1/1 FLC 0+1 FAC 1 Others 4+1/1
Oldham Ath (£600,000 on 17/7/1991) F/PL 117/6 FLC 11/1 FAC 9 Others 1/1
Norwich C (£800,000 on 27/6/1994) P/FL 113+11/5 FLC 11+1 FAC 6
Blackpool (Free on 24/7/2000) FL 25+3/1 FLC 1 Others 1+1

MILLS Daniel (Danny) John
Born: Norwich, 18 May 1977
Height: 5'11" **Weight:** 11.9

International Honours: E: 12; U21-14; Yth
A marauding full back with bags of pace, Danny can also play in the centre of defence. He blossomed into a regular first team player last season, contributing both to club and country with some consistent displays. His bursts of speed down the flank make him a dangerous player going forward and equally adept in defence, where he is very strong and effective. A player who is always 100 per cent committed, he is highly thought of at Elland Road. Danny also became a regular squad member for England and featured regularly in the World Cup finals over the summer.

Norwich C (From trainee on 1/11/1994) FL 46+20 FLC 3+2/1 FAC 2
Charlton Ath (£350,000 on 19/3/1998) P/FL 45/3 FLC 3 FAC 1 Others 2
Leeds U (£4,370,000 on 1/7/1999) PL 64+4/2 FLC 3/1 FAC 2+1 Others 25+1

MILLS Garry Leonard
Born: Faversham, 20 May 1981
Height: 5'9" **Weight:** 11.8
Club Honours: NC '01
Another product of the Rushden youth policy, this young midfielder was somewhat frustrated by injuries last term, restricting his first-team appearances. An undoubted talent, he had the honour of being included in the starting line-up for the club's historic first Football League game, but then dropped back to the substitutes' bench as Shaun Carey got the nod from Brian Talbot. A transfer request was quickly cancelled but the subsequent arrival of Richie Hanlon limited his chances further before injury forced him into a spell on the sidelines.

Rushden & Diamonds (From juniors on 3/7/1999) FL 3+6 FLC 1+1 Others 1

MILLS Rowan Lee
Born: Mexborough, 10 July 1970
Height: 6'1" **Weight:** 13.9
The experienced striker made a couple of early-season appearances for Portsmouth before moving to Coventry City on loan in November. Replacing Jay Bothroyd in the starting line-up he had an immediate impact, scoring in his first two games against Crystal Palace and Wimbledon. He seemed to be a perfect foil for Lee Hughes with his strength in the air and mobility and signed permanently for the Sky Blues, but unfortunately his form never really hit the same heights afterwards. He lost his place to Bothroyd in March and only reappeared in the first team for the final game against Burnley.

Wolverhampton W (Signed from

Stocksbridge PS on 9/12/1992) FL 12+13/2
FLC 1 FAC 3+1/1 Others 3/1
Derby Co (£400,000 on 24/2/1995) FL 16/7
Port Vale (£200,000 on 1/8/1995) FL
81+28/35 FLC 7+3/5 FAC 0+3 Others 6/4
Bradford C (£1,000,000 on 7/8/1998) P/FL
63+2/28 FLC 5+1/1 FAC 4/1 Others 5/3
Manchester C (Loaned on 10/3/2000) FL 1+2
Portsmouth (£1,000,000 + on 11/8/2000) FL
24+2/4 FLC 3/1
Coventry C (Free on 28/11/2001) FL 19+1/5

MILTON Russell Maurice

Born: Folkestone, 12 January 1969
Height: 5'8" **Weight:** 12.1
Club Honours: FAT '98; NC '99
International Honours: E: SP-2
Russell is one of the most skilful players in
the lower divisions and enjoyed a
successful season at Cheltenham in 2001-
02, free from the injury problems that had
troubled his earlier time at Whaddon
Road. He held down a regular place on
the left-hand side of a four-man midfield
where he was able to display the full
range of his creative talents. A fine ball
player with excellent touch and passing
ability, his delivery of set pieces is also a
major weapon in the club's armoury. A
notable highlight was when he set the
Robins on their way to a history-making
FA Cup win over Burnley with the first
goal - a stunning free kick from the edge
of the area.
*Arsenal (From apprentice on 26/2/1987. Free
to Double Flower, Hong Kong during 1988
close season)*
*Cheltenham T (£5,000 from Dover Ath on
12/8/1997) FL 93+3/12 FLC 1 FAC 7+1/3
Others 6/1*

MINTO Scott Christopher

Born: Heswall, 6 August 1971
Height: 5'9" **Weight:** 12.7
Club Honours: FAC '97
International Honours: E: U21-6; Yth
Having been sidelined for many months
with achilles and knee injuries Scott was
able to appear in a couple of London
'derbies' for West Ham in November.
Playing against his former club Charlton
at the Valley he was cheered by both sets
of fans. He can play either full back or as
a wing back and the talented defender
needs a lengthy run in the side to regain
his former fine displays. However, the
remarkable consistency of Nigel
Winterburn made it difficult for him to
play regularly in the first team last season.
*Charlton Ath (From trainee on 2/2/1989) FL
171+9/7 FLC 8/2 FAC 8+2 Others 7/1*
*Chelsea (£775,000 on 28/5/1994) PL 53+1/4
FLC 3/1 FAC 9 Others 5+1 (Free to Benfica,
Portugal on 30/6/1997)*

*West Ham U (£1,000,000 on 15/1/1999) PL
35+4 FLC 2 FAC 1 Others 5*

MINTON Jeffrey (Jeff) Simon Thompson

Born: Hackney, 28 December 1973
Height: 5'6" **Weight:** 11.10
Club Honours: AMC '01
Jeff joined Leyton Orient during the 2001
close season and featured regularly in the
line-up last term. He is a midfield
playmaker who is effective in the tackle
and distributes the ball accurately, but he
can also break up opposition moves and
set up counter attacks. Although he was
joint-second top scorer, he was out of
contract in the summer and was released.
*Tottenham H (From trainee on 11/1/1992)
FL 2/1 FLC 0+1*
*Brighton & Hove A (Free on 25/7/1994) FL
167+7/31 FLC 12/1 FAC 7 Others 5*
*Port Vale (Free on 1/7/1999) FL 34+2/4 FLC
4/2 FAC 3/2 Others 0+2*
Rotherham U (Free on 16/3/2001) FL 5+4/2
*Leyton Orient (Free on 9/7/2001) FL 32+1/5
FLC 1/1 FAC 4 Others 1*

MIRANDA Jose Silvio Lima Gomes

Born: Lisbon, Portugal, 20 April 1974
Height: 5'7" **Weight:** 9.0
This left winger looked as if he could offer
Rotherham a missing ingredient in the
pre-season games last term, and his
promise was rewarded with a two-year
contract. Unfortunately, he failed to
maintain his early form and made just
two League appearances early in the
campaign. Afterwards he was never really
in serious contention for another call up
although he was on the score sheet
regularly for the reserves.
*Rotherham U (Signed from FC Felgueiras,
Portugal on 17/8/2001) FL 2 FLC 0+1*

MISKELLY David Thomas

Born: Newtonards, 3 September 1979
Height: 6'0" **Weight:** 12.9
International Honours: NI: U21-11; Yth
David's first-team opportunities were
again limited at Oldham during the 2001-
02 season. The 22-year-old 'keeper, who
has been capped at youth and U21 level
by Northern Ireland, has spent three
seasons as Gary Kelly's understudy at
Boundary Park. Injury to Kelly gave him an
opportunity to stake his claim in
November, but David was himself badly
injured in making his first start at Stoke.
He returned to fitness and first-team
action in April, playing in the last three
matches of the campaign.
*Oldham Ath (From trainee on 1/7/1997) FL
8+1 FLC 1*

MITCHELL Graham Lee

Born: Shipley, 16 February 1968
Height: 6'1" **Weight:** 12.13
This experienced central defender had
another solid season for Halifax Town in
2001-02, always looking cool when under
pressure. He provided a steadying
influence for the younger members of the
side and helped out with the coaching
responsibilities alongside Neil Redfearn
and Dave Worthington following the
departure of manager Alan Little.
*Huddersfield T (From trainee on 16/6/1986)
FL 235+9/2 FLC 13+2/1 FAC 27/1 Others 24/1*
Bournemouth (Loaned on 24/12/1993) FL 4
*Bradford C (Signed on 23/12/1994) FL
64+1/1 FLC 8 FAC 2 Others 4*
*Raith Rov (Signed on 10/10/1996) SL 22+1
SLC 0+1 SC 1 Others 0+1*
*Cardiff C (Free on 4/8/1998) FL 46 FLC 2 FAC
5 Others 1*
*Halifax T (£45,000 on 20/7/1999) FL
128+2/3 FLC 4 FAC 6/1 Others 3*

MITCHELL Paul Alexander

Born: Stalybridge, 26 August 1981
Height: 5'11" **Weight:** 12.3
After starting the opening matches of the
2001-02 season at right back for Wigan
Athletic, Paul subsequently found himself
relegated to the subs' bench. A hard-
tackling defender, good in the air, his
positive attitude was rewarded when
pressed into an emergency role in
midfield in the away match at Queen's
Park Rangers in February. His strong work
rate and steady performances saw him
enjoy an extended period in the side on
merit.
*Wigan Ath (From trainee on 3/7/2000) FL
16+8 FLC 3+1 FAC 0+1 Others 1+2*
Halifax T (Loaned on 22/3/2001) FL 11

MOHAN Nicholas (Nicky)

Born: Middlesbrough, 6 October 1970
Height: 6'1" **Weight:** 14.0
Club Honours: AMC '00
The big centre back's return to Hull meant
he was reunited with manager Brian
Little, the two having been together
previously at Middlesbrough, Leicester
and Stoke. His vast experience benefited
City's young squad and in Justin Whittle's
absence he was also awarded the
captain's armband. At the end of a
turbulent season however, Nicky was
made available for transfer.
*Middlesbrough (From juniors on
18/11/1987) F/PL 93+6/4 FLC 11 FAC 9+1
Others 11*
Hull C (Loaned on 26/9/1992) FL 5/1
*Leicester C (£330,000 on 7/7/1994) PL 23
FLC 2 FAC 1*

Jeff Minton

Bradford C (£225,000 on 13/7/1995) FL 83/4 FLC 8 FAC 5 Others 5
Wycombe W (Loaned on 14/8/1997) FL 6
Wycombe W (£75,000 on 10/10/1997) FL 52/2 FLC 3 FAC 4 Others 3
Stoke C (Free on 2/3/1999) FL 92+6 FLC 9 FAC 2 Others 12/1
Hull C (Free on 16/7/2001) FL 26+1/1 FLC 2 Others 1

MOILANEN Teuvo (Tepi)
Johannes
Born: Oulu, Finland, 12 December 1973
Height: 6'5" **Weight:** 13.12
Club Honours: Div 2 '00
International Honours: Finland: 3; U21; Yth
Tepi started the 2001-02 season as second choice 'keeper at Preston, and it was not until September that he took over from David Lucas. Dominant in the air and an improving shot stopper, he kept five clean sheets in 11 matches until injury struck against Stockport. He returned to the bench after 6 games out, regaining his place after Lucas's injury in January, and made a world-class stop from Efan Ekoku to preserve North End's lead against Sheffield Wednesday. Sadly a lack of form led to a couple of unfortunate mistakes and he was dropped in February, but ended as first choice following yet another injury to his friend and rival.
Preston NE (£120,000 from FF Jaro, Finland, ex Ilves, on 12/12/1995) FL 141+2 FLC 12 FAC 10 Others 2
Scarborough (Loaned on 12/12/1996) FL 4
Darlington (Loaned on 17/11/1997) FL 16

MOLENAAR Robert
Born: Zaandam, Holland, 27 February 1969
Height: 6'2" **Weight:** 14.4
Robert was a regular in the Bradford City line-up early on last season, but missed all the second half of the campaign with a rib injury. A tough central defender, he formed a solid partnership with David Wetherall until injury intervened. Although not the quickest of players, what he lacks in speed he makes up with strength in the air.
Leeds U (£1,000,000 from FC Volendam, Holland, ex Zilvermeuwen, on 11/1/1997) PL 47+4/5 FLC 4+1 FAC 5/1 Others 4
Bradford C (£500,000 on 1/12/2000) P/FL 42/1 FLC 1+1 FAC 2

MONCUR John Frederick
Born: Stepney, 22 September 1966
Height: 5'7" **Weight:** 9.10
John is an experienced tough-tackling

midfielder who is loved by the West Ham fans. Although he is nearing the end of his career he still has plenty of enthusiasm for the game. He was often brought on as substitute to liven things up and played excellently in the victories over Ipswich and Fulham in March.
Tottenham H (From apprentice on 22/8/1984) FL 10+1/1 FLC 1+2
Doncaster Rov (Loaned on 25/9/1986) FL 4
Cambridge U (Loaned on 27/3/1987) FL 3+1
Portsmouth (Loaned on 22/3/1989) FL 7
Brentford (Loaned on 19/10/1989) FL 5/1 Others 1
Ipswich T (Loaned on 24/10/1991) FL 5+1
Swindon T (£80,000 on 30/3/1992) F/PL 53+5/5 FLC 4 FAC 1 Others 4/1
West Ham U (£900,000 on 24/6/1994) PL 131+37/6 FLC 13+1/2 FAC 7+1/1 Others 5+1

MONK Garry Alan
Born: Bedford, 6 March 1979
Height: 6'0" **Weight:** 13.0
This promising youngster played for Southampton in the Worthington Cup tie against Gillingham last October and also in the following match against Arsenal, but then had to wait until the final day of the season before adding a further appearance from the subs' bench against Newcastle. A powerfully built central defender, he is both strong and very quick.
Torquay U (Trainee) FL 4+1
Southampton (Signed on 23/5/1997) PL 8+2 FLC 1 FAC 0+1
Torquay U (Loaned on 25/9/1998) FL 6
Stockport Co (Loaned on 9/9/1999) FL 2 FLC 2
Oxford U (Loaned on 12/1/2001) FL 5

MONKHOUSE Andrew (Andy) William
Born: Leeds, 23 October 1980
Height: 6'1" **Weight:** 11.6
Probably the most skilful player at Rotherham, Andy simply oozes talent and potential. A tall left winger, he nevertheless remained something of an enigma last term. However, it was not just coincidence that the team's best spell of the season came when he was at the top of his form and he was also instrumental in helping the Millers to record their first League win of the season at Grimsby.
Rotherham U (From trainee on 14/11/1998) FL 22+33/3 FLC 1 FAC 1+4 Others 1+1/1

MONTGOMERY Gary Stephen
Born: Leamington, 8 October 1982
Height: 6'1" **Weight:** 13.8
This young Coventry City goalkeeper was handed a daunting debut against Premiership Chelsea in the Worthington

Cup when Magnus Hedman was injured during the warm-up. Gary did not let the side down and could not be faulted for either goal. He was loaned out to both Crewe (where he made no appearances) and Kidderminster but on both occasions was recalled early because of injury problems at Coventry. He kept a clean sheet for Harriers on his debut against Southend, but was sent off at Bristol Rovers, before being recalled to Highfield Road to cover for injuries.
Coventry C (From trainee on 31/1/2001) FLC 1
Kidderminster Hrs (Loaned on 28/3/2002) FL 2

MONTGOMERY Nicholas (Nick) Anthony
Born: Leeds, 28 October 1981
Height: 5'9" **Weight:** 11.8
It was not until October that Nick made his first appearance in the starting line-up for Sheffield United last term and he went on to play in a variety of roles during the season, mainly in midfield. Early on he was used as a man-to-man marker, being particularly effective in the game at Maine Road. Then came a run of seven matches in November and December, playing an attacking role on the right side of midfield, replacing Paul Devlin. From the turn of the year he was used mainly as a substitute, but played with commitment and energy and was prepared to run at defenders.
Sheffield U (From trainee on 7/7/2000) FL 28+30/2 FLC 1 FAC 1+1

MOODY Adrian James Harkin
Born: Birkenhead, 29 September 1982
Height: 6'0" **Weight:** 12.7
A third-year scholar at Wrexham, Adrian managed only one substitute appearance last season, coming off the bench in the away encounter at Peterborough United in February. A regular in the centre of defence for the club's reserves, he is waiting his chance to break into the first-team squad.
Wrexham (Trainee) FL 2+2

MOODY Paul
Born: Portsmouth, 13 June 1967
Height: 6'3" **Weight:** 14.9
Club Honours: Div 2 '01
Paul had a disappointing time at Millwall last term and after just a couple of first-team appearances he joined Oxford in September. He netted against Plymouth on his debut and ended the campaign as the U's leading scorer, his tally including a hat-trick against Halifax. A popular player with the fans he is a big strong striker with a powerful shot.

Tommy Mooney

Southampton (£50,000 from Waterlooville on 15/7/1991) F/PL 7+5 FLC 1 FAC 0+1
Reading (Loaned on 9/12/1992) FL 5/1 Others 1
Oxford U (£60,000 on 19/2/1994) FL 98+38/49 FLC 10+4/4 FAC 7+1/5 Others 3/3
Fulham (£200,000 on 4/7/1997) FL 29+11/19 FLC 2+2 FAC 1+1 Others 2/1
Millwall (£150,000 on 5/7/1999) FL 45+15/24 FLC 2+1/1 FAC 2/1 Others 3+1
Oxford U (£150,000 on 21/9/2001) FL 29+6/13 FAC 1

MOONEY Thomas (Tommy) John

Born: Billingham, 11 August 1971
Height: 5'10" **Weight:** 12.6
Club Honours: Div 2 '98
This talented striker topped the scoring charts for Birmingham City last term with 15 goals, despite missing two months early on with an ankle injury. Tommy was clever, hard working and a good user of the ball. When Steve Bruce played him wide on the left he responded with four goals in a dozen outings there. He also netted a hat-trick against Norwich in December, including the Blues' 'Goal of the Season', a measured lob with the outside of his left foot.
Aston Villa (From trainee on 23/11/1989)
Scarborough (Free on 1/8/1990) FL 96+11/30 FLC 11+2/8 FAC 3 Others 6/2
Southend U (£100,000 on 12/7/1993) FL 9+5/5 FLC 1+1 Others 2+3
Watford (Signed on 17/3/1994) P/FL 221+29/60 FLC 22/3 FAC 11+1/2 Others 4
Birmingham C (Free on 1/7/2001) FL 29+4/13 FLC 1/2 FAC 1 Others 3

MOOR Reinier Sean

Born: Holland, 12 June 1983
Height: 5'10" **Weight:** 12.0
International Honours: Rol: Yth
Reinier made his debut in senior football for Exeter City when he came on as a substitute for the second half of the home game against Scunthorpe last August and made a further appearance from the bench before fading from the first-team scene following the arrival of new boss John Cornforth. Having been rewarded with a professional contract he will be looking to gain further senior experience in 2002-03.
Exeter C (Trainee) FL 0+2

MOORE Alan

Born: Dublin, 25 November 1974
Height: 5'10" **Weight:** 11.10
Club Honours: Div 1 '95
International Honours: Rol: 8; U21-4; Yth; Sch
Middlesbrough's forgotten man found a

new lease of life at Burnley in 2001-02. After successful pre-season trials, he was signed initially for three months and the move was made permanent when he proved his capabilities at First Division level. Alan provided skills on the left wing to complement those of Glen Little on the right and at his best was dazzling, with the speed and trickery to evade most defenders. His goal at Crewe was arguably the best of Burnley's season and certainly his finest moment so far in claret and blue.
Middlesbrough (From trainee on 5/12/1991) F/PL 98+20/14 FLC 9+6/1 FAC 3+2/2 Others 3+1
Barnsley (Loaned on 30/10/1998) FL 4+1
Burnley (Free on 20/7/2001) FL 23+6/3 FLC 1/1 FAC 2/1

MOORE Darren Mark

Born: Birmingham, 22 April 1974
Height: 6'2" **Weight:** 15.6
International Honours: Jamaica: 3
Darren played consistently well for Portsmouth in the opening games of the 2001-02 season and in September he was sold to West Bromwich Albion. The big central defender became the rock at the heart of the Albion defence. His immense frame, powerful heading, solid tackling and total commitment made him a huge favourite with the fans. A battler to the last, Darren scored twice – his first was a 40-yarder in the away game at Rotherham in mid-November and his second was the vital opener to settle Albion's nerves in their crucial final game at home to Crystal Palace. Darren was selected for the PFA First Division side for 2001-02.
Torquay U (From trainee on 18/11/1992) FL 102+1/8 FLC 6 FAC 7/2 Others 8/2
Doncaster Rov (£62,500 on 19/7/1995) FL 76/7 FLC 4 FAC 1 Others 3/1
Bradford C (£310,000 + on 18/6/1997) FL 62/3 FLC 6/1 FAC 2
Portsmouth (£500,000 + on 15/11/1999) FL 58+1/2 FLC 5 FAC 2
West Bromwich A (£750,000 on 14/9/2001) FL 31+1/2 FAC 4

MOORE David

Born: Salford, 4 April 1985
Height: 5'8" **Weight:** 9.10
This young Wigan striker was one of three trainees who appeared in the line-up for the Worthington Cup tie against Blackpool last August. He spent the remainder of the campaign developing in the club's reserve and youth teams and will be hoping to gain further senior experience in 2002-03.
Wigan Ath (Trainee) FLC 1

MOORE Ian Ronald

Born: Birkenhead, 26 August 1976
Height: 5'11" **Weight:** 12.0
International Honours: E: U21-7; Yth
The only player to appear in all of Burnley's League games in 2001-02, Ian was a consistent performer, and his never-say-die attitude ensured his continuing popularity with the Clarets' faithful. Much more than a pure striker, he is a willing fetcher and carrier and doesn't recognise such a thing as a lost cause. Never the most prolific of goal-scorers, his best strike of the season was probably the one at Crystal Palace, and soon afterwards he scored his first Burnley hat-trick in the FA Cup game against Canvey Island.
Tranmere Rov (From trainee on 6/7/1994) FL 41+17/12 FLC 3+2/1 FAC 1+1 Others 0+1
Bradford C (Loaned on 13/9/1996) FL 6
Nottingham F (£1,000,000 on 15/3/1997) F/PL 3+12/1 FLC 0+2 FAC 1
West Ham U (Loaned on 26/9/1997) PL 0+1
Stockport Co (£800,000 on 31/7/1998) FL 83+10/20 FLC 8/2 FAC 3/1
Burnley (£1,000,000 on 20/11/2000) FL 67+6/16 FLC 0+1 FAC 4/4

MOORE Joe-Max

Born: Tulsa, USA, 23 February 1971
Height: 5'9" **Weight:** 10.10
International Honours: USA: 100; U21
Joe-Max was frustrated to see his first-team opportunities limited at Everton last season. When he did get opportunities, however, he showed his eye for goal was still as sharp as ever. He scored in successive matches against Derby and Leeds, the last a stunning left-foot volley, which showed how lethal he can be in front of goal. He also netted the two goals against Trinidad that took USA to Japan and Korea. Small but lively, he strikes the ball very well and has an impeccable attitude.
Everton (Free from New England Revolution, USA on 7/12/1999) PL 22+30/8 FLC 2+1 FAC 3+6/2

MOORE Stefan

Born: Birmingham, 28 September 1983
Height: 5'10" **Weight:** 11.0
Club Honours: FAYC '02
International Honours: E: Yth
Chesterfield signed this young, pacy forward on loan last October, but he received little opportunity to show his skills before he returned to Villa Park. The Spireites lost him to England youth commitments but one moment of genius – a deft lob to set up a late winner against Bournemouth – served to remind fans of his ability. He went on to captain

the Villa team to success over Everton in the FA Youth Cup final, scoring twice in the 4-1 victory at Goodison in the first leg.
Aston Villa (From trainee on 9/10/2000)
Chesterfield (Loaned on 27/10/2001) FL 1+1 Others 1

MORGAN Alan Meredith
Born: Aberystwyth, 2 November 1973
Height: 5'10" **Weight:** 11.4
International Honours: W: U21-2; Yth; Sch
This versatile and popular player had another frustrating season at Tranmere in 2001-02, when he spent much of his time out of action through injuries. When fit he can play either at full back or in midfield, and it has been known for him to be pressed into service as an emergency striker. A gutsy performer who never shirks a tackle, Alan eventually returned towards the end of the campaign, but managed only two senior appearances.
Tranmere Rov (From trainee on 8/5/1992) FL 42+23/1 FLC 6+2/1 FAC 3+2

MORGAN Christopher (Chris) Paul
Born: Barnsley, 9 November 1977
Height: 5'10" **Weight:** 12.9
As usual gave his all for his hometown club last term. A tough, uncompromising central defender he only missed games when under suspension. Hard-tackling and strong in the air, he was appointed as captain in the closing stages of the season.
Barnsley (From trainee on 3/7/1996) P/FL 146+3/5 FLC 14/1 FAC 8 Others 3

MORGAN Craig
Born: St Asaph, 18 June 1985
Height: 6'1" **Weight:** 12.7
International Honours: W: Yth
This first-year scholar at Wrexham spent most of last season developing in the reserves before stepping up to make his League debut from the subs' bench against Cambridge in April. He also featured from the bench at Stoke and was called up to the Wales U19 squad in the summer. A promising defender, he is the third-youngest player to have appeared for the Robins in League football.
Wrexham (Trainee) FL 0+2

MORGAN Dean
Born: Enfield, 3 October 1983
Height: 5'11" **Weight:** 11.2
This exciting young striker was rewarded for some fine displays in Colchester's U19 and reserve teams with a regular place on

the first-team subs' bench last term. Rated very highly by the club, he finally made his long-awaited first League start at Bury when the U's were safe from relegation. He is comfortable on the ball and has a reputation for scoring some excellent solo goals at junior level.
Colchester U (From trainee on 8/8/2001) FL 1+33 FAC 0+2 Others 1+1

MORGAN Lionel Anthony
Born: Tottenham, 17 February 1983
Height: 5'11" **Weight:** 12.7
International Honours: E: Yth
Unfortunately injury again robbed Lionel of much of last season at Wimbledon. A truly classy midfielder, who plays wide on the left, he netted a sublime free kick in the home win against Rotherham. He represented England at youth-team level during the season and will be hoping for an injury-free campaign in 2002-03.
Wimbledon (From trainee on 10/8/2000) FL 5+11/1 FLC 0+1

MORGAN Mark Paul Thomas
Born: Belfast, 23 October 1978
Height: 6'0" **Weight:** 11.5
International Honours: NI: U21-1
Paul proved an excellent summer signing for Lincoln manager Alan Buckley bringing both skill and strength to the centre of defence. His performances saw him voted 'Away Player of the Year' by the Imps' supporters and earned him a call up to the Northern Ireland squad although he missed out in the end because of a pulled hamstring. The only down side of Paul's season was the number of minor injury problems he picked up.
Preston NE (From trainee on 9/5/1997) FLC 1
Lincoln C (Free on 17/7/2001) FL 32+2/1 FLC 1

MORGAN Simon Charles
Born: Birmingham, 5 September 1966
Height: 5'10" **Weight:** 12.5
Club Honours: Div 2 '99, '02
International Honours: E: U21-2
Simon joined Brighton on a one-year deal in the summer of 2001 and impressed with his professional displays and tremendous attitude in the centre of defence. Despite threatening to score for much of the season, his only goal came in the 2-0 home victory over Northampton in March. A knee problem restricted him at times and it was this that led to him announcing his retirement at the end of the season, but not before assisting the Albion to their second successive divisional title.

Leicester C (From apprentice on 15/11/1984)
FL 147+13/3 FLC 14/1 FAC 4+1 Others 3
Fulham (£100,000 on 12/10/1990) FL 343+10/48 FLC 33/2 FAC 19/3 Others 17/4
Brighton & Hove A (Free on 2/7/2001) FL 42/1 FLC 2 FAC 3

MORISON Steven (Steve)
Born: London, 29 August 1983
Height: 6'2" **Weight:** 12.0
Steve produced a series of consistent performances for Northampton Town's reserve team in 2001-02 and was rewarded with an appearance from the subs' bench during the final game of the season against Cambridge United. The tall quick striker grabbed his chance and almost crowned his debut with a goal, only to see John Hodge's pass cross the line before he could reach it.
Northampton T (Trainee) FL 0+1

MORLEY Benjamin (Ben)
Born: Hull, 22 December 1980
Height: 5'9" **Weight:** 10.1
Ben was originally released by Hull at the end of the 2000-01 campaign, but subsequently signed a new one-year deal and was a regular in the club's reserve side last term. The speedy right back's only first-team action in the opening half of the season was an appearance from the bench in the Worthington Cup tie at Derby. He fought his way back into the senior squad in January but it wasn't until the last game that he made his first League start. It was announced in April 2002 that he would not be offered a new contract.
Hull C (From trainee on 10/12/1998) FL 7+19 FLC 1+2 FAC 2/1 Others 1+2

MORLEY David (Dave) Thomas
Born: St Helens, 25 September 1977
Height: 6'2" **Weight:** 12.7
Dave was switched from defence to midfield by new Carlisle manager Roddy Collins last term, it being felt that his heading and tackling abilities could be allied to a more creative role. He produced some hard-working displays and earned several 'Man of the Match' awards, but when his former boss Ian Atkins took over at Oxford he followed, initially on loan and then permanently. He scored with a soaring header on his debut against Mansfield and weighed in with two more, one a cracking drive at Rushden. He also featured at full back for the U's and missed very few matches after his arrival.
Manchester C (From trainee on 3/1/1996) FL 1+2/1

Ayr U (Loaned on 14/3/1998) SL 4
*Southend U (Signed on 28/8/1998) FL
63+13 FLC 6 FAC 0+2 Others 2*
*Carlisle U (Free on 26/1/2001) FL 37+4/1 FLC
1 FAC 1 Others 1*
Oxford U (Free on 14/12/2001) FL 16+2/3

MORRELL Andrew (Andy) Jonathan

Born: Doncaster, 28 September 1974
Height: 5'11" **Weight:** 12.0
This wholehearted striker never gave
anything less than 100 per cent for
Wrexham last term. Always liable to make
goals for others than score himself, his
unselfish play contributed greatly to Lee
Jones' five-goal haul against Cambridge in
April. Often used from the bench, he was
on the score sheet twice in the 5-1
success over Wigan Athletic in the LDV
Vans Trophy tie in October, and unleashed
a cracker in the final home game of the
campaign against Bournemouth. He was
offered a new deal by the Robins at the
end of the season.
*Wrexham (Free from Newcastle Blue Star on
18/12/1998) FL 31+34/6 FLC 1 FAC 0+2
Others 1+3/2*

MORRIS Glenn James

Born: Woolwich, 20 December 1983
Height: 6'0" **Weight:** 11.3
Glenn spent most of the 2001-02 season
as second choice 'keeper to Scott Barrett
at Leyton Orient before being given his
chance in the senior team for the last two
games. He marked his second appearance
with the man-of-the-match award and
looks to be a goalkeeper with a great
future ahead of him.
Leyton Orient (Trainee) FL 2 Others 1

MORRIS Jody Steven

Born: Hammersmith, 22 December 1978
Height: 5'5" **Weight:** 10.12
Club Honours: ECWC '98; FAC '00; CS
'00
International Honours: E: U21-7; Yth;
Sch
The once-promising career of this talented
midfield player threatens to turn down a
cul-de-sac after some well-publicised off-
the-field problems. Chelsea boss Ranieri is
a proven advocate of a youth policy but
Jody has stiff opposition from
contemporaries Sam Dalla Bona and Frank
Lampard plus the younger Joe Keenan for
a regular central midfield place. A string
of niggling injuries also restricted his
appearances to just a handful during the
season and it is to be hoped that his
career resumes its earlier impetus.
*Chelsea (From trainee on 8/1/1996) PL
63+36/5 FLC 8+1/2 FAC 8+4/1 Others 10+10*

MORRIS Lee

Born: Blackpool, 30 April 1980
Height: 5'10" **Weight:** 11.2
International Honours: E: U21-1; Yth
This young Derby winger rarely featured
in the first team in the early part of last
season, but went on to become a regular
in John Gregory's team in the closing
stages of the campaign. He is a pacy left-
footed player who works hard and has
the ability to ghost past defenders.
*Sheffield U (From trainee on 24/12/1997) FL
14+12/6 FAC 2+5/2 Others 0+1*
*Derby Co (£1,800,000 + on 7/6/1999) PL
15+23/4 FLC 0+2 FAC 0+2*
Huddersfield T (Loaned on 8/3/2001) FL 5/1

MORRISON Clinton (Clint) Hubert

Born: Wandsworth, 14 May 1979
Height: 6'1" **Weight:** 11.2
International Honours: RoI: 7; U21-2
Clint had another excellent season for
Crystal Palace last term when he finished
as the club's leading scorer with 24 goals
in all competitions. He established a fine
partnership with Dougie Freedman, and
scored his 50th goal for the Eagles
against Norwich City. Capped at full
international level by the Republic of
Ireland, he will be looking to fire Palace
into the Premiership in 2002-03.
*Crystal Palace (From trainee on 29/3/1997)
P/FL 141+16/62 FLC 16+3/9 FAC 4/1*

MORRISON John Owen

Born: Londonderry, 8 December 1981
Height: 5'8" **Weight:** 11.12
International Honours: NI: U21-2; Yth;
Sch
This young Sheffield Wednesday winger
had a disappointing season in 2001-02
due to injuries and loss of form. He failed
to impress when given the opportunity
and, apart from one or two flashes of
brilliance, he was unable to build on the
previous season's performances.
Nevertheless he still remained very
popular with the Owls' fans.
*Sheffield Wed (From trainee on 5/1/1999)
P/FL 31+24/8 FLC 8+2/3 FAC 0+2*

MOSES Adrian (Ade) Paul

Born: Doncaster, 4 May 1975
Height: 5'10" **Weight:** 12.8
International Honours: E: U21-2
This versatile defender had a somewhat
stop-start season at Huddersfield last
term. When used he occupied the right-
back berth and even scored his first goal
for the club, a wonderful long range
strike in the FA Cup first round tie against

Gravesend. Ade will be looking to feature
more regularly in 2002-03.
*Barnsley (From juniors on 2/7/1993) F/PL
137+14/3 FLC 15 FAC 15*
*Huddersfield T (£225,000 on 20/12/2000)
FL 23+6 FAC 1+1/1 Others 4*

MOSS Darren Michael

Born: Wrexham, 24 May 1981
Height: 5'10" **Weight:** 11.6
International Honours: W: Yth
Darren joined Shrewsbury Town during
the 2001 close season and was
comfortable playing both at right back
and in midfield. He showed strong
defensive qualities and made some
effective speedy forward runs. Manager
Kevin Ratcliffe was sufficiently impressed
by his progress that his contract was
extended in February for a further three-
and-a-half years, adding to the growing
band of promising youngsters on the
books at Gay Meadow.
*Chester C (From trainee on 14/7/1999) FL
33+9 FLC 1+1 FAC 4 Others 1*
*Shrewsbury T (Free on 24/7/2001) FL
23+8/2 FAC 1 Others 1*

MOSS Neil Graham

Born: New Milton, 10 May 1975
Height: 6'2" **Weight:** 13.10
Neil spent most of the 2001-02 season on
the Southampton bench, but then got his
chance after a training ground injury to
regular 'keeper Paul Jones. An excellent
understudy he always gives his best when
called upon. He played in the last two
games of the campaign and will be
pushing for regular first-team action in
2002-03.
*Bournemouth (From trainee on 29/1/1993)
FL 21+1 FLC 1 FAC 3+1 Others 2*
*Southampton (£250,000 on 20/12/1995) PL
22+2 FLC 2*
*Gillingham (Loaned on 8/8/1997) FL 10
FLC 2*

MUGGLETON Carl David

Born: Leicester, 13 September 1968
Height: 6'2" **Weight:** 13.4
International Honours: E: U21-1
Carl began the 2001-02 season in the
Cheltenham first team but soon lost his
place to Steve Book, before being
relegated to the subs' bench. He later
joined Bradford City on loan where he
made five appearances and produced an
incredible save from Nigel Quashie to deny
Portsmouth a goal. He was released by the
Robins at the end of the season and was
reported to have signed for Chesterfield.
*Leicester C (From apprentice on 17/9/1986)
FL 46 FAC 3 Others 5*

Clint Morrison

*Chesterfield (Loaned on 10/9/1987) FL 17
Others 2*
Blackpool (Loaned on 1/2/1988) FL 2
*Hartlepool U (Loaned on 28/10/1988) FL 8
Others 2*
Stockport Co (Loaned on 1/3/1990) FL 4
*Stoke C (Loaned on 13/8/1993) FL 6 FLC 1
Others 2*
*Glasgow Celtic (£150,000 on 11/1/1994) SL
12 SC 1*
*Stoke C (£150,000 on 21/7/1994) FL 148+1
FLC 17 FAC 5 Others 6*
*Rotherham U (Loaned on 1/11/1995) FL 6
Others 1*
Sheffield U (Loaned on 28/3/1996) FL 0+1
Mansfield T (Loaned on 9/9/1999) FL 9
Chesterfield (Loaned on 9/12/1999) FL 5
Cardiff C (Loaned on 15/3/2001) FL 6
Cheltenham T (Free on 1/7/2001) FL 7 FLC 1
*Bradford C (Loaned on 28/12/2001) FL 4
FAC 1*

MULLIGAN David
Born: Bootle, 24 March 1982
Height: 5'8" **Weight:** 9.13
International Honours: New Zealand: Yth
A product of the Barnsley academy, David
made his debut as a second-half
substitute against Manchester City last
October. He showed enough promise to
retain his position in the starting line-up
for the next game and became a regular
in the right-back position. An excellent
passer with either foot his link-up play
with Kevin Donovan was a feature when
Barnsley went 12 games without defeat
around the turn of the year.
*Barnsley (From trainee on 18/10/2000) FL
27+1 FAC 2*

MULLIN John Michael
Born: Bury, 11 August 1975
Height: 6'0" **Weight:** 11.10
John's only start for Burnley in 2001-02
came in the Worthington Cup game
against Rushden and after a handful of
further appearances from the subs' bench
he was sold to Rotherham. A strong-
running midfield player, he brought a
different dimension to the Millers' team
and once he had settled in he became a
regular in the line-up. Towards the end of
the season he showed his character by
willingly playing in a wider role when he
was obviously happier tucked inside.
*Burnley (From trainee on 18/8/1992) FL
7+11/2 FAC 2*
*Sunderland (£40,000 + on 12/8/1995) P/FL
23+12/4 FLC 5+1 FAC 2+1*
*Preston NE (Loaned on 13/2/1998) FL 4+3
Others 1*
Burnley (Loaned on 26/3/1998) FL 6
*Burnley (Free on 20/7/1999) FL 38+39/8 FLC
2+1 FAC 5+1/1 Others 1*

MULLINS Hayden Ian
Born: Reading, 27 March 1979
Height: 6'0" **Weight:** 11.12
International Honours: E: U21-3
Hayden enjoyed another fine season for
Crystal Palace last term when he was a
near ever present. A midfield player who
also does a fine job in the back four, he
took over the captaincy in Dean Austin's
absence, but missed out on scoring
during the campaign.
*Crystal Palace (From trainee on 28/2/1997)
FL 166+3/16 FLC 18/1 FAC 5 Others 2*

MULRYNE Phillip (Phil)
Patrick
Born: Belfast, 1 January 1978
Height: 5'8" **Weight:** 10.11
Club Honours: FAYC '95
International Honours: NI: 16; B-1;
U21-3; Yth
Phil completed his first season of regular
first-team football in some style with a
string of impressive midfield displays for
Norwich City. Always at the hub of the
Canaries' passing movements he became
an integral part of Nigel Worthington's
side. Steering clear of injuries he proved
that there are few better playmakers
outside the top-flight than this Northern
Ireland international. Although not a
prolific goal-scorer, he improved on his
goals per game ratio, once again proving
how deadly he can be from set-piece
plays. A natural passer of the ball with
excellent vision, he increased his work-
rate, which came with his first extended
run at senior level, to impress many
observers.
*Manchester U (From trainee on 17/3/1995)
PL 1 FLC 3 FAC 0+1*
*Norwich C (£500,000 on 25/3/1999) FL
79+5/9 FLC 5 FAC 2 Others 3*

MUMFORD Andrew Owen
Born: Neath, 18 June 1981
Height: 6'2" **Weight:** 13.6
International Honours: W: Yth; Sch
A change of management at Swansea
saw Andrew employed in a three-man
central defensive unit to great effect. His
ability to pass accurately over distance
was used to set up attacking situations
and he proved effective when bringing
the ball out defence. In November he had
a loan spell with Dr Martens League club
Merthyr and on his return he showed a
much greater level of match fitness. He
was included in a Wales U21 training
camp towards the end of the season.

*Rotherham U (£150,000 on 5/10/2001) FL
27+7/2 FAC 2/2*

MUNROE Karl Augustus
Born: Manchester, 23 September 1979
Height: 6'0" **Weight:** 11.0
A tall central midfield player who provides
a physical presence, Karl was not always a
first-choice player at Macclesfield last
season and his appearances were divided
equally between the starting line-up and
the substitutes' bench. Following the
arrival of new manager David Moss his
play became noticeably more measured
and his disciplinary record improved.
Swansea C (From trainee on 9/7/1998) FL 0+1
*Macclesfield T (Free on 14/10/1999) FL
39+19/1 FLC 4+1/1 FAC 1 Others 1*

MURDOCK Colin James
Born: Ballymena, 2 July 1975
Height: 6'2" **Weight:** 13.0
Club Honours: Div 2 '00
International Honours: NI: 14; B-3; Yth;
Sch
Colin scored Preston's first goal of the
2001-02 campaign, and his first for 18
months, when he equalised against
Walsall, and he followed this with another
in the next game. A tall left-footed centre
back, his strength in the air was missed
when he was absent due to suspension.
He then lost his place until called on as an
emergency left back in October. He
regained a regular spot in the line-up
following Michael Jackson's injury before
a stress fracture ended his season early. A
regular for Northern Ireland, Colin
suffered from the injury curse that
afflicted virtually all of Preston's centre
halves during the campaign.
Manchester U (From juniors on 21/7/1992)
*Preston NE (£100,000 on 23/5/1997) FL
139+14/6 FLC 12 FAC 8+2 Others 10*

MURPHY Christopher (Chris)
Patrick
Born: Leamington Spa, 8 March 1983
Height: 5'6" **Weight:** 9.8
Chris is a diminutive striker with excellent
pace who was looking to gain further
senior experience at Shrewsbury last
season. However he generally lost out to
the prolific Luke Rodgers or Ryan Lowe
for a place in the squad and was
restricted to just a handful of outings
from the subs' bench.
Shrewsbury T (Trainee) FL 0+5

MURPHY Daniel (Danny)
Benjamin
Born: Chester, 18 March 1977
Height: 5'9" **Weight:** 10.8

Club Honours: FLC '01; FAC '01; UEFAC '01; ESC '01; CS '01
International Honours: E: 4; U21-5; Yth; Sch

Playing mostly on the right side of midfield, but occasionally on the left and even more rarely in his favoured position in the centre, Danny was without doubt the most improved player in the Liverpool squad last term. He was called up to the England squad early in the season and made his international debut in the 1-1 friendly with Sweden as a substitute, impressing sufficiently to be given more opportunities later in the season against Italy and Paraguay. Although omitted from the squad of 23 for the World Cup finals, he was placed on standby as first reserve and called up almost immediately as a replacement for his club colleague Steven Gerrard, only to miss out himself after chipping a bone in training.
Crewe Alex (From trainee on 21/3/1994) FL 110+24/27 FLC 7 FAC 7/4 Others 15+3/3
Liverpool (£1,500,000 + on 17/7/1997) PL 59+44/13 FLC 9+1/7 FAC 7+3/1 Others 20+8/3
Crewe Alex (Loaned on 12/2/1999) FL 16/1

MURPHY Daniel (Danny) Thomas
Born: Southwark, 4 December 1982
Height: 5'6" **Weight:** 10.8
International Honours: Rol: Yth
This left-sided defender was a member of Queen's Park Rangers successful U19 team from the 2000-01 campaign. He stepped up to make his first-team debut last December and held on to his place until early February. Although not a tall player he is quick to the tackle and passes the ball well.
Queens Park R (From trainee on 8/12/1999) FL 10+2

MURPHY David Paul
Born: Hartlepool, 1 March 1984
Height: 6'1" **Weight:** 12.3
International Honours: E: Yth
This promising Middlesbrough youngster made his debut in the Worthington Cup tie against Northampton last September and scored in Boro's 3-1 victory. He also made a handful of appearances from the subs' bench when he was mostly used on the left-hand side of midfield.
Middlesbrough (From trainee on 20/7/2001) PL 0+5 FLC 2/1 FAC 0+1

MURPHY John James
Born: Whiston, 18 October 1976
Height: 6'2" **Weight:** 14.0
Club Honours: AMC '02

John had another fine season for Blackpool in 2001-02, finishing with a total of 20 goals in all competitions, including ten in the last ten games of the campaign. He is a big strong striker who is good in the air and holds the ball up well. He was the subject of much transfer speculation before signing an extended contract for the Tangerines.
Chester C (From trainee on 6/7/1995) FL 65+38/20 FLC 6+3/1 FAC 1+2 Others 3+1
Blackpool (Signed on 6/8/1999) FL 111+11/41 FLC 7/5 FAC 8/3 Others 10+2/5

MURPHY Joseph (Joe)
Born: Dublin, Ireland, 21 August 1981
Height: 6'2" **Weight:** 13.6
International Honours: Rol: U21-11; Yth (UEFA-U16 '98)
Joe started the 2001-02 season as first choice in goal for Tranmere, but after a run of 19 consecutive appearances he lost his place to John Achterberg, and it was not until the closing stages when his rival was injured that he won a recall. He possesses excellent handling skills, commands his area well and shows a maturity beyond his years. He was also the regular 'keeper for the Republic of Ireland U21s.
Tranmere Rov (From trainee on 5/7/1999) FL 61+2 FLC 8 FAC 3 Others 1

MURPHY Matthew (Matt) Simon
Born: Northampton, 20 August 1971
Height: 6'0" **Weight:** 12.2
Matt joined Bury during the 2001 close season but rarely seemed to find his best form at Gigg Lane and consequently found his first-team opportunities somewhat limited. He started just five games, mostly in a midfield role, although he also featured up front in the home game against Wigan Athletic. He suffered a knee injury in January that required surgery and was eventually released at the end of the season.
Oxford U (£20,000 from Corby T on 12/2/1993) FL 168+78/38 FLC 10+9/8 FAC 12+3/6 Others 6+3/3
Scunthorpe U (Loaned on 12/12/1997) FL 1+2 Others 1
Bury (Free on 9/8/2001) FL 5+4 Others 1

MURPHY Neil Anthony
Born: Liverpool, 19 May 1980
Height: 5'9" **Weight:** 11.0
International Honours: E: Yth
This young right back made just a single first-team appearance for Blackpool last season, playing in the 4-0 defeat at Brighton back in August. He featured

regularly for the club's reserves during the campaign but was released in the summer.
Liverpool (From trainee on 13/10/1997)
Blackpool (Free on 27/7/2000) FL 4+3 FLC 2

MURPHY Peter
Born: Dublin, 27 October 1980
Height: 5'11" **Weight:** 12.10
International Honours: Rol: Yth
A neat and skilful wing back, Peter provided a dependable presence down the left flank for Carlisle United throughout the 2001-02 campaign. Although not neglecting his defensive duties, he looked at his best going forward and combining well with the midfield and strikers. He took his share of corners and free kicks and was unlucky not to add his name to the score sheet.
Blackburn Rov (From trainee on 15/7/1998)
Halifax T (Loaned on 26/10/2000) FL 18+3/1 FAC 1 Others 2
Carlisle U (Free on 10/8/2001) FL 39+1 FLC 1 FAC 3 Others 1

MURPHY Shaun Peter
Born: Sydney, Australia, 5 November 1970
Height: 6'1" **Weight:** 12.0
Club Honours: AIC '95
International Honours: Australia: 20; U23; Yth
Shaun returned late to pre-season training for Sheffield United last term due to international commitments and took a short while to reach his best form. In October a possible knee operation was delayed whilst he appeared in the World Cup play-offs against Uruguay and on his return he failed to agree terms on a new deal and was placed on the transfer list. He then spent two months on loan at Crystal Palace where he was required as cover for injuries to the club's regular central defenders. On his return to Bramall Lane he found himself back in the first team and eventually signed a new contract for the Blades.
Notts Co (Signed from Perth Italia, Australia on 4/9/1992) FL 100+9/5 FLC 5+2 FAC 6/1 Others 12+1/1
West Bromwich A (£500,000 on 31/12/1996) FL 60+11/7 FLC 3 FAC 4
Sheffield U (Free on 22/7/1999) FL 115/8 FLC 11 FAC 3
Crystal Palace (Loaned on 1/2/2002) FL 11

MURRAY Adam David
Born: Birmingham, 30 September 1981
Height: 5'8" **Weight:** 10.10
International Honours: E: Yth
Adam made a handful of senior

appearances for Derby County early on last term and was subsequently loaned to Third Division club Mansfield Town for the last three months of the season. The all-action central midfield player made a big impression at Field Mill and soon became a favourite with the Stags' fans. He is assured in the tackle, distributes the ball well and has an eye for goal too, as demonstrated by the seven goals he notched during the run-in.
Derby Co (From trainee on 7/10/1998) PL 8+24 FLC 2+1 FAC 3
Mansfield T (Loaned on 26/2/2002) FL 13/7

MURRAY Frederick (Fred)
Anthony
Born: Clonmel, Ireland, 22 May 1982
Height: 5'10" **Weight:** 11.12
International Honours: RoI: Yth
Fred became John Taylor's first signing as manager of Cambridge United, arriving on loan last December and then signing permanently in March. He went on to make an impressive debut at left back against Bristol City and was a near ever present in the line-up for the next three months.
Blackburn Rov (From trainee on 25/5/1999)
Cambridge U (Free on 14/12/2001) FL 21 Others 3

MURRAY Karl Anthony
Born: Islington, 24 June 1982
Height: 5'11" **Weight:** 12.6
This strong-tackling, highly committed midfield player always gives 100 per cent and is a great favourite with the Shrewsbury Town supporters. He was consistently involved throughout last season and produced an excellent performance in the home game against Kidderminster when he made two goals as the Shrews romped to a 4-0 victory.
Shrewsbury T (From trainee on 7/2/2000) FL 60+21/3 FLC 4 FAC 3 Others 1

MURRAY Paul
Born: Carlisle, 31 August 1976
Height: 5'9" **Weight:** 10.5
International Honours: E: B-1; U21-4; Yth
Signed by Southampton after a brief trial period during the summer, Paul impressed in pre-season matches but failed to gain a regular first-team spot. A brief substitute appearance at Tottenham was his only first team outing before he followed Mick Wadsworth to Oldham in December. He produced a series of powerful midfield performances for Athletic, for whom he featured regularly, notching a creditable tally of five goals.

Carlisle U (From trainee on 14/6/1994) FL 27+14/1 FLC 2 FAC 1 Others 6+1
Queens Park R (£300,000 on 8/3/1996) P/FL 115+25/7 FLC 8/1 FAC 9
Southampton (Free on 2/8/2001) PL 0+1
Oldham Ath (Free on 12/12/2001) FL 23+1/5 FAC 1 Others 1

MURRAY Scott George
Born: Aberdeen, 26 May 1974
Height: 5'10" **Weight:** 11.0
Chosen by his fellow professionals as a member of the PFA Second Division team for the second consecutive season, this enthusiastic wing back was given a trial by new Scotland coach Berti Vogts at the end of the season in the squad fixture against Dundee United at Stirling. Earlier he had done well to recover from a fractured cheekbone sustained in the 3-0 home success over Oldham in February. Bristol City fans will long remember his last-minute winner at home to Blackpool as well as his great double strike in a 3-1 success at Cardiff.
Aston Villa (£35,000 from Fraserburgh on 16/3/1994) PL 4
Bristol C (£150,000 on 12/12/1997) FL 148+31/27 FLC 9+3 FAC 10+1/4 Others 10+2/3

MURTY Graeme Stuart
Born: Saltburn, 13 November 1974
Height: 5'10" **Weight:** 11.10
The 2001-02 season was Graeme's best so far with Reading. He was virtually ever-present at right back, and his precision in the tackle, plus immaculate passing and countless brave, last-ditch clearances in front of goal, earned him deserved recognition with selection for the PFA Division Two team. He was also nominated as the supporters' 'Player of the Season', an honour he richly deserved for so many consistent performances. Perhaps his best display of the campaign came in the final game at Brentford, when a typically gritty contribution ensured the draw that brought promotion.
York C (From trainee on 23/3/1993) FL 106+11/7 FLC 10/2 FAC 5+1 Others 6+2
Reading (£700,000 on 10/7/1998) FL 83+9/1 FLC 2 FAC 6+1 Others 4+2

MUSCAT Kevin Vincent
Born: Crawley, 7 August 1973
Height: 5'11" **Weight:** 12.2
International Honours: Australia: 42; U23; Yth
This experienced right back showed mixed form early on last term for Wolves, but after a while he began to

show greater consistency, and his determination was always an asset. An example of his commitment came when he won two sliding tackles against Bradford, won Bradford broke away to score a late goal. A suspension and injury kept him out of the last seven matches. He scored a vital penalty for Australia as they beat Uruguay 1-0 in a play-off for the World Cup, although they lost the tie on aggregate.
Crystal Palace (£35,000 from South Melbourne, Australia on 16/8/1996) FL 51+2/2 FLC 4/1 FAC 2 Others 2
Wolverhampton W (£200,000 on 22/10/1997) FL 178+2/14 FLC 10/1 FAC 11

MUSSELWHITE Paul Stephen
Born: Portsmouth, 22 December 1968
Height: 6'2" **Weight:** 14.2
Club Honours: AMC '93
Having been so influential in Hull's 2000-01 play-off campaign, this vastly experienced 'keeper must have been disappointed to be replaced by summer signing Matt Glennon last term. Nonetheless, he continued to work hard behind the scenes and took his opportunity with both hands when Matt was sidelined with a thigh injury in December. With the form of his outfield colleagues taking an alarming dip, he was given the chance to prove that he remains a very capable 'keeper.
Portsmouth (From apprentice on 1/12/1986)
Scunthorpe U (Free on 21/3/1988) FL 132 FLC 11 FAC 7 Others 13
Port Vale (£20,000 on 30/7/1992) FL 312 FLC 15 FAC 21 Others 19
Sheffield Wed (Free, via trials at Scunthorpe U, Darlington, on 25/8/2000)
Hull C (Free on 19/9/2000) FL 57 FAC 2 Others 4

MUSTAFA Tarkan
Born: Islington, 28 August 1973
Height: 5'10" **Weight:** 11.12
Club Honours: NC '01
International Honours: E: SP-2
2001-02 proved to be an up-and-down season for the Rushden right back who started the campaign as first choice and ended it with serious competition from Andrew Sambrook. After scoring his first goal for the club, a screamer against Burnley in the Worthington Cup, Tarkan's season looked set fair before a serious leg injury sustained at Leyton Orient in September kept him out of competitive action for several weeks. An exciting player who likes to get forward at every opportunity, he regained his place as the season reached its conclusion.
Barnet (Free from Kettering T on 5/8/1997)

Graeme Murty

FL 2+9 FLC 0+1 *(Free to Kingstonian on 9/9/1998)*
Rushden & Diamonds *(Signed on 6/6/2000)*
FL 21+2/1 FLC 2/1 Others 3

MUSTOE Neil John
Born: Gloucester, 5 November 1976
Height: 5'9" **Weight:** 12.10
Club Honours: FAYC '95
This hard-working left-sided midfielder again found himself out of favour at Cambridge United at the beginning of last season and he spent a couple of months out on loan at neighbours Cambridge City. A change of manager saw him recalled but he only managed a handful of appearances from the subs' bench and was released in the summer.
Manchester U *(From trainee on 1/7/1995)*
Wigan Ath *(Signed on 7/1/1998) Others 0+1*
Cambridge U *(Free on 9/7/1998)* FL 71+28/4 FLC 7 FAC 6+1 Others 4+1

MUSTOE Robin (Robbie)
Born: Witney, 28 August 1968
Height: 5'11" **Weight:** 11.12
Club Honours: Div 1 '95
This dynamic box-to-box midfielder was again a regular in the Middlesbrough line-up last term, featuring in all but two Premiership matches. An all-action player who drives the team forward and is constantly prodding and probing, he contributed two goals for Boro' during the season.
Oxford U *(From juniors on 2/7/1986)* FL 78+13/10 FLC 2 FAC 2 Others 3
Middlesbrough *(£375,000 on 5/7/1990)* F/PL 327+38/25 FLC 44+3/7 FAC 29+1/2 Others 12+1/1

MYERS Andrew (Andy) John
Born: Hounslow, 3 November 1973
Height: 5'10" **Weight:** 13.11
Club Honours: FAC '97; ECWC '98
International Honours: E: U21-4; Yth
Andy had an outstanding season at centre back for Bradford City and won several different supporters' clubs 'Player of the Year' awards. He started the campaign vying with Wayne Jacobs for the left-back spot, but after injuries to the centre backs he stepped in and played most of the season there. He is effective in the tackle and very good in the air, but the strongest point of his game is his speed. He was seriously missed when absent in the closing stages with a hamstring injury.
Chelsea *(From trainee on 25/7/1991)* F/PL 74+10/2 FLC 2+1 FAC 9+3 Others 4+3
Bradford C *(£800,000 on 16/7/1999)* P/FL 53+12/3 FLC 4 FAC 1 Others 3+1
Portsmouth *(Loaned on 23/3/2000)* FL 4+4

N

[NARADA] BERNARD
Narada Michael
Born: Bristol, 30 January 1981
Height: 5'2" **Weight:** 10.5
Narada is a left-sided defender who likes to push forward and is an excellent crosser of the ball. In his two years at Bournemouth, he has been desperately unlucky with injuries, typified by his appearance against Wrexham at the new stadium opening when after coming on as a substitute, he was carried off minutes later with an ankle injury. He had a run in the reserves late in the season where his performances earned him a new contract.
Arsenal (From trainee at Tottenham H on 9/7/1999)
Bournemouth (Free on 31/7/2000) FL 10+12 FAC 1 Others 2+1

NARDIELLO Daniel (Danny)
Antony
Born: Coventry, 22 October 1982
Height: 5'11" **Weight:** 11.4
International Honours: E: Yth; Sch
This budding young Manchester United striker made his senior debut in the Worthington Cup tie against Arsenal in the Worthington Cup last November. Meanwhile his education took a more upward step when he became a star pupil at Ashton-on-Mersey School, where he picked up an advanced GNVQ in Leisure and Tourism Studies, a couple of weeks later. Danny is the son of former Coventry City winger Donato Nardiello.
Manchester U (From trainee on 1/11/1999) FLC 0+1

NASH Carlo James
Born: Bolton, 13 September 1973
Height: 6'5" **Weight:** 14.1
Club Honours: Div 1 '02
Carlo began the 2001-02 season as first choice 'keeper for Manchester City ahead of his rival Nicky Weaver, but he had the misfortune to suffer bruising to his ribs in the second match at Norwich and lost his place. It was not until the Worthington Cup defeat against Blackburn that he regained his first-team spot and he then continued to enjoy alternate spells between the posts. Things will be different in 2002-03 following the arrival of Peter Schmeichel at Maine Road.
Crystal Palace (£35,000 from Clitheroe on 16/7/1996) FL 21 FLC 1 Others 3
Stockport Co (Free on 7/6/1998) FL 89 FLC 5 FAC 4

Manchester C (£100,000 on 12/1/2001) P/FL 28+1 FLC 1 FAC 1

NAVARRO Alan Edward
Born: Liverpool, 31 May 1981
Height: 5'11" **Weight:** 11.7
This hard-working player spent time on loan at Crewe in the early part of the 2001-02 season, covering at full back during an injury crisis. He returned to Anfield briefly but in November he was out on loan again, this time at Tranmere for whom he eventually signed on a permanent basis. He made an immediate impact at Prenton Park and went on to feature regularly for the remainder of the campaign. He is a tough-tackling but creative midfielder who can play in any position across the middle, and shows the potential to become the cornerstone of the team.
Liverpool (From trainee on 27/4/1999)
Crewe Alex (Loaned on 22/3/2001) FL 5+3/1
Crewe Alex (Loaned on 9/8/2001) FL 7 FLC 2
Tranmere Rov (£225,000 on 9/11/2001) FL 21/1 FAC 3/1

NAYLOR Anthony (Tony)
Joseph
Born: Manchester, 29 March 1967
Height: 5'7" **Weight:** 10.8
Club Honours: AMC '01
The arrival of Tony Naylor at Cheltenham Town in the summer of 2001 was greeted with much excitement among supporters who saw it as a statement of intent that the fledgling League club was prepared to invest in a player with an established track record and lofty reputation. After a somewhat hesitant start he went on to transform the team with his finishing, intelligent movement and clever ball-work. His presence brought the best out of the players around him in particular his strike-partner, Julian Alsop. Tony finished the 2001-02 season with 18 goals in all competitions including both in the historic 2-1 FA Cup third round win over Oldham Athletic.
Crewe Alex (£20,000 from Droylsden on 22/3/1990) FL 104+18/45 FLC 7+2/5 FAC 9/7 Others 12/9
Port Vale (£150,000 on 18/7/1994) FL 207+46/71 FLC 15+1/8 FAC 12+1/2 Others 12+1/8
Cheltenham T (Free on 16/8/2001) FL 43+1/12 FLC 1 FAC 5/5 Others 4/1

NAYLOR Glenn
Born: Goole, 11 August 1972
Height: 5'10" **Weight:** 11.10
Glenn spent virtually the whole of the 2001-02 campaign out of action with a

serious knee injury and only returned to the Darlington line-up for the last few games. However he did manage to score his 50th goal for club in the final match of the season at Oxford United. His experience, unselfish running and goals were sorely missed during his long absence.
York C (From trainee on 5/3/1990) FL 78+33/30 FLC 2+4 FAC 4+1/2 Others 3+4
Darlington (Loaned on 13/10/1995) FL 3+1/1 Others 1+1
Darlington (Signed on 26/9/1996) FL 156+40/43 FLC 6+1/2 FAC 12+2/5 Others 6+4

NAYLOR Lee Martyn
Born: Walsall, 19 March 1980
Height: 5'9" **Weight:** 11.8
International Honours: E: U21-3; Yth
Lee failed to find a consistent level of form for Wolves last term. His attacking flair was inhibited slightly by having a fine left winger, Mark Kennedy, in front of him. An error at Watford cost Wolves a win and shortly afterwards he was dropped and he did not see the first team again, until the last few minutes of the final League match. He is a left back who can cross the ball well and is also young enough to come good again.
Wolverhampton W (From trainee on 10/10/1997) FL 125+17/4 FLC 12 FAC 9/1

NAYLOR Richard Alan
Born: Leeds, 28 February 1977
Height: 6'1" **Weight:** 13.7
2001-02 was another season when injuries and increased competition for striking berths meant that Richard had little opportunity to put together a first-team run at Ipswich. When he played he always gave 100 per cent and his abrasive style meant his opponents knew that he was around. He scored in the first home game of the new season, flicking home a cross from close range, but spent much of the second half of the campaign out on loan at Millwall and then Barnsley.
Ipswich T (From trainee on 10/7/1995) P/FL 58+67/21 FLC 6+8/1 FAC 1+5 Others 3+6/1
Millwall (Loaned on 29/1/2002) FL 2+1
Barnsley (Loaned on 4/3/2002) FL 7+1

NAYSMITH Gary Andrew
Born: Edinburgh, 16 November 1979
Height: 5'7" **Weight:** 11.8
Club Honours: SC '98
International Honours: S: 6; U21-22; Sch
A gutsy, committed and ever willing left back, Gary also possesses the technical

ability which saw him established as a full Scottish international. When playing that role he loves to get forward and attack, and for a large part of last season he was even asked to play left midfield. He proved to be one of Everton's most potent goal creators from the left flank, but strangely failed to find the net himself last term. He wasn't helped in that objective, though, by a painful ankle injury that ended his season early in February and required surgery.

Heart of Midlothian (From Whitehill Welfare on 17/6/1996) SL 92+5/3 SLC 5/1 SC 10 Others 7/1

Everton (£1,750,000 on 20/10/2000) PL 40+4/2 FAC 5

NDAH George Ehialimolisa

Born: Dulwich, 23 December 1974
Height: 6'1" **Weight:** 11.4
International Honours: E: Yth
George began the 2001-02 campaign on the injury list at Wolves and although he made one early-season appearance from the bench, his next action came in December when he was again used as sub. The speedy, slender striker continued to be on the fringe of the first team and in February he came on and headed the winner against Rotherham. He only made one start, at home to Norwich, but looked dangerous when coming on from the bench. A few weeks from the end of the season he had a suspected hernia.

Crystal Palace (From trainee on 10/8/1992) F/PL 33+45/8 FLC 7+6/2 FAC 3+1/1 Others 4+1

Bournemouth (Loaned on 13/10/1995) FL 12/2 Others 1

Gillingham (Loaned on 29/8/1997) FL 4

Swindon T (£500,000 on 21/11/1997) FL 66+1/14 FLC 4/1 FAC 3

Wolverhampton W (£1,000,000 on 21/10/1999) FL 30+21/7 FLC 0+1 FAC 0+1

N'DIAYE Seyni

Born: Dakar, Senegal, 6 January 1973
Height: 6'2" **Weight:** 12.11
A bustling forward, Seyni has an impressive physical presence but his uncompromising style occasionally led to his enthusiasm being mistaken for malice by officialdom. He scored twice early on for Tranmere last term, but failed to win a regular place in the line-up and in February he moved north to join Dunfermline Athletic.

Tranmere Rov (Free from Caen, France, ex Vitry-Chatillon, Paris St Germain, Neuchatel Xamax, on 19/3/2001) FL 11+8/4 FLC 2 FAC 0+1 Others 0+1

NDLOVU Peter

Born: Bulawayo, Zimbabwe, 25 February 1973
Height: 5'8" **Weight:** 10.2
International Honours: Zimbabwe
Peter was used in a variety of positions for Sheffield United during the 2001-02 season: left wing, right wing and on occasions as one of two front men. He is an enigmatic player, able to score spectacular goals, as against Stockport, and yet also capable of not putting away lesser chances. Quick and tricky with exceptional ball control and balance, he has the ability to beat his opponent but then tends to over-elaborate, delaying the final ball or going for goal himself when others are better placed. He missed few games during the season, and played with energy and commitment for the full 90 minutes, not only in his attacking role but also helping out in defence. His two goals in the final minutes against Millwall turned a 1-2 deficit into a 3-2 win.

Coventry C (£10,000 from Highlanders, Zimbabwe on 16/8/1991) F/PL 141+36/37 FLC 10/2 FAC 5+4/2 Others 0+1

Birmingham C (£1,600,000 on 15/7/1997) FL 78+29/22 FLC 17+2/4 FAC 3+1/1 Others 2+2

Huddersfield T (Loaned on 8/12/2000) FL 6/4

Sheffield U (Free on 2/2/2001) FL 56+4/8 FLC 1+1/1 FAC 2/1

NEAL Lewis

Born: Leicester, 14 July 1981
Height: 6'0" **Weight:** 11.2
Lewis continued to make steady progress at Stoke City last term when he gained further senior experience both in midfield and from the subs' bench. Blessed with being genuinely two footed and with the stamina to get up and down the pitch, it was no surprise when the management offered to extend his contract.

Stoke C (Free from juniors on 17/7/1998) FL 6+6 FAC 0+1 Others 1+2/1

NEDERGAARD Steen

Born: Denmark, 25 February 1970
Height: 6'0" **Weight:** 11.13
This experienced right back or right-side midfield player had a marginal influence on proceedings in his first season at Norwich in 2000-01, but won over all of his doubters with some terrific displays for the Canaries last season. A tremendous athlete, he switched between the two right-flank positions with great aplomb. He strikes the ball very cleanly and was always competing with Phil Mulryne for

the direct free-kick duties. His consistency earned him a one-year extension to his contract and runner-up in the fans' 'Player of the Season' vote.

Norwich C (Free from Odense BK, Denmark on 3/7/2000) FL 47+8/3 FLC 1+2 FAC 2

NEGOUAI Christian

Born: Fort de France, Martinique, 20 January 1975
Height: 6'4" **Weight:** 13.11
This tall midfielder signed for Manchester City last November. He made his debut at Portsmouth and also featured against Rotherham at Maine Road, when he scored a disputed equaliser for the Blues. His last start was in the Worthington Cup tie at Blackburn when he was sent off for two yellow-card offences, and after this he only featured occasionally from the subs' bench.

Manchester C (£1,500,000 from RSC Charleroi, Belgium, ex Vaux en Velin, Lyon, Namur, on 16/11/2001) FL 2+3/1 FLC 1 FAC 0+1

NEIL Alexander (Alex)

Born: Bellshill, 4 May 1978
Height: 5'8" **Weight:** 12.10
Alex scored his first ever League goal for Barnsley in the victory over Crewe Alexandra last season. He lost his place in the team towards the end of September but came back in immediately after the departure of manager Nigel Spackman, but the arrival of new midfielders then severely restricted his opportunities. He is a hard-working midfielder who came to Oakwell as a wide man but has since developed into more of a central player.

Airdrieonians (Free from Dunfermline Ath juniors on 8/7/1999) SL 15+1/5 SC 0+1

Barnsley (£25,000 on 11/7/2000) FL 36+21/2 FLC 2+2 FAC 2

NEILL Lucas Edward

Born: Sydney, Australia, 9 March 1978
Height: 6'1" **Weight:** 12.0
Club Honours: Div 2 '01
International Honours: Australia: 2; U23-12; Yth
It was inevitable that Lucas would eventually leave Millwall, such is his quality, and after just a handful of appearances last term he was sold to Blackburn. He immediately settled in to the right-back position where his coolness and athleticism enabled him to play with panache. His main weakness was inconsistency but he was unruffled and tackled strongly, often being on hand to cover on the edge of the area. He also

featured for Rovers on the right-hand side of a back three, where he looked extremely comfortable.

Millwall (Free from Australian Academy of Sport on 13/11/1995) FL 124+28/14 FLC 6+1 FAC 4 Others 11+1
Blackburn Rov (£1,000,000 on 7/9/2001) PL 31/1 FAC 4

NEILSON Alan Bruce
Born: Wegburg, Germany, 26 September 1972
Height: 5'11" **Weight:** 12.10
International Honours: W: 5; B-2; U21-7
This experienced defender was unable to break into the first team at Fulham and

joined Grimsby Town last October as cover for the absent John McDermott. However, injuries restricted his appearances for the Mariners and he never really settled at Blundell Park. He was released in February and signed for Luton Town, where he went straight in the line-up at left back. His experience

Lucas Neill (foreground)

301

helped steady the Hatters' defence so that only two goals were conceded in the eight games he played and the team had a 100 per cent record. He subsequently signed a further contract at Kenilworth Road.
Newcastle U (From trainee on 11/2/1991) F/PL 35+7/1 FLC 4 Others 4
Southampton (£500,000 on 1/6/1995) PL 42+13 FLC 7 FAC 1+1
Fulham (£250,000 on 28/11/1997) FL 24+5/2 FLC 4+2 FAC 4 Others 2
Grimsby T (Free on 19/10/2001) FL 8+2 FLC 1 FAC 1
Luton T (Free on 22/2/2002) FL 8

NELSON Michael John
Born: Gateshead, 28 March 1980
Height: 6'2" **Weight:** 13.12
This promising central defender signed a permanent contract for Bury during the summer of 2001 and was the Shakers' most impressive defender during the opening weeks. Unfortunately, he then suffered horrendous injuries, including two broken ribs and a collapsed lung, after colliding with his own goalkeeper against Wigan in September. He was expected to be out for three months, but resumed training in just four weeks, although he struggled to recapture his best form for some time. He signed a further extension to his contract in February.
Bury (Free from Bishop Auckland on 22/3/2001) FL 30+3/3 FLC 1 FAC 2 Others 2

NEMETH Szilard
Born: Kamarna, Slovakia, 14 September 1972
Height: 5'10" **Weight:** 10.10
International Honours: Slovakia: 32
This experienced striker was hampered by a hernia problem at the beginning of last term and it was not until Middlesborough's visit to Charlton in October that he made his first appearance in the starting line-up. However, he never really established himself in the line-up and made most of his appearances from the subs' bench.
Middlesbrough (Signed from Inter Bratislava, Slovakia, ex Slovan Bratislava, Kosice, on 30/7/2001) PL 11+10/3 FLC 2/2 FAC 2+2/1

NETHERCOTT Stuart David
Born: Ilford, 21 March 1973
Height: 6'1" **Weight:** 13.8
Club Honours: Div 2 '01
International Honours: E: U21-8
Stuart was an ever present for Millwall last season. He was a rock in the centre of defence and led the team admirably as

skipper. He scored some important goals, mainly from set pieces, and formed a formidable partnership with Sean Dyche at the back. Tremendous in the air he is without doubt one of the best central defenders outside the Premiership.
Tottenham H (From trainee on 17/8/1991) PL 31+23 FAC 5+3/1
Maidstone U (Loaned on 5/9/1991) FL 13/1 Others 1
Barnet (Loaned on 13/2/1992) FL 3
Millwall (Signed on 22/1/1998) FL 161+4/7 FLC 6 FAC 5 Others 13

NEVILLE Gary Alexander
Born: Bury, 18 February 1975
Height: 5'11" **Weight:** 12.8
Club Honours: FAYC '92; PL '96, '97, '99, '00, '01; FAC '96, '99; CS '96; EC '99
International Honours: E: 52; Yth (UEFA-U18 '93)
Gary's versatility for United might have been overshadowed by his performances for England during the early part of last season, but he continued to be a vital and persistent cog down United's right flank during a difficult spell in the Premiership between October and November. A near ever present throughout the campaign, he was a steadying influence when the alarm bells were jangling, and he took over the 'problem' position of centre half with consummate ease for a short while. He earned his 50th cap for England in the friendly against Holland in February, but missed out on a place in the squad for the World Cup finals after breaking a metatarsal in his left foot.
Manchester U (From trainee on 29/1/1993) PL 230+7/3 FLC 4+1 FAC 25+2 Others 75+4

NEVILLE Philip (Phil) John
Born: Bury, 21 January 1977
Height: 5'11" **Weight:** 12.0
Club Honours: FAYC '95; PL '96, '97, '99, '00, '01; FAC '96, '99; CS '96, '97; EC '99
International Honours: E: 37; U21-7; Yth; Sch
This versatile defender took some time to win a regular place in the Manchester United starting line-up last term but once back he also began to develop a talent for scoring goals. He notched the first of two efforts in United's 6-1 demolition of Southampton at Old Trafford in December, and a second in the 4-1 drubbing of Sunderland in February. However, he eventually lost his place in the side as the season reached its climax.
Manchester U (From trainee on 1/6/1994) PL 150+38/4 FLC 8+1 FAC 17+4 Others 32+17/1

NEWBY Jonathan (Jon) Philip Robert
Born: Warrington, 28 November 1978
Height: 6'0" **Weight:** 12.4
Club Honours: FAYC '96
Jon was Bury's only ever-present player last term, choosing to remain at Gigg Lane despite several offers from other clubs, a decision that made him a great favourite with the Shakers' fans. He showed intelligent running and movement, and a great willingness to work for the team, be it in central attack or out on the wing. His total of just seven goals was perhaps disappointing, but his consistent high level of performance and work-rate each match made a massive contribution to the team in a very difficult season. Jon was voted as the fans 'Player of the Season' and also the 'Players' Player of the Season'.
Liverpool (From juniors on 23/5/1997) PL 0+1 FLC 0+1 FAC 0+2
Crewe Alex (Loaned on 3/3/2000) FL 5+1
Sheffield U (Loaned on 4/8/2000) FL 3+10
Bury (£100,000 on 2/2/2001) FL 63/11 FLC 1 FAC 2 Others 2/1

NEWMAN Robert (Rob) Nigel
Born: Bradford on Avon, 13 December 1963
Height: 6'2" **Weight:** 13.4
Club Honours: AMC '86
After stepping up from his role as coach to become manager of Southend United mid-way through last season Rob restricted his playing appearances to a minimum. Although still showing great dominance when playing at centre half, it was his enforced appearances in the forward line that showed his great character. His ability to hold the ball up and lay it off proved invaluable at the time, although he will be hoping that he doesn't have to play too often in the coming season.
Bristol C (From apprentice on 5/10/1981) FL 382+12/52 FLC 29+1/2 FAC 27/2 Others 33/5
Norwich C (£600,000 on 15/7/1991) F/PL 181+24/14 FLC 22+2/2 FAC 13/1 Others 7
Motherwell (Loaned on 12/12/1997) SL 11 SC 3
Wigan Ath (Loaned on 26/3/1998) FL 8
Southend U (Free on 28/7/1998) FL 63+9/11 FLC 4/1 FAC 4 Others 5

NEWTON Adam Lee
Born: Grays, 4 December 1980
Height: 5'10" **Weight:** 11.6
Club Honours: FAYC '99
International Honours: E: U21-1
Adam was unable to win a place in the first team at West Ham last season and

joined Leyton Orient on loan for the final six weeks of the campaign. An exciting prospect who likes to take on defenders with his pace and trickery, he can feature either as a wing back or in a wide-right midfield role. He scored his first goal for the club in the last home game of the season before returning to Upton Park and he was reported to have signed for Peterborough United during the summer.

West Ham U (From trainee on 1/7/1999) PL 0+2 Others 0+1

Portsmouth (Loaned on 2/7/1999) FL 1+2 FLC 2

Notts Co (Loaned on 22/11/2000) FL 13+7/1 FAC 2

Leyton Orient (Loaned on 8/3/2002) FL 10/1

NEWTON Shaun O'Neill

Born: Camberwell, 20 August 1975
Height: 5'8" **Weight:** 11.7
Club Honours: Div 1 '00
International Honours: E: U21-3

This right winger signed for Wolves shortly before the start of the 2001-02 campaign and promptly scored on his debut. His hard-working displays endeared him to the crowd and he scored in three successive matches in September. In fact a header at Watford meant he was still top scorer for Wolves at Christmas with six. His willingness to tackle back also made him an important player although towards the end of the season he did not have quite the same impact.

Charlton Ath (From trainee on 1/7/1993) P/FL 189+51/20 FLC 19+1/3 FAC 11+6/2 Others 7+1/2

Wolverhampton W (£850,000 + on 8/8/2001) FL 45/8 FLC 1 FAC 1 Others 2

NGOTTY Bruno

Born: Lyon, France, 10 June 1971
Height: 6'1" **Weight:** 13.8
International Honours: France: 6

Initially signed by Bolton on a season's loan, Bruno proved to be a revelation in defence and the deal was made permanent in January. Equally adept at playing the right-back or centre-back role, his experience shone through in every single game he played. Excellent on the ball, with superb passing skills and fantastic awareness of the game, he is the epitome of coolness every time he steps foot onto the pitch. Despite being built like the proverbial barn door, he is surprisingly agile and has been known to make some speedy runs down the wing when required.

Bolton W (Loaned from Marseilles, France, ex Lyon, Paris St Germain, AC Milan, Venezia, on 11/9/2001) PL 24+2/1 FLC 2+1

NICHOLLS Kevin John Richard

Born: Newham, 2 January 1979
Height: 6'0" **Weight:** 11.0
International Honours: E: Yth

Kevin was an instant hit at Luton after arriving during the 2001 close season. Installed as team captain he showed incredible spirit and leadership on the field, which would suggest he has the ability to go a long way in the game. A combative midfield player with fine vision, he was a near ever present for the Hatters and showed his nerve with several vital penalty kicks, none more so than in the home game against promotion rivals Plymouth Argyle.

Charlton Ath (From trainee on 29/1/1996) FL 4+8/1 FLC 2+2

Brighton & Hove A (Loaned on 26/2/1999) FL 4/1

Wigan Ath (£250,000 + on 22/6/1999) FL 19+9 FLC 2 Others 4/1

Luton T (£25,000 + on 3/8/2001) FL 42/7 FLC 1

NICHOLLS Mark

Born: Hillingdon, 30 May 1977
Height: 5'10" **Weight:** 10.4
Club Honours: FLC '98

Former Chelsea starlet had a brief trial at Partick in the summer before joining Torquay United on a short-term contract. He put in some useful performances, either as a striker or an attacking midfielder, without ever really threatening to solve the Gulls' goal-scoring problems. He failed to secure a longer deal and after a couple of games for Hamilton he signed for Clydebank.

Chelsea (From trainee on 1/7/1995) PL 11+25/3 FLC 4+3 FAC 1+3 Others 0+5

Reading (Loaned on 30/12/1999) FL 4+1/1 Others 2/2

Grimsby T (Loaned on 24/2/2000) FL 6

Colchester U (Loaned on 5/10/2000) FL 3+1

Torquay U (Free, via trial at Partick Thistle, on 7/9/2001) FL 4+5/1 FLC 0+1 Others 1

NICHOLSON Kevin John

Born: Derby, 2 October 1980
Height: 5'8" **Weight:** 11.5
International Honours: E: Yth; Sch

Having been out of favour, out of position, and out of form at Notts County for much of 2001-02, Kevin finished the season as a hero and the club's saviour. Eventually given the task of stand-in left back to cover a suspension, he made the position his own and stayed in the team through to the end of the campaign. Warmly appreciated by the fans he brought the house down with a truly memorable individual goal in the final

game against Huddersfield, which clinched safety from relegation for the Magpies.

Sheffield Wed (From trainee on 22/10/1997) FL 0+1

Northampton T (Free on 26/1/2001) FL 6+1

Notts Co (Free on 8/3/2001) FL 24+11/3 FLC 2 FAC 0+1 Others 2

NICHOLSON Shane Michael

Born: Newark, 3 June 1970
Height: 5'10" **Weight:** 12.2
Club Honours: GMVC '88

Shane joined Sheffield United during the 2001 close season but was unavailable for the opening games due to suspension. His debut came in the Worthington Cup defeat at Grimsby and he was a regular until injured in January, appearing mainly at left wing back although occasionally in midfield. Rob Ullathorne then became first choice and Shane's appearances were somewhat limited, although he was a regular on the bench. He is a reliable defender, solid in the tackle and able to create openings with his crosses when coming forward.

Lincoln C (From trainee on 19/7/1988) FL 122+11/6 FLC 8+3 FAC 6/1 Others 7+1

Derby Co (£100,000 on 22/4/1992) FL 73+1/1 FLC 4 FAC 4/1 Others 5

West Bromwich A (£150,000 on 9/2/1996) FL 50+2 FLC 2 FAC 2 Others 4

Chesterfield (Free on 21/8/1998) FL 23+1 Others 1

Stockport Co (Free on 4/6/1999) FL 73+4/3 FLC 3 FAC 3

Sheffield U (Free on 18/7/2001) FL 21+4/3 FLC 1

NIELSEN Allan

Born: Esbjerg, Denmark, 13 March 1971
Height: 5'8" **Weight:** 11.2
Club Honours: FLC '99
International Honours: Denmark: 44; U21

Allan began the 2001-02 season in right midfield for Watford and made a promising start with two early goals. However, a serious ankle injury sustained in September left him sidelined for three months. Surprisingly transfer-listed in February, he made it clear he had no wish to leave and underlined his professionalism and leadership qualities with a series of influential performances. His season ended after he suffered a torn thigh muscle in March.

Tottenham H (£1,650,000 from Brondby, Denmark, ex Esbjerg, Bayern Munich, Sion, Odense, FC Copenhagen, on 3/9/1996) PL 78+18/12 FLC 10+1/3 FAC 5+2/3 Others 1

Kevin Nicholls

*Wolverhampton W (Loaned on 23/3/2000)
FL 7/2*

*Watford (£2,250,000 on 3/8/2000) FL
64+3/16 FLC 4+2 FAC 2*

NIELSEN David

Born: Denmark, 1 December 1976
Height: 6'0" **Weight:** 11.13
David was not quite as effective for
Wimbledon last term as he had been in
the 2000-01 campaign, although he
was often used out wide rather than
through the centre. He joined Norwich
on loan in December 2001 and made a
real impact by scoring five goals in his
first five games, including a double in
the 5-0 away win at Hillsborough. This
soon led to City making the move
permanent. An unorthodox striker, he
possesses a real turn of foot enabling
him to spring clear of the closest of
markers and a bag of tricks to confound
any defender.

*Grimsby T (Loaned from FC Copenhagen,
Denmark on 12/10/2000) FL 16+1/5 FAC
1+1/1*
*Wimbledon (Signed on 27/3/2001) FL
15+8/4 FLC 1*
*Norwich C (£200,000 on 14/12/2001) FL
22+1/8 Others 3*

NILSSON Nilsennart **Roland**

Born: Helsingborg, Sweden, 27
November 1963
Height: 5'11" **Weight:** 11.12
Club Honours: FLC '91
International Honours: Sweden: 116
Roland returned to Coventry as a coach
in early 2001 and was persuaded to start
playing again by Gordon Strachan. The
legendary Swedish international
appeared in eight games at right back at
the start of last season until he picked
up an injury, by which time he had been
appointed caretaker-manager following
Strachan's departure in early September.
Despite the right-back position being a
'problem' one for the Sky Blues, Roland
resisted putting on his boots until the
crucial game at Preston in April. The
team lost heavily and he announced his
retirement from playing soon afterwards.
Just over a week later he was sacked as
manager following the club's failure to
reach the play-offs.

*Sheffield Wed (£375,000 from IFK
Gothenburg on 8/12/1989) F/PL 151/2 FLC
16/1 FAC 15 Others 3+1 (Transferred to
Helsingborgs, Sweden on 9/5/94)*
*Coventry C (£200,000 on 29/7/1997) PL 60
FLC 3 FAC 6 (Free to Helsingborgs, Sweden
during 1999 close season)*
Coventry C (Free on 4/7/2001) FL 9 FLC 1

NISHIZAWA Akinori

Born: Shizuoka, Japan, 18 June 1976
Height: 5'11" **Weight:** 11.2
International Honours: Japan: 25
Akinori move to Bolton Wanderers in the
2001 close season was sadly not a
successful one. He did not make a single
Premiership appearance, and his career at
the Reebok consisted of three
Worthington Cup starts. He showed
enough in those games to suggest that
he might force his way into the first team,
but this was not to be. He did, however,
score in the Worthington Cup win over
Walsall.

*Bolton W (Loaned from Cerezo Osaka, Japan
on 8/8/2001) FLC 3/1*

NIXON Eric Walter

Born: Manchester, 4 October 1962
Height: 6'4" **Weight:** 14.12
Club Honours: AMC '90
Eric was employed as Tranmere's
goalkeeping coach last season, but came
out of retirement to help Kidderminster
when first-choice 'keeper Stuart Brock
was suspended. In the three games that
he played for Harriers, he kept two clean
sheets and only conceded one goal in the
other game. Remarkably, he also
managed an appearance for Tranmere too
later on in the campaign. Named on the
bench for the visit to Cambridge, Joe
Murphy obliged by getting himself injured
and Eric came on for the final ten
minutes. Despite his age he still showed
full command of his penalty area!

*Manchester C (£1,000 from Curzon Ashton
on 10/12/1983) FL 58 FLC 8 FAC 10 Others 8*
*Wolverhampton W (Loaned on 29/8/1986)
FL 16*
Bradford C (Loaned on 28/11/1986) FL 3
Southampton (Loaned on 23/12/1986) FL 4
Carlisle U (Loaned on 23/1/1987) FL 16
*Tranmere Rov (£60,000 on 24/3/1988) FL
341 FLC 34 FAC 19 Others 45+1*
Reading (Loaned on 9/11/1996) FLC 1
*Blackpool (Loaned on 5/2/1996) FL 20
Others 2*
Bradford C (Loaned on 13/9/1996) FL 12
*Stockport Co (£100,000 on 28/8/1997) FL
43 FLC 2 FAC 2*
Wigan Ath (Loaned on 28/8/1998) FL 1
Wigan Ath (Free on 24/3/1999) FL 2
*Tranmere Rov (Free on 20/7/1999) FL 1+2
FLC 0+1*
*Kidderminster Hrs (Loaned on 12/10/2001)
FL 2 Others 1*

NOBLE David James

Born: Hitchin, 2 February 1982
Height: 6'0" **Weight:** 12.4
Club Honours: FAYC '00

International Honours: E: Yth
David came to Watford on a season-long
loan from Arsenal and made a fine early
impression with his skill on the ball and
precise passing. He made sporadic
appearances in the first team without
ever pinning down a regular place, and
scored his first senior goal at Grimsby in
October. An England U20 international,
he faded towards the end of the
campaign before returning to Highbury.
Arsenal (From trainee on 13/3/2001)
*Watford (Loaned on 10/7/2001) FL 5+10/1
FLC 3*

NOEL-WILLIAMS Gifton
Ruben Elisha
Born: Islington, 21 January 1980
Height: 6'1" **Weight:** 14.6
Club Honours: Div 2 '98
International Honours: E: Yth
Watford's popular centre forward was a
regular in the first team when fit last
term, and has now made more than 150
League appearances for his only club.
Gifton has always been particularly good
at holding up the ball, but last season he
worked hard to improve his mobility and
was rewarded with nine goals, including a
spectacular header against Arsenal in the
FA Cup. His season came to a premature
end in March when he sustained serious
knee ligament damage that needed
surgery.
*Watford (From trainee on 13/2/1997) P/FL
99+54/33 FLC 10+2/3 FAC 9/5*

NOGAN Lee Martin
Born: Cardiff, 21 May 1969
Height: 5'9" **Weight:** 11.0
Club Honours: AMC '98
International Honours: W: 2; B-1; U21-1
Lee finished the 2001-02 campaign as
York City's second-top scorer with 13
League goals to his credit and played a
huge part in the club's climb to safety. He
also passed the landmark of 100 career
League goals during the season. Apart
from his scoring, Lee's tireless work rate
and all-round ability proved invaluable to
the Bootham Crescent side.
*Oxford U (From trainee on 25/3/1987) FL
57+7/10 FLC 4+1 FAC 2+1/1 Others 4+1/1*
Brentford (Loaned on 25/3/1987) FL 10+1/2
*Southend U (Loaned on 17/9/1987) FL 6/1
FLC 2 Others 1/1*
*Watford (£350,000 on 12/12/1991) FL
97+8/26 FLC 5+2/3 FAC 2/1 Others 1+2*
Southend U (Loaned on 17/3/1994) FL 4+1
*Reading (£250,000 on 12/11/1995) FL
71+20/26 FLC 5+1/1 FAC 2 Others 3/2*
Notts Co (Loaned on 14/2/1997) FL 6
Grimsby T (£170,000 on 24/7/1997) FL

63+11/10 FLC 9+1/2 FAC 4/2 Others 8/2
Darlington (Free on 21/7/1999) FL 37+12/6
FLC 3/2 FAC 3 Others 1+2/1
Luton T (Free on 23/11/2000) FL 7/1 FAC 3/1
Others 0+1
York C (Free on 12/2/2001) FL 56+2/19 FLC 1
FAC 5 Others 1

NOLAN Ian Robert
Born: Liverpool, 9 July 1970
Height: 6'0" **Weight:** 12.1
International Honours: NI: 18
Ian signed for Wigan Athletic after
impressing in a pre-season tour. A
versatile defender capable of playing in

either full-back position, he suffered a
stress fracture of the leg early on at
Brighton and this prevented him from
making a real impact with the Latics. A
steady but unspectacular performer with
stamina and good crossing ability, he
continued to represent Northern Ireland at

Lee Nogan (left)

international level. Out of contract in the summer, he was released on a free transfer.

***Tranmere Rov** (£10,000 from Marine on 2/8/1991) FL 87+1/1 FLC 10/1 FAC 7 Others 9*
***Sheffield Wed** (£1,500,000 on 17/8/1994) PL 164+1/4 FLC 15+1 FAC 15 Others 3*
***Bradford C** (Free on 6/7/2000) PL 17+4 FLC 2/1 Others 4*
***Wigan Ath** (Free on 9/8/2001) FL 5+3*

NOLAN Kevin Anthony Jance
Born: Liverpool, 24 June 1982
Height: 6'1" **Weight:** 13.5
International Honours: E: Yth
The 2001-02 campaign proved to be the stuff dreams are made of for Kevin. He announced his arrival on the first day of the season, when he scored two of the goals in the 5-0 demolition of Leicester and went on to become recognised as one of the best young midfielders in the country. A near ever present for Bolton, he notched an impressive nine goals from midfield, including a 30-yard free kick which proved to be the winner against Aston Villa. A fearsome battler, with a tigerish tackle and a lethal shot, it was a mystery to everyone at the Reebok why he failed to break in to the England U21 side.
***Bolton W** (From trainee on 22/1/2000) P/FL 59+11/9 FLC 1+1 FAC 4+2/2 Others 2*

NORMANN Runar
Born: Harstad, Norway, 1 March 1978
Height: 6'3" **Weight:** 12.11
International Honours: Norway: U21-3; Yth
This left winger was out in the cold at Coventry under Gordon Strachan but Roland Nillson gave him an opportunity with two substitute appearances. Unfortunately, he did little to convince the management that he was first-team material and apart from a brief trial with Lyn Oslo he spent last season in the reserves at Highfield Road.
***Coventry C** (£1,000,000 from Lillestrom, Norway, ex Harstad, on 3/8/1999) P/FL 1+9 FAC 1*

NORRIS David Martin
Born: Stamford, 22 February 1981
Height: 5'7" **Weight:** 11.6
Although he did not make any Premiership appearances, this skilful and pacy midfielder appeared in the FA and Worthington Cups for Bolton last season. In March he joined Hull City on loan to gain some first-team action and made an immediate impact on his debut by scoring within four minutes of coming on as a

half time substitute against Mansfield. He went on to prove that he was more than capable of coping with the physical demands of Division Three.
***Bolton W** (£50,000 from Boston U on 2/2/2000) FLC 3+1 FAC 1/1*
***Hull C** (Loaned on 4/3/2002) FL 3+3/1*

NORVILLE Jason
Born: Trinidad, 9 September 1983
Height: 5'11" **Weight:** 11.2
Jason is a left-footed striker who made his debut for Watford as a substitute at Bradford in October. He made only one further substitute appearance for the first team, but was a regular scorer for the juniors and reserves.
***Watford** (Trainee) FL 0+2*

NOSWORTHY Nyron Paul Henry
Born: Brixton, 11 October 1980
Height: 6'0" **Weight:** 12.0
This former trainee established himself in the Gillingham team at right back last November and went on to give some impressive performances. Strong in the tackle, with good control and sublime pace, he missed the last few matches with a thigh strain. He will be looking to fulfil his potential during the course of the 2002-03 season.
***Gillingham** (From trainee on 30/12/1998) FL 52+19/1 FLC 1+2 FAC 3+7 Others 0+3*

NOTMAN Alexander (Alex) McKeachie
Born: Edinburgh, 10 December 1979
Height: 5'7" **Weight:** 10.11
International Honours: S: U21-11; Yth; Sch
Alex must be one of the unluckiest footballers of last season for whenever he was given a first-team opportunity his best efforts in front of goal either found the woodwork or the opposition goalkeeper in outstanding form. A clever striker who is at his best dropping short off the front-line to create space and then using his skill and vision to create goal-scoring opportunities for himself and his colleagues. Nearly always in the 16-man squad, he was Norwich's most used substitute during the campaign, often doing an excellent job helping the team retain possession late on in games.
***Manchester U** (From trainee on 17/12/1996) FLC 0+1*
***Aberdeen** (Loaned on 11/2/1999) SL 0+2*
***Sheffield U** (Loaned on 20/1/2000) FL 7+3/3*
***Norwich C** (£250,000 on 28/11/2000) FL 16+29/1 FAC 2+1 Others 0+3*

NOWLAND Adam Christopher
Born: Preston, 6 July 1981
Height: 5'11" **Weight:** 11.6
Adam joined Wimbledon from Blackpool during the 2001 close season and spent much of last season developing in the reserves, for whom he scored a cracker from 40 yards in the game at Arsenal. A quick-footed and hard-working young forward, most of his senior appearances came from the subs' bench and he will be aiming to feature more regularly in 2002-03.
***Blackpool** (From trainee on 15/11/1999) FL 18+51/6 FLC 1+5/1 FAC 2+2/1 Others 0+2*
***Wimbledon** (Signed on 29/6/2001) FL 1+6*

NUGENT David James
Born: Liverpool, 2 May 1985
Height: 5'11" **Weight:** 12.11
2001-02 was very much a fairy-tale season for Bury striker David Nugent, who started the campaign as a first-year scholar and ended up forcing his way into the first team at the age of just 16. He made his debut as a late substitute in the 1-1 home draw with Port Vale in March and made three more appearances from the bench before making his full League debut in the 3-1 defeat at Peterborough on the final day of the campaign. He terrorised defenders with his speed and determination to chase every ball and finished off with a hat-trick to help the Shakers' reserves clinch promotion in the Avon Insurance League.
***Bury** (Trainee) FL 1+4*

NUGENT Kevin Patrick
Born: Edmonton, 10 April 1969
Height: 6'1" **Weight:** 13.3
International Honours: RoI: Yth
Kevin managed just a single appearance in the Second Division for Cardiff last term and also featured in two LDV Vans Trophy ties, scoring against Peterborough. He subsequently joined Leyton Orient along with Matt Brazier, returning after a ten-year absence. An excellent target man and effective leader of the line his experience will be useful in bringing on the youngsters on the books at Brisbane Road.
***Leyton Orient** (From trainee on 8/7/1987) FL 86+8/20 FLC 9+3/6 FAC 9/3 Others 9+1/1*
***Plymouth Arg** (£200,000 on 23/3/1992) FL 124+7/32 FLC 11/2 FAC 10/3 Others 5+3*
***Bristol C** (Signed on 29/9/1995) FL 48+22/14 FLC 2+2 FAC 3+2/1 Others 2+1*
***Cardiff C** (£65,000 on 4/8/1997) FL 94+5/29 FLC 8+1/1 FAC 9/6 Others 1+1/1*
***Leyton Orient** (Free on 31/1/2002) FL 7+2/1*

Kevin Nolan

O

OAKES Andrew (Andy) Mark
Born: Northwich, 11 January 1977
Height: 6'4" **Weight:** 12.4
This talented young goalkeeper continued to make good progress for Derby County last term. He played in over half the Rams' Premiership games when covering for the injured Mart Poom and produced a series of steady performances.
Hull C (Signed from Winsford U on 8/12/1998) FL 19 Others 1
Derby Co (£460,000 on 7/6/1999) PL 26 FLC 2 FAC 1

OAKES Michael Christian
Born: Northwich, 30 October 1973
Height: 6'2" **Weight:** 14.6
Club Honours: FLC '96
International Honours: E: U21-6
Michael had a reasonably good season in 2001-02, and was Wolves' number one goalkeeper by a long way. In September he began a four-match spell in which he did not conceded a single goal. By March he was the only ever-present left at Molineux and he went on to play in all their 50 fixtures. When Wolves beat Wimbledon 1-0 to keep their automatic promotion chances alive, he made a fine diving save when it mattered. When the team was doing well certain players took the plaudits, but it was often Michael who proved to be the vital last line of resistance.
Aston Villa (From juniors on 16/7/1991) PL 49+2 FLC 3 FAC 2 Others 5
Scarborough (Loaned on 26/11/1993) FL 1 Others 1
Wolverhampton W (£400,000 + on 29/10/1999) FL 120 FLC 5 FAC 5 Others 2

OAKES Scott John
Born: Leicester, 5 August 1972
Height: 5'11" **Weight:** 11.13
International Honours: E: U21-1
Scott joined Leyton Orient during the 2001 summer break and featured regularly at first-team level before suffering a serious knee injury against Mansfield in October. He failed to make a full recovery and left the club before the end of the season. He is an attacking midfielder who is an excellent passer of the ball. Scott is the brother of Stefan Oakes and son of the Showaddywaddy guitarist Trevor Oakes.
Leicester C (From trainee on 9/5/1990) FL 1+2 Others 1

Luton T (Signed on 22/10/1991) FL 136+37/27 FLC 3+3/1 FAC 12+2/5 Others 3+3/1
Sheffield Wed (£425,000 + on 1/8/1996) PL 7+17/1 FLC 0+1 FAC 0+2
Cambridge U (Free on 29/8/2000) FL 7+11 Others 2
Leyton Orient (Free on 9/7/2001) FL 11 FLC 1

OAKES Stefan Trevor
Born: Leicester, 6 September 1978
Height: 5'11" **Weight:** 12.4
Club Honours: FLC '00
This left-footed midfielder began to make progress again at Leicester last term after a quiet season in 2000-01. It was an injury to Dennis Wise that really opened the door for him, once Dave Bassett had succeeded Peter Taylor as manager, and he took the opportunity to demonstrate that he has a promising future with his hometown club. He scored a late consolation goal at White Hart Lane with a driven free kick and is becoming something of a set-piece specialist for the Foxes.
Leicester C (From trainee on 3/7/1997) PL 38+21/2 FLC 7/2 FAC 5+2

OAKLEY Matthew (Matt)
Born: Peterborough, 17 August 1977
Height: 5'10" **Weight:** 12.1
International Honours: E: U21-4
Fulfilling his potential as a key member of the Saints midfield, Matt has become an influential and commanding figure getting through vast amounts of work and being instrumental in most of the side's moves. An automatic choice on the team sheet his goal-scoring record was somewhat disappointing, although he did notch up a memorable effort with a right-foot volley against Derby in March. He sustained a serious knee injury in April which curtailed his season.
Southampton (From trainee on 1/7/1995) PL 168+19/11 FLC 19+2/2 FAC 9+2/1

OATWAY Anthony Charlie Philip David Terry Frank Donald Stanley Gerry Gordon Stephen James
Born: Hammersmith, 28 November 1973
Height: 5'7" **Weight:** 10.10
Club Honours: Div 3 '99, '01; Div 2 '02
Charlie started the 2001-02 season on the substitutes' bench for Brighton and then missed the next three games due to suspension. He returned to the side against Blackpool and made an immediate impact by scoring the opening goal in a 4-0 home victory, retaining his

place until the arrival of Junior Lewis. This created increased competition for midfield positions and for much of the final third of the season he had to settle for a place on the bench. A terrier like midfielder, Charlie has become a firm fans' favourite at Withdean.
Cardiff C (Free from Yeading on 4/8/1994) FL 29+3 FLC 2/1 FAC 1+1 Others 3+1
Torquay U (Free on 28/12/1995) FL 65+2/1 FLC 3 FAC 1
Brentford (£10,000 on 21/8/1997) FL 37+20 FLC 1+2/1 FAC 4 Others 0+1
Lincoln C (Loaned on 21/10/1998) FL 3
Brighton & Hove A (£10,000 on 9/7/1999) FL 105+7/5 FLC 5 FAC 9/1 Others 2

O'BRIEN Andrew (Andy) James
Born: Harrogate, 29 June 1979
Height: 6'3" **Weight:** 12.4
International Honours: RoI: 5; U21-8; E: U21-1; Yth
Last season saw Andy establish himself as Nikos Dabizas' partner at the centre of Newcastle's back four with a series of solid and dependable displays. An ankle injury meant he missed the Inter Toto Cup matches, but he was on the bench for the start of the Premiership at Chelsea and after returning to the staring line-up his subsequent form ensured he remained first choice for the rest of the campaign. Cool under pressure he is always unhurried on the ball, and he enjoys joining his attack when the opportunity arises. He had the dubious distinction of scoring for both sides in the FA Cup tie at Peterborough.
Bradford C (From trainee on 28/10/1996) P/FL 113+20/3 FLC 5 FAC 8 Others 4
Newcastle U (£2,000,000 on 28/3/2001) PL 40+3/3 FLC 3+1 FAC 4+1/1 Others 0+1

O'BRIEN Michael (Mick) George
Born: Liverpool, 25 September 1979
Height: 5'5" **Weight:** 10.6
Club Honours: FAYC '98
International Honours: E: Sch
During the previous season many had felt that Mick had not been given sufficient opportunity to put his good passing skills and dead ball expertise to use in Torquay's midfield. However, he was given only monthly contracts at the start of the new season to prove himself, and only made one substitute appearance before moving on to Chester City.
Everton (From trainee on 7/10/1997)
Torquay U (Free on 29/7/1999) FL 32+20/5 FLC 3+1 FAC 4+2/2 Others 1+1

O'CALLAGHAN Brian Patrick
Born: Limerick, 24 February 1981
Height: 6'1" **Weight:** 12.1
International Honours: RoI: U21-4; Yth
Brian had limited first-team opportunities
at Barnsley last term but stepped up to
make his debut for Republic of Ireland at
U21 level against Denmark in March. He
was used on a number of occasions in
central midfield and at right back by the
Reds but always seemed more at home in
the centre of defence.
*Barnsley (Signed from Pike Rov on
16/7/1998) FL 21+11 FLC 3+2 FAC 1*

O'CALLAGHAN George
Born: Cork, 5 September 1979
Height: 6'1" **Weight:** 10.10
International Honours: RoI: Yth
This tall gangly Port Vale midfield player
began the 2001-02 season in fine style,
scoring in the 4-2 win over Notts County
on the opening day. His languid approach
and white boots always made him stand
out and he scored again at Bristol City,
but seven defeats out of eight led to
changes and George found himself
dropped. Apart from appearances on the
bench and a game in the FA Cup defeat
at Cardiff he did not make the senior side
again and was released on a free transfer
on the transfer deadline day in March. He
was reported to have signed for Cork City
in the summer.
*Port Vale (From trainee on 10/7/1998) FL
22+12/4 FLC 2 FAC 1+2 Others 0+2*

O'CONNOR Garreth
Born: Dublin, 10 November 1978
Height: 5'7" **Weight:** 11.0
At one stage last season, it looked as if
Garreth's days at Bournemouth were
numbered as he was a regular in the
reserve side and on the verge of moving
to Carlisle on loan. He was recalled to the
first team in the fine win against Stoke
and put in an excellent performance,
which earned him an extended run in the
side. He excelled in the middle of the park
during this spell before injury put paid to
his season.
*Bournemouth (Free from Bohemians on
5/6/2000) FL 13+37/1 FLC 1 FAC 0+4/1
Others 3/1*

O'CONNOR James Kevin
Born: Dublin, 1 September 1979
Height: 5'8" **Weight:** 11.6
Club Honours: AMC '00
International Honours: RoI: U21-9; Yth
James' committed performances again
made him a firm favourite with the Stoke
City fans last term. Previous problems

over the number of yellow cards received
were put behind him, even though his
competitive approach to the game was
undiminished. A strong-tackling
midfielder he continued to represent the
Republic of Ireland at U21 level.
*Stoke C (From trainee on 5/9/1996) FL
133/16 FLC 8/3 FAC 5+1 Others 16+1/3*

O'CONNOR Kevin Patrick
Born: Blackburn, 24 February 1982
Height: 5'11" **Weight:** 12.0
Kevin started the 2001-02 season in a
striking role for Brentford before
switching to the right wing and eventually
found himself a regular on the subs'
bench. He scored a fine left-footed
winner in the Worthington Cup tie
against Norwich but this turned out to be
his only goal of the campaign. A skilful
and technically sound striker, he needs to
work on improving his scoring rate.
*Brentford (From trainee on 4/3/2000) FL
24+18/1 FLC 1+1/1 FAC 1+1 Others 1+4*

O'CONNOR Martin John
Born: Walsall, 10 December 1967
Height: 5'9" **Weight:** 11.8
International Honours: Cayman Isles: 2
Eyebrows were raised when Steve Bruce
released his captain to join Walsall. Bruce
wanted to lower the age of the team and
took a calculated gamble. Martin
remained a true professional to Blues,
even when it was clear his future was in
doubt. He provided the link between
defence and attack and led by example,
playing a vital role as the Saddlers avoided
relegation. Keeping things tight in
midfield, tackling firmly and driving his
side on, he got the goal that earned a
point at Portsmouth in March and
skippered the side on several occasions.
*Crystal Palace (£25,000 from Bromsgrove
Rov on 26/6/1992) FL 2 Others 1+1*
*Walsall (Loaned on 24/3/1993) FL 10/1
Others 2/1*
*Walsall (£40,000 on 14/2/1994) FL 94/21
FLC 6/2 FAC 10/2 Others 3/1*
*Peterborough U (£350,000 on 12/7/1996)
FL 18/3 FLC 4 FAC 2*
*Birmingham C (£500,000 + on 29/11/1996)
FL 181+6/16 FLC 22+1/3 FAC 7 Others 6*
Walsall (Free on 8/2/2002) FL 12+1/1

O'DONNELL Philip (Phil)
Born: Bellshill, 25 March 1972
Height: 5'10" **Weight:** 10.10
Club Honours: SC '91, '95; SPD '98
International Honours: S: 1; U21-8
This unlucky left-sided player endured
another frustrating injury-hit season for
Sheffield Wednesday in 2001-02. He

looked the part in the few games he
was called upon and scored in the
Worthington Cup rout of Watford. It
now appears he may have run out of
time to make an impact at the club and
seems certain to move on in the
summer.
*Motherwell (From juniors on 30/6/1990) SL
123+1/15 SLC 6 SC 11+1/2 Others 3*
*Glasgow Celtic (£1,750,000 on 9/9/1994) SL
77+13/15 SLC 6+1 SC 12+4/4 Others 7+1/1*
*Sheffield Wed (Free on 9/7/1999) P/FL 13+7
FLC 2+3/1*

ODUNSI Saheed **Adeleke**
(Leke)
Born: Lambeth, 5 December 1980
Height: 5'9" **Weight:** 11.8
Leke found first-team opportunities few
and far between at Millwall last term. A
powerful central midfielder, he managed
just two appearances from the subs'
bench, but did well when called up and
showed some good support work and
strong running.
*Millwall (From trainee on 24/2/1999) FL
5+12 FLC 1+2 Others 2+1*

OFODILE Adolfus
Born: Fungu, Nigeria, 15 December 1979
Height: 5'7" **Weight:** 12.1
This pacy little striker arrived at Walsall
with a fine scoring record with his
previous club FC Magdeburg and netted
twice in a pre-season game at
Dunfermline, fans likening him to Chris
Waddle with his skill on the ball.
However, his first-team opportunities
were limited to the Worthington Cup
game at Exeter and a substitute
appearance against Crystal Palace in
November.
*Walsall (Free from FC Magdeburg, Germany,
ex Leca, on 31/7/2001) FL 0+1 FLC 1*

O'HALLORAN Keith James
Born: Dublin, 10 November 1975
Height: 5'10" **Weight:** 12.3
International Honours: RoI: U21-3; Yth;
Sch
Keith is a hard-working, right-sided
midfielder for Swindon Town. His 2001-
02 season was brought to a premature
close in September when he suffered a
broken leg while playing against
Bournemouth at Dorchester. The club's
leading scorer at the time of his injury,
having netted three penalties, he will be
looking to make a comeback in 2002-03.
*Middlesbrough (Signed from Cherry
Orchard on 6/9/1994) F/PL 3+1 FAC 2 Others 1*
*Scunthorpe U (Loaned on 25/3/1996) FL
6+1*

*Cardiff C (Loaned on 29/11/1996) FL 8
Others 2*
*St Johnstone (Free on 27/3/1997) SL
56+19/3 SLC 3+2/1 SC 2+3 Others 2*
*Swindon T (Free on 27/7/2000) FL 46/7 FLC
5/1 FAC 2+1/2 Others 2*

O'HARE Alan Patrick James
Born: Drogheda, Ireland, 31 July 1982
Height: 6'2" **Weight:** 12.2
The young left back joined Chesterfield
on loan last February and remained ever
present until the season concluded. He
showed a lot of maturity and calmness for
a lad without a first-team pedigree, being
comfortable in the air, and when his
tackling and distribution improves he will
become an asset to any central defence.
Bolton W (From trainee on 24/11/2001)
Chesterfield (Loaned on 25/1/2002) FL 19

O'KANE Aidan
Born: Belfast, 24 November 1979
Height: 5'10" **Weight:** 11.3
This young left-sided midfielder struggled
at times to come to terms with Third
Division football after joining York City
shortly after the start of the 2001-02
campaign. After a long period out of the
first team he returned in the closing
weeks and began to show the potential
and promise that had persuaded manager
Terry Dolan to sign him up.
*York C (Signed from Cliftonville, NI, on
13/8/2001) FL 11+1 FLC 1*

O'KANE John Andrew
Born: Nottingham, 15 November 1974
Height: 5'10" **Weight:** 12.2
Club Honours: FAYC '92; Div 2 '97;
AMC '02
This versatile player joined Blackpool in
the 2001 close season and was a regular
in the line-up throughout the campaign,
featuring in a variety of roles, although he
was best used at right back. He scored
four valuable goals and was a member of
the team that defeated Cambridge United
to take the LDV Vans Trophy at the
Millenium Stadium.
*Manchester U (From trainee on 29/1/1993)
PL 1+1 FLC 2+1 FAC 1 Others 1*
Wimbledon (Loaned on 22/6/1995) Others 3
Bury (Loaned on 25/10/1996) FL 2+2/2
Bury (Loaned on 16/1/1997) FL 9/1 Others 1
Bradford C (Loaned on 31/10/1997) FL 7
*Everton (£250,000 + on 30/1/1998) PL 14
FAC 1+2*
Burnley (Loaned on 31/10/1998) FL 8
*Bolton W (Signed on 19/11/1999) FL 32+6/2
FLC 4 FAC 3+1/1*
*Blackpool (Free on 4/7/2001) FL 34+4/4 FLC
2 FAC 2+1 Others 4+1*

OKON Paul Michael
Born: Sydney, Australia, 5 April 1972
Height: 5'11" **Weight:** 11.12
International Honours: Australia: 25;
U23; Yth
Paul was never really in contention for
Middlesbrough last term, making just
one appearance in the starting line-up in
Premiership matches. In January he
moved on to join Watford on a short-
term contract until the end of the
season. He performed effectively as a
midfield anchor man for the Hornets,
proving adept at doing the simple things
very well.
*Middlesbrough (Free from Fiorentina, Italy,
ex Marconi Fairfield, Brugge, Lazio, on
4/8/2000) PL 24+4 FAC 2*
Watford (Free on 10/1/2002) FL 14+1

OLDFIELD David Charles
Born: Perth, Australia, 30 May 1968
Height: 5'11" **Weight:** 13.4
International Honours: E: U21-1
David was used more sparingly by
Peterborough United last term but
remained a vital member of the first-team
squad. He worked tirelessly in midfield
and his experience proved useful in
bringing on the youngsters in the side. He
was out of contract during the summer
and his future was uncertain at the time
of writing.
*Luton T (From apprentice on 16/5/1986) FL
21+8/4 FLC 4+2/2 FAC 0+1 Others 2+1/2*
*Manchester C (£600,000 on 14/3/1989) FL
18+8/6 FLC 2+1/2 Others 0+1/1*
*Leicester C (£150,000 on 12/1/1990) F/PL
163+25/26 FLC 10+1/1 FAC 6/3 Others
11+3/2*
Millwall (Loaned on 24/2/1995) FL 16+1/6
*Luton T (£150,000 on 21/7/1995) FL
99+18/18 FLC 11/2 FAC 2 Others 7+2/4*
*Stoke C (Free on 2/7/1998) FL 50+15/7 FLC
4+1 FAC 2 Others 1+1*
*Peterborough U (Free on 23/3/2000) FL
68+10/4 FLC 3 FAC 8+2/1 Others 4+1*

O'LEARY Kristian (Kris) Denis
Born: Port Talbot, 30 August 1977
Height: 6'0" **Weight:** 13.4
Club Honours: Div 3 '00
International Honours: W: Yth
Kris played alongside numerous partners
in the centre of defence during a
turbulent year both on and off the field at
Swansea. A strong, resolute tackler, who
is effective in the air, he was appointed
club captain following Nick Cusack's
elevation to a managerial role.
Unfortunately, he received three red cards
during the campaign and this is an area

of his game where he needs to show
improvement.
*Swansea C (From trainee on 1/7/1996) FL
113+23/7 FLC 7 FAC 5+1 Others 6+2*

OLEKSEWYCZ Stephen (Steve) Michael
Born: Sowerby Bridge, 24 February 1983
Height: 5'7" **Weight:** 10.7
Steve was only ever on the fringe of the
first team at Halifax in the 2001-02
season and he spent time on loan at
Unibond League clubs Frickley Athletic
and Worksop Town to gain further
experience. His first-team opportunities
were restricted to just two outings from
the bench towards the end of the
campaign at home to Carlisle United and
away at Darlington. He is a promising
young striker who still needs to gain more
senior experience.
*Halifax T (Free from juniors on 11/8/2000) FL
0+5*

OLI Dennis Chiedozie
Born: Newham, 28 January 1984
Height: 6'0" **Weight:** 12.4
This tall striker was yet another of
Queen's Park Rangers successful U19 side
from 2000-01 to be introduced to the
senior team last term. He made his debut
as a substitute against Wigan in February
and also featured from the bench in the
home game with Peterborough the
following month.
*Queens Park R (From juniors on 24/10/2001)
FL 0+2*

OLIVER Michael
Born: Middlesbrough, 2 August 1975
Height: 5'10" **Weight:** 12.4
Michael was given the central midfield
role for Rochdale at the start of 2001-02
in the absence of the suspended David
Flitcroft, and he performed so well that
he won an automatic place in the line-up
for the whole season. He became
increasingly influential after Gary Jones'
departure and weighed in with an
excellent tally of goals. Indeed his
powerful shooting made him the side's
joint-second highest scorer, his tally
including the vital header that settled the
FA Cup replay against a stubborn
Tamworth side.
*Middlesbrough (From trainee on 19/8/1992)
Others 0+1*
*Stockport Co (£15,000 on 7/7/1994) FL
17+5/1 FLC 0+2 FAC 2 Others 1*
*Darlington (Free on 30/7/1996) FL
135+16/14 FLC 7+1/1 FAC 10+1 Others 6+3*
*Rochdale (Free on 14/7/2000) FL 70+13/7
FLC 4 FAC 4/1 Others 4*

OMMEL Sergio

Born: Den Haag, Holland, 2 September
1977
Height: 6'2" **Weight:** 12.12
This experienced Dutch striker appeared
in European Champions' League action
for KR Reykjavik at the start of last
season. He subsequently joined Bristol
Rovers and after scoring four times during
a trial period he was given a contract until
the end of the season. Tall and with a
good touch he formed a useful goal-
scoring partnership with Nathan Ellington
and netted some important goals himself
including a superb 25-yarder against
Cheltenham and the all-important winner
in the penultimate home match against
Kidderminster, which ensured Rovers were
not relegated from the Third Division. He
was one of several players released in the
summer.
*Bristol Rov (Free from KR Reykjavik, Iceland,
ex Groningen, on 23/11/2001) FL 18+5/8 FAC
2+1/1 Others 1+1/1*

OMOYINMI Emmanuel
(Manny)

Born: Nigeria, 28 December 1977
Height: 5'6" **Weight:** 10.7
International Honours: E: Sch
Although popular with the fans for his
speed and trickery, Manny never really
established himself at Oxford United in
2001-02 and was in and out of the side.
High points were his goals at Bristol
Rovers (when he gave United a lead inside
20 seconds) and at Torquay when he
helped gain a point. He is best used in a
wide role where he can use his skills
effectively and cut inside to create
opportunities.
*West Ham U (From trainee on 17/5/1995) PL
1+8/2 FLC 0+2 FAC 1+1*
Bournemouth (Loaned on 30/9/1996) FL 5+2
*Dundee U (Loaned on 20/2/1998) SL 1+3 SC
0+1*
*Leyton Orient (Loaned on 19/3/1999) FL
3+1/1*
*Gillingham (Loaned on 3/9/1999) FL 7+2/3
FLC 2*
*Scunthorpe U (Loaned on 21/12/1999) FL
6/1 Others 1*
Barnet (Loaned on 25/2/2000) FL 1+5
*Oxford U (Free on 10/7/2000) FL 27+20/6
FLC 2 FAC 1+1 Others 2*

ONE Armand

Born: Paris, France, 15 March 1983
Height: 6'4" **Weight:** 14.0
This giant striker struggled early on to
adapt to the pace of the English game
but as the 2001-02 season progressed
opposition teams soon found him to be a
handful. Two-footed, fast and skilful, he

scored the two goals at Bristol City that
earned Cambridge the right to play in the
LDV Vans Trophy final at the Millennium
Stadium. If he maintains this form in
2002-03 he is sure to attract attention
from bigger clubs.
*Cambridge U (£30,000 from Nantes, France
on 7/9/2001) FL 18+14/4 FAC 0+2 Others
4+3/5*

O'NEIL Brian

Born: Paisley, 6 September 1972
Height: 6'1" **Weight:** 12.4
International Honours: S: 6; U21-7;
Yth; Sch
Brian had another frustrating time with
injuries for Derby County last term and
after appearing in the opening few games
he was sidelined until early in the new
year. He is a versatile player who is at
home either in defence or in a midfield
'holding' role.
*Glasgow Celtic (Free from Porirua Viard U
on 10/7/1991) SL 92+27/8 SLC 6+4/1 SC
10/9 Others 8+3/1*

Nottingham F (Loaned on 18/3/1997) PL 4+1
*Aberdeen (Free on 3/7/1997) SL 24+4/1 SLC
4 SC 1 (Transferred to Wolfsburg, Germany
on 23/7/1998)*
*Derby Co (Signed on 16/11/2000) PL 11+3
FLC 0+1 FAC 2*

O'NEIL Gary Paul

Born: Bromley, 18 May 1983
Height: 5'10" **Weight:** 11.0
International Honours: E: Yth
One of the finest prospects to emerge
from the Portsmouth youth system in
recent seasons, Gary made excellent
progress last season starting 31 games.
He is an exciting midfield player with fine
vision, composure and the ability to create
space for himself. He scored with a great
looping volley against Millwall and
crowned an excellent campaign when he
captained England U19s during their
European Championship matches.
*Portsmouth (From trainee on 5/6/2000) FL
34+10/2 FLC 2+2 FAC 1*

Gary O'Neil

O'NEILL Keith Padre Gerard
Born: Dublin, 16 February 1976
Height: 6'1" **Weight:** 12.7
International Honours: RoI: 13; U21-1; Yth; Sch
Signed by Coventry City on the eve of the 2001-02 campaign, Keith went straight into the line-up for the opening game at Stockport. He started the first five games on the left side of midfield but did not look fully fit and picked up a niggling back injury. He then indicated his preference for a more defensive role and got his chance in December when he showed some good tackling skills and aerial power. A pelvic injury struck soon afterwards and he was sidelined until the end of the season when he suffered a double fracture of his left leg in a freak training ground incident.
Norwich C (From trainee on 1/7/1994) P/FL 54+19/9 FLC 8+3/1 FAC 3
Middlesbrough (£700,000 + on 19/3/1999) PL 32+5 FLC 3+1 FAC 1
Coventry C (£1,000,000 on 9/8/2001) FL 7+4

O'NEILL Paul Dennis
Born: Farnworth, 17 May 1982
Height: 5'11" **Weight:** 11.2
Paul was again a regular in the Macclesfield reserve team last term, his occasional first-team outings coming when he deputised as a central defender in the back four. He also enjoyed a short spell out on loan at Bangor in January. He has shared the captaincy of Macc's second string and always working resolutely, remaining cool and confident even when under pressure.
Macclesfield T (From trainee on 5/7/2000) FL 12+12 FAC 1 Others 1

ONUORA Ifem (Iffy)
Born: Glasgow, 28 July 1967
Height: 6'1" **Weight:** 13.10
The perfect foil for his co-striker Marlon King, Iffy may be advancing in years, but he once again showed what an important member of the Gillingham squad he was. Despite suffering a nasty knee injury against Southampton in the Worthington Cup, he bounced back to claim 12 goals during the course of the season. Regarded by many Gills' fans as a human battering ram, he showed that he still has the ability to lead the front line for at least another year.
Huddersfield T (Signed from Bradford University on 28/7/1989) FL 115+50/30 FLC 10+6/4 FAC 11+3/3 Others 13+3/3
Mansfield T (£30,000 on 20/7/1994) FL 17+11/8 FAC 0+1 Others 1

Gillingham (£25,000 on 16/8/1996) FL 53+9/23 FLC 6/1 FAC 4/2 Others 1
Swindon T (£120,000 on 13/3/1998) FL 64+9/25 FLC 4 FAC 2+1
Gillingham (£125,000 on 3/1/2000) FL 69+17/26 FLC 3/1 FAC 4+1/1 Others 3/1

OPARA Lloyd
Born: Enfield, 6 January 1984
Height: 6'1" **Weight:** 13.0
This bustling pacy striker made his senior debut for Colchester when he came off the subs' bench in the closing stages of the Second Division game at Blackpool last October. He featured from the bench on a couple more occasions later in the season and will be hoping to gain more first-team experience in 2002-03. He is the brother of the former U's player KK Opara.
Colchester U (Trainee) FL 0+1 FAC 0+1 Others 0+1

ORMEROD Anthony
Born: Middlesbrough, 31 March 1979
Height: 5'10" **Weight:** 11.12
International Honours: E: Yth
A right winger with a good turn of speed, Anthony joined Hartlepool on loan last September with a view to making a permanent move. However he only managed a couple of first-team appearances in a two-month spell at Victoria Park and failed to impress manager Chris Turner sufficiently to obtain a contract. He was reported to have signed for Scarborough during the close season.
Middlesbrough (From trainee on 16/5/1996) FL 8+11/3 FLC 2+2 FAC 2
Carlisle U (Loaned on 18/1/1999) FL 5+1 Others 1+1
York C (Loaned on 24/9/1999) FL 9+3 Others 1
Hartlepool U (Loaned on 21/9/2001) FL 2

ORMEROD Brett Ryan
Born: Blackburn, 18 October 1976
Height: 5'11" **Weight:** 11.4
Club Honours: AMC '02
This prolific striker netted 20 goals for Blackpool last term including two hat-tricks before being sold to Southampton. A former colleague of James Beattie in Blackburn's youth team, he mostly featured from the bench, but when selected used his strength and pace to good effect. A medial ligament injury sustained in a reserve game in January sidelined him for a month, before he scored on his full debut at Ipswich in March.
Blackpool (£50,000 from Accrington Stanley

on 21/3/1997) FL 105+23/45 FLC 8/4 FAC 5+1/5 Others 7+2/8
Southampton (£1,750,000 on 7/12/2001) PL 8+10/1

OSBORN Mark
Born: Bletchley, 18 June 1981
Height: 6'2" **Weight:** 14.4
Wycombe's reserve 'keeper last appeared in the first team in October 1999 but was given a run out in the two LDV Vans Trophy games last season, proving to be a more than capable deputy. He was loaned out to Conference side Farnborough Town in April after the FA gave special dispensation due to an injury crisis. With first choice Martin Taylor signing a new two-year contract, Mark will probably find first-team opportunities limited once more in 2002-03.
Wycombe W (From trainee on 13/3/1999) FL 1 FLC 0+1 Others 2

OSBORN Simon Edward
Born: Croydon, 19 January 1972
Height: 5'9" **Weight:** 11.4
This skilful midfield player joined Port Vale on trial last September and although not fully fit began to prove what a quality player he could be. Unfortunately Vale were struggling at the time, losing five out of six games and when his month was up there was no permanent deal on offer so he elected to join Gillingham. He made an instant impact for the Gills with his vision and passing ability and was always capable of notching important goals, netting stunning strikes against Sheffield Wednesday and Stockport County. Although he missed the latter part of the season with an achilles problem, it is hoped that a fully fit Simon will show his full range of skills during 2002-03.
Crystal Palace (From trainee on 3/1/1990) F/PL 47+8/5 FLC 11/1 FAC 2 Others 1+3
Reading (£90,000 on 17/8/1994) FL 31+1/5 FLC 4 Others 3
Queens Park R (£1,100,000 on 7/7/1995) PL 6+3/1 FLC 2
Wolverhampton W (£1,000,000 on 22/12/1995) FL 151+11/11 FLC 7/3 FAC 11+1 Others 2
Tranmere Rov (Free on 22/3/2001) FL 9/1
Port Vale (Free on 7/9/2001) FL 7 FLC 1
Gillingham (Free on 12/10/2001) FL 23+5/4 FAC 2+1

OSEI-KUFFOUR Jonathan (Jo)
Born: Edmonton, 17 November 1981
Height: 5'7" **Weight:** 10.6
Club Honours: FAYC '00
This exciting young Arsenal striker joined

Swindon Town on a three-month loan deal last August. He made his League debut as a substitute in the 2-0 home defeat by Oldham, before scoring the first in the 3-0 victory at Bury on his full debut two days later. He returned to Highbury where he was a regular scorer for the Gunners' reserves.
Arsenal (From trainee on 18/7/2000)
Swindon T (Loaned on 24/8/2001) FL 4+7/2 FLC 1 Others 1

O'SHAUGHNESSY Paul Joseph
Born: Bury, 3 October 1981
Height: 6'4" **Weight:** 11.12

This promising Bury midfielder made his Football League debut as a half-time substitute in the home game with Chesterfield last October. However he then struggled with injuries, picking up a knee problem and then a foot injury. His only other appearance during the season came from the subs' bench at Brighton in March.
Bury (From trainee on 10/7/2001) FL 0+2

O'SHEA John Francis
Born: Waterford, 30 April 1981
Height: 6'3" **Weight:** 11.12
International Honours: Roi: 1; U21-13;

Yth; (UEFA-U16 '98)
This composed young central defender received his introduction to first-team football for Manchester United last autumn and showed sufficient promise to indicate that he could well go on to become a star in the future. Of course he needs to gain more experience at senior level but his progress was sufficient to earn him a new contract at Old Trafford.
Manchester U (Signed from Waterford U on 2/9/1998) PL 4+5 FLC 4 Others 0+3
Bournemouth (Loaned on 18/1/2000) FL 10/1 Others 1

Brett Ormerod

OSTENSTAD Egil

Born: Haugesun, Norway, 2 January 1972
Height: 6'0'' **Weight:** 13.0
Club Honours: FLC '02
International Honours: Norway: 18; U21-27; Yth
The striker was sparingly used by Blackburn last term and seemed to have lost much of his sharpness, although he performed competently for the club's reserve team. At the time of writing it was thought that he was likely to leave Ewood Park during the summer.
Southampton (£800,000 from Viking Stavanger, Norway on 3/10/1996) PL 80+16/28 FLC 9/3 FAC 3+1/2
Blackburn Rov (Signed on 18/8/1999) P/FL 30+15/11 FLC 4+3/1 FAC 3+1
Manchester C (Loaned on 9/2/2001) PL 1+3

OSTER John Morgan

Born: Boston, 8 December 1978
Height: 5'9'' **Weight:** 10.8
International Honours: W: 4; B-1; U21-9; Yth
Out of contention at Sunderland, John joined Barnsley on a month's loan last October and made his debut in the thrilling 3-3 draw against Burnley at Turf Moor. However, he only made one more appearance for the Reds before manager Nigel Spackman was replaced and returned to Wearside soon afterwards. During his short stay at Oakwell he played on the left side of midfield and although comfortable on the ball looked a little short of match fitness.
Grimsby T (From trainee on 11/7/1996) FL 21+3/3 FAC 0+1/1
Everton (£1,500,000 on 21/7/1997) PL 22+18/1 FLC 4+1/1 FAC 2+3/1
Sunderland (£1,000,000 on 6/8/1999) PL 6+12 FLC 6+1/1 FAC 1+1
Barnsley (Loaned on 19/10/2001) FL 2

OUADDOU Abdeslam

Born: Morocco, 1 November 1978
Height: 6'3" **Weight:** 12.5
Fulham supporters got their first glimpse of Abdeslam in the opening game of the 2001-02 campaign when he appeared as a substitute against Manchester United, but his first-team chances were limited early on by the form of regular central defenders Andy Melville and Alain Goma. A comfortable player both in the air and with the ball at his feet, he moves forward with purpose, looking to turn defence into attack. Having gained experience during his first season in the Premiership it is to be expected that he will establish himself in a more regular role in 2002-03.

Fulham (£2,000,000 from Nancy, France on 10/8/2001) PL 4+4 FLC 2 FAC 1+1

OULARE Souleymane

Born: Conakry, Guinea, 16 October 1972
Height: 5'11" **Weight:** 12.11
International Honours: Guinea:
The Stoke management team chased hard to bring this experienced striker to the Britannia Stadium. A former Belgian 'Player of the Year' his career was dogged with injury enabling City to snap him up despite keen interest from a number of Premiership clubs. Unfortunately he contracted deep vein thrombosis after just one appearance from the subs' bench and his life lay in the balance for a time. He recovered and his deflected goal at Cardiff in the play-off semi-final suggests that his luck may have turned for the better.
Stoke C (Free from Fenerbahce, Turkey, ex Lycee Cbession, Horoya, Eeklo, St Niklaas, Beveren, Waregem, Genk, Fenerbahce, Las Palmas, on 28/12/2001) FL 0+1 Others 0+1/1

OVENDALE Mark John

Born: Leicester, 22 November 1973
Height: 6'2" **Weight:** 13.2
Suspended for the first two games of the season, Mark had to spend most of the 2001-02 season on the bench at Luton Town. He managed a total of 13 first-team appearances, of which only two matches were lost, but rarely featured in the second half of the campaign. A good shot stopper and very efficient on crosses he was a more than capable second choice goalkeeper.
Northampton T (Free from Wisbech on 15/8/1994) FL 6 Others 2 (Free to Barry T during 1995 close season)
Bournemouth (£30,000 on 14/5/1998) FL 89 FLC 10 FAC 7 Others 5
Luton T (£425,000 on 10/8/2000) FL 39 FLC 4 FAC 2 Others 2

OWEN Michael James

Born: Chester, 14 December 1979
Height: 5'9" **Weight:** 11.2
Club Honours: FAYC '96; FLC '01; FAC '01; UEFAC '01; ESC '01; CS '01
International Honours: E: 29; U21-1; Yth; Sch
This exceptional striker started the 2001-02 season with a rush of goals, netting nine in his first eight games for Liverpool. But even this achievement was eclipsed by his superlative hat-trick for England against Germany in Munich to put his country in the driving seat of their group for World Cup qualification. Shortly afterwards he was sidelined with

a hamstring injury for a month but he returned in great form with five goals in five games and in December he was voted 'European Footballer of the Year' by France Football magazine. A week later he notched up his 100th senior goal for Liverpool at West Ham and he was then awarded the England captaincy, in the absence of the injured David Beckham, for the friendly match with Paraguay in April. He went on to have a useful World Cup, winning the vital penalty that helped bring about the defeat of Argentina.
Liverpool (From juniors on 18/12/1996) PL 132+20/83 FLC 9+1/7 FAC 9+1/7 Others 30+3/14

OWERS Gary

Born: Newcastle, 3 October 1968
Height: 5'11" **Weight:** 12.7
Club Honours: Div 3 '88
This experienced midfield player mostly operated in the centre of the park for Notts County last term, although he can also play on the flank and even at right back on occasion. As ever he performed like a true professional, getting on with the job whatever the circumstances, but unfortunately he was one of several players released during the summer as the Magpies sought to cut their wage bill.
Sunderland (From apprentice on 8/10/1986) FL 259+9/25 FLC 25+1/1 FAC 10+2 Others 11+1/1
Bristol C (£250,000 on 23/12/1994) FL 121+5/9 FLC 9/1 FAC 9 Others 9/2
Notts Co (£15,000 on 30/7/1998) FL 147+7/12 FLC 10+1 FAC 13/2 Others 2

OWUSU Lloyd Magnus

Born: Slough, 12 December 1976
Height: 6'1" **Weight:** 14.0
Club Honours: Div 3 '99
After a quiet couple of years this extremely popular Brentford striker burst back onto the scene in 2001-02. With Ben Burgess taking some of the knocks Lloyd was able to score consistently throughout the campaign, registering doubles against Bury, Swindon and Blackpool. Pacy and hard working, he created chances for his team-mates and netted 20 League goals in a season for the second time in his career. A highlight was scoring the winner in the play-off semi-final against Huddersfield with a snap shot from the edge of the box to set up the Bees' trip to the Millennium Stadium.
Brentford (£25,000 from Slough T on 29/7/1998) FL 148+16/64 FLC 3+4/3 FAC 8/2 Others 13+3/4

Michael Owen

P

PACKHAM William (Will)
Joseph
Born: Brighton, 13 January 1981
Height: 6'2" **Weight:** 13.0
Will started his first senior game for
Brighton in the FA Cup defeat against
Preston North End last January but then
returned to the reserves. However he
stuck to his task and he received a
second start in the away game at Port
Vale on the last day of the season, when
he kept a clean sheet. He was rewarded
for his efforts with a new one-year
contract.
*Brighton & Hove A (From trainee on
29/6/1999) FL 1+1 FAC 1*

PACQUETTE Richard Francis
Born: Paddington, 28 January 1983
Height: 6'0" **Weight:** 12.7
This strongly built striker was on the
substitutes' bench for Queen's Park
Rangers early on last season but never
really established himself as a first-team
regular. However, he made several starts
during Andy Thomson's absence in
February and scored his first goal for the
club in the home win over Bury.
*Queens Park R (From trainee on 1/2/2000)
FL 9+9/2 FLC 0+1 FAC 0+1 Others 0+1*

PAGE Robert John
Born: Llwynpia, 3 September 1974
Height: 6'0" **Weight:** 12.5
Club Honours: Div 2 '98
International Honours: W: 25; B-1;
U21-6; Yth; Sch
Discarded by the new regime at Watford,
Robert initially joined United on a month's
loan, playing at right back. He returned to
Vicarage Road before signing permanently
for the Blades and soon became a
committed and reliable central defender,
firstly partnering Shaun Murphy and then
Keith Curle. Perhaps lacking a little pace,
Robert shows very good anticipation, he
is commanding in the air, a good tackler
and makes few mistakes. Although
regularly in the opposition penalty area at
set pieces he has yet to register his first
goal for the club. He came second in the
Supporters' Club 'Player of the Year'
award and also played regularly for Wales
during the season.
*Watford (From trainee on 19/4/1993) P/FL
209+7/2 FLC 17 FAC 12+1 Others 6/1*
*Sheffield U (£350,000 on 8/8/2001) FL 43
FAC 2*

PAHARS Marians
Born: Latvia, 5 August 1976
Height: 5'9" **Weight:** 10.9
International Honours: Latvia: 53
A pocket sized, hard working attacker,
Marians has formed a near-perfect
partnership with James Beattie at
Southampton and finished the campaign
as Saints' leading scorer. At his most
dangerous when cutting in from the right,
his ability to trouble defenders and put in
perfect crosses made him a cult hero with
the St Mary's faithful.
*Southampton (£800,000 from Skonto Riga,
Latvia on 25/3/1999) PL 94+12/39 FLC 6+1/1
FAC 7/1*

PALMER Carlton Lloyd
Born: Rowley Regis, 5 December 1965
Height: 6'2" **Weight:** 13.3
International Honours: E: 18; B-5;
U21-4
Carlton rejoined Sheffield Wednesday on
loan last September but made little
impact this time around and in November
he took over as player-manager of
Stockport County. He gave an immediate
boost to all at Edgeley Park, memorably
scoring on his debut with a sweet volley
in the 2-1 victory over Norwich City. He
played at the back, in midfield and up
front showing total commitment and
earning him almost cult status at the club.
He delighted everyone connected with
the Hatters when he reversed an earlier
decision to retire and confirmed that he
would carry on playing for one more
season.
*West Bromwich A (From apprentice on
21/12/1984) FL 114+7/4 FLC 7+1/1 FAC 4
Others 6*
*Sheffield Wed (£750,000 on 23/2/1989)
F/PL 204+1/14 FLC 31/1 FAC 18/2 Others
8+1/1*
*Leeds U (£2,600,000 on 30/6/1994) PL
100+2/5 FLC 12 FAC 12/1 Others 4/1*
*Southampton (£1,000,000 on 26/9/1997) PL
44+1/3 FLC 5 FAC 2*
*Nottingham F (£1,100,000 on 21/1/1999)
P/FL 14+2/1*
*Coventry C (£500,000 on 17/9/1999) PL
27+3/1 FLC 2 FAC 3*
Watford (Loaned on 15/12/2000) FL 5
Sheffield Wed (Loaned on 13/2/2001) FL 12
Sheffield Wed (Loaned on 7/9/2001) FL 10
*Stockport Co (Free on 13/11/2001) FL
20+1/3 FAC 1*

PALMER Stephen (Steve)
Leonard
Born: Brighton, 31 March 1968
Height: 6'1" **Weight:** 12.13
Club Honours: Div 2 '92, '98

International Honours: E: Sch
This central defender joined Queen's Park
Rangers in the summer of 2001 and was
immediately appointed club captain.
Although not a quick player he made up
for his lack of pace by reading the game
well and marshalling the players around
him. He scored several important goals
when coming up for set pieces and was
the only ever present for Rangers last
term.
*Ipswich T (Signed from Cambridge University
on 1/8/1989) F/PL 87+24/2 FLC 3 FAC 8+3/1
Others 4+2*
*Watford (£135,000 on 28/9/1995) P/FL
222+13/8 FLC 18+1/1 FAC 9+2 Others 7*
*Queens Park R (Free on 17/7/2001) FL 46/4
FLC 1 FAC 1 Others 1*

PANAYI Sofroni James
(Jimmy)
Born: Hammersmith, 24 January 1980
Height: 6'1" **Weight:** 14.0
A young central defender or left back,
Jimmy was on the fringes of the Watford
first team at the start of the 2001-02
season, but fell out of favour as the club
signed new centre halves. He
subsequently had a trial at Shrewsbury in
April before earning a shock first-team
recall because of injuries, before being
granted a free transfer at the end of the
season.
*Watford (From trainee on 3/7/1998) P/FL
10+3 FLC 0+1*

PANOPOULOS Mikael
(Mike)
Born: Melbourne, Australia, 9 October
1976
Height: 6'1" **Weight:** 11.7
A versatile player who can appear either
at wing back or in midfield, Mike is strong
on the ball and a neat tackler. Apart from
a couple of early-season appearances he
saw no first-team action for Portsmouth
last term and had a spell on loan with
Dunfermline at the turn of the year. He
was one of several Pompey players to be
placed on the transfer list.
*Portsmouth (£500,000 from Aris Salonika,
Greece on 8/9/1999) FL 45+9/7 FLC 3 FAC 1*
*Dunfermline Ath (Loaned on 28/12/2001)
SL 7+2 SC 0+1*

PAPADOPOULOS Demitrios
Born: Kazakhstan, 20 September 1981
Height: 5'11" **Weight:** 10.8
International Honours: Greece: U21
Signed by Burnley in the summer of 2001,
Demitrios arrived with a weight of
expectation, but was hardly given a
chance to live up to it during his first

Scott Parker

season at Turf Moor. It was October before he even made it to the bench for a League match, and his appearances as a substitute were infrequent and usually too brief to deliver any real impression of his abilities, although pace is clearly one of his main assets. He knocked in his share of goals for the reserves, and made an impression on a wider scale with his penalty for the Greek U21 side against England at nearby Ewood Park.
Burnley (£500,000 from Akratitos, Greece on 25/7/2001) FL 0+6 FLC 1 FAC 0+1

PARKER Kevin James
Born: Plymouth, 20 September 1979
Height: 5'10" **Weight:** 11.6
After the previous season had been disrupted by injuries, the speedy left winger or striker was on monthly contracts at Torquay United at the start of 2001-02. However he managed just two appearances from the bench and left Plainmoor at the end of September, signing for Weymouth shortly afterwards.
Norwich C (From trainee on 2/6/1999)
Torquay U (Free on 4/8/2000) FL 8+9/2 FLC 2

PARKER Scott Matthew
Born: Lambeth, 13 October 1980
Height: 5'7" **Weight:** 10.7
Club Honours: Div 1 '00
International Honours: E: U21-11; Yth; Sch
Scott has now developed into one of the most influential and skilful players at the Valley. He has an excellent touch, reads the game well and is a strong tackler. He is very self-assured with good vision, and distributes the ball well. He likes to get forward and was rewarded with a goal against Ipswich Town at the Valley. Now a key member of the Charlton team, he has also become a regular for England at U21 level.
Charlton Ath (From trainee on 22/10/1997) P/FL 56+24/3 FLC 6+2 FAC 3+3
Norwich C (Loaned on 31/10/2000) FL 6/1

PARKIN Jonathan (Jon)
Born: Barnsley, 30 December 1981
Height: 6'4" **Weight:** 13.7
Jon was on the fringes of the squad at Barnsley last term and was not until Lee Crooks was sidelined by injury that he got his chance. When new manager Steve Parkin took over he went on trial to Bristol Rovers and then on loan to Hartlepool United where he spent two months, but managed only one appearance from the subs' bench. He was immediately snapped up by York City,

where he had much better fortunes. He scored on his debut in a 1-0 win at Southend when used as a striker, but also featured in the centre of defence when required.
Barnsley (From trainee on 5/11/1999) FL 8+2 FLC 1+1 FAC 0+1
Hartlepool U (Loaned on 7/12/2001) FL 0+1
York C (Free on 7/2/2002) FL 18/2

PARKIN Samuel (Sam)
Born: Roehampton, 14 March 1981
Height: 6'2" **Weight:** 13.0
International Honours: E: Sch
Sam spent the whole of the 2001-02 season on loan at Northampton Town and featured regularly for the Cobblers throughout the campaign. His early efforts produced just a single goal, albeit in the Worthington Cup against Premiership opposition in the form of Middlesbrough. When Kevan Broadhurst took over as manager he changed the team's style of play and Sam's game improved noticeably. His powerful running and strength in the air made him the perfect strike partner for Jamie Forrester, while his last gasp equaliser against Stoke was talked about for weeks after.
Chelsea (From juniors on 21/8/1998)
Millwall (Loaned on 12/9/2000) FL 5+2/4
Wycombe W (Loaned on 24/11/2000) FL 5+3/1 FAC 0+3/1 Others 2/1
Oldham Ath (Loaned on 22/3/2001) FL 3+4/3
Northampton T (Loaned on 4/7/2001) FL 31+9/4 FLC 2/1 FAC 0+2 Others 2

PARKINSON Andrew (Andy)
John
Born: Liverpool, 27 May 1979
Height: 5'8" **Weight:** 10.12
This slightly built forward signed a new two-year deal for Tranmere in the summer of 2001 but had a rather frustrating season when he spent a large proportion of the time on the bench. Blessed with blistering pace and the ability to create goals from almost nothing, Andy never gave less than his best when called upon. He is at his most threatening when playing out wide on the right, where his skill and vision frequently cause panic among the opposition defence.
Tranmere Rov (From trainee at Liverpool on 12/4/1997) FL 101+53/18 FLC 15+8/5 FAC 12+2/2 Others 1

PARKINSON Gary Anthony
Born: Thornaby, 10 January 1968
Height: 5'11" **Weight:** 13.5
Club Honours: AMC '02
This experienced full back featured fairly

regularly for Blackpool in the first half of 2001-02 before dropping out of the first-team scene. A hard-tackling defender with a powerful shot, he scored his only goal of the campaign in the LDV Vans Trophy win over Stoke City. He was released at the end of the season.
Middlesbrough (From Everton juniors on 17/1/1986) FL 194+8/5 FLC 20/1 FAC 17/1 Others 19
Southend U (Loaned on 10/10/1992) FL 6
Bolton W (Free on 2/3/1993) FL 1+2 Others 4
Burnley (Signed on 27/1/1994) FL 134+1/4 FLC 12 FAC 10 Others 6/1
Preston NE (£50,000 on 30/5/1997) FL 82+2/6 FLC 6 FAC 8/1 Others 6/1
Blackpool (£20,000 on 22/3/2001) FL 22+2 FLC 1 Others 5/1

PARKINSON Philip (Phil)
John
Born: Chorley, 1 December 1967
Height: 6'0" **Weight:** 12.8
Club Honours: Div 2 '94
Despite being well into the veteran stage of his career, Phil remained as much an inspiration in the Reading midfield last term as in each of his previous ten years with the club. He scored the first goal of the promotion season, with a header in the 2-0 win at Blackpool, and was still there in the final match at Brentford, driving on his team-mates in his role as skipper. He also found time to complete his Open University BA degree in Social Sciences during the year. His loyalty to Reading FC was recognised with a testimonial game in May. Typically, he decided to give a large share of the profit to local charities.
Southampton (From apprentice on 7/12/1985)
Bury (£12,000 on 8/3/1988) FL 133+12/5 FLC 6+1 FAC 4/1 Others 13/1
Reading (£37,500 on 10/7/1992) FL 332+24/20 FLC 27+1/3 FAC 21/1 Others 11+3

PARLOUR Raymond (Ray)
Born: Romford, 7 March 1973
Height: 5'10" **Weight:** 11.12
Club Honours: FLC '93; ECWC '94; PL '98, '02; FAC '93, '98, '02; CS '98, '99
International Honours: E: 10; B-1; U21-12
This experienced midfielder was a key influence in Arsenal's double-winning team last season. A hard-working player who likes to get forward and link up with the attack he scored a cracking effort to set the Gunners on their way to victory over Chelsea in the FA Cup final.

Ray Parlour

Arsenal (From trainee on 6/3/1991) F/PL 252+43/22 FLC 20+3 FAC 32+3/4 Others 39+9/6

PARRISH Sean
Born: Wrexham, 14 March 1972
Height: 5'10" **Weight:** 11.8
This alert and combative midfielder missed his share of the 2001-02 season at Chesterfield through injury, but usually gave more than the required 100 per cent when he did play. With the Spireites' midfield under threat from better opponents last season he was unable to get forward with the same effect as previously, but used his tackling, aggression and determination to force opponents off their game. As the season climaxed a run of good performances proved that a fully-fit Sean Parrish can cut the mustard at Second Division level.
Shrewsbury T (From trainee on 12/7/1990) FL 1+2 FLC 1 Others 3 (Free to Telford during 1992 close season)
Doncaster Rov (£20,000 on 28/5/1994) FL 64+2/8 FLC 3+1 FAC 2/1 Others 3
Northampton T (£35,000 + on 2/8/1996) FL 103+6/13 FLC 8+1/1 FAC 2 Others 5/2
Chesterfield (Free on 19/7/2000) FL 44+11/11 FLC 4/1 FAC 4 Others 4+1

PARTON Andrew (Andy)
Born: Doncaster, 29 September 1983
Height: 5'10" **Weight:** 11.12
Second-year trainee Andy received a surprise call-up to Scunthorpe's first team last March, making his debut against Mansfield Town when he produced a decent showing for an hour before being replaced. A goal-scoring centre forward in the juniors, he broke into the reserves as a left winger where he showed off his attributes of pace and accurate crossing.
Scunthorpe U (Trainee) FL 1

PARTRIDGE David William
Born: Westminster, 26 November 1978
Height: 6'1" **Weight:** 13.6
David featured regularly for Dundee United early on last season before joining Leyton Orient on loan as a replacement for Mikele Leigertwood. However he lost his place due to suspension after half-a-dozen games and eventually returned north of the border. He is a no-nonsense defender who is good in the air and effective on the floor.
West Ham U (From trainee on 9/7/1997)
Dundee U (Free on 12/3/1999) SL 59+3 SLC 8 SC 5+1
Leyton Orient (Loaned on 18/1/2002) FL 6+1 FAC 1

PARTRIDGE Scott Malcolm
Born: Leicester, 13 October 1974
Height: 5'9" **Weight:** 11.2
Club Honours: Div 3 '99
This skilful striker played for the last minute of Brentford's opening League game at Wigan and an hour of the Worthington Cup tie against Norwich before joining Rushden on a free transfer. He proved to be a hard-working, unselfish front man and made an excellent contribution to Diamonds' first season in the League, despite scoring only five goals in over 40 appearances.
Bradford C (From trainee on 10/7/1992) FL 0+5 FLC 1+1
Bristol C (Free on 18/2/1994) FL 24+33/7 FLC 2+3/1 FAC 1+3
Torquay U (Loaned on 13/10/1995) FL 5/2
Plymouth Arg (Loaned on 22/1/1996) FL 6+1/2
Scarborough (Loaned on 8/3/1996) FL 5+2
Cardiff C (£50,000 on 14/2/1997) FL 29+8/2 FLC 2 FAC 2 Others 1
Torquay U (Loaned on 26/3/1998) FL 33+1/12 FLC 2 FAC 2/1 Others 2/1
Brentford (£100,000 on 19/2/1999) FL 79+13/21 FLC 3+3 FAC 2+1 Others 7+1/2
Rushden & Diamonds (Free on 13/9/2001) FL 26+11/5 FLC 2 Others 3

PATMORE Warren James
Born: Kingsbury, 14 August 1971
Height: 6'2" **Weight:** 13.12
International Honours: E: SP-7
Warren's name will forever be written into the Rushden history books, even though his career with the club lasted no more than six competitive games. Signed from Yeovil Town in the summer of 2001, he was determined to make a go of full-time football once more. An exceptionally strong and robust forward, he scored the only goal of the club's first-ever League game, against York City, and all seemed set for a fruitful season. However he decided that the full-time game was not for him and in mid-September he returned to Conference life with Woking.
Cambridge U (Signed from Northwood on 25/3/1992) FL 1
Millwall (Free on 27/8/1993) FL 0+1
Northampton T (Free on 19/11/1993) FL 12+9/2 (Freed in February 1995)
Rushden & Diamonds (Free from Yeovil on 15/6/2001) FL 4/1 FLC 2

PATTERSON Darren James
Born: Belfast, 15 October 1969
Height: 6'2" **Weight:** 12.10
International Honours: NI: 17; B-3; U21-1; Yth

Darren spent virtually all of the 2001-02 season recovering from an achilles injury and did not make his first appearance for Oxford United until the end of March. An experienced defender who reads the game well, he appeared just twice before being released in the summer.
West Bromwich A (From trainee on 5/7/1988)
Wigan Ath (Free on 17/4/1989) FL 69+28/6 FLC 7+1/3 FAC 5+4/1 Others 7
Crystal Palace (£225,000 on 1/7/1992) PL 22/1 FLC 5 FAC 6
Luton T (£100,000 on 21/8/1995) FL 52+4 FLC 0+1 FAC 2+1 Others 9
Preston NE (Loaned on 4/10/1996) FL 2
Dundee U (Free on 13/7/1998) SL 23+2 SLC 2 SC 4/1
York C (Free on 1/12/2000) FL 4+2 FAC 2 Others 1
Oxford U (Free on 15/2/2001) FL 20/1

PATTERSON Mark
Born: Leeds, 13 September 1968
Height: 5'10" **Weight:** 12.4
2001-02 was a frustrating season for this experienced Gillingham right back. He lost his place to Nyron Nosworthy in November due to a viral infection, and once he got back in the side he pulled his hamstring during the warm up at Rotherham in late February and was out for the remainder of the campaign.
Carlisle U (From trainee on 30/8/1986) FL 19+3 FLC 4 Others 1
Derby Co (£60,000 on 10/11/1987) FL 41+10/3 FLC 5+2 FAC 4 Others 5+1/2
Plymouth Arg (£85,000 on 23/7/1993) FL 131+3/3 FLC 3 FAC 8 Others 9
Gillingham (£45,000 on 30/10/1997) FL 117+5/2 FLC 8+1 FAC 5+2 Others 4

PAYNE Stephen (Steve) John
Born: Pontefract, 1 August 1975
Height: 5'11" **Weight:** 12.5
Club Honours: GMVC '95, '97; FAT '96
International Honours: E: SP-1
Steve performed with great determination and skill in defence for Chesterfield last term. He began as a centre-back partner to Ian Breckin, but after Steve Blatherwick returned and Stuart Howson emerged, he adjusted to a right-back role. He applied himself equally well wherever he played, reading the game well and becoming a valued and versatile member of the team. Steve won the 'Player of the Year' award in the club's official website poll.
Huddersfield T (From trainee on 12/7/1993)
Macclesfield T (Free on 23/12/1994) FL 71+6/2 FLC 6 FAC 5 Others 2
Chesterfield (Signed on 8/7/1999) FL 92+5/5 FLC 3+1 FAC 2 Others 5+2/2

PAYNTER William (Billy) Paul
Born: Liverpool, 13 July 1984
Height: 6'1" **Weight:** 12.0
Although still a trainee at Port Vale, Billy was quite often on the substitutes' bench last season and made his full debut at home to Wrexham in March. Unfortunately Vale lost 3-1 but he held his place for the next game against Tranmere and did quite well. A promising striker, he scored regularly for the club's reserve team and will be aiming to feature more regularly at senior level in 2002-03.
Port Vale (Trainee) FL 2+6 FAC 0+1

PAYTON Andrew (Andy) Paul
Born: Whalley, 23 October 1967
Height: 5'9" **Weight:** 11.13
Burnley's local hero failed to make a first-team start this time around, but was a regular on the bench before Christmas and notched four goals, including two late efforts in the dramatic 3-3 draw against Crewe. He was loaned out to Blackpool following off-the-field problems, and scored for the Tangerines at Bury, but on his return to Turf Moor he suffered a horrific leg injury whilst playing for the reserves. Many thought his first-team days were over, but he returned to make a few more substitute appearances near the end of the season.
Hull C (From apprentice on 29/7/1985) FL 116+28/55 FLC 9+2/1 FAC 8 Others 3/1
Middlesbrough (£750,000 on 22/11/1991) FL 8+11/3 FAC 1+3
Glasgow Celtic (Signed on 14/8/1992) SL 20+16/15 SLC 3+2/5 SC 1+1 Others 3
Barnsley (Signed on 25/11/1993) FL 100+8/41 FLC 7/3 FAC 6+1/1
Huddersfield T (£350,000 on 4/7/1996) FL 42+1/17 FLC 7/3 FAC 2
Burnley (Signed on 16/1/1998) FL 115+40/68 FLC 4+2/6 FAC 6+1/3 Others 6/3
Blackpool (Loaned on 6/12/2001) FL 4/1

PEACOCK Gavin Keith
Born: Eltham, 18 November 1967
Height: 5'8" **Weight:** 11.8
Club Honours: Div 1 '93
International Honours: E: Yth; Sch
Gavin was signed on a three-month loan deal at the start of last season to offset Charlton's injury crisis. He was hoping to secure a permanent contract and but for injury probably would have. He made five appearances in midfield and looked very assured and comfortable on the ball. Gavin reads the game well and had just established himself in the squad when he sustained a back injury and his loan

period ran out before he could recover so he returned to Queen's Park Rangers where he was a regular in the line-up for the remainder of the campaign. He is the son of Charlton's assistant manager Keith Peacock.
Queens Park R (From apprentice on 19/11/1984) FL 7+10/1 FAC 0+1
Gillingham (Loaned on 5/10/1987) FL 6 Others 2
Gillingham (£40,000 on 16/12/1987) FL 63+1/11 FLC 4 FAC 2 Others 3/1
Bournemouth (£250,000 on 16/8/1989) FL 56/8 FLC 6 FAC 2 Others 2
Newcastle U (£275,000 on 30/11/1990) FL 102+3/35 FLC 6/5 FAC 6/2 Others 3/4
Chelsea (£1,250,000 on 12/8/1993) PL 92+11/17 FLC 6/1 FAC 14+4/9 Others 7
Queens Park R (£1,000,000 on 22/11/1996) FL 182+8/35 FLC 9/3 FAC 8+1/3
Charlton Ath (Loaned on 6/8/2001) PL 1+4

PEACOCK Lee Anthony
Born: Paisley, 9 October 1976
Height: 6'0" **Weight:** 12.8
Club Honours: AMC '97
International Honours: S: U21-1; Yth
Lee missed much of the early part of the 2001-02 season due to a shoulder injury received on holiday, but still managed to finish the campaign with a respectable tally of 17 goals in all competitions for Bristol City. However, despite this the established striker rarely seemed to find his best form and often seemed to lack the mobility he had previously shown. He will be aiming to have a better season at Ashton Gate in 2002-03.
Carlisle U (From trainee on 10/3/1995) FL 52+24/11 FLC 2+3 FAC 4+1/1 Others 6+4
Mansfield T (£90,000 on 17/10/1997) FL 79+10/29 FLC 4/1 FAC 4 Others 4/2
Manchester C (£500,000 on 5/11/1999) FL 4+4 FAC 1+1
Bristol C (£600,000 on 10/8/2000) FL 59+7/28 FLC 1/1 FAC 5/1 Others 6/2

PEAD Craig George
Born: Bromsgrove, 15 September 1981
Height: 5'9" **Weight:** 11.6
International Honours: E: Yth
Craig starred as a midfield player for Coventry's outstanding youth team and after almost two years of injuries he bounced back in 2001-02 to become a regular at left back for the reserves. His steady performances earned him his senior debut at Burnley on the final day of the season and he gave a good account of himself. Craig was honoured with a late call-up to the England U20 party for the Toulon tournament and is a strong prospect for the future.
Coventry C (From trainee on 17/9/1998) FL 1

PEARCE Dennis Anthony
Born: Wolverhampton, 10 September 1974
Height: 5'10" **Weight:** 11.0
Club Honours: Div 3 '98
After signing for Peterborough United in the summer of 2001, Dennis was injured before the new campaign began and apart from the last seven games of the season he was rarely seen. A dependable left back who is comfortable on the ball, he will be hoping to secure a regular place in the line-up in 2002-03.
Aston Villa (From trainee on 7/6/1993)
Wolverhampton W (Free on 3/7/1995) FL 7+2 FLC 1 FAC 1
Notts Co (Free on 21/7/1997) FL 108+10/3 FLC 7+1 FAC 12+1 Others 3
Peterborough U (Free on 10/5/2001) FL 8+1 FAC 1

PEARCE Alexander **Gregory (Greg)**
Born: Bolton, 26 May 1980
Height: 5'10" **Weight:** 11.7
Greg's supporters will argue that he didn't receive a fair crack of the whip at Chesterfield in 2001-02, especially in the early part of the season, when the likes of David Reeves were tried at centre half while Greg looked on from the stand. Intelligent, composed and good in the air, he let nobody down when he got a chance.
Chesterfield (From trainee on 24/3/1998) FL 14+5 FLC 1 Others 0+1

PEARCE Ian Anthony
Born: Bury St Edmunds, 7 May 1974
Height: 6'3" **Weight:** 14.4
Club Honours: PL '95
International Honours: E: U21-3; Yth
If ever there is a player who deserves a bit of luck then it is Ian Pearce. The popular defender returned to the West Ham team against Middlesboro in February after being out injured for ten months. He is a powerful right-sided defender and his height makes him good in the air. Welcomed back by the fans, his presence helped the Hammers to wins over Middlesboro and Everton. He became the hero at Tottenham in April when he hit a volley into the top corner to equalise in the last minute. Hopefully his injury worries are now behind him.
Chelsea (From juniors on 1/8/1991) F/PL 0+4 Others 0+1
Blackburn Rov (£300,000 on 4/10/1993) PL 43+19/2 FLC 4+4/1 FAC 1+2 Others 6+1
West Ham U (£1,600,000 + on 19/9/1997) PL 85+3/6 FLC 6 FAC 7+1/1 Others 1+1

PEARCE Stuart
Born: Hammersmith, 24 April 1962
Height: 5'10" **Weight:** 13.0
Club Honours: FLC '89, '90; FMC '89, '92; Div 1 '02
International Honours: E: 78; U21-1
The first signing Kevin Keegan made as the Manchester City manager was the former England defender Stuart Pearce. He was installed as club captain and brought all his experience and leadership qualities to the club. Any doubts about his fitness were to be proved groundless as he went on to make 41 appearances in what was to be his final season as a player, his only significant absence coming as a result of a hamstring injury which caused him to miss the December fixtures. The last game of the season was a memorable occasion for him and he brought the curtain down on a wonderful playing career when he lifted the First Division trophy.
Coventry C (£25,000 from Wealdstone on 20/10/1983) FL 52/4 FAC 2
Nottingham F (£200,000 on 3/6/1985) F/PL 401/63 FLC 60/10 FAC 37/9 Others 24/6
Newcastle U (Free on 21/7/1997) PL 37 FLC 2 FAC 7 Others 5+1/1
West Ham U (Free on 5/8/1999) PL 42/2 FLC 4 FAC 4/1
Manchester C (Free on 11/7/2001) FL 38/3 FLC 3 FAC 1+1

PEARSON Gary
Born: Seaham, 7 December 1976
Height: 5'10" **Weight:** 12.5
This strong tackling central defender joined Darlington shortly before the start of last season and was thrown in at the deep end, coming on as a substitute after only 15 minutes of the FA Cup third round replay at Peterborough in January. He rose to the occasion and gave a mature display which led to a run of six games in the side before an injury halted his progress. He possesses a powerful shot and blasted in a 25-yard free kick against Shrewsbury in February to open his scoring account for the Quakers.
Sheffield U (From trainee on 3/7/1995. Free to Stalybridge Celtic on 22/3/1996)
Darlington (Signed from Durham C, ex Gateshead, Spennymoor U, Seaham RS, Whitby T, on 8/8/2001) FL 9/1 FAC 0+1 Others 1

PEDERSEN Henrik
Born: Denmark, 10 June 1975
Height: 6'1" **Weight:** 13.5
International Honours: Denmark: 1
Henrik made his debut for Bolton on the left-hand side of midfield at Leeds, where he looked ideally suited to the nature of the English game. However, he then flitted in and out of the side for the remainder of the season and, although he scored twice in cup matches, he has yet to break his Premiership duck. He returned on loan to Silkeborg late in the season to gain match practice and help his old club in their fight against relegation from Denmark's top flight.
Bolton W (£650,000 from Silkeborg, Denmark on 11/7/2001) PL 5+6 FLC 1+1/1 FAC 2/1

PEJIC Shaun Melvyn
Born: Hereford, 16 November 1982
Height: 6'1" **Weight:** 12.3
A third-year scholar at Wrexham, Shaun continued to make good progress last season and featured regularly in the last quarter of this campaign. He slotted in exceptionally well alongside Dennis Lawrence in the centre of the defence, showing himself to be hard working and composed on the ball. He received the Robins' 'Young Player of the Year' award for his efforts. Shaun is the son of the Wrexham physio Mel Pejic, and nephew of Mike the Stoke City stalwart of the 1970s.
Wrexham (Trainee) FL 12+1

PEMBERTON Martin Calvin
Born: Bradford, 1 February 1976
Height: 5'11" **Weight:** 12.6
Martin started the 2001-02 season as second choice to Allen Tankard at left back for Mansfield, but took his chance with some sterling performances when the latter was injured. He is a strong tackler who likes to get forward in support of the forwards and is not afraid to have a shot at goal, as magnificent strikes against Luton and Lincoln testified. Unfortunately he lost his place in the side after a suspension, before returning in midfield following an injury to Craig Disley.
Oldham Ath (From trainee on 22/7/1994) FL 0+5 FLC 0+1 Others 0+1
Doncaster Rov (Free on 21/3/1997) FL 33+2/3 FLC 0+1
Scunthorpe U (Free on 26/3/1998) FL 3+3
Hartlepool U (Free on 3/7/1998) FL 0+4 FLC 0+1 (Free to Harrogate T on 30/9/1998)
Mansfield T (£10,000 + from Bradford PA on 3/8/2000) FL 49+7/5 FLC 1 FAC 2+1 Others 2

PEMBRIDGE Mark Anthony
Born: Merthyr Tydfil, 29 November 1970
Height: 5'8" **Weight:** 12.0
International Honours: W: 42; B-2; U21-1; Sch
This Welsh international midfielder kicked off the 2001-02 campaign operating at left-wing-back for Everton, before being restored to his more natural position further forward. But a calf injury, which had plagued him for 18 months, returned to blight his season once again. There were flashes, during fleeting returns to first-team football, of the influence he could exert on the team. Most notable were a goal-scoring performance against Southampton and an inspirational display in an FA Cup tie at Crewe. Predictably, injury prevented him from building on that performance, but he was back in action for the reserve team towards the end of the season.
Luton T (From trainee on 1/7/1989) FL 60/6 FLC 2 FAC 4 Others 4
Derby Co (£1,250,000 on 2/6/1992) FL 108+2/28 FLC 9/1 FAC 6/3 Others 15/5
Sheffield Wed (£900,000 on 19/7/1995) PL 88+5/12 FLC 6/1 FAC 7/1 Others 1 (Free to Benfica, Portugal on 1/7/1998)
Everton (£800,000 on 6/8/1999) PL 59+7/3 FAC 8+1

PENDLEBURY Ian David
Born: Bolton, 3 September 1983
Height: 5'5" **Weight:** 11.1
This promising left-sided defender made his senior debut for Wigan Athletic against Wrexham last October and also featured a couple of days later at Tranmere. He later showed his versatility appearing on the left side of midfield in two further outings. He was voted as the Latics' 'Young Player of the Year' and signed a 12-month professional contract in the summer.
Wigan Ath (Trainee) FL 4

PENNANT Jermaine
Born: Nottingham, 15 January 1983
Height: 5'6" **Weight:** 10.0
Club Honours: FAYC '00, '01
International Honours: E: U21-13; Yth; Sch
This talented young wide-right midfield player featured for Arsenal in all three Worthington Cup ties last term and also had a couple of outings from the subs' bench in the European Champions League. In January he went on loan to Watford and soon became a crowd favourite with his pace, skill and willingness to take on opponents. A current member of the England Under-21 squad, Jermaine scored his first senior goal against Burnley.
Notts Co (Associated Schoolboy) FAC 0+1 Others 0+1

Sixto Peralta

Arsenal *(From trainee on 16/3/2000, having been signed for £1,500,000 on 14/1/1999) FLC 4+1 Others 0+2*
Watford *(Loaned on 10/1/2002) FL 9/2*

PENNOCK Adrian Barry
Born: Ipswich, 27 March 1971
Height: 6'1" **Weight:** 13.5
2001-02 was a season to forget for Adrian. The experienced Gillingham centre back suffered a serious knee injury at Birmingham in October and was instantly ruled out for the rest of the season. Since then he has worked hard to get back into shape and is looking to get back into first-team action in 2002-03.
Norwich C *(From trainee on 4/7/1989) FL 1*
Bournemouth *(£30,000 on 14/8/1992) FL 130+1/9 FLC 9 FAC 12/1 Others 8*
Gillingham *(£30,000 on 4/10/1996) FL 162+3/2 FLC 9 FAC 11/1 Others 11/1*

PENNOCK Anthony (Tony)
Born: Swansea, 10 April 1971
Height: 6'0" **Weight:** 12.6
Tony arrived at Rushden in the summer of 2001 with high hopes of dislodging Billy Turley from the regular custodian's spot, but it wasn't to be. He had to wait until the end of September before he had a chance to stake his claim. He did nothing wrong in the one win and two draws, but Turley was immediately back in the line-up when available again. He made no further League appearances until the last game of the regular season at Halifax Town when he came on as sub with a play-off place already secured. A loan spell at Farnborough Town also gave this model professional the chance to keep match-fit.
Stockport Co *(Free from Clydach U on 20/8/1990)*
Wigan Ath *(Loaned on 28/12/1990) FL 2 FAC 2*
Wigan Ath *(Free on 5/6/1991) FL 8 FAC 1 Others 2*
Hereford U *(Free on 25/7/1994) FL 13+2 FLC 2 FAC 2 Others 3 (Freed during 1995 close season)*
Rushden & Diamonds *(Free from Yeovil T on 15/6/2001) FL 3+2*

PEPPER Colin Nigel
Born: Rotherham, 25 April 1968
Height: 5'10" **Weight:** 12.4
Tough-tackling midfielder Nigel started the 2001-02 season still recovering from a badly broken leg sustained in August 2000. He returned to the reserves in November but a number of niggling strains meant he was unable to reach full match fitness. He played just two minutes as a substitute at senior level for

Scunthorpe all season and was released at the end of the campaign.
Rotherham U *(From apprentice on 26/4/1986) FL 35+10/1 FLC 1/1 FAC 1+1 Others 3+3*
York C *(Free on 18/7/1990) FL 223+12/39 FLC 16+2/3 FAC 12/2 Others 15+1*
Bradford C *(£100,000 on 28/2/1997) FL 47+5/11 FLC 4/1 FAC 1*
Aberdeen *(£300,000 on 26/11/1998) SL 11+3 SLC 1*
Southend U *(Loaned on 24/12/1999) FL 9+3/2*
Scunthorpe U *(Free on 21/7/2000) FL 2+1*

PERALTA Sixto Raimundo
Born: Argentina, 16 April 1979
Height: 5'10" **Weight:** 11.8
International Honours: Argentina: Yth
Sixto joined Ipswich on a year's loan from Inter Milan and became an instant favourite with the fans once he established himself in the first team with his battling qualities and never-say-die spirit. He has the ability to turn a game with flash of inspiration – a slide rule pass or a mazy dribble, for instance. He scored his first goal for the club on Boxing Day when he cut into the box and passed the ball into the net. His skill set up the goal for Alun Armstrong in the UEFA Cup tie against Inter, thus rather ironically making him responsible for the exit from the competition of his own club.
Ipswich T *(Loaned from Inter Milan, Italy, ex Torino, on 24/8/2001) PL 16+6/3 FLC 1 FAC 2/1 Others 2+2*

PEREZ Lionel
Born: Ardeche, France, 24 April 1967
Height: 5'11" **Weight:** 13.4
One of the most popular players to wear a Cambridge United shirt, Lionel gave some superb performances in what was otherwise a most disappointing season for Cambridge United. He produced some excellent saves in the LDV Vans Trophy final against Blackpool and again in the final match of the campaign against Tranmere, when he came up field to take (and miss) a penalty kick. He was out of contract in the summer and at the time of writing his future was uncertain.
Sunderland *(£200,000 from Bordeaux, France, ex Nimes, on 21/8/1996) P/FL 74+1 FLC 2 FAC 4 Others 3*
Newcastle U *(Free on 2/7/1998)*
Scunthorpe U *(Loaned on 8/10/1999) FL 13*
Cambridge U *(Free on 23/3/2000) FL 87+1 FLC 3 FAC 4 Others 8+1*

PERPETUINI David Peter
Born: Hitchin, 26 September 1979
Height: 5'8" **Weight:** 10.8

Gillingham's only close-season capture, David proved to be a real find and enjoyed a long run in the team from December until February. He has a cultured left foot, which was put to good effect from corners and free kicks. A left-sided player he was sound in defence, and liked to get forward at every opportunity.
Watford *(From trainee on 3/7/1997) P/FL 17+2/1 FLC 1+1*
Gillingham *(£100,000 on 9/8/2001) FL 25+9/1 FLC 1+1 FAC 3*

PERRETT Russell
Born: Barton on Sea, 18 June 1973
Height: 6'3" **Weight:** 13.2
Luton took a bit of a gamble when they signed Russell last summer in view of his injury problems over the previous two seasons, but he showed he had made a full recovery by appearing in almost every match for the Hatters in 2001-02. A rock solid figure in the centre of defence, he was reliable and showed good organisation skills. His game came on to such an extent that he went on to score four League goals.
Portsmouth *(Signed from Lymington on 30/9/1995) FL 66+6/2 FLC 5 FAC 4*
Cardiff C *(£10,000 on 21/7/1999) FL 28+1/1 FAC 5/1 Others 1*
Luton T *(Free on 10/8/2001) FL 39+1/3 FLC 1*

PERRY Christopher (Chris) John
Born: Carshalton, 26 April 1973
Height: 5'8" **Weight:** 11.1
This defender had a solid season at Tottenham in 2001-02. Terrific in the air and authoritative in the tackle, he added organisation and stability to the back line. He reads the game well and has the pace to recover quickly when out of position. Chris is extremely confident on the ball and adds a threat at set pieces.
Wimbledon *(From trainee on 2/7/1991) PL 158+9/2 FLC 21 FAC 24/1*
Tottenham H *(£4,000,000 on 7/7/1999) PL 96+6/2 FLC 12 FAC 8 Others 4/1*

PERRY Mark James
Born: Ealing, 19 October 1978
Height: 5'11" **Weight:** 12.10
International Honours: E: Yth; Sch
This right-sided defender or midfielder started the 2001-02 season in midfield for Queen's Park Rangers and held his place until injury struck in November. Although he regained fitness and appeared in the reserve side he was unable to win a regular place in the first-team starting line-up.

Manu Petit

Queens Park R (From trainee on 26/10/1995) FL 54+12/1 FLC 5 FAC 3 Others 1

PESCHISOLIDO Paolo (Paul) Pasquale

Born: Scarborough, Canada, 25 May 1971
Height: 5'7" **Weight:** 10.12
Club Honours: Div 2 '99
International Honours: Canada: 45; U23-11

Paul made a slow start to the 2001-02 campaign for Sheffield United, finding goals hard to come by despite chances coming his way. After a few games absent through injury he returned with a vengeance in November, scoring five goals in six games. A toe problem prevented him joining Canada for the CONCACAF Gold Cup in January but he made a substitute appearance the following month, before enjoying a run of eight games in the line-up. He produced some excellent performances full of commitment, anticipation and selfless running and added a further cap for Canada when he came on from the subs' bench against Malta in November.

Birmingham C (£25,000 from Toronto Blizzards, Canada on 11/11/1992) FL 37+6/16 FLC 2/1 FAC 0+1 Others 1+1
Stoke C (£400,000 on 1/8/1994) FL 59+7/19 FLC 6/3 FAC 3 Others 5+1/2
Birmingham C (£400,000 on 29/3/1996) FL 7+2/1
West Bromwich A (£600,000 on 24/7/1996) FL 36+9/18 FLC 4+1/3 FAC 1
Fulham (£1,100,000 on 24/10/1997) FL 69+26/24 FLC 7+1/4 FAC 9+1/2 Others 2
Queens Park R (Loaned on 3/11/2000) FL 5/1
Sheffield U (Loaned on 19/1/2001) FL 4+1/2
Norwich C (Loaned on 22/3/2001) FL 3+2
Sheffield U (£150,000 + on 10/7/2001) FL 19+10/6 FLC 2

PETERS Mark

Born: Flint, 6 July 1972
Height: 6'0" **Weight:** 11.8
Club Honours: NC '01

This exceptionally reliable defender was a rock at the heart of Rushden's defence in 2001-02. He immediately settled into Third Division life, and his signing of a new one-year contract at the season's end was widely welcomed by everyone associated with the club. Although never a prolific goal-scorer, he will remember his one from last season with much pleasure, coming as it did in the shock 3-2 defeat of Burnley in the Worthington Cup. Not short of pace, Mark's partnership with Andy Tillson played no

small part in Diamonds reaching the play-off final.

Manchester C (From trainee on 5/7/1990)
Norwich C (Free on 2/9/1992)
Peterborough U (Free on 10/8/1993) FL 17+2 FLC 2 Others 2
Mansfield T (Free on 30/9/1994) FL 107+1/9 FLC 5/1 FAC 8 Others 7
Rushden & Diamonds (Free on 3/7/1999) FL 40 FLC 2/1 FAC 2 Others 4

PETHICK Robert (Robbie) John

Born: Tavistock, 8 September 1970
Height: 5'10" **Weight:** 11.12
Club Honours: Div 2 '02

Robbie made his debut for Brighton as a substitute in the Worthington Cup victory at home to Wimbledon and although he spent much of last season on the bench he featured at right back, in midfield and occasionally at centre half. He showed many attacking qualities and was keen to move forward with the ball and deliver into the box.

Portsmouth (£30,000 from Weymouth on 1/10/1993) FL 157+32/3 FLC 13+3 FAC 9 Others 3+1
Bristol Rov (£15,000 on 19/2/1999) FL 60+3/2 FLC 5 FAC 1 Others 2+1
Brighton & Hove A (Free on 10/7/2001) FL 13+11 FLC 0+1 FAC 1 Others 3

PETIT Emmanuel (Manu)

Born: Dieppe, France, 22 September 1970
Height: 6'1" **Weight:** 12.8
Club Honours: PL '98; FAC '98; CS '98, '99
International Honours: France: 60 (WC '98, UEFA '00)

The major overhaul of Chelsea's midfield during the summer of 2001 brought French World Cup winner Manu Petit back to London after his miserable time in Spain. One of four ex-Barcelona players in the Blues' squad, he arrived at Stamford Bridge carrying a niggling groin strain and was unable to show his true form, and when he picked up an ankle ligament injury in November he seemed resigned to becoming a peripheral figure. However, he came back for an extended run in the second half of the season as he overcame his injury problems and showed his true form at the heart of midfield.

Arsenal (£3,500,000 from AS Monaco, France, ex ES Argues, on 25/6/1997) PL 82+3/9 FLC 3 FAC 13/2 Others 16+1
(£15,000,000 to Barcelona, Spain on 28/7/2000)
Chelsea (£7,500,000 on 23/7/2001) PL 26+1/1 FLC 2 FAC 6 Others 3

PETRESCU Daniel (Dan) Vasile

Born: Bucharest, Romania, 22 December 1967
Height: 5'9" **Weight:** 11.9
Club Honours: FAC '97; FLC '98; ECWC '98
International Honours: Romania: 95; U21

Dan found himself a forgotten man at Southampton last term when he was limited to just two appearances from the subs' bench. The experienced right back remained a true professional and a reliable member of the squad.

Sheffield Wed (£1,250,000 from Genoa, Italy, ex Steava and Foggia, on 6/8/1994) PL 28+9/3 FLC 2 FAC 0+2 Others 1/1
Chelsea (£2,300,000 on 18/11/1995) PL 134+16/18 FLC 8/2 FAC 20+1/1 Others 24+5/3
Bradford C (£1,000,000 on 2/8/2000) PL 16+1/1 FLC 2 FAC 0+1
Southampton (£100,000 on 12/1/2001) PL 8+3/2

PETTEFER Carl James

Born: Burnham, 22 March 1981
Height: 5'7" **Weight:** 10.5

Carl signed a new contract for Portsmouth last August following some impressive displays in the reserves. One of a crop of talented youngsters at Fratton Park, he is sharp, pacy and has an eye for goal. A midfielder who shuts down opponents well, he made his senior debut against Crystal Palace in March.

Portsmouth (From trainee on 23/11/1998) FL 1+2

PETTINGER Paul Alan

Born: Sheffield, 1 October 1975
Height: 6'1" **Weight:** 13.7
Club Honours: FAYC '93
International Honours: E: Yth; Sch

Paul signed for Lincoln City in the summer of 2001 with hopes of replacing Alan Marriott as first-choice 'keeper. He made his debut for the Imps at the start of September but after a run of three games in which he gave creditable performances he found himself back on the bench. Paul suffered a fractured finger in training the following month and when fit again found himself third choice behind both Marriott and Darren Horrigan. He finished the season loaned out to Dr Martens League club Kettering Town.

Leeds U (From trainee on 16/10/1992)
Torquay U (Loaned on 23/12/1994) FL 3
Rotherham U (Loaned on 11/8/1995) FL 0+1
Gillingham (Free on 28/3/1996)
Carlisle U (Free on 2/8/1996)

Rotherham U (Free on 1/8/1997) FL 16 FLC
2 Others 1
Lincoln C (Free on 11/7/2001) FL 3

PETTY Benjamin (Ben) James
Born: Solihull, 22 March 1977
Height: 6'0" **Weight:** 12.5
Club Honours: AMC '00
Ben joined Hull City in the 2001 close
season along with Nicky Mohan, and was
well known to boss Brian Little who had
previously signed him for both Aston Villa
and Stoke. He was subsequently given an
extended run in the centre of midfield
following the injury to Mark Greaves,
then proved his value to the squad by
playing at centre back and right back –
the latter probably being his strongest
role.
Aston Villa (From trainee on 10/5/1995)
Stoke C (Free on 27/11/1998) FL 26+20 FLC
4+1 FAC 3 Others 7+4/1
Hull C (Free on 18/7/2001) FL 22+5 FLC 1+1
FAC 2 Others 3

PHELAN Leeyon
Born: Hammersmith, 6 October 1982
Height: 5'11" **Weight:** 12.6
This young striker was only on the fringes
of the first team at Wycombe last term
and was loaned out to Ashford Town in
December, however he returned early
after tearing ligaments in this thumb.
Leeyon has always scored consistently for
the reserves but with just two substitute
appearances in the season, he decided his
future lay elsewhere and decided to leave
the club in March.
Wycombe W (From trainee on 10/7/2001) FL
0+3 Others 1+1

PHELAN Terence (Terry)
Michael
Born: Manchester, 16 March 1967
Height: 5'8" **Weight:** 10.6
Club Honours: FAC '88
International Honours: RoI: 41: B-1;
U23-1; U21-1; Yth
Terry joined Sheffield United on a three-
month contract last August as cover for
injuries and suspension, and played at left
back in the first six games. Although not
fully match fit he used his experience and
anticipation to give some creditable
performances before suffering a groin
injury in training. He played three more
games in October before leaving Bramall
Lane and later signed for US-A League
club Charleston Battery.
Leeds U (From apprentice on 3/8/1984) FL
12+2 FLC 3 Others 2
Swansea C (Free on 30/7/1986) FL 45 FLC 4
FAC 5 Others 3

Wimbledon (£100,000 on 29/7/1987) FL
155+4/1 FLC 13+2 FAC 16/2 Others 8
Manchester C (£2,500,000 on 25/8/1992) PL
102+1/1 FLC 11 FAC 8/1
Chelsea (£900,000 on 15/11/1995) PL 13+2
FLC 0+1 FAC 8
Everton (£850,000 on 1/1/1997) PL 23+2
FLC 1+1 FAC 1
Crystal Palace (Loaned on 23/10/1999) FL
14
Fulham (Free on 3/2/2000) FL 18+1/2 FLC 1
Sheffield U (Free on 10/8/2001) FL 8 FLC 1

PHILLIPS Gareth Russell
Born: Pontypridd, 19 August 1979
Height: 5'8" **Weight:** 9.8
International Honours: W: U21-3; Yth;
Sch
A powerful worker in the engine room
for Swansea City, Gareth was also used
in a right wing-back role on a number of
occasions last season. He featured
regularly in the line-up scoring two
goals, but also accumulated a number of
yellow cards and this is an area of his
game that he needs to work on. He
added further caps for Wales U21s
during the campaign, making his first
start against Belarus in Cardiff.
Swansea C (From trainee on 9/7/1998) FL
40+21/2 FLC 1+1 FAC 0+2 Others 2

PHILLIPS Kevin Mark
Born: Hitchin, 25 July 1973
Height: 5'7" **Weight:** 11.0
Club Honours: Div 1 '99
International Honours: E: 8; B-1
Last season was an extremely frustrating
campaign for Sunderland's England
international striker, whose good form
was one of the few bright spots of a
miserable campaign. A total of 11
League and Cup goals was scant reward
for a player who was, at times, forced to
plough a lone furrow up front. Excellent
strikes, especially against Leeds, showed
him at his best: a forward with pace,
body strength, capable of turning sharply
when tightly marked and an ability in the
air that belies his small stature. Kevin is
without question a striker who can live
with the very best and he played
through the pain barrier for Sunderland
on more than one occasion last term,
suffering from hip, stomach, groin, and
ankle injuries at various stages of the
season.
Watford (£10,000 from Baldock on
19/12/1994) FL 54+5/23 FLC 2/1 FAC 2
Others 0+2
Sunderland (£325,000 + on 17/7/1997) P/FL
175+1/107 FLC 9+1/5 FAC 10/7 Others 3/2

PHILLIPS Mark Ian
Born: Lambeth, 27 January 1982
Height: 6'2" **Weight:** 13.0
This tall central defender made his debut
for Millwall early last season against
Preston after some good performances in
the reserves. However, his appearances
were limited after he suffered an injury,
which proved to be long term.
Millwall (From trainee on 3/5/2000) FL 1

PHILLIPS Martin John
Born: Exeter, 13 March 1976
Height: 5'10" **Weight:** 11.10
Club Honours: Div 3 '02
Martin had a fine season with Third
Division champions Pilgrims last term. His
tricky old-fashioned wing skills created
many goal-scoring opportunities for his
team-mates and he contributed six goals
himself. One cross that will stick in the
mind of many a Plymouth fan was his
tremendous effort in injury time at Exeter
which led to the winning goal against
arch Devon rivals.
Exeter C (From trainee on 4/7/1994) FL
36+16/5 FLC 1+2 FAC 2+2 Others 1+5
Manchester C (£500,000 on 25/11/1995)
P/FL 3+12 FLC 0+1
Scunthorpe U (Loaned on 5/1/1998) FL 2+1
Others 1
Exeter C (Loaned on 19/3/1998) FL 7+1
Portsmouth (£50,000 + on 27/8/1998) FL
4+20/1 FLC 2+2 FAC 0+1
Bristol Rov (Loaned on 24/2/1999) FL 2
Plymouth Arg (£25,000 on 11/8/2000) FL
73+8/7 FLC 3 FAC 6/2 Others 2

PHILLIPS Steven (Steve)
John
Born: Bath, 6 May 1978
Height: 6'1" **Weight:** 11.10
With the arrival of Mike Stowell, it looked
as though Steve would be on the sidelines
for Bristol City last season, but injuries
allowed him back into the side. He was
then unlucky to lose his place when
Stowell regained fitness in late autumn,
but he had another lengthy run in the
side in the latter half of the campaign.
Despite being a brilliant shot-stopper, he
occasionally seems uncertain on crosses.
Bristol C (Signed from Paulton Rov on
21/11/1996) FL 99+1 FLC 5 FAC 8 Others 7

PHILLIPS Waynne
Born: Bangor, 15 December 1970
Height: 5'10" **Weight:** 11.2
International Honours: W: B-1
Waynne is an up-and-down the field box-
to-box midfielder who will always give his
best shot. He returned to first-team duty
for Wrexham last December and remained

a regular in the line-up until the end of the campaign, finally seeming to have shaken off the injury troubles that have plagued him in recent seasons. He enjoyed a fine game against Tranmere Rovers at the Racecourse in February. He has been offered a month-to-month deal for the 2002-03 season.

Wrexham *(From trainee on 23/8/1989) FL 184+23/16 FLC 17+1 FAC 12+2/1 Others 18+6/1*
Stockport Co *(£200,000 on 13/2/1998) FL 14+8 FLC 1 FAC 1*
Wrexham *(£50,000 on 23/7/1999) FL 34+3/2 FLC 1*

PHILPOTT Lee
Born: Barnet, 21 February 1970
Height: 5'10" **Weight:** 12.9
Club Honours: Div 3 '91
After being a near ever-present in his first season at Hull, Lee was frustrated by injuries in 2001-02. He struggled with thigh and groin problems in the early weeks of the campaign, and then an achilles tendon injury kept him out of action until February. The highlight of his season was his opening goal in the 4-1

defeat of Mansfield in March. He was made available for transfer in the summer.

Peterborough U *(From trainee on 17/7/1986) FL 1+3 FAC 0+1 Others 0+2*
Cambridge U *(Free on 31/5/1989) FL 118+16/17 FLC 10/1 FAC 19/3 Others 15/2*
Leicester C *(£350,000 on 24/11/1992) F/PL 57+18/3 FLC 2+1 FAC 6+2 Others 4+1*
Blackpool *(£75,000 on 22/3/1996) FL 51+20/5 FLC 5/1 FAC 4 Others 0+2*
Lincoln C *(Free on 21/7/1998) FL 33+14/3 FLC 1+2 FAC 1+2 Others 1+3*
Hull C *(Free on 10/8/2000) FL 45+8/2 FLC 1 FAC 2 Others 0+2*

PILKINGTON Kevin William
Born: Hitchin, 8 March 1974
Height: 6'1" **Weight:** 13.0
Club Honours: FAYC '92
International Honours: E: Sch
Kevin took over as Mansfield Town's regular 'keeper on the departure of Bobby Mimms in the summer of 2001. On the whole he showed himself to be a very good shot stopper, and despite the occasional blunder he produced some sterling performances throughout the League programme.

Manchester U *(From trainee on 6/7/1992) PL 4+2 FLC 1 FAC 1*
Rochdale *(Loaned on 2/2/1996) FL 6*
Rotherham U *(Loaned on 22/1/1997) FL 17*
Port Vale *(Free on 1/7/1998) FL 23 FLC 1 FAC 1 (Freed during 2000 close season)*
Wigan Ath *(Free, via a trial at Macclesfield, on 31/8/2000) FL 0 (Freed on 4/9/2000)*
Mansfield T *(Free from Aberystwyth T on 8/9/2000) FL 47 FLC 1 FAC 3 Others 1*

PINAULT Thomas
Born: Grasse, France, 4 December 1981
Height: 5'10" **Weight:** 11.1
The 2001-02 season saw this popular youngster make the grade as a professional at Colchester. A classy midfielder, competitive in the tackle and astute with his passing, he formed a youthful partnership with Kem Izzet and deservedly won a number of 'Man-of-the-Match' awards for some fine displays at Layer Road. The only disappointing aspect of his campaign was his failure to score a goal, despite countless shots from long range.

Colchester U *(Free from AS Cannes, France on 5/7/1999) FL 41+10/1 FLC 2+1 FAC 2 Others 2*

Matt Piper (second left)

PIPER Matthew (Matt) James
Born: Leicester, 29 September 1981
Height: 6'1" **Weight:** 13.5
This exciting young Leicester City striker was loaned to Mansfield Town last November and did well in an extended period at Field Mill. Playing mostly on the right-hand side, he impressed with some tricky ball skills and on his return to Filbert Street he made his debut for the Foxes against Leeds. Subsequently given an extended run by Dave Bassett, he emerged as a shining light in a season of darkness. His first goal for City proved to be the last one ever scored at Filbert Street and his selection as the club's 'Young Player of the Season' was well merited.
Leicester C (From trainee on 12/8/1999) PL 14+2/1 FLC 1 FAC 0+1
Mansfield T (Loaned on 20/11/2001) FL 8/1

PIRES Robert
Born: Reims, France, 29 October 1973
Height: 6'1" **Weight:** 12.4
Club Honours: PL '02
International Honours: France: 54 (UEFA '00)
This quick and skilful wide midfield player was in scintillating form for Arsenal last term, scoring 13 goals and setting up numerous chances for his colleagues. Unfortunately he missed the exciting climax to the Gunners' season and also the World Cup finals after suffering cruciate ligament damage to his left knee. He has since undergone surgery and will be hoping to return to action shortly after the beginning of the 2002-03 season. He was voted as the Football Writers' Association 'Footballer of the Year' for 2001-02 and also won a place in the PFA's Premiership team.
Arsenal (£6,000,000 from Olympique Marseille, France, ex Metz, on 24/7/2000) PL 56+5/13 FAC 9+2/4 Others 23+1/4

PISTONE Alessandro (Sandro)
Born: Milan, Italy, 27 July 1975
Height: 5'11" **Weight:** 12.1
International Honours: Italy: U21 (UEFA-U21 '96)
This pacy defender once again saw a large chunk of his campaign wiped out through injury in 2001-02. However, either side of his two-month absence with knee ligament damage he displayed his class and versatility. A left back who is right-footed, Sandro kicked off the season at centre half. He also played with equal comfort at right back, and scored his first goal for Everton with a stunning right-

foot drive against Bolton on Easter Monday. A good reader of the game, he possesses pace, crispness in the tackle and a willingness to get forward to support his team's attacking momentum.
Newcastle U (£4,300,000 from Inter Milan, Italy, ex Vicenza, Solbiatese, Crevalcore, on 31/7/1997) PL 45+1/1 FLC 1+1 FAC 8 Others 7
Everton (£3,000,000 on 12/7/2000) PL 30+2/1 FLC 1 FAC 1

PITCHER Geoffrey (Geoff)
Born: Sutton, 15 August 1975
Height: 5'7" **Weight:** 11.6
After joining Brighton during the 2001 close season, Geoff made his debut when coming on as a substitute in the goalless draw at Tranmere, when he nearly stole the points late on with a tremendous shot from outside of the area. His first and only goal was a close range side foot in the home victory over Wycombe in the LDV Vans Trophy. He spent much of the second half of the campaign on an extended loan with Conference side Woking but will be aiming to feature more regularly for the Seagulls in 2002-03.
Millwall (From trainee on 18/3/1993)
Watford (Signed on 13/7/1994) FL 4+9/2 FLC 1+1 FAC 2 (Free to Kingstonian during 1996 close season)
Brighton & Hove A (£55,000 on 20/6/2001) FL 2+8 Others 3/1

PITT Courtney Leon
Born: Westminster, 17 December 1981
Height: 5'7" **Weight:** 10.12
Courtney jumped at the chance of first-team football for Portsmouth last term and his speedy wing play excited Pompey fans. Very useful in the middle too, his best position is out wide. The only disappointment of an excellent first campaign was a return of just two goals. He generally operated down the left hand side but can switch effectively if required.
Chelsea (From trainee on 4/7/2000)
Portsmouth (£200,000 on 5/7/2001) FL 29+10/3 FLC 1 FAC 1

PLATT Clive Linton
Born: Wolverhampton, 27 October 1977
Height: 6'4" **Weight:** 13.0
Rochdale's lofty striker was again an automatic choice in the line-up in 2001-02, missing just a handful of games through suspension. Superb at holding the ball up for his colleagues and excellent in the air, he occasionally featured as a lone striker in early season games. He later struck up new and productive partnerships with both Kevin

Townson and Lee McEvilly, although he never scored quite the number of goals that his efforts deserved. His value to the side was emphasised when the one game he missed through injury ended in Dale's defeat in the play-offs.
Walsall (From trainee on 25/7/1996) FL 18+14/4 FLC 1+2/1 FAC 0+1 Others 1+6
Rochdale (£70,000 + on 5/8/1999) FL 111+16/24 FLC 4/1 FAC 7/2 Others 7/1

PLUMMER Christopher (Chris) Scott
Born: Isleworth, 12 October 1976
Height: 6'3" **Weight:** 12.9
International Honours: E: U21-5; Yth
This tall central defender missed the start of the 2001-02 season for Queen's Park Rangers whilst recovering from a long-term injury. He eventually returned to the side in November, but then broke his ankle in only his second game back and was on the sidelines for the remainder of the campaign.
Queens Park R (From trainee on 1/7/1994) F/PL 54+6/2 FLC 2 FAC 7

PLUMMER Dwayne Jermaine
Born: Bristol, 12 May 1978
Height: 5'9" **Weight:** 11.8
2001-02 proved to be a frustrating season for this Bristol Rovers midfielder. He picked up a knee injury in a pre-season friendly match which ruled him out for the opening three months and it was not until October that he returned to action. His strong tackling and accurate distribution were valuable assets but sfurther injuries kept him out of much of the closing stages of the campaign.
Bristol C (From trainee on 5/9/1995) FL 1+13 FLC 1+2 Others 0+1 (Free to Stevenage Borough on 18/11/1998)
Bristol Rov (£15,000 + from Chesham U on 7/9/2000) FL 29+6/1 FLC 0+2 FAC 4 Others 3

POLLET Ludovic (Ludo)
Born: Valenciennes, France, 18 June 1970
Height: 6'1" **Weight:** 12.11
This popular Frenchman was a victim of the fact that Wolves had three of the best central defenders in the First Division last term. When he did come on in the second half against Barnsley he produced a truly outstanding 45 minutes. Suspensions to both Paul Butler and Joleon Lescott gave him a four-match run in mid-season, but he did not quite do enough to break up the successful partnership. When he came in for Butler against Norwich in March he made a vital saving tackle, only to go off shortly afterwards with a head injury.

Wolverhampton W (Free from Le Havre, France on 10/9/1999) FL 72+4/7 FLC 1 FAC 5

POLLITT Michael (Mike) Francis

Born: Farnworth, 29 February 1972
Height: 6'4" **Weight:** 14.0
This big goalkeeper returned to Rotherham after a one-year absence in the summer of 2001, but initially found the step up from Third to First Division football a little demanding. However, once he had adjusted he again proved to be one of the best 'keepers outside the Premiership. He pulled off a string of vital saves, none better than an injury-time penalty save against Stockport which ensured a vital win. Mike was the Millers' only ever present in 2001-02, playing in all 50 League and cup games.
Manchester U (From trainee on 1/7/1990)
Bury (Free on 10/7/1991)
Lincoln C (Free on 1/12/1992) FL 57 FLC 5 FAC 2 Others 4
Darlington (Free on 11/8/1994) FL 55 FLC 4 FAC 3 Others 5
Notts Co (£75,000 on 14/11/1995) FL 10 Others 2
Oldham Ath (Loaned on 29/8/1997) FL 16
Gillingham (Loaned on 12/12/1997) FL 6
Brentford (Loaned on 22/1/1998) FL 5
Sunderland (£75,000 on 23/2/1998)
Rotherham U (Free on 14/7/1998) FL 92 FLC 4 FAC 7 Others 5
Chesterfield (Free on 15/6/2000) FL 46 FLC 3 FAC 1 Others 4
Rotherham U (£75,000 on 29/5/2001) FL 46 FLC 2 FAC 2

POOLE Kevin

Born: Bromsgrove, 21 July 1963
Height: 5'10" **Weight:** 12.11
Club Honours: FLC '97
Although released by Birmingham at the end of the 2000-01 campaign, Kevin was re-signed on a short-term basis to help cover a goalkeeping crisis and made a solitary appearance in the Worthington Cup tie at Bristol Rovers when on-loan 'keeper Alan Kelly was unavailable. In October he joined Bolton Wanderers where he went on to make three appearances as cover for Jussi Jaaskelainen.
Aston Villa (From apprentice on 26/6/1981) FL 28 FLC 2 FAC 1 Others 1
Northampton T (Loaned on 8/11/1984) FL 3
Middlesbrough (Signed on 27/8/1987) FL 34 FLC 4 FAC 2 Others 2
Hartlepool U (Loaned on 27/3/1991) FL 12
Leicester C (£40,000 on 30/7/1991) F/PL 163 FLC 10 FAC 8 Others 12

Birmingham C (Free on 4/8/1997) FL 56 FLC 7 FAC 2 Others 2
Bolton W (Free on 25/10/2001) PL 3

POOM Mart

Born: Tallin, Estonia, 3 February 1972
Height: 6'4" **Weight:** 13.6
International Honours: Estonia: 80
This experienced goalkeeper had a rather frustrating time with injuries last term and had two lengthy spells on the sidelines as a result. A commanding 'keeper who is capable of some tremendous saves, he was unable to save the Rams from relegation. He continued to represent Estonia during the campaign.
Portsmouth (£200,000 from FC Wil, Switzerland, ex Flora, on 4/8/1994) FL 4 FLC 3 (Signed by Tallin SC, Estonia on 9/5/1996)
Derby Co (£500,000 on 26/3/1997) PL 130+3 FLC 10 FAC 8

POPOVIC Anthony (Tony)

Born: Australia, 4 July 1973
Height: 6'4" **Weight:** 13.11
International Honours: Australia: 39; U23; Yth
With Fan Zhiyi absent on World Cup duty with China, Crystal Palace manager Steve Bruce stepped in to sign this experienced left-sided central defender last August. Once a work permit had been sorted out he settled in well, and one of his best performances came in the 5-0 win over Grimsby Town when he contributed two goals.
Crystal Palace (£600,000 from Sanfrecce Hiroshima, Japan on 24/8/2001) FL 20/2 FLC 3 FAC 1

PORTER Christopher (Chris) Ian

Born: Sunderland, 10 November 1979
Height: 6'2" **Weight:** 13.2
This young goalkeeper spent the summer of 2001 with Icelandic Second Division club Leiftur but his spell was cut short after he suffered a broken arm. He returned to England and after a brief trial with Chesterfield signed non-contract forms for Darlington where he had been on loan from Sunderland two seasons previously without making an appearance. He finally made his Football League debut against Swansea City in March and kept a clean sheet before going on to play in the final seven matches of the season.
Sunderland (From trainee on 1/8/1998. Freed on 8/3/2000)
Darlington (Free from Leiftur, Iceland on 21/3/2002) FL 7

POTTER Graham Stephen

Born: Solihull, 20 May 1975
Height: 6'1" **Weight:** 11.12
International Honours: E: U21-1; Yth
Graham was a regular in the York City team in 2001-02 and was at his best in a wide left-sided midfield role. He scored in the FA Cup ties against Colchester United and Reading and also netted the winner in a vital victory over Oxford late in the season. He has good pace and delivers excellent crosses, particularly from free kicks and corners.
Birmingham C (From trainee on 1/7/1992) FL 23+2/2 FAC 1 Others 6
Wycombe W (Loaned on 17/9/1993) FL 2+1 FLC 1 Others 1
Stoke C (£75,000 on 20/12/1993) FL 41+4/1 FLC 3+1 FAC 4 Others 5
Southampton (£250,000 + on 23/7/1996) FL 2+6 FLC 1+1
West Bromwich A (£300,000 + on 14/2/1997) FL 31+12 FLC 0+3 FAC 1
Northampton T (Loaned on 24/10/1997) FL 4 Others 1
Reading (Loaned on 2/12/1999) FL 4 Others 1
York C (Free on 7/7/2000) FL 71+4/4 FLC 3 FAC 10/3

POUTON Alan

Born: Newcastle, 1 February 1977
Height: 6'0" **Weight:** 12.8
This tenacious midfielder had his best season since joining Grimsby Town in 2001-02, beginning to show the full potential that had been promised since his arrival at Blundell Park. Alan is an uncompromising tackler who works hard and is strong on the ball. He was absent in mid season due to a broken ankle but returned from injury at a vital time to help the Mariners to safety. A highlight was his hat-trick in the 6-2 victory over Wimbledon in March when he scored twice from the penalty spot.
Oxford U (From trainee at Newcastle U on 7/11/1995)
York C (Free on 8/12/1995) FL 79+11/7 FLC 5+1 FAC 5/1 Others 2
Grimsby T (£150,000 on 5/8/1999) FL 70+21/7 FLC 10+2 FAC 1+1

POWELL Christopher (Chris) George Robin

Born: Lambeth, 8 September 1969
Height: 5'10" **Weight:** 11.7
Club Honours: Div 1 '00
International Honours: E: 5
Chris added two more international caps to his collection last season, thus making him Charlton's most capped England player with five appearances. A skilful and unflappable left-sided defender, he can

play as an orthodox left back or as a left wing back, and loves to push forward down the flank and deliver crosses from the by-line, or cut inside. He scored his first Premiership goal for the Addicks at White Hart Lane earning Charlton a 1-0 win over Tottenham. As ever Chris was a model of consistency throughout the campaign.
Crystal Palace (From trainee on 24/12/1987) FL 2+1 FLC 0+1 Others 0+1
Aldershot (Loaned on 11/1/1990) FL 11
Southend U (Free on 30/8/1990) FL 246+2/3 FLC 13 FAC 8 Others 21
Derby Co (£750,000 on 31/1/1996) F/PL 89+2/1 FLC 5 FAC 5/1
Charlton Ath (£825,000 on 1/7/1998) P/FL 144+3/1 FLC 7+1 FAC 8/1

POWELL Darren David
Born: Hammersmith, 10 March 1976
Height: 6'3" **Weight:** 13.2
Club Honours: Div 3 '99
Darren showed a return to the form he had displayed in his early days at Brentford last term. A tall, commanding centre half he formed a tremendous partnership alongside Ivar Ingimarsson in the heart of the defence and the two went from strength to strength as the campaign progressed. He suffered a hamstring injury against Chesterfield in March which saw him miss four games, but returned to head the vital equaliser against Huddersfield in the play-off semi-final.
Brentford (£15,000 from Hampton on 27/7/1998) FL 128/6 FLC 7 FAC 4 Others 10+1/2

POWELL Darryl Anthony
Born: Lambeth, 15 November 1971
Height: 6'0" **Weight:** 12.10
International Honours: Jamaica: 17
Darryl was again a regular in the line-up for Derby County last term, but had the misfortune to suffer a knee injury in February and this kept him out of action until the end of the season. He is an enthusiastic central midfield player who grafts hard in the middle of the park.
Portsmouth (From trainee on 22/12/1988) FL 83+49/16 FLC 11+3/3 FAC 10 Others 9+5/4
Derby Co (£750,000 on 27/7/1995) F/PL 187+20/10 FLC 11+1/1 FAC 7+1

POWELL Paul
Born: Wallingford, 30 June 1978
Height: 5'8" **Weight:** 11.6
Paul was again one of Oxford's most skilful players but he had an up-and-down season in 2001-02. He took a while to win over Mark Wright but became a

virtual ever present under Ian Atkins. Although best used as a left winger, he also featured at left back and as a wing back. Quick and tricky, he showed the ability to beat defenders and also contributed four valuable goals.
Oxford U (From trainee on 2/7/1996) FL 139+25/15 FLC 6+2 FAC 8+1/3 Others 2+3/3

POWER Graeme Richard
Born: Harrow, 7 March 1977
Height: 5'10" **Weight:** 10.10
International Honours: E: Yth; Sch
Graeme was a near ever-present in the left-back berth for Exeter City last term and he grew in confidence as the season progressed. He formed a very useful partnership with Andy Roscoe on the left flank and was more involved in attacking moves than had previously been the case. His only goal of the campaign was a delightfully struck effort that proved to be the winner at Shrewsbury. Unfortunately his season came to a premature end when he suffered a fractured leg in a freak accident against Lincoln in March.
Queens Park R (From trainee on 11/4/1995)
Bristol Rov (Free on 15/7/1996) FL 25+1 FAC 1 Others 1+2
Exeter C (Free on 6/8/1998) FL 138+3/2 FLC 3 FAC 10 Others 6

POYET Gustavo (Gus) Augusto
Born: Montevideo, Uruguay, 15 November 1967
Height: 6'2" **Weight:** 13.0
Club Honours: ECWC '98; ESC '98; FAC '00; CS '00
International Honours: Uruguay: 31; Yth
Undoubtedly Glenn Hoddle's best buy last year, Gus was an immediate hit at Spurs. Gutsy, passionate and committed in midfield, he seemed to be enjoying every minute of his move to White Hart Lane. His determination is best demonstrated in his tireless running on and off the ball and he is always quick to find and create space. An attack-minded player, he netted a creditable tally of 14 goals during the campaign.
Chelsea (Free from Real Zaragoza, Spain, ex River Plate, Grenoble, Bella Vista, on 15/7/1997) PL 79+26/36 FLC 3+1/2 FAC 8+1/7 Others 20+7/4
Tottenham H (£2,250,000 on 10/7/2001) PL 32+2/10 FLC 5/1 FAC 4/3

PREECE Andrew (Andy) Paul
Born: Evesham, 27 March 1967
Height: 6'1" **Weight:** 12.0
Bury's player-manager struggled with a

back injury during the early months of las season and required an operation in October to rectify the problem. He returned to action in December, mainly appearing on the subs' bench. His four League starts all came towards the end of the campaign when he hoped, in vain, that his experience would help to pull the Shakers away from trouble at the foot of Division Two. Still as enthusiastic as ever on and off the pitch, Andy's mobility is not quite what it used to be and at 35 it cannot be too long before he contemplates concentrating solely on management.
Northampton T (Free from Evesham on 31/8/1988) FL 0+1 FLC 0+1 Others 0+1 (Free to Worcester C during 1989 close season)
Wrexham (Free on 22/3/1990) FL 44+7/7 FLC 5+1/1 FAC 1/2 Others 5/1
Stockport Co (£10,000 on 18/12/1991) FL 89+8/42 FLC 2+1 FAC 7/3 Others 12+2/9
Crystal Palace (£350,000 on 23/6/1994) PL 17+3/4 FLC 4+2/1 FAC 2+3
Blackpool (£200,000 on 5/7/1995) FL 114+12/35 FLC 4/2 FAC 2+3/2 Others 12/2
Bury (Free on 6/7/1998) FL 66+59/18 FLC 6+4 FAC 2+2 Others 2

PREECE David William
Born: Bridgnorth, 28 May, 1963
Height: 5'6" **Weight:** 11.6
Club Honours: FLC '88
International Honours: E: B-3
David came to Torquay as assistant manager, and it was something of a surprise when a slump in the team's form led him to dust off his boots and return to action at the age of 38. Playing either in the centre or on the left of midfield, he showed surprising stamina combined with common sense simple but effective passing.
Walsall (From apprentice on 22/7/1980) FL 107+4/5 FLC 18/5 FAC 6/1 Others 1
Luton T (£150,000 on 6/12/1984) FL 328+8/21 FLC 23/3 FAC 27/2 Others 8+1/1
Derby Co (Free on 11/8/1995) FL 10+3/1 FLC 2
Birmingham C (Loaned on 24/11/1995) FL 6 Others 1
Swindon T (Loaned on 21/3/1996) FL 7/1
Cambridge U (Free on 6/9/1996) FL 40+35/2 FLC 3+2 Others 2+2
Torquay U (Free on 17/10/2001) FL 4+2

PRENDERVILLE Barry
Born: Dublin, 16 October 1976
Height: 6'0" **Weight:** 12.8
Barry was unfortunate to find himself transfer-listed by Oldham Athletic last December, just six months after having agreed a new one-year contract. A former

Coventry City youngster, he is a utility player who was deployed at right-back at Boundary Park. He made ten first-team appearances last term before the surprise departure of Andy Ritchie. New boss Mick Wadsworth informed the player that he was not in his plans and in January he returned to Ireland to sign for Shelbourne.
Coventry C (Signed from Cherry Orchard on 5/8/1994)
Hibernian (Loaned on 11/9/1998) SL 13/2
Ayr U (Free on 7/6/1999) SL 3+2 SLC 1 Freed on 20/10/1999)
Oldham Ath (Free from St Patricks on 7/9/2000) FL 16+5 FLC 3+1 FAC 1

PRESSMAN Kevin Paul
Born: Fareham, 6 November 1967
Height: 6'1" **Weight:** 15.5
International Honours: E: B-3; U21-1; Yth; Sch
This one-club stalwart had a fine season for Sheffield Wednesday in 2001-02, during which he reached the landmark figure of 400 appearances for the Owls.

He remained a good shot stopper and a fine reader of the game, while his trusty left-foot clearance saved his team on numerous occasions.
Sheffield Wed (From apprentice on 7/11/1985) F/PL 342+3 FLC 44 FAC 18 Others 4
Stoke C (Loaned on 10/3/1992) FL 4 Others 2

PRICE Jason Jeffrey
Born: Pontypridd, 12 April 1977
Height: 6'2" **Weight:** 11.5
Club Honours: Div 3 '00
International Honours: W: U21-7
Jason joined Brentford in the 2001 close season on a three-month trial and played in the first 18 games of the season, initially on the right-hand side of midfield and then at right back. In November he moved north, signing for Tranmere Rovers where he was used as a striker. Remarkably he scored seven goals in his first six games, and his final tally of 11 included doubles in the FA Cup tie against Brigg Town and the Second Division match with Cambridge United.

Swansea C (Free from Aberaman on 17/7/1995) FL 133+11/17 FLC 10/1 FAC 4/1 Others 4+1/1
Brentford (Free on 6/8/2001) FL 15/1 FLC 1 Others 1
Tranmere Rov (Free on 8/11/2001) FL 20+4/7 FAC 5/4

PRICE Michael David
Born: Wrexham, 29 April 1982
Height: 5'8" **Weight:** 11.4
International Honours: W: U21-6
Michael became Hull's 11th signing of the 2001 close season when he signed a three-month contract for the Tigers and did well enough to be offered a two-year deal. However, the attacking left back found first-team opportunities limited and took advantage of a trial at Bournemouth in January 2002, then a loan spell with local Unibond League team North Ferriby United, before being made available for transfer in the summer.
Everton (From trainee on 17/1/2000)
Hull C (Free on 7/7/2001) FL 0+1 FLC 0+1 Others 0+1

Michael Price (right)

PRIEST Christopher (Chris)
Born: Leigh, 18 October 1973
Height: 5'9" **Weight:** 10.10
Chris missed the first three matches of the 2001-02 season with an ankle injury, but then remained a regular in the Macclesfield side until the closing weeks of the campaign. He found it difficult to find a consistent level of form early on, but in the latter part of the season he gave some very competent performances. While he only scored one goal it proved to be an important strike, earning Macc a last-minute draw against high-flying Plymouth Argyle. He is a hard-working central midfielder who operates from box to box.
Everton (From trainee on 1/6/1992)
Chester C (Loaned on 9/9/1994) FL 11/1 Others 2
Chester C (Free on 11/1/1995) FL 151+5/25 FLC 6 FAC 6/1 Others 6
Macclesfield T (Free on 5/7/1999) FL 80+4/9 FLC 2/1 FAC 6 Others 2

PRIMUS Linvoy Stephen
Born: Forest Gate, 14 September 1973
Height: 6'0" **Weight:** 14.0
A powerful and accomplished Portsmouth defender, Linvoy weighed in with three goals last season. A clean tackler with good pace, he is strong on the ball, dominant in the air, dangerous from corners and plays with a confident and relaxed style. He missed two months with a patella tendonitis problem at the beginning of 2001-02 and hamstring trouble also restricted his appearances.
Charlton Ath (From trainee on 14/8/1992) FL 4 FLC 0+1 Others 0+1
Barnet (Free on 18/7/1994) FL 127/7 FLC 9+1 FAC 8/1 Others 4
Reading (£400,000 on 29/7/1997) FL 94+1/1 FLC 9 FAC 6 Others 4
Portsmouth (Free on 4/8/2000) FL 44+1/2 FLC 3 FAC 1

PRINGLE Ulf Martin
Born: Sweden, 18 November 1970
Height: 6'2" **Weight:** 12.3
Club Honours: Div 1 '00
International Honours: Sweden: 2; B-1
Having finally recovered from his injury problems, Martin joined Grimsby Town on loan as newly appointed player-manager Paul Groves sought to strengthen his firepower. However, he had the misfortune to suffer a badly broken leg during his second game for the Mariners, at home to Stockport, and it is feared that this may end his playing career. When fully fit Martin is a quick striker who uses his pace to create chances for his colleagues.

Charlton Ath (£800,000 from Benfica, Portugal on 8/1/1999) P/FL 28+30/8 FLC 2 FAC 3
Grimsby T (Loaned on 21/2/2002) FL 2

PRIOR Spencer Justin
Born: Southend, 22 April 1971
Height: 6'3" **Weight:** 13.4
Club Honours: FLC '97
Spencer was signed by Cardiff City during the 2001 close season with a view to providing some experience in the defensive line. He missed the opening games after fracturing a cheekbone in a training accident and then struggled to find his best form. A rock-solid, tough-tackling defender, he eventually came good and shone in the 14-match unbeaten run that took City through to the Second Division play-offs.
Southend U (From trainee on 22/5/1989) FL 135/3 FLC 9 FAC 5 Others 7/1
Norwich C (£200,000 on 24/6/1993) P/FL 67+7/1 FLC 10+1/1 FAC 0+2 Others 2
Leicester C (£600,000 on 17/8/1996) PL 61+3 FLC 7 FAC 5 Others 2
Derby Co (£700,000 on 22/8/1998) PL 48+6/1 FLC 5 FAC 4
Manchester C (£500,000 + on 23/3/2000) P/FL 27+3/4 FLC 4 FAC 2+1
Cardiff C (£650,000 on 3/7/2001) FL 33+4/2 FAC 3 Others 2

PRITCHARD David (Dave) Michael
Born: Wolverhampton, 27 May 1972
Height: 5'8" **Weight:** 11.12
International Honours: W: B-1
Dave finally returned to action for Bristol Rovers for the opening match of the 2001-02 season against Torquay having been out of action with knee problems since January 2000. It was an emotional return for the tough tackling midfielder when he came off the subs' bench late in the match but he made only one start, at Carlisle in October, before deciding to retire at the age of 29. He subsequently assisted boss Garry Thompson by managing the reserve team for a few games.
West Bromwich A (From trainee on 5/7/1990) FL 1+4 (Free to Telford during 1992 close season)
Bristol Rov (£15,000 on 25/2/1994) FL 157+6/1 FLC 11 FAC 12+1 Others 10+1

PROCTOR Michael Anthony
Born: Sunderland, 3 October 1980
Height: 5'11" **Weight:** 12.7
Michael spent the whole of the 2001-02 season on loan at York City to gain further experience of senior football. He

finished the campaign as the Minstermen's top scorer with 14 League goals including a brace in the 3-1 success at Lincoln. He impressed throughout with his skill on the ball and liveliness up front.
Sunderland (From trainee on 29/10/1997) FLC 0+1
Halifax T (Loaned on 14/3/2001) FL 11+1/4
York C (Loaned on 9/8/2001) FL 40+1/14 FLC 1 FAC 6 Others 1

PROKAS Richard
Born: Penrith, 22 January 1976
Height: 5'9" **Weight:** 11.4
Club Honours: Div 3 '95; AMC '97
Richard made a handful of appearances for Cambridge United last term but found himself out of favour following a change in management. He is a tough-tackling midfielder who adds bite in the centre of the park to any team.
Carlisle U (From trainee on 18/7/1994) FL 184+20/3 FLC 11+1 FAC 10 Others 19+5/1
Cambridge U (Signed on 22/3/2001) FL 9+3/1 Others 0+2

PROSINECKI Robert
Born: Schwenningen, Germany, 12 November 1969
Height: 5'11" **Weight:** 11.12
International Honours: Croatia: 49; Yugoslavia: 15
Robert was superb in midfield for Portsmouth last season, producing a series of master-class displays that brought the fans flocking to Fratton Park. Deadly at free kicks, his jinking runs tormented opposition defenders and were a treat to see at First Division level. A final tally of nine goals helped keep the South Coast club away from relegation, and he managed a brilliant hat-trick in the 4-4 draw with Barnsley. He was deservedly selected for a place in the PFA's First Division team for the season.
Portsmouth (Free from Standard Liege, Belgium, ex Red Star Belgrade, Real Madrid, Oviedo, Barcelona, Seville, Croatia Zagreb, on 17/8/2001) FL 30+3/9 FLC 1 FAC 1

PROUDLOCK Adam David
Born: Telford, 9 May 1981
Height: 6'0" **Weight:** 13.0
International Honours: E: Yth
This big striker did not register a goal for Wolves until the 2001-02 season was several matches old, but came good with a fine hat-trick at Bradford. However, hopes that this would be the turning point proved groundless and struggled to keep his place, before suffering an injury in December. His next first-team action was on loan at Nottingham Forest but he

played only three times before being recalled to Molineux because of injuries and he appeared in the final match of the regular season.
Wolverhampton W (From trainee on 15/7/1999) FL 40+14/11 FLC 4+1/2 FAC 2/1 Others 0+1
Clyde (Loaned on 1/8/2000) SL 4/4 SLC 2/1
Nottingham F (Loaned on 19/3/2002) FL 3

PRUTTON David Thomas
Born: Hull, 12 September 1981
Height: 6'1" **Weight:** 11.10
International Honours: E: U21-14; Yth
This talented youngster continued to make excellent progress last season both at club and international level, establishing himself in the England U21 team. He was a near ever present for Nottingham Forest, playing mainly as a right-sided midfielder, but when Jermaine Jenas moved to Newcastle he was used more in a central role where he looked equally effective. He also proved his versatility by playing one game as a centre back where he did not look out of place.
Nottingham F (From trainee on 1/10/1998) FL 117+2/6 FLC 6 FAC 4

PULLEN James
Born: Chelmsford, 18 March 1982
Height: 6'2" **Weight:** 14.2
This young 'keeper joined Blackpool on loan at the start of the 2001-02 campaign and eventually stayed all season. He made his League debut at Oldham at the beginning of September and then retained his place in the side until the FA Cup game against Newport County, after which he returned to the bench. The experience he gained at Blackpool will serve him well on his return to Ipswich.
Ipswich T (Free from Heybridge Swifts on 1/10/1999)
Blackpool (Loaned on 10/8/2001) FL 16 FLC 1 FAC 1 Others 1

PURCHES Stephen (Steve) Robert
Born: Ilford, 14 January 1980
Height: 5'11" **Weight:** 12.0
Operating as a full back on either flank, Steve was a steady performer for Bournemouth throughout the 2001-02 season. He finally grabbed his first senior goal in the 3-1 win over Stoke City and also scored against Northampton. A brave player with a big heart, relegation hit him hard and he will be determined to succeed during 2002-03.
West Ham U (From trainee on 6/7/1998)
Bournemouth (Free on 4/7/2000) FL 66+9/2 FLC 3 FAC 4

PURSE Darren John
Born: Stepney, 14 February 1977
Height: 6'2" **Weight:** 12.8
International Honours: E: U21-2
Darren continued to blossom in the heart of the Birmingham City defence last season. He was hard in the tackle and dominant in the air. After turning down a new contract Steve Bruce removed the captaincy from him in February but Darren responded by scoring the opening goal in a 3-2 win over Watford the next day. His form lifted when it was agreed negotiations would be put off until the summer.
Leyton Orient (From trainee on 22/2/1994) FL 48+7/3 FLC 2 FAC 1 Others 7+1/2
Oxford U (£100,000 on 23/7/1996) FL 52+7/5 FLC 10+1/2 FAC 2
Birmingham C (£800,000 on 17/2/1998) FL 115+24/8 FLC 16+2/2 FAC 3 Others 6+1

David Prutton

Darren Purse

Q

QUAILEY Brian Sullivan
Born: Leicester, 21 March 1978
Height: 6'1" **Weight:** 13.11
International Honours: St Kitts & Nevis: U23
A goal return of eight from just 15 League starts proved Brian's worth as Scunthorpe's reserve striker last season. Very quick and direct, if a little inconsistent, he did a job whenever called upon and his best run saw him score in three successive matches in February and March before a hamstring injury limited him to just two substitute appearances in the closing weeks.

West Bromwich A (Signed from Nuneaton Borough on 22/9/1997) FL 1+6 FLC 0+1
Exeter C (Loaned on 23/12/1998) FL 8+4/2 Others 2/1
Blackpool (Loaned on 3/12/1999) FL 1 Others 1
Scunthorpe U (Free on 3/2/2000) FL 39+32/16 FLC 0+1 FAC 0+2 Others 0+3/1

QUASHIE Nigel Francis
Born: Peckham, 20 July 1978
Height: 6'0" **Weight:** 12.4
International Honours: E: B-1; U21-4; Yth
A very talented midfield player with Portsmouth, Nigel's vision, tackling and first touch made him one of the better players in a very dismal season last term. He still needs to find greater consistency, but his ability was unquestionable on the left or in the centre of midfield. However, he also accumulated too many yellow cards and this is an area of his game that he needs to improve.
Queens Park R (From trainee on 1/8/1995) P/FL 50+7/3 FLC 0+1 FAC 4/2
Nottingham F (£2,500,000 on 24/8/1998) P/FL 37+7/2 FLC 7/1 FAC 1+1
Portsmouth (£200,000 + on 7/8/2000) FL 62+4/7 FLC 5 FAC 2

QUEUDRUE Franck
Born: Paris, France, 27 August 1978
Height: 6'0" **Weight:** 12.4
This talented left-sided defender broke into the Middlesbrough line-up soon after the start of last season and retained his place for the remainder of the campaign. He immediately endeared himself to the Riverside faithful by scoring on his home debut against Sunderland and in May signed a permanent contract for Boro'.
Middlesbrough (Loaned from RC Lens, France, ex Meaux, on 12/10/2001) PL 28/2 FAC 6

QUINN Alan
Born: Dublin, 13 June 1979
Height: 5'9" **Weight:** 11.7
International Honours: RoI: U21-8; Yth (UEFA-U18 '98)
Despite having a good long run in the side, interrupted only by a brief injury, Alan had a fairly flat season at Sheffield Wednesday last term. He brought bags of drive, skill and enthusiasm to his left-sided midfield role, but never quite reached his full potential.
Sheffield Wed (Signed from Cherry Orchard on 6/12/1997) P/FL 91+5/7 FLC 11/1 FAC 5+1

QUINN Barry Scott
Born: Dublin, 9 May 1979
Height: 6'0" **Weight:** 12.2
International Honours: RoI: 3; U21-17; Yth (UEFA-U18 '98)
The young Coventry City midfield player was a first-team regular at full back during 2000-01, but struggled to win a place in the line-up last term. The form of Marc Edworthy kept him on the sidelines and he played only two games as a midfield ball-winner during the first half of the season. He regained his full-back spot in January and put in some solid performances, but was rested for the run-in after a few below par performances.
Coventry C (From trainee on 28/11/1996) P/FL 54+11 FLC 4 FAC 2+1

QUINN Stephen James
Born: Coventry, 15 December 1974
Height: 6'1" **Weight:** 12.10

Franck Queudrue

International Honours: NI: 25; B-2; U21-1; Yth

For the second season running James hardly figured in West Bromwich Albion manager Gary Megson's plans at the Hawthorns. He started only one League game although he was named as a substitute around a dozen times early on in the campaign. In November he joined Notts County on loan to help out in an injury crisis and although the team was going through a bad spell he still netted three goals in six games. He subsequently had another loan spell at Bristol Rovers in March, impressing on his debut against Exeter and helping the club steer away from any relegation worries. He was released by Albion in the summer and was reported to have signed for Dutch club Willem II.

Birmingham C (Trainee) FL 1+3
Blackpool (£25,000 on 5/7/1993) FL 128+23/37 FLC 10+4/5 FAC 5+1/4 Others 7+4/2

Stockport Co (Loaned on 4/3/1994) FL 0+1
West Bromwich A (£500,000 on 20/2/1998) FL 85+29/9 FLC 3+4/1 FAC 2
Notts Co (Loaned on 30/11/2001) FL 6/3 Others 1
Bristol Rov (Loaned on 22/3/2002) FL 6/1

QUINN Niall John
Born: Dublin, 6 October 1966
Height: 6'4" **Weight:** 15.10
Club Honours: FLC '87; Div 1 '99
International Honours: RoI: 91; B-1; U23-1; U21-6; Yth; Sch

This giant striker has near legendary status at Sunderland and although he was not expected to play a major role last term, suffering as he is from a persistent back injury, his contributions were crucial. He netted a number of vital goals, but perhaps his most important strike, however, was the only goal of a victory at fellow strugglers Derby in February. Niall also created a new scoring record for his country when he bagged his 21st

international goal for the Republic of Ireland against Cyprus in October. In April he received a PFA Merit Award and he was awarded a benefit match by the club, with all proceeds being donated to children's charities – a typically generous gesture from an outstanding individual.

Arsenal (From juniors on 30/11/1983) FL 59+8/14 FLC 14+2/4 FAC 8+2/2 Others 0+1
Manchester C (£800,000 on 21/3/1990) F/PL 183+20/66 FLC 20+2/7 FAC 13+3/4 Others 3/1
Sunderland (£1,300,000 on 17/8/1996) F/PL 168+27/61 FLC 5+1/4 FAC 8+1/2 Others 2/2

QUINN Robert (Rob) John
Born: Sidcup, 8 November 1976
Height: 5'11" **Weight:** 11.2
Club Honours: Div 3 '99
International Honours: RoI: U21-5; B-1

Rob was a fringe player for Oxford United in 2001-02 and was only used sparingly at first-team level, mostly as a replacement for injured colleagues. A defensive midfield player who is more of a destroyer than a creator, he added some steel in the centre of the park and produced some effective displays when called upon.

Crystal Palace (From trainee on 11/3/1995) F/PL 18+5/1 FLC 2+1/1 Others 2+1
Brentford (£40,000 on 9/7/1998) FL 98+11/2 FLC 9+1 FAC 6/2 Others 7/1
Oxford U (£75,000 on 12/1/2001) FL 23+6/2

QUINN Wayne Richard
Born: Truro, 19 November 1976
Height: 5'10" **Weight:** 11.12
International Honours: E: B-1; U21-2; Yth

Wayne is a left sided player able to function at either full back or left midfield, which is where he began the 2001-02 season with a series of sound displays in the Inter Toto Cup matches. After missing out on the start of the Premiership he was back in the side for the Worthington Cup tie at home to Brentford in September, but suffered a groin strain, which sidelined him for several weeks. He returned for the reserves in November but tore a muscle in his right thigh, and by the time he had recovered he found his rivals had established themselves ahead of him, so he appeared only one further time, as a substitute in the FA Cup tie at Peterborough.

Sheffield U (From trainee on 6/12/1994) FL 131+8/5 FLC 14+1 FAC 12+1 Others 2
Newcastle U (£750,000 + on 1/1/2001) PL 14+1 FLC 1 FAC 0+1 Others 6/1

Niall Quinn

R

RACHUBKA Paul Stephen
Born: California, USA, 21 May 1981
Height: 6'1" **Weight:** 13.5
International Honours: E: Yth
Goalkeeper Paul joined Oldham Athletic
on a three-month loan from Manchester
United last November. He went on to
feature regularly for Athletic, impressing
with his command of the penalty box,
assured handling and positive distribution.
The club agreed a fee to make the move
permanent, but the California-born player
opted to wait until the summer to assess
options. He was reported to have signed
for Premiership outfit Charlton Athletic in
May.
*Manchester U (From trainee on 7/7/1999) PL
1 FLC 0+1 Others 0+1*
*Oldham Ath (Loaned on 23/11/2001) FL 16
Others 1*

RADZINSKI Tomasz
Born: Poznan, Poland, 14 December 1973
Height: 5'9" **Weight:** 11.7
International Honours: Canada: 15
A small but pacy striker, Tomasz arrived at
Goodison last summer and was seen as
the perfect foil for the more powerful
Kevin Campbell or Duncan Ferguson. Pre-
season performances were bright, until a
hamstring injury got his new career off to
the worst possible start. He didn't make
his full debut until the end of September,
but while he celebrated the occasion with
a goal against West Ham he was always
playing catch-up with his fitness. He did
score a spectacular solo strike against
Southampton at Goodison Park, but
further injuries disrupted his campaign.
*Everton (£4,500,000 from Anderlecht,
Belgium, ex Germinal Ekeren, on 20/8/2001)
PL 23+4/6 FAC 2/1*

RAE Alexander (Alex) Scott
Born: Glasgow, 30 September 1969
Height: 5'9" **Weight:** 11.12
Club Honours: Div 1 '99
International Honours: S: B-4; U21-8
This combative midfielder made his only
appearance for Sunderland last term in a
1-0 win against Blackburn in September
before joining Wolverhampton Wanderers
in September. Once he had regained full
fitness he was always selected for the
team and established himself as the most
consistent player at Molineux. He would
control the ball, beat a player and pass to
a colleague and make football look an
easy game to play, and even scored with

Tomasz Radzinski

Fabrizio Ravanelli

an overhead kick against Burnley. He also had a knack of getting vital goals, including a last-minute effort for the winner at Millwall. It was no surprise when Wolves' supporters chose him as their 'Player of the Season'.

Falkirk *(Free from Bishopbriggs on 15/6/1987) SL 71+12/20 SLC 5/1 SC 2+1*
Millwall *(£100,000 on 20/8/1990) FL 205+13/63 FLC 13+2/1 FAC 13/6 Others 10/1*
Sunderland *(£750,000 on 14/6/1996) F/PL 90+24/12 FLC 12+1/3 FAC 7 Others 0+2*
Wolverhampton W *(£1,200,000 on 21/9/2001) FL 31+5/7 FLC 1 Others 2*

RAMMELL Andrew (Andy)
Victor
Born: Nuneaton, 10 February 1967
Height: 6'1" **Weight:** 13.12
Wycombe's top scorer had a good first half of the season in 2001-02, notching up 12 goals by the start of December. The highlights included two well-taken goals at Hayes in the FA Cup and a second-half double in the stunning 5-3 win against leaders Brentford. He suffered a major injury blow in the Christmas fixture at Queen's Park Rangers, needing an operation on a damaged ankle, but recovered well to start the final seven games of the campaign, scoring one more goal. The Chairboys relied heavily on his power game, especially his ability to hold up and lay off the ball, not to mention his aerial threat.

Manchester U *(£40,000 from Atherstone U on 26/9/1989)*
Barnsley *(£100,000 on 14/9/1990) FL 149+36/44 FLC 11+3/1 FAC 12+1/4 Others 8/1*
Southend U *(Signed on 22/2/1996) FL 50+19/13 FLC 3+3/1 FAC 2+1 Others 1*
Walsall *(Free on 15/7/1998) FL 60+9/23 FLC 3/1 FAC 3+1 Others 5/1*
Wycombe W *(£75,000 on 7/9/2000) FL 52+1/21 FLC 3/1 FAC 11/4 Others 3*

RAMSAY Scott Alan
Born: Hastings, 16 October 1980
Height: 6'0" **Weight:** 13.0
Scott was placed on the Brighton transfer list at the start of the 2001-02 season and went on loan to Yeovil before returning when Peter Taylor took over as manager. He made just one first-team appearance during the campaign, coming on as a substitute in the LDV Vans Trophy game at Cambridge, before moving on to Conference club Dover Athletic. He is a young striker who is strong on the ball and works hard.

Brighton & Hove A *(From trainee on 29/6/1999) FL 10+25/2 FAC 0+2 Others 2+1*

RANKIN Isaiah (Izzy)
Born: Edmonton, 22 May 1978
Height: 5'10" **Weight:** 11.6
Although Izzy scored a last minute winner against Nottingham Forest on his first appearance for Barnsley last season, his opportunities in the senior team grew less frequent as the season went by and he had trials with Luton and Bournemouth. He is a pacy striker who finished the campaign as leading scorer for the Reds' reserves.

Arsenal *(From trainee on 12/9/1995) PL 0+1*
Colchester U *(Loaned on 25/9/1997) FL 10+1/5 Others 1*
Bradford C *(£1,300,000 on 14/8/1998) P/FL 15+22/4 FLC 2/1 FAC 0+2 Others 1+1/1*
Birmingham C *(Loaned on 19/1/2000) FL 11+2/4*
Bolton W *(Loaned on 11/8/2000) FL 9+7/2 FLC 2*
Barnsley *(£350,000 on 19/1/2001) FL 8+10/2 FLC 0+1*

RANKINE Simon Mark
Born: Doncaster, 30 September 1969
Height: 5'9" **Weight:** 12.11
Club Honours: Div 2 '00
A poor start to the 2001-02 season saw Preston's combative midfielder dropped after only two league games, and a sciatic injury then kept him out for a month. His return saw him influential in central midfield for the win at Birmingham, and he scored three times, including a goal in his 600th senior game against Barnsley. However a broken foot in January kept him out until towards the end of March. Never the quickest of players, Mark excels as the central pivot around whom the more mobile players can go forward, while he is also very effective at closing down opponents.

Doncaster Rov *(From trainee on 4/7/1988) FL 160+4/20 FLC 8+1/1 FAC 8/2 Others 14/2*
Wolverhampton W *(£70,000 on 31/1/1992) FL 112+20/1 FLC 9+1 FAC 14+2 Others 7+2*
Preston NE *(£100,000 on 17/9/1996) FL 206+8/12 FLC 15+1/1 FAC 13/1 Others 6/1*

RAPLEY Kevin John
Born: Reading, 21 September 1977
Height: 5'9" **Weight:** 10.8
Club Honours: Div 3 '99
Kevin an excellent season with Colchester last term, beginning in fine style with five goals in the first seven League games. Although he took the rest of the season to double that tally, he established a potent strike force with Scott McGleish for the U's. One of his best performances came against Queen's Park Rangers in

March when he bagged two goals to help secure a vital win.

Brentford *(From trainee on 8/7/1996) FL 27+24/12 FLC 3+5/3 FAC 0+2 Others 1*
Southend U *(Loaned on 20/11/1998) FL 9/4*
Notts Co *(£50,000 on 23/2/1999) FL 21+31/5 FLC 0+3 FAC 1+1/1 Others 1*
Exeter C *(Loaned on 1/11/2000) FL 6+1 FAC 1 Others 1*
Scunthorpe U *(Loaned on 17/3/2001) FL 1+4*
Colchester U *(Free on 3/8/2001) FL 26+9/9 FLC 2 FAC 2 Others 1*

RAVANELLI Fabrizio
Born: Perugia, Italy, 11 December 1968
Height: 6'1" **Weight:** 13.6
International Honours: Italy: 22
This experienced striker got off to a great start for Derby County last term, netting in the first two Premiership games of the campaign. He proved to be an inspirational signing, finishing the season as joint-top scorer with nine goals, but he missed the closing matches through injury as the Rams slipped into the First Division.

Middlesbrough *(£7,000,000 from Juventus, Italy, ex Perugia, Avellino, Casertana, on 15/8/1996) F/PL 35/17 FLC 8/9 FAC 7/6 (£5,300,000 to Marseilles, France on 3/10/1997)*
Derby Co *(Free from Lazio, Italy on 3/8/2001) PL 30+1/9 FLC 2/1 FAC 1/1*

RAVEN Paul Duncan
Born: Salisbury, 28 July 1970
Height: 6'1" **Weight:** 12.12
International Honours: E: Sch
Paul had a disappointing season for Grimsby Town in 2001-02. Out of the side through injury at the start of the campaign, he then failed to win a regular place in the Mariners' line-up despite their defensive problems. He is an effective central defender who never let the side down on the occasions he was called upon.

Doncaster Rov *(From juniors on 6/6/1988) FL 52/4 FLC 2 FAC 5 Others 2*
West Bromwich A *(£100,000 on 23/3/1989) FL 249+10/15 FLC 20/2 FAC 10/3 Others 15/1*
Doncaster Rov *(Loaned on 27/11/1991) FL 7*
Rotherham U *(Loaned on 29/10/1998) FL 11/2*
Grimsby T *(Free on 13/7/2000) FL 15+9 FLC 2 FAC 0+1*

RAWLE Mark Anthony
Born: Leicester, 27 April 1979
Height: 5'11" **Weight:** 12.0
2001-02 proved to be an up and down season at Southend for Mark as he showed plenty promise, but ended up

Paul Read (foreground)

frustrated. Although a striker, he played many of his games in an unfamiliar wide-right position but still managed a tally of seven goals. A player with good ball skills and an eye for goal, he missed much of the second half of the campaign due to injury, only making his comeback in the final game.

Southend U *(£60,000 + from Boston U on 23/2/2001) FL 36+8/6 FLC 1 FAC 3+1/1 Others 2/1*

REA Simon
Born: Kenilworth, 20 September 1976
Height: 6'1" **Weight:** 13.2
Simon had a somewhat stop-start season at Peterborough last term due to injuries. A left-sided central defender who is very effective in the air, he is not afraid to put his head in where it hurts and shows good control on the ground.
Birmingham C *(From trainee on 27/1/1995) FL 0+1 Others 1+1*
Peterborough U *(Free on 24/8/1999) FL 73+7/4 FLC 3+1 FAC 8 Others 4/1*

READ Paul Colin
Born: Harlow, 25 September 1973
Height: 5'10" **Weight:** 12.11
International Honours: E: Sch
Paul was very much a second choice striker for Exeter City in the 2001-02 campaign, virtually all of his senior appearances coming from the subs' bench. He failed to get on the score sheet and was released by the club in the summer.
Arsenal *(From trainee on 11/10/1991)*
Leyton Orient *(Loaned on 10/3/1995) FL 11 Others 1*
Southend U *(Loaned on 6/10/1995) FL 3+1/1 Others 1*
Wycombe W *(£130,000 on 17/1/1997) FL 32+25/9 FLC 4/2 FAC 1+2/1 Others 1 (Freed during 1999 close season)*
Luton T *(Free from OFK Ostersunds, Sweden on 6/12/1999) Others 0+1 (Free to OFK Ostersund in January 2000)*
Exeter C *(Free on 10/11/2000) FL 13+13/1 FAC 0+1*

REBROV Sergei
Born: Donetsk, Ukraine, 3 June 1974
Height: 5'7" **Weight:** 11.1
International Honours: Ukraine: 51
2001-02 proved to be a season of mixed fortunes for this talented forward. Spurs boss Glenn Hoddle seemed reluctant to give him many opportunities and the season was rife with rumours of his impending departure. Sergei is a pacy, intelligent striker who needs good service, preferably on the ground to be most

productive in terms of goals scored.
Tottenham H *(£11,000,000 from Dynamo Kiev, Ukraine on 6/6/2000) PL 37+22/10 FLC 4+4/3 FAC 7+1/3*

REDDINGTON Stuart
Born: Lincoln, 21 February 1978
Height: 6'2" **Weight:** 13.6
After ending the previous campaign on loan with Mansfield, Stuart signed permanently for the Stags during the summer and began the 2001-02 campaign in excellent form. Although he lost his place to Adam Barrett for a while he returned in place of the injured Les Robinson and had a fine season at Field Mill. He is an effective central defender who prefers to play the ball out of defence but will use the 'big boot' when required.
Chelsea *(Signed from Lincoln U on 24/8/1999)*
Mansfield T *(£20,000 on 16/3/2001) FL 43+4/1 FLC 1 Others 1*

REDDY Michael
Born: Kilkenny City, Ireland, 24 March 1980
Height: 6'1" **Weight:** 11.7
International Honours: RoI: U21-8; Yth
Michael became the first example of Hull implementing their agreement with Sunderland that allows the younger Black Cats to gain senior experience with the Boothferry club when he joined the Tigers on loan in September. Mainly used from the bench, the striker recorded an amazing scoring rate of a goal in every 30 minutes he played. With his speed in and around the area taking the eye, he mostly played alongside Gary Alexander who he had partnered during his loan spell at Swindon. He later joined Barnsley on loan, but pulled a hamstring in his first training session and immediately returned to the Stadium of Light.
Sunderland *(£50,000 from Kilkenny C on 30/8/1999) PL 0+10/1 FLC 2+1/1 FAC 0+1*
Swindon T *(Loaned on 27/1/2001) FL 17+1/4 Others 1+1/1*
Hull C *(Loaned on 21/9/2001) FL 1+4/4*

REDFEARN Neil David
Born: Dewsbury, 20 June 1965
Height: 5'9" **Weight:** 13.0
Club Honours: Div 2 '91
Neil endured a frustrating season at Halifax Town last term when his presence on the field was often sorely missed. When selected he proved that he still has what it takes and scored a total of six goals. He took on the role of player-

manager towards the end of the campaign, but with the club due to play in the Conference in 2002-03 his future was uncertain at the time of writing.
Bolton W *(From Nottingham F juniors on 23/6/1982) FL 35/1 FLC 2 FAC 4*
Lincoln C *(£8,250 on 23/3/1984) FL 96+4/13 FLC 4 FAC 3/1 Others 7*
Doncaster Rov *(£17,500 on 22/8/1986) FL 46/14 FLC 2 FAC 3/1 Others 2*
Crystal Palace *(£100,000 on 31/7/1987) FL 57/10 FLC 6 FAC 1 Others 1*
Watford *(£150,000 on 21/11/1988) FL 22+2/3 FLC 1 FAC 6/3 Others 5/1*
Oldham Ath *(£150,000 on 12/11/1990) FL 56+6/16 FLC 3/1 FAC 7+1/3 Others 1*
Barnsley *(£150,000 on 5/9/1991) F/PL 289+3/71 FLC 21/6 FAC 20/6 Others 5*
Charlton Ath *(£1,000,000 on 1/7/1998) PL 29+1/3 FLC 2/1 FAC 1*
Bradford C *(£250,000 on 3/8/1999) PL 14+3/1 FLC 1+1 FAC 2*
Wigan Ath *(£112,500 on 17/3/2000) FL 18+4/7 FAC 1 Others 5*
Halifax T *(Free on 16/3/2001) FL 39+3/6 FLC 1 FAC 3 Others 1*

REDKNAPP Jamie Frank
Born: Barton on Sea, 25 June 1973
Height: 6'0" **Weight:** 12.10
Club Honours: FLC '95; ESC '01
International Honours: E: 17; B-1; U21-19; Yth; Sch
After three injury-plagued seasons at Anfield, Jamie continued to be troubled by calf and thigh problems last term and made nor further appearances after October. The talented midfield playmaker was out of contract in the summer and was reported to have signed a long-term contract for Tottenham Hotspur.
Bournemouth *(From trainee on 27/6/1990) FL 6+7 FLC 3 FAC 3 Others 2*
Liverpool *(£350,000 on 15/1/1991) F/PL 207+30/30 FLC 26+1/5 FAC 17+1/2 Others 20+6/4*
Tottenham H *(Free on 18/4/2002)*

REDMILE Matthew (Matt) Ian
Born: Nottingham, 12 November 1976
Height: 6'3" **Weight:** 14.10
Club Honours: Div 3 '98
Matt was a rock in the centre of defence for Shrewsbury last season when he showed excellent form from start to finish. He quickly formed an effective partnership with Mick Heathcote and missed only two games throughout. Strong in the air and comfortable on the ball, Matt's game showed a composure that was not evident in his first season at Gay Meadow.

Carl Regan (foreground)

*Notts Co (From trainee on 4/7/1995) FL
140+7/7 FLC 11 FAC 13/1 Others 4*
*Shrewsbury T (£30,000 on 3/11/2000) FL
68/5 FLC 1 FAC 1 Others 1*

REDMOND Stephen (Steve)
Born: Liverpool, 2 November 1967
Height: 5'11" **Weight:** 11.7
Club Honours: FAYC '86
International Honours: E: U21-14; Yth
Bury's assistant-manager is now very
much at the veteran stage of his career,
but his experience continued to prove
vital for the Shakers last term. He
featured as a sweeper in a very young
back five for much of the season before
suffering a hernia injury at Stoke in
February, and this kept him sidelined until
the summer.
*Manchester C (From apprentice on
3/12/1984) FL 231+4/7 FLC 24 FAC 17
Others 11*
*Oldham Ath (£300,000 on 10/7/1992) P/FL
195+10/4 FLC 20 FAC 10+2 Others 1+1*
*Bury (Free on 3/7/1998) FL 119+5/4 FLC 7
FAC 7 Others 4*

REED Adam Maurice
Born: Bishop Auckland, 18 February
1975
Height: 6'1" **Weight:** 12.0
Adam had a frustrating season for
Darlington last term he twice forced
his way into the team only for injury to
immediately rule him out again. He is
now a very experienced defender who is
strong in the air and reads the game well
and he can always be relied upon to
stand-in extremely capably.
*Darlington (From trainee on 16/7/1993) FL
45+7/1 FLC 1 FAC 1 Others 3*
Blackburn Rov (£200,000 on 9/8/1995)
Darlington (Loaned on 21/2/1997) FL 14
*Rochdale (Loaned on 5/12/1997) FL 10
Others 2/1*
*Darlington (Free on 17/7/1998) FL 80+13/2
FLC 6 FAC 6+1 Others 2+3*

REES Jason Mark
Born: Aberdare, 22 December 1969
Height: 5'5" **Weight:** 10.6
International Honours: W: 1; B-1; U21-
3; B-1; Yth; Sch
A combative and committed ball-winner,
Jason was a regular in the centre of
midfield for Torquay for much of last
season, but lost out in the later games to
players capable of more accurate
distribution. He was rather unfortunate to
be released in the summer.
*Luton T (From trainee on 1/7/1988) FL
59+23 FLC 3+2 FAC 2+1 Others 5+1/2*

*Mansfield T (Loaned on 23/12/1993) FL 15/1
Others 1*
*Portsmouth (Free on 18/7/1994) FL 30+13/3
FLC 2+1 FAC 0+1*
Exeter C (Loaned on 31/1/1997) FL 7
*Cambridge U (Free on 8/8/1997) FL 17+3
FLC 2 Others 1*
*Exeter C (Free on 29/7/1998) FL 86+1/5 FLC
4 FAC 8 Others 6 (Freed during 2000 close
season)*
*Torquay U (Free from Tiverton on
13/12/2000) FL 51+7/2 FLC 2 Others 1*

REEVES Alan
Born: Birkenhead, 19 November 1967
Height: 6'0" **Weight:** 12.0
Swindon's veteran central defender and
team captain experienced mixed fortunes
during the 2001-02 campaign. When fit
and available he continued to give his
usual battling performances always
willing to put himself into the thick of
the action and weighing in with a couple
of important goals against Wrexham and
Chesterfield. Unfortunately, he received
three red cards during the season. He is
the twin brother of Oldham striker David
Reeves.
Norwich C (Free from Heswall on 20/9/1988)
Gillingham (Loaned on 9/2/1989) FL 18
*Chester C (£10,000 on 18/8/1989) FL 31+9/2
FLC 1+1 FAC 3 Others 3*
*Rochdale (Free on 2/7/1991) FL 119+2/9 FLC
12/1 FAC 5 Others 5*
*Wimbledon (£300,000 on 6/9/1994) PL
52+5/4 FLC 2+2 FAC 8*
*Swindon T (Free on 23/6/1998) FL 132+4/8
FLC 8+1/2 FAC 4 Others 2*

REEVES David Edward
Born: Birkenhead, 19 November 1967
Height: 6'0" **Weight:** 12.6
Club Honours: Div 3 '95
David gave his all for Chesterfield in
2001-2, which is the least you'd expect,
but with time catching up on him, he
appeared less physically effective than in
the past. His hard work off the ball and
down the right flank was valuable, but in
December he moved on to Oldham
Athletic, initially on loan before a
permanent deal was struck. However, the
season quickly turned sour for the
experienced striker after he suffered a
freak eye injury in the warm-up at Bury in
March. He sustained a damaged retina
when a stray ball struck him in the face
and took no further part in the campaign.
David is the twin brother of Swindon's
Alan Reeves.
*Sheffield Wed (Free from Heswall on
6/8/1986) FL 8+9/2 FLC 1+1/1 FAC 1+1
Others 0+1*

*Scunthorpe U (Loaned on 17/12/1986) FL
3+1/2*
*Scunthorpe U (Loaned on 1/10/1987) FL
6/4*
*Burnley (Loaned on 20/11/1987) FL 16/8
Others 2/1*
*Bolton W (£80,000 on 17/8/1989) FL
111+23/29 FLC 14+1/1 FAC 8+5/5 Others
9+2/7*
*Notts Co (£80,000 on 25/3/1993) FL 9+4/2
FLC 1+1*
*Carlisle U (£121,000 on 1/10/1993) FL
127/48 FLC 9/5 FAC 9/4 Others 23/7*
*Preston NE (Signed on 9/10/1996) FL
45+2/12 FLC 3+1/3 FAC 2/3 Others 1*
*Chesterfield (Signed on 6/11/1997) FL
160+8/46 FLC 10+1/4 FAC 6+1/1 Others 10/5*
Oldham Ath (Free on 19/12/2001) FL 11+2/3

REEVES Martin Lee
Born: Birmingham, 7 September 1981
Height: 6'0" **Weight:** 11.12
This youngster prefers to play in midfield
but made his debut for Leicester City
from the bench as a striker for the closing
minutes of the Premiership fixture at
Southampton. He also appeared in the
latter stages of the win over Blackburn at
Easter before making his first Premiership
start at Sunderland. He will have
benefited from his involvement with the
senior squad and could be a surprise
package in 2002-03.
*Leicester C (From trainee on 1/11/2000) PL
1+4*

REGAN Carl Anthony
Born: Liverpool, 9 September 1980
Height: 6'0" **Weight:** 11.5
Club Honours: FAYC '98
International Honours: E: Yth
Carl was one of a number of Barnsley
players who had a stop-go season in
2001-02. He played a number of games
early on but a sending off against
Sheffield Wednesday in Nigel Spackman's
last match in charge and a disappointing
display against Manchester City brought
his first-team opportunities to an end. A
pacy right back, he was appointed
captain of the reserves.
Everton (From trainee on 19/1/1998)
*Barnsley (£20,000 on 15/6/2000) FL 31+6
FLC 5*

REID Andrew (Andy) Matthew
Born: Dublin, 29 July 1982
Height: 5'7" **Weight:** 11.12
International Honours: RoI: U21-7; Yth
(UEFA-U16 '98)
Andy made his debut for Nottingham
Forest as a striker in 2000-01, but last
term he played as a left winger where he

appeared more comfortable. An excellent crosser of the ball, he is a little reminiscent of former Forest star John Robertson in his style of play.
Nottingham F (From trainee on 16/8/1999) FL 28+15/2 FLC 1+1 FAC 1

REID Brian Robertson
Born: Paisley, 15 June 1970
Height: 6'2" **Weight:** 11.12
Club Honours: AMC '02
International Honours: S: U21-4
Brian had a rather frustrating time at Blackpool during the 2001-02 campaign as a series of niggling injuries restricted his appearances. When fully fit he is an effective left-sided central defender who is good in the air. He signed an extended contract for the Tangerines and will be looking to put his injury problems behind him in 2002-03.
Morton (Free from Renfrew Waverley on 27/7/1988) SL 57/1 SLC 2 SC 7 Others 2/1
Glasgow R (Signed on 25/3/1991) SL 5
Morton (Signed on 11/3/1996) SL 68/3 SLC 4 SC 3 Others 5
Burnley (Signed on 4/9/1998) FL 30+1/3 FAC 1 Others 1
Dunfermline Ath (Free on 7/7/1999) SL 23+4/3 SLC 2 SC 1 Others 1
Blackpool (Free on 6/10/2000) FL 55/2 FLC 1 FAC 5 Others 7/1

REID Paul Mark
Born: Carlisle, 18 February 1982
Height: 6'2" **Weight:** 12.4
International Honours: E: Yth
Although capped by England at U20 level during the 2001-02 campaign, Paul was unable to win a place in the Rangers first-team squad and in February he joined Preston North End on loan until the end of the season. He made just a single appearance from the subs' bench at Deepdale when he also managed to score. A talented young central defender he played with determination and looked particularly effective in the air.
Carlisle U (From trainee on 19/2/1999) FL 17+2 Others 3
Glasgow R (£200,000 on 1/7/2000)
Preston NE (Loaned on 29/1/2002) FL 0+1/1

REID Paul Robert
Born: Oldbury, 19 January 1968
Height: 5'9" **Weight:** 11.8
This left-sided midfielder and Bury captain endured something of a disappointing season in 2001-02. An accumulation of bookings led to suspension as early as October and he then lost the captaincy to Martyn Forrest. He subsequently found himself competing with young David

Borley for a place in the team. After picking up a groin injury in a reserve game he required a hernia operation and did not return until late January. He battled his way back into the side but at the end of the campaign he became a victim of the club's financial pruning and was released.
Leicester C (From apprentice on 9/1/1986) FL 140+22/21 FLC 13/4 FAC 5+1 Others 6+2
Bradford C (Loaned on 19/3/1992) FL 7
Bradford C (£25,000 on 27/7/1992) FL 80+2/15 FLC 3/2 FAC 3 Others 5/1
Huddersfield T (£70,000 on 20/5/1994) FL 70+7/6 FLC 9/1 FAC 5+1 Others 1
Oldham Ath (£100,000 on 27/3/1997) FL 93/6 FLC 4/1 FAC 8 Others 1
Bury (Free on 2/7/1999) FL 102+8/9 FLC 5/1 FAC 5+1 Others 5

REID Steven John
Born: Kingston, 10 March 1981
Height: 6'1" **Weight:** 12.4
Club Honours: Div 2 '01
International Honours: RoI: 7; U21-3; E: Yth;
Steven's consistent performances for Millwall over the past two seasons have made him one of the hottest properties outside the Premiership. He was a regular member of the Republic of Ireland squad and scored his first international goal against Russia. He is a tall elegant player who can appear either in midfield or up front. He has good skill and great pace and is a favourite at the Den. He has a stinging shot with which he has scored some excellent goals, none better than that against Norwich on the first day of the 2001-02 season.
Millwall (From trainee on 18/5/1998) FL 96+23/12 FLC 5+2 FAC 6 Others 10+1

REILLY Alan
Born: Dublin, 22 August 1980
Height: 5'11" **Weight:** 12.6
This young left winger never found himself in favour with the different management structures at Halifax Town during the 2001-02 season and just when he was finding his best form in the reserves he was sidelined with an injury. His first-team action was limited to just two appearances from the subs' bench in the home games against Oxford United and Leyton Orient.
Manchester C (From trainee on 23/9/1998)
Halifax T (Free on 3/12/1999) FL 30+15/2 FLC 1 Others 1+2

REO-COKER Nigel Shola Andre
Born: Thornton Heath, 14 May 1984
Height: 5'8" **Weight:** 10.5

A product of Wimbledon's U19 team, Nigel broke into the reserves at the end of last season playing in a central midfield role. Terry Burton then gave him a run out for the final quarter of an hour in the last game of the season at home to Barnsley. He will be looking to build on his senior experience in 2002-03.
Wimbledon (Trainee) FL 0+1

REPKA Tomas
Born: Zlin, Czechoslovakia, 2 January 1974
Height: 6'0" **Weight:** 12.7
International Honours: Czech Republic: 46
This central defender soon settled to the pace of the English game after joining West Ham last September. He is strong in the tackle and his fierce determination shone in victories over Chelsea and Manchester United. He has matured as a defender who is respected by opponents and fans alike. Technically sound, he brought a new dimension to the team, while his partnership with Christian Dailly developed in to one of the best in the Premiership.
West Ham U (£5,500,000 from Fiorentina, Italy, ex Banik Ostrava, Sparta Prague, on 14/9/2001) PL 3 FAC 3

REUSER Martijn Franciscus
Born: Amsterdam, Holland, 1 February 1975
Height: 5'9" **Weight:** 11.7
International Honours: Holland: 1; U21-12
Martijn was another player who was unable to really establish himself in the Ipswich Town side last term because of injury and the general lack of confidence that affected the whole team. A favourite with the fans, he is a good dead-ball kicker, can use either foot and can play as a midfield provider or an out-and-out striker. He is also a more than useful crosser of a ball.
Ipswich T (£1,000,000 + from Vitesse Arnhem, Holland, ex Ajax, on 23/3/2000) P/FL 33+25/9 FLC 4+4/2 FAC 3 Others 1+5/2

REVELL Alexander (Alex) David
Born: Cambridge, 7 July 1983
Height: 6'3" **Weight:** 12.0
Alex made good progress at Cambridge last season, featuring in over half the club's Second Division games, although he was mostly used from the subs' bench. A tall, pacy and impressive striker he contributed his first senior goals and will be looking to win a regular place in the starting line-up in 2002-03.
Cambridge U (From trainee on 21/4/2001) FL 9+19/2 FAC 0+2 Others 1+3

Claudio Reyna

REYNA Claudio
Born: Livingston, New Jersey, USA, 20 July 1973
Height: 5'8" **Weight:** 11.3
Club Honours: SPD '00; SC '99
International Honours: USA: 92
This industrious central midfielder joined Sunderland last December for a fee equal to the club record. He made an immediate impact at the Stadium of Light, scoring on his home debut against Everton, and went on to enjoy a season of roller-coaster emotions. After being stretchered off against Aston Villa on New Year's Day with an ankle injury, he returned to score two brilliant goals in a vital 2-1 win against Leicester. A dead-ball expert, Claudio was a member of the USA squad at the World Cup finals.
Glasgow R (£2,000,000 from VFL Wolfsburg, Germany, ex Virginia University, Beyer Leverkusen, on 31/3/1999) SL 57+6/9 SLC 2/1 SC 6+1 Others 25/1
Sunderland (£4,500,000 on 7/12/2001) PL 17/3

RHODES Benjamin (Ben)
Born: York, 2 May 1983
Height: 5'10" **Weight:** 11.12
Ben was a third-year trainee at York City last season and stepped up to make his debut in senior football when he came on as a substitute at Darlington in December. Although he is a promising young midfielder he was released in the summer.
York C (Trainee) FL 0+1

RICARD Cuesta **Hamilton**
Born: Colombia, 12 January 1974
Height: 6'2" **Weight:** 14.5
International Honours: Colombia: 29; U21
This enigmatic Middlesbrough striker never found himself as a regular in the first-team squad last term and failed to score a single goal. He moved on to join CSKA Sofia last March in search of regular action and helped his new club reach the final of the Bulgarian Cup where they were defeated by rivals Levski Sofia.
Middlesbrough (£2,000,000 + from Deportivo Cali, Colombia on 13/3/1998) P/FL 92+23/33 FLC 11+2/8 FAC 6/2

RICHARDS Dean Ivor
Born: Bradford, 9 June 1974
Height: 6'2" **Weight:** 13.5
International Honours: E: U21-4
Dean's anxiety to leave Southampton for a bigger club did not win him any friends at St Marys last term. However, he got his way in September when he was sold to Tottenham for a substantial fee, thus

linking up once more with his former boss Glenn Hoddle. The towering central defender added experience and aerial command to the back line. A player who loves to get forward and support the attack he scored twice for Spurs during the season.
Bradford C (From trainee on 10/7/1992) FL 82+4/4 FLC 7/1 FAC 4/1 Others 3+2
Wolverhampton W (£1,850,000 on 25/3/1995) FL 118+4/7 FLC 11 FAC 10/1 Others 2
Southampton (Free on 28/7/1999) PL 67/3 FLC 7/2 FAC 4+1/2
Tottenham H (£8,100,000 on 24/9/2001) PL 24/2 FAC 4

RICHARDS Justin
Born: West Bromwich, 16 October 1980
Height: 5'10" **Weight:** 11.0
Justin became something of a forgotten man at Bristol Rovers last term and managed just a single appearance from the subs' bench at Mansfield. The promising striker had a one-month loan spell at Newport County and also a brief trial at Swindon Town but will be hoping to see much more senior action in 2002-03.
West Bromwich A (From trainee on 8/1/1999) FL 0+1 FAC 0+1
Bristol Rov (£75,000 on 19/1/2001) FL 3+5 Others 0+1

RICHARDS Marc John
Born: Wolverhampton, 8 July 1982
Height: 6'0" **Weight:** 12.7
International Honours: E: Yth
This young Blackburn Rovers striker spent large periods of the 2001-02 campaign out on loan to further his footballing education. He joined Crewe Alexandra at the start of the season, and made five appearances, all but one from the subs' bench, scoring in the Worthington Cup tie at York. In October he joined Oldham Athletic where he often featured as a lone striker and although failing to score he impressed with some bustling performances. Finally in February he had a spell at Halifax Town, where his experience of a relegation dogfight will surely have done him no harm. He will be aiming to make a breakthrough at Ewood Park in the 2002-03 campaign.
Blackburn Rov (From trainee on 12/7/1999) FLC 1
Crewe Alex (Loaned on 10/8/2001) FL 1+3 FLC 0+1/1
Oldham Ath (Loaned on 12/10/2001) FL 3+2 Others 1/1
Halifax T (Loaned on 12/2/2002) FL 5

RICHARDS Tony Spencer
Born: Newham, 17 September 1973
Height: 5'11" **Weight:** 13.1
Tony never really got started at Southend United last season, suffering a series of injuries that restricted his appearances. Signed by manager David Webb during the close season, he scored twice against Halifax Town in a 4-1 victory in August before the injury set backs started. An old-fashioned striker, his build and style caused problems for defenders, something he hopes will happen more often in 2002-03.
West Ham U (From trainee on 14/8/1992. Free to Hong Kong R during 1993 close season)
Cambridge U (Signed from Sudbury T on 10/8/1995) FL 29+13/5 FLC 1 Others 3
Leyton Orient (£10,000 on 21/7/1997) FL 47+16/11 FLC 3+3/1 FAC 2/3 Others 5
Barnet (Free on 11/8/2000) FL 27+6/8 FLC 1/1 FAC 1/1 Others 1
Southend U (£36,000 on 24/7/2001) FL 9+8/2 FLC 0+1 FAC 0+1 Others 0+1

RICHARDSON Barry
Born: Wallsend, 5 August 1969
Height: 6'1" **Weight:** 12.8
This experienced and popular 'keeper began the 2001-02 season in the Conference with Doncaster Rovers before returning to Third Division action with Halifax as a replacement for the departed Lee Butler. He made a number of good saves but was occasionally caught out at set pieces.
Sunderland (From trainee on 20/5/1988)
Scunthorpe U (Free on 21/3/1989)
Scarborough (Free on 3/8/1989) FL 30 FLC 1 Others 1
Northampton T (Free, via trial at Stockport Co, on 10/9/1991) FL 96 FLC 4 FAC 5 Others 8
Preston NE (£20,000 on 25/7/1994) FL 20 FLC 2 FAC 3 Others 2
Lincoln C (£20,000 on 20/10/1995) FL 131 FLC 5 FAC 11 Others 3
Mansfield T (Loaned on 5/8/1999) FL 6 FLC 2 (Free to Doncaster Rov on 16/8/2000)
Halifax T (Free on 21/12/2001) FL 24

RICHARDSON Ian George
Born: Barking, 22 October 1970
Height: 5'10" **Weight:** 11.1
Club Honours: Div 3 '98
International Honours: E: SP-1
Notts County's own 'Captain Courageous' had another useful season at Meadow Lane in 2001-02. A left-sided central defender, he was always fast to cover back, while his prodigious leap regularly led to his scoring spectacular goals. He

was offered a new deal to extend his stay with the Magpies after a proposed move to Wimbledon fell through.
Birmingham C *(£60,000 from Dagenham & Redbridge on 23/8/1995)* FL 3+4 FLC 3+1 FAC 2 Others 1+2
Notts Co *(£200,000 on 19/1/1996)* FL 157+12/7 FLC 12 FAC 17/1 Others 7

RICHARDSON Jay Grant
Born: Bromley, 14 November 1979
Height: 5'9" **Weight:** 12.0
After being released by Chelsea at the end of the previous campaign, Jay signed for Exeter City during the 2001 close season. He stepped up to make his senior debut in the opening game of the campaign against Hull, when he came on from the subs' bench. Although mostly operating as a substitute he showed considerable promise in his first-team outings producing a series of composed displays in midfield for the Grecians. With a year left of his contract he will be hoping to win a regular place in the line-up in 2002-03.
Chelsea *(From trainee on 20/2/1998)*
Exeter C *(Free on 4/7/2001)* FL 5+13 Others 0+1

RICHARDSON Jonathan (Jon) Derek
Born: Nottingham, 29 August 1975
Height: 6'0" **Weight:** 12.6
Jon would be content with a place on the bench for Oxford United at the start of last season, playing only when others were injured or suspended. He featured more regularly when Ian Atkins came in as manager, but was mainly used at right back where he showed some good defensive skills and tried hard to get forward. He missed the last few games of the season through injury and was released in the summer.
Exeter C *(From trainee on 7/7/1994)* FL 242+5/8 FLC 11/3 FAC 15/1 Others 13
Oxford U *(Free on 8/8/2000)* FL 57+2/2 FLC 2 FAC 2 Others 1

RICHARDSON Leam Nathan
Born: Leeds, 19 November 1979
Height: 5'7" **Weight:** 11.4
This promising defender or midfielder had a somewhat disappointing campaign for Bolton last term when he featured at first-team level on just three occasions. He spent the latter stages of the season on loan at Notts County where he settled down at right back and went on to produce some fine performances.
Blackburn Rov *(From trainee on 31/12/1997)* FLC 1

Bolton W *(£50,000 on 13/7/2000)* P/FL 5+8 FLC 3+1 FAC 1
Notts Co *(Loaned on 9/11/2001)* FL 20+1 FAC 1

RICHARDSON Lee James
Born: Halifax, 12 March 1969
Height: 5'11" **Weight:** 11.0
Lee is at his best playing just behind the midfield, where his tenacity and ability to read a game provides a solid platform for team-mates. With the departure of manager Nicky Law from Chesterfield in the new year, Lee became assistant to new boss Dave Rushbury. This meant a starting slot on the bench, at best, but he was available to come on and calm things down if needed. The club will keep Lee on the playing and management staff for 2002-03.
Halifax T *(From trainee on 6/7/1987)* FL 43+13/2 FLC 4 FAC 4+2 Others 6
Watford *(£175,000 on 9/2/1989)* FL 40+1/1 FLC 1+1 FAC 1
Blackburn Rov *(£250,000 on 15/8/1990)* FL 50+12/3 FLC 1 Others 2+2
Aberdeen *(£152,000 on 16/9/1992)* SL 59+5/6 SLC 2/1 SC 8/2 Others 3/1
Oldham Ath *(£300,000 on 12/8/1994)* FL 82+6/21 FLC 6/2 FAC 2 Others 4
Stockport Co *(Loaned on 15/8/1997)* FL 4+2
Huddersfield T *(£65,000 on 24/10/1997)* FL 29+7/3 FAC 0+2
Bury *(Loaned on 27/8/1999)* FL 5/1
Livingston *(Free on 3/2/2000)* SL 6 SC 1
Chesterfield *(Free on 11/8/2000)* FL 43+1/1 FLC 2 FAC 2 Others 4

RICHARDSON Marcus Glenroy
Born: Reading, 31 August 1977
Height: 6'2" **Weight:** 13.2
Marcus started the 2001-02 season up front for Cambridge United but after a handful of appearances he moved on to join Torquay United, managed by ex-U's boss Roy McFarland. Strength, pace and willingness were his plusses, but a lack of ball control limited his success as the target man that the Gulls badly needed. After a period out of the starting line-up, he returned late in the season looking more the part, scoring three goals in his last four matches to fuel hopes that he can develop into a productive striker.
Cambridge U *(Free from Harrow Borough on 16/3/2001)* FL 7+9/2 FLC 1
Torquay U *(£5,000 on 18/9/2001)* FL 18+12/6 FAC 1 Others 0+1

RICHARDSON Nicholas (Nick) John
Born: Halifax, 11 April 1967
Height: 6'1" **Weight:** 12.6

Club Honours: Div 3 '93; WC '93
This hard-working and creative player brought plenty of midfield experience to the York City side last season. His best spell was in mid-term as he helped the club reach the fourth round of the FA Cup for the first time since 1985-86. He eventually lost his place in the closing weeks of the campaign and was released in May.
Halifax T *(Free from Emley on 15/11/1988)* FL 89+12/17 FLC 6+4/2 FAC 2+1/1 Others 6/1
Cardiff C *(£35,000 on 13/8/1992)* FL 106+5/13 FLC 4 FAC 6 Others 12+2/2
Wrexham *(Loaned on 21/10/1994)* FL 4/2
Chester C *(Loaned on 16/12/1994)* FL 6/1
Bury *(£22,500 on 8/8/1995)* FL 3+2 FLC 1
Chester C *(£40,000 on 7/9/1995)* FL 158+11/11 FLC 11/1 FAC 8/2 Others 5/1
York C *(Free on 16/2/2001)* FL 33+6/1 FAC 4+1/1

RICKERS Paul Steven
Born: Pontefract, 9 May 1975
Height: 5'10" **Weight:** 11.0
Oldham Athletic's longest-serving player, Paul is a product of the club's youth system. He was told he could leave the club on a free transfer in May 2002 after starting only one game since the arrival of Mick Wadsworth. Paul was recovering from a broken ankle at the time and may yet stay at Boundary Park if terms can be agreed. The versatile 27-year-old has played over 300 League and cup matches for the club in a number of defensive and midfield roles.
Oldham Ath *(From trainee on 16/7/1993)* FL 242+19/20 FLC 13/2 FAC 17+2 Others 5+2

RICKETTS Michael Barrington
Born: Birmingham, 4 December 1978
Height: 6'2" **Weight:** 11.12
International Honours: E: 1
Michael literally exploded on to the Premiership stage last term, scoring 11 goals by the beginning of December, and 12 in total. Whilst it is true that the goals, and his form, did dry up somewhat after Christmas, the brilliance of his first season as a Premiership striker cannot be ignored. He scored some fantastic goals, the most memorable being a wonderfully executed strike at Highbury in September and a screamer from the edge of the penalty box against Stockport in the Worthington Cup in January. He also went on to win his first England cap against Holland in February.
Walsall *(From trainee on 13/9/1996)* FL 31+45/14 FLC 2+4 FAC 2+2 Others 3+1/1
Bolton W *(£500,000 on 17/7/2000)* P/FL 50+26/31 FLC 0+4/3 FAC 3+3/3 Others 1+2/2

RICKETTS Rohan Anthony
Born: Clapham, 22 December 1982
Height: 5'9" **Weight:** 11.0
Club Honours: FAYC '01
International Honours: E: Yth
This young Arsenal midfield player has developed through the ranks at Highbury and featured in their successful youth team in recent seasons. He stepped up to make his senior debut when he came on from the subs' bench in the Worthington Cup tie against Manchester United.
Arsenal (From trainee on 8/9/2001) FLC 0+1

RICKETTS Samuel (Sam)
Derek
Born: Aylesbury, 11 October 1981
Height: 6'0" **Weight:** 11.12
Sam was another Oxford United player to feature more under Mark Wright than Ian Atkins in 2001-02. A promising youngster, he featured in a number of positions – full back, wing back, midfield and as a centre back – and tried hard in all of those. He scored his first senior goal when he arrived at the back post to hit the second against Southend. Sam is the son of show jumper Derek Ricketts and a nephew of former jockey Johnny Francome.
Oxford U (From trainee on 20/4/2000) FL 32+11/1 FLC 1 Others 2

RIDEOUT Paul David
Born: Bournemouth, 14 August 1964
Height: 5'11" **Weight:** 12.10
Club Honours: FAC '95; CS '95
International Honours: E: U21-5; Yth; Sch
Despite having a coaching career lined up in the USA, Paul opted for one more domestic season to help Tranmere's efforts towards promotion back to Division One. Buoyed by his goal-scoring feats of the previous term, he remained a versatile player, still able to operate as both a striker and in central or wide midfield, while his 19 years of experience gave much help and guidance to his more youthful colleagues. Paul picked up a series of niggling injuries, which prevented him having an extended first-team run, but he still netted five times. He has since moved on to his new job in Kansas.
Swindon T (From apprentice on 15/8/1981) FL 90+5/38 FLC 3/2 FAC 7/1
Aston Villa (£200,000 on 1/6/1983) FL 50+4/19 FLC 4+2/3 FAC 1+1 Others 1
(£400,000 to Bari, Italy on 1/7/1985)
Southampton (£430,000 on 5/7/1988) FL 68+7/19 FLC 13/2 FAC 5+2 Others 1
Swindon T (Loaned on 28/3/1991) FL 9/1
Notts Co (£250,000 on 16/9/1991) FL 9+2/3 FLC 2 FAC 1 Others 2

Glasgow R (£500,000 on 10/1/1992) SL 7+5/1 SLC 0+1 SC 1
Everton (£500,000 on 14/8/1992) PL 86+26/29 FLC 11+2/3 FAC 9+1/3 Others 5/1 (£250,000 to Huang Dong Vanguards, China on 16/4/1997)
Tranmere Rov (Free from Shengzhen, China on 14/7/2000) FL 42+4/6 FLC 5/2 FAC 8/4

RIDLER David (Dave) George
Born: Liverpool, 12 March 1976
Height: 6'1'' **Weight:** 12.2
Dave was a near ever-present for Macclesfield last term and apart from a short period when Steve Macauley arrived on loan, he was first choice to partner Darren Tinson in the centre of the defence. His disciplinary record was much improved, although this meant that he adopted a more cautious attitude in his play.
Wrexham (Free from Rockys on 3/7/1996) FL 104+12/1 FLC 5 FAC 10+2 Others 8+2/1
Macclesfield T (Free on 16/7/2001) FL 37+2 FLC 1 FAC 3+1 Others 1

RIDLEY Lee
Born: Scunthorpe, 5 December 1981
Height: 5'9" **Weight:** 11.2
The form of first-team left back Andy Dawson meant that Lee was restricted to just three starts for Scunthorpe United in 2001-02, the first coming in the Lion's Den at Millwall in the FA Cup third round. A tidy defender who never let his side down, he continued to make good progress in the reserves where he was switched to centre half for a few games. He was given a new one-year deal in the summer and will be hoping to get more first-team opportunities next term.
Scunthorpe U (From trainee on 3/7/2001) FL 3+3 FAC 1 Others 0+1

RIGGOTT Christopher (Chris)
Born: Derby, 1 September 1980
Height: 6'3" **Weight:** 12.2
International Honours: E: U21-9; Yth
Chris firmly established himself in the Derby County line-up last term and missed only one Premiership game all season. A big, powerful centre back who formed a useful partnership with Danny Higginbotham in the heart of the defence, but proved unable to prevent the Rams from sinking to relegation.
Derby Co (From trainee on 5/10/1998) PL 66+3/3 FLC 5/1 FAC 2/1

RIIHILAHTI Aki
Born: Helsinki, Finland, 9 September 1976
Height: 6'1" **Weight:** 12.6

International Honours: Finland: 31
Aki was a near ever present for Crystal Palace last season, only missing one League match during the campaign. A tall and skilful midfield player, one of the high points of his year was scoring with a brilliant 35-yard shot into the top corner against Wimbledon.
Crystal Palace (£200,000 from Valerenga, Norway, ex HJK Helsinki, on 22/3/2001) FL 54/6 FLC 2+1/1 FAC 1

RIISE Jon Arne
Born: Molde, Norway, 24 September 1980
Height: 6'1" **Weight:** 12.6
Club Honours: ESC '01; CS '01
International Honours: Norway: 15; U21-17; Yth
Jon Arne arrived at Anfield in the summer of 2001 as a squad player to provide cover on the left flank, but took advantage of Markus Babbel's long-term absence to establish himself at left back in the side. As a natural left footer, he provided more balance to the team's play and he was always willing to lend support to the attack. His tally of eight goals included a 30-yard rocket in the 3-1 home victory over Manchester United in November.
Liverpool (£3,770,000 from AS Monaco, France, ex Aalesund, on 26/7/2001) PL 34+4/7 FAC 2 Others 15+1/1

RILEY Paul Anthony
Born: Nottingham, 29 September 1982
Height: 5'9" **Weight:** 10.7
Paul made his senior debut for Notts County in the LDV Vans Trophy tie against Oldham last December and burst into a struggling team like a breath of fresh air with his exciting bursts down the left flank. But sadly no sooner had he started then he fell victim to an injury jinx, but battled back to fitness by the end of the season. It remains to be seen whether his permanent position will be at left back or in midfield.
Notts Co (From trainee on 4/12/2001) FL 3+3 Others 1

RIOCH Gregor (Greg) James
Born: Sutton Coldfield, 24 June 1975
Height: 5'11" **Weight:** 12.10
In his first full season at Shrewsbury Town Greg was involved in over 30 consecutive games until he lost his place through suspension. He returned to play an integral part in the run-in, principally occupying a full back role but moved into midfield as different formations were tried during games. He also possesses a bullet-like shot as was demonstrated when he

scored the first of his two goals at Torquay. He was surprisingly released in the summer.

Luton T *(From trainee on 19/7/1993)*
Barnet *(Loaned on 17/9/1993) FL 3 FLC 2 Others 1*
Peterborough U *(Free on 11/8/1995) FL 13+5 FLC 2 FAC 2+1 Others 2+1*
Hull C *(Free on 10/7/1996) FL 86+5/6 FLC 7/3 FAC 5/1 Others 3*
Macclesfield T *(Free on 5/7/1999) FL 58+1/6 FLC 2 FAC 2 Others 2*
Shrewsbury T *(Free on 22/3/2001) FL 46/2 FLC 1 FAC 1 Others 1*

RIPLEY Stuart Edward
Born: Middlesbrough, 20 November 1967
Height: 5'11" **Weight:** 13.0
Club Honours: PL '95
International Honours: E: 2; U21-8; Yth
Stuart managed just one full appearance for Southampton last term when he returned to the side in manager Gordon Strachan's first game against Ipswich in October. Unfortunately he was injured in that match and was then sidelined for almost three months with a knee problem. A reliable and capable winger when fit he was unable to break back into the side.

Middlesbrough *(From apprentice on 23/12/1985) FL 210+39/26 FLC 21+2/3 FAC 17+1/1 Others 20+1/1*
Bolton W *(Loaned on 18/2/1986) FL 5/1 Others 0+1*
Blackburn Rov *(£1,300,000 on 20/7/1992) PL 172+15/13 FLC 18 FAC 14/3 Others 8+1*
Southampton *(£1,500,000 on 10/7/1998) PL 36+17/1 FLC 4+1 FAC 2+1*
Barnsley *(Loaned on 7/11/2000) FL 8+2/1*
Sheffield Wed *(Loaned on 22/3/2001) FL 5+1/1*

RISBRIDGER Gareth John
Born: High Wycombe, 31 October 1981
Height: 5'10" **Weight:** 11.5
After joining Southend United during the summer of 2001, Gareth made his debut as a substitute in the opening game of last season, but failed to make another senior appearance. A tall and gangly midfielder, he performed admirably in the reserves, but was released in January and after a brief spell with Salisbury City he signed for Ryman League club Aylesbury United.

Southend U *(Free from Yeovil T on 4/7/2001) FL 0+1*

RITCHIE Paul Simon
Born: Kirkcaldy, 21 August 1975
Height: 5'11" **Weight:** 12.0
Club Honours: SC '98

International Honours: S: 6; B; U21-7; Sch
Paul's pelvic and groin problems from the previous season carried into the first half of 2001-02 campaign and it was only after a visit to a specialist that he was able to resume training. The experienced defender finally got back in the first team squad at the end of November but with competition for places fierce he made only two appearances in the starting line-up, both in the FA Cup.

Heart of Midlothian *(From Links U on 31/7/1992) SL 132+1/5 SLC 10+1 SC 11/3 Others 6*
Bolton W *(Free on 22/12/1999) FL 13+1 FLC 1 FAC 3+1 Others 2*
Glasgow R *(Free on 26/2/2000)*
Manchester C *(£500,000 on 22/8/2000) P/FL 11+9 FLC 3+1 FAC 3*

RIVERS Mark Alan
Born: Crewe, 26 November 1975
Height: 5'11" **Weight:** 11.2
Mark sustained a niggling knee injury during the pre-season and this kept him out of action for Norwich until early September and by his own admission he never really recovered his full fitness level all season. He can operate on the right flank or in a central striking role and his pace, particularly when running with the ball can unsettle the best of defenders. A regular goal-scorer throughout his career, he will be hoping to start afresh, fully fit, for the forthcoming season and build upon his excellent performance against Birmingham City in the play-off final.

Crewe Alex *(From trainee on 6/5/1994) FL 177+26/43 FLC 14+1/8 FAC 12/4 Others 6+3/3*
Norwich C *(£600,000 on 28/6/2001) FL 19+13/2 FAC 0+2 Others 3/1*

RIX Benjamin (Ben)
Born: Wolverhampton, 11 December 1982
Height: 5'10" **Weight:** 11.11
Ben is another talented youngster to develop through the academy scheme at Crewe. He made his debut as a substitute at Coventry and from then onwards became a regular member of the first-team squad. A stylish midfielder with a fine future ahead of him, he netted his first senior goal in the FA Cup tie against Sheffield Wednesday.

Crewe Alex *(From trainee on 6/2/2001) FL 6+15 FAC 1+3/1*

ROACH Neville
Born: Reading, 29 September 1978
Height: 5'10" **Weight:** 11.1

Neville spent the first three months of last season at Torquay. His lively turn of pace and work rate meant that he was always a threat to defences, often coming off the bench to add life to the attack. However his small stature and lack of goals led to his being released and he subsequently signed for Ryman League club Slough Town.

Reading *(From trainee on 10/5/1997) FL 5+11/1 FLC 1+4/1 FAC 0+1 Others 0+1*
Southend U *(£30,000 on 26/2/1999) FL 13+3/2 FLC 1+1 Others 0+1 (Freed during 2000 close season)*
Oldham Ath *(Free from Eastern Pride, Australia, via St Albans C, on 20/3/2001) FL 0+1*
Torquay U *(Free on 9/8/2001) FL 5+7/1 FLC 1+1*

ROBERT Laurent
Born: Saint-Benoit, France, 21 May 1975
Height: 5'9" **Weight:** 11.2
Laurent added an extra dimension to the Newcastle attack last term with his penetrating runs at pace and his explosive shooting. Playing wide on the left he provides an important balance to the team, and he delivers telling crosses at pace which have proved very difficult to defend against. He was a regular in the side throughout the season, and contributed his share of goals from both open play and set pieces, his free kicks against Manchester United and Southampton being outstanding examples of the latter.

Newcastle U *(£10,500,000 from Paris St Germain, France, ex Montpellier, Nancy, on 10/8/2001) PL 34+2/8 FLC 3/1 FAC 3/1*

ROBERTS Andrew (Andy) James
Born: Dartford, 20 March 1974
Height: 5'10" **Weight:** 13.0
Club Honours: FAYC '91
International Honours: E: U21-5
Andy made the starting line-up for the first 19 games for Wimbledon last season, but then fell out of favour, only playing occasionally for the reserves. He subsequently had a loan spell at Norwich to cover for suspensions and injuries, and slotted quietly and effectively into the central midfield area. He seldom gave the ball away and showed an eye for the long-range effort on goal. Out of contract at Wimbledon this summer he will be hoping to find a club for the new season.

Millwall *(From trainee on 29/10/1991) FL 132+6/5 FLC 12/2 FAC 7 Others 4/1*
Crystal Palace *(£2,520,000 on 29/7/1995) F/PL 106+2/2 FLC 7+1 FAC 8 Others 6/1*

Wimbledon (£1,200,000 + on 10/3/1998)
P/FL 92+9/6 FLC 12+1/1 FAC 3+2
Norwich C (Loaned on 28/1/2002) FL 4+1

ROBERTS Benjamin (Ben)
James
Born: Bishop Auckland, 22 June 1975
Height: 6'1" **Weight:** 13.0
International Honours: E: U21-1
Ben joined Reading as a loan goalkeeper
from Charlton Athletic when Marcus
Hahnemann was recalled by Fulham, and
kept a clean sheet for the first three of his
six appearances. He was a reliable stand-
in, playing with all the enthusiasm of a
youngster, frequently diving yards across
his goal line to make sure the ball was
going wide of the woodwork. His total of
appearances for the Royals would have
been more but for his aggravating a
shoulder injury in the warm-up at
Swindon, when he was replaced by Phil
Whitehead at short notice.
Middlesbrough (From trainee on 24/3/1993)
F/PL 15+1 FLC 2+1 FAC 6 Others 1
Hartlepool U (Loaned on 19/10/1995) FL 4
Others 1
Wycombe W (Loaned on 8/12/1995) FL 15
Bradford C (Loaned on 27/8/1996) FL 2
Millwall (Loaned on 12/2/1999) FL 11
Others 4
Luton T (Loaned on 24/2/2000) FL 14
Charlton Ath (Free on 19/7/2000)
Reading (Loaned on 17/1/2002) FL 6

ROBERTS Christian (Chris)
John
Born: Cardiff, 22 October 1979
Height: 5'10" **Weight:** 12.8
International Honours: W: U21-1; Yth
Chris was a virtual ever-present for
Exeter last season and finished as the
club's top scorer with 11 League goals.
However, he broke the hearts of the City
faithful by transferring to Bristol City just
prior to the deadline day in March.
Whilst a little raw, he showed good pace
during a handful of outings at Ashton
Gate but failed to register a goal for his
new club. He is a promising striker with
a good scoring record to date, who is
always willing to take on opposition
defenders.
Cardiff C (From trainee on 8/10/1997) FL
6+17/3 FLC 2 FAC 2+3 Others 0+2
Exeter C (Free on 24/7/2000) FL 67+12/18
FLC 2+1 FAC 2+1 Others 2
Bristol C (Signed on 26/3/2002) FL 4

ROBERTS Gareth Wyn
Born: Wrexham, 6 February 1978
Height: 5'7" **Weight:** 12.6
Club Honours: FAYC '96

International Honours: W: 4; B-1; U21-
10
Gareth turned in another season of
reliable and steady performances for
Tranmere last term. He was equally
comfortable at left back or in a wing-back
role, and developed into a strong tackler
who never admits that he is beaten.
Always fully committed to the cause, his
calm unruffled, and solid defensive play
contributed much to Rovers' promising
but ultimately unsuccessful attempt to
reach the Division Two play-offs, and also
began to establish himself at international
level for Wales.
Liverpool (From trainee on 22/5/1996) .
£50,000 to Panionios, Greece on 15/1/1999)
Tranmere Rov (Free on 5/8/1999) FL
114+2/3 FLC 15 FAC 10+1

ROBERTS Iwan Wyn
Born: Bangor, 26 June 1968
Height: 6'3" **Weight:** 14.2
International Honours: W: 15; B-1; Yth;
Sch
Appointed as Norwich City's captain for
the 2001-02 season, Iwan finished the
campaign as the club's top scorer for the
fourth season in a row, ending with City's
goal in the First Division play-off final
against Birmingham. His final goals tally
would have been much higher if it hadn't
have been for an injury that forced him to
miss 15 games. His experience and ability
to hold the ball up have long been central
to the Canaries' preferred method of
playing and those attributes were
definitely missed when he was
unavailable. Iwan continued to figure
regularly in Mark Hughes' Welsh squads
during the season.
Watford (From trainee on 4/7/1988) FL
40+23/9 FLC 6+2/3 FAC 1+6 Others 5
Huddersfield T (£275,000 on 2/8/1990) FL
141+1/50 FLC 13+1/6 FAC 12/4 Others 14/8
Leicester C (£100,000 on 25/11/1993) P/FL
92+8/41 FLC 5/1 FAC 5/2 Others 1
Wolverhampton W (£1,300,000 + on
15/7/1996) FL 24+9/12 FLC 2 FAC 0+1
Others 2
Norwich C (£900,000 on 9/7/1997) FL
186+8/69 FLC 14+3/10 FAC 3/2 Others 0+3/1

ROBERTS Jason Andre Davis
Born: Park Royal, 25 January 1978
Height: 5'11" **Weight:** 12.7
International Honours: Grenada: 6
After injuring himself in pre-season
training, Jason spent the first half of the
2001-02 campaign recovering from a
fractured foot. He returned to the West
Bromwich Albion line-up in December,
looking sharp and aggressive with his eye

on goal! He quickly developed a fine
understanding with his new strike-partner
Danny Dichio and went on to score some
fine goals. However, after a series of
superb performances he broke the same
bone in his right foot in the game at
Preston in late February and this brought
his season to a premature end.
Wolverhampton W (£250,000 from Hayes
on 12/9/1997)
Torquay U (Loaned on 19/12/1997) FL
13+1/6 Others 1
Bristol C (Loaned on 26/3/1998) FL 1+2/1
Bristol Rov (£250,000 on 7/8/1998) FL
73+5/38 FLC 6/3 FAC 6/7 Others 3
West Bromwich A (£2,000,000 on
27/7/2000) FL 44+13/21 FLC 3+1/2 FAC 4
Others 2/1

ROBERTS Neil Wyn
Born: Wrexham, 7 April 1978
Height: 5'10" **Weight:** 11.0
International Honours: W: 1; B-1; U21-
2; Yth
Neil drifted in and out of the Wigan
Athletic side last season and didn't really
figure in the plans of new manager Paul
Jewell. Although not a prolific scorer, he
impressed with his high work-rate, an
ability to hold the ball up and a
willingness to probe hard for openings.
He netted twice in a rare start at
Cambridge, the first a delightful lob over
the keeper. He joined Hull City on loan in
January as cover for the suspended Gary
Alexander but failed to register a goal. He
finished the campaign on something of a
high as top scorer for the Latics' reserve
team and coming off the bench to score
twice in the final match at Colchester. Neil
is the older brother of Wrexham central
defender Steve Roberts.
Wrexham (From trainee on 3/7/1996) FL
58+17/17 FLC 1/1 FAC 11+1/4 Others 2+2/2
Wigan Ath (£450,000 on 18/2/2000) FL
30+30/11 FLC 0+1/1 FAC 2/1 Others 2+1
Hull C (Loaned on 25/1/2002) FL 3+3

ROBERTS Sean Joseph
Born: Durban, South Africa, 2 January
1983
Height: 6'2" **Weight:** 12.8
This young 'keeper joined Sheffield
Wednesday as cover last October when
the club were experiencing an injury crisis
amongst their goalkeeping staff.
However, he managed just one
appearance from the subs' bench,
replacing Kevin Pressman when the
regular 'keeper was injured at Burnley.
Sheffield Wed (Signed from Southern
Gauteng, South Africa on 19/10/2001) FL
0+1

ROBERTS Stephen (Steve)
Wyn
Born: Wrexham, 24 February 1980
Height: 6'0" **Weight:** 12.7
International Honours: W: U21-4; Yth
Steve continued to show improvement at Wrexham in 2001-02, and although missing the final stages of the campaign after damaging the back of his knee in the away encounter at Brighton, he enjoyed an excellent season. A thoughtful and composed central defender, he always looked comfortable in possession. He scored his only goal at Chesterfield in September and was offered new terms for the forthcoming season by the Robins. He is the younger brother of Neil Roberts.
Wrexham (From trainee on 16/1/1998) FL 46+4/1 FLC 1 FAC 4/1 Others 2+1

ROBERTS Stuart Ian
Born: Carmarthen, 22 July 1980
Height: 5'7" **Weight:** 9.8
International Honours: W: U21-13
Stuart made an impressive start to the 2001-02 season at Swansea and was leading scorer in mid-October when he was sold to Second Division Wycombe Wanderers for a bargain fee. He immediately excited the Adams Park faithful with his forceful wing play. Blessed with two good feet and lightning acceleration, he likes to tear down the wings and deliver hard crosses. He was first choice until February but was then rested by the manager due to a certain loss of confidence, but is expected to return again in 2002-03.
Swansea C (From trainee on 9/7/1998) FL 58+34/14 FLC 4+3 FAC 4 Others 7+2
Wycombe W (£102,500 on 19/10/2001) FL 18+8 FAC 2+1 Others 0+1

ROBINS Mark Gordon
Born: Ashton under Lyne, 22 December 1969
Height: 5'8" **Weight:** 11.11
Club Honours: FAC '90; ECWC '91; ESC '91; FLC '97
International Honours: E: U21-6
Mark was once again Rotherham's leading scorer last season. He began well, netting nine of the team's first 12 League and cup goals to emphasise his importance, but later found himself relegated to the substitutes' bench. A rich vein of form in February and March saw him notch five goals in six games. He is an experienced striker who has the knack of being in the right place at the right time.
Manchester U (From apprentice on 23/12/1986) FL 19+29/11 FLC 0+7/2 FAC 4+4/3 Others 4+3/1

Norwich C (£800,000 on 14/8/1992) PL 57+10/20 FLC 6+3/1 Others 1+1
Leicester C (£1,000,000 on 16/1/1995) P/FL 40+16/12 FLC 5+4/5 FAC 4+2 Others 1+1
Reading (Loaned on 29/8/1997) FL 5
(Signed by Deportivo Orense, Spain on 15/1/1998)
Manchester C (Free from Panionios, Greece on 25/3/1999) FL 0+2
Walsall (Free on 5/8/1999) FL 30+10/6 FLC 4/1 FAC 2/1
Rotherham U (Free on 5/7/2000) FL 76+7/39 FLC 4/2 FAC 3 Others 1/1

ROBINSON Carl Phillip
Born: Llandrindod Wells, 13 October 1976
Height: 5'10" **Weight:** 12.10
International Honours: W: 9; B-2; U21-6; Yth
Carl continued to have to fight for his place at Molineux last term, despite a fine strike at Coventry that helped Wolves win their first away match. The signing of Alex Rae seemed to be the end for him, yet such was his improved form that he kept the brilliant Scotsman out for a further six matches. However, the workmanlike midfielder's involvement became more occasional and his campaign petered out as he had exploratory surgery on his knee in the spring.
Wolverhampton W (From trainee on 3/7/1995) FL 129+35/19 FLC 12+1/1 FAC 14/3
Shrewsbury T (Loaned on 28/3/1996) FL 2+2 Others 1

ROBINSON John Robert
Campbell
Born: Bulawayo, Rhodesia, 29 August 1971
Height: 5'10" **Weight:** 11.7
Club Honours: Div 1 '00
International Honours: W: 29; U21-5
John is a clever right-footed winger who can play on either flank or as a right wing back and is Charlton's record international appearance holder. He made his 30th appearance for Wales during the season. He works tirelessly, loves to take players on and can cross with either foot. He was in and out of the Addicks' side during the season but always gave his best when selected. He scored his only goal with a long-range shot against Ipswich at the Valley.
Brighton & Hove A (From trainee on 21/4/1989) FL 57+5/6 FLC 5/1 FAC 2+1 Others 1+2/2
Charlton Ath (£75,000 on 15/9/1992) P/FL 286+33/35 FLC 20+3/5 FAC 17+3/3 Others 5+1

ROBINSON Leslie (Les)
Born: Shirebrook, 1 March 1967
Height: 5'9" **Weight:** 12.4
Les started the 2001-02 season in rather shaky form for Mansfield Town, but soon recovered to lead the Stags to automatic promotion at the end of the campaign. He is an effective central defender who is now approaching the veteran stage of his career.
Mansfield T (From Nottingham F juniors on 6/10/1984) FL 11+4 Others 1
Stockport Co (£10,000 on 27/11/1986) FL 67/3 FLC 2 FAC 4 Others 4
Doncaster Rov (£20,000 on 24/3/1988) FL 82/12 FLC 4 FAC 5 Others 5/1
Oxford U (£150,000 on 19/3/1990) FL 379+5/3 FLC 38/3 FAC 22+1 Others 13
Mansfield T (Free on 13/7/2000) FL 80 FLC 5 FAC 5 Others 1

ROBINSON Mark
Born: Guisborough, 24 July 1981
Height: 5'9" **Weight:** 11.0
This highly rated young defender established himself as Hartlepool's first choice left back during the 2001-02 season. As the campaign progressed he grew in maturity, and did not let the side down as he gained valuable experience. Seen as a player for the future, he signed an extension to his contract during the season.
Hartlepool U (From trainee on 2/7/1999) FL 38+5 FLC 1 Others 2

ROBINSON Mark James
Born: Rochdale, 21 November 1968
Height: 5'9" **Weight:** 12.4
Club Honours: Div 2 '96
Mark spent the early part of the 2001-02 campaign on the sidelines at Swindon while recovering from a bilateral hernia. He had to wait until November before appearing as a substitute at Blackpool but then found it harder and harder to recover after each game, and after seeking specialist advice he announced his retirement in January. He continued to assist the club in a scouting capacity until the close of the season.
West Bromwich A (From apprentice on 10/1/1987) FL 2 FLC 0+1
Barnsley (Free on 23/6/1987) FL 117+20/6 FLC 7+2 FAC 7+1 Others 3+2/1
Newcastle U (£450,000 on 9/3/1993) F/PL 14+11 FAC 1
Swindon T (£600,000 on 22/7/1994) FL 255+14/4 FLC 21+1 FAC 14+1 Others 9+1

ROBINSON Marvin Leon St
Born: Crewe, 11 April 1980
Height: 6'0" **Weight:** 12.9

John Robinson

International Honours: E: Sch
This promising young Derby County striker made a successful recovery from a broken leg and returned to action for the reserves last term. He eventually made the subs' bench in the closing stages coming on during the final two matches and scoring for his first senior goal for the Rams in the 1-1 draw at Sunderland on the last day of the season.
Derby Co (From trainee on 8/7/1998) PL 3+8/1
Stoke C (Loaned on 13/9/2000) FL 3/1

ROBINSON Matthew Richard
Born: Exeter, 23 December 1974
Height: 5'11" **Weight:** 11.8
Matthew was a fixture in the Reading team in the early part of the 2001-02 season, offering a potent attacking threat down the left flank from his position at full back, but a series of injuries coupled with loss of form saw him lose his place to the emerging talent of Nick Shorey. Following the home defeat by Brentford in October he only played in the Avon Combination side and occasionally warmed the first-team bench as a non-playing substitute. He was given a free transfer at the end of the season.
Southampton (From trainee on 1/7/1993) PL 3+11 FAC 1+2
Portsmouth (£50,000 on 20/2/1998) FL 65+4/1 FLC 3+2 FAC 3
Reading (£150,000 on 28/1/2000) FL 62+3 FLC 3+1 FAC 2 Others 4

ROBINSON Paul Derrick
Born: Sunderland, 20 November 1978
Height: 5'11" **Weight:** 11.12
Paul has struggled to find his feet since his big money move from Newcastle two years ago. He only got to play 19 minutes of senior football for Wimbledon last term, coming on as a substitute in the away game at Crystal Palace. He led the line in commanding style for the Dons reserves before joining Grimsby Town on loan on the transfer deadline. Signed by the Mariners as back-up for their regular strikers he made five appearances, mostly as a substitute.
Darlington (From trainee on 14/7/1997) FL 7+19/3 FLC 0+1 FAC 2+4/1 Others 0+1
Newcastle U (£250,000 + on 27/3/1998) PL 2+9 FLC 0+1 Others 0+4/1
Wimbledon (£1,500,000 on 9/8/2000) FL 0+4 FLC 1+1
Burnley (Loaned on 10/10/2000) FL 0+4
Dundee (Loaned on 21/2/2001) SL 2+4
Grimsby T (Loaned on 28/3/2002) FL 1+4

ROBINSON Paul Peter
Born: Watford, 14 December 1978
Height: 5'9" **Weight:** 11.12
Club Honours: Div 2 '98
International Honours: E: U21-3
Watford's regular left back enjoyed his best campaign to date with the club in 2001-02. Locally born, Paul is a strong tackler and a wholehearted competitor whose efforts are much admired by the fans. Although he was sent off in the opening match at Manchester City, his overall disciplinary record was much improved on previous seasons and he demonstrated a new maturity while not losing any of his commitment. His four goals – which included a spectacular effort against Charlton in the Worthington Cup – represented his best-ever return.
Watford (From trainee on 13/2/1997) P/FL 154+18/5 FLC 13+1/1 FAC 6+2 Others 5

ROBINSON Stephen (Steve)
Born: Lisburn, 10 December 1974
Height: 5'9" **Weight:** 11.3
International Honours: NI: 5; B-4; U21-1; Yth; Sch
Steve's lack of opportunities at Preston saw him placed on the transfer list last November after which he was effectively invisible on the first-team scene, with his only contributions amounting to four substitute appearances, totalling only 73 minutes. In March he joined Bristol City on loan, making six first-team appearances and producing some stirring performances in the closing stages of the season before returning to Deepdale. Preston fans have never really had an opportunity to assess the attacking midfielder's talents, but following the change of manager it is hoped he will challenge for a regular place in the line-up during 2002-03.
Tottenham H (From trainee on 27/1/1993) PL 1+3
Bournemouth (Free on 20/10/1994) FL 227+13/51 FLC 14/1 FAC 15+1/5 Others 16/3
Preston NE (£375,000 on 26/5/2000) FL 6+18/1 FLC 3+1 FAC 0+1
Bristol C (Loaned on 18/3/2002) FL 6/1

ROBINSON Steven (Steve) Eli
Born: Nottingham, 17 January 1975
Height: 5'9" **Weight:** 11.3
An energetic, hard-working midfielder, Steve was a regular member of the Swindon midfield during the 2001-02 campaign. A predominantly right-sided player he worked tirelessly throughout the season and his never-say-die attitude was a constant feature of his displays.

Birmingham C (From trainee on 9/6/1993) FL 53+28 FLC 6+2/1 FAC 2+2/1 Others 2
Peterborough U (Loaned on 15/3/1996) FL 5
Swindon T (£50,000 on 12/2/2001) FL 55+3/2 FLC 1 FAC 3 Others 1

ROCHE Lee Paul
Born: Bolton, 28 October 1980
Height: 5'10" **Weight:** 10.12
International Honours: E: U21-1; Yth
After spending the whole of the previous season on loan at Wrexham, this promising young Manchester United defender was hoping to see some senior action at Old Trafford in 2001-02. He was not disappointed, featuring in an experimental line-up for the Worthington Cup defeat at Arsenal in November, but this was his only senior call-up during the season.
Manchester U (From trainee on 11/2/1999) FLC 1
Wrexham (Loaned on 24/7/2000) FL 41 FLC 2 FAC 1 Others 1

RODGER Simon Lee
Born: Shoreham, 3 October 1971
Height: 5'9" **Weight:** 11.9
Club Honours: Div 1 '94
Crystal Palace's longest-serving player featured fairly regularly once more for the Eagles last term. A hard-working midfielder who is strong in the tackle, he is out of contract in the summer, but has a testimonial match against Spurs lined up for July.
Crystal Palace (£1,000 from Bognor Regis T on 2/7/1990) F/PL 242+34/11 FLC 30+1/2 FAC 9+4 Others 5+3
Manchester C (Loaned on 28/10/1996) FL 8/1
Stoke C (Loaned on 14/2/1997) FL 5

RODGERS Luke John
Born: Birmingham, 1 January 1982
Height: 5'7" **Weight:** 11.2
This young striker enjoyed a magnificent season for Shrewsbury Town bagging a total of 22 goals, including a hat-trick in the 4-0 home victory against Kidderminster. His other feats included scoring in each of the first six home League games (a new club record) and netting in six consecutive starts. Luke showed a single-minded approach to goal scoring, many of his strikes coming from his ability to beat defenders before unleashing his shot. He formed an excellent strike partnership with Nigel Jemson from whom he learned a great deal.
Shrewsbury T (From trainee on 10/7/2000) FL 51+19/30 FLC 1 FAC 1+1 Others 1+2

RODRIGUES Daniel (Dani)
Ferreira
Born: Madeira, Portugal, 3 March 1980
Height: 6'0" **Weight:** 11.8
International Honours: Portugal: U21
This promising Southampton youngster
recovered from serious injury suffered the
previous season and returned to Bristol
City for another loan spell last December.
Unfortunately he achieved little impact
this time and it seems he needs further
time to recuperate. When full fit Dani is a
skilful striker with electric pace.
*Bournemouth (Loaned from CS Farense,
Portugal on 1/10/1998) FL 0+5 Others 0+2*
*Southampton (£170,000 on 3/3/1999) PL
0+2*
Bristol C (Loaned on 3/10/2000) FL 3+1
*Bristol C (Loaned on 31/12/2001) FL 0+4
Others 0+1*

RODWELL James (Jim)
Richard
Born: Lincoln, 20 November 1970
Height: 6'1" **Weight:** 14.2
Club Honours: NC '01
Jim had been a major part of Rushden's
remarkable rise through the non-league
pyramid, and, with Ray Warburton
injured, he started the season as a regular
choice alongside Mark Peters in the centre
of the defence. He showed no difficulty in
adjusting to the higher standard of
football until he suffered a suspension in
October and Barry Hunter arrived at the
club. After that point, Jim was consigned
to a bit-part role and eventually Boston
United were attracted to his robust, no-
nonsense style of play and he helped
them to promotion from the Conference
earning him a second consecutive
championship-winning medal.
*Darlington (Trainee on 1/1/1989) FL 1 (Free
to Nettleham during 1989 close season)*
*Rushden & Diamonds (£40,000 from
Halesowen T, ex Boston U, Bedworth U,
Hednesford T, Nuneaton Borough, on
15/8/1996) FL 8+1 FLC 2 Others 1*

ROGERS Alan
Born: Liverpool, 3 January 1977
Height: 5'9" **Weight:** 12.6
Club Honours: Div 1 '98
International Honours: E: U21-3
Pacy left-sided midfielder returned for
Nottingham Forest after a long injury lay-
off, but after just a handful of
appearances he was sold to Leicester City
in November. However, he struggled
again with injury and match fitness
problems during his early appearances
before a knee injury in February
threatened to bring his season to a

premature end. A speedy recovery
enabled him to return for the final two
fixtures.
*Tranmere Rov (From trainee on 1/7/1995) FL
53+4/2 FLC 1 FAC 1*
*Nottingham F (£2,000,000 on 10/7/1997)
P/FL 135+2/17 FLC 15/2 FAC 2+1/1*
*Leicester C (£300,000 on 16/11/2001) PL
9+4 FAC 2*

ROGERS David (Dave)
Raymond
Born: Liverpool, 25 August 1975
Height: 6'1" **Weight:** 12.4
Dave began the 2001-02 season with
Portadown before joining Carlisle United
where he soon found his niche in central
defence. A committed performer who
captained the side on occasions, he was
not afraid to press forward when the
occasion demanded. He was reported to
have signed a two-year contract with
Dutch club Cambuur in the summer.
Tranmere Rov (From trainee on 6/7/1994)
*Chester C (Free on 7/8/1995) FL 18+7/1 FLC
2+2 FAC 0+1 Others 1 (Free to Southport on
25/11/1996)*
*Dundee (Free on 6/8/1997) SL 38+5/1 SLC 2
SC 4+1 Others 1*
*Ayr U (Free on 23/6/1999) SL 13+3/1 SLC 2
SC 1 Others 1*
Partick Thistle (Loaned on 31/3/2000) SL 6
*Peterborough U (Loaned on 6/10/2000) FL
1+2 Others 1*
*Scunthorpe U (Free on 2/3/2001) FL 1 (Free
to Portadown during 2001 close season)*
*Carlisle U (Free on 17/9/2001) FL 26+1/1
FAC 3 Others 1*

ROGERS Kristian Raleigh John
Born: Chester, 2 October 1980
Height: 6'3" **Weight:** 12.6
International Honours: E: Sch
Although Kristian enjoyed the lion's share
of goalkeeping appearances for Wrexham
last term, he had to share the number
one spot with David Walsh and Marius
Røvde. Kristian began the season as first
choice, but lost his place following an
injury in October and on recovering
fitness was forced to share duties with his
rivals. A feature of his game was his
bravery and he contributed several
outstanding saves in the penultimate
match of the campaign at Stoke.
*Wrexham (From Chester C juniors on
14/8/1998) FL 33 FLC 2 FAC 1 Others 1*

ROGERS Mark Alvin
Born: Guelph, Ontario, Canada, 3
November 1975
Height: 6'1" **Weight:** 12.12
International Honours: Canada: 4

After establishing himself in the Wycombe
team at the end of the previous season,
Mark carried on where he left off in
2001-02, capably filling in at right back
until an injury to Jason Cousins saw him
move back to his more usual central-
defensive role. He formed a solid
partnership with Paul McCarthy, giving
safe no-nonsense performances, allowing
strikers little space. The highlight of his
season was adding a further three caps
for Canada in the Gold Cup including an
appearance in the third-place match
against South Korea when the bronze
medal was secured.
*Wycombe W (Free from Burnaby Canadians,
Canada on 23/12/1998) FL 77+11/3 FLC 5/1
FAC 12+1/1 Others 4*

ROGERS Paul Anthony
Born: Portsmouth, 21 March 1965
Height: 6'0" **Weight:** 12.0
Club Honours: Div 3 '97, '01; Div 2 '02;
AMC '99
International Honours: E: SP-6
Paul again served Brighton as club
captain in 2001-02 and was instrumental
in maintaining the high level of team
spirit which was an important factor in
the Seagulls' second successive
promotion season. A central midfield
player who likes to get forward, he
surprisingly scored just once during the
campaign, netting the first goal of Peter
Taylor's reign as manager in the 3-0
home victory over Oldham. He was
rewarded with a new one-year contract
in the summer.
*Sheffield U (£35,000 from Sutton U on
29/1/1992) F/PL 120+5/10 FLC 8+1/1 FAC 4
Others 1*
*Notts Co (Signed on 29/12/1995) FL 21+1/2
FAC 1 Others 6/1*
*Wigan Ath (Loaned on 13/12/1996) FL
7+2/3*
*Wigan Ath (£50,000 on 7/3/1997) FL
85+6/2 FLC 6 FAC 3 Others 8/1*
*Brighton & Hove A (Free on 8/7/1999) FL
104+11/15 FLC 5+1 FAC 6/1 Others 6*

ROGET Leo Thomas Earl
Born: Ilford, 1 August 1977
Height: 6'1" **Weight:** 12.2
This powerful central defender made over
20 appearances for Stockport County last
season but a poor performance at West
Brom on New Year's Day saw him drop
down the pecking order at Edgeley Park.
He subsequently had a spell on loan at
Reading where his only first-team game
was in the 0-0 draw at Swindon on
Valentine's Day. He performed solidly and

stayed in the Royals' squad for the remainder of the season, being chosen as a non-playing substitute on four further occasions. He was released by County in the summer.

Southend U *(From trainee on 5/7/1995) FL 105+15/7 FLC 8 FAC 6/1 Others 3/1*
Stockport Co *(Loaned on 1/3/2001) FL 28+3/1 FLC 2*
Reading *(Loaned on 14/2/2002) FL 1*

ROMO David

Born: Nimes, France, 7 August 1978
Height: 6'0" **Weight:** 12.6
International Honours: France: Yth
David attended a French Olympic training squad in Lebanon over the summer of 2001, but by September he had asked to go on the transfer list at Swansea after failing to secure a place in the starting line up. Despite his undoubted technique, he was unable to come to terms with the more physical side of the Football League, and he made only rare appearances throughout the season. He scored his only League goal for the Swans after coming on as substitute against Mansfield, netting a 25-yard scorcher with only his second touch of the ball.

Swansea C *(Free from Guingamp, France on 13/10/2000) FL 31+12/1 FLC 1 FAC 1+1 Others 3+1*

ROOKE Steven (Steve) Alan

Born: Carlisle, 21 September 1982
Height: 5'10" **Weight:** 10.12
A defender who has come up through the youth ranks, Steve made his first-team debut for Carlisle in the final match of the 2001-02 season at Mansfield. Despite this he was released by the club in the summer.

Carlisle U *(From trainee on 27/6/2001) FL 0+1*

ROPER Ian Robert

Born: Nuneaton, 20 June 1977
Height: 6'3" **Weight:** 13.4
After starting the 2001-02 season on the transfer list at Walsall, Ian came back for the game against Sheffield United in November only to be unluckily sent off. Again he battled back to win a first-team place on merit and gave some tremendous displays at the heart of the defence. He was one of the first players to be signed on for 2002-03 and is one of the key figures around whom Colin Lee is aiming to build an established First Division side.

Walsall *(From trainee on 15/5/1995) FL 131+24/2 FLC 4+6 FAC 6+2/1 Others 11+3*

ROSCOE Andrew (Andy) Ronald

Born: Liverpool, 4 June 1973
Height: 5'11" **Weight:** 12.0
Club Honours: AMC '96
Andy put in a set of impressive displays on the left flank for Exeter City in the 2001-02 campaign, supplying an endless supply of crosses for the front two players. An experienced midfield player he is also something of a dead-ball specialist and his goal from a free kick from the edge of the box at Oxford will be long remembered. He remained a firm favourite with the St James' Park faithful.

Bolton W *(From trainee at Liverpool on 17/7/1991) FL 2+1 Others 1+1*
Rotherham U *(£70,000 on 27/10/1994) FL 184+18/18 FLC 10 FAC 10/2 Others 11/2*
Mansfield T *(Free on 5/8/1999) FL 29+10/2 FLC 2 FAC 1 Others 0+1/1*
Exeter C *(Free on 18/7/2000) FL 68+13/8 FLC 2 FAC 4/1 Others 2*

ROSE Karl Barrie

Born: Barnsley, 12 October 1978
Height: 5'10" **Weight:** 11.8
Karl trained with Rochdale at the start of the 2001-02 season and after scoring an excellent goal for the reserves against Halifax he was signed on non-contract forms to play in the LDV Trophy match against Port Vale. He performed creditably as a stand-in for striker Clive Platt but was then released and later signed for Conference club Scarborough.

Barnsley *(From juniors on 7/11/1995) FL 2+2 FAC 1+2*
Mansfield T *(Loaned on 25/3/1999) FL 0+1*
Rochdale *(Free on 25/10/2001) Others 1*

ROSE Matthew David

Born: Dartford, 24 September 1975
Height: 5'11" **Weight:** 11.1
Club Honours: FAYC '94
International Honours: E: U21-2
Matthew was one of only two players to be offered a new contract after being released by Queen's Park Rangers in the summer of 2001. He was initially given a six-month deal, but after some solid performances, this was renewed for the remainder of the campaign. He was a regular throughout the season in central midfield or defence and contributed three valuable goals.

Arsenal *(From trainee on 19/7/1994) PL 2+3*
Queens Park R *(£500,000 on 20/5/1997) FL 131+9/4 FLC 6 FAC 3 Others 1*

ROSE Richard Alan

Born: Pembury, 8 September 1982
Height: 6'0" **Weight:** 11.9
After his creditable performances at the end of the previous season, Richard failed to maintain his form in 2001-02 despite being a virtual ever present in Gillingham's Avon Combination side. He moved to League of Ireland club Longford Town on loan during the season to gain the experience of regular first-team football. Injuries gave him a chance to appear in the final two games of the season and once again he did not let his side down.

Gillingham *(From trainee on 10/4/2001) FL 3+4*

ROSENIOR Liam James

Born: Wandsworth, 9 July 1984
Height: 5'9" **Weight:** 11.8
This young Bristol City midfielder made his senior debut when coming on as substitute in the final game of the 2001-02 season against Stoke. He created a good impression, and it was his incisive pass that set up Aaron Brown to fire in City's equaliser. Liam is the son of the former Fulham and Bristol City player Leroy Rosenior.

Bristol C *(From trainee on 15/8/2001) FL 0+1*

ROSLER Uwe

Born: Magdeburg, Germany, 15 November 1968
Height: 6'0" **Weight:** 12.4
International Honours: East Germany: 5
Although starting the 2001-02 season with two goals in the opening fixture at St Mary's, Uwe was again unable to win a regular first-team place at Southampton due to the form of Marian Pahars and James Beattie. A loan spell at West Bromwich Albion saw him score the winner against Forest, before he returned briefly to Southampton and in January he went back to Germany to sign for SpVgg Unterhaching.

Manchester C *(£375,000 from FC Nurnberg, Germany on 2/3/1994) P/FL 141+11/50 FLC 10+1/5 FAC 14/9 (Free to Kaiserslautern, Germany during 1998 close season)*
Southampton *(Free from Tennis Borussia, Germany on 24/7/2000) PL 9+15 FLC 1+2/1 FAC 0+2*
West Bromwich A *(Loaned on 30/10/2001) FL 5/1*

ROSS Neil James

Born: Birmingham, 10 August 1982
Height: 6'0" **Weight:** 12.10
Neil found first-team appearances limited at Stockport County last season due

Uwe Rosler

mainly to injuries. He had a loan spell at Bristol Rovers early on in the campaign but damaged ankle ligaments and had to return to Edgeley Park. He recovered to make his full debut at Gillingham in January where he equalised with a header at the far post. He then added a couple of appearances before going on loan to Chinese side Wuhan. He is a promising young striker who will be looking to make a breakthrough to regular first-team football in 2002-03.

Leeds U (From trainee on 12/8/1999)
Stockport Co (Free on 28/1/2000) FL 2+3/1
Bristol Rov (Loaned on 23/10/2001) FL 2+3 Others 1

ROUGIER Anthony (Tony) Leo

Born: Tobago, 17 July 1971
Height: 6'0" **Weight:** 14.1
International Honours: Trinidad & Tobago

Tony only played the full 90 minutes in two of his 37 first-team games for Reading last term, but his partnership with Nicky Forster produced the Royals' best strike force of the season. The club's seven consecutive wins came during their spell together, and although Tony only netted once– a diving header at Tranmere – he possessed ample guile and tricks to unnerve most defences. He is not the most aggressive of attackers, but he added to his tally of international caps for Trinidad & Tobago during the campaign.

Raith Rov (Free from Trinity Prospect, Trinidad on 9/3/1995) SL 47+10/2 SLC 3/3 SC 4+1/1 Others 4+1/1
Hibernian (Signed on 10/7/1997) SL 34+11/4 SLC 4
Port Vale (£175,000 on 4/1/1999) FL 41+10/8 FLC 2/1 FAC 1
Reading (£325,000 on 11/8/2000) FL 34+30/3 FLC 2+2 FAC 2+1 Others 3+3

ROUSSEL Cedric

Born: Mons, Belgium, 6 January 1978
Height: 6'2" **Weight:** 12.5
International Honours: Belgium: U21

The well-built striker promised better things having suffered personal problems during his first few months at Molineux. On the opening day he equalised against Portsmouth with a classic header and he appeared in the first five League games. After that he struggled to score and mostly featured from the subs' bench. He continued to score for the reserves before a knee injury ended his season.

Coventry C (£1,200,000 from KAA Ghent,

Belgium on 19/10/1999) PL 28+11/8 FLC 1 FAC 2+1/3
Wolverhampton W (£1,530,000 + on 15/2/2001) FL 9+17/2 FLC 0+1 FAC 0+1

ROUTLEDGE Wayne Neville

Born: Sidcup, 7 January 1985
Height: 5'6" **Weight:** 10.7
This highly rated young striker stepped up from the Academy side to make his debut for Crystal Palace from the subs' bench against West Bromwich Albion last October and later added a second senior appearance as a substitute. He has plenty of time to develop, but will be hoping to see more first-team action in 2002-03.

Crystal Palace (Trainee) FL 0+2

RØVDE Knut Marius

Born: Trondheim, Norway, 26 June 1972
Height: 6'1" **Weight:** 12.7
With Wrexham badly needing some experience in the goalkeeping department Marius was signed from Ayr United last January, his wages being partly funded by the Wrexham Independent Supporters (WINS) due to the club's serious financial position. He established a good understanding with his defenders and was effective in one-on-one situations, producing many instinctive stops. Despite his efforts the Robins were relegated in early April, and when Norwegian club Lillestrom came to him with an SOS due to an injury crisis he decided to accept.

Ayr U (Signed from L/F Honefoss, Norway on 31/3/2000) SL 14+1 SLC 0+1 SC 2 Others 1
Wrexham (Free on 25/1/2002) FL 12

ROWAN Jonathan (Jonny) Robert

Born: Grimsby, 29 November 1981
Height: 5'10" **Weight:** 11.4
Jonny received regular first-team action at the start of the 2001-02 campaign when he formed a strike force in partnership with newcomer Phil Jevons. However, a change in management saw him lose out to Mick Boulding during the second half of the season. He remains a promising young striker and his tally of five goals shows that he is capable of finding the net when given the opportunity.

Grimsby T (From trainee on 12/7/2000) FL 21+8/4 FLC 2+3/2

ROWE Rodney Carl

Born: Huddersfield, 30 July 1975
Height: 5'8" **Weight:** 12.8
A hero of Hull's play-off run the previous season, Rodney started last

term as a squad player behind the new strike force of Lawrie Dudfield and Gary Alexander. He forced his way into the side for the visit of York in September then suffered an ankle injury, and further injury problems meant that he did not complete a full 90 minutes in 2001-02. He was released by the Tigers in April.

Huddersfield T (From trainee on 12/7/1993) FL 14+20/2 FLC 0+2 FAC 6+1/2 Others 3/1
Scarborough (Loaned on 11/8/1994) FL 10+4/1 FLC 4/1
Bury (Loaned on 20/3/1995) FL 1+2
York C (£80,000 on 19/2/1997) FL 74+23/20 FLC 5+1/2 FAC 2+3/3 Others 2/2
Halifax T (Loaned on 24/9/1999) FL 7+2/2 FAC 1
Gillingham (£45,000 on 25/11/1999) FL 8+14/4 FLC 0+1 Others 1
Hull C (Free on 2/1/2001) FL 19+16/8 FLC 0+1 Others 1+1

ROWETT Gary

Born: Bromsgrove, 6 March 1974
Height: 6'0" **Weight:** 12.10
This right back or central defender was injured in the second fixture of 2001-02 at Highbury and was then rushed back into action prematurely after a cartilage operation. The consequence was further knee trouble that kept him out of action for several months. Gary was not able to resume training until March, by which time Leicester City were doomed, and he finally reappeared from the bench on Easter Saturday to help clinch a long overdue victory against Blackburn. A handful of further outings helped to improve his fitness levels in readiness for next season.

Cambridge U (From trainee on 10/9/1991) FL 51+12/9 FLC 7/1 FAC 5+2 Others 5/3
Everton (£200,000 on 21/5/1994) PL 2+2
Blackpool (Loaned on 23/1/1995) FL 17
Derby Co (£300,000 on 20/7/1995) P/FL 101+4/2 FLC 8/2 FAC 5+2
Birmingham C (£1,000,000 on 17/8/1998) FL 87/6 FLC 9/3 FAC 3/1 Others 4/1
Leicester C (£3,000,000 + on 7/7/2000) PL 47+2/2 FLC 2 FAC 4/1 Others 2

ROWLAND Keith

Born: Portadown, 1 September 1971
Height: 5'10" **Weight:** 10.0
International Honours: NI: 18; B-3; Yth
Chesterfield fans saw very little of this creative left-sided player last term. He suffered a cruciate ligament injury in training in September but recovered to make occasional starts by March. In the few games in which he appeared he showed himself to be both imaginative

and comfortable on the ball, but also prepared to get stuck in. Keith will return to contention in August after a full pre-season.

Bournemouth *(From trainee on 2/10/1989)* FL 65+7/2 FLC 5 FAC 8 Others 3
Coventry C *(Loaned on 8/1/1993)* PL 0+2
West Ham U *(£110,000 on 6/8/1993)* PL 63+17/1 FLC 3+2 FAC 5+1
Queens Park R *(Signed on 30/1/1998)* FL 32+24/3 FLC 1+1 FAC 1+1
Luton T *(Loaned on 27/11/2001)* FL 12/2
Chesterfield *(Free on 10/8/2001)* FL 6+3 FLC 1/1

ROWLAND Stephen John
Born: Wrexham, 2 November 1981
Height: 5'10" **Weight:** 12.4
This promising Port Vale defender graduated through the club's youth scheme to become a regular member of the line-up last season. A versatile defender, he made his debut on the left-hand side at Wigan Athletic in October and did well enough to retain his place for the majority of the campaign. He scored one goal, a cracking 20-yard shot against Colchester, and was a joint-winner of the club's 'Young Player of the Year' award.
Port Vale *(From trainee on 2/7/2001)* FL 25/1 FAC 2 Others 2

ROWLANDS Martin Charles
Born: Hammersmith, 8 February 1979
Height: 5'9" **Weight:** 10.10
Club Honours: Div 3 '99
International Honours: RoI: U21-8
Martin suffered a leg injury at the start of the 2001-02 campaign and, after a couple of starts and some appearances from the bench for Brentford, he required a hernia operation in December. He finally shook off his injury problems to start the last 11 League games of the season, scoring six goals from the right side of midfield, including two at Wrexham and the goal that gave the Bees the lead against Reading in the final League game. He is a skilful attacking midfielder with excellent distribution.
Brentford *(£45,000 from Farnborough T on 6/8/1998)* FL 115+16/19 FLC 8+3/1 FAC 5+2 Others 15/2

ROWSON David Andrew
Born: Aberdeen, 14 September 1976
Height: 5'10" **Weight:** 11.12
David joined Stoke City in the summer of 2001 and showed early on that he could play in either a holding midfield role or at right back. It took him some time to

make a first-team place his own and then a series of injuries robbed him of an opportunity to prove his qualities to the fans.
Aberdeen *(Signed from FC Stoneywood on 5/10/1994)* SL 120+20/10 SLC 9+3 SC 7/1 Others 2
Livingston *(Loaned on 24/3/2000)* SL 6/1
Stoke C *(Free on 2/7/2001)* FL 8+5 FLC 1 FAC 1+2 Others 1

ROYCE Simon Ernest
Born: Forest Gate, 9 September 1971
Height: 6'2" **Weight:** 12.8
Simon began the 2001-02 season as Leicester's third choice 'keeper behind Tim Flowers and Ian Walker before linking up with his former manager Peter Taylor at Brighton for a loan period. He made an impressive debut for Albion in the goalless draw at QPR on Boxing Day and saved a penalty in the next game at Blackpool, but couldn't prevent the Albion letting slip a two-goal lead. He subsequently returned to Filbert Street when his loan spell was over and continued to feature in the Foxes' reserves in the latter half of the campaign.
Southend U *(£35,000 from Heybridge Swifts on 15/10/1991)* FL 147+2 FLC 9 FAC 5 Others 6
Charlton Ath *(Free on 2/7/1998)* PL 8
Leicester C *(Free on 17/7/2000)* PL 16+3 FLC 1 FAC 4
Brighton & Hove A *(Loaned on 24/12/2001)* FL 6

RUBINS Andrejs
Born: Latvia, 26 November 1978
Height: 5'9" **Weight:** 10.5
International Honours: Latvia: 32
2001-02 proved to be a disappointing season for this small speedy winger who failed to make a single appearance in the Crystal Palace starting line-up. He had a trial with French club Troyes in January, but remains at Selhurst Park and will be hoping for better fortunes in 2002-03. Despite his lack of first-team football he continued to represent Latvia at international level.
Crystal Palace *(£2,000,000 from Skonto Riga, Latvia on 17/10/2000)* FL 17+12 FLC 3+1/2 FAC 2

RUDDOCK Neil
Born: Wandsworth, 9 May 1968
Height: 6'2" **Weight:** 12.12
Club Honours: FLC '95
International Honours: E: 1; B-1; U21-4; Yth
Brought in as a player-coach to assist Swindon boss Roy Evans, this veteran

central defender used his experience to good effect during the first half of the 2001-02 campaign when he often led by example with some solid defending. He marked his Town debut with a tremendous free kick to earn victory over Colchester and become a cult figure with the fans in the process. However, following the departure of Evans and the return of Andy King he was affected by injuries and lack of fitness, although he returned to action with the reserve team during March.
Millwall *(From apprentice on 3/3/1986)* Others 3+1/1
Tottenham H *(£50,000 on 14/4/1986)* FL 7+2 FAC 1+1/1
Millwall *(£300,000 on 29/6/1988)* FL 0+2/1 FLC 2/3 Others 1+1
Southampton *(£250,000 on 13/2/1989)* FL 100+7/9 FLC 14+1/1 FAC 10/3 Others 6
Tottenham H *(£750,000 on 29/7/1992)* PL 38/3 FLC 4 FAC 5
Liverpool *(£2,500,000 on 22/7/1993)* PL 111+4/11 FLC 19+1/1 FAC 11 Others 5+1
Queens Park R *(Loaned on 26/3/1998)* FL 7
West Ham U *(£100,000 + on 31/7/1998)* PL 39+3/2 FLC 4+1 FAC 3 Others 5+1/1
Crystal Palace *(Signed on 28/7/2000)* FL 19+1/2 FLC 5/1 FAC 0+1
Swindon T *(Free on 10/8/2001)* FL 14+1/1 FLC 1 FAC 2/1 Others 0+1

RUDONJA Mladen
Born: Koper, Yugoslavia, 26 July 1971
Height: 5'9" **Weight:** 11.6
International Honours: Slovenia: 61
Mladen has switched successfully to a left-sided midfield player at Portsmouth, but experienced another frustrating season at Fratton Park when he made just three first-team appearances despite continuing to collect international caps for Slovenia. He was released at the end of the season by Pompey.
Portsmouth *(£200,000 from St Truiden, Belgium, ex Belvedur Izola, NK Zagreb, Koper, Olympija, Marsonia, HIT Gorica, Lugano, Primorje, on 11/8/2000)* FL 4+10 FLC 1+2 FAC 1

RUFUS Richard Raymond
Born: Lewisham, 12 January 1975
Height: 6'1" **Weight:** 11.10
Club Honours: Div 1 '00
International Honours: E: U21-6
Richard missed the majority of last season with a cruciate ligament injury sustained in the second game of the campaign at Ipswich Town. He returned to the side in the televised game against Tottenham Hotspur in March, and immediately put in some crunching tackles, proving that he

was back as strong as ever. He is a strong and determined tackler, very calm under pressure and extremely quick. He reads the game very well, has good distribution and is dominant in the air. He likes to get forward for set pieces and corners and scored Charlton's only goal in the 1-1 draw with Southampton at the Valley.
Charlton Ath (From trainee on 1/7/1993) P/FL 255+3/10 FLC 13 FAC 14 Others 5/1

RUNDLE Adam
Born: Durham, 8 July 1984
Height: 5'10" **Weight:** 11.2
This exciting young left winger broke into the Darlington first team in the new year and immediately became a great favourite with his dazzling direct runs down the flank. He was extremely unlucky not to score on a number of occasions and is a great prospect for the future.
Darlington (Trainee) FL 5+7

RUSHBURY Andrew (Andy) James
Born: Carlisle, 7 March 1983
Height: 5'10" **Weight:** 11.7
This young forward made three senior appearances from the subs' bench for Chesterfield early in the 2001-02 season. Understandably raw, he demonstrated good pace and a willingness to get stuck in, but a struggling side is no place for the inexperienced, and Andy's first-team involvement petered out as more forwards came in during December. In March he was loaned to Unibond League club Matlock Town for the rest of the season, but signed a professional contract with the Spireites for 2002-03. He is the son of Chesterfield boss Dave Rushbury.
Chesterfield (Trainee) FL 0+5 FLC 0+1 FAC 0+1

RUSSELL Alexander (Alex) John
Born: Crosby, 17 March 1973
Height: 5'9" **Weight:** 11.7
After following manager Roy McFarland from Cambridge to Torquay, Alex soon settled in as midfield kingpin. An intelligent user of the ball, he is prepared to track back but is also capable of getting forward to good effect. The Gulls' mid-season slump coincided with his absence through injury and their climb to safety was a consequence of his return to fitness. Most notable of many impressive performances was when he scored a fine hat-trick at Darlington.
Rochdale (£4,000 from Burscough on 11/7/1994) FL 83+19/14 FLC 5/1 FAC 1+1 Others 2+3

Cambridge U (Free on 4/8/1998) FL 72+9/8 FLC 7+1 FAC 7 Others 3
Torquay U (Free on 9/8/2001) FL 33/7 FLC 2

RUSSELL Darel Francis Roy
Born: Stepney, 22 October 1980
Height: 5'11" **Weight:** 11.9
International Honours: E: Yth
Darel is a combative, hard running midfield player whose energetic approach to the game has won him many admirers at Norwich. A difficult player to play against, he never gives up and can make long attacking runs which are often hard to pick up. Competing for a place with the equally energetic Gary Holt, Darel was often included as a substitute, but his commitment to the Canary cause was never in question when he was called upon.
Norwich C (From trainee on 29/11/1997) FL 83+28/7 FLC 8/2 FAC 3+1

RUSSELL Kevin John
Born: Portsmouth, 6 December 1966
Height: 5'9" **Weight:** 10.12
Club Honours: Div 2 '93
International Honours: E: Yth
'Rooster' Russell only appeared in a dozen matches for Wrexham last season, the majority of these during the reign of the former boss Brian Flynn. The reason for this was that from October onwards he assisted the new incumbent Denis Smith in a coaching capacity, although his role as assistant manager had not been made official. No doubt he may have to retain his player registration, as necessary cut backs by the cash strapped North Wales club will mean a small squad for 2002-03, but his vast experience should mean that he will still be a very useful member of the squad.
Portsmouth (From apprentice at Brighton & Hove A on 9/10/1984) FL 3+1/1 FLC 0+1 FAC 0+1 Others 1+1
Wrexham (£10,000 on 17/7/1987) FL 84/43 FLC 4/1 FAC 4 Others 8/3
Leicester C (£175,000 on 20/6/1989) FL 24+19/10 FLC 0+1 FAC 1 Others 5/2
Peterborough U (Loaned on 6/9/1990) FL 7/3
Cardiff C (Loaned on 17/1/1991) FL 3
Hereford U (Loaned on 7/11/1991) FL 3/1 Others 1/1
Stoke C (Loaned on 2/1/1992) FL 5/1
Stoke C (£95,000 on 16/7/1992) FL 30+10/5 FLC 3 FAC 2 Others 4+1/1
Burnley (£150,000 on 28/6/1993) FL 26+2/6 FLC 4/1 FAC 4 Others 1/1
Bournemouth (£125,000 on 3/3/1994) FL 30/1 FLC 3/1 FAC 2/1
Notts Co (£60,000 on 24/2/1995) FL 9+2

Wrexham (£60,000 on 21/7/1995) FL 171+26/17 FLC 6+2/2 FAC 18+5/4 Others 10+1

RUSSELL Lee Edward
Born: Southampton, 3 September 1969
Height: 5'11" **Weight:** 12.0
Lee had marshalled Torquay's defence so effectively at the end of the previous season, that it was a surprise when new manager McFarland decided to reconstruct the back line without him. A true professional, he continued to give his all in training and never let the side down when called into the centre of defence to cover for injuries. With limited first-team prospects, his contract was cancelled by mutual consent on transfer deadline day.
Portsmouth (From trainee on 12/7/1988) FL 103+20/3 FLC 8+2 FAC 4+2 Others 5+2
Bournemouth (Loaned on 9/9/1994) FL 3
Torquay U (Free on 25/3/1999) FL 78+4 FLC 2 FAC 4+1 Others 1

RYAN Keith James
Born: Northampton, 25 June 1970
Height: 5'11" **Weight:** 12.8
Club Honours: FAT '91, '93; GMVC '93
This veteran utility player and club captain had a less influential season than usual at Wycombe Wanderers in 2001-02, spending a fair amount of time on the bench. Whenever called on, however, he never let the team down, and played as a central defender, midfielder and striker, the latter role often injecting a much-needed physical power on ground and air. He has a great engine and the manager regards his total commitment as a paradigm for the other players.
Wycombe W (Signed from Berkhamstead T during 1990 close season) FL 221+39/24 FLC 13+1/3 FAC 19+5/5 Others 15+1/1

RYAN Robert (Robbie) Paul
Born: Dublin, 16 May 1977
Height: 5'10" **Weight:** 12.0
Club Honours: Div 2 '01
International Honours: RoI: U21-12; Yth; Sch
Very few wingers get the better of this strong-tackling Millwall defender last term, and that is why Robbie is considered to be one of the best full backs in Division One. He was an ever present until an injury kept him sidelined towards the end of the season and he then sat on the subs' bench for the last few games.
Huddersfield T (Free from Belvedere YC on 26/7/1994) FL 12+3 FLC 2
Millwall (£10,000 on 30/1/1998) FL 145+10 FLC 8 FAC 6 Others 5

Louis Saha

S

SABIN Eric
Born: Paris, France, 22 January 1975
Height: 6'1" **Weight:** 12.4
This attacking midfielder featured as a striker for Swindon throughout the 2001-02 season and apart from not delivering the hoped for goals, he was a great success. His electrifying pace and ability to run at defenders with the ball often caused problems for the opposition and he made an excellent all-round contribution to the team effort.
Swindon T (Free from Wasquehal, France on 13/7/2001) FL 33+1/5 FLC 1 FAC 3

SADLIER Richard Thomas
Born: Dublin, 14 January 1979
Height: 6'2'' **Weight:** 12.10
Club Honours: Div 2 '01
International Honours: RoI: U21-2; Yth
This tall centre forward had a great season at Millwall last term. He started well and improved with every match in all areas of his game. He was on course to be the club's leading scorer when he sustained a hip injury in early March that really put paid not only to his season at the Den, but also to his World Cup hopes for the Republic of Ireland. He scored 17 goals in all competitions during the campaign.
Millwall (Signed from Belvedere YC on 14/8/1996) FL 101+37/33 FLC 6/2 FAC 4+1/2 Others 7+2/3

SAFRI Youssef
Born: Morocco, 1 March 1977
Height: 5'10" **Weight:** 11.8
International Honours: Morocco:
Youssef was Gordon Strachan's last signing as Coventry manager and proved to be an inspired recruit to the squad at Highfield Road. His introduction, perversely for his international colleague Youssef Chippo, coincided with an 11-match unbeaten run and he impressed with his excellent ball control and passing ability. Playing mainly in the deeper central midfield role he had limited scoring chances but did find the net with a tremendous free kick against Sheffield Wednesday. Youssef is a regular in midfield for his country and is expected to be a target for several Premiership clubs in the summer.
Coventry C (Free from Raja Casablanca, Morocco on 25/8/2001) FL 32+1/1 FLC 2

SAHA Louis
Born: Paris, France, 8 August 1978
Height: 5'11" **Weight:** 11.10

Club Honours: Div 1 '01
International Honours: France: U21; Yth (UEFA-U18 '97)
Once again Louis was amongst the top goal-scorers for Fulham last term, although he never reached the prolific strike-rate achieved in the previous season. It all started well enough with a two-goal burst in the opening game at Old Trafford, giving him a tally of four goals in the opening four games. Louis also scored the Fulham 'Goal of the Season' with a 25-yard rocket against his old club Newcastle, against whom he again proved a thorn in the side, adding another vital goal in the draw at St James' Park. His pace and skills are always likely to prove a handful for opposition defences.
Newcastle U (Loaned from Metz, France on 8/1/1999) PL 5+6/1 FAC 1/1
Fulham (£2,100,000 on 29/6/2000) P/FL 67+12/35 FLC 3+3/6 FAC 6+1

SALAKO John Akin
Born: Nigeria, 11 February 1969
Height: 5'10" **Weight:** 12.8
Club Honours: FMC '91; Div 1 '94, '00
International Honours: E: 5
John was in the starting line-up for Charlton's opening two games of the season and came off the bench for the next two games, but played no further part in the campaign. Frustrated with the lack of opportunities he was loaned to Reading where he did well and went straight into the side to fill the problem position on the left flank. His ability to go past the full back and send over pinpoint crosses contributed greatly to the Royals' impressive mid-season surge to top spot. After being on loan for three months he signed permanently, but although his form then dipped he still played a vital role in the run-in to promotion.
Crystal Palace (From apprentice on 3/11/1986) F/PL 172+43/22 FLC 19+5/5 FAC 20/4 Others 11+3/2
Swansea C (Loaned on 14/8/1989) FL 13/3 Others 2/1
Coventry C (£1,500,000 on 7/8/1995) PL 68+4/4 FLC 9/3 FAC 4/1
Bolton W (Free on 26/3/1998) PL 0+7
Fulham (Free on 22/7/1998) FL 7+3/1 FLC 2/1 FAC 2+2 Others 1
Charlton Ath (£150,000 + on 20/8/1999) P/FL 10+37/2 FLC 1+2 FAC 3+4/1
Reading (£75,000 + on 2/11/2001) FL 31/6 Others 1

SALL Abdou Hamed
Born: Senegal, 1 November 1980
Height: 6'3" **Weight:** 14.2

This giant young defender joined Kidderminster during the 2001 close season as a prospect for the future with a lot of rough edges. After scoring on his debut against York in October he immediately became a firm favourite with the Harriers' fans and made himself a cornerstone of a back four that had the second best defensive record in the Third Division.
Kidderminster Hrs (Free from Toulouse, France on 10/8/2001) FL 27/2 FAC 1 Others 1

SALVATI Marc Robert
Born: Middlesbrough, 5 March 1983
Height: 5'9" **Weight:** 12.0
Marc scored on his full League debut for York City in a 2-1 defeat at Carlisle last September and enjoyed an extended run in the senior squad in the first half of the campaign, although mostly appearing on the subs' bench. A lively and direct right winger he was released at the end of the campaign.
York C (Trainee) FL 1+7/1

SAM Hector McLeod
Born: Mount Hope, Trinidad, 25 February 1978
Height: 5'9" **Weight:** 11.5
International Honours: Trinidad & Tobago: U-
This enigmatic Wrexham striker looked to be on the verge of establishing himself in the starting line-up last season, only to flatter to deceive. His strength was again his unpredictability and he had his best spell in the side during January and February. This included a brace of goals in the 2-2 draw at Bury, and a vital last-minute winner at Peterborough shortly afterwards. He also scored a cracker from 20 yards at Wigan in October.
Wrexham (£125,000 from CL Financial San Juan Jabloteh, Trinidad on 8/8/2000) FL 26+23/11 FLC 2 FAC 2 Others 3

SAMBROOK Andrew (Andy) John
Born: Chatham, 13 July 1979
Height: 5'10" **Weight:** 12.4
This right back joined Rushden in the 2001 pre-season, initially on a monthly deal, and went on to establish himself in manager Brian Talbot's first-team plans. He grabbed the opportunity when Tarkan Mustafa was injured in September and went on to play over 25 League games, although injury ruled him out of the play-off final.
Gillingham (Associated Schoolboy) FL 0+1

Rushden & Diamonds (Free from Hartwick College, USA on 9/8/2001) FL 25+1 FAC 2 Others 1

SAMPSON Ian
Born: Wakefield, 14 November 1968
Height: 6'2" **Weight:** 13.3
Ian completed his eighth full season with Northampton Town in 2001-02 and is now fourth in the club's all-time appearance records. He too fell under the club's injury curse, but his return coincided with the Cobblers' rise from the bottom of the division. He is a reliable central defender who is effective in the air and a constant danger to opposition defences when he moves up to help out in attack.
Sunderland (Signed from Goole T on 13/11/1990) FL 13+4/1 FLC 1 FAC 0+2 Others 0+1
Northampton T (Loaned on 8/12/1993) FL 8
Northampton T (Free on 5/8/1994) FL 306+6/23 FLC 16/1 FAC 11/1 Others 17/2
Tottenham H (Loaned on 22/6/1995) Others 3/1

SAMUEL JLloyd
Born: Trinidad, 29 March 1981
Height: 5'11" **Weight:** 11.4
International Honours: E: U21-1; Yth
This pacy Aston Villa player has the versatility to play at full back, in the centre of defence and in midfield. In October he went on loan to Gillingham where he produced some classy displays only to be recalled as cover for injuries. He initially deputised for Mark Delaney at right back before switching to the opposite flank as a replacement for Alan Wright and retained his place until the end of the campaign.
Aston Villa (From trainee on 2/2/1999) PL 23+12 FLC 0+1 FAC 2 Others 3+2
Gillingham (Loaned on 26/10/2001) FL 7+1

SANCHEZ-LOPEZ Carlos
Born: Madrid, Spain, 22 July 1979
Height: 5'10" **Weight:** 12.5
Carlos began last season in the lower reaches of the Spanish League with Getafe before joining Bristol Rovers on a short-term contract in February. He made a promising debut against Hartlepool in an attacking right-wing-back role, showing good technical touches and a willingness to have a shot on goal. Unfortunately he suffered with a shin problem early on and then a knee injury sidelined him. He was released at the end of the season.
Bristol Rov (Free from Getafe, Spain on 8/2/2002) FL 6

SAND Peter
Born: Aalborg, Denmark, 17 July 1972
Height: 6'0" **Weight:** 12.3
Peter made his debut for Barnsley in the Worthington Cup tie against Newcastle and he scored in his next game against Birmingham. A tall, hard-working midfielder, he suffered because he came into a struggling team and shortly afterwards there was a change of manager. The arrival of new players after Steve Parkin was appointed put his place in jeopardy and in February he was sold to Norwegian club Stabaek for a substantial fee.
Barnsley (£250,000 from Midtjylland, Denmark, ex Hadsund, Brondby, Olstykke, Fremad Amager, on 5/10/2001) FL 4+2/1 FLC 1 FAC 0+1

SANDFORD Lee Robert
Born: Basingstoke, 22 April 1968
Height: 6'1" **Weight:** 13.4
Club Honours: AMC '92; Div 2 '93
International Honours: E: Yth
Having overcome his serious neck problem, Lee got off to a slow start at Sheffield United last term after suffering a recurrence of a calf injury. With opportunities limited at Bramall Lane he went on loan to Stockport to regain match fitness and help shore up a leaking defence, but he made little impression at Edgeley Park. On returning to the Blades he made few appearances, although was a regular on the bench. When called upon, he used his experience and anticipation to give reliable performances in the centre of the back four.
Portsmouth (From apprentice on 4/12/1985) FL 66+6/1 FLC 11 FAC 4 Others 2+1
Stoke C (£140,000 on 22/12/1989) FL 255+3/8 FLC 19 FAC 16/2 Others 31/4
Sheffield U (£500,000 on 22/7/1996) FL 142+9/4 FLC 12+1 FAC 16+1/1 Others 3+1
Reading (Loaned on 5/9/1997) FL 5
Stockport Co (Loaned on 11/10/2001) FL 7

SANTOS Georges
Born: Marseille, France, 15 August 1970
Height: 6'3" **Weight:** 14.0
Georges missed much of the pre-season training for Sheffield United last term while recovering from a serious facial injury suffered the previous March. He was a regular member of the squad from the start of the campaign, but apart from a spell towards the end of the year he was mainly on the bench, although often called into action. On these occasions he generally appeared in midfield or defence, occasionally in attack. An effective ball winner, he always gave 100 per cent,

while his passing created decisive openings for his colleagues. Dismissed for a challenge in the notorious match against West Bromwich Albion, his two-minute substitute appearance in that game marked the end of his career with the Blades.
Tranmere Rov (Free from Toulon, France on 29/7/1998) FL 46+1/2 FLC 6 FAC 1
West Bromwich A (£25,000 on 23/3/2000) FL 8
Sheffield U (Free on 5/7/2000) FL 37+24/6 FLC 2+3 FAC 1+1

SANTUS Paul Graham
Born: Wigan, 8 September 1983
Height: 5'11" **Weight:** 11.4
This Wigan trainee received his debut in senior football last term when he came on as a late substitute in the 2-2 draw at Cambridge United. A right-sided attacking midfield player with good pace and crossing ability, he spent the remainder of the season developing in the club's reserve and youth teams. He was one of three scholars to be awarded a 12-month professional contract in the summer.
Wigan Ath (Trainee) FL 0+1

SAUNDERS Mark Philip
Born: Reading, 23 July 1971
Height: 5'11" **Weight:** 11.12
Mark found first-team opportunities limited at Gillingham, but when called upon never let anybody down with his all-action displays, whether it be in midfield, at right back or occasionally as an emergency striker. Currently on the transfer list, most Gills fans will be sad to see him leave for pastures new.
Plymouth Arg (Signed from Tiverton T on 22/8/1995) FL 60+12/11 FLC 1+1 FAC 2+3 Others 2
Gillingham (Free on 1/6/1998) FL 78+36/11 FLC 4+2 FAC 7+1/1 Others 3+3

SAVAGE Basir (Bas) Mohammed
Born: London, 7 January 1982
Height: 6'3" **Weight:** 13.8
Reading's scouting system spotted Bas while he was turning out for Walton & Hersham in the Ryman League, and he was signed for a bargain fee plus the promise of a pre-season friendly. The lanky striker found the adjustment to full-time training difficult at first, but after several impressive reserve-team appearances he was promoted to the first-team bench for two games at the end of the campaign. His only taste of action came during the four minutes of

Robbie Savage

injury time in the promotion decider at Brentford when he replaced Martin Butler.
Reading (£20,000 from Walton & Hersham on 7/2/2002) FL 0+1

SAVAGE David (Dave) Thomas Patrick
Born: Dublin, 30 July 1973
Height: 6'1" **Weight:** 12.7
International Honours: RoI; 5; U21-5
Dave arrived at Oxford just a few days prior to the start of the 2001-02 season and missed just five games during the campaign. A probing midfielder, he spent most of his time in a central role but started the odd game out in a wide position. He opened his goal account for the U's with a close-range header in the 6-1 win over Halifax.
Brighton & Hove A (Signed from Kilkenny on 5/3/1991. Free to Longford T in May 1992)
Millwall (£15,000 on 27/5/1994) FL 104+28/6 FLC 11/2 FAC 6+2/2 Others 2/1
Northampton T (£100,000 on 7/10/1998) FL 98+15/18 FLC 3 FAC 5 Others 2+1
Oxford U (Free on 18/8/2001) FL 42/1 FLC 1 FAC 1 Others 1

SAVAGE Robert (Robbie) William
Born: Wrexham, 18 October 1974
Height: 6'1" **Weight:** 11.11
Club Honours: FAYC '92; FLC '00
International Honours: W: 25; U21-5; Yth; Sch
This right-footed midfielder or wing back continued to be a crowd favourite at Filbert Street last season, never giving less than 100 per cent effort. However, his form seemed to fluctuate during the campaign as the team struggled. He continued to wear his heart on his sleeve throughout the campaign and was never prouder than when asked to take a temporary hold of the captain's armband and he also won the 'Man of the Match' plaudits for an outstanding midfield display for Wales against Argentina. He was reported to have signed for Premiership new boys Birmingham City in the summer.
Manchester U (From trainee on 5/7/1993)
Crewe Alex (Free on 22/7/1994) FL 74+3/10 FLC 5 FAC 5 Others 8/1
Leicester C (£400,000 on 23/7/1997) PL 160+12/8 FLC 15+2 FAC 12/1 Others 2+1

SAVARESE Giovanni
Born: Caracas, Venezuela, 14 July 1971
Height: 6'0" **Weight:** 13.2
International Honours: Venezuela: 23
This experienced striker showed great skill and composure on the ball during a three-month contract with Millwall at the beginning of last season. A proven goal-scorer elsewhere, he made just a single first-team appearance from the subs' bench before returning to Venezuela in November where he linked up with Deportivo Italchacao.
Swansea C (Free from San Jose Earthquakes, USA, ex New England Revolution, on 13/10/2000) FL 28+3/12 FAC 0+1 Others 3/2
Millwall (Free on 8/8/2001) FL 0+1

SCHEMMEL Sebastien
Born: Nancy, France, 2 June 1975
Height: 5'10" **Weight:** 11.12
International Honours: France: U21
This West Ham wing back enjoyed a marvellous season in 2001-02, culminating in him being named as 'Hammer of the Year' by the fans. Playing on the right-hand side he provided excellent support to the forward line, while his determination and passion made him a firm favourite with the supporters.

Sebastien Schemmel

He scored his first goal for the club against Derby County on Boxing Day and celebrated with great joy.
West Ham U (£465,000 from Metz, France, ex Nancy, on 19/1/2001) PL 45+2/1 FLC 1 FAC 6

SCHMEICHEL Peter Boleslaw
Born: Gladsaxe, Denmark, 18 November 1963
Height: 6'4" **Weight:** 16.0
Club Honours: ESC '91; FLC '92; PL '93, '94, '96, '97, '99; FAC '94, '96, '99; CS '93, '94, '96, '97; EC '99
International Honours: Denmark: 129 (UEFA '92)
One of Europe's best goalkeepers of recent times, Peter was a surprise signing for Aston Villa during the 2001 close season. He proved to be a big hit at Villa Park to begin with and was in commanding form early on, producing a string of inspired displays. He also showed a tendency to come up for corners late in the game and scored at Everton with a fierce right-foot volley. He missed just a handful of games through injury, but in April he made the decision to join Manchester City for 2002-03. Peter was made an honorary MBE for his services to football last December.
Manchester U (£550,000 from Brondby, Denmark on 12/8/1991) P/FL 292 FLC 17 FAC 41 Others 48/1 (Free to Sporting Lisbon, Portugal on 1/7/1999)
Aston Villa (Free on 20/7/2001) PL 29/1 FLC 2 FAC 1 Others 4

SCHOFIELD Daniel (Danny) James
Born: Doncaster, 10 April 1980
Height: 5'10" **Weight:** 11.3
This talented youngster won a regular place in the Huddersfield Town line-up last term, featuring either as a striker or on the wing. Wherever he played he showed excellent close control, accurate passing and good crossing skills, and taunted many an opposition defence. He scored 12 times in all competitions, including the 'Goal of the Season' in the LDV Vans Trophy game against Blackpool. He deservedly received the 'Players' Player of the Year' award.
Huddersfield T (£2,000 from Brodsworth on 8/2/1999) FL 40+4/8 FLC 0+2 FAC 2+1 Others 6/4

SCHOLES Paul
Born: Salford, 16 November 1974
Height: 5'7" **Weight:** 11.10
Club Honours: PL '96, '97, '99, '00, '01; FAC '96, '99; CS '96, '97

International Honours: E: 49; Yth (UEFA-U18 '93)
This all-action central midfield player was asked to change his role for Manchester United and play just behind Ruud van Nistelrooy, instead of in his customary deep-midfield slot in the early part of last season. He went on to have another fine season at Old Trafford and contributed his usual quota of goals beginning with his strike against Deportivo in the European Champions' League qualifier. At international level he produced a sublime performance for England in the 5-1 thrashing of Germany and went on to perform well in the final stages of the tournament.
Manchester U (From trainee on 29/1/1993) PL 175+52/55 FLC 6+2/5 FAC 10+6/4 Others 61+10/17

SCHWARZ Stefan Hans
Born: Malmo, Sweden, 18 April 1969
Height: 5'10" **Weight:** 12.6
International Honours: Sweden: 69; U21
A left sided midfielder, Stefan's experience was crucial to Sunderland in the Premiership last term. A strong tackler, he surprisingly found himself out of favour for a while and his calm demeanour and impeccable distribution was missed as the Black Cats struggled against relegation. His only goal of the campaign was arguably the goal of the season at Sunderland: a brilliant 20-yard lob against his old club Arsenal in October, which saved a vital point in a 1-1 draw.
Arsenal (£1,750,000 from Benfica, Portugal, ex Malmo, on 31/5/1994) PL 34/2 FLC 4 FAC 1 Others 10/2 (£2,500,000 to Fiorentina, Italy on 27/7/1995)
Sunderland (£3,500,000 from Valencia, Spain on 9/8/1999) PL 62+5/3 FLC 1 FAC 6

SCHWARZER Mark
Born: Sydney, Australia, 6 October 1972
Height: 6'5'' **Weight:** 13.6
International Honours: Australia: 19; Yth
Mark fought of the challenge posed by Mark Crossley to retain the goalkeeper's jersey for Middlesbrough for much of last term. A big, commanding 'keeper, he is also an excellent shot stopper.
Bradford C (£350,000 from Kaiserslautern, Germany, ex Blacktown, Marconi, Dynamo Dresden, on 22/11/1996) FL 13 FAC 3
Middlesbrough (£1,500,000 on 26/2/1997) F/PL 165 FLC 16 FAC 11

SCIMECA Ricardo
Born: Leamington Spa, 13 June 1975
Height: 6'1" **Weight:** 12.9
Club Honours: FLC '96

International Honours: E: B-1; U21-9
Nottingham Forest's club captain showed his versatility last term when he appeared at right back, the centre of defence and midfield, before settling in at centre back which looks to be his best position. Strong in the tackle and effective pushing forward, he formed a useful defensive partnership with Jon Hjelde.
Aston Villa (From trainee on 7/7/1993) PL 50+23/2 FLC 4+3 FAC 9+1 Others 5+2
Nottingham F (£3,000,000 on 23/7/1999) FL 107+4/4 FLC 6 FAC 4

SCOTHERN Ashley John
Born: Pontefract, 11 September 1984
Height: 6'0" **Weight:** 11.2
Ashley made his debut for Barnsley as a late substitute at Nottingham Forest last January. Another product of the club's academy and a prolific scorer at U17 level, he was one of the stars of the U18 team that reached the semi final of the FA Youth Cup.
Barnsley (Trainee) FL 0+1

SCOTT Andrew (Andy)
Born: Epsom, 2 August 1972
Height: 6'1" **Weight:** 11.5
Club Honours: Div 3 '99
Andy proved to be a useful foil for Paul Moody up front for Oxford United last term and scored nine times. A hard-working striker, he often played out wide. He missed a number of games with a pulled hamstring and was not always a regular when he returned to fitness due to the emergence of Jamie Brooks, but his hard work will surely see him bounce back in 2002-03.
Sheffield U (£50,000 from Sutton U on 1/12/1992) P/FL 39+36/6 FLC 5/2 FAC 2+1 Others 3+1/3
Chesterfield (Loaned on 18/10/1996) FL 4+1/3
Bury (Loaned on 21/3/1997) FL 2+6
Brentford (£75,000 on 21/11/1997) FL 109+9/28 FLC 8+1/4 FAC 3 Others 6/3
Oxford U (£75,000 on 12/1/2001) FL 46+5/13 FLC 1/1

SCOTT Dion Elijah
Born: Birmingham, 24 December 1980
Height: 5'11" **Weight:** 11.3
This young Walsall defender made just one first-team appearance last season, coming on as substitute for Matthew Gadsby in the last minute of the game at Sheffield Wednesday in October. He was, however, a prominent member of the reserve side that topped the Avon Insurance League Division One and also had a spell on loan with Conference club

Boston United. He was released during the summer and is likely to be in demand by clubs looking for a mobile defender who is also impressive going forward.
Walsall *(From trainee on 18/5/1999) FL 0+2 Others 2*

SCOTT Robert (Rob)
Born: Epsom, 15 August 1973
Height: 6'1" **Weight:** 11.10
Rob is a versatile defender who is equally at home playing on the right side of a back four or as a sweeper where he can use his anticipation and speed to great effect. An automatic choice at Rotherham for most of last season, he missed a few games due to injury in the closing stages of the campaign. Ever-willing to join in with the attack, he netted three goals including one against his former club Sheffield United. Although originally signed as a striker, he is now firmly established as a defender.
Sheffield U *(£20,000 from Sutton U on 1/8/1993) FL 2+4/1 FLC 0+1 Others 2+1*
Scarborough *(Loaned on 22/3/1995) FL 8/3*

Northampton T *(Loaned on 24/11/1995) FL 5 Others 1*
Fulham *(£30,000 on 10/1/1996) FL 65+19/17 FLC 3+5 FAC 3/1 Others 2+2/1*
Carlisle U *(Loaned on 18/8/1998) FL 7/3*
Rotherham U *(£50,000 on 17/11/1998) FL 112+5/7 FLC 5+1 FAC 8/1 Others 6*

SCOWCROFT James (Jamie)
Benjamin
Born: Bury St Edmunds, 15 November 1975
Height: 6'1" **Weight:** 12.2
International Honours: E: U21-5
Signed for Leicester in the summer of 2001, Jamie can operate either as a striker or in a withdrawn midfield role. He took a while to establish himself in the line-up due to early season injuries, but eventually emerged as a surprisingly effective header of the ball. A high point was his sweetly taken strike past Nigel Martyn to earn a surprise point at Elland Road, which was voted the club's 'Goal of the Season'. Dave Bassett often used Jamie in a wide midfield role, from where

he could ghost effectively into the centre to pose an additional threat, but a March calf injury brought his season to an early close.
Ipswich T *(From trainee on 1/7/1994) P/FL 163+39/47 FLC 21+4/7 FAC 9+1 Others 7+4/1*
Leicester C *(£3,000,000 on 31/7/2001) PL 21+3/5 FLC 1 FAC 1/2*

SCULLY Anthony (Tony)
Derek Thomas
Born: Dublin, 12 June 1976
Height: 5'7" **Weight:** 11.12
International Honours: RoI: B-1; U21-10; Yth; Sch
Tony had the misfortune to suffer a pre-season injury soon after signing for Cambridge in the summer of 2001 and it was not until November that he made his debut for the U's. He subsequently appeared on a regular basis adding width and pace to the midfield and contributing two goals in the closing stages of the campaign.
Crystal Palace *(From trainee on 2/12/1993) FL 0+3*

Mark Schwarzer

Bournemouth *(Loaned on 14/10/1994) FL 6+4 Others 2*
Cardiff C *(Loaned on 5/1/1996) FL 13+1*
Manchester C *(£80,000 on 12/8/1997) FL 1+8*
Stoke C *(Loaned on 27/1/1998) FL 7*
Queens Park R *(£155,000 on 17/3/1998) FL 20+20/2 FLC 4+1 FAC 0+1*
Cambridge U *(Free on 9/7/2001) FL 19+6/2 FAC 2 Others 2*

SEAMAN David Andrew
Born: Rotherham, 19 September 1963
Height: 6'4" **Weight:** 14.10
Club Honours: Div 1 '91; PL '98, '02; FAC '93, '98, '02; FLC '93; ECWC '94; CS '98
International Honours: E: 73; B-6; U21-10
David had another fine season in goal for Arsenal and England in 2001-02, despite missing several weeks in the middle of the campaign due to a shoulder injury. A fine shot stopper with excellent positional sense he led the Gunners to a domestic double and then did well for his country in the World Cup finals until beaten by a long-range effort in England's defeat by Brazil.
Leeds U *(From apprentice on 22/9/1981)*
Peterborough U *(£4,000 on 13/8/1982) FL 91 FLC 10 FAC 5*
Birmingham C *(£100,000 on 5/10/1984) FL 75 FLC 4 FAC 5*
Queens Park R *(£225,000 on 7/8/1986) FL 141 FLC 13 FAC 17 Others 4*
Arsenal *(£1,300,000 on 18/5/1990) F/PL 377 FLC 32 FAC 49 Others 63+1*

SEARLE Damon Peter
Born: Cardiff, 26 October 1971
Height: 5'11" **Weight:** 10.4
Club Honours: WC '92, '93; Div 3 '93
International Honours: W: B-1; U21-6; Yth; Sch
Although not as consistent as in the previous season, Damon proved to be a staunch performer for Southend United during 2001-2002, making the left-back berth his own. A stylish performer, his surging overlaps allowed him to deliver a stream of excellent crosses, a skill that persuaded Rob Newman to try him in midfield during the latter part of the campaign. A new 12-month contract should give him the chance to show his value to the Blues once more during 2002-03.
Cardiff C *(From trainee on 20/8/1990) FL 232+2/3 FLC 9/1 FAC 13 Others 29*
Stockport Co *(Free on 28/5/1996) FL 34+7 FLC 2+1 FAC 2 Others 1*

Carlisle U *(Free on 6/7/1998) FL 57+9/3 FLC 4 FAC 1 Others 4+1/1*
Rochdale *(Loaned on 17/9/1999) FL 13+1*
Southend U *(Free on 10/7/2000) FL 87+2/2 FLC 3 FAC 8 Others 8/1*

SEDDON Gareth Jonathan
Born: Burnley, 23 May 1980
Height: 5'11" **Weight:** 11.2
Gareth enjoyed a relatively successful season at Bury last term and finished up as the club's leading scorer with a total of eight goals. He started brightly, forming an effective partnership up front with Jon Newby and he scored the first senior goals of his career in the 2-1 home win against Chesterfield. His progress was restricted by a series of injuries but when fully fit he is undoubtedly an asset to the Shakers.
Bury *(Free from RAF Codsall, via trail at Everton, ex Accrington Stanley, Atherstone U, on 9/8/2001) FL 23+12/6 FLC 1 FAC 1/1*

SEDGEMORE Benjamin (Ben) Redwood
Born: Wolverhampton, 5 August 1975
Height: 5'11" **Weight:** 12.10
International Honours: E: Sch
Ben's hard work throughout the 2001-02 season paid off as he won a regular first-team place despite being on Lincoln's transfer list from the start of the campaign. He battled well in the centre of a midfield four and with better luck could have added to his total of just two goals. Out of football he continued his studies for a degree in psychology and law through distance learning.
Birmingham C *(From trainee on 17/5/1993)*
Northampton T *(Loaned on 22/12/1994) FL 1*
Mansfield T *(Loaned on 25/8/1995) FL 4+5 Others 1*
Peterborough U *(Free on 10/1/1996) FL 13+4 FAC 1*
Mansfield T *(Free on 6/9/1996) FL 58+9/6 FLC 1 FAC 2+1 Others 2*
Macclesfield T *(£25,000 on 19/3/1998) FL 84+18/6 FLC 8/2 FAC 7/1 Others 2*
Lincoln C *(Signed on 16/2/2001) FL 36+17/3 FLC 1 FAC 3 Others 1+1*

SEDGWICK Christopher (Chris) Edward
Born: Sheffield, 28 April 1980
Height: 5'11" **Weight:** 10.10
A flying right winger who is a product of Rotherham's youth policy, Chris steadily grew in confidence last season. He paid more attention to his defensive duties, a factor that proved to be a key element throughout the campaign, and if there was anything lacking in his game it was

goals, for he found the net only once despite packing a powerful shot.
Rotherham U *(From trainee on 16/8/1997) FL 94+46/12 FLC 2+2 FAC 5+5 Others 2+2/1*

SELLARS Scott
Born: Sheffield, 27 November 1965
Height: 5'8" **Weight:** 10.0
Club Honours: FMC '87; Div 1 '93, '97
International Honours: E: U21-3
Scott returned to add his experience to Mansfield Town's promotion push following a spell in Denmark with AGF Aarhus. He scored on his full debut at Luton on Easter Monday as the Stags made a few changes in an attempt to get their promotion push back on track, and looked effective in the closing stages of the campaign, impressing with his set pieces from which he hit the woodwork on several occasions.
Leeds U *(From apprentice on 25/7/1983) FL 72+4/12 FLC 4/1 FAC 4 Others 2/1*
Blackburn Rov *(£20,000 on 28/7/1986) FL 194+8/35 FLC 12/3 FAC 11/1 Others 20/2*
Leeds U *(£800,000 on 1/7/1992) PL 6+1 FLC 1+1 Others 1*
Newcastle U *(£700,000 on 9/3/1993) F/PL 56+5/5 FLC 6+1/2 FAC 3 Others 4/1*
Bolton W *(£750,000 on 7/12/1995) P/FL 106+5/15 FLC 8+1 FAC 5/1 Others 0+1*
Huddersfield T *(Free on 30/7/1999) FL 29+19/1 FLC 1+2/1 FAC 1+1 (Free to Aarhus, Denmark on 17/4/2001)*
Port Vale *(Free on 11/1/2002)*
Mansfield T *(Free on 22/3/2002) FL 5+1/1*

SELLEY Ian
Born: Chertsey, 14 June 1974
Height: 5'10" **Weight:** 11.0
Club Honours: FLC '93; FAC '93; ECWC '94
International Honours: E: U21-3; Yth
Ian found himself out of the reckoning at Wimbledon last season and in February he joined Southend United on loan. He stayed with the Blues for the remainder of the campaign, settling into a midfield role alongside Kevin Maher. A hard-working player with good distribution skills, he tried his best to prompt the team forward, although he also accumulated a number of yellow cards.
Arsenal *(From trainee on 6/5/1992) PL 35+6 FLC 5+1 FAC 3 Others 8+2/2*
Southend U *(Loaned on 3/12/1996) FL 3+1*
Fulham *(£500,000 on 17/10/1997) FL 3*
Wimbledon *(Free on 8/8/2000) FL 1+3*
Southend U *(Loaned on 13/2/2002) FL 14*

SENDA Daniel (Danny) Luke
Born: Harrow, 17 April 1981
Height: 5'10" **Weight:** 10.0

Gareth Seddon (left)

International Honours: E: Yth
Last season marked a coming of age for Danny at Wycombe when he was asked to fill in at right back early in the campaign. Nominally a right winger, he immediately looked at home in his new defensive position and kept his place until the end of the season. He has terrific pace, and Second Division forwards struggled to cope with his perfectly timed darting tackles. He likes to get forward and cross whenever possible and without another natural right back in the squad he should be first choice again in 2002-03.
Wycombe W (From Southampton juniors on 26/1/1999) FL 55+52/3 FLC 0+3 FAC 4+3 Others 2+4

SENIOR Michael Graham
Born: Huddersfield, 3 March 1981
Height: 5'9" **Weight:** 11.6
This promising Huddersfield Town midfielder made a single first-team appearance last term, coming on from the subs' bench in the closing stages of the LDV Vans Trophy victory over Scunthorpe. He spent the remainder of the campaigning developing in the reserves and will be looking to gain more senior action in 2002-03.
Huddersfield T (From trainee on 8/7/1999) FL 0+4 FLC 0+1 Others 0+1

SERENI Matteo
Born: Parma, Italy, 11 February 1975
Height: 6'1" **Weight:** 12.11
International Honours: Italy: U21
Matteo became Ipswich's record signing when he joined the club just before the start of the season. An agile 'keeper, he is an excellent shot-stopper and in the first half of the campaign was called upon many times to keep his side in the game. He received a red card at Leicester, which was later rescinded, and asked to be rested from the FA Cup game at Dagenham – a not unusual request in Italy. Unfortunately, he did not get his place back in the next Premiership game but had to sit and watch from the substitutes' bench.
Ipswich T (£4,500,000 from Sampdoria, Italy, ex Piacenza, Empoli, on 17/8/2001) PL 25 FLC 2 Others 6

SETCHELL Gary John
Born: Kings Lynn, 8 May 1975
Height: 6'1" **Weight:** 14.0
Club Honours: NC '01
Rushden & Diamonds' utility man, Gary is a manager's dream - won't let anyone down when he is in the side, won't moan to anyone when he isn't. Essentially a

left-sided player, be it in defence or midfield, Gary almost managed more League appearances from the bench last season than he did in the starting line-up, and he found his way onto the score sheet just the once – away at Shrewsbury Town.
Rushden & Diamonds (Signed from Kettering T, ex Kings Lynn, Wisbech, Fakenham T, on 6/6/2000) FL 13+9/1 FAC 0+1 Others 0+1

SHAIL Mark Edward David
Born: Sandviken, Sweden, 15 October 1966
Height: 6'1" **Weight:** 13.3
International Honours: E: SP-1
This veteran old-fashioned central defender found himself relegated to a supporting role at Kidderminster last season and was only called into action when Craig Hinton was out injured. He was released by the club in January and returned to Worcester City, the club where he began his career.
Bristol C (£45,000 from Yeovil on 25/3/1993) FL 117+11/4 FLC 5+1 FAC 11/1 Others 4
Kidderminster Hrs (Free on 14/7/2000) FL 40/1 FLC 2 FAC 3 Others 3

SHARP James
Born: Reading, 2 January 1976
Height: 6'1" **Weight:** 14.6
2001-02 proved to be a disappointing season for this Hartlepool player who looked destined for great things exactly a year earlier. He began suffering with a shin splints injury, but soon recovered sufficiently to become a regular. However, he lost his place following a period of suspension and found himself unable to get back in the team. He is a strong left-sided defender, who puts pressure on opposition defences with his extremely long throw.
Hartlepool U (Free from Andover on 10/8/2000) FL 44+5/2 FLC 2 Others 5+1

SHARP Kevin Phillip
Born: Ontario, Canada, 19 September 1974
Height: 5'9" **Weight:** 11.11
Club Honours: FAYC '93; Div 3 '97; AMC '99
International Honours: E: Yth (UEFA-U18 '93); Sch
This reliable left back made just one starting appearance for Wigan Athletic in the League last season and in November he was released by the club. He subsequently joined Wrexham on a non-contract basis and enjoyed an impressive debut at home to Cardiff City, always

lending support to the forwards. He was pushed into midfield on occasions during the season where he looked more comfortable and scored his only goal in the 3-1 defeat at Swindon. He was not on the Robins' retained list at the end of April.
Leeds U (£60,000 from Auxerre, France on 20/10/1992) PL 11+6 Others 0+1
Wigan Ath (£100,000 on 30/11/1995) FL 156+22/10 FLC 7+2/1 FAC 7+3 Others 18+1/1
Wrexham (Free on 2/11/2001) FL 12+3/1

SHARP Neil Anthony
Born: Hemel Hempstead, 19 January 1978
Height: 6'1" **Weight:** 12.10
Neil joined Swansea City last October after impressing for Merthyr in a pre-season friendly against the club. Once he had adjusted to the demands of League football, he showed consistent form in a central defensive role and soon became a regular in the line-up. Strong in the air, he was also a danger at set pieces, striking the woodwork on a number of occasions, before scoring his first senior goal against Kidderminster. A groin strain saw him miss a few games towards the end of the season.
Swansea C (Free from Merthyr Tydfil, ex Kansas C, Hayes, Boreham Wood, Barry T, on 25/10/2001) FL 22+3/1

SHARPE Lee Stuart
Born: Halesowen, 27 May 1971
Height: 6'0" **Weight:** 12.12
Club Honours: ECWC '91; FLC '92; PL '93, '94, '96; CS '94
International Honours: E: 8; B-1; U21-8
Lee missed the first four months of the 2001-02 season for Bradford City after undergoing knee surgery, then after a brief run in the side he suffered a rib injury and missed three more games. He is a very exciting player when he is running down the left wing, taking on players and crossing the ball for the forwards to latch on to. He played a couple of games in the middle of midfield and looked very strong, his passing of the ball was excellent and he was also useful when taking free kicks.
Torquay U (From trainee on 31/5/1988) FL 9+5/3 Others 2+3
Manchester U (£185,000 on 10/6/1988) F/PL 160+33/21 FLC 15+8/9 FAC 22+7/3 Others 18+2/3
Leeds U (£4,500,000 on 14/8/1996) PL 28+2/5 FLC 3/1 FAC 0+1 Others 1+2
Bradford C (£200,000 on 25/3/1999) P/FL 36+20/4 FLC 3+1 FAC 2+1 Others 3
Portsmouth (Loaned on 2/2/2001) FL 17

SHARPS Ian William
Born: Warrington, 23 October 1980
Height: 6'4" **Weight:** 13.8
A tall central defender who is both strong in the air and difficult to shake off the ball, Ian featured regularly for Tranmere in 2001-02 and was handed the captaincy for the final match against Cardiff. He revelled in the role, amply demonstrating his vision and accurate distribution skills, and will no doubt be a major part of manager Dave Watson's plans for the 2002-03 campaign.
Tranmere Rov (From trainee on 5/7/1999) FL 25+5 FLC 1 FAC 2 Others 1

SHAW Paul
Born: Burnham, 4 September 1973
Height: 5'11" **Weight:** 12.4
International Honours: E: Yth
After struggling for form the previous season, Paul found his feet at Gillingham during the course of the 2001-02 season and grew in stature as the goals came along. He is most comfortable playing just

behind the front two and his subtle footwork was always capable of unlocking any defence.
Arsenal (From trainee on 18/9/1991) PL 1+11/2 FAC 0+1
Burnley (Loaned on 23/3/1995) FL 8+1/4
Cardiff C (Loaned on 11/8/1995) FL 6
Peterborough U (Loaned on 20/10/1995) FL 12/5 Others 2
Millwall (£250,000 on 15/9/1997) FL 88+21/26 FLC 6/2 FAC 2 Others 5+6
Gillingham (£450,000 on 11/7/2000) FL 54+16/8 FLC 0+3 FAC 5/3

SHAW Richard Edward
Born: Brentford, 11 September 1968
Height: 5'9" **Weight:** 12.8
Club Honours: FMC '91; Div 1 '94
At the start of the 2001-02 campaign it looked as if Richard's position in Coventry's back four was under major threat. After one game however he was back in the side because of injury and went on to make 32 League appearances, mostly at full back. He had a good steady

season and was rarely exposed by tricky wingers. Richard never gave less than 100 per cent and remained the best man-to-man marker at the club. He has now played almost 250 games for the Sky Blues without scoring a goal and was offered a one-year deal by new boss Gary McAllister.
Crystal Palace (From apprentice on 4/9/1986) F/PL 193+14/3 FLC 28+2 FAC 18 Others 12+1
Hull C (Loaned on 14/12/1989) FL 4
Coventry C (£1,000,000 on 17/11/1995) P/FL 204+7 FLC 16+1 FAC 15+1

SHEARER Alan
Born: Newcastle, 13 August 1970
Height: 6'0" **Weight:** 12.6
Club Honours: PL '95
International Honours: E: 63; B-1; U21-11; Yth
Newcastle captain Alan received the OBE for services to football in July 2001. He spent the summer recovering from surgery to cure his tendonitis problem and

Alan Shearer

then had another good season bagging his usual crop of goals. With the arrival of Craig Bellamy and Laurent Robert he adjusted his style to become the focal point of the attack rather than its spearhead, exploiting his ability to take the ball under pressure and lay it off to his speedy colleagues. He received a euphoric reception when he returned to the side as a substitute against Sunderland, and then scored twice in his first start at Middlesbrough. Further landmarks came with his 400th league appearance and 100th goal for the Magpies.
Southampton (From trainee on 14/4/1988) FL 105+13/23 FLC 16+2/11 FAC 11+3/4 Others 8/5
Blackburn Rov (£3,600,000 on 24/7/1992) PL 132+6/112 FLC 16/14 FAC 8/2 Others 9/2
Newcastle U (£15,000,000 on 30/7/1996) PL 166+5/92 FLC 12/6 FAC 26/18 Others 13/4

SHEERAN Mark John
Born: Newcastle, 9 August 1982
Height: 6'0" **Weight:** 11.10
Mark became an instant hero for Darlington last season when he came off the bench in successive home games to snatch last-minute winners against Luton Town and Lincoln City in the space of four days in January. His darting runs and eye for goal make him an exciting prospect for the future and manager Tommy Taylor wisely resisted the temptation to plunge him into Third Division football too early, using him almost exclusively as a substitute. He still managed to contribute six goals, all in the League.
Darlington (Trainee) FL 1+21/6 Others 0+1

SHELDON Gareth Richard
Born: Birmingham, 31 January 1980
Height: 5'11" **Weight:** 12.0
2001-02 was a disappointing season for Scunthorpe striker Gareth as injuries and lack of fitness restricted him to just six starts. A hamstring problem ruled him out for six weeks early in the season and then in early December he broke a bone in his leg in a 50-50 challenge at Huddersfield, which kept him out for another three months. A direct, quick right winger who can also play up front, he looked set to leave in the summer.
Scunthorpe U (From trainee on 4/2/1999) FL 52+35/6 FLC 4 FAC 4+1/1 Others 3+4/4

SHERIDAN Darren Stephen
Born: Manchester, 8 December 1967
Height: 5'5" **Weight:** 11.5
Darren joined Oldham on a free from

Wigan last summer, teaming up with older brother John. He started the 2001-02 season in fine form, enhancing midfield with his combative style and ability to craft a telling pass. However, his campaign was disrupted by injuries and a series of suspensions, and he faces a seven-match ban at the beginning of 2002-03.
Barnsley (£10,000 from Winsford U on 12/8/1993) F/PL 149+22/5 FLC 9+4/1 FAC 9+2/1 Others 1+1
Wigan Ath (Free on 2/7/1999) FL 50+8/3 FLC 5 FAC 1+2 Others 5/1
Oldham Ath (Free on 24/7/2001) FL 25+3/2 FLC 2 FAC 4 Others 3

SHERIDAN John Joseph
Born: Stretford, 1 October 1964
Height: 5'10" **Weight:** 12.0
Club Honours: FLC '91; Div 1 '97
International Honours: Rol: 34; B-1; U23-2; U21-2; Yth
Despite his advancing years, John again showed flashes of the passing ability and set-piece delivery that have been his career trademark. Although suffering a series of niggling injuries, the former Republic of Ireland international still played regularly, scoring three times during the 2001-02 campaign. Sadly Athletic have to prepare for the day when they can no longer call on John's services as he is expected to retire before the end of next season and concentrate on coaching duties. He is the brother of team-mate Darren Sheridan.
Leeds U (From Manchester C juniors on 2/3/1982) FL 225+5/47 FLC 14/3 FAC 11+1/1 Others 11/1
Nottingham F (£650,000 on 3/8/1989) FLC 1
Sheffield Wed (£500,000 on 3/11/1989) F/PL 187+10/25 FLC 24/3 FAC 17+1/3 Others 5/2
Birmingham C (Loaned on 9/2/1996) FL 1+1 FLC 2
Bolton W (£180,000 on 13/11/1996) F/PL 24+8/2 FLC 2 FAC 2 (Free to Doncaster Rov in 1998 close season)
Oldham Ath (Free on 20/10/1998) FL 110+8/9 FLC 1+1 FAC 12+1/2 Others 1

SHERINGHAM Edward (Teddy) Paul
Born: Highams Park, 2 April 1966
Height: 5'11" **Weight:** 12.5
Club Honours: Div 2 '88; FMC '92; CS '97; PL '99, '00, '01; FAC '99; EC '99
International Honours: E: 51; U21-1; Yth
Teddy returned to White Hart Lane in order to secure regular first-team football and thus keep his place in the national squad. Immediately awarded the captain's

armband, he performed like he had never been away form the club. Possessing a brilliant footballing brain, he loves to play in a role just dropping off the front line and filling the gap between midfield and attack. He bagged a credible 13 goals in total and acted as creator for many more. Despite a dip in form, which was significant in Spurs change of fortunes, Teddy secured his place for England squad as a 'Super Sub', proved by his immediate impact in the final World Cup qualifying game against Greece.
Millwall (From apprentice on 19/1/1984) FL 205+15/93 FLC 16+1/8 FAC 12/5 Others 11+2/5
Aldershot (Loaned on 1/2/1985) FL 4+1 Others 1
Nottingham F (£2,000,000 on 23/7/1991) FL 42/14 FLC 10/5 FAC 4/2 Others 6/2
Tottenham H (£2,100,000 on 28/8/1992) PL 163+3/75 FLC 14/10 FAC 17/13
Manchester U (£3,500,000 on 1/7/1997) PL 73+31/31 FLC 1/1 FAC 4+5/5 Others 23+16/9
Tottenham H (Free on 16/7/2001) PL 33+1/10 FLC 5+1/2 FAC 2/1

SHERON Michael (Mike) Nigel
Born: St Helens, 11 January 1972
Height: 5'10" **Weight:** 11.13
International Honours: E: U21-16
Mike had a strange season at Barnsley last term. He was generally used as a substitute early on, but when Steve Parkin became manager he was thrown back into the starting line up with amazing success. He scored the majority of his goals during December and January when the team were unbeaten. His overall play during this period was of the highest order and his ability to bring other people into the game was often seen. However the Reds soon found themselves in relegation trouble once more and Mike returned to the bench.
Manchester C (From trainee on 5/7/1990) F/PL 82+18/24 FLC 9+1/1 FAC 5+3/3 Others 1
Bury (Loaned on 28/3/1991) FL 1+4/1 Others 2
Norwich C (£1,000,000 on 26/8/1994) P/FL 19+9/2 FLC 6/3 FAC 4/2
Stoke C (£450,000 on 13/11/1995) FL 64+5/34 FLC 4/5 FAC 1 Others 2
Queens Park R (£2,750,000 on 2/7/1997) FL 57+6/19 FLC 2+2/1 FAC 2
Barnsley (£1,000,000 on 27/1/1999) FL 86+32/24 FLC 10+1/7 FAC 4+2

SHERWOOD Timothy (Tim) Alan
Born: St Albans, 6 February 1969
Height: 6'0" **Weight:** 12.9
Club Honours: PL '95

International Honours: E: 3; B-1; U21-4
This extremely resilient midfielder had the misfortune to miss a large portion of the 2001-02 campaign through injury. A commanding figure in the centre of the park, he still adds creativity to the attack as the provider of service to both wings, and enjoys the responsibility of being the first line of defence. He scored one goal during the season – a stunning half volley in the 5-1 drubbing of Chelsea in the second leg of the Worthington Cup semi final.
Watford (From trainee on 7/2/1987) FL 23+9/2 FLC 4+1 FAC 9 Others 4+1
Norwich C (£175,000 on 18/7/1989) FL 66+5/10 FLC 7/1 FAC 4 Others 5+1/2
Blackburn Rov (£500,000 on 12/2/1992) F/PL 239+7/25 FLC 24+1/2 FAC 15+2/4 Others 12
Tottenham H (£3,800,000 on 5/2/1999) PL 81+12/12 FLC 6+3/2 FAC 13/1 Others 3/1

SHIELDS Anthony (Tony) Gerald
Born: Londonderry, 4 June 1980
Height: 5'7" **Weight:** 10.10
This talented youngster was again only on the fringes of the first-team squad at Peterborough last season. A tough-tackling midfield dynamo, he was loaned to Conference club Stevenage Borough early in the new year. He was out of contract in the summer and at the time of writing his future was uncertain.
Peterborough U (From trainee on 6/7/1998) FL 55+27/2 FLC 3+1/1 FAC 3+3/1 Others 0+2

SHIELDS Greg
Born: Falkirk, 21 August 1976
Height: 5'9" **Weight:** 11.2
Club Honours: Div 1 '00
International Honours: S: U21-2; Yth; Sch
This Charlton Athletic defender had a successful month's loan with Walsall in February and March, doing some excellent work in the goalless draw against Manchester City, and in the closing minutes of his last game moving forward to provide the cross for Don Goodman's winner. He later had a spell at Kilmarnock, also on loan, in the closing stages of the campaign.
Glasgow R (From juniors on 1/7/1993) SL 7 SLC 1+1 Others 2
Dunfermline Ath (Signed on 30/6/1997) SL 75 SLC 6 SC 4 Others 1
Charlton Ath (£580,000 on 26/8/1999) P/FL 23+2/2 FLC 4 FAC 3
Walsall (Loaned on 19/2/2002) FL 7
Kilmarnock (Loaned on 28/3/2002) SL 5

SHILTON Samuel (Sam) Roger
Born: Nottingham, 21 July 1978
Height: 5'10" **Weight:** 11.6
Sam was unable to hold down a regular place on the left-hand side of the Kidderminster midfield last season. He often found himself relegated to the substitutes' bench and was only allowed to start once between October and March. When on form he caused havoc in opposition defences with his crosses, but this was a side to his game that was seen far too infrequently throughout the campaign.
Plymouth Arg (Trainee) FL 1+2 FAC 0+1
Coventry C (£12,500 on 31/10/1995) PL 3+4 FLC 1+1 FAC 0+1
Hartlepool U (Free on 9/7/1999) FL 45+9/7 FLC 1+1 FAC 3+1 Others 3+1
Kidderminster Hrs (Free on 11/7/2001) FL 12+12 FLC 1 FAC 0+1 Others 1

SHIPPERLEY Neil Jason
Born: Chatham, 30 October 1974
Height: 6'1" **Weight:** 13.12
International Honours: E: U21-7
Neil forged an excellent partnership with David Connolly up front for Wimbledon last season. His tally of 12 goals included four against champions Manchester City. His first at Maine Road showed his power to hold off defenders before curling the ball into the net. At the end of the final home game he threw his shirt and boots into the crowd at full time, hopefully this will not be the last the Dons' faithful see of him.
Chelsea (From trainee on 24/9/1992) PL 26+11/7 FLC 4+2/1 FAC 3/1 Others 2
Watford (Loaned on 7/12/1994) FL 5+1/1
Southampton (£1,250,000 on 6/1/1995) PL 65+1/12 FLC 5+1/2 FAC 10/5
Crystal Palace (£1,000,000 on 25/10/1996) F/PL 49+12/20 FLC 3 FAC 2 Others 5/1
Nottingham F (£1,500,000 on 22/9/1998) PL 12+8/1 FAC 1
Barnsley (£700,000 on 7/7/1999) FL 70+8/27 FLC 4+1/3 FAC 2 Others 3/1
Wimbledon (£750,000 on 25/7/2001) FL 36+5/12 FLC 1 FAC 2

SHITTU Daniel (Danny) Olusola
Born: Lagos, Nigeria, 2 September 1980
Height: 6'3" **Weight:** 16.0
International Honours: Nigeria: 1
This big, solid central defender initially joined Queen's Park Rangers on loan last October and soon established himself as the first-choice partner for Steve Palmer in the centre of defence. He eventually signed permanently after the deal was funded by two fans, and was a regular in the line-up for the remainder of the

campaign. He went on to make his debut for Nigeria against Paraguay in a game played at Loftus Road.
Charlton Ath (Free from Carshalton Ath on 15/9/1999)
Blackpool (Loaned on 16/2/2001) FL 15+2/2 Others 2
Queens Park R (£250,000 on 23/10/2002) FL 37/2

SHORE Andrew (Drew) Jonathan
Born: Poole, 8 August 1982
Height: 5'11" **Weight:** 11.10
This left-sided midfielder made a surprise first-team debut for Bristol Rovers against local rivals Bristol City in the Southern semi-final of the LDV Vans Trophy in front of over 17,000 fans. Initially signed on a six-month contract, he made sufficient progress to gain an extension until the end of the season and featured on several more occasions during the closing stages of the campaign.
Bristol Rov (From trainee on 4/7/2001) FL 9 Others 1

SHOREY Nicholas (Nicky)
Born: Romford, 19 February 1981
Height: 5'9" **Weight:** 10.10
Nicky made his Reading debut in the Worthington Cup tie at home to Luton last August, but had to wait until October to make the left-back spot his own. Once he had replaced Matthew Robinson, his composure, timing and intelligent anticipation made him an automatic choice, and he now looks to be one of Alan Pardew's best buys. A string of outstanding displays brought him to the attention of several big clubs, but the Royals secured his future when he signed a four-year contract in February.
Leyton Orient (From trainee on 5/7/1999) FL 12+3 FAC 1
Reading (£25,000 on 9/2/2001) FL 32 FLC 2 FAC 2 Others 2

SHORT Craig Jonathan
Born: Bridlington, 25 June 1968
Height: 6'1" **Weight:** 13.8
Club Honours: FLC '02
Craig missed around a dozen games through suspension last term, but when available he was a tower of strength in the centre of the Blackburn defence. Manager Graeme Souness has said that you could build a block of flats on top of this man and certainly anyone who believed that his shortcomings in speed would be exposed were proved wrong. Committed and competitive he missed

Larus Sigurdsson (left)

out on the Worthington Cup triumph due to suspension.

Scarborough (Free from Pickering T on 15/10/1987) FL 61+2/7 FLC 6 FAC 2 Others 7/1
Notts Co (£100,000 on 27/7/1989) FL 128/6 FLC 6/1 FAC 8/1 Others 16/2
Derby Co (£2,500,000 on 18/9/1992) FL 118/9 FLC 11 FAC 7/4 Others 7
Everton (£2,700,000 on 18/7/1995) PL 90+9/4 FLC 7 FAC 4 Others 3
Blackburn Rov (£1,700,000 + on 3/8/1999) P/FL 73+1/1 FLC 3/1 FAC 5

SHTANIUK Sergei

Born: Minsk, Belarus, 13 August 1973
Height: 6'3" **Weight:** 12.11
International Honours: Belarus: 34
After failing to obtain a work permit for Sergei during the previous season, Stoke tried again in the summer of 2001 and this time were successful on appeal. He was a truly outstanding acquisition and deservedly picked up a number of 'Player of the Season' awards for a string of consistent performances in the heart of defence. Excellent in the air and blessed with good distribution he is capable of playing in a higher division, hopefully with City.
Stoke C (£200,000 from Dinamo Moscow, Russia, ex Belarus Minsk, Dinamo Minsk, on 3/8/2001) FL 40/2 FLC 1 FAC 4 Others 3

SHUKER Christopher (Chris) Alan

Born: Liverpool, 9 May 1982
Height: 5'5" **Weight:** 10.1
This young midfielder made his debut for Manchester City when he came off the bench to replace Eyal Berkovic in the Worthington Cup tie at Notts County. He arrived in dramatic fashion, scoring with a great header within minutes of coming on the field. He later made two more appearances as a substitute and will be looking to gain further senior experience in 2002-03.
Manchester C (From trainee on 21/9/1999) FL 0+2 FLC 0+1/1
Macclesfield T (Loaned on 27/3/2001) FL 6+3/1

SHUTTLEWORTH Barry

Born: Accrington, 9 July 1977
Height: 5'8" **Weight:** 11.10
Barry joined Macclesfield on non-contract forms last October, but was very much a fringe player at Moss Rose, his only start coming in the LDV Vans Trophy tie at Darlington. A left-sided defender who can push forward, he failed to impress sufficiently to earn a full contract and moved on to Altrincham in March.

Bury (From trainee on 5/7/1995)
Rotherham U (Free on 1/8/1997) FAC 0+1 Others 1
Blackpool (Free on 7/8/1998) FL 16+3/1 FLC 3 FAC 1 (Free to Scarborough during 2000 close season)
Macclesfield T (Free on 12/10/2001) FL 0+3 FAC 0+1 Others 1

SIBON Gerald

Born: Dalen, Holland, 19 April 1974
Height: 6'5" **Weight:** 13.5
Gerald finished as Sheffield Wednesday's leading scorer last season with 13 goals in all competitions. A tall and languid player who can appear in midfield or up front, he can be an inspiration when the mood takes him and is terrific with free kicks. He has a fine range of all-round skills and great vision and will be hoping to display these in a successful Wednesday team in 2002-03.
Sheffield Wed (£2,000,000 from Ajax, Holland, ex Twente, VVV Groningen, Roda JC, on 16/7/1999) P/FL 75+29/30 FLC 9+2/2 FAC 6+1/2

SIDIBE Mamady

Born: Mali, 18 December 1979
Height: 6'4" **Weight:** 12.4
The tall striker impressed during a trial period at Swansea in the 2001 close season before signing a one-year contract. He showed pace, good control, and the ability to win the ball in aerial challenges. Despite being sidelined on a number of occasions with hamstring and ankle injuries he impressed the Swans supporters with his skill on the ball.
Swansea C (Free from CA Paris, France, ex Racing Club Paris, on 27/7/2001) FL 26+5/7 FLC 0+1 FAC 2/1 Others 1

SIDWELL Steven James

Born: Wandsworth, 14 December 1982
Height: 5'10" **Weight:** 11.2
Club Honours: FAYC '00, '01
This Arsenal youngster joined Brentford on loan last October and eventually stayed for the remainder of the season. Originally signed to stand in for the injured Paul Evans he then moved to the right-hand side of midfield before forming an effective partnership with Evans in the centre of the park. He also weighed in with four goals, the first a stunning 25-yarder against Blackpool. He is a good all-round midfielder who can tackle, pass and shoot with equal ability. He was selected for the England U20 side during the season.
Arsenal (From trainee on 2/7/2001)
Brentford (Loaned on 23/10/2001) FL 29+1/4 FAC 2 Others 3

SIGERE Jean-Michel Paul

Born: France, 26 January 1977
Height: 6'0" **Weight:** 12.7
Club Honours: NC '01
This striker never really did himself justice during his time with Rushden last term. His goal-scoring record – nine from 32 first-team games – would suggest otherwise, but maybe Jean-Michel was just in the wrong place at the wrong time. He made just five starts in 2001-02 and can look back on one Football League goal to his credit. He moved on to Stevenage Borough with Simon Wormull in October.
Rushden & Diamonds (Free from Bordeaux, France on 29/3/2000) FL 4+3/1 FLC 1

SIGURDSSON Larus Orri

Born: Akureyri, Iceland, 4 June 1973
Height: 6'0" **Weight:** 13.11
International Honours: Iceland: 34; U21-16; Yth
Larus Sigurdsson played superbly well on the right side of West Bromwich Albion's back 'three' last term alongside Darren Moore in the centre and Phil Gilchrist on the left. A fine reader of the game, his positional sense was first-class and his vast experience showed through while his work-rate never waned.
Stoke C (£150,000 from Thor, Iceland on 21/10/1994) FL 199+1/7 FLC 15 FAC 6+1 Others 6
West Bromwich A (£325,000 on 17/9/1999) FL 76+6/1 FLC 3 FAC 5 Others 0+1

SILVESTRE Mikael Samy

Born: Tours, France, 9 August 1977
Height: 6'0" **Weight:** 13.1
Club Honours: PL '00, '01
International Honours: France: 11; U21; Yth (UEFA-U18 '96)
This stylish and pacy left-sided defender was once again a regular for Manchester United last term, both in Premiership and Champions' League action. Mikael showed he could combine his defensive duties with an attacking option down the flank, linking up with the original 'left sided flyer' Ryan Giggs. A consistent performer throughout the campaign, his only goal came in the Champions' League qualifier against Nantes in February.
Manchester U (£4,000,000 from Inter Milan, Italy on 10/9/1999) PL 86+10/1 FAC 4 Others 30+6/1

SIMMS Gordon Henry

Born: Larne, 23 March 1981
Height: 6'2" **Weight:** 12.6
International Honours: NI: U21-7; Yth; Sch

Mikael Silvestre

Gordon began the 2001-02 campaign as an established Northern Ireland U21 international, despite not yet having made his first-team debut for Hartlepool. He did not have long to wait, and in the early months of the season looked to be challenging the established players for a regular place in the centre of defence. He was unlucky with minor injuries, but was restricted to reserve football in the second half of the season.
Wolverhampton W (From trainee on 9/4/1998)
Hartlepool U (Free on 10/3/2001) FL 6+4 FAC 1

SIMONSEN Steven (Steve)
Preben
Born: South Shields, 3 April 1979
Height: 6'3" **Weight:** 13.2
International Honours: E: U21-4; Yth
Steve had to wait patiently for an extended spell of Premiership football with Everton last term. He was finally handed his big chance at Bolton in November – and grabbed at the opportunity gratefully. One outstanding tip over in the dying stages of that game earned him plenty of plaudits, and he kept three successive clean sheets after that. A smart shot-stopper and confident in his cross-taking, experience is the only quality lacking from his game.
Tranmere Rov (From trainee on 9/10/1996) FL 35 FLC 4 FAC 3
Everton (£3,300,000 on 23/9/1998) PL 25+2 FLC 2 FAC 5

SIMPKINS Michael (Mike)
James
Born: Sheffield, 28 November 1978
Height: 6'1" **Weight:** 12.0
This left-sided Cardiff City defender started the 2001-02 season tentatively, but grew in confidence and kept his place for the first 12 matches of the campaign. Injury then struck, he lost his place and then found it impossible to get back in the line-up. He is a competent, athletic defender with good stamina.
Sheffield Wed (From trainee on 4/7/1997)
Chesterfield (Free on 26/3/1998) FL 22+4 FLC 2+1 FAC 1 Others 2
Cardiff C (Free on 29/5/2001) FL 13+4 FLC 1

SIMPSON Fitzroy
Born: Trowbridge, 26 February 1970
Height: 5'8" **Weight:** 12.0
International Honours: Jamaica: 37
This experienced midfield player was in and out of the Walsall side early in the 2001-02 season, although he scored a spectacular goal at Crewe. He was then

out for a long spell until Colin Lee brought him back for the goalless draw against Manchester City in February. He held his place during the successful run-in, excelling with his tenacious tackling and use of the ball, and he netted a fine opening goal from a free kick in the Easter Monday win at Nottingham Forest.
Swindon T (From trainee on 6/7/1988) FL 78+27/9 FLC 15+2/1 FAC 2+1 Others 3+2
Manchester C (£500,000 on 6/3/1992) P/FL 58+13/4 FLC 5+1 FAC 4+1
Bristol C (Loaned on 16/9/1994) FL 4
Portsmouth (£200,000 on 17/8/1995) FL 139+9/10 FLC 12+1 FAC 8
Heart of Midlothian (£100,000 on 8/12/1999) SL 7+4 SLC 0+1 SC 2
Walsall (Free on 2/3/2001) FL 29+9/3 FLC 2 Others 1

SIMPSON Michael
Born: Nottingham, 28 February 1974
Height: 5'9" **Weight:** 10.8
Club Honours: AIC '95
Michael had yet another fine season in Wycombe's central midfield in 2001-02, even better than the previous season's grand effort. Very much the heart of the team since Lawrie Sanchez became manager, he is a very busy player and the main channel in midfield for receiving the ball. His deft passing set up countless attacks throughout the campaign although his defensive qualities were just as important. A tigerish tackler, he relentlessly closed down players, and it is no exaggeration to say that his midfield partnership with Dannie Bulman has been the foundation for Wycombe's recent success.
Notts Co (From trainee on 1/7/1992) FL 39+10/3 FLC 4+1 FAC 2+1 Others 7+3
Plymouth Arg (Loaned on 4/10/1996) FL 10+2
Wycombe W (£50,000 on 5/12/1996) FL 187+18/9 FLC 10+1 FAC 20+2/4 Others 8

SIMPSON Paul David
Born: Carlisle, 26 July 1966
Height: 5'6" **Weight:** 11.10
Club Honours: AMC '02
International Honours: E: U21-5; Yth
Paul featured fairly regularly for Blackpool last term, although he did not have as much success as in the previous campaign. He gained an LDV Vans Trophy winners' medal when he came off the bench in the 4-1 victory over Cambridge but was transferred to Rochdale soon afterwards. Signed to boost Dale's promotion campaign, he netted five goals in seven games to ensure a play-off spot and then added a brilliant long-range effort in the semi-final first leg against

Rushden. He is a creative left-sided midfield player who is also a specialist with set-piece kicks.
Manchester C (From apprentice on 4/8/1983) FL 99+22/18 FLC 10+1/2 FAC 10+2/4 Others 8+3
Oxford U (£200,000 on 31/10/1988) FL 138+6/43 FLC 10/3 FAC 9/2 Others 5/2
Derby Co (£500,000 on 20/2/1992) P/FL 134+52/48 FLC 12+3/6 FAC 4+4/1 Others 14+2/2
Sheffield U (Loaned on 6/12/1996) FL 2+4
Wolverhampton W (£75,000 on 10/10/1997) FL 32+20/6 FLC 2+1 FAC 2+5
Walsall (Loaned on 17/9/1998) FL 4/1
Walsall (Loaned on 11/12/1998) FL 6
Blackpool (Free on 11/8/2000) FL 69+7/13 FLC 5+1 FAC 6/1 Others 4+2/1
Rochdale (Free on 25/3/2002) FL 7/5 Others 2/1

SINCLAIR Frank Mohammed
Born: Lambeth, 3 December 1971
Height: 5'9" **Weight:** 12.9
Club Honours: FAC '97; FLC '98, '00
International Honours: Jamaica: 21
A right-footed wing back or central defender, Frank was one of the few Leicester City players to emerge from the 2001-02 season with a generally creditable assessment. He played reasonably consistently throughout, whether in a right-back role or in the centre of defence alongside a variety of partners to win 'Player of the Season' honours. Yet, ironically, his season will probably be remembered for a spectacular 40-yard own goal after just 3 minutes at Middlesbrough, when under no pressure, that left Ian Walker grasping at air. For the record, Frank then went on to be the team's best player that day.
Chelsea (From trainee on 17/5/1990) F/PL 163+6/7 FLC 17+1/1 FAC 18/1 Others 13/3
West Bromwich A (Loaned on 12/12/1991) FL 6/1
Leicester C (£2,000,000 on 14/8/1998) PL 111+6/1 FLC 16 FAC 7/1

SINCLAIR Trevor Lloyd
Born: Dulwich, 2 March 1973
Height: 5'10" **Weight:** 12.10
International Honours: E: 9; B-1; U21-14; Yth
West Ham's fast and tricky right winger had an excellent season in 2001-02. He showed his versatility by occasionally appearing on the left and also played as a striker on occasions. One of his best performances was against Derby County on Boxing Day when he scored with a spectacular 12-yard volley. Trevor gained his first cap for England in their 1-1 draw

Trevor Sinclair

with Sweden in December and went on to become one of the stars in the team in the World Cup finals in the summer.
Blackpool (From trainee on 21/8/1990) FL 84+28/15 FLC 8 FAC 6+1 Others 8+5/1
Queens Park R (£750,000 on 12/8/1993) P/FL 162+5/16 FLC 13/3 FAC 10/2
West Ham U (£2,300,000 + on 30/1/1998) PL 139/29 FLC 9+1 FAC 6 Others 10/1

SINGH Harpal
Born: Bradford, 15 September 1981
Height: 5'7" **Weight:** 10.9
This left-footed winger joined Bury on loan last September and went straight into the Shakers' team. He immediately looked a Premiership-class player, with incredible speed and trickery, being capable of taking on and beating four or five players before delivering a dangerous cross. A hamstring problem briefly interrupted his progress but he returned to the side, scoring an excellent individual strike at home to Bristol City. He subsequently moved to Ashton Gate on loan in March and made an inspiring debut against Cambridge but never really settled and returned to Elland Road before his loan period had fully elapsed.
Leeds U (From trainee on 26/9/1998)
Bury (Loaned on 11/9/2001) FL 11+1/2 FAC 2/1 Others 1
Bristol C (Loaned on 8/3/2002) FL 3

SINTON Andrew (Andy)
Born: Cramlington, 19 March 1966
Height: 5'8" **Weight:** 11.5
Club Honours: FLC '99
International Honours: E: 12; B-3; Sch
This veteran left-winger was very much on the fringes of the Wolves' first-team squad last season following the arrival of Mark Kennedy. He scored a goal in the 2-1 win at Preston, but only made three starts during the campaign. He showed he was still capable of progressing down the wing and getting in a dangerous centre, and hopefully he will see more first-team action in his career.
Cambridge U (From apprentice on 13/4/1983) FL 90+3/13 FLC 6/1 FAC 3 Others 2/1
Brentford (£25,000 on 13/12/1985) FL 149/28 FLC 8/3 FAC 11/1 Others 14/2
Queens Park R (£350,000 on 23/3/1989) F/PL 160/22 FLC 14 FAC 13/2 Others 3/1
Sheffield Wed (£2,750,000 on 19/8/1993) PL 54+6/3 FLC 13 FAC 5 Others 2+1
Tottenham H (£1,500,000 on 23/1/1996) PL 66+17/6 FLC 6+3 FAC 4+4/1
Wolverhampton W (Free on 13/7/1999) FL 62+10/3 FLC 3+2 FAC 5

SKELTON Aaron Matthew
Born: Welwyn Garden City, 22 November 1974
Height: 5'11" **Weight:** 12.6
Aaron returned to Luton Town in the 2001 close season after a four-year absence, but was again beset by injury problems. A versatile player who can appear at centre back or in midfield, he scored his only goal of the campaign at home to Lincoln City.
Luton T (From trainee on 16/12/1992) FL 5+3 FLC 0+1 FAC 2 Others 2
Colchester U (Free on 3/7/1997) FL 114+11/17 FLC 4 FAC 5+1 Others 5+1
Luton T (Free on 6/7/2001) FL 9/1 FAC 1

SKINNER Stephen (Steve) Karl
Born: Whitehaven, 25 November 1981
Height: 6'0" **Weight:** 12.3
After being released by Carlisle at the end of the previous season, Steve joined Unibond club Gretna, but made a surprise return to Brunton Park last October. A well-built striker, he made a number of substitute appearances as well as one start in the following month. Despite some telling contributions, he was unable to secure a long-term deal and returned to Gretna.
Carlisle U (From trainee on 6/6/2000) FL 0+2
Queen of the South (Free on 25/10/2000) SL 1+5 SC 2 (Free to Gretna during 2001 close season)
Carlisle U (Loaned from Gretna on 5/10/2001) FL 1+5 Others 0+1

SKORA Eric
Born: France, 20 August 1981
Height: 6'1" **Weight:** 11.10
Having failed to break into the first team with Nancy, this young midfielder signed a short-term contract for Preston following a successful trial period. Eric made an impressive debut at Walsall, which he followed with a first goal on his FA Cup debut at Brighton in only his second start. He hit a post with a header in his home league debut against Gillingham before being forced out of contention by a foot injury in the next match. It is hoped he will be offered a longer deal, as he showed considerable promise, being mobile, an intelligent distributor of the ball, and with the ability to get into the box.
Preston NE (Free from Nancy, France on 22/10/2001) FL 2+2 FAC 2/1

SLAVEN John
Born: Edinburgh, 8 October 1985
Height: 6'0" **Weight:** 10.11

When this promising striker came off the subs' bench at Scunthorpe, he entered the history books as Carlisle's youngest debutant at 16 years 159 days. Formerly on the books at Rangers and Livingston, his first home appearance came two weeks later and he looks to have a promising future in the game.
Carlisle U (Trainee) FL 0+2

SMART Allan Andrew Colin
Born: Perth, 8 July 1974
Height: 6'2" **Weight:** 12.10
Club Honours: AMC '97
Allan started the 2001-02 season on loan with Hibernian and then Stoke City, before joining Oldham Athletic for a substantial fee in November. The experienced striker added aerial strength and leadership to the forward line, notching six goals in 21 League appearances. However, following two breaches of the club's disciplinary code, Athletic cancelled his contract in May. Allan was able to talk to other clubs and was reported to have signed for Dundee United during the summer.
St Johnstone (From juniors on 24/1/1991)
Brechin C (Free on 30/12/1991)
Inverness Caledonian Thistle (Free on 28/7/1993) SL 2+2 SLC 1+1
Preston NE (£15,000 on 22/11/1994) FL 17+4/6 FAC 2/1 Others 1+1
Carlisle U (Loaned on 24/11/1995) FL 3+1
Northampton T (Loaned on 13/9/1996) FL 1
Carlisle U (Signed on 9/10/1996) FL 41+3/16 FLC 1/1 FAC 4 Others 4+1
Watford (£75,000 + on 2/7/1998) P/FL 48+9/12 FLC 1+2 FAC 1 Others 0+3/1
Hibernian (Loaned on 14/8/2001) SL 2+3/1
Stoke C (Loaned on 6/11/2001) FL 0+2
Oldham Ath (£225,000 on 30/11/2001) FL 14+7/6 FAC 1 Others 2/1

SMICER Vladimir (Vlad)
Born: Czechoslovakia, 24 May 1973
Height: 5'11" **Weight:** 11.3
Club Honours: FLC '01; FAC '01; UEFAC '01
International Honours: Czech Republic: 56; U21-7. Czechoslovakia: 1
Vlad was a valuable squad player for Liverpool last term. Playing mostly on the right side of midfield, he also filled in on the left in the absence of his compatriot Berger, and occasionally as support striker. His strength is his confidence when running at defences with the ball, although he often seems to take too long in delivering his pass.
Liverpool (£3,750,000 from RC Lens, France, ex SK Slavia Praha, on 14/7/1999) PL 42+28/7 FLC 8+1/4 FAC 7+1/1 Others 14+8/1

SMITH Adrian (Adie)
Jonathan
Born: Birmingham, 11 August 1973
Height: 5'10" **Weight:** 12.0
Club Honours: NC '00
International Honours: E: SP-3
One of the most versatile players in the Kidderminster squad, Adie found himself employed in the centre of defence, at right back and also in midfield last season, often swapping position during a game. He scored just twice in the campaign – netting in consecutive games against Mansfield and Carlisle.
Kidderminster Hrs (£19,000 from Bromsgrove Rov on 17/6/1997) FL 65+5/7 FLC 1+1 FAC 3 Others 1/1

SMITH Alan
Born: Rothwell, 28 October 1980
Height: 5'9" **Weight:** 11.10
International Honours: E: 3; U21-10; Yth
This talented Leeds United striker began last season in fine form, coming on as a substitute to score an excellent goal in the 2-0 victory over Southampton on the opening day, but then had his campaign curtailed by injury and suspensions. He picked up an ankle at Arsenal in the second game, which caused him to miss seven games, and then had an enforced absence due to suspension after receiving two red cards. He featured on the right-hand side of midfield in the latter part of the campaign, where he performed really well.
Leeds U (From trainee on 26/3/1998) PL 80+24/26 FLC 2+2 FAC 6+4/3 Others 22+7/9

SMITH Alexander (Alex)
Philip
Born: Liverpool, 15 February 1976
Height: 5'7" **Weight:** 11.10
Club Honours: AMC '01
Alex joined Reading from Port Vale during the 2001 close season, signing a two-year contract. At first things looked bright as he made the left-midfield spot his own, scoring some well-taken goals, but he was then replaced by the on-loan John Salako. Thereafter Alex was confined to reserve-team football, and though he did reasonably well in a variety of positions, he was told he could leave the Royals if he could find another club willing to take him.
Everton (From trainee on 1/7/1994)
Swindon T (Free on 12/1/1996) FL 17+14/1
Huddersfield T (Free on 6/2/1998) FL 4+2
Chester C (Free on 8/7/1998) FL 32/2 FLC 4/1 Others 1

Port Vale (£75,000 on 25/3/1999) FL 52+6/2 FLC 2+1 FAC 2 Others 7/1
Reading (Free on 19/7/2001) FL 12+1/2 FLC 2/1 FAC 1 Others 1

SMITH Benjamin (Ben) Peter
Born: Chelmsford, 23 November 1978
Height: 5'8" **Weight:** 11.0
Ben arrived at Southend during the 2001 close season but his only senior appearance came in a brief outing from the subs' bench in the 4-1 home victory over Halifax Town in August. A talented midfielder he then suffered knee and ankle problems that eventually required corrective surgery.
Reading (Free from trainee at Arsenal on 16/4/1997) FL 0+1 (Free to Yeovil T on 6/3/1998)
Southend U (Free on 8/6/2001) FL 0+1

SMITH Christopher (Chris)
Alan
Born: Derby, 30 June 1981
Height: 5'11" **Weight:** 11.6
Chris joined York City during the 2001 close season and although he played a number of times for the first team he never managed to establish himself as a regular in the line-up. A steady and composed central defender he impressed when called upon and always used the ball constructively.
Reading (From trainee on 22/6/1999)
York C (Free on 2/7/2001) FL 12+3 FAC 3 Others 1

SMITH Craig Mark
Born: Bradford, 8 June 1984
Height: 5'8" **Weight:** 10.10
Craig is yet another exciting Halifax Town prospect who earned himself a first-team call up during the 2001-02 season. He came on from the subs' bench for the final two home fixtures against Hartlepool and Rushden, showing himself to be a midfield player with silky skills and good distribution.
Halifax T (Trainee) FL 0+2

SMITH Daniel (Danny) Lee
Born: Southampton, 17 August 1982
Height: 5'11" **Weight:** 11.4
This young central defender started just two games for Bournemouth last season and made two more appearances from the subs' bench. Unfortunately he failed to fulfil the promise he had shown in the previous campaign and was released in the summer.
Bournemouth (From trainee on 12/4/2000) FL 8+10 FLC 2 FAC 0+1 Others 3

SMITH David
Born: Stonehouse, 29 March 1968
Height: 5'8" **Weight:** 10.7
Club Honours: AMC '98
International Honours: E: U21-10
The 2001-02 season proved another disappointing time for this veteran Grimsby left wing back who found himself behind both Tony Gallimore and young Ben Chapman in the pecking order for a place in the first-team line-up. He played only a limited part in the Mariners' campaign, rarely even making the substitutes' bench. When called upon he showed he still has plenty to offer but it seems likely that his future at Blundell Park is now limited.
Coventry C (From apprentice on 7/7/1986) P/FL 144+10/19 FLC 17 FAC 6 Others 4+1
Bournemouth (Loaned on 8/11/1993) FL 1
Birmingham C (Signed on 12/3/1993) FL 35+3/3 FLC 4 FAC 0+1 Others 1
West Bromwich A (£90,000 on 31/1/1994) FL 82+20/2 FLC 4+2 FAC 1+3 Others 4+1
Grimsby T (£200,000 on 16/11/1998) FL 101+11/9 FLC 9+3/1 FAC 2+1 Others 7/1

SMITH David (Dave)
Christopher
Born: Liverpool, 26 December 1970
Height: 5'9" **Weight:** 12.9
This central midfielder made most of his appearances for Stockport County last season before the arrival of Carlton Palmer. In February he joined Macclesfield Town on loan as cover for the injured Kevin Keen and impressed with his precise passing. He was recalled to the County side on his return and played a key role in the 1-0 victory over Bradford City in March. Unfortunately he picked up an injury in that game and he was forced on to the sidelines for the remainder of the campaign. He subsequently left Edgeley Park after his contact was mutually terminated in the summer.
Norwich C (From trainee on 4/7/1989) F/PL 13+5 FAC 2+1 Others 1+1
Oxford U (£100,000 on 5/7/1994) FL 193+5/2 FLC 23+1/1 FAC 9+1 Others 7
Stockport Co (Free on 4/2/1999) FL 64+7/3 FLC 3+1 FAC 2
Macclesfield T (Loaned on 1/2/2002) FL 8

SMITH Dean
Born: West Bromwich, 19 March 1971
Height: 6'1" **Weight:** 12.10
Dean was again club captain for Leyton Orient in 2001-02 and once more proved to be an inspirational leader of the team. He missed only one game all season and achieved the feat of scoring at each end in the memorable FA Cup victory at

Alan Smith (left)

Portsmouth, his goal for the O's being a 25-yard free kick. He is a powerful and effective central defender and was voted the fans' 'Player of the Season'.

Walsall *(From trainee on 1/7/1989) FL 137+5/2 FLC 10 FAC 4 Others 10*
Hereford U *(£75,000 on 17/6/1994) FL 116+1/19 FLC 10/3 FAC 7 Others 11+1/4*
Leyton Orient *(£42,500 on 16/6/1997) FL 212/29 FLC 16 FAC 17/4 Others 10/1*

SMITH Grant Gordon
Born: Irvine, 5 May 1980
Height: 6'1" **Weight:** 12.7
Grant joined Sheffield United during the summer of 2001 and began the season in midfield for the Blades' reserves. In September he moved on loan to Halifax Town where he made 12 consecutive appearances on the left-hand side of midfield before returning to Bramall Lane. He made his senior debut for United as a substitute against Millwall and featured up front on a number of occasions in the closing stages. He is the son of Gordon Smith the former Glasgow Rangers and Brighton player.
Reading *(Free from trainee at Wycombe W on 7/8/1998)*
Heart of Midlothian *(Free on 19/3/1999)*
Livingston *(Free on 4/7/2000) SL 0+2 SLC 1 Others 1*
Clydebank *(Free on 2/12/2000) SL 16+1/2*
Sheffield U *(Free on 13/7/2001) FL 1+6*
Halifax T *(Loaned on 7/9/2001) FL 11 Others 1*

SMITH James (Jamie) Jade Anthony
Born: Birmingham, 17 September 1974
Height: 5'7" **Weight:** 11.4
Jamie had another fine season at Crystal Palace in 2001-02. An exciting right back he was impressive pushing forward and provided many crosses for his colleagues to latch on to. He also managed to score four goals himself during the campaign.
Wolverhampton W *(From trainee on 7/6/1993) FL 81+6 FLC 10+1 FAC 2 Others 4/1*
Crystal Palace *(Signed on 22/10/1997) P/FL 121+11/4 FLC 15/2 FAC 6+1 Others 1+1*
Fulham *(Loaned on 25/3/1999) FL 9/1*

SMITH Jason Leslie
Born: Bromsgrove, 6 September 1974
Height: 6'3" **Weight:** 13.7
Club Honours: Div 3 '00
International Honours: E: Sch
2001-02 proved to be another disappointing season for Jason at Swansea and injuries restricted him to just

eight League appearances. He underwent a series of operations and scans in an effort to find the cause of his ankle problems, and then picked up a foot injury at the end of the season! When fully fit he is an influential figure at the heart of the defence and is particularly effective in the air.
Coventry C *(Signed from Tiverton T on 5/7/1993. Free to Tiverton T on 15/7/1995)*
Swansea C *(£10,000 on 1/7/1998) FL 114+1/5 FLC 7 FAC 8/1 Others 8/1*

SMITH Jay Mark
Born: Hammersmith, 29 December 1981
Height: 5'11" **Weight:** 11.7
This stylish central midfielder had a somewhat disappointing season for Brentford in 2001-02. He came on from the subs' bench for Paul Evans in the LDV Vans Trophy tie at Wycombe but, despite sitting on the bench in a number of other games he received no further senior opportunities during the campaign.
Brentford *(From trainee on 5/7/2000) FL 2+1 Others 0+1*

SMITH Jeffrey (Jeff)
Born: Middlesbrough, 28 June 1980
Height: 5'10" **Weight:** 11.8
Jeff was a consistent performer for Bolton's reserve team in 2001-02 and made one Worthington Cup start before he was given his Premiership debut as a substitute in the final match of the season at West Ham. He played the last 30 minutes of that game in an unfamiliar left-back role and certainly did not look out of place.
Hartlepool U *(From trainee on 3/7/1998) FL 2+1 Others 1 (Free to Barrow in October 1999)*
Bolton W *(Free from Bishop Auckland on 21/3/2001) P/FL 1+1 FLC 1*
Macclesfield T *(Loaned on 23/11/2001) FL 7+1/2*

SMITH Mark Jonathan
Born: Bristol, 13 September 1979
Height: 6'0" **Weight:** 13.10
After having previously appeared in the Bristol Rovers first team back in December 1998, Mark stepped in as a replacement for the injured Che Wilson at right back last November. He subsequently enjoyed a decent run in the side, mostly as a wing back, and was particularly impressive in Rovers shock 3-1 victory at Derby County in the FA Cup. He was released at the end of the season.
Bristol Rov *(From trainee on 9/7/1998) FL 28+5 FLC 1 FAC 5+2 Others 3*

SMITH Neil James
Born: Lambeth, 30 September 1971
Height: 5'9" **Weight:** 12.12
Club Honours: FAYC '90; Div 2 '99
An abundance of midfield players meant that Neil had few first-team opportunities at Reading last term, and the majority of those were as a second-half substitute. Even the high point of his season – a neatly taken goal against Tranmere – was spoilt when a team-mate jumped on his back during the celebration and cracked a rib, putting Neil out of the side once more. From then on it was mainly reserve-team football, though he continued to play with just as much enthusiasm. He was out of contract in the summer, and was not offered a new contract as the Royals moved to a higher level.
Tottenham H *(From trainee on 24/7/1990)*
Gillingham *(£40,000 on 17/10/1991) FL 204+9/10 FLC 14+1/1 FAC 18/2 Others 7+1/2*
Fulham *(Signed on 4/7/1997) FL 62+11/1 FLC 3+1 FAC 6+3/1 Others 1+1*
Reading *(£100,000 on 20/8/1999) FL 33+32/3 FLC 4+1 FAC 2+1 Others 3+1/1*

SMITH Ian Paul
Born: Easington, 22 January 1976
Height: 6'0" **Weight:** 13.3
Out of favour at Burnley, Paul was a target for Hartlepool manager Chris Turner during the 2001 close season, but it was not until November that the transfer deal was agreed. His arrival proved a turning point for Pool, as the team rose steadily from bottom place in Division Three to finish the season in a play-off position. He is a tall and powerful left-sided player, who is particularly effective going forward from midfield.
Burnley *(From trainee on 10/7/1994) FL 79+33/5 FLC 3+1 FAC 6+1 Others 5*
Oldham Ath *(Loaned on 22/9/2000) FL 3+1 FLC 1*
Hartlepool U *(Free, via trial at Torquay U, on 1/11/2001) FL 30+1/4 FAC 1 Others 2*

SMITH Paul Antony
Born: Hastings, 25 January 1976
Height: 5'11" **Weight:** 11.7
This right-sided midfield man suffered a serious back injury in pre-season which resulted in him undergoing a major operation. Paul returned to light training in January and made such good progress that by the end of the following month he was back in the first team. He provided some balance to Lincoln's midfield four but still lacked full fitness and his season ended early due to a hamstring problem.
Nottingham F *(£50,000 from Hastings T on 13/1/1995)*

Lincoln C (£30,000 on 17/10/1997) FL 101+19/17 FLC 5+1/1 FAC 8/1 Others 7

SMITH Paul Daniel

Born: Epsom, 17 December 1979
Height: 6'4" **Weight:** 14.0
Paul is an effective shot-stopping goalkeeper with excellent quick distribution. Apart from playing for Brentford in the LDV Vans Trophy tie at Wycombe he sat on the sub's bench for every match until the end of January when he replaced Oli Gottskalksson against Brighton. He was then an ever present for the rest of the season keeping 10 clean sheets in 18 games and adding a further shut out at Huddersfield in the first leg of the play-off semi-final.
Charlton Ath (Free from Walton & Hersham on 2/7/1998. Free to Walton & Hersham during 1999 close season)
Brentford (Free from Carshalton Ath on 27/7/2000) FL 19+1 Others 4+1

SMITH Paul William

Born: East Ham, 18 September 1971
Height: 5'11" **Weight:** 13.0
Paul won Gillingham's 'Player of the Year' trophy for the third time in 2001-02, being the first player to achieve this feat for the club. As captain, he led by example with his tireless running and battling performances. His form was so good, it was surprising that no Premiership clubs have taken a look at him. A true professional, he was an ever present during the season and during that time became only the ninth player to appear in 100 consecutive League games for the Gills.
Southend U (From trainee on 16/3/1990) FL 18+2/1 Others 0+1
Brentford (Free on 6/8/1993) FL 159/11 FLC 12/1 FAC 12/3 Others 15/2
Gillingham (Signed on 25/7/1997) FL 222+1/15 FLC 12/1 FAC 15 Others 9+2/2

SMITH Gareth Shaun

Born: Leeds, 9 April 1971
Height: 5'10" **Weight:** 11.0
Shaun enjoyed a testimonial season at Crewe last term, when he was once again a near ever present in the line-up. A hard-tackling defender with a no-nonsense attitude, he is now closing in on Tommy Lowry's all-time record of 436 League appearances for the Railwaymen.
Halifax T (From trainee on 1/7/1989) FL 6+1 Others 1 (Free to Emley in May 1991)
Crewe Alex (Free on 31/12/1991) FL 380+22/41 FLC 24+1/4 FAC 19+2/4 Others 19+2/3

SMITH Thomas (Tommy) William

Born: Hemel Hempstead, 22 May 1980
Height: 5'8" **Weight:** 11.4
International Honours: E: U21-1; Yth
Leading scorer with 11 goals, Tommy was also Watford's most consistently dangerous player with his speed, invention, and ability to run at and beat opponents. Operating either wide on the right or at centre forward, he benefited from the guidance of manager Gianluca Vialli, who predicted a bright future for his protege, and he was again included in the England U21 squad. His reluctance to sign a new contract fuelled predictable transfer speculation, but there was definite news about younger brother Jack, a centre half, who signed his first professional contract with Watford after coming through the academy ranks.
Watford (From trainee on 21/10/1997) P/FL 89+25/26 FLC 6+3/1 FAC 2+1

SNEEKES Richard

Born: Amsterdam, Holland, 30 October 1968
Height: 5'11" **Weight:** 12.2
This classy midfielder failed to reproduce the form that had earned him a reputation as one of the First Division's most skilful players when he joined Stockport County last September, and he was released at the end of his three-month contract. He was re-united with his former West Bromwich Albion boss Brian Little at Hull in November and although dropping down two divisions, he was well suited to City's free-flowing style despite having to adapt to the hustle and bustle of Division Three.
Bolton W (£200,000 from Fortuna Sittard, Holland, ex Ajax, Volendam, on 12/8/1994) P/FL 51+4/7 FLC 11+1/3 FAC 2/1
West Bromwich A (£385,000 on 11/3/1996) FL 208+19/30 FLC 14+3/2 FAC 7/2 Others 2
Stockport Co (Free on 5/9/2001) FL 8+1 FLC 1
Hull C (Free on 29/11/2001) FL 17+5 FAC 0+1 Others 1+1

SODJE Efetobore (Efe)

Born: Greenwich, 5 October 1972
Height: 6'1" **Weight:** 12.0
Club Honours: GMVC '96
International Honours: Nigeria: 9
This stylish defender was again a regular in the heart of the back line for Crewe last term. A tremendous worker who is composed on the ball, he featured for Nigeria in the 2002 World Cup finals.
Macclesfield T (£30,000 from Stevenage Borough on 11/7/1997) FL 83/6 FLC 6 FAC 6/1 Others 1

Luton T (Free on 12/8/1999) FL 5+4 FLC 2 FAC 2+1 Others 1
Colchester U (Free on 23/3/2000) FL 3
Crewe Alex (Free on 21/7/2000) FL 63+5/2 FLC 4+2 FAC 6

SOLANO Nolberto (Nobby) Albino

Born: Lima, Peru, 12 December 1974
Height: 5'8" **Weight:** 10.8
International Honours: Peru: 58; Yth
Apart from the Premiership Nobby started in every game for Newcastle last term. United clearly benefited from his decision not to pursue his international career, and he had a fine season, creating danger with his runs down the flank leading to dangerous crosses or drifting inside to find space in the penalty area for strikes on goal. His dead-ball expertise was an important option in the side's attack, and he supplemented his fine team play with his share of goals to round off an impressive contribution to the club's progress during the season.
Newcastle U (£2,763,958 from Boca Juniors, Argentina, ex Cristal Alianza Lima, Sporting, Deportivo Municipal, on 17/8/1998) PL 121+8/22 FLC 9+1 FAC 16/2 Others 13+1/5

SOLEY Stephen (Steve)

Born: Widnes, 22 April 1971
Height: 5'11" **Weight:** 12.8
International Honours: E: SP-1
Not for the first time this hard-working midfielder's season was affected by injuries and he appeared in less than half of Carlisle's matches in 2001-02. Always looking to get on the score sheet, he managed a run of five goals in ten appearances including match-winning efforts against both Barnet (in the FA Cup) and Exeter. He was one of several players who were released by the club at the end of the campaign.
Portsmouth (£30,000 from Leek T on 22/7/1998) FL 1+7 FLC 0+4
Macclesfield T (Loaned on 19/3/1999) FL 5+5
Carlisle U (Signed on 6/8/1999) FL 75+8/16 FLC 2 FAC 3/1 Others 4+1/2

SOLKHON Brett Michael

Born: Canvey Island, 12 September 1982
Height: 5'11" **Weight:** 12.6
This centre half made just the one League appearance for Rushden in 2001-02, and the circumstances could have been more favourable. Called into action after Jim Rodwell's dismissal at Oxford, Diamonds were soon three goals behind as the home side capitalised on their numerical advantage. However, Brett continued to

perform consistently well for the reserve and youth sides, scoring his fair share of goals from set pieces and earning the club's 'Young Player of the Year' award.
Rushden & Diamonds (From juniors on 7/7/2000) FL 0+1

SOLLITT Adam James
Born: Sheffield, 22 June 1977
Height: 6'0" **Weight:** 11.4
International Honours: E: SP-3
Adam took over as first-team goalkeeper for Northampton Town when Keith Welch was injured after just two games of the 2001-02 campaign. However, he had the misfortune to play behind an ever-changing defensive line and once Welch was fit he resumed his place in the line-up. He is a tall and agile 'keeper who will be hoping to receive more regular senior action in the coming season.
Barnsley (From trainee on 4/7/1995. Free to Gainsborough Trinity during 1997 close season)
Northampton T (£30,000 from Kettering T on 25/7/2000) FL 14+2 FLC 2 FAC 1 Others 1

SOLSKJAER Ole Gunnar
Born: Kristiansund, Norway, 26 February 1973
Height: 5'10" **Weight:** 11.10
Club Honours: PL '97, '99, '00, '01; FAC '99; EC '99
International Honours: Norway: 48; U21-19
Despite not being guaranteed a place in the starting line-up at Old Trafford, Ole Gunnar signed a new long-term contract for Manchester United last October. A supremely dedicated striker, he is the most clinical of finishers. He started the campaign with a double against Ipswich and went on to score 25 goals in all competitions. High points included a hat-trick against Bolton, a double in the Champions' League victory over Nantes (on his 29th birthday) and a sensational effort in the FA Cup tie against Aston Villa. Most importantly his striking partnership with Ruud van Nistelrooy developed along truly prolific lines.
Manchester U (£1,500,000 from Molde, Norway on 29/7/1996) PL 106+57/74 FLC 6/5 FAC 8+9/5 Others 29+38/14

SOLTVEDT Trond Egil
Born: Voss, Norway, 15 February 1967
Height: 6'1" **Weight:** 12.8
International Honours: Norway: 4
This hard-working midfield player had a good season for Sheffield Wednesday last term after being given the captaincy from the start of the campaign. He switched to central defence towards the end of the season to cover for injuries and did well in his new role only to miss the final matches after himself succumbing to injury.
Coventry C (£500,000 from Rosenborg, Norway, ex Ny-Khronborg, Viking Stavanger, Brann, on 24/7/1997) PL 47+10/3 FLC 1+4/1 FAC 5+2
Southampton (£300,000 on 13/8/1999) PL 20+10/2 FLC 6/3 FAC 2+1
Sheffield Wed (Free on 13/2/2001) FL 53/2 FLC 6/2

SOMA Ragnvald
Born: Norway, 10 November 1979
Height: 6'2" **Weight:** 12.2
International Honours: Norway: U21-3; Yth
Although he did not feature much for the West Ham first team last term, Ragnvald was a regular in the reserve line-up. Apart from a couple of substitutions the young defender only started the one League game, this being the unfortunate 7-1 defeat at Blackburn in October.
West Ham U (£800,000 from Bryne, Norway on 19/1/2001) PL 3+4 FAC 1+1

SONG Bahanag Rigobert
Born: Nkanglicock, Cameroon, 1 July 1976
Height: 5'9" **Weight:** 11.10
International Honours: Cameroon: 70 (ANC 2000)
Rigobert started the 2001-02 season well, playing in the West Ham midfield against Liverpool and Leeds. However following the purchase of Tomas Repka at the Cameroon captain was unable to gain a place in the side and subsequently went on loan to 1FC Koln for the remainder of the season.
Liverpool (£2,720,000 from Salernitana, Italy, ex Tonnerre Yaoundi, Metz, on 29/1/1999) PL 27+7 FLC 2 FAC 0+1 Others 1
West Ham U (£2,500,000 on 29/11/2000) PL 23+1 FLC 2 FAC 1

SONNER Daniel (Danny) James
Born: Wigan, 9 January 1972
Height: 5'11" **Weight:** 12.8
International Honours: NI: 7; B-4
This experienced midfielder started the 2001-02 season despite a nagging heel problem which required surgery in November, the week after he was sent-off for Birmingham against West Brom in a 1-0 St Andrew's defeat. He recovered, but failed to break back into the team with Steve Bruce in charge.
Burnley (From trainee at Wigan Ath on 6/8/1990) FL 1+5 FLC 0+1/1 Others 0+2 (Free to Preussen Koln, Germany during 1993 close season)
Bury (Loaned on 21/11/1992) FL 5/3 FAC 3 Others 1/1
Ipswich T (Free from FC Erzgebirge Aue, Germany on 12/6/1996) FL 28+28/3 FLC 6+4/1 FAC 1+1 Others 0+1
Sheffield Wed (£75,000 on 15/10/1998) PL 42+11/3 FLC 3+1/1 FAC 4+2
Birmingham C (Free on 4/8/2000) FL 32+9/2 FLC 12/1 FAC 1 Others 2

SORENSEN Thomas
Born: Denmark, 12 June 1976
Height: 6'4" **Weight:** 13.10
Club Honours: Div 1 '99
International Honours: Denmark: 19; B-1; U21-6
Thomas found himself overworked as Sunderland's goalkeeper at times last season as the Black Cats struggled against relegation. He is lightning-quick when coming off his line and commands his penalty area with an assured authority, constantly keeping his back four on their toes. Although he did not enjoy a vintage season, any mistakes he made were more than cancelled out by several match-saving performances, most notably at Newcastle in August when a string of late saves prevented the Magpies from claiming all three points.
Sunderland (£500,000 + from Odense BK, Denmark on 6/8/1998) P/FL 150 FLC 13 FAC 9

SORVEL Neil Simon
Born: Whiston, 2 March 1973
Height: 6'0" **Weight:** 12.9
Club Honours: GMVC '95, '97; FAT '96
This hard-working midfield player was again a key member of the Crewe Alexandra line-up in 2001-02. Although he missed a couple of matches for the first time since his return to Gresty Road, he again showed great stamina although he failed to register a goal despite possessing a powerful shot.
Crewe Alex (From trainee on 31/7/1991) FL 5+4 FAC 1+1 Others 4
Macclesfield T (Free on 21/8/1992) FL 79+7/7 FLC 4+1 FAC 5 Others 0+1
Crewe Alex (Free on 9/6/1999) FL 119+11/7 FLC 12 FAC 6+1

SOUTHALL Leslie Nicholas (Nicky)
Born: Stockton, 28 January 1972
Height: 5'10" **Weight:** 12.12
Nicky signed for Bolton on a 'Bosman' free at the beginning of last season and turned out to be a great buy. A skilful and tenacious player, he can play anywhere in

Ole Gunnar Solskjaer (right)

the midfield and also as a wing back when the 3-5-2 formation is adopted. He reached double figures as far as Premiership starts were concerned and his versatility was a tremendous asset for Sam Allardyce. His only goal was a 30-yard screamer in the 3-2 defeat at Newcastle.
Hartlepool U (From Darlington juniors on 21/2/1991) FL118+20/24 FLC 6+1/3 FAC 4+4 Others 6+2
Grimsby T (£40,000 on 12/7/1995) FL 55+17/5 FLC 3+3/1 FAC 4+3/2
Gillingham (Free on 9/12/1997) FL 141+13/17 FLC 6+1/1 FAC 10/3 Others 12
Bolton W (Free on 2/7/2001) PL 10+8/1 FLC 4 FAC 2

SOUTHGATE Gareth
Born: Watford, 3 September 1970
Height: 6'0" **Weight:** 12.8
Club Honours: Div 1 '94; FLC '96
International Honours: E: 49
Gareth settled in well at Middlesbrough following his arrival at the Riverside during the 2001 close season. He went on to be a near ever present in defence for Boro' and deservedly finished the campaign by being voted 'Player of the Year'. He also continued to remain part of the England set-up and was a member of the final 23 for the World Cup finals.
Crystal Palace (From trainee on 17/1/1989) F/PL 148+4/15 FLC 23+1/7 FAC 9 Others 6
Aston Villa (£2,500,000 on 1/7/1995) PL 191/7 FLC 17/1 FAC 20/1 Others 15
Middlesbrough (£6,500,000 on 14/7/2001) PL 37/1 FLC 1 FAC 6

SPARROW Matthew (Matt)
Born: Wembley, 3 October 1981
Height: 5'11" **Weight:** 10.6
Unfortunately, the Scunthorpe midfielder was unavailable for the start of last season, a situation that was well documented, but eventually returned to first-team action in January. He kept his place for the rest of the campaign, scoring once – a stunning last-minute winner away to high-flying Luton. Mainly used as a central midfielder though he can play on the right, he has a great work-rate and tackles strongly. He was offered a new three-year contract at the end of the season.
Scunthorpe U (From trainee on 30/7/2001) FL 31+15/5 FLC 0+3 FAC 1 Others 0+1

SPEDDING Duncan
Born: Camberley, 7 September 1977
Height: 6'1" **Weight:** 11.1
Duncan was again troubled by injuries last term and as a result he spent two lengthy spells on the sidelines. Mostly employed

as a left wing back or on the left-hand side of midfield, he was occasionally used in the centre of defence during emergencies. He is particularly effective when foraging down the wing from where he can deliver an accurate cross into the box.
Southampton (From trainee on 24/5/1996) PL 4+3 FLC 0+1
Northampton T (£60,000 on 14/7/1998) FL 98+14/2 FLC 7+2 FAC 4 Others 5

SPEED Gary Andrew
Born: Deeside, 8 September 1969
Height: 5'10" **Weight:** 12.10
Club Honours: Div 2 '90, Div 1 '92; CS '92
International Honours: W: 68; U21-3; Yth
This hard-working player was a key element in the Newcastle midfield engine room last season, although hamstring injuries in August and March plus a broken toe in January disrupted his campaign. His vision coupled with his distribution skills enabled him to change the direction of attacks with sweeping balls to the wings, while he was often to be seen driving forward into the opponents' penalty area where his heading ability made him a constant threat. He continued to captain Wales who experimented with him in the novel role of left back.
Leeds U (From trainee on 13/6/1988) F/PL 231+17/39 FLC 25+1/11 FAC 21/5 Others 14+3/2
Everton (£3,500,000 on 1/7/1996) PL 58/16 FLC 5/1 FAC 2/1
Newcastle U (£5,500,000 on 6/2/1998) PL 146+5/24 FLC 9+1/1 FAC 20/5 Others 14/3

SPENCER James Matthew
Born: Stockport, 11 April 1985
Height: 6'5" **Weight:** 15.2
The local youngster became Stockport County's youngest ever goalkeeper last April when he was surprisingly named in the starting line-up. At just 16 years of age, James made a number of good saves during the game and prevented Watford from grabbing a late equaliser when he superbly kept out Heidar Helguson's point-blank header. He made a second appearance at Norwich three weeks later, coming on after Andy Dibble's early dismissal and made a string of top class saves to deservedly collect the 'Man of the Match' nomination.
Stockport Co (Trainee) FL 1+1

SPILLER Daniel (Danny)
Born: Maidstone, 10 October 1981
Height: 5'9" **Weight:** 12.3

After a long-term injury, it was nice to see young Danny back in action in Gillingham's colours last season. A regular in the club's Avon Combination team, like his colleague Richard Rose, he was loaned out to League of Ireland club Longford Town. His only action in the Gills' League side was as a late substitute in the club's 5-1 thrashing at Bradford City in September.
Gillingham (From trainee on 10/7/2000) FL 0+1

SPRING Matthew John
Born: Harlow, 17 November 1979
Height: 5'11" **Weight:** 11.5
Matthew was again a regular in midfield for Luton Town last term, giving 100 per cent in every game he played. Without doubt his best performance for the Hatters was against Kidderminster Harriers when he scored twice and was nominated as 'Man of the Match'. He was reported to have signed a new two-year contract in the summer.
Luton T (From trainee on 2/7/1997) FL 178+7/19 FLC 12 FAC 13+1/2 Others 2

STALLARD Mark
Born: Derby, 24 October 1974
Height: 6'0" **Weight:** 13.6
This skilful Notts County striker had to contend with a nagging injury that was initially wrongly diagnosed for much of last season. He bravely insisted on playing on, often in pain, to try to help the team out of their difficulties before eventually having to endure a spell on the sidelines. Now fully recovered, he is expected to be challenging for his place back in 2002-03.
Derby Co (From trainee on 6/11/1991) FL 19+8/2 FLC 2+1/2 FAC 2+1 Others 3/2
Fulham (Loaned on 23/9/1994) FL 4/3
Bradford C (£110,000 on 12/1/1996) FL 33+10/10 FLC 2/1 FAC 0+1 Others 3/2
Preston NE (Loaned on 14/2/1997) FL 4/1
Wycombe W (£100,000 on 7/3/1997) FL 67+3/23 FLC 5+1/1 Others 2/1
Notts Co (£10,000 on 3/3/1999) FL 107+11/38 FLC 10/5 FAC 7/3 Others 1

STAM Jakob (Jaap)
Born: Kampen, Holland, 17 July 1972
Height: 6'3" **Weight:** 14.0
Club Honours: EC '99; FAC '99; PL '99, '00, '01
International Honours: Holland: 45
This cool and accomplished central defender made just two first-team appearances for Manchester United at the start of last season before he was sold to Lazio in one of the shock moves of the campaign. The reasons for the sudden

Gareth Southgate

move were never really made clear, but he was sorely missed at Old Trafford for some time, despite the valiant efforts of his replacement Laurent Blanc to shore up United's leaking back line.

Manchester U (£10,750,000 from PSV Eindhoven, Holland, ex Zwolle, Cambuur, Willem II, on 17/7/1998) PL 79/1 FAC 7+1 Others 39+1

STAMP Neville

Born: Reading, 7 July 1981
Height: 5'11" **Weight:** 12.7
Neville had misfortune to suffer a series of injuries during the 2001-02 campaign that severely restricted his senior appearances for York City. A strong-tackling left-sided defender he was eventually released by the Minstermen in the summer.

Reading (From trainee on 22/6/1999) FL 0+1
York C (Free on 10/10/2000) FL 17+3 FAC 1+2 Others 2

STAMP Philip (Phil) Lawrence

Born: Middlesbrough, 12 December 1975
Height: 5'10" **Weight:** 13.5
International Honours: E: Yth
This powerful, fast and skilful midfielder joined Millwall on a month's loan last September, but had the misfortune to suffer a groin injury on his debut and returned to the Riverside soon afterwards. Very much a long-term prospect for Middlesbrough, injuries hampered his prospects of enjoying a brief run in the side and he made only four appearances in the starting line-up last term.

Middlesbrough (From trainee on 4/2/1993) P/FL 75+41/6 FLC 13+4/1 FAC 9+6/1 Others 5+1
Millwall (Loaned on 5/9/2001) FL 0+1 FLC 1

STAMPS Scott

Born: Birmingham, 20 March 1975
Height: 5'10" **Weight:** 11.10
Club Honours: NC '00
One of the best left-backs in the Third Division, Scott was finally given some competition for the position at Kidderminster last term following the arrival of Ian Joy. He responded with a string of excellent performances and was only kept out of the team late on by injury and a suspension, which caused him to miss the last two games. His solid defending and dangerous attacking wing play earned him a two-year extension to his contract at the end of the season.

Torquay U (From trainee on 6/7/1993) FL 80+6/5 FLC 5 FAC 2 Others 2+1/1
Colchester U (£10,000 on 26/3/1997) FL 52+4/1 FLC 4 FAC 3+1 Others 1+1

Kidderminster Hrs (Free on 17/9/1999) FL 70+1 FLC 2 FAC 4 Others 2

STANIC Mario

Born: Sarajevo, Yugoslavia, 10 April 1972
Height: 6'2" **Weight:** 12.12
Club Honours: CS '00
International Honours: Croatia: 45
Following an injury-blighted first season at Chelsea, Mario Stanic played a more prominent role for the Blues in 2001--02. The Croatian international made sporadic substitute appearances in the early part of the season - one of which resulted in his third Chelsea goal at Southampton. Jesper Gronkjær's knee injury in October gave Mario the chance to hold down the wide-right berth in a four-man midfield and he impressed with his hard-running, determined style. Later in the season injuries to left-sided players saw Mario switch flanks and his mazy right-footed dribbling gave the Blues another attacking dimension.

Chelsea (£5,600,000 from Parma, Italy, ex Zeljeznicar Sarajevo, Croatio Zagreb, Sporting Gijon, Benfica, Brugge, on 12/7/2000) PL 26+13/3 FLC 1+1 FAC 4+2/1 Others 3

STANTON Nathan

Born: Nottingham, 6 May 1981
Height: 5'9" **Weight:** 11.3
International Honours: E: Yth
After playing mainly as a central defender for Scunthorpe, Nathan was switched to right back for most of 2001-02. He took a while to settle into the role but had a strong second half of the season using his tremendous pace to make driving runs forward as well as helping out defensively. He appeared in all but four League games during the season and remained one of the club's most consistent players.

Scunthorpe U (From trainee on 19/3/1999) FL 103+16 FLC 4 FAC 8+1 Others 5+1

STAUNTON Stephen (Steve)

Born: Drogheda, Ireland, 19 January 1969
Height: 6'1" **Weight:** 12.12
Club Honours: FAC '89; Div 1 '90; FLC '94, '96
International Honours: RoI: 102; U21-4; Yth
This vastly experienced and versatile defender featured sparingly for Aston Villa in the early part of the 2001-02 campaign. His first spell in the line-up commenced at the end of September when he replaced the injured Olof Mellberg, but with the subsequent long-term injury to Alpay, his run in the side continued through to the end of the

season. Playing as a central defender in a back four formation he produced a string of solid performances throughout the season and has become most capped player in the club's history.

Liverpool (£20,000 from Dundalk on 2/9/1986) FL 55+10 FLC 6+2/4 FAC 14+2/1 Others 1/1
Bradford C (Loaned on 13/11/1987) FL 7+1 FLC 2 Others 1
Aston Villa (£1,100,000 on 7/8/1991) F/PL 205+3/16 FLC 17+2/1 FAC 19+1/1 Others 15+1
Liverpool (Free on 3/7/1998) PL 38+6 FLC 5/1 FAC 2 Others 5+2
Crystal Palace (Loaned on 20/10/2000) FL 6/1
Aston Villa (Free on 7/12/2000) PL 43+4 FLC 2 FAC 4 Others 2

STEELE Lee Anthony James

Born: Liverpool, 7 December 1973
Height: 5'8" **Weight:** 12.7
Club Honours: Div 3 '01; Div 2 '02
2001-02 proved to be another roller coaster season for Lee at Brighton. He began the season on the transfer list but early-season goals against Wigan and Blackpool led Micky Adams to take him off the list. However as the campaign wore on he found that his opportunities were few and far between. Just when all seemed lost, he scored the crucial last-minute winner against Bristol City on Easter Monday, which took Albion to the top of the Second Division.

Shrewsbury T (£30,000 + from Northwich Vic on 23/7/1997) FL 104+9/37 FLC 5/3 FAC 4+1 Others 3
Brighton & Hove A (Free on 19/7/2000) FL 24+36/11 FLC 1+1 FAC 1+4 Others 4/1

STEELE Luke David

Born: Peterborough, 24 September 1984
Height: 6'2" **Weight:** 11.12
A product of Peterborough United's youth system, Luke stepped up to make his senior debut at Reading last April and also appeared in the final game of the season at home to Bury. Once he had conquered his nerves he showed what a good goalkeeper he is, a fact confirmed shortly afterwards when he was transferred to Manchester United for a substantial fee.

Peterborough U (From trainee on 26/9/2001) FL 2

STEPANOVS Igors

Born: Ogre, Latvia, 21 January 1976
Height: 6'4" **Weight:** 13.7
International Honours: Latvia: 49
This big, strong imposing central defender struggled to make an impact at Arsenal

Marcus Stewart

last term due to the intense competition for places in the back line. He made only six Premiership starts during the campaign, and will be aiming to finally make a breakthrough in 2002-03.
Arsenal *(£1,000,000 from Skonto Riga, Latvia, ex FK Ventspils, on 5/9/2000)* PL 15 FLC 3+1/1 FAC 4 Others 3+1

STEPHENSON Paul
Born: Wallsend, 2 January 1968
Height: 5'10" **Weight:** 12.12
International Honours: E: Yth
2001-02 proved to be a disrupted season for this stylish midfielder who is now Hartlepool's most experienced player. He had a lengthy spell out of the side due to a bad knee injury, and at times struggled to maintain his fitness. Still a player with much to offer, he is a playmaker with the ability to control the pace of a game from the centre of midfield.
Newcastle U *(From apprentice on 2/1/1986)* FL 58+3/1 FLC 3+1 FAC 2 Others 2
Millwall *(£300,000 on 10/11/1988)* FL 81+17/6 FLC 3/1 FAC 9/2 Others 8/1
Gillingham *(Loaned on 21/11/1992)* FL 12/2 Others 2
Brentford *(£30,000 on 4/3/1993)* FL 70/2 FLC 6/1 FAC 1+1 Others 5
York C *(£35,000 on 7/8/1995)* FL 91+6/8 FLC 9+2 FAC 5 Others 2+2/1
Hartlepool U *(Free on 20/3/1998)* FL 136+9/9 FLC 5+1/2 FAC 4+1 Others 13+1

STEVENS Ian David
Born: Malta, 21 October 1966
Height: 5'10" **Weight:** 12.6
Club Honours: AMC '89
Ian's career at Carlisle looked to be at an end when he lost his place last August. Several clubs were reported to be interested in his services before a surprise recall to the colours in late November. The manager's faith was soon rewarded and his first half hat-trick in the 6-1 rout of Leyton Orient in January was one of the best individual performances of the season, earning him the PFA 'Player of the Month' award. A striker whose appetite for scoring has not lessened over the years, he remains a popular figure with the supporters.
Preston NE *(From apprentice on 22/11/1984)* FL 9+2/2 Others 1
Stockport Co *(Free on 27/10/1986)* FL 1+1 FAC 0+1 Others 0+1 *(Free to Lancaster C on 27/11/1986)*
Bolton W *(Free on 25/3/1987)* FL 26+21/7 FLC 1+2 FAC 4/2 Others 3+1
Bury *(Free on 3/7/1991)* FL 100+10/38 FLC 3+1 FAC 2+2 Others 7+1/2
Shrewsbury T *(£20,000 on 11/8/1994)* FL

94+17/37 FLC 2+1 FAC 4+2/2 Others 10+2/12
Carlisle U *(£100,000 on 13/5/1997)* FL 64+14/26 FLC 2 FAC 2/1 Others 3/2
Wrexham *(Free on 5/7/1999)* FL 14+2/4 FLC 2 FAC 1+1
Cheltenham T *(Loaned on 21/3/2000)* FL 1
Carlisle U *(Free on 7/8/2000)* FL 64+3/20 FLC 3/1 FAC 5/4

STEVENSON Jonathan (Jon) Ashlee
Born: Leicester, 13 October 1982
Height: 5'6" **Weight:** 11.11
A young striking prospect who signed professional forms in February 2001, Jon made a surprise debut for Leicester City from the bench at Upton Park when he picked up a suspected broken nose. He was regularly involved with the squad in the latter stages of the campaign, again appearing as a substitute on a number of occasions and netting his first senior goal to earn a draw against Aston Villa.
Leicester C *(From trainee on 26/3/2001)* PL 0+6/1

STEWART Gareth John
Born: Preston, 3 February 1980
Height: 6'0" **Weight:** 12.8
International Honours: E: Yth; Sch
Gareth firmly established himself as Bournemouth's number one 'keeper in 2001-02, missing just one League match all season. A confident goalkeeper who is capable of pulling off some fine saves, he won many points for the Cherries during a difficult campaign and headed the local newspaper's merit table for his performances.
Blackburn Rov *(From trainee on 11/2/1997)*
Bournemouth *(Free on 2/7/1999)* FL 83 FLC 1 FAC 5

STEWART Jordan Barrington
Born: Birmingham, 3 March 1982
Height: 5'11" **Weight:** 11.12
A promising product of the Leicester academy Jordan suffered the frustration of establishing himself as a first choice left-back under two different managers last term only for his first-team runs to be cut short by a dislocated shoulder on each occasion. He is highly rated as a left-footed midfielder or full back.
Leicester C *(From trainee on 22/3/2000)* PL 9+4 FLC 1 FAC 2+1
Bristol Rov *(Loaned on 23/3/2000)* FL 1+3

STEWART William Paul **Marcus**
Born: Bristol, 7 November 1972
Height: 5'10" **Weight:** 11.0
International Honours: E: Sch

The 2001-02 season for Marcus was a complete contrast from the previous campaign. He started well, opening his account at Leicester and clearly enjoyed his European experience scoring three goals in four appearances. He converted a penalty in Moscow to give his side a crucial two-goal lead and netted a double in Helsingborg. The first was a header and the second a delicate chip over the 'keeper as he ran on to a through ball. Marcus broke his jaw in training in November and although he scored in his comeback game at Dagenham, he seemed to have lost some of his confidence and with it his place in the starting line-up.
Bristol Rov *(From trainee on 18/7/1991)* FL 137+34/57 FLC 11/5 FAC 7+1/3 Others 16+1/14
Huddersfield T *(£1,200,000 + on 2/7/1996)* FL 129+4/58 FLC 18/7 FAC 9/3
Ipswich T *(£2,500,000 on 1/2/2000)* P/FL 62+10/27 FLC 4+2/1 FAC 4/2 Others 7/6

STEWART Michael James
Born: Edinburgh, 26 February 1981
Height: 5'11" **Weight:** 11.11
International Honours: S: 3; U21-7; Sch
This combative young midfield player showed some excellent touches when he came off the subs' bench for Manchester United at Sunderland in October. He went on to feature in a handful of first-team games, including the end-of-season matches against Ipswich and Charlton. Already capped for Scotland at U21 level, he made his senior debut against Nigeria in April and also featured in the summer tour of the Far East.
Manchester U *(From trainee on 19/3/1998)* PL 5+1 FLC 1+2 Others 0+1

STILLIE Derek Daniel
Born: Irvine, 3 December 1973
Height: 6'0" **Weight:** 12.0
International Honours: S: U21-14
Derek started the 2001-02 season as first choice goalkeeper at Wigan Athletic following the summer sale of Roy Carroll to Manchester United. A good shot stopper and excellent at taking crosses, he played in the opening two matches before losing his place to Stewart Kerr. A reliable performer who always gave 100 per cent, he regained the 'keeper's shirt in October but suffered an abductor muscle injury in the 1-1 home draw against Notts County in December which brought his campaign to a premature end. Out of contract at the end of the season, he was allowed to leave the club.

Aberdeen (From juniors on 3/5/1991) SL 22+1 SLC 2 SC 3
Wigan Ath (Free on 5/8/1999) FL 42+2 FLC 3+1 FAC 5 Others 4

STIRLING Jude Barrington
Born: Enfield, 29 June 1982
Height: 6'2" **Weight:** 11.12
Despite a much-publicised incident at Brentford at the end of the 2000-01 campaign, Jude was given another contract by Luton Town for the 2001-02 season. However he featured only twice at first-team level, appearing as part of a patched-up defence at Bristol Rovers and then as a substitute in the LDV Vans Trophy tie against Dagenham & Redbridge. The Hatters allowed him to leave in March and he signed for Stevenage Borough where he went on to make an appearance in their FA Trophy final defeat by Yeovil Town.
Luton T (From trainee on 9/7/1999) FL 6+4 FAC 0+2 Others 0+1

STOCK Brian Benjamin
Born: Winchester, 24 December 1981
Height: 5'11" **Weight:** 11.2
This highly rated midfielder started to live up to his promise during the 2001-02 season despite spending time on the sidelines due to injury. A free-kick specialist, he opened his senior account with a stunning winner over Bury at Dorchester's Avenue Stadium and wrote his name in to the club's history books by scoring the first ever goal at the new Fitness First Stadium.
Bournemouth (From trainee on 25/1/2000) FL 23+9/2 FAC 2 Others 2+1

STOCKDALE Robert (Robbie) Keith
Born: Redcar, 30 November 1979
Height: 5'11" **Weight:** 11.3
International Honours: S: 3; E: U21-1
Robbie's fortunes have undergone an amazing change over the last 12 months. Firstly he stepped in to gain a regular midfield place for Middlesbrough during the season, and secondly he made his full debut for Scotland in the friendly against Nigeria last April, having previously featured for England U21s at the beginning of 2001-02.
Middlesbrough (From trainee on 2/7/1998) P/FL 50+9/2 FLC 7 FAC 7
Sheffield Wed (Loaned on 13/9/2000) FL 6

STOCKLEY Samuel (Sam) Joshua
Born: Tiverton, 5 September 1977
Height: 6'0" **Weight:** 12.0

Sam joined Oxford during the 2001 close season and showed up well under both managers, missing just a handful of games during the campaign. He was mainly used as a wing back on the right side or as right back from where he pushed forward effectively.
Southampton (From trainee on 1/7/1996)
Barnet (Free on 31/12/1996) FL 177+5/2 FLC 10 FAC 4 Others 11
Oxford U (£150,000 on 13/7/2001) FL 39+2 FLC 1 FAC 1 Others 1

STOCKWELL Michael (Micky) Thomas
Born: Chelmsford, 14 February 1965
Height: 5'9" **Weight:** 11.4
Club Honours: Div 2 '92
Micky again defied his years with another outstanding season for Colchester in 2001-02 when he was voted as the club's 'Player of the Year'. He featured chiefly as an attacking midfield player, although occasionally appearing at right back, and weighed in with a total of 11 goals in all competitions.
Ipswich T (From apprentice on 17/12/1982) F/PL 464+42/35 FLC 43+5/5 FAC 28+3/2 Others 22+4/2
Colchester U (Free on 27/7/2000) FL 91+1/20 FLC 6/1 FAC 3 Others 2+1/1

STOLCERS Andrejs
Born: Latvia, 8 July 1974
Height: 5'10" **Weight:** 11.4
Club Honours: Div 1 '01
International Honours: Latvia: 58
Though a regular on the subs' bench, Andrejs rarely seemed to actually get on to the field of play for Fulham last term. Able to operate either in a wide role on either flank or as a central midfielder or striker, he was a regular in the reserve side where he tended to play in the middle of the park. A player with some neat touches he has yet to force his way into a regular spot in the Fulham side despite remaining a regular for Latvia.
Fulham (£2,000,000 + from Shakhtjor Donetsk, Ukraine, ex Olympija Riga, Skonto Riga, on 7/12/2000) P/FL 8+12/2 FLC 0+1 FAC 0+2

STONE Daniel (Danny) John Cooper
Born: Liverpool, 14 September 1982
Height: 5'11" **Weight:** 12.4
This young defender joined Notts County shortly after the start of the 2001-02 campaign and made his senior debut in the LDV Vans Trophy tie at Bury in October. He went on to make a handful more appearances, mostly in the first half

of the season, and will be hoping to feature more regularly in 2002-03. He is a promising right back, but was also used in a central defensive role on occasions.
Notts Co (Free from trainee at Blackburn Rov on 25/8/2001) FL 5+1 FAC 1+1 Others 1+1

STONE Steven (Steve) Brian
Born: Gateshead, 20 August 1971
Height: 5'8" **Weight:** 12.7
Club Honours: Div 1 '98
International Honours: E: 9
This pacy Aston Villa winger is deceptively fast but possesses a very accurate cross. He loves to run at defenders and pops up in attacking positions too. However, he struggled to secure a regular place in the side last season, although he enjoyed a brief run-out in November as a replacement for the injured Moustapha Hadji.
Nottingham F (From trainee on 20/5/1989) F/PL 189+4/23 FLC 14+1/2 FAC 9 Others 12/2
Aston Villa (£5,500,000 on 12/3/1999) PL 66+24/4 FLC 5+3/1 FAC 5+5/2 Others 9+3

STONEBRIDGE Ian Robert
Born: Lewisham, 30 August 1981
Height: 6'0" **Weight:** 11.4
Club Honours: Div 3 '02
International Honours: E: Yth
Ian played a vital role in the success of Plymouth Argyle throughout their Third Division championship season. Very much a fans' favourite, his all-round play showed improvement and he weighed in with some important goals, notably a superb 25 yarder that clinched an important 1-0 victory over Lincoln City in March. He generally played as a lone striker in Argyle's 4-5-1 away formation when he used his strength to hold off opposing defenders and link up the play to his team-mates. Towards the end of the season, he featured in a slightly withdrawn role behind the two forwards, a move that proved to be a success.
Plymouth Arg (From trainee at Tottenham H on 13/7/1999) FL 73+31/28 FLC 2+1/1 FAC 11+2/2 Others 3+1/1

STONEMAN Paul
Born: Tynemouth, 26 February 1973
Height: 6'1" **Weight:** 13.6
Club Honours: FC '98
Paul featured regularly in the Halifax Town line-up last term and never gave less than 100 per cent. A stalwart defender he ran into disciplinary problems in the second half of the campaign and this is an area of his game where he needs to show improvement. He scored his only goal of the season with a header at Torquay.

Blackpool (From trainee on 26/7/1991) FL 38+5 FLC 5 FAC 3 Others 3
Colchester U (Loaned on 23/12/1994) FL 3/1
Halifax T (Free on 12/7/1995) FL 137+2/11 FLC 8 FAC 4 Others 5

STOWELL Michael (Mike)
Born: Portsmouth, 19 April 1965
Height: 6'2" **Weight:** 14.2
With Billy Mercer's continuing injury problems, this experienced 'keeper was signed up by Bristol City during the 2001 close season. He did well for the Robins in the opening games before being laid up with a thigh strain sustained early in the game at Huddersfield at the end of September. On regaining fitness he displaced an in-form Steve Phillips, before further injury problems brought about another spell on the sidelines.
Preston NE (Free from Leyland Motors on 14/2/1985)
Everton (Free on 12/12/1985) Others 1
Chester C (Loaned on 3/9/1987) FL 14 Others 2
York C (Loaned on 24/12/1987) FL 6
Manchester C (Loaned on 2/2/1988) FL 14 FAC 1
Port Vale (Loaned on 21/10/1988) FL 7 Others 1
Wolverhampton W (Loaned on 17/3/1989) FL 7
Preston NE (Loaned on 8/2/1990) FL 2
Wolverhampton W (£250,000 on 28/6/1990) FL 377+1 FLC 30 FAC 22 Others 11
Bristol C (Free on 27/7/2001) FL 25 FLC 2 FAC 1

STRACHAN Gavin David
Born: Aberdeen, 23 December 1978
Height: 5'11" **Weight:** 11.7
International Honours: S: U21-8; Yth
Gavin played only 21 minutes of first-team football for Coventry City last term, featuring in an early-season game with Wolves. The central midfielder was a regular for the reserves until February when he spent a brief period on loan to Motherwell. He is the son of the Southampton manager Gordon Strachan.
Coventry C (From trainee on 28/11/1996) P/FL 5+10 FLC 1+3/1 FAC 2+2
Dundee (Loaned on 27/1/1999) SL 4+2

STREET Kevin
Born: Crewe, 25 November 1977
Height: 5'10" **Weight:** 10.8
One of the many players to develop through the youth system at Crewe, Kevin was only ever on the fringes of the first-team squad in 2001-02. In November he joined Third Division Luton Town on loan

but was injured in his first full appearance for the Hatters and returned to Gresty Road to recuperate. He is a hard-working attacking midfield player who generally operates on the right-hand side.
Crewe Alex (From trainee on 4/7/1996) FL 57+58/9 FLC 4+3 FAC 1+1
Luton T (Loaned on 20/11/2001) FL 1+1

STRINGER Christopher (Chris)
Born: Sheffield, 19 September 1983
Height: 6'6" **Weight:** 12.0
Chris had a frustrating time with injuries at Sheffield Wednesday last term after making a promising start in the opening game of the season. That was his only first-team appearance during the campaign as Kevin Pressman re-established himself as the club's number one 'keeper while Chris was on the sidelines. He will be hoping to regain his place in the line-up in 2002-03.
Sheffield Wed (From trainee on 20/6/2000) FL 5+1 FLC 0+1 FAC 1

STRUPAR Branko
Born: Croatia, 9 February 1970
Height: 6'3" **Weight:** 13.7
International Honours: Belgium: 17
This big old-fashioned centre forward was kept out of action by a series of niggling injuries in the first half of the 2002-02 campaign and it was not until February that he made a comeback in Derby County's reserve team. He eventually returned to first-team duties and went on to score four goals in the closing stages of the campaign. His form won him a recall to the Belgian national squad and he featured for his country on two occasions in the World Cup finals.
Derby Co (£3,000,000 from KRC Genk, Belgium, ex Spansko, on 17/12/1999) PL 28+8/15 FLC 1

STUART Graham Charles
Born: Tooting, 24 October 1970
Height: 5'9" **Weight:** 11.10
Club Honours: FAC '95; Div 1 '00
International Honours: E: U21-5; Yth
Graham had another good season in the heart of Charlton Athletic's midfield and took over the captaincy during Mark Kinsella's prolonged absence through injury. He is a hard-working attacking midfielder who likes to play just behind the front two. He is a strong tackler and excellent distributor of the ball and scored five goals during the campaign, making him joint-second-top scorer. He built up a great partnership with Scott Parker in the centre of the park and most of the side's

attacking moves stemmed from these two.
Chelsea (From trainee on 15/6/1989) F/PL 70+17/14 FLC 11/2 FAC 5+2/1 Others 3+2/1
Everton (£850,000 on 19/8/1993) PL 116+20/22 FLC 9/3 FAC 10+3/5 Others 2+1/1
Sheffield U (£850,000 on 28/11/1997) FL 52+1/11 FLC 4 FAC 10+1/1 Others 0+1
Charlton Ath (£1,100,000 on 25/3/1999) P/FL 106+6/19 FLC 4 FAC 7/2

STUART Jamie Christopher
Born: Southwark, 15 October 1976
Height: 5'10" **Weight:** 11.0
International Honours: E: U21-4; Yth
After being released by Millwall, Jamie had a trial at Cambridge before signing for Bury as a replacement for left back Chris Armstrong. He slotted straight into the Shakers defence and proved to be a consistent performer throughout the season. A tough-tackling defender who is impressive going forward, he suffered some disciplinary problems but was eventually rewarded with an extended contract in February. He missed the closing stages of the campaign with an ankle ligament injury.
Charlton Ath (From trainee on 18/1/1995) FL 49+1/3 FLC 8+1 FAC 3 Others 0+1
Millwall (Free on 25/9/1998) FL 42+3 FLC 2 FAC 1 Others 6 (Freed during 2001 close season)
Bury (Free, via trial at Cambridge U, on 8/10/2001) FL 24/1 FAC 1+1 Others 2

STUBBS Alan
Born: Liverpool, 6 October 1971
Height: 6'2" **Weight:** 13.10
Club Honours: SPD '98, '00; SLC '97, '99
International Honours: E: B-1
Alan fulfilled a lifetime's dream when he signed for the club he had supported as a boy, and the Everton fans were equally quick to show their appreciation of one of their own. Initially starting the season at the heart of a back- three, he was later used with equal effectiveness as a central defender in a flat back-four. A spirited competitor he also displays a fine range of passing from the back and he can crash in free kicks from 20 yards or more, as he showed at Bolton and Derby in the Premiership and Stoke in the FA Cup.
Bolton W (From trainee on 24/7/1990) P/FL 181+21/9 FLC 23/4 FAC 16+3/2 Others 12+1
Glasgow Celtic (£3,500,000 on 10/7/1996) SL 101+5/3 SLC 8+1 SC 11 Others 14+1/2
Everton (Free on 13/7/2001) PL 29+2/2 FLC 1 FAC 5/1

STURRIDGE Dean Constantine
Born: Birmingham, 27 July 1973
Height: 5'8" **Weight:** 12.1

Dean Sturridge

This speedy and nimble striker was the Leicester City's leading scorer with three early strikes when new manager Dave Bassett made it clear that he was surplus to requirements at Filbert Street. He subsequently joined Wolves where he hit the winner on his debut at Wimbledon, and followed up with a hat-trick against Barnsley. A permanent deal was then arranged and he responded in style by scoring at almost a goal a game for the Molineux club.
Derby Co (From trainee on 1/7/1991) P/FL 142+48/53 FLC 9+4/4 FAC 8/2 Others 2+1
Torquay U (Loaned on 16/12/1994) FL 10/5
Leicester C (£350,000 on 19/1/2001) PL 20+2/6 FLC 1 FAC 2/1
Wolverhampton W (£375,000 on 23/11/2001) FL 27/20 FAC 1 Others 2/1

STURROCK Blair David
Born: Dundee, 25 August 1981
Height: 6'0" **Weight:** 11.1
Club Honours: Div 3 '02
Blair signed for Plymouth last October and made his debut in the FA Cup second round tie against Bristol Rovers at Home Park. A right-sided player, he was mostly used from the subs' bench and his attacking forays down the flanks proved to be very profitable. A high point was his performance against Rushden in December when he spun away from his marker and delivered a perfect cross that was converted from close range to clinch a 1-0 victory. He is the son of the Argyle manager Paul Sturrock.
Dundee U (From juniors on 5/9/1999)
Brechin C (Loaned on 8/8/2000) SL 20+7/6 SC 1+2 Others 3+1/3
Plymouth Arg (Free on 26/10/2001) FL 4+15/1 FAC 0+2

SUFFO Kengne Herve Patrick
Born: Ebolowa, Cameroon, 17 January 1978
Height: 5'9" **Weight:** 12.12
International Honours: Cameroon: 29 (ANC '02)
After a shaky start to the 2001-02 season, Patrick was given his chance by Sheffield United boss Neil Warnock in September and showed a more focused approach to his play. Two excellent goals against Grimsby, when he showed control, the ability to beat a man and shooting power, endeared him to the crowd. However an injury kept him out of the side and, after a few appearances towards the end of the year, he was absent for nearly two months with the Cameroon side in the African Nations' Cup. Although not a regular in their line-up, he scored in the

final penalty shoot-out to help secure a winner's medal. On his return to Bramall Lane his second appearance, as a substitute, lasted two minutes before he was sent off in the infamous game against West Bromwich Albion. He was placed on the transfer list and in April moved on loan to Spanish club Numancia with a view to a permanent transfer.
Sheffield U (£150,000 from Nantes, France, ex Tonerre Yaounde, Barcelona, on 20/11/2000) FL 16+20/5 FLC 0+1/1 FAC 0+1

SULLIVAN Neil
Born: Sutton, 24 February 1970
Height: 6'0" **Weight:** 12.1
International Honours: S: 27
Neil had a terrific season for Tottenham in 2001-02, maturing into a top-class 'keeper. Commanding in the air and extremely agile, he benefited from having a sturdy defence in front of him and this brought his organisational qualities to the fore. Although ending the season sidelined by injury, he was a central figure in changing the team's fortunes round, not least helped by his keeping a total of 15 clean sheets.
Wimbledon (From trainee on 26/7/1988) F/PL 180+1 FLC 18 FAC 25
Crystal Palace (Loaned on 1/5/1992) FL 1
Tottenham H (Free on 5/6/2000) PL 64 FLC 8 FAC 9

SUMMERBEE Nicholas (Nicky) John
Born: Altrincham, 26 August 1971
Height: 5'11" **Weight:** 12.8
Club Honours: Div 1 '99
International Honours: E: B-1; U21-3
This skilful right winger had a brief period on a monthly contract at Manchester City at the start of last season, but failed to win a place in the first team and in November he joined Nottingham Forest on non-contract forms. He gave Forest balance on the right-hand side and was on the verge of being offered a more permanent deal when he was sidelined with a groin injury, making no further appearances for the club.
Swindon T (From trainee on 20/7/1989) F/PL 89+23/6 FLC 9+1/3 FAC 2+4 Others 7/1
Manchester C (£1,500,000 on 24/6/1994) P/FL 119+12/6 FLC 11+2/2 FAC 12/2
Sunderland (£1,000,000 on 14/11/1997) P/FL 87+6/7 FLC 6+1 FAC 4+1 Others 3/1
Bolton W (Free on 4/11/2001) FL 9+3/1 FAC 3
Nottingham F (Free on 9/11/2001) FL 17/2 FAC 1

SUMMERBELL Mark
Born: Durham, 30 October 1976
Height: 5'9" **Weight:** 11.9

Mark was out of the first-team picture at Middlesbrough last term and joined Bristol City on loan at the end of September. He did well in his month at Ashton Gate and later also had a loan spell at Portsmouth. He is an attacking midfielder, who works hard at chasing and harrying opponents.
Middlesbrough (From trainee on 1/7/1995) F/PL 35+16/1 FLC 4+3/3
Bristol C (Loaned on 28/9/2001) FL 5
Portsmouth (Loaned on 28/3/2002) FL 5

SUTCH Daryl
Born: Beccles, 11 September 1971
Height: 6'0" **Weight:** 12.0
International Honours: E: U21-4; Yth
Daryl is Norwich City's longest serving player with over 350 senior appearances to his credit, elevating him into the club's top-15 all-time appearance makers. Excluded from the senior squad for the first part of the campaign, he was involved more often after Christmas and returned to the level of performance that had won him so many plaudits in previous seasons. Something of a utility player, Daryl turned out in central midfield, on the right flank and in both full-back positions during the course of the 2001-02, giving of his best every time he was selected.
Norwich C (From trainee on 6/7/1990) F/PL 255+50/9 FLC 24+3 FAC 10+3 Others 2+5

SVARD Sebastian
Born: Hividovre, Denmark, 15 January 1983
Height: 6'1" **Weight:** 12.11
Club Honours: FAYC '01
International Honours: Denmark: Yth
This promising young Arsenal defender made his senior debut as a substitute in the Worthington Cup tie against Manchester United last November. A strong and quick centre half he has already been capped by Denmark at youth international level.
Arsenal (Signed from FC Copenhagen, Denmark on 1/11/2000) FLC 0+1

SVENSSON Anders
Born: Sweden, 17 July 1976
Height: 5'10" **Weight:** 12.11
International Honours: Sweden: 29
Anders arrived at Southampton in the summer of 2001 and although deployed initially by Stuart Gray as a left-sided midfielder he came good when played in his preferred central role. Under new manager Gordon Strachan his creative ability blossomed and served as a strong backbone to a resurgent Saints' side.

Southampton (£750,000 from IF Elfsborg, Sweden, ex Hestrafors, on 16/7/2001) PL 33+1/4 FLC 3/2 FAC 1

SVENSSON Mathias (Matt)

Born: Boras, Sweden, 24 September 1974
Height: 6'0" **Weight:** 12.4
Club Honours: Div 1 '00
International Honours: Sweden: 3
Matt missed the first half of the 2001-02 campaign after stretching ligaments in his knee, but won his place back in the Charlton side taking over from Jonatan Johansson for six games during February and March before losing out again. Matt is a strong, aggressive striker who is excellent in the air, works very hard and is unselfish. Although he failed to score during the season he was instrumental in creating chances for others and is without doubt one of the best strikers at the club.
Portsmouth (£200,000 from Elfsborg, Sweden on 6/12/1996) FL 34+11/10 FLC 1/1 FAC 3+2/1 (£100,000 to Tirol Innsbruck, Austria on 15/7/1998)
Crystal Palace (£100,000 on 29/9/1998) FL 26+6/10 FLC 2 FAC 1
Charlton Ath (£600,000 on 28/1/2000) P/FL 37+15/7 FAC 2+2/1

SWAILES Christopher (Chris)
William
Born: Gateshead, 19 October 1970
Height: 6'2" **Weight:** 12.11
If ever there was a player who epitomised the never-say-die attitude that helped Rotherham United to avoid relegation last term it must be Chris. He is a rugged central defender who always gives maximum effort and on several occasions he played on despite nasty cuts to his head. At one stage of the season, he was the Millers' second highest scorer with six goals, all of which came when he moved into the opposing penalty area for set pieces, indeed in one golden spell he netted five times in six games.
Ipswich T (From trainee on 23/5/1989)
Peterborough U (£10,000 on 28/3/1991. Free to Boston U in August 1991)
Doncaster Rov (Free from Bridlington T on 27/10/1993) FL 49 FLC 2/1 FAC 1 Others 2
Ipswich T (£225,000 on 23/3/1995) P/FL 34+3/1 FLC 3 Others 2
Bury (£200,000 on 14/11/1997) FL 125+1/10 FLC 9 FAC 8 Others 3/1
Rotherham U (Free on 1/7/2001) FL 44/6 FLC 2 FAC 2

SWAILES Daniel (Danny)
Born: Bolton, 1 April 1979
Height: 6'3" **Weight:** 13.0

Danny was in and out of the Bury line-up for much of last season and spent two months on the sidelines in the new year with a knee ligament problem. A promising central defender who is effective in the air, he signed a new long-term contract in February.
Bury (From trainee on 9/7/1997) FL 54+9/4 FLC 0+3 FAC 6+1 Others 4/1

SWALES Stephen (Steve)
Colin
Born: Whitby, 26 December 1973
Height: 5'8" **Weight:** 10.6
Steve had a rather frustrating time with injuries at Halifax in 2001-02 but when called upon he always performed dependably. He featured in a variety of defensive and midfield roles during the season and scored his first goal for Town in the 1-1 draw at home to Exeter in September.
Scarborough (From trainee on 3/8/1992) FL 51+3/1 FAC 5 Others 3
Reading (£70,000 on 13/7/1995) FL 33+10/1 FLC 6+1 FAC 6
Hull C (Free on 7/12/1998) FL 57+11 FLC 4+1 FAC 1 Others 3
Halifax T (Free on 2/8/2001) FL 20+4/1 FLC 1 FAC 1 Others 0+1

SWEENEY Antony Thomas
Born: Stockton, 5 September 1983
Height: 6'0" **Weight:** 11.9
Although still a trainee, Antony was included in the Hartlepool first-team squad for the pre-season games last term and was eventually rewarded with a couple of appearances from the subs' bench. A member of the club's youth team that did so well before going out to Manchester United in the FA Youth Cup fifth Round, he signed a professional contract in January. He is an attacking midfielder who is a tireless runner.
Hartlepool U (From trainee on 10/1/2002) FL 0+2

SWEENEY Peter Henry
Born: Glasgow, 25 September 1984
Height: 6'0" **Weight:** 12.0
A left-sided midfielder who is a product of Millwall's youth policy, Peter spent much of last season developing in the U19s. He managed the occasional appearance for the reserves but showed enough promise to earn a place on the subs' bench for the first team and made his senior debut for the final two minutes of the game against Stockport County.
Millwall (Free from juniors on 13/12/2000) FL 0+1

SYMONS Christopher (Kit)
Jeremiah
Born: Basingstoke, 8 March 1971
Height: 6'2" **Weight:** 13.7
Club Honours: Div 2 '99; Div 1 '01
International Honours: W: 36; B-1; U21-2; Yth
This experienced Fulham central defender lost his place to Alain Goma after making only a handful of appearances last term, before departing for Crystal Palace in November. He became Trevor Francis' first signing for the Selhurst Park club, but was soon out injured after falling victim to a complicated muscle strain following a fall in the game against Coventry.
Portsmouth (From trainee on 30/12/1988) FL 161/10 FLC 19 FAC 10 Others 13+1/1
Manchester C (£1,600,000 on 17/8/1995) P/FL 124/4 FLC 6 FAC 9
Fulham (Free on 30/7/1998) P/FL 96+6/13 FLC 14+1/1 FAC 12
Crystal Palace (£400,000 on 7/12/2001) FL 9 FAC 1

SYROS George
Born: Athens, Greece, 8 February 1976
Height: 6'3" **Weight:** 13.7
This left-sided central defender joined Bury on a six-month contract last August and stepped into the first team when Michael Nelson picked up an injury in September. He showed impressive form in his early appearances, particularly excelling in a home game against Stoke, but his performance level then slipped and he lost his place following the heavy defeat at Brentford, ironically after scoring the Shakers' consolation goal. He failed to agree a new contract and returned to his former club Akratitos early in the new year.
Bury (Free from Akratitos, Greece on 16/8/2001) FL 9/1 FAC 0+1

SZMID Marek Andrezj
Born: Nuneaton, 2 March 1982
Height: 5'8" **Weight:** 11.6
International Honours: E: Yth
A midfielder of small stature, Marek battled hard in Southend reserves last term, but rarely forced his way into the first team and was subsequently released at the end of the season. The ex-Manchester United youth player was a useful passer of the ball and promised much, but ultimately was unable to produce, thus leaving him with only one full and one substitute appearance to his name.
Manchester U (From trainee on 27/9/1999)
Southend U (Free on 9/11/2001) FL 1+1

T

TABB Jay Anthony
Born: London, 21 February 1984
Height: 5'5" **Weight:** 9.7
An exciting young left winger with pace and skill. Jay spent most of the 2001-02 season developing in the Brentford reserve and U19 sides. He made three appearances from the subs' bench in Second Division games, the first of which came in the Bees 4-0 win over Brighton.
Brentford (From trainee on 23/7/2001) FL 1+4

TAGGART Gerald (Gerry) Paul
Born: Belfast, 18 October 1970
Height: 6'1" **Weight:** 13.12
Club Honours: Div 1 '97; FLC '00
International Honours: NI: 50; U23-2; Yth; Sch
This left-footed central defender spent most of the 2001-02 season recovering from a serious knee injury sustained in the previous campaign. He finally returned for the closing 15 minutes of the last ever game at Filbert Street, when he was given a rapturous reception by the fans.
Manchester C (From trainee on 1/7/1989) FL 10+2/1 Others 1
Barnsley (£75,000 on 10/1/1990) FL 209+3/16 FLC 15/1 FAC 14/2 Others 6/1
Bolton W (£1,500,000 on 1/8/1995) F/PL 68+1/4 FLC 8/1 FAC 4
Leicester C (Free on 23/7/1998) PL 63+8/8 FLC 12+2/2 FAC 8+1 Others 2/1

TAIT Paul
Born: Newcastle, 24 October 1974
Height: 6'1" **Weight:** 11.10
Paul was only on the fringes of the first-team squad at Crewe Alexandra last term, but always gave 100 per cent effort when included in the team. He had a spell on loan at Hull City in November to cover for injuries and suspensions but received few opportunities as the regular men came back earlier than expected. He is a tall target man with good control who produces some neat flick-ons.
Everton (From trainee on 8/7/1993)
Wigan Ath (Free on 22/7/1994) FL 1+4 (Free to Runcorn on 16/2/1996)
Crewe Alex (Signed from Northwich Vic on 9/6/1999) FL 31+32/6 FLC 0+1 FAC 1+1
Hull C (Loaned on 5/11/2001) FL 0+2

TAIT Paul Ronald
Born: Sutton Coldfield, 31 July 1971
Height: 6'1" **Weight:** 10.10

Club Honours: Div 2 '95; AMC '95
Paul was once again Oxford's best midfield player last season, but injuries restricted his appearances and the team suffered as a result. He covered the pitch well and created a number of chances for his colleagues, although he failed to score himself. He was released in the summer.
Birmingham C (From trainee on 2/8/1988) FL 135+35/14 FLC 13+2 FAC 6+2 Others 13+5/4
Northampton T (Loaned on 24/12/1997) FL 2+1
Oxford U (Free on 15/1/1999) FL 86+5/3 FLC 8 FAC 4 Others 2

TAL Idan
Born: Petach Tikva, Israel, 13 September 1975
Height: 5'10" **Weight:** 11.8
International Honours: Israel: 28
A tricky, hard-working winger in the old-fashioned mould, Idan endured a frustrating campaign last term. He came on as a substitute in three of Everton's first four games of the season, then was handed a starting appearance in a Worthington Cup tie against Crystal Palace. He successfully converted a penalty kick in the shoot-out at the end of that tie, but started just one more game all season after that. Towards the end of the campaign he wasn't even troubling the substitutes' bench and he will surely consider his future during the summer.
Everton (£700,000 from Maccabi Petach Tikva, Israel, ex Hapoel Tel Aviv, on 20/10/2000) PL 13+16/2 FLC 1 FAC 0+3

TALBOT Daniel Brian
Born: Enfield, 30 January 1984
Height: 5'9" **Weight:** 10.9
This young left back was still learning his trade at Rushden last term, but nevertheless featured on a couple of occasions at first-team level. He possesses an astute football brain and has no fear of attacking at every opportunity, his pace enabling him to recover his ground when needed. Has a big task ahead if he is to establish himself as the regular choice at Nene Park, but the pedigree is certainly there for him to succeed. He is the son of Diamonds' boss Brian Talbot.
Rushden & Diamonds (From juniors on 10/2/2001) FL 2+1 Others 1

TALBOT Stewart Dean
Born: Birmingham, 14 June 1973
Height: 5'11" **Weight:** 13.7
Having played a major part in the previous season's promotion campaign, Stewart continued to be one of

Rotherham's driving forces at the heart of the midfield in 2001-02. A powerful tackler, he was difficult to knock off the ball, but he will have been disappointed with his lack of goals after netting just one all season. However, that one was crucial as it gave Rotherham a 1-0 win at Stockport to earn three very valuable points. He was appointed as club captain and led the team by example at all times.
Port Vale (Signed from Moor Green on 10/8/1994) FL 112+25/10 FLC 4+3 FAC 4+1 Others 2+3/1
Rotherham U (Free on 13/7/2000) FL 73+3/6 FLC 3 FAC 4+1

TANKARD Allen John
Born: Fleet, 21 May 1969
Height: 5'10" **Weight:** 12.10
Club Honours: AMC '01
International Honours: E: Yth
This experienced defender initially linked up with Mansfield for training during the 2001 close season but was persuaded to stay and he began the campaign in the left-back position. He shared the spot with Martin Pemberton until suffering a torn hamstring in the game at Gay Meadow and this put him out for a lengthy spell. His ball-winning skills and assured passing were particularly invaluable in a very young side.
Southampton (From apprentice on 27/5/1987) FL 5 Others 2
Wigan Ath (Free on 4/7/1988) FL 205+4/4 FLC 15/1 FAC 13 Others 20
Port Vale (£87,500 on 26/7/1993) FL 261+14/11 FLC 21 FAC 16/1 Others 11+1/1
Mansfield T (Free on 2/8/2001) FL 22+8/2 FLC 1 FAC 3 Others 1

TANN Adam John
Born: Kings Lynn, 12 May 1982
Height: 6'0" **Weight:** 11.5
International Honours: E: Yth
The 2001-02 season saw the continued progress of this composed defender at Cambridge United. After making his debut in the last game of the previous campaign he was given his chance in December and hardly missed a game from then onwards. He took over as team captain towards the end of the season and was deservedly voted as the fans' 'Player of the Year'.
Cambridge U (From trainee on 7/9/1999) FL 25+1 Others 6

TARDIF Christopher (Chris) Luke
Born: Guernsey, 19 September 1979
Height: 5'11" **Weight:** 12.7

Chris made a single first-team appearance for Portsmouth against Grimsby last August, but otherwise had to wait patiently in the reserves or on the subs' bench in 2001-02. Several outstanding performances for the second string marked him out as a great prospect, but nevertheless he was one of several players made available for transfer as the season ended.

Portsmouth *(From trainee on 3/7/1998) FL 3+2 FAC 1*

TARICCO Mauricio Ricardo

Born: Buenos Aires, Argentine, 10 March 1973
Height: 5'9" **Weight:** 11.7
This pacy, tenacious wing back suffered from an uncharacteristic disciplinary record at Tottenham last season. At his best Mauricio adds width to support to the midfield and is a great crosser of the ball. Extremely fit and usually composed, he will be looking to be a regular in

the line-up once more in 2002-03.
Ipswich T *(£175,000 from Argentinos Juniors, Argentina on 9/9/1994) FL 134+3/4 FLC 18/3 FAC 8 Others 7*
Tottenham H *(£1,800,000 on 4/12/1998) PL 73+4 FLC 8 FAC 6+2 Others 3*

TATE Christopher (Chris) Douglas

Born: York, 27 December 1977
Height: 6'0" **Weight:** 11.10
Chris played in the opening game of the 2001-02 season for Leyton Orient and then made a couple of substitute appearances before joining Stevenage Borough on loan in September. He also had a spell on loan at Chester later on, but ended the campaign in the O's second string. He is a big and strong striker, although he occasionally turned out as an emergency centre half in reserve matches.
Sunderland *(From trainee at York C on 17/7/1996)*

Scarborough *(Free on 5/8/1997) FL 21+28/13 FLC 0+1 FAC 0+1 Others 2+1*
Halifax T *(£150,000 on 5/7/1999) FL 18/4 FLC 2 FAC 2/1 (£80,000 to Scarborough on 16/12/1999)*
Leyton Orient *(£25,000 on 3/11/2000) FL 10+19/3 FAC 1+2/1 Others 1+2/1*

TAVLARIDIS Efstathios

Born: Greece, 25 January 1980
Height: 6'2" **Weight:** 12.11
International Honours: Greece: U21
This talented youngster appeared for Arsenal in all three of their Worthington Cup ties last term. A promising central defender he is also featured for Greece at U21 level during the campaign.
Arsenal *(£600,000 from Iraklis, Greece on 21/9/2001) FLC 3*

TAYLOR Cleveland Ken Wayne

Born: Leicester, 9 September 1983
Height: 5'8" **Weight:** 11.5
Primarily a right winger, Cleveland is one

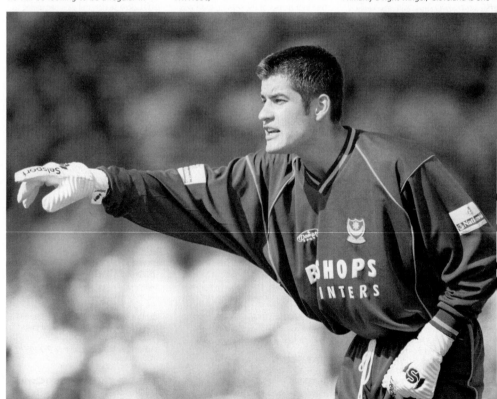

Chris Tardif

of the many youngsters who are starting to come through the ranks at Bolton, thanks to Sam Allardyce's insistence on developing the talent at this level within the club. Cleveland made his debut as a substitute in the FA Cup victory at Stockport, and is certainly a name to look out for in the future.
Bolton W (Trainee) FAC 0+1

TAYLOR Craig
Born: Plymouth, 24 January 1974
Height: 6'1" **Weight:** 13.2
Craig struggled to regain his centre-back place at Plymouth last season after recovering from the broken leg he suffered at the end of the 2000-01 campaign. He finally made his one and only appearance of the season from the subs' bench in the 1-0 victory over York City at Home Park, coming on after David Worrell had been sent off. At the time of writing his future was unclear.
Exeter C (From trainee on 13/6/1992) FL 2+3 FLC 1 Others 2+2 (Free to Bath C on 18/3/1994)
Swindon T (£25,000 from Dorchester T on 15/4/1997) FL 47+8/2 FLC 0+1 FAC 3
Plymouth Arg (Loaned on 16/10/1998) FL 6/1
Plymouth Arg (£30,000 on 20/8/1999) FL 79+2/6 FLC 2 FAC 7 Others 1/1

TAYLOR Gareth Keith
Born: Weston super Mare, 25 February 1973
Height: 6'2" **Weight:** 13.8
International Honours: W: 9; U21-7
Following his successful loan spell at the end of 2000-01, Gareth became a fully-fledged Burnley player and continued in much the same vein, ending the season as the Clarets' leading scorer. He is very much in the traditional mode of big strikers, almost all of his goals coming from headers. His style is limited but effective, although a tendency to lean into defenders brought more than his share of yellow cards. The arrival of David Johnson saw him relegated to the bench at the end of the season, but his arrival into the action for the final game at home to Coventry very quickly brought the only goal of the game.
Bristol Rov (From trainee at Southampton on 29/7/1991) FL 31+16/16 FLC 3+1 FAC 1+1 Others 5
Crystal Palace (£750,000 on 27/9/1995) FL 18+2/1 FAC 2/1
Sheffield U (Signed on 8/3/1996) FL 56+28/25 FLC 8+3/2 FAC 5+2 Others 1+2
Manchester C (£400,000 on 26/11/1998) FL 28+15/9 FLC 2+1/1 FAC 3 Others 1+3
Port Vale (Loaned on 21/1/2000) FL 4

Queens Park R (Loaned on 14/3/2000) FL 2+4/1
Burnley (Free on 20/2/2001) FL 50+5/20 FLC 1 FAC 2

TAYLOR Ian Kenneth
Born: Birmingham, 4 June 1968
Height: 6'1" **Weight:** 12.4
Club Honours: AMC '93; FLC '96
Ian is an industrious, powerful box-to-box player who is one of the most influential players in Aston Villa's midfield. He had the misfortune to suffer an injury-blighted season last term and struggled to secure a first-team place. He eventually returned from a knee injury in October, only to be sidelined the following month with a niggling groin injury.
Port Vale (£15,000 from Moor Green on 13/7/1992) FL 83/28 FLC 4/2 FAC 6/1 Others 13/4
Sheffield Wed (£1,000,000 on 12/7/1994) PL 9+5/1 FLC 2+2/1
Aston Villa (£1,000,000 on 21/12/1994) PL 193+27/28 FLC 18+2/7 FAC 14+2/2 Others 15+1/4

TAYLOR Maik Stefan
Born: Hildesheim, Germany, 4 September 1971
Height: 6'4" **Weight:** 14.2
Club Honours: Div 2 '99; Div 1 '01
International Honours: NI: 21; B-1; U21-1
A fine goalkeeper of outstanding ability, Maik is an excellent shot stopper and almost unbeatable in one-on-one situations. Maik found his expectations of a return to Premiership football dashed by the arrival of Edwin van der Saar two weeks before the start of the 2001-02 season. His only Premiership appearance came in the final game at Blackburn, a game sadly that he will wish to forget, otherwise he was limited to just three Worthington Cup ties and the FA Cup third round games against Wycombe. Despite his absence from the first team Maik retained his place in the Northern Ireland line up but is unlikely to be content to play second fiddle to van der Saar for another season.
Barnet (Free from Farnborough on 7/6/1995) FL 70 FLC 6 FAC 6 Others 2
Southampton (£500,000 on 1/1/1997) PL 18
Fulham (£800,000 + on 17/11/1997) P/FL 165 FLC 20 FAC 16 Others 3

TAYLOR Martin
Born: Ashington, 9 November 1979
Height: 6'4" **Weight:** 15.0
Club Honours: FLC '02

International Honours: E: U21-1; Yth
Martin had many opportunities at Blackburn last term covering in the centre of defence when Craig Short was suspended. Despite his height he is less than assured in the air but possesses amazingly quick feet and an ability to work the ball. He also played in both full back positions with some success though he found the discipline of keeping wide a challenge. He had a particularly memorable game in the Worthington Cup final, which was only his second outing at right back.
Blackburn Rov (From trainee on 13/8/1997) P/FL 29+15/3 FLC 13 FAC 10+1/1 Others 0+1
Darlington (Loaned on 18/1/2000) FL 4
Stockport Co (Loaned on 23/3/2000) FL 7

TAYLOR Martin James
Born: Tamworth, 9 December 1966
Height: 6'0" **Weight:** 14.6
Martin had another very strong season in goal for Wycombe in 2001-02 and became the first player to be voted as the club's 'Player of the Season' three years in a row. He may not have had the high profile publicity of an FA Cup run this time but he went quietly about his business, saving numerous points for the club, and was more often than not 'Man of the Match' away from home. As ever his reaction saves were his forte and at Second Division level he probably has no equal. He is famous for his hatred of losing and although 35 years old now, he is as sharp and fit as ever.
Derby Co (Signed from Mile Oak Rov on 2/7/1986) FI/PL 97 FLC 7 FAC 5 Others 11
Carlisle U (Loaned on 23/9/1987) FL 10 FLC 1 FAC 1 Others 2
Scunthorpe U (Loaned on 17/12/1987) FL 8
Crewe Alex (Loaned on 20/9/1996) FL 6
Wycombe W (Free on 27/3/1997) FL 227 FLC 13 FAC 23 Others 7

TAYLOR Matthew Simon
Born: Oxford, 27 November 1981
Height: 5'10" **Weight:** 11.10
Matthew was a near ever present for Luton last term and again impressed with his obvious class. Employed on the left-hand side either as a full back or a wing back, he has two good feet, tackles well and has the ability to pass a ball accurately. It seems only a matter of time before he moves on to a higher division club, a fact underlined by his selection for the PFA Third Division team for the season.
Luton T (From trainee on 9/2/1999) FL 127+2/16 FLC 6 FAC 10/1 Others 1

TAYLOR Robert (Bob)
Born: Horden, 3 February 1967
Height: 5'10" **Weight:** 12.12
After starting alongside new signing Scott Dobie for West Bromwich Albion in the first three games of last season, this veteran striker reverted to the subs' bench but was always there, waiting in the wings, eager to come and produce the goods. He had to wait some time but 'Super Bob' was eventually called into action and he duly produced the goods, scoring four vital goals – including one in the final game of the season against Crystal Palace when promotion was clinched.
Leeds U (Free from Horden Colliery on 27/3/1986) FL 33+9/9 FLC 5+1/3 FAC 1 Others 4+1/1
Bristol C (£175,000 on 23/3/1989) FL 96+10/50 FLC 6+1/2 FAC 9+1/5 Others 3/1
West Bromwich A (£300,000 on 31/1/1992) FL 211+27/96 FLC 16/6 FAC 6+2/3 Others 16+3/8
Bolton W (Free on 8/1/1998) P/FL 57+20/21 FLC 6+5/2 FAC 4+1/2 Others 3/2
West Bromwich A (£90,000 on 23/3/2000) FL 43+39/17 FLC 5+1 FAC 0+2/1 Others 0+2

TAYLOR Robert Anthony
Born: Norwich, 30 April 1971
Height: 6'1" **Weight:** 13.8
Out of favour at Wolves, Robert began the 2001-02 season on loan at Queen's Park Rangers where he re-established a striking partnership with his former Gillingham colleague Andy Thomson. However, he played only three times for the Loftus Road club and then had a three-month loan spell with the Gills. It took a short while for him to get match fit, but despite getting a few opportunities, he never showed the form of three years previously and was allowed to return to Molineux in early January. He then went out again on loan to Grimsby Town as the Mariners sought to remedy their lack of goal power. However, after a few outings at Blundell Park he suffered a torn achilles tendon, bringing his campaign to a premature close.
Norwich C (From trainee on 26/3/1990)
Leyton Orient (Loaned on 28/3/1991) FL 0+3/1
Birmingham C (Signed on 31/8/1991)
Leyton Orient (Free on 21/10/1991) FL 54+19/20 FLC 1+1 FAC 2+1 Others 2+1
Brentford (£100,000 on 24/3/1994) FL 172+1/56 FLC 16/6 FAC 10/8 Others 14/4
Gillingham (£500,000 on 6/8/1998) FL 56+2/31 FLC 2+1/1 FAC 3/2 Others 7/5
Manchester C (£1,500,000 on 30/11/1999) FL 14+2/5

Wolverhampton W (£1,550,000 on 15/8/2000) FL 5+4 FLC 3/3
Queens Park R (Loaned on 30/8/2001) FL 3+1
Gillingham (Loaned on 8/10/2001) FL 3+8
Grimsby T (Free on 18/1/2002) FL 4/1

TAYLOR Scott Dean
Born: Portsmouth, 28 November 1970
Height: 5'9" **Weight:** 11.8
Club Honours: Div 2 '94; FLC '97
Scott finally recovered from a serious injury suffered the previous season and joined Cambridge United on non-contract forms last November. He showed some good touches when coming on as substitute against Bristol City but after a couple more appearances from the bench he was allowed to leave the Abbey Stadium. When fully fit he is a lively midfield player.
Reading (From trainee on 22/6/1989) FL 164+43/24 FLC 7+5/1 FAC 11+2/3 Others 12+4/1
Leicester C (£250,000 on 12/7/1995) P/FL 59+5/6 FLC 7+3 FAC 2+1 Others 3
Wolverhampton W (Free on 23/9/1999) FL 21+11/3 FLC 2
Cambridge U (Free on 21/11/2001) FL 0+3 Others 0+1

TAYLOR Scott James
Born: Chertsey, 5 May 1976
Height: 5'10" **Weight:** 11.4
Club Honours: AMC '02
This pacy right-sided forward became an instant hit with the Stockport County fans last term, scoring seven times in his first 11 games. Despite his early success he was often kept on the bench and this seemed to affect his confidence. He made his final appearance on New Year's Day at West Brom and signed for Blackpool soon afterwards. He subsequently featured as a striker and out wide for the Tangerines in the closing stages of the campaign.
Millwall (£15,000 from Staines on 8/2/1995) FL 13+15 FLC 0+2/2 FAC 1+1
Bolton W (£150,000 on 29/3/1996) P/FL 2+10/1 FLC 0+4/1 FAC 1/1
Rotherham U (Loaned on 12/12/1997) FL 10/3 Others 1
Blackpool (Loaned on 26/3/1998) FL 3+2/1
Tranmere Rov (£50,000 on 9/10/1998) FL 78+30/17 FLC 16/5 FAC 2+5
Stockport Co (Free on 10/8/2001) FL 19+9/4 FLC 2/3 FAC 0+1
Blackpool (Free on 25/1/2002) FL 13+4/2 Others 3/2

TAYLOR Stuart James
Born: Romford, 28 November 1980
Height: 6'4" **Weight:** 13.4
Club Honours: PL '02
International Honours: E: U21-3; Yth

Stuart was again Arsenal's third choice 'keeper last term, but enjoyed a brief run in the side last autumn after David Seaman and Richard Wright were both sidelined by injury. Altogether he started 13 games for the Gunners and will be looking to build on this experience in the 2002-03 campaign.
Arsenal (From trainee on 8/7/1998) PL 9+1 FLC 3 FAC 1 Others 2+1
Bristol Rov (Loaned on 24/9/1999) FL 4
Crystal Palace (Loaned on 9/8/2000) FL 10
Peterborough U (Loaned on 15/2/2001) FL 6

TEALE Gary
Born: Glasgow, 21 July 1978
Height: 6'0" **Weight:** 11.6
Gary is a wide right-sided midfield player who causes defenders all sorts of problems with his blistering pace and mazy runs down the flanks. He impressed Wigan Athletic manager Paul Jewell in a pre-season friendly but it was not until December that he eventually made the move south. At his best when running at opposition defences, he netted his only League goal to date in the away win at Notts County in February. He is expected to benefit from a close season with the Wigan Warriors Rugby League club for body building exercises.
Clydebank (From juniors on 19/6/1996) SL 52+16/14 SLC 3+1 SC 1 Others 4
Ayr U (£70,000 on 2/10/1998) SL 94+7/13 SLC 5+1/1 SC 10/3 Others 4/1
Wigan Ath (£200,000 on 14/12/2001) FL 22+1/1

TEBILY Olivier
Born: Abidjan, Ivory Coast, 19 December 1975
Height: 6'1" **Weight:** 13.4
Club Honours: SLC '99
International Honours: Ivory Coast: 4; France: U21
Olivier never really established himself during his spell at Celtic and was recruited by Birmingham City boss, Steve Bruce (who had previously signed him for Sheffield United), after Darren Purse rejected a new contract and Steve Vickers got injured. He became a crowd favourite straight away after a powerful debut in the centre of defence against Coventry when he also set up Geoff Horsfield's equaliser. He always showed strength and pace in abundance.
Sheffield U (£175,000 from Chateauroux, France on 24/3/1999) FL 7+1
Glasgow Celtic (£1,250,000 on 8/7/1999) SL 29+9 SLC 4+1/1 SC 2+1 Others 5/1
Birmingham C (£700,000 on 22/3/2002) FL 7 Others 3

Gary Teale

TELFER Paul Norman
Born: Edinburgh, 21 October 1971
Height: 5'9" **Weight:** 11.6
International Honours: S: 1; B-2; U21-3
A 'Bosman' free transfer, Paul followed his former manager to St Mary's in October. A combative midfielder, hard running and a neat passer, he settled quickly into a struggling side and contributed well to the team's impressive revival at the turn of the year. He is equally at home in the right-back berth and covered the position well during the absence of Jason Dodd in March.
Luton T (From trainee on 7/11/1988) FL 136+8/19 FLC 5 FAC 14/2 Others 2/1
Coventry C (£1,500,000 on 11/7/1995) PL 178+13/6 FLC 15/2 FAC 15+4/4
Southampton (Free on 2/11/2001) PL 27+1/1 FLC 1 FAC 1

TERRY John George
Born: Barking, 7 December 1980
Height: 6'0" **Weight:** 12.4
Club Honours: FAC '00
International Honours: E: U21-9
The meteoric rise of John Terry continued apace despite some adverse publicity following two off-field incidents. His magnificent displays allowed Chelsea to overcome the loss of international centre-backs Frank Leboeuf and Jes Hogh and the indisposition through injury of Winston Bogarde. His exceptionally fine season was recognised by the Blues' fans who voted him as the club's 'Player of the Season' despite his relative lack of experience.
Chelsea (From trainee on 18/3/1998) PL 53+8/2 FLC 7+1 FAC 10+5/3 Others 5/1
Nottingham F (Loaned on 23/3/2000) FL 5+1

TESSEM Jo
Born: Orlandet, Norway, 28 February 1972
Height: 6'3" **Weight:** 12.10
International Honours: Norway: 5; B-1
Jo found himself out of favour at Southampton last term after losing his place in the side in October. Following a long period on the sidelines he forced his way back into the squad with several impressive appearances from the bench and contributed an important headed goal at Highbury. Recalled to the side as a striker without success, his value to the Saints from the bench has been important, giving the side that extra something when needed.
Southampton (£600,000 from Molde, Norway, ex Lyn, on 19/11/1999) PL 57+23/10 FLC 4+1/1 FAC 5+1/1

THATCHER Benjamin (Ben) David
Born: Swindon, 30 November 1975
Height: 5'10" **Weight:** 12.7
International Honours: E: U21-4; Yth
This no-nonsense left back put his long-term injury problems behind him when he appeared for Tottenham in last season's Worthington Cup final. He looked fit and lean on his return and had lost none of his pace or strength in the challenge, and he will undoubtedly be itching to get the 2002-03 campaign underway.
Millwall (From trainee on 8/6/1992) FL 87+3/1 FLC 6 FAC 7 Others 1
Wimbledon (£1,840,00 on 5/7/1996) PL 82+4 FLC 12 FAC 5
Tottenham H (£5,000,000 on 12/7/2000) PL 21+3 FLC 5+1 FAC 2

THELWELL Alton Anthony
Born: Islington, 5 September 1980
Height: 6'0" **Weight:** 12.7
International Honours: E: U21-1
This versatile Tottenham defender struggled to make an impact at White Hart Lane last term. He managed just three appearances from the subs' bench and will be looking to see more action in the 2002-03 campaign.
Tottenham H (From trainee on 27/1/1999) PL 13+5 FAC 0+3

THEOBALD David John
Born: Cambridge, 15 December 1978
Height: 6'3" **Weight:** 12.0
This tall commanding centre half found himself reserve to Darren Powell and Ivar Ingimarsson at Brentford last season. He played in the LDV Vans Trophy tie at Wycombe and in the League game at Cambridge as cover for suspensions, before appearing in a run of five games late on when Powell was injured.
Ipswich T (From trainee on 2/6/1997)
Brentford (Free on 8/7/1999) FL 26+5 Others 6

THIRLWELL Paul
Born: Washington, 13 February 1979
Height: 5'11" **Weight:** 11.4
International Honours: E: U21-1
A central midfielder at Sunderland, Paul played his part as an important squad player when called upon last season. Most comfortable in the 'holding' role, where his tenacity, industry, and ability to win the ball and distribute it without any fuss, are best utilised, Paul also filled in on either flank when needed. Whilst he is eager to earn a regular starting place at

the Stadium of Light, he has proved himself invaluable when called upon to do a job at short notice.
Sunderland (From trainee on 14/4/1997) P/FL 22+7 FLC 5+1/1 FAC 1+1
Swindon T (Loaned on 8/9/1999) FL 12

THOGERSEN Thomas
Born: Copenhagen, Denmark, 2 April 1968
Height: 6'2" **Weight:** 12.10
Thomas rarely featured for Portsmouth last term and in October he went on loan to Walsall. He looked promising early on for the Saddlers, netting a vital goal at Stockport, but returned to Fratton Park when his loan period was up. A versatile player who can switch from a midfield role to the right-wing-back position with ease, he possesses a tremendous right-foot shot and distributes the ball well. He was released by Pompey in May.
Portsmouth (£100,000 from Brondby, Denmark, ex Frem, on 5/8/1998) FL 95+13/8 FLC 9 FAC 1+1
Walsall (Loaned on 26/10/2001) FL 7/2

THOM Stuart Paul
Born: Dewsbury, 27 December 1976
Height: 6'2" **Weight:** 11.12
A tall central defender who is strong in the air, Stuart started the 2001-02 season as a regular in the Scunthorpe team, celebrating his first goal for the club in the home win against Shrewsbury in September. However a calf problem ruled him out for two months at the end of October and the trouble returned in January, leading to an operation which ruled him out for the rest of the season. He was released in the summer.
Nottingham F (From trainee on 11/1/1994)
Mansfield T (Loaned on 24/12/1997) FL 5 Others 2
Oldham Ath (£45,000 on 21/10/1998) FL 28+6/3 FLC 1 FAC 1 Others 1
Scunthorpe U (Free on 10/8/2000) FL 34+7/2 FLC 1 FAC 0+2 Others 1

THOMAS Andrew (Andy)
Born: Stockport, 2 December 1982
Height: 5'8" **Weight:** 10.2
Another product of the Stockport County youth system, Andy was handed his debut in early February at Rotherham. The young defender rarely put a foot wrong all afternoon and deservedly kept his place in the side, finishing the season with nine League appearances under his belt.
Stockport Co (From trainee on 11/7/2001) FL 7+3

THOMAS Daniel (Danny) Justin
Born: Leamington, 1 May 1981
Height: 5'7" **Weight:** 11.2
Danny signed for Bournemouth last February on a short-term contract until the end of the season. A left-sided midfielder with an abundance of skill and pace he was mostly restricted to appearances from the bench as he came to terms with the requirements of Second Division football.
Leicester C (From trainee at Nottingham F on 13/5/1998) PL 0+3
Bournemouth (Signed on 8/2/2002) FL 3+9

THOMAS Geoffrey (Geoff) Robert
Born: Manchester, 5 August 1964
Height: 6'1" **Weight:** 13.2
Club Honours: FMC '91; Div 1 '98
International Honours: E: 9; B-3
This widely travelled player rejoined Crewe Alexandra after a 15-year absence during the 2001 close season. His experience in midfield proved a bonus for the club but injuries forced him to miss quite a number of games, nevertheless he remained a popular figure with the fans.
Rochdale (Free from Littleborough on 13/8/1982) FL 10+1/1 Others 0+1
Crewe Alex (Free on 22/3/1984) FL 120+5/20 FLC 8 FAC 2 Others 2+1
Crystal Palace (£50,000 on 8/6/1987) F/PL 192+3/26 FLC 24/3 FAC 13+1/2 Others 15+1/4
Wolverhampton W (£800,000 on 18/6/1993) FL 36+10/8 FLC 1 FAC 1 Others 6
Nottingham F (Free on 18/7/1997) P/FL 18+7/4 FLC 2/1
Barnsley (Free on 1/7/1999) FL 14+24/4 FLC 2+2 FAC 1 Others 0+2
Notts Co (Free on 1/3/2001) FL 8/1
Crewe Alex (Free on 3/8/2001) FL 8+6/2 FLC 1 FAC 1+1/1

THOMAS James (Jamie) Alan
Born: Swansea, 16 January 1979
Height: 6'0" **Weight:** 13.0
International Honours: W: U21-21
Jamie found few opportunities to break into Blackburn Rovers first team last season and after an earlier trial match at Bristol Rovers before Christmas, when he impressed despite getting injured, he eventually joined the Third Division outfit on loan in March. A willing worker who holds the ball up well, he showed promising glimpses of his ability but returned to Ewood Park when his loan period was concluded.
Blackburn Rov (From trainee on 2/7/1996) FL 1+3/1 FLC 1/2

West Bromwich A (Loaned on 29/8/1997) FL 1+2
Blackpool (Loaned on 21/3/2000) FL 9/2
Sheffield U (Loaned on 24/11/2000) FL 3+7/1 FAC 0+1
Bristol Rov (Loaned on 22/3/2002) FL 7/1

THOMAS Jerome William
Born: Wembley, 23 March 1983
Height: 5'10" **Weight:** 11.10
Club Honours: FAYC '00, '01
This exciting young Arsenal winger did well in the Gunners' reserves last season and went on loan to Queen's Park Rangers in March to gain some experience of senior football. He impressed in his brief spell at Loftus Road and scored a memorable winner at Swindon before returning early to Highbury with an ankle injury.
Arsenal (From trainee on 3/7/2001)
Queens Park R (Loaned on 27/3/2002) FL 4/1

THOMAS Martin Russell
Born: Lymington, 12 September 1973
Height: 5'8" **Weight:** 12.6
Club Honours: Div 3 '00
Martin joined Oxford during the 2001-02 season and was soon installed as captain by manager Mark Wright. An all-action midfielder he was a regular under Wright producing some excellent runs into the box and being rewarded with a fine goal against Rushden. However he did not feature at all under Ian Atkins and seems set to depart despite having more time in his contract.
Southampton (From trainee on 19/6/1992)
Leyton Orient (Free on 24/3/1994) FL 5/2
Fulham (Free on 21/7/1994) FL 59+31/8 FLC 6+1 FAC 4/1 Others 7+1/2
Swansea C (Free on 30/7/1998) FL 70+21/8 FLC 8 FAC 5/2 Others 4/1
Brighton & Hove A (Free on 22/3/2001) FL 1+7
Oxford U (Free on 9/7/2001) FL 13+1/2 FLC 1

THOMAS Mitchell Anthony
Born: Luton, 2 October 1964
Height: 6'2" **Weight:** 13.0
International Honours: E: B-1; U21-3; Yth
Injury ensured that the veteran defender spent much of the 2001-02 season on the sidelines, and it was only in the last six weeks of the season that he returned to regular action for Burnley, partly as a result of injuries to Steve Davis and Ian Cox. During that spell Mitchell proved that he had lost none of his old skills, and his experience and composure kept the

Clarets out of trouble on more than one occasion. However he was released in the summer.
Luton T (From apprentice on 27/8/1982) FL 106+1/1 FLC 5 FAC 18
Tottenham H (£233,000 on 7/7/1986) FL 136+21/6 FLC 28+1/1 FAC 12/1
West Ham U (£525,000 on 7/8/1991) FL 37+1/3 FLC 5 FAC 4 Others 2
Luton T (Free on 12/11/1993) FL 170+15/5 FLC 12+1 FAC 6 Others 5+1
Burnley (Free on 2/7/1999) FL 95+4 FLC 6 FAC 6 Others 1

THOMAS Stephen (Steve)
Born: Hartlepool, 23 June 1979
Height: 5'10" **Weight:** 12.0
International Honours: W: U21-5; Yth
Steve has always shown plenty of promise at Wrexham in the past, but injuries had previously held up his progress. Last term was his most productive season to date and he featured in the majority of games, only missing the closing stages of the campaign due to a thigh strain. A combative midfield player who excels in breaking up attacks from the opposition, he got on the score sheet against Brighton at the Racecourse in September with a fine 20-yard strike.
Wrexham (From trainee on 4/7/1997) FL 35+16/3 FLC 1+1 Others 2/1

THOMAS Wayne Junior Robert
Born: Gloucester, 17 May 1979
Height: 5'11" **Weight:** 11.12
Wayne can look back on his 2001-02 season at Stoke with great satisfaction. Signed as a central defender, necessity saw him fill the right-back role following the injury to Mikael Hansson but he played his heart out. Deservedly recognized with a number of 'Player of the Season' awards at the end of the campaign, he was one of the team's great success stories. Physically strong and fit, with good aerial ability and tackling skills, he will need to reduce the number of yellow cards he receives next term.
Torquay U (From trainee on 4/7/1997) FL 89+34/5 FLC 2+1/1 FAC 7/1 Others 6+4
Stoke C (£200,000 + on 5/6/2000) FL 73+1/2 FLC 4+1 FAC 4 Others 10

THOME Emerson August
Born: Porto Alegre, Brazil, 30 March 1972
Height: 6'1" **Weight:** 13.4
This powerful Brazilian centre back was ravaged by injury in 2001-02 and his rock-like presence at the heart of Sunderland's defence was at times badly missed. After establishing a solid partnership with Jody Craddock early in

the campaign, epitomised best by a real backs-to-the-wall rearguard action at Newcastle in August when he was the team's 'Man of the Match', he scored his only goal of the season on New Year's Day to save a point against Aston Villa before a knee injury curtailed his campaign. Dominant in the air and a fearsome tackler, a fully fit Emerson will be a bonus for the Black Cats next term.
Sheffield Wed (Free from Benfica, Portugal on 23/3/1998) PL 60+1/1 FLC 5+1 FAC 4/1
Chelsea (£2,700,000 on 23/12/1999) PL 19+2 Others 1
Sunderland (£4,500,000 on 1/9/2000) PL 42+1/2 FLC 2 FAC 3

THOMPSON Andrew (Andy) Richard
Born: Cannock, 9 November 1967
Height: 5'5" **Weight:** 10.1
Club Honours: Div 4 '88, Div 3 '89; AMC '88
This experienced full back was very much on the fringe of the first team at Cardiff last term and was restricted to just two senior appearances, both in LDV Vans Trophy matches. He eventually joined Shrewsbury Town on loan in January but returned to South Wales with an ankle injury, before joining the Shrews permanently in March. He showed plenty of determination for the Gay Meadow club, notably in the vital away game at Southend when he gave a commanding performance to help secure victory.
West Bromwich A (From apprentice on 16/11/1985) FL 18+6/1 FLC 0+1 FAC 2 Others 1+1
Wolverhampton W (£35,000 on 21/11/1986) FL 356+20/43 FLC 22 FAC 20/1 Others 33/1
Tranmere Rov (Free on 21/7/1997) FL 91+5/4 FLC 13+1 FAC 5+1
Cardiff C (Free on 11/8/2000) FL 5+2 FAC 0+1 Others 2+1
Shrewsbury T (Loaned on 18/1/2002) FL 9+1
Shrewsbury T (Free on 28/3/2002) FL 4

THOMPSON Christopher (Chris) David
Born: Swindon, 15 August 1982
Height: 6'0" **Weight:** 11.12
This promising young right back made his bow in senior football for Northampton Town when he came off the subs' bench for the final two minutes of the Worthington Cup tie against Middlesbrough, thus equalling Aaran Cavill's record for the shortest Cobblers' first-team career. He spent the remainder of the 2001-02 campaign developing in

the U19 and reserve teams but will be aiming to experience further senior action in the coming season.
Northampton T (Trainee) FLC 0+1

THOMPSON Christopher (Chris) Michael
Born: Warrington, 7 February 1982
Height: 5'11" **Weight:** 12.3
Despite finishing the 2000-01 campaign as leading scorer for Liverpool reserves, Chris was surprisingly released during the close season and signed for Grimsby Town following successful trials. He seemed to be on the verge of a breakthrough at the turn of the year after making four League appearances and playing in both FA Cup matches against York City, but then found himself left out following a change in management. He continued to impress for the Mariners' reserves as they narrowly missed out on promotion to the Premier Division of the Avon Insurance League and will be hoping to receive more first-team opportunities in 2002-03.
Grimsby T (Free from trainee at Liverpool on 12/7/2001) FL 4+4 FAC 2

THOMPSON David Anthony
Born: Birkenhead, 12 September 1977
Height: 5'7" **Weight:** 10.0
Club Honours: FAYC '96
International Honours: E: U21-7; Yth
David had an outstanding season for Coventry City in 2001-02 and deservedly won the 'Player of the Season' award. Operating as a wide midfield player he performed consistently at a high level and looked too good for the Nationwide League. He started out on the right, but later switched to the left where his ability to cut inside and shoot with his right foot was seen at its best. He scored some stunning goals from distance including the winner at Walsall, both goals at home to Preston and another winner at Wimbledon. He was at the fulcrum of a large amount of City's attacking force and was sorely missed when unavailable through injury and suspension.
Liverpool (From trainee on 8/11/1994) PL 24+24/5 FLC 5 FAC 0+1 Others 2
Swindon T (Loaned on 21/11/1997) FL 10
Coventry C (£3,000,000 on 8/8/2000) P/FL 57+5/15 FLC 3+1/1 FAC 2

THOMPSON John
Born: Dublin, 12 October 1981
Height: 6'1" **Weight:** 11.11
International Honours: RoI: U21-1; Yth
This young Nottingham Forest defender made his debut at right back at Sheffield

United last January, but was later moved to centre back, which looked to be his best position. Tall, commanding and unflappable, he was just settling into the side when he suffered a knee injury in the away game at Rotherham and this ruled him out for the remainder of the campaign.
Nottingham F (Signed from Home Farm, ex River Valley R, on 6/7/1999) FL 8

THOMPSON Philip (Phil) Paul
Born: Blackpool, 1 April 1981
Height: 5'11" **Weight:** 12.0
This promising young central defender made a number of appearances for Blackpool last term but never established himself as a regular in the first-team line-up. Injury forced him to miss the closing stages of the season and he was released in the summer.
Blackpool (From trainee on 4/9/1998) FL 37+10/3 FLC 4 FAC 0+2 Others 2+1

THOMSON Andrew (Andy)
Born: Motherwell, 1 April 1971
Height: 5'10" **Weight:** 10.13
Andy finished the 2001-02 campaign as leading scorer for Queen's Park Rangers with a total of 21, all scored in Second Division matches. His goals came in bursts with eight in seven matches in September, another seven in seven games in November. He missed several fixtures due to a back injury and it was clear that he was not always fully fit when playing.
Queen of the South (Free from Jerviston BC on 28/7/1989) SL 163+12/93 SLC 8/3 SC 7+2/5 Others 9/8
Southend U (£250,000 on 4/7/1994) FL 87+35/28 FLC 4+1 FAC 3+2 Others 1+2
Oxford U (Free on 21/7/1998) FL 25+13/7 FLC 1 FAC 0+1
Gillingham (£25,000 on 5/8/1999) FL 32+20/14 FLC 5+1/3 FAC 5+1/4 Others 0+1/1
Queens Park R (Free on 22/3/2001) FL 36+10/25 Others 1

THOMSON Andrew (Andy) John
Born: Swindon, 28 March 1974
Height: 6'3" **Weight:** 14.12
This experienced central defender made his 100th League appearance for Bristol Rovers early in the 2001-02 season but was relieved as captain following the departure of manager Gerry Francis at Christmas. He showed his versatility by playing in a central-midfield role but fell out of favour towards the end of the campaign and moved on to Wycombe Wanderers on transfer deadline day. He added some welcome height and

strength at the back for the Chairboys and played in the final three games of the season.
Swindon T *(From trainee on 1/5/1993) P/FL 21+1 FLC 5/1 Others 3*

Portsmouth *(£75,000 on 29/12/1995) FL 85+8/3 FLC 4 FAC 6+1*
Bristol Rov *(£60,000 on 15/1/1999) FL 124+3/6 FLC 8 FAC 6 Others 5*
Wycombe W *(Free on 28/3/2002) FL 3*

THOMSON Peter David
Born: Bury, 30 July 1977
Height: 6'3" **Weight:** 12.6
This tall and uncompromising striker never came anywhere near first-team football

Peter Thomson

Tony Thorpe

for Luton last term apart from an appearance in the LDV Vans Trophy. With the in-form Steve Howard ahead of him he never looked likely to challenge for a first-team spot and in November he joined Rushden on loan. He came off the bench to score for the Diamonds on his debut against Halifax, but otherwise failed to impress. He was eventually released at the end of January and after a trial at Chester he signed for Conference club Morecambe.

Bury *(Signed from Stand Ath on 3/11/1995. Free to Chorley during 1997 close season)*
Luton T *(£100,000 from NAC Breda, Holland on 8/9/2000) FL 4+7/2 FLC 1+1 FAC 1+1 Others 2/1*
Rushden & Diamonds *(Loaned on 5/11/2001) FL 1+1/1 FAC 0+1*

THOMSON Steven (Steve)
Born: Glasgow, 23 January 1978
Height: 5'8" **Weight:** 10.4
International Honours: S: Yth
Steve had his best season to date for Crystal Palace in 2001-02, featuring in over half the club's fixtures, although he was often used as a substitute. A small midfielder with a competitive streak, he is strong in the tackle and an excellent ball winner.
Crystal Palace *(From trainee on 9/12/1995) FL 50+28 FLC 7+3/2 FAC 3/1 Others 1+1*

THORDARSON Stefan
Born: Reykjavik, Iceland, 27 March 1975
Height: 6'1" **Weight:** 12.1
International Honours: Iceland: 5; U21-8; Yth
Stefan was plagued by a serious back injury last season and he was out of first-team contention at Stoke for more than four months. Although previously seen as a left-sided player with a languid style, he played principally as an out-and-out striker. Most of his outings came from the subs' bench and but for his injury he would have made a more regular appearance in the starting line-up.
Stoke C *(Free from Bayer Uerdingen, Germany, ex IA Akranes, Osters IF, BK Brann Bergen, on 26/6/2000) FL 18+33/8 FLC 5+2/2 FAC 2 Others 3+2/1*

THORNE Peter Lee
Born: Manchester, 21 June 1973
Height: 6'0" **Weight:** 13.6
Club Honours: Div 2 '96; AMC '00
Peter got off to a fine start at Stoke City last term, netting four goals before being surprisingly sold to Second Division rivals Cardiff City. Unfortunately injuries then kept him out of action for a significant

portion of the campaign, but even so he managed to score eight times for the Bluebirds. He moved from playing as an out-and-out striker to a position in the 'hole' behind the front two with some success. He is very effective with his back to goal, powerful in the air and composed under pressure.
Blackburn Rov *(From trainee on 20/6/1991) Others 0+1*
Wigan Ath *(Loaned on 11/3/1994) FL 10+1*
Swindon T *(£225,000 on 18/1/1995) FL 66+11/27 FLC 5+1/4 FAC 4+2 Others 1+1/1*
Stoke C *(£350,000 + on 25/7/1997) FL 147+11/65 FLC 12+1/6 FAC 5+1 Others 9+3/9*
Cardiff C *(£1,700,000 on 13/9/2001) FL 23+3/8 Others 2*

THORNTON Sean
Born: Drogheda, Ireland, 8 May 1983
Height: 5'10" **Weight:** 11.0
International Honours: RoI: Yth
Tranmere found another great prospect in this youngster who came up through the ranks. Sean is the most exciting player to emerge at Prenton Park for some time, and impressed all with his dynamic runs and accurate passing. He is an inventive and energetic central midfielder who causes plenty of problems for the opposition.
Tranmere Rov *(Trainee) FL 9+2/1 FAC 0+1 Others 0+1*

THORPE Anthony (Tony)
Born: Leicester, 10 April 1974
Height: 5'9" **Weight:** 12.6
After indicating that he would not be re-signing for Bristol City at the end of the 2001-02 season, Tony was in and out of the line-up during the campaign. Despite this he still topped the club's scoring charts with 19 goals and he will be a difficult man to replace. He is a nippy striker with quick reflexes and an excellent scoring record.
Luton T *(From trainee at Leicester C juniors on 18/8/1992) FL 93+27/50 FLC 5+4/5 FAC 4+3/2 Others 4+3/3*
Fulham *(£800,000 on 26/2/1998) FL 5+8/3 Others 1+1*
Bristol C *(£1,000,000 on 23/6/1998) FL 102+26/50 FLC 5+2/4 FAC 6+1/3 Others 9/4*
Reading *(Loaned on 5/2/1999) FL 6/1*
Luton T *(Loaned on 25/3/1999) FL 7+1/4*
Luton T *(Loaned on 26/11/1999) FL 3+1/1*

THORPE Lee Anthony
Born: Wolverhampton, 14 December 1975
Height: 6'1" **Weight:** 12.4
Lee topped Lincoln's scoring charts for the fifth consecutive season with his tally

of 13 League goals. His skill and pace inside the box always caused plenty of problems for opposing defenders, but he let himself down on two occasions when red carded in consecutive games. After serving a lengthy suspension he worked hard on his self-control and produced some good individual performances in a struggling team. During the summer he moved to Third Division rivals Leyton Orient.
Blackpool *(From trainee on 18/7/1994) FL 2+10 FLC 0+1 FAC 1 Others 1*
Lincoln C *(Free on 4/8/1997) FL 183+9/58 FLC 5+1/1 FAC 14/1 Others 9+1/7*

THORRINGTON John
Born: Johannesburg, South Africa, 17 October 1979
Height: 5'8" **Weight:** 10.12
International Honours: USA: 1
This talented winger burst onto the scene at Huddersfield as a second-half substitute in the Worthington Cup first round tie against Rochdale last August and never looked back. He is a lively player who can attack with pace and purpose, and provides a real threat with his close control and accurate crossing. He scored a wonderful solo effort in the televised win over Wycombe in September. Ankle and hamstring injuries kept him out during the winter months, but he soon returned to the line-up.
Manchester U *(Signed from Mission Viejos Pateadores, California, USA, on 7/10/1997. Free to Bayer Leverkusen, Germany during 1999 close season)*
Huddersfield T *(Free on 16/3/2001) FL 29+2/6 FLC 0+1 Others 3*

THURGOOD Stuart Anthony
Born: Enfield, 4 November 1981
Height: 5'7" **Weight:** 11.8
The type of player all lower division clubs need, Stuart was never found wanting in the Southend United team during the 2001-02 season, regardless of whether he was asked to play in central midfield, wide on the left or right, or even up front. A natural midfielder, he hustled and bustled his way through matches, forever running up and down the pitch, providing the engine room of the Blues' midfield.
Southend U *(Free from Shimuzu-S-Pulse, Japan on 30/1/2001) FL 42+10/1 FLC 1 FAC 4 Others 0+2*

THURSTAN Mark Richard
Born: Cockermouth, 10 February 1980
Height: 6'2" **Weight:** 11.8
Mark's only senior appearance for Carlisle United last term came in the opening day

defeat against Luton. He later had a trial at Southend before moving on loan to Gretna. Time though is still on the side of this defender/midfielder and he will be looking to feature more regularly in 2002-03.

Carlisle U (From juniors on 6/7/1998) FL 4+2 FAC 1+1 Others 1

THWAITES Adam
Born: Kendal, 8 December 1981
Height: 5'10" **Weight:** 11.0
A versatile left sided player, Adam's only first-team appearance for Carlisle United last season came in the final match of the campaign at Mansfield when he came off the subs' bench. Still only 20, he will be hoping to make a greater impact in 2002-03.

Carlisle U (From trainee on 6/6/2000) FL 0+1 FLC 0+1 FAC 0+1 Others 1

TIATTO Daniele (Danny)
Amadio
Born: Melbourne, Australia, 22 May 1973
Height: 5'7" **Weight:** 12.0
Club Honours: Div 1 '02
International Honours: Australia: 19; U23
Danny switched from wing back to a more central midfield role for Manchester City last season under new manager Kevin Keegan. Although seeming to accumulate too many yellow cards, on the positive side he scored a cracking goal from 20 yards out against Coventry at Maine Road. He played a major part, alongside Ali Benarbia, Eyal Berkovic and Kevin Horlock in City's creative midfield, which provided the springboard for the team's successes in front of goal.

Stoke C (Loaned from FC Baden, Switzerland on 25/11/1997) FL 11+4/1
Manchester C (£300,000 on 15/7/1998) P/FL 101+21/3 FLC 10/1 FAC 3+1 Others 1

TILER Carl
Born: Sheffield, 11 February 1970
Height: 6'3" **Weight:** 13.10
International Honours: E: U21-13
This tall, dominant centre half waited patiently for first-team opportunities at Portsmouth last term but was restricted to a brief run in the line-up at the turn of the year. He lost his place after receiving a red card in the defeat at Bradford City and was placed on the transfer list at the end of the season. He is the son of the former Chesterfield and Brighton defender Ken Tiler.

Barnsley (From trainee on 2/8/1988) FL 67+4/3 FLC 4 FAC 4+1 Others 3+1
Nottingham F (£1,400,000 on 30/5/1991)

F/PL 67+2/1 FLC 10+1 FAC 6 Others 1
Swindon T (Loaned on 18/11/1994) FL 2
Aston Villa (£750,000 on 28/10/1995) PL 10+2/1 FLC 1 FAC 2
Sheffield U (£650,000 on 26/3/1997) FL 23/2 FLC 5 Others 3
Everton (£500,000 on 28/11/1997) PL 21/1 FLC 1 FAC 1
Charlton Ath (£700,000 on 30/9/1998) P/FL 38+7/2 FAC 1+1
Birmingham C (Loaned on 9/2/2001) FL 1
Portsmouth (£250,000 on 13/3/2001) FL 16+1/1 FAC 1

TILLSON Andrew (Andy)
Born: Huntingdon, 30 June 1966
Height: 6'2" **Weight:** 12.10
After starting the season at the heart of the Walsall defence Andy underwent an operation for an ankle injury but returned on New Year's Day and got the goal that earned a point at Norwich. He then moved on to join former Saddlers' team-mates Paul Hall at Rushden. He quickly formed a useful defensive partnership with Mark Peters that lasted all the way to the play-off final. He signed a new one-year contract during the summer and will be aiming to be a regular again in 2002-03.

Grimsby T (Free from Kettering T on 14/7/1988) FL 104+1/5 FLC 8 FAC 10 Others 5
Queens Park R (£400,000 on 21/12/1990) FL 27+2/2 FLC 2 Others 1
Grimsby T (Loaned on 15/9/1992) FL 4 Others 1
Bristol Rov (£370,000 on 7/11/1992) FL 250+3/11 FLC 16/1 FAC 11 Others 19+1/2
Walsall (£10,000 on 9/8/2000) FL 50+1/2 FLC 4 FAC 4/2 Others 3
Rushden & Diamonds (Free on 8/2/2002) FL 14 Others 3

TINDALL Jason
Born: Mile End, 15 November 1977
Height: 6'1" **Weight:** 11.10
Jason completed another season as a centre half for Bournemouth in 2001-02, having seemingly made a permanent switch from his former midfield role. His transformation from a squad player to a regular in the side was highlighted when he moved back to midfield for a number of games and showed the huge leaps he has made as a player. Jason scored three excellent goals during the campaign, including a spectacular effort in the Cherries first game in their new stadium against Wrexham.

Charlton Ath (From trainee on 18/7/1996)
Bournemouth (Free on 3/7/1998) FL 98+16/5 FLC 3+2 FAC 5 Others 2+1

TINKLER Eric
Born: Capetown, South Africa, 30 July 1970
Height: 6'2" **Weight:** 13.0
International Honours: South Africa: 38 (ANC '96)
Eric returned to the Barnsley line-up last term after missing the entire previous season through injury. However he injured a knee towards the end of September and was sidelined for several weeks and was then unavailable for a month while captaining South Africa in the African Nations' Cup finals. At his best he was still able to perform at the highest level as a strong and powerful ball-winning midfielder. His contract was cancelled by mutual consent in March.

Barnsley (£650,000 from Cagliari, Italy on 23/7/1997) P/FL 78+21/9 FLC 9+1/1 FAC 6 Others 3

TINKLER Mark Roland
Born: Bishop Auckland, 24 October 1974
Height: 5'11" **Weight:** 13.3
Club Honours: FAYC '93
International Honours: E: Yth (UEFA-U18 '93); Sch
2001-02 was an excellent season for this player who is the engine room of the Hartlepool team. A tough tackling midfielder who always plays at a fast pace, he responded positively to Chris Turner's request for more goals. Chosen as the 'Away Player of the Year', he was virtually ever present until an end-of-season knee injury kept him out of the side.

Leeds U (From trainee on 29/11/1991) PL 14+11 FLC 1 Others 0+1
York C (£85,000 on 25/3/1997) FL 88+2/8 FLC 6 FAC 5 Others 2
Southend U (£40,000 on 13/8/1999) FL 55+1/1 FLC 2+1 FAC 1 Others 1
Hartlepool U (Free on 2/11/2000) FL 67+1/12 FLC 1 FAC 1 Others 6/1

TINNION Brian
Born: Stanley, 23 February 1968
Height: 6'0" **Weight:** 13.0
Brian had a somewhat disappointing season for Bristol City in 2001-02. He took time to recover from a knee operation, and then received a red card in Bristol City's visit to Chesterfield, which ruled him out of the closing stages of the campaign. He occasionally showed flashes of his old brilliance, and all at Ashton Gate hope that he will do so more consistently in 2002-03.

Newcastle U (From apprentice on 26/2/1986) FL 30+2/2 FLC 5 Others 1+1
Bradford C (£150,000 on 9/3/1989) FL

137+8/22 FLC 12/1 FAC 9/4 Others 7+1/2
Bristol C *(£180,000 on 23/3/1993) FL*
334+17/24 FLC 23 FAC 22+2/5 Others 12+3

TINSON Darren Lee
Born: Birmingham, 15 November 1969
Height: 6'0" **Weight:** 13.12
Club Honours: GMVC '97
Darren was yet again the mainstay of the
Macclesfield defence in 2001-02.
Operating as a central defender in either
a back four or five formation he provided
a strong physical presence and was
excellent in the air, while his long throw-
ins proved most effective. One of Macc's
most respected players, he was the only
member of the squad to be ever present
during the campaign.
Macclesfield T *(£10,000 from Northwich Vic
on 14/2/1996) FL 218/5 FLC 13 FAC 11
Others 4*

TIPTON Matthew John
Born: Bangor, Wales, 29 June 1980
Height: 5'10" **Weight:** 11.7
International Honours: W: U21-6; Yth
Although expected to cement a first-team
berth last season, Matthew's goal-scoring
form was disappointing and insufficient to
convince new Oldham boss Mick
Wadsworth of his claims. Known for his
tough-tackling style, Matthew was
unhappy with reserve-team football and
opted to move to Macclesfield. He initially
struggled at Moss Rose, and failed to
score in his first seven matches, but
ended the campaign in encouraging form
– notching three goals in six games.
Oldham Ath *(From trainee on 1/7/1997) FL
51+61/15 FLC 3+4 FAC 4+7/1 Others 3+3/1*
Macclesfield T *(Free on 13/2/2002) FL
12+1/3*

TOD Andrew (Andy)
Born: Dunfermline, 4 November 1971
Height: 6'3" **Weight:** 12.0
Club Honours: S Div 1 '96
Andy originally joined Bradford City in a
three-month loan deal last August before
signing a permanent contract. He arrived
as a centre back, but with the injury to
Ashley Ward he played up front and
scored six goals in 11 games in that role.
He also occasionally featured in midfield
but always gave 100 per cent wherever
he played. In March he joined SPL club
Hearts on loan until the end of the
season.
Dunfermline Ath *(Signed from Kelty Hearts
on 4/11/1993) SL 211+15/35 SLC 14 SC
12+3/2 Others 8+1/2*
Stockport Co *(Loaned on 6/10/2000) FL 11/3*

Bradford C *(£100,000 on 21/8/2001) FL
25+5/4 FLC 2+1/2 FAC 1*
Heart of Midlothian *(Loaned on 28/3/2002)
SL 3/1*

TODD Andrew (Andy) John James
Born: Derby, 21 September 1974
Height: 5'10" **Weight:** 11.10
Club Honours: Div 1 '97, '00
Andy is a versatile player, equally
comfortable at right back, central defence
or in midfield for Charlton. He made a
handful of appearances in central defence
at the beginning of the season but fell
out of favour and then underwent a
minor operation on a troublesome knee.
When fit he was loaned to Grimsby for
the closing stages of the campaign and
his assured displays in the centre of
defence helped eased the Mariners to
safety. He is the son of the former
England defender Colin Todd.
Middlesbrough *(From trainee on 6/3/1992)
FL 7+1 FLC 1+1 Others 5*
Swindon T *(Loaned on 27/2/1995) FL 13*
Bolton W *(£250,000 on 1/8/1995) P/FL
66+18/2 FLC 14+5/1 FAC 1 Others 3*
Charlton Ath *(£750,000 on 18/11/1999)
P/FL 27+13/1 FLC 4 FAC 6+1*
Grimsby T *(Loaned on 21/2/2002) FL 12/3*

TODD Christopher (Chris)
Born: Swansea, 22 August 1981
Height: 6'0" **Weight:** 11.4
Chris spent the summer of 2001 coaching
in the USA before returning to Swansea
at the start of last season. Although
prone to lapses of concentration during
the early part of the campaign he battled
on showing commitment and a
willingness to learn. A promising central
defender who is dangerous at set pieces,
he was most effective in a three-man
defensive line up. Towards the end of the
season he was included in a training
camp for Wales U21s.
Swansea C *(From trainee on 6/7/2000) FL
39+4/4 FLC 1 FAC 1 Others 1*

TODD Lee
Born: Hartlepool, 7 March 1972
Height: 5'6" **Weight:** 11.2
After a superb 2000-01 campaign for
Rochdale, Lee suffered a miserable time
with injuries last term, never managing
more than three games in a row before
breaking down again. Despite glimpses of
his undoubted class when he was fit, the
emergence of young Matt Doughty as the
Dale's regular left back meant that he
was released in the summer.

Stockport Co *(From trainee at Hartlepool U
on 23/7/1990) FL 214+11/2 FLC 24+2 FAC
17/2 Others 33+1*
Southampton *(£500,000 on 28/7/1997) PL
9+1 FLC 1*
Bradford C *(£250,000 + on 6/8/1998) FL
14+1 FLC 2 Others 2*
Walsall *(Loaned on 17/9/1999) FL 1 FLC 1*
Rochdale *(Free on 9/8/2000) FL 48+2/3 FLC
3 FAC 1*

TODOROV Svetoslav
Born: Bulgaria, 30 August 1978
Height: 6'0" **Weight:** 11.11
International Honours: Bulgaria: 25;
Yth
This direct striker never really established
himself for West Ham in the face of some
stiff competition from within the squad
and in March he was sold to First Division
Portsmouth. A good finisher with neat
technique and touch, he was sent off at
Preston shortly after signing but scored a
goal against Burnley in only his third
match for Pompey.
West Ham U *(£500,000 + from Liteks
Lovech, Bulgaria on 30/1/2001) PL 4+10/1
FLC 1 FAC 0+2/1*
Portsmouth *(£750,000 on 20/3/2002) FL 3/1*

TOFTING Stig
Born: Aarhus, Denmark, 14 August 1969
Height: 5'9" **Weight:** 12.0
International Honours: Denmark: 41
This experienced midfielder signed for
Bolton in a cut-price deal last February.
Nicknamed 'The Lawnmower', due to his
no-nonsense style of play, he made a very
impressive debut in the home win against
West Ham in February. He appeared in
four consecutive games until an injury in
the game at Charlton looked like it had
ended his season. However, he made a
quick recovery and he appeared for 45
minutes in the final game of the season
at West Ham.
Bolton W *(£250,000 from Hamburger SV,
Germany, ex Aarhus GF, Hamburger SV,
Odense BK, Duisburg, on 8/2/2002) PL 6*

TOLLEY Jamie Christopher
Born: Ludlow, 12 May 1983
Height: 6'0" **Weight:** 11.3
International Honours: W: U21-2
Jamie had a frustrating time with injuries
during the first half of the 2001-02
campaign and it was not until November
that he made his first start in the
Shrewsbury Town line-up. He needed time
to regain his form and fitness and it was
only after Christmas that Town's
supporters saw the best from him. A
strong-tackling, whole-hearted midfield

Michael Tonge

player he scored a vital last-minute goal to clinch victory at Lincoln in April and retain hopes of a play-off place.
Shrewsbury T (From trainee on 9/1/2001) FL 41+8/3 FLC 0+1 FAC 0+3 Others 1

TOMLINSON Graeme Murdoch
Born: Watford, 10 December 1975
Height: 5'10" **Weight:** 12.7
Graeme partnered Steve Flack up front for Exeter City for the majority of last season, generally performing the role of providing chances rather than scoring goals himself. An effective target man who is adept at holding the ball up and fending off challenges, financial circumstances at the club led to him released in the summer. He showed his respect for boss John Cornforth by saying that he had enjoyed playing under him more than just about any other manager in his career.
Bradford C (Trainee) FL 12+5/6 FAC 0+1
Manchester U (£100,000 on 12/7/1994) FLC 0+2
Wimbledon (Loaned on 22/6/1995) Others 4
Luton T (Loaned on 22/3/1996) FL 1+6
Bournemouth (Loaned on 8/8/1997) FL 6+1/1
Millwall (Loaned on 26/3/1998) FL 2+1/1
Macclesfield T (Free on 9/7/1998) FL 22+24/6 FLC 2+2 FAC 4+2/4 Others 1
Exeter C (Free on 21/7/2000) FL 38+18/6 FLC 2+1 FAC 3/1 Others 0+1

TONER Ciaran
Born: Craigavon, 30 June 1981
Height: 6'1" **Weight:** 12.4
International Honours: NI: U21-12; Yth; Sch
This promising young central midfielder began the 2001-02 campaign in Tottenham's reserve team before joining Peterborough United on loan in December. He played seven times for Posh but never really impressed and soon after his return to White Hart Lane he was released. He subsequently joined Bristol Rovers on a short-term contract where he did well, showing a high work rate and tackling well. Although offered a longer deal by the Pirates, he opted for a return to London and was reported to have signed for Leyton Orient in the summer.
Tottenham H (From trainee on 14/7/1999)
Peterborough U (Loaned on 21/12/2001) FL 6 FAC 1
Bristol Rov (Free on 28/3/2002) FL 6

TONGE Michael William
Born: Manchester, 7 April 1983
Height: 6'0" **Weight:** 11.10
Michael broke into the Sheffield United first team last September and went on to play a key midfield role for most of the

season, being rested on occasions as he adjusted to the demands of senior football. His form was a revelation. He played with confidence and vision, being comfortable on the ball and winning tackles. Never overawed he produced excellent performances in the 'derby' match at Hillsborough and against eventual champions Manchester City at Maine Road. Michael is a fine prospect for the future and in November he signed a new two-year deal with the Blades. He was voted the Supporters' Club 'Young Player of the Year'.
Sheffield U (From trainee on 16/3/2001) FL 28+4/3 FAC 2

TORPEY Stephen (Steve) David James
Born: Islington, 8 December 1970
Height: 6'3" **Weight:** 14.6
Club Honours: AMC '94
Suspension meant Steve missed the first five matches of the 2001-02 season but the Scunthorpe target man returned to have a terrific six months. Always a first choice in the team, he added goal-scoring to his recognised strengths of aerial power and ability to hold the ball up, by netting 15 times by mid-February, including his 100th career League goal against Exeter in January. His season ended disappointingly with no goals in his final 12 matches and a red card that will rule him out of the first two games of the 2002-03 campaign.
Millwall (From trainee on 14/2/1989) FL 3+4 FLC 0+1
Bradford C (£70,000 on 21/11/1990) FL 86+10/22 FLC 6 FAC 2+1 Others 8/6
Swansea C (£80,000 on 3/8/1993) FL 151+11/44 FLC 9+2/2 FAC 10/5 Others 18+3/6
Bristol C (£400,000 on 8/8/1997) FL 53+17/13 FLC 4+1/1 FAC 3 Others 3+1
Notts Co (Loaned on 7/8/1998) FL 4+2/1 FLC 1+1/1
Scunthorpe U (£175,000 on 3/2/2000) FL 92+2/24 FLC 2/1 FAC 7/1 Others 3/2

TORPEY Stephen (Steve) Robert
Born: Kirkby, 16 September 1981
Height: 5'9" **Weight:** 10.8
International Honours: E: Yth
This promising left-sided midfield player joined Port Vale on a monthly contract at the start of the 2001-02 campaign and made his senior debut from the subs' bench against Reading. Although he coped reasonably well he was released soon afterwards and later had a brief association with Conference club Scarborough.

Liverpool (From trainee on 13/5/1999)
Port Vale (Free on 24/8/2001) FL 0+1

TOURE Alioune
Born: Saint-Denis, France, 9 September 1978
Height: 5'8" **Weight:** 10.6
International Honours: France: Yth
Alioune joined Manchester City last September, but his season at Maine Road was over before it really got started. He suffered a deep vein thrombosis attack during the long coach trip to Portsmouth in November and was ordered by doctors not to play for six months while having treatment to thin his blood. The French striker eventually made his debut at home to Wimbledon as a second-half replacement for Richard Dunne and his only other first-team appearance came at Blackburn in the Worthington Cup tie.
Manchester C (Signed from Nancy, France on 14/9/2001) FL 0+1 FLC 0+1

TOWNSEND Benjamin (Ben)
Born: Reading, 8 October 1981
Height: 5'10" **Weight:** 11.3
After impressing so much the previous season, it was perhaps surprising young Ben did not make the right-back spot his own at Wycombe in 2001-02. With Danny Senda in such fine form Ben was finally given his first outing in October in the LDV Vans Trophy but fell badly and cracked his fibula. It took him three months to recover but then started two League games at left back towards the end of the campaign. Ben is highly regarded at the club, having a certain presence on the ball, and should have a bigger part to play in 2002-03.
Wycombe W (From trainee on 13/1/2001) FL 12+1 FAC 5+1 Others 2

TOWNSON Kevin
Born: Liverpool, 19 April 1983
Height: 5'8" **Weight:** 10.3
International Honours: E: Yth
Kevin had a terrific pre-season for Rochdale scoring eight times in eight games. Used almost always as a substitute when the 2001-02 campaign began, he hit his first senior goal when coming on against Exeter and sensationally scored twice as a late substitute against Premiership Fulham in the Worthington Cup. His goals from the bench earned him a 'super sub' tag and a place in the starting line-up. Sharp and elusive, he scored twice more in the remarkable 5-4 victory against York and finished as Dale's top scorer with 17 overall. The speedy striker ended his season on a high with a call-up to the England U19 team.

Rochdale (Free from Everton juniors on 6/7/2000) FL 18+26/14 FLC 0+1/2 FAC 1+1 Others 3+1/1

TRACEY Richard Shaun
Born: Dewsbury, 9 July 1979
Height: 5'11" **Weight:** 11.0
Richard was given several opportunities in the Macclesfield first team in the opening weeks of the 2001-02 season and scored twice in the exciting 4-3 home win against Scunthorpe. However he was dropped from the starting line-up at the beginning of October and in March his contract was cancelled by mutual consent. He subsequently signed for Conference club Scarborough. Richard featured on the left side of midfield for Macc, displaying a good work rate and accurate passing.
Sheffield U (From trainee on 4/6/1997)
Rotherham U (Free on 24/2/1998) FL 0+3 FAC 1+1
Carlisle U (Free on 12/3/1999) FL 39+14/11 FLC 3+1 FAC 1 Others 1+1
Macclesfield T (Free on 25/1/2001) FL 21+12/5 FLC 1 FAC 3

TRACEY Simon Peter
Born: Woolwich, 9 December 1967
Height: 6'0" **Weight:** 13.12
Simon began his 14th season at Bramall Lane with a new challenger for the goalkeeper's jersey in the shape of Wilko de Vogt. Nevertheless, he remained first choice for Sheffield United, having another fine season when he generally looked sure with crosses into the box and his shot stopping was as good as ever. He was the first of the three Blades to be sent off in the remarkable game against West Bromwich Albion – bringing his total of dismissals for the club to a record five. He topped 300 League appearances during the season and now stands 18th in the all-time appearance list for United.
Wimbledon (From apprentice on 3/2/1986) FL 1 Others 1
Sheffield U (£7,500 on 19/10/1988) F/PL 329+3 FLC 22 FAC 18 Others 10
Manchester C (Loaned on 27/10/1994) PL 3
Norwich C (Loaned on 31/12/1994) PL 1 FAC 2
Wimbledon (Loaned on 2/11/1995) PL 1

TRAORE Demba
Born: Stockholm, Sweden, 22 April 1982
Height: 6'1" **Weight:** 11.10
This young and pacy striker featured on a handful of occasions for Cambridge United last term but was unable to establish himself in the line-up. In December he went on loan to Ryman

League club Aylesbury United and he was eventually released in the summer.
Cambridge U (Free from Vasalunds IF, Sweden on 28/12/2000) FL 2+6 FLC 1 Others 0+1

TRAORE Djimi
Born: Paris, France, 1 March 1980
Height: 6'3" **Weight:** 13.10
International Honours: France: U21; Yth
Overtaken by his compatriot Gregory Vignal as first reserve for the left back slot at Anfield, Djimi's chances of first-team action for Liverpool were further reduced by the arrival of Jon Arne Riise in the summer of 2001. He was however granted one senior opportunity, partnering Sami Hyypia in central defence in the second leg of the Champions' League qualifying round against Haka of Finland. A week later he was loaned out to Lens for the remainder of the season.
Liverpool (£550,000 from Laval, France on 18/2/1999) PL 8 FLC 3 Others 3+1

TRAYNOR Gregory (Greg)
Born: Salford, 17 October 1984
Height: 5'9" **Weight:** 10.4
This battling midfielder joined Wigan Athletic as a first-year trainee in the summer of 2001. A good passer of the ball who has bags of potential, he became one the youngest players to represent the club coming on as a substitute in the away match at Brighton. He went on to make his first ever start a couple of days later in the Worthington Cup tie at Blackpool when he showed maturity beyond his years to give an accomplished performance. He spent the remainder of the season developing in the club's reserve and youth sides.
Wigan Ath (Trainee) FL 0+1 FLC 1

TRETTON Andrew (Andy) David
Born: Derby, 9 October 1976
Height: 6'0" **Weight:** 12.9
Andy found himself replaced by new signing Mick Heathcote in the centre of the Shrewsbury defence last season and most of his appearances came as cover for injury or suspension. A centre half who is strong in the air and reads the game well, he never let the side down when called upon. Nevertheless he was released by the club in the summer.
Derby Co (From trainee on 18/10/1993)
Shrewsbury T (Free on 12/12/1997) FL 105+6/6 FLC 2 FAC 4 Others 2

TROLLOPE Paul Jonathan
Born: Swindon, 3 June 1972
Height: 6'0" **Weight:** 12.6
Club Honours: Div 2 '99
International Honours: W: 6; B-1
Paul joined Coventry on a short-term contract last March after being out of the Fulham first team for over a year. He made a promising start against Birmingham but faded in subsequent matches and never appeared in a winning City side. His re-emergence did however earn him a recall to the Wales squad and he won his sixth cap against the Czech Republic. An experienced midfield player who can also play at full back, he is the son of the former Swindon Town stalwart John Trollope.
Swindon T (From trainee on 23/12/1989)
Torquay U (Free on 26/3/1992) FL 103+3/16 FLC 9+1/1 FAC 7 Others 8+1
Derby Co (£100,000 on 16/12/1994) F/PL 47+18/5 FLC 3+2/1 FAC 3+1
Grimsby T (Loaned on 30/8/1996) FL 6+1/1
Crystal Palace (Loaned on 11/10/1996) FL 0+9
Fulham (£600,000 on 28/11/1997) FL 54+22/5 FLC 9+2 FAC 3+5 Others 4/1
Coventry C (Free on 22/3/2002) FL 5+1

TROUGHT Michael (Mike) John
Born: Bristol, 19 October 1980
Height: 6'2" **Weight:** 13.2
This central defender impressed Bristol Rovers manager Gerry Francis in pre-season and he started the 2001-02 season at left back, his first appearance in the club's senior team since January 2000. He featured fairly regularly in the squad during the first half of the season, only to fall out of favour following a managerial change. He returned for the Southern semi-final of the LDV Vans Trophy against Bristol City but was eventually released in the summer.
Bristol Rov (From trainee on 18/3/1999) 25+8 FLC 1 FAC 6+2 Others 4

TRUNDLE Lee Christopher
Born: Liverpool, 10 October 1976
Height: 6'0" **Weight:** 13.3
As is often the case when a player makes the move up from non-league football, the second year is always more difficult than the first, as Lee discovered at Wrexham last season. He continued to excite the fans, creating a buzz whenever he made one of his runs. A predominantly left-footed striker who can turn an opponent on the proverbial sixpence, he finished as second-highest scorer for the Robins in all competitions.

Shane Tudor (left)

Wrexham (£60,000 from Rhyl, ex Burscough, Chorley, Stalybridge Celtic, Southport, on 16/2/2001) FL 42+8/16 Others 1+1/2

TUDOR Shane Anthony
Born: Wolverhampton, 10 February 1982
Height: 5'8" **Weight:** 11.2
This nippy right winger joined Cambridge United on loan last October and then on a full contract a month later. He featured regularly from then on, and was at his best when running with the ball at opposition defences. He also occasionally featured in a more central midfield role.
Wolverhampton W (From trainee on 9/8/1999) FL 0+1
Cambridge U (Free on 22/11/2001) FL 31+1/3 FAC 2/1 Others 6/1

[TUGAY] KERIMOGLU Tugay
Born: Istanbul, Turkey, 24 August 1970
Height: 5'9" **Weight:** 11.6
Club Honours: SPD '00; SC '00; FLC '02
International Honours: Turkey: 76
Tugay may be approaching the veteran stage but he proved a great success in the midfield 'holding' role for Blackburn last term. While not the hardest of tacklers, he nevertheless knows how to get goal side and block attacks. At ease in possession of the ball he has a full range of passing abilities and can unlock defences with the killer ball. His long-range shooting is controlled and effective, his goal against West Ham probably being the pick of his goals.
Glasgow R (Signed from Galatasaray, Turkey on 15/1/2000) SL 26+16/4 SLC 2+1 SC 3+4 Others 6
Blackburn Rov (£1,300,000 on 20/7/2001) PL 32+1/3 FLC 5+1 FAC 3+1

TULLY Stephen (Steve) Richard
Born: Paignton, 10 February 1980
Height: 5'9" **Weight:** 11.0
Steve always delivers honest commitment from the right-back position, and is particularly at home when given license to charge forward as a wing back. He lost his place in the Torquay line-up to Paul Holmes in the second half of last season, and did not have his contract renewed in the summer.
Torquay U (From trainee on 18/5/1998) FL 90+16/3 FLC 5+1 FAC 4+1 Others 8

TURLEY William (Billy) Lee
Born: Wolverhampton, 15 July 1973
Height: 6'4" **Weight:** 15.0
Club Honours: NC '01
This influential Rushden goalkeeper played a major part in the club's run to

the Third Division play-off final in their first season in the Football League. Time and again, he pulled off vital saves, particularly early on when the team was taking time to adjust to their new environment. A very commanding presence in the penalty area, he missed just three competitive first-team games all season, and that was due to suspension.
Northampton T (Free from Evesham on 10/7/1995) FL 28 FAC 2 Others 4
Leyton Orient (Loaned on 5/2/1998) FL 14
Rushden & Diamonds (£135,000 on 15/6/1999) FL 43 FLC 2 FAC 2 Others 4

TURNER John Samuel (Sam)
Born: Pontypool, 9 September 1980
Height: 6'1" **Weight:** 12.6
This young goalkeeper was given his first-team debut for Stockport County at Crewe last October and an assured performance saw him keep the club's first clean sheet of the season, a feat that he almost repeated until he was beaten by Tommy Smith's stoppage-time goal at Watford in Carlton Palmer's first game in charge. The former Charlton 'keeper slipped down the pecking order following the emergence of 16-year-old James Spencer and was released at the end of the season.
Charlton Ath (From trainee on 25/5/1999)
Stockport Co (Free on 12/7/2000) FL 4+2

TUTTLE David (Dave) Philip
Born: Reading, 6 February 1972
Height: 6'1" **Weight:** 12.10
Club Honours: FAYC '90
International Honours: E: Yth
Started last season as third choice central defender for Millwall, making most of his appearances from the subs' bench until an injury to Sean Dyche gave him a run in the first team, where his experience was of great value. He went on loan to Wycombe in March where he shone as a commanding centre half before returning to the Den early after suffering a groin strain.
Tottenham H (From trainee on 8/2/1990) F/PL 10+3 FLC 3+1 Others 1/1
Peterborough U (Loaned on 21/1/1993) FL 7
Sheffield U (£350,000 on 1/8/1993) P/FL 63/1 FLC 2 FAC 3
Crystal Palace (Signed on 8/3/1996) F/PL 73+8/5 FLC 7 FAC 2 Others 6
Barnsley (£150,000 on 18/8/1999) FL 11+1 FAC 1
Millwall (£200,000 on 2/3/2000) FL 18+4 FLC 2+1 Others 3
Wycombe W (Loaned on 22/2/2002) FL 4

TWIGG Gary
Born: Glasgow, 19 March 1984
Height: 6'0" **Weight:** 11.12
This promising youngster has scored regularly with Derby County academy and reserve teams in recent seasons and stepped up to make his senior debut when he came off the subs' bench in the final match of 2001-02 at Sunderland. An exciting prospect, he was voted as the club's 'Young Player of the Year' in 2000-01.
Derby Co (From trainee on 20/3/2001) PL 0+1

TYLER Mark Richard
Born: Norwich, 2 April 1977
Height: 6'0" **Weight:** 12.9
International Honours: E: Yth
The 2001-02 season proved yet another excellent campaign for Peterborough's first-choice 'keeper. He rarely missed a match and impressed throughout with some fine saves. Agile and a fine shot stopper he was out of contract in the summer and his future was unclear at the time of writing and Mark was deservedly honoured by his fellow professionals in the PFA Second Division team for the season.
Peterborough U (From trainee on 7/12/1994) FL 196+1 FLC 10 FAC 17 Others 15

TYSON Nathan
Born: Reading, 4 May 1982
Height: 5'10" **Weight:** 11.12
Nathan made a brief appearance for Reading from the subs' bench in the Worthington Cup tie against Luton before joining Swansea City on loan last August. He was carried off with a knee injury in his second game for the Swans but returned to produce some impressive play on the flank for the Vetch Field club. On his return to the Royals he made a couple more appearances from the bench before joining Third Division Cheltenham Town, also on loan, in March. He made an instant impression at Whaddon Road showing lightning-quick pace and scoring the winning goal in the 2-1 victory over local rivals Kidderminster Harriers. He has good potential as a pacy front player or wide midfielder, and is very much a part of Reading's plans for the future.
Reading (From trainee on 18/3/2000) FL 0+2 FLC 0+1 FAC 0+1 Others 0+1
Swansea C (Loaned on 30/8/2001) FL 7+4/1
Cheltenham T (Loaned on 22/3/2002) FL 1+7/1

UV

UHLENBEEK Gustav (Gus) Reinier

Born: Paramaribo, Surinam, 20 August 1970
Height: 5'10" **Weight:** 12.6
Club Honours: Div 2 '99

Gus started the season on the transfer list at Sheffield United and playing in the reserves. He had few chances early on, but regained his place in December and became first choice until his loan move to Walsall on transfer deadline day. He gave an outstanding display in the Saddlers' last away game against his former club Sheffield United when a 1-0 win ensured the club's First Division safety. He is an all-action defender who is particularly dangerous going forward.

Ipswich T (£100,000 from Tops SV, Holland, ex Ajax, Cambuur, on 11/8/1995) FL 77+12/4 FLC 5+3 FAC 4+3 Others 7+1
Fulham (Free on 22/7/1998) FL 22+17/1 FLC 4+1 FAC 3+2 Others 1
Sheffield U (Free on 10/8/2000) FL 47+4 FLC 5 FAC 3
Walsall (Loaned on 28/3/2002) FL 5

ULLATHORNE Robert (Rob)

Born: Wakefield, 11 October 1971
Height: 5'8" **Weight:** 11.3
International Honours: E: Yth

After turning down a contract offer at the end of the 2000-01 season Rob returned to train with Sheffield United and played in some reserve games. When Shane Nicholson suffered an injury he was then engaged on a non-contract basis and made the left-wing-back position his own. He used his experience, pace and anticipation in defence, and worked hard in attack down the flank, linking well with Michael Brown and producing searching crosses. In March he signed on a permanent basis until the summer of 2003. It was Rob's injury in the infamous game against West Bromwich Albion that reduced the Blades to six players, thus causing the match to be abandoned.

Norwich C (From trainee on 6/7/1990) F/PL 86+8/7 FLC 10+2/1 FAC 7+1 Others 1 (Free to Osasuna, Spain during 1996 close season)
Leicester C (£600,000 on 18/2/1997) PL 28+3/1 FLC 8+1 FAC 2/1
Sheffield U (Free, following an injury and trials at Huddersfield T, Real Zaragoza, Tenerife, Newcastle, on 1/12/2000) FL 27+1 FAC 2

UNDERWOOD Paul Victor

Born: Wimbledon, 16 August 1973
Height: 5'11" **Weight:** 12.8
Club Honours: NC '01

This hugely talented Rushden left back made the transition to League football with consummate ease last term. He assumed the mantle of club captain in the absence of the injured Ray Warburton, but took the responsibility on without hesitation and continued to turn in consistent performances week-in, week-out. Quick in attack, strong in defence, he was voted 'Player of the Year' by the Diamonds' supporters.

Rushden & Diamonds (£50,000 from Enfield, ex Kingstonian, Molesey, Sutton U, Carshalton Ath, on 6/6/1997) FL 40 FLC 2 FAC 2 Others 4

UNSAL Hakan

Born: Sinop, Turkey, 14 May 1973
Height: 5'10" **Weight:** 12.5
International Honours: Turkey: 28

A true left-wing back, Hakan signed for Blackburn, a team that normally plays a flat back-four. He has fine attacking skills, he can beat a player in little space and rake a cross field pass with the best, but he ran into occasional disciplinary troubles.

Blackburn Rov (£1,000,000 from Galatasaray, Turkey, on 1/3/2002) PL 7+1

UNSWORTH David Gerald

Born: Chorley, 16 October 1973
Height: 6'1" **Weight:** 14.2
Club Honours: FAC '95; CS '95
International Honours: E: 1; U21-6; Yth

David has long been recognised as one of Everton's most honest, committed and dedicated players - even if a succession of managers have failed to decide upon his most effective position! He started his career at centre-half, but under Walter Smith was used more and more frequently as a left back or left wing back. When David Moyes arrived as boss he was asked to play left midfield - and responded with a stunning goal 27 seconds into the new manager's reign. Another goal the following weekend, again expertly delivered with his left foot, showed he possesses the technical ability to go with his undoubted commitment.

Everton (From trainee on 25/6/1992) F/PL 108+8/11 FLC 5+2 FAC 7 Others 4/1
West Ham U (£1,000,000 + on 18/8/1997) PL 32/2 FLC 5 FAC 4
Aston Villa (£3,000,000 on 28/7/1998) PL 110+9/15 FLC 6 FAC 12+1/4
Everton (£3,000,000 on 22/8/1998) PL 110+9/15 FLC 6 FAC 12+1/4

UNSWORTH Lee Peter

Born: Eccles, 25 February 1973
Height: 5'11" **Weight:** 11.8

An early-season injury to Matt Barrass enabled Lee take over as the regular right back for Bury last term, and apart from occasional injuries and suspensions he retained his place for the remainder of the campaign. He signed an extension to his contract in February and had a short spell in his preferred position at centre half in the closing fixtures.

Crewe Alex (Signed from Ashton U on 20/2/1995) FL 93+33 FLC 10+1/1 FAC 5+1/1 Others 8+2
Bury (Free on 4/8/2000) FL 46+4/1 FLC 2 FAC 3 Others 3

UPSON Matthew James

Born: Stowmarket, 18 April 1979
Height: 6'1" **Weight:** 11.4
Club Honours: PL '02

This talented Arsenal defender was beginning to win more regular first-team action last term when he had the misfortune to be sidelined after suffering a broken fibula playing against Everton in February. He is a strong and intelligent centre half who is comfortable on the ball and has good distribution skills.

Luton T (From trainee on 24/4/1996) FL 0+1 Others 1
Arsenal (£1,000,000 on 14/5/1997) PL 20+14 FLC 8 FAC 2+1 Others 8+2
Nottingham F (Loaned on 8/12/2000) FL 1
Crystal Palace (Loaned on 2/3/2001) FL 7

VAESEN Nico Jos-Theodor

Born: Ghent, Belgium, 28 September 1969
Height: 6'3" **Weight:** 12.8

Nico started the 2001-02 season as first choice in goal for Birmingham City, but was then sidelined by a poisoned elbow. He was dropped by caretaker managers Mick Mills and Jim Barron, but returned under Steve Bruce, saving a penalty on his comeback in a vital win at Norwich. He ended the season in superb form, making vital saves at important times as Blues clinched place in the Premiership, via the play-offs.

Huddersfield T (£80,000 from SC Eendracht Aalst, Belgium on 10/7/1998) FL 134 FLC 12 FAC 7
Birmingham C (£800,000 on 19/6/2001) FL 22+1 FLC 2 Others 3

VALAKARI Simo

Born: Helsinki, Finland, 28 April 1973
Height: 5'10" **Weight:** 11.10
International Honours: Finland: 19

Jean-Louis Valois

Simo again found himself on the fringes of the first-team squad at Derby County last term and featured in only nine Premiership matches during the season. A combative midfield player, he was generally employed in a 'holding' role by the Rams.

Motherwell (Signed from MyPa, Finland on 6/2/1997) SL 98+6 SLC 3+1 SC 7+2
Derby Co (Free on 6/7/2000) PL 15+5/1 FLC 4

VALOIS Jean-Louis
Born: Saint-Priest, France, 15 October 1973
Height: 5'11" **Weight:** 11.8
Jean-Louis turned down a chance of playing UEFA Cup action for Lille to join Luton Town last September. He made his debut for the Hatters against Torquay United and got off to a bright start, scoring a brilliant goal. With his close ball control, classy dribbling and spectacular shooting skills he soon became a cult figure with the fans, but the rigours of English football affected him and it was not until the spring that he returned to his best form again. At the time of writing he was considering a new contract.

Luton T (Free from Lille, France, ex Auxerre, Guegnon, on 21/9/2001) FL 32+2/6

VAN BLERK Jason
Born: Sydney, Australia, 16 March 1968
Height: 6'1" **Weight:** 13.0
International Honours: Australia: 27; Yth
This left-sided defender was given a three-month contract by Stockport County after surprisingly being released by West Bromwich Albion at the end of the 2000-01 campaign. Unfortunately, he was unable to win the plaudits of the County faithful, though, and he made his final appearance at Preston in early November. After an unsuccessful trial at Wrexham he signed for Third Division Hull City, linking up once more with his former boss Brian Little. The stylish left back soon made his mark at Boothferry Park when – in the space of seven minutes of his second appearance – he netted the winner then was sent-off in the vital promotion game with Rushden. He was rather unlucky to be released by the Tigers at the end of the season.

Millwall (£300,000 from Go Ahead Eagles, Holland on 8/9/1994) FL 68+5/2 FLC 5 FAC 6+1 Others 1+1
Manchester C (Free on 9/8/1997) FL 10+9 FLC 0+1 FAC 0+1
West Bromwich A (£250,000 on 13/3/1998) FL 106+3/3 FLC 8+1 FAC 1 Others 2
Stockport Co (Free on 16/8/2001) FL 13 FLC 1
Hull C (Free on 3/1/2002) FL 10/1

VAN BRONCKHORST Giovanni
Born: Rotterdam, Holland, 5 February 1975
Height: 5'10" **Weight:** 11.10
Club Honours: SPD '99, '00; SC '99, '00; SLC '98; PL '02
International Honours: Holland: 26
This left-footed midfielder joined Arsenal from Rangers during the 2001 close season. A skilful payer who is capable of breaking with the ball from the centre of the park, he never really established a regular presence in the line-up and will be looking to feature more regularly in first-team action next term.

Glasgow R (£5,000,000 from Feyenoord, Holland on 15/7/1998) SL 72+1/13 SLC 6/1 SC 10+1/3 Others 28/5
Arsenal (£8,500,000 on 22/6/2001) PL 13+8/1 FLC 3 FAC 2 Others 6+1

VAN DER GEEST Franciscus (Frank) Wilhelmus
Born: Beverwijk, Holland, 30 April 1973
Height: 6'2" **Weight:** 13.0
Frank only managed two senior appearances for Darlington last term, both in the LDV Vans Trophy, and he was released in January to return to Holland. At the time it seemed there was little prospect of him replacing first-choice 'keeper Andy Collett, but ironically Collett then suffered a serious injury almost immediately afterwards that ruled him out for the remainder of the campaign.

Darlington (Free from Heracles, Holland, ex AZ Alkmaar, Sparta Rotterdam, on 21/8/2000) FL 2 FLC 2 Others 5

VAN DER GOUW Raimond (Rai)
Born: Oldenzaal, Holland, 24 March 1963
Height: 6'3" **Weight:** 13.10
Club Honours: EC '99; FAC '99; PL '00, '01
A highly experienced goalkeeper who oozes presence, Rai found himself relegated to third choice 'keeper for Manchester United last term following the arrival of Ronnie Carroll. He received just a single first-team opportunity in the Worthington Cup tie against Arsenal in November. With his United playing days now seemingly numbered, one can only look back on some great memories, and say a big thank you for his wonderful service to the club.

Manchester U (Free from Vitesse Arnhem, Holland, ex Go Ahead Eagles, on 12/7/1996) PL 26+11 FLC 8+1 FAC 1 Others 13

VAN DER SAR Edwin
Born: Leiden, Holland, 29 October 1970
Height: 6'5" **Weight:** 13.6
International Honours: Holland: 66

The first choice Dutch international goalkeeper arrived at Craven two weeks before the start of the 2001-02 season. As expected he went straight into the side for the opening game and kept his place throughout the campaign except for the final Premiership game and Worthington Cup ties. A big man, Edwin dominates his penalty area although at times early on he appeared a little suspect at corners, but this was soon ironed out as he got used to Premiership action. His huge kicks often turn defence into attack and he is seldom beaten in one to one situations. He pulled off a fine penalty save from Alan Shearer in the home game against Newcastle.

Fulham (£7,000,000 from Juventus, Italy, ex Noordwijk, Ajax, on 10/8/2001) PL 37 FAC 4

VAN DEURZEN Jurgen
Born: Genk, Belgium, 26 January 1974
Height: 5'7" **Weight:** 11.0
Signed by Stoke City on a season's loan from Belgian club Turnhout, Jurgen acquitted himself well and formed an excellent pairing with Clive Clarke on the left-hand side. He showed his adaptability when switched to play at full back or in a central midfield role for the benefit of the side and his committed style made him popular with the City faithful.

Stoke C (Signed from KFC Turnhout, Belgium on 8/8/2001) FL 37+3/4 FLC 1 FAC 4 Others 0+3

VAN HEUSDEN Arjan
Born: Alphen, Holland, 11 December 1972
Height: 6'3" **Weight:** 14.7
Arjan was again the first-choice 'keeper for Exeter City in 2001-02. He produced a string of fine displays demonstrating some clean catching and his ability as a shot stopper. A hip injury kept him out for several games, but it was a measure of the faith boss John Cornforth had in him that he returned to the line-up almost as soon as he was fit again. He was reported to have been offered a new one-year deal for the 2002-03 season, but at the time of writing he had yet to agree terms.

Port Vale (£4,500 from VV Noordwijk, Holland on 15/8/1994) FL 27 FLC 4 Others 2
Oxford U (Loaned on 26/9/1997) FL 11 FLC 2
Cambridge U (Free on 4/8/1998) FL 41+1 FLC 6 FAC 1 Others 4
Exeter C (Free on 31/7/2000) FL 74 FLC 2 FAC 4 Others 1

VAN NISTELROOY Rutgerus (Ruud)
Born: Oss, Holland, 1 July 1976
Height: 6'2" **Weight:** 12.13

International Honours: Holland: 18
After the on-off saga of his transfer from PSV, Ruud more than justified his billing as a top-class striker for Manchester United last term. The archetypal centre forward, he is technically sound, powerful in the air and packs a fearsome shot with either foot. He began with a goal in the Charity Shield match against Liverpool and finished a prolific season with a grand total of 36 in all competitions. Along the way he set a new Premiership record when he netted in eight successive matches, a feat that also equalled a club record set by Liam Whelan back in 1956-57. He forged productive partnerships with both Ryan Giggs and Ole Gunnar Solksjaer and despite his huge successes in 2001-02 there is a feeling at Old Trafford that the best is yet to come. Ruud was deservedly selected by his fellow professionals as the PFA 'Player of the Year' for the season, and also won a place in the PFA Premiership team.
Manchester U (£19,000,000 from PSV Eindhoven, Holland, ex Den Bosch, Heerenveen, on 5/7/2001) PL 29+3/23 FAC 0+2/2 Others 15/11

VARGA Stanislav (Stan)
Born: Czechoslovakia, 8 October 1972
Height: 6'2" **Weight:** 14.8
International Honours: Slovakia: 39

This strong centre back found himself down the pecking order at Sunderland last season. A giant of a man, Stan is not only good in the air but also possesses fine distribution skills, however with opportunities limited at the Stadium of Light, he opted to move on loan to West Bromwich Albion in the new year. He went on to play his part in the Baggies' successful promotion campaign, deputising for the suspended Laris Sigurdsson at a crucial stage in the campaign.
Sunderland (£650,000 + from SK Slovan Bratislave, Slovakia, ex Tetran Presov, on 14/8/2000) PL 18+3/1 FLC 3+1 FAC 5
West Bromwich A (Loaned on 25/3/2002) FL 3+1

VASSELL Darius
Born: Birmingham, 13 June 1980
Height: 5'7" **Weight:** 12.0
International Honours: E: 8; U21-10; Yth
Darius is a striker with terrific pace and an eye for goal who is a real handful for opposition defenders in the penalty area. He earned himself a regular place in the Aston Villa starting line-up last term, forming a successful strike partnership with Juan Pablo Angel. One of the revelations of the Premiership campaign, he scored regularly and his effort against

Blackburn was voted 'Goal of the Month' for September by viewers of 'The Premiership'. He went on to feature at full international level with some success, scoring spectacularly against Holland, and was voted the 'Sunday Mercury Midlands Football Young Player of the Year'.
Aston Villa (From trainee on 14/4/1998) PL 36+40/16 FLC 1+7 FAC 3+3/1 Others 2+10/4

VAUGHAN Anthony (Tony) John
Born: Manchester, 11 October 1975
Height: 6'1" **Weight:** 11.2
International Honours: E: Yth; Sch
Tony was very much a forgotten figure at Nottingham Forest last term and managed only a handful of first-team appearances. He joined Scunthorpe on loan in March and played in the final five matches of the season for the Third Division club. An experienced left-sided centre half, he started well but only once finished on the winning side at Glanford Park and returned to the City Ground at the end of the season.
Ipswich T (From trainee on 1/7/1994) P/FL 56+11/3 FLC 4+2 FAC 2 Others 4
Manchester C (£1,350,000 on 9/7/1997) FL 54+4/2 FLC 6+1 FAC 3 Others 3+1
Cardiff C (Loaned on 15/9/1999) FL 14 Others 1

Darius Vassell (centre)

Nottingham F (£350,000 on 8/2/2000) FL 38+5/1 FLC 2 FAC 1
Scunthorpe U (Loaned on 26/3/2002) FL 5

VAUGHAN David Owen
Born: Rhuddlan, 18 February 1983
Height: 5'7" **Weight:** 10.10
International Honours: W: Yth
This left-sided player is another youngster who came up through the ranks at Crewe. After making his debut in the 2000-01 campaign, he continued to make progress last term and began to make his mark at first-team level. He scored his first goal for the Railwaymen in the FA Cup tie against Rotherham.
Crewe Alex (From trainee on 6/2/2001) FL 12+2 FAC 3/1

VEGA Ramon
Born: Zurich, Switzerland, 14 June 1971
Height: 6'3" **Weight:** 13.0
Club Honours: FLC '99
International Honours: Switzerland: 24; B-1
Ramon became Gianluca Viallli's first signing for Watford, joining on a free transfer from Celtic. The Swiss international centre half proved an enthusiastic competitor, especially in opposing penalty areas, and weighed in with three useful goals. However he occasionally lacked concentration in defence, and was dropped after conceding an own goal at Wolves. He was recalled, only to be sent off at Millwall in January, and then transfer-listed the following month. He made no further appearances.
Tottenham H (£3,750,000 from Cagliari, Italy, ex Trimbach, Grasshoppers, on 11/1/1997) PL 53+11/7 FLC 9+2/1 FAC 8+1
Glasgow Celtic (Loaned on 15/12/2000) SL 18/2 SLC 2 SC 6/2
Watford (Free on 12/7/2001) FL 23+4/1 FLC 5/2 FAC 1

VENUS Mark
Born: Hartlepool, 6 April 1967
Height: 6'0" **Weight:** 13.11
Club Honours: Div 3 '89
Mark scooped the majority of the 'Player of the Year' awards for Ipswich last season despite the fact that Town had the worst defensive record in the Premiership! However, it is probably his contribution to the attack through his free kicks and corners that earned him the honours. He has a high number of assists to his credit a fact highlighted in the game at Southampton when he notched Ipswich's first goal with a screaming 25-yard thunderbolt and proceeded to lay on two further goals for Marcus Stewart.

Hartlepool U (From juniors on 22/3/1985) FL 4 Others 0+1
Leicester C (Free on 6/9/1985) FL 58+3/1 FLC 3 FAC 2 Others 2+1
Wolverhampton W (£40,000 on 23/3/1988) FL 271+16/7 FLC 17+1/1 FAC 15+1 Others 17/2
Ipswich T (£150,000 on 29/7/1997) P/FL 136+4/16 FLC 16/3 FAC 4 Others 12

VERNAZZA Paolo Andrea Pietro
Born: Islington, 1 November 1979
Height: 6'0" **Weight:** 11.10
International Honours: E: U21-2; Yth
Paolo endured a frustrating season through injury, though he had the consolation of being included in the England U21 squad in the early part of the campaign. He was sent off at Wolves in September, and then sustained a serious thigh injury in a domestic incident, but made a speedy recovery and returned to the Watford midfield in November. A fine passer of the ball, he was just re-establishing himself when he suffered a cartilage injury that required an operation in February and brought his season to an early end.
Arsenal (From trainee on 18/11/1997) PL 2+3/1 FLC 4 Others 1+2
Ipswich T (Loaned on 2/10/1998) FL 2
Portsmouth (Loaned on 14/1/2000) FL 7
Watford (£350,000 + on 15/12/2000) FL 41+3/2 FLC 3/1 FAC 2

VERON Juan Sebastian
Born: Buenos Aires, Argentina, 9 March 1975
Height: 6'1" **Weight:** 12.7
International Honours: Argentina: 50
Juan Sebastian became Britain's most expensive signing when he arrived at Old Trafford in the summer of 2001. A supremely talented midfield playmaker with a sublime range of passing skills, he also has the knack of scoring spectacular goals. Despite one or two minor injury problems he featured regularly throughout the campaign, netting five goals, all in Premiership action. He also made Argentina's squad for the World Cup finals, where they were a major disappointment, being eliminated in the first round group stage. He is the son of Juan Ramon Veron who starred for Estudiantes and Argentina in the late 1960s.
Manchester U (£28,100,000 from Lazio, Italy, ex Estudiantes, Boca Juniors, Sampdoria, Parma, on 13/7/2001) PL 24+2/5 FAC 1 Others 13

VIANDER Jani
Born: Tuusula, Finland, 18 August 1975
Height: 6'3" **Weight:** 13.10
International Honours: Finland: 11

A tall and commanding goalkeeper with an impressive reputation, Jani signed for Bolton on a three-month loan deal in the second half of the season. Whilst his build and nationality brought obvious comparisons with Jussi Jaaskelainen, Jani found it difficult to emulate his fellow countryman and made just one FA Cup start before returning to HJK. He later signed for Stoke but failed to make an appearance.
Bolton W (Loaned from HJK Helsinki, Finland, TuPs, K-Up, FinnPa, Ilves, Jaro, Jazz, Kortrijk, on 16/11/2001) FAC 1
Stoke C (£300,000 from HJK Helsinki, Finland on 14/2/2002)

VICKERS Stephen (Steve)
Born: Bishop Auckland, 13 October 1967
Height: 6'1" **Weight:** 12.12
Club Honours: AMC '90; Div 1 '95
Steve managed just two starts for Middlesbrough last term and in September he joined Crystal palace on loan. However despite featuring regularly for the Eagles, no permanent deal could be agreed. He subsequently linked up with Steve Bruce once more at Birmingham City, arriving initially on loan and then signing a permanent deal. He had a big influence on the Blues' defence and showed he could read the game well. Unfortunately he suffered a badly gashed knee that put him out of action for several weeks.
Tranmere Rov (Signed from Spennymoor U on 11/9/1985) FL 310+1/11 FLC 20+1/5 FAC 19/3 Others 36/1
Middlesbrough (£700,000 on 3/12/1993) P/FL 248+11/8 FLC 27+2/3 FAC 17+1 Others 2
Crystal Palace (Loaned on 21/9/2001) FL 6 FLC 1
Birmingham C (£400,000 on 16/11/2001) FL 13+1/1 FAC 1 Others 2

VICTORY Jamie Charles
Born: Hackney, 14 November 1975
Height: 5'10" **Weight:** 12.0
Club Honours: FAT '98; NC '99
International Honours: E: SP-1
After missing almost all of the previous campaign with a serious cruciate ligament injury, Jamie returned to play a part in every one of Cheltenham Town's first-team games in 2001-2002. He took some time to readjust to Third Division football and was dropped for the first time in his six-year career with the Robins only to appear from the bench after 30 minutes. Predominantly left-footed, he featured at left back last term. He is an athletic player who moves forward to support the attack whenever possible while his unhurried

Juan Veron

style of defending contributed to an excellent disciplinary record.
West Ham U *(From trainee on 1/7/1994)*
Bournemouth *(Free on 1/7/1995) FL 5+11/1 FLC 1+1 Others 1+1*
Cheltenham T *(Free on 1/7/1996) FL 94+1/12 FLC 4/1 FAC 7 Others 7/1*

VIDUKA Mark Anthony
Born: Australia, 9 October 1975
Height: 6'2" **Weight:** 13.9
Club Honours: SLC '00
International Honours: Australia: 19; U23; Yth
The complete centre forward, Mark is strong in the air, very skilful on the ground and expert at holding the ball up and bringing others into play. He seemed to score his goals in patches last term, but nevertheless finished with a total of 16 in all competitions in what was a rather disappointing season for the Elland Road club. He has a full repertoire of skills for a big man, highlighted none more so than with his winning goal at Aston Villa in April when he dummied a defender and beat the on-coming goalkeeper with the outside of his foot.
Glasgow Celtic *(Signed from NK Croatia Zagreb, Croatia, ex Melbourne Knights, on 2/12/1998) SL 36+1/30 SLC 4/1 SC 3/3 Others 4/1*
Leeds U *(£6,000,000 on 25/7/2000) PL 67/28 FLC 2/1 FAC 3/2 Others 23/7*

VIEIRA Patrick
Born: Dakar, Senegal, 23 June 1976
Height: 6'4" **Weight:** 13.0
Club Honours: PL '98, '02; FAC '98, 02; CS '98, '99
International Honours: France: 56 (WC '98, UEFA '00)
Patrick had another very effective season for Arsenal last term when he helped the Gunners towards the domestic double of the Premiership and FA Cup. A skilful and determined central midfield player who always seems to have boundless energy. Patrick was once more honoured by his fellow professionals by being voted into the PFA Premiership team for the season.
Arsenal *(£3,500,000 from AC Milan, Italy, ex Cannes, on 14/8/1996) PL 187+7/16 FLC 5 FAC 30+2/2 Others 45/1*

VIGNAL Gregory
Born: Montpellier, France, 19 July 1981
Height: 6'0" **Weight:** 12.4
Club Honours: FAC '01; UEFAC '01; ESC '01
International Honours: France: Yth (UEFA-U18 '00)
This youthful left back enjoyed a run of

eight consecutive games for Liverpool early in the 2001-02 season due to the absence of Markus Babbel. He acquitted himself well but suffered a foot injury in the Worthington Cup tie with Grimsby, which sidelined him for two months and when fit again found that Jon Arne Riise had taken over the left-back slot. The arrival of Abel Xavier in February further reduced his chances and he played no further part in the Reds' campaign.
Liverpool *(£500,000 from Montpellier, France on 29/9/2000) PL 7+3 FLC 1 FAC 0+1 Others 4*

VINCENT Jamie Roy
Born: Wimbledon, 18 June 1975
Height: 5'10" **Weight:** 11.8
Jamie established himself as a regular in the Portsmouth defence last season. A solid left back who defends strongly and is always willing to support the attack with an accurate cross, he performed consistently throughout the campaign and scored a goal in the 4-1 win at Barnsley.
Crystal Palace *(From trainee on 13/7/1993) FL 19+6 FLC 2+1/1 FAC 1*
Bournemouth *(Loaned on 18/11/1994) FL 8*
Bournemouth *(£25,000 + on 30/8/1996) FL 102+3/5 FLC 7+1 FAC 8 Others 9/1*
Huddersfield T *(£440,000 + on 25/3/1999) FL 54+5/2 FLC 3+2 FAC 2*
Portsmouth *(£800,000 on 23/2/2001) FL 43+5/1 FLC 1*

VINE Rowan Lewis
Born: Basingstoke, 21 September 1982
Height: 6'1" **Weight:** 12.2
A product of Portsmouth's youth system, Rowan produced several outstanding displays in the Bradford City reserve team in 2001-02, and made 11 first-team appearances, including three in the starting line-up. Tall, strongly built and eager, he was left to head the first-team strike force in difficult circumstances after Peter Crouch was sold in March, despite being a defender!
Portsmouth *(From trainee on 27/4/2001) FL 3+10*

VINNICOMBE Christopher (Chris)
Born: Exeter, 20 October 1970
Height: 5'9" **Weight:** 10.12
Club Honours: SPD '91
International Honours: E: U21-12
2001-02 proved to be another marvellous season for the Wycombe left back, crowned by winning the Official Supporters Club 'Player of the Season' award and confirming that he really is the best left back the club have had for many

years. With great levels of stamina he likes to push forward and deliver far post crosses but it is his defending which seems to get better by the year. Sticking to his man like a limpet he is adept at man-marking and, although small in stature, his bravery in the tackle is legendary. His only goal was the best seen at Adams Park last season, rifling home from 30 yards against Brentford.
Exeter C *(From trainee on 1/7/1989) FL 35/4/1 FLC 5/1 Others 2*
Glasgow R *(£150,000 on 3/11/1989) SL 14+9/1 SLC 1+2 Others 1*
Burnley *(£200,000 on 30/6/1994) FL 90+5/3 FLC 9 FAC 2 Others 7+1/1*
Wycombe W *(Free on 6/8/1998) FL 156+4/2 FLC 10 FAC 16 Others 4*

VIRGO Adam John
Born: Brighton, 25 January 1983
Height: 6'2" **Weight:** 13.7
Adam found first-team chances difficult to come by at Brighton last term due to the impressive form of the central defensive pairing of Danny Cullip and Simon Morgan and he managed to start just a handful of games. A product of the club's Centre of Excellence, he has developed into a fine centre half who has strong heading ability and a keen positional sense.
Brighton & Hove A *(From juniors on 4/7/2000) FL 6+6 Others 1+2*

VIVEASH Adrian Lee
Born: Swindon, 30 September 1969
Height: 6'2" **Weight:** 12.13
It was not until last October that Adrian managed to win a regular place in the Reading first team at centre-back, but a 13-match run ended when a groin injury saw him replaced by John Mackie in the FA Cup tie at York City. He returned to the starting line-up for the run-in to promotion and once again proved to be the door, experienced defender that the side needed for the vital last few games. He captained the team for several matches, but the real highlight of his season came when he netted the deciding penalty in the shoot-out against West Ham United in a Worthington Cup tie.
Swindon T *(From trainee on 14/7/1988) FL 51+3/2 FLC 6+1 FAC 0+1 Others 2*
Reading *(Loaned on 4/11/1993) FL 5 Others 1/1*
Reading *(Loaned on 20/1/1995) FL 6*
Barnsley *(Loaned on 10/8/1995) FL 2/1*
Walsall *(Free on 16/10/1995) FL 200+2/13 FLC 12 FAC 15/2 Others 13/1*
Reading *(Free on 6/7/2000) FL 58/3 FLC 3+1 FAC 5 Others 7*

Patrick Vieira

W

WAINWRIGHT Neil
Born: Warrington, 4 November 1977
Height: 6'0" **Weight:** 11.5
After a successful loan spell at Darlington at the end of the 1999-2000 season Neil finally signed permanently for the Quakers in August 2001 and went straight into the side operating mainly on the right flank. His mazy running down the wing was a threat to defenders all season and when he cut inside he managed to notch up six goals. When a couple of niggling injuries restricted his appearances the team's fortunes suffered in his absence.
Wrexham (From trainee on 3/7/1996) FL 7+4/3 FAC 1 Others 1
Sunderland (£100,000 + on 9/7/1998) FL 0+2 FLC 5+1
Darlington (Loaned on 4/2/2000) FL 16+1/4
Halifax T (Loaned on 13/10/2000) FL 13 FAC 1 Others 2
Darlington (£50,000 on 17/8/2001) FL 32+3/4 FAC 3+1/2 Others 2

WALKER Andrew (Andy)
William
Born: Bexleyheath, 30 September 1981
Height: 6'0" **Weight:** 11.10
Andy joined Exeter City shortly before the start of the 2001-02 campaign but was only ever second choice to Arjan van Heusden and made only one senior appearance, in the 4-2 defeat at Swansea in September. He was released soon after John Cornforth took over as the Grecians' boss and after a spell with Dr Martens League outfit Tonbridge he signed for Doncaster Rovers in January.
Colchester U (Trainee) FL 3 FLC 1+1 (Free to St Albans C in March 2001)
Exeter C (Free on 8/8/2001) FL 1

WALKER Ian Michael
Born: Watford, 31 October 1971
Height: 6'2" **Weight:** 13.1
Club Honours: FAYC '90; FLC '99
International Honours: E: 3; B-1; U21-9; Yth
This experienced goalkeeper joined Leicester City during the 2001 close season and was kept busy throughout the campaign, but played well enough to earn inclusion in a number of Sven Goran Eriksson's England squads. Unusually, in the defeat at West Ham in January, he had the distinction of firing City's only on target shot during the entire game, when he ventured up field for a late corner.
Tottenham H (From trainee on 4/12/1989) F/PL 257+2 FLC 22+1 FAC 25 Others 6
Oxford U (Loaned on 31/8/1990) FL 2 FLC 1
Leicester C (£2,500,000 on 26/7/2001) PL 35 FLC 2 FAC 2

WALKER James Barry
Born: Sutton in Ashfield, 9 July 1973
Height: 5'11" **Weight:** 13.5
James had another highly successful season at Walsall last term, despite being briefly left out of the side in August and September. His brave penalty save was a major factor in Walsall's shock FA Cup win at Charlton and he also made a 'Save of the Season' in the last minute against Manchester City in February to hold on to a vital point. He was voted the supporters' 'Player of the Season' and the Saddlers may have difficulty holding on to him as offers come in during the summer.
Notts Co (From trainee on 9/7/1991)
Walsall (Free on 4/8/1993) FL 317+2 FLC 19+1 FAC 25 Others 19

WALKER Joshua (Josh) George
Born: Solihull, 20 December 1981
Height: 6'1" **Weight:** 11.6
There were high expectations for Josh following his arrival at Shrewsbury in the 2001 close season, but these were largely unfulfilled. He made his senior debut coming off the bench at Plymouth in the opening game but only featured in three more games, all from the subs' bench. The hard-tackling midfielder was released in the summer.
Manchester U (From trainee on 9/9/1999)
Shrewsbury T (Free on 6/7/2001) FL 0+3 FLC 0+1

WALKER Justin Matthew
Born: Nottingham, 6 September 1975
Height: 5'11" **Weight:** 12.12
International Honours: E: Yth; Sch
Justin missed out on much of Lincoln's pre-season training due to an ankle injury and then struggled to get fully fit when the League campaign started. He came more into the picture after Christmas and as well as winning his place in centre midfield he had a spell in which he netted three goals in four games. These included a stunning stoppage-time free kick at Bristol Rovers which earned the Imps a rare away victory. At the end of the season he was released along with other out-of-contract players when Lincoln went into administration.
Nottingham F (From juniors on 10/9/1992)
Scunthorpe U (Signed on 26/3/1997) FL 126+6/2 FLC 8 FAC 6 Others 7/1
Lincoln C (Free on 12/7/2000) FL 68+8/4 FLC 1+2 FAC 3+1 Others 6/1

WALKER Richard Martin
Born: Birmingham, 8 November 1977
Height: 6'0" **Weight:** 12.0
Club Honours: AMC '02
Richard joined Wycombe Wanderers for a three-month loan period last September and looked a classy player during his stay at Adams Park, scoring an impressive double in the home game with Port Vale. He subsequently joined Blackpool in a permanent deal where he established a promising partnership up front with John Murphy. A quick striker who holds the ball up well, the highlights of his season came in the LDV Vans Trophy where he netted a hat-trick at Oldham and eventually gained a winners' medal after coming off the bench in the final against Cambridge.
Aston Villa (From trainee on 13/12/1995) PL 2+4/2 FLC 1+1 FAC 0+1 Others 1
Cambridge U (Loaned on 31/12/1998) FL 7+14/3 Others 1+2/1
Blackpool (Loaned on 9/2/2001) FL 6+12/3
Wycombe W (Loaned on 13/9/2001) FL 10+2/3 FAC 1/1
Blackpool (£50,000 + on 21/12/2001) FL 16+5/8 Others 1+1/3

WALKER Richard Neil
Born: Derby, 9 November 1971
Height: 6'0" **Weight:** 12.0
Club Honours: NC '99
Richard was one of the early successes at Cheltenham in the early part of last term before losing his place and only returning for the play-offs when he partnered Michael Duff in the centre of defence. He is a useful all-round defender who is effective both in the air and as a man-marker. He was rewarded with the offer of an extended contract towards the end of the season.
Notts Co (From trainee on 3/7/1990) FL 63+4/4 FLC 10 FAC 1+2 Others 8+1 (Free to Hereford U on 24/7/1997)
Mansfield T (Loaned on 23/3/1995) FL 4
Cheltenham T (Signed on 23/10/1998) FL 52+3/1 FLC 3 Others 3

WALKER Richard Stuart
Born: Stafford, 17 September 1980
Height: 6'2" **Weight:** 13.0
Another youngster who has come up through the ranks at Crewe, Richard managed just a single appearance from the subs' bench last season. He is a confident central defender who will be aiming to make a breakthrough in the 2002-03 campaign.
Crewe Alex (From trainee on 6/7/1999) FL 2+2

Dave Walsh

WALLACE Adam John
Born: Ashford, 5 October 1981
Height: 5'11" **Weight:** 12.2
This slightly built striker was unable to breakthrough to the first team at Southampton and was released early in the new year. He subsequently had a brief spell with Dr Martens League club Salisbury City before joining Southend United on a short-term contract in March. However, although he performed admirably in the reserves he managed only two substitute appearances at senior level before being released at the end of the season.
Southampton (From trainee on 2/8/2001)
Southend U (Free on 28/3/2002) FL 0+2

WALLACE Rodney (Rod)
Seymour
Born: Greenwich, 2 October 1969
Height: 5'7" **Weight:** 11.6
Club Honours: Div 1'92; CS'92; SPD '99, '00; SC '99, '00; SLC '98
International Honours: E; B-2; U21-11
Released by Rangers the previous summer Rod struggled to find another club who required his services before Sam Allardyce signed him for Bolton in September. In making his debut as a substitute at Blackburn he capped a remarkable performance by scoring with a header after spending just six minutes on the pitch. He made his full debut at home to Sunderland and continued to feature in the starting line-up with justified regularity for the rest of the season, scoring three goals.
Southampton (From trainee on 19/4/1988) FL 111+17/45 FLC 18+1/6 FAC 10/3 Others 3+1/2
Leeds U (£1,600,000 on 7/6/1991) F/PL 187+25/53 FLC 18+1/8 FAC 16+5/4 Others 1+4/1
Glasgow R (Free on 17/7/1998) SL 73+4/39 SLC 6/4 SC 10+1/4 Others 24+2/7
Bolton W (Free on 17/9/2001) PL 14+5/3 FLC 1+2/1 FAC 1

WALLING Dean Anthony
Born: Leeds, 17 April 1969
Height: 6'0" **Weight:** 12.2
Club Honours: Div 3 '95; AMC '97
International Honours: St Kitts & Nevis
This experienced central defender returned to League football with Cambridge last August and was a regular in the line-up until the end of November. However he fell out of favour following a change in management and made no further appearances before being released in the summer.
Rochdale (Free from apprentice at Leeds U

on 30/7/1987) FL 43+22/8 FLC 3 FAC 0+1 Others 1+1 (Free to Kitchener, Toronto, Canada during 1990 close season)*
Carlisle U (Free from Guiseley, ex Franklin, Toronto, Canada, on 1/7/1991) FL 230+6/22 FLC 18/3 FAC 14+1/1 Others 35/5
Lincoln C (£75,000 on 30/9/1997) FL 35+3/5 FAC 4/3 (£25,000 to Doncaster Rov on 29/5/1999)
Cambridge U (Free from Northwich Vic on 9/8/2001) FL 20 FLC 1 FAC 2 Others 1

WALLWORK Ronald (Ronnie)
Born: Manchester, 10 September 1977
Height: 5'10" **Weight:** 12.9
Club Honours: FAYC '95; PL '01
International Honours: E: Yth
This very talented young striker received few chances to shine for Manchester United last term and his only appearances in the starting line-up came in the Worthington Cup tie at Arsenal in November and the FA Cup defeat by Middlesbrough. A brilliant striker of the ball, especially with his left foot, he is at the stage of his career where he really needs to experience regular first-team football, and at the time of writing seemed likely to be leaving Old Trafford in the summer.
Manchester U (From trainee on 17/3/1995) PL 4+15 FLC 3+2 FAC 1+1 Others 1+1
Carlisle U (Loaned on 22/12/1997) FL 10/1 Others 2
Stockport Co (Loaned on 18/3/1998) FL 7

WALSH Daniel (Danny)
Gareth
Born: Pontefract, 23 September 1979
Height: 5'11" **Weight:** 12.6
After being released by Oldham, Danny had a short trial at Lincoln and a brief association with Guiseley before joining Emley last September. He subsequently moved on to Chesterfield in December but made just one appearance from the bench, against Brighton. A right-sided midfielder, he joined Ossett Town in March 2002.
Oldham Ath (From trainee on 7/1/1998) FL 0+2 (Free to Guiseley during 2001 close season)
Chesterfield (Free from Emley on 21/12/2001) FL 0+1

WALSH David (Dave)
Born: Wrexham, 29 April 1979
Height: 6'1" **Weight:** 12.8
International Honours: W: U21-8
Dave was unable to make the goalkeeper's jersey his own at Wrexham

last term, originally sharing duties with Kristian Rogers and then dropping further down the pecking order following the arrival of Marius Røvde. Although he showed sound positional sense and was a good shot stopper, he did not seem to inspire enough confidence among his defenders and was released in the summer.
Wrexham (From trainee on 4/7/1997) FL 12+2 Others 3

WALSH Gary
Born: Wigan, 21 March 1968
Height: 6'3" **Weight:** 15.10
Club Honours: ECWC '91; ESC '91; FAC '94
International Honours: E: U21-2
Gary started last season as first choice goalkeeper for Bradford City, but suffered a torn thigh on Boxing Day. He then damaged his knee in a reserve match while on his way to recovery and this proved to be his last game of the campaign. He was outstanding in the opening matches and won four 'Man of the Match' awards. He is very strong in the air, and dominates not only the six-yard box, but the whole penalty area.
Manchester U (From juniors on 25/4/1985) F/PL 49+1 FLC 7 Others 6
Airdrie (Loaned on 11/8/1988) SL 3 SLC 1
Oldham Ath (Loaned on 19/11/1993) PL 6
Middlesbrough (£500,000 on 11/8/1995) PL 44 FLC 9 FAC 4
Bradford C (£500,000 + on 26/9/1997) P/FL 128+1 FLC 7 FAC 4 Others 1
Middlesbrough (Loaned on 15/9/2000) PL 3

WALSH Michael Shane
Born: Rotherham, 5 August 1977
Height: 6'0" **Weight:** 13.2
Club Honours: AMC '01
This Port Vale central defender had another very good season in 2001-02, despite missing almost half of it through injury. He began the campaign in the side before a knee injury meant that he started just one game between September and December. Michael began to get back into his stride as the new year commenced and had his best spell during Vale's run of seven wins in eight games which banished any thoughts of a relegation struggle.
Scunthorpe U (From trainee on 3/7/1995) FL 94+9/1 FLC 4 FAC 9 Others 5
Port Vale (£100,000 on 30/7/1998) FL 93+5/3 FLC 4+1 FAC 2 Others 7

WALTERS Mark Everton
Born: Birmingham, 2 June 1964
Height: 5'10" **Weight:** 12.8

Club Honours: FAYC '80; ESC '82; SPD '89, '90, '91; SLC '89, '91; FAC '92; FLC '95
International Honours: E: 1; B-1; U21-9; Yth; Sch
This experienced and popular winger returned to the Bristol Rovers starting line-up last October but the majority of his appearances were from the subs' bench. He could always be relied upon to add attacking flair to any game and his ability to cross accurately with both feet was evident. He scored an important equaliser at Plymouth Argyle in the second round of the FA Cup, his only goal of the season. Mark has now completed 20 seasons as a professional but seems likely to be seeking new pastures for the start of the 2002-03 campaign.
Aston Villa (From apprentice on 18/5/1982) FL 168+13/39 FLC 20+1/6 FAC 11+1/1 Others 7+3/2
Glasgow R (£500,000 on 31/12/1987) SL 101+5/32 SLC 13/11 SC 14/6 Others 10/2
Liverpool (£1,250,000 on 13/8/1991) F/PL 58+36/14 FLC 10+2/4 FAC 6+3 Others 8+1/1
Stoke C (Loaned on 24/3/1994) FL 9/2
Wolverhampton W (Loaned on 9/9/1994) FL 11/3
Southampton (Free on 18/1/1996) PL 4+1 FAC 4
Swindon T (Free on 31/7/1996) FL 91+21/25 FLC 9+1/2 FAC 3+1/2
Bristol Rov (Free on 17/11/1999) FL 46+36/13 FLC 0+5 FAC 0+5/1 Others 0+4

WALTON David (Dave) Lee
Born: Bedlington, 10 April 1973
Height: 6'2" **Weight:** 14.8
Club Honours: Div 3 '94
This defender has been rather unlucky with injuries at Crewe over the last two seasons. Nevertheless he managed to appear in over half the games in 2001-02, scoring two goals. He is a commanding centre half who is particularly effective in the air.
Sheffield U (Free from Ashington on 13/3/1992)
Shrewsbury T (Signed on 5/11/1993) FL 127+1/10 FLC 7 FAC 10/1 Others 11/1
Crewe Alex (£500,000 + on 20/10/1997) FL 119+8/2 FLC 8/1 FAC 3

WALTON Mark Andrew
Born: Merthyr Tydfil, 1 June 1969
Height: 6'4" **Weight:** 15.8
International Honours: W: U21-1
Mark missed the start of the 2001-02 season through injury and then found new signing Neil Alexander has established himself as Cardiff City's number one goalkeeper. His only senior

appearance during the campaign came in the LDV Vans Trophy defeat by Peterborough, but nonetheless he signed a new 12-month contract for the Bluebirds.
Luton T (From juniors on 21/2/1987)
Colchester U (£15,000 on 5/11/1987) FL 40 FLC 3 FAC 8 Others 5
Norwich C (£75,000 on 15/8/1989) FL 22 FLC 1 FAC 5
Wrexham (Loaned on 27/8/1993) FL 6
Dundee (Free on 27/1/1994)
Bolton W (Free on 2/3/1994) FL 3 (Free to Wroxham on 9/9/1994)
Fulham (Free from Fakenham T on 12/8/1996) FL 40 FLC 5 Others 3
Gillingham (Loaned on 6/2/1998) FL 1
Brighton & Hove A (£20,000 on 15/7/1998) FL 58 FLC 2 FAC 4 Others 2
Cardiff C (Free on 11/8/2000) FL 40 FLC 2 FAC 4 Others 2

WANCHOPE Pablo (Paulo) Cesar
Born: Costa Rica, 31 July 1976
Height: 6'4" **Weight:** 12.6
Club Honours: Div 1 '02
International Honours: Costa Rica: 52
Paulo had a very mixed season for Manchester City last term. On the one hand he scored 13 goals in 18 appearances in all competitions and on the other he was plagued by a knee injury for most of the campaign. When teaming up with Shaun Goater the pair were prolific. He scored some fine goals, but the knee problem kept on returning and he was eventually forced on to the sidelines in February as he strove to get fully fit for the World Cup finals.
Derby Co (£600,000 from CS Heridiano, Costa Rica on 27/3/1997) PL 65+7/23 FLC 6+1/5 FAC 4
West Ham U (£3,250,000 on 28/7/1999) PL 33+2/12 FLC 3 FAC 0+1 Others 7+1/3
Manchester C (£3,650,000 on 16/8/2000) P/FL 39+3/21 FLC 4/1 FAC 3/1

WANLESS Paul Steven
Born: Banbury, 14 December 1973
Height: 6'1" **Weight:** 13.12
This hard-working midfielder had another season affected by injury at Cambridge United in 2001-02. His experience helped bring on the younger players in the squad and he had the distinction of scoring United's goal from the penalty spot in the LDV Vans Trophy final against Blackpool. This was to be his last game of the season as he then had to undergo surgery to correct an ankle problem.
Oxford U (From trainee on 3/12/1991) FL 12+20 FLC 0+3/1 Others 2+2
Lincoln C (Free on 7/7/1995) FL 7+1 Others 2

Cambridge U (Free on 8/3/1996) FL 237+8/39 FLC 12 FAC 13+2/1 Others 11/2

WARBURTON Raymond (Ray)
Born: Rotherham, 7 October 1967
Height: 6'0" **Weight:** 13.6
Club Honours: NC '01
If any member of the Rushden squad deserved another crack at League football it was Ray. A truly inspirational figure in the Conference-winning season, there was a sense of huge injustice when it became clear that his last appearance in a Diamonds shirt would be at Carlisle United on a wet Tuesday night in January. As club captain, Ray led by example, yet a series of injuries robbed him of a return to the level he had previously enjoyed. He worked his way back to a level of fitness to earn a move to Boston United and it was fitting that he scored the winning goal at Hayes to secure the Pilgrims' elevation to the Football League.
Rotherham U (From apprentice on 5/10/1985) FL 3+1 FAC 2 Others 2
York C (Free on 8/8/1989) FL 86+4/9 FLC 8/1 FAC 6/1 Others 7
Northampton T (£35,000 on 4/2/1994) FL 186/12 FLC 10 FAC 7/1 Others 17/3
Rushden & Diamonds (£60,000 on 23/10/1998) FL 1

WARD Ashley Stuart
Born: Manchester, 24 November 1970
Height: 6'2" **Weight:** 13.10
Ashley started the first four games of the 2001-02 campaign for Bradford City before being sidelined with an ankle injury and although he returned to the team a recurrence of the same problem saw him out of action once more. He eventually recovered and finished the season with a creditable tally of 11 goals. He is an experienced and hard-working striker.
Manchester C (From trainee on 5/8/1989) FL 0+1 FAC 0+2
Wrexham (Loaned on 10/1/1991) FL 4/2 Others 1
Leicester C (£80,000 on 30/7/1991) FL 2+8 FLC 2+1 FAC 0+1 Others 0+1
Blackpool (Loaned on 21/11/1992) FL 2/1
Crewe Alex (£80,000 on 1/12/1992) FL 58+3/25 FLC 4/2 FAC 2/4 Others 7/5
Norwich C (£500,000 on 8/12/1994) P/FL 53/18 FLC 6/3 FAC 1
Derby Co (£1,000,000 on 19/3/1996) F/PL 32+8/9 FLC 1+1 FAC 2/1
Barnsley (£1,300,000 + on 5/9/1997) P/FL 45+1/20 FLC 9/4 FAC 6/1
Blackburn Rov (£4,250,000 + on 31/12/1998) P/FL 52+2/13 FLC 2 FAC 4+1

Bradford C (£1,500,000 on 18/8/2000) P/FL 51+9/14 FLC 3+1/3 FAC 1

WARD Darren
Born: Worksop, 11 May 1974
Height: 6'2" **Weight:** 14.2
Club Honours: Div 3 '98
International Honours: W: 2; B-1; U21-2

Darren made the short trip across the River Trent soon after the end of the 2000-01 season, signing for Nottingham Forest on a 'Bosman- free'. Widely regarded as one of the best goalkeepers in the Nationwide League, he played in all 46 League games, and joined the small band of players who have appeared for all three of Nottinghamshire's League clubs. He had a solid first season at the City Ground and will be looking to win a regular place in the full Wales national squad in 2002-03.
Mansfield T (From trainee on 27/7/1992) FL 81 FLC 5 FAC 5 Others 6
Notts Co (£160,000 on 11/7/1995) FL 251 FLC 18 FAC 23 Others 10
Nottingham F (Free on 21/5/2001) FL 46 FLC 3 FAC 1

WARD Darren Philip
Born: Harrow, 13 September 1978
Height: 6'0" **Weight:** 12.6

Out of favour at Watford following the arrival of Ramon Vega and Filippo Galli, Darren signed for Millwall last October and went straight into the side against West Bromwich Albion playing in a three-man defence, a system rarely used by the Lions. He was outstanding operating on the right-hand side and helped his new team to a 2-0 victory. However, he spent most of the season on the subs bench due to the excellent partnership of Sean Dyche and Stuart Nethercott, only returning to the side late in the campaign when Dyche was injured.
Watford (From trainee on 13/2/1997) P/FL 56+3/2 FLC 6/1 FAC 2 Others 0+1
Queens Park R (Loaned on 17/12/1999) FL 14 FAC 1
Millwall (£500,000 on 3/10/2001) FL 10+4 FAC 1 Others 2

WARD Gavin John
Born: Sutton Coldfield, 30 June 1970
Height: 6'3" **Weight:** 14.12
Club Honours: Div 3 '93; WC '93; AMC '00

This popular 'keeper spent most of the 2001-02 season in the treatment room after being sidelined by a back injury in November. A fine goalkeeper with a commanding presence and excellent shot-stopping abilities, he was sorely missed during his long absence. By April Stoke had decided not to renew his contract and he was freed with the hope that he could quickly tie up a deal with another club.
Shrewsbury T (From trainee at Aston Villa on 26/9/1988)
West Bromwich A (Free on 18/9/1989)
Cardiff C (Free on 5/10/1989) FL 58+1 FAC 1 Others 7
Leicester C (£175,000 on 16/7/1993) F/PL 38 FLC 3 FAC 0+1 Others 4
Bradford C (£175,000 on 13/7/1995) FL 36 FLC 6 FAC 3 Others 2
Bolton W (£300,000 on 29/3/1996) F/PL 19+3 FLC 2 FAC 4
Burnley (Loaned on 14/8/1998) FL 17
Stoke C (Free on 25/2/1999) FL 79 FLC 7 FAC 2 Others 12

WARD Iain
Born: Cleethorpes, 13 May 1983
Height: 6'0" **Weight:** 10.10

Iain is a product of Grimsby College Academy scheme and a second year junior professional at Blundell Park. The promising defender had an impressive season for the Mariners reserves in 2001-02 resulting in a call-up for his senior debut as a replacement for the suspended Tony Gallimore in the final match of the campaign at Millwall. Despite the 3-0 reverse the youngster did nothing to undermine the management's confidence in him as part of Grimsby Town's future.
Grimsby T (From juniors on 22/11/2000) FL 1

WARD Mark Steven
Born: Sheffield, 27 January 1982
Height: 6'0" **Weight:** 11.2
International Honours: E: Sch

The former England Schools striker had to be content with reserve-team football for Sheffield United last term apart from a single appearance from the subs' bench in the home game with Crewe in October. Despite being on the fringe of the senior side throughout the campaign his contract was not renewed in the summer.
Sheffield U (Signed from Sheffield Colleges on 7/7/2000) FL 0+2

WARD Mitchum (Mitch) David
Born: Sheffield, 19 June 1971
Height: 5'8" **Weight:** 11.7

Mitch endured an eventful start to the 2001-02 season for Barnsley. He received a red card in the opening game and then injured his knee. On his return he replaced Steve Chettle as skipper but he was hampered by ankle problems after the injury flared up at the end of October he required surgery that kept him out for almost three months. On his comeback he found his opportunities limited under a new manager and when he played it was usually in an unfamiliar position wide on the left. He was transfer-listed by the Reds in March.
Sheffield U (From trainee on 1/7/1989) F/PL 135+19/11 FLC 8+3/2 FAC 7+2/2 Others 5+1/1
Crewe Alex (Loaned on 1/11/1990) FL 4/1 FAC 1/1 Others 2
Everton (£850,000 on 25/11/1997) PL 18+6 FLC 2+1 FAC 2
Barnsley (£20,000 on 14/7/2000) FL 46+5 FLC 4+1 FAC 2

WARDLEY Stuart James
Born: Cambridge, 10 September 1975
Height: 5'11" **Weight:** 12.7

Stuart is mainly a right-sided midfield player, but is extremely versatile and even took over in goal for Queen's Park Rangers when Chris Day was injured. He made a limited number of appearances for the club before joining Rushden on loan in January. That deal was subsequently extended by two more months before Stuart put pen to paper on a two-year deal. He scored on his home debut for Diamonds against Macclesfield and netted four more times during the season, including a crucial strike in the first leg of the play-off semi-final against Rochdale.
Queens Park R (£15,000 from Saffron Walden T on 22/7/1999) FL 72+15/4 FLC 2 FAC 3+2/3 Others 1
Rushden & Diamonds (Loaned on 25/1/2002) FL 18/4 Others 3/1

WARE Paul David
Born: Congleton, 7 November 1970
Height: 5'9" **Weight:** 11.8

Paul had a frustrating season at Rochdale last season when he was affected by a string of injuries throughout the campaign. He enjoyed a brief run of four matches early in the New Year but was then injured against York. He managed to get in a few reserve outings before the end of the season but didn't make the first-team squad again and was subsequently released.
Stoke C (From trainee on 15/11/1988) FL 92+23/10 FLC 7+1 FAC 4+1 Others 12+2/4
Stockport Co (Signed on 8/9/1994) FL 42+12/4 FLC 6+1/1 FAC 2 Others 3/1 (Free to Hednesford T on 15/7/1997)
Cardiff C (Loaned on 29/1/1997) FL 5
Macclesfield T (Free on 14/7/1999) FL 9+9/2 FLC 1

Gavin Ward

Rochdale (Free on 10/7/2000) FL 21+17/2 FLC 2+1 FAC 1 Others 1

WARHURST Paul
Born: Stockport,, 26 September 1969
Height: 6'1" **Weight:** 13.6
Club Honours: PL '95
International Honours: E: U21-8
One of the classiest and most consistent Bolton players in recent years, Paul had a season of mixed emotions last year. Playing primarily as a defensive midfielder, whilst occasionally slotting into the back four, he was his usual commanding self. Strong in the tackle and comfortable on the ball, he is a reassuring sight in the famous white shirt. However, a few minor injuries, including a recurrence of his calf problem, prevented him from playing as often as he should have done.
Manchester C (From trainee on 1/7/1988)
Oldham Ath (£10,000 on 27/10/1988) FL 60+7/2 FLC 8 FAC 5+4 Others 2
Sheffield Wed (£750,000 on 17/7/1991) F/PL 60+6/6 FLC 9/4 FAC 7+1/5 Others 5/3
Blackburn Rov (£2,700,000 on 17/8/1993) PL 30+27/4 FLC 6+2 FAC 2+1 Others 4+2
Crystal Palace (£1,250,000 on 31/7/1997) P/FL 27/4 FLC 2 FAC 1
Bolton W (£800,000 on 25/11/1998) P/FL 76+8 FLC 3+3 FAC 3+1 Others 2+2

WARNE Paul
Born: Norwich, 8 May 1973
Height: 5'9" **Weight:** 11.2
There can be no more willing worker than this striker who battled tirelessly for his Rotherham colleagues last season. After being an automatic choice for the previous two years, he found himself down the pecking order somewhat, although the early part of the campaign saw him miss out through injury. However he was an extremely valuable member of the squad and was very popular with the supporters. Never a prolific scorer, his only goal came in the FA Cup defeat at the hands of Crewe Alexandra.
Wigan Ath (£25,000 from Wroxham on 30/7/1997) FL 11+25/3 FLC 0+1 FAC 1 Others 1+2/1
Rotherham U (Free on 15/1/1999) FL 116+15/25 FLC 3+1 FAC 7/1 Others 5

WARNER Anthony (Tony)
Randolph
Born: Liverpool, 11 May 1974
Height: 6'4" **Weight:** 13.9
Club Honours: Div 2 '01
This tall, intimidating 'keeper was an ever present in goal for Millwall last season when he produced many fine performances. His all-round game showed

considerable improvement and he also developed a talent for saving penalties. He remains a great favourite of the Millwall faithful.
Liverpool (From juniors on 1/1/1994)
Swindon T (Loaned on 5/11/1997) FL 2
Glasgow Celtic (Loaned on 13/11/1998) SL 3
Aberdeen (Loaned on 31/3/1999) SL 6
Millwall (Free on 16/7/1999) FL 126 FLC 8 FAC 5 Others 5

WARNER Philip (Phil)
Born: Southampton, 2 February 1979
Height: 5'10" **Weight:** 11.10
This young right back joined Cambridge United during the 2001 close season, but had the misfortune to be sidelined with an ankle ligament problem early on in the campaign. On his recovery he never really established himself in the line-up and he will be looking for better fortunes in 2002-03.
Southampton (From trainee on 23/5/1997) PL 5+1 FLC 1
Brentford (Loaned on 9/7/1999) FL 1+13 FLC 0+1 FAC 1
Cambridge U (Free on 4/6/2001) FL 11+1 FAC 1+1 Others 2

WARREN Christer Simon
Born: Weymouth, 10 October 1974
Height: 5'10" **Weight:** 11.10
This left-sided midfield player was one of four players tried in the left-back position by Queen's Park Rangers last term. He came into the side when Paul Bruce was injured but was unable to hold on to his place and only featured on the bench in the second half of the season.
Southampton (£40,000 from Cheltenham T on 31/3/1995) PL 1+7 FLC 1
Brighton & Hove A (Loaned on 11/10/1996) FL 3
Fulham (Loaned on 6/3/1997) FL 8+3/1
Bournemouth (£50,000 on 8/10/1997) FL 94+9/13 FLC 4+3 FAC 10/1 Others 7
Queens Park R (Free on 15/6/2000) FL 24+12 FLC 1 FAC 1

WARREN David John Paul
Born: Cork, Ireland, 28 February 1981
Height: 5'10" **Weight:** 11.10
International Honours: RoI: Yth (UEFA-U16 '98)
David began the 2001-02 season as the regular right back for Wrexham, but after suffering knee ligament damage in September he had to undergo a cartilage operation. This put paid to any further first-team activity for the rest of the campaign, although he returned to action with the club's reserves in the Avon

Insurance League before the end of the season. He was released by the Robins in the summer.
Wrexham (Free from Mayfield U, Ireland on 4/8/1999) FL 6 FLC 1

WARREN Mark Wayne
Born: Clapton, 12 November 1974
Height: 6'0" **Weight:** 12.2
International Honours: E: Yth
This quick and tough central defender was once again a great favourite of the Notts County fans last term. Unfortunately a series of injuries dogged him throughout the campaign, severely restricting his appearances, and he was released by the club in the summer.
Leyton Orient (From trainee on 6/7/1992) FL 134+18/5 FLC 8+1/2 FAC 5+1 Others 10+4/1
Oxford U (Loaned on 24/12/1998) FL 4
Notts Co (Signed on 28/1/1999) FL 76+8/1 FLC 9 FAC 1 Others 4

WATERMAN David (Dave)
Graham
Born: Guernsey, 16 May 1977
Height: 5'10" **Weight:** 13.2
International Honours: NI: U21-14
Dave was only on the fringes of the first team at Portsmouth last term, but when required he came in and performed competently in the centre of the defence, showing excellent man-marking skills. He left to join Oxford United on the transfer deadline day and was used mainly in a defensive midfield role by the U's, although he also made one appearance at right back.
Portsmouth (From trainee on 4/7/1995) FL 60+20 FLC 4+1 FAC 3
Oxford U (Free on 28/3/2002) FL 4+1

WATKIN Stephen (Steve)
Born: Wrexham, 16 June 1971
Height: 5'10" **Weight:** 11.10
Club Honours: WC '95; Div 3 '00
International Honours: W: B-2; Sch
Steve suffered an ankle injury shortly after the start of the 2001-02 season and this kept him on the sidelines for a number of matches. However he quickly returned to action and he went on to finish the season as the Swans leading scorer with nine goals. Always a difficult opponent for defenders with his ability to hold the ball up as a striker, he also linked up well with Steve Brodie when he was used in an attacking midfield role.
Wrexham (From juniors on 24/7/1989) FL 167+33/55 FLC 11+3/4 FAC 16+6/12 Others 17+5/4
Swansea C (£108,000 on 26/9/1997) FL 152+28/42 FLC 8/1 FAC 6+3/2 Others 2+2/1

WATSON Alexander (Alex) Francis

Born: Liverpool, 5 April 1968
Height: 6'1" **Weight:** 13.0
Club Honours: CS '88
International Honours: E: Yth

Alex joined Exeter City from local rivals Torquay United during the 2001 close season and soon established a formidable partnership with Chris Curran in the heart of the Grecians' defence, helping to shore up a back line that had previously seemed to haemorrhage goals. A powerful and commanding central defender, he scored his first goal for City in the 1-1 draw with Rochdale last December.

Liverpool *(From apprentice on 18/5/1985)* FL 3+1 FLC 1+1 FAC 1+1 Others 1
Derby Co *(Loaned on 30/8/1990)* FL 5
Bournemouth *(£150,000 on 18/1/1991)* FL 145+6/5 FLC 14/1 FAC 12/1 Others 5
Gillingham *(Loaned on 11/9/1995)* FL 10/1
Torquay U *(£50,000 on 23/11/1995)* FL 201+1/8 FLC 11 FAC 10 Others 7/1
Exeter C *(Free on 30/7/2001)* FL 42+1/1 FLC 1 FAC 3 Others 1

WATSON Gordon William George

Born: Sidcup, 20 March 1971
Height: 5'11" **Weight:** 13.2
International Honours: E: U21-2

Gordon finally made a full recovery from his long-term injury troubles last season. An inspirational signing by Hartlepool manager Chris Turner, he provided an immediate answer to the team's goal-scoring problems, netting on his debut against Kidderminster, and then adding a hat-trick in a welcome 4-0 win over Hull. He was Pool's top scorer with 18 goals, having much success with a shoot-on-sight policy, and signed a new contract in May 2002.

Charlton Ath *(From trainee on 5/4/1989)* FL 20+11/7 FLC 2/1 FAC 0+1 Others 1+1
Sheffield Wed *(£250,000 on 20/2/1991)* F/PL 29+37/15 FLC 6+5/3 FAC 5+2/2 Others 2+2/1
Southampton *(£1,200,000 on 17/3/1995)* PL 37+15/8 FLC 6+3/5 FAC 5+1/1
Bradford C *(£550,000 on 17/1/1997)* FL 8+13/5 FLC 1+3
Bournemouth *(Free on 23/8/1999)* FL 2+4 FLC 0+1 FAC 1+2 Others 0+1 *(Freed during 2000 close season)*
Hartlepool U *(Free after recovering from injury and trialling with Portsmouth on 21/9/2001)* FL 31+1/18 FAC 1 Others 3

WATSON Kevin Edward

Born: Hackney, 3 January 1974
Height: 6'0" **Weight:** 12.6

Kevin found it difficult to find his best form in a struggling Rotherham team at the start of the 2001-02 campaign, and in November he joined Reading on loan. He impressed in his role as a 'holding' midfielder during his spell, but returned to Millmoor and regained his first-team place. Reading boss Alan Pardew then came back to sign him on a permanent basis and he proved to be a decisive addition to the squad. A tidy passer of the ball and dead-ball specialist, he scored his only goal for the Royals against Bristol City with a well-struck free kick from all of 30 yards.

Tottenham H *(From trainee on 15/5/1992)* PL 4+1 FLC 1+1/1 FAC 0+1 Others 4
Brentford *(Loaned on 24/3/1994)* FL 2+1
Bristol C *(Loaned on 2/12/1994)* FL 1+1
Barnet *(Loaned on 16/2/1995)* FL 13
Swindon T *(Free on 15/7/1996)* FL 39+24/1 FLC 2+2 FAC 1+2
Rotherham U *(Free on 31/7/1999)* FL 109/7 FLC 6/1 FAC 7 Others 3
Reading *(Loaned on 2/11/2001)* FL 6
Reading *(£150,000 + on 14/3/2002)* FL 6/1

WATSON Paul Douglas

Born: Hastings, 4 January 1975
Height: 5'8" **Weight:** 10.10
Club Honours: Div 3 '99, '01; Div 2 '02

Paul comfortably made the step up to Division Two football with Brighton in 2001-02 and was a near ever-present, his absence in the home game against Cardiff breaking a run of 107 consecutive league appearances. Although left footed he is more comfortable playing at right back, but he also played a few games at left back during the season. A free-kick expert, he scored a number of important goals including the winners against Port Vale and Queen's Park Rangers.

Gillingham *(From trainee on 8/12/1992)* FL 57+5/2 FLC 4 FAC 6 Others 5+3
Fulham *(£13,000 on 30/7/1996)* FL 48+2/4 FLC 3/1 FAC 2 Others 2
Brentford *(£50,000 on 12/12/1997)* FL 37 FLC 2 FAC 2 Others 0+1
Brighton & Hove A *(£20,000 on 9/7/1999)* FL 131+2/14 FLC 5/1 FAC 9/3 Others 5

WATSON Stephen (Steve) Craig

Born: North Shields, 1 April 1974
Height: 6'0" **Weight:** 12.7
International Honours: E: B-1; U21-12; Yth

One of Everton's most resolute and reliable defenders, Steve also showed his versatility during 2001-02. Most comfortable at right back, where he started the season, he was asked to

operate as an emergency centre forward during the height of an injury crisis. He did so diligently for a six-match spell, before gratefully reverting to his more familiar role. Sadly he only enjoyed four more games in that position before an ankle injury wiped three months from his season. He returned for the final half-dozen games - and showed his eye for goal with a match winner at Southampton.

Newcastle U *(From trainee on 6/4/1991)* F/PL 179+29/12 FLC 10+6/1 FAC 13+4 Others 18+4/1
Aston Villa *(£4,000,000 on 15/10/1998)* PL 39+2 FLC 8+1/1 FAC 4
Everton *(£2,500,000 on 12/7/2000)* PL 58+1/4 FLC 3 FAC 2/1

WATTS Steven (Steve)

Born: Lambeth, 11 July 1976
Height: 6'1" **Weight:** 13.7

Steve started the 2001-02 season as a first choice striker for Leyton Orient, replacing the departed Carl Griffiths, and was soon among the goals. He netted the winner in the FA Cup tie at Bristol City, but then appeared to lose his touch and failed to score at all in the New Year. Although he finished the season as the O's leading scorer he was placed on the transfer list in the summer.

Leyton Orient *(Signed from Fisher on 14/10/1998)* FL 67+59/29 FLC 5+2/2 FAC 8+2/4 Others 7/1

WEARE Ross Michael

Born: Ealing, 19 March 1977
Height: 6'2" **Weight:** 13.6

Ross followed his former boss Gerry Francis to Bristol Rovers in the 2001 close season. He got off to a promising start scoring in the second game of the season at Scunthorpe but this proved to be the only goal he managed due to a persistent and longstanding back injury that severely restricted his appearances. After a spell at Lilleshall to assess the problem he returned to action with an outing from the bench at Hartlepool but suffered a reaction in the following match and did not appear again. He announced his retirement in the summer.

Queens Park R *(£10,000 from East Ham U on 25/3/1999)* FL 0+4 FAC 0+1
Bristol Rov *(Free on 18/7/2001)* FL 9+1/1 FLC 2 FAC 1

WEAVER Luke Dennis Spencer

Born: Woolwich, 26 June 1979
Height: 6'2" **Weight:** 13.2
International Honours: E: Yth; Sch

Luke began the 2001-02 campaign as

Steve Watson

Carlisle manager Roddy Collins' first choice goalkeeper. His first three League games included two clean sheets but there were no more after that and he lost his place following the 3-2 reverse at Southend at the end of September. Although he was subsequently linked with other clubs he remained at Brunton Park until the end of the season.
Leyton Orient (From trainee on 26/6/1996) FL 9 FAC 1 Others 1
Sunderland (£250,000 on 9/1/1998)
Scarborough (Loaned on 10/12/1998) FL 6
Carlisle U (Free on 6/8/1999) FL 53 FLC 5 Others 1

WEAVER Nicholas (Nicky)
James
Born: Sheffield, 2 March 1979
Height: 6'3" **Weight:** 13.6
Club Honours: Div 1 '02
International Honours: E: U21-9
After picking up a thigh strain in pre-season, Nicky lost out to Carlo Nash for the opening of the new campaign, but injury robbed his rival of a place in the team. Carlo then had an unbroken run of 19 games in the Manchester City before yielding the jersey and the two followed in similar fashion throughout the campaign. His season came to a premature end for him after he picked up an injury that required corrective surgery against Birmingham City at St Andrew's. The arrival of Peter Schmeichel at Maine Road will surely mean that things are different in 2002-03.
Mansfield T (Trainee) FL 1
Manchester C (£200,000 on 2/5/1997) P/FL 145+1 FLC 14 FAC 11 Others 3

WEBB Daniel (Danny) John
Born: Poole, 2 July 1983
Height: 6'1" **Weight:** 11.8
Club Honours: Div 2 '02
This combative striker spent the first half of the 2001-02 season flitting in and out of the Southend United first team. Blessed with undoubted talent and excellent ball skills, Danny was often let down by his temperament, which caused him to pick up a number of unnecessary yellow cards. He joined Brighton on loan in December with a view to a permanent move, but had to wait until March before scoring his first goal, a fine header in the 2-2 draw against Notts County. However, he returned to Southend United following the departure of Peter Taylor. He is the son of former Chelsea star David Webb.
Southend U (From trainee at Southampton on 4/12/2000) FL 16+15/3 FLC 1 FAC 1+1 Others 3+2/1

Brighton & Hove A (Loaned on 12/12/2001) FL 7+5/1 FAC 1

WEBBER Daniel (Danny)
Vaughn
Born: Manchester, 28 December 1981
Height: 5'9" **Weight:** 10.8
International Honours: E: Yth
This quick-witted and highly mobile forward has the potential to become one of the best young strikers in the Premiership. He was given a rare opportunity to shine in Manchester United's trip to Arsenal in the Worthington Cup in November, when he showed some promising touches and soon afterwards he had a loan spell at Port Vale. Later in the season he also went on loan to Watford where he impressed with his hard-working attitude and notched his first senior goal against Stockport.
Manchester U (From trainee on 7/11/1999) FLC 1+1
Port Vale (Loaned on 23/11/2001) FL 2+2 Others 0+1
Watford (Loaned on 28/3/2002) FL 4+1/2

WEIR David (Davie) Gillespie
Born: Falkirk, 10 May 1970
Height: 6'2" **Weight:** 13.7
Club Honours: S Div 1 '94; B&Q '94
International Honours: S: 34
Everton's 'Player of the Season' – yet again – Davie continued to prove one of the bargain buys of the decade. He was even linked with a summer move to Manchester United such was the level of consistency he showed at the heart of the Toffees' defence throughout a difficult campaign. A reliable and composed centre half, he is also a threat in the opposition penalty area at set pieces.
Falkirk (From Celtic BC on 1/8/1992) SL 133/8 SLC 5 SC 6 Others 5
Heart of Midlothian (Signed on 29/7/1996) SL 92/8 SLC 10/2 SC 9/2 Others 6
Everton (£250,000 on 17/2/1999) PL 119+3/7 FLC 4 FAC 12

WELCH Keith James
Born: Bolton, 3 October 1968
Height: 6'2" **Weight:** 13.7
Keith was once again a great favourite of the Northampton fans last term, putting

Keith Welch

in some sterling performances between the posts. His cool, unflappable approach played a large part in the club's revival and one particular highlight was saving two spot kicks against Wrexham. He was a near ever-present for the Cobblers, only injury and suspension preventing him from reaching his 700th senior appearance during the campaign.
Rochdale (From Bolton W juniors on 3/3/1987) FL 205 FLC 12 FAC 10 Others 12
Bristol C (£200,000 on 25/7/1991) FL 271 FLC 20 FAC 13 Others 14
Northampton T (Free on 7/7/1999) FL 117 FLC 3 FAC 4 Others 3

WELCH Michael Francis
Born: Crewe, 11 January 1982
Height: 6'3" **Weight:** 11.12
International Honours: RoI: Yth
A former Republic of Ireland youth international, Michael joined Macclesfield Town in the 2001 close season, but had to wait until the away match at Hartlepool in March before making his senior debut. A tall strong central defender, he remained in the team to the end of the campaign gaining in confidence with each match.
Macclesfield T (Free from trainee at Barnsley on 9/8/2001) FL 6

WELLENS Richard Paul
Born: Manchester, 26 March 1980
Height: 5'9" **Weight:** 11.6
Club Honours: AMC '02
International Honours: E: Yth
This young Blackpool midfielder turned in some impressive performances during the 2001-02 season. He is a fierce tackler, although he has some neat touches, but could benefit from a few more goals. A highlight of his campaign was an appearance in the LDV Vans Trophy final against Cambridge.
Manchester U (From trainee on 19/5/1997) FLC 0+1
Blackpool (Signed on 23/3/2000) FL 70+10/9 FLC 4+1 FAC 3 Others 8+1/1

WELLER Paul Anthony
Born: Brighton, 6 March 1975
Height: 5'8" **Weight:** 11.2
It was another good season for Burnley's versatile worker, a player who can never be found guilty of lack of effort and quite often a creative force, most commonly in tandem with Glen Little down the right. Usually performing as a link between defence and attack, Paul more than makes up for his lack of inches with enthusiasm and battling qualities. While never quite reaching the heights of the

previous season, he remained a first choice. Although most often used on the right of midfield, he can also play in the centre or on the left and has also helped out in defence.
Burnley (From trainee on 30/11/1993) FL 148+37/11 FLC 7+2 FAC 6+3/1 Others 7

WELSH Andrew (Andy)
Born: Manchester, 24 November 1983
Height: 5'8" **Weight:** 9.8
This tricky left-winger was another of the youngsters to break into the Stockport County first team last season and at times he looked very skilful. He made a total of 16 appearances for the Hatters and showed he was capable of terrorising opposing players with his marauding runs.
Stockport Co (From trainee on 11/7/2001) FL 9+6 FAC 1

WEST Dean
Born: Morley, 5 December 1972
Height: 5'10" **Weight:** 12.2
Club Honours: Div 2 '97
After being overlooked for almost all of the previous season, Dean seemed an unlikely starter for Burnley following the signing of Mark McGregor, but he ended the campaign almost unanimously recognised as the club's player of the year. It was sheer consistency that did it – Dean was the right-back par excellence, primarily a solid and wholly reliable defender, secondly a builder of attacks down the right side, with Paul Weller and Glen Little usually in front of him. They were a formidable unit at their best, and his contribution, though seldom recognised with 'Man of the Match' awards, received its due reward when the whole picture was taken into account.
Lincoln C (From trainee on 17/8/1991) FL 93+26/20 FLC 11/1 FAC 6/1 Others 5+2/1
Bury (Signed on 29/9/1995) FL 100+10/7 FLC 6 FAC 3 Others 2+1
Burnley (Free on 26/7/1999) FL 79+6 FLC 1+1 FAC 6 Others 1

WESTCARR Craig Naptali
Born: Nottingham, 29 January 1985
Height: 5'11" **Weight:** 11.8
International Honours: E: Yth
This young striker created a piece of history last season when he became the youngest player to appear for Nottingham Forest in senior football. He was just 16 years and 257 days old when he came on as a substitute in the home game against Burnley in November. He almost had a dream debut after finding himself in a one-on-one with the Burnley 'keeper, but fired his shot straight at him. In all made eight substitute appearances.

Nottingham F (From trainee on 31/1/2002) FL 0+8

WESTERVELD Sander
Born: Enschede, Holland, 23 October 1974
Height: 6'3" **Weight:** 13.12
Club Honours: FLC '01; FAC '01; UEFAC '01; ESC '01; CS '01
International Honours: Holland: 6; U21; Yth
After seeming to be a permanent fixture for Liverpool following their triumphs of the previous season, Sander had a somewhat traumatic start to the 2001-02 campaign and quickly found himself as the club's third choice 'keeper following the arrival of Jerzy Dudek and Chris Kirkland. He eventually slipped quietly out of Anfield to join Real Sociedad shortly before Christmas.
Liverpool (£4,000,000 from Vitesse Arnhem, Holland, ex Twente, on 18/6/1999) PL 75 FLC 5 FAC 8 Others 15

WESTON Rhys David
Born: Kingston, 27 October 1980
Height: 6'1" **Weight:** 12.3
International Honours: W: 1; U21-4; E: Yth; Sch
Rhys slowly won over the Cardiff City fans last season, steadily growing in confidence and finished the campaign on a high note. He was a regular in the line-up featuring either at right back or in a central defensive role. By the end of the season he was a hugely popular figure among supporters and he will be much stronger for the experience.
Arsenal (From trainee on 8/7/1999) PL 1 FLC 1+1
Cardiff C (£300,000 on 21/11/2000) FL 60+5 FLC 1 FAC 5+1 Others 3

WESTWOOD Ashley Michael
Born: Bridgnorth, 31 August 1976
Height: 6'0" **Weight:** 12.8
Club Honours: FAYC '95
International Honours: E: Yth
This enthusiastic central defender had a somewhat up and down season for Sheffield Wednesday in 2001-02. At times he looked very commanding and was also useful when coming up to support the attack for set pieces. He always gave 100 per cent but needs to improve his consistency to win a regular place in the line-up.
Manchester U (From trainee on 1/7/1994)
Crewe Alex (£40,000 on 26/7/1995) FL 93+5/9 FLC 8 FAC 9/2 Others 10
Bradford C (£150,000 on 20/7/1998) P/FL 18+6/2 FLC 1 FAC 2+1 Others 1+1

Sheffield Wed (£150,000 + on 10/8/2000)
FL 57+2/3 FLC 10+1/4 FAC 1

WESTWOOD Christopher (Chris) John

Born: Dudley, 13 February 1977
Height: 6'0" **Weight:** 12.2
Chris had another solid season for
Hartlepool in 2001-02, despite missing
some games early on after undergoing a
hernia operation. A central defender who
also occasionally appeared at left back, he

was a model professional turning in
consistent performances week-in week-
out.
Wolverhampton W (From trainee on
3/7/1995) FL 3+1/1 FLC 1+1 (Released during
1998 close season)
Hartlepool U (Signed from Telford U on
24/3/1999) FL 117+5/2 FLC 3 FAC 4 Others 12

WETHERALL David

Born: Sheffield, 14 March 1971
Height: 6'3" **Weight:** 13.12

International Honours: E: Sch
David had a horrendous time with injuries
at Bradford City last season. He missed
the opening games with a groin problem
and after a brief run in the side he was
sidelined again by a similar injury. He
eventually travelled to see a specialist in
Denmark before being given the all-clear
to play. He came back into the first team
in March and starred for the rest of the
season. He is a strong and dominating
central defender, and often found himself

Dean West

pushed up front late in games to try and get a goal.

Sheffield Wed (From trainee on 1/7/1989)
Leeds U (£125,000 on 15/7/1991) F/PL
188+14/12 FLC 19+1/2 FAC 21+3/4 Others 4
Bradford C (£1,400,000 on 7/7/1999) P/FL
73+2/5 FLC 6/2 FAC 1 Others 3

WHALLEY Gareth

Born: Manchester, 19 December 1973
Height: 5'10" **Weight:** 11.12
This skilful central midfield player was a regular for Bradford City at the beginning of last season, but then missed four months out with a groin injury. He returned to the side when fit but then went on loan to Crewe shortly before the transfer deadline day. He is a player who dominates the centre of the park and has excellent distribution.

Crewe Alex (From trainee on 29/7/1992) FL
174+6/9 FLC 10+1/1 FAC 15+1/4 Others 24/3
Bradford C (£600,000 on 24/7/1998) P/FL
99+4/3 FLC 10+2/2 FAC 2 Others 5+1
Crewe Alex (Loaned on 28/3/2002) FL 7

WHEATCROFT Paul Michael

Born: Bolton, 22 November 1980
Height: 5'9" **Weight:** 9.11
International Honours: E: Yth; Sch
Paul was unable to win a place in the Bolton Wanderers first team last term and went out on loan to Rochdale where he had an eventful time, scoring three goals and also being sent off against Cheltenham. He returned to the Reebok Stadium with an injury, but then had a second loan spell at Mansfield, where he never really settled. He was subsequently released by Wanderers in May. He is a nippy young striker who will be looking to find regular first-team football in 2002-03.

Manchester U (From trainee on 8/7/1998)
Bolton W (Free on 6/7/2000) FLC 0+1 FAC
0+2
Rochdale (Loaned on 27/9/2001) FL 6/3
Mansfield T (Loaned on 26/2/2002) FL 1+1

WHELAN Noel David

Born: Leeds, 30 December 1974
Height: 6'2" **Weight:** 12.3
Club Honours: FAYC '93
International Honours: E: U21-2; Yth (UEFA-U18 '93)
This experienced striker again missed time with injuries at Middlesbrough last term, but still managed to net a total of seven goals in all competitions to finish as the club's second-top scorer for the season. He is a lively front runner with excellent skills on the ball.

Leeds U (From trainee on 5/3/1993) PL
28+20/7 FLC 3+2/1 FAC 2 Others 3
Coventry C (£2,000,000 on 16/12/1995) PL
127+7/31 FLC 6/1 FAC 15+1/7
Middlesbrough (£2,200,000 on 4/8/2000)
PL 31+15/5 FLC 3/1 FAC 5+2/3

WHELAN Philip (Phil) James

Born: Stockport, 7 March 1972
Height: 6'4" **Weight:** 14.7
International Honours: E: U21-3
Phil was a near ever present for Southend United during the 2001-2002 season, his dominance and calm in the centre of defence proving invaluable. His partnership with new-boy Leon Cort was only broken towards the end of the campaign when he was forced into an unfamiliar centre-forward role due to squad injuries. His strength in the air allied to good skills on the floor made him an obvious club captain, a role he relished.

Ipswich T (From juniors on 2/7/1990) F/PL
76+6/2 FLC 6+1 FAC 3+1 Others 1
Middlesbrough (£300,000 on 3/4/1995) PL
18+4/1 FLC 5 FAC 3
Oxford U (£150,000 on 15/7/1997) FL
51+3/2 FLC 3/1 FAC 5 Others 3
Rotherham U (Loaned on 12/3/1999) FL
13/4
Southend U (Free on 4/7/2000) FL 83+3/6
FLC 2+1 FAC 7/1 Others 7/1

WHITAKER Daniel (Danny) Phillip

Born: Wilmslow, 14 November 1980
Height: 5'10" **Weight:** 11.4
After some superb performances in the Macclesfield reserve side Danny made his senior debut from the substitutes' bench in the home match against Exeter City last February scoring his first senior goal (and Macc's 250th Football League goal) just 25 minutes after his introduction. He is now a permanent member of the first-team squad, normally featuring in a wide-right midfield role where he works tirelessly. He has a good first touch, excellent pace and passes the ball with accuracy. He also occasionally appeared on the left flank and in the centre of midfield where he performed equally well.

Macclesfield T (Signed from Wilmslow Sports on 5/7/2000) FL 15+1/2

WHITBREAD Adrian Richard

Born: Epping, 22 October 1971
Height: 6'1" **Weight:** 12.12
Adrian had an unfortunate season at Reading last term in that he was a regular and valuable member of the back four in

the early part of the campaign before losing his place through injury. He shrugged off knocks suffered in the 4-3 win at Notts County to play the following week at Oldham, where he excelled in another narrow victory, but a block tackle in the last minute brought him serious knee and ankle injuries. Despite extensive rehabilitation work by physio John Fearn he only returned for one further first-team match, the FA Cup tie against Welling.

Leyton Orient (From trainee on 13/11/1989)
FL 125/2 FLC 10+1 FAC 11/1 Others 8
Swindon T (£500,000 on 29/7/1993) P/FL
35+1/1 FAC 3
West Ham U (£650,000 on 17/8/1994) PL
3+7 FLC 2+1 FAC 1
Portsmouth (Loaned on 9/11/1995) FL 13
Portsmouth (£250,000 on 24/10/1996) FL
133+1/2 FLC 8/1 FAC 3
Luton T (Loaned on 23/11/2000) FL 9 FAC 4
Reading (Free on 8/2/2001) FL 33 FLC 3 FAC 1

WHITE Alan

Born: Darlington, 22 March 1976
Height: 6'1" **Weight:** 13.2
In and out of the team during the first half of the 2001-02 season, centre half Alan became an established figure in Colchester United's back-line from December onwards. He grabbed a precious winner at home to Peterborough, and boosted his tally to three goals with efforts at Huddersfield and Notts County. His contract expired in the summer, but he was hopeful of still being at Layer Road for the 2002-03 campaign.

Middlesbrough (From trainee on 8/7/1994)
Others 1
Luton T (£40,000 on 22/9/1997) FL 60+20/3
FLC 3+3 FAC 2 Others 4
Colchester U (Loaned on 12/11/1999) FL 4
Others 1
Colchester U (Free on 19/7/2000) FL 57+8/3
FLC 4+1 FAC 1+1

WHITE Andrew (Andy)

Born: Swanwick, 6 November 1981
Height: 6'4" **Weight:** 13.4
This tall young striker was given an extended run in the Mansfield Town line-up last term and was never overawed; he always gave 100 per cent and scored some useful goals. He dropped out of the first team when more senior players became available but then managed another run in the side towards the end of the season and weighed in with some vital goals.

Mansfield T (Signed from Hucknall T on 13/7/2000) FL 16+10/4 FLC 1/1 FAC 0+3

WHITE Jason Gregory

Born: Meriden, 19 October 1971
Height: 6'0" **Weight:** 12.10

This experienced striker never really settled at Cheltenham last term and spent most of the season on the transfer list. He made a handful of appearances from the bench but mostly featured for the club's reserves. He had a spell on loan at Mansfield in September where he replaced young Andy White but had little effect at Field Mill. A highlight was a superb hat-trick for the Robins' second string against Wycombe.

Derby Co *(From trainee on 4/7/1990)*
Scunthorpe U *(Free on 6/9/1991)* FL 44+24/16 FLC 2 FAC 3+3/1 Others 4+4/1
Darlington *(Loaned on 20/8/1993)* FL 4/1
Scarborough *(Free on 10/12/1993)* FL 60+3/20 FLC 2+1 FAC 5/1 Others 1
Northampton T *(£35,000 on 15/6/1995)* FL 55+22/18 FLC 1+4 FAC 3 Others 5+2
Rotherham U *(£25,000 on 9/9/1997)* FL 52+21/22 FLC 2 FAC 3+1/1 Others 3/1
Cheltenham T *(Free on 10/7/2000)* FL 8+23/1 FLC 1+1 FAC 0+1 Others 1
Mansfield T *(Loaned on 22/9/2001)* FL 6+1 Others 1

WHITEHEAD Damien Stephen

Born: Whiston, 24 April 1979
Height: 5'10" **Weight:** 11.7

Damien was still recovering from a hernia operation at the beginning of the 2001-02 season, but once fit he rarely featured in the Macclesfield senior team. He spent the second half of the campaign on loan assisting League of Ireland First Division side Drogheda United to win promotion with six goals in ten matches. He is a young striker who shows pace in the box and causes problems for defenders, but still needs to develop aspects of his all-round game.

Macclesfield T *(Signed from Warrington T on 6/8/1999)* FL 20+38/14 FLC 0+2 FAC 0+2 Others 1+1

WHITEHEAD Dean

Born: Oxford, 12 January 1982
Height: 5'11" **Weight:** 12.1

Dean missed just five games for Oxford United last season as he established himself firmly in the side. A hard-working destroyer and tough tackler in midfield, he also worked hard on the attacking side of his game. He scored his first senior goal with an excellent finish against Rushden but that was the only time he found the net during the campaign.

Oxford U *(From trainee on 20/4/2000)* FL 46+14/1 FLC 2+1 FAC 1+1 Others 1+1

WHITEHEAD Philip (Phil) Matthew

Born: Halifax, 17 December 1969
Height: 6'3" **Weight:** 15.10

A commanding last line of defence for Reading, Phil was a regular between the posts in 2001-02 apart from a mid-season spell when he was absent through injury. He was able to inspire his team with some fine reaction saves, often when he had not touched the ball for long periods, but his best game was the 0-0 draw at Swindon. He had gone to the match as a spectator, but was called out of the stands to play when Ben Roberts injured a shoulder in the pre-match warm-up. Phil made his 100th appearance for the Royals in the 3-3 draw at Bristol City and looks to be a fixture in the side for some time to come.

Halifax T *(From trainee on 1/7/1988)* FL 42 FLC 2 FAC 4 Others 4
Barnsley *(£60,000 on 9/3/1990)* FL 16
Halifax T *(Loaned on 7/3/1991)* FL 9
Scunthorpe U *(Loaned on 29/11/1991)* FL 8 Others 2
Scunthorpe U *(Loaned on 4/9/1992)* FL 8 FLC 2
Bradford C *(Loaned on 19/11/1992)* FL 6 Others 4
Oxford U *(£75,000 on 1/11/1993)* FL 207 FLC 15 FAC 13 Others 3
West Bromwich A *(£250,000 on 1/12/1998)* FL 26 FLC 1/1 FAC 1
Reading *(£250,000 on 7/10/1999)* FL 90 FLC 5 FAC 6 Others 3

WHITEHEAD Stuart David

Born: Bromsgrove, 17 July 1976
Height: 5'11" **Weight:** 12.4

After spending the bulk of his Carlisle United career in central defence, Stuart found himself used more in a midfield role last term. However he adapted positively to the change and missed only a handful of games until sidelined by an ankle injury in the closing weeks of the campaign. He remained club captain and will be hoping to have fully recovered by the start of the new season.

Bolton W *(Signed from Bromsgrove Rov on 18/9/1995)*
Carlisle U *(Free on 31/7/1998)* FL 139+4/2 FLC 6 FAC 4 Others 2

WHITLEY James (Jim)

Born: Zambia, 14 April 1975
Height: 5'9" **Weight:** 11.0
International Honours: NI: 3; B-1

Jim joined Wrexham on non-contract terms last October and took the right-back position by storm. His contribution to the team was outstanding, and this was duly recognised when he was voted 'Player of the Year' by the club's supporters. A tenacious tackler with no little skill, it is hoped he will be persuaded to stay to help the club's attempt to regain Second Division status next term.

Manchester C *(From juniors on 1/8/1994)* FL 27+11 FLC 3+1/1 FAC 2+1 Others 0+1
Blackpool *(Loaned on 20/8/1999)* FL 7+8 FLC 1
Norwich C *(Loaned on 24/8/2000)* FL 7+1/1
Swindon T *(Loaned on 15/12/2000)* FL 2 FAC 1
Northampton T *(Loaned on 27/2/2001)* FL 13
Wrexham *(Free on 11/10/2001)* FL 34 FAC 1 Others 2

WHITLEY Jeffrey (Jeff)

Born: Zambia, 28 January 1979
Height: 5'8" **Weight:** 11.2
International Honours: NI: 6; B-2; U21-17

Jeff began the 2001-02 season in good form and featured in both of Manchester City's first two games. Unfortunately he suffered a broken fibula bone in his ankle on his second appearance and it was not until the closing stages of the campaign that he returned to match fitness. The skilful midfielder then joined Notts County for the last month of the season and played a key part in helping the Magpies avoid relegation.

Manchester C *(From trainee on 19/2/1996)* P/FL 96+27/8 FLC 9+1 FAC 2+2 Others 4
Wrexham *(Loaned on 14/1/1999)* FL 9/2
Notts Co *(Loaned on 21/3/2002)* FL 6

WHITLOW Michael (Mike) William

Born: Northwich, 13 January 1968
Height: 6'0" **Weight:** 12.12
Club Honours: Div 2 '90, Div 1 '92; FLC '97

A model professional, and one of the characters in the Bolton dressing room, Mike had a phenomenal season last year. Having spent much of the previous campaign in the treatment room with a groin problem, he started out in a central defensive partnership with Gudni Bergsson and was a revelation. The duo produced a string of top-notch performances that belied their advancing years (combined age of 69) and proceeded to frustrate some of the finest strikers in the Premiership. Their pairing was retained throughout the season (minor injuries aside), until Mike was stretchered off with a nasty ankle injury against Derby County in March, but he made a miraculous comeback for the vital end of season run in.

Leeds U *(£10,000 from Witton A on 11/11/1988) FL 62+15/4 FLC 4+1 FAC 1+4 Others 9*
Leicester C *(£250,000 on 27/3/1992) F/PL 141+6/8 FLC 12/1 FAC 6 Others 14*
Bolton W *(£500,000 + on 19/9/1997) P/FL 110+5/2 FLC 13+2 FAC 9 Others 2+3*

WHITMORE Theodore (Theo)
Born: Jamaica, 5 August 1972
Height: 6'2" **Weight:** 11.2
International Honours: Jamaica
With 28 full international appearances during his time at the Yorkshire club, Hull's most capped player had a truly topsy-turvy 2001-02 season. After being transfer listed in the summer, he rediscovered his form to turn in some outstanding performances both on the right-hand side of City's midfield and in a more familiar central role. With his contract due to end in the summer he rejected the offer of a two-year extension in February and was subsequently released. Theo was one of the most naturally gifted players to adorn the Tigers' shirt in many years and will be fondly remembered by the Hull fans.
Hull C *(Free from Seba U, Jamaica on 22/10/1999) FL 63+14/9 FLC 3/1 FAC 7+1 Others 5/1*

WHITTLE Justin Phillip
Born: Derby, 18 March 1971
Height: 6'1" **Weight:** 12.12
The Hull skipper retained the right-sided centre half spot in 2001-02, despite the competition from the numerous new arrivals to Boothferry Park. He was soon at his commanding best, but was briefly sidelined in the autumn with a hamstring injury and then suffered a longer absence in January when the same problem flared up again against Exeter. Justin was runner-up in the Tigers' 'Player of the Year' awards.
Glasgow Celtic *(Free from Army during 1994 close season)*
Stoke C *(Free on 20/10/1994) FL 66+13/1 FLC 3+4 FAC 2 Others 2*
Hull C *(£65,000 on 27/11/1998) FL 135+1/1 FLC 7 FAC 6+2 Others 6/1*

WHITWORTH Neil Anthony
Born: Wigan, 12 April 1972
Height: 6'2" **Weight:** 12.6
International Honours: E: Yth
This powerful central defender was unable to win a regular place in the Exeter City line-up in 2001-02 and was mainly used as cover for suspensions and injuries. When called upon his experience

proved invaluable and he will be hoping to regain his place in the line-up in the coming season.
Wigan Ath *(Trainee) FL 1+1*
Manchester U *(£45,000 on 1/7/1990) FL 1*
Preston NE *(Loaned on 16/1/1992) FL 6*
Barnsley *(Loaned on 20/2/1992) FL 11*
Rotherham U *(Loaned on 8/10/1993) FL 8/1 Others 2*
Blackpool *(Loaned on 10/12/1993) FL 3*
Kilmarnock *(£265,000 on 2/9/1994) SL 74+1/3 SLC 3 SC 4 Others 1*
Wigan Ath *(Loaned on 11/3/1998) FL 1+3*
Hull C *(Free on 16/7/1998) FL 18+1/2 FLC 4 FAC 1*
Exeter C *(Free on 4/8/2000) FL 46+3/1 FLC 3 FAC 1 Others 1*

WICKS Matthew Jonathan
Born: Reading, 8 September 1978
Height: 6'2" **Weight:** 13.5
Club Honours: Div 3 '01
International Honours: E: Yth
With Brighton well served by central defenders, Matthew had problems breaking into the first team last season. He managed just five starts – three in LDV Vans Trophy games and two deputising for the injured Danny Cullip – before moving down a division to join Hull City. Matthew was soon drafted in by the Tigers to solve their problems on the left side of central defence and this was a task he accomplished with admirable maturity.
Arsenal *(From trainee at Manchester U on 23/1/1996)*
Crewe Alex *(£100,000 on 15/6/1998) FL 4+2*
Peterborough U *(Free on 3/3/1999) FL 28+3 FLC 2 FAC 1 Others 1*
Brighton & Hove A *(£25,000 on 1/9/2000) FL 25+1/3 FLC 2 FAC 2/1 Others 4*
Hull C *(Signed on 11/1/2002) FL 14*

WIDDRINGTON Thomas (Tommy)
Born: Newcastle, 1 October 1971
Height: 5'9" **Weight:** 11.12
Club Honours: AMC '01
This hard-tackling midfielder, was signed by Hartlepool in the 2001 close season to add bite and experience to the side. He took some time to settle, then just as his campaign was taking off he received a hamstring injury which brought his season to a premature end in January.
Southampton *(From trainee on 10/5/1990) F/PL 67+8/3 FLC 3+1 FAC 11*
Wigan Ath *(Loaned on 12/9/1991) FL 5+1 FLC 2*
Grimsby T *(£300,000 on 11/7/1996) FL 72+17/8 FLC 10+3 FAC 3+1 Others 1*

Port Vale *(Free on 24/3/1999) FL 77+5/8 FLC 2 FAC 2 Others 3*
Hartlepool U *(Free on 30/7/2001) FL 24/2 FLC 1 FAC 1 Others 1*

WIEKENS Gerard
Born: Tolhuiswyk, Holland, 25 February 1973
Height: 6'0" **Weight:** 13.4
Club Honours: Div 1 '02
Gerard has been involved with either promotion every season since his arrival at Maine Road, and last term was no exception. He played in a 'holding' midfield role in the early part of the campaign before switching to a place in a back three, where he was seen as a calming influence. One of the unsung heroes of Manchester City's success, he got on with what was asked of him and rarely let the side down.
Manchester C *(£500,000 from SC Veendam, Holland on 28/7/1997) P/FL 162+14/10 FLC 13+1 FAC 10+1 Others 3*

WIJNHARD Clyde
Born: Surinam, 9 November 1973
Height: 5'11" **Weight:** 12.4
This powerful striker finally returned for Huddersfield Town last season after 15 months on the sidelines with a serious injury, making an appearance as a substitute in the draw at Colchester United. He generally occupied the bench, featuring late on in games to add an extra dimension to the front line, before being sold to Preston North End to help ease the financial burden of the club. At Deepdale he showed he had lost none of his former power, and marked his home debut with a 'Man of the Match' display, scoring one, winning a penalty and hitting the post. Strong on the ball, he quickly formed a tremendous partnership with Richard Cresswell, and his three goals suggest he may stay permanently.
Leeds U *(£1,500,000 from Willem II, Holland, ex Ajax, Groningen, RKC Waelwijk, on 22/7/1998) PL 11+7/3 FLC 1 FAC 1+1/1 Others 1+3*
Huddersfield T *(£750,000 on 22/7/1999) FL 51+11/16 FLC 7/1 FAC 1 Others 1+1/1*
Preston NE *(Free on 22/3/2002) FL 6/3*

WILBRAHAM Aaron Thomas
Born: Knutsford, 21 October 1979
Height: 6'3" **Weight:** 12.4
Aaron missed four months of the 2001-02 season due to injury but made a welcome return to the team in the final home match when he scored in Stockport County's 3-1 victory over Sheffield

Wednesday. Another injury, however, which really underlined his miserable season, kept him out of the final game of the season at Norwich. The club's leading scorer in 2000-01, he managed just three goals last time round.
Stockport Co (From trainee on 29/8/1997) FL 78+38/20 FLC 4+2/1 FAC 3

WILCOX Jason Malcolm
Born: Farnworth, 15 July 1971
Height: 5'11" **Weight:** 11.10
Club Honours: PL '95
International Honours: E: 3; B-2
Jason's time at Elland Road has been fraught with injuries, and he has had limited opportunities but remains an important squad member. Although his appearances last term were limited, he remains an experienced winger with the ability to go past people, as he showed when setting up Robbie Fowler's goal against Arsenal in January. After a season on the fringes of the first team it remains to be seen if Jason will remain at Elland Road for the start of the 2002-03 campaign.
Blackburn Rov (From trainee on 13/6/1989) F/PL 242+27/31 FLC 16+1/1 FAC 18+2/2 Others 7
Leeds U (£3,000,000 on 17/12/1999) PL 26+24/3 FLC 1 FAC 2+1 Others 6+6/2

WILCOX Russell (Russ)
Born: Hemsworth, 25 March 1964
Height: 6'0" **Weight:** 12.12
Club Honours: Div 4 '87; Div 3 '96
International Honours: E: SP-3
Scunthorpe assistant manager Russ was only used sparingly as a player during the 2001-02 season. He started six games at right back where his vast experience helped a young defence. He played regularly for the reserves to keep his fitness levels up and will remain registered as a player for 2002-03.
Doncaster Rov (Apprentice) FL 1
Northampton T (£15,000 from Frickley Ath on 30/6/1986) FL 137+1/9 FLC 6 FAC 10 Others 8/1
Hull C (£120,000 on 6/8/1990) FL 92+8/7 FLC 5 FAC 5/1 Others 5+1
Doncaster Rov (£60,000 on 30/7/1993) FL 81/6 FLC 5/2 FAC 3 Others 3
Preston NE (£60,000 on 22/9/1995) FL 62/1 FLC 4 FAC 3/1 Others 2
Scunthorpe U (£15,000 on 8/7/1997) FL 106+12/4 FLC 7+2 FAC 11/2 Others 8

WILD Peter
Born: Stockport, 12 October 1982
Height: 5'9" **Weight:** 11.12
Another product of the Stockport County

youth system, Peter was handed a tough debut at home to Wolverhampton Wanderers last February. However, the young midfielder could be pleased with his performance, giving as good as he got against some of the First Division's most experienced players.
Stockport Co (From trainee on 11/7/2001) FL 1

WILDING Peter John
Born: Shrewsbury, 28 November 1968
Height: 6'1" **Weight:** 12.12
Peter was very much a squad man at Shrewsbury in 2001-02 but never let the side down when called upon. He is a hard-working and committed utility player who is equally at home at full back, in central defence or in midfield. He was reported to have been offered a new contract for the 2002-03 campaign and seems likely to remain at Gay Meadow for another year.
Shrewsbury T (£10,000 from Telford on 10/6/1997) FL 142+18/4 FLC 8 FAC 6+1/1 Others 3/1

WILKIE Lee
Born: Dundee, 20 April 1980
Height: 6'4" **Weight:** 13.4
International Honours: S: 1; U21-8
This tall strong centre half played a couple of games for Dundee in the Inter Toto Cup at the start of last season before joining Notts County on loan last August. He looked dominant in the air, but received few opportunities at Meadow Lane before returning north of the border. He subsequently spent a further three months on loan at Falkirk before returning to Dens Park and a regular first-team slot. His season ended on a very positive note when he made his bow for Scotland at international level, featuring in the games against South Africa and a Hong Kong XI.
Dundee (Signed from Downfield Juniors on 8/9/1998) SL 34+6 SLC 3/1 SC 2 Others 2
Plymouth Arg (Loaned on 12/1/2001) FL 2
Notts Co (Loaned on 10/8/2001) FL 2
Falkirk (Loaned on 16/11/2001) SL 9/2

WILKINSON Andrew (Andy) Gordon
Born: Stone, 6 August 1984
Height: 5'11" **Weight:** 11.0
Still on Stoke City's books as a scholar, this bright young prospect made his senior debut when he came on from the subs' bench in the LDV Vans Trophy game at Blackpool last season. A fine defender with pace and athleticism he is one of the

youngest players to feature at senior level for City.
Stoke C (Trainee) Others 0+1

WILKSHIRE Luke
Born: Wollongong, Australia, 2 October 1981
Height: 5'9" **Weight:** 11.5
International Honours: Australia: Yth
This exciting attacking midfield player made his senior debut for Middlesbrough against Southampton last March and went on to feature on a number of occasions in the closing stages of the campaign. He has already been capped by Australia at U20 level and will be looking to feature at first-team level for Boro' more often in 2002-03.
Middlesbrough (Signed from AIS, Australia on 12/5/1999) PL 6+1 FAC 1

WILLEMS Menno
Born: Amsterdam, Holland, 10 March 1977
Height: 6'0" **Weight:** 14.6
The last of former manager Lennie Lawrence's continental signings, this strong-tackling and hard-working player was a near ever-present during the first half of the 2001-02 season but then found himself out of favour at Grimsby following the change of manager. A left-sided midfielder who has a powerful left foot and is a dead-ball specialist, he was placed on the transfer list towards the end of the campaign.
Grimsby T (Signed from Vitesse Arnhem, Holland, ex Den Bosch, Ajax, on 24/11/2000) FL 44+10/2 FLC 2 FAC 3

WILLIAMS Adrian
Born: Reading, 16 August 1971
Height: 6'2" **Weight:** 13.2
Club Honours: Div 2 '94
International Honours: W: 12
Adrian returned to his best form at the heart of the Reading defence last season, even captaining the side on occasions when Phil Parkinson was absent. So consistent was his form that there was even talk of the possibility of a recall to the Welsh squad. Although this did not happen he was more than satisfied with a Second Division runners-up medal for the team he originally joined from school 15 years ago. A no-nonsense-style centre-back, able to compete with the biggest of strikers as he dominates the penalty area, his experience and enthusiasm will be vital to the side in the tough battles ahead in Division One.
Reading (From trainee on 4/3/1989) FL 191+5/14 FLC 16/1 FAC 16/2 Others 14/2

Wolverhampton W (£750,000 on 3/7/1996) FL 26+1 FLC 3 FAC 2+2 Others 2/1
Reading (Loaned on 15/2/2000) FL 5/1 Others 1
Reading (Free on 26/3/2000) FL 48+2/1 FLC 3 FAC 1 Others 3

WILLIAMS Anthony (Tony)
Simon
Born: Bridgend, 20 September 1977
Height: 6'1" **Weight:** 13.5
International Honours: W: U21-16; Yth
Although out of the Hartlepool line-up at the beginning of last season, Tony soon regained his place as the club's first-choice goalkeeper and did not look back as the defence tightened up as the season progressed. Manager Chris Turner, himself an ex-'keeper, rates him highly and in March was pleased to sign him on a contract that will keep him at the Victoria Park until the summer of 2004.
Blackburn Rov (From trainee on 4/7/1996)
Macclesfield T (Loaned on 16/10/1998) FL 4
Bristol Rov (Loaned on 24/3/1999) FL 9
Gillingham (Loaned on 5/8/1999) FL 2 FLC 2
Macclesfield T (Loaned on 28/1/2000) FL 11
Hartlepool U (Free on 7/7/2000) FL 84 FLC 1 FAC 2 Others 8

WILLIAMS Christopher
(Chris) Jonathan
Born: Manchester, 2 February 1985
Height: 5'8" **Weight:** 9.6
Chris became Stockport County's third-youngest ever player when he came off the bench at Watford last November. Following this he made a few substitute appearances and was awarded his only start for County in the thrilling 2-1 victory over Manchester City at Edgeley Park. He is a pacy forward who works extremely hard for the team.
Stockport Co (Trainee) FL 1+4 FAC 0+1

WILLIAMS Daniel (Danny)
Ivor Llewellyn
Born: Wrexham, 12 July 1979
Height: 6'1" **Weight:** 13.0
International Honours: W: U21-9
Danny arrived at Kidderminster during the 2001 close season and quickly established himself as an integral part of the midfield. Playing in the centre of the park his strong tackling was a factor in Harriers' good defensive record and his passing was crucial to the attacking style of the team. He only managed to score one goal, however, in the 4-1 home defeat by Luton Town.
Liverpool (From trainee on 14/5/1997)
Wrexham (Free on 22/3/1999) FL 38+1/3 FLC 4 FAC 4/1 Others 1

Kidderminster Hrs (Free on 11/7/2001) FL 37+1/1 FAC 1 Others 2

WILLIAMS Daniel (Danny)
Josef
Born: Sheffield, 2 March 1981
Height: 5'9" **Weight:** 9.13
This recent graduate from Chesterfield's youth set-up looked set to have a fine season after an early opening was presented on the right side of midfield. Blessed with a lot of skill, he - understandably, given his inexperience - lacked a little of the confidence and composure needed to allow those skills to flourish at Second Division level. Given time, though, those aspects of his game will develop. Danny was pressed into an attacking right-back role later in the season, to little effect, but it was a surprise that he was released in April.
Chesterfield (From trainee on 2/7/1999) FL 23+8 FLC 1+1 FAC 0+2 Others 0+5

WILLIAMS Darren
Born: Middlesbrough, 28 April 1977
Height: 5'10" **Weight:** 11.12
Club Honours: Div 1 '99
International Honours: E: B-1; U21-2
Darren is Sunderland's 'Mr Versatile', constantly called upon in a crisis, and last season was no different as he played at right back, centre back and in midfield, always contributing 100 per cent to the team's cause. A tenacious competitor, he has remained patient and loyal to the Black Cats and many fans believe that he could still establish himself in the right-back role at the Stadium of Light as his pace and tackling strength are ideal for the position.
York C (From trainee on 21/6/1995) FL 16+4 FLC 4+1 FAC 1 Others 3/1
Sunderland (£50,000 on 18/10/1996) F/PL 118+35/4 FLC 15+1/2 FAC 8+1 Others 3

WILLIAMS Eifion Wyn
Born: Anglesey, 15 November 1975
Height: 5'11" **Weight:** 11.12
International Honours: W: B-1
Although clearly a natural goal-scorer, Eifion's Torquay goal drought continued unabated last term. Many felt that he was never given the chance to play with a suitable strike partner, and when he was allowed to move to Hartlepool it seemed that a change of environment might be just what was needed to get the goals flowing again, and this indeed proved to be the case as he went on to help Pools clinch a place in the Third Division play-offs.

Torquay U (£70,000 from Barry T on 25/3/1999) FL 84+27/24 FLC 4+1 FAC 3 Others 3
Hartlepool U (£30,000 on 6/3/2002) FL 5+3/4 Others 2/1

WILLIAMS Gareth John
Born: Glasgow, 16 December 1981
Height: 5'11" **Weight:** 11.10
International Honours: S: 3; U21-1; Yth
This talented young midfielder captained the Nottingham Forest side on many occasions last season when he was a near ever present in the first team. A skilful player who can bring his colleagues into the game with his clever passing, he made his full debut for Scotland against Nigeria towards the end of the campaign.
Nottingham F (From trainee on 23/12/1998) FL 55+8 FLC 2 FAC 3

WILLIAMS James
Born: Liverpool, 15 July 1982
Height: 5'7" **Weight:** 10.8
This versatile young midfielder had a difficult season at Swindon in 2001-02 when he had to undergo two operations to resolve an abdominal problem. His only first-team outing came as a late substitute in the home defeat by Bristol City. Once considered to be an excellent prospect, he was surprisingly released in the summer.
Swindon T (From trainee on 9/12/1999) FL 21+16/1 FAC 0+1 Others 3

WILLIAMS John Nelson
Born: Birmingham, 11 May 1968
Height: 6'1" **Weight:** 13.12
John returned to Swansea in the 2001 close season, but disappointed in the goal-scoring stakes with just four League strikes. Although he had lost some of his electric pace, he still possessed the ability to go past his marker and set up goal-scoring opportunities. He was used to the greatest effect by manager Colin Addison when coming on as a second half substitute to make up a three-man attack.
Swansea C (£5,000 from Cradley T on 19/8/1991) FL 36+3/11 FLC 2+1 FAC 3 Others 1
Coventry C (£250,000 on 1/7/1992) PL 66+14/11 FLC 4 FAC 2
Notts Co (Loaned on 7/10/1994) FL 3+2/2
Stoke C (Loaned on 23/12/1994) FL 1+3
Swansea C (Loaned on 3/2/1995) FL 6+1/2
Wycombe W (£150,000 on 15/9/1995) FL 34+14/8 FLC 4+1/2 FAC 5/4 Others 2
Hereford U (Free on 14/2/1997) FL 8+3/3
Walsall (Free on 21/7/1997) FL 4/2
Exeter C (Free on 29/8/1997) FL 16+20/4
Cardiff C (Free on 3/8/1998) FL 25+18/12 FLC 2/1 FAC 5/3 Others 1

York C *(£20,000 on 12/8/1999) FL 29+13/3 FLC 2 FAC 0+1 Others 1*
Darlington *(Free on 21/12/2000) FL 23+1/5 Others 1*
Swansea C *(Free on 17/7/2001) FL 26+15/4 FLC 1 FAC 2/1 Others 1*

WILLIAMS Lee

Born: Birmingham, 3 February 1973
Height: 5'7" **Weight:** 11.13
International Honours: E: Yth
Lee was unable to break into the Mansfield Town line-up at the start of the 2000-01 season and in September he joined Cheltenham Town on loan. The move proved successful and his skilful play on the wide-right side of midfield added a new dimension to the Robins' play. With Russell Milton on the left and Lee on the right the team had two clever players capable of delivering quality balls from either flank. Lee proved popular with the supporters at Whaddon Road and his move was made permanent after the initial loan expired.
Aston Villa *(From trainee on 26/1/1991)*
Shrewsbury T *(Loaned on 8/11/1992) FL 2+1 FAC 1+1/1 Others 2*
Peterborough U *(Signed on 23/3/1994) FL 83+8/1 FLC 4+1 FAC 5+1/1 Others 7 (Free to Shamrock Rov during 1996 close season)*
Mansfield T *(Free on 27/3/1997) FL 149+28/9 FLC 8 FAC 4+2 Others 4+1*
Cheltenham T *(Free on 21/9/2001) FL 36+2/3 FAC 5 Others 4+1/1*

WILLIAMS Mark Ross

Born: Chatham, 19 October 1981
Height: 5'9" **Weight:** 11.0
Brentford's exciting right winger was again used mainly as a substitute last season, coming on late in the game to run at tiring defences and create chances. A talented player with the ability to take on defenders and deliver a useful cross, he headed his only goal in the 4-0 win over Tranmere in September. His overall tally of appearances from the subs' bench is now just four short of Bob Booker's all-time Brentford League record of 48.
Brentford *(From trainee on 2/11/2000) FL 6+44/3 FLC 0+2 FAC 0+2 Others 0+3*

WILLIAMS Mark Stuart

Born: Stalybridge, 28 September 1970
Height: 6'0" **Weight:** 13.0
Club Honours: Div 3 '94
International Honours: NI: 19; B-1
Mark missed the majority of the 2001-02 season through injury. He suffered a broken leg in the first game of the

season, but played on for a couple of matches before this was diagnosed! The injury jinx continued when he broke down in his reserve comeback against Spurs. Mark gives it his all in every game and the paying public are never disappointed. He returned to the Northern Ireland team after his enforced lay off.
Shrewsbury T *(Free from Newtown on 27/3/1992) FL 96+6/3 FLC 7+1 FAC 6 Others 6/1*
Chesterfield *(£50,000 on 7/8/1995) FL 168/12 FLC 10 FAC 13/1 Others 7/1*
Watford *(Free on 13/7/1999) P/FL 20+2/1 FLC 2*
Wimbledon *(Signed on 26/7/2000) FL 46+1/6 FLC 5/1 FAC 6/1*

WILLIAMS Paul Darren

Born: Burton, 26 March 1971
Height: 6'0" **Weight:** 13.0
International Honours: E: U21-6
Paul started the 2001-02 campaign as a first choice at centre back for Coventry, but lost his place in the line-up following the departure of Gordon Strachan. He subsequently rejoined his mentor at Southampton where he fitted in well as a replacement for Dean Richards and soon became a firm favourite with the Saints fans.
Derby Co *(From trainee on 13/7/1989) FL 153+7/26 FLC 10+2/2 FAC 8/3 Others 14+1/2*
Lincoln C *(Loaned on 9/11/1989) FL 3 FAC 2 Others 1*
Coventry C *(£975,000 on 6/8/1995) P/FL 153+16/5 FLC 16+1/1 FAC 13*
Southampton *(Free on 26/10/2001) PL 27+1 FLC 1 FAC 1*

WILLIAMS Ryan Neil

Born: Sutton in Ashfield, 31 August 1978
Height: 5'5" **Weight:** 11.4
International Honours: E: Yth
The diminutive right winger completed a transfer to Hull in the 2001 close season following protracted negotiations. However, he suffered a horrendous start to his Tigers' career when he damaged medial knee ligaments at Exeter on the opening match of the campaign. He eventually returned to his wing berth in October and bagged his first Tigers' goal against Shrewsbury in January.
Mansfield T *(Trainee) FL 9+17/3 FLC 2 FAC 0+1*
Tranmere Rov *(£70,000 + on 8/8/1997) FL 2+3*
Chesterfield *(£80,000 on 10/11/1999) FL 69+6/13 FLC 3 FAC 1 Others 5+1/1*
Hull C *(£150,000 on 9/7/2001) FL 26+3/2 FAC 1+1 Others 2+1*

WILLIAMS Thomas (Tommy) Andrew

Born: Carshalton, 8 July 1980
Height: 6'0" **Weight:** 11.8
Tommy quickly became a crowd favourite at Peterborough last term, with his charges from full back and skilful play on the ball. A very confident player who always seems to have time to spare, he was sold to Birmingham City in March and made his debut wide on the left at Norwich. He later moved to left back when Martin Grainger was suspended and acquitted himself reasonably.
West Ham U *(£60,000 from Walton & Hersham on 3/4/2000)*
Peterborough U *(Signed on 22/3/2001) FL 32+4/2 FLC 1+1 FAC 4+1 Others 1*
Birmingham C *(£1,000,000 on 12/3/2002) FL 4*

WILLIAMSON Lee Trevor

Born: Derby, 7 June 1982
Height: 5'10" **Weight:** 10.4
Lee began the 2001-02 season as a regular on the right side of the midfield for Mansfield. He seemed to get better and better as the season progressed, and when Les Robinson was injured manager Stuart Watkiss had no qualms about giving him the captain's armband. He is an exciting prospect who is strong in the tackle and possesses a thunderous shot. A fine campaign ended with him being selected for the PFA Third Division side.
Mansfield T *(From trainee on 3/7/2000) FL 54+11/3 FLC 1+3 FAC 4+1 Others 2*

WILLIAMSON Michael (Mike) James

Born: Stoke, 8 November 1983
Height: 6'4" **Weight:** 13.3
This second-year trainee made rapid progress at Torquay last term. A tall centre half, his mature attitude and calmness on the ball marked him out as a star of the future, and these qualities quickly persuaded Southampton to sign him up for a substantial fee in November.
Torquay U *(Trainee) FL 3 Others 1*
Southampton *(£100,000 on 21/11/2001)*

WILLIAMSON Thomas (Tom)

Born: Leicester, 24 December 1984
Height: 5'9" **Weight:** 10.2
This promising young midfielder made his senior debut for Leicester City as a substitute in added time of the final fixture of the season at home to Tottenham and did not even get to touch the ball, thus equalling the feat of Malcolm Clarke back in 1965. Although still a scholar with the Foxes, he can

expect a more worthwhile opportunity in 2002-03.
Leicester C (Trainee) PL 0+1

WILLIS Adam Peter
Born: Nuneaton, 21 September 1976
Height: 6'1" **Weight:** 12.2
Adam always seems to be second choice for one of the centre-back positions at Swindon last term, but whenever called upon he always gave a solid, composed and effective performance. He did not appear until October and when he did get a run in the side he was consistent as a right-sided centre back in either a three or four-man defence, impressing with some terrific tackling. He scored his first League goal in the win over Port Vale at the beginning of March.
Coventry C (From trainee on 1/7/1995)
Swindon T (Free on 21/4/1998) FL 67+10/1 FLC 1+1 FAC 3/1 Others 1
Mansfield T (Loaned on 25/3/1999) FL 10

WILLIS Roger Christopher
Born: Sheffield, 17 June 1967
Height: 6'1" **Weight:** 12.0
Club Honours: GMVC '91
International Honours: E: SP-1
'Harry' had a rather stuttering time in his last season for Chesterfield, with no regular platform of first-team football to show his intelligent and determined forward play. With the signing of Jamie Burt, Mark Allott and Glynn Hurst, he was pushed further down the strikers' list and, although four goals from 11 starts was a good return for him, it was not enough to earn a contract for 2002-03.
Grimsby T (Signed from Dunkirk on 20/7/1989) FL 1+8 FLC 0+1
Barnet (£10,000 on 1/8/1990) FL 39+5/13 FLC 2 FAC 5+1/3 Others 1+4/1
Watford (£175,000 on 6/10/1992) FL 30+6/2 FAC 1
Birmingham C (£150,000 on 31/12/1993) FL 12+7/5 FAC 0+4
Southend U (Signed on 16/9/1994) FL 30+1/7 FAC 1 Others 1
Peterborough U (Free on 13/8/1996) FL 34+6/6 FLC 3 FAC 5+1 Others 5
Chesterfield (£100,000 on 11/7/1997) FL 68+67/21 FLC 12+4/2 FAC 4+3/1 Others 2+4

WILLIS Scott Leon
Born: Liverpool, 20 February 1982
Height: 5'10" **Weight:** 11.5
This young striker spent two months on trial at Carlisle last season and made a single appearance from the subs' bench against Luton. After being released he joined Unibond League club Bamber Bridge before moving on to Droylesden in

the new year. He is the younger brother of both Jimmy (ex-Leicester City) and Paul (formerly of Halifax and Darlington) and a nephew of the television star Cilla Black.
Mansfield T (Free from trainee at Wigan Ath on 23/3/2000. Freed on 23/2/2001)
Carlisle U (Free from Doncaster Rov on 10/8/2001) FL 0+1

WILLMOTT Christopher (Chris) Alan
Born: Bedford, 30 September 1977
Height: 6'2" **Weight:** 11.12
Chris maintained his good progress at Wimbledon last season, building a good partnership with Kenny Cunningham in the centre of defence. His pace and ability in the air were outstanding while his distribution showed improvement. He scored his only goal of the campaign at home to Nottingham Forest on the 'Fans United' day.
Luton T (From trainee on 1/5/1996) FL 13+1
Wimbledon (£350,000 on 14/7/1999) P/FL 45+3/2 FLC 3+1 FAC 2

WILLOCK Calum Daniel
Born: London, 29 October 1981
Height: 5'11" **Weight:** 12.7
International Honours: E: Sch
Calum is a promising young striker whose excellent goal-scoring form for Fulham reserves saw him promoted to the first-team squad and he made his Premiership debut as a substitute in the 2-0 home win over Blackburn in February. A regular in the reserve side his quick thinking puts him into scoring positions. He prefers the ball played to feet where his speed off the mark enables him to get in behind opposition defences.
Fulham (From ADT College, Putney on 18/7/2000) P/FL 0+3

WILLS Kevin Michael
Born: Torquay, 15 October 1980
Height: 5'8" **Weight:** 10.7
Club Honours: Div 3 '02
A product of Plymouth Argyle's youth system, this combative midfield player's performances showed a greater maturity in 2001-02. He regularly appeared in the starting line-up away from home when manager Paul Sturrock used a 4-5-1 formation, and on these occasions he impressed with some authoritative and disciplined midfield displays.
Plymouth Arg (From trainee on 16/7/1999) FL 17+15/1 FLC 1 FAC 1+3 Others 2+1

WILNIS Fabian
Born: Surinam, 23 August 1970
Height: 5'8" **Weight:** 12.6

Fabian found himself behind Chris Makin and Hermann Hreidarsson for the full-back berths from the beginning of last season and struggled to get an opportunity at Ipswich. An elegant full back he is very attack minded and can be as good as an extra forward when he plays. He is also a good crosser of the ball.
Ipswich T (£200,000 from De Graafschap, Holland, ex NAC Breda, on 6/1/1999) P/FL 80+16/3 FLC 7+3 FAC 5 Others 5+1

WILSON Brian
Born: Manchester, 9 May 1983
Height: 5'10" **Weight:** 11.0
Brian is the latest graduate of the talent from Stoke's Academy and made a couple of senior appearances last term. He was outstanding in City's reserve team and looks to have a great future ahead of him playing either at full back or in a more central defensive role.
Stoke C (From trainee on 5/7/2001) FL 0+1 Others 1

WILSON Che Christian Aaron Clay
Born: Ely, 17 January 1979
Height: 5'9" **Weight:** 11.3
Che gained a regular place in the Bristol Rovers defence at right back last season and was appointed captain in the absence of Lewis Hogg towards the end of the campaign. He showed his versatility by successfully switching to centre back in Rovers shock 3-1 FA Cup victory at Pride Park and did a superb man-marking job on Derby's Ravanelli. He was surprisingly released in the summer.
Norwich C (From trainee on 3/7/1997) FL 16+6 FLC 3
Bristol Rov (Free on 13/7/2000) FL 74+1 FLC 7 FAC 6 Others 3+1

WILSON Mark Antony
Born: Scunthorpe, 9 February 1979
Height: 5'11" **Weight:** 13.0
Club Honours: E: Yth; Sch
International Honours: E: U21-2; Yth; Sch
Mark followed Middlesbrough boss Steve McClaren and Jonathan Greening from Old Trafford in the summer of 2001 but he made little impact at the Riverside last term. A promising young midfield player he was restricted to just two starts due to niggling injuries and he will be hoping to make a breakthrough in 2002-03.
Manchester U (From trainee on 16/2/1996) PL 1+2 FLC 2 Others 3+2
Wrexham (Loaned on 23/2/1998) FL 12+1/4
Middlesbrough (£1,500,000 on 9/8/2001) PL 2+8 FLC 2/1 FAC 1+1

Sylvain Wiltord

WILSON Scott Peter
Born: Edinburgh, 19 March 1977
Height: 6'1" **Weight:** 11.8
International Honours: S: U21-7
Club Honours: SPD '99, '00; SC '99, '00
A product of the Rangers youth system, Scott made a number of first-team appearances last term, mostly in the early part of the season. However he was unable to win a regular place in the line-up and in March he joined Portsmouth on loan with a view to a possible permanent transfer in the summer. A cool and calm defender, he impressed in his time at Fratton Park, showing himself to be quick in the tackle and providing a threat when he moved up for set pieces.
Glasgow R (From juniors on 1/7/1993) SL 41+6/1 SLC 6 SC 10+5 Others 7+3
Portsmouth (Loaned on 28/3/2002) FL 5

WILSON Stephen (Steve) Lee
Born: Hull, 24 April 1974
Height: 5'10" **Weight:** 10.12
After signing for Macclesfield at the start of the 2000-01 season Steve took over the 'keeper's jersey from Lee Martin at the beginning of September and remained first choice apart from a brief spell early in the new year when he was recovering from a badly gashed knee. An excellent shot stopper he kept Macc in the match on many occasions, well illustrated in the away wins at Kidderminster and Hartlepool. He was also the 'keeper in the FA Cup first round replay at Forest Green Rovers when he not only saved a spot kick in extra time, but helped his team to victory in what was a new record for a penalty shoot-out competition at senior level.
Hull C (From trainee on 13/7/1992) FL 180+1 FLC 13 FAC 13 Others 11+1
Macclesfield T (Free on 22/3/2001) FL 39 FAC 4 Others 1

WILTORD Sylvain
Born: Paris, France, 10 May 1974
Height: 5'9" **Weight:** 12.2
Club Honours: FAC '02; PL '02
International Honours: France: 42 (UEFA '00)
This young and bustling striker had another good season with and contributed a creditable tally of 17 goals for the Gunners. A member of the team that won a domestic double of the Premiership and the FA Cup, he faced disappointment at the World Cup finals when France were surprisingly eliminated at the first round group stage.
Arsenal (£13,000,000 from Bordeaux, France, ex Rennes, Girondins, on 31/8/2000) PL 43+17/18 FLC 4/4 FAC 11+2/8 Others 11+13/2

WINDASS Dean
Born: Hull, 1 April 1969
Height: 5'10" **Weight:** 12.6
This vastly experienced midfield spent a few days on loan at Sheffield Wednesday last term, but played jut two games before returning to Middlesbrough with an injury. He went straight back in the first-team squad for Boro' and although he made most of his appearances from the subs' bench he still showed himself to be a wholehearted player who knows no fear in his pursuit of goals.
Hull C (Free from North Ferriby on 24/10/1991) FL 173+3/57 FLC 11/4 FAC 7 Others 12/3
Aberdeen (£700,000 on 1/12/1995) SL 60+13/21 SLC 5+2/6 SC 7/3 Others 6/1
Oxford U (£475,000 on 6/8/1998) FL 33/15 FLC 2 FAC 3/3
Bradford C (£950,000 + on 5/3/1999) P/FL 64+10/16 FLC 6/2 FAC 2 Others 6/3
Middlesbrough (£600,000 + on 15/3/2001) PL 16+19/3 FLC 1 FAC 3+3
Sheffield Wed (Loaned on 6/12/2001) FL 2

WINDER Nathan James
Born: Barnsley, 17 February 1983
Height: 6'1" **Weight:** 12.5
This young Halifax Town trainee spent most of the 2001-02 campaign developing with the club's reserve team in the Avon Insurance League. He made one of the briefest senior appearances ever, when he came off the bench with only seconds remaining at Kidderminster in January. He is a promising defender who showed great improvement over the season.
Halifax T (Trainee) FL 0+1

WINSTANLEY Mark Andrew
Born: St Helens, 22 January 1968
Height: 6'1" **Weight:** 12.7
Club Honours: AMC '89
As very much the 'old head' in the Carlisle defence, Mark enjoyed a successful season in 2001-02. His ability to read the game combined with his aerial prowess made him a contender for 'Player of the Season'. One of his best performances was at Bristol Rovers where as captain for the day he led an injury-hit side to a battling goalless draw. Another fine display came against Torquay when he capped his defensive work with a superb headed goal late in the game to open the scoring.
Bolton W (From trainee on 22/7/1986) FL 215+5/3 FLC 19+1 FAC 19 Others 26/3
Burnley (Signed on 5/8/1994) FL 151+1/5 FLC 13 FAC 8 Others 8+1
Shrewsbury T (Loaned on 17/9/1998) FL 8

Preston NE (Free on 22/3/1999)
Shrewsbury T (Free on 22/7/1999) FL 32+1/1 FLC 2 FAC 1
Carlisle U (Free on 7/8/2000) FL 70+2/1 FLC 2 FAC 5+1 Others 1

WINTERBURN Nigel
Born: Nuneaton, 11 December 1963
Height: 5'9" **Weight:** 11.4
Club Honours: Div 1 '89, '91; PL '98; FAC '93, '98; FLC '93; ECWC '94; CS '98 '99
International Honours: E: 2; B-3; U21-1; Yth
Nigel remained as enthusiastic as ever for West Ham last term. Playing in the left-back role he was consistent and committed in every match. At the age of 38 he is a credit to the game and a role model for any youngster. Happily for Hammers fans he was reported to have signed a new deal for the club in the summer.
Birmingham C (From apprentice on 14/8/1981)
Wimbledon (Free on 22/9/1983) FL 164+1/8 FLC 13 FAC 12 Others 2
Arsenal (£407,000 on 26/5/1987) F/PL 429+11/8 FLC 49/3 FAC 47 Others 50+1/1
West Ham U (£250,000 on 5/7/2000) PL 62+2/1 FLC 3 FAC 7

WISE Dennis Frank
Born: Kensington, 15 December 1966
Height: 5'6" **Weight:** 10.10
Club Honours: FAC '88, '97, '00; FLC '98; ECWC '98; ESC '98; CS '00
International Honours: E: 21; B-3; U21-1
This inspirational midfielder never really settled into the midfield anchor role that he had been brought to Filbert Street to occupy. Although scoring with a glancing header against Liverpool, his famed passing touch seemed to be missing too often and he became another to suffer from long-term injury in January, being ruled out for the remainder of the season.
Wimbledon (From trainee at Southampton on 28/3/1985) FL 127+8/27 FLC 14 FAC 11/3 Others 5
Chelsea (£1,600,000 on 3/7/1990) F/PL 322+10/53 FLC 30/6 FAC 38/9 Others 44+1/8
Leicester C (£1,600,000 + on 23/6/2001) PL 15+2/1 FLC 1 FAC 1

WISE Stuart
Born: Middlesbrough, 4 April 1984
Height: 6'1" **Weight:** 13.2
This powerful central defender made his senior debut for York when coming on as a substitute at Luton in February and followed this up with his full debut in the

win at Swansea in April. He is one of a number of promising youngsters who have come through the youth ranks at Bootham Crescent and created a big impression with his strength and purpose.
York C (Trainee) FL 3+3

WISS Jarkko
Born: Finland, 17 April 1972
Height: 6'0" **Weight:** 12.8
International Honours: Finland: 35
This experienced midfielder found it hard to keep his place in the Stockport County first team last season, making just seven starts in all competitions. There was something lacking from his previous competitive displays and he made his final appearance on Boxing Day against Barnsley before moving on a free transfer to Hibernian.
Stockport Co (£350,000 from Moss FK, Norway, ex TPV Tampere, FF Jaro, HJK Helsinki, Molde, Lillestrom, on 10/8/2000) FL 34+7/6 FLC 1+2 FAC 3/1

WOAN Ian Simon
Born: Heswall, 14 December 1967
Height: 5'10" **Weight:** 12.4
Club Honours: Div 1 '98
Ian joined Shrewsbury Town on his return from a spell in the MLS with Columbus Crew. He made his debut against Scunthorpe in February, when his free kick provided the first goal, and found the net himself just a week later at Darlington. A vastly experienced midfield playmaker he is particularly effective with dead ball kicks and did enough to earn an extended contract at Gay Meadow.
Nottingham F (£80,000 from Runcorn on 14/3/1990) F/PL 189+32/31 FLC 15+3/1 FAC 20+1/6 Others 13/2
Barnsley (Free on 25/8/2000) FL 2+1 FLC 3
Swindon T (Free on 27/10/2000) FL 21+1/3 FAC 3 (Free to Columbus Crew, USA during 2001 close season)
Shrewsbury T (Free on 31/1/2002) FL 14/3

WOLLEASTON Robert Ainsley
Born: Perivale, 21 December 1979
Height: 5'11" **Weight:** 12.2
Robert spent the early part of the 2001-02 campaign on loan at Northampton where he featured in a handful of games, mostly from the subs' bench. A central midfield player of great potential, he then returned to Chelsea to continue his development in the club's reserve team.
Chelsea (From trainee on 3/6/1998) PL 0+1 FLC 0+1
Bristol Rov (Loaned on 23/3/2000) FL 0+4
Portsmouth (Loaned on 8/3/2001) FL 5+1

Northampton T (Loaned on 4/7/2001) FL 2+5 FLC 0+1

WOOD Jamie
Born: Salford, 21 September 1978
Height: 5'10" **Weight:** 13.0
International Honours: Cayman Islands: 2
This hard-working young striker joined Halifax Town during the 2001 close season and featured fairly regularly during the first half of the 2001-02 campaign. He scored his only goal in the 2-1 home win over Farnborough Town in the FA Cup but was red carded at Oxford United in December and did not start a game thereafter. He finished the season as leading scorer for Town's reserves.
Manchester U (From trainee on 10/7/1997)
Hull C (Free on 21/7/1999) FL 15+32/6 FLC 2+3 FAC 3+2/1 Others 2+1
Halifax T (Free on 10/8/2001) FL 10+6 FLC 1 FAC 1/1 Others 0+1

WOOD Leigh James
Born: York, 21 May 1983
Height: 6'1" **Weight:** 11.2
This highly rated young York City midfielder established himself in the line-up during the closing weeks of the 2001-02 season as the Third Division side climbed away from the relegation zone. He is a very assured and collected player who reads the game well and uses the ball to great effect, and a very bright future is predicted for him.
York C (From trainee on 7/3/2002) FL 16+3

WOODGATE Jonathan Simon
Born: Middlesbrough, 22 January 1980
Height: 6'2" **Weight:** 13.0
Club Honours: FAYC '97
International Honours: E: 1; U21-1; Yth
Jonathan has made a huge impact at first-team level for Leeds United since developing through the ranks but his career over the last two seasons has been blighted by a series of well-publicised off-the-field matters. It was not until last December that he returned to first-team action at Elland Road and then he was unfortunate to pick up a leg injury at Chelsea in January, forcing him to miss the next seven games. On his return this cultured defender looked as if he had never been away, but another non-football related incident caused him to miss the last four games of the season. Hopefully he can put his problems behind him in 2002-03 and turn all his attention to his football career.
Leeds U (From trainee on 13/5/1997) PL 82+4/4 FLC 6 FAC 10 Others 16

WOODHOUSE Curtis
Born: Beverley, 17 April 1980
Height: 5'8" **Weight:** 11.0
International Honours: E: U21-4; Yth
Curtis' combative qualities added aggression to the Birmingham City midfield but he was often in-and-out of the team. He kept going for the whole 90 minutes and did things simply when on the ball. He failed to dislodge Bryan Hughes and Darren Carter from the central midfield roles towards the end of the campaign, but did a good job filling in wide on the left in tough away matches.
Sheffield U (From trainee on 31/12/1997) FL 92+12/7 FLC 5+3 FAC 10
Birmingham C (£1,000,000 on 2/2/2001) FL 35+10/2 FLC 2+1 FAC 1 Others 2

WOODMAN Andrew (Andy) John
Born: Camberwell, 11 August 1971
Height: 6'3" **Weight:** 13.7
Club Honours: Div 3 '99
Andy began the 2001-02 campaign as Colchester United's number one goalkeeper, starting the first 26 League games, but he was dropped for the visit to Tranmere in January and did not play for the U's again. He subsequently joined Oxford United on loan before making a permanent move on transfer deadline day. An infectious, chirpy character he boosted the atmosphere around the dressing room at the Kassam Stadium and also proved to be an excellent shot stopper with a safe pair of hands.
Crystal Palace (From trainee on 1/7/1989)
Exeter C (Free on 4/7/1994) FL 6 FLC 1 FAC 1 Others 2
Northampton T (Free on 10/3/1995) FL 163 FLC 13 FAC 8 Others 13
Brentford (Signed on 22/1/1999) FL 61 FLC 1 FAC 2 Others 3
Southend U (Loaned on 8/8/2000) FL 17 FLC 2
Colchester U (Free on 10/11/2000) FL 54 FLC 2 FAC 2 Others 1
Oxford U (Free on 18/1/2002) FL 15

WOODMAN Craig Alan
Born: Tiverton, 22 December 1982
Height: 5'9" **Weight:** 9.11
Craig continued to make steady progress at Bristol City last season and made a handful of senior appearances at wing back. He produced some exciting performances and is clearly a highly promising prospect. He will be hoping to feature more regularly at Ashton Gate in 2002-03.

Bristol C (From trainee on 17/2/2000) FL 6+2 Others 4

WOODS Stephen (Steve) John
Born: Northwich, 15 December 1976
Height: 5'11" **Weight:** 12.3
This experienced defender signed at the start of last season to bolster Torquay's back line. Although occasionally used as a full back, his best performances were as the middle of three centre backs where his organisational skills and good positional sense were put to best use.
Stoke C (From trainee on 3/8/1995) FL 33+1 FLC 2 FAC 2 Others 2
Plymouth Arg (Loaned on 26/3/1998) FL 4+1
Chesterfield (Free on 7/7/1999) FL 22+3 FLC 4 Others 0+1
Torquay U (Free on 17/8/2001) FL 38/2 FLC 1 FAC 1

WOODTHORPE Colin John
Born: Ellesmere Port, 13 January 1969
Height: 5'11" **Weight:** 11.8
Stockport County's left-sided utility player once again showed his true professionalism last season when called upon to play in either a defensive or midfield role. With the departure of Mike Flynn in March, Colin became the club's longest serving player, but following the arrival of Martin Pemberton from Mansfield shortly after the end of the season he was told he no longer figured in Carlton Palmer's first-team plans and was made available on a free transfer.
Chester C (From trainee on 23/8/1986) FL 154+1/6 FLC 10 FAC 8+1 Others 18/1
Norwich C (£175,000 on 17/7/1990) P/FL 36+7/1 FLC 0+2 FAC 6 Others 1+1
Aberdeen (£400,000 on 20/7/1994) SL 43+5/1 SLC 5+1/1 SC 4 Others 5+2
Stockport Co (£200,000 on 29/7/1997) FL 114+39/4 FLC 12+1/2 FAC 4+1/1

WOODWARD Andrew (Andy) Stephen
Born: Stockport, 23 September 1973
Height: 5'11" **Weight:** 13.6
Club Honours: Div 2 '97
This versatile defender joined Halifax Town during the 2001 close season and it was hoped that his experience and know-how would lead to brighter things. He made the majority of his appearances at right back but never seemed comfortable in that position. However, once he switched to his preferred central role he excelled and even managed a goal against Carlisle United on Good Friday.
Crewe Alex (From trainee on 29/7/1992) FL 9+11 FLC 2 Others 0+3

Bury (Signed on 13/3/1995) FL 95+20/1 FLC 6+2 FAC 6+1 Others 5
Sheffield U (£35,000 on 23/3/2000) FL 2+1 FLC 1
Scunthorpe U (Loaned on 22/9/2000) FL 9
Scunthorpe U (Loaned on 22/12/2000) FL 3
Halifax T (Free on 3/7/2001) FL 29+1/1 FLC 1 FAC 2

WOOLLEY Matthew (Matt) David
Born: Manchester, 22 February 1982
Height: 5'10" **Weight:** 11.2
Matt is a speedy attacking midfielder who featured mainly in the Macclesfield reserve side in 2001-02. He shared the captaincy of the team, contributing several spectacular goals and deservedly gaining the 'Reserve Team Player of the Year' award. His senior appearances were all from the subs' bench but he will be hoping to win a place in the starting line-up in 2002-03.
Macclesfield T (From trainee at Stockport Co on 19/7/1999) FL 1+4 Others 1+1

WOOTER Nordin
Born: Surinam, 24 August 1976
Height: 5'8" **Weight:** 11.1
International Honours: Holland: U21-15
Nordin, a busy and skilful right winger, had a run of games for the Watford first team in the early part of the 2001-02 season. The fans appreciated his ability to beat players and cross accurately, but he ultimately came to be regarded as too much of a free spirit to benefit the team as a whole. Certainly his failure to score more than once was disappointing. In December, he was made available for transfer, and in January he underwent a cartilage operation, before being granted a free transfer at the end of the season.
Watford (£975,000 from Real Zaragoza, Spain, ex Ajax, on 14/9/1999) P/FL 37+26/3 FLC 4+2 FAC 1

WOOZLEY David (Dave) James
Born: Ascot, 6 December 1979
Height: 6'0" **Weight:** 12.10
Signed on loan from Crystal Palace, Dave looked a class act for Torquay with a series of cool, assured performances on the left of a three-centre-back system. His most memorable moment was crashing a 25-yarder against the bar in a televised cup game with Spurs. The Gulls were very keen to keep hold of him, but he decided to return to Selhurst Park after two months to fight for a first-team spot. After Palace decided to release him, it was a pleasant surprise when Torquay

secured his permanent return on deadline day.
Crystal Palace (From trainee on 17/11/1997) FL 21+9 FLC 3+1 FAC 0+1
Bournemouth (Loaned on 15/9/2000) FL 6
Torquay U (Loaned on 28/8/2001) FL 12 FLC 1
Torquay U (Free on 27/3/2002) FL 3+1

WORMULL Simon James
Born: Crawley, 1 December 1976
Height: 5'10" **Weight:** 12.8
Simon's frustrating spell with Rushden came to an end last October when he moved to Stevenage Borough at the same time as Jean-Michel Sigere. In the space of 18 months, the right-sided midfielder made less than 30 appearances for Diamonds and hardly featured in the first season in the Football League.
Tottenham H (From trainee on 1/7/1995)
Brentford (Free on 14/7/1997) FL 3+2 FLC 1+1 Others 1
Brighton & Hove A (Free on 25/3/1998. Free to Dover Ath on 5/11/1998)
Rushden & Diamonds (Free on 17/3/2000) FL 4+1 FLC 0+1

WORRELL David
Born: Dublin, 12 January 1978
Height: 5'11" **Weight:** 12.4
Club Honours: Div 3 '02
International Honours: RoI: U21-17
David was still recovering from a broken ankle at the start of the 2001-02 season, however, it was not long before he returned to the Plymouth line-up at right back. His consistency, strong defensive skills and excellent positioning helped ensure that Argyle only conceded 28 goals in 46 League games. He produced some good link-up play with the midfield and his forward runs resulted in many goal-scoring opportunities.
Blackburn Rov (Signed from Shelbourne on 12/1/1995)
Dundee U (Free on 30/3/1999) SL 13+4 SLC 2
Plymouth Arg (Signed on 23/11/2000) FL 56 FAC 4 Others 3

WOTTON Paul Anthony
Born: Plymouth, 17 August 1977
Height: 5'11" **Weight:** 12.0
Club Honours: Div 3 '02
Paul enjoyed by far his best season at Plymouth in 2001-02 when he established a formidable centre back partnership with Graham Coughlan. He was always available as an outlet for his team-mates when bringing the ball out of defence, while his passing skills, defensive positioning and strength in the air were

David Wright

all key attributes. A dead-ball specialist he notched six vital goals including a spectacular 40-yard effort into the top right-hand corner against Carlisle in April. He was rewarded for a tremendous season by being voted into the PFA Division Three team of the year by his fellow professionals.
Plymouth Arg (From trainee on 10/7/1995) FL 178+20/12 FLC 6 FAC 16/2 Others 7+1/2

WRACK Darren
Born: Cleethorpes, 5 May 1976
Height: 5'9" **Weight:** 12.10
Darren began the 2001-02 season on the transfer list at Walsall, but forced his way back into the first team through his tireless efforts. He netted goals at Bolton and Burnley in the space of five days in September and was rarely out of the side after that. Although playing mainly in midfield he also gave useful displays up front and in defence when required. Still only 26, he is one of the experienced players around whom the Saddlers are hoping to build an established First Division team.
Derby Co (From trainee on 12/7/1994) FL 4+22/1 FLC 0+3 FAC 0+2
Grimsby T (£100,000 + on 19/7/1996) FL 5+8/1 Others 0+1
Shrewsbury T (Loaned on 17/2/1997) FL 3+1 Others 1
Walsall (Free on 6/8/1998) FL 131+30/25 FLC 9/1 FAC 8+1/1 Others 7+1/1

WRIGHT Alan Geoffrey
Born: Ashton under Lyne, 28 September 1971
Height: 5'4" **Weight:** 9.9
Club Honours: FLC '96
International Honours: E: U21-2; Yth; Sch
Alan is a small and pacy left back who featured regularly early on for Aston Villa last season, passing the landmark figure of 300 starting appearances. However he was kept out of the side by youngster JLloyd Samuel in the new year and rarely even made it to the subs' bench after that.
Blackpool (From trainee on 13/4/1989) FL 91+7 FLC 10+2 FAC 8 Others 11+2
Blackburn Rov (£400,000 on 25/10/1991) F/PL 67+7/1 FLC 8 FAC 5+1 Others 3
Aston Villa (£1,000,000 on 10/3/1995) PL 246+4/5 FLC 19 FAC 24 Others 25

WRIGHT David
Born: Warrington, 1 May 1980
Height: 5'11" **Weight:** 10.8
International Honours: E: Yth
This young Crewe defender missed the

start of the 2001-02 campaign due to injury and it was not until the end of September that he returned to the starting line-up. He soon re-established himself in the side and featured at right back for the remainder of the season.
Crewe Alex (From trainee on 18/6/1997) FL 135+5/1 FLC 7+1 FAC 7

WRIGHT Jermaine Malaki
Born: Greenwich, 21 October 1975
Height: 5'9" **Weight:** 11.9
International Honours: E: Yth
In the 2000-01 season Jermaine tended to be used as the wide midfield player in a 4-4-2 formation for Ipswich, but the arrival of Finidi George meant that he had to move to a central midfield role, which many felt to be his better position. Last season, however, opponents took more notice of him – even man-marking him in some games, which considerably reduced his effectiveness. He missed the last month of the campaign after undergoing a hernia operation.
Millwall (From trainee on 27/11/1992)
Wolverhampton W (£60,000 on 29/12/1994) FL 4+16 FLC 1+3/1 Others 0+1
Doncaster Rov (Loaned on 1/3/1996) FL 13
Crewe Alex (£25,000 on 19/2/1998) FL 47+2/5 FLC 5 FAC 1
Ipswich T (£500,000 on 23/7/1999) P/FL 80+20/4 FLC 10+2 FAC 4+1/1 Others 5+1

WRIGHT Peter David
Born: Preston, 15 August 1982
Height: 5'8" **Weight:** 11.2
This diminutive striker earned himself a 12-month contract with Halifax Town after impressing during the 2001 pre-season. He was not often handed the chance to impress and most of his appearances came from the subs' bench, but nonetheless the youngster kept working hard at his game.
Halifax T (Free from trainee at Newcastle U on 2/8/2001) FL 3+11 FLC 0+1 FAC 0+2

WRIGHT Richard Ian
Born: Ipswich, 5 November 1977
Height: 6'2" **Weight:** 13.0
Club Honours: FAC '02; PL '02
International Honours: E: 2; U21-15; Yth; Sch
Richard made a competent start to his career at Highbury last term when he was essentially the back-up 'keeper to David Seaman. He made his Premiership debut in the 3-1 win over Manchester United last November and always performed competently when called on.
Ipswich T (From trainee on 2/1/1995) P/FL

240 FLC 27 FAC 13 Others 11
Arsenal (£6,000,000 on 13/7/2001) PL 12 FLC 1 FAC 5 Others 4

WRIGHT Stephen (Steve) John
Born: Liverpool, 8 February 1980
Height: 6'2" **Weight:** 12.0
Club Honours: UEFAC '01
International Honours: E: U21-6; Yth
Liverpool's outstanding young prospect at right back made excellent progress last season starting in 14 games and coming on as substitute in three more. He scored his first ever goal for the Reds against Borussia Dortmund in the Champions' League, when he arrived undetected in the penalty area, and later in the campaign he enjoyed a run of seven consecutive starts before returning to the reserves. He also remained a regular for England at U21 level.
Liverpool (From trainee on 13/10/1997) PL 10+4 FLC 1+1 FAC 2 Others 2+1/1
Crewe Alex (Loaned on 6/8/1999) FL 17+6 FLC 1

WRIGHT Thomas (Tommy)
Born: Kirby Muxloe, 28 September 1984
Height: 6'0" **Weight:** 11.12
A prolific striker with Leicester City's academy teams, Tommy gained valuable experience when appearing as a substitute in the closing minutes of the home defeat by Leeds United in March. Having had a taste of first-team action, he will be looking to make rapid progress through the ranks in 2002-03.
Leicester C (Trainee) PL 0+1

WRIGHT-PHILLIPS Shaun Cameron
Born: Greenwich, 25 October 1981
Height: 5'6" **Weight:** 10.1
Club Honours: Div 1 '02
International Honours: E: U21-1
2001-02 proved to be a memorable campaign for Shaun in more ways than one. This will be a season Shaun won't forget in a hurry. He won a First Division championship medal, gained his first England U21 cap and became a father. The small midfielder finally claimed a regular first-team spot at Manchester City and went on to feature in well over half of the Blues' games after a patchy start to the season. A speedy player who can turn on a proverbial sixpence, he linked up well with his colleagues in midfield and contributed eight valuable goals. He is the son of former England striker Ian Wright.
Manchester C (From trainee on 28/10/1998) P/FL 42+12/8 FLC 4+3 FAC 3

Steve Yates

XYZ

XAVIER Abel
Born: Mozambique, 30 November 1972
Height: 6'2" **Weight:** 13.6
International Honours: Portugal: 20; U21; Yth (UEFA-U16 '89; U18 '90)
After an injury-plagued two seasons at Everton, this experienced defender declined the offer of a new contract and was surprisingly sold to local rivals Liverpool in the new year. Pitched into the Reds' first team at Ipswich he couldn't believe his good fortune when he scored his first ever goal in English football. He remained a regular performer at right or left back until the end of the season, scoring another important goal in the second leg of the Champions' League quarter-final against Bayer Leverkusen.
Everton (£1,500,000 from PSV Eindhoven, Holland on 8/9/1999) PL 39+4 FLC 2 FAC 4
Liverpool (£800,000 on 31/1/2002) PL 9+1/1 Others 5/1

YATES Mark Jason
Born: Birmingham, 24 January 1970
Height: 5'11" **Weight:** 13.2
Club Honours: NC '99
International Honours: E: SP-2
Mark was once again an influential figure in the centre of Cheltenham Town's midfield during the 2001-02 campaign. Strong in the tackle and seemingly capable of running all day, he contributed several important goals during the season. He also took over as team captain in the absence of the injured Chris Banks. Highlights during his campaign included the FA Cup win over his former club Burnley and a visit to the Hawthorns for a fifth round tie in the same competition.
Birmingham C (From trainee on 8/7/1988) FL 38+16/6 FLC 5/1 FAC 0+2 Others 5
Burnley (£40,000 on 30/8/1991) FL 9+9/1 FLC 1 FAC 0+2 Others 2+1
Lincoln C (Loaned on 19/2/1993) FL 10+4
Doncaster Rov (Signed on 30/7/1993) FL 33+1/4 FLC 2 FAC 1 Others 1 (Transferred to Kidderminster Hrs on 13/8/1994)
Cheltenham T (Signed on 28/1/1999) FL 136/15 FLC 5 FAC 9 Others 6+1

YATES Stephen (Steve)
Born: Bristol, 29 January 1970
Height: 5'11" **Weight:** 12.2
Club Honours: Div 3 '90
Steve was again a near ever present at right back in the Tranmere defence last season. Always commanding and unflappable, he continued to be effective in the air when under pressure, and although invaluable at the back, he relished any chance to go forward, contributing four goals. He is one of the most popular players at Prenton Park, but with his contract due to end in the summer his future was uncertain.
Bristol Rov (From trainee on 1/7/1988) FL 196+1 FLC 9 FAC 11 Others 21
Queens Park R (£650,000 on 16/8/1993) P/FL 122+12/2 FLC 8 FAC 7
Tranmere Rov (Free on 5/8/1999) FL 109+4/7 FLC 13+1/2 FAC 10/5

[YORDI] GONZALEZ DIAZ Jorge
Born: Cadiz, Spain, 14 September 1974
Height: 6'1" **Weight:** 13.0
This big striker joined Blackburn on loan in the week preceding the Worthington Cup final and made his debut in the second half. His bustling display, in typical old-fashioned centre forward style, earned him good reviews, while the way he held the ball up and his power in the air marked him out as a useful addition. He struggled afterwards but he was always going to be behind Matt Jansen and Andy Cole.
Blackburn Rov (Loaned from Real Zaragoza, Spain, ex Saville, Atletico Madrid, on 22/2/2002) PL 5+3/2 FLC 0+1

YORKE Dwight
Born: Canaan, Tobago, 3 November 1971
Height: 5'10" **Weight:** 12.4
Club Honours: FLC '96; FAC '99; PL '99, '00, '01; EC '99
International Honours: Trinidad & Tobago
A talented athlete with great balance and a wonderful left-foot shot, Dwight failed to establish himself in the Manchester United team last season and made only sporadic appearances in the Premiership and Champions' League. Manager Sir Alex Ferguson had plenty of attacking options, and Dwight was often overlooked unless a touch of experience was called for. His only goal came in the clash with struggling Leicester City in November, while there was much unsettling media coverage over a possible transfer out of Old Trafford, although nothing materialised.
Aston Villa (£120,000 from Signal Hill, Tobago on 19/12/1989) F/PL 195+36/73 FLC 20+2/8 FAC 22+2/13 Others 10/3
Manchester U (£12,600,000 on 22/8/1998) PL 80+16/48 FLC 3/2 FAC 6+5/3 Others 31+11/12

YOUNG Alan James
Born: Swindon, 12 August 1983
Height: 5'6" **Weight:** 10.2
International Honours: E: Yth
Alan missed much of the first half of the 2001-02 season for Swindon as a result of an ankle injury that required surgery. The return of manager Andy King coincided with his regaining fitness and he eventually made his full League debut in the home victory over Port Vale in March. The highlight of his season was surely netting the only goal of the game for the winner in the home victory over Blackpool. He is a slightly built young striker who is always willing to get into the action.
Swindon T (From trainee on 30/10/2000) FL 7+11/1 FAC 0+3/1 Others 1

YOUNG Luke Paul
Born: Harlow, 19 July 1979
Height: 6'0" **Weight:** 12.4
Club Honours: FLC '99
International Honours: E: U21-16; Yth
Signed during the summer of 2001, Luke was used throughout the season as an orthodox right back or right wing back depending on the system Charlton were playing. He is very confident on the ball, a good tackler and able to put in an accurate cross from the by-line. He also possesses a long throw, which was put into good use in the latter part of the season. Luke made four further England U21 appearances during the campaign and is a good prospect for the future.
Tottenham H (From trainee on 3/7/1997) PL 44+14 FLC 1+3 FAC 9+2 Others 2+1
Charlton Ath (£3,000,000 + on 27/7/2001) PL 34 FLC 3 FAC 1

YOUNG Neil Anthony
Born: Harlow, 31 August 1973
Height: 5'9" **Weight:** 12.0
Neil recovered from a nightmare 17 months to make a surprise return to the Bournemouth side against Brighton last term after just a 45-minute run out in the reserves. He kept his place in the side and was appointed captain when Eddie Howe moved to Portsmouth. An enthusiastic right back who likes to get forward he was offered a new one-year contract in the summer.
Tottenham H (From trainee on 17/8/1991)
Bournemouth (Free on 11/10/1994) FL 257+3/3 FLC 19 FAC 16 Others 15

YOUNG Scott
Born: Pontypridd, 14 January 1976
Height: 6'2" **Weight:** 12.6
International Honours: W: B-1; U21-5
Scott was among Cardiff's most consistent performers last term and

battled on despite a persistent and niggling groin strain. The Bluebirds' longest serving player had many highlights: scoring the winner against Leeds United in the FA Cup, earning a Wales call-up (although he was only on the bench against Czech Republic) and signing a new two-year contract.
Cardiff C (From trainee on 4/7/1994) FL 246+19/21 FLC 13+1/1 FAC 20/2 Others 17+3/1

YOUNGS Thomas (Tom)
Anthony John
Born: Bury St Edmunds, 31 August 1979
Height: 5'9" **Weight:** 10.4
Cambridge's longest-serving player finished the 2001-02 campaign as the club's leading scorer for the second season in succession. He is a hard working and unselfish striker and should do well against Third Division defences in 2002-03.
Cambridge U (From juniors on 3/7/1997) FL 87+28/33 FLC 1+3 FAC 4/1 Others 7+3/1

ZABEK Lee Kevin
Born: Bristol, 13 October 1978
Height: 6'0" **Weight:** 12.0
This combative midfield player found it difficult to break into the Exeter City line-up last term and made just two senior appearances, both in the early weeks of the season. Although released by the

Bobby Zamora

Grecians in the summer, his experience and undoubted skill should ensure that he is able to find another club for the 2002-03 campaign.

Bristol Rov (From trainee on 28/7/1997) FL 21+8/1 FLC 2 FAC 2+1/1 Others 4
Exeter C (Free on 10/8/2000) FL 28+5 FLC 2 FAC 1

ZAMORA Robert (Bobby)
Lester
Born: Barking, 16 January 1981
Height: 6'0" **Weight:** 11.0
Club Honours: Div 3 '01; Div 2 '02
International Honours: E: U21-3
Bobby had another superb season with Brighton last term and created a piece of history when he became the first Albion player to hit 30 goals in a season twice. His tally included a hat trick against Cambridge and a new club record when he scored in ten consecutive appearances. He rounded the campaign off in style with the Albion 'Player of the Season' awards, selection for the PFA Second Division representative side and also as the 'Fans' PFA Division Two Player of the Year'. He finished as leading goal-scorer in the Nationwide League for the second successive season and won selection for England at U21 level, making his debut against Portugal in April and featuring in the European Championship finals in the summer.

Bristol Rov (From trainee on 1/7/1999) FL 0+4 FLC 0+1 FAC 0+1
Brighton & Hove A (Loaned on 11/2/2000) FL 6/6
Brighton & Hove A (£100,000 on 10/8/2000) FL 82+2/56 FLC 4/2 FAC 5/4 Others 1/1

ZAMPERINI Alessandro
Born: Rome, Italy, 15 August 1982
Height: 6'2" **Weight:** 12.8
This young central defender joined Portsmouth from Roma last July after becoming a free agent as a result of a registration error by the Italian club. Tall and well built, he had previously been on trial at West Ham when Harry Redknapp signed him for Pompey. He showed himself to be skilful in the tackle and also netted two goals, but lost his place after the 5-0 defeat at West Bromwich Albion.

Portsmouth (Free from AS Roma, Italy on 12/7/2001) FL 16/2 FLC 1

ZAVAGNO Luciano
Born: Rosario, Argentina, 6 August 1977
Height: 6'0" **Weight:** 12.0
Luciano joined Derby County last October and quickly established himself as a

regular in the line-up on the left-hand side of the defence. He held his place in the team until the closing stages of the campaign when he lost out to Richard Jackson.

Derby Co (Signed from ES Troyes, France, ex Santa Fe, Strasbourg, on 19/10/2001) PL 26 FAC 1

ZENDEN Boudewijn
Born: Maastricht, Holland, 15 August 1976
Height: 5'9" **Weight:** 11.5
International Honours: Holland: 36
After being trailed for two years, this top-class winger became Chelsea's second summer signing from Barcelona, following in the footsteps of Emmanuel Petit. He grabbed the headlines in a four-day period in early August; firstly by running the English defence ragged in Holland's 2-0 victory at White Hart Lane and then scoring Chelsea's first goal of the season – albeit slightly fortunately - in his English debut against Newcastle United. The Chelsea crowd warmed immediately to his wing wizardry, particularly his 'Cruyff-turn' developed by his illustrious compatriot a generation earlier. However, his season was severely interrupted when he picked up a nasty groin injury but he reappeared in time to feature in the FA Cup semi-final against Fulham prior to making a brief appearance from the subs' bench in the final.

Chelsea (£7,500,000 from Barcelona, Spain, ex PSV Eindhoven, on 10/8/2001) PL 13+9/3 FLC 2+2 FAC 0+3 Others 3

ZHIYI Fan
Born: Shanghai, China, 6 November 1969
Height: 6'2" **Weight:** 12.1
International Honours: China: 106
This excellent central defender played in the opening games of the 2001-02 season for Crystal Palace before returning to China for his country's World Cup qualifying matches. Soon after his return he was sold to Scottish club Dundee for a substantial fee. At his best he is a superb defender – pacy, hard working and with excellent passing skills.

Crystal Palace (£500,000 from Shanghai, China on 10/9/1998) FL 87+1/4 FLC 11/2 FAC 3

ZIEGE Christian
Born: Germany, 1 February 1972
Height: 6'1" **Weight:** 12.12
Club Honours: FLC '01
International Honours: Germany: 71 (UEFA '96)
This towering defender did all his talking on the pitch last term and notched up an impressive six goals during the season.

Christian became a firm favourite at White Hart Lane, providing a real presence in the team. Composed on the ball with incredible pace and a powerful strike, he commanded the back line at Spurs, adding some much needed steel and determination.

Middlesbrough (£4,000,000 from AC Milan, Italy, ex Bayern Munich, on 6/8/1999) PL 29/6 FLC 3+1/1 FAC 1
Liverpool (£5,500,000 on 29/8/2000) PL 11+5/1 FLC 1+3/1 FAC 2+1 Others 6+3
Tottenham H (£4,000,000 on 1/8/2001) PL 27/5 FLC 4/1 FAC 2/1

ZOLA Gianfranco (Franco)
Born: Sardinia Italy, 5 July 1966
Height: 5'6" **Weight:** 10.10
Club Honours: FAC '97, '00; FLC '98; ECWC '98; ESC '98; CS '00
International Honours: Italy: 35
If one special moment encapsulates the remarkable Franco Zola it came in the FA Cup third round replay against Norwich City last January. He scored a wonderful goal and with a humble gesture typical of this extraordinary man dedicated the goal to an eight-year-old fan, Matthew Aston, who had tragically died shortly before from a brain tumour. The 2001-02 season has been a glorious 'Indian Summer' to Franco's illustrious career as he nears the veteran stage. He often played in the 'hole' behind the two front-runners where his probing and elusive dribbling skills created havoc for opposing defences. He appeared in his third Chelsea FA Cup final and in the post-match 'gloom' immediately lifted everybody at the club by pledging one more year as a player before moving to a coaching role.

Chelsea (£4,500,000 from Parma, Italy, ex Napoli, Torres, Nuorese, on 15/11/1996) PL 155+36/45 FLC 7+3/1 FAC 25+3/9 Others 35+2/9

ZUNIGA Yanez Herlin **Ysrael**
Born: Lima, Peru, 27 August 1976
Height: 5'10" **Weight:** 11.5
International Honours: Peru: 15
The former South American 'Golden Boot' winner made only a handful of appearances for Coventry City last term, all but one of them as a substitute. The diminutive striker rarely looked ready to stake a claim for a first-team place and had a disappointing game in his only start against West Brom in April. He spent a short while on trial with a club in China in the spring before returning to Highfield Road.

Coventry C (£750,000 from FCB Melgar, Peru on 3/3/2000) P/FL 11+18/3 FLC 2/1

Boudewijn Zenden

FA Barclaycard Premiership and Nationwide League Clubs
Summary of Appearances and Goals for 2001-2002.

KEY TO TABLES: P/FL = Premier Football League. FLC = Football League Cup. FAC = FA Cup. Others = Other first team appearances.
Left hand figures in each column list number of full appearances + appearances as substitute. Right hand figures list number of goals scored.

ARSENAL (PREM: 1st)

Player	P/FL App	Goals	FLC App	Goals	FAC App	Goals	Others App	Goals
ADAMS Tony	10				3	1		
ALLIADIERE Jeremie	0 + 1		0 + 2					
BERGKAMP Dennis	22 +11	9	1		4 + 2	3	3 + 3	2
CAMPBELL Sol	29 + 2	2			7	1	10	
COLE Ashley	29	2			4		6 + 1	
DIXON Lee	3 +10				2 + 2		2	
EDU	8 + 6	1	3	1	4 + 1	1	2 + 3	
GRIMANDI Giles	11 +15		2		1 + 3		5 + 3	
HALLS John			0 + 3					
HENRY Thierry	31 + 2	24			4 + 1	1	11	7
INAMOTO Junichi			2				0 + 2	
ITONGA Carlin			0 + 1					
JEFFERS Francis	2 + 4	2	1		1 + 1		0 + 2	
JUAN			1		1			
KANU Nwankwo	9 +14	3	2	1	3 + 2	2	4 + 5	
KEOWN Martin	21 + 1		2		3 + 1		4 + 2	
LAUREN	27	2			3		11	
LJUNGBERG Freddie	24 + 1	12			5	2	8 + 1	3
LUZHNY Oleg	15 + 3		1		4		3	
PARLOUR Ray	25 + 2		1		2 + 2	2	5 + 3	
PENNANT Jermaine			3				0 + 2	
PIRES Robert	27 + 1	9			3 + 2	1	12	3
RICKETTS Rohan			0 + 1					
SEAMAN David	17				1		7	
STEPANOVS Igors	6		2 + 1		1		3 + 1	
SVARD Sebastian			0 + 1					
TAVLARIDIS Efstathios			3					
TAYLOR Stuart	9 + 1		2		1		1 + 1	
UPSON Matthew	10 + 4		1		0 + 1		5 + 1	
VAN BRONCKHORST Giovanni	13 + 8	1	3		2		6 + 1	
VIEIRA Patrick	35 + 1	2			7		11	1
WILTORD Sylvain	23 +10	10	3	4	6 + 1	2	9 + 2	1
WRIGHT Richard	12		1		5		4	

ASTON VILLA (PREM: 8th)

Player	P/FL App	Goals	FLC App	Goals	FAC App	Goals	Others App	Goals
ALPAY	14		2				8	
ANGEL Juan Pablo	26 + 3	12	1		1		2 + 2	4
BALABAN Bosko	0 + 8		1 + 1				1	
BARRY Gareth	16 + 4				0 + 1		6 + 1	
BOATENG George	37		1 + 1		1		8	
CROUCH Peter	7	2						
DELANEY Mark	30		1				8	
DUBLIN Dion	9 +12	4	1 + 1	1	3		5 + 2	1
ENCKELMAN Peter	9						4 + 1	
GINOLA David	0 + 5		1 + 1				3 + 3	2
HADJI Moustapha	17 + 6	2	2		0 + 1		3 + 3	1
HENDRIE Lee	25 + 4	2	2		1		7	2
HITZLSPERGER Thomas	11 + 1	1	1					
KACHLOUL Hassan	17 + 5	2	2				2	
MELLBERG Olof	32				1		2	
MERSON Paul	18 + 3	2			1		5	1
SAMUEL Jlloyd	17 + 6				1		0 + 2	
SCHMEICHEL Peter	29	1	1		1		4	
STAUNTON Steve	30 + 3		2		1		2	
STONE Steve	14 + 8	1	1		0 + 1		5 + 3	
TAYLOR Ian	7 + 9	3	1		1	1		
VASSELL Darius	30 + 6	12	0 + 1		1		2 + 4	2
WRIGHT Alan	23		1		1		7	

BARNSLEY (DIV 1: 23rd)

Player	P/FL App	Goals	FLC App	Goals	FAC App	Goals	Others App	Goals
BARKER Chris	43 + 1	3	3		2			
BARNARD Darren	34 + 4	7	2 + 1		2	1		
BEDEAU Tony	0 + 3							
BERTOS Leo	2 + 2				0 + 1			
BETSY Kevin	10							
CHETTLE Steve	31 + 1		1		2			
CHRISTIE Jeremy	0 + 1				0 + 1			
CORBO Mateo	0 + 1							
CROOKS Lee	20 + 6		2		1			
DONOVAN Kevin	28 + 4	1	2 + 1		2			
DYER Bruce	42 + 2	14	3	3	2	1		
FALLON Rory	2 + 7		1					
FLYNN Mike	7							
GALLEN Kevin	8 + 1	2	0 + 1					
GHENT Matthew	1							
GIBBS Paul	4							
GORRE Dean	14 + 5	2	2					
JONES Gary	25	1						
JONES Lee	2 +11		1 + 1	1	0 + 1			
KAY Antony	0 + 1							
LUMSDON Chris	32	7	1		1			
McSWEGAN Gary	1 + 4							
MARRIOTT Andy	17 + 1		1					
MILLER Kevin	28		2		2			
MORGAN Chris	42	4	3		2			
MULLIGAN David	27 + 1				2			
NAYLOR Richard	7 + 1							
NEIL Alex	17 + 8	2	2 + 1		1			
O'CALLAGHAN Brian	1 + 5							
OSTER John	2							
PARKIN Jon	4		1					
RANKIN Izzy	2 + 7	1	0 + 1		1			
REGAN Carl	6 + 4		2					
SAND Peter	4 + 2	1	1		0 + 1			
SCOTHERN Ashley	0 + 1							
SHERON Mike	23 +10	12	1 + 1		2			
TINKLER Eric	8 + 8		1	1	1			
WARD Mitch	12 + 3		1		1			

BIRMINGHAM CITY (DIV 1: 5th)

Player	P/FL App	Goals	FLC App	Goals	FAC App	Goals	Others App	Goals
BAK Arek	2 + 2				1			
BENNETT Ian	18				1			
BRAGSTAD Bjorn Otto	3							
BURROWS David	9 + 3		1 + 1		1			
CARTER Darren	12 + 1	1					1 + 1	
DEVLIN Paul	11 + 2	1					2	
EADEN Nicky	24 + 5	1	3					
FERRARI Carlos	0 + 4							
FLEMING Curtis	6							
FURLONG Paul	2 + 9	1	0 + 2					
GILL Jerry	14		2		1			
GRAINGER Martin	39 + 1	4	3				3	
HOLDSWORTH David	3 + 1		1					
HORSFIELD Geoff	33 + 7	11	3		1		3	1
HUGHES Bryan	27 + 4	7	2	1	0 + 1		3	1
HUGHES Michael	3							
HUTCHINSON Jon	0 + 3		1					
HYDE Graham	1 + 4							
JOHN Stern	15	7					3	1
JOHNSON Andy	9 +14	3	2		1		0 + 2	
JOHNSON Damien	5 + 4	1					1	
JOHNSON Michael	30 + 2	1	3				1	
KELLY Alan	6							
KENNA Jeff	21						3	
LAZARIDIS Stan	22 +10		1 + 1				0 + 3	
LUNTALA Tresor	9 + 6		1					
McCARTHY Jon	3 + 1							
MARCELO	17 + 4	12	0 + 3		0 + 1		3	1
MOONEY Tommy	29 + 4	13	1	2	1		3	
O'CONNOR Martin	24		0 + 1		1			
POOLE Kevin			1					

	P/FL App	Goals	FLC App	Goals	FAC App	Goals	Others App	Goals
PURSE Darren	35 + 1	3	1		1		2	
SONNER Danny	10 + 5	1	3					
TEBILY Olivier	7						3	
VAESEN Nico	22 + 1		2				3	
VICKERS Steve	13 + 1	1			1		2	
WILLIAMS Tommy	4							
WOODHOUSE Curtis	18 +10		2 + 1		1			

BLACKBURN ROVERS (PREM: 10th)

	P/FL App	Goals	FLC App	Goals	FAC App	Goals	Others App	Goals
BENT Marcus	1 + 8		0 + 1					
BERG Henning	34	1	2		2			
BJORNEBYE Stig Inge	23		4		2			
BLAKE Nathan	0 + 3	1						
COLE Andy	15	9	3	3	2	1		
CURTIS John	10		5		1			
DOUGLAS Jonathan					0 + 1			
DUFF Damien	31 + 1	7	5	1	1 + 1			
DUNN David	26 + 3	7	5		2	1		
DUNNING Darren			1		1			
FILAN John			1					
FLITCROFT Garry	26 + 3	1	2		1			
FRIEDEL Brad	36		6		3			
GILLESPIE Keith	21 +11	2	3 + 1		2 + 1			
GRABBI Corrado	10 + 4	1	1 + 2		1 + 1	1		
GREER Gordon			1					
HIGNETT Craig	4 +16	4	5 + 1	3	2 + 1	1		
HUGHES Mark	4 +17	1	4 + 2	1	1 + 2			
JANSEN Matt	34 + 1	10	4 + 1	6	2 + 1			
JOHANSSON Nils-Eric	14 + 6		5		3	1		
JOHNSON Damien	6 + 1	1	3		2			
KELLY Alan	2				1			
KENNA Jeff			1					
McATEER Jason	1 + 3							
MAHON Alan	10 + 3	1	3 + 3		3			
NEILL Lucas	31	1			4			
OSTENSTAD Egil	2 + 2		0 + 2		1			
SHORT Craig	21 + 1		2	1	2			
TAYLOR Martin	12 + 7		6		3 + 1			
TUGAY	32 + 1	3	5 + 1		3 + 1			
UNSAL Hakan	7 + 1							
YORDI	5 + 3	2	0 + 1					

BLACKPOOL (DIV 2: 16th)

	P/FL App	Goals	FLC App	Goals	FAC App	Goals	Others App	Goals
BARNES Phil	30		1		3		6	
BLINKHORN Matthew	0 + 3				0 + 1			
BULLOCK Martin	37 + 6	2	1 + 1		4		6	3
CALDWELL Steve	6				1		1	
CLARKE Chris	10 + 1				1		1	
CLARKSON Phil	1 + 1				1		1	
COID Danny	24 + 3	3	1		4		5 + 1	
COLLINS Lee	24 + 8	2	1		2		3 + 1	
DAY Rhys	4 + 5				0 + 1		3	
DUNNING Darren	5							
FENTON Graham	6 + 9	5	0 + 1		1		3	
HILLS John	30 + 7	5	1		4	1	6	1
HUGHES Ian	13 + 7	1	1		3		0 + 3	
JASZCZUN Tommy	36 + 4		2		3	1	5	
MacKENZIE Neil	6 + 8	1	1 + 1		1 + 3	1	3	2
MARSHALL Ian	21		1		1		4	
MILLIGAN Jamie	9 + 8		0 + 1		1 + 1		2 + 1	
MILLIGAN Mike	1 + 1				1			
MURPHY John	33 + 4	13	2		3	2	5 + 1	5
MURPHY Neil	1							
O'KANE John	34 + 4	4	2		2 + 1		4 + 1	
ORMEROD Brett	21	13	2	3	2		0 + 2	2
PARKINSON Gary	13 + 2		1				2	1
PAYTON Andy	4		1					
PULLEN James	16		1		1		1	
REID Brian	26		1		3		4	
SIMPSON Paul	25 + 7	1	1 + 1		4	1	1 + 2	1
TAYLOR Scott	13 + 4	2			3		3	2
THOMPSON Phil	10 + 3	1	1		0 + 1		1	

	P/FL App	Goals	FLC App	Goals	FAC App	Goals	Others App	Goals
WALKER Richard	16 + 5	8					1 + 1	3
WELLENS Richard	31 + 5	1	2		2		5	1

BOLTON WANDERERS (PREM: 16th)

	P/FL App	Goals	FLC App	Goals	FAC App	Goals	Others App	Goals
BANKS Steve	1		1					
BARNESS Anthony	19 + 6		2		2			
BERGSSON Gudni	30	1			2	1		
BOBIC Fredi	14 + 2	4						
BUCHANAN Wayne					0 + 1			
CHARLTON Simon	35 + 1		1					
DIAWARA Djibril	4 + 5		2					
DJORKAEFF Youri	12	4						
ESPARTERO Mario	0 + 3							
FARRELLY Gareth	11 + 7		3		2			
FRANDSEN Per	25 + 4	3	1					
GARDNER Ricardo	29 + 2	3	0 + 1		2			
HANSEN Bo	10 + 7	1	2		2			
HENDRY Colin	3		4					
HOLDEN Dean			1					
HOLDSWORTH Dean	9 +22	2	3 + 1	2	0 + 1			
JAASKALAINEN Jussi	34		3		1			
JOHNSON Jermaine	4 + 6		2		1 + 1			
KONSTANTINIDIS Kostas	3							
MARSHALL Ian	0 + 2		2					
N'GOTTY Bruno	24 + 2	1	2 + 1					
NISHIZAWA Akinori			3	1				
NOLAN Kevin	34 + 1	8	1 + 1		1 + 1			
NORRIS David			1 + 1		1	1		
PEDERSEN Henrik	5 + 6		1 + 1	1	2	1		
POOLE Kevin	3							
RICHARDSON Leam	0 + 1		2					
RICKETTS Michael	26 +11	12	0 + 3	2	1 + 1	1		
SMITH Jeff	0 + 1		1					
SOUTHALL Nicky	10 + 8	1	4		2			
TAYLOR Cleveland					0 + 1			
TOFTING Stig	6							
VIANDER Jani			1					
WALLACE Rod	14 + 5	3	1 + 2	1	1			
WARHURST Paul	25		1					
WHITLOW Mike	28 + 1		0 + 1		1			

BOURNEMOUTH (DIV 2: 21st)

	P/FL App	Goals	FLC App	Goals	FAC App	Goals	Others App	Goals
BIRMINGHAM David	3 + 1		1					
BROADHURST Karl	22 + 1		0 + 1		2		1	
COOKE Stephen	6 + 1							
ELLIOTT Wade	40 + 6	8	1		2		1	
ERIBENNE Chukki	6 +18		1				0 + 1	
FEENEY Warren	35 + 2	13	1		2			
FLETCHER Carl	35	5	1		1 + 1			
FLETCHER Steve	1 + 1				0 + 1	1		
FORD James	5 + 2		1					
FOYEWA Amos	1 + 7		0 + 1					
HAYTER Jamie	43 + 1	7	1		2	1	1	
HOLMES Derek	34 + 3	9			0 + 1		1	
HOWE Eddie	38	4	1		2		1	
HUCK William	0 + 7		0 + 1					
HUGHES Richard	16 + 6	2			2	1		
KANDOL Tresor	3 + 9				0 + 2		1	1
McANESPIE Kieran	3 + 4	1						
MAHER Shaun	28 + 3		1					
MELLIGAN JJ	7 + 1				1			
MENETRIER Mickael	1						1	
NARADA	4 + 4						0 + 1	
O'CONNOR Garreth	12 +16		1		0 + 1		1	
PURCHES Steve	41	2	1		2			
SMITH Danny	1 + 2						1	
STEWART Gareth	45		1		2			
STOCK Brian	19 + 7	2			2		1	
THOMAS Danny	3 + 9							
TINDALL Jason	44	3			2		0 + 1	
YOUNG Neil	10 + 1							

BRADFORD CITY (DIV 1: 15th)

	P/FL App	P/FL Goals	FLC App	FLC Goals	FAC App	FAC Goals	Others App	Others Goals
ATHERTON Peter	1							
BLAKE Robbie	19 + 7	10	3	2	1			
BOWER Mark	9 + 1	2	1		0 + 1			
CADAMARTERI Danny	14	2						
CALDWELL Steve	9							
CARBONE Beni	10 + 1	5	1					
COMBE Alan	16							
DAVISON Aidan	9		3					
EMANUEL Lewis	8 + 1		2		0 + 1			
ETHERINGTON Matthew	12 + 1	1						
GRANT Gareth	4 + 6	1	2		0 + 1			
GRAYSON Simon	7							
HALLE Gunnar	31 + 1	1	2 + 1					
JACOBS Wayne	37 + 1	1	1		1			
JESS Eoin	43 + 2	14	2		1			
JORGENSEN Claus	13 + 5	1	2					
JUANJO	5 +12				1			
KEARNEY Tom	5							
LAWRENCE Jamie	13 + 8	2	2	1				
LEE Andy	0 + 1							
LOCKE Gary	26 + 5	2	1		1			
McCALL Stuart	42 + 1	3	0 + 2	1	1			
MAKEL Lee	2 +11		2					
MOLENAAR Robert	21		1 + 1		1			
MUGGLETON Carl	4							
MYERS Andy	28 + 4	2	2					
SHARPE Lee	11 + 7	2	1		1			
TOD Andy	25 + 5	4	2 + 1	2	1			
WALSH Gary	17 + 1							
WARD Ashley	27	10	1	1	1			
WETHERALL David	17 + 2	2	2					
WHALLEY Gareth	21 + 2		0 + 2					

BRENTFORD (DIV 2: 3rd)

	P/FL App	P/FL Goals	FLC App	FLC Goals	FAC App	FAC Goals	Others App	Others Goals
ANDERSON Ijah	33 + 2		2		1		4	
BOXALL Danny	0 + 5						0 + 1	
BRYAN Del	0 + 1							
BURGESS Ben	43	17	2		2	1	4	
CACERES Adrian	5							
DOBSON Michael	38 + 1		2		2	1	3	
EVANS Paul	40	14	2		1		4	
GIBBS Paul	23 + 4	2	2		2	1	0 + 1	
GOTTSKALKSSON Olafur	28		2		2			
HUNT Steve	34 + 1	4	0 + 1		1		4	
HUTCHINSON Eddie	2 + 7				0 + 1		1	
INGIMARSSON Ivar	46	6	2		2		4	
LOVETT Jay	2							
McCAMMON Mark	1 +13				0 + 1		0 + 1	
MAHON Gavin	34 + 1		2		2			
O'CONNOR Kevin	13 +12		1 + 1	1	1 + 1		1 + 2	
OWUSU Lloyd	43 + 1	20	1	1	2		4	1
PARTRIDGE Scott	0 + 1		0 + 1					
POWELL Darren	41	1	2		2		3	1
PRICE Jason	15	1	2				1	
ROWLANDS Martin	13 +10	7	0 + 1		0 + 1		3	
SIDWELL Steven	29 + 1	4			2		3	
SMITH Jay							0 + 1	
SMITH Paul	18						4	
TABB Jay	0 + 3							
THEOBALD David	5 + 1						1	
WILLIAMS Mark	0 +20	1	0 + 1		0 + 1		0 + 1	

BRIGHTON & HOVE ALBION (DIV 2: 1st)

	P/FL App	P/FL Goals	FLC App	FLC Goals	FAC App	FAC Goals	Others App	Others Goals
BROOKER Paul	30 +11	4	2		2 + 1		1	
CARPENTER Richard	45	3	2		3			
CROSBY Andy	0 + 2						3	
CULLIP Danny	44		1		3			
GRAY Wayne	3 + 1	1						
HADLAND Phil	0 + 2							
HART Gary	34 + 5	4	1 + 1		2			
JONES Nathan	29 + 7	2	2		2 + 1		2	
KUIPERS Michel	39		2		2		3	
LEE David	0 + 2							
LEHMANN Dirk	3 + 4		1 + 1				3	1
LEWIS Junior	14 + 1	3						
McPHEE Chris	2						0 + 1	
MAYO Kerry	30 + 3		0 + 1		3		1	
MELTON Steve	5 + 5	1	0 + 1				3	2
MORGAN Simon	42		1		3			
OATWAY Charlie	27 + 5	1	1		3			
PACKHAM Will	1				1			
PETHICK Robbie	13 +11		0 + 1		1		3	
PITCHER Geoff	2 + 8						3	1
RAMSEY Scott							0 + 1	
ROGERS Paul	19 + 6	1	2				3	
ROYCE Simon	6							
STEELE Lee	20 +17	9	1 + 1		1 + 2		3	1
VIRGO Adam	4 + 2						1 + 1	
WATSON Paul	45	5	2		3		1	
WEBB Danny	7 + 5	1			1			
WICKS Matthew	2		1				3	
ZAMORA Bobby	40 + 1	28	2	2	3	2		

BRISTOL CITY (DIV 2: 7th)

	P/FL App	P/FL Goals	FLC App	FLC Goals	FAC App	FAC Goals	Others App	Others Goals
AMANKWAAH Kevin	18 + 6	1	1 + 1	1			3	1
BELL Mickey	41 + 1	7	2		1		3	1
BROWN Aaron	34 + 2	1	2		1		4	
BROWN Marvin	1 + 9				0 + 1		2 + 2	
BURNELL Joe	26 + 4		0 + 2				5	
CAREY Louis	34 + 1		2		1		2	
CLIST Simon	9 +11		2		0 + 1		3	
COLES Danny	20 + 3				1		6	
CORREIA Albano							0 + 1	
DOHERTY Tommy	27 + 7	1	1		1		3	
FORTUNE Clayton	0 + 1						0 + 1	
GOODRIDGE Greg	0 + 2				0 + 1		1 + 1	
HILL Matt	40		1		1		4 + 1	
HULBERT Robin	4 + 7						3 + 2	
JONES Darren	1 + 2						0 + 2	
JONES Steve	17 + 5	5	2		1		0 + 1	
LEVER Mark	26 + 3	1	2		1		1 + 1	
MATTHEWS Lee	6 +16	3	0 + 2				2 + 1	2
MURRAY Scott	34 + 3	8	1 + 1		1		3 + 1	1
PEACOCK Lee	28 + 3	15			1		6	2
PHILLIPS Steve	21 + 1						6	
ROBERTS Chris	4							
ROBINSON Steve	6	1						
RODRIGUES Dani	0 + 4						0 + 1	
ROSENIOR Liam	0 + 1							
SINGH Harpal	3							
STOWELL Mike	25		2		1			
SUMMERBELL Mark	5							
THORPE Tony	36 + 6	16	2	1	1		4	
TINNION Brian	35 + 3	3	1				2 + 1	
WOODMAN Craig	5 + 1						3	

BRISTOL ROVERS (DIV 3: 23rd)

	P/FL App	P/FL Goals	FLC App	FLC Goals	FAC App	FAC Goals	Others App	Others Goals
ARNDALE Neil	0 + 1							
ASTAFJEVS Vitalijs	14 + 5	1			4 + 1	1	1	
BRYANT Simon	8						0 + 1	
BUBB Alvin	3 +10				0 + 1		0 + 2	
CAMERON Martin	10 +15	4	0 + 2		3 + 1		2 + 1	1
CARLISLE Wayne	5							
CHALLIS Trevor	28 + 1				5 + 1		2	
CLARKE Ryan	0 + 1							
ELLINGTON Nathan	27	15	2		5	4	2	2
FORAN Mark	30 + 1	2	1		4		3	
FOSTER Steve	33	1	2		2		1	
GALL Kevin	25 + 6	3	2		2 + 1		2 + 1	
GILROY David	2 + 2							
HAMMOND Elvis	3 + 4		0 + 1		1			
HILLIER David	27	1	2		4			

	P/FL		FLC		FAC		Others	
	App	Goals	App	Goals	App	Goals	App	Goals
HOGG Lewis	22 + 1				4	1	2	1
HOWIE Scott	46		2		6		3	
JONES Scott	14 + 5		2		1		1	
LOPEZ Rik	5 + 2				1			
McKEEVER Mark	6 + 2				0 + 1			
MAUGE Ronnie	14 + 1		2		3		2	
OMMEL Sergio	18 + 5	8			2 + 1	1	1 + 1	1
PLUMMER Dwayne	12 + 3				4		3	
PRITCHARD David	1 + 4							
QUINN James	6	1						
RICHARDS Justin	0 + 1							
ROSS Neil	2 + 3				1			
SANCHEZ-LOPEZ Carlos	6							
SHORE Drew	9						1	
SMITH Mark	17 + 2				3 + 1		1	
THOMAS Jamie	7	1						
THOMSON Andy	29 + 2	1	2		4		2	
TONER Ciaran	6							
TROUGHT Mike	17 + 3		1		3 + 1		2	
WALTERS Mark	7 +19				0 + 4	1	0 + 1	
WEARE Ross	9 + 1	1	2		1			
WILSON Che	38		2		5		1 + 1	

BURNLEY (DIV 1: 7th)

	P/FL		FLC		FAC		Others	
	App	Goals	App	Goals	App	Goals	App	Goals
ARMSTRONG Gordon	11 + 7	2						
BALL Kevin	37 + 5		1		2			
BERESFORD Marlon	13							
BLAKE Robbie	1 + 9							
BRANCH Graham	8 + 2				0 + 1			
BRISCOE Lee	43 + 1	5			2			
CENNAMO Luigi					0 + 1			
COOK Paul	25 + 3	5	0 + 1		0 + 1			
COX Ian	32 + 2	2	1		2			
DAVIS Steve	22 + 1	1	1					
ELLIS Tony	0 +11		1					
GASCOIGNE Paul	3 + 3							
GNOHERE Arthur	31 + 3	3	1		2			
GRANT Tony	26 + 2				2			
JOHNROSE Lenny	0 + 6							
JOHNSON David	8	5						
LITTLE Glen	31 + 6	9	0 + 1		2	1		
McGREGOR Mark	1		1	1				
MAYLETT Brad	0 +10		1		0 + 1			
MICHOPOULOS Nik	33		1		2			
MOORE Alan	23 + 6	3	1		2	1	1	
MOORE Ian	41 + 5	11	0 + 1		2	3		
MULLIN John	0 + 4		1					
PAPADOPOULOS Demitrios	0 + 6		1		0 + 1			
PAYTON Andy	0 +15	4						
TAYLOR Gareth	35 + 5	16	1		2			
THOMAS Mitchell	10 + 2							
WELLER Paul	29 + 9	2			0 + 1			
WEST Dean	43 + 1				2			

BURY (DIV 2: 22nd)

	P/FL		FLC		FAC		Others	
	App	Goals	App	Goals	App	Goals	App	Goals
ARMSTRONG Chris	11		1					
BARRASS Matt	6 + 1							
BHUTIA Bhaichung	3							
BILLY Chris	19 + 2	3	1					
BORLEY David	16 + 5	3			2		1	
BULLOCK Darren	2 + 2							
CLARKSON Phil	4							
CLEGG George	25 + 6	4			0 + 1		0 + 1	
COLLINS Sam	26 + 3		1		1			
CONNELL Lee	9 + 4				0 + 1			
EVANS Gary	1							
FORREST Martyn	31 + 3	1			1		2	
GARNER Glyn	5 + 2				1		1	
GUNBY Steve	0 + 1							
HILL Nicky	3 + 2							
JARRETT Jason	32 + 5	2	0 + 1		2		1	
KENNY Paddy	41		1		1		1	

	P/FL		FLC		FAC		Others	
	App	Goals	App	Goals	App	Goals	App	Goals
LAWSON Ian	12 +12	4			1		1	1
MURPHY Matt	5 + 4						1	
NELSON Michael	28 + 3	2	1		2		2	
NEWBY Jon	46	6	1		2		2	1
NUGENT David	1 + 4							
O'SHAUGNESSY Paul	0 + 2							
PREECE Andy	4 + 9	1	0 + 1					
REDMOND Steve	26		1		2		1	
REID Paul	23 + 5	3	1	1	1 + 1		2	
SEDDON Gareth	23 +12	6	1		1		1	
SINGH Harpal	11 + 1	2			2	1	1	
STUART Jamie	24	1			1 + 1		2	
SWAILES Danny	26 + 2	1	1		2		2	1
SYROS George	9	1			0 + 1			
UNSWORTH Lee	34 + 1	1	1		1		1	

CAMBRIDGE UNITED (DIV 2: 24th)

	P/FL		FLC		FAC		Others	
	App	Goals	App	Goals	App	Goals	App	Goals
ALCIDE Colin	7 + 1		1	1	1		1	
ANGUS Stevland	41		1		1		5 + 1	
ASHBEE Ian	38	2	1		2		5	
AUSTIN Kevin	4 + 2						1	
BRIDGES David	1 + 6	1						
BYRNE Dessie	3 + 1		1					
CHILLINGWORTH Daniel	10 + 2	2					3 + 1	1
CLEMENTS Matt	0 + 1							
COWAN Tom	3 + 2	1						
DUNCAN Andy	20 + 4		0 + 1		2		7	
FLEMING Terry	28 + 6		1		1		3 + 1	
GOODHIND Warren	11 + 3						1 + 3	
GUTTRIDGE Luke	27 + 2	2	0 + 1		1		4	1
JACKMAN Daniel	5 + 2	1					1 + 1	
KANDOL Tresor	2 + 2							
KELLY Leon	1 + 1							
KITSON Dave	30 + 3	9	1		2		4	
McANESPIE Steve	0 + 1							
MARSHALL Shaun	4 + 3							
MURRAY Fred	21						3	
MUSTOE Neil	0 + 5						0 + 1	
ONE Armand	18 +14	4			0 + 2		4 + 3	5
PEREZ Lionel	42		1		2		7	
PROKAS Richard	8 + 1	1					0 + 2	
REVELL Alex	7 +17	2			0 + 2		1 + 3	
RICHARDSON Marcus	4 + 2						1 + 1	
SCULLY Tony	19 + 6	2			2		2	
TANN Adam	24 + 1						5	
TAYLOR Scott	0 + 3						0 + 1	
TRAORE Demba	2 + 5		1					
TUDOR Shane	31 + 1	3			2	1	6	1
WALLING Dean	20				2		1	
WANLESS Paul	28 + 1	6	1		1		6	1
WARNER Phil	11 + 1				1 + 1		2	
YOUNGS Tom	36 + 6	11	0 + 1		2		5 + 1	

CARDIFF CITY (DIV 2: 4th)

	P/FL		FLC		FAC		Others	
	App	Goals	App	Goals	App	Goals	App	Goals
ALEXANDER Neil	46		1		4		2	
BOLAND Willie	40 + 2	1	1		4		2	
BONNER Mark	25 + 4				3 + 1		4	1
BOWEN Jason	21 + 4	5			1 + 1		0 + 1	1
BRAYSON Paul	16 +19	3	1		3 + 1	1		
BRAZIER Matt							1	
CAMPBELL Andy	8	7					0 + 2	
COLLINS James	2 + 5	1			0 + 2		1 + 2	
CROFT Gary	3 + 3	1					2	
EARNSHAW Robbie	28 + 2	11	1	1	3	2	2	1
FORTUNE-WEST Leo	18 +18	9	1		2 + 2	1	3	1
GABBIDON Danny	44	3			4			
GILES Martyn							0 + 2	1
GORDON Dean	7	2						
GORDON Gavin	12 + 3	1	0 + 1		2		1	5
HAMILTON Des	14 + 5				2		2	1
HUGHES David	1 + 1		1				2	
JEANNE Leon	0 + 2							

	P/FL App	P/FL Goals	FLC App	FLC Goals	FAC App	FAC Goals	Others App	Others Goals
JONES Gethin	0 + 1						1 + 1	
KAVANAGH Graham	43	13	1		4	2	2	
KENDALL Lee							1	
LEGG Andy	27 + 8	2	1		4			
LOW Josh	11 +11		0 + 1		0 + 1		2	
McCULLOCH Scott							1	
MAXWELL Layton	5 +12	1			0 + 1		2 + 1	
NUGENT Kevin	1						1 + 1	1
PRIOR Spencer	33 + 4	2			3		2	
SIMPKINS Mike	13 + 4		1					
THOMPSON Andy							1 + 1	
THORNE Peter	23 + 3	8					2	
WALTON Mark							1	
WESTON Rhys	35 + 2		1		2 + 1		2	
YOUNG Scott	30 + 3	4			3	1	4	

CARLISLE UNITED (DIV 3: 17th)

	P/FL App	P/FL Goals	FLC App	FLC Goals	FAC App	FAC Goals	Others App	Others Goals
ALLAN Jonny	10 +19	2	0 + 1		0 + 1			
ANDREWS Lee	37 + 2				3			
BELL Stuart	3 + 2							
BERKLEY Austin	2 + 3		0 + 1					
BIRCH Mark	42		1		3		1	
DICKINSON Michael	0 + 1							
ELLIOTT Stuart	6		1					
FORAN Richie	37	14			3	1	1	
FRIARS Sean	0 + 1							
GALLOWAY Mick							0 + 1	
GREEN Stuart	16	3						
HADDOW Alex	4		0 + 1					
HADLAND Phil	4		1		1			
HALLIDAY Steve	28 +15	6	1		1		1	
HARKIN Mo	2 + 2		1					
HEWS Chay	4 + 1	2						
HOPPER Tony	20 + 9	1	1		1			
HORE John	0 + 3							
JACK Michael	16 +16				2 + 1		0 + 1	
KEEN Peter	36				3		1	
McAUGHTRIE Craig	2 + 3	1					1	
McDONAGH Will	7 + 5	1	1					
McGILL Brendan	27 + 1	2			3		1	
MADDISON Lee	5 + 2		1					
MORLEY Dave	14 + 4		1		1		1	
MURPHY Peter	39 + 1		1		3		1	
ROGERS Dave	26 + 1	1			3		1	
ROOKE Steve	0 + 1							
SKINNER Steve	1 + 5						0 + 1	
SLAVEN John	0 + 2							
SOLEY Steve	19 + 2	4			1	1	1	
STEVENS Ian	23 + 3	8	1		2			
THURSTON Mark	1							
THWAITES Adam	0 + 1							
WEAVER Luke	10		1					
WHITEHEAD Stuart	29 + 3	1	1					
WILLIS Scott	0 + 1							
WINSTANLEY Mark	36	1			2 + 1		1	

CHARLTON ATHLETIC (PREM: 14th)

	P/FL App	P/FL Goals	FLC App	FLC Goals	FAC App	FAC Goals	Others App	Others Goals
BART-WILLIAMS Chris	10 + 6	1			2			
BARTLETT Shaun	10 + 4	1	2		0 + 1			
BROWN Steve	11 + 3	2	2 + 1	1	1 + 1			
COSTA Jorge	22 + 2				2			
EUELL Jason	31 + 5	11	2	1	2	1		
FISH Mark	25		1					
FORTUNE Jon	14 + 5		2	1	2			
JENSEN Claus	16 + 2	1	2					
JOHANSSON JJ	21 + 9	5	2 + 1					
KIELY Dean	38		3		2			
KINSELLA Mark	14 + 3		1					
KISHISHEV Radostin	0 + 3				0 + 1			
KONCHESKY Paul	22 +12	1	0 + 3	1	2			
LISBIE Kevin	10 +12	5	0 + 2		1 + 1			
MacDONALD Charlie	0 + 2	1	0 + 1					

	P/FL App	P/FL Goals	FLC App	FLC Goals	FAC App	FAC Goals	Others App	Others Goals
PARKER Scott	36 + 2	1	3					
PEACOCK Gavin	1 + 4							
POWELL Chris	35 + 1	1	3		2			
ROBINSON John	16 +12	1	3	1	2			
RUFUS Richard	10	1						
SALAKO John	2 + 1		0 + 1					
STUART Graham	31	3	2		2	2		
SVENSSON Matt	6 + 6				0 + 1			
TODD Andy	3 + 2		2					
YOUNG Luke	34		3		1			

CHELSEA (PREM: 6th)

	P/FL App	P/FL Goals	FLC App	FLC Goals	FAC App	FAC Goals	Others App	Others Goals
BABAYARO Celestine	18		3 + 1		4		2	
BOSNICH Mark	5						2	
COLE Carlton	2 + 1	1						
CUDICINI Carlo	27 + 1		5		8			
DALLA BONA Sam	16 + 8	4	3 + 2		4 + 2		0 + 3	
DE GOEY Ed	6						2	
DESAILLY Marcel	24	1	3		8		2	
FERRER Albert	2 + 2		1 + 1		3 + 1			
FORSSELL Mikael	2 +20		0 + 4	2	2 + 4	3	0 + 3	
GALLAS William	27 + 3	1	4		4	1	3	
GRØNKJAER Jesper	11 + 2				3			
GUDJOHNSEN Eidur	26 + 6	14	5	3	6 + 1	3	3	3
HASSELBAINK Jimmy Floyd	35	23	4	3	7	3	2	
HUTH Robert	0 + 1							
JOKANOVIC Slavisa	12 + 8		2 + 1		1 + 4		3	
KEENAN Joe	0 + 1				0 + 1			
KITAMIRIKE Joel							1	
KNIGHT Leon							0 + 1	
LAMPARD Frank	34 + 3	5	4		7 + 1	1	4	1
LE SAUX Graeme	26 + 1	1	3		8	1	2	
MELCHIOT Mario	35 + 2	2	4		5 + 1		3	
MORRIS Jody	2 + 3		2		1 + 1		0 + 1	
PETIT Manu	26 + 1	1	2		6		3	
STANIC Mario	18 + 9	1	1 + 1		4		1	
TERRY John	32 + 1	1	5		3 + 2	2	4	1
ZENDEN Boudewijn	13 + 9	3	2 + 2		0 + 3		3	
ZOLA Franco	19 +16	3	2 + 3		4 + 2	1	3 + 1	1

CHELTENHAM TOWN (DIV 3: 4th)

	P/FL App	P/FL Goals	FLC App	FLC Goals	FAC App	FAC Goals	Others App	Others Goals
ALSOP Julian	38 + 3	20	0 + 1		5	4	5	2
BANKS Chris	38		1		5		2	
BOOK Steve	39				5		5	
BROUGH John	9 +12	1			0 + 2			
DEVANEY Martin	8 +17	1	1		0 + 2	1	2 + 2	1
DUFF Michael	45	3	1		5		5	
FINNIGAN John	12	2					3	1
GRAYSON Neil	13 +21	1	1	1	1 + 4		1 + 3	1
GRIFFIN Antony	21 + 3		0 + 1		4		3	
HIGGS Shane	0 + 1							
HILL Keith	2 + 3							
HOPKINS Gareth	0 + 3							
HOWARTH Neil	18 + 8	1	1		1		2	
HOWELLS Lee	31	2			5	1	2	
JACKSON Michael	0 + 1							
JONES Steve	2 + 3							
LEE Martyn	2 + 3						1 + 1	
McAULEY Hugh	3 + 4				0 + 1		1 + 1	
MILTON Russell	37 + 2	2	1		4	1	3	
MUGGLETON Carl	7		1					
NAYLOR Tony	43 + 1	12	1		5	5	4	
TYSON Nathan	1 + 7	1						
VICTORY Jamie	45 + 1	7	1		5		5	1
WALKER Richard	11 + 1	1	1				3	
WHITE Jason	0 + 4	1	0 + 1					
WILLIAMS Lee	36 + 2	3			5		4 + 1	1
YATES Mark	45	7	1		5		4	

CHESTERFIELD (DIV 2: 18th)

	P/FL App	P/FL Goals	FLC App	FLC Goals	FAC App	FAC Goals	Others App	Others Goals
ABBEY Nathan	46		1		3		3	
ALLOTT Mark	19 + 2	4						

	P/FL		FLC		FAC		Others	
	App	Goals	App	Goals	App	Goals	App	Goals
BECKETT Luke	20 + 1	6			2	2	2	
BLATHERWICK Steve	4 + 1							
BOOTY Martyn	40	2	1		3		3	
BRECKIN Ian	42	1	1		3		3	
BUCHANAN Wayne	3							
BURT Jamie	18 + 6	7						
D'AURIA David	10 + 4	1			3	1	2 + 1	1
EBDON Marcus	29 + 2	2			1		2	
EDWARDS Rob	30 + 1	1			3		3	
HEWITT Jamie	1							
HITZLSPERGER Thomas	5						1	
HOWARD Jon	12 + 8	5	1		2 + 1		1	
HOWSON Stuart	13	1						
HURST Glynn	22 + 1	9						
HYDE Graham	8 + 1	1						
INGLEDOW Jamie	12 + 5		1		1		2	
INNES Mark	22 + 1	2						
JONES Mark	1 + 5						0 + 2	
MOORE Stefan	1 + 1						1	
O'HARE Alan	19							
PARRISH Sean	11 + 9	1			3		2	
PAYNE Steve	44	1	1		2		2 + 1	
PEARCE Greg	5 + 2		1					
REEVES Alan	20 + 2	4	1		3		3	1
RICHARDSON Lee	13 + 1	1			2		2	
ROWLAND Keith	6 + 3		1	1				
RUSHBURY Andy	0 + 3		0 + 1		0 + 1			
WALSH Danny	0 + 1							
WILLIAMS Danny	19 + 5		1		0 + 2		0 + 2	
WILLIS Roger	11 +13	4	1		2 + 1		1	

COLCHESTER UNITED (DIV 2: 15th)

	P/FL		FLC		FAC		Others	
BARRETT Graham	19 + 1	4						
BLATSIS Con	7							
BOWRY Bobby	27 + 9	1	0 + 2		1		2	
BROWN Simon	19						2	
CANHAM Marc	0 + 1							
CHAMBERS Triston	0 + 1							
CLARK Simon	19 + 2		2				2	
COOTE Adrian	5 +14	4						
DUGUID Karl	36 + 5	4	1		2	1	1	
DUNNE Joe	6 + 2	2	1		0 + 1			
FITZGERALD Scott	36 + 1		2		2		2	
GREGORY David	15 + 1		2				1	
HALLS John	6							
HADRAVA David							0 + 1	
IZZETT Kem	36 + 4	3	2	1	1		2	1
JOHNSON Gavin	19 + 1	1			2		2	
JOHNSON Ross	13 + 3	1			2		1	
KEITH Joe	33 + 8	4	2	1	2		1 + 1	
KNIGHT Richard	1							
MacDONALD Charlie	2 + 2	1						
McGLEISH Scott	44 + 2	15	2		2	1	2	
MORGAN Dean	1 +29				0 + 2		1 + 1	
OPARA Lloyd	0 + 1				0 + 1		0 + 1	
PINAULT Thomas	37 + 5		2		2		2	
RAPLEY Kevin	26 + 9	9	2		2		1	
STOCKWELL Micky	45 + 1	9	2	1	2		1 + 1	1
WHITE Alan	28 + 5	3	0 + 1		0 + 1			
WOODMAN Andy	26		2		2			

COVENTRY CITY (DIV 1: 11th)

	P/FL		FLC		FAC		Others	
ANTONELIUS Tomas	3 + 2				1			
BETTS Robert	4 + 5				1			
BOTHROYD Jay	24 + 7	6	1 + 1		1			
BREEN Gary	30		2		1			
CARBONARI Horacio	5							
CARSLEY Lee	25 + 1	2	2	1	1			
CHIPPO Youssef	29 + 5	4	1					
DAVENPORT Calum	1 + 2							
DELORGE Laurent	21 + 7	4	0 + 1		0 + 1			
EDWORTHY Marc	18 + 2		1		1			

	P/FL		FLC		FAC		Others	
	App	Goals	App	Goals	App	Goals	App	Goals
EUSTACE John	5 + 1							
FLOWERS Tim	5							
FOWLER Lee	5 + 8							
GORAM Andy	6 + 1							
GUERRERO Ivan	3 + 1							
HALL Marcus	27 + 2	1	1					
HEALY Colin	17	2						
HEDMAN Magnus	34		1		1			
HUGHES Lee	35 + 3	14	1 + 1		1			
JOACHIM Julian	4 +12	1	1		1			
KIRKLAND Chris	1							
KONJIC Mo	38	2	2		1			
McSHEFFREY Gary	1 + 7	1	0 + 1					
MARTINEZ Jairo	5 + 6	3	1		0 + 1			
MILLS Lee	19 + 1	5						
MONTGOMERY Gary	1		1					
NILSSON Roland	9		1					
NORMANN Runar	0 + 2							
O'NEILL Keith	7 + 4							
PEAD Craig	1							
QUINN Barry	18 + 4		1		0 + 1			
SAFRI Youssef	32 + 1	1	2					
SHAW Richard	29 + 3		1 + 1		1			
STRACHAN Gavin	0 + 1							
THOMPSON David	35 + 2	12	2	1	1			
TROLLOPE Paul	5 + 1							
WILLIAMS Paul	4 + 1							
ZUNIGA Ysrael	1 + 6							

CREWE ALEXANDRA (DIV 1: 22nd)

	P/FL		FLC		FAC		Others	
ASHTON Dean	29 + 2	7	0 + 1		3 + 1	3		
BANKOLE Ade	28		1		2			
BARRETT Graham	2 + 1		0 + 1					
BRAMMER Dave	29 + 1	2	2	1	4			
CHARNOCK Phil	21 + 2	1	1 + 1		1			
COLLINS Wayne	13 + 7	2	1					
FOSTER Steve	29 + 5	5	1		2 + 1	1		
GRANT John	1							
HULSE Rob	40 + 1	12	3	1	3			
INCE Clayton	18 + 1		2		2			
JACK Rodney	24 + 9	7	3		2 + 2			
JONES Steve	1 + 5							
LITTLE Colin	8 + 9	1	2	1				
LUNT Kenny	45	5	2 + 1		4			
MACAULEY Steve	9		1					
McCREADY Chris	0 + 1							
NAVARRO Alan	7		2					
RICHARDS Marc	1 + 3		0 + 1		1			
RIX Ben	6 +15				1 + 3	1		
SMITH Shaun	41 + 1	1	3	1	3			
SODJE Efe	34 + 2	2	2 + 1		4			
SORVEL Neil	31 + 7		3		2 + 1			
STREET Kevin	2 + 7	1						
TAIT Paul	3 + 9							
THOMAS Geoff	8 + 6	2	1		1 + 1	1		
VAUGHAN David	11 + 2				3	1		
WALKER Richard	0 + 1							
WALTON Dave	29 + 2	1	2	1	2			
WHALLEY Gareth	7							
WRIGHT David	29 + 1				4			

CRYSTAL PALACE (DIV 1: 10th)

	P/FL		FLC		FAC		Others	
AKINBIYI Ade	9 + 5	2						
AUSTIN Dean	27 + 8		2 + 1					
BENJAMIN Trevor	5 + 1	1						
BERHALTER Gregg	6 + 8	1	1 + 1					
BLACK Tommy	5 +20		1 + 1	2				
CARASSO Cedric	0 + 1							
CARLISLE Wayne	1		1					
CLARKE Matt	28		2					
EDWARDS Chris	9							
FLEMING Curtis	17							

Player	P/FL App	P/FL Goals	FLC App	FLC Goals	FAC App	FAC Goals	Others App	Others Goals
FRAMPTON Andy	1 + 1							
FREEDMAN Dougie	39 + 1	20	2	1				
GOODING Scott	0 + 1							
GRANVILLE Danny	16				1			
GRAY Julian	35 + 8	2	3		1			
HARRISON Craig	4 + 2							
HOPKIN David	13 + 7	3	0 + 1		1			
KABBA Steve	1 + 3							
KIROVSKI Jovan	25 +11	5	2		1			
KOLINKO Alex	18 + 1		1		1			
MORRISON Clint	45	22	3	2	1			
MULLINS Hayden	43		3		1			
MURPHY Shaun	11							
POPOVIC Tony	20	2	3		1			
RIIHILAHTI Aki	45	5	2 + 1	1	1			
RODGER Simon	29 + 7	1	3	1	0 + 1			
ROUTLEDGE Wayne	0 + 2							
RUBINS Andrejs	0 + 7		0 + 1					
SMITH Jamie	28 + 4	4	2					
SYMONS Kit	9				1			
THOMSON Steve	10 +13		1 + 1		1			
VICKERS Steve	6				1			
ZHIYI Fan	2							

DARLINGTON (DIV 3: 15th)

Player	P/FL App	P/FL Goals	FLC App	FLC Goals	FAC App	FAC Goals	Others App	Others Goals
ATKINSON Brian	35	1			3		1	
BETTS Simon	29		1		4		2	
BRIGHTWELL David	22		1		4		1	
BRUMWELL Phil	16 + 6				3		0 + 2	1
CALDWELL Gary	4							
CAMPBELL Paul	8 + 8	1			1 + 1	1		
CHILLINGWORTH Daniel	2 + 2	1			1	1		
CLARK Ian	28	13			2 + 1			
COLLETT Andy	28		1		4			
CONLON Barry	35	10	1		1	1	1	
CONVERY Mark	6 +11	1	1		0 + 2			
FINCH Keith	11 + 1							
FORD Mark	34 + 1	7	1		2			
HARPER Steve	15 + 8	1	1				0 + 1	
HEALY Brian	1 + 1	1			1			
HECKINGBOTTOM Paul	40 + 2	3			4		2	
HODGSON Richard	24 +12	2	1		3		2	
JACKSON Kirk	1 +10		0 + 1		1 + 1		2	
JEANNIN Alex	11						2	
KELTIE Clark	0 + 1							
KILTY Mark	1				1			
LIDDLE Craig	31	2	1		1		1	
McGURK David	10 + 2				0 + 1			
MADDISON Neil	24 + 6	1	1		1 + 2		2	
MARCELLE Clint	0 + 3						1	
MARSH Adam	1		0 + 1				0 + 1	
MELLANBY Danny	22 + 2	4	1		3			
NAYLOR Glenn	6	1						
PEARSON Gary	9	1			0 + 1		1	
PORTER Chris	7							
REED Adam	7				1			
RUNDLE Adam	5 + 7							
SHEERAN Mark	1 +21	6					0 + 1	
VAN DER GEEST Frank							2	
WAINWRIGHT Neil	32 + 3	4			3 + 1	2	2	

DERBY COUNTY (PREM: 19th)

Player	P/FL App	P/FL Goals	FLC App	FLC Goals	FAC App	FAC Goals	Others App	Others Goals
BARTON Warren	14							
BOERTIEN Paul	23 + 9		1		1			
BOLDER Adam	2 + 9				1			
BURLEY Craig	11		2		1			
BURTON Deon	8 + 9	1	2	2				
CARBONARI Horacio	3							
CARBONE Beni	13	1			1			
CHRISTIE Malcolm	27 + 8	9	0 + 1		1			
DAINO Danny	2		1 + 1					
DUCROCQ Pierre	19							
ELLIOTT Steve	2 + 4							
EVATT Ian	1 + 2							
FEUER Ian	2							
FOLETTI Patrick	1 + 1							
GRENET Francois	12 + 3				1			
HIGGINBOTHAM Danny	37	1	2					
JACKSON Richard	6 + 1							
JOHNSON Seth	7		1					
KINKLADZE Georgi	13 +11	1	1		1			
LEE Rob	13							
MAWENE Youl	17	1	2		1			
MORRIS Lee	9 + 6	4			0 + 1			
MURRAY Adam	3 + 3		2					
OAKES Andy	20		2					
O'NEIL Brian	8 + 2		0 + 1					
POOM Mart	15				1			
POWELL Darryl	23	1	1					
RAVANELLI Fabrizio	30 + 1	9	2	1	1	1		
RIGGOTT Chris	37		2					
ROBINSON Marvin	0 + 2	1						
STRUPAR Branko	8 + 4	4						
TWIGG Gary	0 + 1							
VALAKARI Simo	6 + 3		1					
ZAVAGNO Luciano	26				1			

EVERTON (PREM: 15th)

Player	P/FL App	P/FL Goals	FLC App	FLC Goals	FAC App	FAC Goals	Others App	Others Goals
ALEXANDERSSON Niclas	28 + 3	2			3 + 1			
BLOMQVIST Jesper	10 + 5	1			2 + 1			
CADAMARTERI Danny	2 + 1							
CAMPBELL Kevin	21 + 2	4	1		3	3		
CARSLEY Lee	8	1						
CHADWICK Nicky	2 + 7	3	0 + 1		0 + 1			
CLARKE Peter	5 + 2				3			
CLELAND Alex	0 + 3							
FERGUSON Duncan	17 + 5	6	1	1	2	1		
GASCOIGNE Paul	8 +10	1	1		3 + 1			
GEMMILL Scot	31 + 1	1	1		5			
GERRARD Paul	13		1					
GINOLA David	2 + 3				2			
GRAVESEN Thomas	22 + 3	2			0 + 1			
HIBBERT Tony	7 + 3		0 + 1		1			
LINDEROTH Tobias	4 + 4				2 + 1			
McLEOD Kevin			1					
MOORE Joe-Max	3 +13	2	1		2 + 2			
NAYSMITH Gary	23 + 1				4			
PEMBRIDGE Mark	10 + 4	1			1 + 1			
PISTONE Sandro	25	1			1			
RADZINSKI Tomasz	23 + 4	6			2	1		
SIMONSEN Steve	25				5			
STUBBS Alan	29 + 2	2	1		5			
TAL Idan	1 + 6				0 + 1			
UNSWORTH David	28 + 5	3	1		3 + 1			
WATSON Steve	24 + 1	4	1					
WEIR Davie	36	4	1		5			
XAVIER Abel	11 + 1		1		1			

EXETER CITY (DIV 3: 16th)

Player	P/FL App	P/FL Goals	FLC App	FLC Goals	FAC App	FAC Goals	Others App	Others Goals
AFFUL Les	0 + 2				0 + 1			
AMPADU Kwame	33 + 3		1		3			
BARLOW Martin	26 + 4		1		3		1	
BIRCH Gary	5 +10						1	
BRESLAN Geoff	21 +12	2	0 + 1		0 + 1		1	
BUCKLE Paul	19 + 6	1			2		1	
BURROWS Mark	6 + 3							
CAMPBELL Jamie	14 + 2	1	1		1 + 1		1	
CRONIN Glenn	24 + 6				0 + 2		0 + 1	
CURRAN Chris	35 + 2	1	1		2	1		
DIALLO Cherif	0 + 2							
ELLIOTT Stuart	0 + 1							
FLACK Steve	27 + 9	6	1		1 + 2			
FRASER Stuart	10 + 2							
GOFF Shaun	2							

	P/FL App	P/FL Goals	FLC App	FLC Goals	FAC App	FAC Goals	Others App	Others Goals
GREGG Matt	2							
GROSS Marcus	1							
KERR Dylan	5	1	1					
McCARTHY Sean	18 + 8	6	1		1			
McCONNELL Barry	30 + 2	3	0 + 1		3		1	
MOOR Reinier	0 + 2							
POWER Graeme	36 + 1	1			3		1	
READ Paul	3 +12				0 + 1			
RICHARDSON Jay	5 +13						0 + 1	
ROBERTS Chris	34 + 3	11	1		2		1	
ROSCOE Andy	35 + 3	7			3	1	1	
TOMLINSON Graeme	25 + 7	5	0 + 1		3	1		
VAN HEUSDEN Arjan	33		1		3			
WALKER Andy	1							
WATSON Alex	42 + 1	1	1		3		1	
WHITWORTH Neil	12 + 3		1					
ZABEK Lee	2							

FULHAM (PREM: 13th)

	P/FL App	P/FL Goals	FLC App	FLC Goals	FAC App	FAC Goals	Others App	Others Goals
BETSY Kevin	0 + 1							
BOA MORTE Luis	15 + 8	1	2 + 1	1	2 + 1			
BREVETT Rufus	34 + 1		1 + 1	1	6			
CLARK Lee	5 + 4		3					
COLLINS John	29 + 5		2	1	5			
DAVIS Sean	25 + 5		3		3 + 1			
FINNAN Steve	38		3		6			
GOLDBAEK Bjarne	8 + 5	1	2		0 + 2			
GOMA Alain	32 + 1		1		6			
HARLEY Jon	5 + 5		2		0 + 1			
HAYLES Barry	27 + 8	8	3	2	2 + 3	2		
KNIGHT Zat	8 + 2		2		3			
LEGWINSKI Sylvain	30 + 3	3	1 + 1	1	5	1		
LEWIS Eddie	1							
MALBRANQUE Steed	33 + 4	8	1 + 2	1	6	1		
MARLET Steve	21 + 5	6	1		5 + 1	3		
MELVILLE Andy	35		1 + 1		5 + 1			
OUADDOU Abdeslam	4 + 4		2		1 + 1			
SAHA Louis	28 + 8	8	0 + 2	1	5 + 1			
STOLCERS Andrejs	0 + 5				0 + 1			
SYMONS Kit	2 + 2							
TAYLOR Maik	1		3		2			
VAN DER SAR Edwin	37				4			
WILLOCK Calum	0 + 2							

GILLINGHAM (DIV 1: 12th)

	P/FL App	P/FL Goals	FLC App	FLC Goals	FAC App	FAC Goals	Others App	Others Goals
ASHBY Barry	28	1	2		3			
BARTRAM Vince	36		3		3			
BROWN Jason	10							
BROWNING Marcus	38 + 4	3	2 + 1		2 + 1			
BUTTERS Guy	21 + 2	1	1					
EDGE Roland	14		2					
GOODEN Ty	20 + 5	1	2		2 + 1	1		
HESSENTHALER Andy	10 + 7		1 + 1		0 + 1			
HOPE Chris	46	4	3		3			
IPOUA Guy	20 +20	8	1 + 2		0 + 3			
JAMES Kevin	0 +10							
KING Marlon	38 + 4	17	2 + 1	2	3	1		
NOSWORTHY Nyron	29				1 + 1			
ONUORA Iffy	31 + 2	11	3	1	3			
OSBORN Simon	23 + 5	4			2 + 1			
PATTERSON Mark	17 + 3		3		2			
PENNOCK Adrian	9 + 1		3					
PERPETUINI David	25 + 9	1	1 + 1		3			
ROSE Richard	2 + 1							
SAMUEL JLloyd	7 + 1							
SAUNDERS Mark	6 +13	1	1					
SHAW Paul	27 +10	7	0 + 3		3	1		
SMITH Paul	46	2	3		3			
SPILLER Danny	0 + 1							
TAYLOR Robert	3 + 8							

GRIMSBY TOWN (DIV 1: 19th)

	P/FL App	P/FL Goals	FLC App	FLC Goals	FAC App	FAC Goals	Others App	Others Goals
ALLEN Bradley	19 + 9	4	1 + 2	1				
BEHARALL David	13 + 1		1					
BOULDING Michael	24 +11	11	0 + 2		0 + 2			
BROOMES Marlon	13 + 2		3	2				
BURNETT Wayne	18 +14	2	2		2			
BUSSCHER Robby	0 + 1							
BUTTERFIELD Danny	43 + 3	2	4		2			
CAMPBELL Stuart	32 + 1	3	4		1			
CHAPMAN Ben	12 + 5		3		2			
COLDICOTT Stacy	19 + 7				1			
COOKE Terry	3	1						
COYNE Danny	45		4		2			
CROUDSON Steve	1							
FALCONER Willie	1 + 1							
FORD Simon	8 + 5	1	0 + 1		2			
GALLIMORE Tony	38		3		2			
GROVES Paul	43	2	4		2			
JEFFREY Mike	4 +14	1	1 + 1	1	0 + 1			
JEVONS Phil	25 + 6	6	4	2	2			
LIVINGSTONE Steve	0 + 3							
McDERMOTT John	24		2					
NEILSON Alan	8 + 2		1		1			
POUTON Alan	35	5	3					
PRINGLE Martin	2							
RAVEN Paul	4 + 5				0 + 1			
ROBINSON Paul	1 + 4							
ROWAN Jonny	19 + 5	4	2 + 1	1				
SMITH David	4	1			0 + 1			
TAYLOR Robert	4	1						
THOMPSON Chris	4 + 4				2			
TODD Andy	12	3						
WARD Iain	1							
WILLEMS Menno	27 + 3	1	2		1			

HALIFAX TOWN (DIV 3: 24th)

	P/FL App	P/FL Goals	FLC App	FLC Goals	FAC App	FAC Goals	Others App	Others Goals
BUSHELL Steve	25	1						
BUTLER Lee	21 + 1		1		3		1	
CLARKE Chris	24		1		3			
CLARKE Matthew	22 + 9	1			3		1	
CROOKES Peter	1							
FARRELL Andy	7 + 2				3			
FITZPATRICK Ian	26 + 3	8			3			
HARSLEY Paul	45	11	1		3	1	1	
HEINEMANN Nicky	3							
HERBERT Robert	11 + 1				0 + 2			
HOUGHTON Scott	7							
JONES Gary	20 +15	4	0 + 1		1 + 2		1	
JULES Mark	34 + 1		1		1 + 1		1	
KERRIGAN Steve	23 + 7		1		2		1	
LUDDEN Dominic	2				1			
MIDDLETON Craig	21 + 8	2	0 + 1		1	1	1	
MIDGLEY Craig	12 +12	3	1		2		0 + 1	
MITCHELL Graham	41 + 2				3		1	
OLEKSEWYCZ Steve	0 + 2							
REDFEARN Neil	27 + 3	6	1		3		1	
REILLY Alan	0 + 2							
RICHARDS Marc	5							
RICHARDSON Barry	24							
SMITH Craig	0 + 2							
SMITH Grant	11						1	
STONEMAN Paul	32	1	1				1	
SWALES Steve	20 + 4	1	1		1		0 + 1	
WINDER Nathan	0 + 1							
WOOD Jamie	10 + 6		1		1	1	0 + 1	
WOODWARD Andy	29 + 1	1	1		2			
WRIGHT Peter	3 +11		0 + 1		0 + 2			

HARTLEPOOL UNITED (DIV 3: 7th)

	P/FL App	P/FL Goals	FLC App	FLC Goals	FAC App	FAC Goals	Others App	Others Goals
ARNISON Paul	11 + 8						2	1
BARRON Michael	39	1	1		1		3	

	P/FL App	P/FL Goals	FLC App	FLC Goals	FAC App	FAC Goals	Others App	Others Goals
BASS Jon	19 + 1	1	1		1			
BOYD Adam	10 +19	9					2	
CLARK Ian	5 + 2	2	1					
CLARKE Darrell	24 + 9	7	0 + 1		1	1	2	
COPPINGER James	14	2						
EASTER Jermaine	0 +12	2						
HENDERSON Kevin	13 +10	2	1				0 + 2	
HOLLUND Martin	3		1					
HUMPHREYS Richie	42 + 4	5	1		1		3	
LEE Graeme	38 + 1	4	1		0 + 1		3	
LORMOR Anth	4 +13	1	0 + 1					
ORMEROD Anthony	2							
PARKIN Jon	0 + 1							
ROBINSON Mark	33 + 4						2	
SHARP James	13 + 2						1	
SIMMS Gordon	6 + 4				1			
SMITH Paul	30 + 1	4			1		2	
STEPHENSON Paul	23 + 6		1				1 + 1	
SWEENEY Antony	0 + 2							
TINKLER Mark	39 + 1	9	1		1		1	
WATSON Gordon	31 + 1	18	1		1		3	
WESTWOOD Chris	35		1		1		2	
WIDDRINGTON Tommy	24	2	1		1		1	
WILLIAMS Eifion	5 + 3	4					2	1
WILLIAMS Tony	43		1				3	

HUDDERSFIELD TOWN (DIV 2: 6th)

	P/FL App	P/FL Goals	FLC App	FLC Goals	FAC App	FAC Goals	Others App	Others Goals
ARMSTRONG Craig	7 + 4	1	1				1 + 1	
BALDRY Simon	3 + 1		0 + 1				1 + 1	
BEECH Chris	6 + 3	1	1					
BOOTH Andy	30 + 6	11	1		2		7	3
CLARKE Nathan	36		1				4	
DELANEY Damien	1 + 1							
DYSON Jon					1			
EVANS Gareth	35		1				5	
FACEY Delroy	11 + 2	2					2	
GRAY Kevin	44	1	1		2		8	
HAY Chris	19 +12	5	1		0 + 1		2 + 4	1
HEARY Thomas	21 +11		1		2		8	
HOLLAND Chris	35 + 2	1	1		2		7 + 1	1
IFIL Jerel	1 + 1						2	
IRONS Kenny	34 + 7	7	1		1		7	
JENKINS Steve	40		1		1		5	
KNIGHT Leon	31	16			2	1	4	
LUCKETTI Chris	2							
MACARI Paul	0 + 6		0 + 1				0 + 2	
MARGETSON Martyn	46		1		2		8	
MATTIS Dwayne	21 + 8	1	0 + 1		2		3	
MOSES Ade	13 + 4				1 + 1	1	4	
SCHOFIELD Danny	39 + 1	8			2		6	4
SENIOR Michael							0 + 1	
THORRINGTON John	29 + 2	6	0 + 1				3	
WIJNHARD Clyde	2 +11	1					1 + 1	1

HULL CITY (DIV 3: 11th)

	P/FL App	P/FL Goals	FLC App	FLC Goals	FAC App	FAC Goals	Others App	Others Goals
ALEXANDER Gary	43	17	2	1	2	2	3	3
BERESFORD David	33 + 8	1	2		1		3	
BLOOMER Matt	0 + 3		1					
BRADSHAW Gary	3	1			0 + 1			
CACERES Adrian	1 + 3							
DUDFIELD Lawrie	32 + 6	12	2		2	2	3	
EDWARDS Michael	38 + 1	1	2		2		2	
FOLAN Caleb	0 + 1							
GLENNON Matty	26		2		2		2	
GOODISON Ian	14 + 2		1		2		2	
GREAVES Mark	25 + 1	1	1	1			0 + 1	
HOLT Andy	24 + 6		1				2 + 1	
JOHNSSON JJ	38 + 2	4	2		2	1	2 + 1	
LEE David	2 + 9	1	0 + 1		0 + 1		0 + 1	
LIGHTBOURNE Kyle	3 + 1							
MATTHEWS Rob	9 + 6	3	0 + 1		2	1	1 + 1	
MOHAN Nicky	26 + 1	1	2				1	

	P/FL App	P/FL Goals	FLC App	FLC Goals	FAC App	FAC Goals	Others App	Others Goals
MORLEY Ben	1 + 2		0 + 1					
MUSSELWHITE Paul	20						1	
NORRIS David	3 + 3	1						
PETTY Ben	22 + 5		1 + 1		2		3	
PHILPOTT Lee	9 + 2	1						
PRICE Michael	0 + 1		0 + 1				0 + 1	
REDDY Michael	1 + 4	4						
ROBERTS Neil	3 + 3							
ROWE Rodney	5 + 9	2	0 + 1					
SNEEKES Richard	17 + 5				0 + 1		1 + 1	
TAIT Paul	0 + 2							
VAN BLERK Jason	10		1					
WHITMORE Theo	23 +11	2	2	1	2		3	1
WHITTLE Justin	35 + 1		1		2		2	1
WICKS Matthew	14							
WILLIAMS Ryan	26 + 3	2			1 + 1		2 + 1	

IPSWICH TOWN (PREM: 18th)

	P/FL App	P/FL Goals	FLC App	FLC Goals	FAC App	FAC Goals	Others App	Others Goals
AMBROSE Darren	0 + 1							
ARMSTRONG Alun	21 +11	4	2	1	0 + 1		1 + 2	2
BENT Darren	2 + 3	1	0 + 1	1			0 + 1	
BENT Marcus	22 + 3	9			2	1		
BRAMBLE Titus	16 + 2				2		4	
BRANAGAN Keith	0 + 1							
BROWN Wayne					1			
CLAPHAM Jamie	22 +10	2	2		0 + 1		4 + 2	
COUNAGO Pablo	1 +12		1		0 + 1		2 + 2	
GAARDSOE Thomas	3 + 1	1	0 + 1				0 + 1	
GEORGE Finidi	21 + 4	6					4	1
HOLLAND Matt	38	3	1		1		6	
HREIDARSSON Hermann	38	1	1		2		6	1
LE PEN Ulrich	0 + 1				0 + 1			
McGREAL John	27		2		1		3	
MAGILTON Jim	16 + 8				1	1	5	
MAKIN Chris	30		2		1		4 + 1	
MARSHALL Andy	13				2			
MILLER Tommy	5 + 3		2		0 + 1		0 + 2	
NAYLOR Richard	5 + 9	1	0 + 2		0 + 1		3 + 2	
PERALTA Sixto	16 + 6	3	1		2	2	2 + 2	
REUSER Martijn	18 + 6	1	1	2	2		1 + 2	
SERENI Matteo	25						6	
STEWART Marcus	20 + 8	6	1		2	1	4	3
VENUS Mark	29		1				5	
WILNIS Fabian	6 + 8		1 + 1		1		2	
WRIGHT Jermaine	24 + 5	1	2		2		4 + 1	

KIDDERMINSTER HARRIERS (DIV 3: 10th)

	P/FL App	P/FL Goals	FLC App	FLC Goals	FAC App	FAC Goals	Others App	Others Goals
APPLEBY Richie	18 + 1	4			1			
AYRES Lee	5 + 1		1					
BENNETT Dean	39 + 3	8			1		2	
BIRD Tony	14 +12	2	1	2	1		1	
BLAKE Mark	23 + 1	4	1		1		1 + 1	
BROCK Stuart	42		1		1		1	
BROUGHTON Drewe	23 +15	8	1				2	
CLARKSON Ian	36 + 3				1		2	
CORBETT Andy	0 + 2							
DANBY John	0 + 2							
DAVIES Ben	9		1					
DOYLE Daire	0 + 1		0 + 1					
DUCROS Andy	7 + 7	2			0 + 1			
FOSTER Ian	21 +12	8	1				2	
HADLEY Stewart	5 + 5		0 + 1				0 + 1	
HENRIKSEN Bo	24 + 1	8			1			
HINTON Craig	41		1		1		2	
JOY Ian	13 + 3						1	
LARKIN Colin	31 + 2	6					1 + 1	1
LEWIS Matthew	0 + 2							
MEDOU-OTYE Parfait	2		1					
MONTGOMERY Gary	2							
NIXON Eric	2						1	
SALL Abdou	27	2			1		1	
SHAIL Mark	4						1	

	P/FL App	Goals	FLC App	Goals	FAC App	Goals	Others App	Goals
SHILTON Sam	12 +12		1		0 + 1		1	
SMITH Adie	33 + 3	2						
STAMPS Scott	36 + 1		1		1		1	
WILLIAMS Danny	37 + 1	1	1		1		2	

LEEDS UNITED (PREM: 5th)

	P/FL App	Goals	FLC App	Goals	FAC App	Goals	Others App	Goals
BAKKE Eirik	20 + 7	2	2	1			6	1
BATTY David	30 + 6		1		1		5 + 1	
BOWYER Lee	24 + 1	5	1		1		3	2
DACOURT Olivier	16 + 1		2				6	
DUBERRY Michael	3		0 + 2		0 + 1		1	
FERDINAND Rio	31		2				7	
FOWLER Robbie	22	12			1			
HARTE Ian	34 + 2	5	2		1		8	1
JOHNSON Seth	12 + 2							
KEANE Robbie	16 + 9	3	2	3			6	3
KELLY Garry	19 + 1		0 + 1		1		3	
KEWELL Harry	26 + 1	8	1	1			7	2
McPHAIL Stephen	0 + 1		0 + 2				1	
MARTYN Nigel	38		2		1		8	
MATTEO Dominic	32		1				7	
MAYBURY Alan	0 + 1							
MILLS Danny	28	1	2		1		8	
SMITH Alan	19 + 4	4	1 + 1		1		4 + 1	1
VIDUKA Mark	33	11	1	1	1	1	7	3
WILCOX Jason	4 + 9		1				1 + 2	
WOODGATE Jonathan	11 + 2		1		1			

LEICESTER CITY (PREM: 20th)

	P/FL App	Goals	FLC App	Goals	FAC App	Goals	Others App	Goals
AKINBIYI Ade	16 + 5	2	1	1	1 + 1			
ASHTON Jon	3 + 4							
BENJAMIN Trevor	4 + 7		0 + 1		1			
DAVIDSON Callum	29 + 1		1 + 1		0 + 1			
DEANE Brian	13 + 2	6			1			
DELANEY Damien	2 + 1		1					
DICKOV Paul	11 + 1	4						
ELLIOTT Matt	31		2		1			
FLOWERS Tim	3 + 1							
GUNNLAUGSSON Arnie	0 + 2							
HEATH Matthew	3 + 2				0 + 1			
IMPEY Andy	20 + 7		0 + 2		2			
IZZET Muzzy	29 + 2	4	2		2			
JONES Matthew	6 + 4	1	1 + 1		1			
LAURSEN Jacob	10							
LEWIS Junior	4 + 2		1					
MARSHALL Lee	29 + 6		1		2			
OAKES Stefan	16 + 5	1			1			
PIPER Matt	14 + 2	1	1		0 + 1			
REEVES Martin	1 + 4							
ROGERS Alan	9 + 4				2			
ROWETT Gary	9 + 2		1					
SAVAGE Robbie	35		2		1			
SCOWCROFT Jamie	21 + 3	5	1		1	2		
SINCLAIR Frank	33 + 2		2		1			
STEVENSON Jon	0 + 6	1						
STEWART Jordan	9 + 3		1		1			
STURRIDGE Dean	8 + 1	3	1					
TAGGART Gerry	0 + 1							
WALKER Ian	35		2		2			
WILLIAMSON Tom	0 + 1							
WISE Dennis	15 + 2	1	1		1			
WRIGHT Tommy	0 + 1							

LEYTON ORIENT (DIV 3: 18th)

	P/FL App	Goals	FLC App	Goals	FAC App	Goals	Others App	Goals
BARNARD Donny	6 + 4				0 + 1			
BARRETT Scott	32				4			
BAYES Ashley	12 + 1		1					
BEALL Matthew	7 + 4				1			
BRAZIER Matt	8							
CANHAM Scott	23 + 1	4			1	1	0 + 1	
CASTLE Steve	0 + 1		0 + 1					
CHRISTIE Iyseden	9 + 6	3			0 + 1	1		

	P/FL App	Goals	FLC App	Goals	FAC App	Goals	Others App	Goals
CONSTANTINE Leon	9 + 1	3					0 + 1	
DORRIAN Chris	2 + 1				2			
DOWNER Simon	11 + 1		1					
FLETCHER Gary	3 + 6							
GOUGH Neil	1 +10		1					
GRAY Wayne	13 + 2	5			2	1		
HADLAND Phil	0 + 5	1	0 + 1					
HARRIS Andy	45				4		1	
HATCHER Danny	2 + 6				0 + 1			
HERRERA Robbie	2				0 + 1		1	
HOUGHTON Scott	10 +11	5	1	1				
HUTCHINGS Carl	9 + 1	1						
IBEHRE Jabo	21 + 7	4	1		2 + 1	1	0 + 1	
JONES Billy	16				3 + 1			
JOSEPH Matthew	29 + 1	1	1		3			
LEIGERTWOOD Mikele	8				2			
LOCKWOOD Matt	20 + 4	2	1		1			
McELHOLM Brendan	0 + 2						1	
McGHEE Dave	39 + 1	2			4		1	
McLEAN Aaron	4 +23	1			0 + 3		1	1
MARTIN Johnny	29 + 2	2			3 + 1		1	
MINTON Jeff	32 + 1	5	1	1	4		1	
MORRIS Glenn	2						1	
NEWTON Adam	10		1					
NUGENT Kevin	7 + 2	1					1	
OAKES Scott	11		1					
PARTRIDGE David	6 + 1				1			
SMITH Dean	45	2	1		4	1	1	1
TATE Chris	1 + 6							
WATTS Steve	22 + 8	9	1		4	3	1	

LINCOLN CITY (DIV 3: 22nd)

	P/FL App	Goals	FLC App	Goals	FAC App	Goals	Others App	Goals
BAILEY Mark	18				2		1	
BARNETT Jason	23 + 3	2	1				0 + 1	
BATTERSBY Tony	28 +11	5	1	1	1 + 1			
BETTS Robert	1 + 2						0 + 1	
BIMSON Stuart	34 + 1		1		1 + 1		1	
BLACK Kingsley	30 + 1	5	1		1 + 1		1	
BLOOMER Matt	4 + 1							
BROWN Grant	32 + 4				3		1	
BUCKLEY Adam	19 +12				3		0 + 1	
CAMERON David	23 +21	6	0 + 1		3	1	1	1
CAMM Mark	5 +11				1 + 2			
FINNIGAN John	21 + 2		1		0 + 1			
GAIN Peter	35 + 7	2	1		2 + 1		1	
HAMILTON Ian	26				3	1		
HOLMES Steve	18 + 2	4	1		2	1	1	
HORRIGAN Darren	0 + 1							
LOGAN Richard	0 + 2							
MARRIOTT Alan	43		1		3		1	
MAYO Paul	11 + 3				1 + 1			
MORGAN Paul	32 + 2	1	1					
PETTINGER Paul	3							
SEDGEMORE Ben	33 +10	2	1		3		1	
SMITH Paul	6 + 2							
THORPE Lee	37	13	1		2		1	
WALKER Justin	24 + 7	3	0 + 1		2 + 1		1	

LIVERPOOL (PREM: 2nd)

	P/FL App	Goals	FLC App	Goals	FAC App	Goals	Others App	Goals
ANELKA Nicolas	13 + 7	4			2	1		
ARPHEXAD Pegguy	1 + 1						2	
BABBEL Markus	2						3 + 1	
BARMBY Nick	2 + 4		1				4 + 1	
BAROS Milan							0 + 1	
BERGER Patrik	12 + 9	1			0 + 1		1 + 8	
BISCAN Igor	4 + 1						1 + 4	
CARRAGHER Jamie	33		1		2		16 + 1	
DIOMEDE Bernard							1	
DUDEK Jerzy	35						12	
FOWLER Robbie	8 + 2	3					2 + 5	1
GERRARD Steven	26 + 2	3			2		14 + 1	1
HAMANN Dietmar	31		1		2		14	

	P/FL App	Goals	FLC App	Goals	FAC App	Goals	Others App	Goals
HENCHOZ Stephane	37				2		17	
HESKEY Emile	26 + 9	9	0 + 1		1 + 1		18	5
HYYPIA Sami	37	3	1		2		17	2
KIPPE Frode			0 + 1					
KIRKLAND Chris	1		1				2	
LITMANEN Jari	8 +13	4	1		0 + 1		4 + 5	3
McALLISTER Gary	14 +11		1	1			6 + 6	1
MURPHY Danny	31 + 5	6	1		1 + 1		14 + 3	2
OWEN Michael	25 + 4	19			2	2	12	7
REDKNAPP Jamie	2 + 2	1	0 + 1				1 + 2	1
RIISE Jon Arne	34 + 4	7			2		15 + 1	1
SMICER Vlad	13 + 9	4	1		1		8 + 3	1
TRAORE Djimi							1	
VIGNAL Gregory	3 + 1		1				4	
WESTERVELD Sander	1						2	
WRIGHT Steve	10 + 2		1				2 + 1	1
XAVIER Abel	9 + 1	1					5	1

LUTON TOWN (DIV 3: 2nd)

	P/FL App	Goals	FLC App	Goals	FAC App	Goals	Others App	Goals
BAYLISS Dave	15 + 3							
BOYCE Emmerson	30 + 7		1					
BRENNAN Dean					1		1	1
BRKOVIC Ahmet	17 + 4	1			1	1		
COYNE Chris	29 + 2	3						
CROWE Dean	32 + 2	15			1			
DOUGLAS Stuart	2 + 7		0 + 1					
DRYDEN Richard	2 + 1		0 + 1		1		1	
EMBERSON Carl	33		1		1			
FORBES Adrian	15 +25	4	1		1	1		
FOTIADIS Andrew	0 + 8	1			0 + 1		1	
FRASER Stuart							1	
GEORGE Liam	2 + 2				0 + 1		1	
GILLMAN Robert							1	
GRIFFITHS Carl	10	7	1					
HILLIER Ian	11 +12	1			1			
HOLMES Peter	4 + 3	1	0 + 1		1		1	
HOWARD Steve	42	24	1					
HUGHES Paul	12 +10	2	1					
JOHNSON Marvin	11 + 7	1	1				1	
KABBA Steve	0 + 3							
LOCKE Adam	1 + 2							
McSWEGAN Gary	2 + 1							
MANSELL Lee	6 + 5	1	1				1	
NEILSON Alan	8							
NICHOLLS Kevin	42	7	1				1	
OVENDALE Mark	13							
PERRETT Russell	39 + 1	3	1					
SKELTON Aaron	9	1			1			
SPRING Matthew	42	6			1			
STIRLING Jude	1						0 + 1	
STREET Kevin	1 + 1							
TAYLOR Matthew	43	11	1		1			
THOMSON Peter					1		1	
VALOIS Jean-Louis	32 + 2	6						

MACCLESFIELD TOWN (DIV 3: 13th)

	P/FL App	Goals	FLC App	Goals	FAC App	Goals	Others App	Goals
ABBEY George	15 + 2				1		1	
ADAMS Danny	38 + 1		1		4			
ASKEY John	1 +17	1			0 + 1			
BULLOCK Matthew	2 + 1							
BYRNE Chris	26 + 6	6	1		4	2		
CAME Shaun	1							
EYRE Richard	12 + 2		1				1	
GLOVER Lee	38 + 5	9	1	1	3 + 1	2	1	1
HITCHEN Steve	28 + 2	1	1		3		1	
KEEN Kevin	29 + 1		1		4	1	1	
LAMBERT Rickie	32 + 3	8	1		4	2	1	
LIGHTBOURNE Kyle	22 + 7	4	1					
MACAULEY Steve	12				1			
McAVOY Andy	4 + 6		0 + 1		2 + 1			
MARTIN Lee	8 + 1		1					
MUNROE Karl	19 +11		0 + 1					

	P/FL App	Goals	FLC App	Goals	FAC App	Goals	Others App	Goals
O'NEILL Paul	7 + 4							
PRIEST Chris	32 + 1	1			4		1	
RIDLER Dave	37 + 2		1		3 + 1		1	
SHUTTLEWORTH Barry	0 + 3				0 + 1		1	
SMITH Dave	8							
SMITH Jeff	7 + 1	2						
TINSON Darren	46	1	1		4		1	
TIPTON Matthew	12 + 1	3						
TRACEY Richard	10 +10	2	1		3			
WELCH Michael	6							
WHITAKER Danny	15 + 1	2						
WHITEHEAD Damien	1 + 1				0 + 1			
WILSON Steve	38				4		1	
WOOLLEY Matt	0 + 3						0 + 1	

MANCHESTER CITY (DIV 1: 1st)

	P/FL App	Goals	FLC App	Goals	FAC App	Goals	Others App	Goals
BENARBIA Ali	38	8	2		2			
BERKOVIC Eyal	20 + 5	6	2 + 1		3	1		
CHARVET Laurent	3							
COLOSIMO Simon	0 + 6		1					
DICKOV Paul	0 + 7		0 + 1	1				
DUNNE Richard	41 + 2	1	3		3			
EDGHILL Richard	9 + 2				1 + 1			
ETUHU Dixon	11 + 1		1					
GOATER Shaun	42	28	2	2	1 + 1	2		
GRANT Tony	2 + 1		1					
GRANVILLE Danny	12 + 4		1 + 1					
HAALAND Alfie	0 + 3				0 + 1			
HORLOCK Kevin	33 + 9	7	2		3	1		
HOWEY Steve	34	3	2		2			
HUCKERBY Darren	30 +10	20	2 + 1	5	3	1		
JENSEN Niclas	16 + 2	1			2			
JIHAI Sun	2 + 5							
KILLEN Chris	0 + 3							
MACKEN Jon	4 + 4	5						
MEARS Tyrone	0 + 1							
METTOMO Lucien	17 + 6	1	1 + 1					
MIKE Leon	1 + 1							
NASH Carlo	22 + 1		1		1			
NEGOUAI Christian	2 + 3	1	1		0 + 1			
PEARCE Stuart	38	3	3		1 + 1			
RITCHIE Paul	0 + 8		0 + 1		2			
SHUKER Chris	0 + 2		0 + 1	1				
TIATTO Danny	36 + 1	1	2		1			
TOURE Alioune	0 + 1		0 + 1					
WANCHOPE Paulo	14 + 1	12	1		2	1		
WEAVER Nicky	24 + 1		2		2			
WHITLEY Jeff	0 + 2							
WIEKENS Gerard	24 + 5		2		1			
WRIGHT-PHILLIPS Shaun	31 + 4	8	1 + 1		3			

MANCHESTER UNITED (PREM: 3rd)

	P/FL App	Goals	FLC App	Goals	FAC App	Goals	Others App	Goals
BARTHEZ Fabien	32				1		16	
BECKHAM David	23 + 5	11			1		14	5
BLANC Laurent	29	1			2		15	2
BROWN Wes	15 + 2						5 + 2	
BUTT Nicky	20 + 5	1			2		9 + 1	
CARROLL Roy	6 + 1		1		1		1	
CHADWICK Luke	5 + 3		1		1 + 1			
CLEGG Michael			0 + 1					
COLE Andy	7 + 4	4					1 + 3	1
DAVIS Jimmy			1					
DJORDJIC Bojan			1					
FORLAN Diego	6 + 7						1 + 4	
FORTUNE Quinton	8 + 6	1					3 + 2	
GIGGS Ryan	18 + 7	7			0 + 1		14	2
IRWIN Denis	10 + 2						9 + 2	
JOHNSEN Ronny	9 + 1	1					8 + 1	
KEANE Roy	28	3			2		12 + 1	1
MAY David	2						1	
NARDIELLO Danny			0 + 1					
NEVILLE Gary	31 + 3				2		14	

	P/FL App	P/FL Goals	FLC App	FLC Goals	FAC App	FAC Goals	Others App	Others Goals
NEVILLE Phil	21 + 7	2	1		2		4 + 4	
O'SHEA John	4 + 5		1				0 + 3	
ROCHE Lee			1					
SCHOLES Paul	30 + 5	8			2		14	1
SILVESTRE Mickael	31 + 4				2		11 + 3	1
SOLSKJAER Ole Gunnar	23 + 7	17			2	1	5 +10	7
STAM Jaap	1						1	
STEWART Michael	2 + 1		1				0 + 1	
VAN DER GOUW Rai	0 + 1		0 + 1					
VAN NISTELROOY Ruud	29 + 3	23			0 + 2	2	15	11
VERON Juan	24 + 2	5			1		13	
WALLWORK Ronnie	0 + 1		1		1			
WEBBER Danny			1					
YORKE Dwight	4 + 6	1			0 + 1		1 + 3	

MANSFIELD TOWN (DIV 3: 3rd)

	P/FL App	P/FL Goals	FLC App	FLC Goals	FAC App	FAC Goals	Others App	Others Goals
ASHER Alistair	1 + 9				0 + 2		1	
BACON Danny	1 + 7	1	0 + 1		1			
BARRETT Adam	26 + 3				3		1	
BINGHAM Michael	1 + 1						1	
BRADLEY Shayne	7 + 9	3			2		1	
CLARKE Jamie	1							
CORDEN Wayne	46	8	1		3	1	1	
DISLEY Craig	31 + 5	7	1		2			
GREENACRE Chris	43 + 1	21	1	2	3	5		
HARRIS Richard	0 + 6							
HASSELL Bobby	43		1		3		1	
JERVIS David	0 + 3						0 + 1	
KELLY David	11 + 6	4						
LAWRENCE Liam	32	2	1		3		0 + 1	
MURRAY Adam	13	7						
PEMBERTON Martin	33 + 5	4			1 + 1		1	
PILKINGTON Kevin	45		1		3			
PIPER Matt	8	1						
REDDINGTON Stuart	34 + 4	1	1				1	
ROBINSON Les	36		1		3			
SELLARS Scott	5 + 1	1						
TANKARD Allen	22 + 8	2	1		3		1	
WHEATCROFT Paul	1 + 1							
WHITE Andy	16 + 6	4	1	1	0 + 3			
WHITE Jason	6 + 1						1	
WILLIAMS Lee	0 + 2							
WILLIAMSON Lee	44 + 2	3	1		3		1	

MIDDLESBROUGH (PREM: 12th)

	P/FL App	P/FL Goals	FLC App	FLC Goals	FAC App	FAC Goals	Others App	Others Goals
BERESFORD Marlon	0 + 1							
BOKSIC Alen	20 + 2	8	1		2 + 1			
CAMPBELL Andy	0 + 4				0 + 1	1		
CARBONE Beni	13	1						
COOPER Colin	14 + 4	2	1 + 1		1			
CROSSLEY Mark	17 + 1		1		3			
DEANE Brian	6 + 1	1						
DEBEVE Michael	1 + 3				1 + 1			
DOWNING Stewart	2 + 1							
EHIOGU Ugo	29	1	2		2	1		
FESTA Gianluca	8	1			3 + 1			
FLEMING Curtis	8							
GAVIN Jason	5 + 4		1 + 1		1 + 1			
GORDON Dean	0 + 1							
GREENING Jonathan	36	1	1		3 + 1			
HUDSON Mark	0 + 2							
INCE Paul	31	2	1		4	1		
JOB Josephe-Desire	3 + 1		0 + 1					
JOHNSTON Allan	13 + 4	1	1		2 + 1			
MARINELLI Carlos	12 + 8	2	1 + 1		3 + 2			
MURPHY David	0 + 5		2		0 + 1			
MUSTOE Robbie	31 + 5	2	1 + 1		6			
NEMETH Szilard	11 +10	3	2	2	2 + 2	1		
OKON Paul	1 + 3							
QUEUDRUE Franck	28	2			6			
RICARD Hamilton	6 + 3		0 + 1		1			
SCHWARZER Mark	21		1		3			

	P/FL App	P/FL Goals	FLC App	FLC Goals	FAC App	FAC Goals	Others App	Others Goals
SOUTHGATE Gareth	37	1	1		6			
STAMP Phil	3 + 3				1 + 2			
STOCKDALE Robbie	26 + 2	1	2		6			
VICKERS Steve	2							
WHELAN Noel	18 + 1	4			5	3		
WILKSHIRE Luke	6 + 1				1			
WILSON Mark	2 + 8		2	1	1 + 1			
WINDASS Dean	8 +19	1	1		3 + 3			

MILLWALL (DIV 1: 4th)

	P/FL App	P/FL Goals	FLC App	FLC Goals	FAC App	FAC Goals	Others App	Others Goals
BIRCHAM Marc	22 + 2				1			
BRANIFF Kevin	0 + 1				0 + 1			
BULL Ronnie	20 + 6		0 + 1				2	
CAHILL Tim	43	13	2		2		2	
CLARIDGE Steve	39 + 2	17	1 + 1	1	0 + 1		1 + 1	
DUBLIN Dion	5	2					2	
DUNNE Alan	0 + 1							
DYCHE Sean	35	3	2		2			
GREEN Ryan	12 + 1							
GUERET Willy	0 + 1				1			
HARRIS Neil	9 +12	4			2		1	
HEARN Charley	0 + 2							
IFILL Paul	27 +13	4	2		1		2	
KINET Christophe	11 + 6	3	0 + 1		0 + 1		2	
LAWRENCE Matty	24 + 2		1 + 1		2		2	
LIVERMORE David	43		2		2			
McPHAIL Stephen	3							
MOODY Paul	0 + 1		1	1				
NAYLOR Richard	2 + 1							
NEILL Lucas	2 + 2	1	1					
NETHERCOTT Stuart	46	3	2		2		2	
ODUNSI Leke	0 + 2							
PHILLIPS Mark	1							
REID Steven	33 + 2	5	1		2		2	
RYAN Robbie	32 + 5		2		2			
SADLIER Richard	36 + 1	14	2	1	1	2		
SAVARESE Giovanni	0 + 1							
STAMP Phil	0 + 1		1					
SWEENEY Peter	0 + 1							
TUTTLE Dave	5		0 + 1					
WARD Darren	10 + 4				1		2	
WARNER Tony	46		2		1		2	

NEWCASTLE UNITED (PREM: 4th)

	P/FL App	P/FL Goals	FLC App	FLC Goals	FAC App	FAC Goals	Others App	Others Goals
ACUNA Clarence	10 + 6	3	1 + 1		3 + 2	1	0 + 1	
AMEOBI Shola	4 +11		2 + 1	2	0 + 1		6	3
BARTON Warren	4 + 1		1				6	
BASSEDAS Christian	1 + 1		1				3 + 1	
BELLAMY Craig	26 + 1	9	2 + 1	4	3		6	
BERNARD Olivier	4 +12	3	2		2		0 + 3	
CALDWELL Steve							0 + 3	
CORT Carl	6 + 2	1			2			
DABIZAS Nikos	33 + 2	3	2		3		6	
DISTIN Sylvain	20 + 8		2		5			
DYER Kieron	15 + 3	3	0 + 1		2			
ELLIOTT Robbie	26 + 1	1	2 + 1		3 + 1		6	1
GIVEN Shay	38		1		5		6	
GRIFFIN Andy	3 + 1		1					
HARPER Steve			3					
HUGHES Aaron	34		3		5	1	6	1
JENAS Jermaine	6 + 6							
KERR Brian					0 + 2			
LEE Rob	15 + 1	1	3				3	
LUA LUA Lomano	4 +16	3	0 + 3		0 + 3		0 + 6	2
McCLEN Jamie	3				3	1	0 + 2	
O'BRIEN Andy	31 + 3	2	3 + 1		4 + 1	1	0 + 1	
QUINN Wayne	1				0 + 1		6	1
ROBERT Laurent	34 + 2	8	3	1	3	1		
SHEARER Alan	36 + 1	23	4	2	5	2		
SOLANO Nobby	37	7	4		5	1	6	4
SPEED Gary	28 + 1	5	3		2		6	2

NORTHAMPTON TOWN (DIV 2: 20th)

	P/FL		FLC		FAC		Others	
	App	Goals	App	Goals	App	Goals	App	Goals
ASAMOAH Derek	3 +37	3	0 + 2		0 + 1		0 + 2	
BURGESS Daryl	36	1			2		2	
CARRUTHERS Chris	6 + 7	1					1	
CAVILL Aaran	0 + 1							
DEMPSEY Paul	13 + 7		1 + 1				1	
EVATT Ian	10 + 1		2					
FORRESTER Jamie	40 + 3	17	2	1	2		1	
FRAIN John	25 + 2		1		2		2	
GABBIADINI Marco	30 + 5	7	1		2	2	1 + 1	
HARGREAVES Chris	38 + 1	3	2		1		1	
HODGE John	4 +15	1					0 + 2	
HOPE Richard	35 + 8	6	2		2		2	
HUNT James	38	4	2		2		2	1
HUNTER Roy	38 + 2	4	1		2		1	
LAVIN Gerard	2		1					
McGREGOR Paul	37 + 2	3	1 + 1	1	0 + 2		2	1
MARSH Chris	26				1		1	
MORISON Steve	0 + 1							
PARKIN Sam	31 + 9	4	2	1	0 + 2		2	
SAMPSON Ian	24 + 3				2			
SOLLITT Adam	8 + 2		2					
SPEDDING Duncan	22 + 1		2		2		1	
THOMPSON Chris	0 + 1		0 + 1					
WELCH Keith	38				2		2	
WOLLEASTON Robert	2 + 5		0 + 1					

NORWICH CITY (DIV 1: 6th)

	P/FL		FLC		FAC		Others	
	App	Goals	App	Goals	App	Goals	App	Goals
ABBEY Zema	6	1	1					
BENJAMIN Trevor	3 + 3							
CRICHTON Paul	5 + 1							
DRURY Adam	35		1		1		3	
EASTON Clint	10 + 4	1			0 + 1		3	
EMBLEN Neil	1 + 1							
FLEMING Craig	46		1		2		3	
GREEN Robert	41		1		2		3	
HOLT Gary	46	2	1		2		3	
KENTON Darren	30 + 3	4			2		3	
LIBBRA Marc	17 +17	7	1		2		0 + 1	
LLEWELLYN Chris	5 + 8				0 + 2			
McGOVERN Brian	5 + 4		1					
MACKAY Malky	44	3	1		2		3	1
McVEIGH Paul	37 + 5	8	1		2		3	1
MULRYNE Phil	39 + 1	6	1		1		3	
NEDERGAARD Steen	37 + 3	2			2			
NIELSEN David	22 + 1	8					3	
NOTMAN Alex	6 +24				2		0 + 3	
RIVERS Mark	19 +13	2			0 + 2		3	1
ROBERTS Andy	4 + 1							
ROBERTS Iwan	29 + 1	13	0 + 1				0 + 3	1
RUSSELL Darel	13 +10		1		1 + 1			
SUTCH Daryl	6 +13				1		0 + 2	

NOTTINGHAM FOREST (DIV 1: 16th)

	P/FL		FLC		FAC		Others	
	App	Goals	App	Goals	App	Goals	App	Goals
BART-WILLIAMS Chris	17	3	2	1				
BOPP Eugene	12 + 7	1	0 + 2					
BRENNAN Jim	41		3		1			
CASH Brian	0 + 5							
DAWSON Kevin	3							
DAWSON Mike	1							
DOIG Chris	8		1					
EDDS Gareth	0 + 1							
EDWARDS Chris	2 + 4		1					
FOY Keith	2							
GRAY Andy	8 + 8	1	1 + 1					
HAREWOOD Marlon	20 + 8	11	1 + 1					
HJELDE Jon Olav	42				1			
JENAS Jermaine	28	4	2		1			
JOHN Stern	20 + 6	13	1	1	1			
JOHNSON Andy	0 + 1							
JOHNSON David	17 + 5	3	2		0 + 1			
JONES Gary	2 + 3	1						
LESTER Jack	23 + 9	5	2	1	1			
LOUIS-JEAN Matthieu	37 + 1	1	2					
PROUDLOCK Adam	3							
PRUTTON David	43	3	2		1			
REID Andy	19 +10		1 + 1					
ROGERS Alan	3		1					
SCIMECA Ricardo	35 + 2		2		1			
SUMMERBEE Nicky	17	2			1			
THOMPSON John	8							
VAUGHAN Tony	5 + 3				1			
WARD Darren	46		3		1			
WESTCARR Craig	0 + 8							
WILLIAMS Gareth	44		2		1			

NOTTS COUNTY (DIV 2: 19th)

	P/FL		FLC		FAC		Others	
	App	Goals	App	Goals	App	Goals	App	Goals
ALLSOP Danny	43	19	2	4	3	2	2 + 1	3
BARACLOUGH Ian	30 + 3	3	2		3		3	
BOLLAND Paul	16 + 3		0 + 1		2		0 + 1	
BROUGH Michael	14 + 7				2 + 1		2	
CAS Marcel	39 + 1	6	2		2		2	
CASKEY Darren	39 + 3	5	2		3		2 + 1	1
CHILVERS Liam	9	1			2			
FENTON Nicky	41 + 1	3	2		3		2	
GARDEN Stuart	21						2	
GRAYSON Simon	10	1	1				2	
HACKWORTH Tony	9 +24	1	0 + 1		2 + 1		3	1
HAMILTON Ian	6 + 3		0 + 1				1 + 1	
HEFFERNAN Paul	18 + 5	6	0 + 1		1		0 + 2	
HOLMES Richard	1				0 + 1		1	
IRELAND Craig	26 + 1	1	1					
JORGENSEN Henrik	0 + 2		0 + 1		0 + 2		1	
LIBURD Richard	22 + 3	2	0 + 1				0 + 1	
McNAMARA Niall	0 + 4							
MILDENHALL Steve	25 + 1		2	1	3		2	
NICHOLSON Kevin	15 + 9	1	2		0 + 1		2	
OWERS Gary	26 + 4	1	2		1	1	1	
QUINN James	6	3					1	
RICHARDSON Ian	21 + 3	2			3			
RICHARDSON Leam	20 + 1				1			
RILEY Paul	3 + 3						1	
STALLARD Mark	21 + 5	4	2	1	1		1	
STONE Danny	5 + 1				1 + 1		1 + 1	
WARREN Mark	12 + 5		2				2	
WHITLEY Jeff	6							
WILKIE Lee	2							

OLDHAM ATHLETIC (DIV 2: 9th)

	P/FL		FLC		FAC		Others	
	App	Goals	App	Goals	App	Goals	App	Goals
ADEBOLA Dele	5							
ALLOTT Mark	9 + 6	4			1 + 1		0 + 2	
APPLEBY Matty	16 + 1	2						
ARMSTRONG Chris	31 + 1				3		3	
BALMER Stuart	35 + 1	6	2		4		2	
BAUDET Julien	13 + 7	1			1 + 2		1	
BEHARALL David	18	1			2		2	
BOSHELL Danny	2 + 2							
CARSS Tony	7 + 7	1	1					
CLEGG Michael	5 + 1							
COLUSSO Christian	6 + 7	2						
CORAZZIN Carlo	24 + 9	9	0 + 1		2		1	
DUDLEY Craig	6 + 3	1	0 + 1		0 + 2		0 + 2	
DUXBURY Lee	34 + 6	4	2		4	2	2	1
EYRE John	11 + 9	5	2		2 + 1		2 + 1	1
EYRES David	40 + 5	9	2		4	3	1	1
GARNETT Shaun	4 + 4		1					
GILL Wayne	3							
GORAM Andy	4							
GRIFFIN Adam	0 + 1							
HAINING Will	1 + 3							
HALL Fitz	4	1						
HARDY Lee	0 + 1							
HOLDEN Dean	20 + 3	2			1		3	

	P/FL		FLC		FAC		Others	
	App	Goals	App	Goals	App	Goals	App	Goals
HOTTE Mark			0 + 2					
INNES Mark	0 + 5		0 + 1		0 + 2		2	
KELLY Gary	22 + 1		2		4		2	
McNIVEN Scott	32 + 3		2		3		1 + 2	
MISKELLY David	4							
MURRAY Paul	23 + 1	5			1		1	
PRENDERVILLE Barry	10 + 2		2					
RACHUBKA Paul	16						1	
REEVES David	11 + 2	3						
RICHARDS Marc	3 + 2						1	1
RICKERS Paul	13 +11	2	2		1 + 1		1 + 1	
SHERIDAN Darren	25 + 3	2	2		4		3	
SHERIDAN John	24 + 3	2			4	1		
SMART Allan	14 + 7	6			1		2	1
TIPTON Matthew	11 +11	5	1 + 1		2 + 2		2	

OXFORD UNITED (DIV 3: 21st)

	P/FL		FLC		FAC		Others	
	App	Goals	App	Goals	App	Goals	App	Goals
BEAUCHAMP Joey	2 + 1	1	0 + 1					
BOLLAND Phil	20	1	1		1		1	
BOUND Matthew	22							
BROOKS Jamie	18 + 7	10			1		1	
CROSBY Andy	22 + 1	1						
DOUGLAS Stuart	1 + 3							
FOLLAND Rob	0 +10		0 + 1				1	
GRAY Phil	14 + 7	4	1					
GUYETT Scott	20 + 2		1		1		1	
HACKETT Chris	5 +10				0 + 1		0 + 1	
HATSWELL Wayne	21		1		1		1	
KING Simon	1 + 1							
KNIGHT Richard	3							
LOUIS Jefferson	0 + 1							
McCALDON Ian	28		1		1		1	
MADDISON Lee	11							
MOODY Paul	29 + 6	13	1					
MORLEY Dave	16 + 2	3						
OMOYINMI Manny	11 +12	3			1		1	
PATTERSON Darren	2							
POWELL Paul	33 + 3	4			1		0 + 1	
QUINN Rob	11 + 5							
RICHARDSON Jon	16 + 2							
RICKETTS Sam	19 +10	1	1		1		1	
SAVAGE Dave	42	1	1		1		1	
SCOTT Andy	25 + 5	8	1	1	1		1	
STOCKLEY Sam	39 + 2		1		1		1	
TAIT Paul	13 + 1		1					
THOMAS Martin	13 + 1	2	1					
WATERMAN Dave	4 + 1							
WHITEHEAD Dean	30 +10	1	0 + 1		1		1	
WOODMAN Andy	15							

PETERBOROUGH UNITED (DIV 2: 17th)

	P/FL		FLC		FAC		Others	
	App	Goals	App	Goals	App	Goals	App	Goals
BULLARD Jimmy	36 + 4	8	1		5	1	2	2
CLARKE Andy	19 + 9	5	1 + 1	1	5 + 1	2	1	
CLARKE Lee	0 + 1						0 + 1	
CONNOR Dan	0 + 1		1					
COWAN Tom	4 + 1	1	1					
CULLEN Jon	10 + 3	1			0 + 2		1	
DANIELSSON Helgi	20 +11	2	2		1	1	2	
EDWARDS Andy	44		2		5		1	
FARRELL Dave	35 + 3	6	2		5	2	1	
FENN Neale	25 +11	6	1 + 1	1	6	1	2	
FORINTON Howard	13 + 4	2			0 + 3			
FORSYTH Richard	30 + 2		2	1	4		1	
FRENCH Daniel	1 + 9	1					0 + 1	
GILL Matthew	11 + 1	2						
GREEN Francis	12 +11	3	1 + 1		2		0 + 1	1
HANLON Richie	0 + 1							
HOOPER Dean	7 + 6				2 + 2		1	
JELLEYMAN Gareth	6 + 4				1		2	
JOSEPH Marc	44	2	2		5		2	
KIMBLE Alan	3							
MacDONALD Gary	7 + 1	1	2		1			

	P/FL		FLC		FAC		Others	
	App	Goals	App	Goals	App	Goals	App	Goals
McKENZIE Leon	28 + 2	18	1		3	1	1	1
OLDFIELD David	27 + 3	1	1		3 + 2		1 + 1	
PEARCE Dennis	8 + 1				1			
REA Simon	27 + 3	1	1		5		1	
SHIELDS Tony	6 + 9				1		0 + 1	
STEELE Luke	2							
TONER Ciaran	6				1			
TYLER Mark	44				6		2	
WILLIAMS Tommy	31 + 3	2	1 + 1		4 + 1		1	

PLYMOUTH ARGYLE (DIV 3: 1st)

	P/FL		FLC		FAC		Others	
	App	Goals	App	Goals	App	Goals	App	Goals
ADAMS Steve	40 + 6	2	1		2 + 2		1	
ADAMSON Chris	1							
BANGER Nicky	3 + 7	2						
BENT Jason	16 + 5	3			2 + 1	1	1	
BESWETHERICK Jon	27 + 5				1 + 2		1	
BROAD Joe	1 + 6		0 + 1					
COUGHLAN Graham	46	11	1		4		1	
CROWE Dean	0 + 1							
EVANS Micky	30 + 8	7	1		3		0 + 1	
EVERS Sean	3 + 4		1		0 + 1			
FRIIO David	41	8	1		4	2	1	1
GRITTON Martin	0 + 2		0 + 1					
HEANEY Neil	1 + 7							
HODGES Lee	42 + 3	6	1		4		1	
KEITH Marino	13 +10	9			0 + 2			
LARRIEU Romain	45		1		4		1	
McGLINCHEY Brian	26 + 3	1	1		3		0 + 1	
PHILLIPS Martin	37 + 2	6	1		4	2		
STONEBRIDGE Ian	29 +13	8	0 + 1		4	1	1	
STURROCK Blair	4 +15	1			0 + 2			
TAYLOR Craig	0 + 1							
WILLS Kevin	13 + 5		1		1 + 1		0 + 1	
WORRELL David	42				4		1	
WOTTON Paul	46	5	1		4	1	1	

PORTSMOUTH (DIV 1: 17th)

	P/FL		FLC		FAC		Others	
	App	Goals	App	Goals	App	Goals	App	Goals
BARRETT Neil	23 + 3	2						
BEASANT Dave	27		1					
BIAGINI Leonardo	6 + 2	2						
BRADBURY Lee	17 + 5	7	0 + 1					
BRADY Garry	1 + 5							
BURCHILL Mark	5 + 1	4						
BUXTON Lewis	27 + 2							
COOPER Shaun	3 + 4							
CROUCH Peter	37	18	1	1	1			
CROWE Jason	18 + 4	1			0 + 1			
CURTIS Tom	3 + 6							
DERRY Shaun	12				0 + 1			
EDINBURGH Justin	7		1					
HARPER Kevin	37 + 2	1	0 + 1		1			
HILEY Scott	28 + 5		1		1			
HOWE Eddie	1							
ILIC Sasa	7							
KAWAGUCHI Yoshi	11				1			
LOVELL Steve	8 +12	2			1			
MIGLIORANZI Stefan	1 + 2		0 + 1					
MILLS Lee	2							
MOORE Darren	2		1					
O'NEIL Gary	27 + 6	1	1		1			
PANOPOULOS Mike	1 + 1		1					
PETTEFER Carl	1 + 1							
PITT Courtney	29 +10	3	1		1			
PRIMUS Linvoy	21 + 1	2			1			
PROSINECKI Robert	30 + 3	9	1		1			
QUASHIE Nigel	33 + 2	2	1		1			
RUDONJA Mladen	2 + 1				1			
SUMMERBELL Mark	5							
TARDIF Chris	1							
THOGERSEN Thomas	2 + 3				1			
TILER Carl	7 + 1				1			
TODOROV Svetoslav	3		1					

	P/FL App	Goals	FLC App	Goals	FAC App	Goals	Others App	Goals
VINCENT Jamie	29 + 5	1	1					
VINE Rowan	3 + 8							
WATERMAN Dave	8 + 1							
WILSON Scott	5							
ZAMPERINI Alessandro	16	2	1					

PORT VALE (DIV 2: 14th)

	P/FL App	Goals	FLC App	Goals	FAC App	Goals	Others App	Goals
ARMSTRONG Ian	20 +11	3			1		2	2
ATANGANA	1 + 1							
BIRCHALL Chris	0 + 1		0 + 1					
BRIDGE-WILKINSON Marc	15 + 4	6						
BRISCO Neil	34 + 3		2		1		3	
BROOKER Stephen	41	9	2		2	1	3	1
BURGESS Richard	1 + 1				0 + 1	1		
BURNS Liam	30 + 3		1		1 + 1		2	
BURTON-GODWIN Sagi	33 + 4		1		2		2	1
BYRNE Paul	1 + 1						0 + 1	
CARRAGHER Matt	41		2		2		2	
CUMMINS Michael	46	8	2		2	1	3	
DELANEY Dean	3 + 1							
DODD Ashley	5 + 4	1	0 + 1		1 + 1		1	
DONNELLY Paul	1 + 5						1 + 1	
DURNIN John	18 + 1	1						
GIBSON Alex	1						1	
GOODLAD Mark	43		2		2		3	
HARDY Phil	8	1	2					
INGRAM Rae	22 + 2		2		2		2	
KILLEN Chris	8 + 1	6					1	
McCLARE Sean	19 + 4	1			1		2	
McPHEE Steve	44	11	2	2	2		3	1
MAYE Daniel	0 + 2						0 + 1	
O'CALLAGHAN George	8 + 3	3	2		1		0 + 1	
OSBORN Simon	7		1					
PAYNTER Billy	2 + 5				0 + 1			
ROWLAND Stephen	25	1			2		2	
TORPEY Steve	0 + 1							
WALSH Michael	27 + 1		1					
WEBBER Danny	2 + 2						0 + 1	

PRESTON NORTH END (DIV 1: 8th)

	P/FL App	Goals	FLC App	Goals	FAC App	Goals	Others App	Goals
AINSWORTH Gareth	3 + 2	1			1			
ALEXANDER Graham	45	6	2		3	1		
ANDERSON Iain	16 +15	5	2		3			
BARRY-MURPHY Brian	2 + 2				0 + 1			
BASHAM Steve	0 +16	1	0 + 1		1 + 1			
CARTWRIGHT Lee	34 + 2	1	1		1 + 1			
CRESSWELL Richard	27 +13	13	1 + 1	1	1 + 1	2		
EATON Adam	6 + 6		1					
EDWARDS Rob	36	2	1		3			
ETUHU Dixon	16	3						
GALLACHER Kevin	1 + 4	1	0 + 1	1				
GREGAN Sean	40 + 1	1	2		2			
GUDJONSSON Thordur	4 + 3				0 + 1			
HEALY David	35 + 9	10	2		2 + 1			
HENDRY Colin	2							
JACKSON Michael	12 + 1		1	1				
KEANE Michael	17 + 3	2	0 + 1		3			
KIDD Ryan	5 + 1		1					
LUCAS David	23 + 1		1		1			
LUCKETTI Chris	40	2	1		3			
MACKEN Jon	28 + 3	8	1	1	2 + 1	1		
McKENNA Paul	37 + 1	4	1		2			
MOILAINEN Tepi	23 + 1		1		2			
MURDOCK Colin	22 + 1	2	2		2			
RANKINE Mark	24 + 2	4	1					
REID Paul	0 + 1	1						
ROBINSON Steve	0 + 2		0 + 1		0 + 1			
SKORA Eric	2 + 2				2	1		
WIJNHARD Clyde	6	3						

QUEENS PARK RANGERS (DIV 2: 8th)

	P/FL App	Goals	FLC App	Goals	FAC App	Goals	Others App	Goals
AGOGO Junior	0 + 2							

	P/FL App	Goals	FLC App	Goals	FAC App	Goals	Others App	Goals
BARR Hamid							0 + 1	
BEN ASKAR Aziz	18		1				1	
BIGNOT Marcus	41 + 4		1		1		1	
BONNOT Alex	17 + 5	1	1		1		1	
BRUCE Paul	13	1	1		0 + 1		1	
BURGESS Oliver	4	1			0 + 1			
CONNOLLY Karl	24 + 9	4			1		1	
DALY Wes	1							
DAY Chris	16		1				1	
DE ORNELAS Fernando	1 + 1							
DIGBY Fraser	19				1			
DOUDOU	20 +16	3	1		1		0 + 1	
EVANS Rhys	11							
FITZGERALD Brian	0 + 1							
FOLEY Dominic	3 + 2	1						
FORBES Terrell	43		1		1			
GALLEN Kevin	25	7						
GRIFFITHS Leroy	23 + 7	3			1			
KOEJOE Sammy	0 + 2		0 + 1					
LANGLEY Richard	15 + 3	3						
LEABURN Carl	0 + 1							
McEWEN Dave	2 + 3		0 + 1					
MURPHY Danny	10 + 2							
OLI Dennis	0 + 2							
PACQUETTE Richard	8 + 8	2	0 + 1		0 + 1		0 + 1	
PALMER Steve	46	4	1		1		1	
PEACOCK Gavin	19 + 1	2						
PERRY Mark	13 + 3		1		1		1	
PLUMMER Chris	1				1			
ROSE Matthew	37 + 2	3					1	
SHITTU Danny	27	2						
TAYLOR Robert	3 + 1							
THOMAS Jerome	4	1						
THOMSON Andy	29 + 9	21					1	
WARDLEY Stewart	5 + 5		1					
WARREN Christer	8 + 6		1		1			

READING (DIV 2: 2nd)

	P/FL App	Goals	FLC App	Goals	FAC App	Goals	Others App	Goals
ASHDOWN Jamie	1				1		2	
BRANCH Michael	0 + 2							
BUTLER Martin	14 + 3	2	2					
CURETON Jamie	24 +14	15	1 + 1		2	1		
FORSTER Nicky	36 + 6	19	2		1		2	
GAMBLE Joe	2 + 4		0 + 1		1		2	
HAHNEMANN Marcus	6							
HARPER Jamie	19 + 7	1	3		1		1 + 1	
HENDERSON Darius	2 +36		1 + 2	2	1 + 1		2	2
HUGHES Andy	34 + 5	6			2		1	
IGOE Sammy	27 + 8	1	2		0 + 2		1 + 1	
JONES Keith	10 + 6				1			
MACKIE John	27				0 + 2		1 + 1	
MURTY Graeme	43		2		2		1	
PARKINSON Phil	32 + 1	2	3	1			0 + 1	
ROBERTS Ben	6							
ROBINSON Matthew	14		1 + 1					
ROGET Leo	1							
ROUGIER Tony	20 +13	1	1 + 2		1		1 + 1	
SALAKO John	31	6					1	
SAVAGE Bas	0 + 1							
SHOREY Nicky	32		2		2		2	
SMITH Alex	12 + 1	2	2	1	1		1	
SMITH Neil	3 +11	1	1		1		1	1
TYSON Nathan	0 + 1		0 + 1		0 + 1		0 + 1	
VIVEASH Adrian	18	1	1 + 1		2		2	
WATSON Kevin	12	1						
WHITBREAD Adrian	14		3		1			
WHITEHEAD Phil	33		3		1			
WILLIAMS Adrian	33 + 2	1	3		1		1	

ROCHDALE (DIV 3: 5th)

	P/FL App	Goals	FLC App	Goals	FAC App	Goals	Others App	Goals
ATKINSON Graeme	8 + 3				0 + 1			
BANKS Steve	15							

	P/FL App	P/FL Goals	FLC App	FLC Goals	FAC App	FAC Goals	Others App	Others Goals
BAYLISS Dave	9		1		1		1	
COLEMAN Simon	8 + 3	1	1				0 + 1	
CONNOR Paul	11 + 6	1	1		2 + 1		0 + 1	
DOUGHTY Matt	32 + 4	1	0 + 1		3	1	4	
DUFFY Lee	1 + 5						1 + 1	
DUNNING Darren	4 + 1							
DURKAN Keiron	16 +14	1	2		3		1	
EDWARDS Neil	7		1		1		2	
EVANS Wayne	43		2		3		3	
FLITCROFT Dave	21 +14		1 + 1		1 + 1		4	
FORD Tony	17	2	2	1			1	
GILKS Matty	19		1		2			
GRIFFITHS Gareth	41	4	2		2		3	
HAHNEMANN Marcus	5						2	
JOBSON Richard	34 + 1	3			3		4	
JONES Gary	20	5	2		2		1	1
JONES Steve	6 + 3	1						
McAULEY Sean	23		1 + 1		3		2	
McCOURT Paddy	10 +13	4			0 + 2		0 + 3	
McEVILLY Lee	13 + 5	4					2	1
McLOUGHLIN Alan	15 + 3	1					2	
OLIVER Michael	45	7	2		3	1	3	
PLATT Clive	41 + 2	7	2		3		2	1
ROSE Karl							1	
SIMPSON Paul	7	5					2	1
TODD Lee	8 + 2		1					
TOWNSON Kevin	17 +24	14	0 + 1	2	1 + 1		3 + 1	1
WARE Paul	4 + 4		0 + 1					
WHEATCROFT Paul	6	3						

ROTHERHAM UNITED (DIV 1: 21st)

	P/FL App	P/FL Goals	FLC App	FLC Goals	FAC App	FAC Goals	Others App	Others Goals
BARKER Richie	11 +24	3	1 + 1		2	1		
BEECH Chris	2 + 6	1						
BRANSTON Guy	10	1	0 + 1					
BRYAN Marvin	19		0 + 1					
BYFIELD Darren	3	2						
DAWS Nick	21 +14	1	2		0 + 1			
GRAY Ian	0 + 1							
HUDSON Danny			0 + 2					
HURST Paul	45		1		2			
LEE Alan	37 + 1	9	2		0 + 1			
LOWNDES Nathan	2							
McINTOSH Martin	39	4	2		2			
MIRANDA Jose	2		0 + 1					
MONKHOUSE Andy	21 +17	2	1		1 + 1			
MULLIN John	27 + 7	2			2	2		
POLLITT Mike	46		2		2			
ROBINS Mark	34 + 7	15	2	1	2			
SCOTT Rob	35 + 3	3	2		2			
SEDGWICK Chris	39 + 5	1	1		2			
SWAILES Chris	44	6	2		2			
TALBOT Stewart	36 + 2	1	1		1 + 1			
WARNE Paul	14 +11				2	1		
WATSON Kevin	19	1	2					

RUSHDEN & DIAMONDS (DIV 3: 6th)

	P/FL App	P/FL Goals	FLC App	FLC Goals	FAC App	FAC Goals	Others App	Others Goals
ANGELL Brett	3 + 2	2					0 + 2	
BELL David	0 + 1						0 + 1	
BRADY Jon	9 +13	1	2		1 + 1		0 + 1	
BURGESS Andy	28 + 4	4	1		1 + 1		2 + 1	
BUTTERWORTH Garry	28 + 1	1	1		2		3	1
CAREY Shaun	7 + 1		2					
CARR Darren	1							
DARBY Duane	17 +13	7	0 + 1	1	1			
DEMPSTER John	0 + 2							
DOUGLAS Stuart	4 + 5							
DUFFY Robert	1 + 7	1	0 + 1		0 + 1			
FOLAN Caleb	1 + 5							
GRAY Stuart	12		1				1 + 1	
HALL Paul	34	8			2		4	3
HANLON Richie	33 + 2	6	0 + 1		2	2	1	
HUNTER Barry	23	1						

	P/FL App	P/FL Goals	FLC App	FLC Goals	FAC App	FAC Goals	Others App	Others Goals
JACKSON Justin	5		1					
LEE Christian	1							
LOWE Onandi	25	19			1		3	1
McELHATTON Mike	4 + 3	1						
MILLS Garry	3 + 6		1 + 1				1	
MUSTAFA Tarkan	21 + 2	1	2	1			3	
PARTRIDGE Scott	26 +11	5			2		3	
PATMORE Warren	4	1	2					
PENNOCK Tony	3 + 2							
PETERS Mark	40		2	1	2		4	
RODWELL Jim	8 + 1		2				1	
SAMBROOK Andy	25 + 1				2		1	
SETCHELL Gary	13 + 9	1			0 + 1		0 + 1	
SIGERE Jean-Michel	4 + 3	1	1					
SOLKHON Brett	0 + 1							
TALBOT Daniel	2 + 1						1	
THOMSON Peter	1 + 1	1			0 + 1			
TILLSON Andy	14						3	
TURLEY Billy	43		2		2		4	
UNDERWOOD Paul	40		2		2		4	
WARBURTON Ray	1							
WARDLEY Stuart	18	4					3	1
WORMULL Simon	4 + 1		0 + 1					

SCUNTHORPE UNITED (DIV 3: 8th)

	P/FL App	P/FL Goals	FLC App	FLC Goals	FAC App	FAC Goals	Others App	Others Goals
ANDERSON Mark	0 + 1							
BARWICK Terry	7 + 3		1				0 + 1	
BEAGRIE Peter	39 + 1	11	1		3		2	2
BRADSHAW Carl	18 + 3	1	1				1	
BROUGH Scott	5 +14	1	0 + 1				1 + 2	
CALVO-GARCIA Alex	33 + 1	6			3	2	3	
CARRUTHERS Martin	30 + 3	13	1		2	3	3	1
COTTERILL James	8 + 2						1	
CROUDSON Steve	4		1					
DAWSON Andy	44		1		3		3	
DUDLEY Craig	1 + 3							
EVANS Tommy	42				3		3	
GRANT Kim	3 + 1	1	1					
GRAVES Wayne	16 + 1	3	0 + 1		1			
HODGES Lee	26 + 9	6			3	1	3	1
JACKSON Mark	45	3	1		3		3	
JEFFREY Mike	4 + 2	1						
KELL Richard	16	1			2		3	
McCOMBE Jamie	11 + 6				3	1	2	1
McGIBBON Pat	6							
PARTON Andy	1							
PEPPER Nigel	0 + 1							
QUAILEY Brian	15 +15	8			0 + 2		0 + 2	
RIDLEY Lee	2 + 2				1		0 + 1	
SHELDON Gareth	6 + 8	2	1				0 + 1	
SPARROW Matt	20 + 4	1			1			
STANTON Nathan	39 + 3		1		3		2 + 1	
THOM Stuart	17 + 3	2	1		0 + 1			
TORPEY Steve	37 + 2	13			3		3	2
VAUGHAN Tony	5							
WILCOX Russ	6 + 3		0 + 1					

SHEFFIELD UNITED (DIV 1: 13th)

	P/FL App	P/FL Goals	FLC App	FLC Goals	FAC App	FAC Goals	Others App	Others Goals
ASABA Carl	26 + 3	7	2		2			
BROWN Michael	36	5	2		2	1		
CRYAN Colin	0 + 1							
CURLE Keith	30 + 2	1	1		1			
DEVLIN Paul	14 + 5	2	2	1	1			
DE VOGT Wilko	5 + 1				2			
D'JAFFO Laurent	23 + 9	5	0 + 2	1	1 + 1			
DOANE Ben	14	1						
FORD Bobby	20 + 6		2		2			
FURLONG Paul	4	2						
JAGIELKA Phil	14 + 9	3	1					
JAVARY Jean-Phillipe	6 + 1	1						
KILLEEN Lewis	0 + 1							
KOZLUK Rob	6 + 2							

	P/FL App	Goals	FLC App	Goals	FAC App	Goals	Others App	Goals
LITTLEJOHN Adrian	1 + 2							
LOVELL Steve	3 + 2	1						
MALLON Ryan	0 + 1							
MONTGOMERY Nick	14 +17	2			0 + 1			
MURPHY Shaun	27		2					
NDLOVU Peter	41 + 4	4	1 + 1	1	2	1		
NICHOLSON Shane	21 + 4	3	1					
PAGE Robert	43				2			
PESCHISOLIDO Paul	19 +10	6	2					
PHELAN Terry	8		1					
SANDFORD Lee	5 + 1				1 + 1			
SANTOS Georges	14 +16	2	1 + 1		0 + 1			
SMITH Grant	1 + 6							
SUFFO Patrick	10 +10	4	0 + 1	1				
TONGE Michael	27 + 3	3			2			
TRACEY Simon	41		2					
UHLENBEEK Gus	19 + 1		1		2			
ULLATHORNE Rob	14				2			
WARD Mark	0 + 1							

SHEFFIELD WEDNESDAY (DIV 1: 20th)

	P/FL App	Goals	FLC App	Goals	FAC App	Goals	Others App	Goals
ARMSTRONG Craig	7 + 1							
BONVIN Pablo	7 +16	4	2 + 4	1	0 + 1			
BROMBY Leigh	26	1	6		1			
BROOMES Marlon	18 + 1				1			
BURROWS David	8							
CRANE Tony	4 +11		0 + 3	1	0 + 1			
DI PIEDI Michele	2 +10	1	1 + 1	1				
DJORDJIC Bojan	4 + 1							
DONNELLY Simon	14 + 9	4	2					
EKOKU Efan	21 + 6	7	5 + 1	5	1			
GALLACHER Kevin	0 + 4							
GEARY Derek	29 + 3		6		1			
HAMSHAW Matthew	13 + 8		3 + 1	1	1	1		
HASLAM Steve	39 + 2		7		1			
HEALD Paul	5		1					
HENDON Ian	9		1					
HINCHCLIFFE Andy	1		0 + 1					
JOHNSON David	7	2						
JOHNSON Tommy	8	3	1					
KUQI Shefki	17	6						
LESCOTT Aaron	2 + 5		0 + 1					
McCARTHY Jon	4							
McLAREN Paul	29 + 6	2	5 + 1	1	1			
MADDIX Danny	33 + 3	1	5		1			
MORRISON Owen	11 +13	2	3 + 2	1				
O'DONNELL Phil	6 + 2		2 + 2	1				
PALMER Carlton	10							
PRESSMAN Kevin	40		6		1			
QUINN Alan	35 + 3	2	6		1			
ROBERTS Sean	0 + 1							
SIBON Gerald	31 + 4	12	4		1			
SOLTVEDT Trond Egil	38	1	6		2			
STRINGER Chris	1							
WESTWOOD Ashley	25 + 1	1	5 + 1	1	1			
WINDASS Dean	2							

SHREWSBURY TOWN (DIV 3: 9th)

	P/FL App	Goals	FLC App	Goals	FAC App	Goals	Others App	Goals
AISTON Sam	22 +13	2			0 + 1			
ATKINS Mark	42	2	1		1		1	
CARTWRIGHT Mark	14		1					
DRYSDALE Leon	22 + 4		1					
DUNBAVIN Ian	32 + 2		1				1	
FALLON Rory	8 + 3							
FREESTONE Chris	3 + 4		0 + 1					
GUINAN Steve	4 + 1							
HEATHCOTE Mick	33 + 1	2	1		1		1	
JAGIELKA Steve	25 + 6	5	1		1		1	
JEMSON Nigel	28	10	1	1	1		1	
JENKINS Iain	3 + 2				0 + 1			
LORMOR Anth	7	2						
LOWE Ryan	22 +16	7					1	

	P/FL App	Goals	FLC App	Goals	FAC App	Goals	Others App	Goals
MOSS Darren	23 + 8	2			1		1	
MURPHY Chris	0 + 4							
MURRAY Karl	25 + 9	2	1		1		1	
REDMILE Matt	44	2	1				1	
RIOCH Greg	38	2	1		1		1	
RODGERS Luke	38	22	1		1		1	
THOMPSON Andy	13 + 1							
TOLLEY Jamie	19 + 4	1			0 + 1			
TRETTON Andy	15 + 4				1			
WALKER Josh	0 + 3		0 + 1					
WILDING Peter	12 +10		1					
WOAN Ian	14	3						

SOUTHAMPTON (PREM: 11th)

	P/FL App	Goals	FLC App	Goals	FAC App	Goals	Others App	Goals
BEATTIE James	24 + 4	12	3		2			
BENALI Francis	0 + 3							
BLEIDELIS Imants	0 + 1							
BRIDGE Wayne	38		3		1			
DAVIES Kevin	18 + 5	2	2 + 1	1	0 + 1			
DELAP Rory	24 + 4	2	1					
DELGADO Agustin	0 + 1				1			
DODD Jason	26 + 3		2		1			
DRAPER Mark	1 + 1		0 + 1					
EL KHALEJ Tahar	12 + 2	1	1 + 1	1				
FERNANDES Fabrice	6 + 5	1			1			
JONES Paul	36		3		1			
LE TISSIER Matt	0 + 4				0 + 1			
LUNDEKVAM Claus	34		2		1			
McDONALD Scott	0 + 2		1					
MARSDEN Chris	27 + 1	3	2		1			
MONK Garry	1 + 1		1					
MOSS Neil	2							
MURRAY Paul	0 + 1							
OAKLEY Matt	26 + 1	1	3					
ORMEROD Brett	8 +10	1						
PAHARS Marians	33 + 3	14	2	1	1	1		
PETRESCU Dan	0 + 2							
RICHARDS Dean	4		1					
RIPLEY Stuart	1 + 4		0 + 1					
ROSLER Uwe	3 + 1		0 + 1					
SVENSSON Anders	33 + 1	4	3	2	1			
TELFER Paul	27 + 1	1	1		1			
TESSEM Jo	7 +15	2	1 + 1		1			
WILLIAMS Paul	27 + 1		1		1			

SOUTHEND UNITED (DIV 3: 12th)

	P/FL App	Goals	FLC App	Goals	FAC App	Goals	Others App	Goals
ALDERTON Rio	0 + 2							
BARRY-MURPHY Brian	8	1						
BEARD Mark	5 + 9				0 + 1		1 + 1	
BELGRAVE Barrington	32 + 2	5			2 + 1	2	2	
BRAMBLE Tes	32 + 3	9	0 + 1		4	3	2	1
BROAD Stephen	30 + 2	2	1		3		1	
CLARK Anthony	0 + 2							
CLARK Steve	9 + 3	1						
CORT Leon	43 + 2	4	1		4		1	
DSANE Roscoe	1 + 1							
FLAHAVAN Darryl	41		1		4		2	
FORBES Scott	3 +10				1 + 1			
GAY Danny	5 + 1							
HARRIS Jason	2 + 3							
HOLNESS Dean	1 + 1							
HUTCHINGS Carl	28 + 1	4	1		3		2	1
JOHNSON Leon	24 + 4	2	1		1 + 2		2	
KERRIGAN Danny	6 + 5						1 + 1	
LUNAN Daniel	0 + 1							
McSWEENEY Dave	13 + 8		0 + 1		1		1	
MAHER Kevin	36	5	1		4		2	
NEWMAN Rob	10 + 1	2			3			
RAWLE Mark	25 + 5	5	1		3 + 1	1	2	1
RICHARDS Tony	9 + 8	2	0 + 1		0 + 1		0 + 1	
RISBRIDGER Gareth	0 + 1							
SEARLE Damon	41 + 2	1	1		4		2	

	P/FL App	Goals	FLC App	Goals	FAC App	Goals	Others App	Goals
SELLEY Ian	14							
SMITH Ben	0 + 1							
SZMID Marek	1 + 1							
THURGOOD Stuart	34 + 5		1		4		0 + 1	
WALLACE Adam	0 + 2							
WEBB Danny	10 + 6	2	1				0 + 2	1
WHELAN Phil	43 + 1	5	1		3	1	2	

STOCKPORT COUNTY (DIV 1: 24th)

	P/FL App	Goals	FLC App	Goals	FAC App	Goals	Others App	Goals
ARPEXHAD Pegguy	3							
BECKETT Luke	17 + 2	7						
BRIGGS Keith	30 + 2				1			
BRYNGELSSON Fredrik	3							
BYRNE Mark	1 + 4							
CARRATT Phil	0 + 2							
CHALLINOR Dave	18							
CLARE Robert	21 + 2		1		1			
CLARK Peter	12 + 2							
DALY Jon	11 + 2	1			1	1		
DELANEY Damien	10 + 2	1						
DIBBLE Andy	13		0 + 1		1			
ELLISON Kevin	6 + 5				1			
FLOWERS Tim	4							
FLYNN Mike	26	2	2					
FRADIN Karim	18 + 2	2	1		1			
GIBB Ally	40 + 1		2		1			
HANCOCK Glynn	0 + 1							
HARDIKER John	11 + 1	3						
HARDY Neil	4 + 6	2	1 + 1					
HELIN Petri	10 + 3		1 + 1		0 + 1			
HOLT David	0 + 1							
HURST Glynn	12 + 3	4	0 + 1					
JONES Lee	21 + 3		2					
KUQI Shefki	15 + 3	5	2	1				
LESCOTT Aaron	17				1			
McLACHLAN Fraser	11	1						
McSHEFFREY Gary	3 + 2	1						
PALMER Carlton	20 + 1	3			1			
ROGET Leo	20 + 2	1	2					
ROSS Neil	2 + 1	1						
SANDFORD Lee	7							
SMITH Dave	9 + 2		1					
SNEEKES Richard	8 + 1		1					
SPENCER James	1 + 1							
TAYLOR Scott	19 + 9	4	2		3		0 + 1	
THOMAS Andy	7 + 3							
TURNER Sam	4 + 2							
VAN BLERK Jason	13		1					
WELSH Andy	9 + 6				1			
WILBRAHAM Aaron	19 + 2	3	1					
WILD Peter	1							
WILLIAMS Chris	1 + 4				0 + 1			
WISS Jarko	7 + 4		0 + 2					
WOODTHORPE Colin	22 +12		2		1			

STOKE CITY (DIV 2: 5th)

	P/FL App	Goals	FLC App	Goals	FAC App	Goals	Others App	Goals
BRIGHTWELL Ian	3 + 1						0 + 1	
BURTON Deon	11 + 1	2					2 + 1	2
CLARKE Clive	42 + 1	1	0 + 1		3		4	
COMMONS Kris					1			
COOKE Andy	26 + 9	9	0 + 1		2 + 2	1	1 + 2	
CUTLER Neil	36		1		3		3	
DADASON Rikki	6 + 5	4			0 + 2		0 + 1	
DINNING Tony	5						3	
FLYNN Mike	11 + 2							
GOODFELLOW Marc	11 +12	5	1		1 + 2		2	
GUDJONSSON Bjarni	46	3	1		4	1	3	
GUNNARSSON Brynjar	21 + 2	5			3	2	1	
GUNNLAUGSSON Arnie	9	3					2	
HALL Laurence							0 + 1	
HANDYSIDE Peter	34		1		3	1	3	
HENRY Karl	9 +15		1		2		1	

	P/FL App	Goals	FLC App	Goals	FAC App	Goals	Others App	Goals
HOEKSTRA Peter	20 + 4	3	1		2 + 1			
IWELUMO Chris	22 +16	10	0 + 1		3 + 1	1	4	1
MARTEINSSON Petur	2 + 1							
MILES John	0 + 1							
NEAL Lewis	6 + 5				1 + 1		1	1
O'CONNOR James	43	2			4		3	1
OULARE Souleymane	0 + 1						0 + 1	1
ROWSON David	8 + 5		1		1 + 2		1	
SHTANIUK Sergei	40	2	1		4		3	
SMART Allan	0 + 2							
THOMAS Wayne	40	2	1		3		4	
THORDARSON Stefan	3 +18	4	1					
THORNE Peter	5	4						
VAN DEURZEN Jurgen	37 + 3	4	1		4		0 + 3	
WARD Gavin	10				1		1	
WILKINSON Andy							0 + 1	
WILSON Brian	0 + 1						1	

SUNDERLAND (PREM: 17th)

	P/FL App	Goals	FLC App	Goals	FAC App	Goals	Others App	Goals
ARCA Julio	20 + 2	1	1		1			
BELLION David	0 + 9		1					
BJORKLUND Joachim	11 + 1							
BUTLER Thomas	2 + 5							
CRADDOCK Jody	30	1			0 + 1			
GRAY Michael	35		1					
HAAS Bernt	27		0 + 1		1			
HUTCHISON Don	2							
INGHAM Michael	1							
KILBANE Kevin	24 + 4	2	1		0 + 1			
KYLE Kevin	0 + 6		0 + 1		0 + 1			
LASLANDES Lilian	5 + 7		0 + 1	1				
McATEER Jason	26	2			1			
McCANN Gavin	29		1		1			
McCARTNEY George	12 + 6		1		1			
MACHO Jurgen	4							
MBOMA Patrick	5 + 4	1						
PHILLIPS Kevin	37	11	1	1	1	1		
QUINN Niall	24 +14	6			1			
RAE Alex	1 + 2							
REYNA Claudio	17	3						
SCHWARZ Stefan	18 + 2	1						
SORENSEN Thomas	34				1			
THIRLWELL Paul	11 + 3		1		1			
THOME Emerson	12	1						
VARGA Stan	9				1			
WILLIAMS Darren	23 + 5		1		1			

SWANSEA CITY (DIV 3: 20th)

	P/FL App	Goals	FLC App	Goals	FAC App	Goals	Others App	Goals
APPLEBY Richie	3 + 7		0 + 1				0 + 1	
BOUND Matthew	18	2			2		1	
BRODIE Steve	21 + 5	2			1			
CASEY Ryan	6 +10							
COATES Jonathan	44 + 1	5	1		2		1	1
CUSACK Nicky	33 + 2	2	0 + 1		2	2	1	
DE-VULGT Leigh	7 + 3						1	
DRAPER Craig	0 + 2							
DUFFY Richard					0 + 1			
EVANS Steve	4				2			
EVANS Terry	16				2			
FREESTONE Roger	43		1		2		1	
HOWARD Mike	42	1	1		1		1	
JENKINS Lee	14 + 1	1	1					
JONES Jason	3							
KEEGAN Michael	0 + 2							
LACEY Damian	5 +11	1			1			
MAZZINA Nicolas	3		1					
MUMFORD Andrew	28 + 4	5						
O'LEARY Kris	30 + 1	2	1		1		1	
PHILLIPS Gareth	29 + 6	2	1		0 + 2		1	
ROBERTS Stuart	13	5						
ROMO David	3 + 7	1	1		0 + 1		0 + 1	
SHARP Neil	22 + 3	1						

	P/FL		FLC		FAC		Others	
	App	Goals	App	Goals	App	Goals	App	Goals
SIDIBE Mamady	26 + 5	7	0 + 1		2	1	1	
SMITH Jason	7 + 1				1			
TODD Chris	28 + 4	3	1		1		1	
TYSON Nathan	7 + 4				1			
WATKIN Steve	25 + 6	8	1		0 + 1	1		
WILLIAMS John	26 +15	4	1		2		1	
SWINDON TOWN (DIV 2: 13th)								
BRAYLEY Bertie	0 + 7		0 + 1		0 + 1		0 + 1	
CARLISLE Wayne	10 + 1	2			2			
COBIAN Juan	0 + 1							
DAVIES Gareth	0 + 2							
DAVIS Sol	15 + 6		2		0 + 1			
DUKE David	36 + 6	2	2		3		1	
EDWARDS Nathan	2 + 5						1	
EDWARDS Paul	14 + 6		0 + 1		1	1	1	
FOLEY Dominic	5 + 2	1						
GRAZIOLI Guiliano	24 + 7	8	0 + 2		1 + 1		1	
GRIEMINK Bart	45		2		3		1	
GURNEY Andy	43	6	2		2		1	
HALLIDAY Kevin							0 + 1	
HERRING Ian	0 + 1							
HEWLETT Matt	38 + 1	1	2		1			
HEYWOOD Matty	42 + 2	3	2		3	1	1	
HOWE Bobby	33 + 6	1	2	1	2	1	1	
INVINCIBILE Danny	40 + 4	6	2		3	2		
McAREAVEY Paul	8 +11				1 + 1		1	
McKINNEY Richard	1							
O'HALLORAN Keith	6		1					
OSEI-KUFFOUR Jo	4 + 7	2	1				1	
REEVES Alan	24 + 1	2	1 + 1		1		1	
ROBINSON Mark	6 + 2				1 + 1			
ROBINSON Steve	37 + 3	1	1		3			
RUDDOCK Neil	14 + 1	1	1		2	1	0 + 1	
SABIN Eric	33 + 1	5	1		3			
WILLIAMS James	0 + 1							
WILLIS Adam	19 + 3	1						
YOUNG Alan	7 + 7	1						
TORQUAY UNITED (DIV 3: 19th)								
AGGREY Jimmy	2							
ASHFORD Ryan	1 + 1	1						
BANGER Nicky	1							
BEDEAU Tony	9 +12	4						
BENEFIELD Jimmy	3 + 5		0 + 1		0 + 1		0 + 1	
BRABIN Gary	6				1			
BRANDON Chris	22 + 5	3	2	1	1		1	
BROWN David	2				1			
CANOVILLE Lee	10 + 2	1			1		1	
DEARDEN Kevin	46		2		1		1	
DOUGLIN Troy	5 + 1		2		1		1	
FOWLER Jason	14		1					
GOODRIDGE Greg	9 + 8	1						
GRAHAM David	31 + 5	8	2		1			
GREYLING Anton	0 + 2							
HANKIN Sean	27				1		1	
HANSON Christian	6							
HAZELL Reuben	19							
HEALY Brian	2							
HERRERA Robbie	2 + 1							
HILL Kevin	40 + 4	2	2		1	1	1	
HOCKLEY Matt	12				1			
HOLMES Paul	17 + 1							
LAW Gareth	0 + 5				0 + 1			
LOGAN Richard	16	4						
MacDONALD Charlie	5							
McNEIL Martin	16		2					
MARTIN Andy	5							
NICHOLLS Mark	4 + 5	1	0 + 1				1	
O'BRIEN Mick	0 + 1							
PARKER Kevin	0 + 2							
PREECE David	4 + 2							

	P/FL		FLC		FAC		Others	
	App	Goals	App	Goals	App	Goals	App	Goals
REES Jason	26 + 7		2				1	
RICHARDSON Marcus	18 +12	6			1		0 + 1	
ROACH Neville	5 + 7	1	1 + 1					
RUSSELL Alex	33	7	2					
RUSSELL Lee	7 + 4				0 + 1			
TULLY Steve	17 + 1		2				1	
WILLIAMS Eifion	8 +17	1	1 + 1				1	
WILLIAMSON Mike	3						1	
WOODS Steve	38	2	1		1			
WOOZLEY Dave	15 + 1		1					
TOTTENHAM HOTSPUR (PREM: 9th)								
ANDERTON Darren	33 + 2	3	6	1	3	1		
BUNJEVCEVIC Goran	5 + 1		1 + 1					
CLEMENCE Stephen	4 + 2							
DAVIES Simon	22 + 9	4	6 + 1	3	3			
DOHERTY Gary	4 + 3		1					
ETHERINGTON Matthew	3 + 8		0 + 1		1 + 1	1		
FERDINAND Les	22 + 3	9	5	5	3	1		
FREUND Steffen	19 + 1		5					
GARDNER Anthony	11 + 4		3		1			
IVERSEN Steffen	12 + 6	4	1 + 2	2	1 + 2	1		
KELLER Kasey	9		2					
KING Ledley	32		7	1	3			
LEONHARDSEN Oyvind	2 + 5		2 + 2		0 + 2			
PERRY Chris	30 + 3		7		2			
POYET Gus	32 + 2	10	5	1	4	3		
REBROV Sergei	9 +21	1	2 + 4	3	2 + 1			
RICHARDS Dean	24	2			4			
SHERINGHAM Teddy	33 + 1	10	5 + 1	2	2		1	
SHERWOOD Tim	15 + 4		2 + 3	1	4			
SULLIVAN Neil	29		5		4			
TARICCO Mauricio	30		6		3 + 1			
THATCHER Ben	11 + 1		2 + 1		2			
THELWELL Alton	0 + 2				0 + 1			
ZIEGE Christian	27	5	4	1	2			
TRANMERE ROVERS (DIV 2: 12th)								
ACHTERBERG John	25				4			
ALLEN Graham	30 + 1	1	2		4			
ALLISON Wayne	13 +14	4	0 + 1		2	1	1	
BARLOW Stuart	31 + 7	14	3	2	1 + 3	1		
CHALLINOR Dave	6		1				1	
FLYNN Sean	30 + 1	5	3	2	4	3		
HARRISON Daniel	1						1	
HAWORTH Simon	12	5						
HAY Alex	2 + 1		1				1	
HAZELL Reuben	6		1				1	
HENRY Nick	39	1	3	1	5		0 + 1	
HILL Clint	30	2	1		5			
HINDS Richard	6 + 4		0 + 1				1	
HUME Iain	1 +13		0 + 2				1	
JOBSON Richard	1							
KOUMAS Jason	38	8	1	1	4	4		
MELLON Micky	23 + 4	1	3	1	2 + 1		1	
MORGAN Alan	1 + 1							
MURPHY Joe	21 + 1		3		1		1	
NAVARRO Alan	21		1		3	1		
NDIAYE Seyni	6 + 5	2	2		0 + 1		0 + 1	
NIXON Eric	0 + 1							
PARKINSON Andy	14 +17	2	2		1		1	
PRICE Jason	20 + 4	7			5	4		
RIDEOUT Paul	14 + 1	4			3	1		
ROBERTS Gareth	45	2	3		5			
SHARPS Ian	25 + 4		1		2		1	
THORNTON Sean	9 + 2	1			0 + 1		0 + 1	
YATES Steve	36 + 1	3	3		4	1		
WALSALL (DIV 1: 18th)								
ANDRE Carlos	5				2			
ANGELL Brett	13 + 7	3			1 + 1	1		
ARANALDE Zigor	43 + 2	2	2		3			

	P/FL App	P/FL Goals	FLC App	FLC Goals	FAC App	FAC Goals	Others App	Others Goals
BARRAS Tony	25 + 1	4	2	1				
BENNETT Tom	34 + 6				3	1		
BIANCALANI Frederic	13 + 5	2	0 + 1		2			
BIRCH Gary	0 + 1							
BRIGHTWELL Ian	25 + 2		2		2			
BYFIELD Darren	24 +13	4	0 + 1	1	2 + 1	1		
CARBON Matt	22	1			2			
CHETTLE Steve	6							
CORICA Steve	13	3			0 + 1			
CURTIS Tom	3 + 1							
GADSBY Matthew	17 + 5		2					
GARROCHO Carlos	2 + 2		0 + 1					
GOODMAN Don	7 +10	1	1					
HALL Paul			0 + 1					
HARPER Lee	3		2					
HAWLEY Karl	0 + 1							
HERIVELTO Moriera	11 +13	4	2	1	1 + 1			
HOLDSWORTH David	9	1			2			
KEATES Dean	6 + 7	1	1		1 + 2			
LEITAO Jorge	24 +14	8	1		2 + 1	2		
MARCELO	9	1						
MATIAS Pedro	25 + 5	5	1		2 + 1			
O'CONNOR Martin	12 + 1	1						
OFODILE Adolfus	0 + 1	1						
ROPER Ian	24 + 3		1 + 1		1 + 1			
SCOTT Dion	0 + 1							
SHIELDS Greg	7							
SIMPSON Fitzroy	21 + 7	2	2					
THOGERSEN Thomas	7	2						
TILLSON Andy	8 + 1	1			1			
UHLENBEEK Gus	5							
WALKER James	43		0 + 1		3			
WRACK Darren	40 + 3	4	2	1	3			

WATFORD (DIV 1: 14th)

	P/FL App	P/FL Goals	FLC App	FLC Goals	FAC App	FAC Goals	Others App	Others Goals
BAARDSEN Espen	14		3					
BLONDEAU Patrick	24 + 1		2		1			
BROWN Wayne	10 + 1	3						
CHAMBERLAIN Alec	32		2		1			
COOK Lee	6 + 4							
COX Neil	39 + 1	2	4		1			
DOYLEY Lloyd	11 + 9		1					
FISKEN Gary	12 + 5	1	2 + 2		1			
FOLEY Dominic	1		1					
GALLI Filippo	27 + 1	1	1					
GAYLE Marcus	28 + 8	4	3 + 1	2	1	1		
GIBBS Nigel	0 + 1							
GLASS Stephen	29 + 2	3	2					
HAND Jamie	4 + 6				0 + 1			
HELGUSON Heidar	11 +23	6	0 + 5	1	0 + 1			
HUGHES Stephen	11 + 4		2					
HYDE Micah	37 + 2	4	4	2				
ISSA Pierre	12 + 3	1	2		1			
McNAMEE Anthony	2 + 5	1						
MAHON Gavin	6							
NIELSEN Allan	19 + 3	6	0 + 2		1			
NOBLE David	5 +10	1	3					
NOEL-WILLIAMS Gifton	15 +14	6	5	2	1	1		
NORVILLE Jason	0 + 2							
OKON Paul	14 + 1							
PANAYI Jimmy	0 + 2		0 + 1					
PENNANT Jermaine	9	2						
ROBINSON Paul	38	3	5	1				
SMITH Tommy	35 + 5	11	2 + 2		1			
VEGA Ramon	23 + 4	1	5	2	1			
VERNAZZA Paolo	21		3	1	1			
WARD Darren	0 + 1		1					
WEBBER Danny	4 + 1	2						
WOOTER Nordin	7 +10	1	2 + 1					

WEST BROMWICH ALBION (DIV 1: 2nd)

	P/FL App	P/FL Goals	FLC App	FLC Goals	FAC App	FAC Goals	Others App	Others Goals
APPLETON Michael	18		3					

	P/FL App	P/FL Goals	FLC App	FLC Goals	FAC App	FAC Goals	Others App	Others Goals
BALIS Igor	32 + 2	2	0 + 1		3			
BENJAMIN Trevor	0 + 3	1						
BUTLER Tony	14 + 5		3		0 + 1			
CHAMBERS Adam	24 + 8		3		4			
CHAMBERS James	1 + 4		0 + 1					
CLEMENT Neil	45	6	3		4	2		
CUMMINGS Warren	6 + 8		0 + 2					
DICHIO Danny	26 + 1	9			4	1		
DOBIE Scott	32 +11	10	3	2	1 + 3			
FOX Ruel	2 +18	1	0 + 1		0 + 2			
GILCHRIST Phil	43		3		4			
HOULT Russell	45		3		4			
JENSEN Brian	1							
JOHNSON Andy	28 + 4	4			4	1		
JORDAO	19 + 6	5	0 + 1	1				
LYTTLE Des	13 +10		3		1 + 1			
McINNES Derek	45	3	3		4			
MOORE Darren	31 + 1	2			4			
QUINN James	1 + 6		0 + 2					
ROBERTS Jason	12 + 2	7			3			
ROSLER Uwe	5	1						
SIGURDSSON Larus	42 + 1	1	3		4			
TAYLOR Bob	18 +16	7	3		0 + 1			
VARGA Stan	3 + 1							

WEST HAM UNITED (PREM: 7th)

	P/FL App	P/FL Goals	FLC App	FLC Goals	FAC App	FAC Goals	Others App	Others Goals
BYRNE Shaun	0 + 1							
CAMARA Titi	0 + 1							
CARRICK Michael	30	2	1		1			
COLE Joe	29 + 1		1		3	1		
COURTOIS Laurent	5 + 2		0 + 1					
DAILLY Christian	38		1		3			
DEFOE Jermain	14 +21	10	1		2 + 1	4		
DI CANIO Paolo	26	9			1			
FOXE Hayden	4 + 2				0 + 1			
GARCIA Richard	2 + 6		0 + 1					
HISLOP Shaka	12		1					
HUTCHISON Don	24	1			3			
JAMES David	26				3			
KANOUTE Frederic	27	11			1	1		
KITSON Paul	3 + 4	3			2			
LABANT Vladimir	7 + 5				0 + 2			
LOMAS Steve	14 + 1	4			1 + 1			
McCANN Grant	0 + 3							
MINTO Scott	5		1					
MONCUR John	7 +12		1		1			
PEARCE Ian	8 + 1	2						
REPKA Tomas	31				3			
SCHEMMEL Sebastien	35	1	1		3			
SINCLAIR Trevor	34	5	1		2			
SOMA Ragnvald	1 + 2				1			
SONG Rigobert	5		1					
TODOROV Svetoslav	2 + 4	1			0 + 1			
WINTERBURN Nigel	29 + 2				3			

WIGAN ATHLETIC (DIV 2: 10th)

	P/FL App	P/FL Goals	FLC App	FLC Goals	FAC App	FAC Goals	Others App	Others Goals
ADAMCZUK Dariusz	3		1					
ASHCROFT Lee	14 + 2	3			1			
BRANNAN Ged	31 + 2		1	1				1
BUKRAN Gabor	1							
COOK Paul	6							
CROFT Gary	7							
DALGLISH Paul	17 +12	2			1			
DE VOS Jason	19 + 1	5	1					
DE ZEEUW Arjan	42	2	1		1			1
DINNING Tony	32 + 1	5			1			
ELLINGTON Nathan	3	2						
FILAN John	25							
GREEN Scott	35 + 4	3			1			1
HAWORTH Simon	19 + 8	10	1		1			1
JACKSON Matt	26							
JARRETT Jason	5							

	P/FL		FLC		FAC		Others	
	App	Goals	App	Goals	App	Goals	App	Goals
KENNA Jeff	6	1			1			
KENNEDY Peter	29 + 2		1				1	
KERR Stewart	8							
KILFORD Ian	7 +13				0 + 1	1		
LIDDELL Andy	33 + 1	18			1		0 + 1	
McCULLOCH Lee	24 +10	6			1		0 + 1	
McGIBBON Pat	18	1	1	1			1	
McLOUGHLIN Alan	1 + 2				1			
McMILLAN Steve	29							
MITCHELL Paul	16 + 7		1				0 + 1	
MOORE David			1					
NOLAN Ian	5 + 3							
PENDLEBURY Ian	4							
ROBERTS Neil	5 +12	4				1		
SANTUS Paul	0 + 1							
SHARP Kevin	1 + 1		1		1		1	
STILLE Derek	13		1		1		1	
TEALE Gary	22 + 1	1						
TRAYNOR Greg	0 + 1		1					
WIMBLEDON (DIV 1: 9th)								
AGYEMANG Patrick	17 +16	4	0 + 1		0 + 2			
AINSWORTH Gareth	0 + 2							
ANDERSEN Trond	27 + 3				2			
ARDLEY Neal	27 + 2	3	1		2			
BROWN Wayne	17	1						
BYRNE Dessie	0 + 1							
CONNOLLY David	35	18	1		2			
COOPER Kevin	39 + 1	10	1		2			
CUNNINGHAM Kenny	34				2			
DARLINGTON Jermaine	25 + 4		1					
DAVIS Kelvin	40							
FRANCIS Damien	21 + 2	1			2			
FUEUR Ian	2 + 2		1		2			
GIER Rob	3		0 + 1					
GORE Shane								
HAWKINS Peter	25 + 4				2			
HEALD Paul	4							
HOLLOWAY Darren	32				2			
HUGHES Michael	24 + 2	4			2			
JUPP Duncan	1 + 1		0 + 1					
KARLSSON Par	1 + 6							
KIMBLE Alan	7 + 2		1					
LEIGERTWOOD Mikele	1							
McANUFF Joel	22 +16	4			0 + 2			
MILD Hakan	8 + 1							
MORGAN Lionel	4 + 7	1						
NIELSEN David	6 + 6	2	1					
NOWLAND Adam	1 + 6							
REO-COKER Nigel	0 + 1							
ROBERTS Andy	18		1	1				
ROBINSON Paul	0 + 1							
SHIPPERLEY Neil	36 + 5	12	1		2			
WILLIAMS Mark	4 + 1		1		1			
WILLMOTT Chris	25 + 2		1	1				
WOLVERHAMPTON WANDERERS (DIV 1: 3rd)								
ANDREWS Keith	4 + 7							
BLAKE Nathan	38 + 1	11			1		2	
BRANCH Michael	5 + 2							
BUTLER Paul	43	1	1		1		2	
CAMARA Mohamed	23 + 4		1		1		2	
CAMERON Colin	38 + 3	4	1		1		2	
CONNELLY Sean	5 + 3							
COOPER Kevin	4 + 1						2	1
DINNING Tony	4		1	1				
HALLE Gunnar	4 + 1						2	
KENNEDY Mark	35	5	1		1		0 + 1	
KETSBAIA Temuri	0 + 2		1					
LESCOTT Joleon	44	5			2			
MILLER Kenny	5 +15	2			0 + 1		0 + 2	
MUSCAT Kevin	37				1			

	P/FL		FLC		FAC		Others	
	App	Goals	App	Goals	App	Goals	App	Goals
NAYLOR Lee	26 + 1							
NDAH George	1 +14	1						
NEWTON Shaun	45	8	1		1		2	
OAKES Michael	46		1		1		2	
POLLET Ludo	5 + 3		1		1			
PROUDLOCK Adam	12 + 7	3	1				0 + 1	
RAE Alex	31 + 5	7			1		2	
ROBINSON Carl	15 + 8	2	1					
ROUSSEL Cedric	6 +11	2	0 + 1		0 + 1			
SINTON Andy	3 + 4	1	0 + 1					
STURRIDGE Dean	27	20			1		2	1
WREXHAM (DIV 2: 23rd)								
BARRETT Paul	10 + 5						0 + 1	
BENNETT Danny	5 + 1							
BLACKWOOD Michael	21 +10	2	1		1		1	
CAREY Brian	16 + 2	2	1				0 + 1	
CHALK Martyn	17 + 7	3	1		1		1	
EDWARDS Carlos	10 +16	5	0 + 1					
EVANS Mark	0 + 4							
FAULCONBRIDGE Craig	36 + 1	12	1	1	1		2	
FERGUSON Darren	37 + 1	3	1		1		2	
GIBSON Robin	11 + 7				1			
HILL Keith	12		1		1		2	
HOLMES Shaun	39 + 1		1		1		1	
JONES Lee	3 + 1	5						
LAWRENCE Denis	29 + 3	2	1		0 + 1			
MILLER Willie	5						1	
MOODY Adrian	0 + 1							
MORGAN Craig	0 + 2							
MORRELL Andy	13 +12	2			0 + 1		0 + 2	2
PEJIC Shaun	11 + 1							
PHILLIPS Wayne	27		1					
ROBERTS Steve	24		1		1		2	
ROGERS Kristian	27		1		1		1	
ROVDE Marius	12							
RUSSELL Kevin	8 + 2		0 + 1	1			1	
SAM Hector	15 +14	5	1		1		2	
SHARP Kevin	12 + 3	1						
THOMAS Steve	30 + 8	3	1				2	1
TRUNDLE Lee	30 + 6	8					1 + 1	2
WALSH Dave	7 + 2						1	
WARREN David	5		1					
WHITLEY Jim	34				1		2	
WYCOMBE WANDERERS (DIV 2: 11th)								
BAIRD Andy	1 + 5							
BROWN Steve	31 + 8	8	1		3 + 1	1		
BULMAN Dannie	37 + 9	5	1		3 + 1	1	2	
CARROLL Dave	1 +11				1 + 3		2	
COUSINS Jason	13 + 6		1		1 + 2		1	
CURRIE Darren	44 + 2	3	1		4	3		
DEVINE Sean	19 + 1	5			0 + 1			
EMBLEN Paul	5 + 7	1	1		0 + 1		2	1
HARRIS Richard	2 + 1							
HOLLIGAN Gavin	11 + 9	4			2		2	1
JOHNSON Roger	7	1					1 + 1	
LEACH Marc	1							
LEE Martyn	2 + 5				0 + 1		2	
LOPEZ Carlos	1							
McCARTHY Paul	28	3	1		3			
McSPORRAN Jermaine	19 +13	7	0 + 1		2	1	1	
MARSH Chris	0 + 1		0 + 1					
OSBORN Mark							2	
PHELAN Leeyon	0 + 1						1 + 1	
RAMMELL Andy	27	11	1		2	2		
ROBERTS Stuart	18 + 8				2 + 1		0 + 1	
ROGERS Mark	39 + 2	2	1		4		1	
RYAN Keith	12 +23	1	0 + 1		1 + 1		2	
SENDA Danny	38 + 5				3		2	
SIMPSON Michael	43	1	1		4			
TAYLOR Martin	46		1		4			

	P/FL		FLC		FAC		Others	
	App	Goals	App	Goals	App	Goals	App	Goals
THOMSON Andy	3							
TOWNSEND Ben	2						1	
TUTTLE Dave	4							
VINNICOMBE Chris	42	1	1		4			
WALKER Richard	10 + 2	3			1	1		
YORK CITY (DIV 3: 14th)								
BASHAM Mike	26 + 3	2	1		4		0 + 1	
BRACKSTONE Steve	6 + 3							
BRASS Chris	41	2	1	1	5	1	1	
BULLOCK Lee	39 + 1	8	1	1	5 + 1			
COOPER Richard	23 + 2	1	1		5 + 1		1	
DARLOW Kieran	1 + 1							
DUFFIELD Peter	7 + 4	3			0 + 1			
EDMONDSON Darren	34 + 2		1		5			
EMMERSON Scott	0 + 6		0 + 1					
EVANS Michael	1 + 1							
FETTIS Alan	45		1		6			
FIELDING John	9	1	1				1	
FOX Christian	5 + 7						1	

	P/FL		FLC		FAC		Others	
	App	Goals	App	Goals	App	Goals	App	Goals
GRANT Lee	0 + 1							
HOBSON Gary	14 + 2				4			
HOCKING Matt	29 + 4				5		1	
HOWARTH Russell	1 + 1						1	
JONES Scott	7 + 1	1						
MALEY Mark	11 + 2				2 + 1		1	
MATHIE Alex	11 +12	2			0 + 2		0 + 1	
NOGAN Lee	40 + 2	13	1		5		1	
O'KANE Aidan	11 + 1		1					
PARKIN Jon	18	2						
POTTER Graham	37	2	1		6	2		
PROCTOR Michael	40 + 1	14	1		6		1	
RHODES Ben	0 + 1							
RICHARDSON Nick	17 + 5				4 + 1	1		
SALVATI Marc	1 + 7	1						
SMITH Christopher	12 + 3				3		1	
STAMP Neville	5 + 2				1		1	
WISE Stuart	3 + 3							
WOOD Leigh	12 + 2							

Paul Gascoigne

Where Did They Go?

Below is a list of all players who were recorded in the previous edition as making a first-team appearance in 2000-2001, but failed to make the current book. They are listed alphabetically and show their approximate leaving dates as well as their first port of call if known. Of course, they may well have moved on by now, but space does not allow further reference.

* Shows that the player in question is still with his named club but failed to make an appearance in 2001-2002, the most common reason being injury.

\+ Players retained by Barnet, who were relegated to the Conference.

Name	Club	Date	Destination
ABBEY Ben	Southend U	07.01	Crawley T
ABIDALLAH Nabil	Ipswich T	*	
ADAMS Neil	Oldham Ath	07.01	Retired
AGNEW Steve	York C	07.01	Gateshead
ALDRIDGE Paul	Tranmere Rov	03.02	Macclesfield T (trial)
ALEKSIDZE Rati	Chelsea	*	
AL JABER Sami	Wolverhampton W	01.02	Al-Hilal (Saudia Arabia)
ALOISI John	Coventry C	08.01	Osasuna (Spain)
ANDREASSON Marcus	Bristol Rov	08.01	Bryne (Norway)
ANDREWS John	Mansfield T	10.01	
ANGEL Mark	Darlington	11.00	Queen of the South
ANTHROBUS Steve	Oxford U	07.01	TNS Llansantffraid
ANTONY Paul	Carlisle U	02.02	Gateshead
ARBER Mark	Barnet	+	
ARMSTRONG Chris	Tottenham H	07.02	
ARMSTRONG Joel	Chesterfield	07.02	
ARMSTRONG Stephen	Watford	07.01	South Africa
ARNOTT Andy	Colchester U	03.01	Stevenage Bor
ARTELL David	Rotherham U	*	
ASHINGTON Ryan	Torquay U	*	
ASHTON Jon	Exeter C	07.01	Hayes
ASPIN Neil	Hartlepool U	07.01	Harrogate T
ASPINALL Warren	Brighton & Hove A	11.00	Retired
AWFORD Andy	Portsmouth	01.01	Retired
AXELDAHL Jonas	Cambridge U	07.01	
AYRES James	Luton T	01.01	Enfield
BAGHERI Karim	Charlton Ath	05.01	Iran
BAILEY Alan	Stockport Co	07.01	Burton A
BAKALLI Adrian	Swindon T	07.01	
BAKER Steve	Middlesbrough	11.01	Scarborough
BALL Michael	Everton	08.01	Glasgow Rangers
BAMBER Mike	Macclesfield T	03.02	
BANCE Danny	Plymouth Arg	*	
BAPTISTE Rocky	Luton T	07.01	Farnborough T
BARNES Paul	Bury	07.01	Doncaster Rov
BARNETT Gary	Kidderminster Hrs	05.02	Retired
BARRETT Danny	Chesterfield	07.02	
BARRICK Dean	Bury	02.01	Doncaster Rov
BARROWCLOUGH Carl	Barnsley	*	
BASSILA Christian	West Ham U	07.01	Strasbourg (France)
BATES Jamie	Wycombe W	05.01	Retired
BAZELEY Darren	Wolverhampton W	*	
BEADLE Peter	Bristol C	*	
BEAUMONT Chris	Chesterfield	07.01	Ossett T
BEAVERS Paul	Darlington	07.01	Morpeth T
BEETON Alan	Wycombe W	03.01	Chesham U
BELL Leon	Barnet	+	
BENNION Chris	Scunthorpe U	05.02	
BERGERSEN Kent	Stockport Co	04.01	Moss FK (Norway)
BERRY Trevor	Rotherham U	09.01	Retired
BETTNEY Chris	Macclesfield T	10.00	Worksop T
BIDSTRUP Stefan	Wigan Ath	05.01	Aalborg (Denmark)
BISHOP Ian	Manchester C	03.01	Miami Fusion (USA)
BLACK Michael	Southend U	07.01	Barking & East Ham U
BLACKWELL Dean	Wimbledon	07.02	
BLAKE Noel	Exeter C	07.02	Retired
BLOOMER Bob	Cheltenham T	07.01	Retired
BOGARDE Winston	Chelsea	*	
BOGIE Ian	Kidderminster Hrs	03.01	Bedlington Terriers
BOHINEN Lars	Derby Co	01.01	Lyngby (Denmark)
BOLIMA Cedric	Rotherham U	01.01	St Malo (France)
BOUANANE Emad	Wrexham	07.01	France
BOULD Steve	Sunderland	11.00	Retired
BOWLING Ian	Mansfield T	11.00	Kettering T
BOYD Walter	Swansea C	07.01	Jamaica
BRACEY Lee	Hull C	07.01	Ossett T
BRADSHAW Mark	Halifax T	07.01	Droylsden
BRADY Matt	Wycombe W	07.01	Boreham Wood
BREACKER Tim	Queens Park R	07.01	Retired
BREBNER Grant	Stockport Co	01.01	Hibernian
BREITENFELDER Freidrich	Luton T	04.01	Austria
BRIDGES Michael	Leeds U	*	
BRISSETT Jason	Leyton Orient	12.00	Stevenage Bor
BROWN Danny	Barnet	+	
BROWN Keith	Barnsley	02.02	
BROWN Mickey	Shrewsbury T	07.01	Boston U
BUBB Byron	Millwall	07.01	Hendon
BUGGIE Lee	Bury	07.01	Accrington Stanley
BULLOCK Tony	Lincoln C	07.01	Ross Co
BURLEY Adam	Sheffield U	07.02	
BURNS Jacob	Leeds U	*	
BUSBY Hubert	Oxford U	02.01	Vancouver (Canada)
BUTTERWORTH Adam	Cambridge U	05.02	
BYWATER Steve	West Ham U	*	
CADIOU Frederic	Leyton Orient	12.00	France
CAIG Tony	Charlton Ath	07.01	Hibernian
CALDERWOOD Colin	Nottingham F	05.01	Retired
CAPLETON Mel	Southend U	11.01	Grays Ath
CARLISLE Clarke	Queens Park R	*	
CARR Stephen	Tottenham H	*	
CARRIGAN Brian	Stockport Co	05.02	
CARTER Alfie	Walsall	10.00	Bromsgrove Rov
CARTERON Patrice	Sunderland	07.01	France
CASTLEDINE Stewart	Wycombe W	04.02	
CAU Jean-Michel	Darlington	06.01	France
CHALQI Khalid	Torquay U	08.01	
CHARLERY Kenny	Barnet	09.00	Boston U
CHARLES Gary	West Ham U	*	
CHARLES Julian	Brentford	07.02	
CLARE Daryl	Grimsby T	07.01	Boston U
CLARK Ben	Sunderland	*	
CLARKE Tim	Kidderminster Hrs	07.01	Halesowen T

Name	Club	Date	Destination
COCHRANE Justin	Queens Park R	07.02	
COLEMAN Chris	Fulham	*	
COLLINS James	Crewe Alex	07.01	Northwich Vic
COLLINS Lee	Stoke C	06.01	Halesowen T
COLLINS Simon	Macclesfield T	07.01	Frickley Ath
COLLIS Dave	Charlton Ath	06.02	Grays Ath
COLLYMORE Stan	Bradford C	02.01	Real Oviedo (Spain)
CONNELL Darren	Macclesfield T	07.01	Scarborough
CONNELLY Gordon	Carlisle U	07.01	Queen of the South
CONNOLLY Paul	Plymouth Arg	*	
COOK Jamie	Oxford U	02.01	Boston U
CORDONE Daniel	Newcastle U	07.01	Argentina
CORNFORTH John	Exeter C	07.01	Retired
CORNWALL Luke	Fulham	*	
COTTEE Tony	Millwall	07.01	Retired
COWE Steve	Swindon T	07.01	Newport Co
CRAMB Colin	Crewe Alex	07.01	Fortuna Sittard (Holland)
CROFTS Andrew	Gillingham	*	
CROSS Garry	Southend U	01.01	Chelmsford C
CULKIN Nick	Manchester U	*	
CUNNINGHAM Craig	Wigan Ath	06.02	
DAGNOGO Moussa	Bristol Rov	10.00	
DANILEVICIUS Tomas	Arsenal	03.01	Beveren (Belgium)
DARBY Julian	Carlisle U	07.01	Retired
D'ARCY Ross	Barnet	+	
DAVIDSON Ross	Shrewsbury T	07.01	Ashford T
DAVIES Alex	Swansea C	06.02	
DAVIES Simon	Rochdale	07.01	Bangor C
DAWSON Andy	Carlisle U	02.01	Scarborough
DAY Jamie	Bournemouth	07.01	Dover Ath
DE BILDE Gilles	Sheffield Wed	07.01	Anderlecht (Belgium)
DE BLASIIS Jean Yves	Norwich C	07.01	Istres (France)
DERVELD Fernando	Norwich C	06.01	Odense BK (Denmark)
DE WAARD Raymond	Norwich C	02.01	AZ Alkmaar (Holland)
DEWHURST Rob	Scunthorpe U	05.01	North Ferriby U
DIAWARA Kaba	West Ham U	07.01	
DICKSON Hugh	Wigan Ath	10.01	
DI MATTEO Robbie	Chelsea	02.02	Retired
DOLAN Joe	Millwall	*	
DOMI Didier	Newcastle U	01.01	Paris Saint Germain (France)
DOMINGUEZ Jose	Tottenham H	11.00	Kaiserslautern (Germany)
DOOLAN John	Barnet	+	
DORIGO Tony	Stoke C	07.01	Retired
DOWIE Iain	Queens Park R	07.01	Retired
DOWNEY Chris	Bolton W	*	
DOZZELL Jason	Colchester U	09.01	Retired
DREYER John	Cambridge U	08.01	Stevenage Bor
DUDGEON James	Barnsley	*	
DUNFIELD Terry	Manchester C	*	
DUNN Mark	Notts Co	*	
DYER Alex	Notts Co	11.00	Kingstonian
EADIE Darren	Leicester C	*	
ECKHARDT Jeff	Cardiff C	07.01	Newport Co
EDWARDS Craig	Southend U	09.01	Grays Ath
EDWARDS Paul	Shrewsbury T	07.01	Telford U
EKELUND Ronnie	Walsall	05.01	San Jose (USA)
ELLIS Clint	Bristol Rov	07.01	
ENHUA Zhang	Grimsby T	04.01	Dalian Shide (China)
EPESSE-TITI Steeve	Exeter C	07.01	
ERANIO Stefano	Derby Co	07.01	Retired
ESSANDOAH Roy	Wycombe W	07.01	Cambridge C
EUSTACE Scott	Lincoln C	10.00	Hinckley U
EVANS Kevin	Cardiff C	02.02	Boston U
EYJOLFSSON Sigi	Walsall	11.00	Harelbeke (Belgium)
FABIANO Nicolas	Swansea C	07.01	Paris Saint Germain (France)
FARRELL Sean	Notts Co	07.01	Burton A
FEAR Peter	Oxford U	07.01	Kettering T
FERGUSON Barry	Coventry C	03.02	
FICKLING Ashley	Scunthorpe U	07.01	Scarborough
FITZPATRICK Lee	Hartlepool U	07.01	Rossendale U
FITZPATRICK Trevor	Southend U	05.01	Shelbourne
FLAHAVON Aaron	Portsmouth	08.01	Deceased
FLO Tore Andre	Chelsea	11.00	Glasgow Rangers
FLYNN Lee	Barnet	+	
FOLAN Tony	Brentford	11.01	Bohemians
FORD Mike	Oxford U	09.00	Retired
FORD Ryan	Manchester U	03.02	Ilkeston T
FORDE Fabian	Watford	*	
FORGE Nicolas	Leyton Orient	05.01	France
FORREST Craig	West Ham U	07.02	
FOSTERVOLD Knut	Grimsby T	02.01	Molde FK (Norway)
FRANCIS Kevin	Hull C	07.01	Hednesford T
FREDGAARD Carsten	Sunderland	07.01	FC Copenhagen (Denmark)
FREEMAN Darren	Brighton & Hove A	06.02	Margate
FREEMAN David	Nottingham F	07.02	
FREEMAN Mark	Cheltenham T	05.01	Boston U
FULLARTON Jamie	Crystal Palace	11.00	Dundee U
FULLER Ricardo	Crystal Palace	07.01	
FUTCHER Ben	Oldham Ath	01.02	Stalybridge Celtic
GANNON Jim	Crewe Alex	07.01	Shelbourne
GARNER Darren	Rotherham U	*	
GARRATT Martin	Lincoln C	03.01	Hednesford T
GAUGHAN Steve	Halifax T	07.01	Barrow
GAUNT Ian	Walsall	06.02	
GAVILAN Diego	Newcastle U	01.02	Los Tecos (Mexico)
GAYLE John	Torquay U	07.01	Moor Green
GELLERT Brian	Notts Co	07.01	
GIALLANZA Gaetano	Norwich C	07.02	
GIBBENS Kevin	Southampton	03.02	Oxford U (trial)
GIBSON Paul	Notts Co	07.01	Northwich Vic
GILKES Michael	Millwall	07.01	Slough T
GLASS Jimmy	Oxford U	01.01	Crawley T
GLEDHILL Lee	Barnet	+	
GOPE-FENEPEJ John	Bolton W	12.00	Creteil (France)
GOUGH Richard	Everton	07.01	Northern Spirit (Australia)
GOULD James	Northampton	07.01	Boston U
GOWER Mark	Barnet	+	
GRAHAM Gareth	Brentford	07.01	Margate
GRANT Peter	Bournemouth	*	
GRAY Martin	Darlington	09.01	Retired
GREEN Richard	Northampton T	07.01	Retired
GREENE David	Cambridge U	05.01	
GRIFFIN Charlie	Swindon T	11.00	Woking
GUDMUNDSSON Johann	Watford	02.01	Lyn Oslo (Norway)
GUNNLAUGSSON Bjarke	Preston NE	12.01	Retired
GUPPY Steve	Leicester C	08.01	Glasgow Celtic
HALFORD Steve	Bury	08.01	Bury T
HALL Gareth	Swindon T	07.01	Havant & Waterlooville
HALL Wayne	York C	07.01	Gainsborough Trinity
HAMILTON Gary	Blackburn Rov	07.01	
HAMMOND Dean	Brighton & Hove A	*	
HANMER Gareth	Shrewsbury T	07.01	Telford U
HANSEN John	Cambridge U	08.01	
HANSSON Mikael	Stoke C	02.02	Sweden
HARDY Adam	Bradford C	10.01	Doncaster Rov

Name	Club	Date	Destination
HARKNESS Steve	Sheffield Wed	05.02	
HARRISON Gerry	Halifax T	09.00	Leigh RMI
HARRISON Lee	Barnet	+	
HARTSON John	Coventry C	08.01	Glasgow Celtic
HAWE Steve	Blackburn Rov	07.01	
HAY Danny	Leeds U	07.02	
HAYWARD Steve	Barnsley	*	
HEALD Greg	Barnet	+	
HEATH Robert	Stoke C	08.01	Stafford R
HEGGEM Vegard	Liverpool	*	
HEGGS Carl	Carlisle U	07.01	Forest Green Rov
HEINOLA Antti	Queens Park R	02.01	Finland
HEISELBERG Kim	Swindon T	11.00	Denmark
HEMMINGS Tony	Carlisle U	07.01	Ilkeston T
HENRY Anthony	Lincoln C	07.01	Folkestone Invicta
HERNANDEZ Dino	Wigan Ath	12.00	Cambuur Leeuwarden (Holland)
HICKS Stuart	Mansfield T	03.02	Hucknall T
HIGGINS Alex	Queens Park R	04.01	Emley
HILL Danny	Cardiff C	07.01	Dagenham & Redbridge
HIMSWORTH Gary	Darlington	01.02	
HJORTH Jesper	Darlington	07.01	Denmark
HODGES John	Plymouth Arg	07.01	
HOLDER Jordan	Oxford U	03.02	Oxford City
HOLLAND Paul	Bristol C	03.02	Retired
HOLLOWAY Chris	Exeter C	07.01	Rotherham U
HOLT Grant	Halifax T	07.01	Barrow
HORNE Barry	Walsall	07.01	Belper T
HOWELL Dean	Crewe Alex	07.01	Southport
HOWEY Lee	Northampton T	07.01	Forest Green Rov
HUDSON Mark	Fulham	*	
HUGHES Ceri	Cardiff C	*	
HUGHES Garry	Northampton T	07.01	Kettering T
HULME Kevin	York C	03.01	Altrincham
HUNT Andy	Charlton Ath	03.02	Retired
HUNT Jon	Wimbledon	07.01	
HUNT Nicky	Bolton W	*	
HUNTER Leon	Southend U	07.02	
INGLETHORPE Alex	Exeter C	07.01	Leatherhead
INGLIS John	Carlisle U	01.01	Raith Rov
JACOBSEN Anders	Notts Co	07.01	Skeid Oslo (Norway)
JAMES Lutel	Bury	07.01	Accrington Stanley
JARMAN Lee	Oxford U	07.01	Barry T
JEPSON Ronnie	Burnley	07.01	Retired
JOHANSEN Rune	Bristol Rov	12.00	Tromso (Norway)
JOHNSON Ian	Wigan Ath	07.02	
JOHNSON Joel	Wigan Ath	07.02	
JOHNSON Lee	Brighton & Hove A	03.01	
JOHNSON Richard	Watford	*	
JONES Barry	York C	07.01	Southport
JONES Eifion	Blackpool	07.02	
JONES Marcus	Cheltenham T	02.01	Yeovil T
JONES Matthew	Shrewsbury T	07.01	
JONES Paul	Oldham Ath	07.02	
JONES Stuart	Torquay U	10.01	Hereford U
JONK Wim	Sheffield Wed	07.01	Retired
JORDAN Andy	Cardiff C	*	
JORDAN Scott	York C	03.01	Scarborough
JOSEPH David	Notts Co	07.01	France
KAAK Tom	Darlington	10.00	Clydebank
KANCHELSKIS Andrei	Manchester C	04.01	Glasgow Rangers
KAREMBEU Christian	Middlesbrough	08.01	Olimpiakos (Greece)
KARIC Amir	Ipswich T	*	
KARLSEN Kent	Luton T	10.01	Åsane (Norway)
KAY Ben	Wigan Ath	07.02	
KEARTON Jason	Crewe Alex	08.01	Brisbane (Australia)
KEEBLE Chris	Colchester U	*	
KEELER Justin	Bournemouth	03.01	Dorchester T
KEISTER John	Shrewsbury T	01.01	Margate
KELLER Marc	Blackburn Rov	07.01	
KENNEDY Jon	Sunderland	*	
KENNEDY Richard	Brentford	03.01	Barry T
KERR Scott	Hull C	*	
KIWOMYA Chris	Queens Park R	07.01	Aalborg (Denmark)
KNOWLES Darren	Hartlepool U	07.01	Northwich Vic
KORSTEN Willem	Tottenham H	10.01	Retired
KRISTINSSON Birkir	Stoke C	11.01	IBV (Iceland)
KULCSAR George	Queens Park R	05.01	Retired
LAMBOURDE Bernard	Chelsea	06.01	SC Bastia (France)
LAMEY Nathan	Cambridge U	01.01	Moor Green
LANCASHIRE Graham	Rochdale	07.01	Hednesford T
LARUSSON Bjarne	Scunthorpe U	05.01	Iceland
LAURENCO	Bristol C	05.01	Sporting Lisbon (Portugal)
LEADBITTER Chris	Plymouth Arg	07.01	Guisborough T
LEBOEUF Frank	Chelsea	07.01	Marseilles (France)
LEE David	Carlisle U	01.01	Morecambe
LEE Jason	Peterborough U	*	
LEMARCHAND Stephane	Rotherham U	01.01	France
LENNON Neil	Leicester C	12.00	Glasgow Celtic
LEWIS Graham	Lincoln C	10.00	Northwich Vic
LIGHTFOOT Chris	Crewe Alex	07.01	Morecambe
LILLEY Derek	Oxford U	12.00	Dundee U
LINDLEY Jim	Notts Co	07.01	Gresley Rov
LINIGHAN Andy	Oxford U	05.01	Retired
LOCK Tony	Colchester U	03.01	Dagenham & Redbridge
LOMAS Jamie	Mansfield T	05.01	Matlock T
LONERGAN Andy	Preston NE	*	
LOPES Richie	Northampton T	07.02	
LOVELL Mark	Gillingham	07.02	
LOWE Danny	Northampton T	*	
LUKIC John	Arsenal	07.01	Retired
LYONS Simon	Torquay U	03.02	Barnstaple T
McBRIDE Brian	Preston NE	03.01	Columbus Crew (USA)
McCORMICK Luke	Plymouth Arg	*	
McDERMOTT Andy	Notts Co	06.01	Northern Spirit (Australia)
McDONALD Tom	Southend U	01.01	Barking
McFLYNN Terry	Queens Park R	07.01	Margate
McGAVIN Steve	Colchester U	07.01	Dagenham & Redbridge
McGOWAN Gavin	Luton T	07.01	Bromley
McGOWAN Neil	Oxford U	03.01	Clydebank
McGRATH John	Aston Villa	*	
McGUCKIN Ian	Oxford U	08.01	Barrow
McHUGH Frazer	Swindon T	07.01	Tamworth
McINTYRE Jimmy	Reading	07.01	Dundee U
McKINLAY Billy	Bradford C	07.01	Retired
McLAUGHLIN Brian	Wigan Ath	08.01	
McMAHON David	Newcastle U	07.01	Durham C
McMAHON Francis	Wigan Ath	07.01	Runcorn
McNIVEN David	York C	07.01	Chester C
MALESSA Antony	Bristol C	07.01	
MALZ Stefan	Arsenal	06.01	Kaiserslautern (Germany)
MAMOUM Blaise	Scunthorpe U	01.01	Werder Bremen (Germany)
MANCINI Roberto	Leicester C	02.01	Fiorentina (Italy)
MANN Neil	Hull C	*	
MANNINGER Alex	Arsenal	*	
MANSLEY Chad	Leyton Orient	02.01	Newcastle Breakers (Australia)

Name	Club	Date	Destination
MARCELINO	Newcastle U	*	
MARDON Paul	West Bromwich A	07.01	Retired
MARGAS Javier	West Ham U	01.01	Retired
MARSH Simon	Birmingham C	04.01	
MARSHALL Scott	Brentford	*	
MARTIN Lilian	Derby Co	05.01	Marseilles (France)
MARTINEZ Roberto	Wigan Ath	07.01	Motherwell
MAWSON Craig	Halifax T	07.01	Morecambe
MEAKER Michael	Plymouth Arg	07.01	Northwich Vic
MEIJER Erik	Liverpool	12.00	Hamburger SV (Germany)
MENDES-RODRIGUEZ Alberto	Arsenal	*	
MENDY Jules	Torquay U	08.01	France
MIDGLEY Neil	Barnet	+	
MIKLOSKO Ludo	Queens Park R	07.01	Retired
MILLEN Keith	Bristol C	07.02	
MILLER Alan	Blackburn Rov	*	
MILLER Charlie	Watford	11.01	Dundee U
MILLER Paul	Lincoln C	07.01	Hucknall T
MILLS Jamie	Swindon T	07.01	Clevedon T
MIMMS Bobby	Mansfield T	07.01	Retired
MOLLER Peter	Fulham	07.01	Real Oviedo (Spain)
MONINGTON Mark	Rochdale	07.01	Boston U
MONKOU Ken	Huddersfield T	03.01	Retired
MOREAU Fabrice	Notts Co	05.01	France
MORGAN Bari	Swansea C	07.01	Aberystwyth T
MORGAN Steve	Halifax T	10.00	TNS Llansantffraid
MORINI Emanuele	Bolton W	*	
MORRIS Andy	Wigan Ath	07.01	Prescot Cables
MORRISON Andy	Manchester C	03.02	Retired
MORRISON Peter	Scunthorpe U	07.01	
MORROW Andy	Northampton T	07.01	
MORROW Steve	Queens Park R	07.01	Retired
MOUNTY Carl	Swansea C	07.01	
MUDGE James	Exeter C	*	
MULLER Adam	Sheffield Wed	05.02	
MURRAY Dan	Peterborough U	*	
MURRAY Jay	Leyton Orient	01.02	Barking & East Ham U
MURRAY Neil	Grimsby T	02.01	Mainz 05 (Germany)
MURRAY Shaun	Notts Co	07.01	Kettering T
MUTTON Tommy	Swansea C	01.01	Caernarfon T
MYERS Peter	Halifax T	07.01	Frickley Ath
MYHRE Thomas	Everton	11.01	Besiktas (Turkey)
NAISBITT Danny	Barnet	+	
NANCEKIVELL Kevin	Plymouth Arg	03.01	Tiverton T
NEIL Gary	Torquay U	05.01	
NEWELL Mike	Blackpool	07.01	Retired
NEWMAN Ricky	Reading	*	
NEWTON Eddie	Barnet	09.00	Singapore
NGONGE Michel	Queens Park R	07.01	Kilmarnock
NIGHTINGALE Luke	Portsmouth	*	
NILIS Luke	Aston Villa	01.01	Retired
NIVEN Stuart	Barnet	+	
NOGAN Kurt	Cardiff C	07.02	
NORTHMORE Ryan	Torquay U	*	
NUNEZ Milton	Sunderland	07.01	Nacional (Honduras)
NUTTER John	Wycombe W	05.01	Aldershot T
NYARKO Alex	Everton	08.01	AS Monaco (France)
O'BRIEN Burton	Blackburn Rov	*	
O'CONNOR Jon	Blackpool	07.02	
ODEJAYI Kay	Bristol C	07.02	
O'HANLON Kelham	Preston NE	*	
OLAOYE Del	Port Vale	*	
OLIVER Adam	West Bromwich A	*	
OLSEN Ben	Nottingham F	03.01	D.C. United (USA)
OLSEN James	Tranmere Rov	*	
O'NEILL John	Bournemouth	10.00	Queen of the South
OPARA KK	Leyton Orient	11.01	Billericay T
OPINEL Sasha	Leyton Orient	07.01	Billericay T
ORD Michael	Halifax T	02.01	Harrogate T
O'SULLIVAN Wayne	Plymouth Arg	07.01	Australia
OWEN Gareth	Wrexham	07.01	Doncaster Rov
OWUSU Ansah	Wimbledon	07.02	
PADULA Gino	Wigan Ath	07.01	
PAINTER Robbie	Halifax T	07.01	Gateshead
PALLISTER Gary	Middlesbrough	07.01	Retired
PANUCCI Christian	Chelsea	01.01	AS Monaco (France)
PARKIN Brian	Bristol Rov	05.01	Retired
PARKS Tony	Halifax T	07.02	Retired
PARNABY Stuart	Middlesbrough	*	
PARTRIDGE Richie	Liverpool	*	
PASSI Franck	Bolton W	07.01	France
PEACOCK Darren	Blackburn Rov	12.00	Retired
PEACOCK Richard	Lincoln C	07.01	Stalybridge Celtic
PEAKE Jason	Plymouth Arg	03.01	Nuneaton Bor
PEER Dean	Shrewsbury T	07.01	Moor Green
PEETERS Tom	Sunderland	11.01	Royal Antwerp (Belgium)
PEPPER Carl	Darlington	10.00	Blyth Spartans
PERKINS Chris	Lincoln C	07.01	Stalybridge Celtic
PERRY Jason	Hull C	07.01	Newport Co
PETTERSON Andy	West Bromwich A	07.02	
PEYTON Warren	Bury	07.01	Nuneaton Bor
PHILLIPS Lee	Plymouth Arg	03.01	Weymouth
PHILLIPS Michael	Gillingham	*	
PIERCY John	Tottenham H	*	
PILVI Tero	Cambridge U	07.01	Finland
PINAMONTE Lorenzo	Brentford	07.01	
PINKNEY Grant	Lincoln C	*	
PITTS Matthew	Carlisle U	10.00	Whitby T
PLATT David	Nottingham F	07.01	Retired
PLATTS Mark	Torquay U	10.00	Worksop T
PLUCK Lee	Barnet	+	
POLLOCK Jamie	Crystal Palace	*	
POPE Craig	Barnet	+	
POTTER Lee	Halifax T	07.01	Radcliffe Bor
POTTS Steve	West Ham U	07.02	
PURSER Wayne	Barnet	+	
RADEBE Lucas	Leeds U	*	
RAMAGE Craig	Notts Co	07.01	
RAWLINSON Mark	Exeter C	07.01	Weymouth
READY Karl	Queens Park R	07.01	Motherwell
REED Martin	York C	03.01	Scarborough
REZAI Carl	Halifax T	*	
RIBEIRO Bruno	Sheffield U	07.01	Uniao Leiria (Portugal)
RICHARDS Ian	Halifax T	07.01	Bradford Park Avenue
RIEDLE Karl-Heinz	Fulham	07.01	Retired
RISOM Henrik	Stoke C	07.01	Aarhus GF (Denmark)
RITCHIE Andy	Oldham Ath	07.01	Retired
RIZA Omer	West Ham U	07.02	
ROBERTS Darren	Exeter C	01.01	Barrow
ROBERTSON John	Oxford U	05.01	Ayr U
ROBERTSON Mark	Burnley	03.01	Dundee
ROBINSON Paul	Leeds U	*	
ROCHE Barry	Nottingham F	*	
ROWBOTHAM Jason	Torquay U	01.01	Weymouth
ROY Eric	Sunderland	01.01	ES Troyes (France)
RUDI Petter	Sheffield Wed	07.01	Lokeren (Belgium)
SAHNOUN Nicolas	Fulham	07.01	Bordeaux (France)
SALLI Janne	Barnsley	*	
SALT Phil	Oldham Ath	02.02	Scarborough